MEDIEVAL ISLAMIC CIVILIZATION

AN ENCYCLOPEDIA

Volume 2
L – Z
INDEX

MEDIEVAL ISLAMIC CIVILIZATION

AN ENCYCLOPEDIA

Volume 2

L – Z

INDEX

Josef W. Meri

Editor

Routledge
Taylor & Francis Group
New York   London

Published in 2006 by
Routledge
Taylor & Francis Group
270 Madison Avenue
New York, NY 10016

Published in Great Britain by
Routledge
Taylor & Francis Group
2 Park Square
Milton Park, Abingdon
Oxon OX14 4RN

Printed in the United States of America on acid-free paper
10 9 8 7 6 5 4 3 2 1

International Standard Book Number-10: 0-415-96691-4 (Vol 1), 0-415-96692-2 (Vol 2), 0-415-96690-6 (Set)
International Standard Book Number-13: 978-0-415-96691-7 (Vol 1), 978-0-415-96692-4 (Vol 2), 978-0-415-96690-0 (Set)
Library of Congress Card Number 2005044229

Library of Congress Cataloging-in-Publication Data

Medieval Islamic civilization : an encyclopedia / Josef W. Meri, editor ; advisory board, Jere L. Bacharach ... [et al.].
    p. cm.
    Includes bibliographical references and index.
    ISBN 0-415-96691-4 (v. 1 : alk. paper) -- ISBN 0-415-96692-2 (v. 2 : alk. paper) -- ISBN 0-415-96690-6 (set : alk. paper)
    1. Civilization, Islamic--Encyclopedias. 2. Islamic Empire--Civilization--Encyclopedias. I. Meri, Josef W. II. Bacharach, Jere L., 1938-

    DS36.85.M434 2005
    909'.09767'003--dc22   2005044229

Taylor & Francis Group is the Academic Division of T&F Informa plc.

Visit the Taylor & Francis Web site at
http://www.taylorandfrancis.com

and the Routledge Web site at
http://www.routledge-ny.com

CONTENTS

MAPS

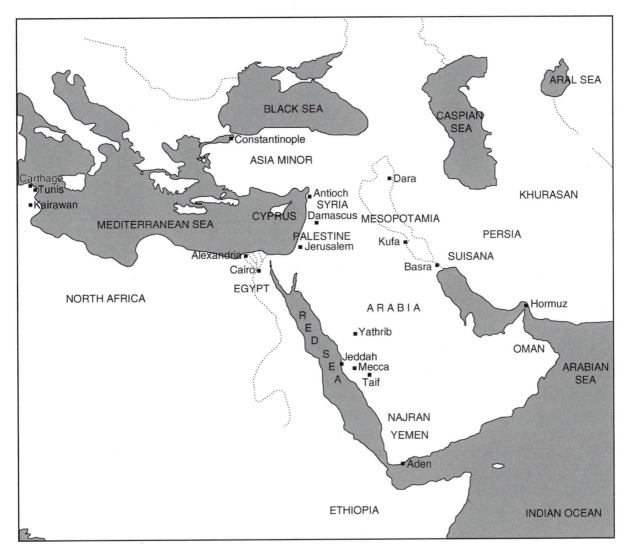

Arabia, ca. 600 CE

MAPS

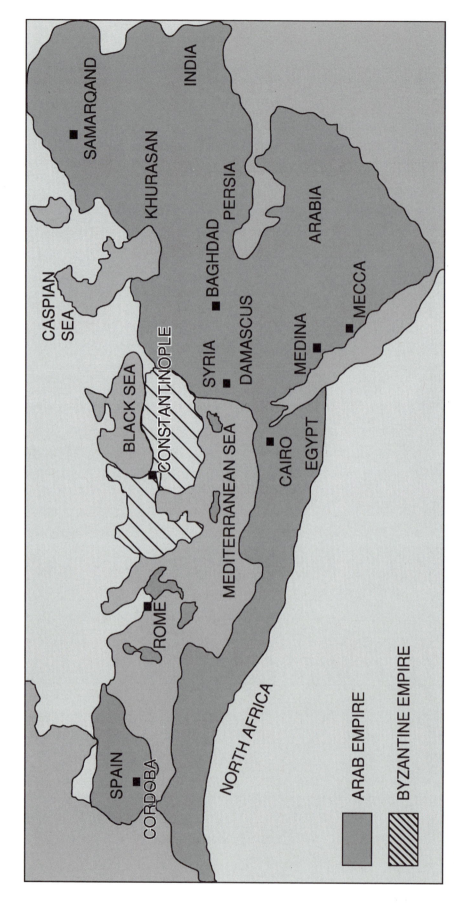

Arab Empire, 700–850 CE

ARAB EMPIRE

BYZANTINE EMPIRE

viii

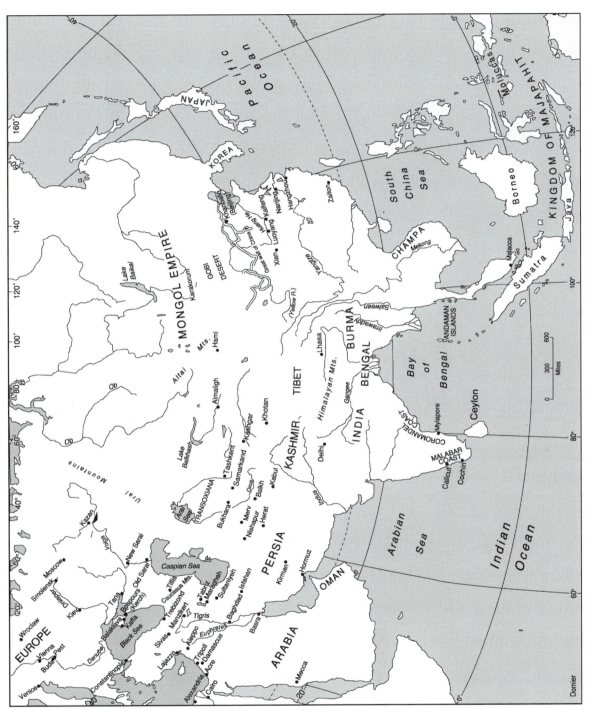

Asia, 1211–1239 CE

INTRODUCTION

The study of Islam as a religion and the languages of the Middle East, especially Arabic and Persian, has gained in prominence. In the West, a common misperception exists that there is something intrinsic in Islam as a religion that engenders acts of violence and terrorism and that Islamics history is replete with instances of pogroms against non-Muslims. On the contrary, the origin of violent acts lies not in the ontology of any given religion whether Islam, Judaism, or Christianity, in any given Scripture whether the Qur'an, Torah, or Bible, or in any given civilization whether Islamic, Greek, or Roman, but rather in a number of factors, including the psychology of human behavior and the often desperate and trying human conditions that compel humans to carry out desperate acts in times of war and peace, sometimes in the name of religion. The historian of any civilization or historical epoch is keenly aware that no premodern (medieval) society was left unscathed by warfare and political conflicts. Lamentably, until now the paucity of easily accessible English language reference sources about the medieval Islamic world has led to a situation in which some discourses concerning the clash of civilizations, current affairs, and modern ideologies and nationalisms have become synonymous with the whole of Islamic civilization. By contrast, the scholar is able to communicate the defining characteristics of a civilization and is moreover, able to critically understand and engage the Islamic world on its own terms—as heir to one of the world's greatest civilizations, not simply as heir to a world religion whose adherents have historically been in conflict with adherents of other faiths.

Despite increased and indeed, highly successful efforts in the academy to teach about Islam as a religion and the Arabic language, the larger civilizational contextual framework of which both are a part is often ignored and marginalized. Medieval Islamic civilization left an indelible mark on Europe in the transmission of knowledge and ideas in such diverse fields as science, medicine, mathematics, literature, and philosophy.

Medieval Islamic Civilization: An Encyclopedia represents a collaborative effort at bridging the gap between that which we perceive Islam and Islamic civilization to be about and what it really is by providing the reader with an easily accessible reference work presented in a concise language.

Such fundamental questions as to what Islamic civilization is and what Muslims did to contribute to European understanding of the sciences, mathematics, arts, literature, philosophy, and government remain largely unanswered. What was the nature of "interfaith" relations in the Islamic world, and what roles did Jews and Christians play in medieval Islamic societies? As a number of the entries highlight, Jews and Christians attained prominent government posts under various Islamic dynasties from Andalusia and Egypt to Iraq and contributed to the preservation and translation of philosophical and theological texts from Greek, Syriac, and Hebrew into Arabic and other Islamic languages, as well as to the creation of new literary and cultural syntheses borne of a common Islamic cultural milieu. These are among the themes that the entries in this work seek to explore. It is our hope that this work will go a long way toward filling the gaps in knowledge.

Audience

The English-speaking world lacks a single reference work that presents Islamic civilization in a manner intelligible to the nonspecialist. Specialist reference works are numerous and offer more detailed and technical articles about various aspects of Islam from pre-Islamic times to the present. The nonspecialist who desires to understand Islamic civilization is left with few choices except to consult general reference works or works devoted to the European Middle Ages, which only give a fragmented picture of medieval Islamic civilization.

It is to be hoped that the nonspecialist reader, as well as university and secondary school students and teachers, will benefit from this work.

Conception and Genesis

Medieval Islamic Civilization was conceived to share our knowledge as experts in the field of Islamic history and civilization and to correct the misconceptions and misinformation that exist. This impetus encouraged me to take up the challenge of helping to produce a unique reference work. However, it must be emphasized that this is very much an international collaborative effort that includes contributions by leading experts in their fields from North America, Europe, and Asia. Contributors come from various academic backgrounds and employ a diversity of approaches. Each of the entries adopts a unique approach to a given topic and is written dispassionately without regard to current political exigencies or political considerations. *Medieval Islamic Civilization* presents cutting-edge research into such pivotal themes relating to daily life, the ethnic and religious communities of the Islamic world, their beliefs and practices, interfaith relations, popular culture and religion, cultural, economic, and political contacts and exchanges with Europe and Asia, learning and universities, and travel and exploration. It provides a comprehensive portrait of the artistic, intellectual, literary, medical, and scientific achievements of Muslims, Jews, Christians, and others who contributed to the flourishing of one of the greatest civilizations known to humankind. Most of the authors are the leading international experts in their field. Yet all the contributions represent the highest standards in scholarship on the Islamic world.

Choice of Entries

While it is impossible to discuss every facet of Islamic civilization in a two-volume reference—nonspecialist encyclopedias are selective by nature—the choice of entries reflects the diversity of the subjects that are covered herein. The editorial board discussed the entries extensively, and certain additions and emendations were made to compensate for underrepresented themes. Unlike other volumes in this highly acclaimed Routledge series on the Middle Ages that are more geographically specific and are focused on the European Middle Ages from the fifth through sixteenth centuries CE, *Medieval Islamic Civilization* posed a considerable challenge given the geographical expanse of the Islamic world, from the Iberian Peninsula and North Africa to the Middle East, South and Southeast Asia from roughly the sixth through seventeenth centuries. Unlike other reference works, *Medieval Islamic Civilization* has de-emphasized historical themes in favor of an original synthesis that gives greater prominence to aspects of daily life and to the non-Arab elements of Islamic civilization.

The Islamic Middle Ages is taken to represent the period from 622 CE, or the first year of the Hijra of the Prophet Muhammad to Medina, which also marks the first year of the Islamic calendar, though we have also included entries that deal with pre-Islamic themes, peoples, and societies down until the seventeenth century in the case of Southeast Asia, where no significant written records exist for earlier periods.

Indeed, the seventeenth and early eighteenth centuries represent the most significant period for written records in Southeast Asia. However, this demarcation is somewhat arbitrary. Indeed, it may be argued that certain continuities existed in Islamic civilization down until the advent of modern secular and national ideologies in the nineteenth century CE.

Acknowledgments

The Board is pleased that so many of our colleagues from around the world recognized the value of *Medieval Islamic Civilization* as not simply another reference work and so enthusiastically answered the call to contribute. We are especially grateful for their inspiring level of commitment and dedication to this initiative and their high-quality contributions.

I would also like to thank the advisory board members for their unstinting dedication, the associate editors Julia Bray and Lutz Richter-Bernburg for expending considerable efforts in commenting on and suggesting revisions to various entries, and to Jere Bacharach for his overall invaluable contributions to *Medieval Islamic Civilization*. I am also grateful to Asma Afsaruddin and Donald Whitcomb for their recommendations. I am especially grateful to the former for agreeing to write a number of significant entries.

This work would not have been possible without the indefatigable efforts and abiding enthusiasm of the editors and publishers at Routledge, in particular Marie-Claire Antoine and Jamie Ehrlich. Also, thanks to the various Routledge staff members who were involved in the early stages of the project.

Finally, it is only fitting that I should pen these words from the Middle East after last having lived here nearly eight years ago.

Josef (Yousef) Waleed Meri
Amman, Jordan

MEDIEVAL SERIES NOTE

The Routledge Encyclopedias of the Middle Ages

Formerly the Garland Encyclopedias of the Middle Ages, this comprehensive series began in 1993 with the publication of *Medieval Scandinavia*. A major enterprise in medieval scholarship, the series brings the expertise of scholars specializing in myriad aspects of the medieval world together in a reference source accessible to students and the general public, as well as to historians and scholars in related fields. Each volume focuses on a geographical area or theme important to medieval studies and is edited by a specialist in that field, who has called upon a board of consulting editors to establish the article list and review the articles. Each article is contributed by a scholar and followed by a bibliography and cross-references to guide further research.

Routledge is proud to carry on the tradition established by the first volumes in this important series. As the series continues to grow, we hope that it will provide the most comprehensive and detailed view of the medieval world in all its aspects ever presented in encyclopedia form.

Vol. 1   *Medieval Scandinavia: An Encyclopedia.* Edited by Phillip Pulsiano.
Vol. 2   *Medieval France: An Encyclopedia.* Edited by William W. Kibler and Grover A. Zinn.
Vol. 3   *Medieval England: An Encyclopedia.* Edited by Paul E. Szarmach, M. Teresa Tavormina, and Joel T. Rosenthal.
Vol. 4   *Medieval Archaeology: An Encyclopedia.* Edited by Pamela Crabtree.
Vol. 5   *Trade, Travel, and Exploration in the Middle Ages.* Edited by John Block Friedman and Kristen Mossler Figg.
Vol. 6   *Medieval Germany: An Encyclopedia.* Edited by John M. Jeep.
Vol. 7   *Medieval Jewish Civilization: An Encyclopedia.* Edited by Norman Roth.
Vol. 8   *Medieval Iberia: An Encyclopedia.* Edited by E. Michael Gerli.
Vol. 9   *Medieval Italy: An Encyclopedia.* Edited by Christopher Kleinhenz.
Vol. 10   *Medieval Ireland: An Encyclopedia.* Edited by Seán Duffy.
Vol. 11   *Medieval Science, Technology, and Medicine: An Encyclopedia.* Edited by Stephen J. Livesey.
Vol. 12   *Key Figures in Medieval Europe: An Encyclopedia.* Edited by Richard K. Emmerson.

The present volume, *Medieval Islamic Civilization: An Encyclopedia*, edited by Josef W. Meri, is Volume 13 in the series.

EDITOR

Josef W. Meri
Fellow and Special Scholar in Residence
Aal al-Bayt Foundation for Islamic Thought, Amman, Jordan

EDITORIAL BOARD

CONTRIBUTORS

Rachid Aadnani
Wellesley College

Asma Afsaruddin
University of Notre Dame

Roger Allen
University of Pennsylvania

Adel Allouche
Yale University

Ilai Alon
Tel Aviv University and University of Chicago

Suat Alp
Hacettepe University

Zumrut Alp
Istanbul Bilgi University

Joseph P. Amar
University of Notre Dame

Mohammad Ali Amir-Moezzi
Université de Paris-Sorbonne

Reuven Amitai
Hebrew University of Jerusalem

Glaire D. Anderson
Massachusetts Institute of Technology

Ali Asani
Harvard University

Mahmut Ay
Ankara University

Sussan Babaie
University of Michigan

Patricia L. Baker
Independent Scholar

Anne K. Bang
University of Bergen

Meir M. Bar-Asher
Hebrew University of Jerusalem

Carol Bargeron
Texas State University

Cedric Barnes
University of London

Doris Behrens-Abouseif
University of London

Persis Berlekamp
University of Texas, Austin

Lutz Richter-Bernburg
University of Tubingen

Zvi Aziz Ben-Dor
New York University

Thierry Bianquis
University of Lyon

Hans Hinrich Biesterfeldt
Ruhr-Universität Bochum

Michal Biran
Hebrew University of Jerusalem

Nader El-Bizri
Institute of Ismaili Studies

Khalid Yahya Blankinship
Temple University

Jonathan M. Bloom
Boston College

Michel Boivin
EHESS/CNRS, Paris

CONTRIBUTORS

Stuart J. Borsch
Assumption College

Ross Brann
Cornell University

Julia Bray
University of Paris, St. Denis

William M. Brinner
University of California, Berkeley

Sebastian Brock
University of Oxford

Rainer Brunner
Universität Freiburg

Richard W. Bulliet
Columbia University

Birsen Bulmus
Georgetown University

Charles E. Butterworth
University of Maryland

Amila Buturovic
York University

Carmen Caballero-Navas
University College London

Pierre J. Cachia
Columbia University

Giovanni Canova
Universita di Napoli

Stefano Carboni
Metropolitan Museum of Art

Michael G. Carter
University of Oslo

Paola Carusi
Università degli Studi di Roma

Brian A. Catlos
University of California, Santa Cruz

Driss Cherkaoui
College of William and Mary

Jamsheed Choksy
Indiana University

Aboubakr Chraibi
Institut National des Langues et Civilisations, Paris

Niall Christie
University of British Columbia

Paul M. Cobb
University of Notre Dame

Mark R. Cohen
Princeton University

David Cook
Rice University

Michael Cooperson
University of California, Los Angeles

Farhad Daftary
Institute of Ismaili Studies

Touraj Daryaee
California State University, Fullerton

Olga M. Davidson
Harvard University

Richard Davis
Ohio State University

Cristina de la Puente
Institute of Philology, CSIC, Madrid

Jesus De Prado Plumed
Universidad Complutense, Madrid

Jonathan P. Decter
Brandeis University

Khalid Dhorat
Dar-al Salam Islamic Center

Eerik Dickinson
Hebrew University of Jerusalem

Amikam Elad
Hebrew University of Jerusalem

Alexander E. Elinson
Queens College, City University of New York

Amira El-Zein
Tufts University

Gerhard Endress
Ruhr-Universität Bochum

Daphna Ephrat
Open University of Israel

Muhammad H. Fadel
Independent Scholar

Rizwi Faizer
Independent Scholar

Sunni M. Fass
Indiana University

Paul B. Fenton
Université de Paris-Sorbonne

Maribel Fierro
Institute of Philology, CSIC, Madrid

Reuven Firestone
Hebrew Union College

Finbarr Barry Flood
New York University

Daniel Frank
Ohio State University

Yehoshua Frenkel
University of Haifa

Bruce Fudge
New York University

Adam Gacek
McGill University

Roland-Pierre Gayraud
Le Laboratoire d'Archéologie Médiévale Méditerranéenne

Eric Geoffroy
Université Marc Bloch

Kambiz GhaneaBassiri
Reed College

Antonella Ghersetti
Università Ca' Foscari

Claude Gilliot
University of Aix-en-Provence

Robert Gleave
University of Bristol

Valerie Gonzalez
Clark University

Matthew S. Gordon
Miami University

William Granara
Harvard University

Frank Griffel
Yale University

Christiane Gruber
University of Pennsylvania

Beatrice Gruendler
Yale University

Li Guo
University of Notre Dame

Kim Haines-Eitzen
Cornell University

Leor Halevi
Texas A&M University

Philip Halldén
Lund University

Abbas Hamdani
University of Wisconsin, Milwaukee

Marlé Hammond
University of Oxford

Andras Hamori
Princeton University

Eric Hanne
Florida Atlantic University

Tilman Hannemann
Universität Bremen

Gerald R. Hawting
University of London

CONTRIBUTORS

Bernard Haykel
New York University

Gisela Helmecke
Staatliche Museem zu Berlin

Konrad Hirschler
Universität Kiel

Jan P. Hogendijk
University of Utrecht

Livnat Holtzman
Bar-Ilan University

Th. Emil Homerin
University of Rochester

James Howard-Johnston
University of Oxford

Rachel T. Howes
*California State University,
Northridge*

Qamar-ul Huda
Boston College

Colin Imber
University of Manchester

Tariq al-Jamil
North Carolina State University

Jan Jansen
Universiteit Leiden

Steven C. Judd
Southern Connecticut State University

Yuka Kadoi
University of Edinburgh

Hossein Kamaly
Columbia University

Ahmad Karimi-Hakkak
University of Maryland

Hassan Khalilieh
University of Haifa

Nurten Kilic-Schubel
Kenyon College

Hilary Kilpatrick
University of Zurich

Leah Kinberg
Tel Aviv University

David A. King
Johann Wolfgang Goethe University

Verena Klemm
University of Leipzig

Alexander Knysh
University of Michigan

Philip G. Kreyenbroek
University of Göttingen

Kathryn Kueny
Lawrence University

Scott A. Kugle
Swarthmore College

Michael Laffan
Princeton University

Arzina R. Lalani
Institute of Ismaili Studies

Ruth Lamdan
Tel Aviv University

Hermann Landolt
Institute of Ismaili Studies

George Lane
University of London

Margaret Larkin
University of California, Berkeley

Gary Leiser
Independent Scholar

Judith Lerner
Independent Art Historian

P. Lettinck
*International Institute for Islamic Thought and
Civilization, Kuala Lumpur*

Yaacov Lev
Bar-Ilon University

Keith Lewinstein
Bridgewater State College

Joseph E. Lowry
University of Pennsylvania

Scott C. Lucas
University of Arizona

Al-Husein N. Madhany
University of Chicago

Roxani Eleni Margariti
Emory University

Louise Marlow
Wellesley College

Andrew Marsham
University of Cambridge

Ulrich Marzolph
Enzyklopädie des Märchens

Christopher Melchert
University of Cambridge

John L. Meloy
American University of Beirut

Charles P. Melville
University of Cambridge

Josef W. Meri
Aal al-Bayt Foundation for Islamic Thought

Alan Mikhail
University of California, Berkeley

Isabel Miller
Institute of Ismaili Studies

Colin Paul Mitchell
Dalhousie University

Jawid Mojaddedi
Rutgers University

James E. Montgomery
University of Cambridge

Shmuel Moreh
Hebrew University of Jerusalem

Michael G. Morony
University of California, Los Angeles

David Morray
University College, Dublin

Robert Morrison
Whitman College

Suleiman A. Mourad
Middlebury College

Hasan M. al-Naboodah
United Arab Emirates University

Azim Nanji
Institute of Ismaili Studies

John A. Nawas
Katholieke Universiteit Leuven

Angelika Neuwirth
Freie Universität Berlin

Andrew J. Newman
University of Edinburgh

Mehri Niknam
The Maimonides Foundation

York Allan Norman
Georgetown University

Alastair Northedge
Université de Paris-Sorbonne

Erik S. Ohlander
Indiana University/Purdue University, Fort Wayne

Mehmet Sait Özervarli
Center for Islamic Studies, Istanbul

Oya Pancaroglu
University of Oxford

Irmeli Perho
Finnish Institute in the Middle East

Andrew Petersen
United Arab Emirates University

Daniel C. Peterson
Brigham Young University

CONTRIBUTORS

Karen Pinto
American University of Beirut

Peter E. Pormann
University of London

Venetia Porter
The British Museum

David Stephan Powers
Cornell University

Tahera Qutbuddin
University of Chicago

Intisar Rabb
Yale University

Babak Rahimi
University of California, San Diego

Leonhard E. Reis
Österreichische Akademie der Wissenschaften

Gabriel Said Reynolds
University of Notre Dame

Lutz Richter-Bernburg
Universität Tübingen

Sajjad H. Rizvi
University of Exeter

Cynthia Robinson
Cornell University

James I. Robinson
University of Chicago

Michael J. Rogers
The Nour Foundation

Leyla Rouhi
Williams College

David J. Roxburgh
Harvard University

D. Fairchild Ruggles
University of Ilinois, Urbana-Champaign

Adam Sabra
Western Michigan University

Noha Sadek
Institut Francais du Proche Orient

Marlis J. Saleh
University of Chicago

Walid Saleh
University of Toronto

Paula Sanders
Rice University

Nil Sari
Istanbul Universitesi

Huseyin Sarioglu
Istanbul Universitesi

Mufit Selim Saruhan
University of Ankara

Tsugitaka Sato
University of Tokyo

Sara Scalenghe
Georgetown University

Sabine Schmidtke
Freie Universität Berlin

Fred Scholz
Freie Universität Berlin

Warren C. Schultz
DePaul University

Stuart D. Sears
Roger Williams University

Recep Senturk
Center for Islamic Studies, Istanbul

Delfina Serrano Ruano
Institute of Philology, CSIC, Madrid

Mustafa Shah
University of London

Reza Shah-Kazemi
Institute of Ismaili Studies

Ayman Shihadeh
University of Glasgow

Boaz Shoshan
Ben-Gurion University of the Nagrev

Kemal Silay
Indiana University

Adam Silverstein
University of Cambridge

John Masson Smith
University of California, Berkeley

Pieter Smoor
Universiteit van Amsterdam

Manu P. Sobti
Georgia Institute of Technology and Southern Polytechnic State University

Jochen Sokoly
Virginia Commonwealth University School of the Arts, Qatar

Bruna Soravia
Luiss University

Denise A. Spellberg
University of Texas, Austin

Peter Starr
Living Human Heritage, Zurich

Devin J. Stewart
Emory University

Paula R. Stiles
University of St. Andrews

Norman A. Stillman
University of Oklahoma

Ian B. Straughn
University of Chicago

Gotthard Strohmaier
Freie Universität Berlin

Sarah Stroumsa
Hebrew University of Jerusalem

Fahmida Suleman
Institute of Ismaili Studies

Mark N. Swanson
Luther Seminary

Samy Swayd
San Diego State University

Richard C. Taylor
Marquette University

Baki Tezcan
University of California, Davis

Marina A. Tolmacheva
Washington State University

Shawkat M. Toorawa
Cornell University

Houari Touati
EHESS, Paris

Alain Touwaide
Smithsonian National Museum of History

William F. Tucker
University of Arkansas

Richard Turnbull
Fashion Institute of Technology

John P. Turner
Kennesaw State University

Geert Jan van Gelder
University of Oxford

Maria Jesus Viguera-Molins
Universidad Complutense, Madrid

Knut S. Vikør
University of Bergen

Paul E. Walker
University of Chicago

Seth Ward
University of Wyoming

Rachel Ward
The British Museum

Anthony Welch
University of Victoria, British Columbia

Brannon Wheeler
University of Washington

CONTRIBUTORS

Clare E. Wilde
Georgetown University

Stéfan Winter
Université du Québec à Montréal

Jonathan David Wyrtzen
Georgetown University

Huseyin Yazici
Istanbul Universitesi

Yetkin Yildirim
University of Texas, Austin

Netice Yildiz
Eastern Mediterranean University

Douglas Young
Stanford University

Hayrettin Yucesoy
Saint Louis University

Homayra Ziad
Yale University

LIST OF ENTRIES A TO Z

A

'Abbasids
'Abd al-Latif al-Baghdadi
'Abd al-Malik ibn Marwan
'Abd al-Rahman III
Abu Bakr
Abu Hanifa
Abu 'l-'Ala' al-Ma'arri
Abu 'l-Fadl al-Bayhaqi
Abu 'l-Fadl 'Allami
Abu Nuwas
Abu Shama
Abu Tammam
Abyssinia
Adab
Aden
'Adud al-Dawla
Adultery
Afterlife
Aghlabids
Agra Red Fort
Agriculture
'A'isha bint Abi Bakr
Akbar
Alchemy
Alcohol
Aleppo
Alexander
Alexandria
Algebra
Alhambra
'Ali al-Rida
'Ali ibn Abi Talib
Almohads
Almoravids
Alp Arslan
Alphabets
Amir Khusraw
Amuli, al-
Andalus
Angels
Animal Husbandry
'Antara ibn Shaddad
Apostasy
Apprenticeship

Aqsa Mosque
Aqueducts
Arabia
Arabic
Arabs
Aramaeans
Aramaic
Architecture, Secular—Palaces
Architecture, Secular—Military
Archives and Chanceries
Aristotle and Aristotelianism
Arwa
Ascetics and Asceticism
Askiya Muhammad Touare
Assassins, Ismaili
Astrolabes
Astrology
Astronomy
'Attar, Farid al-Din
Autobiographical Writings
Aya Sophia
'Ayn Jalut
Ayyubids
Azhar, al-

B

Babar
Backgammon
Badr al-Jamali
Badshahi Mosque, Lahore
Baghdad
Bahrain
Bakri, al-, Geographer
Balkans
Baraka
Barani, Zia' al-Din,
Basra
Baths and Bathing
Baybars I, Mamluk Sultan
Beauty and Aesthetics
Berber, or Tamazight
Berbers
Beverages
Bible

THEMATIC LIST OF ENTRIES

Agriculture, Animal Husbandry, and Hunting

Agriculture
Animal Husbandry
Aqueducts
Camels
Horticulture
Hunting
Nomadism and Pastoralism
Sedentarism

Arts and Architecture

Agra Red Fort
Alhambra
Aqsa Mosque
Architecture, Secular—Military
Architecture, Secular—Palaces
Aya Sophia
Badshahi Mosque, Lahore
Baths and Bathing
Beauty and Aesthetics
Books
Carpets
Ceramics
Dome of the Rock
Furniture and Furnishings
Gardens and Gardening
Glassware
Houses
Jewelry
Madrasa
Metalwork
Mosaics
Mosque of Ibn Tulun, Cairo
Mosques
Music
Musical Instruments
Painting, Miniature
Painting, Monumental and Frescoes

Paper Manufacture
Performing Artists
Poetry
Qutb Minar
Sculpture
Selimiye Mosque, Edirne
Shadow Plays
Shahnama
Sinan
Singing
Süleymaniye Mosque
Sunni Revival
Taj Mahal
Talismans and Talismanic Objects
Textiles
Theater
Umayyad Mosque, Damascus
Urbanism
Women, Patrons
Ziryab

Commerce and Economy

Cartography
Chess
Credit
Land Tenure and Ownership, or Iqta'
Markets
Merchants, Jewish
Merchants, Muslim
Minerals
Mining
Money Changers
Navigation
Road Networks
Ships and Shipbuilding
Silk Roads
Slaves and Slave Trade, Eastern Islamic World
Slaves and Slave Trade, Western Islamic World
Spices
Technology, Mills, Water, and Wind

Geography

History and Historical Concepts

Language

Sibawayh
Syriac
Turkish and Turkic Languages
Urdu

Law and Jurisprudence

Abu Hanifa
Adultery
Apostasy
Bukhari, al-
Commanding Good and Forbidding Evil
Constitution of Medina
Consultation, or Shura
Crime and Punishment
Customary Law
Disability
Divorce
Ethics
Heresy and Heretics
Idolatry
Ibn Hanbal
Inheritance
Ja'far al-Sadiq
Judges
Land Tenure and Ownership
Law and Jurisprudence
Maimonides
Malik ibn Anas
Marriage, Islamic
Marriage, Jewish
Mawardi, al-
Muhammad al-Baqir
Muslim ibn al-Hajjaj
Prisons
Reform, or Islah
Renewal (Tajdid)
Schools of Jurisprudence
Sa'adyah Gaon
Schools of Jurisprudence
Shafi'i, al-
Shari'a
Shawkani, al-
Shi'ism
Usury and Interest
Waqf
Zaydis

Learning

Azhar, al-
Degrees, or Ijaza

Education, Islamic
Education, Jewish
Humanism
Libraries
Madrasa
Manuscripts
Primary Schools, or Kuttab
Scholarship
Seeking Knowledge
Translation, Arabic to Hebrew
Translation, Arabic to Persian
Translation, Pre-Islamic Learning into Arabic

Literature

Adab
Amir Khusraw
'Antara ibn Shaddad
'Attar, Farid al-Din
Autobiographical Writings
Biography and Biographical Works
Decadence
Elegy
Epic Poetry
Epics, Arabic
Epics, Persian
Epics, Turkish
European Literature, Perception of Islam
Excellences Literature
Ferdowsi
Folk Literature, Arabic
Folk Literature, Persian
Folk Literature, Turkish
Foreigners
Hafsa bint al-Hajj al-Rukuniyya
    (Andalusian Poetess)
Harizi, Judah, al-
Humor
Ibn Gabirol
Ibn Hamdis
Ibn al-Muqaffa
Ibn Naghrela, Samuel
Ibn Qutayba
Ibn Quzman
Ibn Sa'd
Ibn Shahin, Nissim ben Jacob
Jahiz, al-
Jami
Judah ha-Levi
Jurjani, Al-
Kalila wa Dimna
Love poetry
Maqama

Mirrors for Princes
One Thousand and One Nights
Poetry, Arabic
Poetry, Hebrew
Poetry, Persian
Poetry, Indian
Popular Literature
Prophets, Tales of
Rhetoric
Shahnama
Sira
Translation

Magic and Divinatory Arts

Astrology
Divination
Dreams and Dream Interpretation
Talismans and Talismanic Objects

Medicine

Black Death
Death and Dying
Disability
Folk Medicine
Food and Diet
Hunayn ibn Ishaq
Ibn al-Haytham, or Alhazen
Ibn al-Nafis
Ibn Sina
Maimonides
Majusi, Al-
Medical Literature, Hebrew
Medical Literature, Persian
Medical Literature, Syriac
Medical Literature, Turkish
Mental Illness
Ophthalmology
Optics
Pharmocology
Razi, al-, or Rhazes
Surgery and Surgical Techniques

Mythical Beings and Places

Angels
Jinn
Mythical Places

Natural Disasters and Weather

Climate, Theories of
Earthquakes
Floods
Meteorology

Personal Hygiene and Cosmetics

Baths and Bathing
Cosmetics
Perfume
Personal Hygiene

Persons

Individuals

'Abd al-Latif al-Baghdadi
'Abd al-Malik ibn Marwan
'Abd al-Rahman III
Abu 'l-'Ala' al-Ma'arri
Abu Bakr
Abu'l-Fadl 'Allami
Abu 'l-Fadl al-Bayhaqi
Abu Hanifa
Abu Nuwas
Abu Shama
Abu Tammam
'Adud al-Dawla
Akbar
Alexander
'Ali al-Rida
'Ali ibn Abi Talib
Alp Arslan
Amir Khusraw
Amuli, al-
'Antara ibn Shaddad
Arwa
Askiya Muhammad Touare
Awliya', Nizam al-Din
Babar
Badr al-Jamali
Bakri, al-, Geographer
Barani, Zia' al-Din, Historian of
    Pre-Mughal India
Bayazid, Yildirim
Baybars I, Mamluk Sultan
Bilal al-Habashi
Biruni, al-

Razi, al-, or Rhazes
Razia Sultana
Sa'adyah Gaon
Saladin, or Salah al-Din
Salman al-Farisi
Shafi'i, al-
Shah Abbas
Shajar al-Durr
Shawkani, al-
Shirazi, al-, Sadr al-Din
Sibawayh
Sibt ibn al-Jawzi
Sinan
Sirhindi, Ahmad
Suhrawardi, al-, Shihab al-Din 'Umar
Sunni 'Ali
Tabari, al-
Tamerlane, or Timur
Tawhidi, al-, Abu 'l-Hayyan
Tusi, al-, Nasir al-Din
'Umar ibn 'Abd al-'Aziz
'Umar ibn al-Farid
'Umar ibn al-Khattab
Usama ibn Munqidh
'Uthman ibn 'Affan
Waqidi, al-
Ya'qub ibn Killis
Yaqut
Zayd ibn Thabit
Ziryab

Peoples

Arabs
Aramaeans
Berbers
Circassians
Copts
Jews
Kurds
Mongols
Persians
Turks

Philosophy and Thought

Amuli, al-
Aristotle and Aristotelianism
Brethren of Purity
Freethinkers
Gnosis
Kirmani, al-, Hamid al-Din

Ibn al-Rawandi
Ibn Rushd
Ibn Sina
Ibn Tufayl
Ibn Zur'a
Illuminationism
Farabi, al- (Alfarabius or Avennasar)
Kindi, al-
Maimonides
Mu'ayyad fi al-Din, Al-
Mulla Sadra
Plato, Platonism, and Neoplatonism
Philosophy
Razi, al-, or Rhazes
Shirazi, al-, Sadr al-Din
Tawhidi, al-, Abu Hayyan
Tusi, al-, Muhammad ibn Hasan
Time, Notions of

Places and Place Study

Abyssinia
Aden
Aleppo
Alexandria
Andalus
Arabia
Baghdad
Bahrain
Balkans
Basra
Bijapur
Brunei
Bukhara
Cairo
Central Asia, History
China
Cordoba
Cyprus
Damascus
Egypt
Fez
Fustat
Ghana
Gibraltar
Granada
Hebron
Herat
India
Isfahan
Istanbul
Java
Jerusalem

Ka'ba, or Kaaba
Karbala
Khurasan
Kilwa
Kufa
Malay Peninsula
Mecca
Mediterranean Sea
Medina
Nile
Nishapur
Oman
Palestine
Qayrawan
Samarqand
Samarra
Seville
Sicily
Sindh
Sudan
Syria, Greater Syria
Transoxiana
Tus
Yemen

Professions, Groups, and Societies

Apprenticeship
Eunuchs
Franks, or Ifranj
Guilds, Professional
Merchants, Christian
Merchants, Jewish
Merchants, Muslim
Money Changers
Peasants
Performing Artists
Qur'an, Reciters and Recitation
Scholars
Scribes, Copyists
Singing
Tribes and Tribal Customs
Urbanism

Religion and Theology

Abu 'l-Fadl al-Bayhaqi
Kulayni, al-
Afterlife
Angels
Aramaeans

Ascetics and Asceticism
Ash'aris
Assasins, Ismaili
Awliya', Nizam al-Din
Bible
Buddhism and Islam
Bukhari
Caliphate and Imamate
Christians and Christianity
Copts
Dates and Calendars
Dhimma
Disability
Druze
Emigration, or Hijra
Eschatology
Funerary Practices, JewishMuslim
Funerary Practices, Muslim
Ghazali, al-
Hadith
Hajj
Heresy and Heretics
Hilli, al-, al-'Allama
Ibadis
Ibn Babawayh
Ibn Hanbal
Ibn Taymiyya
Idolatry
Imam
Islam
Ismailis
Ja'far al-Sadiq
Jesus
Jews
Jihad
Ka'ba
Kabbala
Karaites
Kharijis
Khuza'i, Ahmad ibn Nasr
Majlisi, al-
Malik ibn Abas
Malikism
Marriage, Islamic
Marriage, Jewish
Martyrdom
Mawardi, al-
Mecca
Medina
Messianism
Mir Damad
Monasticism, Arab
Mu'ayyad fi al-Din, al-
Muhammad, the Prophet
Muhammad al-Baqir

L

LAND TENURE AND OWNERSHIP, OR *IQTA'*

Iqta' is an Arabic term designating the land or tax revenues allocated by the great amir or sultan to soldiers in return for military service *(khidma)*. *Khubz* (bread) was synonymous with this term in Ayyubid and Mamluk Egypt and in Syria. Its holder was called *muqta'* in Arabic and *iqta'dar* in Persian.

Qati'a and Day'a in the Early Islamic Period

Three Sunnite schools of law (the Shafi'is, Malikis, and Hanbalis), but not the Hanafis, regard that the land conquered by force belonged to the Muslim community as *fay'*, which was not to be assigned to the Arabs. However, since the early Islamic period it was often granted as *qati'a* to the people who rendered distinguished services to the state. According to al-Mawardi (d. 1058 CE), the iqta's in Islamic law are classified into two types. The first type is an "iqta' of private ownership" *(iqta' al-tamlik)*, which means privately owned land assigned by the state, provided that owners pay the land tax *(kharaj)* or the tithe *('ushr)* according to land category. The second type is an "iqta' of usufruct" *(iqta' al-istighlal)*, by which revenue from a piece of land is apportioned in place of a salary (al-Ahkam al-sultaniya: 190–198). The first type of iqta' is termed *qati'a* in the early historical sources, while the second type of iqta' designates the military iqta' since the middle of the tenth century.

Apart from the qati'a, the privately owned land that was valid for the duration of life was called *tu'ma*, and other privileged landownership appeared, such as *ighar*, carrying with it partial immunity from taxation, and taswigh, having complete immunity from taxation. As C. Cahen suggests, based on such privileged landownership, large-scale landownership developed gradually from the Umayyad to the 'Abbasid periods. A.A. al-Duri further advanced this topic, showing that the land system was connected closely with the origin of the iqta' system (1969:3–22). He states that in the early Islamic period there rose a new aristocracy who held the qati'a assigned from treasury lands *(sawafi)*. Besides, since the cultivated land was evaluated as a source for stable income during the 'Abbasid period, tax collectors aimed at obtaining private domains *(day'a)*, and merchants also invested their commercial profits to purchase day'a. According to J. Shimada, large-scale day'as were invented by such means as reclamation, promise of protection, and enclosure *(hawz)*, whereas small-scale qati'as were apportioned by the person superior in rank (caliph or provincial governor). The state coffers thus suffered as such privileged landownership by merchants, high officials, and the Turkish commanders developed, particularly in Iraq after the ninth century.

As Turkish soldiers (mamluks or ghulams) extended their power after the middle of the ninth century, the authority of the 'Abbasid caliphate declined significantly. In addition, the independence of local governors—for example, the Samanids (875–999) in Iran and the Tulunids (869–905) in Egypt—led to decreases in state revenue, which caused great fiscal difficulties. Other than the development of privileged landownership, pecuniary waste by the ‘Abbasid court also added to these difficulties. Al-Maqrizi (d. 1442), an Egyptian historian, explains that the ‘ata’ (salary) system was conducted in the early Islamic period, paying salaries to the soldiers and officials out of the state treasury (Khitat I:95). However, these serious problems made it more difficult to maintain the ‘ata’ system by the early tenth century. Accordingly, when the Buwayhid army entered Baghdad at the beginning of the year 946, the military iqta‘ system was first introduced in Islamic history.

Establishment and Development of the Iqta‘ System

Miskawayh (d. 1030) relates that Mu‘izz al-Dawla, the Buwayhid great amir, granted iqta‘s to his officers *(quwwad)*, his associates *(khawass)*, and his Turkish chivalry (Tajarib al-Umam, II, 96). A few years later, when the whole of Iraq came to be apportioned into iqta‘, small iqta‘s were granted to Daylamite foot soldiers as well. The peasants under the iqta‘ system, who now paid the land tax not to the government but to their muqta‘ (iqta‘ holder), had to bear hardships of the unjust rule of the muqta‘. According to B. Johansen, the distinction between tax *(kharaj)* and rent *(ujra)* first became vague through the spread of the iqta‘ system, which led to the fundamental changes of the rural society in the Middle East.

The Seljukids, who entered Baghdad in 1055, inherited the Buwayhid iqta‘ system almost as it was. When Tughril Bek advanced from Nishapur to Baghdad, he consolidated his authority through iqta‘ assignments to the local rulers and their subordinates. A. K. S. Lambton observes that the iqta‘ system in Islamic society was quite different from feudalism in Europe, in the sense that the element of mutual obligation inherent to European feudalism was notably absent in the iqta‘ system. Under the Seljukid rule the administrative iqta‘s, as opposed to the military iqta‘s, were granted to amirs who conducted both rights of administration and tax collection. As disclosed in Siyasat nama, Nizam al-Mulk, a Persian vizier of the Seljukids, intended to clarify the muqta‘s rights and duties, to change their iqta‘s every 2 to 3 years, and to send, if needed, supervisors to the local provinces. However, as the sultan's authority decreased after Malik Shah died in 1092, the atabeks and amirs gained independence by means of inheriting iqta‘s from their ancestors.

In Syria and Jazira, iqta‘ grants by the Zankid rulers followed the breakup of the Seljukid empire. ‘Imad al-Din Zanki (1127–1146), who entered Mosul in 1127, allocated iqta‘s to his amirs and soldiers and introduced similar allotments into Jazira and northern Syria. I. Khalil relates that each amir was assigned a district including local towns, while soldiers were granted small iqta‘s. The rights of muqta‘ during the Zankid period, as in the Seljukid period, was legally restricted to the levying of taxes on their iqta‘s; but soldiers, who wished to hold stable iqta‘s, insisted that iqta‘s were privately owned land (milk) to be inherited from father to son. Accepting this argument, Nur al-Din al-Zanki (1146–1174) consented to the inheritance of iqta‘ holdings and ordered that a guardian be chosen if the heir was still a child (Ibn al-Athir, al-Ta’rikh al-bahir, 169). This Zankid iqta‘ system was soon introduced into Egypt by Saladin (Salah al-Din).

In Fatimid Egypt, amirs and high officials held privately owned lands called qati‘a or iqta‘. According to H. Rabie, the muqta‘s were not required to provide military service except in a few cases, but they had to pay the tithe to the government. In this sense the Fatimid iqta‘ system was still different from the military iqta‘ system during the Buwayhid or Seljukid periods. When Salah al-Din was installed as the Fatimid vizier in March 1169, he began to confiscate the iqta‘s held by the Fatimid soldiers and assigned the confiscated lands to his followers in the form of iqta‘ (Abu Shama, Kitab al-rawdatayn, II, 450). As al-Maqrizi relates, from the reign of Salah al-Din, all the Egyptian lands have been distributed to the sultan, amirs, and soldiers as iqta‘s (Khitat, I, 97). In Ayyubid Syria also, the iqta‘ assignment was the most crucial factor for maintaining the Ayyubid state order. However, one of the characteristics peculiar to the Ayyubid iqta‘ system was that demands to the sultan were made concerning iqta‘ holdings. This was due to the fact that the rules and regulations of granting iqta‘s were not yet established, particularly at the early stages of the Ayyubid period.

Because iqta‘s in the early Mamluk period were often granted according to the amir's requests, iqta‘ assignments had features similar to those of the Ayyubid period. However, by the end of the thirteenth century the power of the royal Mamluks had eventually emerged. The sultans saw the necessity of getting rid of the old amirs and strengthening the basis of their power by means of their own Mamluks. To achieve this objective they twice carried out countrywide cadastral surveys, al-Rawk al-Husami (1298) and al-Rawk al-Nasiri (1313–1325). These rawks, especially al-Rawk al-Nasiri, resulted in the iqta‘ revenue *(‘ibra)* of the royal Mamluks being increased sharply at the expense of the freeborn *(halqa)* chivalry (al-Maqrizi, Khitat, I, 88). Amirs from these Mamluks operated advantageous iqta' holdings, which they used as a basis of strengthening their control over the agricultural communities in Egypt and Syria. Al-Rawk al-Nasiri has considerable historical significance in the sense that it brought about great change in the organization of the iqta' system and prescribed the state structure during the middle of the Mamluk period.

TSUGITAKA SATO

See also Waqf

Further Reading

Cahen, C. "L'evolution de l'iqta' du IX au XIII siecle." *Annales: ESC* 8 (1953): 25–52.

Al-Duri, A. A. "The Origins of Iqta' in Islam." *al-Abhath* 22 (1969): 3–22; do. *Ta'rikh al-'Iraq al-iqtisadi al-'Arabi.* Beirut, 1974.

Humphreys, R. S. *Saladin to the Mongols.* Albany, NY, 1977.

Johansen, B. *The Islamic Law on Land Tax and Rent.* London, 1988.

Khalil, I. *'Imad al-Din Zangi.* Beirut, 1967.

Lambton, A. K. S. *Landlord and Peasant in Persia.* London, 1953; do. "Reflections on the IQTA'." In *Arabic and Islamic Studies in Honor of Hamilton,* edited by G. Maqdisi, 358–376. Leiden: A.R. Gibb, 1965.

Lev, Y. *State and Society in Fatimid Egypt.* Leiden, 1991.

Rabie, H. *The Financial System of Egypt A.H. 564-741/A. D. 1169-1341.* London, 1972.

Sato, T. *The State and Rural Society in Medieval Islam: Sultans, Muqta's and Fallahun.* Leiden, 1997.

Shimada, J. *Studies on the Early Islamic State* (in Japanese: Shoki Isuramu Kokkano Kenkyu). Tokyo, 1996.

Turkhan, I. A. *al-Nuzum al-iqta'iyya fi 'l-sharq al-awsat fi 'l-'usur al-wusta.* Cairo, 1968.

LAW AND JURISPRUDENCE

Law *(fiqh,* lit. "understanding") and jurisprudence *(usul al-fiqh,* lit. "roots of understanding"). *Fiqh* is the technical term for Islamic substantive law. Developed largely by scholars, Islamic law has been described as a paradigmatic example of "jurists' law." Medieval treatises of Islamic law typically began with ritual law (purity [*tahara*], ritual prayer [*salat*], fasting [*siyam*], alms-tax [*zakat*], and pilgrimage [*hajj*]) and then proceeded to various topics of private law, such as family law, transactional law, and tort law, and various topics of public law, such as criminal law, the law of war, and constitutional law. Jurists of the medieval period also authored specialized treatises that addressed particular topics in much greater detail than could be done in the generalized treatises that were the foundational texts of both legal education and the administration of the law.

Fiqh should not be confused with Islamic ethical norms or morality. Legal treatises are principally concerned with the positive rules of Islamic law *(al-ahkam al-wad'iyya),* in contrast to rules of obligation *(al-ahkam al-taklifiyya).* Whereas the latter category of rules speaks to the status of an act (such as obligatory, forbidden, favored, disfavored, or indifferent), the former speaks to the consequences of an act (such as valid, invalid, binding, void, voidable). They are addressed not to the generality of believers but rather to legal specialists *(fuqaha')* for use in resolving judicial cases *(qada'),* and the delivery of formal legal opinions *(fatwa).*

Usul al-fiqh is, in the first instance, a philosophical and epistemological discipline that seeks to understand the source of moral obligation (for example, reason or revelation), how moral judgments may be reached (legitimate methods of moral reasoning), and the reliability of moral judgments (for example, certain or probable).

Revelation, all Muslim scholars agreed, was an infallible source of moral knowledge and as a general matter. They also agreed that the divine commands could be found in three sources: the Qur'an (the revealed word of God), the teachings and practice of the Prophet Muhammad (known generically as the *sunna*), and consensus *(ijma').* Only the contents of the Qur'an, however, were universally acknowledged. Otherwise, significant differences—both doctrinal and empirical—characterized Muslim approaches to the sunna and the doctrine of ijma'.

Usul al-fiqh also included techniques of practical reason that were to be used to determine the moral status of an act. The most important such tool was analogy *(qiyas).* Various utility-related arguments were also widely discussed (and often used), but their legitimacy was more controversial.

Finally, because of the primacy of revelation as a source of ethical knowledge, hermeneutics was a matter of central concern in usul al-fiqh. As a general matter, Muslim scholars accorded only presumptive weight to the apparent meaning of revelation, which was sufficient, in their moral theory, to give rise to moral obligation. The apparent meaning of revelation, however, could be overcome if other evidence existed demonstrating that the apparent sense was not intended. It is only the rare revelatory text that is considered, from a hermeneutical perspective, to be conclusive.

MOHAMMAD H. FADEL

See also Customary Law

Further Reading

Hallaq, Wael B. *Authority, Continuity and Change in Islamic Law*. Cambridge: Cambridge University Press, 2001.

———. *A History of Islamic Legal Theories*. Cambridge: Cambridge University Press, 1997.

Schacht, Joseph. *An Introduction to Islamic Law*. Oxford: The Clarendon Press, 1964.

LIBRARIES

Maktaba is the Arabic word normally used to mean "library," but in classical Islam, corresponding appellations were used: "treasure house of books" *(khizanat al-kutub)* or "abode of books" *(dar al-kutub,* an expression that is still in favor for a national library, such as the one in Cairo)*. In Iran, *kitab-khana,* and in modern Turkey, *kütüphane,* are the equivalents. These institutions were never one and the same in the Middle Ages as real public libraries, but the most important were part of institutions of learning created on the initiative of sovereigns or officials of the caliphal government and the different dynasties. For that reason they were also often designated by the name of institutions: House or Abode of Wisdom *(bayt or dar al-hikma),* Abode of Knowledge *(dar al-'ilm)*. From the AH fifth/eleventh CE century onward, they were often a part of the higher colleges, called *madrasas*. Individual scholars or officials, sometimes families, had also private libraries.

Since antiquity, small libraries existed in the great mosques of the most important towns of the empire, and many a scholar bequeathed his library to the mosque of his city. With time, however, many mosques also had large libraries. We shall only mention three of them. In Baghdad, we have considerable information of the library of the mosque of Abu Hanifa. Among many other famous people who bequeathed their private book collections, the grammarian, Mu'tazilite theologian, and exegete al-Zamakhshari can be mentioned (d. 538/1143).

The library of the mosque of Qayrawan in Tunisia had its time of glory under the Zirid al-Mu'izz b. Bads (r. 406–54/1015–1062), but the tribesmen of Banu Hilal destroyed most of the book collections.

Built in 245/859, the Qarawiyyin mosque of Fez had a library founded by the Marinid sultan al-Mutawakkil Abu 'Inan, which opened its doors in 750/1349. However, an earlier sultan of the same dynasty, Abu Yusuf Ya'qub (r. 656–685/1258–1290), is credited with founding a book collection at the same mosque, which had also the Mansuriyya library, established ca. 996/1587 by the scholar-king of the Sa'di dynasty, Ahmad al-Mansur al-Dhahabi.

Three Great Libraries

According to the secretary of the Mamluk chancellery, al-Qalqashandi (d. 82/1418), there were three great libraries in Islam: the House of Wisdom in Baghdad, the library of the Fatimids in Egypt, and the Spanish Umayyad in Cordoba.

Before then the historical data on public or semipublic libraries are not well supported; for instance, the establishment of the so-called House of Wisdom *(bayt al-hikma)* in Damascus by the Umayyad caliph Mu'awiya (r. 41–60/661–680). This library should have been herited by his grandson Khalid b. Yazid, who never became a caliph, and who the legend has made an alchemist. The Umayyad central administration in Damascus followed Byzantine practices by and large, and the language of administration, until the reform of 'Abd al-Malik (r. 65–86/685–705), was Greek. Umayyad employed Christians in their administration, the most famous of them being St. John of Damascus, and they could benefit from them in collecting books and translating some of them into Arabic. However, because as in the seventh century the Byzantine high culture was indifferent to pagan Greek learning. As hellenism was the defeated enemy, it was probably impossible in this intellectual climate to conceive of a translation movement, supported by Greek-speaking Christians, of secular Greek works into Arabic, as D. Gutas has shown. So it is possible to put in doubt the importance of the so-called House of Wisdom in Damascus, and its library.

With the 'Abbasid revolution, the foundation of Baghdad, and the transfer of the caliphate to Mesopotamia, the situation of the Arab empire changed drastically. A new multicultural society developed in Baghdad: Aramaic speakers, Christians and Jews, Persian-speakers, and Arabs were concentrated in the cities. The 'Abbasids had to rely on the local Persians, Christian Arabs, and Arameans for their administration. The culture of these people in the employ of the 'Abbasids was hellenized, but without the animosity of the Orthodox Christian Byzantine circles in Damascus against the ethnic Greek learning. For these reasons, the transfer of the caliphate form Damascus to Iraq had the paradoxical consequence of allowing the preservation of the classical Greek heritage, and this was not without consequences for matters of the library.

It is said that the institution of the House of Wisdom underwent its greatest development in Baghdad in the time of the 'Abbasid caliph al-Ma'mun (r. 198–208/813–833), who is considered responsible for it. The library should have come into being in conjunction with the House of Wisdom, probably on the model of the Academy of Gundishapur. However, it is also possible that a library *(khizana)* could have already existed during the time of his father, Harun al-Rashid (r. 170–193/786–809) and his viziers, the Barmakids, who had begun to have Greek works translated (see Pre-Islamic Learning into Arabic).

In fact, we know nothing about the construction, the location, and the date of foundation of the House of Wisdom. For some scholars, such as D. Gutas: "In reality we have absolutely no mention in our most reliable sources of any such 'founding.'" In Sasanian times, the palace library functioned as an idealized national archive. The term House of Wisdom is a translation of the Sasanian designation for a library, as it appears clearly from a statement of Hamza al-Isfahani (d. after 350/961). It seems that the Islamic House of Wisdom was a library, most likely established as a bureau under al-Mansur (r. 136–158/754–175). It may have been a part of the 'Abbasid administration, modeled on that of the Sasanians. It was devoted to the translation of texts from Persian to Arabic, and to the preservation of the translated books. Under al-Ma'mun it seems to have gained another function related to astronomical and mathematical activities. For the same scholar, the Greco-Arabic translation movement does not seem to have been related to any of the activities of the House of Wisdom. It was also not an academy for teaching the ancient sciences. According to al-Qalqashandi, the greatest lustre shines on the second great library—the library of the Fatimids in Cairo, a branch of the Ismailis. The Fatimid rulers aimed to create rivals to the Baghdad tradition. They founded a completely new Cairo alongside the old, erecting a magnificent palace and a mosque, al-Azhar. They fitted out libraries in the palace and also in the mosque, including their own House of Wisdom, called also Abode of Knowledge *(dar al-'ilm)* in the vast palace covering half of their new capital city of Cairo. According to a contemporary writer, al-Musabbihi (d. 420/1030), caliph al-Hakim (r. 386–411/996–1021) endowed the dar al-ilm with books on a range of subjects, from his palace treasury, and paid for the scholars to teach there and, crucially, for support staff and furnishings. The institution was open to all who wished to study there and included writing materials. The institution came under the jurisdiction of the government's head of propaganda *(da'i al-du'at)*, who invited learned men to meet there twice weekly. A new catalogue prepared in 435/1045 listed at least six and a half thousand volumes on astronomy, architecture, and philosophy. The palace and academy libraries flourished during prosperous years preceding the reign of caliph al-Muntasir (r. 427–487/1036–1094), but the

library was looted during the civil wars in 461/1068. It was closed when the Fatimid dynasty came to an end (567/1171). Salah al-Din sold the palace treasures, including the books, but fortunately some of them were repurchased by enlightened men such as Salah al-Din's learned counselor and secretary (not his vizier), the bibliophile al-Qadi al-Fadil al-Baysani (d. 596/1200). It is said that he gave one hundred thousand volumes to the school he had established, al-Madrasa al-Fadiliyya. According to another report, he collected seventy thousand volumes on diverse subjects. The great Mu'tazilite exegete and theologian 'Abd al-Salam al-Qazwini (d. 488/1095), who had lived for a long time in Cairo, had a collection of forty thousand volumes, of which some had been purchased from people who had plundered the Fatimid palace. As usual, the figures quoted by Arabic authors for the Fatimid library vary widely. Al-Maqrizi gives three figures: 120,000, 200,000, and 601,000 volumes, but Abu Shama says two million!

The third great library, according to al-Qalqashandi, was that of the Umayyad in Spain. When the Fatimids made their entry in Cairo, al-Hakam (II) al-Mustansir (r. 350–366/961–976), occupied a prominent place among the scholars and bibliophile princes of Islam. He created a vast library at Cordoba on the model of the 'Abbasid libraries of Baghdad, with some four hundred thousand volumes and a catalogue in forty-four registers of twenty sheets each. The problem in these hyperbolic figures is in the fact that among these "volumes" could have been also "fascicles" *(juz's)*. The library was in the palace of Cordoba, under the management of the eunuch Bakiya. The splendor of the library was dimmed under al-Hakam's son and successor, Hisham, in order to please the orthodox Maliki religious scholars—what was, above all, distasteful to them was the collection of books pertaining to the ancient sciences, that is, works of philosophy, astronomy, and so forth. The all-powerful al-Mansur allowed them to remove and burn these books. In 1011, when Cordoba was locked in battle with the Berbers, the minister Wadih sold the major part of the library to obtain money for the war; the rest of the books were despoiled.

Other Libraries

Besides the three libraries enhanced by al-Qalqashandi, other great libraries existed. The Buyids, a Persian house that nourished Shi'i sympathies and exercised hegemony over Iraq and Western Persia (334–447/945–1055), took into their service men with an interest in books. Rukn al-Dawla, who ruled Rayy in Western Persia, had in his service Abu l-Fadl Ibn al-'Amid (d. 360/970), a celebrated scholar with a large library, of which the historian Misakawayh was the librarian. The disciple, secretary, and then successor of Ibn al-'Amid, the man of letters al-Sahib Ibn 'Abbad (d. 385/995) had a library in Rayy; the theological works alone amounted to four hundred camel-loads (or two hundred and six thousand volumes). When Mahmud (b. Sebüktigin) of Ghazna, the defender of the "orthodox" Sunni faith, invaded Rayy, he had some of these books burnt as "heretical literature" and some sent to his capital city in 420/1029. He also plundered all the treasures of the last Buyid Majd al-Dawla, including 50 loads of books, excluding those that had Mu'tazilite content or dealt with philosophy and which were therefore burnt under the corpses of the crucified "heretics." A third Buyid vizier, the servant of Baha' al-Dawla, Zaydit Abu Nasr Sabur b. Ardashir (d. 416/1025), founded an Abode of Knowledge (ca. 383/993), in the Baghdadi quarter of "Between the two walls" (quarter of al-Karkh). Its library should have counted ten thousand volumes (according to other sources, one hundred thousand to four hundred thousand), including one hundred exemplars of the Qur'an in the handwriting of Banu Muqla. After the death of Sabur, it seems that the Shi'i poet, grammarian, and theologian al-Sharif al-Murtada (d. 436/1044) was in charge of it. It was used by many scholars, such as the Syrian man of letters Abu l-'Ala' al-Ma'arri, during his brief sojourn in Baghdad (399–400/1009–1010). This library was destroyed by fire during Tughril Beg's march on Baghdad in 451/1059. Bahram b. Mafanna (d. 433), the vizier of Abu Kalijar, which was the penultimate Buyid Amir in Baghdad, established at Firuzabad in Fars: a library consisting of seven thousand volumes, of which four thousand were folios in the handwriting of Abu 'Ali Ibn Muqla and Abu 'Abd Allah Ibn Muqla.

Almost every college (madrasa) in Baghdad had a small or large library of its own. Those attached to the Nizamiyya college (inaugurated in 459/1067), founded by the famous Saljukid vizier Nizam al-Mulk (d. 485/1092), and to the Mustansiriyya college, founded in 631/1234 by the caliph Mustansir, were particularly remarkable for their large size, as well as the value of their books. Other towns such as Nishapur, Samarqand, Tus, Bukhara, Shiraz, Isfahan, Herat, Najaf, Kerbela, Damascus, Jerusalem, Cairo, Tunis, Mecca, Medina, and Oman also had colleges with libraries, or libraries without colleges. Later, Istanbul also had libraries (such as Sülemaniye Kütüphanesi, established in 1557; Köprülü, 1661; Nurosmaniye, 1755; Raghib Pasha, 1763; and Murat Molla, 1775). In India, the first Rohilla chief of Rampur, Nawab Sayyad Faizullah Khan (r. 1175–1193), was a great patron of learning. He was at the origin of a library that was enlarged by his successors. Many private collections of books are still extant among Khariji Ibadi families (or now in public libraries) of the Algerian Mzab. The Zaydi imams of Yemen also had libraries that contained many Mu'tazili works.

Bibliophiles' Collections and Scholars' Libraries

Despite the high prices of books, many individual bibliophiles and scholars collected fine libraries. Of the traditionist and soldier of the Holy War, a model for pious Muslims—'Abd Allah b. Mubarak (d. 181/797)—it is said that: "the number of his books from which he transmitted [hadith] was twenty thousand." Here we cannot speak of a library; the so-called books were more notebooks written to help with memory. When the historian al-Waqidi died in 207/822, he left six hundred bookcases (qimatr). Ibn Hanbal's (d. 241/855) library amounted to twelve and a half camel loads, whereas that of his contemporary (who was also a traditionist like Ibn Hanbal) Yahya b. Ma'in (d. 233/847) filled one hundred and fourteen or one hundred and thirty bookcases and four large jars. Of course, for these two scholars the books or notebooks of their library consisted of hadith materials or related matters like statements on the reliability of hadith transmitters. The library of the son of the Buyid Mu'izz al-Dawla (d. 356/957) in Basra comprised some fifteen thousand volumes, in addition to fascicles and unbound sheets. Al-Qadi al-Fadil's brother is reported, with some hyperbole as usual, to have amassed two hundred thousand titles, each title in a number of copies. Al-Qifti (d. 646/1248), too, was a fervent book collector. His collection is said, again with some hyperbole, to have been the largest ever amassed. He traveled to faraway places and paid large sums (he never married and had no children) for books. He bequeathed his books (worth some fifty thousand dinars) to the ruler of Aleppo, the Ayyubid al-Malik al-Nasir. The library of the physician Sa'id al-Samiri (executed in 649/1251) contained ten thousand volumes. The Cordoban Maliki judge Abu l-Mutarrif Ibn Futays 'Abd al-Rahman (d. 402/1011) was a great collector of books. He always had six copyists working for him. He never lent a work but would willingly get it copied and make a gift of it.

The historian Ghars al-Ni'ma Muhammad b. Hilal (d. 480/1088), of the celebrated al-Sabi' family (physicians, and then official and literary men under the 'Abbasids and Buyids), collected at Baghdad a small library of one thousand volumes (with a waqf, in 452/1060), in various Islamic sciences, to which admission was granted to a limited number of students. He had the hope of replacing the library founded by Baha' al-Dawla. After the death of Ghars al-Ni'ma, the "vile and avaricious" superintendent of the library sold the books on the excuse that the installment of the Nizamiyya college in Baghdad had made Ghars al-Ni'ma's library superfluous.

The libraries of the Shi'i scholars were no less impressive than those of the Sunni. For instance, six hundred Jarudi Zaydi, author of the Kufan Ibn 'Uqda (Ahmad, d. 333/944) wanted to move his books. They amounted to six hundred loads, and the costs was accordingly one hundred dinars. We have already encountered previously the case of al-Sahib Ibn 'Abbad. Al-Sharif al-Murtada, already mentioned, left at his death thirty thousand *juz's* (fascicles), whereas others say eighty thousand volumes.

"Traveling in quest of knowledge," or seeking knowledge, offered to scholars the opportunity of visiting many libraries and of collecting books. The Iranian Avicenna (d. 428/1037), for instance, benefited from the libraries of the Iranian princes. His first visit to the royal library was in Bukhara on the invitation of the Samanid King Nuh (II) b. Mansur. He describes this personal event in the following words: "I found there many rooms filled with books which were arranged in cases row upon row. One room was alloted to works on Arabic philology and poetry; another to jurisprudence, and so forth, the books of each particular science having a room to themselves. I inspected the catalogue of ancient Greek authors and looked for the books which I required: I saw in this collection books of which few people have heard even the names, and which I myself have never seen either before or since." He also used the libraries of the town of Gurgang in Khwarizm, of the Buyids in Rayy and in Hamadhan (Shams al-Dawla), of the Kakuyids ('Ala' al-Dawla Muhammad) in Isfahan, and so forth. The example of the celebrated man of letters, bookseller and copyist Yaqut al-Rumi is also representative of that. He had extended visits to the library of Ibn al-Qiti in Aleppo, the two libraries of the family al-Sam'ani in Marw, and so on.

Books in Figures

It must be said that almost all the figures of books that are provided in this article thus far cannot, as a rule, be accepted at face value; a lot of them are hyperbolic. Many of these libraries, both "public" and private, had catalogues, but none of the six first centuries of Islam are known to have come to us. Perhaps the earliest extant known to us is the catalogue of the library of the Qayrawan mosque, dated 693/1294. A manuscript dated 694/1295 and entitled *The Selection of [the books] in the Libraries of Aleppo* was not, as its title indicates, the catalogue of a special library. One of the methods to ascertain accuracy consists in the writing of exhaustive monographies on authors. This was done, for instance, for the Shi'i scholar Ibn Tawus (d. 664/1266), who was born in Hilla and established himself in Baghdad. He wrote a catalogue of his library, which is now lost. However, thanks to a precise study, we know that his library contained some one thousand five hundred titles. It included works on all major branches of knowledge of his time. He had a ten volume copy of Koranic commentary of the Mu'tazilite Abu 'Ali al-Jubba'i (d. 303/915). Apart from the number of volumes, which is a problem, there is another one that is encountered when speaking of figures in Islamic libraries: the term *juz'* (fascicle), which can refer to several things: a gathering of sheets (often some twenty folios or more), forming a separate volume; a number of booklets bound together; a volume consisting of a number of booklets; or a notebook.

CLAUDE GILLIOT

Primary Sources

Ibn al-Nadim. *The Fihrist of Ibn al-Nadim: A Tenth-Century Survey of Muslim culture.* 2 vols. Ed. and transl. Bayard Dodge. New York: Columbia University Press, 1970.

Further Reading

Balty-Guesdon, M.G. "Le Bayt al-Hikma de Baghdad." *Arabica* XXXIX (1992): 131–50.
Bilici, F. "Les bibliothèques vakif-s à Istanbul au XVIe siècle, prémices des grandes bibliothèques publiques." *REMMM* 47–88 (1999): 39–59.
Bloom, Jonathan Max. *Paper Before Print: The history and impact of paper in the Islamic world.* New Haven: Yale University Press, 2001.
Busse, Heribert. *Chalif und Grosskönig: Die Buyiden im Irak (945–1055).* Wiesbaden: Steiner (in Kommission), Beirut: Institut der DMG, 1969; reprint Wurzburg: Ergon Verlag, 2004 (pp. 523–529, for the libraries).
Déroche, François, *Le livre manuscrit arabe: Prélude à une histoire.* Paris: Bibliothèque Nationale de France, 2004.
Eche, Youssef. *Les Bibliothèques Arabes Publiques et Semi-Publiques en Mésopotamie, en Syrie et en Égypte au Moyen Âge.* Damas: IFEAD, 1967.
Endress, Gerhard. "Hanschriftenkunde." In *Grundriss der arabischen Philologie*, I. Ed. Wolfdietrich Fischer. Wiesbaden: Ludwig Reichert Verlag, 1982, 271–296.

Gutas, Dimitri. *Greek Thought, Arabic Culture: The Greco-Arabic translation movement in Baghdad and early 'Abbasid society (second–fourth/eighth–tenth centuries)*. London and New York: Routledge, 1998.

Hamada, Muhammad Mahir. *The Libraries in Islam* (in Arabic). Beirut: Mu'assasat al-Risala, 1981 (1970) (originally Hamadeh, M.M. "Islamic Libraries during the Middle Ages". Ph.D dissertation, University of Chicago, 1962).

Al-Jawahiri, Khayal M. Mahdi. *On the History of Libraries in the Arabic Countries* (in Arabic). Damascus: Ministry of Education, 1992.

Kohlberg, Etan. *A Medieval Muslim at Work: Ibn Tawus and his library*. Leiden: Brill, 1992.

Kraemer, Joel L. *Humanism in the Renaissance of Islam: The Cultural Revival during the Bouyid Age*. 2d revised edition. Leiden: E. J. Brill, 1992 (1986¹).

Makdisi, George. "Muslim Institutions of Learning in Eleventh-Century Baghdad." *BSOAS* XXIV (1961): 1–56. Reprint in Id., *Religion, Law and Learning in Classical Islam*. nr. VIII.

———. *Religion, Law and Learning in Classical Islam*. London: Variorum, 1991.

Pedersen, Johannes. *The Arabic Book*. Transl. Geoffrey French. Princeton, NJ: PUP, 1984 (in Danish, Copenhagen, 1946).

———. "Some Aspects of the History of the madrasa." *Islamic Culture* III (1929): 525–537.

Pinto, Olga. "The Libraries of the Arabs during the Time of the Abbasides." Transl. F. Krenkow. *Islamic Culture* III (1929): 210–248.

Sibai, Mohamed Makki. *Mosque Libraries: An historical study*. London and New York: Mansell, 1987 (originally a Ph.D dissertation, Indiana University, 1984).

Touati, Houari. *L'armoire à sagesse: Bibliothèques et collections en Islam*. Paris: Aubier (Collection historique), 2003.

Walker, Paul. "Fatimid Institutions of Learning." *Journal of the American Research Center in Egypt* 34 (1997): 179–200.

Wasserstein, D.J. "The Library of al-Hakam II al-Mustansir and the Culture of Islamic Spain." *Manuscripts of the Middle East* 5 (1990–1991, 1993): 99–105.

LINGUISTICS, ARABIC

"In Arabic—the only Semitic language that has remained the language of a whole civilization—ideas spring forth from the matrix of the sentence like sparks from the flint." If Louis Massignon finds the Arabic language inseparable from the civilization it enveloped, then Arabic linguistics played an indispensable role in setting Islamic scholarship ablaze.

Following the advent of the Qur'an in the seventh century CE, the intellectual fervor spurred by the direct contact Arabs and non-Arab Muslims alike had with other civilizations made it impossible for the learned among them not to reflect on the sacrosanct language of the Qur'an. The exchange of knowledge and ideas in the first Islamic centuries between the Arabs and the Byzantines, Greeks, Indians, and Persians—initially in the garrison towns of Basra and Kufa and later in the imperial capitals of Damascus and Baghdad—occurred alongside the development of the Arabic linguistic tradition. As other fields advanced, they borrowed heavily from the logic and methodology of the linguistic sciences. Certainly law and jurisprudence, the prose, poetry and polite learning of the Islamic period *(adab)*, scriptural exegesis, and theology all have their methodological roots in Arabic linguistics. In addition, medicine, mathematics, and the natural and applied sciences were expounded upon and expanded primarily in the Arabic language. Thus the Arabic language became the primary tool for research and a sine qua non to the development of Islamic civilization.

Pietistic and pragmatic concerns also necessitated the development of the linguistic sciences. Most, if not all, Arabic linguists were employed as reciters of the Qur'an in their official capacities. One motivation for linguistic analysis of the Arabic language was to explain the recitational variants of the Qur'an, which Muslims throughout the world use in their obligatory *salah* (prayers). Moreover due to the rapid expansion of the Arab empire, and with it of Islam, the need emerged for teaching correct readings and recitations of the Qur'an to the newest members of the faith, because mistakes in pronunciation can significantly alter the Qur'an's meanings. Extant manuscripts exhibit a native Arabic-speaking laity and their charges making basic grammatical errors (see Arabic, Middle Arabic), which suggests that Arabic grammars became necessary for teaching Arabic to the Arabs and the faithful for practical reasons.

Indeed, by the 800s, little more than one and a half centuries after the death of Islam's "unlettered Prophet," the Arabic linguistic sciences constituted a paradigm or "normal science" as defined by Thomas Kuhn, which is an established method that facilitates problem solving and attracts scholars to the field. This paradigm is not a single grammarian's possession but is rather constitutive of the entire Arabicist assemblage, and is still accepted as authoritative by modern scholarship, so much so that when researchers today find results that contradict the normal science, they ascribe the divergences to their own error rather than to any shortcomings of the paradigm.

Although paradigms of Arabic phonology, morphology, grammar, and lexicography were first articulated in the works of al-Khalil ibn Aḥmad (d. ca. 786), random data collection, field research, error analysis, corpus collection, anomaly study, and symbolic generalization had been pursuits of the scientific community to which Al-Khalil belonged since the writing of the Qur'an more than one hundred years earlier and the collection of pre-Islamic poetry a little later. However, before al-Khalil's systematized Arabic linguistic paradigm, only facts about Arabic existed, and all facts were equally relevant. Al-Khalil condensed and formalized morphological rules into symbols from which all word patterns derive. Based on these patterns, he devised the first Arabic dictionary, the *Kitab al-'Ayn*, that served as a comprehensive and systematic accounting for all the Arabic lexemes. His most famous student, Sibawayh (d. ca. 793), authored *Al-Kitab*, which is regarded to this day as the prototypical descriptive grammar for Arabic. In this way, normal science developed while continually complementing—but not superseding—what was inherited from previous generations. Hence the Arabic linguistic tradition presaged the rise of the Arabic language as the lingua franca of the Islamic world, a state of affairs that lasted well into the medieval period.

AL-HUSEIN N. MADHANY

See also Grammar and Grammarians; Poets; Qur'an; Scholars; Scribes

Primary Sources

Ibn al-Nadim, Muhammad Ibn Ishaq. *The Fihrist of al-Nadim: A Tenth-Century Survey of Muslim Culture.* Vol. 1, ch. 2 (Grammarians and Scholars of Language). Ed. and transl. Bayard Dodge. New York: Columbia University Press, 1970.

Solomn, Sara. "Sibawayhi's Al-Kitab Chapters 1–6: Translation & Notes." *Journal of Arabic Linguistics Tradition* 1 (2003): 35–52. Available online at www.jalt.net/ (2003–2005).

———. "Sibawayhi's Al-Kitab Chapters 7–13: Translation & Notes." *Journal of Arabic Linguistics Tradition* 2 (2004): 13–27. Available online at www.jalt.net/ (2003–2005).

Further Reading

Bakalla, Muhammad Hasan. *Arabic Linguistics: An Introduction and Bibliography.* London: Mansell, 1983.

Bohas, Georges, Jean-Patrick Guillaume, and Djamel Eddin Kouloughli. *The Arabic Linguistic Tradition.* London: Routledge, 1990.

Carter, Michael. "Les Origines de la Grammaire Arabe." *Revue des Études Islamiques* 40 (1972): 69–97.

Dilworth B. Parkinson. "Arabic Linguistics Society Bibliography of Arabic Linguistics: Supplement to Bakalla (1983)." Available online at www.lib.umich.edu/area/Near.East/ALSLING.html (1994).

Kuhn, Thomas S. *The Structure of Scientific Revolutions.* Chicago: University of Chicago Press, 1962.

Massignon, Louis. "Aspects and Perspectives of Islam." In *Testimonies and Reflections: Essays of Louis Massignon,* ed. and transl. Herbert Mason. Notre Dame: University of Notre Dame Press, 1989.

Owens, Jonathon. *Early Arabic Grammatical Theory: Heterogeneity and Standardization.* Amsterdam: John Benjamins, 1990.

Ryding, Karin C. "The Search for a Paradigm: Linguistic Analysis in Medieval Mesopotamia." *The International Journal of Islamic and Arabic Studies,* 6 (1989): 31–37.

Versteegh, Kees. *The Arabic Language.* New York: Columbia University Press, 1997.

LOVE POETRY

Pre-Islamic poetry knows no independent love poems, but *qasīdas* (poems that traverse a sequence of major themes) commonly open with an elegiac remembrance of a love affair *(nasīb)*. Often the vestiges of an encampment trigger a memory. The woman, it may be, belonged to another tribe and left with it. She may have sent the poet packing once she saw his hair turning gray. The essential motif is that of a past parting. With fine descriptions of the desert setting, the *nasīb* is often beautiful in itself, but its function in the *qasīda* is to contrast the elegiac with the poet's self-possessed brio in other episodes (desert journeys, war, feasts, and so on), and the personal with his life as a member of the tribe.

Love poetry proper *(ghazal)* appeared in the Umayyad period. It was now possible to write about love in the present and future. 'Umar ibn abī Rabī'a (d. ca. 103/721) is the foremost representative of the ijāzī school, based in the cities of Mecca and Medina. Whether he is describing jolly, amorous encounters occasioned by the pilgrimage, or tears exacted by caprice, his poetry is usually distinguished by a lightness of spirit, an urban atmosphere, and a delicious diction incomparably simpler than that of pre-Islamic poetry. Some of the poets of Kūfa—not quite a school, perhaps—wrote with pleasant frivolity about slave girls and libertinism. Very different is the 'Udhrī ghazal. The Banū 'Udhra were said to be a people who die when they love. 'Udhrī poetry (among whose principal representatives are Jamīl ibn Ma'mar and Qays ibn al-Mulawwa, known as Majnūn Laylā) is informed by chaste yearning for an unattainable woman, often leading to melancholy, madness, or death. The romancing biographies of these poets were widely read.

In the early 'Abbasid period, Bashshār ibn Burd (d. ca. 167/783), Abū Nuwās (d. ca. 200/815), and the other "moderns" embraced the diverse strains inherited from the Umayyad age, and enriched the ghazal with wit and rhetorical charm. The classical ghazal (which was to last through all of premodern Arabic literature) abounds in conventions of form and image but can reach great sophistication in its psychological insight—tender or ironic—into the lover's condition.

In the 'Abbasid age and thereafter, love poetry, written to boys as often as to women, could be sly or even earthy. More often, however, in an exaltation of sensibility, the poet would revel in checked desire and the torments laid on him by a proud or skittish object of his affections. Ibn Azm of Cordoba (d. 456/1064), the author of a famous treatise on love, soberly reminds us that there is no shame in the lover's humble submission, for in reality the beloved is his social inferior. Aspects of Arabic love poetry have been compared to courtly love, but it has also been noted that these same aspects could also be found in Ovid. The troubadours' emphasis on the joy of love is on the whole absent from Arabic love poetry, and while Arabic treatises on love do speak of the virtues induced in a lover, the ennobling effect of love was not a major theme for the poets.

ANDRAS HAMORI

Further Reading

Bauer, Thomas. *Liebe und Liebesdichtung in der arabischen Welt des 9. und 10. Cambridge History of Arabic Literature.* Wiesbaden: Jahrhunderts, 1998.

M

MADRASA

A *madrasa* is a college of Islamic law. The madrasa was an educational institution in which Islamic law (fiqh) was taught according to one or more Sunni rites: Maliki, Shafi'i, Hanafi, or Hanbali. It was supported by an endowment or charitable trust (waqf) that provided for at least one chair for one professor of law, income for other faculty or staff, scholarships for students, and funds for the maintenance of the building. Madrasas contained lodgings for the professor and some of his students. Subjects other than law were frequently taught in madrasas, and even Sufi seances were held in them, but there could be no madrasa without law as technically the major subject. In theory—but not always in practice—professors held their positions for life. Most madrasas were endowed by persons of wealth and power, such as sultans, viziers, amirs (military commanders), merchants, and qadis (judges) or their wives.

There is no consensus on the origin of the madrasa. Various scholars have tried to show that it was inspired by Buddhist monasteries in Central Asia, that it derived from the Turkish muyanliq (a charitable fortified hospice, or ribat in Arabic) in Central Asia, that it was stimulated by the growth of libraries, that it was the outgrowth of the function of the mosque (where law was also taught), or that it arose from inns (khans) that were built near mosques. In the latter case, these inns served as residences for the students. The mosque–inn complex thus represented the transition to the madrasa.

The first madrasas appeared during the late tenth century in the eastern Islamic world. By the early eleventh century, there were several in Nishapur. The Seljuk vizier Nizam al-Mulk (1064–1092) greatly promoted their spread. He founded the renowned Nizamiyya Madrasa in Baghdad in 1065 for the Shafi'is and proceeded to establish similar colleges in other cities of the Seljuk Empire. His primary objective was to use this institution to strengthen Sunnism against Shi'ism and to gain influence over the religious class. Madrasas rapidly spread from east to west. By the middle of the thirteenth century, they were found in profusion in Anatolia, Syria, and Egypt. They reached Andalus by 1349, but they apparently did not take root there.

In addition to being centers of instruction in law, madrasas could be used to exercise influence over the religious class, because the founder of a madrasa could specify in his deed of endowment the subjects to be taught and the salaries to be paid. The ruling elite often took advantage of this. However, madrasas played other roles in Muslim society that often differed according to time and place. In Anatolia, their waqfs often came from conquered Christian property; they thus developed there at the expense of the Church. In Syria, they probably stiffened Muslim resistance to the Crusaders by helping to rally the faithful. In Egypt, they added to the pressure on Copts to convert to Islam. Altogether, they were probably the most important Muslim religious institution after the mosque. There is evidence that the Western college originated from the madrasa.

GARY LEISER

See also **Buddhism and Islam; Christians and Christianity; Law and Jurisprudence; Malikism; Merchants, Muslim; Schools of Jurisprudence; Seljuks; Sufism and Sufis; Sultan; Sunni Revival**

Further Reading

Esin, Emel. "The Genesis of the Turkish Mosque and Madrasa Complex." *Annali dell'Instituto Orientale di Napoli* 32 (1972): 151–85.

Leiser, Gary. "The *Madrasah* and the Islamization of Anatolia before the Ottomans." In *Law and Education in Medieval Islam: Studies in Memory of George Makdisi*, eds. Joseph Lowry et al., 174–91. Cambridge: Gibb Memorial Trust, 2004.

———. "Notes on the Madrasa in Medieval Islamic Society." *The Muslim World* 67 (1986): 16–23.

Makdisi, George. *The Rise of Colleges: Institutions of Learning in Islam and the West*. Edinburgh: Edinburgh University Press, 1981.

MAHMUD OF GHAZNA

Abu'l-Qasim Mahmud (971–1030 CE, r. 998–1030) was the second ruler of the Ghaznavid dynasty in the eastern Islamic lands. The eldest son of Sebuktigin (a Turkish commander under the Samanid dynasty of Transoxiana) and the daughter of a chief of Zabulistan, Mahmud fought along with his father in the internecine warfare that characterized the end of the Samanid empire and was awarded honorifics and command of the army of Khurasan. In 994, Mahmud secured direct investiture of Khurasan from the 'Abbasid Caliph al-Qadir, consolidated Samanid domains south of the Oxus, including Ghazna, and brought under control the dynasties of the upper Oxus that had paid tribute to the Samanids.

Mahmud's reign saw constant campaigning, an unbroken string of victories, and the establishment of the largest empire in the eastern Muslim world since the 'Abbasids. His massive centralized administration, financed by often excessive taxation of Khurasan and Afghanistan, laid the foundations for a Persianate state in India and provided a military-state model for later Muslim rulers. Mahmud's empire building combined direct conquest with the creation of tribute-paying states. He defeated the Qarakhanids near Balkh (1008), the Khwarazmshahs in Gurganj (1017), the Ismaili rulers of Multan (1010), and the Buyids in northern Persia (1029), and he made vassal states out of the Farighunids in Juzjan (998), the Shers of Gharchistan (998), the Saffarids in Sistan (1003), and the rulers of Makran and Kushdar in Baluchistan (998 and 1011, respectively). The 1008 defeat of a confederacy of Hindushahis, headed by Anandpal of Waihind, also ensured success in northern and central India. Mahmud's signature campaigns against Hindu religious centers, including the Somnath temple in Gujarat in 1020, brought an influx of bullion to Ghazna and further financed Mahmud's sophisticated bureaucracy and professional army. Despite financial success, however, Mahmud established Muslim dominion in India only up to Lahore, where he left a governor in 1020 and which remained a frontier for campaigns for two centuries.

Although it was the subject of controversy, the religious impetus of Mahmud's Indian campaigns was minimal; he fought equally tenaciously against Muslim rivals and maintained many Hindu troops as a check on their Turkish counterparts. However, Mahmud did project himself as a staunch Sunni and supporter of the 'Abbasid caliphs. The dynasty as a whole favored the Hanafi school, but some sources reveal Mahmud's sympathy for the Karramiyya sect as well as his later decision to become a Shafi'i.

Ghazna inherited Samanid administrative and cultural traditions and, under Mahmud, became second only to Baghdad in importance. Keen to join the larger Muslim tradition of sponsoring scholarship and the arts, Mahmud founded an academy and a royal museum that were enriched by the libraries of conquered cities. Although Mahmud spoke Turkish, his court oversaw new developments in Persian, most notably in lyrical romances and romantic epics as well as a budding Turkish literature. Well after his death, Mahmud's Indian campaigns inspired epic and hagiographical literature, and his relationship with a slave created the famous poetical pairing of "Mahmud and Ayaz." Luminaries of Mahmud's court included the poets Firdawsi (of *Shahnama* fame), Farrukhi, Manuchihri, and Unsuri, and the polymath al-Biruni.

HOMAYRA ZIAD

See also **'Abbasids; Abu Hanifa; Al-Biruni; Al-Shafi'i; Buyids; Epics, Persian; Firdawsi; Ghaznavids; India; Iran; Ismailis; Khurasan; Lahore; Persian; Poetry, Indian; Poetry, Persian; Samanids; Shahnama; Sindh; Turkish and Turkic Languages; Turks**

Further Reading

Bosworth, Clifford E. *The Ghaznavids*. Edinburgh: Edinburgh University Press, 1963.

———. "Mahmud of Ghazna in Contemporary Eyes and in Later Persian Literature." *Iran* 4 (1966): 85–92.

———. "Farrukhi's Elegy on Mahmud of Ghazna." *Iran* 29 (1991): 43–9.

Habib, Mohammed. *Sultan Mahmud of Ghaznin*, 2nd ed. Delhi: S. Chand, 1967.

Nazim, Muhammad. *The Life and Times of Sultan Mahmud of Ghazna*. Cambridge, UK: Cambridge University Press, 1931.

MAHMUD-AL-KATI, AFRICAN SCHOLAR

Mahmud-al-Kati was a scholar of Soninke origin who died near Timbuktu in 1593. He married one of the daughters of Akiya Dawud, who reigned in the Songhay Empire from 1549 until 1582. He wrote a work about the history of the Songhay Empire that was later incorporated in the *Ta'rikh al-Fattash,* a compilation of texts to which sons and in-laws later added data or edited the existing text. This compilation is currently one of the most important sources for the history of the Sudan and for that of the Songhay Empire in particular. The authorship and interpretation of some parts of this compilation are still points of scholarly debate.

JAN JANSEN

Further Reading

Hopkins, John F.P., and Nehemiah Levtzion. *Corpus of Early Arabic Sources for West African History.* Cambridge, UK: Cambridge University Press, 1981.

MAIMONIDES, RABBI MOSES BEN MAIMON (1135–1204)

Maimonides is one of the most illustrious and influential Jewish figures of the medieval period. He was born in Cordoba, where tolerant and enlightened Muslim rulers had turned the city into a center of excellence for Jewish and Muslim knowledge. His lineage was scholarly—his father, Maimon, was dayyan (judge of the religious court) of the city—and Maimonides received the best of Jewish education and Islamic sciences.

As the result of religious persecution by the Almohads of North Africa, who invaded the caliphate of Cordoba, Maimon and his family left Cordoba in 1148 and wandered in Spain and North Africa for eight or nine years, finally settling in Fez in 1160. It was during this difficult period of wandering that Maimonides began his halakhic activity. His commentary on the Mishnah, written in Arabic, is an attempt to explain the meaning of the Mishnah without expecting the reader to have knowledge of the minutiae of the Talmudic discussions and commentaries. Also, it is the beginning of his lifelong efforts to harmonize Aristotelian philosophy with revelation. In the book, he discusses his Thirteen Principles of Faith, the first such creed in Jewish law, which include the three principles of Unity, Incorporeality, and Immutability of God.

In Fez, Maimonides continued his general studies but concentrated specifically on medicine. He also began his continued and consequential response with Sephardi Jewish communities, which lasted until his death. Maimonides' personal experiences of religious persecution and wandering had caused him to have an empathic awareness of human suffering. His consoling and educating outlook in these matters is well demonstrated by his famous letters to communities under religious persecution. In his *Iggeret ha-Shemmad (Letter on Forced Conversion),* also known as *Iggeret Kidush ha-Shem (Letter of the Sanctification of the Divine Name),* while utterly condemning religious persecution, he did not advocate martyrdom for the persecuted Jews. His religious decision was that Jews must leave the country where they are obliged to negate the divine law; this was certainly the decision that Maimonides and his family followed. Despite bitter experiences with religious persecution, Maimonides did not become an anti-Muslim and declined to classify Muslims as idolaters.

Around 1165, Maimonides and his family were again put under pressure to convert. They left Morocco and took a hazardous boat journey to Acre, which was at the time under Christian rule. The family sailed for Egypt, and, after a short stay in Alexandria, settled in the Jewish quarter in Fostat near Cairo.

In Fostat, Maimonides took up the honorary position of becoming the religious leader of the community as well as continuing his intellectual output. His first wife had died young, so in Egypt he married his second wife and had his only son, Abraham, to whose education he devoted himself. He completed his commentary on the Mishnah in 1168. A year later, the tragic drowning of his beloved brother, David, a merchant who had supported Maimonides in his studies, dealt him a heavy blow. Maimonides rejected the idea of earning his living as a paid rabbi. Being a religious leader was an honor, not a means of employment. He advised his student that it was better to earn a meager living as a weaver than as a paid rabbi. Maimonides chose to practice medicine, and, in 1170, he became personal physician to the family of Sultan Salladin of Egypt, a position that he kept until his death.

The two most scholarly and influential books of Maimonides are *Mishneh Torah (Repetition of the Law)* and *Dalālat al-Hā'irin (The Guide of the Perplexed).*

Mishneh Torah, the only work that Maimonides wrote in Hebrew, is an authoritative legal code that revolutionized the study of Jewish law. Written in a lucid and succinct Hebrew for an educated and believing Jew, it is the first attempt in Jewish history at an innovative systemization and categorization of the Jewish Law based on rational philosophy.

The greatest Jewish Aristotelian and the supreme rationalist, Maimonides' magnum opus is *The Guide,* which was completed in 1200. Written in terse philosophical language, it is a systematic exposition of Aristotelian philosophy and its synthesis with Jewish faith. The book addresses a faithful and religious Jew, who, having studied philosophy, is troubled by the anthropomorphic biblical references to God. Maimonides demonstrated that all such readings should be understood allegorically and went on to present God as an Aristotelian first cause and self-intellectualizing intellect. Furthermore, Maimonides posits the theory that the human individual's share in divine providence is proportionate to his intellectual perfection.

MEHRI NIKNAM

Further Reading

Encyclopaedia Judaica, vol. xi.
Goitein, S.D. *A Mediterranean Society*, vol. v. University of California Press.
Pines, Shlomo. *The Guide of the Perplexed*. Chicago, University of Chicago Press.
Twersky, Isadore. *A Maimonides Reader*. Behrman House, Inc., Library of Jewish Studies.

MAJLISI, AL-

Al-Majlisi Muhammad Baqir ibn Muhammad Taqi (1627/28–1699/1700) was one of the most authoritative and prolific hadith (tradition) scholars within Shi'ism. During the reign of the last Safavid Shahs, he was appointed Shaykh al-Islam of Isfahan (1686/87) and thereby also assumed an unprecedented political importance. Western judgment of both his activities and his character has remained extremely controversial until today, ranging from a cautiously benevolent assessment (Donaldson) to outright condemnations for his fanaticism (Browne, Lockhart, Turner). Among Shi'i authors, by contrast, al-Majlisi's decisive role in spreading Shi'ism thought in Iran is nearly universally acknowledged. Al-Majlisi managed to popularize his teachings by writing numerous works in an easily understandable Persian style in which he summarized the essential doctrines for the common people. At the same time, he used his power to fight anything that he considered to be a heresy. Apart from non-Muslims (above all Hindus), his main enemies came from within Islam, and he propagated a relentless persecution of Sunni Muslims as well as of Sufism.

Al-Majlisi's most important field of interest was the hadith, which in Shi'ism is not restricted to the traditions of the Prophet Muhammad but also comprises the sayings of the twelve Imams, most important among them being Muhammad al-Baqir and Ja'far al-Sadiq. His encyclopedic compilation *Bihar*

al-anwar (Oceans of Lights) is the monumental continuation and perfection of earlier works, such as al-Kulayni's *al-Kafi*. Far more than a mere collection of legal prescriptions, the 110 volumes of this work may be regarded as the cornerstone of Shi'i identity. The scope of topics ranges from epistemology, theology, and law to cosmography, medicine, social behavior, ritual purity, and the Qur'an. Most important, however, is the doctrine of the Imamate: approximately one-third of the entire work is devoted to the Shi'i understanding of history, the virtues of the Imams, and eschatology as embodied by the hidden twelfth Imam, the Mahdi. Apart from this compilation, al-Majlisi composed a number of other works about the hadith, most notably *Hilyat al-Muttaqin (The Adornment of the God-fearing)*, *Haqq al-Yaqin (The Absolute Truth)*, and *Hayat al-Qulub (The Life of the Hearts)*.

RAINER BRUNNER

See also Eschatology; Hadith; Isfahan; Safavid; Shi'ism; Sufism

Primary Sources

al-Majlisi, Muhammad Baqir. *Bihar al-Anwar*, 110 vols. Beirut, 1983.
———. *Hilyat al-Muttaqin*. Tehran, 1964.
———. *Haqq al-Yaqin*. Tehran, 1959.
———. *'Ayn al-Hayat*. Tehran, 1955.
———. *Hayat al-Qulub*. Qom, 1963.
———. *The Life and Religion of Mohammed, as Contained in the Sheeah Traditions of the Hayât-ul-Kuloob*. Translated from the Persian by Rev. James L. Merrick. Boston: Philips, Sampson, and Company, 1850.

Further Reading

Arjomand, Said Amir. *The Shadow of God and the Hidden Imam: Religion, Political Order and Societal Change in Shi'ite Iran from the Beginnings to 1890*. Chicago and London: The University of Chicago Press, 1984.
Babayan, Kathryn. *Mystics, Monarchs, and Messiahs: Cultural Landscapes of Early Modern Iran*. Cambridge, Mass, and London: Harvard University Press, 2002.
Browne, Edward G. *A Literary History of Persia. Volume IV: Modern Times (1500–1924)*. Cambridge, UK: Cambridge University Press, 1959.
Brunner, Rainer. "The Role of *Hadith* as Cultural Memory in Shiite History." *Jerusalem Studies in Arabic and Islam* 30 (2005): in print.
Cole, Juan. *Sacred Space and Holy War: The Politics, Culture and History of Shi'ite Islam*, Chapter 4. London and New York: I.B. Tauris, 2002.
Donaldson, Dwight M. *The Shiite Religion: A History of Islam in Persia and Irak*. London: Luzac & Company, 1933.
Hairi, Abdul-Hadi. "Madjlisi, Mulla Muhammad Bakir." In *Encyclopaedia of Islam*, vol. 5, 1086–88. Leiden: Brill, 1986.

Kohlberg, Etan. "Bihar al-Anwar." In *Encyclopedia Iranica*, vol. 4, 90–3. London and New York: Routledge & Kegan Paul, 1990.

Lockhart, Laurence. *The Fall of the Safavid Dynasty and the Afghan Occupation of Persia.* Cambridge, UK: Cambridge University Press, 1958.

Pampus, Karl-Heinz. *Die Theologische Enzyklopädie Bihar al-Anwar des Muhammad Baqir al-Madjlisi (1037–1110 AH = 1627–1699 A.D. Ein Beitrag zur Literaturgeschichte der Safawidenzeit.* PhD dissertation. Bonn, 1970.

Turner, Colin. *Islam Without Allah? The Rise of Religious Externalism in Safavid Iran.* Richmond, VA: Curzon, 2000.

MAJUSI, AL-, OR HALY ABBAS

'Alī ibn al-'Abbās al-Majūsī (fl. AH 364/975 CE) eminent name in Islamic medicine as the author of a single known work, *al-Kitāb al-Malakī: Kāmil al-Òināʿa al-Ôibbīya (The Royal Book: Completion of Medical Art;* the title has often been abridged to just one of its two components), one of the most renowned Arabic medical compendia.

Life

Apart from the few data that can be gleaned from his names and his unique book, no reliable biographical evidence about al-Majūsī is extant; this suggests that he never made it to the caliphal and (political turmoil notwithstanding) cultural capital of Baghdad. Rather, al-Majūsī ("the Magian"; his name indicates a Zoroastrian family background, as his father's and his own fairly nondenominational given names may do also) appears to have studied and practiced in his native Iranian province of Fārs—or rather its administrative center Shīrāz—at the time the residence of the ambitious and powerful Būyid governor 'Aud al-Dawla. Al-Majūsī's teacher of medicine, Mūsā ibn Sayyār, having operated within the Būyid orbit, he himself inscribed his work to 'Aud al-Dawla, indeed presenting it to him exclusively; perhaps only after the dedicatee's death did it become accessible to the wider public. On the basis of 'Aud al-Dawla's royal *(malakī)* title as extant in al-Majūsī's work, its presentation to him can be dated to the interval 363–367/974–978, the only approximately precise date in al-Majūsī's life (the presumed year of his death, 384/994, cannot be ascertained).

The Royal Book

The Royal Book: Completion of Medical Art ranks as one of the foremost examples of classical Islamic Galenism, primarily because of its extensive scholarship, lucid exposition, and dominant rationalism (i.e., the near-total absence of occult material) but also because of its wide reception in subsequent centuries; despite its being overshadowed by Avicenna's *Canon Medicinae (Kitāb al-Qānūn fī l-Ôibb, Canon of Medicine)*, it continued to be perused not merely within Islamic civilization but also in Hebrew and Latin Europe. In Constantine the African's pioneering adaptation (ca. 1080 CE), it was titled *Pantegni*, whereas Stephen of Pisa/Antioch stayed closer to the original in his own translation of 1127 and its title, *Liber Regius* (and variants). According to a pattern established since late antiquity, the author presents the entire syllabus of medical learning in one book; however, not merely in his own view, his work surpasses his predecessors both quantitatively and qualitatively. It is neatly divided into two sections—theory and practice—of ten treatises each and that cover the areas of anatomy, physiology, dietetics and preventive medicine, etiology and symptomatology of localized and general ailments, diagnosis by the pulse and uroscopy, medicinal therapy and surgery, and, finally, pharmacy.

LUTZ RICHTER-BERNBURG

See also Medicine

Further Reading

Burnett, Charles, and Danielle Jacquart, eds. *Constantine the African and 'Alī ibn al-'Abbās al-MaÊūsī: The* Pantegni *and Related Texts. Studies in Ancient Medicine*, vol. 10. Leiden: Brill, 1994.

Micheau, Francoise, "'Alī ibn al-'Abbās al-MaÊūsī et son Milieu." Ibid., 1–15.

Richter-Bernburg, L. "Observations on al-Majūsī, the Author of *Liber Regius.*" *Journal for the History of Arabic Science* 4 (1980): 341–2, 363–75.

Sezgin, Fuat, ed. *The Complete Medical Art—Kāmil al-Òināʿa al-Ôibbīya—by 'Alī ibn al-'Abbās al-Majūsī,* 2 vols., Publications of the Institute for the History of Arabic-Islamic Science; Ser. C, vol. 16, 1–2. Frankfurt am Main: Institute for the History of Arabic-Islamic Science, 1985.

Ullmann, Manfred, *Islamic Medicine.* Edinburgh: Edinburgh University Press, 1978.

———. *Die Medizin im Islam*, 140–6. Leiden and Köln: E.J. Brill, 1970.

MALAY PENINSULA

Early Knowledge and Trade

From around the second century CE, the Malay Peninsula was a major meeting point along the maritime counterpart to the Silk Road. During the early tenth century, Abu Zayd of Siraf even described the narrow isthmus at Kra as the midpoint between the lands of the Arabs and China. Although there is evidence of some overland traffic at Kra—carried between Krabi on the west coast and Chaiya in the east—the vast bulk of international shipping, with holds filled with Chinese ceramics and Middle Eastern glass and glass products (some of which are thought to have contained unguents or perfumes), seems to have passed through the Straits of Malacca to the south. For this reason, the history of the peninsula is inextricably linked to the major island Sumatra and most especially to East Sumatra, which is the site of a series of kingdoms. Of these, the eighth- and ninth-century rulers of Srivijaya claimed some authority over the Straits and as far north as Kra from their bases in Palembang and Jambi.

At various points in the region, Chinese, Indian, and Middle Eastern vessels would harbor to take on supplies and await the appropriate monsoonal winds to carry them further on their respective journeys. Indications are that eastward-bound vessels would have skirted the Sumatran coast, calling at Lamreh in present-day Aceh before docking at the major ports in East Sumatra. Then, after gaining the appropriate shift in winds, they would head north through the Riau Archipelago and on to Tioman island, the coast of Champa, and southern China beyond.

At all of these points, the prestige goods of the archipelago's seas and forests were exchanged. These included shells, alluvial gold, ambergris, forest products such as resins and rare birds, camphor wood, textiles, and—perhaps most famously—spices. Some spices, such as cloves, were in use in both Rome and China by the second century. These, like nutmeg and mace, had already been brought from their sources farther afield in the Moluccas and the Banda archipelago by archipelagic shipping.

Muslim knowledge of the straits passage varied in accordance with the security and prosperity of both the maritime routes and the mainland Silk Road. Much of what was known until the time of al-Idrisi reflected information gathered during the ninth century, at a time when the 'Abbasids were actively pursuing the Indian Ocean trade with China from the Persian Gulf port of Siraf. It is in these accounts that there are clear references to peninsular Kra, the north Sumatran Lamreh (known in the texts as Ramni or Rami), and echoes of the claims of the eighth-century rulers of Srivijaya, known to Abu Zayd as Sribuza or even as Zabaj, a term long used as a coverall for the lands of the Malay peoples inhabiting both sides of the Straits.

Although the name *Zabaj* has clear salience and importance in the early Arab accounts, its etymology has been disputed. Some have seen it as a distant pronunciation of an Indian adjectival form, Javaka, meaning "peoples of Java," whereby Java is understood to refer to both Sumatra and Java. However, comparison with reconstructed forms of the Chinese gloss for an older archipelagic state based in Sumatra called Jaba (Jia-ba-dej; i.e., Jabadesh) and the phonetic agreement of this form with Greek names for the same entity (Zabai, Iabadiou) are much closer to Zabaj.

Even so, by the time al-Idrisi did record information relating to the areas once covered by Zabaj and Kra, Palembang—the former chief entrepôt of Srivijaya—had long been reduced by a raid from the Tamils of southern India in 1025. In any case, as Jacq-Hergoualc'h has suggested, various entrepôts on the east coast of the Malay Peninsula, such as Tambralinga, already exercised a degree of independence well before the eleventh-century raids, especially during periods of relative quiet in the China trade. One might also draw the same conclusions for many of the Malay and Khmer ports in the region. Certainly various toponyms are emphasized in the geographies of al-Biruni and al-Idrisi at the expense of Zabaj and Sribuza, including Malayu (Jambi), Fansur, and Rami, as well as the more stable mainland entities of Cambodia (Qmar) and Champa (Sanf).

During the late thirteenth century, the region of Sumatra and the Malay peninsula came under the hegemony of the Javanese kingdoms of Singasari and then Majapahit after a Mongol intervention in 1293. Both dynasties actively sought to monopolize both intra- and extraregional trade. It is also apparent that Javanese claims of suzerainty were accepted by both the southern Song and the later Yuan (Mongol) dynasties. The view of a Java-dominated world was also accepted in the Indian Ocean. The geographies of Yaqut and his successors refer more and more to Java as a regional construct and relegate Zabaj and its affinates to the fields of cosmography and the bizarre.

Although Arab geographic knowledge vacillated in accordance with the rumors of shifting patterns of authority in a distant region, the success and continuity of trade was not tied exclusively to the durability of the states that sought advantage from it. One scholar has remarked about the relative durability of trading guilds—often tied to ethnic and religious networks, whether Tamil, Arab, or Chinese—as compared with the kingdoms that rose and fell along the same coasts. Although it seems clear that most Muslim vessels were bound for China, this was not the only West Asian trade to touch on insular Southeast

Asia. Documents from the Geniza trove, found in Cairo during the late nineteenth century, suggest that there was also direct contact between Egypt, Kra, and the west coast of Sumatra at Fansur between the tenth and thirteenth centuries. This was handled by Jewish merchants and their Malay partners, and it facilitated the movement of the all-important spices from the Indian Ocean into the Mediterranean through the port of Alexandria.

Java, Spice, and Conversion

Today the area that constitutes the nation-states of Indonesia, Brunei, and Malaysia is largely Muslim and Shafi'i in orientation. Although the presence of Muslim traders seems certain from at least the ninth century, there is great uncertainty about how or when Islam came to prevail in the western reaches of the archipelago. The first epigraphic evidence of any Muslim ruler comes from the northern tip of Sumatra, the site of the former port kingdom of Samudra (also known as Pasai). Here is to be found the restored tomb of a sovereign called Malik al-Salih, conventionally dated to 1297. Even so, Samudra is not remembered by Malay accounts as the first Muslim kingdom of the archipelago. Malay literature speaks instead of the neighboring port of Perlak as the first Muslim kingdom and the agent of the conversion of Samudra Pasai. This chronology is confirmed by the account of Marco Polo, who passed through the Straits in approximately 1291 and mentioned the existence of a major island called Java Minora that consisted of eight separate kingdoms. Of these he described Ferlec (Perlak), Basma, Samara, Dagroian (Indragiri), Lambri (Lamreh), and Fansur and remarked that, although most were under the rule of the Great Khan (of Java), Ferlec had been recently won over by the Muslim merchants who frequented the place.

Although trade must have played a vital role in the conversion of Sumatra's entrepôt ports, indigenous accounts stress the role of saints from the Middle East who had ventured to the islands via ports in southern India. The great lag between first contact and royal conversion—as opposed to the local instances that must have occurred betwen traders and locals—has caused some scholars to suggest the possibility of a new missionary impulse led by Sufis after the Mongol sack of Baghdad. A. H. Johns once proposed that these activities were perhaps entwined with the activities of trade guilds, whereas others have pointed to the complex nature of conversion in the archipelago involving merchants of many ethnic groups (Tamil, Persian, Chinese, and Arab) who came to play a greater role at courts.

One possible argument for the slow spread of Islam in the region after the late thirteenth century is that it was connected to a weakening in previous structures in the face of the spread of Javanese power and then a vacuum caused by its decline. According to the account of Prapanca, which was written during the mid-fourteenth century, the Javanese sent military expeditions into the Straits in the 1270s, and the various statelets of Sumatra and the Malay Peninsula remained loyal vassals. However, it is possible that the Javanese appointed relatively disinterested outsiders as local governers or tax collectors with ties to the all-important international trade and most probably with Ayyubid Yemen and Egypt. The fact that Malik al-Salih adopted an Ayyubid-style name and that the first known individual in the Middle East with a patronymic connection to Southeast Asia was a mystic active in Aden and the Red Sea Coast linked to the spice trade, Abu 'Abd Allah Mas'ud b. 'Abd Allâh al-Jawi (fl. ca. 1277–ca. 1315) points to such a connection. Furthermore, the hagiographic stories about 'Abd al-Qadir al-Jilani, which were collected and edited by an adept of al-Jawi, 'Abd Allâh b. As'ad al-Yafi'i (1298–1367), were later reworked as Malay, Javanese, and Sundanese recensions, and they appear to have influenced one of the earliest stories of royal conversion in the archipelago. One legend of al-Jilani speaks of his gaining the gift of eloquence from the sputum of the Prophet. The king of Pasai was said to have been converted in a dream in which the Prophet also spat in his mouth and gave him the ability to recite the Qur'an in its entirety.

When Ibn Battuta passed through the region in around 1345, he, too, commenced his account of the island of Sumatra by remarking that it was the island of the Javanese people. He also made sure to note that it was the source of the famous incense Luban Jawi (benzoin). Meanwhile, within the area of Java, which he seems to have located as the lands below the Peninsula in toto, Ibn Battuta detailed his experiences in two kingdoms. One of these was Samudra, which then consisted of a walled settlement upriver under the authority of a ruler called Malik al-Zahir, a form that echoes that of his predecessor Malik al-Salih. The next court he visited—and where he received a much more cursory welcome—was called Mul Jawa. Although his slighting description of its non-Muslim king could have been applied to any number of potentates east of Samudra and indeed is most often identified with Java or the Peninsula, this was most likely Jambi given that Ibn Battuta was following the same well-worn route that his predecessors had followed for more than five centuries.

Whatever the roots and reasons for royal conversion, the spread of Islamic rule and its concomitant symbolic forms—including dress, Arabic script, and titles—gathered momentum during the fourteenth and fifteenth centuries, although this process often contained clear reference to the previously prevailing Indianized traditions. For example, the next major known inscription after the tomb of Malik al-Salih comes from the eastern side of the Malay Peninsula at Trengganu. This inscription, datable to either 1303 or 1387, takes the form of a large stone engraved in Malay written in a modified Arabic script and records the adoption of new Islamic rules. Even so, although the rules and script pay tribute to Islamic models, much of the terminology—including the name of God—is drawn from Sanskrit and Malay. Certainly rules and rulings were adopted by local sovereigns. According to Ibn Battuta, the ruler of Samudra was an avid discussant on matters of Shafi'i law, the school that now predominates in the region to the practical exclusion of all other forms.

The Malacca Sultanate

As Islam spread down the coasts of Sumatra—being adopted by the courts of Aru and Deli in the 1400s—it also gained adherents on the peninsula. It may also have served a useful purpose for escapees from Javanese hegemony seeking international support. According to what is often regarded as the preeminent account of Malay royal lineage, the *Sulalat al-Salatin (Malay Annals)*, the dynasty of Malacca was founded around 1400 by a refugee prince from Palembang after an interim period in Temasek, now occupied by the city of Singapore.

Oliver Wolters has presented the Malaccan story as an account stressing the continuum of authority from long-lost Srivijaya, although much interpretation is required to extract the precise details from the narrative. What is clear, however, is that the city came, in the fifteenth century, to play the role once performed by Palembang and Jambi as the key mediator for the China trade in the Straits, with its rulers continuing the practice of monopolistic protection, close partnership with the sea peoples who both patrolled the islands and gathered its hinterland products, and good harbor facilities with low taxation.

Most relevant to present concerns, however, is that the ruler of Malacca appears to have adopted Islam with the encouragement of the lord of Pasai. The subsequent history of Islam during this period is often presented by Malaysian national and colonial historiography as a golden age, with Malacca playing the dominant role in Straits shipping.

It is clear that Malacca became an important hub for trade with the wider region through its ties to international commerce. Recognition from the Chinese emperor in 1405 combined with statements of loyalty to both the neighboring powers of Tai Ayudhya and Java's Majapahit, would also have served this end. Ultimately, it surpassed Samudra in influence, although it, Aru, and Kedah on the peninsula remained strong rivals. Sultan Muzaffar Shah (d. ca. 1459) even managed to incorporate much surrounding territory—Dinding, Selangor, Muar, and Bintan—and secured the allegiance of Pahang on the east coast of the peninsula. Malaccan influence was also felt across the strait, in Inderagiri and Kampar, which had access to the mineral wealth and pepper plantations of the Minangkabau highlands. The successors of Sultan Muzaffar then added Bernam and Perak on the peninsula, the Riau archipelago, and Siak. By the time of the last ruler, Mahmud Shah (r. 1488–1528), the Sultanate took in Pahang on the east coast, the west coast between Perak and Johor, large swathes of the east coast of Sumatra, and insular possessions in the South China Sea and the Riau archipelago. Even so, it was never in total control of the passage and always had to contend with the rivalry of other Malay states to the north under the influence of the Thais and the still-active Sumatran entities of Aru and Samudra-Pasai.

At the beginning of the sixteenth century, Malacca was the principal Muslim power that was responsible for the wider dissemination of the faith to the further reaches of the archipelago (e.g., in the spice-gathering zones of the Moluccas) and indeed the propagation of its form of Malay as the prestige language of interethnic communication. Its ruler was confident enough to pledge his fealty to China and Ayudya, but he no longer regarded Java as a threat. Indeed, Malacca was now the primary magnet for both intra-archipelagic and international trade. Its regional foci were reflected in the appointment of four different harbormasters to deal with the traffic from Gujerat; the peoples of southern India, Bengal, Pasia, and Pegu; those from Java, Palembang, Banda, and the Moluccas; and those of China, Champa, and the Ryukyu archipelago.

Because of the volume of trade and its strategic location, Malacca was identified by the Portuguese as the key regional prize after their arrival in the Indies in 1509. The city was captured by Albuquerque in 1511.

Some have seen this moment as one of galvanization for the Muslims of the archipelago against Christian aggression, but such claims are overstated.

Significantly, the displaced Sultan Mahmud appealed to China for aid. By the same token, the taking of Malacca did not guarantee any Portuguese monopoly in the region but rather a chance to compete with the emerging states of importance. Among these, Aceh, which overwhelmed most of north Sumatra—including Samudra—gained in influence in the 1520s. The Acehnese also seem to have engaged in a degree of trade with the Portuguese, just as the rulers of Samudra had done, even allowing a Portuguese factory to be established there. Peninsular Johor also maintained trade relations, although only after a long period of intermittent attacks. It was then forced into an uneasy alliance with Malacca after 1536. Despite Acehnese ambitions of regional hegemony and trading relations with the Ottoman Empire, it would appear that it was only in the middle of the century—and perhaps with encouragement from local Ottoman spice procurers—that Aceh engaged Malacca in open warfare. To this end, the Acehnese rulers requested aid from the Ottomans, and a fleet was even dispatched in the 1560s. However, it was forced to deal with an uprising in Yemen, and what forces did arrive were primarily in the form of large cannon and artillery experts.

Aceh remained a regional force well into the seventeenth century in the company of the comprador states of Banten in Java and Johor on the peninsula. It was also during the seventeenth century that the Atlantic nations became more actively involved in the spice trade to the cost of their Portuguese and Spanish predecessors. Both the Dutch and the English sought to establish factories in Aceh, but they were refused and settled instead in ports further to the east at Batavia and Bencoolen. In the emerging struggle, Portugal was slowly excluded, even if Portuguese retained its importance alongside Malay as a language of regional importance. Malacca itself was finally taken by the Dutch in 1641.

The Doctrinal Importance of Aceh

Whereas Malacca holds center stage in modern Malay accounts of Islam and Islamization, it was Aceh that played the preeminent role in determining the future course of Malay Islam and indeed the mystically leaning Islam of many of the courts of the archipelago, such as Banten and Cirebon on West Java. Unlike earlier periods, there is a great deal of textual evidence surviving from the seventeenth century showing that north Sumatra was regarded as the leading site for interpretations of Sufism in the archipelago, especially as compared with Malacca, for

which there is little evidence of great scholarly concern with Islamic matters outside of those of trade and legislation. Some of the earliest known Malayo-Muslim writings were composed by Hamzah al-Fansuri, whose patronym indicates that he came from the west Sumatran region of Fansur, which was long noted as a source of excellent camphor. Indeed, camphor is often referred to in his poetry, which also hints at induction into a Sufi order in Ayodhya and further travels to Mecca and Jerusalem. Although al-Fansuri was long thought to have died in Aceh during the late sixteenth century, the evidence—again based on a headstone—points instead to his passing in Mecca in 1527.

Whereas al-Fansuri was clearly a member of a mystical order, he left no known writings of an expository nature regarding his belief or his scholarly affiliations. Instead, the first such indigenous writings come from the pen of a scholar who acknowledged his intellectual debt to al-Fansuri, Shams al-Din al-Samutra'i (often spelled al-Samutrani; d. 1630), who highlighted the place of Malay as the primary language of exegesis of Arabic and Persian works.

Certainly Southeast Asia remained interlinked with an Indian Ocean world. The earliest accurately datable Malay work, the *Taj al-Salatin,* which was composed in Johor in 1601, makes repeated references to events and persons in India and to Arabic and Persian books read there. Even so, the intellectual motor of change lay not so much in the historical links with India itself but with the ongoing interaction with expatriate communities throughout the entire Indian Ocean, whether among Malays abroad in the Yemen and the Hejaz or with peripatetic scholars linked by trade and patronage of the courts.

One of the most famous such émigrés was apparently a Hadrami from India, Nur al-Din al-Raniri (d. 1656), who rose to prominence at the Acehnese court around 1637 under Sultan Iskandar II (r. 1636–1641) and who is often remembered for his condemnation of the works of al-Fansuri and al-Samutra'i as constituting deviant or heterodox understandings of Sufism. Under al-Raniri, a form of local inquisition was instigated, which resulted in the public burning of these works, and, apparently, of some of the followers. However, al-Raniri is also remembered more widely for his major contribution to Malayo-Islamic juridical literature, the *Sirat al-Mustaqim,* which remains one of the most important works of Shafi'i jurisprudence used in Malay-literate religious networks; it is often regarded as a work that sits in good company with the works of al-Ghazali. It is also noteworthy that, although the Islamization legends of Kedah (on the east coast of the Malay Peninsula) backdate Islamization to a putative connection with Pasai, the name of the primary saint and the works cited in this regard are clearly linked to al-Raniri and his *Sirat*.

The contentious ascendancy of al-Raniri was undone in 1641, when a local challenger who was remembered as a scholar and mystic from the Minangkabau highlands gained the favor of the reigning sultana, Taj al-Alam Safiyat al-Din Shah (1641–1675); this was not unsual for Southeast Asia, with queens having ruled over Islamic states such as Pasai and later in Patani.

Although al-Raniri instituted a campaign against ostensibly deviant forms of mysticism, he was himself a Sufi. One Indonesian scholar, Azyumardi Azra, sees him as a key leader in a centuries-long program of reform and further Islamization in the archipelago as a whole. Still, the message of teachers like al-Raniri appears to have gained greater acceptance over time but in a more accommodationist local guise. This was presented by Abd al-Ra'uf al-Sinkili (1615–1693), who served under Iskandar II's female successor, Sultana Safiyat al-Din, and composed the first complete Malay exegesis of the Qur'an. This work, the *Tarjuman al-Mustafid*, was based heavily on the tafsir of "the two Jalals," al-Mahalli (1389–1459) and al-Suyuti (1445–1505). Although al-Sinkili's work is now increasingly rare, he laid the groundwork for the lasting importance and popularity of the Jalalayn in Southeast Asia.

MICHAEL LAFFAN

See also 'Abd al-Qadir al-Jilani; Al-Biruni; Ghazali; Ibn Battuta; Ibn Khurradadhbih; Al-Idrisi; Java; Merchants, Guilds; Merchants, Jewish; Scriptural Exegesis, Islamic; al-Shafi'i; Silk Roads; Southeast Asia, Languages and Literatures: Malay and Javanese; Sufism and Sufis; Sumatra and the Malay Peninsula; Sufism and Sufis; al-Suyuti; Yaqut; Yemen, Hadramaut; Hejaz; Ayyubids; Rasulids

Further Reading

Andaya, Barbara Watson, and Leonard Andaya. *A History of Malaysia*, 2nd ed. Houndmills: Palgrave, 2001.
Azra, Azyumardi. *The Origins of Islamic Reformism in Southeast Asia: Networks of Malay-Indonesian and Middle Eastern 'Ulamâ' in the Seventeenth and Eighteenth Centuries*. Honolulu: University of Hawaii Press, 2004.
Coedès, George. *The Indianized States of Southeast Asia*. Honolulu: East West Center Press, 1968.
Cortesão, Armando, ed. and transl. *The Suma Oriental of Tomé Pires (...) and the Book of Fransisco Rodriguez (...)*. London: The Hakluyt Society, Second Series no. 89, 1944.
Goitein, S.D. *Letters of Medieval Jewish Traders*. Princeton, NJ: Princeton University Press, 1973.
Ibn Battuta. *The Travels of Ibn Battûta A.D. 1325–1354*, eds. and transl. H.A.R. Gibb and C.F. Beckingham, vol. IV, 874–87. London: Hakluyt Society, 1994.
Jacq-Hergoualc'h, Michel. *The Malay Peninsula: Crossroads of the Maritime Silk Road*. Leiden: Brill, 2002.
Jones, Russell. "Ten Conversion Myths from Indonesia." In *Conversion to Islam*, ed. Nehemia Levtzion, 129–58. London, Methuen.
Prapañca, Mpu. *DeSawarnana (Nâgarakrtâgama)*, ed. Stuart Robson. Leiden: KITLV Press, 1995.
Reid, Anthony. *Southeast Asia in the Age of Commerce*, 2 vols. New Haven, CT: Yale University Press, 1988–1993.
Riddell, Peter G. *Islam and the Malay-Indonesian World: Transmission and Responses*. Honolulu: University of Hawaii, 2001.
Tibbetts, G.R. *A Study of the Arabic Texts Containing Material on South-East Asia*. Leiden and London: Brill, 1979.
Wolters, Oliver. *Early Indonesian Commerce: A Study of the Origins of Śrîvijaya*. Ithaca, NY: Cornell University Press, 1962.
Yule, Henry, and Henri Cordier. *The Book of Ser Marco Polo*, 2 vols. Philo Press, Amsterdam, 1975.

MALI EMPIRE

The Mali Empire gained fame from descriptions of Arab authors such as Ibn Battuta and Ibn Khaldun as well as from the fact that the founding of the Empire by Sunjata has been transmitted since the Middle Ages in the so-called Sunjata epic. As Ghana collapsed, Mali established itself as the leading power in the western Sudan, and it was famous for its riches derived from its gold mines. In the fourteenth century, the Mali Empire covered large parts of the African savannah. The heyday of the Mali Empire was either the period of Sunjata (probably the first half of the thirteenth century) or the reign of Mansa Musa (the first half of the fourteenth century). Around 1380, the Mali Empire lost influence to the rapidly growing Songhay Empire. In the Middle Niger, references to the Mali Empire seemed to have faded away occasioned by the rise of the rulers of Ségou in the seventeenth century. However, it is also possible that the rulers of Mali never had as strong a hold in this area as they did in the Upper Niger region. Currently, the Mali Empire is particularly remembered by the Maninka (Malinké) who live south of the city of Bamako (the capital of the present-day republic of Mali) and in northeastern Guinea.

The history of the Mali Empire has not been well documented in contemporary written sources. Most of the few available sources were written either after the heyday of the empire or/and from the perspective of a successor state of the Empire. Current scholarship envisions the Upper and Middle Niger area during the Middle Ages as going through centuries of a trend toward the creation of state organizations with central agencies of redistribution and possessing a majority or monopoly of power and authority, at least episodically, for the duration of one or more regimes. Rulers accomplished centralization by absorbing—first politically through conquest or clientship and then culturally—regions into the Empire. Whether Mali was an "empire" depends to a large extent of the definition of the word.

Historiographically, the Mali Empire is the most illustrious empire of the medieval west Sudan. To understand the importance of the Mali Empire, a closer look at scholarly interpretations is necessary. The French colonial regime, according to the oral traditions, emphasized Sunjata's role as the alleged founder of the dynasty of rulers of Mali. Although Sunjata's name is mentioned in the Arab sources, data about his deeds come from oral accounts that were written down after 1850. These accounts, known as the Sunjata epic (Austen, 1999; Johnson, 2003) narrate Sunjata's quest for the throne of Mande. He was said to have been sent in exile by his older brother Dankaran Tuman, a weak figure who was subsequently defeated by the sorcerer-king Sumaoro Kanté of Susu (a kingdom that is not related to the present-day Soso ethnic group, who live in Guinea). After the occupation of Mande by Sumaoro, the people of Mande sent a delegation in search of Sunjata, a delegation that convinced him to return to Mande. The actual confrontation between Sunjata and Sumaoro Kanté is a wonderful story full of witchcraft and magic. Sumaoro is said to have transformed himself into the rocks near Koulikoro, which is one hundred kilometers east of Bamako. Sunjata thus liberated the people of Mande and became ruler. He gave each family a task in society at a meeting at the plain of Kurukanfugan (five kilometers north of present-day Kangaba, along the river Niger), thus establishing Mande society. Inherent to present-day Mande society is a tripartite division of its population into status categories: noblemen, artisans, and servants: This is a social system that was probably already in existence during the Middle Ages. In the village of Kangaba, every seven years, a ceremonial restoration and reroofing of the Kamabolon sanctuary takes place. During this ceremony, which evokes the imagination of many people in Mali and beyond, the authoritative recitation of the Sunjata epic is performed by the *jeliw* of the village of Kela. However, this recitation is a "secret" family affair; it takes place inside the sanctuary, and the hundreds of attendees are only allowed to watch the event from a distance. The Kamabolon ceremony is clear proof of the importance of the memory of the Mali Empire in present-day historical imagination.

Inevitably, Arab writers, when writing about the foundation of Mali, refer to the Sunjata epic. Moreover, this narration has functioned for centuries as a political charter for the Maninka (Jansen 2001). Sunjata also has a major appeal to political elites in West African nation states such as Mali (a name chosen by the political elite of Soudan Français in the 1950s, at the eve of independence), Guinea, and the Gambia. These countries base national histories on the Sunjata epic, and each considers the Mali Empire its historical predecessor, which sometimes leads to doubtful strategies to appropriate Sunjata into their own nation's medieval history (Conrad 1994).

Academic history, which considers the reign of Mansa Musa as the heyday of the Mali Empire, has traditionally emphasized information from written sources. It rejected history reconstructed by the French colonial regime on the basis of its solely oral traditions. However, this academic search for external validity seems to be in the process of falling victim to decreasing popularity, particularly among scholars of African origin, who are in search of a paradigm that may allow for an intensive use of twentieth-century oral tradition for African medieval history (Diawara, 2003). Hence, a politically inspired struggle regarding epistemologies is at the moment of this writing central in the scholarly appreciation of the Mali Empire.

The position of Islam in the Mali Empire is an issue of academic debate. It is generally accepted that most of the rulers of Mali adhered to Islam. Moreover, long-distance traders adhered to Islam; whether the common people adhered to Islam is not well known. Arab sources suggest that the rulers of Mali had economic interests that were achieved by not striving actively for the conversion to Islam of the local populations; after conversion, these individuals would work less in the gold mines.

JAN JANSEN

See also Ibn Battuta; Ibn Khaldun; Mansa Musa

Further Reading

Conrad, David C. "A Town Called Dakajalan: The Sunjata Tradition and the Question of Ancient Mali's Capital." *Journal of African History* 35 (1994): 355–77.
Diawara, Mamadou. *L'Empire du Verbe et L'Éloquence du Silence*. Cologne: Rüdiger Köppe Verlag, 2003.
Hopkins, John F.P., and Nehemiah Levtzion. *Corpus of Early Arabic Sources for West African History*. Cambridge, UK: Cambridge University Press, 1981.
Jansen, Jan. *Epopée-Histoire-Sociéte: Le Cas de Soundjata (Mali-Guinée)*. Paris: Karthala, 2001.
Johnson, John W. *Son-Jara: The Mande Epic*, 3rd ed. Bloomington, Ind.: Indiana University Press, 2003.
Levtzion, Nehemia. *Ancient Ghana and Mali*, 2nd ed. New York: Africana, 1980.

MALIK IBN ANAS

Malik ibn Anas was a Medinan jurist whose teachings laid down the foundations of the Maliki school of law. He died in AH 179/796 CE in Medina at the age of eighty-five. He cultivated the study of hadith, fiqh, and qira'a.

Malik spent most of his life in Medina, where his scholarly activities appear to have been highly valued. In 144/761, the 'Abbasid caliph al-Mansur entrusted him to transmit the Hassanids of Mecca a demand to hand over the Shi'i pretenders Muhammad and Ibrahim b. 'Abd Allah. The mission failed, and, in 145/762, Muhammad seized power in Medina. This rebellion seems to have been supported by Malik, because he issued a fatwa declaring that the homage paid to al-Mansur was not binding because it had been given under compulsion. When the rebellion failed, Malik was flogged by the 'Abbasid governor of Medina, an action that strengthened his religious prestige. Subsequently, Malik came to terms with the government.

The most important writing attributed to him is the *Muwatta'*, although the authorship and chronology of this book have been the subject of debate. The *Muwatta'* consists of a compilation of about two thousand Prophetic reports organized in sixty-one chapters dealing with questions of ritual *('ibadat)* and legal transactions *(mu'amalat)*. Its somehow hybrid character between hadith and fiqh is reflected in the fact that the *Muwatta'* is considered a legal textbook as well as—at least according to some scholars—one of the canonical collections of hadith. As the term *Muwatta'* suggests, Malik's compilation was intended to "level the path" to the implementation of justice and law. A distinctive feature of the *Muwatta'* is the role given to the practice of the people of Medina, which is put forward as an additional source of law as well as the decisive criterion in the interpretation of Qur'an and hadith.

Malik had hundreds of disciples who spread his teachings in all directions. The historian Ibn Jaldun mentions three geographical lines in this transmission: (1) Qayrawani; (2) Andalusian; and (3) Eastern (including Iraqi and Egyptian branches).

Qadi 'Iyad b. Musa pointed out the existence of twenty different versions of the *Muwatta'*, the most famous and widespread being the riwaya of the Andalusian Yahya b. Yaya al-Laythi. Worthy of mention are also the transmissions of al-Shaybani, Ibn Bukayr, 'Ali b. Ziyad, al-Qa'nabi, Abu Mus'ab al-Zuhri, Suwayd al-Hadathani, Ibn al-Qasim, and 'Abd Allah Ibn Wahb. Other relevant names in the spread and early development of Maliki doctrine are those of Ashhab, Ibn 'Abd al-Hakam, Asad b. Furat, Ibn al-Majishun, Mutarrif, Asbagh b. al-Faraj, Ibn Habib, and al-'Utbi.

Malik was also venerated as a trustworthy hadith scholar. The names of al-Awza'i, al-Layth b. Sa'd, al-Shafi'i, and al-Thawri stand out from among the mass of scholars who are reported to have transmitted prophetic reports from him.

DELFINA SERRANO RUANO

Further Reading

B. Anas, Malik. *Muwatta' Iman Malik*, transl. M. Rahimuddin. Lahore: Sh. Muhammad Asraj, 1985.
———. *Al-Muwatta' of Imam Malik ibn Anas: The First Formulation of Islamic Law*, transl. A.A. Bewley. London: Kegan Paul, 1989.
Brunschvig, R. "Polémiques Médiévales Autour du Rite de Mâlik." *Al-Andalus* 15 (1950): 377–413.
Calder, N. *Studies in Early Muslim Jurisprudence*. Oxford, UK: Clarendon Press, 1993.
Cottart, N. "Mâlikiyya." In *EI²*.
Dutton, Y. *The Origins of Islamic Law: The Qur'ân, the Muwatta and Medinan Amal*. Richmond, Va: Curzon, 1999.
Fierro, M. "El Derecho Mâlikí en al-Andalus: Ss. II/VIII–V/XI." *Al-Qantara* 12 (1991): 119–32.
Hallaq, W. "On Dating Malik's *Muwatta*." *UCLA Journal of Islamic and Near Eastern Law* 1 (2001–2002): 47–65.
Lagardère, V. "L'Unificateur du Malikisme Oriental et Occidental à Alexandrie: Abû Bakr at-Turtûsi." *Revue de l'Occident Musulman et de la Mediterranée* 31 (1981): 47–61.
Mansour, M.H. *The Maliki School of Law: Spread and Domination in North and West Africa, 8th–14th Centuries*. San Francisco: Austin & Winfield, 1994.
Melchert, Ch. *The Formation of the Sunni Schools of Law, 9th–10th Centuries CE*. Leiden, New York, and Cologne: Brill, 1997.
Motzki, H. "The Prophet and the Cat: On Dating Malik's *Muwatta* and Legal Traditions." *Jerusalem Studies in Arabic & Islam* 22 (1998): 18–83.
Mukhtar, Ahmad, al-'Umar al-Jabruti az-Zayla', Ibrahim. "Maliki Scholars and Technical Terms." Available at: http://ourworld.compuserve.com/homepages/ABewley/malikis.html. Accessed May 24, 2005.
Muranyi, M. *Beiträge zur Geschichte der Hadit- und Rechtsgelehrsamkeit der Malikiyya in Nordafrika bis zum 5. Jh. d.H.: Biobibliographische Notizen aus der Moscheebibliothek von Qairawan*. Wiesbaden: Harrassowitz, 1997.
Mûsà 'Iyâd b. *Tartîb al-Madârik wa-Taqrîb al-Masâlik li-Ma'rifat a'Lâm Madhhab Mâlik*, 3 vols., ed. A.B. Mahmûd. Beirut: Dâr Maktabat al-Hayât, 1387–1388/1967–1968.
Saifullah, M.S.M., Hesham Azmy, and Muhammad Ghoniem. "On The 'Versions' of Malik's Muwatta'." Available at: http://www.islamic-awareness.org/Hadith/muwatta.html. Accessed May 24, 2005.
Schacht, J. "Mâlik b. Anas." In *EI²*.
Turki, A.M. "La Vénération pour Mâlik et la Physionomie du Mâlikisme Andalou." In *Théologiens et Juristes de l'Espagne Musulmane. Aspects Polémiques*, 43–67. Paris, Maisonneuve & Larose, 1982.

MALIKISM

Malikism is a juridical–religious school the origins of which can be traced back to the teachings of Malik ibn Anas (d. Medina, AH 179/795 CE) as compiled in the *Muwatta'*. The legal arguments of this legal school are based on the Prophetic traditions *(hadith)* and the juridical practice *('amal)* of Medina, backed in many cases by Malik's personal opinion. As is true of other legal schools, Malikis base their doctrine on the Qur'an, Prophetic traditions, and *ijma'* (consensus). Malik was accused of limiting the concept of ijma' to the practice of the people of Medina, and he was accused as well of putting this practice on a level with the Prophetic traditions and with the precedents of the Righteous Caliphs and the opinions of the prominent Companions. He was additionally criticized for excessive resort to the *ra'y* (personal judgment) to restrict the application of certain hadiths or even to leave them aside. Finally, another criticism made to him was his application of the analogy *(qiyas)* to the ijma'. Malikis of later generations faced these criticisms by making an effort to "traditionalize" jurisprudence, although no significant changes were made in practice. It has to be said as well that diverse tendencies within the Maliki school existed (i.e., Iraqi, Andalusi, and Ifriqi) that were not reunited until the twelfth century. According to the historian Ibn Khaldun, this reunification was possible thanks to the efforts of the jurist Abu Bakr al-Turtushi (d. 1126).

From Medina, Malik's doctrines were disseminated in Egypt, Iraq, Khurasan, Syria, Yemen, the Maghrib, al-Andalus, and, much later, in Sudan and the Islamicized areas of the west of black Africa. Currently this is the prevalent legal school in Sudan, Morocco, Mauritania, Nigeria, and all of the Islamicized areas of sub-Saharan Africa, with the exception of the Indian Ocean coastline. Malikism coexists with Ibadi and Hanafi centers in Algeria, Tunisia, and Libya. Finally, there are some Maliki groups in the cities of Hijaz and the United Arab Emirates.

DELFINA SERRANO RUANO

Further Reading

Brockopp, J.E. *Early Maliki Law: Ibn 'Abd al-Hakam and His Major Compendium of Jurisprudence.* Leiden, New York, and Köln: Brill, 2000.
Brunschvig, R. "Polémiques Medievales Autour du Rite de Malik." *Al-Andalus* 15 (1950): 377–413.
Cottart, N. "Malikiyya." In EI².
Fierro, M. "The Legal Policies of the Almohad Caliphs and Ibn Rushd's *Bid$ayat al-Mujtahid*." *Journal of Islamic Studies* 10 (1999): 226–48.
———. "Proto-Maliki, Malikis and Reformed Malikis in al-Andalus." In *The Madhhab, Proceedings of the 3rd International Conference on Islamic Legal Studies.* Cambridge, Mass: Harvard, 2000.
Jackson, S.A. *Islamic Law and the State: The Constitutional Jurisprudence of Shihab al-Din al-Qarafi.* Leiden, New York, and Cologne, 1996.
Lagardère, V. "L'Unificateur du Malikisme au XIᵉ et XIIᵉ Siécles, Abu Bakr al-Turtushi." *Revue de l'Occident Musulman et de la Méditerranée* 31 (1981): 47–61.
Mansour, M.H. *The Maliki School of Law: Spread and Domination in North and West Africa, 8th–14th Centuries.* San Francisco, Austin, and Winfield, 1994.
Melchert, Ch. *The Formation of the Sunni Schools of Law, 9th–10th Centuries CE.* Leiden, New York, and Cologne: Brill, 1997.
Müller, Ch. *Gerichtspraxis im Stadtstaat Córdoba: Zum Recht der Gesellschaft in Einer Malikitisch-Islamischen Rechtstradition des 5./11. Jahrhunderts.* Leiden, New York, and Cologne: Brill, 1999.
Muranyi, M. *Beiträge zur Geschichte der Hadit- und Rechtsgelehrsamkeit der Malikiyya in Nordafrika bis zum 5. Jh. d.H.: Biobibliographische Notizen aus der Moscheebibliothek von Qairawan.* Wiesbaden: Harrassowitz, 1997.
Powers, D. *Law, Society and Culture in the Maghrib, 1300–1500.* Cambridge, UK: Cambridge University Press, 2002.
Scholz, P. *Malikitisches Verfahrensrecht: Ein Studie zu Inhalt und Methodik der Scharia mit Rechtshistorischen und Rechtsvergleichenden Anmerkungen am Beispiel des Malikitischen Verfahrensrechts bis zum 12.* Jahrhundert and Frankfurt: Lang, 1997.
Turki, A.M. *Polémiques Entre Ibn Hazm e Bagi sur les Principes de la loi Musulmanes.* Argel, 1973.
Urvoy, D. *Pensers d'al-Andalus. La Vie Intellectuelle à Cordoue et à Séville au Temps des Empires Berbères (Fin XIᵉ Siècle-Début XIIIᵉ Siècle).* Toulouse, 1990.

MALIKSHAH

Malikshah was the third sultan (r. 1072–1092 CE) of the Great Seljuk Empire. Born in 1055, he was a son of Sultan Alp Arslan, who named him his successor in 1066. Malikshah was with his father when he was assassinated in Transoxiana in 1072 and was immediately proclaimed sultan. Alp Arslan's grand vizier, Nizam al-Mulk, facilitated Malikshah's succession and retained the vizierate. Nizam was the guiding force behind Malikshah throughout his rule and managed the empire while the sultan expanded its borders and brought it to the height of its power and glory.

As soon as Malikshah became sultan, his uncle Qavurt, the ruler of Kirman, challenged his rule. Malikshah crushed Qavurt's revolt in Hamadan in 1074 and executed him. While Malikshah was dealing with Qavurt, the Qarakhanid ruler Shams al-Mulk pushed south from Transoxiana into Tukharistan. The sultan rushed to drive him back in 1073 and 1074, and he then gave his brother Tekish control of Tukharistan. At the same time, Malikshah shored up his borders in the same region against Ghaznavid irredentism. Malikshah returned to suppress a rebellion of Tekish in 1080 and 1081 and again in 1084. In 1089, the sultan invaded Qarakhanid territory, taking Seljuk arms to their farthest point east and forcing the submission of the Qarakhanid ruler of Kashghar and Khotan.

In the west, Malikshah had to deal with a hostile Georgia, independent Kurdish and Arab emirates, and various Turkmen leaders. He campaigned twice in the Caucasus, during 1078/1079 and 1085, keeping Georgia on the defensive and the Kurds under control. In 1084, he destroyed the Kurdish Marwanid dynasty in Diyarbakr. Meanwhile, various independent Turkmen bands had been forcing back the Byzantine frontier. Malikshah's cousin Sulayman ibn Qutulmish was the leader of one such group. He captured Nicaea in 1075 and took control of much of western and central Anatolia. Malikshah was suspicious of him and around 1077 or 1078 sent an army to subdue him but without success. Sulayman's descendants later created the Seljuk Sultanate of Anatolia or Rum, which survived until 1307. For Malikshah, more important than Anatolia were Syria and Jazira. There he strove to ensure that the influence of the Shi'i Fatimids in Egypt was neutralized, that the major cities were in Sunni Muslim hands, and that the local Arab emirates were obedient. In 1084 and 1085, he campaigned in Syria and reached the Mediterranean.

Malikshah also devoted some attention to Arabia. Through diplomacy, he had the Friday sermon (khutba) in Mecca changed so that it was given in the name of the 'Abbasid caliph rather than the Fatimid. In 1076/1077, one of his commanders invaded the eastern coast of Arabia as far as Bahrain, attacking the Shi'i Qarmathians en route. Around 1091 or 1092, he sent a force to Yemen, which briefly occupied it and Aden.

Malikshah used Isfahan exclusively as his capital until his second trip to Baghdad in 1091, when he decided to make that city his winter capital and began large-scale building projects there. He generally excluded the 'Abbasid caliphs from affairs of state. Nizam al-Mulk had the task of enforcing Seljuk policy toward the caliphs. In 1087, he arranged a marriage between the caliph al-Muqtadi and a daughter of Malikshah. Relations between the sultan and caliph cooled, however, and, by 1091, Malikshah was planning to depose al-Muqtadi. Nothing came of this, because, in 1092, less than two months after Nizam al-Mulk was assassinated, the sultan suddenly died of fever. He was buried in Isfahan. At his death, the empire plunged into turmoil as his sons struggled for the throne.

Malikshah managed to unite most of the heartland of the Middle East, from Transoxiana to Syria, into one state, although this unity did not survive him. More important, he gave his full support to a revival of Sunnism, ensuring its triumph over Shi'ism. This revival was carried out on two fronts: one military and the other ideological. The sultan continuously campaigned to forcefully crush centers of Shi'ism; generally he was successful, but pockets of it persisted in remote areas. The Isma'ili propagandist Hasan-i Sabbah, for example, seized the fortress of Alamut in the Alburz mountains in Iran in 1090. At the same time, Nizam al-Mulk promoted Sunnism with the full financial and political resources of the state. He was especially renowned for establishing colleges of Sunni law (the Nizamiyya madrasas) in most of the major cities of the empire; these colleges flourished and had a lasting effect on Islam.

GARY LEISER

Primary Sources

Ibn al-Athir. *The Annals of the Saljuq Turks*, transl. D.S. Richards. London: RoutledgeCurzon, 2002.
Din Nishapuri, Zahir, al-. *The History of the Seljuq Turks*, transl. Kenneth Luther. London: Curzon, 2001.

Further Reading

Bosworth, C.E. "The Political and Dynastic History of the Iranian World (AD 1000–1217)." In *The Cambridge History of Iran, Vol. 5, The Saljuq and Mongol Periods*, ed. J.A. Boyle, 1–202. Cambridge, UK: Cambridge University Press, 1968.

MAMLUKS

The Mamluk Sultanate of Egypt and Syria (1250–1517 CE) had its origins in the tempestuous middle decades of the thirteenth-century eastern Mediterranean region: the Ayyubid confederation, founded by Saladin in 1169, was troubled by intrafamily conflicts across the lands it controlled in Egypt, Syria, and upper Mesopotamia; the remnants of the Latin Crusader states were clustered around the Levantine port cities of Acre, Tripoli, and Antioch; and hostile Mongol armies were advancing from the East. In the face of challenges from fellow Ayyubids, al-Malik al-Salih Ayyub, the last major Ayyubid ruler of Egypt (r. 1240–1249), had recruited a corps of approximately eight hundred to one thousand military slaves (mamluks; literally "owned") to serve as a loyal bastion of his military forces (see Slavery, Military). These mamluks were referred to in the sources as either the "Bahri" corps (so named because their barracks were on an island in the river Nile [bahr al-Nil]) or the "Salihi" mamluks after their king's royal title. They subsequently played a key role in defeating

Fifteenth Century CE. The Dome of Sultan al-Ashraf Qaytbay's tomb and mosque. Exterior. Late Mamluk dynasty, 1474–75. Credit: Erich Lessing/Art Resource, NY. Mosque of Sultan Qaytbay, Cairo, Egypt.

the Egyptian Crusade of King Louis IX of France in 1248 through 1250. Al-Malik al-Salih Ayyub died during that campaign, and shortly thereafter his Mamluks murdered Ayyub's son and heir, who had threatened their lives and positions.

During the ensuing turbulent decade, this Mamluk corps fought with Ayyubid forces and each other. After they had consolidated their control of Egypt, they faced a Mongol invasion of Syria mounted after the latter's sack of Baghdad in 1258. An army led by these Salihi Mamluks and the Mamluk Sultan Qutuz (r. 1259–1260) defeated Mongol forces at 'Ayn Jalut in northern Palestine in 1260. On the return journey to Egypt, the Salihi Mamluk Baybars I assassinated Qutuz and became sultan.

Baybars (r. 1260–1277) was the true establisher of the Mamluk Sultanate, which soon became the major power in the eastern Mediterranean region. Under Baybars, the Mamluks established control over the Ayyubid Syrian provinces and began a concerted effort to eliminate the Crusaders from the eastern Mediterranean littoral; this goal was achieved by 1291. Until the mid-fourteenth century, the sultanate was engaged in a protracted struggle on its eastern borders with the Il-Khanid Mongols. The Mamluks then survived the campaigns into Syria by Timur at the beginning of the fifteenth century, and they later struggled with the Ottomans on their northern borders. The sultanate was conquered by the Ottomans in 1517, and, although their Mamluk system of rule ended, memories of Mamluk ideals and legacies played a subsequent role in the politics and society of Ottoman Egypt.

The Salihi Mamluks and their successors established a ruling system that was based on militarily defined ranks. Although actual practice over the more than two and half centuries of Mamluk history was often different, ideally the Mamluk sultan was at the top of a hierarchy of ranks and responsibilities open only to mamluks. Mamluk society valued loyalty to both the master who purchased, trained, and supported an individual mamluk and to the group of fellow mamluks belonging to that master. Because both the sultan and leading mamluk amirs (holders of military rank) would purchase mamluks of their own, the jockeying for power among the resulting factions was complex and frequently violent. A typical mamluk career might begin in the cavalry ranks and then progress through the posts of Amir of ten (number of mamluks in his retinue), Amir of forty, and Amir of one hundred. In addition to these promotions, a mamluk might receive positions in the military-political administration, from offices in the court to appointments as governors of towns or cities to commander of the army or even viceroy. As rank and position increased, a Mamluk would count on receiving an *iqta'* (a right of revenue from agricultural districts of varying size and wealth). Detailed land surveys were carried out early during the Mamluk sultanate to aid in the process of revenue determination and iqta' distribution. Although rewards would increase with higher rank, so to would risk. The Mamluk chronicles frequently relate the confiscation of wealth, imprisonment, and/or death of Amirs who had fallen from favor.

As freeborn Muslims, the sons of Mamluks, known collectively as *awlad al-nas* ("sons of the people"; i.e., the sons of those who matter), were to be excluded from this ruling system. It frequently occurred, however, that Mamluk Sultans attempted to bequeath office to their sons. Although it appears that there were family dynasties of sultans—the largest and most famous being the descendents of al-Malik al-Mansur Qalawun (r. 1280–1290)—most of these rulers were essentially place holders, controlled by leading Mamluk amirs who were themselves maneuvering to claim the throne. A notable exception to this was al-Malik al-Nasir Muhammad ibn Qalawun, whose third reign (1309–1340) is often described as the zenith of Mamluk power.

The leading cities of the sultanate, Cairo and Damascus, were centers of learning in the medieval Islamic world. Both sultans and leading amirs patronized the construction of mosques, madrasas, hospitals, convents, dormitories, tombs, and other structures, many of which still survive. Financial support for these institutions and those who worked in them was often detailed in endowment deeds *(waqfs)*. These legal documents would typically identify the revenue sources dedicated for the expenses of the institution. One result of Mamluk patronage of the religio-educational segment of society was the composition of large number of works in many genres. Large numbers of texts survive and provide a wealth of primary source material unparalleled in other Muslim states of the time.

The revenue needed to cover the expenses of the Mamluk military system and to provide this high level of patronage came from many sources. The first and most important was the income generated by the tremendous agricultural fertility of Egypt; a second was the revenue generated from trade. The Mamluk domains were astride the lucrative trade routes linking the Mediterranean region to the Indian Ocean and points east. Mamluk Cairo and the Syrian coastal cities were thus hubs of commerce attracting goods and merchants from far beyond the Mamluk borders, many of whom did their business in commercial buildings constructed by the order of Mamluk sultans.

WARREN C. SCHULTZ

See also Maqrizi; Ibn Taghri Birdi; Ibn Battuta; Ibn Khaldun; Ibn Qadi Shuhba; Ibn Taymiyya; Ibn Wasil

Primary Sources

Holt, P.M. *The Memoirs of a Syrian Prince: Abu'l-Fida, Sultan of Hamah (672–732/1273–1331)*. Wiesbaden: Franz Steinder Verlag, 1983.

Lyons, U., and M.C. *Ayyubids, Mamelukes, and Crusaders: Selections from the Ta'rikh al-Duwal wa'l-Muluk of Ibn al-Furat*, vol. 2. Cambridge: W. Heffer and Sons Ltd, 1971.

Ibn Sasra. *A Chronicle of Damascus, 1389–1397*, vol. 1, ed. and transl. William M. Brinner. Berkeley: University of California Press, 1963.

Ibn Taghri Birdi. *History of Egypt, 1382–1469 AD, Translated from the Arabic Annals of Abu l-Mahâsin ibn Taghrî Birdî*, 8 vols., transl. William Popper. Berkeley and Los Angeles: University of California Press, 1954–1963. University of California Publications in Semitic Philology, vols. 13–14, 17–19, 22–24.

Further Reading

An extensive bibliography of Mamluk History is available online at: http://www.lib.uchicago.edu/e/su/mideast/mamluk/. The reader may also consult the journal *Mamluk Studies Review*, which was published annually from 1997 and biannually since 2003.

Ayalon, David. *Studies on the Mamluks of Egypt (1250–1517)*. London: Variorum Reprints, 1977.

———. *The Mamluk Military Society*. London: Variorum Reprints, 1979.

Holt, P.M. *The Age of the Crusades: The Near East from Eleventh Century to 1517*. London: Longman, 1986.

Irwin, Robert. *The Middle East in the Middle Ages: The Early Mamluk Sultanate 1250–1382*. Carbondale, Ill: Southern Illinois University Press, 1986.

MA'MUN, AL-

'Abd Allah al-Ma'mun was the seventh 'Abbasid caliph (r. 813–833 CE). He assumed office after a brutal civil war against his brother, Muhammad al-Amin, shortly after the death of their father, Harun al-Rashid (d. 809). Al-Rashid's controversial succession arrangement had designated Muhammad as caliph and 'Abd Allah as governor of Khurasan. The ensuing conflict, informed by a debate about relations between Baghdad and the provinces and fueled by sibling antagonism and provocative gestures on the part of both brothers, led to an early rout (811) of al-Amin's forces by Tahir ibn al-Husayn (d. 822) and the subsequent assassination of al-Amin (813) in Baghdad. Years of fighting in and around the capital followed. This second round of upheaval undercut central authority in nearly every province. It was sparked by opposition to al-Fadl ibn Sahl (d. 817), al-Ma'mun's chief advisor, and al-Ma'mun's nomination of 'Ali al-Rida (d. 817) as his successor (Al-Rida, an 'Alid notable,

became in due course the eighth imam of the Twelver Shi'is). The latter decision, which was quickly reversed, appears to have been an effort by al-Ma'mun to mend fences with the 'Alids and their supporters.

Relative calm in Iraq was established with al-Ma'mun's return to Baghdad (818–819). Efforts in Syria and Egypt by 'Abd Allah ibn Tahir (d. 844), followed by further campaigns (including that in Egypt led by al-Ma'mun' himself), contributed to the restoration of central control over most of the empire. The Tahirids and a mix of new Iranian, Central Asian, and Turkish forces recruited by al-Ma'mun and his influential brother, Abu Ishaq, largely replaced the Khurasani forces that had brought the dynasty to power decades earlier. (Abu Ishaq was to succeed his brother, adopting the regnal title al-Mu'tasim, in 833). These forces took part in campaigns on the Byzantine frontier, an effort to which al-Ma'mun devoted considerable energy. The period also witnessed a difficult conflict against the Zutt (a community of north Indian origin) in southern Iraq as well as turmoil in Khurasan. It was in relation to the latter troubles that the Tahirid family consolidated control over Khurasan.

The eldest of al-Rashid's sons, al-Ma'mun had received a classical education in Arabic, literature, the arts, and the Islamic religious sciences. His long reign, which was marked by a devotion to culture, is associated with two specific initiatives. The first was the Arabic translation of pre-Islamic works from Greek, Persian, Syriac, and Sanskrit. The effort, which was begun under the later Umayyads and then accelerated by the second 'Abbasid ruler, Abu Ja'far al-Mansur, became a hallmark of al-Ma'mun's reign. The effort, which provided Arab/Islamic urban culture with an array of vital works of science, medicine, philosophy, political theory, and literature, paved the way to a remarkable interplay of Hellenistic, Iranian, and Indian ideas with Arab/Islamic thought. The second initiative, which occurred very late in al-Ma'mun's reign, was closely associated with the Mu'tazili chief qadi, Ahmad ibn Abi Du'ad (d. 854). The Mihnah, a campaign in which leading Muslim scholars were required to declare support for the doctrine of the "createdness" of the Qur'an, was probably rooted in al-Ma'mun's desire to bring weight to the religious authority of the caliphate.

MATTHEW S. GORDON

Further Reading

Kennedy, Hugh. *The Prophet and the Age of the Caliphates*, 2nd ed. Harlow, UK: Pearson Education Ltd., 2004.

Rekaya, M. "Al-Ma'mun." In *The Encyclopedia of Islam*, 2nd ed.

MANSA MUSA

By the fourteenth century, when the Mali empire reached its peak under the rule of Mansa Musa (also called Kankan Musa; r. 1312–1327 CE), Mali's reputation had spread throughout the Muslim world, not only because of commerce in gold, slaves, and other commodities but also because of the ruler's impressive pilgrimage to Mecca in 1324/1325. There is no direct eyewitness of this pilgrimage, but most often referred to is al-'Umari's report from 1337, according to which Mansa Musa was accompanied by an entourage of thousands. An oft-quoted anecdote reports Mansa Musa's generous gifts of gold during his stay in Cairo, which resulted in the huge inflation of the local gold price. Writers of later chronicles (e.g., Ibn Khaldun, Mahmud al-Kati) drew on al-'Umari, Ibn Battuta, and oral sources. It is of note that, although Ottoman reigning Sultans did not go on pilgrimage, they often made lavish endowments to the Holy Places, and there is a long tradition of royal pilgrimages in West Africa. Although Mansa Musa certainly struck the imagination of many generations after him, there is no direct evidence of his exploits in present-day West African oral tradition. However, it has often been suggested that the tradition of Nfa Jigin's pilgrimage to Mecca and his subsequent return with the amulets that are currently preserved in Komo secret societies was inspired by Mansa Musa's pilgrimage.

JAN JANSEN

See also Mali Empire; Ibn Battuta

Further Reading

Hopkins, John F.P., and Nehemiah Levtzion. *Corpus of Early Arabic Sources for West African History.* Cambridge, UK: Cambridge University Press, 1981.
Masonen, Pekka. *The Negroland Revisited—Discovery and Invention of the Sudanese Middle Ages.* Helsinki, The Finnish Academy of Science and Letters, 2000.

MANUSCRIPTS

Islamic civilization, perhaps like no other, is a civilization of the book. Indeed, books were copied by hand for more than thirteen centuries in the main Islamic lands, and there are still places in the Islamic world where this activity is very much alive. The number of surviving manuscripts in Arabic, Persian, and Ottoman Turkish may be estimated at several million. The manuscript age produced a wealth of literature that covered the whole spectrum of the traditional branches of knowledge. The development of the early Islamic book culture, however, is closely connected with the Judeo-Christian culture of the Near East.

The speedy development of many Islamic disciplines was due to one major factor: the codification of the Qur'an. After the revelation given to Muhammad was codified in book form, the Qur'an became a model for the scribe; any innovations therefore in the way it was transcribed and embellished had repercussions on Arabic book production as a whole.

Despite the occasional destruction of books by natural or manmade disaster, early Arab authors often boasted about the number of books in circulation during their time. There was a tendency in medieval Islam to constantly create new disciplines and subdisciplines; this fact becomes evident just by looking at the great variety of types of compositions: short or long, original or abridged, commented on or glossed, versified or paraphrased.

As the intellectual output grew, it was necessary to compile lists of books in circulation, catalogs of collections, and records of study. Much of the output of this early period is documented in the well-known book catalog *al-Fihrist* by Ibn al-Nadim (d. AH 380/990 CE), which lists no fewer than 5,970 titles of books that were known or circulating during the author's time.

Medieval Islamic manuscripts were made in two different forms: the roll and the codex. The type of roll used was the rotulus (which opens vertically and in which the writing of the text runs perpendicular to the length of the roll) as opposed to the volumen (which opens horizontally).

Although most of the Arabic papyri containing literary texts survive as leaves or fragments from codices, rotuli were also used as a vehicle for their copying. A good example here is the work of 'Abd Allah ibn Lahi'ah (d. 174/790), which was made in roll form and preserved in Heidelberg, Germany. Again, although parchment was used more often for the codex, there are some early rotuli fragments of the Qur'an on parchment that have survived. The roll was also used for pilgrimage certificates, amulets (sometimes containing the complete text of the Qur'an), and calendars.

The vast majority of medieval manuscripts, however, were made as codices, consisting of one or a number of quires and each containing one or usually several folded sheets (bifolia). A typical medieval quire was made by nesting the folded sheets, and it consisted of either ten leaves (quinion) or eight leaves (quaternion).

Most of the non-Qur'anic codices from the medieval period were bound in a traditional binding that was characterized by a pentagonal flap that rested on the front of the text block (under the upper cover) and that had a dual function: to protect the fore edge and to serve as a bookmark.

To ensure the correct sequence of gatherings and leaves, signatures (numbering of quires), foliation (numbering of leaves), or catchwords were used, although parchment Qur'ans copied in the ancient scripts never had signatures, and neither did many non-Qur'anic manuscripts.

Originally the quires were marked using the alphanumeric notation (abjad; until the end of the sixth/twelfth century) or Greco-Coptic numerals. Later (i.e., the second half of the fifth/eleventh century), the number of the quire came to be spelled out in full letters. In medieval and later manuscripts, the word *juz'* or *kurrasah* (quire) accompanied by a numeral was used. The usual position of the signature was the top left-hand corner of the first folio of each quire.

It appears that the use of catchwords goes back to the beginning of the third/ninth century (and not, as previously thought, to the early fifth/eleventh century). In some manuscripts, there are no catchwords (properly speaking) in the form of isolated words at the bottom of the recto (i.e., page a). Instead, the last word or words of the bottom line of the verso (i.e., page b) are repeated at the beginning of the top line on the recto of the next leaf. Most codices—and especially early Arabic ones—were not foliated. The practice of foliation seems to have been uncommon until some time after the introduction into the Arab world of the Indian numeric symbols, around the fourth/tenth century.

Although various writing surfaces were used by the early Arabs, papyrus and parchment were the materials most extensively employed during the first centuries of Islam. Furthermore, it seems that most (if not all) Qur'ans were copied on parchment, perhaps following the Jewish tradition of copying the Torah on kosher parchment. On the other hand, the majority of non-Qur'anic medieval manuscripts were written on paper, originally made locally and later (from the eighth/fourteenth century) imported from Europe (mainly Italy).

Most of the non-Qur'anic compositions followed a more or less standard pattern of presentation of the text. Almost invariably all texts began on the verso of the first leaf of the text block with the superscript basmalah and ended traditionally with a colophon. To guide the scribe's hand on the line, a ruling board *(mistarah)* was often used. Like many Western medieval manuscripts, Islamic manuscripts feature rubrics and abbreviations; the latter are often marked with a tilde. The text on the page is mostly justified and is often provided with a frame or a rule border. To justify the left-hand margin, the scribe would use different devices such as elongation or contraction of horizontal strokes within words, as well as word superscription. Rubrics were used extensively for chapter headings, keywords, text commented on or glossed, and abbreviations. Significant sections or elements of the text were also marked by marginal notabilia (side heads).

Deluxe copies of the Qur'an and commissioned non-Qur'anic manuscripts were often illuminated and sometimes—especially in the Turkish and Iranian/Indian contexts—illustrated. The painted decoration often consisted of double-page frontispieces and finispieces (especially in Qur'ans), or title, head, and tail pieces. The incipit page was a favorite area for decoration during the later medieval period.

The colophons were usually written in the language of the main text. However, Persian and Turkish manuscripts were often provided with colophons in the Arabic language (and vice versa). Also, in well-executed manuscripts, colophons are often written in a different script and may have been illuminated. For example, in Iran during the eighth/fourteenth and ninth/fifteenth centuries, colophons were often written in ta'liq script; from the ninth/fifteenth century onward, they were written in riqa' or tawqi'/riqa', nasta'liq, and shikastah nasta'liq scripts.

Apart from a traditional use of the Muslim date, manuscripts were also dated by feasts, regnal years (anno regni), fractions, and various non-Muslim calendar systems, although the dates were sometimes presented in the form of chronograms or chronosticons (using the alphanumeric values of the alphabet).

Except for deluxe copies of the Qur'an, most medieval manuscripts were copied in informal hands that are broadly referred to as *naskhi* (naskh-related) and *maghribi.* Also, many that have survived can be characterized as scholarly hands that were greatly influenced by various chancery scripts and styles.

Throughout the Middle Ages, knowledge was passed on from teacher to pupil in the way that was characteristic of Islamic teaching. The collation of texts and its importance—well-known in the Greco-Syriac tradition—came to be recognized as essential to the accurate transmission of the religious sciences. Many texts of the medieval period (especially those involving the religious disciplines) were transmitted through dictation in front of sometimes very large audiences. Texts were studied in circles and authenticated by means of granting audition certificates *(sama'at)*.

Naturally, as a result of the transmission of works through dictation, holographs, whether drafts or fair copies (i.e., texts written entirely in the author's hand), were extremely rare during the first four Muslim centuries. Drafts, if they existed, did not have the same academic value as an authorized text; their value was more appreciated by bibliophiles than scholars. However, not all books were collated: Abu Rayhan al-Biruni, for instance, writing during the middle of the fifth/eleventh century, complained about the widespread neglect by scribes of collation and of the verification of a text's accuracy.

Most of the errors made in the process of copying were involuntary omissions. In well-executed manuscripts, they were marked by a signe de renvoi (reference marks), which has its origin in the Greek lambda. Some texts were heavily glossed using interlinear space and margins.

With regard to the present knowledge of the extant corpus of Islamic manuscripts, there is no fragment or codex with a non-Qur'anic text that can be attributed to the Umayyad period (41–132/661–750) or earlier. There are no dated manuscripts from the period before the third/ninth century, and those that are datable on paleographic grounds are mainly Qur'anic fragments in Hijazi and early 'Abbasid scripts. There appear to be no more than forty datable manuscripts from the third/ninth century; in this figure are included eleven Christian manuscripts and a number of Qur'anic fragments. Furthermore, there are only some 530 dated or datable manuscripts from the fourth/tenth and fifth/eleventh centuries. The overwhelming majority of manuscripts that have survived span the period from the sixth/twelfth century to the end of the thirteenth/nineteenth century, with most of them belonging to the late Islamic period (tenth/sixteenth–thirteenth/nineteenth centuries).

Most of the surviving Arabic codices are written on parchment and paper, although papyrus was also used for their production during the first centuries of Islam. The oldest surviving papyrus codex, dated 229/844, contains the work *Hadith Dawud* by Wahb ibn Munabbih (d. 110/728). The second oldest, copied before 276/889, is the *Jami' fi al-Hadith* by 'Abd Allah ibn Wahb (d. 197/812). Most of the surviving manuscripts on parchment are Qur'anic fragments. There are a few large fragments of the Qur'an in codex form written in Hijazi scripts and therefore datable to the second half of the first/seventh or early second/eighth century. Some fourteen parchment fragments of the Qur'an are safely datable to the third/ninth century. The earliest non-Qur'anic codex written on parchment is a portion of *Siyar al-Fazari* dated 270/883; the oldest dated codex written on paper is *Gharib al-Hadith* by 'Abu 'Ubayd al-Qasim ibn Sallam (d. 224/838), which was executed in 252/866 and is preserved in the library of the University of Leiden.

ADAM GACEK

Further Reading

Déroche, François, et al. *Manuel de Codicologie des Manuscrits en Écriture Arabe*. Paris: Bibliothèque Nationale de France, 2000.

Gacek, Adam. *The Arabic Manuscript Tradition: A Glossary of Technical Terms and Bibliography*. Leiden and Boston: E.J. Brill, 2001.

———. "Technical Practices and Recommendations Recorded by Classical and Post-classical Arabic Scholars Concerning the Copying and Correction of Manuscripts." In *Manuscrits du Moyen-Orient*, 51–60, plates 20–32., ed. F. Déroche. Istanbul and Paris, 1989.

Guesdon, Marie-Geneviève, and Vernay-Nouri, Annie. *L'Art du Livre Arabe: Du Manuscrit au Livre D'Artiste*. Paris: Bibliothèque Nationale de France, 2001.

Pedersen, J. *The Arabic Book*, 20–53. Princeton, NJ: Princeton University Press, 1984.

MANZIKERT

Manzikert was a town in eastern Anatolia and the site of the famous battle in 1071 CE between the Byzantine emperor Romanus IV Diogenes and the Seljuk sultan Alp Arslan. Throughout much of its known history, Manzikert had been a fortified Armenian town on a major trade and invasion route between central Anatolia and Iran. It was in Byzantine hands in 1054 when Toghril Beg, the first sultan of the Great Seljuk Empire, unsuccessfully besieged it. Alp Arslan, Toghril's successor, captured it in 1070. Meanwhile, acting independently, bands of Turkmen had been raiding Byzantine territory. By 1068, when General Romanus Diogenes became emperor, these raiders had reached the Bosphorus. During his third campaign to put a stop to this growing menace, he set out in March 1071 to capture Manzikert, Akhlat (some thirty five miles to the south), and close major Turkish invasion routes. Alp Arslan learned of this while in Northern Syria and turned to meet him. The emperor had divided his forces between Manzikert and Akhlat; he had just taken the former when Alp Arslan appeared. Many of the emperor's foreign mercenaries then deserted (some to the sultan), and the commander in charge of his read guard plotted against him. Outnumbered, Alp Arslan proposed a peace agreement, but Romanus refused to negotiate. During the ensuing battle (probably on August 26th), the sultan defeated and captured the emperor but released him after dictating peace terms. The emperor was deposed while returning to Constantinople. Byzantine defenses collapsed, leaving Anatolia open to large-scale Turkish invasion. Alp Arslan did not, however, order a systematic conquest of Byzantium; he immediately marched east to face a crisis in Transoxania. Nevertheless, Turkmen tribes began streaming into

Byzantium on their own. Thus began the long process of the Turkification and Islamization of Anatolia.

GARY LEISER

See also Byzantine Empire; Muslim–Byzantine Relations; Seljuks; Seljuk Warfare

Further Reading

Vryonis, Speros. "The Greek and Arabic Sources on the Battle of Mantzikert, 1071 AD," In *Byzantine Studies: Essays on the Slavic World and the Eleventh Century*, ed. Speros Vryonis. New Rochelle, New York: Aristide Caratzas, 1992.
———. "The Greek and Arabic Sources on the Eight Day Captivity of the Emperor Romanos IV in the Camp of the Sultan Alp Arslan after the Battle of Mantzikert." In *Novum Millennium: Studies on Byzantine History and Culture Dedicated to Paul Speck*, eds. Claudia Sode and Sarolta Takács. Aldershot, UK: Ashgate, 2000.
———. "The Battles of Manzikert (1071) and Myriocephalum (1176): Notes on Food, Water, Archery, Ethnic Identity of Foe and Ally." In *Mésogeios* 22–23 (2004).

MAQAMA

The *maqama* (pl. *maqamat*) is a short narrative written in rhymed prose *(saj')* that often consists of a recasting of any number of well-known literary, scholarly, or religious discursive styles. Although the details vary from one author to another, some general characteristics can be described. The maqama features a recurring pair of characters: the narrator and an eloquent trickster. The trickster often appears in disguise and usually speaks in a recognizable style or tone. For example, he may speak as a preacher, an astrologer, a literary critic, or a poet. The climax occurs in the recognition scene, during which the trickster's identity is revealed and the two protagonists part ways, although often not before the gullible crowd, including the narrator, is convinced to hand over considerable sums of money. Studies of the maqama largely agree that it emerged out of the larger field of adab learning, drawing upon the latter's treatment and use of a wide range of themes, motifs, clichés, and images from all manner of literary and intellectual contexts. It has been argued that the original intent of composing the maqama was to lighten the mood of scholarly adab sessions. In its later manifestations, the maqama may have been intended as a pedagogical tool for the secretarial *(katib)* class.

The maqama crystallized in 995 or 997 CE, when Badi' al-Zaman al-Hamadhani (d. 1008) composed his collection of maqamat. However, it was not until the maqama collection of al-Hariri (d. 1122) appeared that the form reached its peak in sophistication,

assumed its relatively standard structure, and was accepted into the literary canon as one of Arabic literature's first admittedly fictional forms. Al-Hariri had a number of imitators, the most notable in Arabic being al-Saraqusti (d. 1143), and in Hebrew, Judah al-Harizi (d. 1225); both of these writers were Andalusians. In addition to these classical imitations, the maqama also provided the inspiration for a number of creative variations. These experiments included the development of character and plot (e.g., the maqamats of Solomon Ibn Saqbel [first half of the twelfth century] and Ibn al-Murabi' al-Azdi [d. 1350]). Although direct lines of influence are difficult to draw with any certainty, strong relationships between the maqama and the Spanish picaresque novel have been discussed extensively.

ALEXANDER E. ELINSON

See also Adab; Andalus; Education; Humanism; al-Hamadhani, Badi' al-Zaman; Judah al-Harizi; Translation, Arabic to Hebrew

Primary Sources

Al-Hamadhani, Badi' al-Zaman. *Sharh Maqamat Badi' al-Zaman al-Hamadhani*, ed. Muhammad Muhyi al-Din 'Abd al-Hamid. Cairo, 1962.
Al-Harizi, Judah. *Tahkemoni*, ed. Y. Toporowsky. Tel Aviv: Mahberot le-Sifrut, 1952.
Al-Saraqusti, Abu al-Tahir Muhammad b. Yusuf. *al-Maqamat al-Luzumiyya*, ed. Hasan al-Waragli. Rabat: Manshurat 'Akkaz, 1995.
Al-Sharishi, Abu al-'Abbas Ahmad ibn 'Abd al-Mu'min. *Sharh Maqamat al-Hariri*, 5 vols., ed. Muhammad Abu al-Fadl Ibrahim. Beirut: Dar al-Fikr, 1992.

Further Reading

Beeston, A.F.L. "Al-Hamadhani, al-Hariri and the *Maqamat* Genre." In *The Cambridge History of Arabic Literature: 'Abbasid Belles-Lettres*, eds. Julia Ashtiany et al., 125–35. Cambridge, UK: Cambridge University Press, 1990.
Drory, Rina. "The Maqama." In *The Cambridge History of Arabic Literature: The Literature of Al-Andalus*, eds. María Rosa Menocal, Raymond P. Scheindlin, and Michael Sells, 190–210. Cambridge, UK: Cambridge University Press, 2000.
De la Granja, Fernando. *Maqamas y Risalas Andaluzas (Traducciones y Estudios)*. Madrid: Hiperión, 1976.
Hamadhani, Badi' al-Zaman, al-. *Maqamat*, transl. W.J. Prendergast. London: Curzon Press, 1973.
Hariri, al-. *Maqamat*, transl. F. Steingass. London: Sampson Low, Marston & Co., 1897.
Harizi, Judah ben Solomon, al-. *The Tahkemoni of Judah al-Harizi*, transl. Victor Emanuel Reichert. Jerusalem: R.H. Cohen's Press, 1965–1973.
———. *The Book of Tahkemoni: Jewish Tales from Medieval Spain*, transl. David Simha Segal. Portland, Ore: Littman Library of Jewish Civilization, 2001.

Ibn Saqbel, Solomon. "Asher in the Harem." In *Rabbinic Fantasies*, eds. David Stern and Mark Mirsky, transl. Raymond P. Scheindlin, 253–267. Philadelphia: The Jewish Publication Society, 1990.

Ibn Shabbetai. "The Misogynist." In *Rabbinic Fantasies*, eds. David Stern and Mark Mirsky, transl. Raymond P. Scheindlin, 269–294. Philadelphia: The Jewish Publication Society, 1990.

Kennedy, Philip F. "The *Maqamat* as a Nexus of Interests." To appear in *Muslim Horizons, A Volume on Approaches to Medieval Arabic Literature*, eds. Julia Ashtiany Bray, Robert Irwin, Robert Hoyland, Julie Meisami, and James E. Montgomery. E.J.W. Gibb Memorial Trust Series, forthcoming.

Kilito, Abdelfattah. *Les Séances: Récits et Codes Culturels Chez Hamadhânî et Harîrî*. Paris: Sindbad, 1983.

Monroe, James T. *The Art of Badi' az-Zaman al-Hamadhani as Picaresque Narrative*. Beirut: American University of Beirut, 1983.

———, ed. and transl. *Al-Maqamat al-Luzumiyah by Abu l-Tahir Muhammad ibn Yusuf al-Tamimi al-Saraqusti ibn al-Aštarkuwi (d. 538/1143)*. Leiden, Boston, and Köln: Brill, 2002.

Nemah, H. "Andalusian Maqamat." *Journal of Arabic Literature* 5 (1974): 83–92.

Scheindlin, Raymond P. "Fawns of the Palace and Fawns of the Field." *Prooftexts* 6 (1986): 189–203.

MAQQARI, AL-

Al-Maqqari Ahmad b. Muhammad Abu 'l-Abbas Shihab al-Din, Algerian scholar and polygraph, was born in Tlemcen in AH 986/1577 CE from a prominent intellectual family that traced its origin to the village of Maqqara, near Masila. After an early training in Tlemcen, the young Ahmad moved to Fez in Morocco and then to Marrakech, following the court of the Sacdid sultan Ahmad al-Mansur, to whom he dedicated his *Rawdat al-As (The Garden of Myrtle)* about the ulemas of Marrakech and Fez. After al-Mansur's death in 1012/1603, al-Maqqari established himself in Fez, where he was the imam at the Karawiyyin mosque and led the standard life of a religious scholar. In 1027/1617, he left for the East, possibly after a quarrel with the local ruler, and took his residence in Cairo, where he composed his best-known work, *Nafh al-Tib*. This work was based on personal recollections and the consultation of a wide array of sources. He performed several pilgrimages to the Holy Sites, and he traveled to other intellectual centers in the East, most notably to Damascus, where he made himself a reputation as a teacher. Al-Maqqari died in Cairo in 1041/1632.

Although he was a prolific writer about various subjects (at least twenty-four works are ascribed to him), al-Maqqari's reputation is consigned to his two works of Andalusian matter: (1) *Azhar al-Riyad (The Gardens' Flowers)*, about a noted Andalusian twelfth-century judge and scholar, Iyad, which offered, in addition to his biography, a wealth of information about Andalusian and Moroccan scholars; and (2) the monumental *Nafh al-Tib fi Gusn al-Andalus al-Ratib (The Wind's Breeze on the Juicy Andalusian Branch)*, which consisted of two sections—the first one an antiquarian compilation of Andalusian geography, history, and literature and the other a biography of the Granada writer and court secretary Lisan al-Din Ibn al-Khatib (fourteenth century), together with a selection of his administrative and literary writings. The first and most popular part of the *Nafh* was partially translated into English in the nineteenth century by P. de Gayangos from the manuscripts owned by the British Museum; it was then edited by a pool of eminent orientalists led by R. Dozy, thereby providing a basis for the scholarly research on and the knowledge of the Iberian peninsula under Islamic domination until well into the twentieth century. Al-Maqqari's importance rests, even today, with his use of a multiplicity of sources that no longer exist; he quoted these at length in his two major works.

BRUNA SORAVIA

Further Reading

Azhar al-Riyad fi Akhbar Iyad, ed. S.A. Arab and A.S. al-Harras, Rabat 1980.

Dozy, R., et al. *Analectes sur L'Histoire et la Littérature des Arabes d'Espagne*. Leiden, 1855–1861.

De Gayangos, P., transl. *The History of the Mohammedan Dinasties in Spain*. London, 1840–1843.

Nafh al-Tib fi Gusn al-Andalus al-Ratib, ed. I. Abbas. Beyrut, 1968.

Rawdat al-as. Rabat 1964.

MAQRIZI, AL-

Taqi al-Din Ahmad b. 'Ali al-Maqrizi (1364–1442 CE) was a noted scholar, author, historian, and occasional civil servant for the Mamluk Sultanate of Egypt and Syria. Born in Cairo and possibly of descent from the Fatimid dynasty, he spent the majority of his early life in that city. In his forties and after an evidently frustrating career in the Mamluk religious administration in which he held the post of Muhtasib (among others), he left for an extended teaching sojourn in Damascus. About this time, al-Maqrizi withdrew from public life, quite possibly because of his disillusionment with Mamluk rule (although one of his later works may have been an attempt to gain a new sultan's attention and influence his policies). Whether this was an active choice by al-Maqrizi or one forced upon him by the vicissitudes of his career, the fact remains that many of his works are noteworthy for their pointed criticism of leading Mamluks, their actions, and their policies.

Al-Maqrizi is best known today for his works of *ta'rikh* (history). He may have been inspired to write history by Ibn Khaldun, whom he knew and studied under. He wrote annalistic chronicles (most notably of the Fatimids *[Itti'az al-Hunafa']* and a longer one devoted to the Ayyubid and Mamluk sultanates *[Kitab al-Suluk]*), biographical works, shorter treatises, works devoted to such topics as criticizing the economic policies of the Mamluks or detailing the differences between the Umayyads and the 'Abbasids, and a thorough topographical and historical description of Cairo and its environs *(Khitat)*. His relationships with his contemporary historians—most notably al-'Ayni (d. 1451), who had replaced him as Muhtasib of Cairo at one point—seem to have been strained. Regardless of the opinions of his contemporaries, al-Maqrizi's works have proven to be a major source of information for scholars of the Mamluk Sultanate.

WARREN C. SCHULTZ

See also 'Abbasids; Ibn Khaldun; Ibn Taghri Birdi; Mamluks; Umayyads

Primary Sources

Allouche, Adel, transl. *Mamluk Economics: A Study and Translation of al-Maqrizi's* Igathah. Salt Lake City, Utah: University of Utah Press, 1994.
Broadhurst, R.J.C., transl. *A History of the Ayyubic Sultans of Egypt. Translated from the Arabic of al-Maqrizi with Introduction and Notes.* Boston: Twayne Publishers, 1980.

Further Reading

Mamluk Studies Review VII (2003), ed. Li Guo.

MARINIDS

The Marinids were the Berber dynasty that ruled Morocco from around 1250 to 1465 CE. Originally affiliated with the Almohad empire, the Marinids (or Banu Marin tribe [Zenata confederation]) began to assert control over the towns of eastern Morocco from the early thirteenth century, crushing an Almohad army in 1216 and eventually seizing Meknes, Fez, and, in 1269, the capital Marrakesh. The reign of Abu Yusuf Ya'qub (1258–1285) saw the construction of numerous mosques, madrasas (Islamic schools), and official buildings, especially in a newly laid-out capital just to the west of old Fez. During this time, the

Marinids, disposing of a Berber cavalry as well as Christian mercenaries and a naval fleet, also began to intervene in Spain in support of the Nasrid emirate of Granada, but they were decisively beaten by Castille at Rio Salado in 1340 and played no part in stemming the *reconquista* after that. They were more successful on the African front, where, after numerous tries, Abu 'l-Hasan 'Ali (r. 1331–1351) conquered Tlemcen and adjoining regions from the Zayyanids in 1337, ostensibly in support of the Hafsid dynasty of Tunis, whom the Marinids recognized as caliphs. Securing control of the eastern trans-Saharan caravan trade was most likely also a reason, because Abu 'l-Hasan went on to occupy Tunis itself from 1347 to 1349 before being confronted by an Arab tribal revolt and returning to Morocco, where he was deposed by his son Abu 'Inan Faris (r. 1348–1358). Abu 'Inan occupied Algeria and Tunis a second time in 1357 before being turned back by another revolt; after his reign, the Marinids increasingly fell prey to internecine struggles that saw real power exercised by their viziers. This factionalism was exploited by the Nasrids and even more so the Portuguese, who, in 1415, annexed Ceuta. Continued Portuguese encroachment saw the rise of a militant Sufism over the next decades that preceded the reestablishment of Idrisid Sharifian rule in Morocco. A subsidiary Marinid lineage, the Wattasids, effectively ruled in regency from 1420 until 1465, when a militant mob killed the last Marinid sultan and the Wattasids began to reign in their own name. If the Marinids ultimately failed to recreate the Almohad empire, they are remembered foremost as great patrons of classical Islamic architecture in Morocco and of famous literary figures such as Ibn Battuta (d. ca. 1368) and Ibn Khaldun (d. 1406).

STEFAN WINTER

See also Almohads; Berbers; Fez; Granada; Hafsids; Ibn Battuta; Ibn Khaldun; Idrisids; Madrasa; Sufism; Sunni Revival

Further Reading

Julien, Charles-André. *Histoire de l'Afrique du Nord : Des origines à 1830.* Paris: Payot, 1951.
Kably, Mohammed. *Société, Pouvoir et Religion au Maroc à la fin du "Moyen-Âge": (XIVe-XVe Siècle).* Paris: Maisonneuve et Larose, 1986.

MARKETS

Muhammad's profession as a merchant has meant that markets and commerce have always played a central role in Muslim life. In particular, Mecca's position as a trading center, in combination with its religious significance, ensured that it retained its commercial importance throughout the medieval period. The link between religion and commerce can be seen in the plan of many traditional Islamic cities; the markets are located around the main Friday mosque, with markets selling more valuable goods (e.g., gold) located closer to the mosque and stalls selling less pure or more polluting goods (e.g., pottery) located further away. The division of markets into different commodities is not unique to the Islamic world and was also found in medieval/Byzantine Constantinople, although the association with religion is more marked in the Islamic world. For example, in many cases, markets were incorporated into the fabric of the mosque and were used to subsidize the functioning of the mosque. Famous examples include the White Mosque in Ramla (ca. 720 CE), the al-Aqmar Mosque (1125) in Cairo, and the Suleymaniyya Mosque (1550–1557) in Constantinople/Istanbul.

The majority of markets were located in urban centers and it could be argued that markets are a prerequisite for an Islamic city or town. There were, however, some exceptions to the urban location of markets, with annual fairs held in remote rural or desert locations throughout the premodern period. These rural markets were often centred on khans or caravanserais (e.g., Khan al-Tujjar/Suq al-Khan and Khan al-Minya, both in Galilee). Markets were usually regulated by an inspector *(mutasahib)* who would ensure that correct weights and measures were used.

Although it is probable that the majority of markets were semipermanent stalls lining a street, in some cases elaborate architecture was built to house the markets. For example, at Baysan/Scythopolis/Baysan, archaeologists have discovered a market hall with a polychrome glass mosaic inscription dated 749 CE and attributed to the Umayyad caliph Walid II. In Baghdad, there is a rare surviving example of a medieval market hall known as Khan Mirjan, which was built by the Ilkhanid rulers in 1359. The building is two stories high and roofed with eight transverse ribs joined by transverse barrel vaults with windows/vents at each end.

ANDREW PETERSEN

Further Reading

Cezar, M. *Typical Commercial Buildings of the Ottoman Classical Period.* Istanbul.
Hillenbrand, R. "Carvansarais." In *Islamic Architecture: Form, Function and Meaning*, 331–76. Edinburgh: Edinburgh University Press, 1994.

MARRIAGE, ISLAMIC

Marriage in Islam finds mystical, sociolegal, and cultural expression. The Qur'an states that, although God generally created everything in pairs (e.g., 51:49), He created the human being first from a single soul in His divine Presence and then fashioned it into a pair (4:1, 75:39, 39:6, passim). In mystical terms, it becomes the constant quest of the masculine and feminine aspects of this single soul to reunite so that they return to the state of completeness of the first moment of creation, when the soul was in close proximity to the divine and unaware of separate existence. This quest is facilitated through the mutual attraction of male and female. According to verse 30:21: "And of His signs is that He created for you mates from amongst yourselves, that you might dwell with them [in comfort and tranquility], and He has placed between you love and mercy."

In sociolegal terms, the union of male and female finds expression in the institution of marriage. A civil contract in form, marriage differs from the ordinary contract in that its core elements are religiously determined. Muhammad reformed the pre-Islamic practice of Arabia with the overall effect of a strengthened nuclear family and an improved status of women relative to his time. Some reforms included a limitation on polygyny and emphasis of women's status as full legal persons with accompanying property rights. For example, the bride-gift (mahr, sadaq) became one of several pecuniary rights to which the woman was entitled upon marriage. Islamic law regulates the valid conclusion and dissolution of marriage and specifies broad contours of spousal rights and duties. For a valid marriage contract, most Sunni jurists require an offer and acceptance of marriage in the presence of two witnesses with the approval or participation of the female's guardian. Shi'i jurists require neither witnesses nor the approval or participation of a guardian. In accordance with classical Islamic law, Muslims jurists still formally permit polygynous marriage, although some Muslim countries have outlawed the practice (e.g., Turkey, Tunisia). Likewise, Shi'i jurists still permit temporary marriage (mut'a), although Sunni jurists abolished it during the generations after Muhammad. Islamic law conceived of divorce as the unilateral right of the husband, and it specified limited ways for a woman to dissolve the marriage. Adherence to Islamic family law has become circumscribed or wholly voluntary, depending on the extent to which a state incorporates that law. Law in most majority-Muslim countries today combines an eclectic hybrid mix of Islamic rules, customary law, and portions of European codes.

Weddings vary widely according to cultural and local traditions, from the Near East and South Asia to China and the Americas. A simple wedding can entail a private, informal meeting during which a man and woman sign a marriage contract before witnesses. More commonly, weddings are public ceremonies that resemble local traditions and that are modified to retain core Islamic elements. Typically, guests assemble in mosques, in halls, or outdoors to listen to a short sermon *(khutba)*. Then the officiant asks the man and the woman (or her representative) whether they accept the other in marriage and whether the woman accepts the dower offered, which has been typically negotiated before the ceremony. The couple may sign the contract; this may be done symbolically if they have done so before the public ceremony. Finally, the guests participate in a celebratory reception *(walima)*, usually with food, drink, and music.

INTISAR RABB

See also Divorce

Further Reading

Abu Zahra, Muhammad. "Family Law." In *Law in the Middle East: Origin and Development of Islamic Law*, eds. M. Khadduri and H. Liebesny, 132–78. Washington, DC: 1955.
Hodgson, Marshall. "Family Law: Pressure Toward Equality in Personal Status." In *The Venture of Islam*, vol. 1, 340–4. Chicago & London: University of Chicago Press, 1974.
Mallat, Chibli, and J. Connors, eds. *Islamic Family Law*. London: Graham and Trotman, 1990.
Murata, Sachiko. *The Tao of Islam: A Sourcebook on Gender Relationships in Islamic Thought*. Albany, NY: State University of New York Press, 1992.
Stern, Gertrude H. *Marriage in Early Islam*. London: Royal Asiatic Society, 1939.

MARRIAGE, JEWISH

In the Hebrew Book of Genesis 2:18, God says: "It is not good for man to be alone; I will make a fitting helper for him." Furthermore, Genesis 2:24 says: "Hence a man leaves his father and mother and clings to his wife, so that they become one flesh." In later Israel, Jews had to leave their land and spread through much of the world, living in many lands: the Middle East, North Africa, Europe, and eventually across the seas to the Americas. Marriage traditions were based on the Pentateuch and other fields of the Bible, such as the prophets of Israel, and they were later solidified by the many rabbis. Early traditions of marriage came from rabbinic leaders in areas such as Iran, Mesopotamia, Syria, Yemen, and North Africa, who accepted polygamy, whereas among the

northern and Eastern European Jews, it became prohibited to have more than one wife. All Jews tended to marry early, and, although divorce could be obtained, it was not common, because the family had been established as the basis of Jewish life.

Traditionally, *kiddushin* was a sacred relationship in which the wife was consecrated to her husband and forbidden to all others throughout the duration of marriage. This was not merely a legal contract; although the husband acquired rights over her "wifehood," he undertook duties toward her: supplying her with food and clothing and denying himself to provide for his wife and children.

Weddings were often performed out of doors, but they were often held indoors because of problems with non-Jews. The following was and is the traditional format of a Jewish wedding: four family members or friends hold up the wedding canopy under which the bride and groom stand. The rabbi recites a blessing with a cup of wine from which the groom and bride drink. The groom then places a ring on the bride's finger, and he states the following: "Behold, you are consecrated to me by this ring, according to the laws of Moses and Israel." The *ketubah* (marriage contract) is then read, after which the rabbi or other leaders then recite seven marriage benedictions. Often, the groom crushes a glass under his right shoe; this is seen by some as a sign of mourning the destruction of Jerusalem or as a token of seriousness even in the happiest moment.

Today, Jewish marriage customs depend on different traditions—especially in the United States—among the Orthodox, Conservative, Reform, and Reconstructionist Jews and several newer groups.

WILLIAM M. BRINNER

See also Divorce

Further Reading

Davidovitch, David. *The Ketuba: Jewish Marriage Contracts Through the Ages*. New York, 1985.
Lewittes, Mendell. *Jewish Marriage: Rabbinic Law, Legend, and Custom*. 1993.
Satlow, Michael L. *Jewish Marriage in Antiquity*. Princeton, NJ, 2001.

MARTYRDOM

Contrary to general assumption, the Qur'an does not have a specific term for *martyr* or *martyrdom*. *Shahid*, which is the word that has become common in Arabic for martyr, is used in the Qur'an interchangeably with *shahid* for humans only in the sense of a legal or eye witness. God is also known as *shahid*, because He witnesses everything. Only in later non-Qur'anic tradition does this word acquire the meaning of "one who bears witness for the faith," particularly by laying down his life. Extraneous—particularly Christian—influence may be suspected here, because this secondary meaning clearly overlaps with the signification of the Greek term *martys*, which is rendered as martyr in English. Scholars have pointed to the probable influence of the cognate Syriac word for martyr–witness, *sahedo*, on the Arabic *shahid* and the latter's subsequent acquisition of the secondary and derivative meaning of martyr.

Among the Qur'anic verses that have been construed to refer to the special status of the military martyr is 3:169, which states, "Do not think that those who were slain in the path of God are dead. They are alive and well provided for by their Lord." Some of the early hadith (tradition) works, however, make clear that the phrase "slain in the path of God" was not understood to be restricted only to those fallen in battle but could be glossed in several ways. For instance, the *Musannaf* of 'Abd al-Razzaq (d. 826 CE) contains a number of Companion reports that relate competing definitions of *shahid*. A few examples will suffice. One report attributed to the Companion Abu Hurayra states that the shahid is one who, were he to die in his bed, would enter heaven. The explanatory note that follows states that it refers to someone who dies in his bed and is without sin *(la dhanb lahu)*. Another report is related by Masruq b. al-Ajda', who states the following: "there are four types of *shahada* or martyrdom for Muslims: the plague, parturition or delivery of a child, drowning, and a stomach ailment." Significantly, there is no mention of martyrdom being earned as a result of dying on the battlefield in this early report. An expanded version of this report, however, originating with Abu Hurayra, quotes the Prophet as adding to this list of those who achieve martyrdom "one who is killed in the way of God *(man qutila fi sabil Allah)*." It is this expanded version containing the full, five definitions of a shahid that is recorded later in the *Sahih* of al-Bukhari (d. 870). The early eighth-century hadith work *al-Muwatta'* of Malik b. Anas (d. 795) states the following: "The martyrs are seven, apart from death in God's way. He who dies as a victim of an epidemic is a martyr; he who dies from drowning is a martyr; he who dies from pleurisy is a martyr; he who dies from diarrhoea is a martyr; he who dies by [being burned in] fire is a martyr; he who dies by being struck by a dilapidated wall falling is a martyr; and the woman who dies in childbed is a martyr."

By the ninth century, however, *shahid* predominantly came to mean a "military martyr," and most standard hadith works typically devote a section that lists the profuse heavenly rewards earned by pious combatants who fell on the battlefield. Frequently cited hadiths relate that all of the martyr's sins are forgiven, except for debts; if the martyr is free of debt, he wins instant admission into Paradise without any reckoning. The earlier, broader semantic range of the term *shahid* became effectively superseded over time, although it was not completely effaced.

According to certain hadiths, the courting of martyrdom is expressly prohibited. Al-Bukhari records reports in which the Prophet warns that it is forbidden for an individual to long for death and to wish for an encounter with the enemy. The willful seeking of martyrdom is regarded as a form of suicide or self-destruction, which is categorically proscribed in the Qur'an (2:195; 4:29) and in hadith.

ASMA ASFARUDDIN

Further Reading

'Abd al-Razzaq al-San'ani. *Al-Musannaf*, ed. Habib al-Rahman al-A'zami. Beirut: 1970–1972.

Al-Bukhari, Muhammad. *Al-Sahih*. Bulaq, 1893–1894.

Jeffrey, Arthur. *The Foreign Vocabulary of the Qur'an*. Baroda, 1938.

Malik b. Anas, al-. *Al-Muwatta'*, ed. 'Abd al-Baqi. Cairo, 1980.

Wensinck, A.J. "The Oriental Doctrine of the Martyrs." In *Semietische Studiën uit de Nalatenschap*. Leiden, 1941.

MAS'UDI, AL-

Al-Mas'udi was an Arab/Muslim historian, geographer, and belletrist who died in 956 CE. The available information about his life is limited to brief entries in later biographical dictionaries and comments on al-Masu'di's part in his two surviving works (see below). Born at the end of the ninth century to a respected Baghdadi family of Kufan origins, he probably died in al-Fustat. The range of his scholarly interests and his association with a number of prominent early tenth-century scholars point to a thorough education in Arabic, the Islamic sciences, and related disciplines. His writings evince a lifelong appetite for reading and extensive travel (to which al-Mas'udi makes frequent reference). There is no evidence, however, of the manner in which he sustained his career (C. Pellat, a modern biographer, has suggested a personal fortune). Imami (Twelver) authors to the present day identify him as one of their own. Sunni sources, most notably al-Dhahabi, refer to him only as a Mu'tazili.

A prolific author, al-Mas'udi contributed perhaps as many as thirty-six works about an impressive range of topics, including history, geography, theology, heresiography, philosophy, and various fields of science. Much debated among modern scholars is the extent to which he is to be considered a historian given his extensive use of material generally defined as cultural and literary (i.e., as properly belonging to *adab* [belles-lettres]). Al-Mas'udi appears to have been largely avoided by later generations of Muslim scholars; Ibn Khaldun (d. 1406), who cites him frequently, was an important exception. This has been attributed to al-Mas'udi's eschewal of the traditionist style of history writing promoted by, most notably, al-Tabari (d. 923), the hallmark of which was contained in narratives supported by isnads (chains of transmission; see Hadith). Like al-Ya'qubi (d. 897), al-Mas'udi made no use of isnads. More to the point is that he defined history in far more expansive terms than did his contemporaries.

His principal surviving work is the ambitious *Muruj al-Dhahab (The Fields of Gold)*, which was written in Egypt around 943 and revised several times thereafter (the surviving version is early, dating to the mid-940s). Modern editions of the *Muruj* run to some half dozen fat volumes, and it is divided into two parts. The first part, whihc is encyclopedic, includes sections about the unfolding of monotheism (sacred history) during the pre-Islamic period; surveys of India and China; material about oceans, seas, and rivers; lists of the kings of Mesopotamia, Egypt, and other regions; and ethnographic data about Slavs, Africans, and the Franks. For this reason, the *Muruj* is often cited, alongside al-Ya'qubi's earlier *Ta'rikh (History),* as a notable example of Arab-Islamic world history. The second and longer part consists mainly of a detailed account of Islamic history. A section about the Prophet's life is followed by accounts of the reigns of the Rightly Guided Caliphs and those of the Umayyad and 'Abbasid houses. Introductory comments on al-Mas'udi's part indicate that these were excerpted from a far longer work, the *Akhbar al-Zaman*, of which no trace survives.

The second surviving work, *Kitab al-Tanbih Wa-l-ishraf*, brings together, in highly concise fashion, much of the information contained in the *Muruj* and, apparently, other works. It is, in this sense, a supplementary work. It appears to have been the last of al-Mas'udi's books, completed just before his death.

MATTHEW S. GORDON

See also Mu'tazilites

Further Reading

Khalidi, Tarif. *Islamic Historiography: The Histories of al-Mas'udi*. Albany, NY: State University of New York Press, 1975.

Pellat, Charles. "Al-Mas'udi." In *The Encyclopedia of Islam*, 2nd ed.

Shboul, A. *Al-Mas'udi and His World*. London, 1979.

MATHEMATICAL GEOGRAPHY

The Muslims inherited Ptolemy's lists of longitudes and latitudes of cities from one end of the known world to the other as well as his maps of the world and of various regions. Tables displaying the geographical coordinates of numerous localities are found in several Islamic works about mathematical geography as well as in the more numerous (approximately two hundred and twenty-five) astronomical handbooks known as *zîjes*. A minority of tables also display the qibla for each locality. Such tables are often engraved on astronomical instruments, especially those from Safavid Iran.

The maps prepared by Muslim scholars based on this geographical data and fitted with coordinate grids represent a tradition that is quite distinct from the better-known (and more colorful) tradition of maps without scales. Alas, most of them have not survived the vicissitudes of history.

The tables of al-Khwârizmî (Baghdad; ca. 825), with 545 pairs of entries, incorporated already a correction of the length of Ptolemy's Mediterranean. The Caliph al-Ma'mûn patronized the measurement of the diameter of the earth; his astronomers measured the number of miles corresponding to one degree of the meridian. The world map prepared for al-Ma'mûn, which had a square coordinate grid, has not survived.

Abu 'l-Rayhân al-Bîrûnî (ca. 1025) presented a new table of coordinates of some 604 localities. He also prepared maps based on these coordinates and discussed several cartographical projections known otherwise only from Renaissance European works. A late copy of a much-corrupted version of his world maps has recently been discovered. In his book *Tahdîd Nihâyât al-Amâkin (The Determination of the Locations of Cities)*, al-Bîrûnî set out to establish the geographical coordinates of Ghazna to compute the qibla there: the result was the most valuable work on mathematical geography from the medieval period.

Some anonymous Iranian scholar, probably during the eleventh century and possibly in Isfahan, prepared a monumental geographical work featuring more than 450 localities; the title of this work has been transmitted as *Kitâb al-Atwâl Wa-'l-'urûd li-'l-Furs (The Book of Longitudes and Latitudes of the Persians)*, and it originally included a map that has not survived. This underlies most of Islamic mathematical geography in Iran after the thirteenth century, because it was used by al-Tûsî in Maragha during the mid-thirteenth century, al-Kâshî, and Ulugh Beg in

Samarqand during the mid-fifteenth century. Shortly thereafter, apparently in nearby Kish, another scholar whose name is unknown produced yet another monumental geographical table; this one, however, was different. In addition to the coordinates of some 274 localities, values of the qibla and distance to Mecca were given—in the main, accurately, to the nearest few seconds—for each locality. The compiler(s) used the earlier Persian geographical tables and those of al-Tûsî and Ulugh Beg. This was the source for virtually all of the geographical information on Safavid instruments.

Since 1989, three seventeenth-century Safavid world maps engraved on brass have been discovered. These are centered on Mecca, and the highly sophisticated mathematical grid enables the user to read off the qibla and distance to Mecca. The geographical data for 150-odd localities is taken from the fifteenth-century Kish tables, but the underlying mathematics has been discovered in two texts from tenth-century Baghdad and eleventh-century Isfahan.

DAVID A. KING

See also Astronomy; Astrolabes; Cartography

Further Reading

Ali, Jamil. *The Determination of the Coordinates of Cities . . . by al-Bîrûnî.* Beirut: American University of Beirut Press, 1967.

Kennedy, Edward Stewart. "Mathematical Geography." In *Encyclopedia of the History of Arabic Science,* 3 vols., eds. Roshdi Rashed and Régis Morelon, vol. I, 185–201. London: Routledge, 1996.

——. *A Commentary Upon Bîrûnî's Kitâb Tahdîd [Nihâyât] al-Amâkin, An 11th Century Treatise on Mathematical Geography.* Beirut: American University of Beirut Press, 1973.

Kennedy, Edward Stewart, and Mary Helen Kennedy. *Geographical Coordinates of Localities from Islamic Sources.* Frankfurt am Main: Institut für Geschichte der Arabisch-Islamischen Wissenschaften, 1987.

King, David A. *World-Maps for Finding the Direction and Distance to Mecca: Innovation and Tradition in Islamic Science.* Leiden: E.J. Brill and Al-Furqan Islamic Heritage Foundation, 1999.

MATHEMATICS

Mathematics and astronomy were the two most important exact sciences in Islamic civilization between 700 and 1700 CE. Henceforth, the term *Islamic mathematics* will be used, with the adjective Islamic referring to civilization. Although a few mathematical problems were motivated by Islam, most mathematics had no relation whatsoever to religion. The majority of the mathematicians were Muslims, but notable contributions to the Islamic mathematical tradition were made by Christians, Jews, and followers of other religions. These mathematicians belong to the Islamic mathematical tradition because they wrote in Arabic, which developed into the language of science during the translation period during the eighth and ninth centuries CE. After 1000 CE, a few mathematical texts were written in Persian, but these texts are full of Arabic mathematical terms. The term *Arabic mathematics* is sometimes used, but it should be remembered that many mathematicians of medieval Islamic civilization were not Arabs; Iranian mathematics account for an estimated one-third of the discoveries.

Most of the current knowledge about Islamic mathematics is based on Arabic manuscripts that are found in libraries all over the world. The most important collections are in Istanbul, Tehran, Cairo, Paris, London, and Leiden (Netherlands). Almost all surviving manuscripts are copies made by scribes who did not have advanced mathematical training. Less than one-third of these manuscripts have been edited in Arabic or translated into a Western language or Russian. Information about Islamic mathematics can also be found in manuscripts about astronomy and optics, and, to a much lesser extent, in texts about astrology, law, and linguistics. A few treatises have been lost in the Arabic original but survive in a medieval Latin or Hebrew translation. Astronomical instruments, sundials, and Islamic mosaics demonstrate the practical skill of some of the mathematicians.

Islamic mathematics can be schematically subdivided into arithmetic, algebra, and geometry. Many treatises were written about commercial arithmetic, with detailed explanations of number systems and computations involving fractions. Algebra was mainly used for recreation and had few practical applications. For algebraic computations, a certain amount of training and mathematical talent was necessary. Geometry was studied at different levels. Some texts contain practical geometrical rules for surveying and for measuring figures. Theoretical geometry was a necessary prerequisite for understanding astronomy and optics, and it required years of concentrated work. Many mathematicians and astronomers produced handbooks of astronomical tables so that the astrologers, who did not understand the geometrical background in detail, could predict the positions of the planets by a few easy additions, subtractions, and multiplications. Some geometers seem to have prepared manuals explaining the practical construction of mosaics for craftsmen.

The early history of mathematics in medieval Islamic civilization is intimately connected with the history of astronomy. Soon after the establishment of the 'Abbasid caliphate and the founding of Baghdad during the mid-eighth century CE, some mathematical knowledge must have been assimilated from the pre-Islamic Iranian tradition in astronomy, which had survived until that time. Astronomers from India were invited to the court of the caliph during the late eighth century, and they explained the rudimentary trigonometrical techniques that were necessary in Indian astronomy. Around 800 CE, the astronomers in Baghdad turned to the more sophisticated astronomy of the Greeks. The fundamental work of Greek astronomy was the *Almagest* of Ptolemy (c. 150 CE), which was translated into Arabic several times. Because the *Almagest* was impossible to understand without an intimate knowledge of the *Elements* of Euclid and other Greek geometrical works, these works were also translated into Arabic during the early decades of the ninth century. During the second half of the ninth century, Islamic mathematicians were already making contributions to the most sophisticated parts of Greek geometry. Islamic mathematics reached its apogee in the Eastern part of the Islamic world between the tenth and twelfth centuries CE.

Little is known about the biographies of most Islamic mathematicians. It is clear that many mathematicians and astronomers had difficulty finding support for their work. Some of the best mathematicians of the Islamic tradition worked at the courts of kings, such as the Buwayhid dynasty in Iran during the tenth century CE and Ulugh Beg in Samarkand around 1420 CE.

From the late tenth century on, mathematical knowledge was transmitted from the Western part of the Islamic world to Christian Europe. The Romans had not been interested in science. As a result, the knowledge of mathematics in Christian Europe was very limited, and the notion of a mathematical proof was nonexistent. During the twelfth century, many Arabic mathematical and astronomical texts (including Arabic translations of Greek texts) were translated into Latin in Spain and, to a lesser extent, in Sicily and other areas. This was the beginning of the development of science in Medieval Europe. Many achievements of Eastern Islamic mathematicians remained unknown in the West, until the European orientalists of the nineteenth and twentieth centuries turned their attention to Arabic scientific manuscripts.

Some important discoveries of Islamic mathematicians are discussed in articles about algebra and geometry. The mathematicians also worked on the theory of numbers and magic squares. Thabit ibn Qurra proved a general formula for finding amicable numbers, using the example 17296, 18416. Each of these numbers is the sum of the divisors of the other number. A magic square of order n is a square in which the numbers $1, 2, \ldots, n^2$ are written in such a way that the sum of the numbers in each row, in each column, and in each of the two diagonals is the same. During the ninth through twelfth centuries, several Eastern Islamic mathematicians (including Ibn al-Haytham) invented elegant methods for finding magic squares of arbitrary order. The name *magic square* is modern, and the medieval Islamic mathematicians, who were generally uninterested in magic, talked about "harmonious dispositions of numbers."

Three problems in Islamic religion can be solved by means of advanced mathematics:

1. The Islamic calendar is a lunar calendar. The day begins in the evening, at sunset, and a new month begins when the lunar crescent is first sighted on the Western horizon. Whether or not the crescent is visible depends on its perpendicular distance to the horizon at sunset, the distance along the horizon between the sun and the moon, the ripeness of the crescent, and also on atmospherical phenomena. From the ninth century onward, Islamic mathematicians and astronomers proposed a multitude of visibility criteria, theories, and tables for the prediction of the first visibility of the lunar crescent.

2. It is a religious duty of the Muslim to pray five times a days towards the qibla (i.e., the direction of Mecca). From the ninth century onward, Islamic mathematicians began to interpret this problem mathematically. In their view, the qibla should be taken along a great circle on the spherical earth through the locality of prayer and the Ka'ba in Mecca. Approximate methods were used in the ninth century, but, from the tenth century onward, exact methods became popular among the mathematicians and astronomers in the Eastern Islamic world. Exact solutions were proposed by al-Biruni, Ibn al-Haytham, and others. The exact determination of the qibla by crude methods from the early Islamic tradition. They did not understand the mathematical methods, and they generally ignored the results of the exact computations.

3. The times of the five daily prayers are determined by the height of the sun above the horizon or its depression under the horizon. From the ninth and tenth centuries onward, Islamic astronomers computed prayer tables, determining the times of prayer in equinoctial or seasonal hours. For these computations, one needs difficult spherical trigonometry. A large amount of material about prayer tables written by the tenth-century Egyptian astronomer Ibn Yanus is still in existence.

Because most Arabic mathematical manuscripts have not yet been published and investigated, the preceding survey is necessarily incomplete, and it may turn out to be misleading in the light of future research. Important new discoveries have been made during the last decades, and there is no evidence that this process has come to an end.

JAN P. HOGENDIJK

See also Geometry; Algebra; Numbers; Ibn Al-Haytham; Al-Biruni

Further Reading

Berggren, Len. *Episodes in the Mathematics of Medieval Islam.* New York: Springer, 1986.
Hogendijk, Jan P., and A.I. Sabra, eds. *The Enterprise of Islamic Science: New Perspectives,* Cambridge, Mass: M.I.T. Press, 2003.
King, David A. *Islamic Mathematical Astronomy.* London: Variorium, 1986.
———. *Astronomy in the Service of Islam.* London: Variorium, 1987.
———. *In Synchrony with the Heavens: Studies in the Astronomical Timekeeping and Instrumentation in Medieval Islamic Civilization.* Leiden: Brill, 2004.

MAWARDI, AL-

Abu 'l-Hasan 'Ali ibn Muhammad ibn Habib al-Mawardi was a Muslim polymath who was born in Basra around 975 CE and who died in Baghdad on May 27, 1058.

Mawardi studied Shafi'i law in Basra and Baghdad. He was appointed to various judgeships but probably appointed deputies to do the actual work. He carried out diplomatic missions on behalf of the Caliph al-Qa'im (r. 1031–1075) to the Buyids, who actually controlled Iraq and Iran, and also once to their rivals, the Seljuks.

In modern times, Mawardi has become most famous for *al-Ahkam al-Sultaniyya,* a treatise describing the Islamic polity. The 'Abbasid caliphs of his own time were in fact fairly weak figures, although they slowly regained power as part of the Sunni Revival; almost their only means of influencing politics was refusing to confirm appointments and titles made or claimed by the warlords and threatening to call in other warlords from further afield, such as the Ghaznavids. Accordingly, Mawardi stresses that all authority flows by delegation from the caliph; he appointed military commanders to maintain order and judges to maintain justice. There is a close verbal parallel to Mawardi's *Ahkam* under the same title by the Hanbali judge Ibn al-Farra' (d. 1065), probably a rebuttal of Mawardi's work. The chief substantial difference between the two is that Ibn al-Farra' does not allow an incompetent caliph to be deposed, whereas Mawardi does.

During the Middle Ages, Mawardi's most famous work was *al-Hawi al-Kabir,* of which only recently has a full text been published. Formally a commentary on the *Mukhtasar of al-Muzani,* it rehearses and defends the ordinances of Shafi'i law at great length (see Law and Jurisprudence). Mawardi systematically adduces Qur'an, prophetic sunna (precedent), consensus, and analogy, in that order. He expressly commends Shafi'i law as the best combination of revelation with reason.

Mawardi's style of argument is notably uneven, and he continually piles flimsy evidence and reasoning on top of apparently sound arguments. It thus marks the transition from a tradition of legal writing that aims to establish the correctness of one school's doctrine to one that aims to establish only its plausibility; this demonstrates that there will always be multiple schools. Implicitly, the different Sunni schools of the eleventh century had become somewhat like modern Protestant denominations; the adherents of each sect may think theirs is the best, but they recognize that theirs is not the only one that is adequate.

Also currently in print is Mawardi's commentary on the Qur'an, *al-Nukat Wa-l-'uyun.* It goes through the entire Qur'an in order, quoting a few verses at a time and then providing short glosses, mainly from exegetes of the eighth century; occasionally textual variants are also used, and there are examples of usage from poetry. It usually presents a range of possibilities and seldom asserts that any one is the best interpretation. Mawardi's views sometimes agree with those of the Mu'tazilites (e.g., the rejection of predestination); however, he does not seem to be a systematic advocate of Mu'tazilism. Finally, there are also several shorter works in print about law, politics, and adab (belles-lettres).

CHRISTOPHER MELCHERT

Further Reading

Gibb, H.A.R. "Al-Mawardi's Theory of the Khilafah." *Islamic Culture* 11 (1937): 291–302.
Laoust, Henri. "La Pensée et L'Action Politiques D'Al-Mawardi." *Revue des Études Islamiques,* 36 (1968): 11–92.
Mawardi. *The Laws of Islamic Governance,* transl. Asadullah Yate. London: Ta-Ha Publishers, 1996.
———. *The Ordinances of Government,* transl. Wafaa H. Wahba. Reading, UK: Garnet, 1996.
———. *The Discipline of Religious and Worldly Matters,* transl. Thoreya Mahdi Allam, rev. Magdi Wahba and Abderrafi Benhallam. Morocco: ISESCO, 1995.

MECCA

The city of Mecca lies in the western area of the Arabian peninsula, and it is situated in an infertile valley of the geographical region traditionally known as the Hijaz. Muslim sources relate that the Prophet Muhammad was born in Mecca in the year 570 CE. He belonged to one of the clans of the tribe of Quraysh; the Quraysh were the respected elders of this oasis town, which prospered as a center of commerce because of its strategic location at the midpoint of an established trade route. The city also had its markets and fairs. Quraysh organized caravans that traded in territories both south and north of the Arabian peninsula. Mecca was also home to the sacred shrine known as the Ka'ba and the ancient spring of Zamzam. The Ka'ba was located in an area known as the *masjid al-haram*. The precincts of Mecca, which are defined by a number of miqat (stations), are considered haram (inviolable). As custodians of the Meccan shrine, Quraysh provided water for visiting pilgrims, regulating rituals and practices associated with the hajj (pilgrimage). Islamic sources record that these ceremonies had assumed an idolatrous and somewhat animistic bent. The perversion of the monotheistic symbolism of the shrine and the pilgrimage provided the setting for the emergence of Islam.

The first verses of the Qur'an were revealed to Muhammad at Mecca in 610 CE. The Prophet preached there for twelve years, encountering determined opposition. He was compelled to leave the city in 622 CE, migrating with his companions to Medina. The Prophet and his followers did return triumphantly in 630 CE, taking the city without bloodshed. The Ka'ba was purged of its idols, and the monotheistic motif of the rituals associated with the pilgrimage was restored. However, the city of Medina became the political center of the fledgling Islamic state, although Mecca retained its importance as the spiritual capital of the Muslim world: it serves as the qibla (direction) that Muslims face to perform their ritual prayers, and it is the focus of the annual pilgrimage. It preserves these religious distinctions until this day, with only Muslims being permitted to enter its sacred boundaries.

MUSTAFA SHAH

See also Arabia; Arabs; Hajj; Islam; Idolatry; Jazira; Ka'ba; Markets; Medina; Muhammad the Prophet; Pagans and Pagan Customs; Pilgrimage; Qur'an; and Umra

Further Reading

Francis, Peters. *Mecca: A Literary History of the Muslim Holy Land.* Princeton, NJ: Princeton University Press, 1994.

Montgomery, Watt. *Muhammad's Mecca: History in the Qur'an.* Edinburgh: Edinburgh University Press, 1988.

MEDICAL LITERATURE, HEBREW

Jewish communities, which during the Middle Ages were largely settled throughout the Mediterranean area, enjoyed under Islamic rule a cultural expansion that, paradoxically, was associated with the adoption of the Arabic language and cultural model. Social tolerance and the influence of a flourishing Arabic cultural development resulted in a complex and rich Jewish intellectual life, the achievements of which were easily transmitted among the Jewish communities that shared the same cultural milieu (i.e., those established within the extensive Islamic territories).

This long chapter of Jewish history is divided into two main periods in terms of time and location: the Islamic East and al-Andalus (as the Islamic part of the Iberian Peninsula was known at the time). During this extensive interlude, Arabic became for Jews not only an adopted mother tongue but also a vehicle for learning and cultural transmission; Hebrew was reserved during this period for writings of a religious and literary character.

Arabic medical knowledge, which flourished from the middle of the eighth century and was available through Arabic translations from the Greek as well as from their own original production, was assimilated, learned, and even taught by Jews. Furthermore, they participated in the task—performed under the auspices of the Islamic cultural expansion—of preserving, transmitting, and commenting on classical philosophical and scientific texts, thereby partaking in the creation of a distinct corpus of Greco-Arabic medicine.

The art of medicine was learned from books, but it was also acquired through the relationship established between a student and a particular master (generally a prominent physician) who transmitted to the student (usually a male, but occasionally a female) both theoretical and practical knowledge. Prospective physicians were trained under the supervision and guidance of the master and, as far as is known, Jews and Muslims without distinction enjoyed the benefits of this system.

According to the sources, medicine seems to have been a favorite occupation among Jews, because the number of Jewish medical practitioners providing care for both the Jewish and the Muslim populations was considerable. Apparently, this professional choice was stimulated by the fact that physicians enjoyed an enhanced social and economic status, which was obviously a desirable aim for a religious minority living under the domination of another people.

Nevertheless, the number of practitioners does not seem proportional to the number of medical authors or, more accurately, known medical texts authored by Jews, whose figures are substantially inferior. This contrast, however unusual it might seem at first sight, is not so if the above-mentioned fact that Jews' proficiency in Arabic made the rich corpus of Greco-Arabic medicine available to them is recalled. The very availability of texts, together with the assumption of the theoretical framework developed by Islamic medicine, seems to have acted as a deterrent for original production.

However scant, Jewish textual production was not unimportant. Some medical authors succeeded in attracting the general acknowledgment of their contemporaries, which secured a place for their works within the corpus that circulated at the time. Among them, two outstanding figures deserve special mention. The first is Isaac ben Solomon Israeli, or Isaac Judaeus (born in Egypt c. 855 CE, died in Kairawan c. 955 CE), who was a leading Jewish philosopher, physician, and medical author. The uncontested acknowledgment of his work resulted in its early translation into Hebrew and Latin, which allowed for its dissemination in the West. Israeli's works on fevers, urine, foods and simple remedies, and medical conduct were extensively read and quoted throughout the Middle Ages and beyond.

Undoubtedly the best-known Jewish figure in the field of medicine, Moses ben Maimon, or Maimonides (born in Cordoba in 1138, died in Egypt in 1204), was a highly prestigious philosopher, exegete, and physician. His medical works were deeply embedded in the Islamic medical tradition, and they shared and transmitted notions of physiology, etiology, and therapeutics that were common to that tradition, bearing a strong influence of what has been called the "Galenization" of Islamic medicine. Maimonides was a prolific author, and at least nine medical works were ascribed to him. He wrote some minor monographs devoted to asthma, hemorrhoids, sexual hygiene and aphrodisiacs, diet, and pharmacology. He also produced three major medical works: a commentary on the Hippocratic *Aphorisms,* a book on *Extracts from Galen,* and his own *Aphorisms,* known as *[Medical] Aphorisms of Moses.* This last work was an extensive synthesis of contemporary medical knowledge (Galenic for the most part) that was apparently conceived as a practical tool for learning or to be carried during practice.

At the end of the twelfth century, there was an upsurge in Hebrew, and it began to be used as a vehicle of science. This prompted the translation into and the original production in this language of medical texts. However, both in and outside Islamic lands, Jews continued to write and read medicine in Arabic up to the fourteenth and fifteenth centuries. In Christian territories, a learned minority who had emigrated from Islamic regions but who still maintained intimate links with Arabic language and science committed themselves to the translation into Hebrew of Arabic medical books, thus contributing to the dissemination and transmission of the bulk of Greco-Arabic medical knowledge to the West.

CARMEN CABALLERO-NAVAS

Further Reading

Ferre, Lola. "The Place of Scientific Knowledge in Some Spanish Jewish Authors." *Micrologus. Natura, Scienze e Società Medievali, IX, Gli Ebrei e le Scienze, The Jews and the Sciences* (2001): 21–34.

Friedenwald, Harry. *Jewish Luminaries in Medical History.* Baltimore: The Johns Hopkins Press, 1946.

García-Ballester, Luís, "A Marginal Learned Medical World: Jewish, Muslim and Christian Medical Practitioners, and the Use of Arabic Medical Sources in the Late Medieval Spain." In *Practical Medicine from Salerno to the Black Death,* eds. Luís García-Ballester et al., 353–94. Cambridge, UK: Cambridge University Press, 1994.

Goitein, S. D. *A Mediterranean Society: The Jewish Communities of the Arab World as Portrayed in the Documents of the Cairo Geniza,* 6 vols., vol. 2, 240–61. Berkeley, Los Angles, and London, University of California Press.

Jacquart, Danielle, and Françoise Micheau. *La Médecine Arabe et L'Occident Médiéval, Editions Maissonneuve et Larose.* Paris, 1990.

Meyerhoff, Max. *Studies in Medieval Arabic Medicine: Theory and Practice,* ed. Penelope Johnstone. London: Variorum Reprints, 1984.

———. "Medieval Jewish Physicians in the Middle Ages." *Isis* 28 (1938). Reprinted in Sezgin, Fuat, ed. *Mūsā ibn Maymūn (Maimonides) (d. 601/1204): Texts and Studies,* 140–68. Frankfurt am Main: Institute for the History of Arabic-Islamic Science at Johann Wolfgang Goethe University, 1998.

Muntner, S. *Moshe ben Maimon (Maimonides). Medical Works,* 3 vols. Jerusalem, Mosad ha-Rav Kook, 1957–1961.

Rosner, Fred, and Samuel Kottek, eds. *Moses Maimonides: Physician, Scientist and Philosopher.* New Jersey, 1993.

Sezgin, Fuat, ed. *Isḥāq ibn Sulaymān al-Isrā'īlī (d. c. 325/935): Texts and Studies.* Frankfurt am Main: Institute for the History of Arabic-Islamic Science at Johann Wolfgang Goethe University, 1996.

———, ed. *Mūsā ibn Maymūn (Maimonides) (d. 601/1204): Texts and Studies.* Frankfurt am Main: Institute for the History of Arabic-Islamic Science at Johann Wolfgang Goethe University, 1998.

Sirat, Collete. *A History of Jewish Philosophy in the Middle Ages.* Cambridge, UK, and New York: Cambridge University Press, 1985.

MEDICAL LITERATURE, PERSIAN

Given the impact of Arabic as the language of religion and the paramount vehicle of learning, even in the

Iranian linguistic area, it may not be amiss to recall the commonplace fact that Persian medical literature is at the same time less and much more than the medical literature of Iran. It is considered less because Arabic writing about medicine flourished well before and then alongside (at times overshadowing) its Persian counterpart in medieval Iran; and it is considered more because of the expansion of Persian as the language of learning into non-Iranian—primarily Turkic and Indic—linguistic regions.

This discussion will neglect vernacular in favor of academic writing and will be divided into the following sections: (1) Background; (2) Formative Period, c. AH 340–440/950–1050 CE; (3) Consolidation, Elaboration, and Islamic Naturalization of Persian Galenism, 440–620/1050–1220; (4) Avicennism, Literary Differentiation, and Inter-Asian Exchanges, 620–900/1220–1500; and (5) After 900/1500.

Background

Given the literary dominance of Arabic in Iran that ensued upon the Muslim/Arab conquest around the middle of the first/seventh century, the middle-Iranian, pre-Islamic tradition of writing survived only within the ever-decreasing Zoroastrian community. Thus, Arabic models, naturally by themselves of multiple derivation (e.g., Arabian, Hellenistic, [Middle] Iranian), had an obvious impact on the emergence of (Neo-)Persian as an Islamic literary language during the fourth/tenth century. With regard to Persian medical literature in particular, the question presents itself of whether, in addition to Arabic Galenism and the so-called prophetic medicine, it was also informed by direct scholastic transmission from Middle Iranian, without an Aramaic–Arabic intermediary; at the level of vernacular healing craft, such survivals were to be expected. Further, the geographic proximity of India facilitated exchanges that left a more noticeable imprint in Iran than further west, whether during the Sasanian period or later, after ca. 300/900.

Formative Period, ca. 340–440/950–1050

Practical utility readily explains the fact that medical works are to be found among the earliest witnesses to Persian literature. Although this period saw a veritable outburst of medical writing in Arabic in the very regions of Persian literary activity, the three incunabula of Persian medicine attest to the diffusion of superior and diverse learning among a readership that was unable or unwilling to acquire Arabic. A student of Abū Bakr al-Rāzī (d. 313/925) at one remove from the Bukhara region, Abū Bakr Akhawaynī, composed a textbook for his son and other adepts of medicine, the first such compendium in Persian (Hidāyat al-Muta‘Allimīn fī l-Tibb [Learners' Guidance to Medicine]). Other genres of Arabic scholarly writing were similarly adopted, such as the didactic versification and the alphabetically arranged materia medica; the former is represented by Hakīm Maysarī's Dānishnāma (Book of Knowledge) of 370/980, and the latter is demonstrated by Abū Mansūr Harawī's Kitāb al-Abniya ‘an Îaqā'iq al-Adwiya (Book of Foundations Concerning the True Essence of Medicines; ca. 380/990), which also drew on near-contemporary Indian scholarship. At the same time, Maysarī's and Harawī's works illustrate the integration of medicine into general education, at least among courtly society and in Samanid dominions, where Persian letters as such first developed.

Nevertheless, the privileged position that Arabic generally maintained in scholarship is, for example, reflected in Avicenna's (before 370/980–428/1037) medical writings; although his magisterial Canon (Kitāb al-Qānūn fī l-Tibb) is in Arabic, he only composed a brief treatise on phlebotomy in Persian (Andar Dānish-i Rag [On the Knowledge of the Veins]).

Consolidation, Elaboration, and Islamic Naturalization of Persian Galenism, 440–620/1050–1220

The lasting impact of Avicenna's Canon was not limited to Arabic domains; its Persian—by no means slavish—reception found monumental and, in turn, similarly influential expression in the medical encyclopedia Dhakhīra-yi Khwārizmshāhī (The Khwārizmshāh's Treasure) by Ismā‘īl Jurjānī (ca. 434–535/ca. 1042–1140), an author of vast erudition and, by the breadth of his writings, acute attention to the varied needs of laymen, learners, practitioners, and complete scholars. Further, he vividly illustrated the Islamic naturalization of Hellenistic science (i.e., in the present context, Galenism). As examples of rather humble and practice-oriented writing, two other works deserve mention here: a catechetic survey of ophthalmology, Nūr al-‘Uyūn (Light of the Eyes) by Abū Rawh Jurjānī ‘Zarrīndast' (in 480/1087 inscribed to the Seljuq Sultan Malikshāh) and a practitioner's manual of theoretical and curative medicine, Mukhtasar Andar ‘ilm-i Tabīb (Abridgment on the Physician's

Science) by the Jewish physician Abū Sa'd 'Zardgilīm' (c. 550/1155).

Both Zarrīndast's *Ophthalmology* for a Seljuq sultan and Ismā'īl Jurjānī's activity in Khwārizm (on the frontier to Turkic) during this period illustrate the afore mentioned expansion of Persian into non-Iranian linguistic realms.

Avicennism, Literary Differentiation, and Inter-Asian Exchanges, 620–900/1220–1500

As a result of Činggis Khān's and his successors' invasions of the Islamic Middle East (c. 618–660/ 1220–1262) as well as Tamerlane's (1370–1405) campaigns, the region's demographic balance further changed in favor of Turkic and Mongol nomadic pastoralists. Their eventual Islamic acculturation consolidated and territorially expanded the position of Persian (e.g., the medical author Shihāb al-Dīn Nāgawrī from India [790–794/1388–1392]). In medicine, increased communication across Asia under shared Mongol rule even resulted in Persian adaptations from the Chinese (*Tansūqnāma-yi Īlkhānī [The Ilkhan's Book of Precious Knowledge]* by Rashīd al-Dīn Fadlallāh [c. 645–718/1247–1318]). Demand for translations from Arabic also rose, as did generally the writing of commentaries and abridgments. Apart from the "medicine of the Prophet" or of the Shi'i Imāms in academic medicine, Avicennism continued to hold sway as is witnessed by, for example, *Qānūnja (Little Canon)* by Mahmūd Čaghmīnī (d. 745/1344) and the Persian version of Ibn al-Nafīs's *Mūjiz al-Qānūn (Abridgment of the* Canon*)* by Qutb Muhammad (c. 906/1500); it is also seen in ostensibly independent works such as *Ghiyāthīya (To Ghiyāth al-Dīn)* by Najm al-Dīn Mahmūd Shīrāzī (before 720/1320) and *Kifāya-yi Mujāhidīya (Adequacy for Mujāhid al-Dīn)* by Mansūr ibn Muhammad (c. 787/1385). The thematic range of specialized treatments kept increasing, and eventually included reproductive and sexual medicine. *Materia medica* for centuries found its authoritative Persian formulation in *Ikhtiyārāt-i Badī'ī (Selections for Badī' al-Jamāl')* by Zayn al-Dīn 'Alī Ansārī (770/1368–1369); in anatomy, the just-mentioned Mansūr supplemented his *Tashrīl-i Mansūrī (Mansūr's Anatomy)* with a series of five illustrations; Abū Zayn Kahhāl included—even highlighting it in the title—surgery in his otherwise conventional survey *Sharāyit-i Jarrāhī (Requirements of Surgery;* mid-ninth/fifteenth century). New manuals of basic curative medicine continually appeared as well. In addition, medicine was included in general encyclopedias of arts and sciences (e.g.,

Dānishnāma-yi Jahān [Book of Knowledge of the World] by 'Alī ibn 'Alī Amīrān Isfahānī, c. 880/1475).

After 900/1500

Although no caesura in medical theory marks the turn of a new period around this date, contemporaneous events and processes did eventually effect Persian medicine. The rise and consolidation, respectively, of new dynasties—the Turkish Ottomans, the Safavids of Iran, the Shaybanids of Uzbekistan, and the Mughals of India—boosted literary activity in Persian and won it new territory. For example, renewed interest in Hindu medicine resulted in Persian versions of Sanskrit texts (*Ma'din al-Shifā-yi Sikandar-Shāhī [The Healing-Mine of Sikandar-Shah]* by Miyān Bhūwa ibn Khawāss Khān, 918/1512); medical handbooks and monographs met with unceasing demand; and, more remarkably, diseases and substances of American, European, and Far Eastern origin called for discussion. Syphilis (ātishak ["firelet"] or ābila-yi farang [Frankish pox]) was instantly noted, at times correctly diagnosed as transmissible and treated by the supposed panacea smilax (čūb-i čīnī [Chinese wood]) if not by mercury (e.g., *Khulāsat al-Tajārib [Choice Experiences]* by Bahā' al-Dawla Nūrbakhshī, 907/1501–1502; *Risāla-yi Ātishak [Essay on Firelet]*; and *Risāla-yi Čūb-i Čīnī [Essay on Chinese Wood]* by 'Imād al-Dīn Maîmūd Shīrāzī, ca. 978/1570). Coffee (qahwa), tea (čāy), and tobacco (tanbākū) were not ignored, either.

LUTZ RICHTER-BERNBURG

Further Reading

De Crussol des Épesse, Thierry, transl. *Discours sur L'Oeil d'Esmā'īl Gorgānī.* Teheran: IFRI & PU d'Iran/Louvain: Peeters, 1998.

Elgood, Cyril. *A Medical History of Persia and the Eastern Caliphate.* Cambridge, UK: Cambridge University Press, 1951.

———. *Safavid Medical Practice.* London: Royal Asiatic Society, 1970.

Keshavarz, Fateme. *A Descriptive and Analytical Catalogue of Persian Manuscripts in the Library of the Wellcome Institute for the History of Medicine.* London: Wellcome Institute, 1986.

Klein-Franke, Felix, and Zhu Ming. "Rashīd ad-Dīn as a Transmitter of Chinese Medicine to the West." *Le Muséon* 109 (1996): 395–404.

Richter-Bernburg, Lutz. "Iran's Contribution to Medicine and Veterinary Science in Islam, AH 100–900/AD 700–1500." In *The Diffusion of Greco-Roman Medicine into the Middle East and the Caucasus,* eds. John A.C. Greppin, E. Savage-Smith, and P. Gueriguian, 139–68. Delmar, NY: Caravan, 1999.

—————. *Persian Medical Manuscripts at the University of California, Los Angeles.* Malibu: Undena, 1978.

Sabra, Abdelhamid I. "The Appropriation and Subsequent Naturalization of Greek Science in Medieval Islam: A Preliminary Statement." *History of Science* 25 (1987): 223–43.

Storey, Cyril A. *Persian Literature: A Bio-Bibliographical Survey*, vol. 2, 2. London: Royal Asiatic Society, 1971.

MEDICAL LITERATURE, SYRIAC

Syriac Christians first gained notoriety for their medical skills in Gundaishapur in southwest Persia, where they came into contact with classical Greek medical thought and began translating the works of Dioscorides, Galen, Hippocrates, and Paul of Aegina into Syriac. The Alexandrian-educated Sergius of Resh'aina (d. 536) was one of the earliest Syriac Christians to distinguish himself both as a translator and a medical practitioner. The Boktishu' family of physicians were among the earliest East Syriac Christians to contribute to the intellectual and scientific efflorescence of 'Abbasid Baghdad. Girgis Boktishu' (ca. 770), dean of medicine in Gundaishapur, was personal physician to the Caliph al-Mansur. Gabriel, the son of Girgis, translated extracts from leading Greek medical theorists from Syriac to Arabic, and he compiled them in a work that he titled *al-Mujaz (The Compendium)*. The renowned Hunayn ibn Ishaq (d. 873), court physician to the Caliph al-Mutawakkil, revised and expanded the Syriac translations of Sergius of Resh'aina and translated them into Arabic; medical treatises by his nephew, Hobaysh ibn al-Hasan, often circulated under the name of Hunayn.

Syriac continued to be used as a medium for scholarship, although its scope and impact were much reduced well after Arabic had established itself as the language of life and letters throughout dar al-Islam (the empire of Islam). A particularly well-executed and lavishly illustrated text (Glasgow University Library, Sp Coll MS Hunter 40) entitled *Taqwim al-Abdan fi Tadbir al-Insan (The Arrangement of Bodies for Treatment)* by the eleventh-century scholar Abu 'Ali Yahya ibn 'Isa ibn Jazla is written in Syriac, Arabic, and karshuni (Arabic in Syriac characters). The work of translation from Greek, through Syriac, and into Arabic was carried on most intensively from the eighth through the tenth century, and it had an immediate as well as a long-term impact on Arab culture. In the first instance, Syriac translations of Greek scientific and philosophical works made available a synthesis of the classical heritage of Greece to an increasingly literate and intellectually sophisticated Arabic-speaking populace. In a broader sense, Syriac translations of classical works into Arabic

expanded the vocabulary, level of diction, and intellectual range of the Arabic language and helped it develop into an adequate medium for intellectual life.

JOSEPH P. AMAR

See also Arabic; Baghdad; Christians and Christianity; Cultural Exchange; Hunayn ibn Ishaq; Syriac; Linguistics; Medical Literature; Physicians; al-Razi (Rhazes); Scholars, Science; Translation

Further Reading

Brock, Sebastian. *A Brief Outline of Syriac Literature.* Kottayam, India: St. Ephrem Ecumenical Research Institute, 1997.

Hourani, Albert. *A History of the Arab Peoples.* Cambridge, Mass: The Belknap Press of Harvard University Press, 1991.

MEDICAL LITERATURE, TURKISH

Turkish medical literature, being spread in a wide territory and written in various dialects, is still a field that is not studied sufficiently. According to research that has been performed so far, examples of the first written Turkish literature, the *Orkhon* and *Yenisei* engravings, are from the fifth to the ninth century; however, the earliest Turkish medical literature that was recorded in forty-five rolls and found in Turfan, Central Asia, was started during the tenth century in Uigur Turkish. The medical prescriptions described in Uigur medical texts, translated from Indian and Chinese medical literature, consist mainly of *materia medica,* and some are local drugs.

After the conversion to Islam in large groups from the tenth century on, Turkish peoples favored writing in Arabic, which was accepted to be the literary language of the Islamic world. If Turkish literature in which medical terminology is used is disregarded (e.g., the *Divan-i Lughati't Turk* of the eleventh century; 581 medical terms are used), the start of Turkish medical literature that came to be continuous was with *Tuhfa-i Mubarizi* by Hakim Barakat, dedicated to Mubaruziddin Khalifat Alp Ghazi, the governor of Amasya. The first Anatolian Turkish medical work known so far, this volume was compiled during the first quarter of the thirteenth century, during the Seljuk period. The rapid accumulation of the Turkish medical literature written during the fourteenth and fifteenth centuries was realized through the support of the rulers of the Anatolian Seljuk states (who expected books to be written in Turkish) and paid importance to knowledge and art; hence, this protected and motivated scholars and physicians. These books were written in a simple style that the common

The forms of instruments necessary for extracting the foetus. (*Sharafaddin Sabunjuoghlu's Jarrahiyatu'l-Haniya.* Part 2, Chapter 77, f. 113a, Millet Library.). © Nil Sari.

people were familiar with; therefore, this is the best literature to be studied as interesting linguistic material. The subjects studied in Turkish medical work were mainly practical applications of the same character as classical Islamic medicine in theory and practice. For example, the classification of illnesses (e.g., fevers, tumors) and their etiology, signs, and symptoms were described in accordance with the humoral theory. Examinations (e.g., feeling for the pulse, performing uroscopy) and treatments such as vomiting, bloodletting, purgation, as well as simple and complex drug therapies were also based on the humoral theory.

The Turkish medical literature of this period was influenced by the preceding literature: the *Al-Qanun fi't Tıb* of Ibn Sina; the *Zahire-i Kharezmshahi* of Jurjani; and the *Kitab al-Jami'i fi-al-Adviyatu al-Mufrada* of Ibn Baytar were the most favored Islamic sources used, whereas Hippocrates, Galen, and Dioscorides were the most frequent references. However, some writers and translators quoted new information and described their own practices and experiences. Such information that was assumed to be original can be evaluated only by comparing it

with the preceding works. The examples that are best known for their contributions are the following: Ishaq ibn Murad's book that consists of Turkish drug names (*Adviya-i Mufrada,* 1389), which was the first Turkish medical work of the Ottoman period; Mehmed ibn Mahmud of Shirvan and his exhaustive book on eye diseases (*Murshid,* 1438); Sharafaddin Sabunjuoghlu's illustrated book about surgery (*Jarrahiyatu'l-Haniya,* 1465); a translation of al-Tasrif's part on surgery by Abu'l-Qasim al-Zahrawi and his book of medical prescriptions describing his own experiences (*Mujarrabnama,* 1468); and Akhi Chalabi's (d. 1524) work on kidney and urinary bladder stones and their treatment (*Risala-i Hasatu'l-Kilya).* The most favored Turkish medical books that comprised all subjects of classical Islamic medicine were the *Muntahab-ı Shifa* of *Hajy Pasha* (d. 1424); the *Yadigar* of *Ibn Sharif* (1425); and the *Manafi'u'n-Nas* (1566) of *Nidai.* Turkish medical compilations and translations of the known and anonymous writers from between the fourteenth and the sixteenth centuries (known so far) comprise about fifty works, most of which have not yet been studied.

NIL SARI

See also Ibn Sina or Avicenna; Jurjani; Abu'l-Qasim al-Zahrawi

Further Reading

Adivar, Adnan. *Osmanli Turklerinde Ilim*, IV. Baski, Remzi Kitabevi. Istanbul, 1982.
Bayat, Ali Haydar. *Tip Tarihi.* Izmir, 2003.
Sehsuvaroglu, Bedii. "Anadolu'da Turkce İlk Tip Eserleri." *Istanbul Universitesi Tip Fakultesi Mecmuasi* 1 (1957): 79–93.
Sesen, Ramazan. "Ortacag Islam Tibbinin Kaynaklari ve XV Yuzyilda Turkce'ye Tercume Edilen Tip Kitaplari." *Tip Tarihi Araştirmalari* 5 (1993) :11–20.
Suveren, Kenan, and Ilter Uzel. "Ilk Turkce Tip Yazmalarına Genel Bir Bakis." *Tip Tarihi Araştirmalari* 2 (1988): 126–42.

MEDINA

The oasis settlement of Medina, Islam's second most holy city, lies in the western region of the Arabian peninsula. It was originally called Yathrib, and it is located 385 kilometers northeast of Mecca in the geographical region known as the Hijaz. Medina provided the platform from which the Prophet was able to place the Islamic faith firmly on the landscape of Arabia and beyond. It is situated on an elevated plain of predominantly fertile land that is renowned for its abundant date palms and vineyards. It was close to the trade routes that passed along the western coast of the Arabian peninsula. Arab and Jewish tribes had

Schematic view of Medina, the center of the cult of Muhammad, whose goal was union with the prophet. Tile. Cairo, Mamluk period, sixteenth century. Credit: Werner Forman/Art Resource, NY. Museum of Islamic Art, Cairo, Egypt.

settled there over the centuries that preceded the emergence of Islam. The Aws and the Khazraj were the settlement's two main Arab tribes. The Jews of Medina, who constituted a sizable element of the city's population, were influential landowners and merchants. Members of the Arab clans, who were mostly pagans, performed the annual pilgrimage to the Meccan sanctuary. During one such occasion, several individuals from Medina were persuaded to convert to the new faith, paving the way for the promulgation of the Prophet's message in the oasis settlement.

When the Prophet was compelled to leave Mecca in 622 CE, he and his followers were welcomed in Medina; the Muslims there were known as the *Ansar* (Helpers). The Prophet purchased a plot of land, constructing a modest mosque *(masjid)* with adjoining apartments in which he lived. It served as the seat of government for him and his immediate successors. The migration *(hijra)* to Medina marked a turning point in the religion's history and development. The Prophet assumed greater political and personal authority in the city, drawing up a constitution that governed relationships among the city's communities. He was also able to challenge Quraysh by threatening their trade caravans.

Islam as a religious institution evolved decisively. Qur'anic revelation in Medina covered themes of a legislative nature; furthermore, ritual prayers, alms giving, fasting, and pilgrimage were made obligatory. When the Prophet passed away, he was buried in the mosque where he had lived. The mosque serves as an important shrine for visiting pilgrims.

MUSTAFA SHAH

See also Arabia; Arabs; Battles; Constitution of Medina; Early Islam; Emigration (Hijra); Hajj; Islam; Land Tenure and Ownership; Markets; Merchants; Mosques; Muhammad the Prophet; Nomadism and Pastoralism; Pacts and Treaties; Pilgrimage; Shari'a

Further Reading

Lecker, M. *Muslims, Jews and Pagans: Studies on Early Islamic Medina.* Leiden: E.J. Brill, 1995.
Watt, Montgomerry, W. *Muhammad Prophet and Statesman.* Oxford, UK: Oxford University Press, 1961.

MEDITERRANEAN SEA

Islamic sources refer to the Mediterranean as *Bahr al-Rūm* (the Sea of the Greeks), *Bahr al-Sham* or *al-Bahr al-Shami* (the Sea of Syria), and/or *Bahr al-Maghrib* (the Sea of the West). The Byzantines' loss of Syria and Egypt to Muslims during the first half of the seventh century CE marks the beginning of Islamic expansion in the Mediterranean arena. Taking advantage of experienced Greek and Coptic sailors, shipwrights, and former Byzantine maritime installations in Syria, Palestine, and Egypt, Mu'awiya, who was then the *wali* (governor) of Syria (640–661 CE), commandeered the first Islamic maritime expedition against Cyprus in AH 28/648 CE. During the subsequent year, he launched a second attack on Arwad (Arados), an island located off the Syrian coast, and he burned the island's city. Islamic fleets—the Syrian one in particular—intensified their activities against Byzantine targets in the eastern basin of the Mediterranean and Aegean and assaulted Crete, Cos, Cyprus, and Rhodes in 33/653–654, ultimately scoring their first naval victory against the Byzantine navy at Phoenix (Dhat al-Sawari) in 34/655. With the establishment of the Umayyad Caliphate and the transfer of the capital from Kufa to Damascus in 40/661, Muslims intensified their naval activities and targeted Byzantine strategic positions on the Mediterranean as well as the Aegean seas. During the spring of 49/669, they launched an unsuccessful attack against Constantinople. During their second attempt to capture the Byzantine capital, they laid an enduring siege to it that lasted for eight years (53–60/673–80), with no success. The third fruitless effort was in 99–100/717–718, which ended with the destruction, capture, and burning of Islamic ships. In addition to these major attacks, Muslims carried out annual expeditions to different targets on the Mediterranean. Although Byzantine supremacy at sea was shattered, the Islamic naval triumph had no immediate overarching results because of the domestic complications in the caliphate itself.

In separate, spontaneous, and uncoordinated expeditions, Muslim sea powers launched attacks against Sicily and Crete during that same year. Although the Aghlabid fleet commandeered by Asad Ibn al-Furat (an old Maliki jurist of Khurasani origin) raided Sicily, an Andalusian flotilla led by Abu Hafs 'Umar al-Balluti landed and held sway over the island of Crete. The assaults on and conquest of Sicily and Crete mark a turning point in Islamic naval history in the Mediterranean. Within a few decades, Islamic fleets captured the Mediterranean islands of Majorca, Minorca, Ibiza, Sardinia, Pantelleria, Malta, and Cyprus. Their military expeditions extended to Christian coastal frontiers and hinterland. A series of more advanced and permanent military and pirate bases were established along the northern shores of the Mediterranean Sea at Fraxinetum in Provence, Monte Garigliano near Naples, and around Bari in Apulia. Navigation in the Adriatic Sea became controlled by independent Islamic flotillas, whereas Byzantine navigation in the Aegean was threatened by the Syrian and Cretan Arabs, who sacked and captured Thessalonica in 904 CE and invaded and landed on several other strategic islands. The Islamic control of the Mediterranean did not, thus, begin during the seventh or eighth century CE but rather during the first half of the ninth century CE, when the Muslim world was fragmented into political entities governed by dynasties of both Arab and non-Arab origin.

The Islamic *imperium* over the Mediterranean Sea lasted for more than two centuries despite the recapture of Crete by Byzantium in 351/961. The actual degeneration of Muslim naval power in the Mediterranean began by the late fourth and early AH fifth centuries/eleventh century CE and continued into the early AH sixth century/twelfth century CE; this resulted from inter-Islamic military struggles and the penetration of Bedouin tribes. In 442/1050, the Hilalis (Banu Hilal) who had ravaged the province of Barqa (Libya) and left it to the Sulaymis continued their advance toward Gabès, Bèja, Qayrawan, al-Mahdiyya, Bougie (Bijaya), and the Central Maghrib. This invasion had formidable impact on the socioeconomic and political life of the region. In addition to destroying the basis of Tunisian agriculture, industry, and sub-Saharan trade, the resulting deterioration of the port cities led to a decline in maritime commerce. Navigational activity along the coast between Gabès to Büna (Bône) seems to have been paralyzed, and therefore the port cities were exposed to hostile attacks by Sicilian and Italian flotillas. Ibn Khaldun (733–809/1332–1406) summarizes that decline as follows:

"Then, the naval strength of the Muslims declined once more, because of the weakness of the ruling dynasties. Maritime habits were forgotten under the impact of the strong Bedouin attitude prevailing in the Maghrib and as a result of the discontinuance of Spanish habits. . . . The Muslims came to be strangers in the Mediterranean. The only exceptions are a few inhabitants of the coastal regions. They ought to have had many assistants and supporters, or they should have had support from the dynasties to enable them to recruit help and work toward the goal of [increasing seafaring activities]." (Ibn Khaldun, *Muqaddimah*, vol. 1, 268–9. English edition, 212.)

HASSAN KHALILEH

See also Trade, Mediterranean

Further Reading

Al-'Abbadi, Ahmad, and Al-Sayyid Salim. *Ta'rikh al-Bahriyya al-Islamiyya fi Misr wa-l-Sham.* Beirut: Dar al-Nahda al-'Arabiyya, 1981.

Ahrweiler, Hélène. *Byzance et la Mer: La Marine de Guerre, la Politique et les Institutions Maritimes de Byzance aux VIIᵉ-XVᵉ Siècles.* Paris, 1966.

Arslan, Shakib. *Ta'rikh Ghazawat al-'Arab fi Faransa wa-Swisra wa-Italya wa-Jaza'ir al-Bahr al-Mutawassit.* Beirut: Dar al-Kutub al-'Ilmiyya, 1933.

Aziz Ahmad. *A History of Islamic Sicily.* Edinburgh: Edinburgh University Press, 1975.

Bury, John B. "The Naval Policy of the Roman Empire in Relation to the Western Provinces from the 7th to the 9th Century." *Centenario Della Nascita di Michele Amari* 2 (1910): 21–34.

Christides, Vassilios. "Raid and Trade in the Eastern Mediterranean: A Treatise by Muhammad bn. 'Umar, the *Faqih* from Occupied Moslem Crete, and the *Rhodian Sea Law*, Two Parallel Texts." *Graeco-Arabica* 5 (1993).

——. *The Conquest of Crete by the Arabs (CA. 824): A Turning Point in the Struggle Between Byzantium and Islam.* Athens, 1984.

——. "The Raids of the Moslems of Crete in the Aegean Sea: Piracy and Conquest." *Byzantion* 51 (1981): 76–111.

Conrad, Lawrence I. "The Conquest of Arwad: A Source Critical Study in the Historiography of the Early Medieval Near East." In *The Byzantine and Early Islamic Near East; Problems in the Literary Source Material,* ed. Averil Cameron & Lawrence Conrad, 317–401. Princeton, NJ: The Darwin Press, 1992.

Delgado, Jorge L. *El Poder Naval de Al-Andalus en la Época del Califato Omeya.* Granada: Universidad de Granada, 1993.

Gabrieli, Francesco. "Islam in the Mediterranean World." In *The Legacy of Islam,* eds. Joseph Schacht and Clifford E. Bosworth, 63–104. Oxford, UK: Clarendon Press, 1974.

——. "Greeks and Arabs in the Central Mediterranean Area." *Dumbarton Oaks Papers* 18 (1964): 59–65.

Ibn Khaldun, 'Abd al-Rahman. *Kitab al-'Ibar wa-Diwan al-Mubtada' wa-l-Khabar fi Ayyam al-'Arab wa-l-'Ajam wa-l-Barbar,* 7 vols. Beirut: Dar al-Kitab al-Lubnani, 1992.

——. *The Muqaddimah,* 9th ed., transl. Franz Rosenthal. Princeton, NJ: Princeton University Press, 1989.

Jenkins, Romilly J. "Cyprus Between Byzantium and Islam, AD 688–965." In *Studies Presented to David Moore Robinson,* eds. G.E. Mylonas and D. Raymond, vol. 2, 1006–14. Saint Louis, Mo: Washington University, 1953.

Kaegi, Walter E. *Byzantium and the Early Islamic Conquests.* Cambridge, UK: Cambridge University Press, 1993.

Kazhdan, Alexander. "Some Questions Addressed to the Scholars Who Believe in the Authenticity of Kaminiates' 'Capture of Thessalonica'." *Byzantinische Zeitschrift* 71 (1978): 301–14.

Kreutz, Barbara M. *Before the Normans: Southern Italy in the Ninth and Tenth Centuries.* Philadelphia: University of Pennsylvania Press, 1991.

Kyrris, Costas. "The Nature of the Arab-Byzantine Relations in Cyprus from the Middle of the 7th to the Middle of the 10th Century AD" *Graeco-Arabica* 3 (1984): 149–75.

Lewis, Archibald. *Naval Power and Trade in the Mediterranean AD 500 to 1100.* Princeton, NJ: Princeton University Press, 1951.

Lewis, Archibald, and Timothy Runyan. *European Naval and Maritime History, 300–1500.* Bloomington, Ind: Indiana University Press, 1990.

Moreno, Eduardo M. "Byzantium and al-Andalus in the Ninth Century." In *Byzantium in the Ninth Century: Dead or Alive,* ed. Leslie Brubaker, 215–27. Aldershot, 1998.

Salim, Al-Sayyid, and Ahmad al-'Abbadi. *Ta'rikh al-Bahriyya al-Islamiyya fi l-Maghrib wa-l-Andalus.* Beirut: Dar al-Nahda al-'Arabiyya, 1969.

Setton, Kenneth M. "On the Raids of the Moslems in the Aegean in the Ninth and Tenth Centuries." *American Journal of Archaeology* 58 (1954): 311–9.

MENTAL ILLNESS

Madness and other mental disorders were present in Islamic societies from the earliest times; however, the explanation of and reaction to states of the mind that were defined as deviating from the norm were manifold and variegated in different contexts. For instance, the suitor consumed by ardent and irrational love for an unobtainable mistress, as exemplified in *Majnun Laila (Laila's Madman)*, or the fool who, in his insanity, speaks words of wisdom—both topics of some prominence in Arabic literature—illustrate ambivalent attitudes toward mental alterity. On the one hand, madness can lead to doom and destruction; on the other, it can lead to clarity and artistic creativity. Although madness appears in a range of positive and negative guises, the focus in this discussion will be on mental illness as a medical concept, with a discussion of the religious and legal ramifications at the end.

Generally speaking, Islamic physicians viewed mental illness as a physiological condition that required treatment. They inherited medical concepts of mental health and disease to a large extent from their Greek predecessors, who developed them within the framework of humoral pathology. Drawing on ideas first expressed in the Hippocratic corpus, Galen, who was the most influential Greek medical author, argued that the "temperaments of the soul follow the mixtures of the body." To put it differently, mental conditions are linked to the state of the body: if one of the four humors dominates, this has a direct effect on the mind. An excess of black bile (marar aswad; Greek *melaina cholê*), for example, was seen to cause "melancholy" (waswas sawdawi; Greek *melancholia*), a severe mental condition characterised by delusions and extreme mood swings. A typical physiological explanation for processes that caused this form of melancholy was the following: black bile that degenerated in the spleen ascended via the stomach and heart in the form of vapors to the brain, where it corrupted the psychic pneuma, which was necessary for all intellectual activities. Other forms of mental disease were similarly explained in terms of humoral pathology and thought to originate in the brain. According to 'Ali ibn Rabban al-Tabari in *Firdaws al-Hikma fi l-Tibb (Paradise of Wisdom on Medicine,* ed. M.Z. Siddiqi, 138. Berlin, 1928; cf. Dols, *Majnun,*

115), they include epilepsy *(sar')*, prophetic illness *(marad kahini)*, despair *(wahsha)*, madness *(waswasa)*, delirium *(hadhayan)*, corruption of imagination and intelligence *(fasad al-khayal wa-l-'aql)*, forgetfulness *(nisyan)*, open animal-like brutality *(tawahhush fi l-barari)*, lethargy *(subat)*, roaring in the head *(dawi)*, vertigo *(duwar)*, inflammation *(waram [harr])*, and headache *(suda')*. The challenge for the practitioner consisted of diagnosing the exact mental condition and determining which humoral imbalance was responsible for it. For instance, the hospital physician al-Kaskari used criteria such the temperament of the patient as indicators to ascertain the nature of the mental disorder: sluggishness and forgetfulness point to a cold temperament, which requires a different treatment from a warm one, which is revealed through insomnia.

After the physician had diagnosed the exact nature of the illness, he or she could prescribe the appropriate treatment, which primarily aimed at restoring the bodily balance by expelling excess humors and replenishing deficient ones, thereby bringing the four cardinal qualities (cold, warm, dry, and moist) into proper alignment. This was achieved not only through medication but also through diet, exercise, and other, more subtle means, such as music therapy. In general, patients suffering from mental disorders would either be treated at home or in hospitals. The latter were associated with mental health care from the ninth century onward, and the word for hospital (bimaristan) later came to mean "insane asylum." Patients were sometimes treated for significant amounts of time in hospitals (there is an example of one person remaining there for years, first as a patient and later, on the way to recovery, as an orderly; see al-Tanukhi, *Nishwar al-Muhadara wa-'Akhbar al-Mudhakara*, ed. 'A. Shaliji, 8 vols., vol. VIII, 233. Beirut, 1971–1973.). Moreover, there are even some cases of famous patients who suffered from insanity staying in a hospital until death (e.g., al-Baladhuri; see *Fihrist*, ed. Flügel, 113).

Unlike the Bible, which contains numerous stories of miraculously cured mental illnesses, such as those about Jesus healing people possessed by demons (e.g., Luke 8: 26–33), the Qur'an has very few references to wondrous cures, and, when they do occur, they chiefly refer to Jesus and draw on a Christian tradition (e.g., 3:49; 5:110); moreover, the Prophet Muhammad is not portrayed as a healer or exorcist. However, in the later tradition, the Qur'an or certain verses taken from it are employed to remove jinns that are believed to be the cause of madness. Such practices are often closely connected to magic, which is also used in the form of amulets, talismans, and magical-medicinal bowls to restore mental health.

In Islamic law, the problem of insanity is discussed in a number of contexts, nearly all in connection with the question of incapacity *(hajr)*. Although the legal schools *(madhahib)* vary with regard to their definition of insanity, there are common traits: the insane person *(majnun)* is someone who is unable to make rational judgments and who lacks intellect *('aql)*; his or her legal status is therefore similar to that of a child. The insane are assigned guardians *(walis)* who can act on their behalf. Likewise, those who are not *compos mentis* cannot be responsible for any crimes, even homicide, because their actions lack intent; however, criminal damages were payable to the victims or their family.

PETER E. PORMANN

See also Hospitals

Primary Sources

Dols, Michael W. Majnun: *The Madman in Medieval Islamic Society*. Oxford, UK: Clarendon Press, 1992.

Further Reading

Cloarec, Françoise. *Bîmâristâns, Lieux de Folie et de Sagesse: La Folie et ses Traitements dans les Hôpitaux Médiévaux au Moyen-Orient*. Paris: L'Harmattan, 1998.
Pormann, Peter E. "Theory and Practice in the Early Hospitals in Baghdad—al-Kaskari on Rabies and Melancholy." *Zeitschrift für Geschichte der Arabisch-Islamischen Wissenschaften* 15 (2003): 197–248.
———. "Islamic Hospitals in the Time of al-Muqtadir." In *Abbasid Studies: Occasional Papers of the School of 'Abbasid Studies, Leuven, 27 June–1 July 2004*, eds. J. Nawas et al. Leuven and Dudley, Mass: Peeters, 2006, forthcoming.

MERCHANTS, JEWISH

The Muslim conquests brought the majority of world Jewry under Arab rule. During the first two centuries of the caliphate, large numbers of Jews went over from the agrarian life depicted in the Talmud to a cosmopolitan one. Unlike feudal Latin Christendom, Islamic society held commerce in high esteem and placed no occupational restrictions upon non-believers. Although the shari'a imposed upon the goods of dhimmi merchants a tariff of five percent (double that paid by Muslims who thus enjoyed a favored trading status), this was only half of what was levied upon traders from outside the domain of Islam. By the ninth century, Jews were benefitting from the general prosperity, entering the growing bourgeoisie, and actively participating in the Islamic Commercial Revolution. Under the 'Abbasids, Jewish merchants from the district of Radhan around Baghdad became prominent in the burgeoning international trade. According to the geographer Ibn Khurradadhbih, who was the head of caliphal posts and intelligence, the Radhanites (al-Radhaniyya) operated as far east as China and as far west as Spain, trading in precious commodities such as aromatics, spices, textiles, furs, and slaves. Who exactly they were and whether they formed a league or association has been hotly debated by scholars, and no definitive resolution is possible without further data.

A concomitant of the Commercial Revolution under the 'Abbasids was the development of merchant banking. Although Christians were most prominent in the profession, Jews were well represented. Their activities included money changing and assaying, granting loans, and issuing instruments of credit such as the *hawala* (bill of exchange), ruq'a (order of payment), *sakka* (payment note), and *suftaja* (bill of exchange comparable to a modern cashier's check). During the ninth and tenth centuries, several Jewish bankers (e.g., the Sons of Netira and the Sons of Aaron) made it to the rank of government bankers *(jahabidha)*. In addition to extending credit to the caliphal court, men like Netira and his sons played a prominent role in Jewish communal affairs. Even before the rise of Islam, there had been intimate bonds connecting the rabbinical and mercantile elites. Members of the mercantile class studied at the great gaonic academies *(yeshivot)* of Sura and Pumbeditha, which by this period were located in Baghdad. Merchant alumni who spread throughout the Islamic world fostered ties between the diaspora communities and the academies and helped further the dissemination of the talmudic form of Judaism. Men like Jacob ibn 'Awkal, his son Joseph in Fustat, and the Berekhya brothers in Qayrawan served as intermediaries and representatives of the academies and facilitated the flow of correspondence and funds, issuing suftajas that were drawn on their banking correspondents in Baghdad.

The heyday of the Jewish mercantile class came during the Fatimid caliphate (909–1161 CE). Shortly after their rise to power in Ifriqiyya (Tunisia), the country became the nexus for land and sea trade and thus the hub of the Mediterranean world. The heterodox Fatimids did not impose the discriminatory tariffs on their non-Muslim subjects, and Jewish merchants, both indigenous Maghrebis and immigrants from the East, prospered in the laissez-faire atmosphere. When the Fatimids transferred their seat of power to Egypt in 973, many merchants reestablished themselves in Fustat, Cairo, and Alexandria. One Jewish merchant, Abu Sa'd al-Tustari, who had been a purveyor to the Fatimid court, rose to the heights of political influence until his assassination in 1047 as advisor to the queen mother and regent for the boy caliph al-Mustansir.

The Cairo Geniza documents, which constitute one of the greatest sources not just for Jewish history but for medieval economic and social history as well, attest to the active role played by Jewish merchants in the flourishing trade that extended from Spain to India. Diversification was one of the hallmarks of medieval merchants. The Jewish merchants, both great and small, who were represented in the Geniza handled a tremendous variety of commodities, ranging from textiles to spices and aromatics, medicinals, foodstuffs, gemstones, and precious metals. The great House of Ibn 'Awkal (990s–ca. 1040) handled no less than eighty-three commodities and their varieties. Textile production was probably the most important industry in the medieval Muslim world, and Jewish merchants were heavily involved in all stages. Businessmen sometimes formed a temporary partnership for very large shipments, purchases, or other transactions. These could be outright partnerships of pooled capital (shirka or khulta) or commenda (qirad) in which one partner provided capital and the other labor and know-how. Most joint ventures, however, were conducted on the basis of informal cooperation (mu'amala or suhba) whereby merchants provided reciprocal services for each other.

Although most Jews throughout the Islamic world were craftsmen and laborers, there were always Jewish merchants involved in commerce at every level.

NORMAN A. STILLMAN

See also Ibn Khurradadhbih; Interfaith Relations; Money Chargers; Spices; Textiles; Trade

Further Reading

Fischel, Walter J. *Jews in the Economic and Political Life of Mediaeval Islam*, 2nd ed. New York: Ktav Publishing House, 1969.
Goitein, S.D. *A Mediterranean Society: The Jewish Communities of the Arab World as Portrayed in the Documents of the Cairo Geniza. Vol. I: Economic Foundations.* Berkeley and Los Angeles: 1967.
———. *Letters of Medieval Jewish Traders.* Princeton, NJ: Princeton University Press, 1973.
Stillman, Norman A. "The Eleventh Century Merchant House of Ibn 'Awkal (A Geniza Study)." *Journal of the Economic and Social History of the Orient* 16 (1973): 15–88.

MERCHANTS, MUSLIM

Merchants played a vital role in the economic life of the urban societies from pre-Islamic Arabia through the late classical era of Islam; the Prophet Muhammad himself acted as a merchant during the earlier part of his life, and so were some of his Companions, namely Abu Bakr, 'Uthman ibn 'Affan, 'Abd al-Rahman ibn 'Awf, and 'Amr ibn al-'As. The Qur'an refers nine times to the term *tijara* (merchandise and/or trafficking) in seven suras (chapters), although no mention is made of the term *tajir* (merchant).

In addition to the Qur'an, Muslim jurists and theologians set forth a series of works—like those of al-Ghazali, al-Dimashqi, and Ibn Khaldūn—pertaining to the ethical theory of trade. In his *Ihya' 'Ulum al-Din*, al-Ghazali (vol. 2, 79–111) lays down seven fundamental principles for a Muslim merchant in his pursuit of profit: a merchant should (1) begin his transactions with good faith and intention; (2) conceive of trade as a social duty; (3) not be the first to enter and the last to leave the market; (4) avoid forbidden and all doubtful and suspicious business; (5) carefully watch his words and deeds in business; (6) not be distracted from fulfilling his religious duties and rituals; and (7) not travel by sea. In addition, al-Ghazali ordains a seller to give emphasis to the quality and quantity of the commodities and must quote the correct price of the day. As a result, al-Ghazali considers the tijara as a form of jihad.

The AH sixth-century al-Dimashqi's composition *al-Ishara ila Mahasin al-Tijara (Beauties of Commerce)* is a pioneering and more practical manual for merchants that consists of two parts, one dealing with the merchant and the other with his goods. Concerning the first part, he classifies merchants into three categories: (1) the wholesaler (*khazzan*; literally, "hoarder"), who stores the goods and sells them when there is a scarcity of them and the prices are high; (2) the traveling merchant (*rakkad*; literally, "peregrinator"), who transports goods from one country to another; and (3) the exporting merchant or shipper (*mujahhiz*) who is himself stationary but who sends the shipments abroad to a reliable agent to whom the commodities are exported, provided that both parties share the profits. The part about goods concerns the essence of wealth, the way to test the gold, various commodities and their prices, ways of distinguishing bad merchandise from good, crafts and industries, advice to merchants, warnings against tricksters, the administration of wealth, and so on. Like al-Ghazali, al-Dimashqi pictures the ideal merchant as a person who fears God and observes equity in his dealings, buys and sells on easy terms, carries goods for the needs of people, and is satisfied with a small profit.

The occupation of trade as viewed by Ibn Khaldun requires people to acquire skills, to have the ability to praise their commodities, and to deal cunningly and stubbornly with their customers. However, unlike the foregoing two figures, he adopts the principle of "buying cheap and selling dear (ishtira' al-rakhis wa-bay' al-ghali).'' Furthermore, where al-Ghazali advises merchants not to risk their properties and lives for the sake of deriving profits, Ibn Khaldun clearly states in his *Muqaddima* (310–3) that it is more advantageous and more profitable for the merchant's enterprise if he brings goods from a country that is far away where there is danger on the road. With the exception of religious prohibitions, merchants are entitled to practice all methods and to transport goods from remote countries and sell them for high prices.

The expansion of Islamic trade in the East and West could not have developed without adopting the trading patterns that prevailed in the former Persian and Byzantine territories and providing a congenial legal environment for its promotion. Investment in commercial enterprises took many forms; among them were the commenda (mudaraba, qirad, and muqarada) and the partnership (sharika). The rules governing a commenda in which the muqarids offer capital to the master and crew of a ship can be epitomized as follows. The agents collect the amount of investment before actually commencing transactions in their capacity as trustees. They maintain it as a trust and thus must take care with it and return it when demanded by the muqarids. However, they will be absolved of liability in the event that the capital is lost unintentionally. The agents of the muqarids are legally responsible for their acts and for the contractual obligations that they carried out within the bounds of their authority. Likewise, they must have a fixed share in the profit, because profit sharing is the purpose of this partnership. However, they can be held liable if they disrespect contract terms. After the contract becomes void, they will receive a comparable wage for their labor, whereas the capital investor exclusively bears the profit or loss. If the entire profit is earmarked for the capital investors, the agents will be entitled to a certain portion of goods in exchange for their labor but will not be eligible for remuneration. Conversely, if the entire profit is attributed to the agents, then the transaction will be regarded as a loan, and they will have the right to the entire profit; however, they will also bear any loss and will still be liable for repayment of the loan to the investor. Partnership, however, varies from commenda in that the parties share the losses and profits proportionately to each one's share, although the partners fix the duration of the transaction, the types of commodities, and the geographic scope. In both situations *(qirad and sharika)*, the investment could be made on credit using either transfer of debt *(hawwala)* or letter of credit *(saftaja)*.

In addition to investment in trade, governmental institutions levied various types of canonical and non-canonical taxes on merchants, whereas jurists promulgated rules pertaining to on-land transport and carriage by sea for dealing with sharing losses and profits, jettison, salvage of goods, and so on.

HASSAN KHALILEH

Further Reading

Bosworth, C.E., W. Heffening, and M. Shatzmiller. "Tidjara." In *The Encyclopaedia of Islam, New Edition.* Leiden: E.J. Brill, 2000.

Chaudhuri, K.N. *Trade and Civilization in the Indian Ocean: An Economic History from the Rise of Islam to 1750.* Cambridge, UK: Cambridge University Press, 1993.

Constable, Olivia R. *Trade and Traders in Muslim Spain: The Commercial Realignment of the Iberian Peninsula 900–1500.* Cambridge, UK: Cambridge University Press, 1994.

Crone, Patricia. *Meccan Trade and the Rise of Islam.* Princeton, UK: Princeton University Press, 1987.

Dimashqi, Abu l-Fadl Ja'far ibn 'Ali. CE *Al-Ishara ila Mahasin al-Tijara wa-Ghushush al-Mudallisin Fiha.* Beirut: Dar Sadir, 1999.

Fischel, Walter. *Jews in the Economic and Political Life of Mediaeval Islam.* New York: Ktav Publishing House, 1969.

Al-Ghazali, Abu Hamid Muhammad ibn Muhammad. *Ihya' 'Ulum al-Din,* 5 vols. Beirut: Dar Sadir, 2000.

Goitein, Shelomo D. *A Mediterranean Society: The Jewish Communities of the Arab World as Portrayed in the Documents of the Cairo Geniza: Economic Foundations.* Berkeley: University of California Press, 1967.

Ibn Khaldun, 'Abd al-Rahman. *The Muqaddimah,* 9th ed., transl. Franz Rosenthal. Princeton, NJ: Princeton University Press, 1989.

Khalilieh, Hassan S. *Islamic Maritime Law: An Introduction.* Leiden: E.J. Brill, 1998.

Lambton, A.K.S. "The Merchant in Medieval Islam." In *A Locust's Leg: Studies in Honour S.H. Taqizadeh,* eds. W.B. Henning and E. Yarshater, 121–30. London, 1962.

Risso, Patricia. *Merchants and Faith: Muslim Commerce and Culture in the Indian Ocean.* Boulder, Colo: Westview Press, 1995.

Udovitch, Abraham L. "An Eleventh Century Islamic Treatise on the Law of the Sea." *Annales Islamologiques* 27 (1993): 37–54.

———. "Merchants and Amirs." *Asian and African Studies* 22 (1988): 53–72.

———. *Partnership and Profit in Medieval Islam.* Princeton, NJ: Princeton University Press, 1970.

———. "Commercial Techniques in Early Medieval Islamic Trade." In *Islam and the Trade of Asia,* ed. D.S. Richards, 37–62. Oxford, UK: Bruno Cassirer, 1970.

———. "The 'Law Merchant' of the Medieval Islamic World." In *Logic in Classical Islamic Culture,* ed. G.E. von Grunebaum, 113–30. Wiesbaden: Otto Harrassowitz, 1970.

———. "At the Origins of the Western *Commenda*: Islam, Israel, Byzantium?" *Speculum* 37 (1962): 198–207.

MESSIANISM

The term *messianism* is derived from *messiah*, a transliteration of the Hebrew word for "the anointed one," which denotes a future consecrated king who will restore the kingdom of Israel and save people from evil. It has become a generic term used to describe the expectation of a deliverer, often associated with a particular sacred family, who will destroy the forces of evil, eradicate injustice, and establish the true faith at the end of times. As such, messianism is often associated with a theory of salvation, a soteriology, in which the messianic figure is also a spiritual redeemer as well as a political authority, and a theory about the end of times, an eschatology, whereby the advent of the messiah ushers in a final apocalyptic struggle against evil before the cosmos comes to an end by divine decree.

In the pre-Islamic Near East, messianism was prevalent. In Judaism, sporadic expectation led to a common process of the flourishing of "false messiahs," who were charismatic figures who failed to fulfill the hope of the community and were seen as inadequate heirs of David. Such movements culminated in apocalyptic and chiliastic conflict and violence and, in some cases, in an esoteric withdrawal and acquiescence with the status quo, most notably with Sabbatai Zevi during the seventeenth century CE and in forms of Hassidism. A clear tension between an apocalyptic and a rational, routinized messianism is visible in Jewish history, as it is in other traditions. Among Christians, the messiah had come in the form of Jesus and provided redemption; however, hope, justice, and the kingdom of heaven were postponed until his second coming at the end of time, to which messianic hope was pinned. Zoroastrians pinned their hope on the future advent of the Saoshyant, "one who will bring benefit," who was to be born of a virgin from the seed of Zoroaster; this human world savior would bring forth righteousness and initiate the cosmic struggle to rid the world of evil. As with other traditions, Zoroastrian expectation was most heightened during times of oppression, hardship, and suffering.

Messianism in Islam is focused on the future appearance of the mahdi, "the rightly guided one" who is believed to be a descendent of the Prophet who will vanquish evil and injustice and restore justice and Islam during the corrupt last days. During the earliest period, it was a concomitant of the eschatological expectation expressed in the Qur'an and in the Prophetic narrations of an impending end of time. The Prophet himself was called the mahdi, and some of his Companions refused to believe that he had truly passed from this world because they believed that they were living during the last days. Revisionists have argued that early Islam was in fact a messianic, Judaic movement with the goal of uniting the monotheists and recapturing the holy land. The movement fixed its expectations not on the Prophet but on the deliverer: al-Faruq, the title associated with 'Umar ibn al-Khattab, the caliph responsible for the conquest of Jerusalem. Be that as it may, the history of messianism in Islam was closely associated with those groups who suffered political defeat and whose charismatic notions of religious authority residing in the holy family of the Prophet were marginalized: the Shi'is.

The defeat of the radical Shi'is who denied legitimacy to the caliphate and fought for the rights of the family of the Prophet led to apocalyptic forms of messianism, first encountered among the Kaysaniyya, who believed in the rightful authority of Muhammad ibn al-Hanafiyya, the son of 'Ali ibn Abi Talib. The failure of the revolt in his name in 686 led by Mukhtar ibn Abi 'Ubayd al-Thaqafi introduced two key notions of Shi'i messianism: the occultation (ghayba) and return (raj'a) of the Imam. Ibn al-Hanafiyya was believed to have disappeared into the mountains north of Mecca, where he was divinely protected, and it was thought that he would return at the end of time to reclaim his right and establish justice. Various 'Alids and even 'Abbasids adopted the title *mahdi* to draw the loyalty and aspirations of the disaffected, but the revolts against caliphal authority failed. Conflicts and splits among the nascent Imami Shi'is were often directly related to the expectation that a particular claimant was the mahdi. Eventually, from among the radical Shi'is who insisted on the infallible authority and charisma of the family of the Prophet, two groups emerged: the Isma'ilis, whose Imams went into hiding in the face of persecution only to emerge as victorious caliphs in North Africa from 909, and the Imamiyya, who were later known as the Ithna'ashariyya (Twelvers) who settled on a divinely established line of twelve imams, the last of whom was Abu'l-Qasim Muhammad ibn al-Hasan, who was born in secrecy in 868 and, after the death of his father, went into occultation. The divine promise of deliverance was postponed both because of the lack of faith of the believers and the paucity of their strength in the face of secular authority. Islamic messianism henceforth was associated with the Twelver Shi'is (although one branch of the Isma'ilis, the Tayyibis, still believed in a line of protected, occulted imams who went into concealment [satr] during the twelfth century).

The Twelver Shi'is divided the period of occultation into a lesser one, during which the imam remained in contact with the community through his agents and that ended in 941, and a greater one, which covers the expanse of time until his appearance (zuhur) at the end of time. Later traditional authorities such as al-Tusi developed a theory of hierarchical access to the imam in the lesser occultation, placing at its head a gate (bab) to the Imam in the form of four individuals, one after the other: (1) 'Uthman al-'Amri; (2) his son Muhammad; (3) al-Husayn ibn Rawh (a member of the powerful Nawbakhti family); and (4) 'Ali ibn Muhammad al-Samarra'i. It was at the death of the latter that the period of the greater occultation began with a letter of the Imam preserved in Shi'i collections announcing that, from that time on, contact with the Imam was severed until his advent.

In this state, the Twelvers dealt with the loss of contact in a series of ways: jurists began to articulate notions of their authority as the true representatives of the Imam, mystics insisted on the spiritual experience of the Imam and established their leaders as the true gate to the Imam, and popular legends accrued about the location of the Imam. The hope and need to keep the link with the Imam, who in Shi'i theology became known as a rational necessity for the knowledge of God, could lead to chiliastic outbreaks. A number of millennarian revolts occurred during the medieval period in the name of a mahdi, often in association with the Twelfth Imam in the face of social oppression and as an expression of dissent. Particular times were seen as ripe for the advent: one thousand years from the advent of Islam expectation accounts partly for the Nuqtavi and Mahdavi uprisings in Safavid Iran and Mughal India, and one thousand years from the occultation of the Imam may explain the heightened expectation of the mid-nineteenth century that led to the Shaykhi, Babi, and Bahai movements in Iran. However, there is one example of a successful messianic, millenarian movement that established a viable and lasting state: the Safavids. However, the shift there from the divine Isma'il who established dynastic power in Iran in 1501 (venerated by his followers as the mahdi and as 'Ali incarnate) to Shah Sultan Husayn at the end of the seventeenth century (a routinized king surrounded by jurists and theologians of the Twelver tradition) is striking.

SAJJAD H. RIZVI

See also Afterlife; 'Ali ibn Abi Talib; Apocalypticism; Imam; Shi'ism; 'Umar ibn al-Khattab

Primary Sources

Amir-Moezzi, Mohammed Ali. *The Divine Guide in Early Shi'ism.* Albany, NY: State University of New York Press, 1994.
Arjomand, Said Amir. "The Crisis of the Imamate and the Institution of the Occultation in Twelver Shi'ism." *IJMES* 28 (1996): 491–515.
———. "The Consolation of Theology: Absence of the Imam and the Transition from Chiliasm to Law." *Journal of Religions* 76 (1996): 548–71.
Bashear, Suliman. "The Title *al-Faruq* and Its association with 'Umar I'" *Studia Islamica* 92 (1990): 47–70.
Blichfeldt, Jan-Olaf. *Early Mahdism: Politics and Religion in the Formative Period of Islam.* Leiden: Brill, 1985.
Boyce, Mary. *Zoroastrians.* London: Routledge, Kegan & Paul, 1979.
Cohn, Norman. *Cosmos, Chaos and the World to Come.* New Haven, Conn: Yale University Press, 2001.
Cook, Michael, and Patricia Crone. *Hagarism: The Making of the Islamic World.* London: Oxford University Press, 1977.
Daftary, Farhad. *The Ismailis.* Cambridge, UK: Cambridge University Press, 1990.
Hussain, Jassim. *The Occultation of the Twelfth Imam.* London: The Muhammadi Trust, 1982.
Madelung, Wilferd. "Abdullah b. al-Zubayr and the Mahdi." *JNES* 40 (1981): 291–306.
———. "The Sufyani Between History and Legend." *Studia Islamica* 63 (1986): 5–48.
al-Murtada, Sayyid. *Risalat al-Ghayba*, transl. A.A. Sachedina in "A Treatise on the Occultation of the Twelfth Imam." *Studia Islamica* 68 (1978): 109–24.
Sachedina, Abdulaziz. *Islamic Messianism: The Idea of the Mahdi in Twelver Shi'ism.* Albany, NY: State University of New York Press, 1981.
Scholem, Gershom. *The Messianic Idea in Judaism and Other Essays on Jewish Spirituality.* New York: Schocken Books, 1995.
al-Shaykh al-Mufid. *Kitab al-Irshad: The Book of Guidance*, transl. I.K.A. Howard, 524–55. London: The Muhammadi Trust, 1981.

METALWORK

Metalworkers across the Islamic world produced a wide range of vessels and objects: from base metal pans to be used in a kitchen to gem-encrusted gold bottles destined for a palace, from precision-forged steel swords to delicate filigree gold earrings. However, statuary—the category of metalwork that was most esteemed in other cultures—is missing, because figural sculpture is prohibited by Islam.

The recyclability of metalwork makes it more susceptible to total destruction than almost any other category of art, and, without a tradition of burying precious or household items with the dead, the survival rate of Islamic metalwork has suffered. Throughout the Islamic period, gold and silver wares were the most expensive and highly esteemed of all metalwork, but most of these have been melted down for their monetary value or to be remade in a more contemporary style. A rare glimpse of the extravagance and technical skill of the finest court goldsmith's work is conveyed by objects displayed in the treasury of the Topkapi Palace in Istanbul, many of them decorated in repoussé and encrusted with emeralds, rubies, jade, or rock crystal plaques.

Most surviving metalwork of the Islamic period consists of brass vessels. The earliest examples were produced by casting, which enabled them to be manufactured in batches. The majority of them are plain and functional, although some are engraved with simple geometric, floral, or animal ornament or Arabic inscriptions with good wishes for the owner.

The most important contribution of the Islamic metalworker was the inlay technique. Between the twelfth and sixteenth centuries, base metal vessels were often transformed into luxury objects by inlaying the engraved brass surface with gold, silver, and copper. The inlay technique was not invented by the Islamic metalworkers, but its decorative potential had never been exploited as fully before. The result was that inlaid brass vessels became immensely prestigious and fashionable, and more time, skill, and money were expended for their manufacture and decoration.

The inlay technique was developed in the workshops of Afghanistan and eastern Iran during the twelfth century. Ewers, buckets, pen boxes, inkwells, and other vessels were made, often in sheet brass in imitation of the shapes of precious metal, and they were finely inlaid with silver and copper sheet and wire. They were decorated with a combination of benedictory inscriptions, arabesque scrolls, and figural scenes; personifications of the zodiac and the planets were especially popular. Historians claim that these wares were highly valued locally and abroad and were even given as diplomatic gifts to foreign rulers. The technique soon spread westward, and a series of inlay centers sprang up in western Iran, Anatolia, and northern Iraq, boosted by the Mongol invasion in the 1220s, which encouraged more metalworkers to travel west in search of patrons.

The most important of these new inlaid brass centers was Mosul in Northern Iraq, where inlays were used to decorate traditionally shaped vessels with scenes of court life such as enthronements, hunting scenes, and musicians, which appealed to the wealthy inhabitants of Mosul. The destruction of Mosul by the Mongols in 1259 forced the metalworkers to move to neighboring countries, most notably Syria, which was already producing fine vessels in a similar style for the courts of the Ayyubid sultans.

After the establishment of the Mamluk regime in Egypt and Syria, these metalworkers and their successors were encouraged to produce vessels inlaid with bold inscription friezes containing the names, titles, and blazons of the elite. However, the increasingly active trade with Europe gave the metalworkers an alternative market that appreciated figural and animal designs and exotic "Saracenic" ornament such as pseudo-Arabic inscriptions and complex arabesques.

Meanwhile, the Mongols injected a range of chinoiserie ornament into the decorative repertoire of the metalwork produced for their courts in Iran as well as an appreciation of poetic inscriptions. A series of inlaid brass wine jugs produced at the court of Timur (Tamerlane) and his successors in Herat, Afghanistan, during the fifteenth century feature verses from contemporary poets such as Hafez, often in praise of the wine that they would have contained.

By the end of the fifteenth century, the fashion for these highly decorated vessels was waning and was replaced by a passion for Chinese porcelain. Brass or copper vessels continued to be produced, sometimes engraved and tinned to resemble silver or gilded to look like gold; however, these base metal wares never regained the kudos of the inlaid brasses of the medieval period.

RACHEL WARD

See also Sculpture

Further Reading

Allan, James, W. *Islamic Metalwork: The Nuhad Es-Said Collection.* London, 1982.
Baer, Eva. *Metalwork in Medieval Islamic Art.* New York, 1983.
Melikian Chirvani, A.S. *Islamic Metalwork From the Iranian World, 8th–18th Centuries.* London: Victoria and Albert Museum, 1982.
Ward, Rachel. *Islamic Metalwork.* London: British Museum Publications, 1993.

METEOROLOGY

Meteorological phenomena have been mentioned and discussed by a variety of authors in the medieval Arabic/Muslim world. Those who tried to explain these phenomena within a theoretical framework linked them up with Greek philosophy and science, particularly with Aristotle's *Meteorology* and with what his pupil Theophrastus and later Greek commentators have written about this subject. The discipline dealing with meteorological phenomena and their explanation was known as the "science of the upper phenomena" ('ilm al-athar al-'ulwiyya); that is, the science of the phenonema that occur in the atmosphere above the earth. These phenomena include not only such things as rain, snow, wind, thunder, lightning, haloes, and rainbows but also comets and the Milky Way, which, according to Aristotle, were not celestial phenomena but rather were occurring in the upper atmosphere. Aristotelian meteorology also included the study of rivers, the sea, earthquakes, and the formation of minerals and metals within the earth.

These were grouped together with the aforementioned phenomena because all of them were explained as being caused by one basic phenomenon: the double exhalation. The sun dissolves by its heat two kinds of exhalations from the earth: a vaporous, moist, cold exhalation from the water on the earth and a smoky, dry, hot exhalation from the earth itself. It is from these two exhalations that fill the atmosphere that all meteorological phenomena arise. For instance, when the moist exhalation rises to higher, colder regions of the atmosphere, it densifies into clouds and condenses into rain. The hot exhalation rises to the upper part of the atmosphere, which is adjacent to the celestial sphere of the moon. There it forms clusters that are ignited by the motion of the celestial sphere, and this is seen as meteors, comets, or the Milky Way. Wind is not moving air, according to Aristotle, but rather dry exhalation that moves horizontally; it is moved along in a circular motion around the earth by the motion of the upper atmosphere, which in turn is moved along by the circular motion of the celestial sphere.

Aristotelian meteorology became known in the Arabic/Muslim world during the ninth century by means of (a rather distorted) Arabic version of Aristotle's *Meteorology* and by the translations of the Greek commentaries by Alexander and Olympiodorus as well as of Theophrastus' *Meteorology*. Subsequently, a number of Arabic/Muslim scholars wrote about meteorological subjects based on the Greek theories, such as al-Kindi, Ibn Suwar ibn al-Khammar, Ibn Sina, Ibn Bajja, and Ibn Rushd. The views expressed by these scholars are mostly adopted from or inspired by the Aristotelian theory, but they also criticized it (e.g., when this theory could not explain clearly observed phenomena); besides that, they also presented ideas that may be considered as original contributions. For instance, they all rejected the view that the Milky Way is a phenomenon in the atmosphere, because this cannot explain the fact that it is stable and always looks the same. Instead, they claimed that it is the light of many stars that are close together, an opinion that was already shared by many Greek thinkers before and after Aristotle. Also, they rejected Aristotle's explanation of the motion of the wind, because it could not explain the obvious fact that winds may blow from different directions; instead, they attempted several other explanations.

The group of scholars who wrote their treatises that were inspired by Aristotle's *Meteorology* generally did not contribute much toward a correct explanation of the phenomena they studied, although they did reject some of his views that could not explain certain facts. Progress toward the correct explanation of the rainbow was made in another tradition by those who did experimental research on optical phenomena, starting from Ptolemaeus' *Optics,* by scholars such as Ibn al-Haytham and Kamal al-Din al-Farisi.

P. LETTINCK

See also Aristotle and Aristotelianism

Primary Source

Petraitis, C., ed. *The Arabic Version of Aristotle's Meteorology.* Beirut, 1967.

Further Reading

Daiber, H. "The Meteorology of *Theophrastus* in Syriac and Arabic Translation." In *Theophrastus; His Psychological, Doxographical and Scienitfic Writings,* eds. W.W. Fortenbaugh and D. Gutas, 166–293. New Brunswick and London, Transaction Publishers, 1992.
Lettinck, P. *Aristotle's Meteorology and its Reception in the Arab World; With an Edition and Translation of Ibn Suwâr's* Treatise on Meteorological Phenomena *and Ibn Bâjja's* Commentary on the Meteorology. Leiden: Brill, 1999.

MINERALS

Taking his cue from the Qur'anic verse "God sent iron down to earth, wherein is mighty power and many uses for mankind" (LVII, "Iron," 25), the great scientist al-Biruni (973–1048 CE) in his *Mineralogy* praises divine providence for humankind, for gold and silver, and for raw materials to serve as currency and thus to facilitate trade and commerce. Sura 9:34, "Repentance," speaks about "those who treasure up gold and silver and do not expend them in the way of God" and threatens them with severe punishment. According to tradition, Muhammad condemned the use of gold and silver for drinking vessels or similar purposes. Therefore, the manufacture of luxury articles was largely confined to sumptuous pottery (e.g., with luster or other polychrome overglaze decoration) and to copper, bronze, and brass objects with inlays of gold and silver only. Although silver was found in many regions of the Muslim world, gold came mainly from sub-Saharan Africa. As a result of the Italian export of luxury goods, some African gold was diverted to Europe, as the historian Ibn Khaldun (1332–1406) testifies. Precious stones (e.g., rubies, emeralds) and pearls were highly valued; pieces of fantastic size were reported to have been in possession of the ruling families. Rock crystal was worked in specialized shops in Basra and Cairo; of about 165 preserved objects, most were found in European ecclesiastical treasuries. Sura 15:19, "The Rock," speaks of "things that are weighed" and that God makes grow in the interior of mountains. Commentators who would not attribute to the Qur'an the popular idea of metals growing like plants interpreted this as referring to fruits to be found on the surface of the mountains. From the fourth book of Aristotle's *Meteorology,* which was translated during the ninth century into Arabic, intellectuals derived the notion that metals were generated out of exhalations from the depths of the earth; later all metals were taken to be compounds of sulfur and mercury. The pseudo-Aristotelian *Book of Stones* explores the occult properties of various substances, among which it includes the—actually observed—magnetic stone. The author also reports how Alexander the Great (introduced as his disciple) succeeded in extracting diamonds from the lair of poisonous snakes. In Arabic literature, there are many such stories about stones with miraculous properties. Al-Biruni, who viewed them as nonsense, approached the matter in a different way. He constructed a device by which he measured the specific gravity of metals and stones with remarkably good results. In alchemical and magical literature, much of which was translated into Latin, the seven Ptolemaic planets are assigned corresponding metals: Saturn, lead; Jupiter, tin; Mars, iron; the Sun, gold; Venus, copper; Mercury, mercury (i.e., "quicksilver," the only such name still in use); and the Moon, silver.

GOTTHARD STROHMAIER

See also Alchemy; Aristotle and Aristotelianism; Astrology; al-Biruni; Jewelry; Magic; Metalwork; Mining; Precious Metals; Weights and Measurements

Further Reading

Ashtor, Eliyahu, et al. "*Ma'din.*" In *The Encyclopaedia of Islam,* 2nd ed., vol. 5, 963–93. Leiden: Brill, 1984.
Ruska, Julius, ed. and transl. *Das Steinbuch des Aristoteles.* Heidelberg: Carl Winter, 1912.
Ullmann, Manfred. *Die Natur- und Geheimwissenschaften im Islam.* Leiden and Cologne: Brill, 1972.
Wulff, Hans E. *The Traditional Crafts of Persia: Their Development, Technology, and Influence on Eastern and Western Civilizations.* Cambridge, Mass, and London: MIT Press, 1966.

MINING

The Late Antique and early Islamic mining boom, which followed an earlier decrease in mining activity, began during the sixth century CE, continued during the seventh century, peaked by the ninth century, and tailed off during the late ninth and tenth centuries. Thus, a marked increase in the exploitation of Central Asian silver mines occurred at the end of the sixth and during the seventh centuries and peaked during the ninth and tenth centuries. During the sixth and early seventh centuries, the mining of gold and copper was revived in central and western Arabia, of silver in Yemen, and of copper in Oman; this lasted until the ninth and tenth centuries. Silver mining was revived in North Africa during the late eighth century; there was a dramatic expansion of iron mining in North Africa during the eighth and ninth centuries; and gold mining had been revived in Upper Egypt by the ninth century. Mining and metallurgical activity in gold, silver, copper, and iron resumed at centralized sites in Visigothic Iberia from the fifth or sixth century onward. Iron mining peaked in the Guadix region during the ninth century and then retracted during the tenth and eleventh centuries.

Mining during the Islamic period included gold, silver, copper, iron, lead, mercury, arsenic, sulfur, zinc, tin, precious and semi-precious gemstones (emeralds, topaz, lapis lazuli), ochres, natron, naptha, asbestos, sal ammoniac, alum, borax, and salt. Steatite, marble, basalt, and granite were quarried. Minerals continued to be mined in the Islamic world after the eleventh century but with reduced output.

Important changes in technology are associated with the new mining. Except for iron, oxidized ores near the surface had been exhausted by ancient miners. Older sites continued to be worked during the Islamic period, but it was now necessary to dig deeper for sulfide ores and quartz veins. Although mining technology varied according to mineral and region, could range from primitive to highly developed in any particular region, and different forms of organization coexisted, early Islamic mining is distinguished by a more extensive use of sloping and horizontal adits, shafts with galleries, mercury amalgamation to extract gold from crushed quartz, cupellation to extract silver from lead ores (galena) and to separate gold from copper and lead ores, cementation to separate gold from silver, and the use of bellows inserted into ceramic tubes built into the furnace wall to maximize the heat. Except for the use of nitric acid to separate gold from silver (parting), none of these methods were new.

The centers of mining activity were in the Caucasus, Armenia, northern Iran, Fars, central Asia, central and western Arabia, Yemen, Oman, the Sofala region in East Africa, the upper Nile region, the oases in Egypt's western desert, central North Africa, Ghana in West Africa, and Iberia. In some places, multiple mineral resources were mined. Gold, silver, copper, iron, and steatite were mined in western Arabia. Armenia was a source of silver, iron, copper, lead, borax, arsenic, mercury, and salt. Tenth-century Fars was self-sufficient in minerals and did not need to import them, although there was little silver. The gold, silver, and mercury mines of Central Asia were among the richest in the Islamic world, whereas mineral-rich Iberia probably had the most diverse resources.

As compared with Late Antiquity, there was more involvement by independent prospectors and by merchants in mining during the Islamic period. Investment and exploitation by private miners, merchants, and government agents were usually mixed at particular mines, and the government normally took a share of the production. Both individual local miners and merchants were active in the silver mines at Panjhir in Central Asia and at the gold mines of Wadi al-'Allaqi in Upper Egypt. There was private ownership of mines at Panjhir, where a new vein of silver belonged to whomever found it, and in Oman, where the owners of copper mines leased them to tenants for 10% of the profit. There were also mining partnerships in Oman, and the risks and profits were shared. In Yemen, the agents of the ruler and private miners jointly exploited the silver mines at Radrad. By the ninth century, an iron mine in Sicily was owned by the Muslim ruler, and the gold mines at Wadi al-'Allaqi in Upper Egypt were run by Fatimid government agents from the tenth century onward. The labor force in early Islamic mining was relatively free and mobile. There are no references to slave labor until the ninth century at Wadi al-'Allaqi and in central Arabia.

MICHAEL G. MORONY

See also Precious Metals; Minerals

Further Reading

Dunlop, D.M. "Sources of Gold and Silver in Islam According to al-Hamdani." *Studia Islamica* 8 (1957): 29–49.
Al-Hasan, Ahmad, and Donald Hill. "Ma'din." In *Encyclopaedia Islamica*, 2nd ed., vol. V, 963–73.
Heck, Gene W. "Gold Mining in Arabia and the Rise of the Islamic State." *Journal of the Economic and Social History of the Orient* 42 (1999): 364–95.
Lombard, Maurice. *Les Metaux dans l'Ancien Mond du Ve au Xie Siecle.* Paris: Mouton, 1974.
Lowick, N. "Silver from the Panjhir Mines." *Metallurgy in Numismatics* 2 (1988): 65–74.
Toll, Christopher. *Die Beiden Edelmetalle Gold und Silber.* Uppsala: Almqvist & Wiksells, 1968.
Weisgerber, G. "Patterns of Early Islamic Mining." *Seminar for Arabian Studies* 10 (1980): 115–26.

MIR DAMAD (d. 1631)

Sayyid Muhammad Baqir Ibn Shams al-Din Muhammad al-Husayni al-Astarabadi, known as Mir Damad, was one of the most subtle Shi'i thinkers of the Safavid period. An illuminationist philosopher known for his novel solution to the problem of time and creation, he also contributed to the study of Shi'i tradition and had an important role in popularizing the collection of supplications known as *al-Sahifa al-Sajjadiyya,* which was attributed to the fourth Shi'i Imam 'Ali ibn al-Husayn Zayn al-'Abidin (d. 714). Born in Astarabad in 1562 but raised in the holy city of Mashhad, little is known about Mir Damad's early life except that he studied philosophy with Fakhr al-Din Sammaki, an illuminationist philosopher of Shiraz, and jurisprudence and the science of tradition with Shaykh al-Husayn ibn 'Abd al-Samad (d. 1576), Sayyid al-Husayn al-Karaki (d. 1593), and his own uncle 'Abd al-'Ali al-Karaki (d. 1585). Popularly known as *Mu'allim-i Thalith* (Third Teacher) after Aristotle and al-Farabi, Mir Damad was a close confidant of Shah 'Abbas I. He progressed to Qazvin, the Safavid capital under Shah Tahmasp (d. 1576), where he met Shaykh Baha' al-Din al-'Amili (d. 1621), the jurist and architect who became a great friend, and Mulla Sadra (d. 1641), perhaps his most famous student. He moved with the court to Isfahan and was a renowned figure among the intellectuals of his time. He became *Shaykh al-Islam* of Isfahan, conducting the coronation of Shah Safi in 1629. He died in Najaf in 1631 while accompanying the Shah on a pilgrimage to the Shi'i holy sites in Iraq.

Mir Damad wrote more than sixty works in notoriously cryptic Arabic about the scriptural and intellectual sciences, and he also wrote commentaries about the works of Ibn Sina and Suhrawardi. Popular anecdotes in the biographical literature contain jokes suggesting that even God has difficulty understanding him. He authored *al-Rawashih al-Samawiyya (Heavenly Percolations)* about the main Twelver Shi'i collection of tradition, *al-Kafi,* laying out his hermeneutics, juristic method, and commentary on the text. *Nibras al-Diya' (Lamp of Illumination)*, about the Shi'i doctrine of bada' (the notion that God seems to change His mind to accommodate historical contingency), was an attempt at defending the doctrine against Nasir al-Din al-Tusi's rejection. He argued that bada' lexically meant the appearance of a view that did not exist previously and that such a notion cannot arise with respect to divine knowledge, volition, or determination. However, it may come about in the current perception of the divine will. He explained the notion by drawing the analogy with the divine law, which changes and is abrogated during each successive dispensation. Similarly, there is an ontological dispensation that changes but that makes it appear as if God has changed his mind.

Mir Damad's major philosophical treatise was *al-Qabasat (Burning Embers)*. In his introduction, he stated that he was asked by one of his students to pen a treatise establishing a philosophical proof for God's singularity as an eternal being and the process by which he brings the cosmos into being through ibda' (creating something from nothing) and takwin (engendering in the world of generation and corruption). The purpose of the text was to explain the nature of the incipience of the cosmos (huduth al-'alam). The work was divided into ten embers or chapters. The first set the "Avicennan scene" by describing the nature of the cosmos' logical posteriority to God (huduth dhati) and Avicenna's three modalities of time: (1) zaman (time), which describes the relationship between mutable entities; (2) dahr (perpetuity), which locates the relationship between mutable and immutable entities; and (3) sarmad (eternity), the sole ontological plane of the divine and the relationship of immutability. The remaining chapters demonstrated that all relationships of prior and posterior, between existents and essences, entail the priority of the divine. The central doctrine of the work was perpetual incipience (huduth dahri). The traditional debate between theologians and philosophers had pitted temporal incipience (huduth zamani; the idea that God had created the world in time) against the notion of essential incipience (huduth dhati; the idea that reduced the world's posteriority of God to a logical consequence of contingency following necessity). Mir Damad argued that both positions are inadequate. Temporal incipience begs the question of the world being created in a time after a time (the lapse between God's time and the world's time). Essential incipience is reductionist and seems to rob God of the agency to create volitionally. He felt that the best solution was to locate creation outside of both time and eternity in the intermediate ontological plane of perpetuity (dahr) that described the relationship between an immutable and timeless God and a mutable and timed world.

Because of the difficulty of his thought and the popularity of Mulla Sadra, Mir Damad's contributions were soon forgotten.

SAJJAD H. RIZVI

See also Ibn Sina or Avicenna; Isfahan; Mulla Sadra; Safavids; Shah 'Abbas; Suhrawardi

Further Reading

Corbin, Henry. *En Islam Iranien*, vol. IV, 9–53. Paris: Gallimard, 1972.
Dabashi, Hamid. "Mir Damad." In *History of Islamic Philosophy*, eds. Nasr and Leaman, vol. I, 597–634. London: Routledge, 1996.
Rahman, F. "Mir Damad's Concept of *Huduth Dahri*: A Contribution to the Study of God-World Relationship in Safavid Iran." *JNES* 39 (1980): 139–51.

MIRRORS FOR PRINCES

An English translation of the German term *fürstenspiegel, Mirrors for Princes* refers to a particular genre of prose composition in which those in authority are invited to reflect on the nature of efficient and ethical rule, most especially in the light of their own behavior. As such, it belongs to a substantial corpus of homiletic and aphoristic literature that is found in many world cultures and that incorporates, among other categories of composition, tales of prophets and religious teachers, collections of proverbs, animal fables, and more practical manuals of advice about conduct and policy.

Within the Arab/Islamic context, one of the earliest examples of the genre takes the form of an epistle written by a pioneer in the development of an Arabic prose style, 'Abd al-Hamid, known as *al-Katib* ("The Secretary"; d. 750). His risalah to 'Abdallah, son of the Umayyad Caliph Marwan (d. 750), begins by reminding the young prince of his dependence on God before directing his attention toward more practical matters of behavior, protocol, administrative and military organization, and so on.

This particular period (the first half of the eighth century CE) was one during which the interests of secretarial staff in the increasingly elaborate caliphal chancellery were focused on the translation of works from other contiguous cultures as a means of developing and refining new modes of writing. 'Abd al-Hamid's epistles have often been seen as reflections of an interest in the works from the Hellenistic tradition, and the *Epistle to the Prince* in particular is regarded as a natural successor to a translation that may have been undertaken earlier by one of 'Abd al-Hamid's own teachers, Abu al-'Ala' Salim, rendering into Arabic the famous exchange of correspondence on the topic of wise rulership between Aristotle and Alexander. The literary tradition of India and Persia was the source of another translated work of this type, in this case in the form of a collection of animal tales. The Persian scholar Ruzbih, one of the more renowned translators of the time who adopted the Arabic name Ibn al-Muqaffa' (d. 757), translated the *Panjatantra* into Arabic; he also translated *Kalilah wa-Dimnah,* a group of fables in which two jackals provide a series of exemplary stories to illustrate to the king the consequences of wise and foolish decisions.

From an initial phase in the relatively short epistle form (including other works by Ibn al-Muqaffa', such as *Risalah fi al-Sahabah [Epistle on Companions]*), the Mirrors for Princes genre developed at the hands of later writers into a series of much larger and more detailed works. Many of the most illustrious names in

Islamic intellectual history wrote examples and in a variety of languages: the *Kitab al-Taj (Book of the Crown)*, a discussion of Persian court procedures, may have been falsely attributed to the great polymath of Arabic writing, al-Jahiz (d. 868), but the renowned Shafi'i jurist al-Mawardi (d. 1058) wrote both a study of the principles of Islamic rulership under the title *Al-Ahkam al-Sultaniyyah (Rules for Authority)* and an advice manual entitled *Nasihat al-Muluk (Advice for Kings)*. Islam's most renowned theologian, al-Ghazzali (d. 1111), also wrote a Mirrors for Princes work under the latter title.

Within an entirely different frame of reference—that of popular forms of expression—it can be observed that the original Asian version of *A Thousand and One Nights*, a collection of some 258 tales of Indo-Persian provenance that reached Baghdad at some point during the ninth and tenth centuries and that was later translated into French by Antoine Galland beginning in 1704 (as opposed to the "European" "complete" version compiled thereafter), can be regarded as a further contribution to the Mirrors for Princes genre. Although the tales included in this world-famous collection can be (and have been) analyzed from numerous points of view, it remains the case that the framing story of the two kings, Shah-Zaman and Shahrayar, and the situation of Shahrazad, the collection's narrator, are centrally concerned with the behavior of kings and the process of making decisions. Indeed, the framing story itself and the tales whereby Shahrazad manages to postpone her imminent death not only reflect on the ethics of violence—particularly that directed at women—but also contain within them exemplary tales of considerable variety.

ROGER ALLEN

Further Reading

Bosworth, C. Edmund. "Administrative Literature." In *Religion, Learning and Science in the 'Abbasid Period. Cambridge History of Arabic Literature*. Cambridge, UK: Cambridge University Press, 1990.
———. "Mirrors for Princes." In *Encyclopedia of Arabic Literature*. London: Routledge, 1998.
Latham, Derek, "The Beginnings of Arabic Prose: The Epistolary Genre." In *Arabic Literature to the End of the Umayyad Period. Cambridge History of Arabic Literature*, 154–79. Cambridge, UK: Cambridge University Press, 1983.

MONASTICISM, ARAB

Monasticism is the Christian institution of a "solitary" life in the service of God, practiced either in community or alone. By the sixth century, male and female monastic communities, both within and outside of cities, existed in Abyssinia, Egypt, greater Syria, and Mesopotamia and had penetrated the Arabian peninsula (Shahid; Byzantium). It is likely this eastern Christian monasticism that, according to the majority reading, the Qur'an considers an innovation (57:27), although it praises monks (5:82; but 9:31, 34) and in numerous passages commends practices that are common to monastic communities (night vigils, fasting; see 3:113f.; 32:16; 33:35; 51:15f.). This Qur'anic ambivalence toward monasticism mirrors Late Antiquity Christian episcopal reservations about the institution (see, for example, Rabbula ["Rules"]).

Although sometimes parodied as places of drunken revelry, monasteries were considered to be safe, sacred, and protected places by both Christians and Muslims (see Ibn Taymiyya's reference to Muslims who sought blessings from Christian priests and monks [Meri, 132]). Although the monasteries along the Persian Gulf and in South Arabia did not survive, those in Egypt, Palestine, the Levant, and Mesopotamia persisted, eventually adopting the language of their new overlords. It was in the monasteries of Palestine that Christians first adopted Arabic as their ecclesiastical, theological, and vernacular language (Griffith). Many apocalyptic accounts of Islamic rule originated in monasteries that came to be Arabic speaking and, although they lament the prevalence of Arabic (particularly in the liturgies), many are themselves written in Arabic (Suermann).

Like the Qur'an, Islamic tradition praises individual monks but questions the monastic institution: a Christian monk is said to have recognized Muhammad as a prophet (Ibn Ishaq, 79–81), but the proclamation of the absence of monasticism in Islam is attributed to Muhammad (as is the saying that jihad is the monasticism of Islam; for the locations of these traditions, see Wensinck, 312; the monastic struggle with personal demons has similarities with greater jihad, see Aphrahat and Landau-Tasseron). Critiques of monastic practices (e.g., lifelong celibacy) appear in anti-Christian polemics and in debates about aspects of Sufism (Islamic mysticism).

CLARE E. WILDE

See also Ascetics and Asceticism; Christians and Christianity; Churches; Education, Christian; Sufism and Sufis; Women: Ascetics and Mystics

Primary Sources

Aphrahat. "Demonstratio VI. Tahwitha d-Bnai Qyama." In *A Select Library of Nicene and Post-Nicene Fathers of the Christian Church. Second Series*, eds. Ph. Schaff and H. Wace, 14 vols., vol. XIII, part 2, 362–75. Grand Rapids, Mich: W.B. Eerdmans, 1952–1957.

Ibn Ishaq. "Sirat Rasul Allah." In *The Life of the Muhammad*, transl. A. Guillaume. London: Oxford University Press, 1955.

Rabbula. "Rules and Zohre for the Priests and the Bnai Qyama." In *Syriac and Arabic Documents Regarding Legislation Relative to Syrian Asceticism*, ed. and transl. A. Voobus, 36–50. Stockholm: Etse, 1960.

al-Tabari, Abu Ja'far Muhammad b. Jarir. *Tafsir [=Jami' al-Bayan 'an Ta'wil al-Qur'an]*, 2nd ed., eds. M. and A. Shakir, 24 vols. Cairo, Dar al-Ma'arif.

Further Reading

Calvet, Y. "Monuments Paléo-Chrétiens à Koweit et dans la Région du Golfe." In *Symposium Syriacum VII* [Orientalia Christiana Analecta, 256], ed. R. Lavenant, 671–85. Rome: Pontificio Istituto Orientale, 1998.

Griffith, S.H. "Monasticism and Monks." In *Encyclopaedia of the Qur'an*, 5 vols., ed. J.D. McAuliffe, vol. III, 405–8. Leiden: Brill, 2001–2005.

Landau-Tasseron, Ella. "Jihad." In *Encyclopaedia of the Qur'an*, 5 vols., ed. J.D. McAuliffe., vol. III, 35–43. Leiden: Brill, 2001–2005.

Meri, J.W. *The Cult of Saints among Muslims and Jews in Medieval Syria*. Oxford, UK: Oxford University Press, 2002.

Shahid, I. *Byzantium and the Arabs in the Sixth Century*, vol. 2, part 1. Washington, DC: Dumbarton Oaks, 2002.

Suermann, H. "Koptische Arabische Apokalypsen." In *Studies on the Christian Arabic Heritage in Honour of Fr. Prof. Dr. Samir Khalil Samir, S.I.*, eds. R. Ebied and H. Teule, 25–44. Leuven: Peeters, 2004.

Troupeau, G. "Les Couvents Chrétiens dans la Littérature Arabe Musulmane." *La Nouvelle Revue de Caire* 1 (1975): 265–79.

Wensinck, A.J. *Concordance et Indices de la Tradition Musulmane*, 8 vols. Leiden: E.J. Brill, 1992.

MONEY CHANGERS

The money changer *(sayrafi)* played a crucial role in medieval Islamic marketplaces. One of his primary duties was the determination of value of the many different coins used in economic transactions. Although coins of local origin and relatively recent age undoubtedly dominated marketplaces, there can be little doubt that coins of older ages and foreign origins were also in circulation, because the intrinsic value of their gold and silver content would never disappear. Thus, it would seem probable that a sayrafi would have an extensive knowledge of the many coinages in circulation as well as the means of weighing and testing hitherto unfamiliar coins. Such a conclusion, although of deductive sense, must remain probable, because there is no known moneychanger's handbook, if such a genre ever existed; nor is it known exactly the mechanisms by which sayrafis profited from their knowledge. Anecdotal evidence of the actions of sayrafis is to be found in contemporary chronicles, and there is extensive mention in the Geniza materials. This material also states that sayrafis played a role in the creation of sealed bags (or purses) containing a certified and known value of coinage. With this, sayrafis were also assisting economic transactions, because the weighing and testing of large numbers of individual coins were undoubtedly time-consuming activities. Warnings about the possible un-Islamic nature of sayrafi practices are common in the normative Hisba manuals of the age; thus the central irony exists that these moneychangers—ubiquitous as they were and whom Goitein labeled the bankers of their time—are known only through the records of those who used their services or suspected them.

WARREN C. SCHULTZ

Primary Sources

Buckley, R.P., transl. "The Book of the Islamic Market Inspector. *Nihayat al-Rutba fi Talab al-Hisba* (The Utmost Authority in the Pursuit of Hisba)." *Journal of Semitic Studies*, Supplement 9. Oxford, UK: Oxford University Press, 1999.

Further Reading

Goitein, S.D. *A Mediterranean Society. Vol. 1, Economic Foundations*. Berkeley, Calif: University of California Press, 1967.

MONGOL WARFARE

One of the main reasons behind the phenomenal success of the expansion of the Mongols in the thirteenth century was the large, well-organized, and effective war machine erected by Genghis (Chinggis) Khan. This army, drawing on earlier Inner Asian Steppe models, combined large numbers, mobility, firepower (i.e., archery), loyalty, endurance, and excellent command to achieve these results. For more than two generations, it was virtually unstoppable. Even after the breakdown of the united Mongol Empire in approximately 1260, the Mongols continued to expand into southern China. In other areas in which the frontier of Mongol control more or less stabilized, the Mongol armies were still a source of fear to their subjects and neighbors for generations to come. In the Islamic world, no ruler was capable of seriously challenging Mongol forces (despite some local successes of the Khwarazm-shah Jalal al-Din) after the first incursion of the Mongols under Genghis Khan in 1219 until the Mongol defeat at the hands of the Mamluks at 'Ayn Jalut in 1260. Even after this victory, the Mamluks took the threat of another invasion by the Ilkhanid Mongols very seriously, leading to a

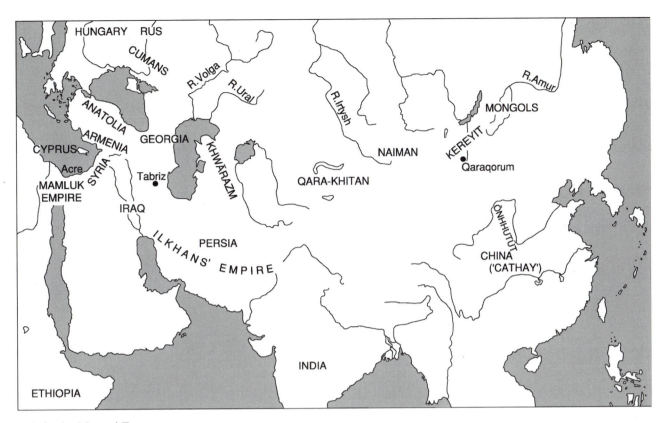

Asia in the Mongol Era.

sixty-year war in Syria and along the Euphrates border.

Like their Steppe predecessors, the Mongol army was based on disciplined masses of light-mounted archers. This type of soldier was a direct result of the lifestyle of the majority of inhabitants on the Steppe: pastorial nomadism, which necessitated mobility based on horsemanship. First, the harsh conditions of the Steppe made for physical robustness and inured its inhabitants to hardships of various kinds. (The fourteenth-century historian and philosopher Ibn Khaldun noted that inhabitants of steppes, deserts, and mountain regions enjoyed these advantages because of the climate and geography of their homelands.) Second, all pastoralists were hence potential cavalry fighters. To this was added the long-standing use of the composite bow, built from wood, horn, sinews, and other materials. This relatively small bow could be wielded effectively from the back of the horse, even allowing the user to shoot backward while the horse galloped ahead (the famous "Parthian shot," which the Romans and others encountered). The development and spread of the stirrup around 500 CE gave the nomads even more control over their horses and shooting. However, success of the Eurasian nomads was not just a matter of the individual soldier. For centuries before the Mongols, the Eurasian Steppe was home to a military tradition of masses of disciplined mounted archers who attacked in wave after wave, each withdrawing to permit the next to advance while shooting. Only when the other side was weakened or fleeing would the nomads engage them in hand-to-hand combat. Another tactic of choice among the nomads was the feigned retreat, either to draw the enemy into an ambush or to disrupt their formation, thereby making them more susceptible to a sudden attack. The armies of the Eurasian nomads were often organized using a decimal system, with units of as large as one thousand members and, on occasion, even ten thousand.

Genghis Khan's genius was to take this superb raw material and already famous (or infamous, depending on one's perspective) military tradition and to turn it into an efficient and virtually unbeatable military machine. This was first achieved by inculcating loyalty with both commanders and common soldiers. Loyalty was awarded, whereas treachery was severely punished. Genghis Khan cultivated a group of fiercely loyal and capable commanders, perhaps the most famous being Jebe and Sübetei. Gradually an imperial (or perhaps imperialist) ideology was developed, claiming that the sky-god (Tengri) had given a mandate to Genghis Khan and his family (and, by extension, the Mongols in general), thereby welding the Mongol nobles and commoners to the royal family. The training of large-scale formations was encouraged by the use of a hunting circle (jerge). A personal guard for the Khan was established, which soon turned into a royal guard corp (keshig) whose soldiers were known as ba'atud (heroes; sing. ba'atur; rendered bahadur in Muslim languages). Regiments of one thousand and divisions of ten thousand (sing. tümen) were established, although it is probably justified to doubt how often these were up to full strength given the wear and tear of campaigning. Of great importance was the sheer number of troops. As the Mongol state expanded, so did its manpower base. Theoretically, all adult males (i.e., between the ages of fifteen to sixty years) were eligible for service and could disappear for years on campaign, leaving the women, the elderly, and the children to manage the pastoral homestead. Eventually the Mongol armies were comprised of almost all of the nomadic manpower of the Eurasian Steppe. The figures of hundreds of thousands for the size of Mongol armies do not necessarily have to be rejected out of hand. In addition to mobility, firepower, tactics, discipline, and leadership, the size of Mongol armies also played an important role in the series of Mongol victories and the resulting expansion.

The most important weapon of the individual Mongol (as well as of the Turkish) trooper was the composite bow, with a bundle of several types of arrows. Additional weapons would have included a knife, a sword, an axe, a club, perhaps a lance, and also a lasso. Personal armor was probably a haphazard affair, particularly during the early stages of the Mongol empire, and was probably mostly composed of leather and cloth, although nobles, commanders, and guardsmen may have been better equipped. As conquest progressed into the sedentary countries (first China, then the Islamic world, and also Rus'), equipment—both weapons and armor—surely improved. This would have been a result of booty and tribute as well as harnessing the manufacturing capabilities of these countries for equipping the army. How far this percolated down the ranks is hard to ascertain. One gets the impression that the portrayal of Mongol troops in the paintings by artists of sedentary provenance, even working under Mongol patronage, may at times reflect artistic and military conventions of the sedentary society and not necessarily current Mongol military reality. The Mongols rode small steppe ponies that were known for their endurance but that soon tired if they galloped quickly or carried large loads. This necessitated each trooper to set out on campaign with a string of several horses, usually around five. These would be rotated both during the

march and in battle itself, although how this actually took place during the fighting is not really clear. In any event, such a large train of mounts necessitated careful logistical planning for water and pasturage. It has been suggested that reasons for the withdrawal of the Mongols from Hungary and Syria were due to the lack of pasturage in these countries.

As soon as raids into sedentary areas turned into campaigns of conquest, it became clear that even the most motivated and organized armies of cavalrymen could not deal with sieges of forts and fortified cities. This called for the employment of engineers to engage in mining operations, to build siege engines and artillery, and to concoct and use incendiary and explosive devices. For instance, Hülegü, who led Mongol forces into the Middle East during the second wave of the invasions in 1250, had with him a thousand squads of engineers, evidently of north Chinese (or perhaps Khitan) provenance. There is some discussion among scholars regarding whether the Mongols employed gunpowder both as an explosive device and to shoot projectiles. Be that as it may, there is no indication whatsoever that the Ilkhanid Mongols, during their sixty-year war with the Mamluks, ever employed any type of gunpowder weapon either against fortifications or on the open field.

Although it may be expected that, after several generations in sedentary areas, the Mongol armies underwent some transformation (not least in the quality and type of weapons and armor), there are clear indications that, at least in the Middle East, the Mongol armies were similar in broad lines in tactics and character of troops to the earlier Mongol armies. Thus, at the battle of Wadi al-Khaznadar fought near Homs between the Mamluks and Mongols under Ghazan in 1299, the mainstay of the Mongol army still appears to be light-mounted archers. Mongol field armies also included contingents from local troops. In China, this could be quite significant, but, in the Middle East, these auxiliary units—be they from subjugated Muslim rulers or Armenian and Georgian "allies"—appear to have been of secondary importance.

Mention should be made of the Mongol use of espionage and reconnaissance as well as subterfuge and psychological warfare. Thus, the Mongols succeeded in establishing contact with the wazirs in both the 'Abbasid and Syrian Ayyubid courts, convincing them to work for their interests and thus planting discord and defeatist attitudes among their opponents long before their troops showed up. Mamluk sources recount the capture of Ilkhanid operatives, although they would not have known of successful Mongol activities. The Mamluks, on the other hand, had a most successful, long-term, secret operation against the Mongols, often giving them advance notice of Mongol aggressive plans and even occasionally wreaking havoc at the Mongol ordu (the Ilkhan's moving camp).

Until the encounter with the Mamluks at 'Ayn Jalut, the Mongols were virtually unbeatable on all fronts in which they were active. What probably stopped the Mongols more than any other factor was their own disagreements and infighting. Even the Mamluks, who continued to best the Ilkhanid Mongols in both the border war and most of the major battles until 1323, when peace was concluded between them, greatly profited from the Ilkhans' wars with their Mongol neighbors. Early Mongol success was brought about by unity within the Mongol tribes (often achieved through war); later Mongol failure was brought about and compounded by the breakdown of this unity.

REUVEN AMITAI

See also 'Ayn Jalut; Ilkhanids; Mamluks; Mongols; Tamerlane

Further Reading

Allsen, Thomas T. *Mongol Imperialism: The Policies of the Grand Qan Möngke in China, Russia and the Islamic Lands.* Berkeley and Los Angeles, Calif: University of California Press, 1987.
———. "The Circulation of Military Technology in the Mongolian Empire." In *Warfare in Inner Asian History,* ed. Nicola Di Cosmo, 265–93. Leiden: E.J. Brill, 2002.
Amitai-Preiss, Reuven. *Mongols and Mamluks: The Mamluk-Ilkhanid War, 126–1281.* Cambridge, UK: Cambridge University Press, 1995.
———. "Whither the Ilkhanid Army? Ghazan's First Campaign into Syria (1299–1300)." In *Warfare in Inner Asian History,* ed. Nicola Di Cosmo, 221–64. Leiden: E.J. Brill, 2002.
Biran, Michal. "The Battle of Herat (1270): A Case of Inter-Mongol Warfare." In *Warfare in Inner Asian History,* ed. Nicola Di Cosmo, 175–219. Leiden: E.J. Brill, 2002.
Di Cosmo, Nicola. "Inner Asian Ways of Warfare in Historical Perspective." In *Warfare in Inner Asian History,* ed. Nicola Di Cosmo, 1–29. Leiden: E.J. Brill, 2002.
Martin, H. Desmond. *Chingis Khan and his Conquest of North China.* Baltimore: The John Hopkins Press, 1950.
Martinez, A.P. "Some Notes on the Il-Xanid Army." *Archivum Eurasiae Medii Aevi* 6 (1986–1988): 129–242.
Morgan, David O. "The Mongol Armies in Persia." *Der Islam* 56 (1979): 81–96.
———. "The Mongols in Syria, 1260–1300." In *Crusade and Settlement,* ed. Peter Edbury. Cardiff, UK: University College Cardiff Press, 1985.
———. *The Mongols.* Oxford, UK: Blackwell, 1986.
———. "Mongols." *Encyclopaedia of Islam, New Edition,* vol. 7, 230–5.
Ratchnevsky, Paul. *Genghis Khan: His Life and Legacy,* ed. and transl. Thomas N. Haining. Oxford, UK: Blackwell, 1991.
Rossabi, Morris. *Khubilai Khan: His Life and Times.* Berkeley and Los Angeles, Calif: University of California Press, 1988.
Saunders, John J. *The History of the Mongol Conquests.* London: Routledge & Kegan, 1971.
Smith, John M., Jr. "'Ayn Jalut: Mamluk or Mongol Success." *Harvard Journal of Asiatic Studies* 44 (1984): 307–45.
———. "Nomads on Ponies vs. Slaves on Horses." *Journal of the American Oriental Society* 118 (1998): 54–62.

MONGOLS

The Mongols were a tribe in the steppe area north of China that gave its name to a larger group of related tribes that were united by Genghis (Chinggis) Khan (ca. 1162–1227 CE) at the end of the twelfth century and the beginning of the thirteenth century. This tribal state rapidly expanded, and, by the middle of the thirteenth century, it controlled most of China (subsequently conquering all of it), the entire Eurasian Steppe (including the southern part of modern-day Ukraine), Iran, and much of the surrounding countries. The Mongols had a profound influence on much of the Islamic world, and West and Central Asia eventually converted to Islam.

By 1206, Genghis Khan, who had been born with the name Temüchin, had succeeded in uniting the Mongol and some Turkish-speaking tribes in the area today known as Mongolia. Most notable of these were the Tatars, hitherto the most prominent tribe in the area, who evidently spoke a language that was similar to Mongolian. The Tatars were the traditional enemies of the Mongols; after their defeat, they were broken up and integrated into the emerging Mongol nation. Ironically, the name *Tatar* became a synonym for *Mongol* in both eastern and western languages, and these are often used interchangeably. (Later, Tatar was used in a more restricted sense for the Turkish-speaking peoples of southern Russia.) In 1206, a *quriltai* (tribal council) was convened in which the title Genghis Khan (perhaps meaning "universal khan") was officially bestowed on Temüchin, who according to the *Secret History of the Mongols,* the main source of information about this period, had already subjugated those who lived in tents of felt—that is, the nomads of the entire region. It is on this basis that institutions were created that would provide the infrastructure for future conquest and rule: the adoption of an alphabet (from the Uighur Turks), a rudimentary legal system (although whether this is the famous Yasa at this stage is perhaps doubtful), the systematic division of the army (see Mongol Warfare for a further discussion of the army), and perhaps the beginnings of an imperial ideology that may have set its sights on the conquest of sedentary areas. The idea of world conquest, which was subsequently clearly articulated in Mongol imperialist ideology, was probably explicitly expressed only later. Scholars are divided as to whether this was already in the period of Genghis Khan or only under his immediate successors.

Regardless, in 1205, raids had commenced against the Hsi-Hsia (of Tibetan origin) in northwest China. By 1209, this state was subjected, and soon afterward raids began against the Jin, who controlled northern China. By 1215, the Mongols had conquered the territory north of the Yellow River. Their campaign against the Jin was to continue until 1234, some seven years after Genghis Khan's death. Over time, the Mongol conquest was to continue, and, by 1278, under the Great Khan Qubilai, the subjugation of the rest of China ruled by the southern Sung was completed. Mongol rule in China, known as the Yuan dynasty in Chinese historiography, lasted until 1366.

While they expanded into China, Mongol forces had also been expanding to the west. By around 1218, the area later known as Kazakhstan was subjugated, bringing the Mongols into direct contact with the realm of the Khwarazm-Shah, the most powerful ruler in the eastern Islamic world. Relations between Genghis Khan and the Khwarazm-Shah soon deteriorated, and, in 1219, Genghis ordered the full-scale invasion of his territory. Together with his sons, Genghis led his armies from Mongolia into Transoxiana and then Khurasan (Turkmenistan, northern Afghanistan, and northeastern Iran of today). The power of the Khwarazm-Shah was broken, and most of the cities of these hitherto prosperous areas, long known as centers of Islamic culture, were left in ruins. Mongol cruelty in this area appears to have resulted from a combination of factors: a lack of acquaintance with and appreciation of Islamic culture; retribution against the Khwarazm-Shah for his killing of Mongol envoys; punishment against the local population for resisting (and thereby contravening the heaven-given mandate to Genghis Khan to conquer the world); and, perhaps, a desire to establish in this area a *cordon sanitaire* to prevent future problems while the Mongols continued their expansion on other fronts.

In 1223, Genghis Khan withdrew with the majority of his army to Mongolia. A small force was left to garrison the newly conquered territory, and soon a rudimentary administration was established. Augmented by reinforcements from the Steppe, this garrison gradually expanded the area of Mongol control. By 1250, most of Iran, the southern Caucasus region (Georgia, Armenia, and northern Azerbaijan), and much of Anatolia was under at least ostensible Mongol rule. In 1255, Hülegü, the brother of the Great Khan Möngke and grandson of Genghis Khan, arrived at the edge of the Islamic world to organize areas already conquered and to expand the territory under Mongol control. Within a year, he had consolidated Mongol rule in areas hitherto ruled by the Mongols and had subjugated most of the Isma'ili (the so-called Assassins) forts in eastern and northern Iran. At the beginning of 1258, Hülegü took Baghdad, putting to death the Caliph al-Musta'sim, thereby ending five hundred years of 'Abbasid rule there. The Mongol advance in the Middle East was stopped in September 1260 by the Mamluks at the battle of 'Ayn Jalut in northern Palestine, and the Mongols withdrew beyond the Euphrates. Hülegü and his successors were known as the Ilkhanids, and they ruled an area comprising modern-day Iran, northern Afghanistan, Turkmanistan, Iraq, most of the Caucasus, and Anatolia until 1335. By about 1300, the Ilkhans, the Mongol elite, and evidently many of the Mongol tribesmen had converted to Islam. In the long run, the majority of Mongols in the Middle East appear to have assimilated into the larger population of Turkish speakers who surrounded and served them.

By around 1260, in the aftermath of the death of the Great Khan Möngke (r. 1251–1259), the great Mongol empire began to fragment into four successor states. The realm of the Ilkhanids has just been described. The Great Khan, who still enjoyed titular authority over the other princes (which did not prevent some of them from going to war with him on occasion), ruled China and the Mongolian homeland and, as said above, was known also as the Yuan emperor by the Chinese. In the steppe region of modern-day Ukraine and European Russia, there emerged the state known in the West as the Golden Horde (from the word *ordu*, "royal camp" in Turkish and Mongolian). Mongol armies had consolidated their control over this area by 1237, and they had subjugated the cities of Rus' (most importantly Kiev). This was a springboard for an amazing campaign into Eastern Europe in 1241, culminating in the double victories at Liegnitz and Pest in April of that year. These smashing victories did not lead, however, to the permanent occupation of Central or Eastern Europe. News had arrived of the death of the Great Khan Ögödei (1229–1241), which necessitated a return of the princes to Mongolia; logistical problems (i.e., the lack of pasturage for the Mongol mounts) perhaps also played a role in this action. Mongol rule solidified in the steppe areas of southern Russia and the Ukraine of today under the leadership of the descendents of Jochi, the eldest son of Genghis Khan. The Golden Horde unequivocally ruled European Russia until the end of the fourteenth century. Even in decline, when the Golden Horde had fragmented, its successor states—whose people were known as Tatars—still played important roles in the history of the region, and it was a matter of centuries until they were finally brought under the control of the expanding Russian empire. Already during the early fourteenth century is seen the double process of Islamization and Turkification in the Golden Horde, which has been noted above for the Mongols in the Middle East.

Central Asia (the area more or less subsequently covered by modern Uzbekistan, Kazakhstan, Kirgizstan, and the Xinjiang province in China) was in the hands of the descendents of Chaghatai, the second son of Genghis Khan. Further east in the steppe was the stomping grounds of Qaidu (d. 1301), a grandson of the second Great Khan Ögödei, who controlled the Chaghataids and also fought the Great Khan Qubilai (1264–1294) to establish his independence and legitimacy. During the early fourteenth century, the Ögödeids were eliminated as an independent force, but the Chaghataids were unable to provide this area with political stability. This was the background for the emergence of Tamerlane (also Timur-lang and Timur the Lame), who, around 1370, unified Transoxiana and used it as a springboard for further campaigns in the Steppe as well as in Iran and beyond. Tamerlane occupied Damascus in 1400 and defeated the Ottomans at the battle of Ankara in 1402. Unlike Genghis Khan, Tamerlane, upon his death in 1405, did not leave his descendents an institutionalized state. Despite the subsequent political confusion, the Timurids achieved well-earned fame for their patronage of the arts. Tamerlane was known as a Mongol, but he was actually a Turkish-speaking Muslim of Mongol descent. In Transoxiana and later in the steppe region to the north and northeast, again is seen the double process of Islamization and Turkification found elsewhere in Mongol-controlled areas in Western Asia.

The Mongols achieved a well-deserved reputation for the destructiveness of their conquests, and at times their rule could be characterized by a rapaciousness toward the local population. At the same time, they were patrons of arts and sciences, established relatively stable administrations, and offered a degree of religious toleration that was previously unknown in either the Islamic world or the Christian West. The unification of most of Asia brought about the widening of horizons. Some of this came in the form of detailed knowledge of East Asia that was brought to Europe; this had some influence on the desire of Europeans to reach these fabled areas, leading indirectly to the "Age of Discovery" and the resulting colonialism and other related developments.

REUVEN AMITAI

See also Assassins; 'Ayn Jalut; Central Asia; Genghis Khan; Ilkhanids; Juvayni; Mamluks; Öljeitü; Rashid al-Din; Tamerlane; Timurids; Tusi, Nasir al-Din

Primary Sources

Bar Hebraeus. *The Chronography of Gregory Abû 'l-Faraj*, ed. and transl. E.A.W. Budge, vol. 1. London: Oxford University Press, 1932.

Dawson, Christopher, ed. *The Mission to Asia: Narratives and Letters of the Franciscan Missionaries in Mongolia and China in the Thirteenth and Fourteenth Centuries*, transl. by a Nun of Stanbrook Abbey. London: Sheed and Ward, 1980.

al-Din, Rashid. *Rashiduddin Fazlullah's Jami'u't-tawarikh: Compendium of Chronicles. A History of the Mongols*, 3 vols., transl. W.T. Thackston. Cambridge, Mass: Harvard University Dept. of Near Eastern Languages and Civilizations, 1998–1999.

Grigor of Akanc' [Akner]. In R.P. Black and R.N. Frye, eds. and transl. "History of the Nation of Archers." *Harvard Journal of Asiatic Studies* 12 (1949): 269–399.

Juvayni, ˌAÔā Malik. *The History of the World Conqueror*, transl. John A. Boyle, 2 vols. Manchester, UK: Manchester University Press, 1957.

Polo, Marco. *The Travels*, transl. Ronald Latham. Hammondsworth: Penguin, 1958.

Rubruck, William of. *The Mission of Friar William of Rubruck: His Journey to the Court of the Great Khan Möngke, 1252–1255*, transl. Peter Jackson. London: Halkuyt Society, 1990.

Spuler, Bertold. *History of the Mongols: Based on Eastern and Western Accounts of the Thirteenth and Fourteenth Centuries*, transl. Helga and Stuart Drummond. London: Routledge and Paul, 1972.

The Secret History of the Mongols: A Mongolian Epic Chronicle of the Thirteenth Century, 2 vols., transl. Igor de Rachewiltz. Leiden: Brill, 2004.

Al-'Umari, Ibn Fadl Allah. *Das Mongolische Weltreich: al-'Umarī's Darstellung der Mongolischen Reiche in Seinem Werk Masālik al-AbÔār fī al-Mamālik al-AmÔār*,d. and transl. Klaus Lech. Wiesbaden: Harrossowitz, 1968.

Further Reading

Allsen, Thomas T. *Mongol Imperialism: The Policies of the Grand Qan Möngke in China, Russia and the Islamic Lands*. Berkeley and Los Angeles, Calif: University of California Press, 1987.

———. *Commodity and Exchange in the Mongol Empire: A Cultural History of Islamic Textiles*. Cambridge, UK: Cambridge University Press, 1997.

———. *Culture and Conquest in Mongol Eurasia*. Cambridge, UK: Cambridge University Press, 2001.

Amitai-Preiss, Reuven. *Mongols and Mamluks: The Mamluk-Ilkhanid War, 126–1281*. Cambridge, UK: Cambridge University Press, 1995.

Barthold, W. *Turkestan Down to the Mongol Invasion*, 4th ed. London: Luzac and Company, 1977.

Biran, Michal. *Qaidu and the Rise of the Independent Mongol State in Central Asia*. London: Curzon, 1997.

Boyle, John Andrew. "Čingiz-Khān." *Encyclopaedia of Islam, New Edition*, vol. 2, 41–4.

————, ed. *Cambridge History of Iran. Vol. 5: The Saljuq and Mongol Periods*. Cambridge, UK: Cambridge University Press, 1968.

Fennell, John L.I. *The Crisis of Medieval Russia, 1200–1304*. London: Longman, 1983.

Fletcher, Joseph. "The Mongols: Ecological and Social Perspectives." *Harvard Journal of Asiatic Studies* 46 (1986): 11–50.

Franke, Herbert, and Denis Twitchett, eds. *The Cambridge History of China*, Vol. 6, Alien Regimes and Border States, 907–1368.

Halperin, Charles J. *Russia and the Golden Horde: The Mongol Impact on Medieval Russian History*. Bloomington, Ind: Indiana University Press, 1985.

Jackson, Peter. "The Dissolution of the Mongol Empire." *Central Asiatic Journal* 95 (1980): 481–513.

————. "The Mongols and Europe." In *The New Cambridge Medieval History*. Vol. 5, c. 1198–1300, ed. D. Abulafia. Cambridge, UK: Cambridge University Press, 1999.

Komaroff, Linda, and Stefano Carboni. *The Legacy of Genghis Khan: Courtly Art and Culture in Western Asia, 1256–1353*. New York: The Metropolitan Museum of Art/New Haven, Conn: Yale University Press, 2002.

Lane, George. *Early Mongol Rule in Thirteenth-Century Iran: A Persian Renaissance*. London: Curzon Press, 2003.

Martin, H. Desmond. *Chingis Khan and his Conquest of North China*. Baltimore: The John Hopkins Press, 1950.

Melville, Charles. "The Fall of Amir Chupan and the Decline of the Ilkhanate, 1327–37: A Decade of Discord in Mongol Iran." *Papers on Inner Asia*, no. 30. Bloomington, Ind: Indiana University Research Institute for Inner Asian Studies, 1999.

Morgan, David O. *The Mongols*. Oxford, UK: Blackwell, 1986.

————. "Mongols." In *Encyclopaedia of Islam, New Edition*, vol. 7, 230–5.

Ratchnevsky, Paul. *Genghis Khan: His Life and Legacy*, ed. and transl. by Thomas N. Haining. Oxford, UK: Blackwell, 1991.

Rossabi, Morris. *Khubilai Khan: His Life and Times*. Berkeley and Los Angeles, Calif: University of California Press, 1988.

Spuler, Bertold. "Čingizids." In *Encyclopaedia of Islam, New Edition*, vol. 2, 44–7.

Saunders, John J. *The History of the Mongol Conquests*. London: Routledge & Kegan, 1971.

MOSAICS

The use of both wall mosaics and floor mosaics is known from the Islamic world between the seventh and fourteenth centuries CE, but whether one can trace a continuous tradition after the 'Abbasid period is doubtful. Instead, it appears that contacts with Byzantium led to occasional uses of mosaics, whereas the Umayyad monuments of Syria also acted as a reservoir (literal and conceptual) for periodic and fleeting revivals of the art that were often linked to campaigns of restoration.

The first mention of mosaics occurs in 684/685 CE, when the interior walls of the Ka'ba were covered with marble and glass mosaics brought from the walls of the Ethiopian cathedral at San'a in Yemen. The same media were employed subsequently in the Dome of the Rock in Jerusalem (692 CE), built by the caliph 'Abd al-Malik. The interior mosaics depict a range of fantastic and naturalistic vegetation, including vines and fruit-bearing trees, stems of acanthus tied with gold jewelry, hybrid plants bearing winged motifs emerging from jeweled vases, and an inscription executed in gold on a dark blue ground. Mosaic trees and winged motifs were also prominent on the exterior of the building, before they were replaced during the sixteenth century.

The mosques built or rebuilt by al-Walid I (r. 705–715 CE) in Damascus, Medina, and Fustat were also decorated with nonfigural mosaics. Surviving fragments of the mosaics in the Umayyad Mosque of Damascus attest to their high quality and iconographic virtuosity. These include a thirty-meter long panel in the courtyard depicting monumental trees, pavilions, and multistoried structures set on a riverbank executed against a shimmering gold background similar to that found in Byzantine mosaics; descriptions of the lost Umayyad mosaics in Medina suggest that they were similar. In both cases, it is evident that assistance was obtained from the Byzantine emperor, but the involvement of local Syrian mosaicists is also probable. The Umayyad mosaics make use of small glass tesserae (usually ten cubic meters or less) and mother of pearl set into a bed of plaster marked to indicate the required distribution of colored tesserae, which were angled to maximize the visual effects of the brilliant vitreous medium.

The Umayyads of Cordoba followed Syrian precedent, and extensive use was made of glass mosaics in al-Hakam II's extension to the Friday Mosque of that city in 965 CE. Technical examination of the Cordoba mosaics tends to confirm textual accounts of some Byzantine involvement in their execution. The remains of contemporary wall mosaics were also found at the nearby Umayyad palace of Madinat al-Zahra.

Evidence for wall mosaics in Umayyad secular structures in Syria (ca. 700–750 CE) is limited but includes the Umayyad palace at Khirbat al-Minya and the bathhouse at Hammam al-Sarakh. More common are the polychrome stone (and occasionally glass) floor mosaics found at 'Amman, Khirbat al-Minya, Qasr al-Hallabat, Qastal, Qusayr 'Amra, al-Muwaqqar, and al-Ramla. The floors made use of interlocking geometric patterns, fruit-bearing trees and plants, and more complex figural scenes closely related to those found in the churches of the region.

Prayer niche from the Beyhekim Mosque, Konya, Anatolia. Third quarter, thirteenth century CE. Above the niche runs a verse from the Koranic Sura 29. Around the three sides in stylized ornamental Kufic the Throne Verse (Sura 2,555). Faience mosaic, 395 × 280 cm. Inv. I 7193. Photo: Georg Niedermeiser. Credit: Bildarchiv Preussischer Kulturbesitz/Art Resource, NY. Museum fuer Islamische Kunst, Staatliche Museen zu Berlin, Berlin, Germany.

The most spectacular examples are found in the bath-house at Khirbat al-Mafjar in Palestine, where the entire floor surface, some nine hundred square meters, is covered with thirty-nine different panels, making it the largest expanse of floor mosaic surviving from antiquity. An adjoining private audience chamber contained a particularly fine mosaic showing a tree flanked on one side by two grazing gazelles and on the other by a lion attacking a gazelle.

The use of glass mosaics continued under the 'Abbasids of Iraq. In 783 CE, the caliph al-Mahdi had the sanctuary at Mecca decorated by mosaicists; al-Mutawwakil (r. 847–861 CE) embellished the Mosque of the Prophet at Medina with mosaics and adorned the Friday Mosque of Samarra in Iraq with the medium along its qibla wall. The ninth-century 'Abbasid palaces at Raqqa and Samarra witnessed a number of striking and apparently unique experiments in the use of vitreous wall cladding, including three-dimensional glass mosaics and translucent glass floor tiles. Scrolling mosaic grapevines bearing pendant mother-of-pearl grapes set against a gold ground ornamented the façades of the Balkuwara Palace at Samarra, suggesting a dependence on Umayyad models when it came to more orthodox forms of glass ornament.

Aside from Norman Sicily, between the ninth and the thirteenth centuries CE, the surviving evidence for the use of wall mosaics in Islamic monuments comes from Jerusalem. The Fatimid Caliph al-Zahir (r. 1021–1036 CE) embellished the mihrab dome of the Aqsa mosque with vegetal mosaics inspired by Umayyad prototypes as part of an extensive restoration of the mosque. After the Ayyubid reconquest of the city in 1187 CE, the main mihrab was provided with inscriptions executed in white, green, black, and gold mosaics and set against a pearl-studded scrolling acanthus. The interior of the mihrab was filled with a network of interlocking circles filled with vines and pendant bunches of grapes comprised of mother of pearl.

The pearl vine (often issuing from a vase) was later employed in the hoods of mihrabs in Cairo, Damascus, Hims, and Jerusalem during a minor renaissance of the art under the Bahri Mamluks of Egypt and Syria (1250–1382 CE). The theme is found as early as 1250 in the tomb of Shajarat al-Durr (Tree of Pearls) in Cairo, although it has been argued that the mosaics are a later addition dating to the period from the reign of Sultan al-Zahir Baybars (r. 1260–1276 CE), when the use of glass mosaic became popular. Mosaics were also used to decorate Mamluk fountains (a usage witnessed slightly earlier in the Artuqid palace at Diyarbakr) and wall surfaces. Extensive interior panels of gold-ground mosaics featuring architectural and landscape scenes appeared in the tomb of Baybars in Damascus (1281 CE), inspired by the mosaics in the nearby Umayyad Mosque. Syrian mosaicists also worked on Mamluk palaces in Damascus and Cairo, where fragmentary wall mosaics found in a Mamluk palace on the citadel of Cairo recall those of Baybars's tomb while also drawing perhaps on contemporary painting.

Mamluk interest in this archaic art can be directly linked to the impact of the Umayyad monuments of Syria, which were repeatedly restored and renovated during this period. Glass mosaics were among a range of features that were integrated into Bahri Mamluk monuments with the intention of appropriating some of the kudos of the early Islamic structures for their medieval successors. Mamluk mosaics are technically cruder than their Umayyad prototypes; however, this fact is recognized even by contemporaries, who note the practice of combining tesserae gleaned from Umayyad monuments with those of more recent manufacture. This florescence of the art comes to an end around 1340 CE, which effectively marks the last occurrence of mosaics in Islamic architecture.

FINBARR BARRY FLOOD

See also Dome of the Rock, Umayyad Mosque (Damascus)

Further Reading

van Berchem, Marguerite. "The Mosaics of the Dome of the Rock at Jerusalem and the Great Mosque in Damascus." In *Early Muslim Architecture, Volume 1, Part 1: Umayyads A.D. 622–750*, ed. K.A.C. Creswell, 213–372. Oxford, UK: Clarendon Press, 1969.

Bonfioli, M. "Syriac-Palestinian Mosaics in Connection With the Decorations of the Mosques at Jerusalem and Damascus." *East & West* 10 (1959): 57–76.

Finster, Barbara. "Die Mosaiken der Umayyaden-Moschee von Damaskus." *Kunst des Orients* 7 (1970–1971): 83–141.

Flood, Finbarr Barry. "Umayyad Survivals and Mamluk Revivals: Qalawunid Architecture and the Great Mosque of Damascus." *Muqarnas* 14 (1997): 57–79.

Hamilton, R.W. *Khirbat al-Mafjar: An Arabian Mansion in the Jordan Valley*. Oxford, UK: Clarendon Press, 1959.

King, G.R.D. "Some Christian Wall-mosaics in Pre-Islamic Arabia." *Proceedings of the 13th Seminar for Arabian Studies held at the Middle East Centre, Cambridge, 25–27th July 1979*, 37–43. London, 1980.

Piccirillo, Michele. *The Mosaics of Jordan*, 343–53. Amman: American Center of Oriental Research, 1993.

Rabbat, Nasser. "The Mosaics of the Qubba al-Zahiriyya in Damascus: A Classical Syrian Medium Acquires a Mamluk Signature." *Aram* 9–10 (1997–1998): 227–39.

Rosen-Ayalon, Myriam. "A Neglected Group of Mihrabs in Palestine." In *Studies in Islamic History and Civilization in Honour of Professor David Ayalon*, ed. M. Sharon, 553–63. Jerusalem and Leiden: Brill, 1986.

Stern, Henri. "Notes sur les Mosaiques du Dome du Rocher et de la Mosquée de Damas, à Propos d'un Livre de Mme Gautier van Berchem." *Cahiers Archéologiques* 22 (1972): 201–25.
———. *Les Mosaiques de la Grande Mosquée de Cordoue.* Berlin: de Gruyter, 1976.

MOSES

The biblical figure of Moses and his interactions with the Israelites dominate the narrative of the Qur'an and occupy much of medieval Muslim exegesis as a model with which the Prophet Muhammad is compared.

The Qur'an contains roughly the same narrative about the life of Moses as does the Bible, including his birth (20:38–40, 28:7–14), Midian (28:22–8), call (19:51–3, 20:9–56, 27:7–14, 28:29–35), dealings with Pharaoh (7:103–37, 10:75–92, 11:96–9, 17:101–3, 20:42–79, 23:45–9, 25:35–6, 26:10–69, 28:31–42, 40:23–46, 43:45–56, 51:38–40, 79:15–26), the theophany (7:142–5), the episode of the golden calf (7:138–56, 20:86–98), and the story of Korah (28:76–82, 29:39). Moses' encounter with Khidr (who is not named) in verse 18:60–82 is associated by Muslim exegetes with the encounter between Moses and his father-in-law Jethro in Exodus 18. Muslim exegetes also conflate the account of Moses in Midian (28:21–8) with the biblical story of Jacob (Genesis 28–2), recounting that Moses lifted a rock off the well in Midian, worked for the marriage of Zipporah, and left only after causing Jethro's flocks to produce speckled sheep.

Moses is called the "Speaker of God" (kalim Allah) in Muslim exegesis, although in Qur'an verse 28:34 he appears to have a speech impediment. His education in the Pharaoh's palace and claim to be most knowledgeable is contrasted by Muslim exegetes with the image of the Prophet Muhammad as an unlettered servant of God.

The contest between Moses and Pharaoh is portrayed in the Qur'an as a contest between the Pharaoh who claimed to be God (79:24) and the true God working through Moses. Only five plagues are mentioned by the Qur'an, which adds that Pharaoh commanded Haman to build a tower like the Tower of Babel and that there was an Egyptian who believed Moses (40:23–46).

Muslim exegesis of the accounts of Moses' wandering with the Israelites in the wilderness focuses on the disobedience of Moses and the Israelites (2:47–61). Echoing Christian exegetical themes, Muslim exegetes explain that the Torah—specifically the laws pertaining to the eating of animals—was revealed as a punishment for the Israelites. Ibn Ishaq reports that God took back part of the Torah because the Israelites worshipped the Golden Calf.

According to traditions preserved in Tabari and other exegetes, Moses was responsible for defeating the giant Og who had survived the Flood of Noah and lived in the land God had commanded the Israelites to take. In contrast with the biblical image of Moses (e.g., Exodus 32:30–5), the Qur'an and Muslim exegesis do not consistently portray Moses as interceding on behalf of the Israelites. Moses' refusal to intercede in Qur'an verse 5:25 is interpreted to mean that Moses asked God to send his people to Hell and is compared directly with the promised intercession of the Prophet Muhammad for all people on the Day of Judgment.

The revelation of certain passages from the Qur'an is interpreted as being directed at the Jews of Medina, reminding them of the Israelites' rebellion against Moses and God. Qur'an verse 2:48 states that the Israelites are to be punished on the Day of Judgment without the allowance of receiving intercession. Despite his prophetic status, Moses is also sometimes portrayed by Muslim tradition as still waiting in his grave for resurrection rather than enjoying Paradise.

BRANNON WHEELER

Further Reading

Bienaimé, Germain. *Moïse et le Don de L'Eau dans la Tradition Juive Ancienne: Targum et Midrash, Analecta Biblica 98.* Rome: Biblical Institute Press, 1984.
Coats, George W. "Moses: Heroic Man, Man of God." *Journal for the Study of the Old Testament*, Supplement Series, 57. Sheffield: Journal for the Study of the Old Testament Press, 1985.
Gressmann, H. *Mose und Seine Zeit: Ein Kommentar zu den Mose-Sagen.* Göttingen: Dandenhoed and Ruprecht, 1913.
Meeks, Wayne. *The Prophet-king: Moses Traditions and the Johannine Christology.* Leiden: E.J. Brill, 1967.
Wheeler, Brannon. *Moses in the Quran and Islamic Exgesis. Curzon Studies in the Quran.* London: Curzon, 2002.

MOSQUE OF IBN TULUN, CAIRO

The mosque built by Ahmad ibn Tulun (835–884), the semi-autonomous governor of Egypt from 868 until his death, is the sole remaining element of al-Qata'i' (The Allotments), a new district that he established northeast of Fustat (the original Muslim settlement) that also included a palace, a maydan, and an administrative center. Built of brick rendered with plaster, the mosque includes a square courtyard (approximately 300 feet/92 meters to a side) surrounded by hypostyle halls with rows of arcaded

General view. Abbasid caliphate, ninth century. Credit: Vanni/Art Resource, NY. Mosque of Ibn Tulun, Cairo, Egypt.

Further Reading

Behrens-Abouseif, Doris. *Islamic Architecture in Cairo: An Introduction*. Leiden: Brill, 1989.
Creswell, K.A.C. *Early Muslim Architecture*. Oxford: The Clarendon Press, 1940. Reprinted New York: Hacker, 1979.

MOSQUES

Origins, Features, and Functions

The mosque is the most ubiquitous building type in Islamic architecture and serves not only as a focal point of prayer and worship but also often functions as a neighborhood center and communal gathering place. The enormous structural and decorative diversity in medieval mosques is suggested in part by the two Arabic terms most often used to define a mosque. *Masjid* simply implies a place of prostration, a necessary requirement for the prayer ritual *(salat)*, and thus any location can technically serve as a masjid (locus for private or individual prayer). The word *jami'*, however, carries with it a suggestion of communal prayer, particularly participation in the Friday noon prayer at which the *khutba* (a combination of prayer and sermon) is delivered by the *imam* (religious leader to the congregation). Although masjid and jami' were not always clearly distinguished during early Islam, by the ninth century the two types of mosques had distinct functions and features.

According to Islamic tradition, the basic form of the mosque derives from the Prophet Muhammad's house in Medina in Saudi Arabia, built in 622, although this house seems from the start to have been something more than just a domestic residence for the Prophet and his wives. The evidence for this structure is literary rather than archaeological and describes a large walled courtyard with entrances on three sides and two covered porticos, the larger of which functioned as a sanctuary for the faithful where they might find shelter from the sun during prayer. The wall of this portico, referred to as the *qibla* wall, was oriented first toward Jerusalem and then later toward Mecca and reinforced the importance of a directional indicator in the mosque, because prayer must be carried out while facing Mecca. The smaller portico at the back of the house provided shelter for Muhammad's poorer followers and in essence divided the congregation, a practice that would be maintained (although for different reasons) in later mosques. Although mosque structure and form would not be standardized until

piers supporting flat wooden roofs. The prayer hall on the southeast is much deeper than the other halls and contains several mihrabs, a minbar (pulpit), and a dikka (tribune) that were added in later periods. The mosque, measuring approximately 400 × 460 feet/122 × 140 meters, is enclosed by high (33 feet/10 meters) walls crowned with elaborate cresting; this in turn is enclosed on three sides by a lower outer wall that creates an outer court *(ziyada)* that serves to separate the mosque from the city. In this space, opposite the mihrab, stands the mosque's most notable feature: a stone minaret with a cubical base, a cylindrical shaft, and an elaborate finial reached by an external spiral staircase. The mosque is relatively plain except for bands of nonrepresentational designs carved in the plaster and long wooden planks placed below the ceiling and carved with texts from the Qur'an. The building is the best surviving example of the architectural style developed at the 'Abbasid court at Samarra in Iraq and brought to Egypt by Ibn Tulun and his retinue.

JONATHAN M. BLOOM

after Muhammad's death in 632, there are clear precedents in the Prophet's Medina dwelling for the most important components of later mosques, namely a courtyard in which the faithful could gather (and perform ritual ablutions), a roofed enclosure or sanctuary where prayer was carried out, and a qibla wall oriented toward Mecca.

Various other components of mosque architecture developed during the early Islamic period and assumed a more defined identity and appearance in medieval mosques. Many of these components are thought to derive from the rich heritage of Roman, Byzantine, and Sasanian architecture in the eastern Mediterranean world, particularly that of palaces. One of the most visible features in the covered sanctuary of a mosque is the *mihrab,* a niche-like structure (and in some cases an entire separate room) usually found in the center of the qibla wall. The mihrab has no specific liturgical function beyond acting as a point of orientation in the mosque (again indicating the direction of Mecca), although because the qibla itself performs this same task in a sense the mihrab is functionally redundant. The mihrab may have derived from the apse of Byzantine churches or Roman palaces, and it came to be a focal point of lavish adornment in the mosque. Mihrabs were often decorated with elaborate carved stucco, mosaics, ceramic tiles, and colored stone inlays and were sometimes made even more visually prominent by the addition of a dome over the area in front of the mihrab.

Another important component of a mosque was the *minbar,* or pulpit, which essentially is a piece of liturgical furniture found in a jami' rather than a masjid, because it is from the minbar that the khutba would be delivered at the Friday noon prayer. The minbar usually took the form of a small raised platform or seat that was accessible by a few narrow stairs and frequently surmounted by a conical or polyhedral canopy. Its function was simply to elevate the imam (or in some cases caliph or ruler) above the assembled congregation so that his voice could more easily carry. The origins of the minbar are uncertain but perhaps derive from either the throne or pulpit reserved for the bishop's use in the Byzantine church or the raised throne used in pre-Islamic Sasanian Iran. Minbars were most often constructed of wood or stone, and intricately carved wooden examples survive from the ninth-century Great Mosque in Qairawan in Tunisia and from the twelfth-century Kutubiyya Mosque in Marrakesh, Morocco.

A somewhat less ubiquitous structure found in some mosques is the *maqsura* or royal enclosure. This is usually located near the mihrab and takes the form of a square space with latticed walls, separating the ruler from the congregation but simultaneously maintaining at least partial visibility to the faithful and vice versa. Perhaps not surprisingly, the maqsura is often more elaborately decorated than any other area in the sanctuary of a mosque save the mihrab itself. The origin of the maqsura is unclear but can be traced both to Byzantine church ceremonies (in which the emperor participated in the mass while housed in a separate enclosure) and perhaps to the more pragmatic fear of assassination and the need to at least partially screen a Muslim ruler from the congregation.

On the exterior of the mosque, easily the most visible feature is the *minaret* (from the Arabic *manar*), the tower from which the call to prayer (adhan) is made. There is more variation in the form and appearance of the minaret than in any other mosque feature, and surviving minarets are square, round, polygonal, conical, and even spiral in shape. There is again uncertainty about the origin of the form and whether the minaret was initially even connected with the activity most often associated with it. It is possible that early minarets were devised as highly visible symbols of a young faith and that they were meant to mark that faith's ascendance and monumentality. Indeed, even today the skyline of any predominantly Muslim town or city is punctuated by the vertical forms of minarets. Outstanding surviving examples from the medieval period include the spiral minaret outside the walls of the ninth-century Great Mosque at Samarra in Iraq; the square minarets of the Kutubiyya Mosque in Marrakesh and the Hassan Mosque in Rabat, both in Morocco and both built during the twelfth century; the cylindrical minaret of the twelfth-century Masjid-i Kalyan in Bukhara, Uzbekistan; and the square Giralda minaret of the Great Mosque in Seville, Spain, built during the twelfth century but later used as the bell tower of that city's cathedral.

Regional and Dynastic Diversity

The enormous geographical range of the medieval Islamic world, which stretched from Morocco and Spain in the west to northern India in the east, precludes anything but a summary treatment of the multifarious forms that mosques took, although three general types of plans can be discerned. Those that descended in form from the Prophet's house in Medina are termed *hypostyle* or *Arab-style* mosques and differ markedly from subsequent Iranian and Turkish examples, which will be examined in turn. In addition to variations in plan and structure, the raw materials of these three types also differed, although this tended to be a byproduct of geography rather than ethnic or national identity. In areas rich in natural deposits of stone (e.g., Egypt, Syria, Anatolia), mosques tended to be built in stone, whereas, in stone-poor regions (e.g., Iraq, Iran) baked brick was by necessity the preferred material. Mosque decoration also varied enormously and was a product of both location and dynastic preference for certain forms of adornment.

Most early mosques in the central Islamic lands (Egypt, Arabia, Syria, and Iraq) were hypostyle in plan with large enclosed courtyards and covered sanctuaries composed of parallel aisles that could easily be enlarged if the population of an urban center increased. Early eighth- and ninth-century mosques at Kufa and Basra in Iraq, Qairawan in Tunisia, and Fustat in Egypt all followed this plan, although all were also largely rebuilt at later dates. Three of the most typical early hypostyle mosques were erected under the patronage of the Umayyad Caliph al-Walid (r. 705–715) during the early eighth century in Damascus, Jerusalem, and Medina. The historical importance of each site reflects the conscious effort of the Umayyad dynasty to formulate and situate a new style of monumental architecture. The Mosque of the Prophet in Medina, which was built on the remains of Muhammad's house (see above), included the Prophet's tomb and was enlarged by al-Walid in 707 and adorned with mosaics (now lost). The Aqsa Mosque in Jerusalem was built on the Haram al-Sharif (Sacred Enclosure), also called the Temple Mount, and was completely reconstructed by al-Walid in 709, although only fragments of the Umayyad mosque remain intact in the present structure. The Great Mosque in Damascus, built by al-Walid from 709 to 715, also occupies a site of great pre-Islamic importance: here had stood the Jewish temple of Hadad, a Roman temple dedicated to Jupiter and the Christian church of St. John the Baptist. Al-Walid's mosque has a typical hypostyle plan with a raised and domed aisle perpendicular to the mihrab on the qibla wall. The mosaics on the outer face of the courtyard and its surrounding arcades—along with those in the Dome of the Rock in Jerusalem—provide evidence of a rich decorative tradition in Umayyad buildings, probably carried out by Byzantine craftsmen.

Large hypostyle mosques were also built by the 'Abbasid rulers of Iraq (r. 749–1258), most notably the Great Mosque at Samarra north of Baghdad with its aforementioned spiral minaret; this was completed by the Caliph al-Mutawakkil in 847. This remains one of the largest mosques in the Islamic world, although today only the baked brick walls and minaret survive intact. Similarly, large hypostyle mosques were constructed in North Africa under the Almoravid (1056–1147) and Almohad (1130–1269) dynasties in Fez (the Qarawiyyin Mosque, begun at an earlier date and subsequently enlarged several times) and Marrakesh (the twelfth-century Kutubiyya Mosque). In these latter examples, the proportions of earlier hypostyle mosques were reversed, and the sanctuary was much larger than the courtyard.

A similar reversal is evident in the Great Mosque at Cordoba, Spain, which was begun in 784 by the westernmost branch of the Umayyad dynasty and enlarged twice during the tenth century to accommodate the needs of a growing population. The mosque in Cordoba is notable for the use of doubled columns (one on top of the other) in the arcades of the sanctuary, extremely complex arch and vault forms in the area in front of the qibla wall, and a mihrab in the form of a separate polygonal chamber. The mosque also serves as a lesson in the reuse of materials; not only were the interior columns taken from pre-Islamic buildings in the region, but the mosque was later converted to a cathedral during the fifteenth century during the Christian Reconquista of Spain.

The hypostyle plan was also used in early mosques in Iran (e.g., in the eighth-century 'Abbasid mosque at Damghan and the tenth-century mosque at Nayin built by the local Buyid dynasty rulers), but there soon appeared a more specifically Iranian form, sometimes referred to as the *kiosk* mosque or, more accurately, the *eyvan* (Arabic, *iwan*) mosque. An *eyvan* is a vaulted open hall with an arched rectangular façade, the origins of which are derived either from Sasanian palaces or the Sasanian fire temple known as the *chahar taq*. The eyvan was also a prominent feature in Iranian madrasas (theological colleges), where it served as a meeting place and classroom for students.

The complex history of medieval Iran, which experienced invasions by Turkic peoples in the eleventh and twelfth centuries (resulting in the establishment of the Saljuq dynasty in Iran and, later, in Anatolia), by the Mongols in the thirteenth century, and by the Timurids in the fourteenth century, is aptly seen in the aggregate nature of the Great Mosque at Isfahan. This mosque dates from the 'Abbasid period during the eighth century, with additions and renovations during the tenth century by the Buyids, during the eleventh and twelfth centuries by the Saljuqs, and at still later dates by the Mongols (Ilkhanids; r. 1256–1353), Muzaffarids (r. 1314–1393), Timurids (r. 1370–1506), and Safavids (r. 1501–1732). Each successive dynasty left its mark on the mosque, be it a new mihrab, portal, vaulting system, or glazed tilework decoration.

Large domed chambers were also prominent in Iranian mosques, often placed in front of the mihrab (e.g., in the fourteenth-century Mongol mosque at Varamin) or providing a massive open space in the sanctuary (as in many Safavid mosques of the sixteenth and seventeenth centuries). This is perhaps best seen in the seventeenth century eyvan-style Masjid-i Shah (Royal or Ruler's Mosque), which was built by Shah 'Abbas (r. 1588–1629) in the Safavid capital of Isfahan. The mosque is situated just off the great square (maydan), which formed the heart of Shah 'Abbas' reconstruction of the city. A portal leads the visitor from the maydan to the off-axis form of the mosque (which was oriented, as usual, toward Mecca, whereas the maydan was not). The Masjid-i Shah also features not only twin minarets on either side of the maydan portal but an additional pair flanking the portal that leads into the mosque proper. The portals and both the exterior and interior of the dome are lavishly decorated with tilework.

Turkish mosques differ from Arab and Iranian models in several ways. The conquest of Anatolia in 1071 by the Saljuqs exposed Turkish architects to Byzantine church architecture and inspired further experiments with domed spaces and, particularly during the Ottoman dynasty (r. date), the use of alternating brick and stone on a building's exterior. Saljuq mosques were often built on the Iranian four-eyvan model, although the harsher Anatolian climate sometimes necessitated closing over the central courtyard with a dome. A clear turning point for Turkish architecture arrived with the Ottoman conquest of Constantinople (later Istanbul) in 1453 and, with it, possession of that city's famous domed church, Hagia Sophia, which Sultan Mehmed I (the Conqueror; r. 1444–1445 and 1451–1481) converted immediately into a mosque. In subsequent imperial mosques throughout the new capital and indeed throughout the Ottoman empire, Hagia Sophia provided a template, with its succession of domed spaces culminating in an enormous central dome. The height of Hagia Sophia's dome (180 feet) would not be eclipsed until the sixteenth-century works of the master architect Sinan, who served several sultans, most notably Kanuni Süleyman (Süleyman the Lawgiver or Süleyman the Magnificent as he was known in Europe). Sinan's experiments with balanced forms and a more sober decorative aesthetic than was seen in the eastern Islamic world culminated in his masterwork, the Selimiye Mosque, which was built for Sultan Selim II (r. 1566–1574) in Edirne in Thrace.

RICHARD TURNBULL

See also 'Abbasids; Almohads; Almoravids; Aqsa Mosque; Architecture, Religious; Aya Sophia; Badshahi Mosque (Lahore); Basra; Buyids; Byzantine Empire; Ceramics; Cairo; Cordoba; Damascus; Dome of the Rock; Egypt; Fez; Furniture and Furnishings; Fustat; Ilkhanids; Isfahan; Istanbul; Jerusalem; Kufa; Medina; Mehmet II, the Conqueror; Mongols; Mosaics; Mosque of Ibn Tulun (Cairo); North Africa; Ottoman Empire; Ottoman Turks; Qayrawan; Safavids; Sasanians: Islamic Traditions; Samarra; Selimiye Mosque (Edirne); Seljuks; Seville; Shah 'Abbas; Sinan; Süleymaniye Mosque (Istanbul); Timurids; Umayyad Mosque (Damascus); Umayyads

Further Reading

Blair, Sheila S., and Jonathan M. Bloom. *The Art and Architecture of Islam 1250–1800.* New Haven and London: Yale University Press, 1994.

Bllom, Jonathan. *Minaret, Symbol of Islam. Oxford Studies in Islamic Art 7.* Oxford, UK, 1989.

Creswell, K.A.C. *Early Muslim Architecture,* 2 vols. Oxford, UK: Oxford University Press, 1932–1940. Reprinted New York, 1979.

———. *The Muslim Architecture of Egypt,* 2 vols. Oxford, UK: Oxford University Press, 1952–1959. Reprinted New York, 1979.

Dickie, James (Yaqub Zaki). "Allah and Eternity: Mosques, Madrasas and Tombs." In *Architecture of the Islamic World,* ed. George Michell. New York: Thames and Hudson, 1984.

Ettinghausen, Richard, Oleg Grabar, and Marilyn Jenkins-Madina. *Islamic Art and Architecture 650–1250.* New Haven, Conn, and London: Yale University Press, 2001.

Goodwin, Godfrey. *A History of Ottoman Architecture.* Baltimore: Johns Hopkins University Press, 1971.

Grabar, Oleg. *The Shape of the Holy: Early Islamic Jerusalem.* Princeton, NJ: Princeton University Press, 1996.

———. *The Great Mosque of Isfahan.* New York: New York University Press, 1990.

Hill, Derek, and Oleg Grabar. *Islamic Architecture and its Decoration.* London: Thames and Hudson, 1964.

Hillenbrand, Robert. *Islamic Architecture. Form, Function and Meaning.* New York: Columbia University Press, 1994.

Kuran, Aptullah. *The Mosque in Early Ottoman Architecture.* Chicago and London: University of Chicago Press, 1968.

MU'AYYAD FI AL-DIN, AL-

Al-Mu'ayyad fi al-Din al-Shirazi (999/1000–1087 CE) was a distinguished and multitalented personality of the Ismaili religious and political mission (the *da'wa*), which reached from Transoxiana to North Africa and from Northern Iran to Yemen. In the heyday of Fatimid power during the eleventh century, he spent most of his life in the service of the Caliph–Imam al-Mustansir bi 'llah (r. 1036–1094). Al-Mu'ayyad excelled as missionary agent *(da'i)* and scholar, bringing the Ismaili spiritual heritage to its pinnacle. As prose author and poet, he showed a masterful command of Arabic literary style and rhetoric.

Al-Mu'ayyad was born into an Ismaili family in Shiraz, the capital of the Buyid province of Fars in southwestern Iran. His full name is Abu Nasr Hibat Allah Ibn Musa Ibn Abi 'Imran b. Da'ud al-Shirazi. His honorific name, al-Mu'ayyad fi 'l-Din ("The one aided"—by God—"in religion"), was probably bestowed upon him when he was appointed head of the Fatimid mission in the province.

Al-Mu'ayyad is the author of a unique work of memoirs, the *Sirat al-Mu'ayyad fi al-Din,* that covers more than twenty years of his career (1038–1060). The *Sira* is a personal and thrilling work of history that mirrors, in the life and destiny of a da'i, the mutual relationship between Fatimids, 'Abbasids, and Buyids under the growing pressure of the Turcoman invasion from Central Asia into the heartlands of the Islamic world. Furthermore, the *Sira* is a rich source for the organization and the norms of the clandestine network of the Ismaili da'wa.

As al-Mu'ayyad tells in his *Sira,* he was attempting to convince the Buyid prince of Fars, Abu Kalijar, that a shift to the Fatimid cause would generate political and religious advantages for him. This highly demanding and dangerous task was skillfully undertaken by the Ismaili missionary in a hostile environment during the days of the Sunni revival. Al-Mu'ayyad initially evaluated his mission as a success, but he soon fell out of favor with Abu Kalijar and was forced to flee to the court of al-Mustansir. The second part of the *Sira* deals with al-Mu'ayyad's experiences after his arrival in Cairo (ca. 1045), where high-handed officials tried to foil the continuation of his religiopolitical career. He thereby used an authentic and courageous critical perspective on the political situation at court and the apparent inability of the young caliph–imam to deal with it. Despite many setbacks, the ambitious refugee gradually worked his way up the hierarchy at court. He was given the post of director of the Fatimid chancery. Next, he was dispatched as head of a diplomatic delegation to northern Syria from 1056 through 1058; this was a very difficult political adventure that al-Mu'ayyad deals with in the third part of his *Sira.* There, at the fringes of the Fatimid empire, he was to build up an alliance under Fatimid command between the rebellious 'Abbasid general Abu'l-Harith al-Basasiri and local Bedouin chiefs against the Turcoman Seljuks, who already had made an end to Buyid rule and taken over power in the 'Abbasid capital in 1055. In the *Sira's* epilogue, al-Mu'ayyad celebrates the triumph of al-Basasiri who—without further support of the Fatimids—occupied Baghdad, exiled the caliph, and established the Friday prayer for al-Mustansir for more than a year (1058–1060).

After his return to Cairo in 1058, al-Mu'ayyad was granted what he had been striving for ever since his dramatic flight from Fars: he was appointed the highest rank of chief missionary (da'i al-du'at) in the central administration of the Fatimid da'wa. From that point on, he devoted his life to administering the affairs of the da'wa, teaching missionaries from both inside and outside of the Fatimid empire, such as the philosopher–poet Nasir-i Khusraw of Badakhshan and Lamak ibn Malik al-Hammadi, a high representative of the loyal Sulayhid state in Yemen. After receiving instruction from al-Mu'ayyad for five years, Lamak organized the introduction of the Ismaili da'wa in the Indian subcontinent, where it has continued to the present day among the Bohra communities in Gujarat and other urban centers in India and Pakistan.

As chief da'i, al-Mu'ayyad was also the author of eight hundred lectures (*majalis al-hikma;* "sessions of wisdom") that he held in front of the community of believers every Thursday in Cairo. These sermons, which make up the largest collection of this genre in the literary heritage of the Ismailis, contain the essence of al-Mu'ayyad's religious and philosophical thinking; he likely stood in the tradition of the Ismaili Neoplatonist philosopher and theologian Abu Ya'qub al-Sijistani (d. ca. 971). Among the (partly) edited majalis are the correspondence with the blind Syrian philosopher–poet Abu 'l-'Ala' al-Ma'arri on the subject of vegetarianism as well as al-Mu'ayyad's refutation of the *Kitab al-Zumurrud* of Ibn al-Rawandi.

In addition to the *majalis,* al-Mu'ayyad is the author of religious–philosophical treatises, prayers, and more than sixty Arabic qasidas that contain a wide range of Fatimid theological and ideological motifs. As recent research shows, he was the founder of a new literary tradition of "da'wa poetry," which was intended to function as a medium of the proclamation of the Fatimid cause and to educate its followers. Al-Mu'ayyad's poems still play a prominent role in ritual liturgy of the Bohras in India today. Among them, he is still praised and respected as a spiritual guide and leader.

VERENA KLEMM

See also Arabic poetry; 'Abbasids; Arwa; Autobiographical Writings; Buyids; Cairo, Egypt; Plato and (Neo)Platonism; Sunna

Primary Sources

Al-Mu'ayyad fi al-Din al-Shirazi, Abu Nasr Hibat Allah: *Diwan al-Mu'ayyad fi al-Din da'i al-Du'at*, ed. M. Kamil Husayn. Cairo, 1949.

———. *al-Majalis al-Mu'ayyadiyya*, vols. 1 and 3, ed. Mustafa Ghalib. Beirut, 1974–1984; vols. 1 and 2, ed. Hatim Hamid al-Din. Oxford and Bombay, 1975–1986.
———. *Sirat al-Mu'ayyad fi al-Din da'i al-Du'at*, ed. M. Kamil Husayn. Cairo, 1949.

Further Reading

Klemm, Verena. *Memoirs of a Mission: The Ismaili Scholar, Statesman and Poet al-Mu'ayyad fi'l-Din al-Shirazi.* London: Tauris, 2003.
Qutbuddin, Bazat-Tahera. "Al-Mu'ayyad fi al-Din al-Shirazi: Founder of a New Tradition of Fatimid Da'wa Poetry." PhD dissertation. Harvard University, 1999.

MUHAMMAD AL-BAQIR (D. CA. AH 117/735 CE)

Abu Ja'far Muhammad b. 'Ali was one of the most learned Muslims of his age. He played a pivotal role in the history of early Islam as an authority on the exegesis of the Qur'an, the Traditions of the Prophet, and on all matters relating to the rites, rituals, and practices of the faith. Born in 57/677 in Medina, al-Baqir had an especially prestigious genealogy as the maternal and paternal grandchild of al-Hasan and al-Husayn, the Prophet's grandsons. He was popularly known as *al-Baqir,* which is short for *baqir al-'ilm,* meaning "one who splits knowledge open"; this signifies his erudition in bringing knowledge to light, a function that he did indeed perform. There are considerable variations regarding his death, and estimates range from 114/732 to 126/744. However, the dates given by al-Waqidi (117/735) and Ibn al-Khayyat (118/736) appear to be more realistic, considering reports about his death in al-Tabari during the rising of his half-brother, Zayd b. Ali.

Sunni and Shi'i sources describe al-Baqir as an eminent scholar. He is well known among the early *fuqaha* (jurists). His traditions appear in major works of tradition, and he is an authority for al-Tabari's historical and exegetical works. In Sufi circles, too, al-Baqir's sayings are quoted. In Shi'i tradition (both Ithna'ashari and Ismaili), al-Baqir is seen as the inaugurator of the legal and religious teachings that were further developed under his son and successor, Ja'far al-Sadiq. Zaydi tradition, too, relied heavily on al-Baqir through his disciple, Abu'l Jarrud.

Al-Baqir lived at a time in history when religious doctrine was at the center of both the intellectual and political life of the community. The late first and early second centuries of Islam were crucial times for the foundation of the studies connected with the Qur'an; this involved interpretation of the Qur'an that relied, in turn, on the recollected actions and sayings of the Prophet Muhammad. Medina, where al-Baqir resided, continued to be the center of religious learning after the time of the Prophet, and it was in this cusp of history that al-Baqir played a remarkably significant role.

Only a few decades before the birth of al-Baqir, his grandfather al-Husayn b. Ali, together with his entourage, were afflicted by the tragedy of Karbala. However, by the end of his lifetime, al-Baqir had given his Shi'is not only a distinct identity with a coherent theory of imamate, but he had also founded a separate legal school, the madhhab ahl al-bayt, that had well-defined views on several aspects of fiqh (jurisprudence). This was the time when the early discussions and differences in the community surrounded the question of who has the right to rule. There were serious theological discussions about aspects of leadership and the imamate, such as imam, Islam, 'ilm, 'amal, and qada wa qadar; many had political undertones. The religious–philosophical movements and communities of the Khawarij, the Murji'a, the Qadariyya, the Kaysaniyya, and the Zaydiyya sought their own answers to problematic questions. The Shi'is, under al-Baqir, did not shy away from these issues but rather proposed their own solutions. They not only entered the arena with confidence but also had their solutions accepted by others.

Contending with several competing groups, al-Baqir put forward a coherent theory of the imamate based on the Qur'an and hadith (tradition). His emphasis on hereditary imamate proved to be timely, because many regarded the imamate as an exclusively political matter that was based either on the *ijma* (consensus) of the people or on the rising of the imam. A stronger argument in favor of al-Baqir's school was its conviction that the Prophet had expressly designated and appointed 'Ali as his successor by *nass al-jali* (explicit designation); this meant that the Imam's authority did not depend on either human electors or the allegiance *(bay'a)* of the people. The hereditary character of the nass was thus the crucial point in al-Baqir's doctrine; it served as a restriction for many who considered claiming the nass a license to leadership.

In addition, in al-Baqir's view, the imam was endowed with the hereditary 'ilm as a result of the nass bestowed on him. Therefore, true knowledge was ultimately confined only to the imam in the Prophet's family and not to every member of the Prophet's family and certainly not to the whole community. The whole tradition of the community was thus not valid as a proper source for law; only traditions of the Imams or those of the Prophet confirmed by the Imams were allowed. This approach of al-Baqir's school toward the majority of the Prophet's companions changed the legal pattern of the Shi'is, and, in so doing, laid the foundation of a distinct school of jurisprudence: the madhhab ahl al-bayt. The basis of Shi'i law and theology emerged and developed itself within the circle of al-Baqir's adherents. A distinctive ruling, for example, that goes back to him is that of wiping one's footwear *(al-mash 'ala'l khuffayn)* before praying as being unacceptable as a substitute for washing the feet. In addition to transmitting this formal kind of knowledge, al-Baqir also played the role of a spiritual guide initiating his followers in experiential knowledge. This is represented in the concept of light in his theory of the imamate, embodying the numinous aspect of the imam's knowledge that sets the inner wisdom in motion.

Therefore, strictly in terms of the scholarly literature that expresses Shi'i doctrines, al-Baqir assumed a dignified position for his century. From the prominence of his traditions and the profound contributions they represent, a truly remarkable personality is perceived—one that deserves recognition as an outstanding figure in the history of the Shi'is and a major force of Islamic thought in general.

ARZINA R. LALANI

Further Reading

Al-Amín, Muhsin b. 'Abd al-Karím. *A'yan al-Shí'a*. Damascus, 1935–1961.

Al-Kulayní, Muhammad b. Ya'qúb. *Al-Usul min al-Kafi*. Teheran, 1388/1968.

Abu Nu'aym, Ahmad al-Isfahani. *Hilyat al-Awliya'*, vol. 3. Cairo, 1932–1938.

Amir-Moezzi, M.A. *The Divine Guide in Early Shi'ism*, transl. David Streight. Albany, NY, 1994.

van Arendonk, C. *Les Débuts de L'Imamat Zaidite au Yémen*. Leiden, 1960.

Al-Ya'qúbí, Ahmad b. Ibn Wadih. *Taríkh*, vol. 2. Beirut.

Hodgson, M.G.S. "How Did the Early Shi'a become Sectarian?" *JAOS* 75 (1955): 1–13.

Ibn Hajar al-'Asqalani, Ahmad b. *Tahdhib al-Tahdhib*, vol. 9. Hyderabad, 1325–1327/1907–1909.

Ibn Sa'd, Muhammad. *Kitab al-Tabaqat*, eds. E. Sachau et al. Leiden, 1905–1940.

Jafri, S., and M. Husain. *Origins and Early Development of Shi'a Islam*. Beirut, 1979.

Kohlberg, Etan. *Belief and Law in Imami Shi'ism*. Great Britain, 1991.

———. "Muhammad b. Ali" In *EI2*, 397–400.

Lalani, Arzina R. *Early Shi'i Thought: The Teachings of Imam Muhammad al-Baqir*. London, 2000.

Madelung, Wilferd. *Der Imam al-Qasim ibn Ibrahim und die Glaubenslehre der Zaiditen*. Berlin, 1965.

———. "al-Baqer, Abï Ja'far Mohammad." *EIR* 3: 725–6.

al-Muradi. *Amali Ahmad b. 'Isa*. Arabo-Biblioteca, Ambrosiana, Milan, H. 135.

al-Qadi al-Nu'man, Abu Hanífa. *Da'a'im al-Islam*, 2 vols., ed. A.A.A. Fyzee. Cairo, 1950 and 1960. (See also Ismail K. Poonawala's revised translation, *The Pillars of Islam*. Oxford, UK, 2002.)

———. *Shahr al-Akhbar fí Fada'il al-a'Imma al-Athar*, 3 vols., ed. Muhammad al-Husayní al-Jalali. Qumm, 1409–1412/1988–1992.

al-Qummí, 'Alí b. Ibrahím. *al-Tafsír*, 2 vols. Najaf, 1386/1966.

al-Tabarí, Abu Ja'far Muhammad b. Jarír. *Ta'ríkh al-Rusúl wa al-Muluk. Annales*, ed. M.J. de Goeje. Leiden, 1879–1901.

———. *Jami' al-Bayan 'an Ta'wíl ay al-Qur'an*.

MUHAMMAD IBN AL-QASIM

Muhammad ibn al-Qasim, one of the most famous Arab generals of the eighth century, was born around 695 CE in Taif, Arabia, to Habibat al-Uzma and al-Qasim. Because his family belonged to the tribe of Banu Thaqif, he was also called Muhammad ibn al-Qasim al-Thaqafiyya. Not much is known about his early childhood, most of which he probably spent in Taif. As a young boy, Muhammad was very fond of a fragrant wild plant called al-Bahar; hence, he came to be affectionately known as Abu al-Bahar. When his father, al-Qasim (who was a cousin of al-Hajjaj, the powerful Arab viceroy of Iraq), was appointed governor of al-Basrah, the family moved there. It was in this important center of the rapidly growing Arab empire that Muhammad was exposed to a cosmopolitan, intellectual, and cultural environment. Because al-Hajjaj was particularly fond of his cousin's young son, Muhammad spent some time with him in Wasit, the capital of the Iraqi province. Presumably the viceroy educated Muhammad in military and administrative affairs, a training that would be prove invaluable for his short but brilliant career.

Around 709 or 710, when Muhammad was fifteen or sixteen years old, al-Hajjaj entrusted his protégé with his first military mission: the subjugation of a group of Kurds in the province of Fars who had become a serious threat to law and order in the region. After his victory over the Kurds, he was made governor of Fars, and he was responsible for developing its administrative structure. Muhammad proceeded to plan and build at Shiraz, a strategically situated new city that would serve as the provincial capital and as an important military base for commanders. He was also responsible for subjugating the area around to the south of Shiraz, called Sabur, and the distant area of Jurjan, near the southeastern shores of the Caspian.

In 711, on the basis of his achievements in Fars, al-Hajjaj appointed the seventeen-year-old Muhammad as the commander of the army that was to be sent to Sind (now in southern Pakistan) to punish and subdue local pirates who had been harassing Arab trading ships and who had taken Arab women and children hostage. Because two previous naval missions had failed, al-Hajjaj entrusted Muhammad with the command of an invasion by land that would result in the annexation of Sind. During a period of approximately three years, Muhammad conquered the coast of Makran, took control over the important seaport of al-Daibul, and began extending his authority inland over the lower Indus valley. By 712, he had defeated Dahar (the ruler of Sind) and taken over the city of Aror, and he began proceeding northward to capture Multan. During subsequent months, he signed treaties with surrounding states in Rajasthan, Kathiawar, and Gujarat. Muhammad was not only a brilliant military commander and strategist but he was also an excellent administrator; he reorganized the civil administration of the region.

Notwithstanding the superior military power at his disposal, Muhammad was an enlightened ruler, seeking to win over the confidence of the local population. By employing local administrators and forgiving the inhabitants of conquered cities, he garnered a great deal of local support, especially from those who were seeking relief from their autocratic rulers. He was also tolerant of local religious beliefs, declaring at Aror that the local Indian temples were equivalent to churches, synagogues, and the fire temples of the Magians. Not surprisingly, in Multan, he did not destroy the famous temple dedicated to the Sun God. In effect, Muhammad recognized the Hindus and Buddhists as equivalent to the *ahl al-kitab* (the people of the Book), who, like Christians and Jews, had the right to practice their faith in return for the payment of *jizya* (tax). He exempted Brahmins from the tax, a custom that was followed by subsequent Muslim rulers in India.

In 715, the new Ummayad Caliph Suleiman came to power determined to seek revenge for the support that al-Hajjaj had given to his brother al-Walid in a dispute about succession to the caliphate. Because al-Hajjaj was already dead, the Caliph's wrath descended on al-Hajjaj's family, the most prominent among them being Muhammad ibn al-Qasim. The new Caliph dismissed Muhammad from his post in Sind, ordering his immediate arrest and repatriation to Iraq. Muhammad was imprisoned at al-Wasit, where he and other members of his clan were tortured and killed. Today, Muhammad ibn al-Qasim is memorialized as a great hero in contemporary Pakistan, especially in religious nationalist circles who see Islam as having been first introduced into the region as a result of his conquest of Sind and the establishment of the first Muslim state that would endure for nearly three centuries. A new international seaport, Port Al-Qasim, near Karachi, has been named in his honor.

ALI ASANI

Further Reading

Baloch, Nabi Bakhsh. "Muhammad ibn al-Qasim: A Study of His Family Background and Personality." *Islamic Culture* Oct (1953): 242–71.

MUHAMMAD, THE PROPHET (571–632 CE)

The last in the line of Abrahamic prophets—or the Seal of Prophets, as the Qur'an calls him—Muhammad was a descendant of Ishmael, son of Abraham. He fought against polytheism and revived monotheism, a legacy that quickly spread around the world after his demise. In the Qur'an, he is named a mercy to the worlds, a bringer of glad tidings, a warner, a lamp spreading light, a universal messenger, and a witness. He is described as compassionate, having a tender heart, and embodying an exalted standard of character, neither seeking reward from the people nor speaking according to his own desires.

The Qur'an explains that Muhammad's mission is not to bring a doctrine that is new among the Messengers of God but whose sole duty instead is to proclaim the divine message, to confirm that which was brought by the Messengers before him, and, through this, to confront religious hypocrisy. The Qur'an stresses that Muslims must obey him as the Messenger of God and greet him each time his name is mentioned by saying, "God's blessings and peace be upon him." Bearing witness that Muhammad is a servant and Messenger of God is a major pillar of faith in Islam, second only to faith in the oneness of God.

Muhammad was born in Mecca in the Year of the Elephant, 571 CE, when Abraha, the Abyssinian governor of Yemen, unsuccessfully attempted to destroy the Ka'ba with an army mounted on huge elephants, intending to divert pilgrims to the magnificent cathedral he built in Sana. Muhammad was born to his mother Amina six months after the death of his father Abdullah, who passed away at a young age. Following the Arab custom, he was sent as a small baby to the desert for four years to grow in good health, away from the epidemics that iteratively afflicted Mecca, and to learn the best and purest usage of the Arabic language from the desert Bedouins. During this time, a woman named Halima from the tribe of Bani Sa'd looked after him and served as his wet nurse. At the age of four, he was returned to his mother in Mecca. At the age of six, Muhammad's mother passed away, and he grew up first in the custody of his grandfather, Abdu l-Muttalib, for two years, and later in the home of his uncle, Abu Talib, with whom he stayed until his marriage.

Muhammad was by ancestry a member of a highly esteemed family, the Sons of Hashim, and a tribe, the Quraysh, in a sacred city, Mecca, in which was found a holy sanctuary, the Ka'ba, which was symbolically the House of God. The Arabs had revered the Ka'ba as a pilgrimage site since Abraham, the Father of Prophets, and his first son Ishmael first built it in compliance with God's command. The economy of Mecca was based on caravan trade, because Mecca was a station on the trade route between Syria and Yemen. The Meccans also raised animals, but for their own need alone, which they pastured on the mountains nearby. The barren landscape of Mecca did not allow farming. Accordingly, the children of Mecca were raised to become merchants, as too was Muhammad.

As a young child, Muhammad's education included training in refined speech, care of animals, travel, martial arts, and trade. The cosmopolitan environment of Mecca, which was constantly visited by pilgrims and tradesmen, exposed him to varying economic, cultural, and religious practices. He learned the best usage of the Arabic language during the time he spent in the desert among the Bedouins, who were renowned for their excellence in poetry. He also spent time as a shepherd, and he later said that all Prophets had the experience in their lives of serving as shepherds.

At the age of nine (or perhaps twelve), Muhammad accompanied his uncle Abu Talib with a caravan to Syria as part of his training as a merchant and trader (such treacherous trips across the desert and the constant threat of armed conflict among neighboring tribes necessitated training in the martial arts; this was held to be another crucial part of the upbringing of the children of Mecca). During the course of this journey, the caravan passed the cell of a Christian monk named Bahira, who observed that Muhammad was continually shaded by a cloud that accompanied him and that the tree beneath which Muhammad took shelter lowered its branches to him. Recognizing in his appearance a description from a manuscript in his possession, Bahira asked to examine the boy's back, where he saw a birthmark confirming that the prophet so long awaited was indeed Muhammad.

This range of experiences in such a cosmopolitan environment fostered an informed perspective from which Muhammad was able to appraise the customary religious practices prevalent among his tribe and fellow citizens of Mecca. The people of Mecca were proud to be descendants of Abraham and servants of the House of God, although by the time Muhammad was born very little of Abraham's legacy remained intact. In particular, monotheism no longer stood unchallenged by polytheism and paganism. The Arabs honored the Ka'ba as the House of God, but they filled it with idols that they expected to serve as intercessors between them and God. Even the place of the holy well, Zamzam, near the Ka'ba, had been long forgotten. The pristine monotheism of Abraham had been almost completely forgotten, although Muhammad was able to join the ranks of those few adherents who remained. These followers of Abraham refrained from worshiping idols, moral corruption, and injustice, but they had no power to reinstitutionalize monotheism. Among them, as among the Meccan community generally, Muhammad acquired a reputation for being singularly trustworthy and therefore became known by the Arabic epithet *al-Amin*.

At the age of twenty-five, Muhammad was approached for marriage by a wealthy widow, Khadija, who entrusted him with her trade caravans; at that time she was forty years old. This led to a marriage that lasted for twenty-five years, until Khadija's death in 619 CE at the age of sixty-five years. The bridegroom moved from the house of his uncle, Abu Talib, to the house of Khadija; she bore two sons and four daughters. Because their first child was Qasim, a son who died in infancy, Muhammad came to be known as Abu l-Qasim, the father of Qasim. The next child was a daughter, Zaynab, who was followed by three other daughters, Ruqayya, Umm Kulthum, and Fatima, and finally by another short-lived son, Abdullah.

When Muhammad reached the age of thirty-five, the tribes of Mecca decided to jointly undertake the physical restoration of the Ka'ba. They cooperated fully in its construction until it came to placing the sacred Black Stone, al-Hajar al-Aswad, back in its original place in one of the Ka'ba's walls: each tribe wanted the honor of this final task exclusively for itself. Tension rose, reaching the point at which outright warfare seemed inevitable. However, because his fairness was well known to all, the leaders of the tribes at length agreed to ask Muhammad to resolve the conflict. Muhammad placed the Black Stone on his cloak and asked a representative of each tribe to join together in raising the stone and carrying it to its place. This ingenious solution pleased all of the tribes and forestalled a civil war; furthermore, it was a significant test of Muhammad's capacity for leadership and peacemaking, which he successfully passed. Because of his commitment to resolving conflict peacefully and promoting justice, Muhammad also participated in an order of chivalry that was meant to aid the oppressed and promote social order and equality for all in Mecca, irrespective of their being dwellers of the city or aliens.

Disturbed by corruption in the city, Muhammad made it his practice to enter spiritual retreat in isolated caves in the mountains surrounding Mecca. At the age of forty, he received the first revelation in a cave he frequented on the mountain of Hira, also known as the Mountain of Light. God sent him the Archangel Gabriel, who gave the following command: "Read: In the name of your Lord Who created, created the human being from a clot. Read: And your Lord is Most Generous, Who taught by the pen, taught the human being what he knew not" (Qur'an, Surat al-'Alaq, 96:1–5).

Receiving direct revelation from God left Muhammad in great anguish, astonishment, and awe. He left his place of retreat, hastening home in the most profound consternation. Khadija tried to comfort her husband and sought consultation with Waraqa, a blind, elderly Christian sage with profound knowledge of the Bible. Waraqa had (like the monk Bahira) long anticipated the coming of a new prophet, even suspecting that he might already be in the Arabs' midst. After listening to Muhammad's experience, Waraqa said: "Holy! Holy! By him in whose hand is the soul of Waraqa, the Angel of Revelation who came to Moses has come to Muhammad. Truly, Muhammad is the Prophet of this people. Bid him rest assured." Waraqa later told Muhammad: "You will be called a liar, and ill-treated, and they will cast you out and make war upon you; and if I live to see that day, God knows I will help His cause." The reassurances of Khadija and Waraqa were followed by reassurances from Heaven in the form of subsequent revelations, which arrived intermittently for twenty-three years until his death. The fact that the first person to embrace Islam was a woman and a merchant has left an enduring impression on the thought of Muslims, who continue to revere Khadija as the Mother of Believers.

The rise of a Prophet among the Arabs of Mecca came as a complete shock to the pagans and polytheists, who first ignored him, later tried to silence him by force, and at last tried to completely eradicate his message. However, Christians and Jews were more familiar with divine Revelation; some had been awaiting the arrival of the last Prophet in the form of the Messiah. Believers in the new revelation came from various ranks of society. Abu Bakr, a businessman and longtime friend, was the next person to embrace it, after Khadija. He was followed by Bilal, an Abyssinian slave, and Ali, the cousin of Muhammad, who was then a young child. Some of the notables of Mecca saw a threat to their power in the steady growth of the Muslim community. In response, they placed the nascent community under an economic boycott, and they also initiated a campaign of propaganda and torture; this led some Muslims to seek refuge in Abyssinia. At length the pagan Meccans established an alliance among themselves to definitively sever all ties with the Muslims, placing them under siege in a section of the city with no contact with the outside world and no access to food. Despite unbearable pressure and a growing number of deaths under torture, none of the believers reverted back to polytheism.

As despair escalated among the believers, the Archangel Gabriel one night awakened the Prophet Muhammad from his sleep and led him on a Night Journey from Mecca to Jerusalem. Together they rode on a beast with white wings named Buraq, whose every stride reached as far as the eye could see. From the Dome of the Rock in Jerusalem, they ascended together to the Seven Heavens, where the Prophet of Islam conversed in the spiritual realm with the Prophets who brought the earlier revelations. Finally, he was accepted to the Divine Presence, where he spoke with God. On this occasion, God gave him a number of commandments that are comparable with the Ten Commandments of Moses, including the following:

"And your Lord has decreed that you worship none save Him, and that you treat your parents with goodness. If one of them, or both of them, reach old age with you, do not say 'oof' to them, and do not reject them, but speak honorable words to them. And lower to them the wing of humility, out of compassion, and say, 'My Lord, have mercy upon them as they brought me up when I was small.' Your Lord is best aware of what is in your souls. If you are righteous [He will forgive you], for surely, He is Ever-Forgiving to those who frequently return in repentance. And give the one near to you his right, and the poor, and the wayfarer, and do not squander your wealth in frivolous squandering. Truly, those who squander are brothers of the devils, and the devil was always ungrateful to his Lord. But if you must turn away from them, seeking the mercy you hope for from your Lord, then speak to them a gentle word. And neither let your hand be tied to your neck [in avarice] nor expand it so wide [in extravagance] that you sit there blamed or destitute. Surely your Lord expands the provision to whomever He wishes or cuts it. Surely He is Fully Aware, All-Seeing. And do not kill your children from fear of poverty. We provide for them and We provide for you. Truly killing them is a great sin. And do not come near to illicit sexual intercourse; surely it is a monstrous obscenity and an evil way. And do not kill any human being whose life Allah has willed to be sacred—save by the right of law. And whoever is killed unjustly, We have given authority to his heir, but let him not exceed the limits [set by law] in taking life. Surely he shall be helped [by God]. And do not come near to the wealth of the orphan save with that which is better, until he comes to strength, and keep the contract. Surely you will be asked about the contract. And give full measure when you measure, and weigh with a straight balance. That is better and more excellent in the end. And do not pursue that of which you have no knowledge. Surely the hearing and the sight and the heart—all of these will be questioned. And do not walk arrogantly upon the earth. Surely you cannot tear the earth apart, and you will never be taller than the mountains. All of that is distasteful in the sight of your Lord."

(Qur'an, Surat al-'Isra 17:23–38)

These verses from the Qur'an summarize the basic teachings given to the Prophet Muhammad during the Meccan period of revelation, which are also reflected in his numerous non-Qur'anic sayings, which are known as *hadith* (tradition). The significant overlap with the Ten Commandments is striking. During the Night Journey and Ascension, God also commanded Muslims to pray five times a day *(salat)*, a ritual that embodies the ascension of the believer to the Divine Presence.

As the number of Muslims grew, the efforts of the notables of Mecca to suppress their movement increased. The escalating tension between these groups and the deteriorating conditions under which the Muslims lived forced the Prophet to search for a place of refuge for his community away from his birthplace. The small yet also rapidly expanding community of Muslim believers in the city of Yathrib, today known as Medina, invited the Prophet and his followers to join them. Finally, in 622 CE, the community of believers undertook the emigration from Mecca to Medina. This is known as the *hijra,* and it was accepted during the time of Caliph Umar as the beginning of the Islamic *(hijri)* lunar calendar.

However, this was only the outer hijra, as the Prophet reminded his followers; the inner hijra takes place in the heart of the person who moves from evil to goodness. Without the inner hijra, the outer one would be meaningless, he instructed, thereby making hijra obligatory for his followers. At length, the entire Muslim community relocated to Medina physically, just as every believer since that time is to make hijra in the heart.

The economy of Medina depended on farming. Initially it was not easy for the Immigrants, who were merchants by profession, to adjust themselves to their new setting. However, their brothers and sisters in Medina, known as the Helpers, made great sacrifices to support them.

The Immigrants and the Helpers constituted the two branches of the Muslim community in Medina. The Prophet Muhammad was not only their leader but also, as the duly appointed ruler of Medina, the leader of the Jews, the pagan polytheists, and the Christians who lived there. These communities joined him in signing the newly drafted constitution of the city-state. The fact that Islam numbered merchants and farmers among its early adherents contributed to its future spread to communities elsewhere that exhibited a range of types of social and economic organization. Likewise, the peaceful experience of the Muslim community in joining with other religious communities as citizens of a single state united under one leadership made a lasting impact on Islamic political philosophy and state structure. The Constitution of Medina, which was concluded jointly among the Prophet and the leaders of other religious communities in Medina, is still available today for study, and it is commonly regarded as the first written constitution for a pluralist society.

The hijra from Mecca to Medina entailed for Muslims not only a change of location but also a change in political and social organization. Whereas they had lived as a violently oppressed minority in Mecca, they became the ruling element in Medina, charged with the protection of other minority groups. This also meant that the Prophet Muhammad joined in his person both religious and political leadership. Like Jesus, he was a supreme spiritual leader; like Moses, David, and Solomon, he was equally a ruler and a law-giving Prophet. In Mecca, he prohibited fighting even in self-defense by his followers, although in Medina the revelation authorized him to permit it. However, all the while—and despite the growing resources under his control as the head of an ever-expanding state—he led the same devout and ascetic life that he always had.

In Medina, the Prophet Muhammad placed the different areas of social life under laws and moral norms, from family to commerce, inheritance to warfare. His Mosque served not only as a place of worship but also as a school, court, and parliament. He devoted special attention to consultation when making decisions: unless there was a clear divine command transmitted to the Prophet through revelation, choices of crucial importance to the community (e.g., whether to wage war) were reached in the Mosque only after a public consultation and debate. He adjudicated cases brought before him in the Mosque not only between Muslims but also occasionally between non-Muslims as well. He even accepted foreign ambassadors in the Mosque, which was, to their astonishment, an extremely humble place. Because the floor had no carpet, worshippers prostrated on the sand; it was roofed over in palm fronds, and no sculpture or picture adorned the walls. The Prophet Muhammad sat on the ground; he never possessed a chair, a throne, or a crown.

His home was also extremely humble, consisting of small rooms attached to the Mosque and entirely without the luxury so commonly thought to befit leaders of such stature. In his home, the Prophet always slept on the floor on a simple mat, as he refused to sleep in a comfortable bed. He frequently fasted and usually ate only one meal a day without completely filling his stomach. He did not wear silk or gold, and he allowed them only for the women in his community. His custom was to carry a silver ring. He helped his wives with the housework, assisting in such matters as milking the goats, sweeping the floor, and sewing his own clothes. He spent at least one-third of the night in solitary prayer. In addition to the congregational prayers mandated for five specific times each day, he constantly offered voluntary players. For the Prophet, the highest level of worship of God was "to worship Him as if you see Him; for even if you do not see Him, He sees you." He preached that Muslims must live in constant awareness of the Divine Presence and act accordingly in daily life.

This high degree of piety did not prevent him from active involvement in family and community affairs and leadership by example in even the most mundane aspects of life. The first Muslims in Mecca were mostly merchants. The Prophet's early career as an international tradesman provided him the experience he needed when legislating about commercial relations. Later, this was coupled with laws governing agrarian economy as befit the new environment of Medina with its traditionally agrarian economy.

At the beginning of his mission, the Prophet Muhammad practiced and preached a steadfast commitment to pacifism. This continued for fourteen years, until in the second year of the hijra polytheists from Mecca attacked Medina in a violent campaign to uproot Islam from its new sanctuary. Only then were the Muslims permitted by divine command to defend themselves and join the aggressors in battle. For the first time, a small Muslim army engaged in armed struggle with the disproportionately larger and more experienced army of polytheists at a location near Medina, known as Badr. This encounter became the first military victory in Islamic history as Muslims triumphed over the polytheists. The defeated army in turn reorganized and attacked Medina for the second time the following year, this time defeating the Muslims at Uhud.

Despite this victory, the polytheists were not happy with the result, because their goal was not just military victory but total eradication of the new religion from the face of the earth. Accordingly, they attacked Medina again with a still greater army. Upon receiving the news of the approaching army, the Prophet Muhammad gathered his Companions in the Mosque for consultation. Eventually, they adopted the proposal of Salman Farisi, a Persian convert who advised the community to dig trenches around Medina and defend the city instead of directly confronting the polytheist army that was approaching with overwhelming numbers. This strategy succeeded, as the polytheist army, attacking in the expectation of a quick victory, stalled in the trenches and grew increasingly impatient. Finally, they ended the siege and returned to Mecca.

The following year, during the time of the pilgrimage, the Prophet Muhammad and his followers went to Mecca for pilgrimage. Customarily, all Arab tribes agreed that, during the period of pilgrimage, fighting was prohibited, and the Ka'ba would be open to anyone who wished to visit it. However, the rulers of Mecca broke this rule for the first time and did not allow Muslims to enter Mecca and perform pilgrimage to the Ka'ba. As an alternative, they proposed a peace treaty with the Muslims; according to the terms of the treaty, the Muslims agreed to return to Medina with the understanding that, during the following year, they would be able to perform pilgrimage in Mecca. The Prophet Muhammad accepted this seemingly humiliating concession, later known as the Treaty of Hudaybiyya. Paradoxically, the treaty worked to the advantage of the Muslims by enabling them to spread Islam more easily among Arab tribes in the newly peaceful environment. It also fostered the consolidation of the Muslim community in Medina. During the following year, Muslims made their first pilgrimage to the Ka'ba under the leadership of Abu Bakr. However, the truce did not last for long, because the polytheists nullified it by violating its conditions.

In response to the termination of the truce, the Prophet decided to enter Mecca, by force if necessary. After lengthy negotiations, the Muslims were able to conquer Mecca peacefully and purge the Ka'ba of its many idols. The House of God and enduring symbols of true monotheism were restored once again according to the Prophet Abraham's initial vision. The Prophet Muhammad and his Companions did not retaliate against those long-time enemies who had tortured them, boycotted their livelihood, harmed their families, expelled them from their homeland, and even pursued and attacked them after they had immigrated to another city. In other words, the final conquest of Mecca was bloodless.

During the following year, the Prophet made his last pilgrimage to the Ka'ba, which was known as the Farewell Pilgrimage. On this occasion, he delivered the so-called Farewell Sermon from the back of his camel to about a hundred thousand Muslims. The message of this sermon has made it one of the most highly esteemed texts of the Islamic tradition to this very day. In this sermon, the Prophet summarized basic tenets of Islamic law, particularly the rights and duties of men and women. For generations, the

Arabs had considered the property and person of the pilgrims inviolable and the time and place of pilgrimage sacred. The Prophet generalized this sanctity as a fundamental rule applicable to all persons, times, and places: "O People, just as you regard this month, this day, this city as Sacred, so regard the life and property of every Muslim as a sacred trust."

He also reminded the community of the prohibition of usury and interest, women's rights, the five daily prayers, fasting during Ramadan, pilgrimage to the Ka'ba, and payment of zakat (an annual charity). He emphasized to them their accountability on the Day of Judgment: "Remember, one day you will appear before God and answer your deeds. So beware, do not stray from the path of righteousness after I am gone."

And he ended his sermon as follows:

"O People, no prophet or apostle will come after me and no new religion will be born. Reason well, therefore, O People, and understand the words that I convey to you. I leave behind me two things, the Qur'an and my example, the *Sunna*, and if you follow these you will never go astray. All those who listen to me shall pass on my words to others and those to others again; and may the last ones understand my words better than those who listen to me directly. Be my witness, O God, that I have conveyed your message to your people."

In the following year, 632 CE, the Prophet passed away. His death caused a short-lived state of confusion and deep consternation among his Companions, who did not want to face the necessity of assuming stewardship of the community in his place. Finally, the Companions decided to appoint Abu Bakr as his successor, the Caliph.

The Qur'an, the Book of God, which contains verbatim revelations from God revealed piecemeal to Muhammad over twenty-three years, was Muhammad's legacy to humanity. His own sayings and the stories about him, known as hadith, have been collected in a separate literature and passed down through generations.

The Prophet Muhammad was husband, father, tradesman, teacher, founder and president of a state, judge, and commander—but he was first and foremost the servant and Messenger of God, who called for monotheism and the restoration of the universal and primordial principles of morality and justice.

RECEP SENTURK

Further Reading

Adil, Hajjah Amina. *Muhammad the Messenger of Islam.* Washington, DC: Islamic Supreme Council of North America, 2002.
Armstrong, Karen. *Muhammad: A Biography of the Prophet.* San Francisco: Harper, 1993.
al-Busiri, Imam Sharaf al-Din. *The Burda: The Poem of the Cloak,* transl. Hamza Yusuf. Essex, UK: Sandala, 2002.
Cleary, Thomas, ed. and transl. *The Wisdom of the Prophet: The Sayings of Muhammad.* Boston: Shambhala, 2001.
Cragg, Kenneth. *The Event of the Qur'an.* London: Oneworld, 1994.
Guillaume, A., ed. and transl. *The Life of Muhammad: A Translation of Ishaq's Sirat Rasul Allah.* London: Oxford University Press, 1955 (reissued 2003).
Ibn Kathir. *The Life of the Prophet Muhammad (Al-Sira al-Nabawiyya),* 2 vols., transl. Trevor Le Gassick. Reading, UK: Garnet, 1998.
Imam Jazuli. *Guide to Goodness: Dala'il al-Khayrat,* transl. Hassan Rosowsky. Chicago: Kazi.
Lings, Martin. *Muhammad: His Life Based on the Earliest Sources.* London: Inner Traditions, 1983.
Malik ibn Anas. *Al-Muwatta: The First Formulation of Islamic Law,* transl. Aisha Bewley. Granada, Spain: Medinah Press, 1989.
Nasr, Seyyed Hossein. *Muhammad: Man of God.* Chicago: Kazi, 1995.
Rodinson, Maxime. *Mohammed,* transl. Anne Carter. London: Pantheon, 1971.
Schimmel, Annemarie. *And Muhammad is His Messenger: The Veneration of the Prophet in Islamic Piety.* Chapel Hill, NC: University of North Carolina Press, 1985.
ash-Shaybani, Muhammad ibn al-Hasan. *The Muwatta of Imam Muhammad.* London: Turath, 2004.
Watt, W. Montgomery. *Muhammad at Mecca.* Chicago: Kazi, 1993.
———. *Muhammad at Medina.* Oxford, UK: Oxford University Press, 1981.
———. *Muhammad's Mecca: History in the Quran.* Edinburgh, UK: Edinburgh University Press, 1988.
al-Yahsubi, Qadi 'Iyad ibn Musa. *Muhammad Messenger of Allah: Ash-Shifa of Qadi 'Iyad,* transl. Aisha Bewley. Inverness, UK: Madinah Press, 1991.

MULLA SADRA (d. 1641 CE)

Sadr al-Din Muhammad ibn Ibrahim Shirazi, also known as Mulla Sadra, is the most significant Islamic philosopher after Avicenna. Born into a courtly family in Shiraz in 1571, his interest in intellectual pursuits was indulged by his father. He moved first to Qazvin and then to Isfahan, the successive capitals of the Safavids, to pursue his studies with the two preeminent teachers of his age, Mir Damad (d. 1621) and Shaykh Baha al-Din al-'Amili (d. 1621), who was Shaykh al-Islam in Isfahan during the reign of Shah 'Abbas I. After completing his training, Mulla Sadra returned to Shiraz to work and teach, but, failing to find an adequate patron, he retreated to Kahak near Qum to meditate and initiate the composition of his works. He acquired the patronage of Imamquli Khan (d. 1612), a notable Georgian ghulam who was in charge of the Safavid military administration and the governor of Sadra's home province of Fars, and he moved to Shiraz, where he taught at the Madrasa-yi Khan, which was founded by Imamquli. There, he trained a generation of philosophers; the most significant were Muhsin Fayd Kashani (d. 1680) and 'Abd al-Razzaq Lahiji (d. 1661), both of whom became his sons-in-law. After an illustrious and prolific career, he died in Basra on the return from his seventh pilgrimage to Mecca in 1641.

Mulla Sadra's magnum opus is a large compendium of philosophy and theology that maps intellectual inquiry upon a mystical metaphor of the soul's journey in this world. Hence, it is popularly known as the *Four Journeys (al-Asfar al-Arba'a)*. The first journey from this world to God provides the seeker with the intellectual principles for understanding philosophy, such as the basic definition of philosophy and the significance of the question of being. In this journey, the seeker moves away from multiplicity and phenomenal deception toward unity and an awareness of the underlying nature of reality. The second journey in God with God is a discourse on the nature of God and the divine attributes, and it significantly includes Mulla Sadra's famous proof for the existence of God. It is the stage of the mystic's absorption in the divine essence and his effacement of the self. The third journey from God to this world explains the God–world relationship, nature, time, creation, and ontological categories in this world. For the mystic, this is the return to sobriety and a realization of the duties of moral agency in this world. The final journey in this world with God is a description of human psychology that focuses on soteriology and eschatology and reveals most clearly the significance of Twelver Shi'ism to his thought. This is the final stage of the mystic's journey, a recognition that everything as a unified whole reflects the ontological unity of the divine.

Mulla Sadra is often described as a metaphysical revolutionary because of his doctrine of existence. Any attempt to conceptualize existence falsifies it through reification. A reified, fixed concept cannot capture the nature of existence, which is dynamic and in flux. One can discern three distinct doctrines of existence that draw upon Mulla Sadra's intellectual influences, which include Avicennan philosophy, the intuitive philosophy of Suhrawardi, and the Sufi metaphysics of Ibn 'Arabi. The first doctrine is the ontological primacy of existence *(asalat al-wujud)*. Essences are not entities waiting for a divine agent to actualize and individuate them through the bestowal of existence, an essentialist doctrine that posits a rather paradoxical existence of an essence before it comes to exist. Rather, the divine agent produces existences in this world that take on the garb of some particular essence. Existence must be ontologically prior not only because of the absurdity of an existence

before existence but also because God is devoid of essence, and his causal link to the world can only be existential if one wishes to avoid the problem of a composite god.

The second doctrine is the modulation of existence *(tashkik al-wujud)*. Existence is a singular reality, of which the phenomenal experience as multiple is illusory. Different existences in this world are different intense degrees of a single whole. The particular degrees of existence are not stable substances in the Aristotelian sense and rather are structures of events in flux. This leads to the third doctrine that all individuals in existence undergo motion and flux *(haraka jawhariyya)*. An existing entity is not a stable substance constant in time to which change occurs as an accident, such as a young Zayd becoming old and graying; rather, it is a structure of unfolding, dynamic events of existence.

Mulla Sadra became *the* philosopher of the Islamic East. His commentary on *al-Hidaya (The Guidance)* of Athir al-Din al-Abhari was the cornerstone of the rationalist curriculum of the Indian madrasa (Islamic school) from the eighteenth century. In Iran, his philosophical school has dominated since the nineteenth century.

SAJJAD H. RIZVI

See also Ibn 'Arabi; Ibn Sina; Iluminationism; Isfahan; Mir Damad; Plato and Neoplatonism; Safavids; Shah 'Abbas; Shi'ism; Suhrawardi

Further Reading

Chittick, William, transl. *The Elixir of the Gnostics*. Provo: Brigham Young University Press, 2003.
Corbin, Henry. *En Islam Iranien*, vol. IV, 54–122. Paris: Gallimard, 1972.
Jambet, C. *L'Acte d'Être*. Paris: Fayard, 2002.
Kh~maneh, M. *Zindag~n,-yi ^adr al-Muta\allihn*. Tehran: Siprin, 2000
Morris, James, transl. *The Wisdom of the Throne*. Princeton, NJ: Princeton University Press, 1981.
Rahman, F. *The Philosophy of Mulla Sadra*. Albany, NY: State University of New York Press, 1975.
Rizvi, S. *Mulla Sadra: Philosopher of Mystics*. Cambridge, UK: The Islamic Texts Society, 2005.

MURALS

See Painting, Monumental and Frescoes

MUSIC

The importance of music across medieval Islamic civilization is widely documented. Although often contested by Islamic law, vocal and instrumental traditions were significant in both scholarship and public life, and these early sounds still flavor the music of the present-day Middle East. Qur'anic recitation and the adhan (call to prayer) are never considered music in Islamic tradition.

General Principles and Issues

Sources

Music in the medieval Islamic empire was largely based in oral practice and oral transmission, with little or no emphasis on written music notation before the Ottoman period. Other types of information, however, exist in such sources as religious texts; philosophical, scientific, and legal treatises; collections of song texts; narratives and biographies; and pictorial evidence, such as engravings and miniatures. These documents and images allow a glimpse into the world of music and musicians, often showing or describing music theory, music-making contexts, musicians, instruments, and performance practice. Although the music likely had at least some basis in pre-Islamic or folk forms, music theory was usually the domain of the educated, literate elite. As such, the use of these texts and treatises tends to limit current knowledge to court traditions and musical practices in urban centers rather than nomadic or rural communities.

In the absence of written scores, it is difficult to determine or describe what this music actually sounded like. It is known that vocal music, singing, and poetry/verse were and are extremely central to Middle Eastern music. Early writings such as the tenth-century *Kitab al-Aghani* describe instrumental ensembles "playing as one," a likely reference to a monophonic (unison) playing style, although there is discussion of the use of *za'ida* (glosses) such as trills, turns, and other more individual ornamentations of melody. Such improvisatory practices are still common in Middle Eastern music today.

Sources also point to the use of an underlying drone (a low sustained or repeated pitch) as well as an emphasis on compound musical forms such as suites (cycles or sequences of vocal and instrumental composed pieces and improvisations). For example, the four-movement chamber music genre of *nuba* is first discussed in the mid-ninth century; writings over the next two centuries suggest the addition of a fifth movement, particularly in the regions of al-Andalus and North Africa. The Turkish *fasıl* suite, described in the fifteenth century, consists of improvisation,

a prelude, a group of composed songs, and an instrumental closing.

Modal Systems

An important feature of Middle Eastern music, from the pre-Islamic period to the present day, is the use of rhythmic and melodic modes as the bases for musical theory and practice. Modes are complex, conceptual frameworks around which all Middle Eastern music is organized. The principles of rhythmic modes (*iqa'at*) have strong links to poetic meter and involve phrases of varying lengths and patterns of beats and rests, whereas melodic modes involve sets of notes, scales, and intervals as well as particular notes of emphasis and emblematic patterns of melodic movement. Both rhythmic and melodic modal systems also have particular emotional correspondences (pleasure, courage, sadness) and expressive, affective properties.

Modal theory is considered in numerous treatises throughout the medieval period, with early writings referring to melodic modes as *asabi'* and only later with the present-day term *maqamat*. These treatises discuss the various classification schemes for modal organization as well as the changes over time and region in the number of modes and their names. For instance, early Arabic writing speaks of eight melodic modes, whereas later Persian theory is organized on the basis of twelve modes; some thirteenth-century writings even add six secondary modes (*awazat*).

Religious Controversy

Despite flourishing musical traditions and courtly patronage of music across Islamic civilization, the practice of music in Islam was and is not without significant controversy on religious and legal levels. There does not appear to have been a ban on music during the earliest days of Islam, and, indeed, the conquerors found it difficult to suppress the pre-Islamic musical customs of the areas they dominated. However, stricter injunctions against music in general began to appear under the orthodox caliphs who ruled after the death of the Prophet; from that time on, music fell variously in and out of favor throughout the medieval period and beyond.

The root of the controversy lies in differing perceptions of music's effect on the listener: the idea that music brings a devotee closer to God (a position prominent in Sufism) versus the fear that music—especially secular entertainment genres—provides a distraction from spiritual endeavors and tempts the listener into sin. Vocal traditions, especially unaccompanied singing, are generally less contentious than instrumental music, and treatises from the medieval period support a range of positions that frequently have their bases in passages or anecdotes from the Qur'an or hadith. These positions range from strict opposition to any secular or instrumental music—such as Ibn Abi'l Dunya's (d. 894 CE) *Dhamm al-Malahi (Disapprobation of Musical Instruments)*—to more liberal interpretations that only seek to ban instruments that cause "pleasure." The deep controversy over the permissibility of music in Islam is also reflected in the terminology used to refer to music and instruments, including the term *malahi,* which can refer either to musical instruments in general or to instruments that are forbidden.

Historical and Geographical Perspectives

Overview

During the early years of Islam in such centers as Mecca and Medina, many musicians could be found among the large populations arriving from newly conquered areas. Both slaves and non-Arab Muslims of the free *malwa* (client) class, often Persians, participated in a system of patronage that included *madjlis* (salons) hosted at private homes. Women, who were not yet sequestered, participated widely in music-making both as patrons (see Women Patrons) and performers, especially in the *qayna* (singing girl) tradition, which involved both singing and accompaniment on stringed instruments such as the *'ud* or *tunbur* (short-necked and long-necked lutes, respectively). Although the 'ud would continue to rise in prominence in Arabic music theory, these earlier instruments were probably carried over from pre-Islamic Sasanian court lute traditions, and they went by several other names: *mizhar* (a skin-backed lute), *muwattar* (probably played with the thumb), and *barbat* (a wood-backed lute). Other instruments mentioned during this period included the *mizmar* (a conical double-reed wind instrument), *daff* (frame drum, with or without metal discs), and *dufuf* (tambourine). There are also references to the use of music at feasts and in festive contexts such as weddings or celebrations.

Although music, especially instrumental music, fell out of favor under the orthodox caliphs, the fourth caliph 'Ali (r. 656–661 CE) provided considerably more protection for the arts and set the stage for the rise of court patronage during the Umayyad period and the development of a courtly art/music-tradition. The mid-seventh century also saw the rise of the male professional musician, who typically came from a more educated background and enjoyed a higher social status than the slave qaynat. There are even accounts of rulers with acknowledged performing skills, such as Caliph al-Walid II, who was accomplished as a singer, composer, and performer on the 'ud and the drum.

With the dawn of the 'Abbasid caliphate came the start of what is often considered the "Golden Age" of intellectual and artistic life. A considerable foreign influence began to pervade the Arab domination of the previous century, and there is early musical evidence of this shift in the eighth- and early ninth-century adoptions of new 'ud tunings and string names according to Persian methods. The primary sites of music-making were still the courts and the houses of wealthy or noble patrons, and the stage for a flowering of the musical arts was set by such rulers as Caliph Al-Mahdi (r. 775–785), who was known to be particularly partial to the musical arts and who was himself a singer.

The 'Abbasid period also marked the start of an extremely fertile era for Arabic music theory, including writings on notes, scales, acoustics, intervals, rhythm, modes, and composition. Although the foundation had been laid by such earlier writers as Yunus al-Katib and al-Khalil ibn Ahmad, some of the most enduring contributions to music theory started with the ninth-century exposure of Islamic scholars to ancient Greek treatises on subjects including mathematics, philosophy, astronomy, and music. Beginning with the establishment of the *Bayt al-Hikmal (House of Wisdom)* by the Caliph al-Ma'mun (r. 813–833) for the purpose of translating these sources into Arabic, these theoretical treatises would constitute the basis for music scholarship and art/music traditions over the next seven centuries and beyond in both the Middle East and Europe.

Music Theory and Theorists

The 'ud, which was considered the "instrument of philosophers," figures prominently in medieval music theory, especially in discussions of modal systems that are often oriented toward particular frets and fingerings. Most treatises deal with the 'ud al shabbut (perfect lute) that was introduced during the early 'Abbasid period: a wood-backed short-necked lute with four strings and played with a plectrum (probably also of wood). Rich in symbolism, ninth-century writings tell of the biblical figure Lamech creating the first 'ud by arranging pieces of wood that corresponded to the size and shape of his dead son's bones; treatises also point to cosmological correspondences between the four strings and the four elements, seasons, or humors of the body. The 'ud was also considered to be one of the most perfect imitators of the human voice, a characteristic that gave it and other stringed instruments primacy in most instrument classification systems of the period. Other instruments described in medieval treatises include the tunbur; bowed strings such as the rabab (spike fiddle) and kamanja (fiddle); the double-reed mizmar, surna, and zammara; flutes and pipes such as the nay, yara'a, and armuniqi (pan-pipes); and zithers called qanun and shahrud. There are also descriptions of long, cylindrical, or hourglass-shaped tubul (drums).

Although there are important treatises dating from the mid to late-ninth century, such as the writings of Al-Kindi (d. 873 CE), two very significant writers appear in the tenth century: Abu al-Faraj al-Isbahani (897–967) and Abu Nasr al-Farabi (870–950). Al-Isbahani's *Kitab al-Aghani (Book of Songs)* is a vast compendium of information about history, social life, and music from the dawn of Islam to the tenth century, including a number of song texts and information on modal theory. Al-Farabi, who was born in Turkey, is often considered one of the greatest Arab philosophers. His major work, *Kitab al-Musiqi al-Kabir (Grand Book on Music)*, marks a fundamental intellectual shift from theory based on Greek philosophy to theory based on actual, local practice. Al-Farabi's work formed the basis for a body of theory shared across the Islamic empire, and his legacy can be found in treatises throughout the rest of the medieval period.

Writers who bear the mark of al-Farabi's influence include Ibn Sina (d. 1037), one of the most prominent theorists of the next generation, and Safi al-Din (d. 1294), who wrote the *Kitab al-Adwar (Book of Musical Modes)*. Safi al-Din's work, which was drawn from the contemporary music of his day, was translated primarily into Persian and Turkish and is considered to have its greatest effect on styles in those regions. *Kitab al-Adwar* represents the first record of the twelve-mode Persian system, which began to rise in the eleventh century and upon which post-'Abbasid Persian and Ottoman Turkish music theory is largely based. Safi al-Din was also one of the first writers to use the term *maqam* in reference to modes; this term persists to the present day. Another writer with a great influence on Persian-speaking areas was 'Abd al-Qadir ibn Ghaybi al-Maraghi (d. 1435), an 'ud player and music theorist who wrote in Persian and made frequent reference to the work of Safi al-Din.

Sufism and Music

The spread of Sufism was an important force in the preservation and development of music in the medieval Middle East, with a particularly strong effect on the evolution of Ottoman Turkish art music. In contrast with the swirl of debate surrounding the practice of music in Islam, Sufi mysticism embraced the use of both vocal and instrumental music and the principles of sama' as a primary means for spiritual engagement. A fundamental concept in Islam, *sama'* can literally indicate "listening" or "audition," but it also has a range of more subtle meanings that relate to intent, spiritual posture, and inward practice on the part of the listener. Particularly in Sufi religious doctrine, this concept incorporates, for example, the ideas of listening as an art form; a state of interior attentiveness; contemplation; and the Qur'anic notion of hearing as a mode of knowledge and as one that is more trustworthy than vision.

Sufi sama' (in Turkish, *sema*) ceremonies incorporate melody, rhythm, poetry, movement, dress, and other sensory and symbolic components. Among the most well-known practitioners are the Mevlevi brotherhood, which was founded in thirteenth-century Seljuk Turkey and rooted in the teachings of Celaleddin-i Rumi (d. 1273). Sources suggest that the first Mevlevi ensembles were comprised of the nay (a vertical seven-holed reed flute) and the kudum (a small, metal, double kettledrum), with the later addition of the tunbur, rabab, and *halile* (cymbals). The nay, which is found throughout the Middle East, is central to Sufi practice and features prominently in Sufi symbolism and poetry. Common metaphors include man as a flute played by Allah or the plaintive sounds of the nay as the flute crying for its reed bed, just as man cries to be rejoined with God.

Other Regions and Styles

Music was also being cultivated and documented in other parts of the empire. In al-Andalus and the Iberian Peninsula, nearly eight centuries of Muslim rule gave rise to a number of musical developments, and a great deal is written about the influence of 'Ali ibn Nafi (also known as Ziryab), who arrived at the Cordovan court from Baghdad in 822. Ziryab is widely acknowledged for his role in blending Christian and Eastern musical forms, and, although accounts differ, he is often credited with creating or improving compound suite forms such as the nuba and making changes to the 'ud that include the addition of a fifth string and the introduction of the eagle-feather plectrum. In addition to Andalusian court settings, music also took place in evening entertainment sessions called *zambra,* which are described in eleventh century writings. These sessions took place in either palaces or private homes and involved instrumental music, song, and dance. Accounts of zambra tell of the use of instruments including the 'ud, tunbur, mi'zaf (zither), and double-reed wind instruments such as the mizmar and buq.

In the Tunisian Fatimid caliphate, which later had its capital in Cairo, sources describe court art/music-traditions as well as a particular emphasis on military bands known as *tabl-khanah* (this term could refer to either the ensemble or its repertoire). These ensembles included trumpets, drums such as the *naqqarat* and *kusat,* and cymbals or castanets *(sunudj)* and whistles *(safafir).* There are also descriptions of military Mehter and Janissary bands in Turkey as early as the 1550s, although these ensembles did not gain real prominence until the Ottoman period. Scholars continue to debate the extent to which Crusaders' exposure to Islamic military bands may have influenced the adoptions of such medieval European instruments as the anafil trumpet and certain types of kettledrum. Similar debates surround the origins of the European lute and rebec, with suggestions that they may have been derived from the 'ud and rabab, respectively.

SUNNI M. FASS

See also Singing; Poetry; Al-Farabi; Ziryab; Sufism; Rumi

Further Reading

Browning, Robert H., et. al, eds. *Maqam: Music of the Islamic World and its Influences.* New York: Alternative Museum, 1984.

Danielson, Virginia, Scott Marcus, and Dwight Reynolds, eds. *The Garland Encyclopedia of World Music, Volume 6: The Middle East.* New York: Routledge, 2002. Chapters by Blum, Danielson, Neubauer, Sawa, Reinhard.

Farmer, Henry George. *A History of Arabian Music to the XIIIth Century.* London: Luzac, 1929. Reprints 1967, 1996.

———. *The Sources of Arabian Music: An Annotated Bibliography of Arabic Manuscripts Which Deal With the Theory, Practice, and History of Arabian Music from the Eighth to the Seventeenth Century.* Leiden: E.J. Brill, 1965.

Shiloah, Amnon. *Music in the World of Islam: A Socio-Cultural Study.* Detroit, Mich: Wayne State University Press, 1995.

MUSLIM COMMUNITY AND POLITY, OR UMMAH

Ummah literally means community at varying scales, ranging from the followers of a particular Prophet to humanity as a whole. Even the different species of animals form an ummah similar to human communities, according to the Qur'an, because they also exhibit communal organization (6:38). Similar to the *millah* (the religious community), the ummah is a community that derives its identity from a commonly shared religion, transcending regional, ethnic, and racial allegiances. Each Prophet had an ummah made up of people whom he was charged by God to invite to the divine message, whether they accepted him as a Messenger of God or not.

In the Qur'an, it was said that God would not hold a community accountable without first sending them a Messenger. This Messenger will testify about their deeds on the Day of Judgment, with the Prophet Muhammad testifying for the other Prophets as a whole (4:41). Therefore, each community received its Prophet (10:47). God sent some Prophets only to a particular region, tribe, or nation, whereas some Prophets were sent to humanity in general. The Qur'an also states that, if God had so willed, He could have made all of humanity a single ummah without distinctions, divisions, or conflicts. By granting human beings the free will to reject divine guidance as well as giving them accountability for their own choices, God permits a diversity of faith among human beings and the rise of religious communities committed to different types of faith (2:213; 10:19). God is the only one who knows exactly when a given community will rise and when it will perish.

Because the Prophet Muhammad was sent to humanity as a whole, all of humankind constitutes his ummah, regardless of whether individual persons have accepted his invitation to Islam or are still being invited. Thus, the Constitution of Medina refers to Jewish and pagan citizens of Medina as members of the Prophet's ummah. However, the term *ummah* is more commonly used to refer to the global Muslim community—the polity united around brotherhood in Islamic faith. This conception signals a revolutionary change from the allegiance to the tribal organization that was then prevalent in Arabia to an allegiance grounded in shared religion. It introduces a faith-based identity and social organization that aims to supersede conventional identities and organizations on the basis of region, language, race, or nation. The global Muslim ummah has been united around the legacy of the Prophet Muhammad and has thus shared a common moral and religious culture. The unity of the ummah around a single point is symbolized by turning toward the Ka'ba in the five daily prayers from everywhere in the world. The annual pilgrimage to the Ka'ba, the hajj, is another manifestation of the unity of the ummah at the global level.

Islamic theology and law require that the unity of the ummah be reflected not only at the level of ritual but also at the level of social and political organization. The global Muslim community should be under the leadership of a single caliph in both religious and political affairs. However, the vast geographic span of the Islamic world has not permitted such a global unity as a single polity since the first century of Islamic history.

The Qur'an draws parallels between an ummah and an individual human being, particularly regarding the time of their birth and death, which are set by divine decree and beyond the reach of human beings to change (7:34). As in the case of each individual, each ummah is accountable for its own deeds (2:141).

In the Qur'an, the ummah of the Prophet Muhammad is praised as the best community as a result of enjoining what is right and forbidding what is wrong (3:110, 104). It was only for the want of this quality that previous communities had been corrupted and destroyed. The Qur'an also describes the Muslim ummah as a moderate or justly balanced community that follows the middle path, away from extremes, such that it can stand as witness over humanity, while the Prophet Muhammad will in turn be a witness over the ummah (2:143).

Consequently, the consensus of the ummah, which is called ijma', is a source of legitimacy in law and policy making. Unlike the church organization in Christianity or parliament in representative democracies, there is no individual or organization that can officially voice the will of the ummah. Instead, overlap in the opinions of independent and loosely affiliated scholars reflects the consensus of the ummah. In cases of disagreement, the majority view does not have the power to automatically rule out or override the minority view. This is based on the principle of free ijtihad, which stipulates that one informed opinion cannot annul another informed opinion. Political authorities, policy makers, and individuals are free to choose among these scholarly opinions regardless of whether the majority of the ummah subscribes to them or not. However, if there is consensus on an issue among the scholars, the state and the ummah as a whole are bound by it.

Admission to the ummah is open, with the single requirement of continual allegiance to Islamic faith, law, and community. New members of the ummah are automatically accepted as full citizens of the Islamic state, regardless of where they live, and they are qualified for the civil rights provided by it. From this perspective, citizenship is defined as belonging to an inclusive political community without territorial borders. While protecting the rights of the members of the ummah, the Hanafi jurists limited law enforcement by Muslim authority only within the territories of the Islamic state (dar al-Islam). However, the rest of the schools of law (maliki, shafii, and hanbali) refused such a territorial limitation to the enforcement of law in instances of protecting the rights of Muslims. Excommunication from the ummah is not a known practice in Islamic history. Although the renunciation of faith privately out of personal conviction was tolerated in Islamic history, public denouncement, sacrilege, and blasphemy against Islam and thus membership in the ummah, with a perceived attempt to undermine Muslim community, was considered an offense. Membership in the ummah is seen as an interminable commitment and allegiance to the community and faith, thereby permanently excluding the possibility of resignation.

RECEP SENTURK

Further Reading

al-Dihlawi, Shah Wali Allah. *Difference of Opinion in Fiqh (Al-Insaf)*. London: Ta Ha, 2003.

Johansen, Baber. *Contingency in a Sacred Law: Legal and Ethical Norms in the Muslim Fiqh*, 238–62. Leiden: Brill, 1999.

Kandhlawi, Muhammad Zakariyya. *The Differences of the Imams (Iktilaf al-A'imma)*. Santa Barbara, Calif: White Thread, 2004.

al-Mawardi, Abu'l-Hasan. *Al-Ahkam as-Sultaniyyah: The Laws of Islamic Governance*. London: Ta Ha, 2000.

MUSLIM IBN AL-HAJJAJ

Muslim ibn al-Hajjaj al-Qushayri was the author of *Sahih Muslim*. After al-Bukhari's *al-Jami' al-Sahih*, Muslim's *al-Jami' al-Sahih* is the most respected collection of the hadith (the accounts of the words, deeds, and opinions of the Prophet Muhammad) in Islam.

In many ways, Muslim's *Sahih* resembles that of al-Bukhari, which has led to comparisons through the ages. Both are roughly the same size; the traditional figures given are that Muslim's work contains twelve thousand hadith with repetitions and three thousand thirty three individual hadith without. Like al-Bukhari, Muslim grouped his hadith according to the legal, theological, or historical issue that they address. In some quarters, his classification and presentation have been regarded as preferable to al-Bukhari's.

Both men were contemporaries and indeed shared many of the same teachers. For reasons that are by no means clear, it is unanimously asserted that al-Bukhari's collection predates that of Muslim. This may well be based on nothing more than a general impression created by the fact that Muslim took some hadith from al-Bukhari, whereas there is no evidence that the reverse ever occurred. Al-Bukhari's collection is also commonly regarded as superior to Muslim's as a repository of authentic hadith, although the highly regarded Abu 'Ali al-Hafiz al-Nisaburi (AH 277/890 CE–349/960) and at least some scholars in North Africa held the opposite opinion.

Muslim's introduction to his collection is a very perplexing document. Among other things (including what was later interpreted as an attack against al-Bukhari), Muslim states that he included hadith from transmitters of varying degrees of reliability in his *Sahih.* For later scholars, reason seemed to necessitate that there exclusively be transmitters of the highest standard of reliability in a collection of authentic hadith. It has been argued Muslim meant to extend his work to cover less-authentic hadith but never had a chance to do so. Others felt that the less-reliable transmitters were only found in the isnads of certain non-core hadith, which were included merely to clarify the authentic hadith. Still others have argued that, although Muslim does include hadith from unreliable transmitters, he also knew the same texts from unimpeachable transmitters and chose to include the former because they happened to have shorter lines of transmission.

Muslim also left behind a number of monographs about subjects that were associated with the study of hadith. Of these, his *Kitab al-Tamyiz,* an account of the actual methods the early authorities used to authenticate hadith, is by far the most significant. There can be no doubt that, when this book receives adequate attention, a number of questions about the great hadith collections will be answered.

Very little is known about Muslim's life. He was born in Nishapur shortly after 200/816. As was the custom of the day, he traveled extensively throughout the Islamic world to collect his hadith, and it is claimed that he knew three hundred thousand. He died in 261/875 in Nasrabadh, outside of Nishapur, pehaps from eating too many dried dates at one sitting.

EERIK DICKINSON

Primary Sources

al-Baghdadi, Al-Khatib. *Ta'rikh Baghdad,* 14 vols., vol. 13, 100–4. Cairo: Maktabat al-Khanji, 1349/1931.
Muslim ibn al-Hajjaj al-Qushayri. *Sahih Muslim,* transl. A. H. Siddiqui, 4 vols. Lahore, 1971.
———. *Kitab al-Tamyiz,* ed. M.M. Azami. Riyadh.

Further Reading

Encyclopaedia of Islam, 2nd ed., vol. 6, 691–2. Leiden: E.J. Brill, 1953.
Juynboll, G.H.A., transl. "Muslim's Introduction to his Sahih." *Jerusalem Studies in Arabic and Islam* 5 (1984): 263–311.
Sezgin, Fuat. *Geschichte des Arabischen Schrifttums*, vol. 1, 136–43. Leiden: E.J. Brill, 1967.

MUSLIM–BYZANTINE RELATIONS

Byzantium was the prime target of Muslim attack by virtue of its geographical position on the northwestern edge of the caliphate. More important, though, was the ideological challenge it presented. Not only was Byzantium a political rival that remembered its imperial past and believed in an imperial future (if only on the eve of the End of Time), but it continued to ascribe to itself a central role in God's providential scheme as the sole authorized managing agent in earthly affairs. Worse still, it clung tenaciously to a version of the true faith—over-intellectualized, it could be argued, and with a polytheistic encrustation—that had been superseded by the Prophet's revelation.

There was much more to relations between Byzantium and the Muslim world than open warfare. Religious polemic could be temporarily set aside. Diplomatic and other conventions grew up that mitigated conflict. After the caliphate dissolved into a number of regional powers, Byzantium could set its Muslim neighbors against each other. There was much commercial and cultural exchange. 'Abbasid magnates sponsored translations of Greek philosophical and scientific texts. The Byzantine court responded by sending intellectuals as ambassadors to Baghdad. Muslim fashions in dress and Muslim decorative motifs were picked up in Byzantium. Monarchical power in Islam as well as Byzantium manifested itself in sumptuously decorated palaces and carefully choreographed ceremonies in which automata as well as living beings played their part. Luxury artifacts with intricate workmanship moved in both directions in the course of diplomatic exchanges. Nonetheless, war was the norm. Byzantium may be characterized above all as a highly militarized society in which the collective life was dominated by war against Islam. That war had six distinct phases.

Warfare, 634–969 CE

(1) 634–718

After the conquest of Iran (642–652 CE), the prime foreign policy aim of the caliphate was the destruction of Byzantium. Hence, there were three concerted attempts to take Constantinople, in 654, the 670s, and 717–718. Apart from a fleeting failure of nerve in 654, when the whole population of Anatolia (the inhabitants of the plateau, the mountains, and the coasts) formally submitted, Byzantium fought back, trading blow for blow, building a powerful fleet, and investing in fixed defenses by land. However, the cost was high; there was serious damage to the urban infrastructure of Asia Minor during the course of forty years of fighting before and after the second fitna.

(2) 718–ca. 840

Byzantium finally acknowledged its de facto loss of imperial status (its self-image was now that of a latter-day Chosen People, belabored from without but guaranteed survival from above), and it abandoned conventional warfare in favor of guerrilla methods. These can be documented from 779, but they were probably developed during preceding decades. They involved the evacuation of civilians and livestock to designated fortresses and refuge zones, the systematic harassing of raiding forays and foraging parties, and the concentration of effort on ambushing the Muslims as they withdrew through the frontier passes. Such tactics succeeded in preserving Byzantium's diminished resource base over several generations. The caliphate still directed major attacks against Byzantium, but there were now longer intervals of relative calm. The aim was now either incremental conquest or the harvesting of booty and prestige, as in 781, when a huge army, numbering just under ninety-six thousand men and under the nominal command of the young Harun al-Rashid, overran Asia Minor and entered Bithynia, where only a resort to hostage-taking secured the army's escape from a Byzantine trap. A system of forward bases *(thughur)* that were well fortified and permanently garrisoned was elaborated along the frontier from Tarsus in Cilicia to Malatya (Melitene) on the Euphrates, flanked to the north by Kalikala (Theodosiopolis) in western Armenia. Twice the Arabs came tantalizingly close to establishing a permanent presence inside Anatolia's mountain rim: in 806, when Harun al-Rashid briefly gained control of the whole length of the Cilician Gates, and in 833, when al-Ma'mun secured a fortified bridgehead at Tyana.

(3) ca. 840–969

During this phase, the task of prosecuting the war against Byzantium increasingly devolved upon the thughur and the volunteers who gathered there,

especially in the well-endowed charitable foundations of Tarsus, a system that aroused Byzantine admiration and envy. The war stabilized into one of Muslim raid, by sea as well as land, and Byzantine counter-raid. Conventions were established to facilitate the exchange and ransoming of prisoners. A cross-cultural sense of affinity and a shared heroic ethos grew up in the borderlands, which, on occasion, led borderers to frustrate the policies of the central authorities by surreptitiously resupplying beleaguered enemy towns. The *Digenes Akrites,* a hybrid epic romance rooted in ninth- and tenth-century reality (although only written down around 1100), captures the attitudes of the frontier milieux. The balance of power and initiative shifted steadily in Byzantium's favor, but this change was attributable more to Arab divisions than Byzantine strength. A first orthodox counteroffensive (871–883) ended in defeat outside Tarsus. After an interlude during which Byzantium was preoccupied with Bulgaria and Armenia (the latter a vital buffer against Islam), a second offensive of unconventional character was launched in the 920s. Precision diplomacy and carefully targeted military action were directed into the thughur. A succession of strategic cities capitulated as each in turn was isolated and suffered a steady erosion of its resources, both physical and moral, through constant raiding. Malatya was the first to be annexed in 934; Tarsus (evacuated by jihad fighters carrying their small arms) and Antioch were the last, in 965 and 969, respectively. These successes, together with the reconquest of Crete (961) and the extrusion of Muslims from joint rule of Cyprus (965), reestablished Byzantium as a great Near Eastern power.

Warfare, 969–1453 CE

(4) 969–1081

The Fatimid conquest of Egypt and much of Syria transformed the geopolitical situation. Whereas Egypt under the Ikhshidids had been neutralized from 937, its massive resources were now in the hands of a hostile, ideologically active power. Byzantium responded first with shows of force in the Jazira and Syria (972–975) and then pursued a cautious policy of expansion in Transcaucasia, mainly through diplomacy; it succeeded in annexing a large swath of land (western Iberia, the kingdoms of Ani and Vaspurakan) between 1000 and 1045. Access was thus secured to a large supplementary reservoir of Christian manpower. Byzantium's eastern advance was abruptly halted and reversed upon encountering the swifter-moving drive to the west of the Turks, the third great power of the eleventh-century Near East. First Armenia and then Anatolia came under attack from Seljukid armies and Turkoman bands. The decisive victory of the Sultan Alp Arslan at Manzikert in 1071 opened Anatolia to unrestricted raiding and settlement over the following decade.

(5) 1081–1204

Pressing problems in the Balkans and involvements further afield in Italy and Hungary may often have distracted Komnenian emperors, but they did not abandon hope of recovering Anatolia. Circumstantial evidence suggests that the conception of launching a Christian *jihad* (holy war) targeted at Jerusalem and of using the Pope as its principal propagandist originated in Byzantium. Latin Christendom formed much of the largest reservoir of Christian manpower on which Byzantium would have to draw if it were to confront the Turks on equal terms. Byzantine hopes of recovering Anatolia while their western allies secured the Holy Land found retrospective expression in the Treaty of Devol (1108). The gains in Anatolia were limited to the coastlands, and Byzantium had to rely on its own diplomatic and military resources to contain, subvert, and confront Turkish power. The defeat of a full expeditionary army at Myriokephalon in 1176 marked the end of this policy. Byzantium itself, weakened by political intrigue and civil war, soon fell prey to its erstwhile Western allies.

(6) 1204–1453

Both rump Byzantine states in Anatolia, the "empires" of Nikaia and Trebizond, had to maneuver for advantage in a Turkish-dominated world. The Nikaian rulers proved to be more successful, and they reconstituted a simulacrum of the Komnenian state, which was first the plaything and then the prey of the Ghazi-driven Ottoman Sultanate. While Byzantines increasingly stressed their Hellenism, the Ottomans laid claim to Rome's Trojan ancestry and finally absorbed Constantinople, the New Rome, in 1453.

JAMES HOWARD-JOHNSTON

Further Reading

Ahrweiler, Hélène. *Byzance et la Mer: La Marine de Guerre, la Politique et les Institutions Maritimes de Byzance aux VIIe–XVe Siècles*. Paris: Presses Universitaires de France, 1966.

Beaton, Roderick, and David Ricks, eds. *Digenes Akrites: New Approaches to Byzantine Heroic Poetry*. Aldershot: Variorum, 1993.

Bonner, Michael. *Aristocratic Violence and Holy War: Studies in Jihad and the Arab-Byzantine Frontier*. New Haven, Conn: American Oriental Society, 1996.

Bryer, Anthony, and Michael Ursinus, eds. *Manzikert to Lepanto: The Byzantine World and the Turks, 1071–1571*. Amsterdam: Hakkert, 1991.

Dagron, Gilbert. "Byzance et le Modèle Islamique au Xe Siècle: À Propos des *Constitutions Tactiques* de L'Empereur Léon VI." *Comptes Rendus de l'Académie des Inscriptions et Belles-Lettres* (1983): 219–42.

Dagron, Gilbert, and Haralambie Mihăescu. *Le Traité sur la Guérilla (De Velitatione) de L'Empereur Nicéphore Phocas (963–969)*. Paris: Centre National de la Recherche Scientifique, 1986.

Eastmond, Antony, ed. *Eastern Approaches to Byzantium*. Aldershot: Ashgate, 2001.

El Cheikh, Nadia M. *Byzantium Viewed by the Arabs*. Cambridge, Mass: Harvard University Press, 2004.

Grabar, Oleg. "The Shared Culture of Objects." In *Byzantine Court Culture from 829 to 1204*, ed. Henry Maguire, 115–29. Washington, DC: Dumbarton Oaks, 1997.

Gutas, Dimitri. *Greek Thought, Arabic Culture: The Graeco-Arabic Translation Movement in Baghdad and Early Abbasid Society (2nd–4th/8th–10th Centuries)*. London and New York: Routledge, 1998.

Imber, Colin. *The Ottoman Empire, 1300–1481*. Istanbul: Isis Press, 1990.

Lilie, Ralph-Johannes. *Die Byzantinische Reaktion auf die Ausbreitung der Araber: Studien zur Strukturwandlung des Byzantinischen Staates im 7. und 8. Jhd*. Munich: Institut für Byzantinistik und Neugriechische Philologie der Universität, 1976.

———. *Byzantium and the Crusader States, 1096–1204*. Oxford, UK: Clarendon Press, 1993.

McGeer, Eric. *Sowing the Dragon's Teeth: Byzantine Warfare in the Tenth Century*. Washington, DC: Dumbarton Oaks, 1995.

Magdalino, Paul. "The Road to Baghdad in the Thought-World of Ninth-Century Byzantium." In *Byzantium in the Ninth Century: Dead or Alive?*, ed. Leslie Brubaker, 195–213. Aldershot: Ashgate, 1998.

Mango, Cyril. "Discontinuity with the Classical Past in Byzantium." In *Byzantium and the Classical Tradition*, eds. Margaret Mullett and Roger Scott, 48–57. Birmingham, Ala: Centre for Byzantine Studies, 1981.

Mango, Marlia. *Byzantine Trade (4th–12th Centuries): Recent Archaeological Work*. Aldershot: Ashgate, 2006.

Runciman, Steven. *The Fall of Constantinople 1453*. Cambridge, UK: Cambridge University Press, 1965.

Shepard, Jonathan, and Simon Franklin, eds. *Byzantine Diplomacy*. Aldershot: Ashgate, 1992.

Vasiliev, A.A. *Byzance et les Arabes*, 3 vols. Brussels: Institut de Philologie et d'Histoire Orientales/Fondation Byzantine, 1935–1968.

MUSLIM–CRUSADER RELATIONS

Politically, Muslim–Crusader relations during the two centuries of encounter in the Near East can be divided into three principal phases. The first lasted from the Frankish capture of Turcoman-held Antioch in AH 491/1098 CE until 'Imad al-Din Zanki's recovery of Edessa (modern Urfa in southern Turkey) from the

Crusaders in AH 539/1144 CE. The period is characterized by frequent accommodation between the two camps. Local Muslim rulers often resorted to arms against the western invaders, whose territory reached its maximum extent during the period. However, they feared co-religionist outsiders more than they did the Franks, with whom they tended to make political and military accords.

The second period, which lasted until the death of Saladin in AH 589/1193 CE, is marked by a rise in Muslim ideological fervor against the invaders. The success of Muslim arms under Zanki and his son Nur al-Din encouraged unity under the banner of jihad (holy war). Uncompromising opposition to the Crusaders reached its peak with the capture of Jerusalem by Saladin in AH 583/1187 CE.

The third and final period, which ended with the capture of Frankish Acre by the Mamluks in AH 690/1291 CE, sees a return to the *détente* of the first phase. After the death of Saladin, competing Ayyubid interests often meant that expediency was put before jihad, most notably when the Ayyubid ruler of Egypt, al-Malik al-Kamil, gave Jerusalem to Frederick II of Sicily in AH 626/1229 CE.

Social relations between the two cultures were marked in the beginning by mutual incomprehension and hostility. Over time, however, second and succeeding generations of Franks were born (sometimes of mixed marriages) who would live all their lives in the East. Compromises began to be made in the matter of customs and personal habit, mostly by the newcomers, and a *modus vivendi* was achieved.

DAVID MORRAY

See also Ibn Jubayr; Jihad; Pacts and Treaties; Peace and Peacemaking; Syria: Greater Syria; Usama ibn Munqidh; Zankids

Further Reading

Hillenbrand, Carole. *The Crusades: Islamic Perspectives*. Edinburgh: Edinburgh University Press, 1999.
Ibn Munqidh, Usama. *Kitab al-I'tibar*, transl. P.K. Hitti as *Memoirs of an Arab-Syrian Gentleman*. Beirut, 1964.

MUSLIM–MONGOL DIPLOMACY

Almost immediately from the time that they shared a border with the Muslim lands, the Mongols employed diplomacy to further their strategy of expansion. Having conquered Muslim territory, Mongol khans and commanders continued to send out missives and envoys to Muslim rulers who had yet to submit. Even after the Mongol efforts at conquest in the Middle East were stalled, after the battle of 'Ayn Jalut, when they were defeated by the Mamluks in 1260 CE, the Ilkhanid Mongols based in Iran continued to dispatch embassies to this enemy calling for their submission as part of the war that lasted for some sixty years. Other Mongol states, especially the Golden Horde, maintained contact with the Mamluks. Around 1320, the Ilkhanate launched a diplomatic *démarche* that led to the conclusion of the war against the Mamluks and inaugurated a period of peace with them. A full discussion of Muslim–Mongol diplomacy should be placed in a wider examination of Mongol diplomacy vis-à-vis other sedentary states, especially those in Europe. Such a discussion is impossible in the present context; please see the bibliography below.

Genghis Khan initiated contacts with the Khwarazm-Shah 'Ala' al-Din Muhammad, the ruler of the eastern Muslim countries, after the latter captured and put to death more than four hundred merchants that arrived at his frontier from Mongol territory. The Khan demanded restitution and punishment for those responsible. The Khwarazm-Shah's answer was to execute the envoys with the exception of one, who was sent back shaven. As is well known, the Khwarazm-Shah was to rue this action; other rulers were to learn that they tampered with the safety of Mongol envoys at their own risk. Genghis Khan, of course, was unable to accept this humiliation, and he launched the campaign (1219–1223) that first brought the Mongols to the Middle East.

As Mongol forces gradually expanded the territory under their control, they came into contact with other Muslim rulers. It appears that, on the whole, diplomatic contact was established by the local Mongol commanders working under the general auspices of the Great Khan in Mongolia. Many Muslim rulers gradually had come to recognize the power of the Mongols, and they saw no alternative to finding an accommodation with them. Thus, in the mid-1240s, contacts were already established between the Mongols and the Caliph al-Musta'sim (1242–1258), who, in 1246, sent envoys to the Great Khan, and it seems already that some type of submission was expressed. Likewise, relations were established around this time or a bit later between the Mongols and some of the princes of Syria, Anatolia, and the Jazira. Thus, in 1254 CE, when the Franciscan William of Rubruck reached the capital of the Great Khan Möngke, he found an envoy of the Ayyubid ruler of Karak, "who wanted to become a tributary and ally of the Tatars" (Jackson and Morgan, 1990). The most important Ayyubid ruler in Syria on the eve of the Mongol invasion of the country, al-Nasir Yusuf (r. 1236–1260 in Aleppo and after 1250 in Damascus), had sent an envoy to the Mongol governor Arghun Aqa as early as 1243 or 1244; the subsequent year, he was paying tribute to the Mongols (and he may have been doing so as early as 1241). In 1245 or 1246, this sultan sent a relative to the Great Khan Güyük (1246–1248), who returned with an order defining the sultan's obligations to the Mongols. In 1250, yet another envoy was dispatched to the Great Khan's court. The Ayyubid ruler of Mayyafariqin, al-Kamil Muhammad, arrived at Möngke's court in 1253, made his submission, and found there Muslim princes from Mosul and Mardin. It is clear, then, that years before Hülegü's arrival in the area the majority of Muslim princes in Iraq, Jazira, and Syria had made some type of submission to the Mongols and that at least some were paying tribute.

This is not the place to examine why many of these rulers, including the caliph, responded belligerently to Hülegü upon his arrival in the area in the mid-1250s, despite their previous expression of submission. Prior to his attacks on Baghdad and Syria, the Ilkhan corresponded with the Caliph al-Musta'sim and al-Nasir Yusuf, and he called on them to submit or face the consequences of attack and destruction. It should be noted that, generally, the Mongols sent such calls for surrender before they attacked; this was in parallel with similar usage in Islamic law. In both cases, the Muslim rulers remained defiant and suffered Mongol attacks and conquests, and both were eventually executed.

In the spring of 1260, Hülegü sent a beautifully crafted missive in Arabic (composed by the savant Nasir al-Din Tusi and based on an earlier letter sent to al-Nasir Yusuf) to Qutuz, the new ruler of Mamluk Egypt. The latter had the envoys cut in half, and he had their heads prominently displayed in Cairo. This was a clear message of defiance to the Mongols, to the army, and to the local population; he made it obvious that he meant business and that there was to be no compromise with the Mongols. Qutuz soon set off on the campaign that led to the victory at 'Ayn Jalut. Qutuz's successor, Baybars (1260–1277), exchanged several letters conveyed by envoys with Abagha Ilkhan (1265–1282). These letters were generally truculent, and it is clear that the intent was more in the realm of psychological warfare than in real attempts at diplomatic relations, let alone ending the war.

The Ilkhan Tegüder (1282–1284) initiated an exchange of letters with Sultan Qalawun (1279–1290). The first impression from these letters is that the new Ilkhan, a convert to Islam, was interested in ending the state of war between the two states. A deeper examination, however, shows that these letters are really a more subtle demand for submission to the Mongols, despite their Islamic style. The Mamluks, it would seem, understood their true tenor, and they were far from enthusiastic about the supposed calls for peace. In any event, Tegüder's short reign ended any chance of a transformation of the essence of Mamluk–Ilkhanid relations. During the reign of Arghun Ilkhan (1284–1291), there was no evidence of any diplomatic contact between the two states. Overtly belligerent letters were exchanged by the Sultan al-Ashraf Khalil (1290–1293) and Geikhatu (1291–1295). The former, fresh from his victories at Acre and Qal'at al-Rum in eastern Anatolia, threatened to invade Iraq. His assassination, however, nipped this plan in the bud. The Ilkhan Ghazan (1295–1304) launched a series of invasions against Syria, even enjoying some success, although he was unable to hold the country after his victory in Wadi al-Khaznadar in central Syria in 1299. Interspersed with these campaigns, he exchanged letters with the young Sultan al-Nasir Muhammad (second reign, 1299–1309). Again, the Ilkhan called on the Mamluks to submit, although his claims are couched largely in Islamic terms. The Mamluks, for their part, rejected all of Ghazan's claims out of hand, disparaging the Islam of the newly converted Mongols in the process. Öljeitü Ilkhan (1304–1316) sent the Mamluks a letter soon after gaining the throne, calling for peace. Here, too, the Mamluk leadership realized that these were hollow claims and responded in kind. Only several years after Abu Sa'id (1316–1335) ascended the Ilkhanid throne did the Mongols of Iran open up with a real peace offensive that recognized the status quo. Initial contacts were carried out by the international slave trader al-Majd al-Sallami, and soon official envoys were bringing letters. A treaty was ratified in 1323, and this led to a period of peaceful coexistence until the demise of the Ilkhanate in 1335.

Under Baybars, diplomatic relations were maintained with the Mongol Golden Horde, which ruled the steppe region north of the Black and Caspian Seas. The Jochid Khans of the Golden Horde were engaged in a war with their Ilkhanid cousins, and both the Jochids and the Mamluk sultans were interested in cooperation, perhaps even in a joint offensive against their common enemy. Islam played a part in these relations, because some of the Jochid Khans were Muslims; however, even those who were pagans maintained warm relations with the Sultans. Evidently, other, more practical matters of state were behind these relations. Given the great distance between the Golden Horde and the Mamluk Sultanate, no joint campaign was ever organized, but the importance of the second front, where the Ilkhans had to fight on occasion and thus could not always devote themselves to the war against the Mamluks, was of great importance to the latter. In addition, diplomatic relations with the Golden Horde guaranteed the continual supply of young mamluks (military slaves) to the sultanate from among the Turkish and even the Mongol tribesmen of this steppe area. The importance of these relations declined somewhat with the improvement of relations between the Mamluks and the Ilkhanate. There were also occasional relations with the Mongol rulers of Central Asia, and these were often at odds with their Ilkhanid relations; however, this was of minor importance in the long run.

REUVEN AMITAI

See also Genghis Khan; Mamluks; Mongols

Further Reading

Allouche, Adel. "Tegüder's Ultimatum to Qalawun." *International Journal of Middle Eastern Studies* 22 (1990): 437–46.
Amitai, Reuven. "The Resolution of the Mongol-Mamluk War." In *Mongols, Turks and Others: Eurasian Nomads and the Sedentary World*, eds. Reuven Amitai and Michal Biran. Leiden: Brill, 2004.
Amitai-Preiss, Reuven. "An Exchange of Letters in Arabic between Abaγa Ilkhan and Sultan Baybars (A.H. 667 / A.D. 1268-9)." *Central Asiatic Journal*. 38 (1994): 11–33.
———. *Mongols and Mamluks: The Mamluk-lkhanid War 1260–1281*. Cambridge, UK: Cambridge University Press, 1995.
Boyle, John A. "The Il-Khans of Persia and the Princes of Europe." *Central Asiatic Journal* 20 (1976): 25–40.
Holt, Peter M. "The Īlkhān AÍmad's Embassies to Qalāwūn: Two Contemporary Accounts." *Bulletin of the School of Oriental and African Studies* 49 (1986): 128–32.
———. *The Age of the Crusades: The Near East from the Eleventh Century to 1517*. Chapter 18. Diplomatic and Commercial Relations of the Mamluk Sultanate. London: Longman, 1986.
Horst, Heribert. "Eine Gesandschaft des Mamlüken al-Malik al-NāÒir im Īlïānhof in Persien." In *Der Orient in der Forschung: Festschrift für Otto Spies*, ed. Wilhelm Hoenerbach. Wiesbaden: Harrassowitz, 1967.
Humphreys, R.S. *From Saladin to the Mongols: The Ayyubids of Damascus 1192–1260*. Albany, NY: State University of New York Press, 1977.
Jackson, P., and D. Morgan. *The Mission of Friar William of Rubruck*, 184. London, 1990.
de Rachewiltz, Igor. *Papal Envoys to the Great Khans*. London: Faber and Faber, 1971.
Ratchnevsky, Paul. *Genghis Khan: His Life and Legacy*, ed. and transl. Thomas N. Haining. Oxford, UK: Blackwell, 1991.

AL-MUTANABBI, ABU'L-TAYYIB AHMAD IBN AL-HUSAYN AL-JU'FI

Arabic poetry during the tenth century remained bound by conventions originating in pre-Islamic Arabia, with poets of the period still expected to employ the traditional *qasida* (ode) form. Abu'l-Tayyib Ahmad ibn al-Husayn al-Ju'fi al-Mutanabbi, whose name for succeeding generations became synonymous with the accolade "great poet," was born in the Iraqi city of Kufa in 915 CE. Despite the apparent poverty of his origins—his father was a water-carrier—al-Mutanabbi was educated at one of the best schools in Kufa (one with decidedly Shi'i leanings). In late 924, in accordance with the custom among poets and philologists of the period who viewed the Bedouin as the true repository of pure Arabic speech and eloquence (and probably also escaping the turmoil in Kufa after the Qarmatian invasion), al-Mutanabbi went to live for a period of two years among the south Arabian Bedouin of the Samawa in the Syrian desert, a sojourn that left its mark on both his psyche and his poetry.

During the early stages of his career, al-Mutanabbi worked in Baghdad and throughout Syria as the intermittent panegyrist of a number of rich bourgeois and Bedouin tribal chiefs. Even at this point, his masterful engaging of the Arab poetic tradition inspired the charge of plagiarism, which would plague him throughout his career. At the same time, several of the hallmarks of his style, including frequent use of antithesis, an emphasis on conciseness of expression, and careful attention to the musical quality of his verses, were already discernible in his poetry. Arrogant by nature and frustrated by the world's indifference, al-Mutanabbi eventually turned to violence as a means to attain the power and wealth that he saw as his due. It is from the insurrection he led in the Samawa region of Syria (ca. 933) that his name *al-Mutanabbi* ("the would-be prophet") derives. This rebellion, perhaps Qarmatian in origin, resulted in a two-year imprisonment for al-Mutanabbi. The poet himself later stated that he had never claimed to be a prophet and that his sobriquet, initiated by others, stemmed from a verse in which he likened himself to the pre-Islamic Arabian prophet, Salih, mentioned in the Qur'an.

The various patrons that al-Mutanabbi eulogized during the early part of his career were but a prelude to his nine-year relationship (middle of 948–middle of 957) with the Hamdanid prince Abu'l-Hasan 'Ali ibn Abi'l-Hayja' Sayf al-Dawla, which must be considered the heyday of al-Mutanabbi's career. Basking in the luxury of an opulent and intellectually vibrant court and indulged by a dynamic patron, al-Mutanabbi produced some of his most celebrated poetry. His panegyrics to Sayf al-Dawla bespeak the poet's pleasure at singing the praises of one he deemed a true Arab leader and a champion of Islam against the Byzantines; these demonstrated a measure of real affection mixed with the conventional praise of premodern Arabic poetry. At the same time, al-Mutanabbi's ability to capitalize on small details or events to diversify his odes helped minimize the monotony that the all-important panegyric form sometimes experienced at the hands of a less-talented artist. The poet's affection for his patron also rendered more emotionally resonant the many elegies that al-Mutanabbi wrote about members of Sayf al-Dawla's family. In addition, al-Mutanabbi directly participated in almost all of his patron's military campaigns, and he recorded these events in poems such as his famous ode about the recapture of the fortress town of Hadath from the Byzantines. This poem conveys an epic quality that is reminiscent of the Amorium poem of Abu Tammam (ca. 805–845), whom al-Mutanabbi admired both for his poetry and for the Yemenite origins that they shared.

The poetry from this period illustrates al-Mutanabbi's ability to stretch the limitations placed on the poet by convention through manipulation—and sometimes omission—of the traditional amatory prelude, which he often replaced with lyrical and philosophical versifying about life and its paradoxes as well as his own feelings of pessimism and frustration. It is perhaps this irrepressible insertion in his poems of a measure of personal feeling and individual presence at a time when conventional taste least encouraged it that is al-Mutanabbi's greatest gift to Arabic poetry, and it at least in part explains the great admiration he inspired in subsequent generations. Many of al-Mutanabbi's gnomic lines have entered popular Arab culture as a result of their concision and the acoustical and semantic symmetry of their construction, which render them easy to remember.

In 957, al-Mutanabbi fled the Hamdanid court, a victim of both the plotting of enemies at court and his own insensitivity and arrogance. He made his way to the court of the Ikhshidid regent of Egypt, Abu'l-Misk Kafur, who represented, in the poet's eyes, the antithesis of the ideal patron. The opulence and intellectual fertility of his new environment were not enough to extinguish al-Mutanabbi's shame at having to eulogize a former slave, whom he considered inherently inferior. Al-Mutanabbi's five years in Egypt yielded not only biting satire focusing on the race, ugliness, and slave origins of the patron he so profoundly resented but also praise poetry that barely disguised a dangerously satirical subtext. By this point in his career, al-Mutanabbi was the recognized master of a school of poetry, and he continued to be the center of enthusiastic circles of admirers and students who discussed, annotated, and preserved his work under the poet's direct guidance. Among his most devoted students was the philologist Abu'l-Fath 'Uthman Ibn Jinni (d. 1002). Eventually, even some of his archenemies—including the literary theorist Abu 'Ali ibn al-Hasan al-Hatimi (d. 998), who had excoriated al-Mutanabbi for his so-called

plagiarisms and borrowings from Hellenistic philosophy—came to acknowledge, albeit grudgingly, his excellence as a poet. Although panegyric was the main focus of al-Mutanabbi's poetry, as the economics of the contemporary poetic culture demanded, he had the distinction of having produced several hunting poems and even lyrical descriptions of nature. Leaving Persia in 965, probably to return to Sayf al-Dawla's court, al-Mutanabbi was attacked outside Wasit in Iraq and killed, along with his son, by a Bedouin chief who was the uncle of the Qarmatian rebel whom al-Mutanabbi had satirized a year earlier. Perhaps no other premodern Arab poet has had such a profound and sustained influence over the evolution of Arabic poetry, even into the modern era. Al-Mutanabbi's poetry provided one of the primary models for the neoclassical poets of the late nineteenth and early twentieth centuries, who were bent on revitalizing Arabic poetry by reconnecting it to its glorious poetic heritage. His influence extended across the Arab East and North Africa and even into Persia.

MARGARET LARKIN

See also Abu Tammam; Elegy; Epic Poetry; Hamdanids; Ikhshidids

Primary Sources

Barquqi, 'Abd al-Rahman. *Sharh Diwan al-Mutanabbi (Explanation of the Collected Poetry of al-Mutanabbi)*, 2 vols., 4 parts. Beirut: Dar al-Kitab al-'Arabi, 1980.

al-Ma'arri, Abu'l-'Ala'. *Sharh Diwan Abi'l-Tayyib al-Mutanabbi: Mu'jiz Ahmad (Explanation of the Collected Poetry of Abu'l-Tayyib al-Mutanabbi: Ahmad's Miracle)*, 4 vols. Cairo: Dar al-Ma'arif, 1988.

al-'Ukbari, Abu'l-Baqa'. *Sharh Diwan Abi'l-Tayyib al-Mutanabbi (Explanation of the Collected Poetry of Abu'l-Tayyib al-Mutanabbi)*, 2 vols., 4 parts. Beirut: Dar al-Ma'rifa, 1978.

al-Wahidi al-Nisaburi, Abu'l-Hasan 'Ali ibn Ahmad. *Diwan al-Mutanabbi: Sharh Abi'l-Hasan 'Ali ibn Ahmad al-Wahidi al-Nisaburi (The Collected Poetry of Abu'l-Tayyib al-Mutanabbi: Commentary by Abi'l-Hasan 'Ali ibn Ahmad al-Wahidi al-Nisaburi)*. Berlin, 1821.

al-Yaziji, Nazif. *al-'Arf al-Tayyib fi Sharh Diwan Abi'l-Tayyib (The Sweet Fragrance in Explaining the Diwan of Abu'l-Tayyib)*, 2 vols. Beirut: Dar Sadir.

The diwan (collected poetry) of al-Mutanabbi with commentary, listed by commentator:

Further Reading

Blachère, Régis. *Un Poète Arabe du IVᵉ Siècle de L'Hégire (Xᵉ Siècle de J.-C.): Abou t-Tayyib al-Motanabbi (Essai D'Histoire Littéraire) (An Arab Poet of the Fourth Century A.H. (Tenth Century A.D.): Abu'l-Tayyib al-Mutanabbi (An Essay in Literary History)*. Paris: Librairie d'Amérique et d'Orient, Adrien-Maisonneuve, 1935.

Hamori, Andras. *The Composition of Mutanabbi's Panegyrics to Sayf al-Dawla*. Leiden: E.J. Brill, 1992.

Heinrichs, Wolfhart. "The Meaning of *Mutanabbi*." In *Poetry and Prophecy: The Beginnings of a Literary Tradition*, ed. James L. Kugel. Ithaca, NY, 1990.

Husayn, Taha. *Ma'a al-Mutanabbi (With al-Mutanabbi)*, 12th ed. Cairo: Dar al-Ma'arif, 1980.

Latham, J.D. "Towards a Better Understanding of al-Mutanabbi's Poem on the Battle of al-Hadath." *Journal of Arabic Literature* X (1979): 1–22.

Shakir, Mahmud Muhammad. *al-Mutanabbi*, 2 vols. Cairo: Matba'at al-Madani, 1976.

MU'TAZILITES

The Mu'tazilites were a group of Muslim theologians that first appeared during the early eighth century and dominated Muslim theology during the ninth and tenth centuries. They emerged from the earlier group of Qadarites, who engaged in the theological dispute about human free will versus divine predestination. Qadarites, who were active in Basra, argued that humans have power (qadar) over their actions and are therefore morally responsible for them. They argued against a conservative group of scholars who held that the power to act lies with God, whose omnipotence determines human actions. Later Mu'tazilites claimed that, around the year 740 CE, the Basrian scholar Wasil ibn Ata' (699–749) disputed with his colleague 'Amr ibn 'Ubayd (699–761) and convinced him that the teaching of the prominent Qadarite Hasan al-Basri (642–728), namely that the grave sinner is an "unbeliever", is wrong. Wasil ibn Ata', together with 'Amr ibn 'Ubayd, is credited with having formed a new group that called itself "those who set themselves apart" *(al-mufitazila)*. The name *Mu'tazilites,* however, referred to a number of theologians and their students, and not all saw themselves as connected to Wasil and 'Amr; what brought them together was their rationalist approach toward Muslim theology. Various positions of this group developed into a school of thought that centered around five principles: (1) God's unity (tawhid); (2) God's justice (fiadl); (3) God's sincerity regarding the promised rewards and punishments for human deeds; (4) grave sinners should not be subject to legal sanctions as long they have committed no crime, although they should still be morally shunned ("the state between the two states"); and (5) the obligation to call for morally good deeds and forbid bad ones.

After the 'Abbasid revolution in 750, the Mu'tazilites became the leading theological direction in Basra and the new capital, Baghdad. Mu'tazilite theologians were favored by the early 'Abbasid caliphs, particularly by al-Ma'mun (r. 813–833) and his successors during the *mihna* (test). Although he himself was not committed to Mu'tazilite theology, al-Ma'mun unsuccessfully tried to force Muslim scholars to accept the Mu'tazilite position that the Qur'an had been created in time as opposed to being eternal. During the first half of the ninth century, leading proponents of the Mu'tazilites in Baghdad—most prominently Abu l-Hudhayl (d. 842) and al-Nazzam (d. ca. 840)—developed Mu'tazilite theology into a system that included explanations of physical processes, God's nature, His relationship with creation, and ethics. A second intellectual peak was reached during the turn from the tenth to the eleventh century, when a circle around the Qadi Abd al-Jabbar (d. 1025) in Rayy (modern Tehran, Iran) formulated the most comprehensive treatment of the school's theology. Although Mu'tazilites continued to be influential in regions on the edge of the Islamic world (in Yemen or in Khwarezm, modern north Uzbekistan), their influence on theological debates in the center diminished during the eleventh century. One of their last proponents was al-Zamakhshari (d. 1144), whose commentary on the Qur'an, *The Reconnoiterer (al-Kashshaf)*, had a great influence on all later books of this genre.

Mu'tazilite theology was part of Kalam, the rationalist technique of defending articles of faith. Although it stood under the influences of concepts in Greek philosophy, it developed quite independently thereof. The systematic character of Mu'tazilite theology focuses on the two principles of God's unity and God's justice. Mu'tazilites rejected all suggestions of anthropomorphism *(tashbih)* in the divine, and they taught that the relationship between God and his attributes *(sifat)* is totally unlike, for instance, that of humans and the attributes they have. God is believed to *be* the perfect mode of attributes like "knowing" or "just" that he ascribes to himself in the Qur'an. Al-Nazzam taught that "God is by himself continuously knowing, living, powerful, hearing, seeing, and eternal, not through a (separate) knowledge, power etc. (that he has)." God is perfect unity, and none of his attributes can be distinct from him. His attributes are not entities, like knowledge, that are inherent in Him as they are in the case of humans. The way in which God is "knowing," "powerful," or "just" is, according to the Mu'tazilites, different from what humans know as knowledge, power, and justice only through their deficiencies. Mu'tazilites maintained that divine justice, for instance, is the perfection of the kind of justice that is innately known to humans. They had to admit that destruction through natural disasters must be just punishment for immoral acts that could have been avoided. Acting according to the morals of the one justice that is both divine and human would, in turn, force God to grant salvation. Although this point led to the heavily moralistic outlook of the Mu'tazilite school, it also made it vulnerable to the attacks of Sunni theologians, mostly of the Ashfiarite school, who argue that humans can have no full knowledge of divine justice, or, more generally, no full knowledge of God's attributes as such.

FRANK GRIFFEL

Further Reading

Dhanani, Alnoor. *The Physical Theory of Kalam: Atoms, Space, and Void in Basrian Mufitazi Cosmology.* Leiden: Brill, 1994.

van Ess, Josef. *Theologie und Gesellschaft im 2. und 3. Jahrhundert Hidschra. Eine Geschichte des Religiösen Denkens im Frühen Islam*, 6 vols. Berlin and New York: De Gruyter, 1991–1997.

———. "Mu'tazilah." In *Encyclopedia of Religion*, ed. Mircea Elieade, vol. 10, 220–9. New York: Macmillian, 1987.

Gimaret, Daniel. "Mu'tazila." In *Encyclopaedia of Islam*, 2nd ed., vol. 7, 783–93. Leiden: Brill, 1993.

Hourani, George F. *Islamic Rationalism: The Ethics of Abd al-Jabbar.* Oxford, UK: Clarendon Press, 1971.

Martin, Richard C., Mark R. Woodward, and Dwi S. Atmaja. *Defenders of Reason in Islam. Mu'tazilism from Medieval School to Modern Symbol.* Oxford, UK: Oneworld, 1997.

Watt, William M. *The Formative Period of Islamic Thought.* Edinburgh: Edinburgh University Press, 1973.

Wolfson, Harry. *The Philosophy of the Kalam.* Cambridge, Mass: Harvard University Press, 1976.

MYSTICISM, JEWISH

Jewish mysticism, which is rooted in ancient biblical and rabbinic literature, is not exclusively limited to Qabbalah, which is the best known of its expressions. There existed pre-Qabbalistic forms of Jewish esotericism, some of which, like many of the later major developments of Qabbalah itself, flourished in an Islamic environment.

Beginnings in the East

Chronologically, it was Jewish mysticism that initially influenced Sufism. Although they recognize Neoplatonic and Christian influence on the evolution of early Sufi practice and doctrine, scholars have neglected the considerable impact of Jewish spirituality and piety on its formative period in Baghdad, the contemporary seat of great centers of Talmudic learning. Sufi hagiography has preserved many isrâ'îliyyât, edifying tales involving "the pious men from among the Children of Israel," which are traceable to rabbinic sources. These were supposedly transmitted through interreligious contacts or Jewish conversions to Islam, some of which took place precisely in Sufi circles in Baghdad, where Jews would attend lectures. Some scholars have dated to the post-Islamic era of the Ge'onim (ninth century CE) the composition of the enigmatic essay of Hebrew cosmogony, known as the Sefer yezirah or Book of Creation, which became the speculative framework of numerous systems of Jewish philosophy and mysticism. L. Massignon linked its cosmic semiotics and mystical phonetics to Arabic grammar and Shi'i gnosticism, a view that was recently defended by S. Wasserstrom. Its first recorded commentaries were composed in Judeo-Arabic between the ninth and thirteenth centuries and were of a philosophical and theological approach.

The Golden Age of Spain

Andalusia was a fertile terrain of intercultural exchange where Sufism flowered early during the tenth century, notably through the teachings of Ibn Masarrah (886–931), whose system involved the "science of letters." These arithmological speculations, known as *gematriyah,* were also a central part of Jewish exegesis and esotericism since Talmudic times (third to fourth centuries). Similarities between these two approaches suggest mutual interaction, probably in Muslim Spain, where this discipline was highly developed by Mulyî al-Dîn ibn Arabî (d. 1240), who reports that he discussed this subject with a Jewish rabbi. Sufi traces are perceptible in the religious poetry of the great Hispano-Hebrew bards, such as Solomon ibn Gabirol (d. ca. 1057) and Judah Halevi (1075–1141). The first Jewish medieval work to betray clear Sufi influence was, however, Balyâ ibn Paqûdâh's *Farâ'i al-Qulûb (Duties of the Hearts),* a treatise about ascetic theology that was composed in Arabic around 1080. It indicates the availability of Sufi sources in Muslim Spain, where it was the first fully fledged Sufi manual to have been composed. To revitalize Jewish ritual formalism, Balyâ devised a spiritual itinerary that follows the stages of the Sufi Path, although it rejects the possibility of union with God and eschews extreme forms of Sufi asceticism. One of the first classics of Judaeo-Arabic literature to be translated into Hebrew, it became an important channel for the percolation of Sufi notions in Jewish spirituality, remaining popular among Qabbalists and mystics right down to the eighteenth century. Drawing on al-Qushayrî's *Risâlah (Epistle)*, one of Sufism's basic textbooks, Joseph ibn 'Aqnîn's allegoric Arabic commentary (twelfth century) about the Song of Songs resembles a Sufi treatise about divine love.

His *Tibb al-Nufûs (Hygiene of the Souls)* quotes al-Junayd (d. 910) and Ibn Adham, referring to them by their Sufi epithets: Shaykh at-Tâ'ifah ("the elder of the community") and al-Ruĺânî al-Akmal ("the perfect spirit").

The Jewish Pietist Movement in Egypt

Through Ayyubid and Mamluk protectors, Sufism prospered in Egypt, attracting a host of charismatic figures, such as Abû'l-Hasan al-Shâdhilî (d. 1258), Muhammad al-Badawî (d. 1276), Abû' l-Abbâs al-Mursî (d. 1287), and Ibn Atâ' Allâh (d. 1309). Progressively institutionalized in the form of brotherhoods and monasteries (khanqâhs) in the urban centers, its infectious religious fervor had repercussions on the local Jewish populations, whose mystical receptivity had been heightened by the contemporary social and intellectual unrest. By the time of the great scholar Moses Maimonides (1135–1204), many Jews, who were referred to in contemporary documents as *hasîdîm* ("pious ones"), had already begun to adopt the Sufi way of life. This attraction is reflected in the numerous Sufi writings discovered in the Cairo Genizah, which include pages from the principal masters copied into Hebrew letters. The same source also yielded Sufi-inspired Jewish ethical manuals, theological treatises, definitions of mystical states, and exegetical works that reinterpreted scriptural narrative in harmony with Sufi doctrine, often portraying biblical figures as masters of the Sufi path. They are not, however, simple Judaized adaptations of Muslim texts but rather original compositions that were dexterously transposed in the biblical and rabbinic texture.

This pietistic tendency gained momentum with the appointment in 1213 of Abraham (1186–1237), the son of Moses Maimonides, as the spiritual leader *(nagîd)* of Egyptian Jewry. An ardent protagonist of Judeo-Sufi pietism, in his commentary on the *Pentateuch,* Abraham Maimonides depicted the ancient biblical characters as pietists in the same way as Sufi literature portrays the Prophet and his companions as Sufis. His *Kifâyat al-Âbidîn (Compendium for the Servants of God),* a monumental legal and ethical treatise, displays a strong propensity for mysticism of a non-Qabbalistic and manifestly Muslim type. He overtly expresses admiration for Sufis in whom he sees the heirs of ancient Israelite traditions. He wistfully acknowledges that the Sufi initiation ritual, which consists of the investiture of the master's cloak *(khirqah)* and the Sufi ascetic discipline as well as the necessity of spiritual guidance under an

accomplished master, were originally practiced by the prophets of Israel. Like al-Ghazâlî, Abraham Maimonides emphasized the spiritual significance of the precepts and their "mysteries," which were partly rediscovered in the traditions preserved by the Sufis. Calling themselves "the disciples of the prophets," the pietists adopted manifestly Muslim customs, believing that they were an integral part of an original "prophetic discipline," the restoration of which would hasten the promised return of prophecy. Clearly inspired by Muslim models, Abraham enacted several ritual "reforms" with the purpose of enhancing the decorum and purport of synagogue worship. Considered especially meritorious by Sufi authors, the ablution of hands and feet, although not strictly required by Jewish law, became a prerequisite to prayer.

Following Muslim custom, worshippers were arranged in rows and faced Jerusalem at all times during the synagogue service. He prescribed various postures during prayer, such as standing, kneeling, frequent bowing, the spreading of the hands, and weeping in supplication. In addition to canonical prayers, nightly vigils and daily fasts were instituted, as was solitary worship *(khalwah),* a practice that was characteristic of Sufism and that required retirement from society for protracted periods in an isolated and dark place. Although contrary to the Jewish tradition of communal prayer, Abraham Maimonides considered it to be of Hebrew origin. The hasidim also refer to *dhikr,* or "spiritual recollection," which is a typically Sufi ritual; so far, however, no details have been discovered describing how it was performed in Jewish circles. Because of their protracted devotions, the pietists established special prayer halls; Abraham Maimonides himself possessed his own private synagogue. Other pietist innovations included ascetic aspects. In contrast with traditional Jewish ethics, they advocated celibacy like certain Sufis, and they considered marriage and family responsibilities to be an impediment to spiritual fulfilment. The association of the Maimonides family with Sufi-type pietism endured for nearly two centuries. Abraham's own son, Obadyah Maimonides (1228–1265), showed strong leanings toward Sufism in his *al-Maqâla al-hawdiyyah (The Treatise of the Pool),* an ethico-mystical manual based on the typically Sufi comparison of the heart to a pool that must be cleansed before it can be filled with the vivifying waters of gnosis.

David ben Joshua (ca. 1335–1415), last known of the Maimonideans, was also interested in Sufism. The progressive, spiritual program presented in his Judeo-Arabic work *al-Murshid ila t-Tafarrud (The Guide to Detachment)* embodies the most far-reaching synthesis of traditional rabbinical and Sufi ethics. For example, since the first step on the path to perfection is motivated by the quest for light, he derives the initial stage, *zehîrût*, originally signifying in Hebrew "precaution," from the root *zhr* ("to shine"), following the Illuminationist notion of ish-râq. Certain Judeo-Sufi personalities were associated with the Maimonidean dynasty. Rabbi Hanan'el ben Samuel al-Amshâtî, not only a member of Abraham Maimonides' rabbinical court but also his father-in-law, authored exegetical works that resound with philosophical and Sufi notions. A committed pietist (several Genizah documents refer to him as *he-Îâsîd* [the pietist]), he actively defended the movement, although its novel practices and doctrines had come under attack. In his mystical commentary on the Song of Songs, Abraham Abû Rabî'a he-Îâsîd (d. 1223) interpreted the book as an allegorical dialogue between the mystic intoxicated with divine love and the object of his desire, the beatific vision. Despite Abraham Maimonides' political and religious prestige, the pietist movement, like many revivalist trends in religious history, met with virulent opposition.

The pietists were accused of introducing "false ideas," "unlawful changes," and "gentile (Sufi) customs," and they were even denounced to the Muslim authorities. Although Abraham excommunicated his opponents, opposition continued during the office as nâgîd of Abraham's son, David Maimonides (1222–1300), who, after the closure of his synagogue, was compelled to leave Egypt, seeking refuge in Akko. As a result of its elitist character, together with this opposition, the movement gradually disappeared with the general decline of Oriental Jewry.

Later Influences

Sufism continued sporadically to fascinate individual Jews. According to the biographer al-Kutubî, the thirteenth-century Sufi al-Hasan Ibn Hûd would study Maimonides' *Guide for the Perplexed* with the Jews of Damascus. The sixteenth-century Egyptian mystic al-Sha'arânî relates in his autobiography that Jews would attend his lectures and ask him to write amulets to protect their children. Qaraite Jews, perhaps through a kinship between Sufi asceticism and their own rather austere brand of ethics, showed an interest in Sufi writings, which they were still copying during the seventeenth century. Jews also maintained contact with Sufis in other localities. Fifteenth-century Yemenite Jews freely used Sufi concepts in their writings and quoted verses from the mystical poetry of the Sufi martyr al-Hallâj. Sufi concepts percolated into Jewish literature through Hebrew translations made in Spain and Provence, especially those of the works of al-Ghazâlî.

There were contacts between Sufis and Qabbalists in Morocco as related by the great Moroccan sixteenth-century Qabbalist David ha-Levi. Hebrew transcriptions of the poetry of Rûmî and Sa'dî contributed to the diffusion of Sufi ideas among Persian Jews, foreshadowing the exquisite rub'ayyât of Sarmad (d. 1661), a Persian Jew who became a wandering dervish in India.

The Early Kabbalists

Thirteenth-century disciples of the Qabbalist Abraham Abû'l-'Afiyah (d. ca. 1291) in the Holy Land show familiarity with Sufi practices that they directly observed. Isaac of Akko (ca. 1270–1340) in particular had knowledge of Sufi techniques, including solitary meditation (*khalwah;* Hebrew, *hitbôdedùt*) and the visualization of letters. He is an important link in the transmission of these methods to the later Qabbalists of Safed. Abû'l-'Afiyah may himself have encountered Sufis during his brief visit to Akko (Acre) around 1260 or elsewhere during the course of his wide travels. The focal point of his meditative discipline, which led to prophetic inspiration, is the practice of *hazkârâh*, a term that is itself strikingly reminiscent of the Arabic *dhikr*.

The Kabbalists of Safed

Evliya Chelebi testifies that sixteenth-century Safed was a vibrant Sufi center. Islamic influence has insufficiently been taken into account in the study of the Safed Qabbalistic school, which flourished under Rabbi Isaac Lurya (1534–1572), himself a native of Egypt. Among the most significant Sufi models that may lie behind some of the mystical rituals initiated by the Qabbalists are saint worship and the visitation of tombs, the formation of spiritual brotherhoods (*habûrôt*) around saints, and spiritual concerts (*baqashshôt*) consisting of the singing of paraliturgical poems (similar to the Sufi samâ' ceremony). Solitary meditation resurges in the *Sullam ha-'Aliyyâh* (*Ladder of Ascension*, a title that smacks of Sufism) by Judah al-Butînî (d. 1519) and the *Pardes Rimmônîm (Orchard of Pomegranates)* by Moses Cordovero (d. 1570). In his meditative method, which is practiced in dark places, the latter advocates Sufi-like techniques such as breathing control. Other techniques, which were subsequently transmitted to East European

Hasidim, include ritual purity, silence, fasting, restriction of sleep, and the ecstatic repetition of divine names.

The Shabbatians

Significant contact between mystics took place in Turkey and its provinces during the Ottoman era. These were intensified during the messianic turmoil roused by Shabbatay Zevi (d. 1675). During his confinement in Adrianople and after his outward conversion to Islam, Zevi would attend dhikr seances in the Bektashi convent at Hizirlik, and it seems that he established contact with the khalwatî mystic Muhammad al-Niyâzî (d. 1694). His apostate followers, known as the Doenme, continued to maintain close relations with the mystical brotherhoods in Turkey and in particular with the syncretistic Bektashis, from whom they borrowed certain rituals, Turkish liturgical poems, and melodies. As late as the nineteenth century, Doenme descendants such as the Mevlevi Ezzet Effendi were prominent in Sufi orders.

PAUL B. FENTON

See also Kabbala

Further Reading

Cohen, G. "The Soteriology of Abraham Maimuni." *Proceedings of the American Academy Jor Jewish Research* 35 (1967): 75–98; 36 (1968): 33–56.
Fenton, P.B. "Some Judaeo-Arabic Fragments by Rabbi Abraham he-Hasid, the Jewish Sufî." *Journal of Semitic Studies* 26 (1981): 47–72.
———. *The Treatise of the Pool, al-Maqâla al-Îawdiyya by 'Obadyah Maimonides.* London, 1981.
———. "The Literary Legacy of David II Maimuni." *Jewish Quarterly Review* 74 (1984): 1–56.
———. *Deux Traités de Mystique Juive.* Lagrasse, 1987.
———. "La Hitbôdedût Chez les Premiers Qabbalistes d'Orient et Chez les Soufis." In *Priere, Mystique et Judaïsme,* ed. R. Goetschel, 133–58. Paris, 1987.
———, ed. *al-Murshid ila t-Tafarrud by David Maimonides.* Jerusalem, 1987.
———. "Shabbatay Sebi and the Muslim Mystic Muhammad an-Niyâzi." *Approaches to Judaism in Medieval Times* 3 (1988): 81–8.
Goitein, S.D. "A Jewish Addict to Sufism in the Time of Nagid David II Maimonides." *Jewish Quarterly Review* 44 (1953–1954): 37–49.
———. "A Treatise in Defence of the Pietists." *Journal of Jewish Studies* 16 (1965): 105–14.
———. "Abraham Maimonides and his Pietist Circle." In *Jewish Medieval and Renaissance Studies,* ed. A. Altmann, 145–64. Cambridge, Mass, 1967.
Goldziher, I. "Ibn Hud, the Muhammadan Mystic, and the Jews of Damascus." *Jewish Quarterly Review* 6 (1893): 218–20.
Idel, M. *Abraham Abulafia and the Mystical Experience.* New York, 1988.
Rosenblatt, S., ed. *The High Ways to Perfection of Abraham Maimonides.* New York and Baltimore, 1927–1938.

MYTHICAL PLACES

Medieval Islamic culture abounded with stories, legends, and beliefs about mythical and imaginary places. Almost all such places were described as the result of travel, whether real or imagined. This helps to explain why most were to be found at the edges of the (then) known world: in the direction of China and Japan to the far east (e.g., Roc Island); in the colder climes of the Nordic lands (e.g., the Sea of Karkar); and especially in the Indian Ocean (viewed by Ptolemy as an "encompassing sea"), both to the south (e.g., Camphor Island) and in Southeast Asia (e.g., Zabaj). Desert and mountain locations include Hush, the land of the jinn, and Mount Qaf, respectively.

The principal medieval Islamic sources for information about mythical places include travel accounts, such as *Akhbar al-Sin wal-Hind (Accounts of China and India)* by Sulayman the Merchant (ca. ninth century), written in 850; mariners' tales and works about navigation, such as *'Aja'ib al-Hind (Book of the Wonders of India)* by Buzurg ibn Shahriyar (d. 1009), written in 953; works of regional and world geography, such as *Kitab al-Buldan (Book of Regions)*, written around 903 by Ibn al-Faqih al-Hamadhani (ca. early tenth century), and the anonymous Persian *Hudud al-'Alam (The Regions of the World)*, written around 982; cosmographical works—more often than not in the marvels and wonders genre ('aja'ib; Latin, mirabilia)—such as *'Aja'ib al-Makhluqat (Wonders of Regions)* by al-Qazwini (d. 1283) and the Ottoman Turkish *Dürr-i Meknun (The Well-Preserved Pearl)* by Yazidi-oghlu Ahmed Bijan (d. ca. 1456); and, finally, popular and folk literature, such as *Alf Layla wa-Layla (The Thousand and One Nights)*.

The mythical places of the medieval Islamic imagination may be classified into three broad categories: (1) places that are liminal, typically at the ends of the earth or at the edge of the known world (e.g., the City of Brass); (2) places where things are topsy-turvy and normative rules are suspended (e.g., the Island of Connubial Sacrifice); and (3) places that are habitats for unusual creatures or inhabitants (e.g., the land of Gog and Magog). These categories are by no means mutually exclusive. The islands of Waqwaq typify the mythical place and occur, moreover, in all types of sources, which place them everywhere, from the southwest Indian ocean to the Indonesia archipelago and even as far as Japan. In most cases, dark or dangerous waters surround the islands. Descriptions of Waqwaq range from a land inhabited by ingenious and treacherous inhabitants to the home of the Waqwaq tree, whose fruit is women. Waqwaq is not, however, to be found in the North, unlike Artha (or Arthaniya), a city described in the *Risala (Epistle)*, an account of a journey up the Volga by the diplomatic envoy Ibn Fadlan (c. early tenth century). In Artha, the sun never sets, and the inhabitants are said to eat strangers, a story that may have circulated to protect valuable trade routes.

Artha and Waqwaq, like so many of the mythical locations described in medieval Islamic sources, probably had their origin in real places but were then transformed into mythical ones with a hold on the imagination that has been both enduring and, from the perspective of medieval literature and art, also richly rewarding.

SHAWKAT M. TOORAWA

See also Folklore and Ethnology; Heaven; Hell; Stories and Storytelling; Trade

Primary Sources

Anonymous. *Hudud al-'Alam (The Regions of the World): A Persian Geography, 372 A.H.–982 A.D.*, transl. V. Minorsky. Oxford: E.J.W. Gibb Memorial Trust; London: Luzac, 1937. Reprinted Karachi: Indus Publications, 1980.

———. *Alf Layla wa-Layla (The Arabian Nights)*, transl. Husain Haddawy (based on the text of the fourteenth-century Syrian manuscript edited by Muhsin Mahdi). New York: Norton, 1990.

———. *Sirat Sayf ibn Dhi Yazan (The Adventures of Sayf Ben Dhi Yazan, an Arab Folk Epic)*, transl. Lena Jayyusi. Bloomington, Ind: Indiana University Press, 1996.

Bijan, Yazidi-oghlu Ahmed. *Dürr-i Meknun (The Well-preserved Pearl)*, ed. Necdet Sakaoghlu. Istanbul: Tarih Vakfı Yurt Yayınları, 1999.

Ibn Fadlan. "al-Risala – 'La Relation du Voyage d'Ibn Fadlân chez les Bulgares de la Volga'," transl. Marius Canard. *Annales de l'Institut d'Etudes Orientales de l'Université d'Alger* (1958): 41–116.

Ibn al-Faqih al-Hamadhani. *Kitab al-Buldan (Book of Regions)*, ed. M. de Goeje. Leiden: E.J. Brill, 1885.

Ibn Muhammad al-Qazwini, Zakariya. *'Aja'ib al-Makhluqat (The Wonders of Creation)*. Cairo: Mustafa al-Babi al-Halabi and Sons, 1956.

Ibn Shahriyar, Buzurg. *Kitab 'Aja'ib al-Hind (The Book of the Wonders of India: Mainland, Sea, and Islands)*, ed. and transl. G.S.P. Freeman-Grenville. London: East-West Publications, 1981.

"Sulayman al-Tajir, Akhbar al-Sin wal-Hind." In *Arabic Classical Accounts of India and China*, transl. S. Maqbul Ahmad. Shimla: Indian Institute of Advanced, 1989.

Further Reading

Allibert, Claude, "L'Ile des Femmes dans les Recits Arabes." *Etudes Océan Indien* 15 (1997): 261–67.

Deluz, Christiane. *Le Livre de Jehan de Mandeville. Une "Géographie" du XIVè Siècle*, 75–86. Louvain-la-Neuve: Institut d'Études Médiévales de l'Université Catholique de Louvain, 1988.

Ferrand, Gabriel. *Relation de Voyages et Textes Géograhpiques Arabes, Persans et Turcs Relatifs à l'Extrême-Orient du VIIIè au XVIIIè Siècles*, 2 vols. Paris: E. Leroux, 1913–1914.

Manguel, Albert, and Gianni Guadalupi. *The Dictionary of Imaginary Places*, 2nd ed. San Diego, Calif: Harcourt Brace, 1999.

Maqbul Ahmed, S., and Fr. Taeschner. "Djughrafiya, Geography." In *Encyclopaedia of Islam*, 2nd ed., eds. H.A.R. Gibb et al., vol. 2: 575–90. Leiden: Brill, 1957.

Miquel, André. *La Géographie Humaine du Monde Musulman Jusqu'au Milieu du 11è Siècle*, 4 vols., vol. 2, 482–513. Paris, The Hague: Mouton & Co., 1973–1988.

Toorawa, Shawkat M. "Wâq al-Wâq: Fabulous, Fabular, Indian Ocean (?) Islands...." *Emergences* 10 (2000): 387–402.

N

NAFS AL-ZAKIYYA

Muhammad b. Abdallah b. al-Hasan b. al-Hasan b. 'Ali b. Abi Kalib is believed to have been born in the year AH 92/710–711 CE. Shi'i sources, however—as well as many Sunni sources—give the year as AH 100, which is dubious because of its messianic connotations.

Abdallah b. al-Hasan, his father, was the head of the Hasanid family and a figure who was respected by the entire Hashimid family. His mother was Hind bnt. Abi 'Ubayda b. Abdallah b. Zam'a b. al-Aswad b. al-Muyyalib b. Asad b. 'Abd al-'Uzza b. Qusayy. Her father, Abu 'Ubayda, was one of the leading figures of Quraysh.

Muhammad had nine brothers and five sisters from three different mothers. Abdallah b. al-Hasan's family had a house in al-Madina, although evidently the family's main place of residence was a large estate near al-Madina called Suwayqa or Farsh Suwayqa. Muhammad had two wives and three concubines, who bore him seven sons and two daughters. The best known among his children was 'Abdallah, called al-Ashtar.

Little is known about Muhammad's education. It seems that his father sought to give his sons Muhammad and Ibrahim a formal knowledge of *hadith* (tradition) and *fiqh*. However, Muhammad was not known for any kind of scholarship; in the books of *rijal* (transmitters) of Hadith he is mentioned as a minor transmitter.

Muhammad is described as having a large body, great strength, and a very dark complexion. On his face he had the scars of smallpox *(al-judari)*. In the middle of his shoulders, he had a black mole that was the size of an egg, and he stuttered when he talked. Some of the physical traits attributed to Muhammad b. 'Abdallah were similar to those of the Prophet Muhammad, and the resemblance to Moses is also apparent (e.g., stuttering). Traditions depicting his physical as well as spiritual–religious traits were disseminated, circulated, and transmitted by pro-Shi'i scholars, family members of the Hasanids (some of them belonging to the most inner and close circle of Muhammad b. Abdallah's supporters), and other sections of the 'Alid family.

The accepted tradition is that Muhammad b. 'Abdallah was already called al-Mahdi ("The Messiah") and al-Nafs al-Zakiyya ("The Pure Soul") during the Umayyad period. Clearly, at the time of his death, both names were in current use.

There is little information about Muhammad from the Umayyad period. What there is deals for the most part with one subject: the political aspirations that Abdallah b. al-Hasan had for his son, Muhammad (or Muhammad and his brother Ibrahim), which included fostering a recognition of Muhammad among Banu Hashim as the most deserving candidate for the caliphate.

It is highly plausible that these traditions were created and disseminated after the rebellion of Muhammad b. Abdallah against the 'Abbasids in 145/762 and possibly already for a short period before the rebellion.

The 'Abbasid Period

In several traditions, it is said that Muhammad never ceased promoting himself as a candidate for the caliphate, even during the rule of Abu 'l-'Abbas al-Saffah (r. 132/750–136/754). He and his brother Ibrahim remained in hiding and did not appear before the caliph, despite the caliph's request for them to do so and despite his most generous attitude toward their father, Abdallah b. al-Hasan, the Hasanid family, and the 'Alids in general.

After the year 136/754, when allegiance was sworn to al-Mansour until the breaking of the revolt in Rajab in 145/762, Muhammad and his brother Ibrahim refrained from appearing before al-Mansour. They remained in hiding and did not swear allegiance to the caliph. At the end of the year 140/758, al-Mansour ordered that Muhammad's father be put under house arrest in al-Madina, along with some of his family members. They remained under arrest in al-Madina until the end of 144/762. Between the years 140 and 144—and especially between 143/760–761 and 145/762, during the governorship of Riyah b. 'Uthman—pursuit of the two brothers intensified. At the end of 144, Abdallah b. al-Hasan, his brothers, and their children were taken to al-Hashimiyya near al-Kufa and put in prison. This brought Muhammad out in open rebellion.

Muhammad strove to give the rebellion as broad a character as possible and to extend it to other regions beyond the borders of the Arab Peninsula. Actual attempts were made in Egypt, Syria (to a small extent), and apparently also in al-Basra and al-Kufa. However, other than those of several individuals, no missions of aid are known to have been sent to Muhammad from these cities.

Muhammad b. Abdallah entered al-Madina, openly proclaiming rebellion, on the twenty-eighth of Jumada II, 145 (23 September 762). His takeover of the city did not meet with any significant resistance. Immediately upon entering the city, he freed the prisoners from jail, arrested the 'Abbasid governor and the mawali of the 'Abbasid family, confiscated the properties of the 'Abbasids in the city, and took over bayt al-mal. Another important source of finance for the rebellion was the money given to Muhammad by one of the dignitaries of al-Madina: the total sadaqa of the Óayyi' and Asad tribes, which he had collected for the 'Abbasids. Muhammad wanted to administer the city as the capital of the caliphate and, to that end, he established a series of administrative and judiciary posts. He sent his brother Ibrahim to al-Basra, where he raised the banner of rebellion on Ramadan 1, 145 (November 762). At the same time, Muhammad sent governors to all parts of the Arabian Peninsula.

Al-Mansour's letter to Muhammad b. Abdallah, suggesting that he accept an aman, evoked a strong reply from Muhammad. These letters may very well be authentic, but even if they are not, they are very early and of great importance in that they reflect the early arguments of the 'Abbasids and the Hasanids with regard to who had the legitimate right to rule.

Al-Mansour sent his nephew, 'Isa b. Musa, to head a strong army that was composed mainly of Ahl Khurasan units against Muhammad. At the beginning of the rebellion, most of the inhabitants of al-Madina supported Muhammad. However, this support was not uniform; there were those who opposed the rebellion, even among his close family, among the rest of the 'Alid families, and among the important families of Quraysh. In the Zubayrid and 'Umari (the descendants of 'Umar b. al-Khassab) families, however, there was general homogeneity with respect to supporting Muhammad, with just a small opposition. The Zubayrids constituted the main military and administrative backbone of the rebellion. Also noted among Muhammad's supporters are families and individuals from Arab tribes: the Juhayna, Sulaym, Bakr, Aslam, Ghifar, Numayr (mawali), and Bahila (mawali).

Several of the important religious scholars (*'ulama*) of this period from al-Madina as well as from other cities supported and joined the rebellion. Some of them had Shi'i tendencies, although a large number were not pro-Shi'i. Noted among them are Malik b. Anas, Sufyan al-Thawri, Abu Hanifa, Hisham b. 'Urwa b. al-Zubayr, and others. When this list of scholars is examined, it becomes clear that, for at least some of them, their leanings toward the rebellion and their support of Muhammad is not at all unequivocal. It is noteworthy that Ja'far al-Sadiq did not support Muhammad and his rebellion, although despite this there are a number of people belonging to Ja'far's immediate family who took an active part in the uprising. First and foremost, his sons Musa and Abdallah and his brother's son Hamza b. Abdallah should be mentioned, but there were also other Husaynids, all uncles and cousins of Ja'far al-Sadiq, who participated in the rebellion.

After their rise to power, tense relations and hostility prevailed between the 'Abbasids and Ja'far al-Sadiq. Their fear no doubt greatly increased seeing that the Husaynid family was neither united in their attitude toward the rebellion nor, evidently, in backing Ja'far al-Sadiq's leadership. They were displeased with Ja'far's quietism during the rebellion. His refraining to appear openly before 'Isa b. Musa as a sign of loyalty to the 'Abbasids led to the confiscation of

Ja'far's estate, 'Ayn Abi Ziyad, with the approval of al-Mansour, who also ordered his house in Medina to be burned down.

Muhammad b. Abdallah was considered the sixth or seventh imam of the Zaydis. During this period, there was a body in al-Kufa that was noted in the sources as Zaydiyya, the nucleus of which was made up of supporters of Zayd b. 'Ali b. al-Husayn b. 'Ali b. Abi Talib. This group constituted the important nucleus of Ibrahim b. Abdallah's army, although no mention is made of it in connection with Muhammad's rebellion. Evaluating the rebellion as a Zaydi–Hasani rebellion fully supported by the Mu'tazila is too general and inaccurate.

With the arrival of 'Isa b. Musa's army at the approaches of al-Madina, most of Muhammad's supporters abandoned him. At various stages of the battle, particularly at the end, several senior commanders and many soldiers ran away. The final battle took place at Ahjar al-Zayt, to the south of Thaniyyat al-Wada', on the fourteenth or fifteenth day of Ramadan 145 (sixth or seventh of December 762). Because of their numeric and qualitative inferiority, the battle quickly ended in the defeat of Muhammad's men. His head was sent to Caliph al-Mansour; his dead warriors were crucified in two rows in the city and left there for three days. Throughout his entire rule, al-Mansour never stopped persecuting members of the Hasanid family and Muhammad b. Abdallah's supporters. He ordered the confiscation of all of the estates of Banu Hasan and an estate of Ja'far al-Sadiq, who only had it returned to him by Caliph al-Mahdi.

Throughout the Umayyad Caliphate and particularly during the reign of Hisham b. 'Abd al-Malik (105/724–125/743), there was a slow decline in the economic and geopolitical status of Medina. With the 'Abbasids' rise to power, this process was accelerated by the deliberate policy of the first two 'Abbasid caliphs.

Despite the limited strategic importance of Medina for the 'Abbasids, they took the rebellion very seriously, because, to a certain extent, Muhammad b. Abdallah succeeded in extending it past the borders of the Arabian Peninsula and thus constituted a real danger to the 'Abbasid regime. Above all, the rebellion was a challenge to their right to rule. Participation of the Quraysh families in al-Madina (particularly the Zubayrids, who had a history of hostility towards the 'Alids), the 'Umaris, the Ansar, and some of the tribes in al-Madina and its environs in the rebellion—as well as the support of scholars who were not known to be pro-Shi'i—all speak against an exclusive Shi'i tinge to the rebellion.

Nevertheless, the fact that the rebellion was headed by Muhammad b. Abdallah was of great importance. His lineage and claim to the right to rule competed successfully with the arguments for the legitimacy of the 'Abbasids, which at that time were in a stage of transition from the legitimacy of the 'Alid-Hashimiyya to that of al-'Abbas, the Prophet's uncle. Muhammad b. Abdallah's rebellion accelerated the development of the 'Abbasid ideology of legitimacy relating to al-'Abbas and was an important turning point in the relationship between the 'Abbasids and the branches of the 'Alid family, particularly the Zaydis and the Hasanids. It is also very likely that it hastened the development of the qu'ud doctrine of the Husaynids.

AMIKAM ELAD

Primary Sources

Al-Tabari. *Taqrikh al-Rusul wa-al-Mulk*, ed. M.J. de Goeje, vol. III, 143–265, 282–318. Leiden. E.J. Brill, 1879–1901. (New printing, Leiden, 1964.)

B. Shabba, 'Umar. *Kitab Muhammad wa-Ibrahim Ibnay Abdallah b. Hasan*, transl. T. Nagel. *Der Islam* XLVI (1970): 227–234.

Muth, F.C. *Der Kalif al-Mansour im Anfang Seines Kalifats (136/754 bis 145/762)*, ed. Peter Lang, 62–198. Frankfurt am Main, 1987.

The History of al-Tabari, Vol. XXVIII. Abbasid Authority Affirmed: The Early Years of al-Mansour AD 753–763/ A.H. 136–145, 84–231, 252–92. New York: State University of New York Press, 1995.

al-Faraj al-Isfahani, Abu. *Maqatil al-Talibiyyin*, 179–399. Cairo, 1949.

Al-Baladhuri, Ahmad b. Yahya. *Ansab al-Ashraf*, vol. II, 507–38, ed. W. Madelung. Beirut and Berlin, 2003.

———. *Ansab al-Ashraf*, vol. III, ed. A.A. Duri. Beirut, 1978.

Idem, vol. III (ed. Muhammad Baqir al-Mahmudi, biographies of the descendants of al-Hasan and Husayn), Beirut, Dar al-Ta'aruf li-al-MaÔbu'At, 1977, Index, esp. 75-141; idem, vol. III (ed. S. Zakkar and R. Zirikli), Beirut, Dar al-Fikr, 1417/1996, pp. 1239–1277.

Anonymous. *Fragmenta Historicorum Arabicorum*, ed. M.J. De Goeje, vol. I, 230–56. 1869.

B. KhayyaÔ al-'Usfuri, Khalifa. *Taqrikh*, ed. Suhayl Zakkar, vol. II, 648–50. Damascus, 1968.

ed. Akram Âiyaq al-'Umari, vol. II, al-Najaf, 1967, pp. 449–451.

B. Habib, Muhammad. *Kitab al-Muhabbar*, ed. Ilse Lichtenstaedter, Index. Hyderabad, 1942.

———. "Asmaa al-Mughtallin min al-Ashraf fi al-Jahiliyya wa-al-Islam wa-Asmaa man Kutila min al-Shu'ara." In *NawAdir al-MakhÔuÔat2*, ed. 'Abd al-Salam Muhammad Harun, vol. VI, 189–90, 192, 207, 271–2. Cairo, 1973.

Al-Mubarrad, Muhammad b. Yazid. *al-Kitab al-Kamil*, ed. W. Wright, Index, 786–90. Leipzig, 1864.

Al-Ya'qubi, Ahmad b. Abi Ya'qub b. Ja'far b. Wahb. *Taqrikh*, vol. II, 445–56. Leiden, 1882.

Ibn Qutayba, Abdallah b. Muslim. *'Uyun al-Akhbar*, Index. Cairo, 1924–1930.

Al-Kindi, Abu 'Umar Muhammad b. Yusuf. *Kitab al-Wulat wa-Kitab al-QuÃat,* ed. R. Guest, 111–6, 361–2. Beirut, 1908; Leiden, E.J. Brill, 1912.

Al-Mas'udi, Abu al-Hasan, 'Ali b. al-Hasan b. 'Ali al-Mas'udi. *Muruj al-Dhahab wa-ma'Adin al-Jawhar,* ed. C. Pellat, vol. IV, 2401–13. Beirut, 1973.

Al-Isfahani, 'Ali b. Husayn Abu al-Faraj al-Isfahani. *Kitab al-Aghani,* Index. Bulaq, 1284–1285 H.; Cairo, Dar al-Kutub al-Misriyya, 1345/1927.

Al-Tanukhi, Abu 'Ali al-Muhsin b. 'Ali, *Kitab al-Faraj ba'da al-Shidda,* ed. 'Abbud al-Shaliji, Index. Beirut, Dar Ñadir, 1978.

Ibn 'Abd Rabbihi, Ahmad b. Muhammad. *Kitab al-'Iqd al-Farid,* Index, vol. 5, 74–89. Cairo, 1940–1953.

Abu al-'Arab, Muhammad b. Ahmad b. Tamim. *Kitab al-Mihan,* ed. Yahya Wuhayb al-Jabburi, Index. Dar al-Gharb al-Islaai, 1983.

Ibn al-Athir, 'Ali b. Muhammad b. al-Athir, 'Izz al-Din. *Al-Kamil fi al-Taqrikh,* ed. C.J. Tornberg, vol. V, 390–425, 428–37. Leiden, 1863–1871.

———. *Al-Kamil fi al-Taqrikh,* vol. V, 513–27, 529–55, 560–71. Beirut, Dar Sadir-Dar Beirut, 1402/1982.

Sibt b. al-Jawzi, Yusuf b. Kizolghlu. *Mirqat al-Zaman.* Manuscript of the British Library. Add. 23, 277, fols. 274b–7b, 280a–5a.

Ibn Kathir, Abu al-Fidaq Isma'il b. 'Umar. *al-Bidaya wa-al-Nihaya fi al-Taqrikh,* vol. X, 80–7. Cairo, MaÔba'at al-Sa'ada, 1351–1358 H.

Al-Maqrizi, Ahmad b. 'Ali. *Kitab al-Niza' wa-al-Takhasum Fima Bayna Bani Umayya wa-Bani Hashim,* 56–9. Leiden, 1888.

Ibn Taghribirdi, Jamal al-Din, Abu 'l-Masasin, Yusuf b. Taghribirdi. *al-Nujum al-Ûahira fi Muluk Misr wa-al-Qahira,* vol. I, 349, 352–3; vol. II, 1–4. Cairo, 1929–1930.

Ibn Sa'd, Muhammad b. Sa'd. *al-Óabaqat al-Kubra (al-Qism al-Mutammim li-Tabi'iyy Ahl al-Madina wa-man ba'Dahum min rub' al-Óabaqa al-Thalitha ila Muntasaf al-Óabaqa al-Sadisa²),* ed. Ziyad Muhammad Mansour, 250–9, 372–81. al-Madina, Maktabat al-'Ulum wa-al-Hikam, 1408/1987.

Ibn Abi Hatim, Abu Muhammad 'Abd al-Rahman b. Abi Hatim al-Razi. *Kitab al-Jari wa-al-Ta'dil.* Hyderabad, 1371–1373 H.; Beirut. Dar IÎyaÞ al-Turath al-'Arabi, 1271/1952.

Ibn 'Asakir, Abu al-Qasim, 'Ali b. al-Hasan [known as] Ibn 'Asakir. *Taqrikh Madinat Dimashq,* ed. 'Umar b. Gharama al-'Amra[w]I), vol. XXVII, 364–90; vol. XXXII, 298–348. Beirut, Dar al-Fikr, li-al-Siba'a wa-al-Nashr wa-al-Tawzi', 1415/1995–2002; Ms. 'Atif Ef., 1817.

Ibn Hajar al-'Asqalani, Ahmad b. 'Ali Shihab al-Din, Abu al-FaÃl, Ibn Hajar al-'Asqalani. *Tahdhib al-Tahdhib.* Hyderabad, 1325–1327 H.; Beirut: Dar al-Fikr, 1404/1984.

Al-Mizzi, Jamal al-Din, Abu al-Hajjaj, Yusuf al-Mizzi. *Tahdhib al-Kamal fi AsmaÞ al-Rijal,* ed. Bashshar 'Awwad Ma'ruf. Beirut, MuÞassasat al-Risala, 1985–1992.

Al-Dhahabi, Muhammad b. Ahmad, Shams al-Din al-DhahAbi. *Mizan al-i'Tidal,* ed. 'Ali Muhammad Mu'awwaÃ and AÎmad 'Abd al-Mawjud. Beirut: Dar al-Kutub al-'Ilmiyya, 1995.

———. *Siyar a'lAm al-nubalAÞ,* vol. VI, 210–24. Beirut, MuÞssasat al-Risala, 1982–1985.

———. *Taqrikh al-Islam wa-Wafayat al-Mashahir wa-al-A'lam,* ed. 'Umar 'Abd al-Salam Tadmuri, 14–44. Beirut: Dar al-Kitab al-'Arabi, 1408/1988.

Further Reading

el-'Ali, Ñalî. "Mulkiyyat al-AraÃi fi al-Hijaz fi al-Qarn al-Awwal al-Hijri." *Majallat al-'Arab* III (1969): 961–1005.

Arazi, A. "Materiaux pour L'Etude du Conflit de Préséance Entre la Mekke et Medine." *Jerusalem Studies in Arabic and Islam* V (1984): 177–235.

Crone, P. "On the Meaning of the Abbasid Call to al-RiÃa." In *The Islamic World from Classical to Modern Times, Essays in Honor of Bernard Lewis,* eds. CE Bosworth et al., 95–111, 99–100, 108. Princeton, NJ, 1989.

Hasan, Sa'd Muhammad. *al-Mahdi fi al-Islam...,* 112–28. Cairo, 1373/1953.

Jafri, Husain M. *Origins and Early Development of Shi'a Islam,* Index, 259–83. London and New York, 1979.

Kennedy, H. *The Early Abbasid Caliphate,* 66–70. London, Croom Helm, 1981.

Lassner, J. "Provincial Administration Under the Early Abbasids: Abu Ja'far al-Mansour and the Governors of the Haramayn." *Studia Islamica* XLIX (1979): 39–54.

———. *The Shaping of Abbasid Rule,* 69–87. Princeton, NJ, 1980.

al-Laythi, Samira Mukhtar. *Jihad al-Shi'a fi al-'Asr al-'Abbasi al-Awwal,* Chapter II. Beirut: Dar al-Jil, 1396/1976.

Madelung, W. *Der Imam al-Qasim Ibn Ibrahim und die Glaubenslehre Zaiditen,* Index. Berlin, 1965.

———. "al-Mahdi." In *EI²*.

Momen, M. *An Introduction to Shi'i Islam: The History and Doctrine of Twelver Shi'ism,* Index. New Haven and London, Yale University Press, 1985.

Nagel, T. "Ein Früher Bricht über den Aufstand von Muhammad b. Abdallah im Jahre 145 h." *Der Islam* XLVI (1970): 227–62.

Nöldeke, T. "Der Chalif Mansour." In *Orientalische Skizzen,* 126–34. Berlin, 1892. (English translation: *Sketches from Eastern History,* 120–9. London, 1892.)

Omar, F. *The Abbasid Caliphate 132/750–170/786,* 223–39, 240–8. Baghdad, 1969.

———. "al-Rasa'il al-Mutabadila Bayna al-Mansour wa-Muhammad Dhi al-Nafs al-Zakiyya." In *Majallat al-'Arab,* vol. V, 17–36. 1970.

———. "al-Rasa'il al-Mutabadila Bayna al-Mansour wa-Muhammad Dhi al-Nafs al-Zakiyya." In *BuÎuth fi al-TaqrIkh al-'Abbasi,* 92–110. Beirut and Baghdad, 1977.

Sharon, M. *Black Banners from the East: The Establishment of the Abbasid State, Incubation of a Revolt,* 87, 90–3, 96–9. Jerusalem, The Magnes Press; Leiden: E.J. Brill, 1983.

———. *Revolt: The Social and Military Aspects of the Abbasid Revolution,* 225–6, 238–9. Jerusalem, The Max Schloessinger Memorial Fund, The Hebrew University, 1990.

Tucker, W. "Rebels and Gnostics, al-Mughira Ibn Sa'id and the MughIriyya" *Arabica* XXII (1975): 33–47.

———. "Abu Mansour al-'Ijli and the Mansouriyya: A Study in Medieval Terrorism." *Der Islam* LIV (1977): 66–76.

Traini, R. "La Corrispondenza tra al-Mansour e Muhammad an-Nafs az-Zakiyya." In *Annali del Instituto Universitario Orientale di Napoli,* vol. XIV, 773–98. 1964.

Van Arendonk, C. *Les Debut de l'Imamat Zaidite au Yemen,* transl. J. Ryckmans, 45–57. Leiden: E.J. Brill, 1960.

van Vloten, G. *Zur Abbasidengeschichte, ZDMG,* vol. LII, 213–22. 1898.

Zaki Ñafwat, A. *Jamharat RasaÞil al-'Arab fi Þl-'Usur al-'ArAbiyya al-Zahira,* vol. III, 84–96. 1356/1937.

NAMES

The parts of a medieval Arabic name are best demonstrated by an example. The great mystical writer Ibn 'Arabi had the proper name *(ism 'alam)* Muhammad, the *kunya* Abu 'Abd Allah ("the father of 'Abd Allah"; "paedonymic" would be the normal English word for this, if one existed), the *nasab* ibn 'Ali ibn Muhammad ("the son of 'Ali the son of Muhammad"), the nickname *(laqab)* Muhyi 'l-Din ("the reviver of the faith"), and the *nisbas* al-Hatimi and al-Ta'i, since his family claimed descent from a man of pre-Islamic Arabia named Hatim of the Tayy tribe. Most biographical dictionaries arrange their subjects in alphabetical order by proper name, then father's name, and so on, but the 'urf by which someone is best known may happen to be any part of the name: Abu Hanifa (kunya), Fatima bint Muhammad (name with nasab), Ibn Sa'd (nasab to the father), Ibn Khaldun (nasab to a remote ancestor), Shajar al-Durr (laqab), al-Mas'udi (nisba to a remote ancestor), al-Qazwini (nisba to a city), and al-Mawardi (nisba to a trade). It was normally most polite to address someone by kunya, and women are often known only by kunya.

Hadith (tradition) recommends the names 'Abd Allah and 'Abd al-Rahman as those God likes best, and it is also advised to name one's children after prophets. Although not otherwise encouraged by Islamic law, Arabic personal names have always been most popular among Muslims, followed by Persian and Turkish personal names (many of which are now common in the Arab world as well).

CHRISTOPHER MELCHERT

Further Reading

Caetani, Leone, and Giuseppe Gabrieli. *Onomasticon Arabicum,* 2 vols. Rome: Casa Editrice Italiana, 1915.
Schimmel, Annemarie. *Islamic Names. Islamic Surveys.* Edinburgh: University Press, 1989.
Sublet, Jacqueline. *Le Voile du Nom.* Paris: Presses Universitaires de France, 1991.

NAVIGATION

The Arabic term that denotes navigation is *milaha,* which signifies in a broader sense seafaring or in a narrower connotation the sailor's act of determining the vessel's position, location, and course to the destination. The sunna of the Prophet (his sayings and doings) and the Qur'an do not prohibit Muslims from sailing the seas. The Qur'an urges Muslims to consider navigating as well as exploiting the rich resources of the sea. Likewise, the sunna comprises hundreds of hadiths that exhort Muslims to organize maritime expeditions, to sail to Mecca on pilgrimage, to exploit marine resources, and to expand overseas trade. Regarding military operations at sea, Prophetic traditions give more credit to Muslim naval warriors and amphibious troops than to holy warriors who fight on land. One hadith says that "a maritime expedition is better than ten campaigns of conquest on land." The Prophet also said that "a day at sea is equivalent to one month on land, and a martyr at sea is like two martyrs on land" and that "those who perish while fighting at sea will receive double the compensation of those fighting on land." Al-Shaybani added that "any Muslim who takes part in a sea expedition would be doubly compensated (rewarded) and that once the soldier puts his foot on ship all his sins are forgiven as if he were born anew." This emphasis on the double reward might reflect the legacy of a traditional fear of the sea and the necessity for encouraging recruitment for a religious war (jihad) at sea. Maritime expeditions were regarded as very risky owing to unreliable weather and the naval power and maneuvers of the enemy, but these factors did not allow a soldier to flee the scene of the battle unless the Muslim admiral commanded his flotilla to withdraw collectively.

Although the Arabs had long been acquainted with the sea and had sailed for centuries through the Red Sea, the Persian Gulf, and the Indian Ocean using different types of ships and nautical techniques, it seems that they emerged as a global sea power after the Islamic military advents on the eastern and western fronts. Within less than a century of the emergence of Islam in Arabia, the Prophet's followers dominated more than half of the maritime possessions of their former neighbors. The eastern, western, and southern shores of the Mediterranean Sea were entirely under Islamic dominion, as were the Red Sea, the Persian Gulf, and parts of the coast of the Indian Ocean. The Islamic expansions in the east and west united the former Persian and Byzantine territories that had been split by the successors of Alexander the Great (356–323 BCE). Owing to this new political unity, commercial activity between the Far East and the Mediterranean greatly expanded. As evidence, al-Biruni reports the following:

"... the power of the Muslim state and its extension from the al-Andalus in the west to the outermost reaches of China and Central India in the east, and from Abyssinia and Bilad al-Zinj (East Africa) in the south to the Slav and

Turkish land in the north enabled many nations to live together in intimacy, without allowing outsiders to bother them or to interrupt traffic. Other peoples who were non-Muslims and still pagans came to regard the Muslim state and its people with respect."

(Nazmi, *Commercial Relations*, p. 54)

Muslim caliphs, especially the Umayyads, maintained all dockyards and naval bases and the former administrative system of Rome and Byzantium in the southern shores of the Mediterranean as well as the marine system in the former Persian provinces; they also established new maritime installations. In AH 18/640 CE, when a severe famine spread in Arabia, Caliph 'Umar ibn al-Khattab ordered a cleaning of Trajan's canal, which connected Babylon with Clysma (sixty-nine miles in length), for the transport of sixty thousand irdabbs of corn from Egypt to Jar, the port of Medina. The real age of Islamic navigation began from the reign of 'Uthman ibn 'Affan. During the Umayyad and 'Abbasid periods, many port cities on the Indian Ocean, the Persian Gulf, and the Arab, Red, and Mediterranean Seas flourished. Among these cities were Basra, Siraf, Aden, Suhar, Shihr, Qais, Bahrain, Hurmuz, Jedda, Jar, Qulzum, 'Aydhab, Tarsus, Ladhiqiyya, Beirut, Sidon, Tyre (Sur), Acre, Alexandria, Rosetta, Damietta, Tinnis, Babylon, Barqa, and Tunis.

Over the course of time, Islamic societies contributed to the art of navigation. Their contributions are reflected in manuals of seafaring, nautical instruments, and the introduction of the lateen sail (a triangular sail suspended from a long yardarm at an angle to the mast) to Mediterranean navigation. Among the oldest Islamic manuals of navigational science that have come down to us are *Kitab al-Fawa'id fi Usul 'ilm al-Bahr wa-l-Qawa'id,* which was composed by Ahmad ibn Majid in 895/1490, and the works of Sulayman ibn Muhammad al-Mahri (d. 917/1511). This should not be interpreted to mean that Muslim navigators did not produce and use portolan charts (sing., *qunbas*) before the days of Ibn Majid. By contrast, Ibn Majid names two Persian navigators, Ahmad ibn Tabruya and Khawsshir Ibn Yusuf al-Ariki, who sailed during the early years of the eleventh century and who wrote navigational works. Another major instrument that Muslim astronomers and mathematicians developed as early as the seventh century was the astrolabe, an instrument for observing or showing the positions of the stars. On the astrolabe, latitude was determined by the height of the sun or the pole star, which was measured by the qis figure system (science of taking latitude measurements). A third nautical instrument that Muslim sailors transferred from China was the compass. This

magnetic instrument was known to Muslim seafarers before the tenth century and probably was not considered very important in the East, because the skies over the Indian Ocean were usually very clear, especially during the times that Muslim mariners sailed with monsoons. The earliest documented Arab use of the compass in the Mediterranean dates to the 1240s. In brief, Muslim navigators mastered astrology; the science of latitude and longitude; the nature and directions of winds; the seasons; the knowledge and locations of coasts, ports, islands, dangerous shoals, and the narrow maritime lanes; the use of various terrestrial instruments; and the art of calculating solar months and days. Most of the Islamic literature about the science of navigation was translated into Latin. For instance, the population of the Balearic Islands—especially the Mallorcan Jewish cartographers—played a vital role in translating Arabic nautical charts, instruments, and books into Latin. By doing so, Western European commercial ships could sail toward the Canary Islands and other destinations along western African coasts.

Islamic ships sailed to every part of the known world, including the major ports on the Mediterranean, Adriatic, Aegean, Marmara, Black, and Caspian Seas, in addition to the western African coasts on the Atlantic Ocean; their ships also sailed as far north as Denmark in 844. In the East, Muslim seafarers navigated the Red and Arab Seas, the Persian Gulf, and the Indian Ocean. Their merchant ships sailed from Near Eastern ports to India and Sri Lanka, Malay, the Philippines, Indonesia, and China in the Far East as well as Zanzibar, Mozambique, and even Madagascar in east and southeast Africa. Certainly the seasons and art of navigation differ for each one of the seas and oceans mentioned above. For instance, the sailing season in the Mediterranean had been observed from the Classical Hellenic period to the late medieval period. Ships habitually set out from the eastern basin of the Mediterranean during the early spring and returned from the west during the Feast of the Cross *('id al-salib)*, which was celebrated on the 26th or 27th of September, whereas the return journey of ships heading eastward took place between the end of July and the beginning of September. However, sailing during inappropriate times was probably limited to military expeditions and instant transport of food supplies. As for the seasons of navigation in the Indian Ocean, navigators took advantage of the seasonal winds (monsoons) that blow in one direction for about six months and in the opposite direction for the rest of the year. With regard to the art of navigation on these waters, Muslim geographers (e.g., al-Mas'udi [d. 346/956]; author of *Muruj al-Dhahab)* point out that navigating on each one of these seas required the previous personal knowledge and expertise of sailors.

The duration of maritime voyages depended on the seaworthiness of the vessel, the professional behavior of the sailors, the distances between ports of origin and destinations, cargo's volume and weight, weather conditions, and the human hostilities that the ship could encounter. After the embarkation and debarkation ports were specified, captains and shipmasters could fix the ship's course, whether it had to cross the high sea, hug the coast, or sail on inland waters (e.g., rivers, artificial canals).

This discussion cannot be concluded without saying a few words about navigation for military purposes. One of the few—but most important—sources about the subject that still survives is *Al-Ahkam al-Mulukiyya fi Fann al-Qital fi l-Bahr wa-l-Dawabit al-Namusiyya*, by Muhammad Ibn Mankali (d. 784/1382). His treatise, which contains explicit references to and fragments of an Arabic translation of Leo VI's *Tactica*, is a mine of information about the technology of Islamic warships and "Greek fire"; rights and duties of sailors, marines, and commanders; navigation under various climatic conditions; and, most importantly, how to plan, manage, and coordinate the battle at sea.

HASSAN KHALILEH

Further Reading

'Abd al-Dayim, al-'Azız M. "*Al-Ahkam al-Mulukiyya fi Fann al-Qital fi l-Bahr wa-l-Dawabit al-Namusiyya*." PhD dissertation. Cairo: Cairo University, 1974.

Abulafia, David. *A Mediterranean Emperium: The Catalan Kingdom of Majorca*. Cambridge, UK: Cambridge University Press, 1994.

Barakat, Wafiq. *Fann al-Harb al-Bahriyya fi l-Ta'rikh al-'Arabi al-Islami*. Aleppo: Ma'had al-Turath al-'Ilmi al-'Arabi, 1995.

Brice, William C. "Compasses, Compassi and *Kanabıs*." *Journal of Semitic Studies* 29 (1984): 169–78.

Castello, Francesc. "Arab Cartography." In *Aspects of Arab Seafaring: An Attempt to Fill in the Gaps of Maritime History*, eds. Yacoub Yousef and Vassilios Christides. Athens, 2002.

Christides, Vassilios. "Milaha." In *The Encyclopaedia of Islam*, vol. 7, 40–6. 1993.

———. "Two Parallel Naval Guides of the Tenth Century—Qudama's Document and Leo VI's *Naumachica*: A Study on Byzantine and Moslem Naval Preparedness." *Graeco-Arabica* 1 (1982): 51–103.

Clark, Alfred. "Medieval Arab Navigation on the Indian Ocean: Latitude Determinations." *American Oriental Society* 113 (1993): 360–73.

Hassan, Ahmad Y., and Donald R. Hill. *Islamic Technology: An Illustrated History*. Cambridge, UK: Cambridge University Press, 1992.

Hourani, George F. *Arab Seafaring in the Indian Ocean in Ancient and Early Medieval Times*. Princeton, UK: Princeton University Press, 1995.

Khalilieh, Hassan S. "The *Ribat* System and Its Role in Coastal Navigation." *Journal of the Economic and Social History of the Orient* 42 (1999): 212–25.

———. *Islamic Maritime Law: An Introduction*. Leiden: E.J. Brill, 1998.

Khoury, Ibrahim. *Al-'Ulum al-Bahriyya 'ind al-'Arab*. Damascus: Majma' al-Lugha al-'Arabiyya, 1972.

Kreutz, Barbara M. "Mediterranean Contributions to the Medieval Mariner's Compass." *Technology and Culture* 14 (1973): 367–83.

Lewis, Archibald. "Maritime Skills in the Indian Ocean." *Journal of the Economic and Social History of the Orient* 16 (1973): 238–64.

Lichtenstadter, Ilse. "Origin and Interpretation of some Qur'anic Symbols." In *Studi Orientaliststici in Onore di Giorgio Levi Della Vida*, vol. 2, 58–80. Roma: Instituto per l'Orient, 1956.

Lombard, Maurice. "Une Carte du Bois la Méditerranée Musulmane (VIIe–Xie Siècle)." *Annales Economies Sociétés Civilisations* 14 (1959): 234–54.

Nadavi, Sayyed Sulaiman. "Arab Navigation." *Islamic Culture* 15 (1941): 435–48; 16 (1942): 72–86, 182–98, 404–22.

Nazmi, Ahmad. *Commercial Relations between Arabs and Slavs*. Warsaw: Wydawnictwo Akademickie, 1998.

Picard, Christophe. *La Mer et les Musulmans d'Occident au Moyen Age*. Paris: Presses Iniversitaires de France, 1997

———. *L'Océan Atlantique Musulman de la Conquête Arabe à l'Époque Almohaed: Navigation et Mise en Valeur de Côtes d'al-Andalus et du Maghreb Occidental*. Paris, 1997.

Prinsep, James. "Note on the Nautical Instruments of the Arabs." *Journal of the Asiatic Society of Bengal* 5 (1836): 784–94.

Pryor, John H. *Geography, Technology, and War: Studies in the Maritime History of the Mediterranean 649–1571*. Cambridge, UK: Cambridge University Press, 1992.

Renaud, H.P.J. "Sur une Tablette d'Astrolabe Apparlenant à M.H. Terrasse." *Hespéris* 26 (1939): 157–69.

Salem, Elsayyed. *Al-Bahr al-Ahmar fi l-Ta'rikh al-Islami*. Alexandria, 1993.

Savage-Smith, Emilie. "Celestial Mapping." In *Cartography in the Traditional Islamic and South Asian Societies*, eds. J.B. Harley and David Woodward. Chicago: The University of Chicago Press, 1992.

Tibbetts, Gerald R. "Milaha." In *The Encyclopaedia of Islam*, vol. 7, 50–3. 1993.

———. "The Beginning of a Cartographic Tradition." In *Cartography in the Traditional Islamic and South Asian Societies*, eds. J.B. Harley and David Woodward. Chicago: The University of Chicago Press, 1992.

———. *Arab Navigation in the Indian Ocean before the Coming of the Portuguese*. London: The Royal Asiatic Society of Great Britain and Ireland, 1971.

———. "Arab Navigation in the Red Sea." *Geographical Journal* 127/3 (1961): 322–34.

Tolmacheva, Marina. "On the Arab System of Nautical Orientation." *Arabica* 27 (1980): 181–92.

Udovitch, Abraham L. "Time, the Sea and Society: Duration of Commercial Voyages on the Southern Shores of the Mediterranean during the High Middle Ages." In *La Navigazione Mediterranea nell'Alto Medioevo*, 503–63. Spoleto: Centro Italiano di Studi sull'Alto Medioevo, 1978.

Yusuf, S.M. "Al-Ranaj: The Route of Arab Mariners across the Bay of Bengal and the Gulf of Siam in the 3rd and 4th Centuries AH—9th and 10th centuries AD" *Islamic Culture* 39 (1955): 77–103.

NAVY

It is commonly believed that Mu'awiya Ibn Abi Sufyan was the first planner and establisher of the Islamic navy. A careful examination of primary sources reveals that the first Islamic naval expedition in history took place in AH 17/638 CE during the caliphate of 'Umar Ibn al-Khattab and was led by al-'Ala Ibn al-Hadrami, governor of Bahrain, against Persia; it ended with a trapped Islamic army nearby Istakhr. Three years later, in 20/641, with the permission of 'Umar, 'Alqama Ibn Mujazziz crossed the Red Sea toward Abyssinia. The expedition was disastrous, and only a few ships returned safely to their home port. In view of these facts, one may justifiably feel that the reluctance of 'Umar Ibn al-Khattab to permit his generals to embark on naval adventures did not result from religious considerations but from his unsuccessful and disastrous attempt against Abyssinia. However, the establishment of the Islamic navy in the Mediterranean Sea occurred during the reign of Uthman Ibn 'Affan. It was through the joint efforts of 'Abd Allah Ibn Abi Sarh, governor of Egypt, and Mu'awiya of Syria that the first maritime expedition on Cyprus in 28/648–649 was launched.

The Islamic expansions in the East and the West were not destructive. Muslim authorities not only preserved all dockyards, naval bases, and systems in the former Byzantine and Persian provinces, but they also founded new maritime installations—arsenals and naval centers—along their maritime possessions. Along the Syro-Palestinian coast were Tarsus, Laodicea, Tripoli, Beirut, Tyre, 'Asqalan, and, most importantly, 'Akka (Acre), from which the first Islamic naval expedition was launched against Cyprus; Egypt had Alexandria, Rosetta, Damietta, Tinnis, Babylon, and Clysma on the Red Sea. As for North Africa and Spain, their most important naval centers were Barqa, al-Mahdiyya, Tunis, Bougie, Ténès, Badis, Ceuta, Cádiz, Algeciras, Seville, Málaga, Almuñécar, Pechina/Almeria, Cartagena, Alicante, Denia, Valancia, and Tortosa. Likewise, they maintained and developed several naval centers in strategic Mediterranean islands, such as the Balearic Islands, Sicily, Crete, and Pantelleria. As a protective measure and until Muslims had acquired supremacy over the sea, the headquarters of their fleets were located in inland waters; the Egyptian navy was in Babylon, whereas the Andalusian one was in Seville.

Amir al-bahr (admiral) was the supreme commander of the maritime frontiers and naval forces. The duties of the construction of warships and the selection of appropriate materials—timber for keels, planking, masts, yards, oars, oakum, metals, skins, cables, pitch and tar, and other fittings—were laid upon him and a team of inspectors, who had to ensure that shipwrights observed technical standards and did not use inferior or inadequate raw materials. Every ship passed a comprehensive technical inspection while it was still in the yard and during the journey to avoid unpleasant consequences. Among the types of warships built in the arsenals for the fighting fleets in the eastern and western basins of the Islamic Mediterranean were *dromon, fattash, ghurab, harraqa, jafn, jariya, qarib, qarqur, qishr, shalandi, shini, tarida,* and *zawraq.*

The responsibility of recruiting highly skilled sailors, patient artisans, brave warriors, alert spies, and physicians rested with the admiral and his chief commanders. Papyri from early Islamic Egypt show that the method of recruitment of sailors for the raiding fleets was compulsory; sailors were drawn from all provinces and included various classes of the population. In case of reluctance or fugitiveness, the local authorities had to pay the wages of men hired from another place. As for the fighting men, they were Arab emigrants and mawalis who settled in the Levantine, Egyptian, and North African frontiers. Only experienced crews and warriors with high morals who were faithful, professional, and fearless in the face of the enemy were taken onboard. Supplies for the ships' human element included bread, butter, wine, oil, and salt.

Only a few Arabic manuals dealing with Islamic naval warfare have survived. Ibn Mankali's handbooks, *Al-Ahkam al-Mulukiyya wal-Dawabit al-Namusiyya fi Fann al-Qital fi al-Bahr* and *Al-Adilla al-Rasmiyya fi al-Ta'abi al-Harbiyya,* give great detail about naval preparedness and tactics. Because Islamic warships could be attacked with all kinds of weapons, their commanders were instructed to carry a large supply of spears, swords, crossbows and arrows, stones and catapults, venomous creatures sealed up in earthenware jars, and combustibles and Greek fire. Ibn Mankali describes how to be prepared against enemies, addressing such things as the following: exercises; prayers offered and speeches delivered before the actual combat; time, place, and disposition of enemy; strategic tactics and arrangement of warships; disposition of the flagship; and the flags to be used during the maritime battle for signaling purposes.

HASSAN KHALILEH

Further Reading

'Abbady, Ahmad, and Elsayyed Salem. *Tarikh al-Bahriyya al-Islamiyya fi Misr wal-Sham.* Beirut: Dar al-Nahda al-'Arabiyya, 1969.

Adawi, Ibrahim A. *Quwwat al-Bariyya al-'Arabiyya fi Miyah al-Bahr al-Mutawassit.* Cairo: Maktabat al-Nahda, 1963.

Ahmad, Ramadan A. *Tarikh Fann al-Qital al-Bahri fi al-Bahr al-Mutawassit 35–978/655–1571*. Cairo: Wizarat al-Thaqafa, 1986.

Christides, Vassilios. "Byzantine Dromon and Arab Shini: The Development of the Average Byzantine and Arab Warships and the Problem of the Number and Function of the Oarsmen." *Tropis* 3 (1995): 111–22.

———. "Naval History and Naval Technology in Medieval Times: The Need for Interdisciplinary Studies." *Byzantion* 58 (1988): 309–32.

———. *The Conquest of Crete by the Arabs CA. 824: A Turning Point in the Struggle Between Byzantium and Islam*. Athens, 1984.

———. "Naval Warfare in the Eastern Mediterranean (6th–14th Centuries): An Arabic Translation of Leo VI's Naumachica." *Graeco-Arabica* 3 (1984): 137–48.

———. "Two Parallel Naval Guides of the Tenth Century—Qudama's Document and Leo VI's Naumachica: A Study on Byzantine and Moslem Naval Preparedness." *Graeco-Arabica* 1 (1982): 51–103.

Delgado, Jorge L. *El Poder Naval de Al-Andalus en la Época del Califato Omeya*. Granada: Universidad de Granada, 1993.

Fahmy, Aly M. *Muslim Sea-Power in the Eastern Mediterranean from the Seventh to the Tenth Century AD*. Cairo: National Publication & Printing House, 1966.

———. *Muslim Naval Organisation in the Eastern Mediterranean from the Seventh to the Tenth Century AD*. Cairo: National Publication & Printing House, 1966.

Nukhayli, Darwish. *Al-Sufun al-Islamiyya 'ala Huruf al-Mu'jam*. Alexandria: Alexandria University Press, 1974.

Picard, Christophe. *La Mer et les Musulmans d'Occident au Moyaen Age*. Paris: Presses Universitaires de France, 1997.

Salem, Elsayyed, and Ahmad 'Abbady. *Tarikh al-Bahriyya al-Islamiyya fi al-Maghrib wal-Andalus*. Beirut: Dar al-Nahda al-'Arabiyya, 1969.

Ziadé, Nicole. "Al-Ustul al-'Arabi fi Ayyam al-Amawiyyin." In *Studies on the History of Bilad al-Sham during the Umayyad Period*, eds. M. Bakhit and M. Abbadi, 37–86. Amman, 1990.

NAWRUZ

Of Persian origin, Nawruz (No Roz; new day), the ancient Iranian festival of the New Year, survived the Arab conquest and continued to be celebrated in Islamic lands many centuries thereafter. Originally the first day of the Persian solar year, it corresponded with the spring vernal equinox, and the duration of its celebration was six days. Medieval Islamic sources give various (folkloric) explanations for the origins of Nawruz, which involve the mythical Persian Jamshid or the biblical patriarchs Abraham and King Solomon. No Roz was the day to wear new clothes and serve food of the new season. People used to rise early in the morning, go to wells and streams, draw water in vases, and pour it over themselves or sprinkle it on each other. Explanations for these customs varied, from considering them a good omen and a means to ward off harm to the cleansing of the smoke off of those attending the rituals of the fire of the preceding winter nights. Shi'i explanation of the significance of Nawruz, which is ascribed to the Imam Ja'far al-Ṣādiq, sees in it the day of God's primal covenant with mankind, the day of the first rising of the sun, the day of the defeat of the Antichrist, and the day of a number of other important events.

During 'Abbasid time, and especially during the reign of al-Mutawakkil (847–861 CE), Nawruz was celebrated with great pomp and rejoicing. Performances of masked actors took place at the caliphal court in Baghdad, a variety of sweet dishes were cooked, and caliphs received gifts from their subjects and exchanged gifts with high officials. In addition, the common people exchanged gifts. They used to illuminate their homes with cotton pods and clay censers. Enthusiasm could reach such a degree that Caliph al-Mutadid's attempt in 284/897 to prevent the unrestrained rejoicing in the streets failed. Other customs reported are the dyeing of eggs and the sprinkling of perfume on a man and treading seven times on him as a means of driving away the evil eye, laziness, and fever. A report from around 900 tells that the Baghdadi people even dared to sprinkle water on policemen. There is a report about Muslims drinking wine in public and eating lentils "like the non-Muslims *(dhimmis)*."

Nawruz was celebrated not only in previously Sasanian territories but also in Islamic Egypt. The circumstances of its arrival there are unknown, however; it could be an effect of the Persian rule of ancient Egypt or, alternatively, an adaptation of the Saturnalia of the Roman era. Be that as it may, in Egypt, unlike in the eastern provinces, although it did mark the beginning of the year, Nawruz was an autumn festival that was celebrated on the first day of the Coptic month of Tūt (September), when the Nile was expected to reach its highest level. Celebrations are first reported in Egypt in the year 912, and some of the reported customs remind one of those that have been related for ancient Iran: the exchange of gifts, the eating of special food, and the wearing of new clothes. Under the Fatimids, Nawruz was expressed in an official celebration in which gifts were bestowed on officials and their families. It appears, however, that a carnival increasingly became its main function. The people drank wine and beer; there were those who ambushed travelers and sprayed them with filthy water or wine, and others threw eggs on one another. Even emirs and dignitaries were exposed to this sort of ridicule, and, to rescue themselves, they had to pay "ransom." Slapping one another with boots or leather mats in public places was possibly a remnant of a pagan ritual. Sexual overtones were expressed in the play of water games, causing men and women to become wet so that naked bodies could be seen through clothes. In 1188, the public gathering of transvestites and prostitutes is reported. Masquerades are reported during the celebration of 975. Puritan scholars of the Mamluk period lamented the adverse effect of the festival on both the common people and the learned. They reported that schools were shut down and turned into playgrounds and that teachers were insulted and sprayed with water. These writers found it detestable that the participants were able "to commit all kinds of evil," that "there was no interdiction [to any sort of behavior] and no authority imposed."

The high mark of Nawruz in medieval Cairo was the procession of the Emir of Nawruz, usually a wanton who was either naked or dressed in colorful clothes, his face besmeared with lime or flour and a beard of fur attached to his face, on his head a special cap made of palm leaves, riding a donkey in the streets. He held a sort of register in his hand, "visited" homes of dignitaries to collect "debts," and punished those who refused to pay. Manifest in this procession is the carnivalesque element of status reversal and riotous revelry á la medieval Christian festivals such as the King of Fools.

Egyptian rulers occasionally outlawed certain elements of the Nawruz festival, such as the spraying of water. The Mamluk Sultan Barquq banned the celebrations in 1385 altogether, and those disobeying were severely punished. Although reports are contradictory regarding what the situation was afterward, it is most likely that the festival vanished from Cairo after approximately 1400. Still, there are indications that it survived in one form or another in Egyptian provinces until modern times.

BOAZ SHOSHAN

See also Festivals and Celebrations

Further Reading

Ahsan, Muhammad Manazir. *Social Life under the Abbasids*. London: Longman, 1979.
Cuypers, Michel. "Le Nowruz en Egypte." *Luqman* 10 (1993–1994): 9–36.
von Grunebaum, G.E. *Muhammadan Festivals*. London: Curzon Press, 1976.
Shoshan, Boaz. *Popular Culture in Medieval Cairo*, Chapter 3, Cambridge, UK: Cambridge University Press, 1993.

NEZAMI

Nezami was born in Ganjeh (Kirovabad under the Soviets, now Gyandzhe) in Azerbaijan in 1141, and he died in the same town in 1209. He is reputed to have left the town only once in his life, at the behest of a local ruler who wished to meet him. The exordia and conclusions to his poems tell us that he was monogamous but married three times due to his wives' deaths; that he was particularly enamored of his first wife, Afaq; that he had a son named Mohammad; and that he was never a court poet, although all of his poems were written with aristocratic patrons in mind, and all of them were apparently well received by their dedicatees.

His fame rests with his *Khamseh (Quintet)*, also known as the *Panj Ganj (Five Treasures)*, which consists of five long poems in the masnavi (couplet) form, using different meters. Three of the five are romances, and they are considered to be the greatest examples of the form in Persian. The first of the five—and the only one that does not consist of a single narrative—is the *Makhzan al-Asrar (Treasury of Secrets)*, which is a compendium of mystical tales; the second poem, *Khosrow o Shirin*, tells the story of the love of the Sasanian King Khosrow for the Armenian Princess Shirin; the third, *Leili o Majnun*, deals with two legendary lovers from different Arab tribes; the fourth, *Haft Paykar (The Seven Portraits)*, is concerned with the loves of the Sasanian King Bahram Gur; and the fifth, *Sekandarnameh*, deals with Alexander the Great.

The sources for three of the four narratives are to be found in Ferdowsi's *Shahnameh* (the exception, *Leili o Majnun*, is an Arab tale with no known Persian source before Nezami). The eleventh-century romance *Vis o Ramin* by Gorgani provided the basis for Nezami's rhetoric, but, in the same way that Nezami considerably elaborates on Ferdowsi's relatively brief anecdotes, he develops Gorgani's rhetoric in complex and sophisticated ways. In particular, despite his evident delight in his skill at writing highly evocative sensuous descriptions, he turns the emphasis of the romance away from carnal love as an end in itself to a concern with spiritual identity and ethical growth. His last poem, which treats Alexander as a seeker of spiritual wisdom, returns to the mystical emphasis of his first work and makes explicit the theme of personal ethical development that is implicit in his love stories.

Nezami is both a learned poet and a humanly endearing one. He is not afraid to deploy his thorough knowledge of the traditional learning of his time (e.g., his extensive use of arcane astrological lore), but his poems are never overwhelmed with such matter, and they have remained enormously popular for their human portraits (particularly of women), their suspenseful (if leisurely) plots, and their sumptuous descriptive passages. Nezami's elegant and highly effective allegorical integration of sensuous and mundane elements on the one hand and mystical and ethical elements on the other is unequaled by any other Persian narrative poet.

RICHARD DAVIS

See also Alexander; Astrology; Ferdowsi; Sasanians; Traditions, Islamic

Further Reading

Burgel, J.C. "The Romance." In *Persian Literature,* ed. E. Yarshater. New York, 1988.
Meisami, Julie Scott. *Medieval Persian Court Poetry.* Princeton, NJ, 1987.
Safa, Zabihollah. *Tarikh-e Adabiyat dar Iran (The History of Literature in Iran)*, 5 vols. Tehran, 1366/1987.
Zarrinkub, Abdolhosayn. *Pir-e Ganjeh dar Jostoju-ye Nakojabad (The Sage of Ganjeh in Search of Never-Never Land).* Tehran, 1372/1993.

NILE

Suffering an almost total lack of rain, Egypt, which has always been a primarily agricultural society, has been uniquely dependent on the flood of the Nile for its survival. This role of the river overshadowed its secondary importance as a means of transportation, especially of goods, as it was in Mamluk time, when boats with a usual capacity of seventy tons (and up to 350 tons) were used for carrying grain.

Knowledge of the Nile among Medieval Muslim geographers was based mostly on legendary or pseudoscientific traditions adopted from Ptolemy's ideas about the sources of the Nile in the legendary "Mountain of the Moon"; they believed it was south of the equator, as reflected in al-Khwarizmi's ninth-century *Surat al-Ard.* A map in an eleventh-century manuscript of this work indicates that the Nile's sinuous course was by then known. Later geographers, gathering pieces of information from traders and travelers, assumed the existence of a few "Niles"; alternatively, they believed there was one long one made out of a few.

The Nile habitually was at its lowest level in Lower Egypt around the beginning of June and would then rise and reach its maximum level in the Coptic month of Tut (29 August to 27 September), coinciding with the ancient New Year. If the level was sixteen to eighteen cubits (dhira') (about 9.3–10.4 meters), crop growth should have been sufficient. However, the whimsical nature of the Nile's inundation impelled most political regimes to measure its rise, and, for this, the ancients invented the Nilometer. Al-Maqrizi, the renowned chronicler of Mamluk Egypt, quotes a popular saying to the effect that God should save from a level of twenty cubits, because it would result in flooding and the destruction of crops. It now

appears, though, that, by the Mamluk period, this level no longer posed a threat of overflooding; over the course of time, the minimum and maximum increased at a steady rate as a result of the sediment on the bed of the river.

Until the nineteenth century, a maintenance-intensive irrigation system remained almost unchanged. When the flood began, the water was harnessed by an extensive network of local irrigation canals of various sizes to draw it into basins along the Nile Valley and in the Delta. Dikes were used to trap the water and to allow moisture to sink into the basins. The alluvium washed down from Ethiopian topsoil settled on the fields and provided rich fertilization. Constant dredging of the canals and the shoring up of dikes were required. Some innovations, like the saqiya (an ox-driven water wheel), the Archimedes screw, and the shaduf (a simple water hoist), appeared already during the late Pharaonic and Ptolemaic eras, and they persisted into the Islamic period.

A too-slow rise of the water between July and September or its sudden recession frequently aroused anxiety among the populace. This was the point when merchants and brokers would consider it in their interest to withhold supplies and push prices of grain up. There are numerous descriptions of crowds at the Nile docks or in front of mills and bakeries, struggling to obtain grain, dough, or bread. Small wonder, then, that medieval rulers attempted to conceal information about the river level; one sultan even contemplated destroying the Nilometer.

The attainment of a level of at least sixteen cubits was the occasion for celebrating the "Plenitude of the Nile"; this has been so since at least the Fatimid time. Announcing to the people the attainment of the desired level, the official in charge of the Nilometer went in procession from the palace along the road of Bayn al-Qasrayn, dressed in a special golden robe, to the sound of trumpets and drums. The preparations for the ceremonies required the relocation of the Fatimid caliph and court officials from the palace to the pleasure pavilions erected along the Canal from Cairo to Fustat. The ceremonies themselves consisted of two parts. The first was the perfuming with saffron of the Nilometer at Rawda Island, which was presided over by the Fatimid caliph and later by Ayyubid and Mamluk sultans, who were sailing in decorated boats. The second part was the "breaking of the dam," which was annually constructed across the Canal (khalij) near its mouth to prevent too early a flooding. The ruler throwing a spear at the dam was a signal for the workmen to rush forward and destroy it. During that ceremony, the Qur'an was recited, and singers performed into the night; the ruler then presided over a banquet. In Fatimid times, there were public observatories near the dam, where seats were rented; at some point during the twelfth century CE, they were destroyed by either overcrowding or fire. Occasionally Mamluk troops performed lancing drills, and merrymaking, wine drinking, and sexual promiscuity were part of the Nile celebrations. At the beginning of the sixteenth century, the traveler Leo Africanus reported in some detail about family trips in decorated boats. There were occasional attempts to ban popular celebrations, and scholars considered the people's "abominations" the reason for the Nile's low level.

Islamic regimes tried to abolish Coptic festivals associated with the Nile. Already, 'Umar ibn al-Khattab, the second caliph, forbade the sacrificial rites and, instead of a virgin known as the "Nile Bride," a piece of paper was thrown to the river. Later, the Fatimids and Mamluks in particular subjected Coptic festivals of the Nile to occasional censorship, especially during droughts, but this met only limited success. Among these festivals, one should mention the Feast of Submersion ('Id al-Ghitas). This occurred on the eve of the Epiphany, which commemorated Christ's baptism and coincided with a seasonal transition shortly after the winter solstice around the middle of January. During the 'Abbasid period, thousands of torches were lit, and large crowds of Copts and Muslims thronged the river banks. Another Coptic Nile festival, the Festival of the Martyr ('Id al-Shahid), was celebrated in May to mark the beginning of the spring. Its focal point was a sacrificial object—a finger of a martyr that was kept during the year in the Shubra church in Cairo—being immersed in the river. The priests of the church orchestrated the ritual that was believed to bring about the Nile's inundation. Large crowds are reported to have been spectators. A description from the height of the Mamluk period reports about the riding of horses, the pitching of tents, the performing of singers and entertainers, and the consuming of much wine (so much, in fact, that the local peasants could pay their land tax from the revenues procured from its sale). Even prostitutes, effeminate males, and reprobates of all types participated, to the point that "numerous sins are performed in excess." This festival persisted to the mid-fourteenth century, a time when the Mamluk regime moved against a perceived threat of increasing Coptic influence.

BOAZ SHOSHAN

Further Reading

Borsch, Stuart J. "Nile Floods and the Irrigation System in Fifteenth-Century Egypt." *Mamluk Studies Review* 4 (2000): 131–45.

Halm, H. "Die Zeremonien der Salbung des Nilometers und der Knaloffnung in Fatimidischer Zeit." In *Egypt and Syria in the Fatimid, Ayyubid and Mamluk Eras,* eds. U. Vermeulen and D. de Smet, 111–23. Leuven: Uitgeverij Peeters, 1995.

Levtzion, Nehemia. "Arab Geographers, the Nile, and the History of Bilad al-Sudan." In *The Nile: Histories, Cultures, Myths,* eds. Haggai Erlich and Israel Gershoni, 71–6. Boulder: Lynne Rienner, 2000.

Lutfi, Huda. "Coptic Festivals of the Nile: Aberrations of the Past?" In *The Mamluks in Egyptian Politics and Society,* eds. Thomas Philipp and Ulrich Haarmann, 254–82. Cambridge, UK: Cambridge University Press, 1998.

Sanders, Paula. *Ritual, Politics, and the City in Fatimid Cairo.* Albany, NY: State University of New York Press, 1994.

Shoshan, Boaz. *Popular Culture in Medieval Cairo.* Cambridge, UK: Cambridge University Press, 1993.

NISHAPUR

Nishapur is a city in northeastern Iran. During its heyday (ca. 950–1050) it was the largest city in the Muslim world (one to two hundred thousand people) that was not situated on navigable water. Although the semiautonomous Tahirid dynasty ruled from Nishapur in the ninth century, its prominence stemmed from trade, manufacturing, and religious learning rather than from being a military garrison or imperial capital. Growing largely through religious conversion, Nishapur supplanted nearby Tus (modern Mashhad), a Sasanid governing center, as the administrative hub of the province of Khurasan. Trade from eastern lands passing south of the Kopet Dagh mountains funneled through Nishapur, and the city became a major producer of cotton cloth and high-quality ceramics. The Ash'ari school of Islamic theology, which featured such noted scholars as Imam al-Haramain al-Juvaini and al-Ghazali, came to be based in Nishapur during the eleventh century. It was simultaneously the home of such noted Sufis as Abu al-Qasim al-Qushairi. Nishapur's great size required high productivity in the surrounding farmlands. The advent of the Seljuq dynasty with its pastoralist followers in 1037 unsettled the agricultural economy and triggered the city's slow decline. A decade of fighting among religious factions (primarily the Hanafis and the Shafi'is), nomadic raids, and earthquakes caused most of the shrunken city to be abandoned in 1162. A smaller walled city rebuilt on the western border of the metropolis was destroyed by the Mongols during the thirteenth century; Nishapur was then relocated two kilometers further west. With the growing pilgrimage city of Mashhad, the new regional metropolis, Nishapur never again attained more than local importance.

RICHARD W. BULLIET

Further Reading

Bulliet, Richard W. *The Patricians of Nishapur.* Cambridge, Mass: Harvard University Press, 1972.

NIZAM AL-DIN

Nizam al-Din Awliya' (1244–1325 CE) was the most renowned Sufi saint of medieval South Asia (India, Pakistan, and Bangladesh). He was a scholar of *hadith* (tradition) and an exponent of juridical independence *(ijtihad)*. He systematized the core practices of the Chishti Sufi community and spread its institutions, making the Chishti community the most characteristically South Asian Sufi group. His contribution to Persianate Islamic culture in Hindustan is vast. His given name was Muhammad Nizam al-Din, and a nickname, Awliya' (Saints), evolved from his early titles: Sultan-i Masha'ikh (Ruler of Spiritual Masters) and Mahbub-i Ilahi (God's Beloved).

Life

Nizam al-Din was born in Badaun, north of Delhi. Mongol invasions exiled his parents' families from Bukhara; his father died during his childhood. Raised by his mother, Bibi Zulaykha, he held her as an exemplar of ascetic and mystical women. She supported him while he studied Qur'an, hadith, and jurisprudence (usul al-fiqh). At sixteen, he migrated to Delhi and studied hadith with Mawlana Kamal al-Din Zahid.

While in Delhi, he heard of a Sufi master named Shaykh Farid al-Din Ganj-i Shakar. The Shaykh's brother commented on his aim to become a judge (qadi), to which he replied, "Don't become a judge—become something else." Listening to Qur'an 57:16, "Has not the time arrived for true believers that their hearts should humbly engage in remembrance of God?," he abandoned his ambition to instead "become something else."

Shaykh Farid al-Din greeted him with a poem: "Burning of separation from you has singed so many hearts/Flooding of desire for you has ravaged so many souls." He initiated Nizam al-Din into the Chishti Sufi practices of rapturous love, disciplined poverty, and poetic sensitivity. Nizam al-Din became his spiritual successor (khalifa) at age twenty-three, and he settled in Ghiyathpür, outside Delhi. He built a popular devotional center (jama 'at-khana or khanaqah), confronted the rulers, and trained disciples. He refused to marry or raise children (see Lawrence, 1994).

Teachings

Mu'in al-Din Hasan Chishti (d. 1236) brought the Chishti order from Afghanistan. Teaching that a Sufi cultivates "generosity like a river, magnanimity like the sun, and humility like the earth," he distilled universal teachings from Islam, attracting Hindu devotees while extolling Muhammad as the perfect human being and Imam 'Ali as the exemplary Sufi. He adapted Hindu devotional hymns to create the Chishti institution of sama'. Musical devotion has roots in Persianate Sufism, but Chishti masters elevated it to a central practice.

Nizam al-Din's teachings can be summarized in three statements. First, service to the needy is better than ritual worship; the way to knowledge of God *(ma'rifa)* is bringing happiness to others. Arguing that this was the best way to imitate the Prophet Muhammad, Nizam al-Din made a pun that equated Prophethood *(payghambari)* with "bearing the sorrows of others" *(pay-i ghamm bari)*. Second, the presence of God is found among the destitute. To this end, Nizam al-Din emphasized a hadith: "All people are God's family, and the most beloved of people are those who do most good for God's family." Third, egoism is idolatry. The following anecdote reveals his compassion and tolerance with regard to interfaith relationships. Walking with Amir Khusraw, wearing his cap tilted, Nizam al-Din observed Hindus praying to the sun; he approved of their worship, paraphrasing Qur'an 22:66: "To every community there is a religious way and a direction for prayer" *(har qawm ra-st rahi dini o qiblah gahi)*. Amir Khusraw spontaneously added, "Every community has a right way and a direction to pray/and I turn in prayer to face the captivating one whose cap's awry" *(man qiblah rast kardam janib-i kaj-kulahi)*. This conversation makes for a rhyming couplet that is sung in Qawwali performances.

Nizam al-Din advocated three practical means to realize these teachings. First, find a spiritual master and serve him *(pir-muridi)*. Second, embrace poverty and renounce hoarding *(tark-i dunya)*. Third, nourish the heart through devotional music *(sama')*. Sultan Ghiyath al-Din Tughluq (r. 1320–1325 CE) entertained criticism from legalistic scholars that Islamic law forbade such music. The Shaykh debated in court and defended the practice with hadith reports.

Community

Nizam al-Din was a skilled organizer who brought into his devotional center disciples of all classes. He codified the rules of living at devotional centers; in finance, he relied on voluntary gifts *(futuh)* rather than royal land grants *(jagirdari)*. Members daily gave away everything beyond basic needs and maintained a communal kitchen *(langar-khanah)* that fed the needy by the thousands. Nizam al-Din refused to meet Sultans face to face, which was in contrast with their Suhrawardi peers in South Asia. Nizam al-Din oversaw the expansion of the Chishti community by sending delegates across the Delhi Sultanate, which expanded to Bengal, Rajastan, and Gujarat and which, by 1310 CE, encompassed the Deccan. Delegates set up devotional centers based on Nizam al-Din's model.

Nizam al-Din attracted followers of high quality. He insisted that his inner circle study Islamic sciences *(usul al-din)* before he granted successorship *(khilafat)*. His chief successor, Shaykh Nasir al-Din (d. 1356), was a scholar of Qur'an and Arabic grammar whose Sufi discourses (see Khayr al-Majalis) are interwoven with hadith reports. Other disciples were more musical, like Burhan al-Din Gharib (d. 1337), who oversaw the spread of the Chishti community in Gujarat through his rapturous dance (see Ernst, 1992).

Nizam al-Din's disciples included courtier poets. Amir Khusraw (d. 1325) created Persian love poems *(ghazal)*, Hindawi poems in praise of Nizam al-Din based on Krishna-devotion imagery, and musical settings of Islamic prayers and praise that defined the tradition of Qawwali singing. Amir Hasan Sijzi (1254–1336) wrote down Nizam al-Din's oral Sufi discourses in a unique record, *Fawa'id al-Fu'ad* (see Lawrence, 1992), spawning a genre of Sufi literature *(malfuzat)* that was adopted by other South Asian Sufi communities.

Legacy

Although Nizam al-Din wrote no books, the historian Barani left a record of his personality. His followers enriched South Asian literature and music. Their Persian prose formed a unique genre at the interface between oral discourses and written records, and their Persian poetry set the standard for ghazals throughout the early modern period. Their sung poetry sparked the use of vernacular South Asian languages in Sufi communities (Hindawi, Punjabi, and Gujarati, and, later, Deccani Urdu).

Nizam al-Din's legacy includes his tomb complex *(dargah)*, built by rulers of the Tughluq dynasty (1320–1451) and the Lodi dynasty (1451–1526), who chose to be buried near it although they ruled from Agra. Mughal rulers (1535–1865) patronized his tomb. In later Mughal times, it became a centerpiece of spiritual life in Delhi through The Procession of the Flower-Sellers (see Lewis, 2002), a parade from the Red Fort to the tomb of Nizam al-Din and on to Mehrauli, near the Qutb Minar. Nizam al-Din's tomb remains one of the most popular Islamic sites in independent India, and the Chishti community he formalized continues to be the most active Sufi community in South Asia.

SCOTT A. KUGLE

See also Chishti; Dancing; Music; Muslims; Singing; South Asia; Saints and Sainthood; South Asia; Sufism and Sufis

Primary Sources

Hussayni, Sayyid Muhammad Akbar. *Jawami' al-Kalim: Malfuzat-i Muhammad Gisu Daraz.* Kanpur: Intizami Press, 1936.
Khurd, Amir. *Siyar al-Awliya'.* Delhi: Chirangi Lal Muhibb-i Hind Press, 1320 A.H.
Qalandar, Hamid. *Khayr al-Majalis: Malfuaat-i Nasir al-Din Chishti.* Aligarh Muslim University, 1959.

Further Reading

Digby, Simon. "Tabarrukat and Succession Among the Great Chishti Shaykhs." In *Delhi through the Ages: Essays in Urban History, Culture and Society,* ed. R.E. Frykenberg. Delhi: Oxford University Press, 1986.
Ernst, Carl. *Eternal Garden: Mysticism, History, and Politics at a South Asian Sufi Center.* Albany, NY: State University of New York Press, 1992.
Ernst, Carl, and Bruce Lawrence. *Sufi Martyrs of Love: The Chishti Order in South Asia and Beyond.* New York: Palgrave Macmillan, 2002.
Habib, Muhammad. *Life and Works of Hazrat Amir Khusro of Delhi.* Aligarh Muslim University, 1927.
Lawrence, Bruce. *Notes From a Distant Flute: The Existent Literature of Pre-Mughal Indian Sufism.* Tehran: Imperial Academy of Philosophy, 1978.
———. "The Early Chishti Approach to Sama'." In *Islamic Society and Culture: Essays in Honor of Aziz Ahmad,* eds. Milton Israel and N.K. Wagle. Delhi: Manohar, 1983.
———, transl. *Nizam al-Din Awliya: Morals for the Heart.* Mawa, NJ: Paulist Press, 1992.
———. "Honoring Women through Sexual Abstinence: Lessons From the Spiritual Practice of a Pre-modern South Asian Sufi Master, Nizam al-Din Awliya." *Journal of Turkish Studies* 18 (1994): 149–61.
Lewis, Charles. *Mehrauli: A View From the Qutb.* Delhi: Harper Collins India, 2002.
Nizami, Khaliq Ahmad. *The Life and Times of Shaikh Nizamuddin Auliya.* Delhi: Idarah-i Adabyat-i Delli, 1991.
Qureishi, Regula Burkhardt. *Sufi Music in India and Pakistan: Sound, Context and Meaning in Qawwali.* Chicago: University of Chicago Press, 1995.
Safi, Omid. "The Sufi Path of Love in Iran and India." In *A Pearl in Wine: Essays on the Life, Music and Sufism of*

Hazrat Inayat Khan, ed. Zia Inayat Khan. New Lebanon: Omega Press, 2001.

Schimmel, Annemarie. *Islam in the Indian Sub-Continent.* Leiden, E.J. Brill, 1980.

Zarcone, Thierry. "Central Asian Influence on the Early Development of the Chishtiyya Sufi Order in India." In *The Making of Indo-Persian Culture,* eds. Muzaffar Alam, Françoise Delvoye, and Marc Garborieau. New Delhi: Manohar, 2000.

NIZAM AL-MULK, ABU 'ALI B. 'ALI AL-TUSI,

Abu 'Ali b. 'Ali al-Tusi Nizam al-Mulk was an influential Seljuk vizier and educational patron. He was born in Tus in Khurasan (eastern Iran) in AH 408/1018 CE, the son of a Ghaznavid tax collector; little is known of his early life. By 445/1054, he was in the service of Alp Arslan, who was then a lieutenant in eastern Khurasan for his father, the Seljuk Sultan Chaghri Beg. Soon after Alp Arslan's accession to the sultanate after the death of his uncle Tughril Beg, Nizam al-Mulk was appointed vizier after he had contrived the execution of his rival al-Kunduri, formerly Tughril Beg's vizier.

The period of Nizam al-Mulk's greatest influence upon the affairs of the Seljuk empire began after the death of Alp Arslan in 465/1072. The early years of the reign of Alp Arslan's successor, the eighteen-year-old Malikshah, were completely dominated by his vizier. Eventually, however, rival interests at court and Malikshah's own desire to be rid of the man who for twenty years was the real ruler of the empire led to Nizam al-Mulk's downfall. He was murdered in 485/1092, apparently by an agent of the assassin leader Hassan-i Sabbah at the instigation of the vizier's enemies at court.

Nizam al-Mulk founded a chain of madrasas (Islamic schools) in the main cities of Persia, Iraq, and the Jazira. His motive was perhaps to assert Seljuk Sunnism against Fatimid and other Shi'i interests by training a cadre of reliable, Sunni-oriented officials to run the Seljuk empire. His political desiderata and the means of achieving them were articulated in the *Siyasat-nama (Treatise on Government),* which was made up of fifty chapters of advice illustrated by historical anecdotes.

DAVID MORRAY

See also Bureaucrats; Madrasa; Mirrors for Princes; Viziers

Further Reading

Bosworth, C.E. "The Political and Dynastic History of the Iranian World (AD 1000–1217)." In *The Cambridge History of the Iranian World,* vol. 5, ed. J.A. Boyle. Cambridge, 1968.

Nizam al-Mulk. *Siya¢sat-Na¢ma (The Book of Government, or Rules for Kings),* transl. H. Darke. London, 1960.

NOMADISM AND PASTORALISM

Through the early middle ages, nomads in the Middle East exploited the dry, inarable steppe and desert inside the Fertile Crescent and below into the Arabian peninsula; they focused on subsistence. The region's arable lands at oases, near rivers, or in rainy zones that enabled irrigated or "dry" farming supported settled communities. The inarable areas provided vegetation (technically, a desert may have vegetation on up to 49% of its surface) for sustaining domestic animals and their human managers, which were Arab Bedouins for the most part and able to move about to reach enough of it. Sheep and cattle that can only move short distances and that require water daily were raised on the better pastures and water sources fringing the settled lands. Camels subsisted on poorer range: they can eat a variety of vegetation (e.g., "camel thorn"), bear infrequent watering, and move at a good pace between widely separated patches of vegetation, wells, oases, and markets. The nomads traded animals and their products for agricultural and manufactured goods from settled communities.

This nomadism entailed (and still does, where it survives) an attenuated society. Communities consisted of camps of a few households of somewhat extended families. Beyond this, clans and tribes—genealogical constructs differing only in size—established personal identity and rights to pasture and water. Tribes descended (in the male line) from a remote ancestor (usually male); a clan's founding ancestor lived more recently; membership in both is by birth (although "clients" may be assimilated). Genealogy gave these units form, although their apparently fixed shape depended on memory that was usually softened by forgetfulness and often altered by falsification enabled by fogginess. Pastoral dispersion discouraged gatherings of the clans and tribes, and genealogical structure provided no obvious political center: apical ancestors were long dead, and living clansmen were only collateral relatives. Leadership involved persuasion and cajolery rather than authority.

Limitations of pasture and water restricted the keeping of horses. Horses require regular and plentiful watering and quality grazing (i.e., no camel thorn); at times they had to be fed the nomads' own food, dates, and camel milk. In addition, horses are endangered by high temperatures and would at times have to share the nomads' tents; these nomads kept few of them.

The small size, isolation, and insecurity of their communities made for the compensatory cultivation of a warrior culture, but shortages of weaponry and horses impaired their military capabilities. The best arms were expensive. Spears and daggers were common; swords and armor were coveted but rarer. Without trees, archery was of little importance. The warriors mostly fought on foot: camels make awkward fighting platforms (Lawrence of Arabia shot his own camel in the head during a camel charge). Nevertheless, the camel was the main military asset, providing mobility and logistics that were superior to their better-armed and better-mounted settled neighbors. Military commanders were chosen ad hoc by consensus, and they had to maintain the voluntary and revocable participation of their followers by persuasion. Raiding was the most common military undertaking.

During the early years of Islam, nomads made up the bulk of the manpower of the Muslim armies, although men from Mecca and Medina led them and worked to settle them in garrison towns. Although these settlements were subdivided by tribe, the army in the field was arrayed in decimal units, and the troops were supported by state stipends rather than pastoralism. As these armies became professional, nomads were relegated to occasional voluntary service in caliphal campaigns.

Beginning in the eleventh century, nomads from Inner Asia—mostly Turks, who were reinforced by Mongols during the thirteenth century—occupied the fine and largely arable grasslands of Anatolia, northern Iran, and Afghanistan. Their nomadism was geared not to try to make use of useless land but to the maintenance of military capabilities enabling seizure and defense of valuable resources. In these regions, the nomads moved up to cool highland meadows in the summer and down to snow-free but rainy and grassy lowlands in winter; this was done to obtain good grazing all year round for their sheep, goats, cattle, camels, and especially horses—lots of horses (actually ponies, because they grazed instead of requiring feeding).

Horses opened the Middle East to these nomads and enabled them to stay. They could raise horses easily, mount all of their warriors, and provide plentiful remounts (five per Mongol soldier) to outnumber and outpace low-horsepower sedentary cavalries. Pastoralism eased logistics: the horses grazed; the soldiers ate horse meat. The sedentaries' armies required food and fodder to be bought and transported. In addition, horses enhanced the nomads' basic weaponry—homemade bows made by compounding bits of wood, bone, and sinew into a light, compact, strong tool to project heavy arrows—enabling the archers to hit hard and then run fast. Finally, these nomads had an advantage in "manpower availability." Subsistence chores could be managed by women and children; in peacetime, men basically had nothing to do (Bedouin pastoralism seems to be somewhat more labor intensive). In war, most men could participate, particularly as cavalrymen. As with the Bedouin, the warrior way of life pervaded these nomads' culture and inspired their actions, but to greater effect.

The social and political arrangements of these originally Inner Asian nomads differed from the Bedouins'. A nuclear family—a man, his wife, and their children—constituted a household. By the nomads' calculation, a hundred milking sheep or their equivalent (one horse or cow was considered to be equal to five sheep or goats) could decently support a household. The community in times of security was a camp of up to ten households, depending on the size of their herds (if there were more animals, there were fewer households). In dangerous times, households might camp together by the thousands within a protective circle of wagons; a large camp's many animals required frequent moves to new pastures.

Clans were like the Arabs': based on genealogy and providing identity and certain rights. Tribes were quite different. Leading and managing large camps and large cavalry forces produced chiefs with powers that were unknown to the indigenous Middle Eastern nomads: absolute and arbitrary authority. The tribe in Inner Asia and its related Middle Eastern regions was not just a large clan that was kin to the chief, but it could include any persons obedient to him of any lineage, religion, economy (non-nomad), language, or culture. These tribes had no membership or size limitations. Mongol tribalism during the thirteenth century produced cavalry armies that numbered in the tens and sometimes hundreds of thousands.

JOHN MASSON SMITH

See also Sedentarism

Further Reading

Barfield, Thomas. *The Nomadic Alternative.* Upper Saddle River, NJ: Prentice Hall, 1993.
Barth, Fredrik. *Nomads of South Persia: The Basseri Tribe of the Khamseh Confederacy.* Prospect Heights, Ill: Waveland, 1986.
Cole, Donald P. *Nomads of the Nomads: The Al Murrah Bedouin of the Empty Quarter.* Arlington Heights, Ill: Harlan Davidson, 1975.
Khazanov, Anatoli M. *Nomads and the Outside World,* 2nd ed., transl. Julia Crookenden. Madison, Wisc: University of Wisconsin Press, 1994.

Smith, John Masson, Jr. "Mongol Nomadism and Middle Eastern Geography: Qishlaqs and Tumens." In *The Mongol Empire and Its Legacy,* eds. Reuven Amitai-Preiss and David O. Morgan, 39–56. Leiden: Brill, 1999.

———. "Mongol Society and Military in the Middle East: Antecedents and Adaptations." In *War and Society in the Eastern Mediterranean, 7th–15th Centuries,* ed. Yaakov Lev. Leiden: Brill, 1997.

NUMBERS

A variety of number systems were used in medieval Islamic civilization:

1. The Hindu–Arabic system is the modern decimal position system for writing integer numbers by means of ten symbols: the modern forms 1, 2, 3, 4, 5, 6, 7, 8, 9, and 0. The system was developed in India around 500 CE and probably transmitted by Indian scholars to Baghdad around 775 CE. The numbers were described in a small treatise about arithmetic by Muhammad ibn Musa al-Khwarizmi around 830 in Baghdad. The name *al-Khwarizmi* indicates that he was from Khwarizm, now Khiwa in modern Uzbekistan. He also authored an influential work about algebra. His treatise about arithmetic is lost in Arabic, but it was transmitted into Latin in the twelfth century. His name was Latinized as *Algorismi,* hence the modern word *algorism* or *algorithm* for methods of computation in general.

   In or after the tenth century, two varieties of the symbols emerged: the Eastern forms, which are still used in Egypt, the Middle East, Iran, and Pakistan; and the Western forms, which were used in North Africa and Spain and which are the immediate precursors of the modern shapes.

   The words *cipher* and *zero* are both derived (via Latin *cipherum* and *zephirum*) from the Arabic word *sifr,* meaning "empty place," which was used for the zero. This Arabic word *sifr* is, in turn, a translation from the Sanskrit term *shunya,* which the Indian mathematicians used for zero. Contrary to what is sometimes believed, the zero was not invented by Islamic mathematicians but rather adopted by them from India.

   The decimal position system never became very popular in medieval Islamic civilization; it was used mainly for the writing of very large numbers. Al-Khwarizmi and later mathematicians illustrated the system by means of the famous chessboard problem: if we put one grain on the first cell of the chessboard, two grains on the second, four grains on the third, eight grains on the fourth, and so on, what is the total number of grains on the chessboard? The total number can be written in the "Indian" system as 18,446,744,073,709,551,615.

   The decimal position system was transmitted to Christian Europe by the Latin translation of al-Khwarizmi's work and also by the Italian mathematician Leonardi Fibonacci. During the late twelfth century, Fibonacci learned the system in the city of Bougie (Algeria) and then on his return wrote an explanation of the system in his *Liber Abaci,* which became influential in Europe. It took until the Renaissance for the system to be firmly established in Europe. The modern forms of the symbols were fixed after the development of printing.

2. The abjad system can be used to write integer numbers between 1 and 1999. In the Arabic alphabet (and also in the Greek alphabet and the alphabets of the other Semitic languages), each letter has a numeric value between 1 and 1000. The name *abjad* is a combination of the letters with values between 1 and 4: *alif* = 1, *ba'* = 2, *jim* = 3, and *dal* = 4. The numeric values of the letters are the integers from 1 to 9, the tens from 10 to 90, the hundreds from 100 to 900, and 1000 for the letter ghayn. Numbers between 1 and 1999 are formed from a combination of these letters, thus 1024 = ghayn-kaf-dal (*kaf* = 20).

3. The medieval Islamic astronomers used the sexagesimal system that had been invented in ancient Babylonia and that is still used today for writing angles in degrees, minutes, and seconds. The system was also used by the later Greek astronomers, including Ptolemy. The Greeks indicated the individual numbers by a system similar to the Arabic abjad system. Each letter of the Greek alphabet has a numeric value, thus alpha = 1, beta = 2, theta = 9, and so on. The Islamic astronomers applied the same system to the Arabic alphabet according to the abjad system, which has been explained above. This system was called the "numbers of the astronomers," and it was very popular. For numbers larger than 1000, the astronomers in the Eastern Islamic world occasionally used the Hindu–Arabic numbers.

4. Examples of other, less-popular systems are the Coptic numbers used in Egypt and the siyaq

numbers used in bookkeeping. In many Arabic texts, numbers are written out in words: for example, "twenty-three." Computation and trading were often done without number symbols; the traders possessed an elaborate system of finger reckoning.

JAN P. HOGENDIJK

See also Mathematics; Geometry; Astronomy; Algebra

Further Reading

Folkerts, M., ed. *Die Alteste Lateinische Schrift ber das Indische Rechnen Nach al-Hwarizmi.* Munchen: Verlag der Bayerischen Academie der Wissenschaften, 1997.
Ifrah, G. *From One to Zero: A Universal History of Numbers.* New York: Viking Press, 1985.
Kunitzsch, Paul. "The Transmission of Hindu-Arabic Numerals Reconsidered." In *The Enterprise of Science in Islam: New Perspectives,* eds. J.P. Hogendijk and A.I. Sabra, 3–21. Cambridge, Mass: MIT Press, 2003.
Saidan, A.S. *The Arithmetic of al-Uqlidisi.* Dordrecht: Kluwer, 1978.

NUR AL-DIN IBN ZANGI

Nur al-Din Mahmud (d. 1174 CE) was the second son of the Turkish warlord Zangi and, like his father, a leading figure in the Muslim opposition to the Crusader states established in the Syrian littoral as a result of the First Crusade (1097–1099). Zangi had been murdered shortly after he had taken Edessa from the Crusaders in 1144, and Nur al-Din, initially operating from his base in Aleppo, made permanent the Muslim reconquest of Edessa in 1146 and then expanded his campaigns against the remaining Latin states. Shortly after the failed Second Crusade, Nur al-Din inflicted a serious defeat on the Principality of Antioch. By 1154, Nur al-Din took over control of Damascus from the Muslim Burid dynasty. From this base, he took several steps to support the ulama and their clarion calls for jihad (holy war) against the Franks. He constructed and endowed centers of learning and worship.

Within a decade after establishing Damascus as the capital of lands under his control, Nur al-Din's attention was drawn to the succession struggles within Fatimid Egypt, which were in turn complicated by Crusader invasions from the Kingdom of Jerusalem. In 1164, 1167, and 1168, Nur al-Din sent armies to Egypt led by his Kurdish General Shirkuh. Shirkuh died on this last campaign, and he was succeeded in command by his nephew Salah al-Din Yusuf ibn Ayyub (subsequently known to the Crusaders as Saladin), who quickly took control of Egypt, ruling it

but recognizing Nur al-Din as his overlord. When Nur al-Din died in 1174, Saladin quickly moved against Nur al-Din's heirs and subordinated their holdings to his growing realm.

WARREN C. SCHULTZ

See also Crusades; Damascus; Jerusalem; Saladin

Further Reading

Eliséeff, Nikita. *Nur al-Din. Un Grand Prince Musulman de Syrie au Temps des Croisades,* 3 vols. Damascus: Institut Français de Damas, 1967.
Holt, P.M. *The Age of the Crusades: The Near East from the Eleventh Century to 1517.* Longman, 1986.

NUR JAHAN

Nur Jahan (born Mihrunnisa) was one of the most powerful figures in seventeenth-century Mughal government, literature, and art. She was born in 1577 CE in Kandahar to a noble and ambitious Persian family, fleeing Persia for better prospects at Akbar's court in Fatehpur-Sikri. In 1594, she was married to 'Ali Quli Khan Istaju, a Persian soldier likewise seeking his fortune in India, with whom she produced a daughter, Ladli Begam. She was widowed in 1607 at the age of thirty and was invited to the Mughal court to be a lady-in-waiting to one of the stepmothers of the Emperor Jahangir.

She met Jahangir in the palace bazaar at the Agra Fort in 1611 and married him two months later. In 1614, he named her Nur Jahan (Light of the World), a sign of her central role in his life and at court. Indeed, he became so incapacitated by addictions that she gained enormous influence over him and de facto power over the empire. One sign of this was her minting gold and silver coins, an act that was traditionally reserved for the sovereign alone. A contemporary European observer wrote that Jahangir "hath one Wife, or Queen, whom he esteems and favours above all other Women; and his whole Empire is govern'd at this day by her counsel." Nur Jahan's success was due equally to an astute sense of politics and diplomacy and to her family's support and parallel rise to power. Her father held the title of I'tmad al-Dawla (Pillar of the Government), and her brother similarly held high office in the court of Jahangir and later Shah Jahan. Although Nur Jahan never bore a child for Jahangir, her family was nonetheless enmeshed with the Mughal line: Ladli Begam married one of Jahangir's sons and produced a daughter, and Shah Jahan married Nur Jahan's niece, for whom he built the Taj Mahal.

As a result of gifts, court stipends, and her own business acumen, Nur Jahan became extremely wealthy and could patronize literature, art, architecture, and fashion with taste that extended to imported European luxury goods. Her innovations in these areas included new weaves and prints for textiles, clothing designs, and gourmet recipes with artistic presentation. In addition, she was a connoisseur of painting and an accomplished poet in both Arabic and Persian. She seems to have played a role in almost all imperial architectural commissions during the period of her marriage to Jahangir. Not only was she the principal patron of the Nur Mahal Serai (Jalandhar) on the Agra–Lahore Road, the renovated Ram Bagh (Agra), the Nur Manzil Garden (Agra), the Tomb of I'tmad al-Dawla (Agra), the Pattar Mosque (Srinagar), and her own tomb near Jahangir's in Shahdara (Lahore), but she also clearly played an important role in the design of the many imperial gardens built along the shores of Lake Dal in Kashmir.

Even before the death of her husband in 1627, Nur Jahan schemed against the future emperor, Shah Jahan, and on his accession she was sent to live her last years in Lahore with her daughter. Her house stood in the same garden enclosure where she built her tomb, and she was buried there upon her death in 1645.

D. FAIRCHILD RUGGLES

See also Mughals; Women Patrons; Women Rulers

Further Reading

Findly, Ellison Banks. *Nur Jahan: Empress of Mughal India.* New York and Oxford: Oxford University Press, 1993.
Pant, Chandra. *Nur Jahan and Her Family.* Allahabad: Dan Dewal Publishing, 1978.

NUSAYRIS

Nusayrism is a syncretistic religion with a close affinity to Shi'ism. Most of its adherents live in Syria and the southeastern regions of present Turkey. In Syria, the Nusayris constitute more than one million (about twelve percent of the population). They live chiefly in the mountainous areas of Latakia, known as Jabal al-'Alawiyyin, on the country's northwest coast, where they represent close to two-thirds of the populace.

The original name of the sect is *Nusayriyya*, after Muhammad ibn Nusayr, a disciple of the Imams 'Ali al-Hadi (d. 868 CE) and al-Hasan al-'Askari (d. 873–4), the tenth and eleventh imams of Twelver Shi'ism. The modern name of the sect is *'Alawis;* this name was adopted at the beginning of the twentieth century to underscore the sect's links with 'Ali ibn Abi Talib, the common ancestor of all of the Shi'i factions.

Despite the important role played by Ibn Nusayr during the formative phase of Nusayrism, the real founder and promulgator of the Nusayri faith seems to have been al-Husayn ibn Hamdan al-Khasibi (d. ca. 957).

During the early years of the twelfth century, the Crusaders conquered part of the mountainous region of Latakia. During the Mamluk period, unsuccessful attempts were made to convert the Nusayris to Sunni Islam.

For most of the Ottoman period, the Nusayris were recognized as a distinctive group with the right to maintain an autonomous judicial apparatus. Modern Western interest in the Nusayri religion began during the mid-nineteenth century. A pioneering monograph about the Nusayris, *Histoire et Religion des Nosairis,* was published by the noted French scholar René Dussaud in Paris in 1900. An important source for the study of Nusayrism in modern times is *al-Bakura al-Sulaymaniyya fi Kashf Asrar al-Diyana al-Nusayriyya,* a description and refutation of the Nusayri religion that was written by Sulayman al-Adhani, a Nusayri convert to Christianity from the town of Adhana in southern Turkey.

The Nusayris again came to the fore during the period of the French mandate over Syria and Lebanon (from 1920). France promoted their integration into the ranks of the French army and even granted them autonomy in the Jabal al-'Alawiyyin region. Their presence in the French army prepared the ground for their later inclusion in the army of an independent Syria. The Nusayris are the only minority to have succeeded in assuming power in their own country.

Like the rival Druze religion, Nusayrism is shrouded in mystery, its secrets being the exclusive prerogative of the initiated *(khassa)*, whereas the uninitiated *('amma)* are kept strictly separate. In essence, Nusayrism is an antinomian religion, and the religious obligations are limited to moral prescriptions.

The Nusayris believe that the deity manifested itself in history in the form of a trinity. This trinitarian revelation is believed to be a theophany that has recurred in seven eras (called *akwar, adwar,* or *qubab*) throughout the course of history. According to the Nusayri trinitarian doctrine, two entities or persons *(aqanim)* emanated from the supreme aspect of the deity. This supreme aspect, called *ma'na* (meaning, essence), is sometimes identified with God Himself. The second is the *ism* (Name) or *hijab* (Veil). The third entity is the *bab* (Gate), which is the gate through which the believer may contemplate the mystery of divinity. This trinity has been incarnated in historical or mythical persons. During the seventh and last cycle, the "Muhammadan cycle" that opens the Muslim era, the trinity was incarnated in three central figures of early Islam: 'Ali as the ma'na, Muhammad as the ism, and Salman the Persian as the bab, from whence comes the acrostic sirr 'A[yn] M[im] S[in] (i.e., the mystery of 'Ali, Muhammad, and Salman).

The syncretistic nature of the Nusayri religion is also evident in its calendar, which is replete with festivals from diverse origins: Christian, Persian, and Muslim (both Sunni and Shi'i). However, being regarded by the Muslim world as heretics has not prevented the Nusayris from seeing themselves as monotheists *(muwahhida* or *muwahhidun)*.

Among the Nusayris in Syria, there are currently two distinct trends. The more conservative members of the community, living mainly in the Jabal al-'Alawiyyin region, adhere steadfastly to the traditional creeds and rituals of the sect. Alternatively, others are becoming assimilated into Twelver Shi'ism and in fact identify themselves as Shi'is. This is taking place mainly in cities, where these individuals have come under the influence of Shi'i communities.

MEIR M. BAR-ASHER

Further Reading

Al-Adhani, Sulayman. *al-Bakura al-Sulyamaniyya.* Beirut. (Partial English translation in Salisbury, E. "'The Book of Sulaimân's First Ripe Fruit Disclosing the Mysteries of the Nusairian Religion' by Sulaimân Effendi of Adhanah." *Journal of the American Oriental Society* 8 (1864): 227–308.)

Bar-Asher, M.M. "Sur Les Éléments Chrétiens de la Religion Nusayrite-'Alawite." *Journal Asiatique* 289 (2001): 185–216.

———. "The Iranian Component of the Nusayri Religion." *Iran* 41 (2003): 217–27.

Bar-Asher, M.M., and A. Kofsky. *The Nusayri-'Alawi Religion: An Enquiry into Its Theology and Liturgy.* Leiden, 2002.

Dussaud, R. *Histoire et Religion des Nosairis.* Paris, 1900.

Lyde, S. *The Asian Mystery: The Ansaireeh or Nusairis of Syria.* London, 1860.

Moosa, M. *Extremist Shi'ites: The Ghulat Sects.* New York, 1988.

Al-Tabarani, Abu Sa'id Maymun ibn Qasim. *Kitab Sabil Rahat al-Arwah wa-Dalil al-Surur wa-l-Afrah ila Faliq al-Asbah al-Ma'ruf bi-Majmu' al-A'yad,* ed. R. Strothmann. *Der Islam* 27 (1944–1946).

Al-Tawil, Muhammad Amin Ghalib. *Ta'rikh al-'Alawiyyin.* Beirut.

OATHS

Known variously as *qasam, half,* and *yamīn,* the oath was ubiquitous in medieval Islam. Apart from its formal use in judicial contexts, the oath—and its close relative, the vow *(nadhr)*—was a common means by which individuals affirmed commitments to one another in all areas of life, from high politics to business negotiation to relationships within the family. The treatment of oaths in the medieval law books attests to not only the ubiquity of this social practice but also the ongoing efforts of religious scholars to shape and control it.

In the most basic sense, oaths can be described as commitments made to another party in which God serves as witness and guarantor ("By God, I shall never set foot in this house again," "By God, I shall not sell this item for less than one dinar"). As such, the legal scholars normally distinguish them from vows in which the commitment is made directly to God ("If God should restore my health, I pledge to make the pilgrimage to Mecca on foot"), although the boundaries between them are easily obscured: vows, for example, might assume the shape of oaths, particularly if they are uttered not for straightforwardly pious purposes but rather to achieve something in a negotiation (for example, "If what I say is not true, I will sacrifice a sheep and distribute its meat as alms," known to the lawyers as a "Vow of Incitement and Anger" and not always considered binding by them). In principle, vows are sworn *to* God, whereas oaths are sworn *by* God. In practice, the latter were also sworn by things other than God, as is suggested by

the repeated strictures of the lawyers against such practices and the number of *hadith,* which insist that valid oaths are sworn only "by God," He alone being worthy of such magnification. People swore "by my father's life" and "by the beard of the Prophet"—and by any number of other things as well—but normative practice insisted that God is the only true guarantor of commitments, and we even read of a teaching ascribed to various Companions that it is preferable to swear falsely by God than truthfully by anything else.

Oaths "by God" contain within themselves no specific penalty for nonfulfillment *(h.inth),* and in most cases such oaths were not judicially enforceable. There were, of course, informal social sanctions that regulated the use of swearing and would have discouraged the habitual swearing of false oaths, but in the immediate sense violation of an oath "by God" was strictly a matter between the individual and God. To swear falsely, or to break an oath-bound commitment, was to make oneself vulnerable to divine punishment. Believers might turn to any of several Qur'anic passages that underscore the importance of fulfilling one's covenants (for example, Q 16:91) and promise a painful doom to those who knowingly swear false oaths (for example, Q 58:14f). Similarly, there is no shortage of *hadith* reminding those who would swear falsely or otherwise sinfully that they will be barred from Paradise and given a seat in the Fire. It was because of the otherworldly nature of the sanction that the practice of swearing at a mosque or a saint's tomb was often adopted. At the same time, some oaths did spell out specific temporal consequences in their very language; for example, "If I do not repay this debt in full by the end of the month, one of my slaves is free," or "If you [that is, my wife] leave this house without my permission, you are divorced." These are essentially conditional statements of manumission and divorce: Once the condition is met, the penalty takes immediate effect and would at least in theory be enforceable by a court.

Unlike such conditional statements, oaths "by God" uttered with deliberation could, when not fulfilled, be expiated along the lines set out in Qur'an 5:89 (feeding or clothing ten paupers, freeing a slave, or, for those who lack such means, a three-day fast). It was even possible, in the eyes of some scholars, to set aside an oath, make no effort to fulfill it, and replace it with an act of atonement (kaffāra), a practice reflected in a prophetic hadith in which Muhammad states that "I never swear an oath unless, upon seeing something better, I expiate it and do the better thing." What is reflected here is the practical acknowledgment that believers needed ways to escape their oath-bound commitments without irreparably damaging their status in the afterlife. This concern is attested to at several places in the Qur'an; for example, 66:1–2 (dissolution of oaths of sexual abstention) and 2:224 (oaths ought not become an obstacle to righteous behavior). In the legal discussions as a whole, it is clear that the scholars were concerned to provide escape routes and otherwise limit the oath's binding power when to insist on it would place the afterlife of believers in jeopardy or undermine ritual practices favored by the law. (Examples of the latter problem would include vows of extreme asceticism or commitments to make pilgrimage to sites not part of the recognized sacred topography of Mecca.) These escape routes include, in addition to expiation, the practice of istithnā' (adding the phrase "If God wills" to the oath) and the recognition of a category of "unintended" (laghw) oaths that are considered neither binding nor—by most jurists—in need of expiation. Finally, the well-known literature of juristic expedients (hiyal) is filled with clever evasions by which one escapes the consequences of an oath while formally respecting it, as well as examples of recourse to misleading language that seem to undermine the very idea of an oath.

KEITH LEWINSTEIN

See also Cursing

Primary Sources

Most collections of hadith and works of jurisprudence contain chapters on oaths and vows (aymān and nudhūr); good examples include:

'Abd al-Razzāq al-S.an'ānī. al-Musannaf. 12 vols. Beirut: 1983–1987), vol. 8.
Shams al-Dīn al-Sarakhsī. al-Mabsūt. 30 vols. Cairo: 1324–1331, in vols. 8 and 9.
Ibn Hazm. al-Muhallā. 11 vols. Cairo, 1928–1933, vol. 8.
Ibn Rushd. Bidāyat al-Mujtahid. 2 vols. Cairo, 1966, vol 1.

Further Reading

Abū Fāris, M. Kitāb al-Aymān wa-'l-Nudhūr. Amman, 1988.
Brunschvig, R. "Voeu ou serment? Droit compare du Judaïsme et de l'Islam." Hommage à Georges Vajda. Louvain, 1980, 125–134.
Calder, N. "Hinth, birr, tabarrur, tah.annuth: an Inquiry into the Arabic Vocabulary of Vows." BSOAS 51 (1988): 214–239.
Encyclopaedia of Islam. 2d ed. s.v. kasam.
Gottschalk, W. Das Gelübde nach älterer arabischer Auffassung. Berlin, 1919.
Hawting, G. "An Ascetic Vow and an Unseemly Oath?: īlā' and zihār in Muslim Law." Bulletin of the School of Oriental and African Studies 57 (1994): 113–125.
Mottahedeh, R. Loyalty and Leadership in an Early Islamic Society. Princeton, 1980, 40–72.
Pedersen, J. Der Eid bei den Semiten. Strassburg, 1914.

ÖLJEITÜ (ULJAYTU)

Öljeitü (Ar. Uljaytu) was the eighth Mongol Ilkhanid ruler of Persia and Iraq. Ghiyath al-Din Muhammad Khudabandah Uljaytu was born in AH 680/1282 CE and succeeded his brother Ghazan as ilkhan on Dhu 'l-Hijja 703/July–August 1304 and reigned until 716/1316. Ghazan, Uljaytu's predecessor, had converted to Islam in 694/1295. Uljaytu continued the practice, begun under his brother, of rebuilding and reestablishing the schools and mosques that had been destroyed by previous Mongol rulers. Shortly after he succeeded his brother as ilkhan in 703/1304, Uljaytu declared Islam as the official religion of all areas within his realm. During his reign, Uljaytu engaged in extensive patronage of religious institutions and scholarship. He was aided in the central administration of the dynasty by three primary officials: the wazirs, Rashid al-Din Fadl Allah Hamadani, Sa'd al-Din Muhammad Sawaj, and Taj al-Din 'Ali Shah Gilani, who replaced Sa'd al-Din after his fall from favor and execution in 711/1312. Uljaytu also relied extensively on Qutlughshah as senior commander of his armies (amir).

Uljaytu's reign as ilkhan was characterized by both the ongoing external effort to win success over the Mamluks by subjugating Syria and Egypt, and the internal struggle to consolidate his kingdom in the face of challenges from several independent Mongol chiefs. Uljaytu's acceptance of Islam did not prevent him from reaching out to European kings and

Christian authorities in Europe for support in his struggle against the Mamluks. He sent letters to Edward I of England, King Philip the Fair of France, and Pope Clement V expressing his desire for a concerted action against the Mamluks. Internally, one of the first steps undertaken by Uljaytu to gain control over independent Mongol provinces came in 705/1306 when he launched an attack on Fakhr al-Din, the ruler *(malik)* of the Kart dynasty that controlled Harat. The expedition was unsuccessful and Uljaytu's commander, Danishmand Bahadur, was killed in a conspiracy organized by one of his officers, Jamal al-Din Muhammad Sam.

In the following year, Uljaytu set out on a campaign against the province of Gilan on the Caspian Sea, not far from his newly established dynastic capital of Sultaniyah. It is likely that Uljaytu saw the conquest of Gilan as necessary for generating revenue for financing his long-term goal of challenging Mamluk dominance of Syria and Egypt. In part due to its harsh climate and difficult-to-navigate geography, the small kingdom of Gilan was able to resist Mongol conquest during the period of Uljaytu's predecessors. In 706/1307, Uljaytu mounted an elaborate invasion of Gilan, ordering his commanders to lead armies into the province from four different points: Chupan entered Gilan from the Northwest, Tughan and Mu'min were sent to the eastern province of Gurjiyan, his senior *amir*, Qutlughshah, descended on the city from Khalkhal, and Uljaytu himself advanced on Gilan through Kurandasht, Lawshan on the Shahrud, Daylaman, and finally entering Lahijan. There is considerable debate concerning the outcome of Uljaytu's expedition to Gilan. Persian contemporary sources have largely described the attempt to subjugate Gilan as successful. In addition, Arabic sources, particularly Mamluk chroniclers, appear to confirm this view, with variation in the time and sequence of events between the two historiographical traditions. It appears that the Mongol armies suffered a number of significant losses during the campaign, including the death of Uljaytu's senior amir, Qutlughshah. The *ilkhan* was ultimately successful in establishing Mongol sovereignty over the province and its resources.

In 712/1312–1313, Uljaytu launched what was to be the last Mongol offensive against Mamluk territory. The Ilkhanid army marched from Mawsil and reached the walls of Rahbat al-Sham on the Euphrates in Ramadan/December of that year. The inhabitants of the city defended the invasion fiercely and after almost three weeks of fighting, lacking the provisions, Uljaytu ordered his troops to withdraw. Following the unsuccessful invasion, Uljaytu began to engage in conciliatory diplomacy with the Mamluks,

and in 723/1323, al-Nasir Muhammad concluded a peace treaty with his son and successor, Abu Sa'id.

Contemporary biographical sources on Uljaytu reveal a high degree of ambiguity concerning the details of his conversion to Islam. His conversion to Islam was preceded by a series of religious affiliations, from being baptized as a Christian, to later becoming Buddhist, before finally accepting Shi'ism. At the time of his conversion to Islam, Uljaytu initially became an adherent to the Hanafi *madhhab*. This is perhaps a result of the early Hanafi influence during his time as governor of Khurasan. Uljaytu later adopted the Shafi'i *madhhab* under the influence of the Shafi'i scholar, Nizam al-Din 'Abd al-Malik al-Maraghi, and his *wazir*, Rashid al-Din. However, Uljaytu continued to encourage religious debates and exchanges at his court and surrounded himself with scholars of all legal schools and theological persuasions. Uljaytu invited the erudite Shi'i scholar al-'Allama al-Hilli to join his court for the purpose of furthering religious debate. In Rajab 709/December 1309, al-'Allama al-Hilli accompanied Uljaytu on a visit to the tomb of Salman al-Farisi at Mada'in. Though the issue of which of the Shi'i scholars in the court of Uljaytu was responsible for the conversion of the *ilkhan* to Shi'ism is contested in the contemporary sources from the period, Uljaytu publicly converted to Shi'ism in Sha'ban 709/January 1310.

The existent documentary and literary sources from the period after Uljaytu's conversion are replete with accounts of his efforts to propagate Islam more generally and Shi'ism in particular. The *ilkhan* sponsored several legal and theological debates between al-'Allamah al-Hilli and Sunni scholars in the court from the years 710/1311 to 716/1316. Shortly thereafter, Uljaytu established the *madrasah sayyarah*, which was a mobile school founded to accompany the *ilkhan* whenever he traveled. Positions in the *madrasah sayyarah* were apparently reserved for scholars with a close relationship with the *ilkhan*. The famous eighth-fourteenth-century traveler, Ibn Battuta, although generally displeased with the degree of what he deemed to be Shi'i heresy on his visit to Iraq and Iran, provides extensive details concerning the endowed religious institutions he observed in Mongol domains during the reigns of Uljaytu and his son, Abu Sa'id. Furthermore, Ibn Battuta and other contemporary observers provided important numismatic evidence related to Uljaytu's efforts to promote Shi'ism. Uljaytu eliminated the names of the Sunni *khulafa' al-rashidun* from coins and ordered coins minted honoring the Twelve Shi'i Imams. He also ordered that the names of the Twelve Imams be in the Friday prayer.

Furthermore, Uljaytu transferred the Ilkhanate capital from Tabriz to Sultaniyah, where he sought to establish a large religious institution in the city to rival the size of the one established by Rashid al-Din in the Rab'-i Rashidi. Uljaytu also completed work on his large and intricately decorated tomb prior to his death, and his magnificent tomb is one of the greatest examples of Mongol architecture that still survives. The funerary complex built by Uljaytu includes several prayer halls, spaces for reciting the Qur'an, and residence halls. The largest copy of the Qur'an made in the period, an enormous (seventy-two by fifty centimeters) thirty-part manuscript transcribed in Baghdad between 706/1306 and 710/1313, was also endowed to Uljaytu's funerary complex at Sultaniya. Although the other contemporary buildings surrounding the tomb did not survive, there was a large congregational mosque with a monumental portal leading to a large central courtyard with four *iwan*s, a domed sanctuary, and an adjacent *khanaqah*.

In addition to the lavish building that Uljaytu engaged in at Sultaniyah and the endowment of formal institutions, he also served as patron for individual scholars. Uljaytu continued to support the renowned observatory and school for the study of philosophy and mathematics at Maragha, endowed first by Hulagu in 657/1258 under the direction of Nasir al-Din al-Tusi and completed during the reign of Hulagu's successor, Abaqa (663–683/1265–1284).

Uljaytu died in his bed at Sultaniyah 17 December 1316/1 Shawwal 716. He was thirty-six years old. Quite extraordinary for a reigning Mongol ilkhan, he is believed to have died of natural causes, related to a protracted struggle with a stomach ailment.

TARIQ AL-JAMIL

Further Reading

al-Abru, 'Abd Allah ibn Lutf Allah Hafiz. *Dhayl-i jami' al-tawarikh-i Rashidi*. Edited by Khan Baba Bayani. Tehran: Intisharat-I Danishgah-i Tehran, 1350/1971.

Abu'l-Fida', Isma'il ibn 'Ali ibn Mahmud ibn Muhammad ibn Taqi al-Din 'Umar ibn Shahanshah ibn 'Ayyub. *al-Mukhtasar fi akhbar al-bashar*. Edited by Muhammad Zaynahum, Muhammad 'Azab, and Yahya Sayyid Husayn. Cairo: Dar al-Ma'arif, 1998–1999.

(*Mukhtasar ta'rikh al-bashar*) *The Memoirs of a Syrian Prince Abu'l-Fida', Sultan of Hamah (672–732/1273–1331)*. Translated by P.M. Holt. Freiburger Islamstudien, vol. 9. Wiesbaden: Steiner, 1983.

al-Amin, Hasan. *Mustadrakat a'yan al-shi'a*. 10 vols. Beirut: Dar al-Ta'aruf lil-Matbu'at, 1419/1999.

al-Amin, Muhsin. *A'yan al-shi'a*. 15 vols. Beirut: Dar al-Ta'aruf lil-Matbu'at, 1420/2000.

Amitai-Preiss, Reuven. "Mongol Imperial Ideology and the Ilkhanid War Against the Mamluks." In *The Mongol Empire & Its Legacy*, edited by Reuven Amitai-Preiss and David O. Morgan. Leiden: Brill, 2000.

Amuli, Shams al-Din Muhammad ibn Mahmud. *Nafa'is al-funun fi ara'is al-'uyun*. Tehran: 1309/1891–1892.

Bausani, Alessandro. "Religion under the Mongols." In *The Cambridge History of Iran*, edited by J. A. Boyle, 397–406. Cambridge: Cambridge University Press, 1968.

Blair, Sheila. "The Mongol Capital of Sultaniyya 'The Imperial'." *Iran, Journal of the BritishInstitute of Persian Studies* 24 (1986): 139–151.

"Sultaniyya." *EI* (2): 9:859b.

Ibn Battutah, Muhammad ibn 'Abd Allah. *Rihlat Ibn Battuta: al-musammat tuhfat al-nuzzar fi ghara'ib al-amsar*. Beirut: Dar al-Kutub al-'Ilmiyya, no date given.

Ibn al-Dawadari, Abu Bakr ibn 'Abd Allah. *Kanz al-durar wa jami' al-ghurar: masadir ta'rikh misr al-islamiyya*. Cairo: Qism al-Dirasat al-Islamiyya, al-Ma'had al-Almani lil-Athar bi-l-Qahira, 1960–1982.

Ibn al-Fuwati, Kamal al-Din 'Abd al-Razzaq. *Kitab al-hawadith li-mu'allif min al-qarn al-thamin*. Edited by Bashshar 'Awwad Ma'ruf and 'Imad 'Abd al-Salam Ra'uf. Beirut: Dar al-Gharb al-Islami, 1997.

al-Hawadith al-jami'a wa-l-tajarib al-nafi'a fi l-mi'a al-sabi'a. Baghdad: Matba'at al-Furat, 1351/1932.

Majma' al-adab fi mu'jam al-alqab. Edited by Muhammad Kazim. Tehran: Mu'assasat al-Tiba'a wa-l-Nashr Wizara al-Thaqafa wa-l-Irshad al-Islami, 1995/1416.

Ibn Hajar al-'Asqalani, Shihab al-Din. *al-Durar al-kamina fi a'yan al-mi'a al-thamina*. 5 vols. Beirut: Dar al-Kutub al-Haditha, 1966–1967.

Ibn Kathir, 'Imad al-Din Isma'il ibn 'Umar. *al-Bidaya wa-l-nihaya fi l-ta'rikh*. 14 vols. Edited by Ahmad Abu Muslim. Beirut: Dar al-Kutub al-'Ilmiyya, 1997.

al-Khwansari, Muhammad Baqir. *Rawdat al-jannat fi ahwal al-'ulama' wa-l-sadat*. 8 vols. Beirut: al-Dar al-Islamiyya, 1991.

al-Isbahani, Mirza 'Abd Allah Afandi. *Riyad al-'ulama' wa hiyad al-fudala'*. 6 vols. Edited by Ahmad al-Husayni. Qum: Matba'at al-Khayyam, 1980.

Riyad al-'ulama' wa hiyad al-fudala'. 7 vols. Edited by al-Sayyid Mahmud al-Mar'ashi and al-Sayyid Ahmad al-Husayni. Qum: Maktabat Ayat Allah al-Mar'ashi al-'Amma, 1401/1980–81.

Ibn Taghri Birdi, Abu'l-Mahasin Yusuf. *al-Nujum al-zahirah fi muluk Misr wa-l-Qahira*. Cairo: Dar al-Kutub al-Misriyya, 1348–1392/1929–1972.

Melville, Charles. "The Ilkhan Oljeitü's Conquest of Gilan (1307): Rumour or Reality." In *The Mongol Empire & Its Legacy*, edited by Reuven Amitai-Preiss and David O. Morgan. Leiden: Brill, 2000.

Qashani, Abu'l-Qasim 'Abd Allah ibn 'Ali. *Ta'rikh-i Uljaytu*. Tehran: Bangah-i Tarjumah va Nashr-i Kitab, 1348/1969.

al-Rashid al-Din, Fadl Allah. *Jami' al-Tawarikh: Ta'rikh al-Maghul*. Translated into Arabic by Muhammad Sadiq Nashat, Muhammad Musa Hindawi, and Fu'ad 'Abd al-Mu'ti al-Sayyad. 2 vols. Cairo: Dar al-Kutub al-'Arabiyya, 1960.

al-Safadi, Salah al-Din Khalil ibn Aybak. *al-Wafi bi-l-wafayat*. 29 vols. Beirut: Dar al-Ihya' lil-Turath al-'Arabi lil-Tiba'a wa-l-Nashr wa-l-Tawzi', 1420/2000.

Spuler, Bertold. *Die Mongolen in Iran: Politik, Verwaltung and Kultur der Ilchanzeit*. Berlin: Academie-Verlag, 1968, 1220–1350.

al-Tihrani, Agha Buzurg. *al-Dhari'a ila tasanif al-shi'a*. 26 vols. Beirut: Dar al-Adwa', 1983.

Tabaqat a'lam al-shi'a. Beirut: Dar al-Kitab al-'Arabi, 1971–1975.

Wassaf, 'Abd Allah ibn Fadl Allah. *Ta'rikh-i Wassaf al-hadra dar ahwal-i salatin mughul [Tajziyat al-amsar wa tazjiyat al-a'sar]*. Tehran: Bunyad-i Farhang-i Iran, 1967.

OMAN

The name 'Oman' has been used since classical times to describe southeastern Arabia. It was referred to thus by early Arab accounts, and the name continued in use throughout the medieval and later periods.

After the death of Muhammad the Prophet (632 CE), Oman became part of the Islamic caliphate. Many of its people, primarily from the Azd tribes, migrated to Basra during the early Islamic period and formed an important part of the Umayyad army. Led by al-Muhallab ibn Abi Sufra, they also played an important role in domestic affairs in Iraq.

During the Umayyad period, the Omani emigrants in Iraq maintained close contact with Oman itself, and many of them returned home after the failure of the Yazid ibn al-Muhallab uprising in 723 CE. In Basra, many Omanis supported the nascent Ibadi movement, named after 'Abdallah ibn Ibad, an early Khariji leader who rejected the use of violence against an unjust ruler. Thus they formed the nucleus of the Ibadi sect.

The Imamate in Oman

After the downfall of the Umayyads in 749–750 CE, the history of Oman can be divided into two geographical areas. The coast was dominated for much of the time by external powers and was heavily influenced by political and military vicissitudes until the arrival of the Portuguese at the beginning of the sixteenth century.

In the interior, the Ibadi Imamate was established in 750 CE, eventually emerging as a separate religious sect adopted by the majority of Omanis. In time, Ibadism became both a sect and a political system, which has profoundly affected the structure of Omani society and history. For Ibadis, spiritual and political authority meets in the body of one person, the Imam of the community and its legal jurist in secular and religious matters. He has full freedom in practice, limited only by the constraints of jurisprudence as interpreted or seen by the Imam.

Despite many attacks, the Ibadi Imamate developed into an institution that was defended strongly by Omanis for centuries. Political conditions and external dangers obliged its adherents to coalesce into an integrated community in order to guarantee their survival.

Oman's history has been greatly influenced by Ibadi thought. Also of importance was the Nabhani period (twelfth to seventeenth centuries CE), when there was a flowering of local literature and culture, which can be seen in the rich literature of the Nabhanis, especially their poetry.

Making use of the monsoon winds, Omani ships sailed to Africa, India, and Southeast Asia, selling local produce such as dates, and pearls, frankincense, and imported goods. On the return voyages they brought items such as perfumes, ivory, silk, sandalwood, spices, and rice.

Because of this active trade, many Omanis settled in East Africa and Southeast Asia, spreading both Arabic culture and Islam. Oman's rising power and economic strength led in due course to the emergence of the Ya'ariba dynasty in 1624 CE. This became a regional power, dominating much of the East African coast and initiating a new era in Oman's modern history.

HASAN M. AL-NABOODAH

See also '**Abbasids; Trade, African; Trade, Indian Ocean; Tribes and Tribal Customs**

Further Reading

al-Rawas, I. *Oman in Early Islamic History*. Reading, UK: Ithaca Press, 2000.

Ennami, A. K. "Studies in Ibadism." Ph.D. dissertation. Cambridge: University of Cambridge, 1971.

Ibn Ruzayq. *History of the Imams and Seyyids of Oman*. Translated by George P. Badger. London: Hakluyt Society, 1871.

Miles, S. B. *The Countries and Tribes of the Persian Gulf*. London: Frank Cass, 1966.

Naboodah, H. "Eastern Arabia in the Sixth and Seventh Centuries A.D." Ph.D. dissertation. United Kingdom: University of Exeter, 1989.

———. "Banu Nabhan in the Omani Sources." *New Arabian Studies* 4 (1997): 181–195.

———. "The Ibadi Movement: A Study of Its Early Development and Ideas." *Digest of Middle East Studies*, 12 (Fall 2003): 1–18.

Potts, D. T. *The Arabian Gulf in Antiquity*. 2 vols. New York: Oxford University Press, 1990 (reprinted 1992).

Sirhan Ibn Sa'id. *Annals of Oman*. Translated by E. C. Ross. Cambridge: The Oleander Press, 1984.

Wilkinson, John C. *The Imamate Tradition of Oman*. Cambridge: Cambridge University Press, 1987.

ONE THOUSAND AND ONE NIGHTS

One Thousand and One Nights is an anonymous collection of Arabic tales. In Baghdad, by the AH second/eighth CE century, a Persian book titled *Hazar Afsaneh (The Thousand Tales)* had been translated into Arabic. It then circulated under a new Arabic

Portrait of Caliph Harun al-Rashid (785–809), hero of the Arabian Nights, shown as a young man. Indian miniature, signed Behzad. Seventeenth century CE. Ms.arabe, 6075, f.9r. Credit: Snark/Art Resource, NY. Bibliotheque Nationale, Paris, France.

title, *Alf Layla wa Layla (A Thousand and One Nights)*.

However, this version no longer exists. The oldest extant manuscripts date from the fifteenth century, and further different versions from the eighteenth and nineteenth centuries. In these, some elements have changed completely (the tales told by Shahrazad) and others slightly (the opening story of the two kings), while the formal organization of the book has not changed. We know this because its overall structure still corresponds to the description given by Ibn al-Nadim in his fourth-/tenth-century bibliography, *al-Fihrist*. It consists of an opening story inside which, each night, other stories are told. The use of embedded stories is a narrative technique that probably comes from India. From a theoretical viewpoint, it raises important questions about the purposes of storytelling.

The frame story, which introduces Shahrazad, continues to fulfill its original function, although the events which it reports are slightly different from those described by Ibn al-Nadim. (More significantly, a comparison of the framework of the *Thousand and One Nights,* as we now know it, with that of the *Hundred and One Nights*, an abridged North African version, shows that the latter is an older version; this is clearly important to an understanding of the development of the *Nights*.)

Entirely new are the tales told by Shahrazad, which immediately follow the opening of the frame *(The Merchant and the Genie, The Fisherman and the Genie)*. They constitute a new corpus, which went through two phases.

The first phase was one of literary conceptualization. In terms of Arabic literary theory, the stories in *Thousand and One Nights* were fictitious (*khurafat,* sing. *khurafa*). When they were adopted into Arabic, the story that was placed at the beginning of the book was the one which, to Arabic thinking, represented the *khurafa* par excellence, that of *The Merchant and the Genie*. All versions of the *Nights* begin with this story, and from the functional, thematic, and ideological points of view, it conditions the choice of stories that form the core of the work in all its extant forms (for example, *The Fisherman and the Genie, The Porter and the Three Ladies, The Story of the Three Apples, The Story of the Hunchback,* and the tales included therein). From the functional viewpoint, the story of didactic intent *(mathal)* yields place to the marvelous tale *('ajab)*, with the added feature, characteristic of the *khurafa*, that each successive tale must be more astonishing. The *Nights* as a whole bear the imprint of this new function; their aim is to surprise and astound, and only incidentally to teach a lesson. From the thematic viewpoint, the

notions of justice and injustice provide a continuous link, with the drama of the tales arising from the fact that the punishment is always incredibly disproportionate to the crime. Lastly, from an ideological viewpoint, the process of embedding is used specifically to express what may be termed a Near Eastern (that is, Islamo-Judeo-Christian) outlook, in which a story is told in irrevocable exchange for a human life, as if it were a righteous deed.

The second phase was one of compilation. As the collection grew in size it came to include various registers of Arabic literature, from historical anecdotes only a few lines long and derived from high literature (*see* Adab) to folk tales (*see* Folk Literature) and tales of chivalry (*see* Sira) stretching over hundreds of pages. The resulting mixture was a middling literature comprising hundreds of story cycles in a diction lying somewhere between classical and colloquial Arabic. It is anonymous and above all freely creative, in the sense that any redactor could make his own changes to it. Consequently, most manuscripts, editions, and even translations of the *Nights* include new stories, in addition to the common core previously mentioned, and sometimes the same story will be found with considerable variations. The most striking instance of this is the translation of Antoine Galland (1704–1715), which includes numerous Arab folktales, such as those of Aladdin and Ali Baba, which had never belonged to the *Nights*. Thus a translation such as that of Richard Burton (1885–1888, online at www.geocities.com/jcbyers2000/toc.htm#burton1) may be considered as representative in its way of the varied *Nights* corpus as the Bulaq edition of 1835 with 1001 nights and Muhsin Mahdi's 1984 edition with only 282.

ABOUBAKR CHRAIBI

Further Reading

Abbott, Nabia. "A Ninth-Century Fragment of the Thousand Nights, New Lighton the Early History of the Arabian Nights." *Journal of Near Eastern Studies* VIII no 3 (July 1949): 129–164, 132–133.

Chraïbi, Aboubakr. *Contes nouveaux des Mille et une nuits.* Paris: Librairie d'Amérique et d'Orient Jean Maisonneuve Successeur, 1996.

———. "Situation, Motivation, and Action in The Arabian Nights." In *The Arabian Nights Encyclopedia,* edited by Ulrich Marzolph and Richard van Leeuwen, with the collaboration of Hassan Wassouf. Denver: ABC-Clio 2004.

Dodge, Bayard (Ed and Trans). *The Fihrist of al-Nadîm: A Tenth-Century Survey of Muslim Culture.* 2 vols. New York: Columbia University Press, 1970.

Gaudefroy-Demombynes, Maurice (Trans). *Les Cent et Une Nuits.* Paris: Sindbad, 1982 (1911).

Gerhardt, Mia. *The Art of Story-Telling.* Leyde: Brill, 1963.

Ghazoul, Ferial. *The Arabian Nights: A Structural Analysis.* Cairo: Cairo Associated Institution, 1980.
Haddawy, Husain (Trans). *The Arabian Nights.* London: W. W. Norton, 1990.
———— (Trans). *The Arabian Nights II : Sindbad and Other Popular Stories.* London: W. W. Norton, 1995.
Irwin, Robert. *The Arabian Nights: A Companion.* London: Allen Lane (The Penguin) Press, 1994.
Mottahedeh, Roy P. "'Ajâ'ib in The Thousand and One Nights." In *The Thousand and One Nights in Arabic Literature and Society*, edited by Richard C. Hovannisian and Georges Sabagh. Cambridge University Press, 1997.

OPHTHALMOLOGY

Ophthalmology is the branch of medicine devoted to the study of diseases of the eye and their cures. Physicians from all religious groups within the medieval Islamic world, where eye diseases were common, avidly studied this branch of medicine. From many sources, they compiled in Arabic considerable information on this topic and added new observations of their own. All this information served as the common body of knowledge on ophthalmology in the Muslim world until the nineteenth century. The earliest treatise on this subject—the Greek, Syriac, and other special textbooks being lost—was written by the Christian court physician in Baghdad, Yuhanna ibn Masawaih (777–857). This book, *Daghal al-'ayn (The Alteration of the Eye)*, which provided the first known description of pannus, was a mixture of information that was soon superceded by the work of Ibn Masawaih's student and coreligionist, Hunayn ibn Ishaq (809–877). Hunayn's *al-'Ashr maqalat fi 'l-'ayn (The Ten Treatises on the Eye)* was the first systematic textbook on ophthalmology. He wrote it over many years, completing it while at the height of his glory as a translator and medical practitioner in Baghdad, under the caliph al-Mutawakkil (r. 847–861). Based primarily on Galen, it described the structure of the eye and its relationship to the brain, vision, health, and disease, the causes of eye diseases, remedies for eye diseases, the treatment of eye diseases, and compound remedies for eye diseases. This book also contained the earliest known anatomy of the eye.

Ophthalmology reached its height of understanding in the works of two other Christians, 'Ali b. 'Isa (d. in the first half of the eleventh century) and his contemporary, 'Ammar al-Mawsili. 'Ali, who practiced in Baghdad, wrote *Tadhkirat al-kahhalin (The Promptuary for Ophthalmologists)*, the most comprehensive book on ophthalmology in Arabic to survive in the original format. Based on Hunayn, Galen, and other authors of antiquity, it described at length the anatomy of the eye, external and internal

diseases of the eye and their treatment (including conjunctivitis, cataracts, and trachoma), and numerous remedies and their effect on the eye. The work *Tadhkira* became the standard resource on the subject. More original, however, was 'Ammar, who was born in Mosul but eventually practiced in Egypt during the reign of al-Hakim (996–1020). His *Muntakhab fi 'ilaj al-'ayn (The Select Work on the Treatment of the Eye)* combined a succinct account of ophthalmology with noteworthy descriptions of cataract surgery. Subsequent work on ophthalmology was overwhelmingly derived from Hunayn, 'Ali, and 'Ammar. It was epitomized, with some notable discussion of trachoma and its sequelae, by the Muslim Ibn al-Nafis (d. 1288), who was born in Damascus and went on to become the personal physician of Sultan Baybars in Egypt (r. 1260–1277), in his *Kitab al-Muhadhdhab fi 'l-kuhl (The Perfected Book on Ophthalmology)*. The works of Hunayn, 'Ali, and probably 'Ammar were translated into Latin in the Middle Ages and formed the basis of ophthalmology in Europe until the first half of the eighteenth century.

GARY LEISER

See also Materia Medica; Medical Literature, Arabic; Optics; Physicians; Surgery and Surgical Techniques; Translation, Pre-Islamic Learning into Arabic

Primary Sources

'Abd al-'Aziz al-Sulami. *Questions and Answers for Physicians.* Translated and edited by Gary Leiser and Noury Al-Khaledy. Leiden: Brill, 2004.
'Ali ibn 'Isa. *Memorandum Book of a Tenth-Century Oculist (His Tadhkira).* Translated by C. A. Wood from the German translation. Chicago: Northwestern University Press, 1936.
'Ammar al-Mawsili. *The Cataract Operations of 'Ammar ibn 'Ali al-Mawsili.* Translated by Max Meyerhof. Barcelona: Masnou, 1937.
Hunayn ibn Ishaq. *The Book of the Ten Treatises on the Eye.* Translated and edited by Max Meyerhof. Cairo: Government Press, 1928.

Further Reading

Savage-Smith, Emilie. "Ibn Nafis's *Perfected Book on Ophthalmology* and His Treatment of Trachoma and Its Sequelae." *Journal for the History of Arab Science*, 4 (1980): 147–187.

OPTICS

Optics, as a scientific discipline that explores the nature and comportment of vision and light, finds its earliest methodic roots in Euclid's elementary treatise the *Optika* (ca. 300 BCE), which eventually was geometrically systematized by Ptolemy (d. ca. 165 CE). According to those polymaths, vision results from the emission of actual light rays from the eye, which take the shape of a cone whose vertex is at the center of the eye and its base on the surfaces of visible objects. This optical theory reconfirmed Plato's account in the *Timaeus*, wherein it was stated that vision is attributed to the soul's nonconsuming fire, which provides the eye with a light that gets emitted into the surrounding air to meet lit objects. This picture was also affirmed in Galen's (d. ca. 200 CE) anatomy of the eye, whereby he argued that vision occurs due to the eye's spirit, which passes through the luminous channels of the optical nerve and is radiated unto the external environment as a light ray that travels at an infinite velocity. A similar observation regarding the speed of light was also made by Heron of Alexandria (d. 75 CE) in his work *Catoptrics*. These mathematical "emission" theories of vision contrasted the physical "intromission" accounts of sight, like what is encountered in Aristotle's *De anima (Tract on the Soul)*, wherein it was ambivalently stated that visual perception results from the introduction of the form of the visible object without its matter into the eye. Although the channels of the transmission of Euclid's Greek *Optika* were indeterminate, its Arabic version was preserved under the title *Kitab Uqlidus fi ikhtilaf al-manazir*. As for Ptolemy's text, it is known from its Greek source, whereas its Arabic rendition is only recoverable from fragments of Latin translations. One of the earliest engagements with optics in Islam may be traced back to Hunayn ibn Ishaq's (d. ca. 873) Galenic studies and al-Kindi's (d. ca. 870 CE) commentaries on Euclid's *Optika*; the latter surviving in Latin under the title *De aspectibus* and were directed by philosophical speculations more than geometric demonstrations. The most remarkable accomplishment in the science of optics is ultimately achieved in Ibn al-Haytham's (Alhazen; d. ca. 1039) monumental *Kitab al-manazir* (*The Optics*; ca. 1027), which was translated into Latin as *De aspectibus* (ca. 1270 CE) and had a focal impact on the unfolding of the perspective tradition in the history of medieval science and Renaissance art. Gathering the findings of the Ancients, Ibn al-Haytham was able to overcome the main dispute over the nature of vision between the Greek mathematicians and physicists. Rejecting the claim that vision occurs by way of the emission of a light ray from the eye, Ibn al-Haytham systematized the intromission account of vision by demonstrating that seeing results from the introduction of the rays of light into the eye in the shape of a virtual conical model. He moreover supplemented his *Optics* with a *Treatise on Light (Risala fi l-Daw')* that studied the radiating dispersion of light across transparent media

in a rectilinear propagation. His optical writings did also incorporate catoptrical explorations of reflection on planar, spherical, cylindrical, parabolic, and conical mirrors. He also integrated the study of lenses and magnification within the science of optics, as well as verify his theoretical hypotheses with controlled tests and experimental installations. The refraction of light also constituted a central subject in his *Optics* that assisted him in his explorations in astronomy and meteorology. Although his optical tradition was comprehensively studied and integrated within the European Latin scientific impetus, it, unfortunately, confronted a period of long interruption in transmission within the medieval Islamic civilization. A parallel engagement in ocular investigations is noted in Ibn Sina's (Avicenna, d. 1037 CE) critical espousal of the Aristotelian theory of vision, which classified optics as a branch of physics rather than mathematics. However, in diverging from Aristotle's *Meteorology*, Ibn Sina ultimately advanced an alternate explanation of the phenomenon of the rainbow. Following his tradition, Nasir al-Din Tusi (d. 1274 CE) wrote a commentary on Euclid's *Optika* that did not show signs of being aware of the optical writings of Ibn al-Haytham. However, the most notable progress in optics, which built on Ibn al-Haytham's results and disseminated them, is creditably attributed to *Tanqih al-manazir (The Revision of the Optics)* by Kamal al-Din al-Farisi (d. 1320 CE). Informed by Ibn Sina's writings, Kamal al-Din revised Ibn al-Haytham's elucidation of the nature of the rainbow and the halo. Using geometrical constructs to demonstrate how the rainbow results from the refraction of light falling on individual raindrops, Kamal al-Din further substantiated his hypothesis by experimentally modeling this process on the passage of light through a spherical vessel filled with water. Following this latest advancement in classical optics, the study of vision in the Muslim world did not progress beyond synoptic summarizations of earlier sources.

NADER EL-BIZRI

See also Aristotle and Aristotelianism; Astronomy; Geometry; Hunayn ibn Ishaq; Ibn al-Haytham, or Alhazen; Ibn Sina, or Avicenna; Kindi, al-, Historian; Mathematics; Meteorology; Plato and (Neoplatonism; Ptolemy; Tusi, Nasir al-Din

Primary Sources

Euclid. *The Arabic Version of Euclid's Optics: Kitab Uqlidus fi Ikhtilaf al-Manazir*. Edited and translated by Elaheh Kheirandish. Berlin: Springer Verlag, 1999.
Ibn al-Haytham. *Kitab al-manazir*. Edited by Abdelhamid I. Sabra. Kuwait: National Council for Culture, Arts and Letters, 1983.

———. *The Optics of Ibn al-Haytham, Books I-III, On Direct Vision*. Translated by Abdelhamid I. Sabra. London: The Warburg Institute, University of London, 1989.

Ibn Sina. *Kitab al-shifa', Kitab al-nafs*. Edited by Fazlur Rahman. Oxford: Oxford University Press, 1960.

Further Reading

Beshara, Saleh O. *Ibn al-Haytham's Optics: A Study of the Origins of Experimental Science*. Minneapolis: Bibliotheca Islamica, 1977.

Gül, Russell. "The Emergence of Physiological Optics." In *Encyclopedia of the History of Arabic Science*. Vol. II. Edited by Roshdi Rashed and Régis Morélon. London and New York: Routledge, 1996.

Lindberg, David C. *Theories of Vision from al-Kindi to Kepler*. Chicago: University of Chicago Press, 1976.

———. "The Western Reception of Arabic Optics." In *Encyclopedia of the History of Arabic Science*. Vol. II. Edited by Roshdi Rashed and Régis Morélon. London and New York: Routledge, 1996.

Rashed, Roshdi. "Geometrical Optics." In *Encyclopedia of the History of Arabic Science*. Vol. II. Edited by Roshdi Rashed and Régis Morélon. London and New York: Routledge, 1996.

———. *Optique et mathématiques, recherches sur la pensée sceintifique en arabe*. Aldershot: Variorum Reprints, 1992.

Sabra, Abdelhamid I. "The Physical and the Mathematical in Ibn al-Haytham's Theory of Light and Vision." In *The Commemoration Volume of Biruni International Congress in Tehran*. Vol. 38. Tehran: High Council of Culture and Arts, 1976.

———. "Sensation and Inference in Alhazen's Theory of Visual Perception." In *Studies in Perception: Interrelations in the History of Philosophy and Science*, Edited by Peter K. Machamer and Robert G. Turnbull. Ohio: Ohio State University Press, 1978.

———. "Optics, Islamic." In *Dictionary of the Middle Ages*. Vol. 9. Edited by Joseph R. Strayer. New York: Charles Scribner's Sons, 1987.

OTTOMAN EMPIRE

The Ottoman Empire was one of the largest and longest-lived Islamic empires. It emerged around 1300 CE as a small principality on former Byzantine territory, to the west of Constantinople. It ceased to exist after defeat in the World War I and the establishment of the Republic of Turkey in 1923. The term *Ottoman*, or *Osmanli*, in Turkish derives from the ruling dynasty, named after Osman (c. 1300–1324), the first ruler of the line.

At the time of its foundation the emirate—not yet an empire—of Osman was one of a large number of Turkish principalities that emerged in western Anatolia following the collapse of Byzantine rule in the late thirteenth century. Several factors favored its rapid expansion. In the second half of the

thirteenth century, central and eastern Anatolia had come under the rule of the Ilkhanids, the Mongol dynasty of Iran. The collapse of this dynasty in the early fourteenth century resulted in a political fragmentation. The Balkan Peninsula underwent a similar disintegration. The Latin victors of the Fourth Crusade in 1204 had divided Byzantine Greece among themselves, and for more than a century most of Greece remained a mosaic of Latin principalities. Much of the northern Balkan Peninsula was briefly united in the fourteenth century under the Serbian Tsar Stephen Dushan, but this political unity did not survive his death in 1355. This lack of a major opposing power was a factor that facilitated Ottoman expansion, as was the ability of the Ottoman rulers to exploit rivalries between their neighbors. Most notably, it was as the ally of the Byzantine pretender John VI Kantakouzenos that the second Ottoman ruler, Orhan (c. 1324–1362), occupied territory on the Gallipoli Peninsula, marking the first stage of the Ottoman conquest of the Balkans. By the end of his reign, Orhan's successor, Murad I (1362–1389), had, through conquest, marriage, and alliances, become the dominant power in much of the Balkans and western Anatolia. By 1402, his son, Bayezid I (r. 1389–1402), had annexed all of western and central Anatolia. In the Balkans he established the Danube as the Empire's northern frontier, provoking hostilities with the kingdom of Hungary. The rout of a Hungarian-led crusading army at Nicopolis in 1396 confirmed Bayezid as the dominant ruler south of the Danube.

In 1402, Timur-i Leng (Tamerlane) defeated Bayezid at Ankara, dismembering his empire in Anatolia and unleashing an eleven-year civil war between his sons. The disaster might have led to the end of the Ottomans. Instead, a hundred years later, the Ottoman Empire was on the verge of becoming a world power, while Timur's empire had disappeared. Three factors probably favored the Ottoman recovery. First, the Ottomans had adopted the principle that Ottoman territory was indivisible. Bayezid's sons fought to the death until a single ruler, Mehmed I (r. 1413–1421), prevailed rather than divide the territory. Second, by the end of the fourteenth century the Ottomans had established, probably on Byzantine and Ilkhanid precedent, a system of registering fiscal and military obligations that allowed administrative continuity in times of political crisis. Third, rivalries among the enemies of the Ottomans prevented a major threat to the warring princes. Mehmed I and his son, Murad II (r. 1421–1451), recovered much of the territory that had been lost in 1402. In central Anatolia, only the emirate of Karaman, reestablished after 1402, escaped reannexation. In the West, the Ottoman annexation of Serbia in 1435 threatened Hungary, triggering Hungarian invasions in 1443 and 1444. It was the Hungarian defeat at Varna in 1444 that ensured that the Balkans would come under Muslim Ottoman rather than Catholic Hungarian rule.

Murad II's successors Mehmed II (r. 1451–1481) and Bayezid II (r. 1481–1512) gave the empire a shape familiar from later centuries. Mehmed II's conquest of Constantinople in 1453 provided the empire with its enduring capital. In thirty years of continuous warfare, he conquered most of the Balkan Peninsula, including Bosnia in 1463, annexed Karaman and other non-Ottoman principalities in Anatolia, and established in these territories direct Ottoman rule rather than rule through vassal dynasties. The work of Mehmed's son, Bayezid, in sponsoring the codification of Ottoman law gave Mehmed's conquests an administrative/legal identity. The strongly Sunni identity of the empire was a product of the following reign.

In 1514, Selim I (r. 1512–1520), after defeating and killing his brothers, routed the Safavid Shah of Iran, Isma'il I, at Chaldiran and, in the following two years, conquered Safavid territory in southeastern Anatolia. The Safavids did not present so much a military as an ideological threat. They were both Shi'i and, more important, heads of a religious order that claimed many Ottoman subjects among its adherents. These religious claims led the Ottoman sultans to emphasize their Sunni orthodoxy as against Safavid heresy. Selim I's conquest (1516–1517) of the Mamluk domains in Syria, Egypt, and the Hejaz reinforced this tendency. Not only did he double the empire's size but he also acquired the holy cities of Mecca and Medina, giving him a claim to leadership of the Islamic world. These were claims that his son, Süleyman I (r. 1520–1566), reinforced. Süleyman opened his reign with the conquest of Rhodes and of Belgrade, on the southern border of Hungary. In 1526, he defeated the Hungarians at Mohács, and from 1526 until 1541, Hungary was a vassal kingdom. The conquest brought Süleyman into conflict with the Habsburg, Ferdinand of Austria, who claimed the Hungarian crown, and his brother, the Holy Roman Emperor and King of Spain, Charles V. To counter Habsburg claims, Süleyman, in 1541, converted central Hungary to an Ottoman province, leaving Transylvania as a vassal kingdom. Nonetheless, continuing Habsburg claims led to intermittent warfare in Hungary until the end of the reign. At the same time, Ottoman and Spanish rivalries in North Africa—Algiers had accepted Ottoman suzerainty in 1519—led to intermittent warfare with the Spanish Habsburgs in the Mediterranean. The third

area of conflict was with the Safavids. From 1533 to 1536, a campaign brought Baghdad, much of Iraq, and eastern Anatolia under Ottoman control; later campaigns between 1548 and 1555 brought no Ottoman gains.

The sixteenth-century wars against the Safavids, and the Habsburgs, brought the Ottomans into conflict with powerful dynastic empires, and it was as a competitive response to these rivals that Süleyman I stressed his Islamic orthodoxy against Safavid heresy and his equivalence to Charles V's status as Holy Roman Emperor, by assuming the title of "Caliph." After a favorable treaty with the Habsburgs of 1547, he adopted the title of "Emperor." The Ottoman dynasty was to use the title Caliph intermittently until 1924.

It was once customary to designate the period from the death of Süleyman in 1566 as the period of the "decline" of the Ottoman empire. Although this designation is an oversimplification—the Ottomans conquered Cyprus from Venice in 1572 and much of the Caucasus and Azerbaijan from the Safavids between 1578 and 1590—the period saw a setback in Ottoman fortunes. The inconclusive war in Hungary from 1593 to 1606 revealed Ottoman military weakness; by 1606, the Ottomans had lost all territory gained from the Safavids after 1578. An eventual peace with Iran in 1639 confirmed the border as fixed in the treaty of 1555. The last major Ottoman conquest, Crete in 1669, came only at the end of a war that lasted nearly twenty-five years. After the failed siege of Vienna in 1683, the Ottomans began to lose territory, the Treaty of Carlowitz in 1699 confirming the loss of Hungary and other possessions. By the outbreak of World War I, almost nothing remained of Ottoman territory in Europe.

To explain these losses, it is more accurate to think in terms of the "rise" of Europe rather than the "decline" of the Ottomans. The changes in European ways of thinking bearing the labels (of convenience) "the Renaissance" and "the Scientific Revolution" led, from the sixteenth century, to developments in military and naval weapons, tactics, and organization, which the Ottomans had difficulty in emulating. The same developments in European thinking created "the Industrial Revolution" of the late eighteenth and nineteenth centuries, which together with the earlier development of mercantile capitalism, led to European domination of the Ottoman economy and the undermining of indigenous industries. Furthermore, after an unsuccessful confrontation with the Portuguese in the Indian Ocean in the sixteenth century, the Ottomans abandoned attempts to control maritime trade westward from India and Southeast Asia, allowing the Atlantic powers to dominate this lucrative field of commerce. Perhaps most significant of all, the import in the nineteenth century of the European concept of nationalism undermined the political unity of an empire based on dynastic and religious identities. The attempts by nineteenth-century reformers to create an Ottoman national identity, and the attempt of Abdulhamid II (r. 1876–1909) to encourage a shared identity among all Muslim subjects, with a loyalty to the sultan/caliph, could not stem the growth of nationalism in the Empire. Even without the defeat in World War I, nationalist separatism would probably by itself have destroyed the Ottoman empire.

COLIN IMBER

Further Reading

Imber, Colin. *The Ottoman Empire, 1300–1650: The Structure of Power.* Houndmills: Palgrave Macmillan, 2002.

Mantran, Robert (Ed). *Histoire de l'Empire Ottoman.* Paris: Fayard, 1989.

Quataert, Donald. *The Ottoman Empire, 1700–1922.* Cambridge: Cambridge University Press, 2000.

P

PAINTING, MINIATURE

Although there remains a persistent belief that the religion of Islam, in its myriad expressions, opposed images and the creation of paintings, painting was consistently practiced in the historical Islamic lands, especially in books. The size of the book, and comparisons to Western medieval manuscripts, led scholars to reference painting in Islamic codices as "miniatures." For Islamic material, however, the term is restricted to painting—generally in polychrome—alone and not to the illuminations in gold and opaque pigments that accompany books.

Islamic painting is an art form of widely different visual expressions and rich in its formal and aesthetic developments, whether one looks at books composed in Arabic, Persian, or Ottoman Turkish. Stimulated by new purposes and needs, the practice of painting had developed outside of the codex by the late 1400s. Artists made single-page paintings, for example, for exchange within the contexts of royal courts. By the late 1500s, artists produced paintings speculatively for sale to a broader sector of the population whose loose collections were often assembled into albums.

Early historical evidence of paintings for books, or even as single sheets, is fragmentary, with few extant examples and only occasional references in written sources. In his preface to *Kalila wa Dimna*, for example, Ibn al-Muqaffa' (d. ca. 758–760 CE) mentions that the function of paintings in his text was to provide pleasure to the reader and also to make the reader more mindful of the book's value. Illustrated copies of *Kalila wa Dimna* do not survive from this early period, though they are attested to, along with other illustrated texts, in primary sources. The extant historical record grows after 1000 CE, becoming steadily more complete with each passing century.

The earliest known books containing paintings are all in Arabic and are principally works of science (for example, astronomy/astrology and specific applications of medicine and mechanics) and belles-lettres (such as wisdom literature, mirrors for princes, and the *Maqamat* of al-Hariri). The earliest dated illustrated codex is al-Sufi's *Book on the Fixed Stars* (1009), which contains line drawings of the constellations. Like other manuscripts of its general type, the images draw from pre-Islamic artistic tradition or contemporary non-Muslim societies (for example, Byzantium) and recast them by subtle adaptations. Prototypes were also selected for paintings that served nonillustrative functions, including the author portraits used as visual frontispieces in copies of Dioscurides's *De Materia Media* of the early 1200s. A number of functions are evident in manuscript paintings between ca. 1000 and 1300. Some paintings were designed to clarify points in the text and thus served a didactic illustrative function. Others went beyond this role to develop visual subjects not strictly required by the text (such as the genre scenes in the Pseudo-Galen *Book of Antidotes*, early 1200s, that show figures working in fields and pharmacists preparing remedies). Others, like the frontispieces to the *De Materia Medica*, visually expressed such cultural practices as the method of learning or the transmission of knowledge and the foundation of its authority.

The Secret Rose Garden, by Mahmud Shabistari (mystic author, thirteenth century CE). Persian miniature. Inv. 994/1586. Photo: Ruth Schacht. Oriental Division. Credit: Bildarchiv Preussischer Kulturbesitz/Art Resource, NY. Staatsbibliothek zu Berlin, Berlin, Germany.

Paintings in these Arabic manuscripts are characterized by direct compositions that arrange starkly silhouetted figures against unpainted paper on a single ground line tufted with plants and flowers. The dramatic contrast between painted compositional elements (and their general shape) and the unpainted paper in thirteenth- and fourteenth-century copies of al-Hariri's *Maqamat (Assemblies)* inspired formal comparisons to the shadow puppetry of the medieval Islamic period. Other paintings arrange figures in schematic depictions of architecture. In both compositional types the image appears as a visual interruption to the text, directly inserted into it.

This painting idiom held sway in the Central Islamic lands only until the late 1200s but continued in Syria and Egypt. Little is known about manuscript painting on the medieval Iberian Peninsula, because books are rare. After 1200, in the aftermath of the Seljuks, painting took on a more prominent role in books.

The permanent presence of the Mongols in Iran after 1258 resulted in numerous changes in painting. The pictorial idiom current in centers such as Baghdad and Maragha was steadily altered, presumably through artists' exposure to Chinese models. These changes are reflected in isolated adoptions of iconography (such as Buddhist types used to represent Gabriel in a copy of al-Biruni's *Chronology of Ancient Nations*, dated 1307); the handling of paint as a wash; and a calligraphic line to render landscape elements and drapery. Compositions of marked horizontal emphasis and the habit of cutting off figures at the frame (suggesting they continue beyond its edge), moreover, indicate a conceptual link to Chinese scroll painting. Geographically remote artistic traditions were absorbed into Mongol Ilkhanid painting, exemplified in the illustrated sections from the world history composed by Rashid al-Din (d. 1318). Experiments with composition and spatial representation, and the development of painting that covered the paper, culminated with the *Great Mongol Book of Kings* (before 1336) and the *Shahnama* composed by Firdawsi (ca. 1010). In addition to these new formal developments, painting under the Ilkhanids occurred in a milieu that witnessed a broad shift toward the Persian language and an understanding that programs of paintings in books could enhance the ideological message of its text. It was also a time when painting joined the canon of artistic forms sponsored by imperial patronage. The importance of painting as a courtly art is attested to by the multiplication of centers after 1350 where painting flourished, though painting continued to be practiced in noncourtly settings.

The next critical development took place in Baghdad under the Jalayirid dynasty. A manuscript composed of three *mathnawi*s, by Khwaju Kirmani in 1396, contains a small number of highly developed compositions that have grown to fill the vertically oriented page format, closely keyed to the relevant text, and which are executed in an exacting technique at a small scale. One painting carries the signature of Junayd amid the architectural decoration; although not the first artist's signature, its prominence signals the artist's growing status. All of these features of the Khwaju Kirmani manuscript constitute a watershed in the practice of painting and were embraced by the Timurids. They became ardent patrons of painting and further perfected earlier traditions.

By the early 1400s, paintings illustrated books of diverse subject matters—history, science, and poetry (epic, lyrical, and romantic)—in Iran and Central Asia. Pictorial idioms were codified for each literary genre, where textual genres were also reflected through differing rates of illustration. Timurid achievements in the art of painting—principally in Herat and Shiraz—manifest in sheer aesthetic power and high technical development were such that contemporary and later dynasties followed their example. One major development that took place in the late 1400s has been attributed to the artist Kamal al-Din Bihzad (d. 1535–1536). Working under Mir 'Ali Shir (d. 1501) and Sultan Husayn (d. 1506), paintings signed by or attributed to Bihzad evidence an increased naturalism in palette, diverse facial expression and gesture (which suggest direct observation), and complex compositions with multiple focal points of activity. Paintings of his design, and those of his contemporaries, came the closest to evoking an image of what the eye might see, though its specific pictorial variety was short lived.

Under the Safavids, successors to the Timurids, painting continued to constitute a principal artistic medium of the court, and it was sponsored through the royal workshops of such patrons as Shah Isma'il (d. 1524) and Shah Tahmasp (d. 1576): Members of the royal house also practiced painting and elevated some artists to the status of intimate. Safavid painting fused the idioms of the Timurids and the Turkmen dynasties of western Iran and Iraq to create a fresh aesthetic distinct from its sources. The same developments later took place in India under the Mughals. Eager to assert their Timurid ancestry, Mughal patrons sought out Timurid manuscripts, which they collected, as well as artists from Iran and Central Asia. In India, imported styles were fused with local Rajput Hindu traditions and later combined with European sources in the form of prints or paintings under Akbar (d. 1605).

Similar processes occurred in Ottoman painting, a tradition that responded equally to Persian and

European idioms. By the early 1500s, Ottoman painting had developed its unique character, one often described as "realistic" or "documentary" in conception and nature. It may well be that these visual aspects result from the principal texts favored by the Ottomans as much as by the particular resources to which artists were exposed or the artists' objectives. Unlike the contemporary Safavids, the Ottomans developed the illustrated history (to unprecedented levels) while they also composed shorter historical narratives describing campaigns, especially during the reigns of Suleyman (d. 1566) and Murad III (d. 1595).

Another unprecedented Ottoman development occurred in the subject matter of topographical painting, images representing cities encountered on various military campaigns. Such images drew from multiple pictorial sources, from works of cartography—both European and Islamic—to pilgrimage guidebooks and scrolls of the Islamic tradition.

DAVID J. ROXBURGH

See also Arabic; Ceramics; Cultural Exchange; Kalila wa Dimna; Ilkhanids; Libraries; Manuscripts; Maqama; Materia Medica; Mughals; Ottoman Turks; Paper Manufacture; Persian; Safavids; Seljuks; Shadow Plays; Shahnama; Timurids; Turkish and Turkic Languages

Primary Sources

Ahmad b. Mir Munshi, al-Husayni. *Calligraphers and Painters: A Treatise by Qadi Ahmad, Son of Mir Munshi, circa AH 1015/AD 1606.* Translated by V. Minorsky. Washington, D.C.: Freer Gallery of Art, 1959.

Thackston, Wheeler M. *Album Prefaces and Other Documents on the History of Calligraphers and Painters.* Leiden: Brill, 2001.

Further Reading

Arnold, Thomas W. *Painting in Islam. A Study of the Place of Pictorial Art in Muslim Culture.* Oxford: Clarendon Press, 1928.

Atasoy, Nurhan, and Filiz Cagman. *Turkish Miniature Painting.* Istanbul: R. C. D. Cultural Institute, 1974.

Atil, Esin. *Kalila wa Dimna: Fables from a Fourteenth-Century Arabic Manuscript.* Washington, D.C.: Freer Gallery of Art, 1981.

Beach, Milo Cleveland. *Early Mughal Painting.* Cambridge, MA: Harvard University Press, 1987.

Blair, Sheila S. *A Compendium of Chronicles: Rashid al-Din's Illustrated History of the World.* London: Nour Foundation in association with Azimuth Editions and Oxford University Press, 1995.

Canby, Sheila R. *Persian Painting.* New York: Thames and Hudson, 1993.

———. *The Rebellious Reformer: The Drawings and Paintings of Riza-yi Abbasi of Isfahan.* London: Azimuth Editions, 1996.

——— (Ed). *Persian Masters: Five Centuries of Painting.* Bombay: Marg, 1990.

Ettinghausen, Richard. *Arab Painting.* Geneva: Skira, 1962.

Grabar, Oleg. *The Illustrations of the Maqamat.* Chicago and London: Chicago University Press, 1984.

———. *Mostly Miniatures: An Introduction to Persian Painting.* Princeton, NJ: Princeton University Press, 2000.

Grabar, Oleg, and Sheila S. Blair. *Epic Images and Contemporary History: The Illustrations of the Great Mongol Shahnama.* Chicago and London: Chicago University Press, 1980.

Gray, Basil (Ed). *The Arts of the Book in Central Asia, 14th–16th Centuries.* Boulder, CO: Shambhala Press, 1979.

Grube, Ernst J. *Persian Painting in the Fourteenth Century: A Research Report.* Naples: Istituto Orientale di Napoli, 1978.

Haldane, Duncan. *Mamluk Painting.* Warminster: Aris and Phillips, 1978.

Jazari, Isma'il b. al-Jazari. *The Book of Knowledge of Ingenious Mechanical Devices.* Translated and annotated by Donald R. Hill. Dordrecht: Reidel, 1974.

Milstein, Rachel, Karin Rührdanz, and Barbara Schmitz. *Stories of the Prophets: Illustrated Manuscripts of Qisas al-Anbiya'.* Costa Mesa, CA: Mazda, 1999.

O'Kane, Bernard. *Early Persian Painting: Kalila and Dimna Manuscripts of the Late Fourteenth Century.* London and New York: I. B. Tauris, 2003.

Robinson, B. W. *Fifteenth-Century Persian Painting: Problems and Issues.* New York and London: New York University Press, 1991.

Rogers, J. M. *Mughal Miniatures.* New York and London: Thames and Hudson, 1993.

Roxburgh, David J. *The Persian Album, 1400–1600: From Dispersal to Collection.* New Haven and London: Yale University Press, 2005.

Simpson, Marianna Shreve. *Sultan Ibrahim Mirza's Haft Awrang: A Princely Manuscript from Sixteenth-Century Iran.* New Haven: Yale University Press, 1997.

Sims, Eleanor. *Peerless Images: Persian Painting and Its Sources.* New Haven and London: Yale University Press, 2002.

Welch, Anthony. *Artists for the Shah. Late Sixteenth-Century Painting at the Imperial Court of Iran.* New Haven and London: Yale University Press, 1976.

Welch, S. C., and Martin Dickson. *The Houghton Shahnameh.* 2 vols. Cambridge: Harvard University Press, 1981.

PAINTING, MONUMENTAL AND FRESCOES

A major problem in assessing the role of monumental painting in Islamic art is the uneven distribution of the evidence. We have a number of frescoes surviving in whole or in part from the first two centuries of Islam, and again from the seventeenth century onward. However, for the intervening centuries we are largely dependent on fragmentary finds and literary evidence. There are also anomalies in the geographical distribution of the evidence, with most of the early paintings coming from Syria and Iraq, the later material concentrated in the eastern Islamic world, and the Maghrib poorly represented.

Detail of a Persian archer, from Shah Abbas I. (1587–1629) leading the Battle against the Ishbeks. Persian fresco from the Great Hall of the Pavilion of the Forty Columns. Credit: SEF/Art Resource, NY. Chihil Sutun (Pavilion of the Forty Columns), Isfahan, Iran.

At the time of the Muslim conquest of Mecca (630 CE), the interior of the Ka'ba was painted with images of Christ and Mary, Old Testament Prophets, trees, and angels. Remains of classically inspired wall paintings recovered from Qaryat al-Faw in Central Arabia also attest the presence of frescoes in a pre-Islamic Arabian secular milieu that may have informed the decoration of the Umayyad palaces in Syria (ca. 700–750 CE), many of which were provided with wall paintings. In some cases (for example, Qasr al-Hayr al-Gharbi and Rusafa) painted dadoes imitate the quarter-sawn marble panels used in Umayyad mosques. In others, more elaborate figural schemes were used. In Qasr al-Hayr al-Gharbi a pair of painted plaster floors were painted with a hunting scene of Sasanian inspiration juxtaposed with a remarkably Classical personification of Earth.

Such eclecticism reaches a crescendo in the interior of the small bathhouse at Qusayr 'Amra, where the walls, vaults, and domes are covered with a spectacular array of painted images whose iconography is poorly understood. These include a royal enthronement scene with Solomonic overtones, the six major kings of the earth, hunting scenes, images of the three ages of man, flying victories, scenes of everyday life (including musicians and carpenters), acrobatic scenes, and an enormous seminaked woman standing beside a pool. The painting of an extraordinary zodiacal dome on the interior of the caldarium dome continues a late antique tradition known from accounts of a bathhouse in Gaza.

Evidence from the ninth-century 'Abbasid palaces at Samarra in Iraq suggests a continuing eclecticism and the use of wall painting to emulate more costly modes of ornament. Frescoes in the Balkuwara Palace were gilded, perhaps in imitation of gold-ground mosaics. In the Jausaq al-Khaqani, scrolling acanthus designs were painted with white dots to imitate the mother-of-pearl discs used in glass mosaics, the scrolls of the acanthus peopled with human and animal figures like the inhabited scrolls of Classical pavements. The so-called Harem in the same palace was extensively decorated with figural paintings, including an enigmatic female figure wrestling a bull, and female attendants. Continual repaintings make it difficult to date these images with any precision.

Fragmentary ninth- or tenth-century wall paintings recovered from Nishapur range from simple red and white geometrical dadoes to inhabited vegetal scrolls, to male and female figures with the severe fringes and dark scalloped curls found in the Samarran frescoes. The paintings included a falconer wearing a coat patterned with large rosettes, a sword, and a belt with lappets similar to those worn by Central Asians and Turks. The component units of a *muqarnas* vault bore flowering plants with eyes at their base. This anthropomorphism also characterized a series of dadoes painted with a bizarre ensemble of feathery wings, vegetation, or cornucopia sprouting hands and eyes, which may have had an apotropaic function.

A penchant for striking visual effects is suggested by textual accounts of illusionistic wall paintings executed in Fatimid Egypt (969–1171 CE), including a pair of dancing girls who, through a skillful use of color, were seen to merge into or emerge from the wall of a palace. A dancing girl is among the images painted in concave *muqarnas* elements recovered from a Fustat bathhouse, which also include a seated figure with a cup. The dancer is comparable to those found on Fatimid lustre ceramics and on the Capella Palatina ceiling (ca. 1142 CE) in Norman Palermo, which may have been decorated by Fatimid artists. The evidence from Nishapur and Fustat highlights the common practice of painting frescoes (sometimes of an erotic character) in medieval bathhouses. The fourteenth-century writer al-Ghuzuli explains that hunting, war, lovers, and gardens are the types of scenes appropriate to a bathhouse, possessing a therapeutic value capable of restoring the animal, spiritual, and natural aspects of man and overcoming the physical debilitation caused by the bath.

Further to the West, evidence for wall painting comes chiefly from the palace of the Alhambra in Granada, much of which was built by the Nasrid sultans (1232–1492 CE) in the course of the fourteenth century CE. The Torre de las Damas was painted with mounted hunting or military scenes, some in superimposed registers, that included a representation of a group seated within an open tent. In the Court of the Lions, three extraordinary concave wooden ceilings were covered with leather and gesso, on which images of the Nasrid sultans were painted, along with themes of courtly love and chivalry derived from contemporary French and Castilian paintings.

The continued development of wall painting in eastern Iran was facilitated by the rise of regional dynasties and courts from the tenth century onward, and descriptions of Ghaznavid architecture include

mention of a palace at Balkh whose walls were decorated with scenes of Sultan Mahmud (r. 998–1030 CE) in battle and also feasting, staples of Islamic courtly art inherited from Sasanian tradition. Mahmud's son is said to have had a palace at Herat decorated with erotic paintings. Frescoes of forty-four life-size Turkish guards clad in rich robes were found in the South Palace at Lashkari Bazaar, confirming the existence of elaborate wall paintings at the Ghaznavid court.

Fragmentary wall paintings reportedly from Rayy depict registers of small-scale figural scenes less than twenty centimeters high, which raise interesting questions about the relationship between wall painting and other arts in Seljuk Iran (1040–1194 CE). In both their style (black outline with bold reds, greens, and blues) and the use of superimposed registers, these fragments recall contemporary Minai (enamel) ceramics, which may themselves imitate a lost tradition of late twelfth- and early thirteenth-century Persian book illustration. In the neighboring Seljuk sultanate of Anatolia, wall paintings ranged from the utilitarian (painting faux masonry over heterogeneous construction materials) to the visual marking of buildings associated with the sultan with prominent red checkerboard and zigzag patterns. The remains of wall paintings depicting seated figures were found at the thirteenth-century Seljuk kiosk at Alara near Alanya.

Combinations of painted and tile decoration were used in monuments erected in the wake of the Mongol conquest such as the palace of Takht-i Sulayman (ca. 1280 CE) in Azerbayjan, and there are reports that the Ilkhanid sultan Abu Said (r. 1316–1335 CE) had a palace near Herat decorated with scenes of his military victories. The painted decoration of the Mausoleum of Uljaytu at Sultaniyya (1313 CE) suggests a relationship with contemporary manuscript illumination, which is also witnessed later in surviving Timurid wall paintings, such as the lapis and gold interior of the Gur-i Amir in Samarqand (1405 CE). Wall paintings represented in Ilkhanid, Jalayirid, and Timurid book painting are executed in a fine calligraphic blue and white style that is quite unlike that of the images in which they appear. Their style and preference for elements of chinoiserie betray the impact of Chinese blue and white ceramics. That they are reliable guides to contemporary wall painting is suggested by frescoes preserved in the Timurid tombs of the Shah-i Zinda complex in Samarqand (late fourteenth century CE), which depict naturalistic landscapes, trees, and ewers or vases containing flowers, executed in dark blue pigment on a white ground.

Literary references indicate the parallel existence of a tradition of Timurid historical wall painting. These include Ibn Arabshah's description of Timur's

(r. 1370–1405 CE) garden palaces at Samarqand, in which he was depicted engaged in hunting or specific military campaigns, receiving homage, and feasting and at leisure, so "that those who knew not his affairs, should see them as though present." Timurid cartoons preserved in later albums contain large-scale figures (some more than forty centimeters tall) pounced for transfer, perhaps to wall surfaces. Conversely, it has been suggested that some historical scenes in Timurid historical manuscripts, such as the *Zafarnama,* may have been modeled after lost wall paintings.

Evidence for wall painting in fifteenth- and sixteenth-century Ottoman architecture comes mainly from mosques such as the Muradiye at Edirne (1434 CE) and the tombs of Ottoman sultans in Bursa, decorated with trees, and vegetal motifs including vases of flowers. Although there are literary references to the Italian artist Gentile Bellini being commissioned to paint frescoes for Sultan Mehmet II (r. 1444–1481 CE) in the Topkapi Palace in Istanbul, no such paintings survive and most extant Ottoman frescoes date from the eighteenth and nineteenth centuries.

Further East, in the Delhi sultanate, a prohibition on figural art imposed by the Tughluqid sultan Firuz Shah (1351–1388 CE) offers incidental evidence for the decoration of palace walls and doors with figural paintings, which were considered especially appropriate to royal places of rest. Textual evidence for wall painting is more plentiful in the Mughal period (1526–1858 CE), especially during the reigns of Akbar (1556–1605) and Jahangir (1605–1627), whose interest in world religions explains a penchant for Christological imagery, which appeared alongside hunting, battle, and garden scenes in the palace at Fatehpur Sikri (1579 CE). Miniature paintings of this period show wall paintings inspired by European prints and Christian imagery decorating the Mughal throne. Remains of paintings executed during the reign of Jahangir were found in the tower of Lahore fort, where a vault was painted with scenes of European inspiration, including angels, birds, and stars. The vault has been interpreted as a Solomonic baldachin, a reminder of the role that monumental painting could play in creating a suitable ambience for the projection of royal authority.

In Turkey, Iran, and India, wall paintings were commonly employed in funerary monuments. The earliest intact funerary frescoes are those in a polygonal tomb-tower at Kharragan in northwestern Iran (1067–1068 CE), depicting peacocks, trees, and hanging lamps. Among the most spectacular Indian examples is the tomb of the Bahmanid ruler Ahmad Shah, which was built near Bidar in the Deccan in 1436 CE, and offers important evidence for pre-Mughal Indian wall painting. The interior surfaces are covered with vibrant paintings of inscriptions, medallions, and cartouches filled with geometrical and vegetal ornament, in which red predominates, with blue, yellow, and white used as subsidiary colors. The paintings derive inspiration from tile dadoes, Indian stone carving, textiles, and even Ottoman carpets, a reminder of the role of textiles in transmitting architectural designs. They are broadly comparable to paintings found in Rasulid and Tahirid mosques and madrasas in the Yemen, a region that has preserved particularly fine examples of medieval painted ceilings. Among these are the Jami' al-Muzaffar (before 1295 CE) and the Madrasa al-Mutabiyya' (1392 CE) in Taizz. In the paintings of the 'Amiriya Madrasa at Rada' (1504 CE) red predominates as in the Deccani tomb.

A number of extant wall paintings in Isfahan and elsewhere indicate the importance of the medium in the architecture of the Safavids (1501–1765 CE). The 'Ali Qapu Palace in Isfahan was originally provided with paintings of tall willowy youths in the style of the famous painter Riza-yi 'Abbasi (d. 1635 CE). The vague eroticism of such paintings is mirrored in the contemporary vogue for epic love stories such as *Yusuf and Zulakha,* or *Farhad and Shrin,* which were included in the carved and painted decoration of a Safavid palace at Nai'in (ca. 1560 CE).

The ancient themes of *bazm va razm* (feasting and fighting) known from reports of Ghaznavid, Timurid, and Turkmen frescoes were also popular at the Safavid court. Examples include the paintings of the Qaysariyya (1620 CE), the entrance to the bazaar in the maidan of Isfahan where Shah 'Abbas I (1587–1629 CE) is depicted battling his Uzbek enemies. Four large paintings (ca. 1660s) in the interior of the Chihil Sutun depict historical scenes involving Safavid engagement with their neighbors, including the Mughals and Uzbeks.

Some of the Safavid wall paintings are said to have been commissioned from European artists, and Europeans (primarily the Dutch and English) feature frequently in wall paintings of the period. They are often associated with small dogs (such as those on the exterior of the Chihil Sutun), a theme also found in single-page paintings of the period. The popularity of such subjects reflects the increasing importance of European powers in the Middle East and India, where contemporary images of Europeans were also painted on the walls of Mughal palaces.

FINBARR BARRY FLOOD

See also Baths and Bathing; Ceramics; Mosaics; Painting, Miniature

Further Reading

Almagro, Martin, Luis Caballero, Juan Zozaya, and Antonio Almagro. *Qusayr 'Amra: Residencia y Baños*

Omeyas en el desierto de Jordania. Madrid: Instituto Hispano-Árabe de Cultura, 1975.

Babaie, Susan. "Shah 'Abbas II, the Conquest of Qandahar, the Chihil Sutun and Its Wall Paintings." *Muqarnas* 11 (1994): 125–142.

Digby, Simon. "The Literary Evidence for Painting in the Delhi Sultanate." *Bulletin of the American Academy of Benares* 1 (1967): 47–58.

Dodds, Jerilynn D. "The Paintings in the Sala de Justicia of the Alhambra: Iconography and Iconology." *The Art Bulletin* 61 (1979): 186–197.

Ettinghausen, Richard. "Painting in the Fatimid Period: A Reconstruction." *Ars Islamica* 9 (1942): 112–124.

Gasparini, Elisabetta. *Le pitture murali della Muradiye di Edirne.* Padua: Sargon, 1985.

Gray, Basil. "The Tradition of Wall Painting in Iran." In *Highlights of Persian Art, Persian Art Series No. 1,* edited by Richard Ettinghausen and E. Yarshater, 313–329. Boulder, CO: Westview Press, 1979.

Grube, Ernst. "Wall Paintings in the Seventeenth Century Monuments of Isfahan." *Iranian Studies* 7 (1974): 511–542.

Herzfeld, Ernst. *Die Malereien von Samarra.* Berlin: D. Reimer, 1927.

Lentz, Thomas W. "Dynastic Imagery in Early Timurid Wall Painting." *Muqarnas* 10 (1993): 253–265.

Morgenstern, Laure. "Mural Painting." In *A Survey of Persian Art,* Volume 3, edited by Arthur Upham Pope and Phyllis Ackerman, 1365–1390. Ashiya, 1981.

Öney, Gönül. "The Interpretation of the Frescoes in the I. Kharragan Mausoleum near Qazwin." *Akten des VII. Internationalen Kongresses Für Iranische Kunst und Archaologie, München 1976.* Berlin: 1979, 400–408.

Philon, Helen. "The Murals in the Tomb of Ahmad Shah near Bidar." *Apollo* 152, no. 465 (2000): 3–10.

Al-Radi, Selma. "The 'Amiriya in Rada' the History and Restoration of a Sixteenth-Century Madrasa in the Yemen." *Oxford Studies in Islamic Art* 13, 1997.

Wilkinson, Charles, K. *Nishapur: Some Early Islamic Buildings and their Decoration.* New York: The Metropolitan Museum of Art, 1986.

Zayadine, F. "The Umayyad Frescoes of Quseir 'Amra." *Archaeology* 31, no. 3 (1978): 19–29.

PALERMO

See Sicily

PALESTINE

The Roman province of Palestine (Palaestina) was created following the suppression of the Bar Kokhba Jewish rebellion of 132–135 CE. It replaced the province of Judea (Iudaea) that existed since 63 BCE, following the conquest of Pompey. Around 400 CE, the province of Palestine was subdivided into three provinces: Palaestina Prima, Secunda, and Tertia. According to Irfan Shahid, the Muslim administrative division of Syria into four provinces (*ajnad,* sing. *jund*) was inspired by the Byzantine theme system that Heraclius created between 628 and 636 CE. The Muslim *ajnad* system included four provinces known as Jund Filastin, Urdunn, Dimashq, and Hims. Jund Filastin consisted of Palaestina Prima, while Palaestina Secunda became Jund Urdunn. Jund Filastin included within its borders the coastal towns of Casearea (Qaysariyya) in the North and Rafah in the South and internal territories, including Jerusalem.

The impact of the Arab–Muslim conquest of the Middle East was manifold, but two issues—Arabization and Islamization—stand out. The main question is: Was Islamization driven by the sedentarization of Arab–Muslim tribes from Arabia in the Middle East, or by mass conversion of the local populations? The evidence for Palestine, irrespective of the Arab–Muslim administrative division of the area, is that Arabization preceded Islamization, and the Christian and Jewish populations adopted Arabic while resisting Islamization. However, in some places the two processes went hand in hand. During the eight and ninth centuries, the town of Ayla (modern-day 'Aqaba) became renowned for its scholarship and families of scholars engaged in the transmission of traditions. Local circumstances must always be taken into account. In Samaria (administratively divided between the *ajnad* of Urdunn and Filastin), for example, mass conversion driven by economic hardship and persecutions took place from the ninth century onward. However, the conversion of the Samaritan population reflected local conditions and says little about other populations. The Muslim conquest of Palestine also had repercussions on the agriculture of the region, with cotton replacing flax as the main cash crop. The spread of cotton facilitated the development of the papermaking industry in Syria and Palestine.

Ramla, the capital of Jund Filastin, was founded by the Umayyad caliph Sulayman ibn 'Abd al-Malik in 715. The caliph is credited with the construction of a palace, a mosque, an extensive water supply and storage system, and the House of the Dyers. The town proved to be a successful urban creation important enough to attract the attention of the caliph Harun al-Rashid, who built there a large underground water reservoir. Two pious endowments (*awqaf,* sing. *waqf*) set up in AH 300/912–913 CE and 301/913–914 revealed the town's prosperity. The first pious endowment was established by the Egyptian administrator Abu Bakr Muhammad ibn 'Ali al-Madhara'i and consisted of water installations for the benefit of the public. The second *waqf* was set up by Fa'iq, a Saqlabi eunuch who was freed of the caliph al-Mu'tamid (870–982). Although the exact nature of this foundation remains elusive, the endowed property consisted of an urban commercial building (*funduq*), which functioned as a place of commerce and an inn.

Several Fatimid officials resided in Ramla during the Fatimid period (early eleventh century), including the governor, who is referred to as *wali*, meaning apparently the governor of Jund Filastin. The governor, through his military slave *(ghulam)*, controlled the police force and kept contact with Cairo through the postal service, or the *barid*. The town was also the seat of the secret policy *(ashab al-akhbar)* and the local Fatimid propagandist *(da'i)*. Two other officials whose presence is attested to in the town were the fiscal administrator *('amil)* and auditor *(zimmam)*, both of whom were nominated by the government in Cairo. The social composition of the population of Ramla remains enigmatic, but there was a local Muslim elite made up of notables, judges, and court witnesses.

Much of our information about Ramla, Jund Filastin, and the other *ajnad* is derived from the chronicle of Musabbihi (977–1029) and concerns the governorship of Anushtakin al-Dizbiri and the Bedouin rebellion of 1024–1029. In Muharram 414/March–April 1023, Anushtakin was appointed as the governor of Jund Filastin, bearing the title of a military governor *(mutawalli harb Filastin)*. The beginnings of his governorship were peaceful and, in April 1024, a large caravan of Khurasani pilgrims from Mecca traveled through Ayla via Ramla and Damascus to Baghdad. The Fatimid regime was quick to take advantage of the need of the Khurasani pilgrims to use the Fatimid territories, due to unsafe roads between Mecca and Baghdad, for propagandistic purposes. The military governors *(wula al-harb)* were ordered to assist the pilgrims. Khurasan was a staunch Sunni region, and Musabbihi testifies that the Fatimids hoped to demonstrate that the hostile propaganda that depicted them as heretics was unfounded. The pilgrims visited Jerusalem, and the regime in Cairo hoped that they would be impressed by the prosperity of the region under Fatimid rule. However, the situation in Jund Filastin quickly changed for the worst. In September 1024, hostilities erupted between Anushtakin and Hassa ibn al-Jarrah, the leader of the Banu Tayy Bedouins, who was authorized to collect taxes (under the terms of an *iqta'* grant) from Bayt Jubrin, in the South of Jund Filastin. This round of hostilities ended with the looting of Tiberias (Tabariyya), the capital of Jund Urdunn, and the occupation of Ramla. The Bedouin conquest of Ramal was a bleak chapter in the history of the town. Hassan executed the soldiers of the Fatimid garrison in the town and confiscated the property and money of several well-to-do people. The town was looted and women and children enslaved. Eventually, after taking vast plunder, Hassan set fire to Ramla. The soap industry suffered ruin, and large quantities of olive oil and soap were destroyed. In spite of the destruction

inflicted on Ramla, Hassan tried to win formal concession from the Fatimids, asking for Nablus and Jerusalem to be recognized as his *iqta'*. Nablus was practically Hassan's stronghold and was officially added to his territories, but the Fatimids refused to cede Jerusalem. Eventually, Anushtakin, with the cooperation of the governors of Tiberias and Jerusalem, was able to defeat Hassan and by the end of 1025, the high tide of the Bedouin uprising was over. However, in 1029, Anushtakin fought and defeated the Bedouin coalition that challenged the Fatimid rule in Palestine and Syria.

The impact of the Bedouin rebellion on Palestine (or more precisely the *ajnad* of Filastin and Urdunn) and Bilad al-Shamm (meaning Damascus and Aleppo) was short-lived. In 1047, the Persian traveler Nasiri Khusrau visited these regions and, on the whole, his impression was very favorable. The towns of the Eastern Mediterranean (that is, those of the Syria–Palestine littoral) prospered under the Fatimid rule. By the mid-eleventh century the Mediterranean trade of the Fatimid state was in its full swing, and Nasiri Khusrau's description of Tripoli, Beirut, Sidon, Tyre, and Acre mirrors this booming commerce. As a person coming from the inland territories of the Muslim world he was much impressed by port facilities *(mina)* that, for his Persian readers, he describes as "a stable for ships." In Tripoli, anchored ships from Byzantium, Sicily, Maghreb, Muslim Spain, and Europe, and the ten percent tax collected from them, financed the Fatimid garrison in the town. The chain in the entry of the port of Acre ('Akka) attracted Nasiri Khusrau's attention, but he is vague about Acre's commerce. The port of Acre had been built during the rule of Ahmad ibn Tulun (868–884), the semi-independent ruler of Egypt, but only during the Fatimid period did the Mediterranean trade make its full impact on the coastal towns Syria and Palestine. It also had significant internal consequences and facilitated the emergence of local commercial elites. Nasiri Khusrau, for example, refers to the Sunni cadi of Tyre Ibn Abi 'Aqil as a rich and influential person. During the second half of the eleventh century and the first decades of the twelfth century, Banu 'Aqil emerged as the local ruler of Tyre and navigated skillfully between the Fatimids, Seljuks, and Franks. Then, in 1124, the town was conquered by the Crusaders.

Nasiri Khusrau's description indicates that the eleventh-century Mediterranean trade had greater significance for the coastal towns of Syria (modern Lebanon) than for those of Urdunn and Filastin. With the exception of Jerusalem, Nasiri Khusrau has little to say about the inland towns of these two *ajnad*. The Jasmine Mosque of Tiberias is fully described, but he has nothing to say about the town itself. Ramla is described as a fortified town with an elaborate system of rainwater collection and storage. An inscription commemorated the 425/1033 earthquake that destroyed many buildings but spared the people. If the soap industry of Ramla recovered from the 1025 destruction remains unknown, but the cultivation of olives continued to prosper and the agriculture of the region abundantly supplied the two stable foods of its population: bread and olives. In 1068, Ramla was hit by an especially destructive earthquake, which destroyed the town and killed fifteen thousand people.

Nasiri Khusrau estimated the population of Jerusalem at twenty thousand and referred to its endowed hospital, which is not alluded to by other sources. He fully describes the holy places of Jerusalem and Hebron, including measurements, and he also provides a detailed description of the Hebron soup kitchen. This charitable institution was financed by an extensive pious endowment and offered meals to the pilgrims. Little escaped Nasiri Khusrau's attention: The international dimension of the holy places of Jerusalem is also noted. He mentions the destruction of the Holy Sepulchre by al-Hakim (1008) and the restoration of the place, following Byzantine diplomatic efforts. Another testimony about the life in Jerusalem and Palestine is supplied by the Andalusi scholar Ibn al-'Arabi, who stayed in Jerusalem between 1092 and 1095. He describes Jerusalem and its Muslim intellectual life, as well as his encounters with scholars in Ascalon and Acre. However, the patterns of life in Syria and Palestine, as described by Nasiri Khusrau and Ibn al-'Arabi, were completely shattered by the Seljukid invasion of the region and the Fatimid attempts of reconquest (1060–1090) and the wars of the Crusades.

YAACOV LEV

See also Syria; Greater Syria

Primary Sources

Ibn al-Qalanisi. *Dhayl Ta'rikh Dimashq.* Edited by H. F. Amedroz. Leiden, 1908.

Muqaddasi. *Kitab Ahsan al-Taqasim (The Best Division for Knowledge of the Regions).* Translated into English by B. A. Collins. Reading, 1994.

Musabbihi. *Akhbar Misr.* Edited by A. F. Sayyid. Cairo, 1978.

Naser-e Khosraw. *Book of Travels (Safarnama).* Translated into English by W. M. Thackston Jr. New York, 1986.

Further Reading

Amar, Zohar. "The History of the Paper Industry in al-Sham in the Middle Ages." In *Towns and Material Culture in the Medieval Middle East*, edited by Y. Lev, 119–135. Leiden, 2002.

Bacharach, Jere L. "Palestine in the Policies of Tulunid and Ikhshidid Governors of Egypt (AH 254–358/868–969 AD)" In *Egypt and Palestine. A Millennium of Association (868–1948)*, edited by A. Cohen and G. Baer, 51–66. New York, 1984.

Cobb, Paul M. "Scholars and Society in Early Islamic Ayla." *JESHO* XXXVIII (1995): 417–428.

Drory, Joseph. "Some Observations During a Visit to Palestine by Ibn al-'Arabi of Seville in 1092–1095." *Crusades* 3 (2004): 101–124.

El'ad, Amikam. "The Coastal Cities of Palestine During the Early Middle Ages." In *The Juraselam Cathedra.* Jerusalem: Detroit, 1982.

Gil, Moshe. *A History of Palestine 634–1099.* Translated into English by Ethel Broido. Cambridge, 1992.

Le Strange, G. *Palestine Under the Moslem.* London, 1890.

Levy-Rubin, Milka. "New Evidence Relating to the Process of Islamization in Palestine in the Early Muslim Period—the Case of Samaria." *JESHO* XLIII (2000): 257–276.

Luz, Nimrod. "The Construction of an Islamic City in Palestine: The Case of Umayyad al-Ramla." *JRAS* 7 (1997): 27–54.

Shahid, Irfan. "Heraclius and the Theme System: New Light from the Arabic." *Byzantion* LVII (1987): 391–406.; "Heraclius and the Theme System. Further Observations." *Byzantion* LIX (1989): 208–243; "Heraclius and the Unfinished Themes of Oriens. Some Final Observations." *Byzantion* LXIV (1994): 352–376.

Sharon, Moshe, "A Waqf Inscription from Ramlah." *Arabica* 13 (1966): 77–84; "Waqf Inscription from Ramla c. 300/912–13." *BSOAS* (1997): 98–108.

PAPER MANUFACTURE

Paper was unknown before the coming of Islam in the 600s CE to Southwest Asia and North Africa, where papyrus and parchment were used for writing documents and books. Muslims learned the technique of papermaking in the eighth century after they conquered Transoxiana, where Buddhist missionaries and merchants along the Silk Road had introduced paper from China. The Chinese had invented paper in the second or first century BCE; it was made from cellulose fibers suspended in water and then collected on a screen and dried. Chinese paper was normally made from bast fibers extracted from such semitropical plants as bamboo and paper mulberry, whereas new sources of cellulose were needed in arid Central Asia. Therefore papermakers there, as well as in the Muslim lands, used such fibers as flax and hemp, as well as waste fibers from rags and old ropes.

Paper mills were established in Baghdad soon after its founding in 762 CE, for the 'Abbasid bureaucracy centered there had an insatiable demand for materials on which to write innumerable documents and records. By the middle of the ninth century the ready availability of relatively inexpensive paper had sparked a cultural revolution throughout 'Abbasid society, as writers on every subject—from theology to cookery—committed their thoughts to paper and began thinking about things in ways they had not done before. Nevertheless, manuscripts of the Koran were copied on parchment codices until the end of the tenth century. Baghdad remained an important center of paper manufacture until the fourteenth century, and the finest papers continued to be manufactured in Iran and India (where it had been introduced in the fourteenth century) into the 1600s.

By ca. 800, paper was available in Damascus, and Syria quickly became known for its quality product. Although papyrus was used in Egypt into the tenth century, it was steadily replaced by paper, either imported from Syria or manufactured locally, and by the end of the century the papyrus industry was dead. Although parchment remained popular for longer than elsewhere in North Africa and the Iberian Peninsula, paper was already used in al-Andalus in the tenth century, and several hundred paper mills are reported in twelfth-century Fez. In the eleventh and twelfth centuries, Andalusi papermakers were responsible for the transfer of the technology to regions under Christian rule, whence it eventually spread to other regions of Europe. The Byzantines used but did not manufacture it, although Istanbul became a center of paper manufacture after the Ottoman conquest of Constantinople in 1453. Early Italian papermakers seem to have also learned their craft in Syria or Egypt, and by the fifteenth century, Europeans were selling cheap but low-quality papers in Southwest Asian and North African markets, initiating the decline and eventual demise of the local paper industry.

JONATHAN M. BLOOM

Further Reading

Bloom, Jonathan M. *Paper before Print: The History and Impact of Paper in the Islamic Lands.* New Haven and London: Yale University Press, 2001.

Le Léannec-Bavavéas, Marie-Thérèse. *Les papiers non filigranés médiévaux de la Perse à l'Espagne. Bibliographie 1950–1995.* Paris: CNRS Editions, 1998.

PARTY KINGDOMS, IBERIAN PENINSULA

The Party Kingdoms, or *Taifa* Kingdoms, emerged out of the anarchy that followed the collapse of the Umayyad caliphate of Córdoba in 1009 CE and the ensuing period of civil war *(fitna)* that lasted until 1031. The Arabic term *muluk al-tawa'if* (factional kings) was applied to the rulers of these petty states, because their existence defied the Islamic ideal of political unity under the authority of a single caliph. The era of the Party Kingdoms, which lasted until 1110 CE, was one of great cultural florescence in al-Andalus, particularly among Muslims and Jews. It was also the period in which native Iberian Muslims lost control of their political destiny; from this time forward they would dominated by Iberian Christian and North African Muslim powers.

The Umayyad caliphate had been run, in fact, if not in name, by the 'Amirid dynasty of "chamberlains" *(hajib)* since Muhammad ibn Abi 'Amir al-Mansur (976–1002) seized power during the reign of Hisham II (976–1009/1010–1113). On his death, al-Mansur was succeeded by two sons, 'Abd al-Malik (r. 1002–1008), and 'Abd al-Rahman (or "Sanjul"), who took power in 1008. Unable to maintain the delicate and volatile balance of factions within the government and Andalusi society, or to counter popular resentment of the growing prestige of Berber groups who had been invited to al-Andalus as part of caliphal military policy, Sanjul provoked the outrage of the Umayyad aristocracy, the religious elite *('ulama')*, and the populace by pressuring the aging and childless Hisham to name him as successor in 1008. Sanjul was deposed by elements of the military, and the people of Córdoba rampaged against local Berbers. As civil war erupted in the capital, power was seized in the various provincial cities by local governors, members of the palace slave *(saqaliba)* contingent, the *'ulama'*, and Berber clans, which had come to dominate the army. The variety of political leadership reflected the divisions that had emerged in Andalusi politics and society since the time of 'Abd al-Rahman III (r. 912–961). Until the death of Hisham III in 1031, each of the rulers maintained a patina of legitimacy by styling himself as the *hajib* ruling in the name of the Umayyad caliph, while struggling against neighboring Party Kingdoms both for survival and a greater share of Andalusi territory.

By the 1040s, most of the smaller states had been swallowed up, leaving several major players, which included: Badajoz, ruled by the Aftasids, an Andalusi dynasty; Toledo, ruled by the Dhi'l-Nun, of Berber origin; Zaragoza, ruled by the Banu Hud, of Arab origin; Seville, ruled by the Andalusi 'Abbasids; Granada, ruled by the Berber Zirid clan; Valencia, ruled by 'Amirids; and Almería, ruled by a succession of factions. By this point the slave regimes were no more; lacking a broader constituency they fell victim to Andalusi and Berber cliques who had a wider popular base or a more cohesive military core. Among the great rivalries that emerged were those of Seville and Granada (which also faced the hostility of Almería), and Toledo and Zaragoza. Zaragoza was further plagued by internal divisions thanks to the custom of Hudid rulers of dividing their patrimony among their heirs.

These rivalries were capitalized on by the Christian kingdoms of the peninsula, particularly Castile and León, which were united under the strong leadership of Fernando I of Castile (r. 1035–1065) and his successor Alfonso VI (r. 1065–1109). Fernando, who exploited Andalusi weakness by pushing far south of the Duero and taking Coímbra in 1064, initiated a policy in which military pressure was used to convert the Party Kingdoms into tributary states. As a consequence, Badajoz, Seville, Toledo, Zaragoza, and Granada were forced to pay large indemnities *(parias)* of gold and silver in exchange for military support and protection from attack. Other Christian principalities, notably Aragon and Barcelona, quickly imitated this. As a result, Christian powers became increasingly embroiled in Andalusi affairs, supporting their *taifa* clients against rival kingdoms and using them in their own internecine struggles. Hence, Castile-supported Toledo fought Aragon-supported Zaragoza, and Zaragoza faced a rebellious Lérida aided by Barcelona. It was in this context that the famous Rodrigo Diaz del Vivar, "El Cid," an exile from Castile, found himself commanding the military forces of Zaragoza against the troops of Aragon and Barcelona. Indeed, "El Cid" had earned his moniker from Sevillan troops in 1064 after he led them to victory against the forces of *taifa* Granada, when they referred to him gratefully as "my lord" *(sidi)*. Such interventions were symptomatic of a general dependence of the *taifa* kingdoms on Christian military strength, which further undermined their autonomy.

The *taifa* kingdoms were able to support the *paria* regime because of the fact that their economic infrastructure had remained largely undamaged by the unrest of the *fitna*. These were economies based on intensive agriculture and market gardening, manufacture and craft and, particularly in the case of the Mediterranean coast, trade. The trans-Saharan gold trade that had fueled the incredible prosperity of the caliphate also continued, providing the *taifa* kings with the funds they needed to meet their tributary obligations. The vibrant Andalusi economy also sustained a cultural renaissance, encouraged by the new political plurality in which rival courts vied as patrons of Arabic letters, science, and theology; the great poet Ibn Hazm (b. Córdoba, 993) is the best-known figure of this age. Jewish culture and letters, including both Arabic- and Hebrew-language literature, also throve, producing remarkable figures such as the poet Isma'il ibn Naghrilla (b. Córdoba, 991), who exercised power as effective head of state of the *taifa* of Granada from 1027 to 1056. This cultural diversity reflected the ethnoreligious composition of the kingdoms, most of which had significant Jewish and Mozarab Christian minorities, members of which not infrequently enjoyed great prestige and wielded considerable political power. For example, Isma'il ibn Naghrilla, *wazir* and military commander of Granada, was succeeded by his son Yusuf. Sisnando Davídez, a Mozarab who later served as Alfonso VI's envoy, had been an administrator in Muslim Badajoz, and a number of *dhimmis* (non-Muslim subjects) served in the government of Zaragoza.

For the most part this diversity was tolerated by the Muslim majority, including the *'ulama'*, although some of the latter were outraged by the prospect that *dhimmis* should hold formal office under a Muslim regime. Their ire, however, came to be directed increasingly at the *taifa* kings themselves, many of whom were Berbers who shared no ethnocultural affiliation with the Andalusi population and who ruled as a foreign military elite. Popular dissatisfaction was aggravated by the increasing burden of taxation, which the *'ulama'* (who tended to come from the commercial class) and the common people were expected to bear as a result of the *paria* system. The *taifa* kings' imposition of uncanonical taxes and their submission as tributaries to Christian powers served as an ideological rallying point for popular revolt. The situation of the *'ulama'* was further exacerbated by the disruption of long-distance trade networks, thanks to incursions of the Normans in the Mediterranean and the Banu Hilal in Tunisia, and by the growing unrest in the Andalusi countryside, where the inter-*taifa* warfare and banditry led to general disorder. In 1085, the populace of Toledo led by the religious elite ejected the *taifa* king al-Qadir from the city. Turning to his patron, Alfonso VI, al-Qadir agreed that if reinstated he would hand the city over to the Castilian king, on the promise of later being installed as king in Valencia. Thus, in that same year, after negotiating a treaty with the local *'ulama'*, Alfonso entered Toledo as king.

This event made evident the corruption and debility of the *taifa* kings, who were derided in learned and pious Andalusi circles as decadent and effete. A well-known contemporary satirical verse mocked them: "They give themselves grandiose names like 'The Powerful,' and 'The Invincible,' but these are empty titles; they are like little pussycats who, puffing themselves up, imagine they can roar like lions." It also demonstrated to the *taifa* kings that Alfonso's aim was conquest; indeed, following up his seizure of Toledo, Alfonso laid siege to the other powerful northern *taifa*, Zaragoza (as a means of blocking the expansion on his Christian rival, the Kingdom of Aragón). By now both the *'ulama'* and the *taifa* rulers agreed outside help was desperately required. The only group to which they could turn was the Almoravids, a dynamic Berber faction that had coalesced on the southern reaches of the African gold routes and had managed to impose their political will on the region of Morocco, having taken Marrakech in 1061 and Fez in 1069. Self-styled champions of a Sunni Islam revival (which resonated with that of the Seljuks in the East), they saw their mission not only as halting the Christian advance in al-Andalus but also of deposing the illegitimate *taifa* rulers.

In 1086, the Almoravid Yusuf ibn Tashfin led a sizeable army to al-Andalus at the invitation of al-Mu'tamid of Seville. With the half-hearted help of the Andalusi troops the Almoravid faced Alfonso VI and his loyal Muslim clients in battle at Zallaqa (or Sagrajas) and issued them a major defeat. He did not follow this up, returning instead to Morocco. For the next two years the *taifa* kings were confident enough to defy Alfonso VI, but when he began to attack them again, they were forced to call on the Almoravids for help once more. Ibn Tashfin waited until 1089 when, having obtained juridical opinions from the *'ulama'* of the East authorizing him to take power in al-Andalus, he returned and set about deposing the remaining *taifa* rulers one by one. By 1094, virtually all of the kingdoms had fallen, their rulers having been either killed or shipped off as prisoners to Almoravid Morocco.

Valencia did not fall until 1002. By 1087, "El Cid," against the opposition of Zaragoza and the various Christian kings, had determined to take the city for himself and was provided with a pretext when an *'ulama'*-led uprising deposed and executed al-Qadir in 1092. Rodrigo besieged the city, which, forsaken by the Almoravids, surrendered in 1093. Having negotiated a treaty with the Muslim population, Rodrigo ruled the city and surrounding territory until his death in 1099—a Christian *taifa* king. Three years later, unable to resist the growing pressure of the Almoravids, Rodrigo's wife and successor, Jimena, and her troops abandoned the city to its inhabitants, setting it ablaze as they left. The remaining Party Kingdom, Zaragoza, remained independent partly because the Almoravids were content to use it as a buffer state and partly because its rulers became so adept at playing off their Christian rivals against each other. As in the case of Toledo, however, the populace and the religious elite became increasingly frustrated by a leadership that was so deeply embroiled with the very Christian powers who seemed determined to defeat them. In 1110, a popular uprising banished the last Hudid king from power, and the city submitted to Almoravid rule. Zaragoza would ultimately fall to Alfonso I of Aragon in 1118, surrendering after a lengthy siege, after the surviving members of the Banu Hud struggled vainly with Alfonso VI's help to regain their patrimony.

The period of the Party Kingdoms marks a turning point in the history of medieval Iberia, when the balance of political and economic initiative shifted from the Muslim-dominated South to the Christian-dominated North. Whether as a consequence of a crisis of *'asabiyya* (group identity) on the part of the Andalusis, or as the result of larger political and economic trends, the destiny of the Muslims of Spain would henceforth be in the hands of foreigners. The politics of the *taifa* period, however, defy the notion that this process or the so-called Christian Reconquest that looms so largely in it was the result of an epic civilizational struggle between Islam and Christendom; the most striking aspect of *taifa* era al-Andalus was the relative absence of religious sectarianism and the profound enmeshment of Christian, Muslim, and Jewish individuals and political factions.

BRIAN A. CATLOS

Further Reading

Benaboud, M'hammad. "'Asabiyya and Social Relations in Al-Andalus During the Period of the Taifa States." *Hesperis-Tamuda* 19 (1980–1981): 5–45.

Clément, François. *Pouvoir et Légitimité en Espagne Musulmane à l'Époque des Taifas (Ve-XIe siècle): L'Imam Fictif*. Paris, 1997.

Wasserstein, David. *The Rise and Fall of the Party-Kings: Politics and Society in Islamic Spain 1002–1086*. Princeton, NJ, 1985.

PEACE AND PEACEMAKING

The relations between Islam and the non-Muslims are dealt with in several literary genres. The earliest arrangements are recorded in the biographies of the Prophet Muhammad *(al-sira al-nabawiyya)* and in chronicles that narrate the stories of the Islamic conquests *(futuhat)*. In these sources two terms attract the reader's attention: *aman* and *sulh*. In the jurisprudence manuals the international law of Islam is condensed in chapters dealing with holy war *(jihad)*. The points of departure of these legal traditions are several Qur'anic verses, sayings by the Prophet Muhammad *(hadith)*, and episodes from his *sira*. Two other terms that frequently occur are *hudna* and *fay*.

Muslim scholars adopted a dualistic vision of earth that seems to be associated with a dualistic division of mankind. Already the Qur'an contrasts the party of God *(hizb Allah)* with the party of Satan *(hizb al-shaytan)*, and the opening chapter *(al-Fatiha)* of the holy book contrasts those who follow the straight path and those who go astray.

With the codification of Islamic holy law (shari'a) Muslim jurists assumed a world vision that divided the earth into two realms: the Abode of Islam (dar al-Islam) and the land of the non-Muslim enemy (dar al-harb: lit., abode of war). Use of the term dar al-Islam is pervasive in the writings of Muslim jurists and theologians to delimit an idealistic entity. It is used to point to an abstract entity rather than to outline a political or administrative system.

Muslim jurists perceived the Abode of Islam as divided into three parts: the holy cities of Arabia (haram), the northern part of the Arabian Peninsula (Hijaz), and the rest of the Muslim territory. All agreed that non-Muslims are forbidden from entering the holy cities (haram) of Mecca and Medina. Others deduced from the deeds of 'Umar (r. 634–644) that the exclusion extends to the rest of Arabia, even though Jews were living in Yemen. However, they did not agree on the ultimate conditions for the residence of nonbelievers (kafir, kuffar) within the boundaries of the caliphate. Some Tabari, for example, maintained that the residence of the protected people (ahl al-dhimma) is dictated by necessity (darura). As long as the Muslims rely on the participation of the people of the book (ahl al-kitab), their stay is tolerated. Whenever the conditions change it is permissible to deport them.

The jurists delineated the relationships between dar al-Islam and dar al-harb, including the conditions for border crossing, either during a military expedition by armies of Islam (jihad) or by Muslims and non-Muslims for civil purposes such as commerce. They also outlined the conditions regulating the entry of non-Muslims into the Abode of Islam (isti'man). The sources of their approach derived from pre-Islamic practices and the procedures that resulted from the reality at the frontiers of the caliphate.

According to the common vision prevailing among the Shafi'i jurists and theologians, the Abode of Islam is land governed by shari'a, where Muslims can openly and freely exercise their beliefs, practices, and communal deeds. Most salient are the public prayers on Fridays, the observance of Islamic festivals, the nomination of Muslim judges, and the collection of land tax (kharaj). Consequently, the adherent of the Shafi'i school of law will not define a territory as an Islamic country unless it is ruled by a Muslim governor.

Hanafi jurists used a less restricting definition. They designated as an Islamic land any territory where a Muslim judge (qadi) could impose the shari'a, even if this land was under alien rule and a non-Muslim governor nominated the qadi. Yet even these jurists distinguished between dar al-Islam proper and Islamic enclaves within dar al-harb. According to them, a Muslim dwelling under a non-Muslim government should not be punished in accordance with shari'a regulations, because proper implementation of a qadi's judgment requires authorization by a Muslim ruler.

War and peace being a common phenomenon in Arabia, the Constitution of Medina ('ahd al-umma) includes clauses concerning hostilities and collaboration between the Believers and their enemies. This was in line with tribal practices. To shelter a person separated from his kin, pre-Islamic (jahiliyya) Arab tribes employed the jiwar institution: They integrated the refugee (tarid; khali') into a clan and provided him with new bonds and security. Tribes concluded agreements and constituted confederations (khilf; 'ilaf).

The Prophet implemented these institutions in the new reality that emerged in Arabia. Several verses in the Qur'an address the issue of war and peace, and together with the Prophetic traditions (hadith) they served as a model for innovative institutions that emerged throughout the rising caliphate in order to cope with the extensive social and political changes that ensued.

With the elaboration of Islamic law, a new term was introduced to regulate the relationships between the powerful and the vulnerable. Islamic law distinguishes between two types of peace and reconciliation arrangements. The first addresses the relations among Muslims and is concerned with stopping conflict and violence among believers. The second category deals with halting hostilities between Muslims and non-Muslims.

Such arrangements are of two sorts: One, which is permanent, is with communities dwelling within the boundaries of dar al-Islam. On the basis of the divine orders, which were briefly mentioned earlier in this entry, jurists established the policy that the caliphate should execute regarding the non-Muslims: They should pay a head tax (jizya). The chronicles of the Islamic conquest record the so-called peace arrangements (sulh) between the victorious Muslims and the populations of the conquered towns and cities that had surrendered without a fight. In these arrangements the Muslims promised to save the life of the conquered people and protect their property (aman) against the payment of taxes. The aman/jizya stipulations outlined one type of peace covenants. This payment by the People of the Book should guarantee them peace, as long as they stuck to the letter of the covenant of 'Umar and paid this yearly taxation.

The second type of arrangement was contracted with those residing outside the Abode of Islam. This type of peace accord concerns inhabitants of *dar al-harb*; the accord with those who are beyond the reach of Islam is considered to be of a temporary nature.

The jurists regarded both types of settlements as a legal contract *('aqd)*. As such, the treaty had to be agreed in a legal session *(majlis)* and bear the signatures of witnesses. It should specify the minute details, including its duration and undertakings by the parties.

The creation of frontiers did not mean that the caliphate's relationship with the powers of the other side on the separation lines was hostile. Political and economic needs drove sultans and Muslim jurists to develop legal mechanisms for concluding a truce *(salm; 'ahd)* with the enemy.

Muslim jurists *(fuqaha')* used the term *thughur* for the frontier zone that separated *dar al-Islam* and *dar al-harb*. Control of territory, they maintained, was not a necessary precondition of territoriality. More important was the hegemony of Islam. This was their fundamental expression of identity; ownership of territories became secondary.

The regulations for fighting against *dar al-harb* are collected in the chapter about holy war *(bab al-jihad)*. In addition to regulations concerning such matters as payment, property, spoils of war *(ghanima)*, plunder *(khums)*, and booty *(fay)*, these chapters in the legal compendia deal with ideas about sovereignty, territory, borders, and just war. Such is the scope of these chapters they might well be considered as guidelines for Islamic international law.

Islam strictly condemns bloodshed and murder, yet the *fuqaha'* do not exclude the use of force as a coercive measure. Ibn Taymiyya (1263–1328) argues that just war or lawful war is a tool of coercion *(al-qital al-mashru' huwa al-jihad)* that should be waged against unbelievers and apostates. Being considered lawful violence, the *jihad* should not stop before reaching its goal; namely, conversion of the polytheists, the surrender of the monotheists, and the final victory of Islam. Other *fuqaha'* hold a less comprehensive view of *jihad*, viewing it as merely a defensive instrument to protect the territory of Islam.

Jihad by no means implies a permanent state of war. Muslim scholars *(ulama')* extended the noun *jihad* to cover questions concerning contracts with others. In the *jihad* chapters *shari'a* treatises outline pacts that the Muslim state has made with foreign states, because political and military needs required Muslim rulers to operate also outside the realm of Islam. Caliphs and sultans corresponded with Christian, Indian, and other rulers and dispatched and received ambassadors and delegations. These negotiations resulted in peace agreements.

The *fuqaha'* considered a provisional truce with these non-Muslim (mainly Christian) adversaries to be a reflection of Islamic weakness; the caliphate lacked the power to impose its terms and the enemy was strong enough to bargain the conditions. In contrast, the *aman/jizya* arrangements reflected the strength of the victorious Muslims: They had the authority to dictate conditions to the vanquished non-Muslim tributaries; the latter were weak and had to accept the terms dictated by the Muslims.

An early example of an arrangement between *dar al-Islam* and *dar al-Harb* is a letter sent by Egypt's governor (in AH 141/758 CE) to the ruler of Nubia encouraging him to act in accordance with the Qur'anic verse "Fulfil the compact *('ahd)* of God when you make a compact and do not break the oath *(ayman)*." The letter includes references to an agreement signed *(suliha)* between the parties and to duties *(baqt,* or *pactum)* that the ruler has undertaken.

A variety of this pact is the settlement between the caliphate and "the land of the covenant" *(dar al-'ahd)* adjacent to some frontier zone—that is, tributary states that submit *(taslim)* to the Muslims and conclude a truce *(yusalihu)* but are not included within the boundaries of the caliphate. The population of these districts would pay land tax *(kharaj)* but not poll tax *(jizya)*. They would not come under the jurisdiction of the imam (caliph), but they would remain governed by their indigenous rulers. They became treaty people and warfare against them was prohibited.

The truce with an enemy that is perceived as strong and powerful is called a *hudna*. Basically it is formulated as a contract that ensures the cessation of fighting between the parties during an agreed upon period, but its duration should not exceed ten years and ten months. The pact negotiated at Hudaybiyya (in 6/628) is a model of this type of assumed of contract. Here the Muslims signed a truce with the people of Mecca; the Qurayshites accepted the offer by the Prophet Muhammad to postpone *(wad')* fighting and to sign a peace accord *(salah)*.

Islamic states have concluded several *hudna* truces and signed trade and other bilateral agreements *(ta'ahhud; u'ahada)* with Christian governments and non-Muslim states. The clerks who drew up these treaties could lean on the Qur'anic verse: "Those of the polytheists with you the Muslims have a covenant." The jurists considered these pacts to be symbolic acts reflecting power relationships between the parties to the contract. In addition to its limited duration, a truce must be advantageous to the Muslims. Finally, the parties to the truce must accept the grandeur of Islam and acknowledge this in the written accord.

The *hudna* contract has to do with hegemony and income rather than with control and exclusivity. Just as the Muslims agreed to sign temporary truces, so they accepted the idea of condominium *(munasafa)*. This sort of arrangement between the Crusaders and the rulers of Syria is recorded throughout the years of the Latin presence in the East.

Documents from the Mamluk chancellery reveal the language and structure of treaties that the sultans concluded with the Crusaders and with Byzantium and other Mediterranean states. The sources shed light on the negotiations that led to the truce. The parties should assemble in contractual meeting. Although the truces were recorded in line with the Islamic tradition, the Arab clerks did not hesitate, in several provisions, to use friendly language. The *hudna* was an instrument used to regulate the arrangements between the Islamic state and non-Muslim territories *(dar al-harb)*.

In conjunct with the *hudna*, Muslim lawyers further developed the idea of safe conduct *(aman)*. The *musta'min* is a non-Muslim (mostly Christian) who enters the Abode of Islam for a brief fixed period to carry out precisely defined deeds. The Muslim authorities pledge to ensure the safety of the visitor that came from *dar al-harb* (predominantly from southern Europe). The *hudna* permitted foreign *(harbi)* merchants and ambassadors to obtain safe conduct while in Islamic territory. Abu Hanifa, for example, argued that if a non-Muslim *(ahl al-harb)* merchant crosses the border to trade within the Abode of Islam he has immunity, even if he transgresses the Islamic law *(hadd)* because he is not of the same status as the protected people *(kitabiyyun)* that are permanent residents of *dar al-Islam*. His student, Abu Yusuf, supports this position by asking: "Could you imagine that an ambassador would be punished for committing adultery?"

During the early Ottoman era the commercial treaties between Muslim rulers and Christian trading partners in the Mediterranean developed to the capitulations treaties *(imtiyaz)*.

YEHOSHUA FRENKEL

Further Reading

Abu 'l-Hasan 'Ali al-Mawardi. *al-Ahkam al-sultaniyya wa-l-wilayat al-diniyya*. Beirut: Dar al-Kutub al-'Ilmiyya, 1416/1996. English translation by W. H. Wahba. *The Ordinances of Government*. London, 1996.

P. Kh. Hitti (Trans.) *The Origins of the Islamic State: Being a Translation from the Arabic, Accompanied with Annotations, Geographic and Historic Notes of the Kitab futuh al-buldan of al-Imam Abu-l 'Abbas Ahmad b. Yahya ibn-Jabir al-Baladhuri (d. ca. 279/892)* reprint. Beirut: Khayats, 1966.

Hinds, Martin. "A Letter from the Governor of Egypt." *Studia Arabica et Islamica* (1981): 209–229 [reprinted in his *Studies in Early Islamic History*, edited by J. Bachrach, L. I. Conrad, and P. Crone. Princeton: The Darwin Press, 1996].

Hunwick, J. O. "al-Maghiliand the Jews of Tuwat: the Demise of a Community." *Studia Islamica* 61 (1985): 155–183.

Khadduri, M. *War and Peace in the Law of Islam*. Baltimore, 1955.

Petry, Carl F. "Holy War, Unholy Peace? Relations between the Mamluk Sultanate and European States prior to the Ottoman Conquest." In *The Jihad and Its Times: Dedicated to Andrew Stefan Ehrenkreutz*, edited by Hadia Dajani-Shakeel and Ronald A. Messier, 95–112. Ann Arbor: Center for Near Eastern and North African Studies, The University of Michigan, 1991.

Sartain, Elizabeth M. "Medieval Muslim–European Relations: Islamic Juristic Theory and Chancery Practice." In *Images of the Other: Europe and the Muslim World before 1700*, edited by David Blanks (ed.), 81–95. Cairo: The American University in Cairo Press, 1996.

Weigert, G. "A Note on *hudna*: Peacemaking in Islam." In *War and Society in the Eastern Mediterranean, 7th–15th Centuries*, edited by Y. Lev, 399–405. Leiden: Brill, 1997.

Taeko, Nakamura. "Territorial Disputes between Syrian Cities and the Early Crusaders." In *The Concept of Territory in Islamic Law and Thought*, edited by Yanagihashi Hiroyuki, 101–124 London: Kegan Paul International, 2000.

PEASANTS

Peasants in Muslim societies were called fallah in Arabic, ra'iyat in Persian, and reaya in Turkish. The fallahun (sing., fallah) in the Arab society were widely used, designating both landed farmers and tenants without land and seed. Particularly, the cultivators who made sharecropping (muzara') contracts with the government or landlords were called muzari'un. The fallahun, in the historical sources, were often called muzari'un and formed the majority of the villagers.

In the Arab–Muslim state formed in the seventh century, the government consented the former land holdings of the indigenous peasants who had to pay both land tax (kharaj) and poll tax (jizya). The 'ushr was levied on the Arab–Muslims who had acquired lands from the prior peasants, but in some cases the kharaj was also levied on them. Based on the Islamic principle of law, even the newly converted Muslims of the non-Arabs (mawali) could have enjoyed the same rights as the Arab Muslims. However, the mawali had to bear the discrimination of state policy in favor of the Arab Muslims, which eventually led to the fall of the Umayyad dynasty. During the following 'Abbasid period, the legal theory of fay' (conquered land belonging to the Muslim community) was established to regulate that both Arab and non-Arab cultivators had to pay the kharaj as rent to the government, which held landownership. However, during this period there developed the privileged landownerships (qati'a and day'a) by merchants, high officials, and Turkish commanders. They enjoyed the right to pay 'ushr only, while the cultivators in qati'a or day'a had to pay their landowners high rent other than the amount for 'ushr.

When the Buyid dynasty was established in the middle of the tenth century, the iqta' system was implemented in Iraq, which expanded to Iran, Syria, and Egypt by around the middle of the twelfth century. Under the new regime, the situation of peasants in rural society has changed considerably. According to Miskawayh (d. 1030), tunna' (sing., tani) in Iraq, who owned the small amounts of land (day'a), had to either leave the village, endure injustice, or take the means of surrendering their landed property to the muqta' (iqta' holder) to escape ill treatment (Tajarib al-umam, II, 97). In Iran also, dihqans (village chiefs), who had converted to Islam promptly to retain their status in rural society, were ruined, leaving their landed property under the rule of muqta's. Consequently, dihqans in the Seljukid Iran came to designate not village chiefs, but only peasants or tenants. When Saladin (Salah al-Din) introduced the iqta' system into Egypt, the Egyptian peasants, who had paid the kharaj to the government and the rent to landowners, came to pay these levies collectively to their muqta's. B. Johansen explains that under the iqta' system the difference between tax and rent ceased to exist, and the Egyptian peasants were transformed into tenants of the muqta's (Johansen 1988).

According to al-Nuwayri (d. 1333), the peasants called fallahun or muzari'un were, after irrigation by the annual flood of the Nile, customarily allocated land to be cultivated according to qabala contracts made not with the government but with their muqta' (Nihayat al-arab, VIII, 247–250). The muqta's employed their private agents (mubashir) to collect tax revenues, as well as lend seed to peasants for cultivation. After the establishment of the iqta' system, the muqta's became responsible for the maintenance of the irrigation system, using corvee (sukhra) levied on their peasants in iqta' every winter. Other than these levies the peasants under the iqta' system, when the muqata's visited their village, were obliged to provide them with tribute goods (diyafa) such as grains, fowl, goats, clover, dough, cakes, and other items. Through the conduct of the Nasiri cadastral surveys (al-Rawk al-Nasiri) in Egypt and Syria during the years 1313–1325, to the annual revenue of the iqta', which had hitherto been calculated on the basis of the kharaj, were added the diyafa and jawali (poll tax).

Al-Maqrizi relates that muqta's thus strengthened their rule over the peasantry through their iqta' holdings and brought about an important change in which the village-based peasants (fallah qarrar) came to be regarded as "serfs" ('abd qinn) subordinate to their muqta's (Khitat, I, 85). 'Abd qinn is legally a slave for life who cannot expect to be sold or emancipated. Egyptian peasants under the iqta' system, however, were not the slaves by law but were likened to 'abd qinn based on their actual situation. Such a situation of Egyptian peasants continued to be unchanged until the advent of the Ottoman rule at the beginning of the sixteenth century.

TSUGITAKA SATO

See also Buyids; Iqta'; Saladin

Further Reading

'Abd al-'Aziz. al-Duri, Ta'rikh al-'Iraq al-iqtisadi fi l-qarn al-rabi' al-hijri. Beirut, 1974.
Bahr, M. A. al-Qarya al-Misriyya fi 'asr salatin al-mamalik. Cairo, 1999.
Frantz-Murphy, G. The Agrarian Administration of Egypt from the Arabs to the Ottomans. Cairo, 1986.
Johansen, B. The Islamic Law on Land Tax and Rent. London, 1988.
Lokkegaard, F. Islamic Taxation in the Classic Period. Copenhagen, 1950.
Lambton, K. S. Landlord and Peasant in Persia. London, 1953.
Morimoto, K. The Fiscal Administration of Egypt in the Early Islamic Period. Kyoto, 1981.
Sato, T. State and Rural Society in Medieval Islam: Sultans, Muqta's and Fallahun. Leiden, 1997.

PERFORMING ARTISTS

Jesting and mockery were forbidden in Islam, as in the case of Judaism and Christianity, yet during the long history of Arabic theater since the rise of Islam, it is possible to detect various types of performing artists. These artists were given different names and terms in different regions and centuries.

During the time of the Prophet Muhammad, there were male and female singers (mughannun, maghani), musicians (arbab al-malahi), dancers (raqqasun), jokers and comedians (mudhikun, muharrijun, masakhira), performers of hobbyhorse (kurraj) plays, slapstick actors (safa'ina), and pantomimes and imitators of gestures, voices of people, and animals (muhaki, hakiya).

During the 'Abbasid period influenced by Persian culture, performing arts flourished not only in caliphs' courts but also among common people. Caliphs and grandees looked for boon companions (nudama'), male and female singers, dancers, musicians, jesters, and buffoons who would entertain them with songs, jocks, anecdotes, verses, and stories of admonition. Masked actors (samaja), live actors, jokers, storytellers (hakawati), and ram-holders were given wages in the royal and grandees' courts. They were given different collective terms, mainly mukhannathun (lit. effeminate men, that is, entertainers or actors), la'ibun, la''abun (entertainer, musician, and actor), and khayali or mukhayil (live actor or performer of shadow plays). From the thirteenth century CE onward, the terms muhabbaz (itinerant or strolling actor), musakhir (masquerade, formerly samaja), muharrij (buffoon), and Ibn Rabiya, were coined. In the Eastern parts of the Arabic-speaking world, these new terms replaced the former terms given for performing artists.

In the hadith there are traditions relating that the Prophet Muhammad allowed his young wife 'A'isha to play with her dolls, and later on allowed her to watch with him the plays of the Abyssinians with spears and shields. It is also told that 'A'isha was entertained by a woman comedian who would perform pantomime dances to entertain her. In the Prophet's camp, hobbyhorse players performed games and plays. In Madina such players were considered effeminate men (mukhannthun) who dyed their feet and palms red with hinna and dressed and toyed like women. Al-Hakam b. Abi 'l-'As was called al-haki (imitator) because he used to imitate Muhammad's manner of walk.

During the Umayyad period, singers and buffoons used to play not only with hobbyhorses but also with animal skins and masks. Many 'Abbasid caliphs encouraged performing artists, especially comedians, musicians, singers, and even fart makers (darratun) to refresh, enliven, and comfort them in their hard times. Some comedians used to perform in hospitals (maristan), giving lunatics "psychological treatment" (Moreh 1992:70).

In the Book of Songs (Kitab al-Aghani), a twenty-one-volume work by Abu 'l-Faraj al-Isfahani (d. 967), there is valuable information on poets, singers, and other types of performing artists. Al-Isfahani tells a story of a singer who recorded, during the reign of al-Amin (809–813), a satirical play mocking a haughty and arrogant judge called al-Khalanji and handed it to actors and dancers to perform. Consequently, the "judge" has to leave Baghdad out of disgrace (Aghani, XI, 338 f.).

The 'Abbasid and the Fatimid caliphs, mainly al-Mutawkkil (r. 847–862), celebrated the Nawruz with masquerading actors (samaja). A gallery was built for al-Mutawakkil to protect him from his enemies. Among his famous performing artists were four comedians. The first was the singer Husayn b. Sha'ra, who was also his jester. The second artist was the poet Abu 'l-'Ibar (d. ca. 865), who is called mimase (actor) in Syriac by Bar Hebreaus in his Laughable Stories. The third artist was his successor, the jester al-Kutanji, who authored many books on follies and fools. The fourth was al-Mutawakkil's boon-companion and comedian, 'Abbada 'l-Mukhannath. The latter used to ridicule 'Ali b. Abi Talib, who was hated by al-Mutawakkil. To please his patron, 'Abbada used to tie a pillow around his belly (under his clothes), take off his head-gear to expose his bald head, and dance in the presence of his patron while the singers sang: "The bald one with the paunch is coming, the caliph of the Muslims!" This performance was among the reasons which al-Muntasir, the son of al-Mutawakkil, regarded the killing of his father as lawful (Ibn al-Athir, Kamil, VII, p. 55f.).

The comedian, Abu al-Ibar, a descendant of the 'Abbasid dynasty, related about himself that when he was a boy he used to frequent professional master comedians to learn with other novice comedians the art of hazl (comedy). Their profession was based on dialogue of contraries and absurdity. They act by doing the opposite of what they were told to do, a kind of jest that was used also in shadow plays.

Ibn al-Haj, in his Madkhal (compiled in 1331), enumerates various types of entertainment during the Nile Festivals, such as the processions of Amir al-Nawruz, which were pre-Islamic festivals and celebrations by live actors (mukhayilin) that were considered bida' (heresy). These actors used to perform "The Play of the Judge" wearing his attire and uttering many rude remarks which they directed to the attire itself.

In Muslim Spain, the Umayyad terms for performing artists continued to be used, as it is possible to understand from Pedro de Alcala's Vocabulista aravigo en lietra castillana (Granada 1505). Umayyad theatrical terms such as la''ab, la''ab al-khiyal, mumathil (actors), and mal'ab (theater), where the props of the actors, such as sacks, gowns, trousers, head cloths, and veils, were hung on a rope. Hobby-horses, plays by live actors, marionettes, and shadow plays were performed until the expulsion of Muslims and Jews from Spain in 1492.

In the late medieval Muslim civilization, performing artists were among the lowest stratum of Muslim society; they were classified with monkey holders, prostitutes, dancers, and acrobats. They performed indecent farces mainly in colloquial dialects to entertain common people. This was an oral popular art and rarely recorded due to the sanctity of the classical written Arabic in which the Qur'an was revealed. Performing art was a revolt against the serious religious and sophisticated *adab* literature written in classical Arabic. It was an outlet for the depressed populace against oppressive rulers, exploiting religious and military officials, heavy taxes, corruption, and bribery. Humor was the best outlet against strict morals and customs, gender separations, and sexual suppression in despotic governments who ruled a depressed and deprived poor society that was exploited by a cruel ruling class whose main aim was collecting taxes and acquiring wealth. Modern education and close contact with European theater changed the status of the performing artists to a respectable artistic profession of high income.

SHMUEL MOREH

See also Festivals and Celebrations; Humor; Music; Shadow Plays; Singing; Storytellers and Storytelling; Theater

Further Reading

And, Metin. *Culture, Performance and Communication in Turkey*. Tokyo: Institute for the Study of Languages and Cultures of Asia and Africa, Tokyo University of Foreign Studies, 1987.
————. *Drama at the Crossroads: Turkish Performing Arts Lind Past and Present*. East and West. Istanbul, 1991.
Bosworth, C. E. *The Medival Islamic Underworld; Banu Sasan in Arabic Society and Literature*. Leiden: 1976.
Lane, W. E. *Manners and Customs of the Modern Egyptians*. London: J. M. Dent & Sons Ltd., 1954 (Everyman's Library, 315, Travel & Topography).
Moreh, S. *Live Theatre and Dramatic Literature in the Medieval Arab World*. New York: New York University Press, 1992.
————. "Acting and Actors, Medieval." and "Abu 'l-'Ibar". In *Encyclopedia of Arabic Literature*, edited by J. Scott Meisami and P. Starkey. 2 vols. London and New York: Routledge, 1998.
————. "Masks in Medieval Arabic Theater." *Assaph* C 9 (1993): pp. 89–94.
Neubauer, E. *Musiker am Hof der fruhen 'Abbasiden*. Frankurt, 1965.
Rowson, E. K. 'The Effeminates of Early Median'." *JAOS* 111 no. 4 (1991): 671–693.
Sadan, J. *Al-Adab al-'Arabi al-Hazil wa-Nawadir al-Thuqala'. (Humour in Classical Arabic Literature and the "Anecdotes on Boring Persons" – A Literary Genre)*. Tel-Aviv: Tel-Aviv University, 1983.
————. "Kings and Craftsmen, a Pattern of Contrasts." *Studia Islamica*, Pt. I, LVI (1982): 5–49; Pt. 2, LXII (1985): 89–120.
Shiloah, A. *Music in the World of Islam*. Hants, 1995, 13.

PERFUME

Perfumes (scent, Arabic *'itr*, pl. *'utur*) as a group constituted an important medieval commodity, used especially in personal hygiene, cuisine, and pharmacology.

The costliest perfumes originated in regions east of the Central Islamic lands; medieval authors identify China and the region around the Indian Ocean as sources of some of the most valuable perfumes—musk and ambergris, for example. Such perfumes had to be transported across great distances, whether on sea or on the land-based "silk routes" that connected China and India to Central Asia, Mesopotamia, the Mediterranean, and Europe, and were considered luxury goods associated with the highest levels of society. More common perfumes, like those derived from flower essences, might be produced locally, and thus be more readily obtainable and less costly.

Judging from references in texts (geographies and medical works, for example), in which the varieties and commercial values of fragrant substances were discussed, musk *(misk)*, ambergris *('anbar)*, and camphor *(kanfur)* were among the most valuable of the variety of perfumes available to medieval consumers. According to a saying attributed to Muhammad, musk was the best of the perfumes. Musk is a sweet-smelling gland secretion of the male musk deer *(Moschus moschiferus* L., *Cervidae)*. Along with ambergris, musk was most often associated with rulers and elites. Ambergris, a secretion found in the intestines of the sperm whale, was similar to musk in odor, burned easily and with a bright flame, and was valued similarly to musk. Camphor derived from the resin of East Asian and Indonesian trees *(Cinnamomum camphora* and *Dryobalanops aromatica)*. Marco Polo's observation that Indonesian camphor was worth its weight in gold suggests perfume's importance to medieval economies.

Literature produced for and about medieval Islamic courts reflects perfume's status as a gift fit for royalty. Likewise, a tenth-century handbook for 'Abbasid courtiers reflects the attention paid by court elites to the fragrances with which they perfumed their bodies, as well as their surroundings (through the use of incense). Some fragrances were preferred over others because of their association with specific genders and/or social classes. For example, the author of the handbook notes that the perfume made from the musk of civet cats (Arabic *zabad* or *ghaliya*) was generally associated with children and female slaves.

Perfumes also played important roles in medieval Islamic culinary culture: to cleanse cooking vessels before food preparation; as spices; or to scent or color finished dishes and drinks. Musk and other, less costly substances were used to cleanse the hands and mouth before and after eating, and to anoint guests at feasts.

Perfumes played a key role in medieval medicine, so much so that perfume or spice merchants *('attar)* came to be synonymous with druggists and chemists. Pharmacological texts describe the effects of particular fragrances on the various parts of the body, and their efficacy in treating particular ailments. To give a few examples, ambergris and musk were believed to stimulate and strengthen the brain, the heart, and the senses, whereas camphor was used to treat the liver, oral inflammations, fevers, and headache.

GLAIRE D. ANDERSON

See also Cosmetics; Health and Hygiene; Medical Literature; Medicine, Diet and Dietetics; Personal Hygiene; Pharmacology; Rosewater

Further Reading

Encyclopedia of Islam, 2d ed. Leiden: Brill, 1960. (See "'Anbar," "Attar," "'Itr," "Misk," "Kafur.")

Van Gelder, G. J. H. "Four Perfumes of Arabia: A Translation of al-Suyui's *al-maqama al-miskiyya*." In *Parfums d'Orient. Textes reunis par R. Gyselen*. Bures-sur-Yvette: Groupe pour l'étude de la civilisation du Moyen-Orient, 1998. 203–212.

PERSIAN

Persian belongs to the Southwest Iranian branch of the Indo-European language family. Sir William Jones, who wrote the first Persian grammar in a European language (1771), and who proposed the existence of this linguistic family, claimed it was his realization that Persian had lexical cognates in both Sanskrit and Greek, which first led him to his discovery. Medieval Persian is continuous with, and both morphologically and lexically very similar to, modern Persian: The two are known collectively as New Persian, to distinguish them from Old Persian (also called Avestan) and Middle Persian (Pahlavi).

The first texts in Old Persian are the cuneiform rock inscriptions of the Achaemenid emperors, which date from the late sixth and early fifth centuries BCE. Even though extant manuscripts of the Avesta date only to the thirteenth century CE, the most ancient parts of the Avesta (the hymns, or Gathas), indicate a more archaic stage of the language than these inscriptions and must therefore be dated to before this period (although there is considerable scholarly dispute as to just how long before). Archaeological and textual evidence indicates that Old Persian was current in an area roughly coterminous with modern Iran and much of Afghanistan, as well as in southern Central Asia, extending as far as the steppes of southern Russia and eastward to Sinkiang.

Middle Persian, or Pahlavi, a term that derives from "Parthava" meaning Parthian—the name of the

dynasty that ruled Iran from the fall of the Seleucids (247 BCE) to the rise of the Sasanians (225 CE)—is mainly represented by Sasanian examples; these include rock inscriptions, inscriptions on coins, and secular and religious texts, including a considerable number of Manichean texts from Central Asia. The Middle Persian script derives from a Parthian script; the northeastern Parthian form of the language differed somewhat from the southern Sasanian form that replaced it. Documents in a related language, Sogdian, have also survived from the same period.

Up to the period of the Arab invasion of Iran in the mid-seventh century CE, Persian had developed within a virtually closed Indo-European linguistic environment, and shows no significant influence from languages outside this family. This situation changed radically with the Arab conquest of the country. As the language of its conquerors, Arabic became the dominant political and administrative language of Iran throughout the Umayyad period (651–750 CE) and during the early 'Abbasid period (750–1258 CE): As the vehicle of the religion of Islam, to which a majority of Iranians had probably converted within two or three hundred years of the conquest, it also occupied a privileged position in any discourse involving theological or philosophical topics. Persian survived as a folk/oral language, and when it reemerged as a written language in the ninth century CE, it had absorbed considerable influence from Arabic. The script was now a modified form of the Arabic script (though the earliest surviving written examples of New Persian are in Hebrew characters and date from the mid-eighth century), and much of the vocabulary, especially as it relates to abstract or "sophisticated" matters, is also Arabic. An analogous situation, familiar to English speakers, is the development of English after the eleventh-century Norman French conquest. Although English retained a core Germanic (Anglo-Saxon) vocabulary, this was overlaid with a predominantly French-derived vocabulary, and the more sophisticated the speaker, and the topic being treated, the more this vocabulary becomes evident. Similarly, the core vocabulary of Persian continued to be derived from Pahlavi, but Arabic lexical items predominated for more abstract or abstruse subjects and often replaced their Persian equivalents in polite discourse. Just as English has been modified to the extent that an untutored English speaker cannot read an Anglo-Saxon text with comprehension, an untutored Persian speaker cannot read Pahlavi with comprehension. This is compounded for Persian because of the change of script from Pahlavi to Arabic, but it would still be the case if the script were readily legible to a modern Persian speaker. However, the parallel breaks down at a certain point: French and English are both Indo-European languages and share many cognates and much of their semantic structure, whereas Arabic and Persian belong to quite separate linguistic families (Semitic and Indo-European, respectively), have virtually no cognates except through loan words from one to the other, and have wholly differing semantic structures. Persian has, in general, confined its borrowings from Arabic to lexical items, and its morphology is relatively unaffected by the influence of Arabic, being confined to a few conventions such as the (usually optional) use of Arabic plurals for Arabic-derived words (as an English speaker may use Latin plurals for Latin loan words in English).

The grammar of New Persian is similar to that of many contemporary European languages: The case system has virtually disappeared and has been replaced largely by a system of prepositions and postpositions; normal sentence word order is subject-object-verb; gender markers are generally absent; and plurals and other modifications to words are generally made by the addition of suffixes, prefixes, or, in the case of Arabic-derived vocabulary, infixes. The theoretical availability of the whole of Arabic to Persian speakers means that the language has a very large vocabulary and is rich in synonyms, near synonyms, and fine shades of distinct meaning in a given semantic area; some Arabic loan words are used in Persian with meanings quite distinct from their meanings in Arabic. Persian is also a highly idiomatic language, and a comprehension of the literal meaning of each word in a phrase by no means guarantees comprehension of the import of the phrase as a whole. For the nonnative speaker, Persian's immense vocabulary, and the prevalence of idioms, are the chief obstacles to achieving fluency.

In the same way that the emergence of New Persian can be seen as a linguistic result of political circumstances, new political conditions ensured the language's literary survival. In the ninth and tenth centuries CE, areas of eastern Iran, under local dynasties, began to achieve de facto independence from the 'Abbasid caliphate centered on Baghdad. The consequent loosening of Arabic cultural ties signaled a reemergence of Persian, and the first recorded poem in New Persian is a panegyric written on the occasion of the conquest of Herat by the Saffarid ruler Ya'qub Lais, in 867 CE. The main impetus for Persian's literary revival was provided by the vigorous patronage of the Samanids, who ruled Khorasan from c. 875 CE to 1005 CE, and who instigated an extensive program of translation from Arabic into Persian, as well as assiduously promoting the writing of Persian poetry. Samanid literary production in Persian clearly looks to Arabic for many of its models, both as regards its chief forms and its rhetoric but is also distinctively Persian in its idiomatic vocabulary and often more or less nationalist preoccupations. Epic poetry, drawing on pre-Islamic native tradition and revived under the Samanids, is particularly Persian in its cultural orientation and owes little or nothing to Arabic models. The success and prestige of Khorasanian New Persian literature meant that subsequent dynasties also encouraged literary production in Persian, and within two centuries or so Persian had become the major literary language of Southwest Asia. The twelfth-century CE author Ibn al-Balkhi claimed that Persian was current "from the Oxus to the Euphrates," and by this period it had also been carried into Northern India by (mainly Turkish) conquerors. By the thirteenth century the acclaim given to the Persian poetry of both Amir Khosrow in India, and Jalal addin Rumi in Asia Minor, indicates that Persian now had a significant literary presence well beyond the confines of Iran. Indeed, in Asia, from ca. the twelfth century CE to the sixteenth century CE, Persian was considered as the Islamic language of belles lettres par excellence, and it became a cliché that just as Arabic was the language of theology and law, and Turkish the language of the administration and the army, so Persian was the language of literate polite society. In the sixteenth century, and subsequently, Persian, especially Persian poetry, was cultivated at both the Ottoman courts in Turkey, and at the Moghul courts in India; in the latter environment especially, it produced a significant local literature. The diffusion of Persian beyond its heartland of Iran and western Afghanistan meant that dialectal differences gradually emerged, and this was particularly true of both the Persian spoken in Northern India and that in Central Asia, where its speakers gradually became an enclave surrounded by Turkish-speaking communities and where the local dialect began, in time, to show considerable Turkish influence. However, the canonical status of Persian literary classics as models, especially works by Ferdowsi, Sa'di, and (later) Hafez, also meant that written Persian during the middle ages differed little from one dialectal area to another.

RICHARD DAVIS

Further Reading

Lazard, Gilbert. *La Langue Des Plus Anciens Monuments de la Prose Perse*. Paris, 1963.
———. *The Origins of Literary Persian*. Bethesda, 1993.
Levy, Reuben; *The Persian Language*. New York, 1951.
Windfuhr, Gernot L. "Persian." In *The World's Major Languages*, edited by Bernard Comrie, 523–546. Oxford, 1990.

PERSIANS

Pre-Islamic Period

The Persians were part of the Indo-Iranian Aryan migrations of the second millennium BCE, and Assyrian inscriptions talk of a "people of Parsua" based in the region of Hamadan as early as the ninth century BCE. By the seventh century BCE, the Persians had emerged as a distinct ethnolinguistic and political group based in the arid, southern climes of the Iranian Plateau among many competing Iranian and Semitic groups (Bactrian, Soghdian, Babylonian, Assyrian). Under the leadership of Cyrus the Great (580–530 BCE), the Achaemenian empire emerged from its home province of Pars—from which "Persia" is derived thanks to the Greek sources—and was extended to comprise the Iranian Plateau, the Mesopotamian river-valleys, and western Khurasan. The Persians incorporated preexisting Median notions of divine rule and various administrative practices, and there is evidence to suggest that they were henceforth exposed to early Avestan texts and Magian traditions. The internationality of the Achaemenian empire is readily apparent in their provincial satrapy system whereby regions such as Phoenicia, Lydia, Cilicia, Babylon, and Egypt remitted regular tribute to the Persians. This far-flung empire was maintained from administrative centers in Ectabana and Susa, and Darius built a majestic ceremonial capital near Persepolis in the early fifth century BCE to formally receive envoys and tribute bearers during the Persian New Year (Nawruz) celebrations. It was also during the Achaemenian period that the earlier teachings and prescriptions of Zarathustra (Greek, Zoroaster) contained in the Avestan scriptures gained great currency in western Asia.

A revolt of Greek colonists in Ionia against the Persian-installed governor ushered in a new era of Irano-Mediterranean geopolitics whereby the Athenian and Persian empires fought a series of devastating wars in the fifth century BCE under Darius and Xerxes. The Persian invasions of Greece, culminating with the battles of Marathon (490 BCE) and Salamis (480 BCE), were in turn followed by a lengthy phase of Greek brinkmanship in the Achaemenian empire, as it stagnated under the rule of Artaxerxes (465–425 BCE) and Artaxerxes II (404–359 BCE). This set the stage for the devastating invasions of Alexander the Great in 334–331 BCE, and the formal termination of the Achaemenian Persian empire. For the next five centuries, Hellenistic culture enjoyed considerable prominence in the Iranian world under the successor Greco-Iranian dynasties of the Seleucids and Parthians. The Persians would be able to reclaim political primacy in the third century CE, when a local notable named Ardashir, from the town of Istakhr (near Shiraz), overthrew Parthian rule in 224 and revived many of the existing Achaemenian political, religious, and cultural traditions under the new dynastic banner of the Sasanians. In addition to carving out a formidable empire that included Central Iran, Iraq, and parts of Transoxiana, this dynasty (224–642 CE) is acknowledged for its intense dedication to the notion of divine kingship and its vigorous sponsorship of Zoroastrianism as a state religion. The peak of Sasanian rule came during the reign of Anushirvan (531–579 CE), who among other things instituted a series of wide-ranging reforms designed to promote social stability, responsible administration, and efficient tax collection. A wide array of treatises on political theory and princely advice literature was produced in Middle Persian in the sixth century, a practice that would reemerge during the Persian literary renaissance of the tenth and eleventh centuries. Indeed, the legacy of the Sasanian administrative infrastructure and the continuity of Persian bureaucratic culture in Islamic times would be key to the later success of the Islamic 'Abbasid caliphate (750–1258 CE).

Islamic Period

The Sasanian empire, with its centralized capital city-complex of Mada'in on the Euphrates and Tigris rivers, was one of the two great land-based empires (the other being Byzantium) capable of opposing the Arab Islamic invasions of the seventh century. However, paralyzing rivalries and strife within the royal Sasanian household and decades of exhausting wars with the Byzantines conspired to undermine any cohesive Persian resistance to the revolutionary movement of Islam. More telling perhaps were the somewhat bigoted policies of the Sasanians toward non-Zoroastrian groups (Christians, Jews, Sabeans, Mazdakites), which no doubt contributed to the social anarchy surrounding the Islamic invasions. Although a series of skirmishes and clashes had taken place, it was the pitched battle at al-Qadisiyya where the Sasanian main host under Yazdgird III was routed by the general of Caliph 'Umar, Sa'd b. Abi Waqqas in 637. Military encampments at Basra and Kufa facilitated further incursions into Iran, and Muslim Arab armies pushed resistance farther north along the

Zagros Mountains into Azerbaijan. Persian communities of Zoroastrians, Christians, and Jews were by and large content to negotiate treaties of surrender with these newly arrived Arab tribal armies, and there is no reason to accept popularly held views that Iran was Islamicized at these early dates. Conversion to Islam for reasons of political expediency was not uncommon, however, and we read of prominent individual Sasanian bureaucrats and various prominent landholders *(dihqans)* who accepted Islam to either ingratiate themselves with the new political order or to escape certain canonical taxes levied on non-Muslims. By the end of the Umayyad caliphate (661–750 CE), the Persian-speaking world of the Iranian Plateau, Azerbaijan, Sistan, Khvarazm, Khurasan, and Transoxiana had been conquered.

During the seventh and eighth centuries, large numbers of Arab tribespeople began settling in these newly conquered regions, particularly in the prosperous province of Khurasan, and converted Persian elite and nobility became "clients" *(mawali)* of various Arab tribal networks. A collaborative taxation system emerged whereby *mawali* Persian administrators established and maintained registers of taxation *(diwan)* on behalf of the Arab governors and military elite in urban settlements and rural garrisons. However, the Umayyad caliphate—based in Damascus—was unsympathetic to complaints from classes of Persian *mawali* who found themselves not only shut out of elite Arab political circles but were also being forced to levy both Muslim and non-Muslim canonical taxes on the Persian population. This regional resentment made Iran, particularly Khurasan, fertile propagandistic terrain for the panoply of Muslim groups who openly challenged and berated the Umayyad rulers on the basis of venality, corruption, and irreligiousness. The most successful of these were led by Abu Muslim in the mid-eighth century, who championed a revolution against the Arab/Syrian-centric Umayyad dynasty and the establishment of a ruling household whose provenance was ideologically and genealogically more palatable. This was a revolution supported by a coalition of groups: disgruntled Arab tribesmen in the East, proto-Shi'i groups, *mawali* Persian administrators, Persian *dihqan*s, and Khurasani peasants and troops. The subsequent establishment of the 'Abbasids in 750, and their relocation of the capital to Baghdad—built near the former Persian Sasanian capital of Ctesiphon—was a profound development for Persian political and administrative culture during the medieval period.

The epicenter of Arabo-Islamic civilization in the ninth and tenth centuries was undoubtedly Baghdad. The greatest claim to fame of early medieval Baghdad was its sponsorship and promotion of extensive translations into Arabic of Greek, Syriac, Pahlavi, and Sanskrit treatises on philosophy, logic, astronomy, mathematics, medicine, and political philosophy. This transmission was to some extent influenced by a number of Persian scholar–bureaucrats who were able to combine their extensive training in Arabic with their Pahlavi roots to translate a number of Sasanian works that were, in fact, translations of much older Greek sources that had made their way to Iran during the sixth-century reign of Anushirvan. Concurrent with this was the rise of courtly *shu'ubiya* literature, whereby non-Arab Muslims, including many Persian literati, used formal Arabic rhetorical poetry to lionize and praise non-Arab traditions in the face of Arab cultural domination. This sense of independence often took militaristic manifestations, and we find a number of hybrid Shi'i/Zoroastrian revolts, such as those by Sunpad in Nishapur, Babak in Azerbaijan, and Ustad Sis in Baghdis, plaguing the 'Abbasid caliphate in the eighth to tenth centuries.

The rise of New Persian and renaissance of Persian literature in the medieval period took place well east of the original home province of Fars. A number of semiautonomous Eastern dynasties (Tahirids, Samanids, Ghaznavids) based in the Iranian-speaking oasis-settlements of Bactria, Herat, Bukhara, and Samarqand were influenced by longstanding Persian mythical and literary traditions. Thanks to the efforts of historians such as al-Bal'ami—who translated al-Tabari's monumental historical chronicle from Arabic into Persian—and poets such as Rudaki and Daqiqi, New Persian had emerged as the administrative and creative language of choice for the Samanid dynasty based in Samarqand. However, the Ghaznavid patronage of men like Abu al-Fazl Baihaqi and Abu al-Qasim Ferdowsi in the city of Ghazna would prove to be pivotal. Ferdowsi's production of the monumental *Shahnam (Shahnameh)*, an epic poem recounting the deeds and glories of Iranian kings and heroes in legend and history, accomplished much for the revival and preservation of Persian language and culture. This Iranicizing of the Eastern Islamic lands was further complemented by the Shi'i Buyid dynasty, originally from Daylam, who had assumed custodianship of Baghdad and the 'Abbasid caliphate in the tenth century. Although Arabic was still the dominant administrative language, Buyid rulers such as Azud al-Daula resuscitated a number of pre-Islamic Iranian practices, most notably the titulature of *shahanshah* (king of kings) and the celebration of the Persian New Year. Thus, the conveyance of the Persian revival from east to west by the Seljuk Turks after their conquest of Baghdad in 1055 was well received by networks of Iranian administrators, poets, and literateurs who had been serving for generations under Arab rule.

The increased use of New Persian for administrative and poetic purposes during the Seljuk period reinforced the importance of Iranian bureaucracy and scholarship in the eleventh through thirteenth centuries. It would also be during the medieval period that rivalry between Persian city dwellers and Turkic nomads would intensify as a result of the large-scale arrival of Turkic tribes in the Iranian Plateau since the ninth century. Iran would undergo considerable Turkification with the arrival of the Seljuks, and the uneasy relationship between the Turkic military, tribal elite (*arbab-i saif*, or "men of the sword") and the Persian administrative/religious classes (*arbab-i qalam*, or "men of the pen") would often turn rancorous. Charged by their Seljuk Turkic overlords with the financial welfare of the state, Persian chief administrators *(vazirs)* used their status to secure power and patronize religious and cultural projects. A case in point is Nizam al-Mulk, who acted as vizier to the Seljuk rulers Arp Aslan and Malikshah during the eleventh century. In addition to promoting the spread of the *madrasa* collegial system, Nizam al-Mulk penned one of the most authoritative political advice manuals of the medieval period, the *Siyasat nama* (Book of Government). Indeed, this celebrated text constituted a revival of Sasanian political culture that demanded leadership from a "just ruler" *(al-sultan al-'adil)* akin to Anushirvan, who in turn guaranteed religious conformity and responsible taxation.

The most harrowing development for medieval Persians was the Mongol shockwave of the mid-thirteenth century. While Eastern Iranian cities such as Herat, Nishapur, and Balkh were ruthlessly sacked by Chingiz Khan in the 1220s, the remainder of Iran would be conquered thirty years later by the Great Khan's nephew, Hulegu. Approximating the demographic and economic impact of the Mongols would be challenging, but it is clear that the urban and agricultural prosperity of Iran regressed considerably after the thirteenth century. Descendants of Hulegu Khan established their own dynasty in Iran, the Il-Khans (1265–1365), and later rulers such as Oljeitu and Ghazan Khan were known for their attempts to implement a number of social and economic reforms in the hopes of rehabilitating the Iranian economy. The Persian bureaucratic elite once again stepped in to serve as intermediaries between the subject population and the Mongol overlords, and the continued adoption of New Persian as the courtly lingua franca saw the rise of a strong Persian historiographical school thanks to administrators like al-Juvaini and Rashid al-Din. The Mongol and post-Mongol eras

witnessed a flourishing of Persian poetry in the province of Fars under Sa'di and Hafez, while the Timurid rulers of Transoxiana and Khurasan actively sponsored scholars producing works on poetry, philosophy, and mysticism in Persian. It was also during the post-Mongol age that we see a dilution of centralized Sunni orthodoxy and the corresponding proliferation of Shi'i and mystical Sufi activity across the Iranian world. Arguably the best example of these syncretist trends was the Persian Safavid millennarian mystical order in Azarbaijan of the fifteenth century. When Shaikh Isma'il conquered Tabriz in 1501, he assumed the ancient Persian Achaemenian title of *shah* (king) while at the same time proclaiming that Twelver Shi'ism was henceforth the state religion. From the sixteenth century onward, Turco-Mongol dominance in Iran would be increasingly repressed by transplanted Caucasus *ghulam* slave troops and an ascending Persian administrative and clerical elite.

COLIN PAUL MITCHELL

See also **Bureaucrats; Buyids; Epics, Persian; Ethics; Ghaznavids; Ilkhanids; Interfaith Relations; Mirrors for Princes; Nawruz; Persian; Poetry, Persian; Political Theory; Safavids; Samanids; Shahnama; Shi'ism; Sufism and Sufis; Timurids; Translation, Arabic to Persian; Viziers; Zoroastrianism**

Further Reading

Bailey, H. (Ed.). *The Cambridge History of Iran.* 8 vols. Cambridge, 1968–1993.
Barthold, W. *An Historical Geography of Iran.* Edited and translated by S. Soucek. Princeton, 1984.
Bausani, Allesandro. *The Persians.* London, 1971.
———. *Religion in Iran: From Zoroaster to Baha'u'llah.* New York, 2000.
Bosworth, C. E. *The Medieval History of Iran, Afghanistan, and Central Asia.* London, 1977.
Briant, Pierre. *From Cyrus to Alexander: A History of the Persian Empire.* Eisenbraun, 2002.
Browne, E. G. *A Literary History of Persia.* 4 vols. Cambridge, 1958.
Corbin, Henri. *Spiritual Body and Celestial Earth: From Mazdean Iran to Shi'ite Iran.* Translated by N. Pearson. Princeton, 1977.
Frye, Richard. *Bukhara: The Medieval Achievment.* Norman, 1965.
———. *The Golden Age of Persia: The Arabs in the East.* London, 1975.
———. *The Heritage of Persia.* London, 1962.
Lambton, Anne K. S. *Continuity and Change in Medieval Persia: Aspects of Administrative, Economic and Social History, 11th–14th Century.* Albany, 1988.
———. "Justice in the Medieval Persian Theory of Kingship." *Studia Islamica* 17 (1962): 91–119.
———. *Landlord and Peasant in Persia.* London, 1953.
———. *Theory and Practice in Medieval Persian Government.* London, 1980.

Lentz, Thomas W., and Lowry, Glenn D. *Timur and the Princely Vision: Persian Art and Culture in the Fifteenth Century.* Washington, 1989.

Lewisohn, L., and Morgan, D. *The Heritage of Sufism.* 3 vols. Oxford, 1999.

———. *The Legacy of Mediaeval Persian Sufism.* London, 1992.

Madelung, Wilferd. *Religious and Ethnic Movements in Medieval Islam.* Aldershot, 1992.

Meisami, Julie Scott. *Medieval Persian Court Poetry.* Princeton, 1987.

Minorsky, Vladimir. *Medieval Iran and Its Neighbours.* London, 1982.

———. *The Turks, Iran and the Caucasus in the Middle Ages.* London, 1978.

Morgan, David. *Medieval Persia, 1040–1797.* London, 1988.

Paul, Jürgen. *Herrscher, Gemeinwesen, Vermittler: Ost Iran und Transoxanian in vormongolischer Zeit.* Stuttgart, 1996.

Rypka, Jan. *History of Iranian Literature.* Edited by K. Jahn. Dordrecht, 1968.

Savory, Roger. *Iran Under the Safavids.* Cambridge, 1980.

Spuler, B. *Iran in der früh-islamischer Zeit: Politik, Kultur, Verwaltung und öffentliches Leben 633–1055.* Wiesbaden, 1952.

PHARMACOLOGY

In contemporary medical sciences, *pharmacology* designates the clinical analysis of the action of medicines on the human body; in historical sciences, it designates the *discipline of medicines (o peri pharmakôn logos [the Discourse on Medicines])*, according to Dioscorides, *De materia medica* (praef., 5). As in antiquity and Byzantium, medicines in the Arabic world were products made of one or more natural substances (materia medica) coming from the three natural realms (vegetal, mineral, and animal).

Origins

Arabic pharmacology arose from the assimilation of previous knowledge, particularly Greek. Assimilation proceeded in a cumulative way: The first translators did not necessarily render all plant names by their exact translation, but transliterated them. Due to the possible misidentification and, consequently, the incorrect therapeutic uses of plants this process could provoke, previous translations were revised or new ones were made to replace transliterated terms with exact translations. Translation proceeded in three main phases:

1. Translations were first made into Syriac. They continued the work of Sergios of Res'ayna (sixth century CE), who translated from Greek books VI–XI from *De simplicium medicamentorum temperamentis et facultatibus (On the Mixtures and Properties of Simple Medicines*, in 11 books) by Galen (129 to after ca. 216 CE) devoted to materia medica. Hunayn ibn Ishaq (800–873 CE) revised Sergios' translation of books VI–XI and translated himself books I–V from Greek into Syriac. Hunayn also translated from Greek into Syriac Galen's other pharmacological treatises: *De compositione medicamentorum per genera (On the Composition of Medicines by Types)*, *De compositione medicamentorum secundum locos (On the Composition of Medicines by [Affected] Places of [the Human] Body)*, and *De antidotis (On Antidotes)*. He completed this corpus with the most important treatise on materia medica of antiquity, *De materia medica* by Dioscoride (first century CE) (five books, with two inauthentic treatises on venoms and poisons), and the medical encyclopedia by Oribasius (fourth century CE), which includes pharmacology.

2. Hunayn, first working alone and later on in collaboration with Istifân ibn Bâsîl and his nephew Hubaish, translated from Greek into Arabic the works previously translated into Syriac by Sergios of Res'ayna or himself: Dioscorides, *De materia medica* (including the two inauthentic treatises on toxicology); Galen, *De simplicium medicamentorum temperamentis et facultatibus*, books VI–XI, *De compositione medicamentorum per genera,* and *De compositione medicamentorum secundum locos*; and the medical encyclopedia of Oribasius. For *De materia medica* by Dioscorides, he translated it twice: In the first version, Istifân translated the seven books and Hunayn revised his work; in the second, Hunayn translated *De materia medica* I–IV, and Istifân the rest, including the two spurious works on poisons and venoms, and Hunayn revised the whole. Hunayn also translated the medical encyclopedia of the Byzantine physician Paul of Egina (seventh century CE).

3. Previous translations of Dioscorides were revised, or new ones were made. In the East, al-Nâtilî (tenth century CE), supposed to be Avicenna's teacher, revised Hunayn's and Istifân's second translation. During the twelfth century CE, two new translations were made from Hunayn's Syriac version. The first was commissioned by the Ortukid king of Kayfa, Fakhr ad-Din Kara Arslan (1148–1174 CE).

Since it was not considered good enough, another one was commissioned to another translator, who did it for Kara Arslan's cousin, Najm al-Din Alpi (r. 1152–1176 CE), at the court of Maridin. In the West, Hunayn and Istifân's first translation was known prior to mid-tenth century CE. 'Abd ar-Rahmân III (912–961 CE), the Emir and, further on (929), Caliph of Cordova, received in 948 CE an illustrated copy of Dioscorides' Greek text from a Byzantine emperor called Romanos, who is not exactly identified because of a contradiction in the report of the story. Local Arabic scientists working with a Byzantine monk sent to Cordova by the emperor upon the Caliph's request identified the plants of the Greek text to local species and revised Hunayn's and Istifân's Arabic text on this basis, without translating afresh the Greek text into Arabic, as has often been affirmed. This work is considered to be at the origin of the so-called Andalusian school of pharmacology.

In many manuscripts of Dioscorides' Arabic translation, the text is illustrated with color plant representations not made from direct observation of nature, but from Greek sources, which they gradually transformed, however, in three major ways, as follows:

a. Drawings of plants were stylized over time by stressing the main characteristics of the plants. Such essentialism led to a simplification that sometimes made drawings unrealistic.
b. Materia medica were represented in a context, be it their natural biota (with such elements as water, rocks, and animals) or a scene with representations of personages (harvesting of plants, preparation of medicines, and pharmacological treatment of sick patients).
c. The layout of such representations evolved from a full-page picture (with some lines of text in the upper or lower part of the page) to only a portion of the page width (on the outer side), as happened in Greek manuscripts also. This new layout did not eliminate the previous one, however, at least in deluxe Arabic manuscripts produced in Baghdad in the thirteenth century CE.

New Works, New Problems, New Medicines

Dioscorides' treatise was widely diffused in the Arabic world, as the high number of preserved manuscript copies indicates, and it deeply influenced pharmacology. As early as the late ninth century CE, scientists of different provenances wrote new and original works in Arabic. The dynamic of their production should not necessarily be attributed to the desire of their authors to be original, as has been suggested, but can result at least in part from the problems the assimilation of Dioscorides' De materia medica created: Its plants, typical of the Eastern Mediterranean, which were not necessarily well known by Arabic scientists, were tentatively equated with local species; their representations, which originally reproduced those of the Greek manuscripts, did not necessarily correspond to species in the Arabic world; plant classification, which relied in part on the names of the plants in Dioscorides' Greek text, became less perceptible after such names had been fully Arabized. The solution of such problems was all the more urgent because knowledge of medicinal plants coming from other cultures (Mesopotamia, Persia, India) was agglutinated in De materia medica.

The new syntheses on pharmacology associated data from Dioscorides (descriptions of the plants, animal and mineral products) and Galen (therapeutic properties), as did Byzantine works. The most significant contributions were by Rhazes (865–925), al-Bîrûnî (943–1078), Ibn Sînâ (980–1037), al-Gâfiqî (twelfth century CE) and Ibn al-Baitâr (ca. 1190–1248), who wrote specific works on pharmacology or devoted significant parts of larger medical encyclopedias to pharmacology. The works by al-Gâfiqî and Ibn al-Baitâr, both from the so-called Andalusian school of pharmacology, are usually considered as the most complete and achieved of the Arabic world in matters of pharmacology.

Even after such new works were produced, lexicology of materia medica remained a field of particular importance. The Andalusian, Ibn Gulgul (944–post 994), and Ibn al-Baitâr commented on Dioscorides' Arabic version in order to clarify untranslated or incorrectly translated plant names, and to accurately identify botanical species.

Medicines made of more than one ingredient (compound medicines), which started to be particularly developed in antiquity in the first century CE and reached their most achieved form with the so-called theriac (made of up to 60+ ingredients), were also used in the Arabic world where their recipes circulated in the form of collections of recipes (the so-called aqrâbâdîn from the Greek grafidion [notebook]). They raised a specific question, which was left unanswered by classical physicians, particularly Galen in his treatises De antidotis and De theriaca ad Pisonem (On the Theriac, to Piso): What is their actual therapeutic property? Is it greater than or equal to the sum of the individual components? The question was all the more complicated because Galen introduced the notion that every property of a drug results from the association of two opposite properties (hot and cold; dry and wet). Several answers were given to that fundamental question: al-Kindî (ca. 800–870) proceeded in a mathematical way, proposing a formula aimed at calculating the final property of compound medicines. Ibn Sînâ distinguished a primary property (that is, the excess of one quality over the other in a couple of opposites) and the specific property (that is, the property of the specific substance of a medicine). On the other hand, he estimated that the properties of medicines should be determined empirically by administering the medicines to the patients. Such empiricism was radical: Properties were considered to vary not only from one patient to another but also for the same patient from one moment to another according to possible individual physiological modifications. Ibn Rushd (1126–1298) (Averroës) criticized the Galenic concept of two opposite properties being associated in one and the same materia medica. Such reflection on the properties of medicines was further used as a paradigm for a philosophical analysis of the transformation of matter. In this way, pharmacology got the status of a heuristic tool in philosophical enquiry, as had already been the case in classical antiquity (first century CE). Such status was transmitted to the Latin Middle Ages, particularly with Robert Grosseteste (d. 1253 CE) and Roger Bacon (d. 1294).

Presentation of data, which first reproduced the discursive way of Greek pharmacological handbooks (including plant representations), was modified by Ibn Butlân (d. 1068) in the *Taqwîn as-sihha*. Data are presented in tables (one for each materium medica) and reduced to single words or short phrases. This layout was largely diffused in the Late Middle Ages with the Latin translation and adaptation of *Taqwîn as-sihha* known as *Tacuinum sanitatis*.

The development of new alimentary products and new technologies had a deep impact on pharmacology. The production of sugar and alcohol made it possible to develop new forms of medicines: syrups and the gums for sugar; extracts obtained by distillation with alcohol. The major novelty of such forms was that they guaranteed a better stability of the products and avoided rapid alteration. New Arabic treatises on pharmacology classified medicines by their pharmaceutical form. Such a prolonged life cycle of medicines might be among the causes that contributed to the development of the pharmaceutical profession in the Arabic world, which, in previous cultures, was mainly concerned with providing fresh drugs and preparing medicines, in a more limited way. Complementarily, the development of glazed ceramic transformed the technique of medicine conservation, particularly for the liquid and semiliquid ones. Earth wares with a porous surface did not guarantee a good conservation of medicines: The substance in contact with the internal wall of containers saturated it and it became oxidized when reaching the external wall by a constant process of evaporation. As a consequence, medicines contained in such pots were quickly altered. Glazed medicine containers had a special oblong shape, better known under its Italian name *albarello*, and allowed a much better conservation of their content by reducing the process of oxidation resulting from absorption of the content in the wall of the container. This kind of ceramic was transmitted from the Arabic world to the West through Sicily and Spain, and, from there, to Italy, where it was particularly developed during the Renaissance.

ALAIN TOUWAIDE

Further Reading

Dietrich, A. *Dioscurides Triumphans. Ein anonyme arabischer Kommentar (E. 12. Jh. n. Chr.) zur Materia medica.* 2 vols, 1988.

———. *Die Dioskurides-Erklärungen des Ibn al-Baitar. Ein Beitrag zur arabischen Planzensynonymik des MA*, 1991.

———. *Die Ergänzungen Ibn Gulgul's zur Materia medica des Dioskurides*, 1993.

Dubler, C. E. *La "Materia medica" de Dioscorides. Transmisión medieval y renacentista.* 6 vols, 1953–1959.

Elkhadem, H. *Le taqwîm al-Sihha (Tacuini Sanitatis) d'Ibn Butlân: un traité médical du XIe siècle. Histoire du texte, édition critique, traduction, commentaire*, 1990.

Grube, E. J. "Materialen zum Dioskurides Arabicus." In *Aus der Welt des Islamischen Kunst*, 1959, 163–194.

Hamarneh, S. *Bibliography on Medicine and Pharmacy in Medieval Islam*, 1964.

———. *Origins of Pharmacy and Therapy in the Near East*, 1973.

Hamarneh, S., and G. Sonnedecker. *A Pharmaceutical View of Albucasis Al-Zahrâwî in Moorish Spain*, 1963.

Kahl, O. *Sâbûr ibn Sahl. The Small Dispensatory. Translated from the Arabic together with a study and glossaries*, 2003.

Leclerc, L. *Traité des simples par Ibn El-Beïthar.* 3 vols, 1877–1883 (repr. 1996).

Levey, M. *Early Arabic Pharmacology*, 1973.

———. *The Medical Formulary or Aqrâbâdhîn of Al-Kindî.* Translated with a study of its materia medica, 1966.

Sadek, M. M. *The Arabic Materia Medica of Dioscorides*, 1983.

Samsó, J. *Las ciencias de los antiguos en Al-Andalus*, 1992.

Sezgin, F. *Geschichte des arabischen Schriftums*, vol. 3, 1970.

Strohmaier, G., and Sadek. "The Arabic Materia Medica of Dioscorides." *Gnomon* 57 (1985): 743–745.

Touwaide, A. "L'intégration de la pharmacologie grecque dans le monde arabe. Une vue d'ensemble." *Medicina nei Secoli* 7 (1995): 159–189.

———. "La traduction arabe du *Traité de matière médicale* de Dioscoride. Etat de la recherché." *Ethnopharmacologia* 18 (1996): 16–41.

———. *Farmacopea araba medievale*. 4 vols, 1992–1993.

———. "Tradition and Innovation in Mediaeval Arabic Medicine. The Translations and the Heuristic role of the Word." *Forum* 5 (1995): 203–213.

———. "Le paradigme culturel et épistémologique dans la science arabe à la lumière de l'histoire de la matière médicale." *Revue du Monde Musulman et de la Méditerranée* 77–78 (1995): 247–273.

———. "Theoretical Concepts and Problems of Greek Pharmacology in Arabic Medicine." *Forum* 6 (1996): 21–30.

Ullmann, M. *Die Medizin im Islam*, 1970.

Vernet, J. *Ce que la culture doit aux arabes d'Espagne*, 1985.

PHILOSOPHY (FALSAFA)

Falsafa is an Arabic term that renders the Greek *philosophia* and is used to describe the Greco-Arabic tradition of philosophy and the wider classical Islamic tradition. The impetus for philosophical speculation in Islam is a much debated issue. Whether one wishes to see solely Hellenic roots for philosophy in the 'Abbasid period or whether one searches as a confessional statement for philosophical inspiration in the Qur'an and the tradition of the Prophet is largely a matter of ideology. The origins of philosophy are far too complex to be reduced to a singular causality. What is clear is that in the 'Abbasid period the speculative desire to understand the nature of the Qur'an, and the relationship between believer and cosmos, was increasingly articulated in arguments of a systematic nature. The standards of argumentation, partly as a result of the need to find a neutral set of rules that could apply in disputation with non-Muslims who did not accept the validity of the Qur'anic revelation, was Aristotelian logic, especially the *Topics* (translated into Arabic in this period as the Book of Dialectic, or *al-jadal*). It has also been suggested that the 'Abbasids encouraged philosophical and scientific speculation, complemented by translations from Greek works as an expression of their imperial ideology. A translation movement developed in the capital of Baghdad, fueled by money from the court and produced mainly by Arab Christian theologians familiar with Greek and with the Syriac tradition of translating the works of Aristotle, Plato, and other Hellenic thinkers into scholarly Near Eastern vernaculars. The works were kept in the library of the chancellery in Baghdad and named *Bayt al-Hikma* (House of Wisdom). This movement intersected with a key intellectual circle associated with arguably the first Muslim philosopher, Abu Yusuf Ya'qub al-Kindi (d. 870 CE). Thus translations and arguments that joined Hellenic debates and took them into fresh avenues of inquiry were largely coeval.

Translation Movement

Important translators such as Hunayn b. Ishaq (d. 873) and Yahya b. 'Adi (d. 974) coordinated translations firstly of the Aristotelian *organon* to establish rules of disputation and standards of rational discourse, and later the metaphysical, natural philosophical, and psychological works of the Stagirite. Aristotle was the philosopher par excellence, and the Neoplatonic curriculum that Islam inherited began the study of philosophy with Aristotle. What they also inherited was the desire to harmonize the work of Plato and Aristotle. Yahya is supposed to have translated Plato's *Timaeus*, the key cosmological text of the Neoplatonic curriculum, and Porphyry's *Isogoge* or introduction to Aristotelian logic was incorporated into the study of logic. Harmonization led to the proliferation of pseudo-Aristotelian works attributed to the Stagirite that were actually of Neoplatonic provenance. Foremost among them were the Theology of Aristotle, a paraphrastic epitome of Plotinus' *Enneads* IV–VI and *Kitab fi Mahd al-Khayr (Liber de Causis),* a work that draws upon Proclus' *Stoikeiôsis Theologikê (Elements of Theology).* Both works were at the forefront of the second translation movement beginning in twelfth-century Spain, when Arabic philosophical works were translated into Latin and influenced the development of the scholastic philosophy of the universities.

The *Theology of Aristotle* was produced by the Nestorian translator 'Abd al-Masih b. 'Abdallah b. Na'ima al-Himsi (d. 835) for the circle of al-Kindi (d. 870) in Baghdad. The *Theology* is also part of a larger corpus of *Plotiniana Arabica,* drawing upon the *Enneads* that includes fragmentary sayings attributed to the "Greek Sage" *(al-Shaykh al-Yunani)* and an *Epistle on Divine Science (Risala fi-l-'Ilm al-Ilahi).* The text purports to be a translation of a theological text of Aristotle, with the commentary of Porphyry (d. 270), and certainly is a valuable expression of the Neoplatonic heritage of classical Islamic philosophy. The misattribution appealed to the taste of early Islamic philosophy that perpetuated the late antique Neoplatonic reconciliation of the philosophies of Plato and Aristotle and filled a perceived lacuna in the system of Aristotle that the Arabs inherited, providing doctrines about the nature of God and eschatology. Nevertheless, the text was adapted to suit the needs of its audience and was always more than a translation, incorporating material akin to Aristotelianism and even drawing upon pseudo-Dionysian doctrines on the "profession of ignorance." The *Theology* is divided into ten *mayamir* (sing., *mimar*), the Syriac Christian word for a chapter of a theological treatise. It is prefaced by a prologue that mentions the author, the translator, the editor (al-Kindi), and the patron (Ahmad, the son of the caliph al-Mu'tasim). It may have been modeled on a text of Porphyry that sets out some of the key issues to be tackled in the text concerning the nature of the soul, its descent into the world of matter, and its reversion to its principle. The *Theology* became the impetus for philosophical speculation and established some of the key features of Islamic Neoplatonism. Commentaries and glosses upon the text were written by Christian, Jewish, and Muslim philosophers, including Ibn Sina and 'Abd al-Latif al-Baghdadi (d. 1231) in the classical period and Qadi Sa'id Qummi (d. 1696) in the later Safavid period.

The doctrines of the *Theology* mainly concern the nature of the soul. The soul descends, like all other beings, from a causal chain of emanation that is produced by a purely good and loving principle, the One or the Creator *(al-Bari')*. It descends from a higher intelligible world to reside within a material body that is part of the sensible world. The cosmos is thus a natural and logical consequence of the One and not a volitional result of a theistic creator. Unlike the Aristotelian doctrine, the soul is not a perfection or entelechy of the body (although in at least one instance this view is approved) but is independent of the body as an eternal, immaterial substance capable of separating itself and ascending momentarily to experience the beatitude of its intelligible origin. This possibility is expressed in the famous "doffing metaphor" of *Theology mimar* I (see *Enneads* IV.8.1). The soul alienated in this world desires to taste the freedom of its origins, transcending the material cage of this world, and wishes to revert to its principle. Philosophers such as Suhrawardi and Sufis such as Ibn 'Arabi later cited this metaphor. Other doctrines and issues broached include time and creation, the nature of God and His agency, the nature of knowledge, and the end of the soul. Because of the coverage of central issues and its ascription to Aristotle, the *Theology* became the seminal text in the classical period of Islamic philosophy.

Indian and Persian Influences

The push eastward brought Muslims in contact with Persian and Indian thought and science, and early on astronomical and medical works were translated from Pahlavi and Sanskrit. The scientist and philosopher al-Biruni (d. 1048) also had the *Yogasutra* of Patanjalᴆ translated from Sanskrit, the only major work of Indian philosophy available in the classical period. Persian texts on *moralia* were transformed into a work such as *Javidan Khirad (Eternal Wisdom)* of Miskawayh (d. 1030). But the most enduring and striking legacy of the East was the physics of atomism that became a central feature of theological speculation about the nature of the cosmos, and the significance and influences of the celestial bodies upon the earth.

Theology and Philosophy

If rational discourse is a standard for judging *falsafa*, then much of the *kalam* tradition ought to be considered to be philosophical. Although the philosophical nature of much of the debate among theologians *(mutakallimun)* is indubitable (such as arguments about occasionalism, atomism, free will, and determinism), there was a tension from an early period between them and philosophers. Theology remained an apologetic defense of dogma as discerned in the Qur'an and the Prophetic tradition, whereas *falsafa* was an attempt at a rational speculation about some more abstract notions about reality. Although it did not fail to serve as the handmaiden of theology when the need arose, the Neoplatonic Aristotelianism of the philosophers *(falasifa)* was considered to be in contravention with sound belief. Ibn Sina (d. 1037) was the central figure in the formation of the new Islamic philosophy. He established key philosophical doctrines about the nature of God as a Necessary Being, described the nature of the human soul and its end in the afterlife, and provided engaging philosophical analyses of the nature of prophecy and revelation. He produced a successful and influential synthesis of theology and philosophy and it was precisely for this reason that he had been subjected to attack. The famous theologian al-Ghazali (d. 1111) in his *Tahafut al-Falasifa (Incoherence of the Philosophers)* revealed the ambivalence of theology toward philosophy. He was quite willing to co-opt Aristotelian logic as a standard for argumentation and use philosophical styles of discourse, but quite averse to the metaphysics to which they committed the practitioner. In this work, al-Ghazali condemned twenty doctrines expressed by philosophers such as Ibn Sina and held them to be incompatible with Muslim dogma, while providing rather philosophical refutations of those positions. On three specific issues, he regarded the philosophers as being guilty of heresy since belief in those doctrines was unbelief. These were the notions that the world was coeternal with God because it was only a logical and not a temporal consequent of him, that God did not know particulars but only knew universals, and that that there was no bodily resurrection. That al-Ghazali was willing to use philosophical arguments to refute philosophy and that he wrote other works that seemed to acknowledge Avicennan cosmology did contribute to his losing the case. One must not accept condemnations of the philosophical as a universal distaste for rational discourse in Islam. The cultural history of the classical period actually suggests that philosophy was far from being a pursuit marginal to intellectual Muslim society.

Islamic Philosophy

The philosophical tradition survived al-Ghazali's assault. Ibn Rushd (d. 1198) wrote a successful refutation of it. He led a revival of an orthodox Aristotelianism in Islam and also penned a famous legal defense justifying rational speculation. However, medieval Islam had no taste for orthodox Aristotelianism. Thinkers were more concerned with perpetuating the late antique process of harmonizing metaphysics with theism and thus forms of Neoplatonism were more in vogue. Philosophy after the polemics culminating in al-Ghazali survived in a number of guises, all revealing the central role of Ibn Sina and acting as reactions to his thought. First, the real success of *falsafa* led to its naturalization within the theological tradition of *kalam*. The rise of philosophical theology meant that discourse not only commenced with philosophical logic but also with its epistemological foundations concerning the nature of knowledge and its metaphysical foundations concerning existence and its divisions. Second, following Ibn Sina, works of *falsafa* included extensive discussions about the nature of God, his attributes, and his relationship with the world and included both the *kalam* cosmological proof for his existence and the Avicennan proof of God as the Necessary Being. Avicennan *falsafa* won the day. Third, followers of Ibn 'Arabi engaged with philosophy and produced a far more systematic metaphysical account of Sufi thought. Fourth, various traditions arose in critique of Ibn Sina, beginning with Suhrawardi (d. 1191) and his school of "illumination," and later in the Safavid period Mulla Sadra (d. 1641) attempted to reconcile Ibn Sina, Suhrawardi, and Ibn 'Arabi. The scope of philosophy and its cultural influence has thus extended far beyond its beginnings in 'Abbasid Baghdad.

SAJJAD H. RIZVI

Primary Sources

Adamson, P. *The Arabic Plotinus*. London: Duckworth, 2002.
Adamson, P., and R. Taylor, eds. *The Cambridge Companion to Arabic Philosophy*. Cambridge: Cambridge University Press, 2005.
Corbin, H. *A History of Islamic Philosophy*. London: Routledge, 1993.
Daiber, H. *A Bibliography of Islamic Philosophy*. 2 vols. Leiden: Brill, 1999.
Fakhry, M. *A History of Islamic Philosophy*. 3rd ed. New York: Columbia University Press, 2004.
al-Ghazali. *The Incoherence of the Philosophers*, transl. M. Marmura. Provo, UT: Brigham Young University Press, 1998.
Gutas, D. *Greek Thought, Arabic Culture*. London: Routledge, 1998.
Ibn Rushd. *The Incoherence of the Incoherence*, transl. S. van den Bergh. London: E.J.W. Gibb Memorial Trust, 1954.
Ibn Sina. *The Metaphysics*, transl. M. Marmura. Provo, UT: Brigham Young University Press, 2006.
Kraye, J. et al., eds. *Pseudo-Aristotle in the Middle Ages*. London: Warburg Institute, 1986.
Leaman, O. *A Brief Introduction to Islamic Philosophy*. Cambridge: Polity Press, 1998.
———. *Classical Islamic Philosophy*. Cambridge University Press, 2001.
Nasr, S. H., and M. Aminrazavi, eds. *An Anthology of Philosophy in Persia*. 5 vols. New York: Oxford University Press/London: I. B. Tauris, 1998–2005.
Nasr, S. H., and O. Leaman, eds. *History of Islamic Philosophy*. 2 vols. London: Routledge, 1996.
Peters, F.E. *Aristoteles Arabus*. Leiden: Brill, 1968.
Rosenthal, F. *The Classical Heritage in Islam*. London: Routledge, 1975.
Sharif, M.M. ed. *History of Muslim Philosophy*. 2 vols. Wiesbaden: Otto Harrassowitz, 1966.
Suhrawardi. *The Philosophy of Illumination*, transl. J. Walbridge and H. Ziai. Provo, UT: Brigham Young University Press, 1998.
Walzer, Richard. *Greek into Arabic*. Oxford: Bruno Cassirer, 1962.

PIGEONS

Pigeons had a presence in the everyday life of medieval Muslims. As pets they were more universal and popular than game birds, such as the falcon, whose keeping was mostly reserved to the upper classes. It is apparent from Jahiz that they were reasonably priced during his time and easily attainable from the city markets, although well-trained zejil (those that were trained to fly to a destination and come back) could be costly. For example, one that had come back to Baghdad from as far as Sham could cost up to a thousand dinars. When reading passages regarding the pigeon from his *Kitab al-Hayawan*, one sees very clearly how Jahiz's zoology is really about humans. Pigeons are scrutinized in such a way as to deduce facts about marriage, coupling, love, passion, monogamy, polygamy, homosexuality, loyalty, sacrifice, jealousy, and the like. They are a mirror of male–female relations in all possible forms.

It is known that pigeons were part of an intricate postal system established by the 'Abbasids and developed to its highest efficiency during the Mamluk period. The Mamluk historian Qalqashandi details how pigeons were dispatched to the towers that were erected for this purpose.

Pigeons have a presence in the imagination of medieval Muslims, not just as an item of conspicuous consumption in the Souq, and as part of the postal system, but also as a strong image of sanctity and courier of wisdom. It is mentioned that the inhabitants of Mecca were witness to the fact that no pigeon has ever landed on the Ka'ba. This alone has convinced many that pigeons are superior to all birds and animals. It is well known that the conqueror of Egypt, Amr b. al-As, changed his plans of constructing the barrack town of Fustat lest he disturb the dove and its chicks that had nested in his tent.

Medieval Muslim authors frequently allude to Noah's pigeon, which is viewed as a guide figure that carries good tidings. The pigeon is awarded by God for his loyalty and services, with the collar on his neck, making him stand out till the dawn of time. It is the pigeon's collar (tawq) that Ibn Hazm of Andalus has named his treatise on love. The most prevalent aspect of the image of the pigeon is that it carries God's words (ta'wil). This is similar to the imagery in the prologue of the gospel according to John, where the dove symbolizes the Holy Ghost, carrier of divine logos. Similarly, in Genesis 1:2, a dove hovering over the waters refers to the spirit of God at the time of creation. Abu Firas's highly acclaimed poem, which epitomizes the pigeon as a bird that reminds the poet of his freedom lost also partakes from this imagery of the messenger of wisdom. The poet, who was taken captive by the Hamadanis in Mousul, sees a pigeon through the bars of his prison, a pigeon that is praying. He calls out to the bird and asks it if it understands his predicament, as if wishing the pigeon to carry away words of his agony.

ZUMRUT ALP

Further Reading

Abu Zayd. 'Ali Ibrahim, al-Hamam fi al-shi'r al-'arabi. Cairo: Dar al-Ma'arif, 1996.
Al-Mas'udi. Kitab al-Tanbih wa'l-Ishraf. Edited by Michael Jan de Goeje. Leigen: E. J. Brill, 1894.
Al-Qazwini. 'Ajaib al-Makhluat wa Gharaib al-Mawjudat. Edited by Ferdinand Wustenfeld. Gottingen: Druck und Verlag der Dieterichschen Buchhandlung, 1848–1849.
Ibn Hazm, 'Ali ibn Ahmad. Tawq al-Hamama fi al-ulfa wa al-ullaj. Edited by al-Tab'ah 1. Dar al-Maktaba al-Hilal, Beirut, 2000.
Jahiz, Abi 'Uthman 'Amr ibn Bahr al-Jahiz (Ed). al-Tab'ah 1. Dar al-Kutub al-Ilmiya, Beirut, 1998.
Moulton, Richard, G. (Ed). Modern Reader's Bible. London: Macmillan & Co. Ltd., 1916.
Qalqashandi, Ahmad ibn 'Ali. Subh al-A'sha fi Sina'at al-ansha.' Cairo: al-Mu'arrasah al-Misriyah al-Ammah li'l-Ta'lif wa'l-Tarjumah wa'l-Tiba'ah wa'l-Nahr, 1964.

PILGRIMAGE

No single word exists for pilgrimage to holy places. Unlike the canonical Pilgrimage to Mecca (Hajj), which is incumbent upon Muslims once in their lifetimes (Qur'an 3:97), the commendable 'Umra, or lesser pilgrimage, the ziyara (Arab. lit. a visit, visiting), or pious visitation to tombs, shrines, and other sacred places and devotional objects, is not prescribed in the Qur'an or in the Hadith of the Prophet Muhammad.

Devotees from all walks of life, including rulers, theologians, scholars, and common people, visited tombs and shrines of holy persons, including the prophets and patriarchs, saints, Sufi shaykhs, and rulers—usually individuals who possessed exemplary learning and piety—and other holy places for a variety of reasons, including to obtain blessings, cures, and relief from adversity; to acquire knowledge about the burial places of the prophets and the earliest generations of Muslims, especially the Companions and Followers of the Prophet; and for the fulfilment of supplication.

In pre-Islamic times, pilgrimage to the tombs and shrines of the prophets and patriarchs and to Christian saints was widespread among Christians and Jews. In Islamic times, Jews and Christians visited their respective shrines, common shrines, and those of Muslims. Particularly from the eleventh and twelfth centuries, when the ziyara and the construction of shrines proliferated across the Islamic world due in no small part to the spread of Sufism, the ziyara assumed, at least outwardly, peculiar Islamic characteristics. Jews and Christians invoked supplications not only in such liturgical languages as Hebrew and Syriac but also in Arabic and Persian. Jews removed their shoes as they entered holy places. Moreover, cupolas like on Muslim shrines surmounted Jewish and Christian shrines.

Among the most venerated pilgrimage sites by region were: (Cairo): Husayn ibn 'Ali (d. 680), the Prophet's granddaughter Zaynab, the Egyptian theologian Al-Shafi'i (d. 820); (Damascus): John the Baptist (Yahya ibn Zakariyya'), the Prophet's granddaughter Zaynab; (Iraq): 'Ali ibn Abi Talib

(d. 661) at Kufa and Husayn ibn 'Ali at Karbala. In Damascus, Muslims, Christians, Jews, and Zoroastrians venerated the eleventh-century Muslim patron saint Shaykh Arslan, while Christians and Muslims venerated the Virgin Mary at the Christian shrine outside the city. In Iraq and Persia, Jews, Muslims, and Christians made ziyara to the regional shrines of the Prophets Daniel, Ezekiel, and Ezra.

Medieval Muslims composed guides for various regions of the Middle East, including Egypt, Syria, and Iraq, which mention those places that are especially efficacious for attaining cures from ailments and for obtaining *baraka,* or blessing. Most pilgrimage guides do not mention a prescribed order for visiting shrines, but rather highlight those shrines that are especially efficacious or blessed. The most important works by region include: 'Ali ibn Abi Bakr al-Harawi's (d. 1215) *Kitab al-Isharat ila Ma'rifat al-Ziyarat (Guide to Knowledge of Pilgrimage Places)*, which is the only known guide that mentions pilgrimage places throughout the Islamic world from North Africa and the Mediterranean to the borders of India, including those of Jews and Christians. Al-Harawi's guide also mentions the antiquities of ancient civilizations, talismanic objects, wells, rivers, and sacred substances such as water and soil. Egyptian guides, such as Ibn 'Uthman's (d. 1218) *Murshid al-Zuwwar (The Pilgrims' Guide)* stress the etiquette of ziyara as do later pilgrimage guides like Ibn al-Hawrani's *Al-Isharat ila Amakin al-Ziyarat (Guide to Pilgrimage Places)*. By contrast, Iraqi Shi'i pilgrimage guides such as Ibn Qawlawayh's (d. 978/9) *Kamil al-Ziyarat (The Complete Pilgrimage Guide)*, which emphasize *ziyara* to the tombs and shrines of the Prophet, his Family, and the Shi'i imams, are more precise in that they instruct pilgrims in the rites prescribed by the fifth and sixth imams Muhammad al-Baqir and Ja'far al-Sadiq which they are to undertake, including purification rituals, prayers, and supplications. Common to all guides is the surrender of the devotee's self to God and reflecting on the hereafter and on the tomb or shrine's inmate.

Ziyara for the purpose of acquiring *baraka* and knowledge was also made to living saints, ascetics, and more generally, individuals renowned for their exemplary piety and learning and was a widespread practice.

Unlike the veneration of saints in the Christian context, the ziyara became controversial. The Hanbali (*see* Schools of Jurisprudence) theologian Ibn Taymiyya (d. 1328) and his disciples regarded the ziyara to tombs and shrines and to living individuals as heretical innovation and polytheism, views to which the majority of Muslim theologians did not subscribe.

Ziyara was also made to copies of the Qur'an in Damascus and elsewhere, particularly those associated with the third and fourth Rightly Guided Caliphs 'Uthman ibn 'Affan and 'Ali b. Abi Talib.

JOSEF W. MERI

See also Hajj; Saints and Sainthood; Christian; Umra

Primary Sources

Harawi, 'Ali ibn Abi Bakr. *A Lonely Wayfarer's Guide to Pilgrimage: 'Ali ibn Abi Bakr al-Harawi's Kitab al-isharat ila ma'rifat al-ziyarat.* Translated by Josef W. Meri. Prineton: Darwin Press, 2004.
Ibn al-Hawrani, "A Late Medieval Syrian Pilgrimage Guide: Ibn al-Hawrani's *Al-Isharat ila Amakin al-Ziyarat (Guide to Pilgrimage Places)."* *Medieval Encounters: Jewish, Christian and Muslim Culture in Confluence and Dialogue* 7 (2001): 3–78.

Further Reading

Meri, Josef W. *The Cult of Saints Among Muslims and Jews in Medieval Syria.* Oxford and New York: Oxford University Press, 2002.
Meri, J. "Ziyara." *EI(2)*, 11:524–529.
———. "The Etiquette of Devotion in the Islamic Cult of Saints." In *The Cult of Saints in Late Antiquity and the Middle Ages: Essays on the Contribution of Peter Brown*, edited by J. Howard-Johnston and P. A. Hayward, 263–286. Oxford, 1999.
Taylor, Christopher S. *In the Vicinity of the Righteous: Ziyara and the Veneration of Saints in Late Medieval Egypt.* Leiden: Brill Academic Publishers, 1999.

PLATO, PLATONISM, AND NEOPLATONISM

Neoplatonism was a philosophical movement that primarily belonged to the Hellenist Alexandrian and Syriac schools of thought. Its founder, Plotinus (ca. 205–270 CE), an Egyptian of Greek culture, was profoundly influenced by Plato's *Republic*, *Phaedo*, and *Symposium*, as well as being inspired by Aristotelian, Stoic, and neo-Pythagorean doctrines. Plotinus' own monumental corpus, the *Enneads*, was partly drafted in response to the objections raised by Aristotle against Plato's theory of ideas. Therein, Plotinus argued that the Platonic forms subsist in what Aristotle referred to as *Nous* (intellect). Giving a metaphysical primacy to abstract ideas, the realm of the intelligible was construed as being the ground of the ultimate reality, which was radically independent from sensible beings. This ontology led to a belief in the existence of absolute values rooted in eternity. Further elaborations of Plotinus's teachings were undertaken by his disciple, Porphyry of Tyre (ca. 232–305 CE), and were supplemented by the work of the latter's pupil, the Syrian Iamblichus (ca. 250–330 CE). However, Proclus (ca. 411–485 CE) introduced the most rigorous systematization of this tradition. The impetus of Neoplatonism in philosophy confronted many challenges following the closing of the Athenian Academy (ca. 526 CE) by the Roman Emperor Justinian. The momentum of this tradition was renewed with the philosophers of the medieval Islamic civilization who imbued it with monotheistic directives. Following Socrates, in a critique of the Sophists, Platonists believed that knowledge cannot be derived from appearances alone, and that it can only be properly attained through universal ideas. Heeding the meditations of Parmenides, they held that the realm of being was unchanging, eternal, and indestructible; while following Heraclitus, they took the sensible realm as being subject to a constant flux of transformational becoming. Establishing a distinction between truth and belief, they asserted that the intelligible was apprehended by reason and the sensible by mere opinion. With this Platonist heritage, the ethical code of goodness became a cosmological principle. Eventually, Neoplatonists held that The One, as the indeterminate perfection of absolute unity, simplicity, and goodness, imparts existence from itself due to its superabundance. This event was grasped as being a process of emanation that accentuated the primacy of Divine transcendence over creation and represented an alternate explication of generation that challenged the *creatio ex nihilo* doctrine. Endowed with vision, the One, as the First undiminished Source of existence, imparts *Nous*, the immanent changeless Intellect, as its own Image. From this effused *Nous* issues forth the World Soul, which acts as a transition between the realm of ideas and that of the senses. Refracting itself in materiality, the Soul generates all sensible composite beings, while matter represents the last station in the hierarchy of existence as the unreal substratum of the phenomenal universe. Emanation, as a processional descent, was itself to be followed by an ascent that expressed the longing of the rational soul to return to its Source and a yearning to inhabit the realm of ideas. This reversible movement acted as the basis of the moral code of the Neoplatonist system, which advocated a dualist separation of mind and body, as well as affirmed the immortality of the soul. Philosophers in medieval Islam came to know Plato through the Arabic translations of his *Laws, Sophist, Timaeus,* and *Republic.* His influence on the history of ideas in Islam is most felt in the domains of ethics and political philosophy, whereby his views offered possibilities for reconciling pagan philosophy with monotheistic religion in the quest for truth and the unveiling of the ultimate

principles of reality. His *Republic* and *Laws* presented an appealing legislative model that inspired political thought in Islam, particularly the line in thinking that is attested in al-Farabi's (ca. 870–950 CE) treatise *al-Madina al-Fadila (The Virtuous City)*, which gave prominence to the role played by philosophy in setting the legal arrangements and mores of the ideal Islamic polity. The *Corpus Platonicum* also impressed humanists like Ibn Miskawayh (ca. 940–1030 CE), who, in his *Tahdhib al-akhlaq (The Cultivation of Morals)* espoused the Platonic tripartite conception of the soul, along with its ethical–political ramifications. As for the Neoplatonist doctrines, these found their way into the intellectual history of Islam through Plato's dialogues, as well as being channeled via the tracts known as *Aristotle's Theology* and *Liber de causis (Kitab al-Khayr al-Mahd)*. Although both texts were erroneously attributed to Aristotle, the former reproduced fragments from Plotinus's *Enneads*, and the latter rested on Proclus' *Elements of Theology*. This misguiding textual transmission led to imbuing Aritotelianism with Neoplatonist leitmotifs, which impacted the thinking of authorities such as al-Kindi (d. ca. 873 CE), Ikhwan al-Safa' (tenth century CE), al-Farabi (d. ca. 950 CE), and Ibn Sina (d. 1037 CE), who in their turn influenced the onto-theological systems of al-Sijistani (fl. 971 CE), al-Kirmani (d. 1020 CE), Suhrawardi (d. 1191 CE), Ibn 'Arabi (d. 1240 CE), and Mulla Sadra (d. 1640 CE).

NADER EL-BIZRI

See also Aristotle and Aristotelianism; Brethren of Purity; al-Farabi (Alfarabius or Avennasar); Ibn 'Arabi; Ibn Sina (Avicenna); Illuminationism; al-Kindi (Philosopher); al-Kirmani, Hamid al-Din; Mulla Sadra; Suhrawardi, Shihab al-Din 'Umar; Tusi, Nasir al-Din

Primary Sources

al-Farabi (Alfarabius). *De Platonis Philosophia.* Edited by Franz Rosenthal and Richard Walzer. London: The Warburg Institute, University of London, 1943.

Galenus, Claudius. *Compendium Timaei Platonis.* Edited by Paul Krauss and Richard Walzer. London: The Warburg Institute, University of London, 1951.

Plato. *Plato Arabus.* Edited by Paul Krauss and Richard Walzer. London: The Warburg Institute, University of London, 1943.

Further Reading

Krauss, Paul. "Plotin chez les arabes." *Bulletin de l'Institut d'Égypte* 23 (1941): 236–295.

Netton, Ian Richard. *Muslim Neoplatonists: An Introduction to the Thought of the Brethren of Purity.* London: G. Allen and Unwin, 1982.

Rosenthal, Franz. "On the Knowledge of Plato's Philosophy in the Islamic World." *Islamic Culture* 14 (1940): 398–402.

Walzer, Richard. "Aflatun." In *The Encyclopaedia of Islam.* Vol I. Leiden: Brill, 1960.

———. *Greek into Arabic: Essays in Islamic Philosophy.* Cambridge, MA: Harvard University Press, 1962.

POETRY, ARABIC

Arabic poetry was originally an evocation of heroic aspects of pre-Islamic Bedouinity, such as fighting, hunting, tribal loyalty, and contending with the harshness of nomadic life (women poets were more or less restricted to one theme, elegy). It was composed in a cross-dialectal poetic *koine*, with a rich and difficult vocabulary, abounding with nature descriptions and extended similes, which, though concrete, are charged with ethical symbolism and are often enigmatic or riddling. The earliest pieces date from perhaps the sixth century CE, and the pre-Islamic corpus is now accepted as authentic, though probably retouched by the 'Abbasid scholars who first put it in writing. It uses a common stock of motifs and compositional devices, which recur in most of the poetry written in Arabic throughout the Middle Ages and beyond, and laid down a system of thought and allusion that permeated Arabic literary sensibility. The form in which the great pre-Islamic set pieces were composed was the polythematic *qasida*; its preeminence continued into the Islamic period. Typically, it could include two or more of the following: an opening description of the deserted encampment—an image of transience—and/or the description of a lost beloved, played against the arduous journey by which the poet asserts his manliness, his self-praise and/or praise of the patron, the whole being held in tension by the poem's function as an affirmation of shared values, of which the poet, who speaks in the first person, is the inspired mouthpiece. The prosodic features of the *qasida* are monorhythm and monorhyme, which limit its length to around a hundred lines on average. Transmuted into the ceremonial court panegyric celebrating the divine right of caliphs or a patron's victories, the Islamic *qasida* found its most dramatic exponents in Abu Tammam (d. ca. AH 232/845 CE) and al-Mutanabbi (d. 354/965). The former liked to dress as a Bedouin and the latter considered himself a man of action; but the genuine tribal warrior poet was now largely a figure of the past, and many poets writing in Arabic were not Arabs; notable exceptions were the Hamdanid prince Abu Firas (320–357/932–968), captured in battle by the Byzantines, and Usama ibn Munqidh (d. 584/1188).

Islam and empire, and above all the growth of a highly literate, urban culture centered on elite patronage, brought changes in the role of poetry and a proliferation of new genres, such as the love poem (*ghazal; see* Umar ibn Abi Rabi'a), wine poem *(khamriyya)* and verse homily *(zuhdiyya),* and the didactic poem in rhymed couplets. Formulaic but fluid macrostructures and microstructures, together with brevity and narrative minimalism, nevertheless continued to characterize most Arabic poetry. However tightly fashioned, Arabic poems were essentially open textured because they were constructed on multiple allusion. Classical Bedouin models and the brilliant conceits of "modern" poets could be evoked—indeed, to do so was inescapable—by a motif, phrase, rhythm, or a single word; so, too, could the Qur'an and hadith. Contemporary realities—concrete, topical, ideological, or intellectual—often clearly dictate the argument or frame of reference (*see* Ibn Hamdis), but the specific is not always easy to distinguish from the generic (for example, in the case of wine poems or homoerotic love poems: such poems are not necessarily autobiographical). The poet's stylistic persona might be consistent and genre-based or split into multiple facets distributed across a range of genres, and here patronage played a crucial role; for an example of how poets could shape their talents to their market, see the entry on Abu Nuwas.

Not all poets were dependent on patrons; nevertheless, there were few genres that were not geared to the elite, its ideology, and pastimes (mystical poetry is one exception; *see* Rabi'a al-'Adawiyya and Ibn 'Arabi), and it was rare to refuse to adapt one's poetry to social requirements, as did al-Ma'arri (d. 449/1058), for poetry was part of social life. There could be no *adab* without poetry, in the form both of the ability to versify elegantly and of knowledge of the classical and modern poets and of the scholarly and critical controversies surrounding them. Poetry was closely associated with music and singing; women slave entertainers were often composers and poets. Poets might be princes, such as Abu Firas, or have risen from humble origins, like Abu Tammam, and vernacular folk poetry seems to have had many themes in common with the learned poetry written in classical Arabic. In Andalus, the combined charm of music and of the vernacular gave rise to new poetic forms, the *muwashshah* and the *zajal*, which were imitated in the Islamic East. Both are strophic, with complex multiple rhythms and rhymes; the *muwashshah* culminates in an envoi *(kharja)* in a vernacular (Ar., Romance); the *zajal* is entirely in colloquial Arabic (*see* Ibn Quzman).

Poetry also held a central place in intellectual life. Grammarians, lexicographers, and commentators of the Qur'an combed the early Arabic corpus for examples and parallels. Poetic criticism (*see* Rhetoric) was a discipline in its own right but could be slanted to dogmatic ends to demonstrate the inimitable expressivity of the Qur'an (see al-Jurjani). Commentaries and supercommentaries (sharh, pl. shuruh) on poetry collections (diwans) or proof-verses were an opportunity to draw together all the learning associated with poetry (see Adab, al-Baghdadi). Together with tribal genealogies, poetry and the stories attached to it provided historians with almost their sole materials for reconstructing the pre-Islamic Arab past; as the only monument surviving from that past, ancient poetry was—and "modern" poetry continued to be—the supreme Arabic art form. Yet its status was ambiguous, for its ethos was non-Islamic and sometimes counter to Islam. Udaba' such as al-Jahiz (d. ca. 255/869), Ibn Qutayba (d. 276/889), and Abu al-Faraj al-Isfahani (d. ca. 363/972; see Adab), argued or demonstrated that the virtues embodied in Arab poetic eloquence not only could not be jettisoned but also must be cherished by good Muslims, while some theorists sidestepped the issue by pleading that poetry, ancient and modern, belonged to the sphere of make-believe, not to that of truth or morality.

Arabic poetry remained largely impervious to outside influences but exerted a decisive influence on Hebrew poetry.

JULIA BRAY

See also Abu Firas; Abu Nuwas; Abu Tammam; Adab; Hebrew Poetry; Ibn Hamdis; Ibn Qutayba; Ibn Quzman; al-Jahiz; al-Jurjani; Love Poetry; al-Mutanabbi; Mystical Poetry; Rabi'a al-Ma'arri; Rhetoric; Umar ibn Abi Rabi'a; Usama ibn Munqidh

Further Reading

Alvarez, L. "Muwashshah' and 'Zajal, medieval.'", In *Encyclopedia of Arabic Literature*, II, edited by Julie Scott Meisami and Paul Starkey, 563–566 snf 818–819. London and New York: Routledge, 1998 (comprehensive coverage of form, history, and scholarly debate).

Ashtiany, Julia et al (Eds). *'Abbasid Belles-Lettres*. 1990.

Bauer, Thomas. *Liebe und Liebesdichtung in der arabischen Welt des 9. und 10. Jahrhunderts: eine literatur- und mentalitätsgeschichtliche Studie der arabischen Ghazal*. Wiesbaden: Harrassowitz, 1998.

Bencheikh, J. E. 'Les secrétaires poètes et animateurs de cénacles au IIe et IIIe siècles de l'Hégire.' *Journal Asiatique* 263 (1975): 265–315.

Frolov, D. *Classical Arabic Verse. History and Theory of 'Arud*. Leiden and Boston: Brill, 2000 (prosody: metrics).

van Gelder, G. J. H. "The Abstracted Self in Arabic Poetry." *Journal of Arabic Literature* 14 (1983): 22–30.

———. *Beyond the Line. Classical Arabic Literary Critics on the Coherence and Unity of the Poem*. Leiden: Brill, 1982.

Heijkoop, Henk, and Otto Zwartjes. *Muwashah, Zajal, Kharja. Bibliography of Strophic Poetry and Music from al-Andalus and Their Influence in East and West*. Leiden and Boston: Brill, 2004.

Jacobi, Renate. "The Camel-Section of the Panegyrical Ode." *Journal of Arabic Literature* 13 (1982): 1–22.

Kilpatrick, Hilary. "Women as Poets and Chattels: Abu l-Faraj al-Isbahani's 'al-Ima' al-Shawa'ir.'" *Quaderni di Studi Arabi* (Venice) 9 (1991): 161–176.

Montgomery, James E. *The Vagaries of the Qasida: The Tradition and Practice of Early Arabic Poetry*. Cambridge: Gibb Memorial Trust, 1997.

———. "Of Models and Amanuenses: The Remarks on the Qasida in Ibn Qutayba's *Kitab al-Shi'r wa-l-Shu'ara.*'" In *Islamic Reflections Arabic Musings. Studies in Honour of Alan Jones*, edited by Robert G. Hoyland and Philip F. Kennedy, 1–47. Oxford: Gibb Memorial Trust, 2004.

———. *The Era of al-Mutanabbi—Proceedings of the Eighth Symposium on Classical Arabic Poetry (1995)*, *Arabic and Middle Eastern Literatures* 2 (i) (1999).

Motoyoshi Sumi, Akiko. *Description in Classical Arabic Poetry. Wasf, Ekphrasis, and Interarts Theory*. Leiden and Boston: Brill, 2004.

Najjar, Ibrahim. *La Mémoire rassemblée. Poètes arabes "mineurs" des IIe/VIIIe et IIIe/IXe siècles*. Paris: La Française d'Édition et d'Imprimerie, 1987 (the social matrix of poetry).

Ouyang, Wen-Chin. *Literary Criticism in Medieval Arabic-Islamic Culture: The Making of a Tradition*. Edinburgh: Edinburgh University Press, 1997.

Pérès, Henri. *La Poésie andalouse en arabe classique au XIe siècle. Ses aspects généraux et sa valeur documentaire*. Paris: Adiren Mainsonneuve, 1937.

Rikabi, Jawdat. *La Poésie profane sous les Ayyûbides, et ses principaux représentants*. Paris: G.-P. Maisonneuve, 1949.

Rosa Menocal, María et al. *The Literature of al-Andalus*. 2000.

Sperl, Stefan. "Islamic Kingship and Arabic Panegyric Poetry in the Early Ninth Century." *Journal of Arabic Literature* 8 (1977): 20–35.

———. *Mannerism in Arabic Poetry: A Structural Analysis of Selected Texts*. Cambridge: Cambridge University Press, 1989.

Sperl, Stefan, and Christopher Shackle (Eds). *Qasida Poetry in Islamic Asia and Africa*. I: *Classical Traditions and Modern Meanings*; II: *Eulogy's Bounty, Meaning's Abundance. An Anthology*. Leiden: Brill, 1996.

Stetkevych, Jaroslav. *The Zephyrs of Najd. The Poetics of Nostalgia in the Classical Arabic Nasib*. Chicago: Chicago University Press, 1993.

Vadet, Jean-Claude. *L'Esprit courtois en Orient dans les cinq premiers siècles de l'Hégire*. Paris: Maisonneuve et Larose, 1968.

"The Cambridge History of Arabic Literature." In *Arabic Literature to the End of the Umayyad Period*, edited by A. F. L. Beeston et al. Cambridge: Cambridge University Press, 1983).

POETRY, HEBREW

Hebrew liturgical poetry, known as the *piyyut,* which used foreign vocabulary, complex grammatical forms, and an opaque style, flourished in Byzantine Palestine prior to the Islamic conquest. By the ninth century, the center of literary activity moved from Palestine to Iraq, where a number of poets continued the *piyyut* tradition. Some literary characteristics of the early *piyyut* persisted through the Islamic Middle Ages, although later poets such as Abraham Ibn Ezra (1092–1167) lampooned the lexicographic and grammatical irregularities of the classical style. Sa'adyah Gaon (882–942), dean of the academy of Jewish learning in Baghdad, initiated a trend toward Hebrew purity based on biblical vocabulary and grammatical forms, although he did not abandon post-biblical vocabulary entirely. Although he tried to limit the amount of poetry recited in prayer, he included original poems in the prayer book he composed. Sa'adyah authored poems for didactic and polemical (that is, nonliturgical) purposes, a point that reflects the impact of his Arabic milieu (he was preceded in this by some Karaite poets). The Arabic environment is also sensed in the philosophical content of some poems and in the cosmopolitan values espoused in his essay for poets, *Kitab usul al-ahi'r al-'ibrani* (*Book of Principles of Hebrew Poetry*).

Because of intensified study of the Bible and Hebrew grammar in al-Andalus (following Muslim engagement with the Qur'an and Arabic grammar), Jews came to value composition using the biblical lexicon only and to regard the Hebrew Bible as a standard of eloquence and style. This near obsession with biblical Hebrew reflects an assertion of Jewish cultural nationalism even as it testifies to deeply ingrained Arabized values.

Menahem Ben Saruq, a mid-tenth-century Andalusian poet patronized by the courtier Hasdai Ibn Shaprut, wrote secular poems, including panegyrics and a famous greeting, written on Hasdai's behalf, to the Jewish king of Khazaria. Menahem was displaced by the rival poet Dunash Ben Labrat (d. c. 990), who revolutionized Hebrew poetry by adopting the prosodic features of Arabic verse (quantitative meter and monorhyme). Dunash thus allowed Jews to participate in one of the hallmark traditions of the age through the medium of their own historic language.

The use of Arabic meter was a subject of ambivalence among Andalusian Jews. Moses Ibn Ezra extolled Arabized Hebrew poetry in his *Kitab al-muhadara wa-l-mudhakara* (*Book of Conversation and Discussion*), a Judeo-Arabic treatise on Hebrew poetics, while Judah Halevi demurred in the *Kuzari* that foreign meters sullied the purity of Hebrew verse (even though he often used Arabic meter in his own poetry). Hebrew poems also imitate the structural principles of Arabic forms such as the *qasida* and the *muwashshah*. The Hebrew *qasida* links disparate themes (such as nature and panegyric) using standard constructions of the "escape verse" (*takhallus*). The Hebrew *muwashshah* follows the strophic pattern of its Arabic counterpart and frequently concludes with a *kharja*, either in Arabic or Hispano-Romance.

Many Hebrew poems fit neatly into Arabic thematic genres (wine poems, garden poems, poems of desire, panegyrics, invective, and so on). Recasting these themes in the language of the Bible allows for ironic and humorous effects through intertextual allusion. Arabic themes and meters also penetrate Hebrew devotional verse in al-Andalus. The pre-Islamic motif of *al-buka' 'ala al-atlal* (*Weeping over the Ruins*), wherein the poet laments the effacement of the tribe's encampment, is evoked by Jewish poets lamenting the decay of the Jewish encampment *par excellence*, the Temple in Jerusalem. Although Andalusian Hebrew poetry is highly conventional, occasional poems reveal poetic individuality: Samuel Ibn Naghrela (993–1056) recounted battles of the Taifa kings; Solomon Ibn Gabirol (1021 to ca. 1055) wrote about his frustrated pursuit of philosophical wisdom; Moses Ibn Ezra (c. 1055 to after 1135) lamented his exile from al-Andalus; and Judah Halevi composed devotional poems during his pilgrimage to Palestine.

Another Arabized literary form that emerged in al-Andalus was the Hebrew rhymed prose narrative, which followed conventions of the Arabic *maqama*. In Solomon Ibn Saqbel's *Asher Son of Judah Spoke* (first half of twelfth century), the protagonist is rushed into marriage, only to have his veiled intended replaced with a bearded man. The story shares the *maqama's* penchants for trickery and denouement through recognition. This narrative was followed in Christian Iberia and in the Islamic world with a variety of rhymed prose narratives that adhere to the classical *maqama* to varying degrees. The most classical Hebrew example is Judah al-Harizi's *Tahkemoni*, which borrows plot materials from al-Hamadhani, al-Hariri, and other Arabic authors. Jews continued to compose poetry and prose in the Arabic style in North Africa, the Islamic East, and in Christian Europe for centuries to come.

JONATHAN P. DECTER

See also Judah Halevi; Judah al-Harizi; Ibn Ezra; Solomon Ibn Gabirol; Samuel Ibn Naghrela; Maqama; Poetry, Arabic; Sa'adyah Gaon

Further Reading

Brann, Ross. *The Compunctious Poet: Cultural Ambiguity and Hebrew Poetry in Muslim Spain.* Baltimore and London: The Johns Hopkins University Press, 1991.

Pagis, Dan. "Variety in Medieval Rhymed Narratives." *Scripta Hierosolymitana* 27 (1978): 79–98.

Scheindlin, Raymond P. *The Gazelle: Medieval Hebrew Poems on God, Israel, and the Soul.* Philadelphia: Jewish Publication Society, 1991.

————. *Wine, Women, and Death: Medieval Hebrew Poems on the Good Life*. Philadelphia: Jewish Publication Society, 1986.

Schirmann, Jefim. *Toledot ha-shirah ha-'ivrit bi-Sefarad ha-muslemit*. Edited, supplemented, and annotated by Ezra Fleischer. Jerusalem: Magnes Press, 1995.

POETRY, INDIAN

Muslims in medieval India composed poetry either in Persian or in the various Indic vernaculars, depending on their socioeconomic class and the literary traditions with which they identified.

Poetry in Persian was principally associated with the *ashraf*, the ruling class and aristocracy of Central Asian or Iranian origin, who governed many regions of the subcontinent from the tenth century onward. Although the *ashraf* occasionally used Turkish and Arabic, they espoused Persian as their principal literary language to maintain a distinct cultural and ethnic identity from the local population. Their use of Persian enabled them to participate in a wider international Turko-Persian culture that, at least until the eighteenth century, provided a shared cultural ethos between the ruling elites of a vast region that now comprises modern-day India, Pakistan, Afghanistan, Iran, Central Asia, and even Turkey. The cosmopolitan nature of this culture meant that literati in Indian cities such as Delhi, Lahore, and Bijapur shared the same literary traditions as their counterparts in Heart, Bukhara, and Isfahan. It also meant that poets and artists could move freely in search of royal patronage in any part of this cultural nexus. Beginning in the sixteenth century, the Mughals enhanced the status of Persian when they declared it as the official language of their empire and used it to create a common literary ethos between heterogeneous religious and social groups. Thus, members of the Hindu administrative and ruling elite became enthusiastic participants in Persian literary culture, many of them becoming significant poets in the language.

As a result of this official patronage, during certain historical periods the total quantity of Persian literature produced in India greatly exceeded that produced in Iran proper. The vast corpus includes every major and minor Persian literary genre. Poetry was by far the most popular form of literary composition in Persian. Poets in medieval India utilized all major poetic forms, including the *qasida* (the panegyric extolling the virtues of a ruler or patron), the *ghazal* (the mystically tinged love lyric) and the *masnawi* (a "double-rhymed" epic form used particularly for narrating epics). The vast majority of Persian poets in India adhered strictly to poetic conventions as they relate to symbols and imagery as developed in Iran and Central Asia. They composed *nazira*s, poems imitating the classical models of renowned Persian authors, as a way of demonstrating their literary skills. From very early on, however, there developed a unique style of Indian Persian called *sabk-i hindi* (the Indian style), which incorporated Indian elements into the world of Persian literary culture. The Indian style began modestly with early poets such as Mas'ud Sa'd Salman (d. ca. 1131) and Amir Khusrau (d. 1325), reaching maturity in the seventeenth century.

The influence of Persian extended far beyond its use as a literary medium among the elite. Persian became such an important cultural element in medieval India that Persian vocabulary features prominently in all major North Indian languages. It also strongly influenced the poetic forms, idioms, and even the writing systems of several Indic languages, such as Urdu, Sindhi, Baluchi, Pashtu, and Panjabi. Indeed, the poetic symbolism of Urdu poetry and its nuances cannot be appreciated without a background in Persian.

Pioneering the use of Indian vernaculars for composing poetry were various Sufis, or mystics. While it may be too simplistic to conceive of them as missionaries who converted substantial portions of the local population to Islam, the evidence strongly suggests that it was Sufis, composing poetry in local languages, who were responsible for the widespread dissemination of ideas among the masses. The most significant characteristic of this poetry was its folk character, drawing on indigenous traditions of folk songs, as a way of communicating with audiences who did not understand Persian or Arabic. Poets freely adopted indigenous literary structures and forms from folk poetic traditions that were predominantly oral in character and meant to be sung or recited with musical accompaniment. Often, these folk poems were incorporated in popular Sufi rituals such as the *sama'* and *qawwali* (concerts of mystical music). As this folk poetic tradition was closely tied to women's traditions, Sufi poetry in the vernaculars extensively adopts forms and symbols of songs sung by women as they performed their daily household chores such as spinning, weaving, grinding grain, and singing lullabies. As Richard Eaton illustrates in his book *Sufis of Bijapur*, Sufi poets incorporated in these songs basic teachings of Islam by drawing parallels between various household activities and Islamic practice or doctrine. The constant humming of the spinning wheel was compared to the Sufi *dhikr,* or ritual repetition of the names of God, while the upright handle of the grindstone (*chakki*) reminded one of the letter *alif* for Allah; the axle recalls the importance of Prophet Muhammad as a pivot of faith and the grain that is being ground resembles the ego self which must be transformed.

Perhaps the most interesting Indian literary convention that Sufi poets incorporated into their poetry is representing the soul as the *virahini*, a woman who is longing for her beloved, who is symbolically God. Though the woman-soul symbol is rare in Persian and Arabic poetry, it is quite common in Indian literature. Its most renowned use is in Hindu devotional poetry addressed to Krishna to whom the *gopi*s, or milkmaids, in particular Radha, express their longing for union. Muslim poets adapted this symbol to various Islamic theological frameworks, varying the identity of the Muslim *virahini*'s beloved according to the context. In some cases the beloved could be God, or the Prophet Muhammad, or even the Sufi *shaykh*. In the *ginan*s, the devotional poems of the subcontinent's Khoja Ismaili communities, the *virahini*'s beloved could even be the Shi'i Imam. Naturally, the genre of folk poetry would vary not only from one Muslim theological context to another but also from region to region. Thus, in the South Indian region of Tamilnadu, the *pillaitamil* (baby poem) which was usually addressed to a Hindu deity such as Krishna in his form as a baby, was adapted for singing the praises of the baby Prophet Muhammad.

Muslim writers in the vernaculars could also express their ideas through other literary devices. In areas of northern India, especially where Hindi dialects such as Awadhi, Braj, and Bhojpuri were spoken, they used the romantic epic as a vehicle to transmit mystical ideas. In this, they were probably inspired by the well-established Persian tradition in which romances such as Yusuf-Zulaykha are retold within a mystical framework. The use of Indian romances can be dated to 1379, when the Hindi poet Maulana Daud, disciple of a Chishti Sufi master, composed the *Chandayan,* in which he retells the romance between Lurak and Chanda as a mystical allegory. This epic was so famous that Badauni, the author of *Muntakhab al-Tawarikh*, records that a Muslim preacher used excerpts from Maulana Daud's epic during his sermon in the mosque because of its great impact on listeners. A pioneering literary work, the *Chandayan* initiated a centuries-long tradition of Islamic mystical romances in various dialects of Hindi, including masterpieces such as Kutuban's *Mrigavati* (composed in 1503), Malik Muhammad Jaisi's *Padmavat* (composed in 1540), and Manjhan's *Madhumalati* (composed in 1545).

Use of popular romances in communicating mystical ideas is also found outside the Hindi-speaking belt. In the late fourteenth century, Shah Muhammad Saghir composed in Bengali the epic of Yusuf and Zulaykha, which was based partly on the Persian tradition. This was the first of many such Islamic poetic epics in Bengali. In the Punjab, poets not only composed such epics in Punjabi, but they also regularly alluded to legendary Punjabi lovers in other poetic genres. Such was also the case in Sind, where we find Qazi Qadan (d. 1551), an early poet, alluding to Sindhi romances in his compositions. This trend was continued by later poets, the technique being perfected in the eighteenth century in the poetry of the Shah Abdul Latif in whose skillful hands the heroines of the romances are transformed into symbols for the soul longing for union with God through suffering and death.

Aside from the major thematic emphasis on portraying the human–divine relationship as one of yearning love, Muslim poetry in the vernaculars is characterized by other overarching themes: the condemnation of intellectualism and bookish learning as a means of approaching God, the main targets of criticism being the religious scholars and jurists who claimed exclusive authority to interpret matters of faith; the uselessness of blindly performed rituals; the centrality of the Prophet Muhammad as a guide, friend, and intercessor for the faithful; and the importance of the *pir* as a source of mystical guidance and instruction. On account of his special relationship as a *wali* (friend of God), and as a representative of the Prophet Muhammad, the *pir* also possesses a special numinous power *(barakah)* that can help the devotee through all sorts of difficulties, worldly or spiritual. The most controversial aspect of this poetry, at least in the eyes of the conservatives, was its expression of ideas associated with the *wahdat al-wujud* (unity of existence) mystical philosophy, traditionally associated with the school of Ibn 'Arabi (d. 1240), the Arabo-Hispanic mystic. This mystical philosophy, which had far-reaching influence in many different Muslim literary traditions, was used in India by Sufi poets to stress the fundamental unity of all that may outwardly appear multiple or different. As a consequence, Muslim poets composed verses indicating that there was no difference between Hindu and Muslim, or Ram and Rahim, or Nimrud and Abraham. Naturally, conservatives were alarmed by these expressions, which they felt blurred the distinction between Creator and creation.

ALI ASANI

Further Reading

Alam, Muzaffar. "The Culture and Politics of Persian in Pre-colonial Hindustan." In *Literary Cultures in History: Reconstructions from South Asia*, edited by Sheldon Pollock, 131–198. Berkeley, 2003.

Asani, Ali S. "Muslim Literatures in South Asia." In *Muslim Almanac*, edited by Azim Nanji, 355–364. Detroit: Gale, 1996.

Eaton, Richard. *Sufis of Bijapur 1300–1700*. Princeton, 1978.

POETRY, PERSIAN

Poetry is one of the great glories of medieval Persian civilization; an enormous amount of verse in various genres, much of it of very high quality, was written throughout the medieval period and much has survived. After the Arab conquest of the seventh century "two centuries of silence" descended on the country; in the ninth century poetry in Persian began to be written again, in the quasi-independent courts of eastern Iran. Vigorous patronage by the Samanids, who ruled in Khorasan from c. 875 CE to the beginning of the eleventh century, meant that the style of the first centuries of Persian poetry's revival is named Khorasani. It is characterized by dignity, relative simplicity, and an immediacy of emotional effect. The earliest poems were panegyrics, and the rhetoric of adulation and supplication endemic to courtly praise poetry pervades virtually all Persian poetic genres, including the erotic and the mystical, with the partial exception of epic. Panegyric remained a major form throughout the medieval period, occupying a place in the court culture similar to that of the official portrait in the later court cultures of Europe.

The major genres of Persian poetry emerged in the period of the Khorasani style (tenth to early twelfth centuries). These include the short poem or epigram, generally in the four line rubai (pl. rubaiyat) form, or as a qate' (fragment, a form often used for satire or personal invective); the medium-length poem of praise (usually in the qasideh form); the lyric (ghazal), which developed from the traditionally lyrical opening of the qasideh; and the long narrative, which could be epic, romance, a didactic/mystical work, or some combination of the three. Narratives were written in couplets; all the other mentioned forms use monorhyme (stanzaic forms exist in Persian but are relatively rare). With the exception of the meter of the rubai, and that normally employed for epic, all Persian meters, of which there are a large number, are derived from meters in Arabic poetry, and like them are scanned quantitatively rather than accentually (pre-Islamic Persian meter appears to have been basically accentual: accentual meters still exist in some folk/popular compositions). The Khorasani style's masterpiece is the *Shahnameh* (c. 1010) of Ferdowsi, which recounts the pre-Islamic myths and romanticized history of Iran from the creation of the world to the Arab conquest. Sanai (d. 1131) is credited with writing the first important mystical masnavi in Persian *(Hadiqat a-Haqiqat, "The Garden of the Truth"),* and he is also one of the earliest writers of the ghazal. Epigrams (as rubaiyat) were widely written in this period; the usual ascription of many of them to Omar Khayyam is historically doubtful.

The most significant works in the majority of Persian verse genres, apart from epic and epigram, were produced in the so-called Eraqi style (mid-twelfth to fifteenth centuries), which flourished throughout Iran but is particularly associated with Shiraz in the southern heartland of the country. Eraqi style is more lush and more cerebral than Khorasani, delighting in decoration, word play, and conspicuous euphony. Many of the tropes current during the period of the Khorasani style had become conventional, and in its elaborate use of such conventions, Eraqi poetry was consciously intertextual and self-referential, presupposing a fairly high level of literary sophistication in its audiences. The influential romances of the Azerbaijani poet Nezami (1141–1209), *Khosrow o Shirin, Leili o Majnun, Haft Paykar*, may be regarded as transitional between the two styles. Nezami's contemporary, Attar (c. 1136–c. 1220), wrote mystical narratives (the best known is the *Manteq al-Tayr, Conference of the Birds*), a form that achieved its most celebrated success in the *Masnavi-e Ma'navi* of Rumi (1207–1273). Two natives of Shiraz, Sa'di (c. 1213–1292) and Hafez (c. 1319–c. 1390), are the acknowledged masters of the ghazal; Sa'di's are written with unrivaled elegance and euphony, while Hafez's combine erotic and mystical motifs with consummate technical sophistication. Jahan Khatun, the daughter of a ruler of Shiraz during Hafez's lifetime, is the only medieval woman poet whose divan (complete short poems) has come down to us, though she was preceded by the tenth to eleventh century Rabe'eh Qozdari, and the twelfth century Mahsati; a few poems by both these woman poets have survived.

As the Eraqi style flourished, Persian poetry was more extensively appreciated and written outside the confines of Persia itself. Poetry in Persian had been written in northern India since the Ghaznavid conquests of the eleventh century, but it is in the time of Sa'di that we find poets of the first rank (for example, Rumi in Turkey and Amir Khosrow [1253–1325] in India) writing outside of Persia. Persian verse retained great prestige in both Turkey and Moslem India, as well as in areas of Central Asia, throughout the later medieval period and beyond. In the sixteenth century the establishment of the Moghul court in northern India, and its adoption of Persian as the court language, gave rise to a distinctive Indian literature written in Persian.

Poetry in the fifteenth century is dominated by the figure of Jami (1414–1492), who set out to excel in virtually all current forms of poetry and belles-lettres and convinced many of his contemporaries that he had done so. His great fame, and the changes that overtook Iranian culture shortly after his death, mean that he is traditionally regarded as the last of the "classical" poets. In the Safavid period (1501–1736) a new style, prefigured in some of Jami's verses, the "Indian Style," emerges. There is debate as to whether the style first appeared in India or Iran, but the name is fitting since many of its best-known practitioners lived in India. This style is rhetorically complex, tends to use startling and original metaphors, and the poems often deal with abstruse subjects: It is thus broadly comparable to the Gongorist style in Europe. It remained current in Persian poetry until the mid-eighteenth century, when a return to earlier and simpler models of rhetoric was advocated.

RICHARD DAVIS

Further Reading

De Bruijn, J. T. P. *Persian Sufi Poetry*. Richmond, 1997.
Meisami, Julie Scott. *Medieval Persian Court Poetry*. Princeton, 1987.
Pagliaro A., and A. Bausani. *Storia della Letteratura Persiana*. Milan, 1960.
Safa, Zabihollah. *Tarikh-e adabiyat dar iran (The History of Literature in Iran)*. 5 vols. Tehran, 1366/1987.
Yarshater, E. (Ed). *Persian Literature*. New York, 1988.

POLICE

The police *(shurta)* as an urban force responsible for suppression of crime evolved from a military formation referred to as *shurtat al-khamis*, which apparently existed in Kufa during the rule of 'Ali (656–660). The association between the *shurta* and the military continued during the Umayyad and early 'Abbasid period. According to Fred M. Donner, the *shurta* was a military force used to fight Muslim rebels, whereas Michael Lecker considers it an elite force. The Egyptian chronicler al-Kindi (897–961) provides a list of people who were nominated as the chiefs of Fustat *shurta* during the Umayyad and 'Abbasid periods, but the precise nature of this force is difficult to ascertain.

In tenth-century Fustat there were two *shurta* forces known as the Upper and Lower *shurta,* and their role as an urban police responsible for the suppression of crime is clearly attested to for the Fatimid period (969–1171). The chiefs of police exercised judicial power and were responsible for the punishment of criminals. By the tenth century the chief of police monopolized the administration of criminal justice to the exclusion of the cadi. According to an administrative text from Baghdad of the early Buyid period (c. 950) the chief of police had to be familiar with the scale of punishments, but legal education was not a qualification required from him. He was advised to study texts such as the *Book of Brigands*, apparently by Jahiz (776–869), and other unspecified works such as *kutub ashab al-shurut wa-siyar al-muluk.*

In Fustat during the Fatimid period, the people nominated as chiefs of police were eunuchs of the court and officers among the Kutama Berbers. In 364/974–975, an attempt to involve jurists *(fuqaha')* in the in the process of the administration of criminal justice was unsuccessful. In 401/1010–1011, on the other hand, the chief cadi Malik ibn al-Fariqi forbade the chiefs of police to intervene in the jurisdiction exercised by the cadi according to the Muslim holy law, the *shari'a*. A certain encroachment of the chief of police on the judicial domain of the cadi is attested to by the sources. For example, cases of apostasy from Islam were dealt with by the cadi and the chief of police. According to the holy law, apostasy is a capital offense. In the Fatimid period the apostates were handed to the chief of policy for the implementation of the death penalty.

The problematic coexistence between the jurisdiction exercised by the cadi and that of the chief of police is illustrated by the appointment, in August 1011, of the military commander Muhammad ibn Nizzal as the chief of the two police forces in the Egyptian capital. His letter of appointment stated that it is his duty to implement the Qur'anic dictum "to command right and to forbid wrong" and, in practical terms, he was entrusted with the implementation of a comprehensive ban on the sale and production of wine. The reference to this Qur'anic dictum as describing the function of the chief of police can be understood as an attempt to Islamize the extra *shari'a* jurisdiction enforced by the chief of police. To what degree there was any congruency between the holy law and the criminal justice administrated by the chief of police is a vexing question. A further complication arises when one takes into account the involvement of the rulers themselves in the administration of criminal justice. In AH 257/870–871 CE, in Baghdad, a serial killer, 'Ali the strangler, was flogged to death on the order of the caliph and, in 321/933–934, a band of highway robbers was punished at the presence of the caliph. Their chief was flogged and executed while the others were punished by having their hands and legs cut off. Public punishment, including execution, of criminals was typical of premodern societies and aimed to deter offenders and restore the moral order. The royal patronage of such events served to manifest the ruler's commitment to uphold the moral order and rule of law. These points are neatly demonstrated by a letter addressed by Fatimid ruler al-'Aziz to his vizier, Ya'qub ibn Killis. In 373/983–984, a foreign merchant was murdered and robbed at a covered market *(qaysariyya)* in Fustat. Rashiq, the slave of the chief of police, made several arrests, but people accused him as being behind the murder and claimed that he had arrested innocent people. A petition to that effect was submitted to al-'Aziz, who wrote to the vizier instructing him "to cleanse this disgrace from our dynasty and the grief it had caused to it." indeed, the chief of the police was temporarily removed from his post. Justice was considered as an Islamic virtue and rulers declared their commitment to the rule of justice. Thus, the involvement of Muslim rulers with the administration of criminal justice is perfectly understood, but it raises the question whether the holy law was strictly implemented in those cases or the emphasis was more on summary justice.

It seems that in the twelfth century the status of the chief of police was on the decline. During the 1120s in Fatimid state receptions and ceremonies, the chiefs of the two police forces in the capital were at the bottom of the list of state functionaries, preceding only the heads of the non-Muslim communities and non-Muslim secretaries. During the thirteenth century the terms *police* and *chief of police* disappeared from the sources, and new appellations *wali* (meaning the chief of police forces in Fustat and Cairo) and *ma'una* (meaning police) became common. The police as an urban institution completely degenerated during the Mamluk period. This development is in line with Ira M. Lapidus' observation that "The Mamluks governed not by administration, but by holding all of the vital social threads in their hands". Thus, many aspects of urban life were left to the discretion of the Mamluk emirs, and the distinction between administrative responsibilities and police functions was blurred. The same process is attested to for Damascus and Aleppo. The existence of a police force *(shurta)* in Damascus during the second half of the tenth century is well attested to by the sources. However, during the twelfth century the term *shurta* disappeared from the sources and was replaced by a new urban official: the *shihna*, who combined in his hands the authority of an urban prefect and a military governor. This new institution was also very prominent in thirteenth-century Aleppo.

YAACOV LEV

Primary Sources

Anonymous. *Siyasat al-Muluk*. Edited by J. Sadan. "A New Source of the Buyid Period." *Israel Oriental Studies* IX (1979): 355–376.

Ibn Jawzi. *Al-Muntazam fi Ta'rikh al-Umam wa-l-Muluk*. Edited by 'Ata, Muhammad 'Abd al-Qadir and 'Ata, Mustafa 'Abd al-Qadir. Beirut, 1992, vol.12, 124; vol.13, 316.

Ibn al-Ma'mun. *Akhbar Misr*. Edited by A. F. Sayyid. Cairo, 1983.

Itti'az al-Hunafa'. Edited by Al-Shayyal, Jamal al-Din. Cairo, 1967, vol. 1, 262–263.

Kindi. *The Governors and Judges of Egypt* (together with fragments of *Raf' al-Isr* by Ibn Hajar). Edited by R. Guest. London, 1912.

Maqrizi. *Kitab al-Muqaffa al-Kabir*. Edited by M. Yalaoui. Beirut, 1991, vol.5, 433–434.

Further Reading

Crone, Patricia. *Slaves on Horses. The Evolution of the Islamic Polity*. Cambridge: Cambridge University Press, 1980, 248, n.474.

Donner, Fred M. "The Shurta in Early Umayyad Syria." In *The Fourth International Conference on the History of Bilad al-Sham*. Amman, 1989, 247–262.

Lapidus, Ira M. *Muslim Cities in the Later Middle Ages*. Cambridge, MA: Harvard University Press, 1967.

Lecker, Michael. "Shurtat al-Khamis and Other Matters: Notes on the Translation of Tabari's Ta'rikh." *Jerusalem Studies in Arabic and Islam* 14(1991): 276–288.

Lev, Yaacov. "Charity and Justice in Medieval Islam." *Rivista degli Studi Orientali* LXXVI (2002): 1–16.

POLITICAL THEORY

The title "Islamic political theory" should be understood as a euphemism only for the sake of convenience and as a shorthand description to signify diverse strains of political thought in medieval Islamic history.

Political theories emerged as responses to various challenges including the debate over the legitimacy of the caliphate, providing advice to sovereigns, guiding the political institution in certain directions, and elaborating an ideal political regime. All strains of thought followed a course of evolution in direct contact with the sociopolitical realities of their surroundings, and therefore not only rationalized the conceptualization of the political process but also contributed with novel particularities to political thought in response to specific challenges. In this necessarily brief survey, only the broad outlines of three traditions will be given: legal paradigm, *siyasa* (practical governance), and political philosophy. Apart from references for the purposes of comparison, political thought of the Shi'is and Mu'tazilites has not been examined here. Also, this treatment cannot offer a comprehensive survey of the diversity and nature of Islamic political theories. Any detailed examination must treat the discussion of reason and revelation as applied in political theory to dispel the mistaken impression that Islamic political thought has been fully and overtly religious, with no room for human morality and rationality. Appropriate attention must also be given to the Mu'tazilites, Shi'is, and Philosophers whose political views surfaced and resurfaced in the ideological and intellectual compromises of the post-Mongolian political milieu.

Qur'an

Most frequently cited Qur'anic terms that are used to construct political views in medieval Islamic history are to possess or to dominate, m-l-k; to judge or to rule over, h-k-m; to succeed, kh-l-f; and finally, to lead, a-m-m, although they occur in the Qur'an in unrelated or only slightly relevant contexts. Although the Qur'an itself does not offer a vision that can be defined as political, it certainly encourages the believers to pursue an organized social and distinctly urban life. The revelations in the Qur'an brought a new sense of community and mission to the faithful, which probably encouraged political organization. Some suggestive broad political maxims in the Qur'an make reference to kingship and even traditional tribal leadership. A number of verses refer to the Egyptian Pharaohs as kings in the context of the stories of Moses and Joseph (al-Zukhruf 51; Yusuf 43, 50, 54, 72). Israelites ask Moses for a king to lead them in warfare (al-Baqara 246); David is given a kingdom (al-Baqara 251); and Israelites were made kings over other nations (al-Maida 20). Except for one verse (al-Naml 34: "When kings enter a country, they despoil it, and make the noblest of its people its meanest; thus do they behave"), the outlook of the Qur'an to kingship may be defined as mirroring a historical institution without a particular stance for or against it. Also significant is the Qur'anic sympathy for city life, especially vis-à-vis nomadic *modus vivendi,* for which the Qur'an displays a clear disdain (al-Quraysh; al-Tawba 101, 120). It is conceivable that the Qur'anic references to city life, to politically organized societies, and to kingship in neutral and even positive terms preconditioned, without pointing out any details and direction, the Muslim community to appreciate and even seek a political framework beyond the nomadic–tribal social organization of North Arabia.

Caliphate

The establishment of the caliphate in 632 was certainly a groundbreaking achievement politically and intellectually in medieval Islamic history. Muhammad was above all a messenger transmitting God's revelations to his community. He was also the leader of his community, in charge of its political organization in Medina. His position in Medina had therefore created a context to which his followers responded in his absence. Indeed, his death prompted a controversy among his followers in respect to his political legacy on two fundamental issues: the form of his political community and the nature of his religious prerogatives—whether transferable to a successor, real or corporeal. The birth of the caliphate (khalifa, or deputy, from khalafa, meaning "to succeed") immediately after his death in 632 was a response to both challenges. This new institution secured the political unity of the community against centrifugal tendencies partially responsible for the first civil war and its aftermath and set the political organization on a path of centralized government. The second matter, however, proved to be a contentious issue for at least the first two centuries in the history of the caliphate. As such, how the early Muslim community understood the meaning and nature of the caliphate remains disputed among scholars. Nonetheless, by the tenth century the caliphate seems to have been stripped of its pretensions to religious prerogatives in a long contestation with religious scholars, although the caliph was privileged with an aura of holiness. One must, however, modify that assertion by at least one condition that it was still possible for the caliph to claim, like his counterpart rulers in the Latin West, religious authority by invoking messianic expectations, which did happen in a number of cases. However, this was more of an exception rather than the rule. As an institution, the caliphate evolved in constant reciprocal relation with its political realities, tribal and sedentary Arabic political traditions, local customs, and Islamic values taking shape within the society. The conventions of appointment and succession, nature of authority, qualifications of the caliph owed much to this multifaceted relationship and affected the content of political thought. The historical political institution for and against which political views were articulated reflected certain features. First of all, the caliphate was confined to the members of Quraysh. Secondly, the method of appointment and succession to rule was not uniform; it ranged from election (shura) to appointment (ahd), to even military cue/usurpation (ghlaba). The caliph was appointed *ad vitam* until his death or removal from office by force. The nature and limits of his authority were not defined and was, in fact, contested by tribal centrifugalism, opposition of religiopolitical movements, and later by military commanders and more significantly sultans. Competing caliphates in Egypt (the Shi'i Fatimids) and Spain (Umayyads) in the tenth century put to the test the unity of the caliphate in both practice and theory. When the Buyids and later the Seljuks occupied Baghdad and turned the caliph into a secondary and increasing shadow figure in the eleventh century, onward they brought with them the discussion of the position of the sultan vis-à-vis the caliph. Seljuk migration from Central Asia in the eleventh century and particularly the Mongol conquests in the thirteenth century brought about a new type of sovereigns who derived their legitimacy not from jurisprudential delegation of authority (although the Seljuks did benefit from such provisions) but from their dynastic birthright. With such dynasties came also new sources of law based on secular nomadic customs rendering impossible to limit the discussion on politics to caliphate. As the succession to the caliphate and policies of caliphs were matters of controversy in an age of rapid expansion and organization, the issue of legitimacy and competition for the office led not only to civil wars but also to ideological disputes within the Muslim community. Right from the beginning, the controversy over the caliphate involved the identity of the rightful candidate for the office. The first civil war during the reigns of Uthman and Ali (656–661) led to the separation of the Kharijites from the rank of Ali, while the second civil war (683–692) helped the crystallization of Shi'i, Umayyad, and anti-Umayyad opposition, squeezing out in the process the initial political discussions around the qualification of the caliph and the legitimacy of his rule. With the consolidation of the conquests, the growth of urban centers and urban classes, the establishment of the 'Abbasid caliphate in 750 onward, and more significantly the religiopolitical developments among the Mu'tazilites, the Shi'is (Imami and Zaydi varieties), and proto-Sunnites (and later Sunnites) supplied new debates and new ideas into political thought on subjects ranging from necessity of the imamate to identity and qualifications of the imam. One must add to this the spread of political ideologies of state bureaucrats, mostly promoting initially Sasanian, but later Turkic and Hellenistic political practices, and of Greek political philosophies, which were elaborated through translations and writings of Muslim philosophers. It was against this rich background that political theories were formulated and reformulated.

Pioneering Debates

One might be surprised to read that the debate over the free will and predestination or the position of the sinner in faith had anything to do with political thought. Yet a position on each one of these questions had ramifications for recognizing or denying the legitimacy of the Umayyad caliphs. As the Umayyads believed their rule to be something ordained by God, they promoted predestinarian views, whereas some of their opposition supported the idea of free will and held Umayyads accountable for their actions. Likewise, if the Umayyads could be described as sinners for a number of reasons (least of which killing and religious laxity), were they still a part of the community of faithful and therefore legitimate caliphs despite their sins? Another front where political views were articulated was the comparative merit or excellence of the first four caliphs. In the seventh and eighth centuries the order of excellence was not yet stable. Whereas the non-Shi'is seem to draw a line between the reign of the first two caliphs (Abu Bakr and Umar) and later ones (Uthman and Ali), the former being the most excellent, and displayed conflicting views about the latter, the Shi'is questioned the legitimacy of the historical caliphate *in toto* as they were in the process of developing the idea of a divinely appointed imam. A corollary debate involved the distinction between the reign of the first four caliphs and later caliphates (caliphate vs. kingship). One of the most important debates among the opposition to the Umayyads concerned the succession to rule, particularly the call for *shura* and election against Umayyad practices of family succession. During 'Abbasid times, however, the call for *shura* remained a distant echo in the Kharijite opposition and, in few instances, in dynastic competition. The Shi'i opposition during the Umayyad caliphate promoted a Hashimite right to the caliphate. However, as the 'Abbasids excluded the Alids from their dynastic lineage the Shi'i opposition became increasingly focused on Alid lineage, eventually settling on a particular imam among the Alids. Since much of the debate about politics in early Islamic centuries involved legitimacy of the caliph and qualification of an ideal candidate for the office, political thought became increasingly focused on the personality of the candidate. The rise of powerful sultanates in the eleventh century onward provided the necessary historical background for an elaborate discussion of the theories of the sultanate, which proliferated especially in the wake of the Mongol conquests. Such developments gradually rendered the classical theory centered on the caliph obsolete and provoked rational responses among religious scholars to modify their views. The modification came as shifting the focus of discussion onto the conduct of the holders of coercive power in the House of Islam, the Amirs and Sultans, who were finally vested after the Mongol conquest with legal political authority instead of the caliph. After the Mongol conquests the discussion of politics no longer involved in any serious measure the caliphate rather the proliferating sultanates. One may examine medieval Islamic political thought in three main groups, which are not necessarily aligned with sectarian divisions: First is the theory formulated by legal scholars and theologians, which we may call legal theory because it was based to a large extent on jurisprudential reasoning. Second is siyasa, which represented the views promoted by bureaucrats or secretaries and which evolved into the genre of mirror for princes and incorporated ethics (akhlaq) into political thought. The third is political philosophy advanced by Muslim philosophers.

Legal Theory

Legal theories of politics were put forth by the proto-Sunni and Sunni religious scholars in an atmosphere of debate and interaction with three major fronts: alternative religiopolitical currents, including the Shi'is, Kharijites, and Mu'tazilites; secretaries; and finally, the caliphate itself. Overall tenor of the legal theories may be described as defending the historical caliphate against its political and sectarian opposition as legal scholars saw the caliphate as the source of unity and welfare of the Muslim community. Yet at the same time political views came about as a conscious attempt to place the caliphate on a trajectory more agreeable to the legal framework already in formation and less amenable to the intellectual legacy of Sasanian imperial tradition—ideological and intellectual background of 'Abbasid secretaries. It is in this delicate balance between recognizing the legitimacy of the historical caliphate and steering it in the direction of the ideal imamate that we find the distinction the legal scholars made between the rightful imamate and kingship. Legal theory holds that appointing an imam is necessary—even a religious obligation for the community—contrary to many Mu'tazilites who thought that the imamate was neither necessary nor religiously obligatory. It is also required that the caliph be Muslim from the tribe of Quraysh, a view that again many Mu'tazilites and Kharijites did not require or even accept. The Shi'is, on the other hand, limited the imamate to the descendants of Ali, at best the politically active members of Banu Hashim (Zaydites). Legal theory emphasized that the imam should be elected. The terms of election were rational enough to accommodate practical necessities. The election could be either through a selection of one well-qualified individual or a group of qualified electors (ahl al-hall wa al-aqd). It could also, as stipulated by al-Ghazali (1111) in the age of Sultanates, be

through the selection of ahl al-shawka, or holders of coercive power, that is, sultans. The imam could also be appointed by his predecessor or win himself the seat through a successful military cue (ghlaba). While the emphasis on election was clearly a response to the Shi'i view of the divinely appointed imam (nass), its ramifications cannot be confined to sectarian competition. The provision that the imam must be the most excellent of the community was generally reserved by the tenth century for the first four caliphs and involved to a large extent the debate over the legitimacy and the comparative merit of the Rightly Guided Caliphs (Rashidun), although it certainly was also intended for improving the historical conditions of the caliphate, which was not always in line with religious scholars' expectations. Zaydites advocated the imamate of the most excellent among the family of the Prophet, whereas the Mu'tazilites allowed the imamate of the less qualified for practical reasons and to prevent dissension. There can be only one imam at a time, although al-Baghdadi (1037) stipulated that it was acceptable to have more than one imam if two regions were separated from each other by a significant barrier such as a large body of water. Legal theory as elaborated by al-Mawardi (1058) and later scholars identified some qualifications for the caliph: knowledge of laws, legal probity, and physical and mental fitness to carry his political and military duties. The duties of the caliph, on the other hand, simply comprised the governance of the caliphate, leading armies in warfare, protecting the community against military threats, assuring the implementation of laws, distribution of justice, and appointing lesser administrators who represented the caliph in their respective responsibilities. (By the time of al-Mawardi, this included the de facto rulers as well). Because legal theory held the unity of the community to be one of the foremost aims of the caliphate, it frowned upon dissension and advocated obedience to the ruling caliph as long as the laws of Shari'a were not violated, in which case obedience becomes not only unnecessary but also prohibited—a condition that allowed, significantly, legitimate dissent to keep the power of the ruler in check. Nevertheless, legal political theory does not, in general, stipulate a regulation for deposing the caliph apart from apostasy, loss of freedom, and of sanity. Political theory of legal scholars was first initiated to some extent in the jurisprudential corpus (such as Abu Yusuf's Kitab al-Kharaj), which was mostly based on Hadiths attributed to the Prophet and the practice of the first four caliphs. It was elaborated in Hadith works of the ninth century and given a prominent place in the works of theology (Kalam), beginning with al-Ash'ari.

Siyasa or Mirror for Princes

Already during the late Umayyad period, but increasingly with the establishment of the 'Abbasid caliphate, the genre of political advice (produced in a range of literary styles from fables to poetry and for the consumption of rulers and educated lay) occupied a substantial place in medieval Islamic political imagination. Expressed and elaborated in treatises of advice to governors, caliphs, princes, and secretaries this genre began largely with transmitting Sasanian imperial practice as exemplified in the activities of Ibn al-Muqaffa (757). However, it gradually became a genre incorporating aspects of practical ethics (akhlaq), jurisprudence, and Greek political philosophy, thus forming an influential political ideology that Amirs and Sultans of the late 'Abbasid period aspired to follow. This genre proliferated in the post-Mongol political and cultural environment and was primarily addressed to rulers for the purpose of improving governance by discussing the necessary moral qualifications of the ruler and of advising him on manners to help in practical politics. Despite all of its practical purposes, it also promoted and advocated a distinct vision of politics and governance. Foremost is the promotion of kingship and king, who must be obeyed at all costs, as the central theme of its political theory. It was the duty of the king to protect his domains against any enemy who committed to disturb the sociopolitical equilibrium. Contrary to paradigmatic legal theory, which saw the caliphate embedded in religious law, siyasa saw royal authority and religion as twins whose survival depends on the welfare of the other. Such concern with balancing religion and kingship for the survival of royal authority is also reflected in the emphasis on social equilibrium, which is accomplished only by keeping every class in its respective place. It is no other than justice, a notion that was largely inherited from Near Eastern imperial traditions and supplanted by experiences from actual practice in Islamic context, that can maintain this equilibrium. The famous circle of justice aptly demonstrates the centrality of the king, the pragmatic organization of social order, the function of each class in society, and the necessary medium to keep this order in balance for the prosperity of all: No royal authority is possible without military; military needs finance and finance depends on taxes levied on subjects; subjects can be maintained only by justice and justice is provided by royal authority. Remarkably, the references to religious law (Shari'a) do not figure prominently in this genre. Shari'a law was certainly taken into account as social conduct and moral attitude derived much from it, but royal authority and justice were not dependent on Shari'a law, as was the case with legal theory. To the extent that the Shari'a law was a part of the society, the ruler and his subjects were obliged to respect its stipulations for maintaining political and social harmony; religion was, after all, one of the twins. First of all, the siyasa was much more interested in practical governance and the ways by which this should be accomplished. Secondly, the reality was that dynastic laws were based on extrareligious traditions and customs and did not derive their legitimacy from religious laws. In fact, siyasa flourished better and was more meaningful and effective in situations where political legitimacy rested on inherited dynastic right or divine mandate, as was the case with Turkic, Persian, and Mongolic sultanates in Central Asia and the Middle East.

Political Philosophy

It would be futile to cramp down the views expressed in political philosophy into highly condensed lines, because political theories vary widely from Philosopher King of al-Farabi to Governance of the Solitary of Ibn Bajja. Rather, a broad sketch of common aspects of political philosophy will be given. Among the work translated from Greek heritage into Arabic, political philosophy formed a portion. Swinging between advice (Epistles of Salim) and theoretical exposition of political authority, political philosophy emerged finally as a creative merger of ancient philosophical heritage, late antique royal legacy, and new Islamic experience. Similar to the legal theory and siyasa, the elaboration of political philosophy needed courtly patronage, yet unlike the genre of siyasa, it did not concern itself primarily with advising the ruler; it did not address them either. Political philosophy offered a theoretical exposition of politics under the rubric of tripartite practical philosophy. Furthermore, contrary to the legal theory and siyasa, political philosophy dealt extensively with raison d'etre and origins of political authority, which gave it, together with philosophy's general orientation, a distinct humanistic and rational dimension. Whereas legal theory and siyasa approached political organization as a given, philosophical exposition started from scratch with the assumption that political authority arose from human's need to organize themselves into peaceful communities. Stage by stage, from household management headed by the male member of the family, human beings organized their respective domains of authority, leading their subordinates closer toward perfection and happiness. Similarly the king/imam, by his personal virtues and intellectual capacity, leads his subjects according to their intellectual and moral capacities to moral and intellectual perfection and happiness. In the body of political philosophy the king figures as central to the whole system: He rests at the top of the social hierarchy and represents the highest moral and intellectual level. Similar to the genre of mirror for princes, political philosophy, too sidestepped Shari'a as a basis for political community. Shari'a laws were certainly incorporated into the legal system required for any political organization since not all of the subjects were of the same social, moral, and intellectual capacity and level. Inspired by the Greek sages, Plato and Aristotle, Muslim philosophers created a political vision that took into account Muslim political experience but did not respond to it directly. Rather, unlike legal theory and mirror for princes, the vision set forth the conditions for the ideal rule.

HAYRETTIN YUCESOY

See also Ibn Khaldun

Further Reading

Black, Anthony. *The History of Islamic Political Thought: From the Prophet to the Present*. Routledge, 2001.
Crone, Patricia. *Gods Rule: Government and Islam*. Columbia University Press, 2004.
———. *Medieval Islamic Political Thought*. Edinburgh University Press, 2004.
Lambton, Ann K. S. *State and Government in Medieval Islam: An Introduction to the Study of Islamic Political Theory: The Jurists*. Oxford University Press, 1981.
———. *Theory and Practice in Medieval Persian Government*. Ashgate Pub Co, June 1, 1980.
Mahdi, Muhsin. *Alfarabi and the Foundation of Islamic Political Philosophy*. University of Chicago Press, 2001.
Rosenthal, Erwin Isak Jakob. *Political Thought in Medieval Islam*. Greenwood Press Reprint, 1985.
Watt, W. M. *Islamic Political Thought*. Edinburgh University Press, 1998.
EI. 2nd ed. Khalifa (A. K.S. Lambton).
EI. 2nd ed. Imama (W. Madelung).
EI. 2nd ed. Nasihat al-Muluk (C. E. Bosworth).

POPULAR LITERATURE

Definitions

The contours of what is "popular" and "polite" literature differ from culture to culture, and the aesthetic assumptions implicit in this binary division have often been questioned. Most scholarly works on the literary history of medieval Islamic literature in Arabic, Persian, and Turkish have followed the already existing format of literary histories of Western languages and cultures, adopting their divisions and terminology without taking into consideration different social structures, priorities, and aesthetic contours, and without allowing for the fact that our knowledge of economic and social life in many parts of the early medieval Islamic world remains extremely patchy and hence prone to wild conjectures. The essential constituents of the study of popular literature—the methods of composition, the performance and location of performance, as well as the different ways of production and memorization, the range of participating audience and solitary readership, and the changes in the content and diction in time and place—have on the whole not received the attention they deserve. With the exception of *The Arabian Nights,* which since the growth of interest in magical realism as a universal genre has become a staple diet of academic courses on comparative literature, popular texts in Arabic and other languages of medieval Islamic culture have been used mostly as quarries for motif-indices without much attention to other contextual, literary, and historical implications. For example, one of the last examples of traditional popular Persian prose narratives, *The Adventures of Amir Arsalan,* was first recited at the Qajar court in Iran in the second half of the nineteenth century and contains many themes of much earlier medieval popular narratives, including incidents illustrating the wiles of women, a favorite and recurrent theme in medieval literature, perennial clashes between good and evil viziers, and that hallmark of most popular adventures from Hellenistic romances to Victorian bodice rippers: the ongoing though constantly interrupted amorous escapade. This and other similar examples encourage us to reexamine the use of terms such as *courtly* and *medieval* as working definitions and labels of demarcation. Moreover, the occurrence of many of the themes of popular literature, such as the "wiles of women," or the importance of the shrewd tutor or governess as an eminence grise in manuals of advice and other less strictly popular genres, shows again how blurred the contours can be in a culture in which the notions of entertainment and instruction, popular piety, and sectarian beliefs were often indistinguishable and yet firmly insisted upon and vociferously stated.

Rise of Islam

These connections and tensions appear from the first centuries of Islamic history and are reflected in the early commentaries on the Qur'an. Two denunciations of "Tales of the ancients" *(asatir al-awwalin)* in the Qur'an (VIII, 31; LXXXIII, 13) provide early exegetes with an opportunity to explain and expand these terse verses in terms of a clash of intentions and worldviews. Nadhr b. al-Harith, a rich merchant from the Quraysh and a staunch foe of the Prophet, is depicted in these commentaries as a purveyor not only of singing slave girls but also of imported stories from Persia, regaling the public with tales of the adventures of the Iranian heroes Rostam and Esfandiyar. This propaganda war against the Prophet, implying that the Qur'anic stories were merely lackluster products of the same genre, came to a bloody end when the hapless impresario was beheaded by no less a figure than 'Ali b. Abi Talib, who himself was to become the archetypal Moslem hero in later popular literature and appear as a latter-day Rostam in many an adventure.

Impact of the Qur'an and its Commentaries

As implied and illustrated earlier in this entry, the impact of Islam on popular literature can be seen through several different perspectives. The contribution of the Qur'an itself was pivotal. Again, as in the case of the "Tales of the Ancients," not only its extended accounts of previous times and past nations, but also its more condensed allusions, became building blocks for many a full-blown vita of ancient prophets and their stories *(Qissas al-anbiya; Isra'i-liyyat)*, which began to appear in Arabic and Persian, and later Uighur and Turkish, commentaries of the Qur'an and soon attracted such attention that they began to feature in more and more popular expanded versions with relatively simple diction and syntax, ideal as part of a preacher's baggage of exempla. One exceptionally extended and self-contained account, the entire Sura XII of the Qur'an, the story of the prophet Joseph, which was referred to in the Qur'an itself as "the best of stories," was retold more than any other and praised by the exegetes for its miraculous encapsulation of all the ingredients of an ideal story, although some thought that its masterly evocation of female sexuality was too potent for the weaker sex and advised its perusal to be limited to men only. On the other hand, the far more nebulous figure of Du'l-Qarnayn, "the two-horned" figure in Sura XVIII, has also had an equally profound but more complex impact on popular stories, through his identification with Alexander the Great and through the fusion of the Qur'anic allusion and its extended explication by commentators with material culled from the Alexander romance of Pseudo-Callisthenes. The mixture of the different strands, Islamic and Hellenic in this particular popular story, and the way its figures and motifs reflect preoccupations and anxieties of different peoples of different regions of the Islamic world, from Egypt and Ethiopia to the farthest corners of Islamic penetration into Southeast Asia, require a multidisciplinary approach and a knowledge of several indigenous cultural histories. The mystical figure of Khizr, for example—never mentioned directly by name in the Qur'an itself—shares many associations with the Green Man or Knight of European medieval literature, as well as the angelic figure of Soroush in pre-Islamic Zoroastrian Iran and later Persian poetic imagery and literature in general, including popular stories. Khizr is not only a major figure in the Alexander legend but also appears in other popular tales in his capacity as an intermediary from above and a helper of the tale's hero at the bleakest hour.

Religious Biographies and Campaigns

Along with the Qur'an, the life of the Prophet himself *(al-sira al-nabawiyya),* and the martial feats of the Prophet and his Companions *(ansar)* against the heathen *(al-maghazi),* the early history of Islam provided much material for popular culture in its different forms, including popular spectacles, religious drama, and popular epics, and always with some reference to already existing traditions. In addition to the already mentioned heroic depiction of 'Ali, the martyrdom of his younger son Hosayn at the battle of Kerbala is reminiscent of the fate of the young princes Iradj and Siyavosh in the Persian *Book of Kings,* who opt for justice and the right conduct while fully prescient of the fatal consequences awaiting them. Another figure from the Prophet's immediate family whose tales of adventure form a considerable corpus of their own is Hamza, Muhammad's paternal uncle, transformed into an indefatigable fighter who surpasses Alexander in the range of his itinerary. Hamza traveled not only in the heartland of the Islamic world but also to such outposts as Central Asia, Greece, and Tangiers, often meeting the legendary prophet Khizr in his capacity as the guide and helper of pious and God-fearing travelers. The sumptuously illustrated manuscript of his adventures, the *Hamza-nama,* commissioned by the Indian Mughal emperor Akbar, which has been the centerpiece of several exhibitions in the West, is yet another reminder of the close interaction between Islamic courts and popular literature.

Caliphs, Sufis, Monarchs, and 'Ayyars

Already in the depiction of Hamza, one detects a distinctly heroic but not necessarily strictly Islamic characterization, a factor that perhaps contributed to the great range of its translations and adaptations, including one into Georgian. This tendency is intensified in the depiction of such later familiar figures in the world of popular literature as Harun al-Rashid, the 'Abbasid caliph who for all intents and purposes appears indistinguishable from other worldly rulers who also frequent popular tales, such as Mahmud of Ghazna or the Safavid Shah Abbas. They are usually depicted as stern but generous and manly figures whose courts provide convenient backdrops to a host of popular episodic anecdotes. The 'Ayyars, those cunning yet chivalrous characters of nearly all Islamic literatures who gave their name as an epithet to the hero of the earliest Persian popular prose narratives, *Samak-e Ayyar*, or even those founding fathers of Sufi sects whose popular hagiographies form a substantial corpus of popular literature, particularly in Persian, are celebrated from different perspectives. Samak, like Rostam in the *Book of Kings*, often appears as Jeeves to his feckless sovereign's Bertie Wooster, while Ahmad-e Jam, a celebrated Persian Sufi with a much-visited shrine and a robust vita, is eulogized for his physical prowess and saintly deeds. His gallant self-control in his dotage, when he refrained from copulating with his nubile peasant bride more than once in the space of a single night out of concern for her well-being, is remarked upon with admiration in his vita.

Language and Style

The nomenclature used in titles of popular stories illustrates both the connections and regional differences in the popular literature of the medieval Islamic world. In Persian for example, the *Book of Kings (Shahnama)* of Pre-Islamic monarchs and heroes became an inexhaustible source of imitation and borrowing and generated secondary verse epics that usually selected a relatively minor character from its rich repertoire, and made him into the main protagonist with the help of new episodes and adventures. The same process was in force in popular prose literature in works such as the *Firuz Shah Nameh* that appears both in Persian and in Arabic versions. The two languages also share the term *Qissat* (Per. *Qessa*) as a designation for a narrative story, as in the famous Arabic *Qissat Abu Zaid al-Hilali wa-l-Na'isa,* though in Persian the word was given different nuances and applied mostly to shorter tales. The Arabic stories, however, also describe themselves as *siras*; and in modern critical terminology the entire genre comes under the heading of *sira sha'biyya* or popular *sira*.

These include such famous stories as *Sira 'Antar, Sirat al-Zahir Baybars, Sirat Bani Hilal al-Kubra, Sirat Saif b. Dhi Yazan,* and others. The Arabic stories are composed in rhyme prose with frequent insertions of poetry, whereas the Persian stories tend to be in simple prose, with some containing occasional lines of poetry. However, in their case, too, the simple prose is at times replaced by interludes of ornate descriptive passages on such literary topics as sunrises and sunsets, or depiction of beautiful women. This has led some editors and commentators to detect the influence of copyists or scribes at the final stage when this basically oral composition was turned into a written format. But the two styles could have well coexisted from the outset; in the case of the popular storyteller, as in the case of his rival the popular preacher, occasional flights of rhetoric and a purple passage or two depicting a well-established topic would have been a way of parading one's skills as a performer. The more racy and simple diction could be reserved for the main part of the narrative where the action demanded all the attention. The same mixture of styles occurs in Turkish folk epics such as *Köroghlu*, except that here regional variations contain different proportions of poetry and prose. *The Book of Dede Korkut*, on the other hand, is entirely in prose but contains passages where rhyming and transliteration occur.

Narration and Wonder

The uneasy dichotomy between "popular" and polite has already been referred to at the outset. But it must be borne in mind that "literature" also has had an eventful semantic history, with both "literature" and "text" as metaphors assuming ever more widening range and connotations. This revision of taxonomies can itself suggest new ways of studying medieval popular literature in terms of its own dynamics and internal structure. Thus in spite of using material culled from different times and cultures—the reign of the Kayanids or Sasanids, glancing back at the heroic age of the Oghuz Turks, or drawing upon the *Days of the Arabs (Ayyam al-Arab)*—the underlying narrative techniques of the episodes and their ways of focalization can be constructively studied together. The supernatural, for example, in its different manifestations, in characterization as magicians and sorcerers, or in location, in exotic lands populated by strange men and beasts, was a frequent feature of most tales, and it was this abandonment of verisimilitude that has given the term *popular* its laudatory and pejorative connotations from the outset. The eleventh-century Persian historian Bayahqi, for example, in a short diatribe against stories in which an old sorceress can turn a man into an ass, while another aged hag can rub an ointment into his ears and turn him back into a human being, dismisses the entire genre as mere superstitions that induce sleep to the ignorant when they are read to them at night. Yet it is this very defiance of verisimilitude and the destabilizing effect of the magical hall of mirrors conjured up at times by these narratives that have found them new audiences in our own time.

OLGA M. DAVIDSON

See also Alexander; Biography and Biographical Works; Dreams and Dream Interpretation; Epic Poetry; Epics, Arabic; Epics, Persian; Epics, Turkish; Folk Literature, Arabic; Folk Literature; Persian; Folk Literature, Turkish; Magic; Maqama; Miracles; Mirrors for Princes; One Thousand and One Nights; Performing Artists; Popular Religion; Saints and Sainthood; Safavids; Sasanians, Islamic Traditions; *Shahnama*; Sira, Stories and Storytelling; Sufism and Sufis; Supernatural Beings; Theatre; Women Warriors

Further Reading

Chadwick, N. K., and V. Zhirmunsky. *Oral Epics of Central Asia.* Cambridge: Cambridge University Press, 1969.
Connelly, B. *Arab Folk Epic and Identity.* Berkeley: University of California Press, 1986.
Encyclopaedia of Islam, 2d ed., articles:
  "Hamâsa" (Ch. Pellat, Arabic; H. Massé, Persian; I. Mélikoff, Turkish; A. T. Hatto, Central Asia; Aziz Ahmad, Urdu), Vol. III, 110–119.
  "Hikâya" (Ch. Pellat, Islamic and Arabic; A. Bausani, Persian; Pertev Naili Boratav, Turkish; Aziz Ahmad, Urdu; R. O. Winstedt, Malayan), Vol. III, 367–377.
  "Kissa" (B. Flemming, In older Turkish Literature; L. P. Elwell-Sutton, Persian; J. A. Haywood, Urdu; A. H. Johns, Malaysia and Indonesia) Vol. V, 193–205.
  "Manâkib" (Ch. Pellat), Vol. VI, 349–357.
  "Marthiya" (Ch. Pellat, Arabic; W. L. Hanaway, Jr. Persian; B. Flemming, Turkish; J. A. Haywood, Urdu), Vol. VI, 602–612.
Sîra Sh'abiyya" (P. Heath), Vol. IX, 664–665.

Gerhardt, M. *The Art of Story Telling.* Leiden: Brill, 1963.
Hanaway, W. L. Jr. (Tr.) *Love and War: Adventures from the Firuz Shâh Nâma of Sheikh Bîghamî.* Persian Heritage Series, vol 19. New York: UNESCO, 1974.
Heath, P. *The Thirsty Sword: Sîrat 'Antar and the Arabic Popular Epic.* Salt Lake City: University of Utah Press, 1996.
Irwin, R. *The Arabian Nights: A Companion.* London: Allen Lane, 1994.
Lewis, G. (Tr.) *The Book of Dede Korkut.* Harmondsworth, United Kingdom: Penguin Books, 1974.
Lyons, M. C. *The Arabian Epic.* 3 vols. Cambridge: Cambridge University Press, 1995.
Norris, H. T. "Fables and Legends." In *The Cambridge History of Arabic Literature: 'Abbasid Belles-Lettres,* edited by J. Ashtiany et al., 136–145. Cambridge: Cambridge University Press, 1990.
Renard, J. *Islam and the Heroic Image.* Columbia, SC: University of South Carolina Press, 1993.
Reynolds, D. F. "Creating an Epic: from Apprenticeship to Publication." In *Textualization of Oral Epics*, edited by L. Honko, 263–277. (Trends in Linguistics: Studies and Monographs, 128). Berlin: Mouton de Gruyter, 2000.

POST, OR BARID

Post, or *Barid,* was the official system of swift overland communication employed by rulers in the premodern Islamic world. The origins of both the term *Barid* and the institution that it represents have been debated by scholars, although it is clear that Byzantine and Sasanian models, which were known to pre-Islamic Arabians through the imperial penetration of the Arabian Peninsula, influenced the creation and early development of the Islamic *Barid.* Elaborate postal systems were in existence in the Near East since ancient times, and the natural and topographical conditions that dictated the creation and maintenance of these systems remained unchanged over millennia. Thus caliphs such as Mu'awiya (r. 661–680 CE) and 'Abd al-Malik (r. 685–705 CE), who are credited with having established the *Barid* throughout Umayyad lands, had only to continue the basic structure of the routes and postal stations that dotted the caliphal landscape.

In general terms, the *Barid* allowed caliphs to communicate swiftly and securely with the remotest provinces of their rule. Messengers to and from the provinces would, upon the presentation of the necessary documentation, be entitled to the use of fresh mounts, lodgings, and other provisions that were available at stations along defined routes. These stations were ideally situated six to twelve miles apart (the former distance applying to eastern regions, the latter to western ones), but local conditions such as the existence (or lack) of water, mountains, deserts, or towns often affected the course of the routes and the location of postal stations. From the early 'Abbasid period, itineraries of the imperial routes and stations were collected for official use, and these influenced the composition of Arabic geographical works.

The *Barid* served rulers in a variety of capacities: messengers transmitted official correspondence—mostly reports and decrees; governors were escorted to their posts; foreign emissaries were transported to the capital; and mounts and soldiers were dispatched to the scenes of battle. Messengers using the *Barid* could cover enormous distances with great speed, thereby allowing rulers to act with efficiency on the reports sent from afar. Thus the *Barid* was a crucial tool of centralization for rulers of far-flung empires such as those of the Umayyads, 'Abbasids, Mamluks, and Ottomans, whose power depended on their ability to control and react to events throughout their lands.

Regional postal administrators coordinated the local activities of the *Barid* and regularly relayed reports to a central postal chief based in the capital. The regional administrators were responsible for the upkeep and management of the local postal stations. Depending on the region and period, funding for the system was derived either from the central treasury or by an arrangement according to which towns and villages that maintained the local postal infrastructure were compensated through a commensurate reduction in taxes levied. However, when manned postal stations were unavailable, couriers would usually requisition mounts and provisions from locals who were barred from using the system. This often led to a general feeling of popular resentment toward the official couriers, and there is a detailed record of the postal reforms instituted by Near Eastern rulers, from Roman to Ottoman times, aimed at curbing the excesses of couriers and the oppression that they are known to have visited upon the towns and villages through which they passed.

Under the Umayyads, the *Barid* was organized on a rudimentary basis, with local (Sasanian or Byzantine) traditions prevailing in different parts of the caliphate. The 'Abbasids rationalized the system and increasingly used it in the context of gathering and relaying information; hence, during this period the *Barid* came to be closely associated with internal surveillance. With the gradual fragmentation of the caliphate in the late ninth and early tenth centuries CE, the need for an empire-wide system of communication diminished, as did the ability of the Baghdad-based rulers to control the postal infrastructure in distant provinces. The central *Barid* declined accordingly, with independent dynasties such as the Fatimids and Ghaznavids maintaining their own postal systems until the Mamluk sultan Baybars I (r. 1260–1277 CE) revived the *Barid,* albeit on a smaller scale. Earlier, in 1234, the second Great Mongol, Khan Ogedei (r. 1229–1241 CE), established the impressive *Yam* postal system, drawing on Chinese precedents and connecting internally the most extensive land-based empire in history. A decree of the Ottoman sultan Mustafah II (r. 1664–1703 CE) ordered that the imperial courier system *(Ulaq)* be privatized, thereby altering the very nature of premodern postal systems of the Near East.

From the tenth century CE, homing pigeons were increasingly used in the Islamic world for transmitting urgent news, particularly during the Mamluk period, although they were not, strictly speaking, part of the *Barid*'s infrastructure.

ADAM SILVERSTEIN

See also Diplomacy; Espionage; Ibn Khurradadhbih; Pigeons; Road Networks

Further Reading

Dvornik, Francis. *The Origins of Intelligence Systems.* New Jersey: Rutgers University Press, 1974.
Morgan, David O. "Reflections on Mongol Communications in the Il-Khanate." In *The Sultan's Turret: Studies in Persian and Turkish Culture.* Leiden: Brill, 2000, 375–385.
Sauvaget, Jean. *La Poste aux Chevaux dans l'Empire des Mamelouks.* Paris, 1943.
Silverstein, Adam. "The Origins and Early Development of the Islamic Postal System *(al-Barīd)*, until ca. 846 CE" Ph.D. dissertation, University of Cambridge, 2002.
———. "A New Source for the Early History of the *Barid.*" *al-Abhath* 50–51 (2002–2003): 121–134.

POVERTY, ISLAMIC

As is the case in a number of premodern cultures, medieval Islamic society viewed poverty both as a social problem and as a form of religious piety. Understanding the attitudes of medieval Muslims toward poverty and the poor, therefore, turns on the distinction between the poor as an identifiable group or groups in society and the adoption of poverty as a spiritual value by elite groups of pious men and women.

Poverty represented a social problem from the very beginnings of the Muslim community. The Qur'an lists the poor *(al-fuqara' wa al-masakin)* among the recipients of the alms-tax *(zakah)*. Later, legal scholars argued about the respective meanings of these two terms, but it was agreed that both referred to persons who possessed too little property to pay zakah themselves. This discussion provides us with the first attempt at a definition of poverty from the point of view of Islamic law. In time, Sufis argued that the first pious, poor Muslims in history were those companions of the Prophet who left their possessions behind when they emigrated from Mecca to Medina, and who took up residence on the portico of the Prophet's mosque. These *ahl-suffa* (people of the portico) provided a model for later ascetics and Sufis, as well as serving as a link that would connect Sufi poverty to the earliest Muslim community under the leadership of the Prophet himself.

The Islamic conquests likely had the effect of enriching many early Muslims, but this was temporary. Over time, the community grew to include people of all social classes and ethnic origins. By the time of the civil war between Harun al-Rashid's sons, al-Ma'mun and al-Amin (809–813 CE), the poor people of Baghdad were sufficiently numerous to enter Muslim political history for the first time. They defended the city and supported al-Amin against his brother. Thereafter, the existence of poor persons among the Muslim community was accepted as a fact of life, and the poor appear to us in the sources in a number of guises. Among these are the *harafish*, who are described as day laborers, beggars, and sometime Sufis. In Mamluk Cairo, the *harafish* were led by a *shaykh* or *sultan* who was responsible to the sultan. The sultans and amirs frequently employed them to build buildings or dig canals.

In one famous classification of the groups making up medieval Islamic society, that of the fifteenth-century Egyptian chronicler al-Maqrizi, the poor appear as the lowest of seven social classes and are classified as "beggars who beg from people and live at their expense." The sixth class, made up of those who work for a wage, includes "wage laborers, porters, servants, stablemen, weavers, masons, construction workers, workmen, and the like." All of these groups belonged to the *'amma* (common people), as opposed to the *khassa* (elite). The chroniclers, as the children of privilege, often express disgust at the rowdy behavior of the lower classes, and fear of their propensity for violence in times of hunger or during epidemics. The chroniclers routinely record the occurrence of bread riots, especially in the troubled years of the late fourteenth and early fifteenth centuries. Also of concern to the wealthy were the activities of young men organized in *futuwwa* groups in the major Muslim cities. Although originally intended as protectors of their urban neighborhoods, the groups sometimes invaded the spaces occupied by the wealthy and engaged in robbery and looting.

In contrast to the negative light in which the chroniclers present the poor, all classes of society seem to have held Muslim ascetics and Sufis in high regard, at least so long as these holy poor did not violate the norms of Muslim law or adopt heretical religious ideas. In the early centuries of Islam, it was ascetics—people who renounced material comfort in order to pursue a life devoted to worship, study, or holy war—who filled this role. As Sufism began to emerge as an independent movement at the end of the ninth century, however, it began to absorb many of the ideas and practices associated with the earlier ascetic movement. There is some dispute as to what degree Sufism opposed the conventional piety and political order, but the Sufis quickly emerged as a spiritual elite, one of whose chief distinguishing characteristics was the practice of pious poverty.

Although the Sufis would have rejected the term for theological reasons, one might describe this type of poverty as voluntary poverty, as opposed to the involuntary poverty of the lower classes. Indeed, the Sufi hagiographies make a point of emphasizing the elite origins of many Sufis, and present their disavowal of wealth as a sign of their rejection of the material world and embrace of spiritual devotion.

As time went on, the Sufi became an easily recognizable figure, with his begging bowl and patched cloak. Sufis began to attract the attention of the rulers of Muslim states and to attract their patronage. From the tenth century onward, Muslim rulers built convents to house Sufis, many of whom were itinerant. Perhaps the best known of these institutions was the *khanqah*, a Sufi convent that was usually built by the ruler as a waqf. Other terms for Sufi institutions included *ribat* and *zawiya*, many of them founded by private persons to benefit their teacher or a particular Sufi order. Indeed, late medieval Sufism was increasingly organized around Sufi orders founded by charismatic teachers, who claimed to pass down teachings originating with the Prophet.

This institutionalization of Sufism had a negative effect on the reputation of the holy poor. Scholars critical of Sufism, such as Ibn al-Jawzi (d. 1200), suggested that the Sufis were living off of the hard work of their fellow Muslims, and thus were undeserving of veneration by ordinary believers. Ibn Taymiyya (d. 1328) rejected assigning any special status to holy poverty, arguing that wealthy persons who spent their money on pious purposes, such as supporting *jihad*, were no less worthy of respect. These neo-Hanbali scholars denied the holy poor any special status and argued that the best Muslims were those who were socially and politically engaged, not those who isolated themselves from society to devote themselves to worship. Indeed, the increased dependence of the Sufis on elite patronage was used to call their motives into question. Some Sufis, known as *Malamati*s, responded to popular veneration by intentionally violating Islamic law in order to attract criticism.

In general, however, the piety of the holy poor continued to inspire the respect of all classes of Muslim society. Even the ordinary beggar received alms with a prayer for his benefactor, and the idea that the poor were especially close to God continued to be persuasive to most Muslims. Many founders of pious endowments, for example, stipulated that those employed by the endowment regularly pray for the souls of the founder and his or her descendants. In this way, the holy poor helped ensure the salvation of their social superiors.

ADAM SABRA

See also 'Abbasids; Burial Customs; Charity; Ethics; Funerary Practices, Muslim; Gifts and Gift Giving; Hospitality; Ibn al-Jawzi; Ibn Taymiyya; Mamluks; al-Maqrizi; Mecca; Medina; Mosques; Public Works; Syria; Sufism and Sufis; Waqf

Further Reading

Amin, Muhammad Muhammad. *Al-Awqaf wa'l-hayah al-ijtima'iyya fi Misr 648–923 H./1250–1517 M*. Cairo: Dar al-Nahda al-'Arabiyya, 1980.

Bonner, Michael. "Definitions of Poverty and the Rise of Muslim Poor." *Journal of the Royal Asiatic Society* 3, 6, 3 (1996): 335–344.

Bonner, Michael, Mine Ener, and Amy Singer (Eds.). *Poverty and Charity in Middle Eastern Contexts*. Albany: State University of New York Press, 2003.

Brinner, William. "The Significance of the Harafish and their Sultan." *Journal of the Economic and Social History of the Orient* 6 (1963): 190–215.

Karamustafa, Ahmet T. *God's Unruly Friends: Dervish Groups in the Islamic Later Middle Period*. Salt Lake City: University of Utah Press, 1994.

McChesney, Robert D. *Charity and Philanthropy in Islam: Institutionalizing the Call to Do Good*. Indianapolis: Indiana University Center on Philanthropy, 1995.

Sabra, Adam. *Poverty and Charity in Medieval Islam, Mamluk Egypt, 1250–1517*. Cambridge: Cambridge University Press, 2000.

Singer, Amy. *Constructing Ottoman Beneficence: An Imperial Soup Kitchen in Jerusalem*. Albany: State University of New York Press, 2002.

Stillman, Norman. "Charity and Social Service in Medieval Islam." *Societas* 5 (1975): 105–115.

POVERTY, JEWISH

For most medieval and even early modern societies, we know about poverty mainly from the point of view of those looking at the poor from the outside—those who thought and wrote about poverty and those who gave relief to the poor. For the Jewish world of the Islamic Middle Ages, letters preserved in the Cairo Geniza (covering mainly the period 1000–1250 CE) illustrate also the point of view of the poor themselves, as their voice is heard in letters of appeal, or indirectly in requests written on their behalf. Some of the letters of appeal, especially those of indigent women, were written by professional letter writers. Nonetheless, they realistically reflect poverty as a lived experience, as well as Judaism's belief that poverty is a misfortune no matter whom it afflicts.

Written in Hebrew or in Judeo-Arabic, most of the letters of appeal were addressed to would-be benefactors in Fustat (Old Cairo). Some wrote from far away (as far away as Europe or distant Islamic lands) and some from nearby. When their correspondence no longer served a function, for instance, after a would-be benefactor responded with a gift, it was discarded in the Geniza chamber of the synagogue, unexpectedly to be discovered centuries later and studied by modern scholars.

The letters reveal strategies of the poor. Biblical epigraphs to letters, perched like conspicuous inscriptions on buildings; introductions composed of biblical verses; and scriptural fragments quoted within the bodies of letters—many of which had received prominence in rabbinic literature in connection with charity—exhort would-be givers to follow the charitable advice of holy writ. Prominent are verses including the word *tzedaqa*, which in the Bible usually means "righteousness" but was understood by Geniza people in its post-biblical meaning of "charity." Favorite biblical quotations include the verses "Happy is he who is thoughtful of the wretched; in bad times may (the Lord) keep him from harm" (Psalm 41:2; see Palestinian Talmud Pe'a 8:8, 21b and elsewhere) and "Charity saves from death" (Proverbs 10:2, 11:4; see Babylonian Talmud, Bava Batra 10a). The Judeo-Arabic refrain, "may God make you always one of the besought rather than a beseecher," and the Hebrew adage based on a midrash, "be one of the givers, not of the takers," both of them pronounced in many a Geniza letter of appeal, similarly play on the belief that one can avert indigence by being charitable.

Mindful of the etiquette of female privacy, women wrote only to communal officials or to the community as a whole. Widows relied especially on a rabbinic dictum that "the court (and by extension, the Jewish community) is the father of orphans and the judge of widows." Men appealed to individuals as well, even ones they did not know or who did not know them.

These people were not beggars (information about actual begging, defined as house-to-house solicitation and frowned upon in Judaism, is nearly nil, though of course it existed). Often making use of the literary form of the Arabic petition, these suppliants for charity wished to avoid both begging and public charity (*see* Charity, Jewish). Their letters reflect a relationship between the petitioner and the petitioned, very much like the ancient and gentlemanly system of patronage pervading Near Eastern society. That relationship was characterized by bonding between the benefactor and the recipient of his protection, who in this case prayed to God on behalf of his or her patron in gratitude for a gift bestowed (or anticipated) and would praise him publicly for his generosity.

Most of the indigents writing these letters belonged to the "working poor," though some came from the more well-to-do, that is, the "good families." Together they made up what modern scholars call the "conjunctural poor." Conjunctural poverty (juxtaposed to "structural" or chronic poverty) results from a particular convergence of circumstances that change a person's economic situation for the worse. This sudden impoverishment, however temporary, is a source of shame. The "shamefaced poor," as they are called in medieval and early modern European texts, resist turning to others for help, let alone resorting to the embarrassment of the public dole or of beggary. Conjunctural poverty was already recognized in early rabbinic Judaism, where the midrash speaks about the "person from a prominent family *(ben gedolim)* who fell from his wealth *(yarad mi-nekhasav)* and was too ashamed to take (alms)." In the Geniza world the category of the shame-faced poor extended downward to include the working poor who, most of the time, lived in self-sufficiency, just above the poverty line.

One of the most interesting concepts of poverty revealed by the Geniza letters is the twin notion of *mastūr* and *kashf al-wajh*. *Mastūr* means, literally, "concealed." *Kashf al-wajh* means "uncovering the face." They are metaphors. *Mastūr* in the medieval Judeo-Arabic context (the word is also found in classical Arabic texts and in modern Arabic dialects) represents the two groups already mentioned, those who are normally well off and those of the working poor. When the *mastūr* or *mastūra* fell temporarily into poverty, he or she was forced to "uncover his/her face" and seek help. In order to limit their shame, to avoid having to resort to public charity by collecting alms at the synagogue compound, along with the chronic poor, these people wrote letters petitioning for private charity. Just how salient the distinction between chronic and conjunctural poverty (with its attendant shame) was in Jewish thinking during the Geniza period can also be judged from the more inert and "silent" evidence of the alms lists, where occasionally a beneficiary is listed as "mastūr," indicating that he or she is normally self-sufficient and not in need of a public handout.

If we want to discuss further the different kinds of victims of poverty, we may begin with the large body of foreign poor coming to Egypt from abroad, or to the capital from the Egyptian countryside. They crop up in letters of appeal written after they arrived and on scores of alms lists, collecting bread, wheat, clothing, or cash through the community's public relief system. The Egyptian countryside abounded in needy foreigners, too.

Wayfarers—strangers from the outside—are among the classic poor in all societies. Typically they moved on after a short stay. Foreigners who sojourned for a long time, or who settled permanently, posed a more serious problem. Until they found good work, they continued to fill the ranks of the poor. Many of the educated foreigners wending their

way to Egypt had to settle for work as elementary school teachers or in other characteristically low-paying professions in the community. As such, they still needed alms.

By nature unknown to the community, foreigners faced the problem of proving they belonged to the "deserving poor." Their right to charity was challenged also by an ancient halakha (Jewish law) that states: "The poor of your household have priority over the poor of your town, and the poor of your town have priority over the poor of another town." Means were devised to determine the deservedness of these outsiders. Foreigners whose eligibility had been established—for instance, when a local resident vouched for their need—appear on lists of the poor receiving alms.

Related to the category of the foreign poor were the captives, Jews kidnapped by pirates or by soldiers during war and presented for ransom to the Jewish community. Usually far from home, stripped of their possessions, and lacking the support of family, they remained poor for a long time after their release and needed to be fed, clothed, and sheltered. Similarly deprived, refugees from war or persecution often found sanctuary in Egypt. Military disruptions and violence in Asia Minor in the late eleventh century brought an influx of refugees (called "Rum") into the Egyptian capital, where they show up prominently on alms lists from the turn of the twelfth century.

Also frequently penniless were refugee proselytes. These were mainly people of European origin (Latin lands or Byzantium) who converted to Judaism and later fled to places such as Egypt to escape abuse in hostile Christian surroundings. In Islamic lands they received refuge and protection as poll-tax-paying non-Muslims and charity from the Jewish community. A remarkable case of an impoverished proselyte who was also a refugee is the widow from southern France who made her way through northern Spain to Egypt, fleeing from her harassing Christian family. People named "son of the prose-lyte" and "son of the captive" also appear on the dole. It is evident that they inherited their parents' poverty.

Just as women—especially widows, divorcées, and abandoned wives—suffered from poverty, so did orphans (fatherless children). The community had no orphanage. Orphans typically lived with widowed mothers, with other family relations, or in some cases with families who had taken them in in a kind of foster-care arrangement. Monies left by fathers in their estates (if there was any) was allotted to their children's guardians (often their widowed mothers) to support these youngsters.

Debt was a typical cause of poverty, including the annual poll tax debt to the government, from which the poor were not exempt during the Geniza period. For them it constituted a heavy burden. The community raised monies to subsidize the poll tax of the indigent. Complaints of people in debt, sometimes fleeing their creditors, are common. Debtors were liable to imprisonment and so their charitable relief was often equated with ransoming of captives. Hunger, dearth of clothing, and illness—three cross-cultural symptoms of poverty—loom large in the Geniza. Many letters complain about hunger, lack of clothing, or illness. Petitioners complain of having large families, often giving the number of mouths to be fed. When an item of clothing is missing, the poor ask for a replacement. The kinds of illness suffered by the poor feature eye disease, particularly ophthalmia. Others who were chronically poor because of illness or infirmity include people suffering from paralysis, the tremors, and those with loss of limb. Finally, old age represents another, typically cross-cultural cause of indigence in this period. What was the percentage of the Jewish poor? On the basis of alms lists and economic data contained in about four hundred engagement and marriage contracts—the amounts of the marriage gift of the groom and of the dowry of the bride—Goitein estimated that 25% of the Jewish community of Fustat during the eleventh and twelfth centuries were destitute. Things got worse in the thirteenth century as general economic conditions in Egypt declined. This is reflected in pleas for help for the poor from the head of the Jews, the Nagid Joshua (1310–1355), the great-great-grandson of Maimonides.

What kinds of occupations often meant living in poverty? Members of the underclass included such poorly paid people as doorkeepers, messengers, water carriers, shoemakers, washers of the dead, gravediggers, porters, night watchmen, and kashrut supervisors. Many people were occasionally poor, rather than chronically. Their appearance sometimes on alms lists and sometimes on donor lists means that they floated back and forth between subsistence (greater or lesser) when they were working, which kept them out of "deep" poverty—to borrow Paul Slack's term in his study of poverty in early modern England—and impoverishment, which led them to the dole. Typical of persons in this category were cantors, tanners, errand boys, ghulams (young men, slaves or freedmen, serving as apprentices or factotums), carpenters, teachers, olive makers or sellers, milkmen, glassmakers, tailors, journeymen, dyers, and money changers.

MARK R. COHEN

Further Reading

Cohen, Mark R. "Four Judaeo-Arabic Petitions of the Poor from the Cairo Geniza." *Jerusalem Studies in Arabic and Islam* 24 (2000): 446—471.
———. *Poverty and Charity in the Jewish Community of Medieval Egypt*. Princeton: Princeton University Press, 2005.
———. *The Voice of the Poor in the Middle Ages: An Anthology of Documents from the Cairo Geniza*. Princeton: Princeton University Press, 2005.
Goitein, S. D. *A Mediterranean Society: The Jewish Communities of the Arab World as Portrayed in the Documents of the Cairo Geniza* (5 vols plus Index volume by Paula Sanders). Berkeley and Los Angeles: University of California Press, 1967–1993, esp. vols. 2 and 5.
Lev, Yaacov. "Charity and Social Practice: Egypt and Syria in the Ninth-Twelfth Centuries." *Jerusalem Studies in Arabic and Islam* 24 (2000): 472–507.
Slack, Paul. *Poverty and Policy in Tudor and Stuart England*. London and New York: Longman, 1988.

PRAYER

Muslims consider prayer as one of the cornerstones of their religion. The following five practices fall under the rubric of prayer in Islam: (1) formal prayer *(salat)*, (2) informal prayer *(du'a)*, (3) invocation *(dhikr)*, (4) litanies *(awrad, ahzab)*, and (5) the bestowal of blessings upon the Prophet Muhammad *(tasliya)*.

1. Formal prayer *(salat)*. The Prophet Muhammad said, according to the two most authentic hadith collections, that the greatest human act is the performance of the formal prayers at their proper times. Both Sunni and Shi'i Muslims agree that the five times at which all sane adult Muslims are obligated to perform the formal prayers are daybreak *(fajr)*, midday *(zuhr)*, afternoon *('asr)*, sunset *(maghrib)*, and nightfall *('isha')*. They agree that the daybreak prayer consists of two units *(rak'as)*, the sunset prayer consists of three units, and the remaining three prayers each consists of four units. There is also consensus that each unit of prayer consists of an initial declaration of "God is greatest" *(Allahu akbar)*, the recitation of the first Sura of the Qur'an followed, in the first two units of every prayer, by a passage of choice from the Qur'an, as well as a single bow, two prostrations, and that every two units of prayer are separated by a period of time seated during which one mentions the twin professions of Islam: There is no god but God, and Muhammad is the messenger and

servant of God *(tashahhud)*. This consensus is striking because the Qur'an articulates neither the precise times, nor the number of units, nor the precise actions of the formal prayers, despite the large number of verses exhorting Muslims to perform their prayers properly. This high degree of consensus across sectarian lines suggests an early date for the establishment of the formal prayer, which traditional Muslim sources link to the pre-Hijra Ascension *(mi'raj)* of the Prophet Muhammad.

Muslims who execute the formal prayer must be in a state of purity *(tahara)*, which can be achieved by either ablutions *(wudu')* or, in the cases of major ritual impurity arising from intercourse or menstruation, a bath *(ghusl)*, and must face Mecca. Although Muslims may perform the formal prayers individually, the Prophet reportedly promised significantly greater rewards for those who pray in a group. Group prayer may take place anywhere that is clean, although the preferred location is the mosque, or *masjid* (place of prostration). The call to prayer *(adhan)* is issued for each obligatory prayer at the mosque, and group prayer must be led by an Imam who, ideally, is the man who has the greatest knowledge of the Qur'an.

There are also nonobligatory formal prayers, usually performed individually, that scholars recommend prior to the five obligatory *(fard)* formal prayers and after the midday, sunset, and nightfall prayers. Other formal prayers include the Friday congregational prayer *(jum'a)*, which substitutes two sermons *(khutba)* for two of the units of the midday prayer and, for Sunnis, extra evening prayers during the month of Ramadan *(tarawih)*. Other formal prayers detailed in legal and hadith books that consist of slightly modified units of prayer include the two Feast prayers *('id)*, funeral prayer *(janaza)*, supplication for rain prayer *(istisqa')*, eclipse prayer *(kusuf)*, and the prayer for guidance while facing a difficult choice *(istikhara)*.

2. Informal prayer *(du'a)*. God informs Believers in the Qur'an that "I reply to the call of every supplicant when he calls me" (2:186), and hadith books contain numerous supplications that are attributed to the Prophet Muhammad and his Companions. Informal prayer may be performed at any time, in any language, by anyone.

3. Invocation *(dhikr)*. While the Qur'anic concept of *dhikr* means "remembrance (of God)," as in "Remember me, and I will remember you" (2:152), Sufis from an early date identified three levels of invocation, namely of the tongue, the heart, and the innermost self *(sirr, lit.* "secret"). Each Sufi order developed its own methods of invocation, the purpose of which was to draw closer to God. The major hadith collections also recommend specific invocations attributed to the Prophet Muhammad after the formal prayers and other times of day.

4. Litanies *(awrad, ahzab)* are distinguished from invocation by their greater complexity, set times, and the fact that they are performed only by Sufis who have been inculcated properly in an order, whereas many invocations can be performed by non-Sufis.

5. Blessings on the Prophet Muhammad *(tasliya)*. The Qur'an states "God and His angels send blessings *(sallu)* on the Prophet: O you who believe, send blessings on him and salute him with all respect" (33:56). Muslims understand this verse as a command to say "May God bless and salute him" immediately following any mention of the Prophet Muhammad; note that the Shi'i and some Sunnis add "and his family" to this statement.

SCOTT C. LUCAS

See also Funerary Practices; Imam; Mosques; Mysticism, Islamic; Popular Religion; Purity, Ritual; Sufism and Sufis

Further Reading

Keller, Nuh Ha Mim. *The Reliance of the Traveller*. Rev. ed. Beltsville, MD: Amana Publications, 1999.

Padwick, Constance E. *Muslim Devotions: A Study of Prayer-Manuals in Common Use*. London: S. P. C. K., 1961.

Trimingham, J. Spencer. *The Sufi Orders in Islam*. New York: Oxford University Press, 1971.

Zayn al-'Abidin 'Ali ibn al-Husayn. *The Psalms of Islam: al-Sahifa al-kamila al-sajjadiyya*. Translated by William Chittick. London: The Muhammadi Trust of Great Britain and Northern Ireland, 1988.

PRECEDENCE

The term *sabiqa* (or *sabq*), meaning "precedence" in general and, more specifically, "precedence in submission and service to Islam," was a key concept in the early sociopolitical history of Islam, invoked to "rank" the faithful according to their excellence. In addition to early conversion, precedence in emigrating for the sake of Islam (both to Abyssinia and to Medina) and in participation in the early battles of Islam also conferred great merit. The two concepts of precedences *(sawabiq)* and "merits" or "excellences" *(fada'il)* became conjoined to create a paradigm of the most excellent leadership. Such a paradigm finds scriptural sanction in Qur'anic verses such as "God is satisfied with those who preceded foremost *(al-sabiqun al-awwalun)* from among the Muhajirun and the Ansar and those who followed them in charity and they are pleased with Him, and He has prepared for them gardens below which flow rivers where they will dwell forever; that is the great victory;" "Those who precede(d) are the ones who precede *(al-sabiqun al-sabiqun)*; they are those who will be brought near [to God] in the gardens of bliss" *(Surat al-Waqi'a,* 56:10–12), and "Those among you who spent and fought before the victory are not of the same rank [as others] but greater in rank than those who spent and fought afterwards" *(Surat al-Hadid,* 57:10).

Sunni sources uniformly assign the highest precedence to the Prophet's Companions from among the Muhajirun and the Ansar, and even among them recognize a certain order of precedence. Among Sunni exegetes, al-Tabari reports that the phrase *"al-Muhajirun al-awwalun"* or *"al-sabiqun al-awwalun"* in verse 9:100 was understood to refer to those Muslims in particular who took the pledge of al-Ridwan (a reference to the treaty of al-Hudaybiyya in AH 6/628 CE), or more generally to all those who had prayed toward the two *qibla*s. The *manaqib* or *fada'il al-sahaba* sections of standard Sunni *hadith* compilations also emphasize the *sabiqa* of the Companions as the criterion for assigning greater excellence to them in general from among the community of the faithful.

It is well known that when the official *diwan* or register of pensions was first established by 'Umar in circa AH 15, the *sabiqa* of each Muslim became an important criterion in determining the amount of stipend he or she would be awarded. Those who were among the earliest converts to Islam and had fought in the early battles of Islam, thus, mainly from among the Muhajirun, were given larger stipends. Although the *diwan* was organized according to tribal affiliation, it was the principle of *sabiqa* that determined its overall function, pointing to the centrality of this concept in the early period.

ASMA AFSARUDDIN

Further Reading

Afsaruddin, Asma. *Excellence and Precedence: Medieval Islamic Discourse onLegitimate Leadership.* 36–79.
Diwan. EI. new ed. Vol 3. Edited by H. A. R. Gibb et al. Leiden and London, 1960, 323.

PREDESTINATION

The doctrine of predestination *(qadar)* is one of the cardinal creeds of Sunni religious orthodoxy. Its core teachings are referenced to the scriptural sources of the Islamic tradition, namely the Qur'an and the Prophetic traditions *(hadith)*. The issue of predestination proved to be a controversial area of discussion in early Islam, featuring prominently in the schisms that appeared in the formative years of this tradition. The circumspect review of topics of this nature propelled the advancement of scholastic theology employed for the consolidation and synthesis of the doctrines of Sunni orthodoxy. The Sunni conception of predestination advocates that God is the omnipotent creator of all that exists. He created the universe, determining precisely not only its fundamental nature but also the form and function of all that exists in it. As a result, everything that comes into existence or has existed is incontrovertibly subject to God's foreknowledge and His sovereign will. The temporal events of the past, present, and future are likewise encompassed by God's eternal knowledge. Indeed, one Prophetic tradition states that these events have been descriptively written on a preserved tablet before the inception of creation. Details of a person's life span, sustenance, and very acts, including whether individuals would be prosperous or dejected, are recorded on this tablet. In the words of the Qur'an, "And all things we created with divine portion" (Q 54:49). However, the profound question for theologians related to whether God's determination of events and their contingencies extended to an individual's inclination to faith and acts of obedience and disobedience.

Notwithstanding the fact that there were theological sects outside of orthodoxy that presented disparate explanations of the doctrine of predestination, there also existed within Sunni orthodoxy a number of fine distinctions regarding the conceptual compass of the creed of *qadar*. Sunni theologians were agreed that God was the sole creator of all that existed, irrespective of whether it is inherently good or evil; there was also consensus regarding God's power over all creation and the fact that His foreknowledge and sovereign will governed all man's acts. They accepted that God determined a person's life span and that individuals could neither exceed their appointed time nor could they curtail it; and a similar set of strictures applied to provisions decreed by God. However, disagreement occurred concerning whether God bestowed individuals with an innate capacity and will of their own, allowing them to perform acts for which they merited either reward or punishment; this would have implications for their capacity to choose between belief and disbelief. The deliberations on this subject were intricate as theologians grappled with the theoretical complexities of this issue. However, from a practical perspective scholars maintained that the doctrine of predestination should not be construed as a pretext for disobedience, laxity, or recklessness. Moral responsibility and accountability were not to be relinquished in the wake of this doctrine, which was essentially a declaration of God's absolute omnipotence.

Early Discussions on Predestination

During the rule of the Umayyad caliphs (661–750 CE), the subject of predestination assumed political importance. The Umayyads emerged as leaders of the Islamic world following years of political upheaval. They established a state with its capital in Damascus, Syria, vigorously pursuing its political and economic advancement. The legitimacy of this ruling dynasty was questioned by a number of scholars due to the unpopularity of its policies. The Umayyads and their supporters invoked the doctrines of qadar to defend their position as caliphs. They argued that God had willed that they should be rulers, implying that opposition to their leadership constituted defiance of God's decree. This situation led prominent individuals to qualify the specific scope of the accepted doctrine of predestination, asserting that it did not excuse injustices carried out during Umayyad rule. These issues are discussed in an epistle attributed to the ascetic figure, Hasan al-Basri (d. 728 CE). It was supposedly part of a dialogue on predestination with the caliph 'Abd al-Malik (r. 685–705 CE). There are no Prophetic traditions in this epistle, which has led Montgomery Watt to argue that such traditions were not in wide circulation at the time and that the subsequent profusion of traditions endorsing a fatalistic espousal of predestination reflected an attempt to buttress a developed doctrine. However, such traditions were always general in character, while the disputable points relating to the subtleties of predestination were of a more specific kind. Scholars who compiled collections of traditions much later often included a separate chapter on predestination.

The Arabic term qadar literally connotes measurement or estimation; it is often paired with the word qada', which denotes God's general decree. The term qadar is used in its derived sense to refer to predestination; however, individuals who opposed key aspects of the doctrine of predestination were paradoxically referred to as Ahl al-Qadar or Qadariyya, namely, proponents of free will. A further term featuring in the discourse on the subject is the word jabr, which signifies compulsion. Those individuals who subscribed to a rigid understanding of predestination were referred to as the Jabariyya and even classified as an active sect. Medieval writers on heresy identified Jahm ibn Safwan (d. 746 CE) as being the leader of the Jabariyya. He argued that man acted under absolute compulsion, claiming that individuals possessed neither the will nor the capacity to act. Jahm professed that attributes such as "creator" that are used to describe God could not be applied to man, deducing that God alone was the true creator of all that exists, including the very acts of man. The analogy of a feather in the wind was employed by Jahm to exemplify the relationship of man to his acts. He even contended that reward and punishment are predetermined.

The proponents of free will were represented by a curious selection of individuals. Medieval writers recognized Ma'bad al-Juhani (d. 705 CE) as one of the first figures to rationalize the doctrine of qadar, referring to the free will of individuals, although his contribution was politically inspired; indeed, he was executed for his insurrectionist activities. A second figure of importance is Ghaylan al-Dimashqi (d. 743 CE). He debated the subject of predestination in the presence of two caliphs, recalling in one instance that God does not will the commission of sins. Ghaylan was also put to death for political insurgency. Predestination featured among the issues critically examined by an emerging faction of Basran scholars who were connected with Hasan al-Basri. This group served as precursors to a significant theological movement outside of Sunni orthodoxy, the Mu'tazilites. The Mu'tazilites were renowned for their rational approach to the teachings of the Islamic tradition, employing modes of thought and argumentation imported from the Greek philosophical tradition. They emphatically rejected key aspects of predestination, claiming that the traditional concept of this doctrine, whereby God is acknowledged as the author of man's deeds, undermined the immutable principle of God's divine justice. Mu'tazilites asserted that God acted in accordance with the dictates of reason. They argued that it would be unfair of God to determine or decree an individual's acts and then subsequently punish or reward that person. God's justice predicated that humans must be free agents and able to choose between belief and disbelief. However, it is essential to bear in mind that the antithesis between orthodoxy and Mu'tazilism on the issue of predestination rested on who was the true creator of man's acts. The Mu'tazilites claimed that God neither created the acts of man nor were these acts subject to His sovereign will; more crucial was their assertion that God had no power over these acts, indicating that His knowledge therein was consequential.

The consequence of such abstraction was that it impinged on the orthodox doctrine of the omnipotence of God, provoking detailed rebuttals. Intriguingly, Sunni theologians and proponents of Mu'tazilism adduced verses from the Qur'an to support their stances. The Qur'an includes verses that are deterministic in tenor, in addition to verses intimating human free will. It states that "No misfortune can take place either in this world or in the life of an individual, except that it had been set down in writing before its passing. Indeed, that is for God so simple" (Q 57:22); it also mentions: "Say, it is the truth from your Lord. So let him who desires to believe do so; and let him who desires to disbelieve do so" (Q 18:29). The Qur'an also comprises verses that speak of God's power to guide and lead astray individuals and His sealing the hearts of disbelievers. The Mu'tazilites argued that such verses were redolent of description, not prescription. Sunni orthodoxy accentuated the contextual strictures that governed the import of these verses, referring to God's foreknowledge and absolute prerogative in such contexts. The Mu'tazilites attained great influence among the 'Abbasid caliphs, particularly during the eighth and ninth centuries CE. The doctrines they defined were approved by the state, despite orthodox opposition. Their stance on predestination, stressing specific aspects of the free will of individuals, is also found in Shi'i expressions of Islam.

Later Developments

A former leading Mu'tazilite by the name of Abu'l-Hasan al-Ash'ari (d. 935 CE) devoted his intellectual energies to refuting Mu'tazilite dogmas, especially their understanding of human free will. His argument was based on the premise that there were limits to the utility of human reason. It was not able to fathom the true nature of God's actions, which, in turn, were not subject to a rationale. The extant literature composed by Ash'ari serves as testimony to the sustained nature of his critique of the Mu'tazilites. He inspired many of his peers and successors to the extent that he became the eponym of a school of theology aptly known as the Ash'arite school. Later adherents of this tradition developed many features of his theological teachings. However, in stressing the absolute sovereign will of God and his omnipotence, Ash'ari and his followers had argued that God was not only the creator of all acts but also that the capacity to carry out an act did not exist prior to the execution of that act; moreover, it

is created by God at the exact time of carrying out that act and not before. Yet, although man may possess limited capacity as provided by God, this capacity has no effective efficacy over the object of its power. This explanation is defined as the concept of *kasb* (acquisition); it postulated that through this process of acquisition, humans merited reward and punishment.

Despite the fact that the concept of *kasb* was significantly revised by later Ash'arite theologians, it was seen as excessively deterministic in substance. Indeed, some scholars associated with the Zahirite and Hanbalite traditions of orthodoxy equated it with the harsh determinism of the *Jabariyya*. Scholars of these orthodox traditions, including Ibn Hazm (d. 1064 CE) and Ibn Taymiyya (d. 1328 CE), rebuked the Ash'arites for their formulation of the doctrine of *kasb*, composing diatribes on this and other Ash'arite theological concepts. They stated that God was certainly the creator of all that exists in the world. However, he had furnished man with the capacity to choose, although His sovereign will governed all acts. A second theological school of Sunni orthodoxy is associated with a figure from Samarqand named al-Maturidi (d. 944 CE). The theology espoused by this scholar attached great importance to reason in the synthesis of doctrine. His definition of predestination presented the notion that God was the creator of man's acts, although man possessed his own capacity and will to act. Man was therefore the true author of his acts and, although they were subject to God's will, in the case of evil acts, they did not occur with the pleasure of God. Over ensuing centuries, Sunni theologians continued to elucidate the doctrine of predestination, authenticating the creed as a distinction of orthodoxy. However, even those groups perceived as being outside the circles of orthodoxy used the basic construct of predestination as an analogue for their own understanding of its significance. The dynamics of the issue left an indelible mark on the discourse of Islamic theology.

MUSTAFA SHAH

See also 'Abbasids; Ash'aris; Caliphate and Imamate; Ethics; Hadith; Al-Hasan al-Basri; Heresy and Heretics; Freethinkers; Ibadis; Ibn Sina; Ibn Taymiyya; Islam; Kharijis; Mu'tazilites; Polemics and Disputation; Qur'an; Al-Razi, Fakhr al-Din; Shi'ism; Theology; Theologians; Umayyads; Zaydis

Further Reading

Abrahamov Binyamin. *Islamic Theology: Traditionalism and Rationalism*, Edinburgh: University Press, 1998.
———. "A Re-examination of al-Ash'ari's Theory of *kasb* According to *Kitab al-luma.*" *Journal of the Royal Asiatic Society*, (1989): 210–221.

Majid, Fakhry. *A Short Introduction to Islamic Philosophy, Theology, and Mysticism.* Oxford: Oneworld Publications, 1997.

Richard, Frank. *Al-Ghazali and the Ash'arite School.* London: Duke University Press, 1994.

Wilferd, Madelung. *Religious Schools and Sects in Medieval Islam.* London: Variorum, 1985.

Watt, Montgomery. *The Formative Period of Islamic Thought.* Oxford: Oneworld Publications, 1998.

———. *Islamic Philosophy and Theology.* Edinburgh: Edinburgh University Press, 1997.

———. *Freewill and Predestination in Early Islam.* London: Luzac & Co., 1948.

Wolfson, Harry Austryn. *The Philosophy of the Kalam.* Cambridge, MA: London: Harvard University Press, 1976.

PRIMARY SCHOOLS, OR *KUTTAB*

Found from remote villages to large urban neighborhoods, the *kuttab* was a type of voluntary educational institution designed to furnish Muslim children with a basic education in religious matters. Important centers for the socialization of recent converts, the earliest primary schools seem to have been organized locally during the Umayyad period and by the ninth century CE were widespread throughout the Islamic world. Typically, the curriculum of a *kuttab* revolved around the memorization of the Qur'an, coupled with practical instruction in basic religious duties, although this was often supplemented with elementary instruction in reading, writing, and arithmetic. Depending on the wishes of a pupil's family and the availability of qualified instructors, subjects such as history, grammar, and poetry could be taught as well. Usually located in a single room within the precincts of a neighborhood mosque or similar building, *kuttab* education was characterized by a strict system of rote learning: students sitting on the floor around their teacher *(mu'allim)* in a semicircle writing their lessons on a tablet *(lawh)* and then repeating it back for correction. Typically, teachers were paid by the pupil's family; poorer students would simply run errands on their behalf. Although there was no precise age for enrollment, students generally began attending around age four and would spend between two and five years studying, normally at their own pace, alongside students of different levels. Generally speaking, boys constituted the overwhelming majority of *kuttab* students, whereas girls were educated, if at all, in separate facilities or by private tutors.

ERIK S. OHLANDER

See also Children and Childhood; Education; Madrasa

Further Reading

Goldziher, Ignaz. "Education (Muslim)." In *The Encyclopaedia of Religion and Ethics*, edited by James Hastings. New York: Charles Scribner's Sons, 1908.

Landau, J. M. "Kuttab." In *The Encyclopaedia of Islam.* 2d ed, edited by H. A. R. Gibb et al. Leiden: E. J. Brill, 1954–2003.

Totah, Khalil A. *The Contributions of the Arabs to Education.* New York: Teachers College, Columbia University, 1925.

PRISONS

Prisons were known to the pre-Islamic Arabs, and some settled communities in Arabia had them. 'Adi b. Zayd (d. about 600 CE) composed poetry on his incarceration by the Lakhmid king, al-Nu'man III (d. 602). Nomads took captives in raids; imprisonment itself was impractical. Imprisonment was neither an official punishment in Roman law nor in Near Eastern provincial laws. It was used instead for pretrial detention. However, debtors and serious criminals such as thieves and murderers were increasingly incarcerated in late antiquity, as were political prisoners. Imprisonment was also among the punishments used in Sasanian Iran.

In the Qur'an the only mention of prison (Ar., sijn) is in the story of Joseph (Q 12:32ff and Q 26:29). House arrest was the punishment for women guilty of fornication, before it was replaced by flogging (Q 4:15 and Q 24:2). The reference to banishment as a punishment for highway robbery was sometimes interpreted as imprisonment (Q 5:33).

Punitive imprisonment had a very limited role in the hudud (punishments by divine ordinance). The main purposes for prisons in the legal literature were pretrial detention and coercion of debtors. An apostate could be imprisoned for three days to allow him to repent and escape execution. However, it was occasionally a punishment (such as for certain categories of murderer and recidivist thieves). These parallels with pre-Islamic laws in the Near East raise unresolved genetic questions about Islamic law. A judge could also impose punitive imprisonment for matters outside the hudud through his power of ta'zir (discretionary punishment). To maintain order, rulers could imprison whomever they wished.

Nearly all cities had prisons. In 762, when al-Mansur (d. 775) founded his new capital at Baghdad, he constructed the Matbaq prison within the Round City, and another, The Prison of the Syrian Gate, outside the walls. Al-Tabari (d. 923) mentions men's and women's prisons in ninth-century Baghdad. Al-Maqrizi (d. 1442) describes seven prisons from different periods of Cairo's history. He says those for criminals, thieves, and highway robbers were cramped and foul-smelling places of torment.

Such terrible conditions were common in robbers' prisons. The historical evidence suggests that robbers' prisons were widespread, although they are rarely mentioned in legal texts. The extent of such incarceration remains uninvestigated. The conditions in debtors' prisons and those in which suspects were held seem to have been less harsh. The adab al-qadi (the conduct of the judge) literature sets out prisoners' rights: people should not be detained without a complainant; guests and even conjugal relations might be permitted; and mistreatment, such as beatings and forced labor, was prohibited. How often these strictures were actually observed is less clear.

Historical sources provide numerous accounts of political prisoners and prisoners of war. Palaces and other such buildings could be reused to hold them, such as the Palace of the Tree in which 'Abbasid princes were detained in Baghdad and the Treasury of the Banners in Cairo, where senior officials were incarcerated until it became a prison for Frankish captives during the Crusades. Many political prisoners and prisoners of war had a worse fate: Castles and citadels often had a jubb (pit); others were held in robbers' prisons; and many were tortured or executed.

ANDREW MARSHAM

See also Courts; Crime and Punishment; Judges; Law and Jurisprudence; Shari'a; Thieves and Brigands; Treason (Hiraba)

Further Reading

Rosenthal, F. *The Muslim Concept of Freedom prior to the Nineteenth Century*. Leiden: Brill, 1960.
Schneider, I. "Imprisonment in Pre-classical and Classical Islamic Law." *Islamic Law and Society* 2 (1995): 157–173.
———. "Sidjn." In *The Encyclopaedia of Islam*. 11 vols. Edited by C. E. Bosworth et al. Leiden: E. J. Brill, 1960–2003. Vol. 9, 547–548.
Ziadeh, F. J. "Adab al-Qadi and the Protection of Rights at Court." In *Studies in Islamic and Judaic Traditions: Papers Presented at the Institute for Islamic-Judaic Studies, Center for Judaic Studies, University of Denver*. 2 vols. Edited by W.M. Brinner and S.D. Ricks. Atlanta: Scholars Press, 1986–1989. Vol. 1, 143–150.

PROCESSIONS, MILITARY

Processions (Ar. *mawkib*; *mawakib*) played an important role in representing the military and, more broadly, the political power of medieval Islamic states and officials. Since the distinction between military and political functions can be ambiguous, what follows will emphasize those examples wherein the representation of power is primary. No doubt the use of processions was common to all medieval Islamic polities; nevertheless, documentation is rather uneven. Sufficient evidence from a number of historical contexts does exist, however, to provide some insight into the political and cultural potency of these occasions.

Processions displayed publicly the symbols and instruments of power. Islamic symbols of sovereignty included such items as the *taj* (crown, but an elaborate and adorned turban), the parasol, sword, mace, inkstand, and others. The Seljuks, displaying their nomadic roots in the Asian steppes, introduced the elaborately decorated saddle-cover *(ghashiyya)* that was carried in front of the parading sultan, and which was also used, along with those other aforementioned symbols, by subsequent rulers, including the Mamluk sultans of both Cairo and Delhi. There is little evidence about processions of the 'Abbasid caliphate, the ceremonial of which seems to have been largely fixed to the court itself; indeed, the term *mawkib* also came to mean audience. However, 'Abbasid officials, along with their enormous entourages, did mount elaborate processions, the conduct of which was governed by strict protocol. According to Hilal al-Sabi', one should ride behind one's superior so as not to subject him to the dust stirred up by one's mount; however, while conversing with the superior one should ride just ahead of him so as not to require him to turn his head. Processions of the Fatimid state are perhaps the most thoroughly documented. The Fatimids used processions regularly to project their power into the cultural and urban fabric of Cairo and Fustat. The most famous occasion was the New Year's procession involving hundreds of officials and thousands of soldiers, which itself became a field of competing power for the participants.

Military power was displayed on occasions when armies departed on campaign or returned from battle. In Mamluk Cairo these often involved the entire political and social establishment. In their last campaign, when they met defeat at the hands of the Ottomans in 1516, the parading army was accompanied by members of the state bureaucracy, Sufi orders, artisan guilds, and various other urban groups. Victory parades offered the opportunity to demean enemies of the state. Victorious soldiers carried severed heads on pikes, violated captured banners, broke war drums, and shackled prisoners, including vanquished rulers. Public processions could also provide popular access to the sultan. When the Mamluk sultan passed through Cairo with his entourage, whether on official business or for pleasure, the masses had the opportunity to voice their concerns to the sultan as he passed by or to express their opprobrium by pelting the royal party with rubbish.

In addition to the representation of power, processions also signaled former enemies' submission to the state and their incorporation into its apparatus. The Spanish Umayyad caliphate staged elaborate processions, requiring days of travel, in which North African supplicants would submit to their authority. After transport across the Mediterranean, the party would be well received and furnished with gifts of horses and equipment necessary for the journey to Cordoba, including litters for women in the group. The party would then undertake the long journey to Cordoba, where they would camp outside the city in preparation for a parade through the city, followed by a formal procession the day after to the caliphate's suburban capital at Madinat al-Zahra' for an audience. The latter parade in particular seems to have been especially spectacular, involving thousands of armed men who lined the route, state officials, and soldiers in ceremonial dress, all of whom required preparations through the preceding night.

The cultural variety inherent in the Islamic world is evident in processional displays of martial power. Ibn Khaldun observed in the North African Marinid state the custom of the Zanata Berber warriors, in which poets and musicians inspired the troops as they marched to battle. Sultan Mahmud of Ghazna, whose Afghanistan-based empire extended into the Punjab, conducted a martial review in which he employed a formation consisting of forty caparisoned elephants standing in front of seven hundred war elephants, all of which would probably have been adorned with protective metal faceplates and headpieces decorated with dangling elements that when clanged would intimidate the enemy. Martial processions were the focal point of independent cultural practices. Ghaznavid expansion into the Gangetic Plain was commemorated, and described by Ibn Battuta in the fourteenth century, in the hero-cult procession of the lance of Sayyid Salar Mas'ud, the legendary warrior and nephew of Sultan Mahmud. The martial displays of the Mamluks, in the context of the Rajab procession of the Mahmal (see Processions, Religious and Festivals and Celebrations) Pop in fifteenth-century Cairo, were parodied by carnivalesque clowns.

JOHN L. MELOY

Further Reading

Hilal al-Sabi'. *Rusum Dar al-Khilafah (The Rules and Regulations of the 'Abbasid Court)*. Translated by Elie Salem. Beirut: American University of Beirut, 1977.
Ibn Battuta. *The Travels of Ibn Battuta, AD 1325–1354*. Translated by H. A. R. Gibb. 3 vols. Hakluyt Society, Second Series, vols. 110, 117, 141. Cambridge: Cambridge University Press, 1958–1971.
Ibn Iyas. *An Account of the Ottoman Conquest of Egypt in the Year AH 922 (AD 1516)*. Translated by W. H. Salmon. Oriental Translation Fund, New Series, vol. 25. London: Royal Asiatic Society, 1921.
Ibn Khaldun. *The Muqaddimah: An Introduction to History*. Translated by Franz Rosenthal. 3 vols. London: Routledge and Kegan Paul, 1958.
Safran, Janina M. "Ceremony and Submission: The Symbolic Representation and Recognition of Legitimacy in Tenth-Century al-Andalus." *Journal of Near Eastern Studies*, 58 (1999): 191–201.
Sanders, Paula. *Ritual, Politics, and the City in Fatimid Cairo*. Albany: State University of New York, 1994.
Sanders, Paula et al. "Mawakib." In *The Encyclopaedia of Islam*, 2d ed., vol. 6, 849–867. Leiden: Brill, 1991.

PROCESSIONS, RELIGIOUS

Religious processions played an important role in daily life across the medieval Islamic world. These ranged from formal to informal, and from those required by religious law to those that reflected local practice. The pilgrimage to Mecca includes procession-like rituals (circumambulation of the Ka'ba, the passage between Safa and Marwa, and the passage to Mina and the Plain of 'Arafa), which are the only ones explicitly sanctioned by religious law and are more fundamentally acts of prayer and worship. Many other processions, although not necessarily sanctioned by the law, nevertheless related explicitly to religious life and are a vivid reminder, along with those of a more profane character, of the Islamic world's cultural variety and vitality.

Political authorities throughout the Islamic lands organized processions on special occasions, which served to associate the regime with significant moments in the religious and cultural calendar. Rulers ranging from the sultans of Delhi to the Umayyad caliphs of Andalusia staged elaborate processions on the Feasts of the Fast-Breaking and Sacrifice, as well other days of religious significance. In the later medieval period, the Meccan sharifs organized processions to commemorate the birthday of the Prophet (Mawlid al-Nabi), which entailed a parade with candles and lanterns from the Ka'ba to the birthplace of the Prophet within the town and processions, one festive with musicians and warriors, during the month of Rajab.

The Fatimid caliphs went to great lengths to associate themselves with the cultural traditions of Egypt. Not only did the Fatimids celebrate occasions of a distinctly Shi'i origin, such as the Festival of Ghadir Khumm commemorating the Prophet's acknowledgement of the legitimate succession of 'Ali ibn Abi Talib and his descendents, but they also staged parades of wider appeal to the largely Sunni population of Egypt during the month of Ramadan, on the occasion of the Islamic New Year, or on the aforementioned feasts. In addition, the Fatimid rulers, as well as their Ayyubid and Mamluk successors, celebrated what were most likely indigenous Egyptian holidays for the Inundation of the Nile (Wafa' al-Nil) with a procession and the ceremonial Opening of the Canal (Kasr al-Khalij), in which the ruler himself often participated.

Processions of the *mahmal* palanquins, dispatched to accompany the pilgrimage caravans from locations such as Egypt, Syria, Iraq, and Yemen, represented the piety and protection of the sponsoring ruler. The most thoroughly documented of these was the mahmal sent by the Mamluk sultans in Cairo, a tradition finally stopped in the twentieth century. The mahmal was paraded through Cairo on three occasions each year: in Shawwal upon its departure for Mecca, in Muharram upon its return, and in Rajab, which included the procession of members of the religious establishment, the Sufi orders, and the soldiers who often performed tricks displaying their equestrian and martial skills. The Rajab procession illustrates vividly the cultural potency of spectacle in any parade; it was especially carnivalesque, particularly in the fifteenth century. Even as a state-sponsored event, the occasion generated such enthusiastic participation on the part of the Cairene crowd that it owed its power more directly to the exuberance of its spectators.

Other groups staged processions as well, although these occasions are less well known. For example, processions occurred in the context of marriages, funerals, circumcisions, and the ritual prayer for rain. The 'Ashura' procession of the symbolic bier of al-Husayn, as practiced in India, may well have a medieval precursor. The Festival of Ghadir Khumm was evidently started as a popular celebration by the residents of Fustat and the North African troops in the Fatimid Army. But then it was appropriated by the state, eventually losing much of its distinctly Shi'i or Isma'ili content and becoming an occasion that attracted the attention of all Muslims in Egypt. The Sufis of Cairo's Salahiyya Khanqah silently paraded every Friday to pray at the Mosque of al-Hakim, led by their shaykh and attendants bearing a Qur'an chest, an occasion that attracted spectators seeking the blessings of the event. The pious visitation *(ziyarat)* of tombs and shrines (pilgrimage) also entailed the use of processions, although this feature was not characteristic of this cultural practice. As is so common in popular religious practice, many of these popular processions blurred confessional boundaries. The procession of Amir Nawruz, as a spring festival in Iran or as a renewal festival in Egypt, included the

practice of charivari and ritual status reversals. Local festivals entailed processions, particularly in Egypt, to celebrate the days *(mawlid)* devoted to the commemoration of venerated individuals in the Muslim, Jewish, or Christian faiths, who were celebrated by members of all three religions.

JOHN TURNER

See also Festivals and Celebrations; Hajj; Nawruz; Pilgrimage; Saints' Days

Further Reading

Ibn Battuta. *The Travels of Ibn Battuta, AD 1325–1354.* Translated by H. A. R. Gibb. 3 vols. Hakluyt Society, Second Series, vols. 110, 117, 141. Cambridge: Cambridge University Press, 1958–1971.

Ibn Jubayr. *The Travels of Ibn Jubayr.* Translated by R. J. C. Broadhurst. London: Jonathan Cape, 1952.

Jomier, Jacques. *Le Mahmal et la caravane égyptienne des pèlerins de la Mecque (XIIIe-XXe siècles).* Cairo: Institut français d'archéologie orientale, 1953.

Lutfi, Huda. "Coptic Festivals of the Nile: Aberrations of the Past?" In *The Mamluks in Egyptian Politics and Society*, edited by Thomas Philipp and Ulrich Haarmann. Cambridge: Cambridge University Press, 1998.

Sanders, Paula. *Ritual, Politics, and the City in Fatimid Cairo.* Albany: State University of New York, 1994.

Sanders, Paula et al. "Mawakib." *The Encyclopaedia of Islam.* 2d ed, vol. 6, 849–867. Leiden: Brill, 1991.

Shoshan, Boaz. *Popular Culture in Medieval Cairo.* Cambridge: Cambridge University Press, 1993.

PROPHETS, TALES OF THE

The "Tales of the Prophets" *(Qisas al-anbiya')* refers to a beloved literature in Islam containing legends and folktales that shed light on the ancient, pre-Islamic prophets and the events and stories of their age. These tales serve not only as exegesis on the Qur'an but also indirectly as Islamic exegesis on the Hebrew Bible and New Testament, since they often relate to biblical narratives and personages that are not referenced in the Qur'an. The "Tales of the Prophets" (TOP) literature also includes material on prophets and peoples that are not known from the Bible.

The singular form of the term *tale* is *qissa*, which is derived from the verb *qassa*, meaning "to narrate" or "tell a story." This verb is found in the Qur'an in the sense of narrating stories of messengers *(rusul)* or prophets *(anbiya')*, specifically including such Islamic prophets as Noah, Abraham, Ishmael, Isaac, Jacob, the tribes, Jesus, Job, David, and Solomon: "We have narrated *(qasasna)* to you about the messengers..." (4:164), as well as prophets and heroes unknown to the Bible, such as Shu'ayb (and the destroyed townships *al-qura*) (Q 7:101, 11:100, 120, and so on).

From the first generation following the Prophet Muhammad, preachers known as *qass* (pl. *qussas*, "storytellers") commented on the Qur'anic narratives concerning biblical characters and the fates of extinct peoples. They were among the first exegetes or commentators on the Qur'an, and their literary products remained an oral endeavor for generations as they told their stories in the market or preached in the mosques. These were popular preachers, and they were beloved among the masses. Religious and legal scholars were sometimes annoyed when they were unable to compete for the crowds and appeal generated by the entertaining style of the storytellers and the folkloristic content of their tales. Their material came from a combination of sources ranging from pre-Islamic Arabian folklore to Jewish *midrash*, and they produced different types and combinations of material, including moral preaching, political satire, fractious propaganda, and their own interpretive, marvelous tales. Their role varied from pious Qur'anic exegete and sermonizer to teller of tales and even buffoon, telling comical and inappropriate stories. Because of their unpredictable nature and potential threat to religious and political elites, they were eventually discouraged and even outlawed by the authorities.

Modern academic studies of oral literatures have attested to the complex individual, creative process of passing along tradition, wherein the faithful transmitter naturally clarifies, develops, expands or narrows, and otherwise contributes personally to the product that moves among and between generations. While faithful, the process is nevertheless not one of literal or unembellished transmission, and the collections that have been preserved include material that reflects Jewish, Christian, Zoroastrian, Gnostic, and other religious realia. Because the content of the prophetic tales was constructed from traditions about the beloved and sacred prophets of ancient times, there was always danger of the tellers or the tales moving populations away from established and approved principles and categories of belief. As a result, a kind of censoring process rose with the emergence of Islamic orthodoxies that removed some materials from the mass of oral tales and organized others into a variety of categories that were more or were less acceptable. Some were eventually branded unacceptable, such as the infamous *isra'iliyyat*, the Israelite tales deriving from what were considered Jewish distortions of divine and prophetic traditions and marked as inappropriate for Islam.

As in all Islamic literatures, the TOP existed in oral form for generations before they were reduced to writing. The earliest compositions have been lost to us, but fragments of some have been found while others can be partially reconstructed from references to them in later works. Among the earliest are the works of Wahb b. Munabbih (d. ca. 732), a Yemenite who is said to have been of at least partial Jewish origin.

The *genre* that is known today as TOP does not find a place among the most noble categories of Islamic literature, such as *hadith*, *tafsir* (Qur'an commentary), and *fiqh* (law), but the actual *content* of the TOP is not infrequently found in *hadith* and *tafsir*. Collections of history *(ta'rikh)* more unabashedly contain TOP, especially the universal histories such as Tabari's *History of Prophets and Kings* (translated into English as *The History of al-Tabari*) that begin with creation and include many tales with biblical or midrashic parallels, but that are unknown from Islamic scripture. Tabari also wrote a massive commentary on the Qur'an, and he carefully sifted through the huge collection of (originally) oral narrative at his disposal, allowing many more prophetic tales in his *History* than in his *Commentary*. He nevertheless includes a great many TOP as appropriate elucidation of Qur'anic verses, phrases, and individual words in his *Tafsir*. The hadith collections also contain TOP in many chapters, and the most highly regarded collection of al-Bukhari contains an entire section called "The Book of the Prophets." More than four centuries after Tabari, Ibn Kathir (d. 1373) follows the organization of universal histories, beginning with Creation in his own history, *Al-Bidaya wal-nihaya*, but he omits much material found in Tabari that, by Ibn Kathir's day, was considered to be unacceptable *isra'iliyat*. The first two volumes of *Al-Bidaya* are sometimes published separately today under the title *Qisas al-anbiya'*.

The two most popular collections of traditional TOP are those of al-Kisa'i *(Qisas al-anbiya')* and al-Tha'labi *('Ara'is al-majalis)*, both of which have been translated into English (see bibliography). Other TOP material may be found within the published histories of al-Azraqi (d. 858), Ibn Qutayba (d. 889), al-Ya'qubi (d. 892), al-Mas'udi (d. 956), and Ibn al-Athir (d. 1232), to name only a few. TOP have been revived in the Islamic world during the twentieth century, perhaps reflecting the resurgence of Islamic religiosity during this period. Two of the most popular Arabic collections are those of 'Abd al-Wahhab al-Najjar (d. 1941), *TOP*, published in the 1930s, and 'Afif 'Abd al-Fattah Tabbarah, *Ma'a al-anbiya' fi-l-Qur'an al-karim (With the Prophets in the Glorious Qur'an)*, published in the 1970s. TOP collections have also been published in many other languages in the Islamic world, including Farsi, Urdu, Turkish, and Malay.

REUVEN FIRESTONE

Primary Sources

Al-Azraqi, Al-. *Akhbar Bakka*. Edited by Wustenfeld as *Chroniken der Stadt Mecca*. Leipzig, 1858; reprint ed., *Akhbar Makka al-musharrafa*. Beirut, n.d.

Ibn al-Athir. *Al-Kamil fi al-ta'rikh*. Beirut, 1965.

Ibn Kathir. *Qisas al-anbiya'*. Beirut, 1982/1402.

———. *Tafsir*. Beirut: Dar al-Andalus, 1985/1405.

Ibn Munabbih, Wahb. *Kitab al-tijan fi muluk Himyar*. San'a', 1979.

Ibn Qutayba. *Al-ma'arif*. Beirut, 1987/1407.

Ibn Sa'd. *Kitab al-tabaqat al-kabir*. 9 vols. Beirut 1997, vol. 1, 37/Haqq (transl.) 2 vols., New Delhi, n.d., vol. 1, 33–34.

Kisa'i, Al-, Eisenberg (Ed). *Vita Prophetarum*. Leiden: Brill, 1922, 110–121/English translation by Wheeler Thackston. Boston: Twayne, 1978.

Mus' 'di, Al-. *Muruj al-dhahab wa ma'adin al-jawahir*. Beirut, 1965.

Najjar, Al-. *Qisas al-anbiya'*. Beirut, n.d.

Tabbarah, 'Afif 'Abd al-Fattah. *Ma' al-anbiya' fi l-Qur'an al-karim* (2d printing). Beirut, 1980.

Tabari, Al-. *Ta'rikh*. Leiden: Brill, 1964/English translation by Ehsan Yar-Shater as *The History of al-Tabari*. Albany: State University of New York Press.

———. *Tafsir*. Beirut: Dar al-Fikr, 1984/1405.

Tha'labi, Al-. *'Ara'is al-majalis*. Beirut, n.d., 57–63/English translation by William M. Brinner. Leiden: Brill, 2002, 114–123.

Ya'qubi, Al-. *Ta'rikh*. Leiden: Brill, 1969.

Further Reading

Athamina, Khalil. "Al-Qasas: Its Emergence, Religious Origin and Its Socio-Political Impact on Early Muslim Society." *Studia Islamica* 76 (1989): 53–74.

Barth, J. *Midraschische Elemente in der muslimischen Tradition. Festschrift zum Siebzigsten Geburtstage A Berliner's*. Frankfurt, 1903, 8–40.

Brinner, William R. "Introduction." *'Ara'is al-majalis fi qisas al-anbiya' (Loves of the Prophets)*. Leiden: Brill, 2002, xi–xxxii.

Firestone, R. *Journeys in Holy Lands: The Evolution of the Abraham-Ishmael Legends in Islamic Exegesis*. Albany, NY: SUNY, 1990.

Goitein, S. "'Isra'iliyat'" (Hebrew). *Tarbitz* 6 (1934–1935): 89–101.

Hirschberg, J. *Judische und Christliche Lehren im Vor-Un Fruhislamischen Arabien*. Krakow, 1939.

Lindsay, J. "'Ali Ibn 'Asakir as a Preserver of *Qisas al-Anbiya*': The Case of David b. Jesse." *Studia Islamica* 82 (1995): 45–82.

Meyouhas, J. *Bible Tales in Arab Folk-Lore*. London: Knopf, 1928.

Newby, G. *Tafsir Isra'iliyyat*. JAAR Thematic Volume.

———. *The Making of the Last Prophet: A Reconstruction of the Earliest Biography of Muhammad*. Columbia, SC: USC Press, 1988.

Rosenblatt, S. "Rabbinic Legends in Hadith." *Muslim World* 35 (1945): 236–252.

Schwarzbaum, H. *Biblical and Extra-Biblical Legends in Islamic Folk-Literature*. Walldorf-Hessen: Verlag Fur Orientkunde Dr. H. Vorndran, 1982.

Tottoli, Roberto. "The Origin and Use of the Term *Isra'iliyyat* in Muslim Literature." *Arabica* 46 (1999): 193–210.

Waldman, M. "New Approaches to 'Biblical' Material in the Qur'an." In *Studies in Islamic and Judaic Traditions*, edited by Brinner and Ricks, 47–64. Atlanta: Scholars Press, 1986.

Wasserstrom, S. "Jewish Pseudepigrapha and *Qisas al-Anbiya*'." In *Judaism and Islam: Boundaries Communication and Interaction: Essays in Honor of William M. Brinner*, edited by Hary, Hayes, and Astren, 237–253. Leiden: Brill, 2000.

Weil, G. *Biblical Legends of The Mussulmans*. New York: Harper, 1846.

PROSTITUTION

Prostitution remained a major social phenomenon in the Islamic world throughout the medieval period. Evidence of the widespread nature of this illicit practice comes from a variety of sources: travel literature, Islamic legal opinions, law codes, and books on judicial theory and by the sixteenth century, even local court records.

Unsurprisingly, this evidence almost entirely focuses on prostitution within an urban context, particularly major metropolitan areas, such as twelfth- and early thirteenth-century Baghdad, fourteenth- and early fifteenth-century Cairo, and Istanbul during its rapid urban development after 1500. Most of these accounts are very scant on detail, naming a number of guilty parties but rarely giving a detailed description. One can only assert that this crime was often so discreet that it eluded documentary scrutiny. We know, for instance, from recent work done on prostitution within the Ottoman era that many female prostitutes worked out of their own private homes. Others worked collectively under pimps or madams, in particular in non-Muslim quarters where the authorities were likely to be far more relaxed about enforcing legal restrictions against prostitution. Other sites included bathhouses and taverns, which also catered to non-Muslims and Muslims alike. By the seventeenth century, male prostitution would often be solicited in coffeehouses; "dancing boys" would offer themselves, along with the opium, tobacco, and coffee that would also be for sale.

Islamic legal discussion of prostitution revolved around the concept of *zina*, or adultery. A male would commit *zina* if he had had sexual relations outside of marriage or his concubine. A female would commit *zina* if she had sex with anyone besides her husband. Although prostitutes could certainly be prosecuted for committing *zina*, a number of legal fictions would be developed in order to leave the institution untouched. For instance, at least one scholar from the *hanefi mezheb* would argue that the sale of a woman to a male client was not a form of *zina*, since the exchange of a fee for sexual favors approximated the dowry a bridegroom would pay for a wife. The male's payment of a prostitute's fee, a dowry, or for that matter the purchase amount for a female slave constituted a right of ownership of the female, which allowed him to have sex at will.

The general attitude of tolerating prostitution as a necessary social evil can be seen throughout the centuries of Islamic history. As early as the caliphates, prostitution was occasionally taxed, a de facto acknowledgment that they had the right to exist. Al-Makrizi makes a similar assertion about Fatimid and Persian tolerance of the illicit sexual trade. Evliya Çelebi, the great Ottoman traveler of the seventeenth century, commented that prostitutes had long formed their own guilds and as such were an accepted part of Ottoman legal structure.

However, one needs also to remember that there were at least two other legal categories that at times approximated prostitution. First is the institution of *mutah*, or temporary marriage, which was contracted between a male who paid a *mahr* to the female party in exchange for sexual relations. The duration of *mutah* was indeed flexible, lasting as short as a day to several months or even years. Yet, *mutah* resembled a marriage contract except for the ability of the woman, as well as the man, to break the contract, the requirement that the female not be a virgin, the female's waiting period before remarriage was considerably less, the wife had no right of inheritance, and her offspring only had such rights if the father consented. *Mutah* had existed prior to Muhammad as a means to regulate the transient tribal relations of the times. Some have argued that the *mutah* originated in pre-Islamic matrilineal Arabic society, as evidenced by the female's equal right to break the marriage contract. While the Prophet Muhammad did not clearly condemn the institution, the Caliph Omar did. From that time onward, *mutah* was only practiced by Twelver Shi'i Muslims, who believed that *mutah* allowed men to vent their biological needs.

Finally, scholars have often pointed to concubinage as a frequent recourse to marital relations. Muslim males had the right to have sexual relations with female slaves at will, and could end them at will, exclusive of whether or not they were married to third parties. This practice can be seen as early as the initial Arab conquest but was particularly popular among the Mamluks and the Ottomans. The purchase of such slaves, most frequently under the Mamluks and Ottomans, tended to be expensive, and the children from such relations became dependents. For those who could not afford concubines, regular prostitutes remained the more attractive option.

BIRSEN BULMUŞ

Further Reading

Keddie, Nikki R. Problems in the Study of Middle Eastern Women. *International Journal of the Middle East Studies* 10, no. 2 (May 1979): 225–240.

Mantran, Robert. *Istanbul au siècle de Soliman le Magnifique*. Paris: Hachette, 1994.

Nielson, Paula I. *The Origin of Mu'tah (Temporary Marriage) in Early Islam*. Unpublished dissertation. The University of Utah, June 1995.

Rapoport, Yossef. *Marriage and Divorce in the Muslim Near East, 1250–1517*. Unpublished dissertation. Princeton University, June 2002.

Semerdjian, Vivian Elyse. *"Off the Straight Path": Gender, Public Morality and Legal Administration in Ottoman Haleppo, Syria*. Unpublished dissertation. Georgetown University, October 2002.

PTOLEMY

Claudius Ptolemy (Ar. Batlamiyus) was active in Alexandria circa 150 CE. He belongs, together with Aristotle, Euclid, and Galen, to the four most well-known scholars of antiquity in the Arabic and Islamic intellectual world. Above all he was a scholar in astronomy, astrology, and geography.

In astronomy, *Almagest* is the Arabic name *(al-Majisti)* for *Megale syntaxis, Syntaxis mathematica (The Mathematical Compilation, The Great Compilation)*. This great treatise of theoretical astronomy, in thirteen books, was written circa 150. It is often presented as being exclusively a work of "mathematical" astronomy. Indeed, it exposed all that is necessary to size quantitatively the movement of stars. But it also contains elements of "physical" astronomy. Early on, it was translated into Arabic by al-Hajjaj b. Yusuf b. Matar (210/826), and revised with the Christian Sarjis b. Hiliya (Serjios/Serjius Eliae) in 214/829. It was translated again by the physician Ishaq b. Hunayn (d. 298/910) in 279/892, a translation that was revised by the mathematician Harran Thabit b. Qurra (d. 288/901), whose maternal language was Syriac and who knew Greek very well, and also wrote a commentary and other books on it. Gerard of Cremona (d. 1187) found in Toledo an Arabic manuscript of it, which was a mix of the versions of al-Hajjaj and Ishaq b. Hunayn, and translated it into Latin.

The *Book of Planetary Hypotheses (Hypothesis ton planomenon)*, comprising two treatises, was composed after *Almagest*. Its purpose is to present an organization of the universe in material spheres. Only the first treatise is extant in Greek. The history of the modern knowledge of this book is complicated, and we must content ourselves in saying here that the two treatises are extant in Arabic: *al-Iqtisas (The*

Exposition). Al-Biruni gives: *Kitab al-Manshurat*: *Sections* [of the spheres]).

The *Book of Phaseis (Phaseis aplanon aspheron)* is brief, dealing with the visibility of the fixed stars. It consists in two treatises, the first of which is not extant in Greek. The Arabic translation of the whole in the AH third/ninth CE century is lost, but a passage of al-Biruni purports to have, partly, the content of the first treatise.

Ptolemy's last astronomical work is the *Easy Tables (Procheiroi kanones)*, a better title than the usual English one: *Handy Tables*, which is known in Arabic as *al-Zij al-muyassar*, or *Zij Batlamiyus (Ptolemy's Tables, Tabulae manuales)*. They are quoted in Arabic since the third/ninth century, having been transmitted in Greek in the version established by Theon of Alexandria (d. end of fourth century), and not Theon (the Old) of Smyrna, as it is often unfortunately said.

In his astrological work *Tetrabiblos*, Ptolemy deals only with general astrology that relates to whole races, countries, and cities, and genealogy, which concerns the individual. It was translated into Syriac, then into Arabic *(Kitab al-Arba'a; Quadipartitum)*. According to al-Nadim, it was translated by Ibrahim b. al-Salt and revised by Hunayn b. Ishaq.

The *Geography (Geographike hypegesis)* of Ptolemy had a great influence on the geographical opinions of the Muslims, but his question as to how the Arabs came into possession of their Ptolemaic information is a crucial one. They give much information on the authority of Ptolemy, which clearly does not come fairly directly from his *Geographia*, and yet there is not extant in Arabic any work that may be described as a translation of it. Therefore no such translation is extant, and it is not clear that it ever existed.

CLAUDE GILLIOT

See also Astrology; Astronomy; Biruni; Geography

Primary Sources

Ibn al-Nadim (or al-Nadim). *The Fihrist of Ibn al-Nadim*. A tenth-century survey of Muslim culture. 2 vols. Edited and translated by Bayard Dodge. New York: Columbia University Press, 1970, II, 639 sqq.

Sai'd al-Andalusi. *Science in the Medieval World: Book of the Categories of Nations*. Translated by I. Salem Semaan and Alok Kumar. Austin: University of Texas Press, 1991.

Ya'qubi, Ibn Wadih qui dicitur al-Ja'qubi Historiae. 2 vols. Edidit indicesque adjecit M. TH. Houtsma. Leiden: Brill, 1883 (reprint, ibid. 1969), I, 150–161, translated by Martin Klamroth in *ZDMG* 42 (1888): 17–27.

Further Reading

De Zénon d'Elée à Poincaré. Recueil d'études en hommage à Roshi Rashed. Edited by Régis Morelon and Ahmad Hasnawi. Louvain-Paris: Peeters (Les Cahiers du MIDEO, 1), 2004.

Endress, Gerhard. "Die wissenschaftliche Literatur." In *Grundriss der arabischen Philologie*, II, edited by Helmut Gätje. Wiesbaden: Ludwig Reichert, 1987, 400–506. Volume III edited by Wolfdietrich Fischer, ibid., 1992, 3–152.

Morelon, Régis. "Fragment arabe du premier livre du Phaseis de Ptolémée." *JHAS*, 1–2 (1981): 3–22.

———. "Une proposition de lecture de l'histoire de l'astronomie arabe." In *De Zénon d'Elée à Poincaré* 237–49.

———. "La version arabe du *Livre des Hypothèses* de Ptolémée, traité 1." *MIDEO* 21 (1993): 7–85.

Pingree, David. "Astrology." *CHAL* III 290–300.

Rosenthal, Franz. "al-Kindi and Ptolemy." In *Studi orientalistici in onore di Giorgio Levi Della Vida*, II, Roma: Istito per l'Oriente, 1956, 436–456, reprint in Id., *Science and Medicine in Islam*, Aldershot: Variorum (CS 322), 1990, nr. IV.

Saliba, George. "Aristotelian Cosmology and Arabic Astronomy." In *De Zénon d'Elée à Poincaré* 251–268.

Sezgin, Fuat. *Geschichte des arabischen Schrifttum*, VI, *Astronomie*. Leiden: Brill, 1978, 83–96.

The Cambridge History of Arabic literature, III. Edited by M. J. L. Young et al. *Religion, Learning and Science in the 'Abbasid Period*. Cambridge, United Kingdom: Cambridge University Press, 1990.

QADI

See Judges

QAYRAWAN

Qayrawan was one of the most important cities of medieval North Africa and still retains a high status as one of the first Muslim cities to be founded in the region. The city is located on an arid plain in the center of modern-day Tunisia (medieval Ifriqiyya). Its location away from the coast has meant that its economy has mostly been based on agriculture and inland trade. Today the city still has a large number of traditional crafts, including leatherworking and textile production.

History

Although Qayrawan is generally regarded as a Muslim foundation, there is considerable evidence of a Byzantine city or town on or nearby the site of the present city. The pre-Islamic town was known as Kuniya or Kamuniya, and remains of an ancient church and a temple have been identified in the vicinity of the modern town. During the Muslim conquests, the area was frequently used as a military camp (kayrawan) for the Arab armies. The area was considered safe for the Arab armies because of its location away from the coast, where it could be attacked by Byzantine sea power, and away from the mountains, which contained troops resisting the invasion. On three occasions in the mid-seventh century (654–655, 661–662, and 665), the Muslim general Mu'awiya Ibn Hudayj set up a military camp in the area near a rocky outcrop known as al-Karn (this may be identified with the hill today known as Batn al-Karn that is twelve kilometers northwest of the city). Some early Arabic chroniclers (Ibn 'Idhari and Ibn Naji) even state that Ibn Hudayj built some permanent structures at the site.

Despite the plentiful evidence of earlier occupation of the site, it is clear that the city of al-Qayrawan was founded by Mu'awiya Ibn Hudayj's successor 'Ukba Ibn Nafi', who was appointed governor of Ifriqiyya in 670. 'Ukba was not satisfied with the location of the military camp and capital at al Karn, and he chose a new site on the flat plain nearby. The first buildings constructed were the Dar al-'Imara (governor's palace) and the Friday mosque, which took more than five years to complete. However, 'Ukba's successor was not satisfied with the location of the town, and he tried to establish a new town three kilometers away; this was to be known as Takirwan. This action did not meet with the approval of the Umayyads, who sent 'Ukba to return the settlement to its original site.

The town suffered a further setback in 684, when 'Ukba and his forces were defeated by the Berber rebel Kusayla. For five years, the Berbers used Qayrawan as their capital until it was recaptured by Umayyad forces in 689. The town remained free of armed conflict until the 740s when it was once again fought over by Berbers and various schismatic religious groups. Central control was restored by the 'Abbasids in 761, when they sent Muhammad ibn al-Ash'ath to be governor of the region. The new governor built a wall around the city to protect it from further attacks, although this did not prevent it from being sacked by the Berbers in 771. Although the town remained nominally under 'Abbasid control, effective rule passed to a local dynasty known as the Aghlabids. Under the Aghlabids, Qayrawan developed as an intellectual, mercantile, and religious center. The Aghlabid conquest of Sicily brought further wealth and prestige to the city.

During the tenth century, Qayrawan was incorporated into the growing domain of the Shi'i Fatimids. However, the inhabitants of the city remained Sunni, which caused constant friction with the Fatimid rulers. Eventually the position of Qayrawan within the Fatimid realm became untenable. First, the city was burnt and pillaged by Fatimid troops; later (1054), the city was subjected to a sacking by the Banu Hilal (from which it has never fully recovered). During the twelfth century, the town was peripheral to the main events in the region, although its prominence increased during the late thirteenth century (1270) when Ifriqiyya was invaded by the Crusaders under Louis IX. The Hafsid ruler considered moving the capital back to Qayrawan.

During the early sixteenth century, the city—along with the rest of Ifriqiyya—became part of a Spanish protectorate under the nominal rule of Mawlay Hassan. Qayrawan was probably of little interest to the Spanish, although they did establish a garrison in the city. In 1575, formal Muslim control of the region was restored when the Ottomans ejected the Spanish. Under Ottoman rule, Qayrawan was neglected, and, in 1701, its citizens suffered the indignity of being forced to destroy their own town. Although the town was rebuilt three years later, it continued to be in a very poor condition until the 1750s, when its citizens were granted tax exemptions and it was supplied with a new city wall. In 1881, the city was incorporated into the French protectorate of Tunisia.

The population of the city varied considerably throughout its history, from an estimated fifty thousand during the seventh century to well over one hundred thousand during the ninth century. Although the majority of the population were Sunni Muslims, there were also significant numbers of Jews and Christians.

Topography

The old city of Qayrawan is located to the north of the French colonial quarter and is enclosed by a circuit of walls built of fired brick that stretch for more than three kilometers. To the east and northeast of the walled town are the ancient suburbs of Guebelia, Jebelia, and Zlass. The Great Mosque is located at the extreme west end of the Old City (Medina), although it probably stood somewhere near the center of the original city as laid out by 'Ukba ibn Nafi'.

The layout and dimensions of the original city are not known, although it is probable that it was roughly square, and, according to al-Bakri, each side measured approximately four kilometers. For the first century of its existence, the city did not have walls, although it was probably enclosed by a ditch and rampart (as were other early Islamic cities such as Basra and Kufa). The interior was divided according to tribal allotments. Although the precise tribal allocations are not known, it is known that the Fihr tribe (a branch of the Quraysh) had an area to the north of the Great Mosque. The chief building material was reused stone taken from the Roman Byzantine buildings in the vicinity, although baked brick was also extensively used.

The high point of the city came with the period of Aghlabid rule, when it benefited from both the links with the high culture of 'Abbasid Baghdad and from the conquest of Byzantine Sicily. The Aghlabids initiated a series of improvements, the most significant of which was the rebuilding of the Great Mosque and its minaret (see Monuments below). In addition to these buildings, they also constructed two fortified palaces in the vicinity of the city: al-'Abbasiyya and al-Rakkada.

A consequence of the phenomenal growth of Qayrawan during the ninth century was that the city's water supply was inadequate for its growing population. It is known, for example, that the city had forty-eight hammams (bathhouses), each of which needed a considerable amount of water. During the Umayyad period, the rulers had relied on a water source (Mams) that was thirty-three kilometers away; water was carried to the city by an aqueduct and distribution system that had been built by the Romans. The Aghlabids renovated this system and increased capacity by building a number of large circular cisterns, the most famous of which stands near the Tunis gate and was built by Abu Ibrahim Ahmed between 856 and 863.

Monuments

The principal monument of Qayrawan—and the only surviving building whose origins can be traced back to the seventh century—is the Great Mosque. This is a large rectangular enclosure (approximately one hundred and twenty by seventy meters) that is aligned southeast by northwest with a prayer hall occupying one-third of the area at the southeast end. At the northwest end of the enclosure, there is a massive square minaret built of fired brick on a stone base. Unfortunately, nothing remains (above ground) of the first mosque built by 'Uqba in 670, and the mosque in its present form dates mostly from the time of the Aghlabids (ninth century). The only early features that remain visible are a mihrab, now functioning as a doorway for the imam, and a cistern, both of which belong to the mosque as rebuilt by Yazid ibn Hatim in 772 CE. The present mihrab dates to the ninth century and comprises a deep concave recess covered by a pointed, horseshoe-shaped arch. Surrounding the mihrab, there are a series of 139 polychrome-luster tiles imported from Baghdad. To the right of the mihrab is the minbar, which is the oldest surviving example of this fixture.

The Mosque of Three Doors is famous for its façade, which is made up of three doorways covered with horseshoe-shaped arches resting on marble columns. Above the arches there is a monumental kufic inscription attributing the construction of the mosque to Muhammad ibn Khayrun al-Ma'arifi in 866. The mosque was substantially altered in 1440, when a minaret was added and the interior remodeled.

Qayrawan also has a large number of religious buildings dating to the later middle ages, including the fourteenth-century Zawiya of Sidi 'Abid al-Gharyani and the Zawiya of Sidi Sahib.

ANDREW PETERSEN

Further Reading

The most important early sources are *al-Bakri* and *Ibn 'Idhari.*

For the Great Mosque, see Creswell, K. A. C., with revisions and additions by J.W. Allan. *Early Muslim Architecture,* 315–30. Aldershott, 1989.

For the history of the city, see Talbi, M. "Al-Kayrawan." In *EI,* 2nd ed., 824–32.

See also visual material at http://archnet.org.

QAZWĪNĪ, AL-, ZAKARĪYA B. MUḤAMMAD B. MAḤMŪD (D. 1283)

Qazwīnī's name appears in various forms in different sources (Wüstenfeld, *al-Qazwīnī,* 1849). He was the author of two well-known works: a cosmography, *The Wonders of Created Things and the Oddities of Existing Things* (*'Ajā'ib al-Makhlūqāt wa-Gharā'ib al-Mawjūdāt*), and a geography with two variant titles, *The Wonders of the Lands* (*'Ajā'ib al-Buldān*) or *The Monuments of the Lands and the Annals of [God's] Servants* (*Āthār al-Bilād wa-Akhbār al-'Ibād*). Judging from the broad dissemination of extant manuscript copies, these two works were the most widely read examples of a medieval Islamic literary genre about wonders ('ajā'ib) (*EI2,* "'Adjā'ib"; *Encyclopedia Iranica,* "Adjā'eb al-Makhlūqāt"). It was a genre that drew on Neoplatonic ideas about creation as emanation and on classical traditions regarding the oddities of distant lands. Qazwīnī was a qāḍī (judge) (Ibn Taghrībirdī; von Hees) and also a professor at al-Madrasa al-Sharābīyya in Wasit (Ibn al-Fuwaṭī; von Hees).

Recent work shows that the established version of Qazwīnī's biography as presented in *The Encyclopaedia of Islam, New Edition,* requires revision. It has long been held (a) that Qazwīnī was a qāḍī at Wasit and Hilla before the Mongol Conquest, (b) that he left this post at the time of the conquest and subsequently turned to scholarship, and (c) that his literary patron was 'Alā' al-Dīn 'Aṭā Malik Juwaynī.

Of these three propositions, only proposition (a) continues to stand unchallenged. It has been based on the clear statement of the biographer Ibn Taghrībirdī (d. 1470), who wrote the following: "He was a judge in Wasit and Hilla in the days of the Caliphate. He was a learned *imām,* a *faqīh,* and he wrote useful compositions including 'The Book of the Wonders of Creation.' He died on the seventh day of Muḥarram in the year 682 [1283 CE]."

Proposition (b), by contrast, can now be shown to be false. It has been based on logical but speculative assumptions concerning the interpretation of a statement in the preface to *The Wonders of Creation.* There, Qazwīnī himself wrote, "When I was tested to go far from home and homeland, and be separated from family and from those who lived nearby, I set myself to studying in accordance with the saying, 'In time, a book is an excellent companion.'" Scholars have assumed that the home referred to here is Wasit, that the reason for Qazwīnī's separation from it is the conquest, and that the reference to studying suggests the writing of books as opposed to the practice of law. However, Syrinx von Hees has recently brought to light new evidence that contradicts these assumptions. The author of *al-Ḥawādith al-Jāmi'a,* who is thought to be Ibn al-Fuwaṭī, mentioned Qazwīnī among the notable personages of Mongol Iraq who died in AH 682. He wrote the following: "He composed a book called *The Wonders of Creation.* . . . He took on the judgeship of Hilla in the year (AH) [6]50, and then transferred to the judgeship of Wasit in the year (AH) [6]52, and was assigned to teach in the Sharābī Madrasa, which he continued to do until his death." Therefore, it now seems that if Qazwīnī's statement in his preface was meant literally, he was referring to his departure from a previous home and that, both before and after the conquest, his life of study in Wasit included the study, practice, and teaching of law as well as the composition of books.

As for proposition (c), it is questionable, but it cannot be summarily dismissed. It is based on a passage extolling Juwaynī that appears in some—but not all—of the surviving manuscripts of *The Wonders of Creation*. The passage does not appear in the only surviving manuscript that was made in Wasit while Qazwīnī lived there (Munich, cod. arab 464). This fact is notable, but it does not prove that Juwaynī could not have been the patron of the text, because there are several comparable instances in which patronage for a text was only secured after the text was completed. The passage does appear in an undated manuscript that was probably produced about twenty years after both Qazwīnī and Juwaynī died (London, Or. 14140). Some subsequent manuscripts include the passage, whereas others do not. On the basis of the available evidence, it is impossible to settle the question. Even so, much can be learned much about the history of the reception of the text if we can identify patterns among those manuscripts that do include the eulogy to Juwaynī and among those that do not.

Qazwīnī's geography has not traditionally been used as a source for his biography, but von Hees has recently approached it as such. By collecting the first-person references in the geography, von Hees makes a strong case that Qazwīnī spent his youth in Qazwin, studied in Mosul, and then pursued his career in Baghdad, Hilla, and Wasit. One might initially be cautious about these conclusions given that the use of the first person in geographic writing is often a stylistic convention rather than a means for the presentation of autobiographical data. However, as a stylistic convention, the use of the first person in geographical writing often serves to validate otherwise questionable passages concerning distant lands. It is striking that Qazwīnī, by contrast, actually uses the first person for passages concerning areas in which he is otherwise known to have lived or in which he may quite conceivably have lived given what is otherwise known of his life. It therefore seems that the first-person references in the geography can indeed be used for the reconstruction of his biography.

Qazwīnī's two works are *The Wonders of Created Things and the Oddities of Existing Things* (*'Ajā'ib al-Makhlūqāt wa-Gharā'ib al-Mawjūdāt*) and *The Wonders of the Lands* (*'Ajā'ib al-Buldān*), of which a variant edition is called *The Monuments of the Lands and the Annals of [God's] Servants* (*Āthār al-Bilād wa-Akhbār al-'Ibād*). Both works were widely disseminated, as demonstrated by numerous surviving manuscripts not only in the original Arabic but also in Persian and Turkish translations and summaries. Both were encyclopedic compendia in which Qazwīnī organized information gathered from numerous previous authorities into an overarching framework. Manuscripts of the cosmography often contain hundreds of illustrations. Before describing the two works further, it is necessary to explain their modern publication histories.

Both texts were first published by Ferdinand Wüstenfeld, whose editions remain the most widely available versions to scholars. As has long been recognized, Wüstenfeld's choice of manuscript sources for these editions renders them problematic. Recent scholarship based on Qazwīnī's own manuscript of the cosmography is beginning to reveal how Wüstenfeld's problematic edition of that text has led to misunderstandings of it in the secondary scholarship. However, parallel scholarship on the early manuscripts of the geography has not yet been undertaken, so it is still unclear what the effects of Wüstenfeld's edition of that book have been.

In the case of the cosmography, Wüstenfeld mixed sections from manuscripts dated from the thirteenth to the eighteenth centuries, the contents of which actually vary considerably. Ruska attempted to quantify this variation by determining exactly how many Arabic editions existed, but his method for classifying the editions was problematic, for two reasons. First, he attempted to count "lost" versions that he presumed must have existed along with surviving versions. Second, he only checked for correspondences and differences at a select few points in the text, and thus falsely identified manuscripts that diverge at other points in the text as belonging to the same edition (von Hees, 91–6). It is not yet possible to say exactly how many manuscript versions there are, but there are clearly many more than the four that Ruska enumerated. However many versions there may be, the general observation can nonetheless be made that the earlier manuscripts place comparatively greater emphasis on natural history, whereas the later ones place comparatively greater emphasis on oddities. Thus, Wüstenfeld's decision to include many passages from later manuscripts in his published version has resulted in an edition that has a much greater emphasis on oddities than Qazwīnī's original cosmography. This has unfortunately led to widespread misunderstandings about the emphases of the original book, since much of the secondary scholarship on it is based on Wüstenfeld's version. There are also less widely available editions published in the Arab world, but none that the present author has found to portray the text as it appears in any single early manuscript. Therefore, it is desirable to study Qazwīnī's cosmography as much as possible from early manuscripts.

It has long been recognized that the manuscript on which an authoritative published version should be based is Munich cod. arab. 464. Dated 1280, it is the only dated manuscript to survive from Qazwīnī's lifetime. The appearance of his name and titles in the opening rosette indicate that it was his personal copy, and it is almost complete. The present author suggests that the missing passages should be filled in by reference to a newly found manuscript dated 1322, Süleymaniye Yeni Cami 813, which is also almost complete (Berlekamp, *Proceedings from the Arab Painting Conference,* ed. Contadini, forthcoming). Folio-by-folio comparison of the texts in the two manuscripts shows that they contain the same version of the text.

On the basis of these two manuscripts, the original outline of the cosmography is as follows. It begins with a preface that contains separate expositions of the key terms of the title, which are also the overarching themes of the book: wonder *(al-'ajab)*, created things *(al-makhlūqāt)*, odd things *(al-gharīb)*, and existing things *(al-mawjūdāt)*. In accordance with this, the bulk of the book consists of encyclopedia entries about separate created wonders that are presented according to the classifications of creation to which they belong, which in turn are organized according to a cosmographic hierarchy. The first part deals with "things above," whereas the second deals with "things below." The "things above" are organized into chapters about the planets, the fixed stars of the northern and southern hemispheres, the lunar mansions, the angels, and time. The "things below" are divided into sections about the four elements of fire, air, water, and earth. The fire section is the shortest and contains no subchapters. The air section treats such phenomena as winds, thunder, lightning, the aureole of the sun, and the rainbow. The water section starts with a preliminary chapter about the surrounding ocean and then continues with additional chapters about other seas (the China Sea, the Indian Ocean, the Persian Sea, the Red Sea, the Sea of Zanzibar, the Mediterranean Sea, and the Caspian Sea), with subsections about the islands and characteristic inhabitants of each; it concludes with a section about sea creatures in general. The earth section includes subchapters addressing differing opinions as to how the earth is laid out, the regions and climes of the earth, earthquakes and the sinking in of the ground, mountains, rivers, springs, and wells. These subchapters are followed by those about beings born of mothers. The first such discuss metals and stones (which were understood to have been born of the earth). These are followed by plants: first trees and then small plants. These in turn are followed by animals, classified as follows: people; riding animals; livestock; predatory animals; birds; creepers (such as insects and rodents); and, finally, a concluding section about strangely formed breeds. In Munich cod. arab. 464, a passage about jinn written on later paper and in a later hand is inserted between those about people and riding animals. In Süleymaniye Yeni Cami 813, the text is continuous from people to riding animals, demonstrating that the passage about jinn was a later addition to the text of Munich cod. arab. 464 rather than a replacement for a lost original folio.

The illustrations found in different manuscripts of the cosmography vary considerably. Their significance varies from one manuscript to the next, shifting with changes in the history of the text and with changes in audience. However, taken together, they do challenge two assertions that are often made about manuscript painting in Islamic societies: that it appears in secular contexts and that its audiences were limited to the princely courts. In its original context and version, the cosmography was a deeply religious text, with each wonder presented as a sign pointing to the greatness of its Creator; illustrations of these created wonders appear throughout Qazwīnī's own copy of this text, although Qazwīnī himself was a judge and professor of Islamic law and was not associated with any princely court. Although the overall character of the text shifts in its later history, subsequent illustrated copies vary widely in their quality, suggesting that they were made for audiences at a variety of social levels.

As for the geography, Wüstenfeld's edition of it is also considered problematic, and rightly so. The version entitled *The Wonders of the Lands ('Ajā'ib al-Buldān)* is recognized as an older version than that entitled *The Monuments of the Lands and the Annals of [God's] Servants (Āthār al-Bilād wa-Akhbār al-'Ibād),* but Wüstenfeld's edition is based on various manuscripts of *The Monuments of the Lands and the Annals of [God's] Servants.* It will not be known what the implications of Wüstenfeld's problematic choice of manuscript sources have been for secondary scholarship on the geography until intensive study of the early manuscripts is undertaken. Meanwhile, the geography as it occurs in Wüstenfeld's edition can be described as follows. It is organized according to the earth's seven climes, with descriptions of the cities, countries, mountains, and rivers of each. Included in the descriptions of the cities and countries are short biographies of the famous luminaries who came from them.

PERSIS BERLEKAMP

Primary Sources

Ibn al-Fuwaṭī, Kamal al-Din. *Al-Ḥawādith al-Jāmi'a,* ed. Muṣṭafa Jawād. Baghdad: al-Maktaba al-'Arabīya, 1351/1932.

Ibn Taghrībirdī, [Abū Muḥasin] Yūsuf. *al-Manhal al-Ṣafī wa-al-Mustawfā baʿda al-Wāfī*, vol. 5. Cairo, 1988.

Katip Çelebi, aka Ḥajjī al-Khalīfa. *Kashf al-Ẓunūn*, 6 vols., vol. 2. Beirut: Dār al-Kutub al-ʿIlmīya, 1413/1992.

Qazwīnī, Zakarīya b. Muḥammad. *Die Wunder des Himmels und der Erde*, transl. Alma Giese. Stuttgard: Thienemann, Edition Erdmann, 1986.

Qazwīnī, Zakarīya b. Muḥammad. "Kitāb ʿAjāʾib al-Makhlūqāt. Die Wunder der Schöpfung." In *Zakarija Ben Muhammed Ben Mahmud el-Cazwini's Kosmographie. Erster Theil*, ed. Ferdinand Wüstenfeld. Göttingen, 1849.

Qazwīnī, Zakarīya b. Muḥammad. "Kitāb Āthār al-Buldān. Die Denkmäler der Länder." In *Zakarija Ben Muhammed Ben Mahmud el-Cazwini's Kosmographie. Erster Theil*, ed. Ferdinand Wüstenfeld. Göttingen, 1848.

Further Reading

"ʿAdjāʾib." In *EI2*.

"Adjāʾeb al-Makhlūqāt." In *Encyclopedia Iranica*.

Badiee, Julie. "Angels in an Islamic Heaven." *Bulletin of the Los Angeles County Museum XXIV* (1978).

———. "The Sarre Qazwini: An Early Aq Qoyunlu Manuscript?" *Ars Orientalis* 14 (1984): 97–113.

———. *An Islamic Cosmography: The Illustrations of the Sarre Qazwini*. PhD dissertation. The University of Michigan, 1978.

Berlekamp, Persis. *Wonders and Their Images in Late Medieval Islamic Culture: 'The Wonders of Creation' in Fars and Iraq, 1280–1388*. PhD dissertation. Cambridge, Mass: Harvard University, 2003.

———. "From Iraq to Fars: Tracking Cultural Transformations Through the 1322 Qazwini *'Ajā'ib* Manuscript, Süleymaniye Yeni Cami 813." *Proceedings of the Arab Painting Conference*, ed. Anna Contadini. Forthcoming.

Bothmer, Hans-Caspar Graf von. *Die Illustrationen des 'Münchener Qazwīnī' von 1280 (cod. Monac. arab 464): Ein Beitrag zur Kenntnis Ihres Stils*. PhD dissertation. Universität München, 1971.

Carboni, Stefano. "Constellations, Giants and Angels from al-Qazwini Manuscripts." In *Islamic Art in the Ashmolean Museum*, ed. James Allan, 83–97. Oxford, UK: Oxford University Press, 1995.

———. "The London Qazwīnī: An Early Fourteenth Century Copy of the 'Ajā'ib al-Makhlūqāt." *Islamic Art* III (1988–1989): 15–31.

———. *The Wonders of Creation and the Singularities of Ilkhanid Painting: A Study of the London Qazwini British Library Ms. Or. 14140*. PhD dissertation. London: School of Oriental and African Studies, University of London, 1992.

Carboni, Stefano, and Anna Contadini. "An Illustrated Copy of al-Qazwīnī's *The Wonders of Creation*." *Sotheby's Art at Auction 1989–1990* (1990): 228–33.

von Hees, Syrinx. *Enzyklopädie als Spiegel des Weltbildes: Qazwīnīs Wunder der Schöpfung- eine Naturkunde des 13. Jahrhunderts. Vol. 4, Diskurse der Arabistik*. Wiesbaden: Harrossowitz Verlag, 2002.

"Kazwīnī." *Encyclopedia of Islam*.

"Kazwīnī." *EI2*.

Rhürdanz, Karin. "Zwei Illustrierte Qazwīnī-Handschriften in Sammlungen der DDR." *Persica* X (1982): 97–114, Abb. 1–9.

de Ruita, Jan Jaap. "Human Embryology in Zakariyā Al-Qazwīnī's 'The Marvels of Creation.'" *Tidjsdrift Voor de Faxhindeus du Geneeskunde, Naturwaterschappen, Wirkunde in Fedurick* 9 (1986): 99–117.

Ruska, Julius. "Über den Falschen und den Echten Kazwīnī." *Mitteilungen zur Geschichte der Medizin und der Naturwissenschaften (Leipzig/Hamburg)* 13 (1914): 183–8.

Sezgin, Fuat, ed. *Studies on Zakarīyā b. Muḥammad al-Qazwīnī (d. 1283)*. Frankfurt am Main, 1994.

QUR'AN

The Qur'an is sacred scriptural text of all forms of Islam, a compilation of the revelations given to the Prophet Muhammad. The term *Qur'an* probably means "reading" or "recitation," and it is etymologically linked both to the Syriac *qeryana* (scripture reading) and the Hebrew *miqra'* (recitation, scripture).

The Qur'an is made up of 114 surahs (chapters), which range in length from three short verses to 286 or 287 relatively long verses (depending upon how those verses are counted). The chapters are arranged roughly in order of decreasing length. Because the length of Muhammad's revelations tended to increase with the passage of time, this means that the later chapters, in terms of the moment of their reception by the Prophet, occur toward the front of the standard editions of the book, whereas the earliest revelations are found toward the back.

The Historical Origins of the Qur'an

According to traditional accounts, the divine messenger of revelation (subsequently identified as the archangel Gabriel) first appeared to Muhammad when the Prophet was approximately forty years old (in or near 610 CE). It is generally agreed that this appearance constitutes Muhammad's call as a messenger of God, and that Qur'an verse 96: 1–5 represents the first portion of the Qur'an revealed to the Prophet. Thereafter, revelation came in various ways. The earliest chroniclers report that Muhammad would enter a trancelike state during which he would receive his divine communications. Sometimes he saw visions, but, overwhelmingly, his revelatory experiences were auditory. One well-known account, for instance, describes a sound like the ringing of bells, which conveyed to him the words that he would dictate and that would eventually be written down.

Establishing the precise chronology of Qur'anic revelations is a very difficult matter. The chapters of the Qur'an have traditionally been divided into those received at Mecca (i.e., prior to Muhammad's hijra in

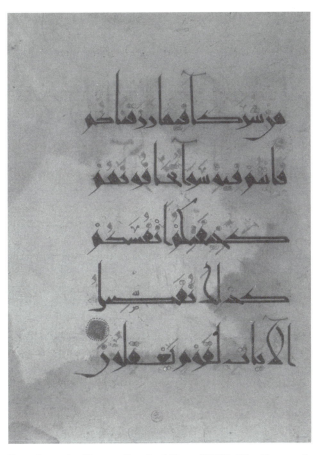

Page from the Koran. Surah al-Rum (XXX, The Romans), verses 24 and 25:...after it (the earth) is dead: verily in that are signs for those who are wise. And among His signs is this, that heaven and earth stand at his command. Then when he calls you by a single call from the earth...Kiric writing. Persian, eleventh century CE. (CT 7886). Credit: Victoria & Albert Museum, London/Art Resource, NY. Victoria and Albert Museum, London, Great Britain.

622 CE) and those received during his exile at Medina. Western scholarship, in turn, has distinguished between early, middle, and late Meccan revelations, but many questions remain and are perhaps insoluble. The process of revelation indisputably ended with Muhammad's death in 632 CE, which closed the Qur'anic canon.

There is some controversy about how early Muhammad's revelations began to be committed to writing. Traditional accounts depict his early followers as memorizing his revelations—memorizing the Qur'an in its entirety remains a highly honored achievement even today—but also portray them as recording the revelations in whatever medium they were able to locate in seventh-century central Arabia (e.g., on the shoulder blades of camel skeletons, on palm fronds). However long the period of principally oral transmission, however (assuming that one

occurred), it was effectively ended by very early efforts to collect and standardize the Qur'anic revelations. These culminated in the promulgation of an official text within approximately two decades of Muhammad's death, under the third caliph, 'Uthman (r. 644–656 CE). With, for the most part, only relatively minor adjustments of versification and orthography, the 'Uthmanic recension has had the field to itself since the mid-seventh century—partially, no doubt, because competing versions were destroyed for the sake of maintaining unity within the rapidly expanding and diversifying Muslim community.

The Theological Status of the Qur'an in Islam

In Muslim belief, the historical earthly Qur'an is a transcript from the umm al-kitab (the "mother of the Book"), the celestial archetype from which the original scriptures of the other "peoples of the Book" (e.g., the Torah of Moses and the Gospel of Jesus) were also derived. (Those original Jewish and Christian scriptures have since become corrupted.) The Qur'an is seen as complementing and completing earlier divine revelations. It is a reaffirmation (musaddiq) of what went before (5:44–8) and a reminder (dhikr) to those who pay heed.

Muslims also believe the Qur'an to be the literal word of God in the highest possible sense, the divine utterance that has existed for all eternity. Accordingly, it is inerrant, and even the physical book that contains the text is holy, to be approached only in purity and with some degree of awe, and to be disposed of, when that is required, with proper reverence. Indeed, given the importance of the Qur'an as the word of the transcendent God made manifest in this world, some have suggested that its analogue in Christian theology is not so much the Bible but rather the divinely incarnate Word (Christ, the Johannine Logos) itself.

Among the central themes of the Qur'an are the divine tawhid (unity, rigorously pure monotheism), demands for ethical behavior and social justice, the coming universal physical resurrection, the inescapable final judgment, and the final rewards of both the faithful and the unfaithful. The Meccan revelations tend to be terse and apocalyptic, frequently drawing notice to the signs of God's awesome power in nature; the Medinan revelations, as befitted Muhammad's new political role in that settlement, tend to greater discursiveness and give greater attention to political and legal topics. The Qur'an is neither a narrative or historical chronicle nor an anthology of the Prophet's meditations but rather a collection of relatively free-standing revelations in which God, speaking in the first-person plural, addresses Muhammad and, through him, the community of the faithful and ultimately the entire world. It is, however, replete with narratives (and, even more commonly, with allusive references to narratives with which the audience is presumed to be familiar) of God's actions in history, the exemplary missions of earlier prophets, and the earthly fates of those who failed to obey.

The Place of the Qur'an in the Muslim Community

Whereas the Jewish people created and shaped the Hebrew Bible and the Christian church created and shaped the New Testament, in a very real sense the Qur'an created and shaped the Muslim community. It played an essential role in the transformation of Arabic culture from orality to a deeply literate civilization, not only because it emphasizes books, pens (as witnessed by that first revealed text, 96:1–5), and writing, but because it established a written text—itself—at the foundation of the Arab/Islamic tradition. Moreover, such disciplines as rhetoric, grammar, and lexicography, which are often referred to as the "Islamic sciences," arose among Muslims first and foremost as tools for a precise understanding of the revealed book of God, a task perhaps made more urgent by the rapid conversion of peoples for whom Arabic was an acquired tongue.

Most fundamentally, however, the Qur'an is and, since the passing of the living prophetic voice from Islam that occurred with the death of Muhammad, has always been the ultimate religious authority within the Muslim community, the principal source for theology, and the unquestioned basis of Islamic law. As might be expected, its oracular statements and allusive references have generated a vast commentary literature as well as large numbers of other books about various aspects of its text and teachings. One notable genre is that of the "tales of the prophets," in which quasi-midrashic accounts of earlier messengers of God (drawn, for the most part, from the Jewish and Christian neighbors of their compilers) are supplied, no doubt—to some extent at least—in an attempt to flesh out the many stories to which the Qur'an alludes but does not fully recount.

Because it is literally the word of God, every individual word and every sound of the Qur'an is sacred to believing Muslims. (The Arabic word *ayah* [pl. *ayat*], which occurs several hundred times within the Qur'an itself, is frequently translated as "verse." Significantly, however, its essential meaning is "sign" or

"miracle.") For the same reason, speaking legally and theologically, the Qur'an is truly the Qur'an only in its original Arabic. In this form, however, it is considered not only inerrant but literarily unapproachable. (This is the doctrine known as the *i'jaz al-Qur'an* [inimitability of the Qur'an].) Thus, like their Arab co-believers, non-Arabic-speaking Muslims around the world study the reading of the Qur'an in its original language to be able to pronounce it correctly, even if their grasp of Arabic vocabulary and grammar remains weak. To recite the Qur'an well is a meritorious act—an entire discipline, called *'ilm al-tajwid,* has been developed to foster and regulate such recitation—and professional Qur'an reciters can and do become popular celebrities. Such recitation carries considerable emotional power for believers, and it is said to have brought more than a few nonbelievers (notable among them is 'Umar, the second of the orthodox caliphs) into Islam.

The Qur'an is used liturgically: in prayer, for recitation at funerals, during the holy fasting month of Ramadan, at the beginning of social and official functions, and, in modern times, at the beginning and end of broadcast days on both radio and television. Beautiful calligraphic renditions of Qur'anic passages adorn mosques and public monuments, and, because careful copying of the Qur'anic text on paper and other media is also recognized as a meritorious act, form one of the more important of the "minor" arts in Islamic civilization. The Qur'an is and has always been virtually omnipresent wherever Muslims live and work.

DANIEL C. PETERSON

See also Muhammad, the Prophet; Qur'an and Arabic Literature; Qur'an and Christians; Qur'an, Manuscripts; Qur'an, Reciters and Recitation; 'Uthman ibn 'Affan

Further Reading

Ayoub, Mahmoud M. *The Qur'an and Its Interpreters*, 2 vols. (to date). Albany, NY: State University of New York Press, 1984.

Burton, John. *The Collection of the Qur'an*. Cambridge, UK, and New York: Cambridge University Press, 1977.

Hawting, G.R., and Abdul-Kader A. Shareef, eds. *Approaches to the Qur'an*. London and New York: Routledge, 1993.

Izutsu, Toshihiko. *God and Man in the Koran: Semantics of the Koranic Weltanschauung.* Tokyo: Koio Institute of Cultural and Linguistic Studies, 1964.

Jeffrey, *The Qur'an as Scripture*. New York: R.F. Moore, 1952.

Jeffery, Arthur. *Materials for the History of the Text of the Qur'an.* Leiden: E.J. Brill, 1937.

Mir, Mustansir. *Dictionary of Qur'anic Terms and Concepts.* New York: Garland, 1987.

Nelson, Kristina. *The Art of Reciting the Qur'an.* Austin: University of Texas Press, 1985.

Nöldeke, Theodor. *Geschichte des Qorans*, revised ed. Hildesheim: Georg Olms Verlag, 1964.

Rahman, Fazlur. *Major Themes of the Qur'an.* Minneapolis: Bibliotheca Islamica, 1980.

Robinson, Neal. *Discovering the Qur'an: A Contemporary Approach to a Veiled Text*, 2nd ed. Washington, DC: Georgetown University Press, 2003.

Wansbrough, John E. *Quranic Studies: Sources and Methods of Scriptural Interpretation.* Oxford: Oxford University Press, 1977.

QUR'AN AND ARABIC LITERATURE

As God's revelation to the Prophet Muhammad, the Qur'an has a central place not only in piety and religious life but in language, education, and culture generally. It is considered the most exemplary model of the Arabic language, and it is not surprising that the influence of both its form and its content is felt throughout Arabic writing.

Medieval Arabic literature consisted mainly of poetry and belles-lettres. The former was well developed and highly regarded among the Arabs during pre-Islamic times and thus continued largely unchanged, enjoying pride of place in literary culture. Although there was little of what could be called fiction, prose genres also flourished, from short narrative anecdotes to highly ornate epistles. In all of these, one may discern Qur'anic phrases, motifs, and symbols, the scripture serving as a major component of the Arab/Islamic literary universe.

Poetry

The Qur'an appears to speak disparagingly of poets in 2:224–7: "And the poets! Attending them are those who lead astray/Have you not seen how they wander distraught in every valley/And they say that which they do not do/Except those who have believed and have done good works and remembered God frequently...." The Qur'an insists on its distinction from human or jinn-inspired poetry and soothsaying, but the above verses seem to acknowledge the permissibility of poetry, and most Qur'anic exegetes found ways of explaining these verses without condemning the art.

The main form of influence is iqtibas (borrowing). Although some legal objections to this practice are recorded, it was acceptable as long as the poet was not trying to imitate or compete with the revelation. The borrowing may consist of an entire Qur'anic verse or a part thereof or a word or phrase that conjures up, in the mind of one well acquainted with the scripture, a specific Qur'anic passage. Of course, the Arab writer could and did "borrow" equally from poetry, history, proverbs, and any other genre in the same fashion, but, as the Word of God, the Qur'an was at once the most familiar and the most prestigious and authoritative.

The basic form of Arabic poetry, the qasida (ode), was established before the rise of Islam and remained largely unchanged, and thus Qur'anic borrowing in poetry was subject to limitations imposed by thematic convention and poetic meter, often requiring alteration of wording or syntax. Nonetheless, from the earliest stages, there are numerous examples of poets employing Qur'anic phrases in their own verse. Sometimes these would be consistent with the themes of the revelation, especially in religious poetry or political polemic, but often it would simply provide a useful simile for the topic at hand. For example, from verse 54:7, "They shall come forth from the tombs as if they were scattered locusts," al-Hutay'a (d. c. 661) transferred the imagery from the eschatological to the military:

And there we were, when the horses came, as if they were scattered locusts, the wind behind them.

Sometimes the usage is tangential—if not antithetical—to the original context. Di'bal al-Khuza'i (d. 860) satirized the eighth 'Abbasid Caliph al-Mu'tasim by referring to the story of the People of the Cave, of whom the Qur'an (18:22) says, "They say, They were seven, and the eighth their dog."

In the books, the kings of the House of Abbas are seven, of an eighth no record has come. Likewise the people of the Cave were seven excellent men, and the eighth was [their] dog.

The "borrowing" could serve a thematic purpose on the level of meaning, or it could handily demonstrate the author's erudition as well as his skill in transforming the form or the context of the quotation, be it from poetry into prose or vice versa. Arab writers employed various kinds of rhetorical devices such as alliteration, antithesis, puns, and various figures of speech, and it was common to employ Qur'anic references for this purpose. For example, when a Kharijite poet says of his comrades, "Most faithful to their obligations when they make them; most abstemious in hardship *('usr)* and in ease *(yusr)*," he is evoking Qur'an verse 94:5–6: "Indeed, after hardship comes ease." However, because the Qur'anic pair of words are rhyming antonyms, he also uses the common devices of antithesis and alliteration. The original context of the verse is lost, but the symbolic resonance and rhetorical qualities of the Qur'anic terms are carried over to the poet's verse.

However, there were two poetic genres in which thematic aspects were especially important: ascetic poems (zuhdiyyat) and wine poems (khamriyyat). The former borrows heavily from those Qur'anic verses that speak of renunciation of worldly things but also extol fear of God and an awareness of mortality. The most famous of the ascetic poets was Abu l-'Atahiya (d. 826), and the following example shows his evocation (but not direct citation) of verse 31:34, "No soul knows in what land it shall die":

Would that I knew, for I know not which day will be the last of my life, Nor in which country my spirit will be taken, nor in which my tomb will be dug.

The ascetic poem flourished during the eighth and ninth centuries, after which Sufi and mystical themes were the main vehicles for piety in poetry. In these, Qur'anic references were also common although perhaps more subject to esoteric transformations.

Wine poetry is best represented by Abu Nuwas (d. c. 814), whose bacchanalian verse might seem an unlikely venue for Qur'anic influence. However, his frequent scriptural references can have thematic significance: his mischievous celebrations of hedonism and his defiance of religious morality are heightened by the irony of Qur'anic allusion.

Prose

The rising importance of Arabic as the language of the state meant that the new class of scribes in the empire's administration had to learn to write and express themselves according to nascent standards of eloquence. The Qur'an became one of—if not *the*—most important source of style, diction, motifs, and themes. The borrowing of scriptural references was especially prominent in the writings of 'Abd al-Hamid (d. 750), secretary of the Umayyad chancery, and his techniques of citing and elaborating Qur'anic passages set a precedent for much of subsequent Arabic prose. Without the restrictions of poetic meter and convention, Arabic prose writers enjoyed greater freedom in their adaptations of Qur'anic phrases, and they found much more room in various epistles and sermons for adopting themes of the Qur'an, such as the power of God, eschatology, ethical and theological topics, and prophetic history. Oratory lacking Qur'anic references could be deemed defective.

The popular "Tales of the Prophets" genre (qisas al-anbiya') consisted of narrative expansions and digressions that were based on the Qur'anic references to the biblical and Arabian prophets who preceded Muhammad. In other narratives, the Qur'an may be quoted as part of some witty repartee, as an expression of wisdom or piety, or as something apparently in between, such as in *The Book of Misers* of al-Jahiz (d. 869), where the Light Verse (24:35) serves as a kind of coda to a lesson about the efficient use of lamps and oil.

In terms of form, the maqamat genre (picaresque tales in complex rhymed prose) recalls the Qur'an not only in rhythm and measured movements but also in the myriad (and ambiguous) thematic and lexical allusions. Finally, Abu l-'Ala al-Ma□arri (d. 1057) and Ibn Shuhayd (d. 1035) deserve mention for works; their style, imagery, and homiletic vision are based squarely on the Qur'an, blending scriptural eschatology with elegant wit.

Literary Theory

The early or "ancient" poetry was held in high regard as an art in itself and, because it represented the pure and uncorrupted Arabic of the Bedouins, it was thought necessary for understanding Qur'anic language, among other things. However, the relationship between Qur'an and poetry became more complex as poetic styles changed and critics sought new ways to evaluate them. With the appearance of "modern" (muhdath) poetry during the latter part of the eighth century, some sought justification for new uses of tropes and figures (e.g., types of metaphor, paronomasia, antithesis) in the Qur'an and other "ancient" poetry or prose.

This use of the Qur'an as standard for literary style marked the beginnings of the doctrine of Qur'anic "inimitability" (i'jaz). The Qur'an asserts its own superiority in a number of places (10:38; 11:13; 52:33–4), but it was not until the late tenth century that the dogma was firmly formulated. In essence, it stated that the miracle of Muhammad's prophecy was the Qur'an, and the nature of that miracle lay in its stylistic perfection.

Among the major authors of works on Qur'anic inimitability were al-Rummani (d. 994), al-Khattabi (d. c. 996), and al-Baqillani (d. 1013), all of whom argued that the scripture's rhetorical features are greatly superior to their counterparts in mundane poetry. The study of Arabic rhetoric was thus of interest not only to literary critics but also to exegetes and theologians seeking explanations of Qur'anic language. For example, were the scripture's references to the "hand" or "face" of God to be taken literally or figuratively? Questions of metaphor could be asked for quite divergent reasons: some were concerned with the uniqueness of God's language, whereas others were interested in the figures and devices it shared with human poetry.

The literary and the theological interests found reconciliation in the work of the great 'Abd al-Qahir al-Jurjani (d. 1078), especially with regard to the theory of imagery and the relationship between syntax and semantics. During subsequent centuries, scholars continued to write poetic commentaries and criticism, but the framework for the more theoretical science of rhetoric was not poetry itself but rather a project of proving the superior eloquence of the Qur'an.

BRUCE FUDGE

Further Reading

von Grunebaum, G. E. "I'djaz." In *The Encyclopedia of Islam*, 2nd ed. Leiden: E.J. Brill, 1960.

———. *A Tenth-Century Document of Arabic Literary Criticism: The Sections on Poetry of al-Baqillani's I'jaz al-Qur'an.* Chicago: The University of Chicago Press, 1950.

Heinrichs, Wolfhart. "Arabic Poetics, Classical." In *The New Princeton Encyclopedia of Poetry and Poetics*, ed. Alex Preminger and T.V.F. Brogan. Princeton, NJ: Princeton University Press, 1993.

Kennedy, Philip F. *The Wine Song in Classical Arabic Poetry: Abu Nuwas and the Literary Tradition.* Oxford, UK: The Clarendon Press, 1997.

al-Qadi, Wadad. "The Impact of the Qur'an on the Epistolography of 'Abd al-Hamid." In *Approaches to the Qur'an*, ed. G.R. Hawting and Addul-Kader A. Shareef, 285–313. London: Routledge, 1993.

al-Qadi, Wadad, and Mustansir Mir. "Literature and the Qur'an." In *The Encyclopedia of the Qur'an*, ed. Jane Dammen McAuliffe. Leiden: E.J. Brill, 2001.

Sanni, Amidu. *The Arabic Theory of Prosification and Versification.* Beirut: Franz Steiner, 1998.

Schimmel, Annemarie. *As through a Veil: Mystical Poetry in Islam.* New York: Columbia University Press, 1982.

Shahid, Irfan. "The Sura of the Poets, Qur'an XXVI: Final Conclusions." *Journal of Arabic Literature* XXXV (2004): 175–220.

Zubaidi, A.M. "The Impact of the Qur'an and *Hadith* on Medieval Arabic Literature." In *The Cambridge History of Arabic Literature: Arabic Literature to the End of the Umayyad Period*, eds. A.F.L. Beeston et al., 322–43. Cambridge, UK: Cambridge University Press, 1983.

QUR'AN, RECITERS AND RECITATION

The most common word for a reciter of the Qur'an is *qari'* (pl. *qurra'*), whereas recitation is most commonly referred to as *tilawa* and *qira'a*. Other terms used for reciters are *ahl al-Qur'an* (people of the Qur'an), *hamalat al-Qur'an* (bearers of the Qur'an), and *huffaz* (those who have memorized the Qur'an; sing. *hafiz*). The later term *muqri'* (pl. *muqri'un*) is used for a proficient—and usually professional—reciter of the Qur'an. The high religious and social status of the Qur'an reciter is indicated in the following hadith

(tradition) related by Anas b. Malik, in which the Prophet states, "Indeed there are people from among the general population who belong to God." The people assembled inquired, "And who are they, O Messenger of God?" He said, "The people of the Qur'an are the people of God and His elect."

The term *qurra'* also appears to refer to an early religiopolitical faction that was active during the first two civil wars. A considerable number of them joined the Khawarij during the Battle of Siffin in AH 37/657 CE that was fought between 'Ali and Mu'awiya.

Chapters in hadith works and individual monographs that deal with the excellences of the Qur'an (fada'il al-Qur'an) often have valuable information to impart about early recitational practices and the religious merits and social status earned by the pious reciter, both professional and nonprofessional. The *S.ahih* of al-Bukhari, for example, records hadiths that deal with a wide variety of topics pertaining to Qur'an recitation in the chapter entitled *Kitab Fada'il al-Qur'an (The Book of the Excellences of the Qur'an).* Some reports discuss the manner of revelation and what was first revealed and that the Qur'an was revealed in the tongue of the Quraysh and in seven variant dialects (sab'at ah ruf). It describes the compilation and recording of the Qur'anic text, and it refers to the Qur'an reciters from among the Companions. Other sections (babs) deal with the merits of individual surahs (chapters), such as al-Fatiha and al-Baqara; sections follow that discuss the descent of godly tranquility (sakina) and the angels on those who recite or read the Qur'an. It is stated that the only bequest of the Prophet was the written Qur'anic text (ma bayna 'l-daffatayn). There is a discussion of the excellence of the Qur'an over the rest of speech, of the desirability of chanting the Qur'an, and of the joy of the people of the Qur'an (ahl al-Qur'an). There are traditions concerning the excellence of those who learn and teach the Qur'an, memorize it, and are faithful to its injunctions. Other traditions warn against forgetting the Qur'an, talk about referring to the Qur'anic chapters by their names, the various modes of recitation, and the amount of the Qur'an to be recited at a time.

Such meticulous attention to the modes and etiquette of recitation as is apparent in the reports recorded by al-Bukhari testifies to the importance of this pious activity in both individual and communal religious practices.

The Professional Qurra'

The historian al-Tabari describes the rise of professional qurra' already by the time of the second caliph,

'Umar (d. 644), who appointed a separate qari' for men and women; it is not clear if they were compensated for their activities. The early literature, however, shows a great deal of ambivalence toward the notion of earning a livelihood through the teaching of the Qur'an. Reports that express pious aversion to this practice are plentiful in the literature. Thus, Ibn 'Abbas is quoted as relating the following from the Prophet: "If one to whom God teaches the Qur'an should complain of poverty, God will inscribe poverty between his eyes until the Day of Resurrection." However, a countertradition explicitly states what the ideal wage should be for the professional Qur'an reciter. In this report from 'Ali, the Prophet remarks, "Whoever recites the Qur'an receives two hundred dinars. If he is not given this amount in this world, then he will be given it in the next." The scholars were in fact divided over this sensitive issue. According to al-Qurtubi (d. 671/1273), al-Zuhri (124/742), Abu Hanifa (d. 150/767), and their companions were against the practice of receiving wages, because teaching the Qur'an is "one of the religious duties" (wajib min al-wajibat), and receipt of wages for it would be as unacceptable as being remunerated for prayer and fasting. On the other hand, Malik, al-Shafi'i, Ahmad b. Hanbal, and Abu Thawr acknowledged the permissibility of receiving wages on the basis of a hadith related by Ibn 'Abbas and recorded by al-Bukhari, which states, "Indeed it is the Book of God for which you have the greatest right to accept wages." These reports preserve for us the vestiges of a pietistic reaction against the increasing "professionalization" and "commercialization" of the teaching of the Qur'an. There is an implicit—and not-so-implicit—assumption that the professional qurra' and the 'ulama' in general master the Qur'an mainly to enhance their scholarly reputations and for monetary aggrandizement, a trend that is vilified in many traditions. Among the professional qurra' must be counted the early qussas (storytellers, popular preachers), who were appointed as religious functionaries in the mosque and whose task, among others, was to publicly recite passages from the Qur'an and interpret them.

Variant Readings of the Qur'an

The literature mentions that the Qur'an in the early period was recited in sab'at ahruf; this phrase is understood to signify the seven "dialects" in which the early Muslims are said to have recited the Qur'an until the Qurayshi dialect became the standard one. Medieval Arabic sources maintain a clear distinction between the ahruf and the qira'at, the latter being the variant readings recognized to this day. The distinction and the connection between these two concepts are not fully understood in the current time and are in need of a meticulous study for a better understanding of the early history of Qur'anic recitational modes. By the fourth/tenth century, the seven most recognized qira'at of the Qur'anic text had developed, to which an additional three are sometimes appended. These readings are occasionally attributed to Companions like Ibn Mas'ud and Ubay b. Ka'b but more commonly to expert reciters of the second/eighth century. The list of the ten experts from which these recognized readings emanate is as follows:

1. Nafi' ibn 'Abd al-Rahman (d. c. 169/785–786), Medinese
2. 'Abd Allah b. Kathir al-Dari (d. 120/737–738), Meccan
3. Abu 'Amr Zabban b. al-'Ala (d. c. 154/770–771), Basran
4. 'Abd Allah b. 'Amir (d. 118/736), Damascene
5. 'Asim b. Abi al-Najud Bahdalah (d. c. 127/744–745), Kufan
6. Hamza b. Habib (d. c.156/772–773), Kufan
7. 'Ali b. Hamza al-Kisa' (d. c. 89/804–805), Kufan
8. Abu Ja'far Yazid b. al-Qa'qa' al-Makhzumi (d. c. 130/747–748), Medinese
9. Ya'qub b. Ishaq al-Hadrami (d. 205/820–821), Basran
10. Khalaf b. Hishm (d. 229/844), Baghdadi

Manner of Recitation

The classic science of Qur'anic recitation is referred to as *tajwid* (literally "making beautiful"), which requires "giving each sound its correct weight and measure." Recitation handbooks such as those composed by Ibn Mujahid (d. 324/936) and al-Dani (d. 444/1052) began to appear during the fourth/eleventh century; these detailed, among other things, the correct vocalization of letters, the proper length of vowels, and the points of articulation of sounds (makharij al-sawt). Consonants with the same points of articulation are often assimilated (idgham), and there are particular rules for nasalization (ghunna). The Qur'anic text (mushaf) indicates many of these conventions through special symbols. Styles of recitation vary from one another, usually on the basis of their relative rapidity. The term *hadr* refers to a faster pace of recitation that is often adopted during the daily prayers (salat) as compared with tartil (murattal), which refers to a slower pace used for studying and memorization.

Some of the sources indicate that ceremonies that frequently marked an individual's conclusory reading/recitation of the Qur'an (khatm al-Qur'an) and its public witnessing were frowned upon during the early period as an unbecoming show of piety. However counter-reports occur in the later literature that counsel, for example, that one's family be invited to witness the conclusion of an individual's Qur'an recitation, indicating a change in attitude. One such a report cited is from Qatada, who related that a man was once reciting the Qur'an in the mosque of the Prophet while Ibn 'Abbas kept watch over him. When the man expressed his desire to complete the Qur'an, Ibn 'Abbas told his seated companions to rise and attend the concluding recitation. Some reports also suggest that early Qur'an recitations left out inflectional endings (i'rab); later scholars discouraged this practice and advocated full inflection.

The following noteworthy hadith related by Ibn 'Umar served as an important proof text in which the Prophet stated, "For whomever recites the Qur'an without full declension, the attending angel records for him 'as revealed' with ten merits for each letter; for whomever declines only part of the Qur'an, two angels are assigned to him who write down for him twenty merits; and for whomever declines the [entire] Qur'an, four angels are assigned to him who record seventy merits for each letter." A certain hardening of the attitude is perceived in some scholars who are not named and who are quoted by al-Qurtubi as saying, "Declension of the Qur'an is a fundament of the religious law *(al-shari'a)* because through it its meaning is established which is the Revelation *(al-shar'a)*." Certainly by the seventh/thirteenth century, when al-Qurtubi lived, the *scriptio plena* had become the normal—and normative—feature of the sacred text, so much so that the absence of its distinctive features—desinential inflection and diacriticization—came to be regarded as a textual deficiency and aberration.

ASMA AFSARUDDIN

Primary Sources

Al-Nawawi. *al-Tibyan fi Adab Hamalat al-Qur'an*, ed. al-Khuli. Cairo, 1976.

Ibn al-Jazari. *Ghayat al-Nihaya fi Tabaqat al-Qurra'*, ed. Gotthelf Bergsträßer. Cairo, 1351–1352/1932–1933.

Further Reading

Afsaruddin, Asma. "The Excellences of the Qur'an." *JAOS* 122 (2002): 1–24.

Denny, Frederick M. "The *Adab* of Qur'ân Recitation: Text and Context." In *International Congress for the Studies of the Qur'ân*, series 1, eds. A.H. Johns and Syed Husain M. Jafri, 143–60. Canberra, 1980.

Juynboll, G.H.A. "The Position of Qur'an Recitation in Early Islam." *JSS* 20 (1974): 240–51.

Melchert, Christopher. "Ibn Mujahid and the Establishment of Seven Qur'anic Readings." *Studia Islamica* 91 (2000): 5–22.

Nelson, Kristina. *The Art of Reciting the Qur'an.* Austin, 1985.

QUTB MINAR

Mosque

A Muslim army occupied Sind in 711, and Islam subsequently expanded its rule along the Indus River. By the beginning of the eleventh century, the Ghaznavid dynasty (977–c. 1150) controlled Afghanistan, the Punjab, and Sind, and between 1007 and 1027 Sultan Mahmud of Ghazna conducted more than twenty raids into northern India, destroyed many Hindu and Jain temples, and acquired enormous booty for his Turkic homeland. The Ghaznavids were energetic patrons of architecture, and two impressive minars still stand in Ghazna.

The successor Ghurid dynasty (c. 1100–1215) embellished its lands with buildings as well, most notably during the late twelfth century with the towering minar of Djam in their capital city of Firuzkuh in Afghanistan. Inscribed with the entire surah Maryam (Qur'an 19:1–98), the minar's epigraphs put particular emphasis on the prophetic tradition leading up to Muhammad and proclaim the unique role of Muhammad as the bearer of the final divine revelation. The Ghurid sultan defeated the Hindu army under Rai Pithora at the second battle of Tarain in 1192, supplanted the Rajput ruler of Delhi, and established a capital there. The new territory was governed as a Ghurid fief by General Qutb al-Din Aybak, a literate and manumitted mercenary slave, until 1206, when he established an independent sultanate. Under his rule, Islamic domain expanded rapidly in northern India.

On the site of the eleventh- and twelfth-century Lal Kot (Red Fort) of Delhi, the Ghurids ordered the construction of a jami' mosque to serve the new Muslim population and to demonstrate the new order of faith and governance. Now known as the Quwwat al-Islam (Might of Islam) mosque or the Qutb mosque, from the twelfth until the middle of the seventeenth century it was more simply identified as the jami' mosque of Delhi, and it served as the city's principal congregational mosque until Shah Jahan constructed his great mosque further to the north in Mughal Delhi's Shahjahanabad in 1650 to 1656.

The old jami' mosque's original courtyard supplanted not only the Hindu fortress but also a Vaishnavite temple. As an inscription on the building testifies, most of the red sandstone building materials for the new mosque came from twenty-seven demolished temples in and around Delhi. Additional epigraphic evidence names Qutb al-Din Aybak as the commander who ordered the construction of the mosque in 1192 and his sovereign Mu'izz al-Din as its patron in 1197. These two dates allow for the establishment of the initial dimensions of the early mosque. Four arcades framed a rectangular courtyard pointing in the direction of prayer, and the pillars supporting the arcades' roof and domes came from Hindu and Jain temples. In keeping with Islam's avoidance of figural imagery in a sacred context, the building's work crews, which were almost entirely Hindu, chiseled away or plastered over the pillars' figural art. Despite this refurbishing, the second Delhi sultan, Iltutmish (1210–1235), decided that the qiblah arcade should be altered to approximate mosque aesthetics in the Ghurid homeland. An enormous five-arched stone screen that was richly decorated with incised ornament and inscriptions in angular and cursive styles was erected in front of the qiblah. The screen's central arch was notably taller than the flanking arches, and some ten meters in front of it was an eleventh-century iron pillar, once topped with an image of Garuda, the Hindu god of victory. With the statue removed, the iron pillar remained in the mosque as a remarkable trophy and permanent testimony to victory.

The epigraphic program of the screen consists of both Qur'anic selections and hadith (tradition) and should be read like a huge open book: it is visual support for the imam leading the community in prayer. Hadith underscores the importance of building mosques, whereas citations from the Qur'an present several themes: divine sovereignty; divine support for Muslim victory; warnings to all nonbelievers and opponents of Islam that their disbelief will bring them defeat and destruction; a promise of paradise to believers; and the obligations of faith and the times of prayer. In essence, this quotation of scripture reinforces Islam's political and social agenda in occupying Delhi and its environs. It presents an appropriate and very careful selection from Qur'an and hadith that must have been the responsibility of the sultan, advised by learned persons such as the Muslim judge (qadi) who accompanied the army. Iltutmish was known for his piety and for his support of the Hanafi madhhab (rite). That very few persons were literate and that the inscriptions were rendered in styles that only the highly educated could read did not pose a problem; for most believers, the visible presence of holy writ was more important than specific content.

Minar

If the mosque's courtyard presented the obligations of the faith to believers, then the great minar was a visible statement of Islam's victory to the surrounding countryside and its former Hindu rulers. With a diameter of 14.32 meters at its base and a height of 72.5 meters, it towered over the entire complex. Like its Ghaznavid and Ghurid predecessors—especially the somewhat shorter minar of Djam—it marked the surrounding landscape as part of the realm of Islam. In the original mosque, it stood outside of the southeast corner, but Iltutmish's extension brought it within the walls. Its five distinct stories delineate much of the history of Islam in Delhi. According to Persian and Arabic historical inscriptions on the lower three stories, the first story was completed under the authority of the Ghurid Sultan Mu'izz al-Din b. Sam and Qutb al-Din Aybak, whereas the second and third stories were constructed under the patronage of Sultan Iltutmish. Most of the fourth and all of the present fifth story were the result of repairs ordered by Sultan Firuz Shah (1351–1388) after the top of the minar was severely damaged by lightning.

Its 379 steps provide access to four overhanging balconies that are supported by elaborate projecting muqarnas (honeycomb or stalactite) brackets. Each of the stories is visually unique. The first story was decorated with alternating wedge-shaped flanges and semicircular fluting. The second story was ringed only with fluting, and the third story was solely ornamented with flanges. The fourth story is circular but clothed in white marble, whereas the final story is a composite design. Ten times the height of the iron pillar, the minar stood as a gigantic symbol of victory, and, with the morning light, its shadow moved across the prayer wall's face and touched the pillar.

Extensive Qur'anic and historical inscriptions cover the exterior of the first two stories, where sharp-eyed and experienced viewers could have read them. Placement and styles of script suggest that the designers came from Khurasan in northeastern Iran. Several themes occur on the first story: God's uniqueness, omniscience, and omnipotence; God's power to create and maintain life; the obligations of prayer and faithful adherence to Islam; Islam's victory; the promise of paradise to the faithful; and warnings to disbelievers and idolators that a terrible fate awaits them (this theme in particular occurs again and again). Notably, Qur'an verses 258–60 refer to the prophet Abraham's devotion to monotheism and his destruction of idols; this is a very pointed object lesson for those that Islam considered polytheists in northern India.

Later History

Successor to the Mu'izzi sultans, the Khalji dynasty's most important ruler, 'Ala' al-Din Muhammad (1296–1318), initiated the construction of a second minar that would have risen to at least twice the height of the Qutb minar. Never completed, its giant stump stands in a northern section of 'Ala' al-Din's expansion of the mosque. Other planned extensions would have included a doubling of the size of the qiblah screen and the construction of four cubic and domed gateways. Only one of these gateways, the 'Alai Gate, still stands on the southern side of the mosque; its red sandstone and marble exterior and interior walls are elaborately inscribed. 'Ala' al-Din's wars in the south had brought unparalleled wealth back to Delhi, and the sultan used much of it to start his massive building program at the early mosque. Qur'anic verses and Persian inscriptions refer repeatedly to the destruction of idolators' temples. Other inscriptions focus on belief and disbelief, paradise, pilgrimage, the truth of the Revelation, and the benefits of prayer. Again and again, nonbelievers are promised dire punishment for eternity, whereas believers are offered the joys of paradise.

In the southwest corner of the complex, 'Ala' al-Din also constructed a madrasa that probably contains his own tomb. Well into the sixteenth century, the Qutb mosque remained the center of belief and a symbol of Islam's power. On its periphery over the course of three centuries were constructed numerous mosques, water tanks, and tombs that make it a virtual necropolis of the wealthy and powerful and one of the richest repositories of Islamic architecture anywhere in the world.

During the British Raj, the Qutb mosque and minar were admired and beautified as picturesque ruins. The old jami' mosque became a popular picnic place, and Indian and British painters produced hundreds of surviving views of the site. This marked the beginning of its transformation into a major tourist site; the Qutb minar has become a revenue generator in India that is second only to the Taj Mahal.

ANTHONY WELCH

See also Afterlife; Abu Hanifa; Arabic; Arabs; Architecture, Religious; Baraka; Conquest; Delhi; Ghaznavids; God; Hadith; Hindus; Imam; India; Khurasan; Madrasa; Mahmud of Ghazna; Mosques; Muhammad, the Prophet; Muslim Community and Polity (Umma); Persian; Persians; Prayer; Qur'an; Razia Sultana; Scriptural Exegesis, Islamic; Slavery (Military); Slaves and Slave Trade, Eastern Islamic World; Sunni Revival; Turkestan; Turks

Further Reading

Brown, Percy. *Indian Architecture (The Islamic Period)*. Bombay: D.B. Taraporevala Sons, 1942.

Maricq, André, and Gaston Wiet. *Le Minar de Djam*, Paris: Mémoires de la Delegation Archéologique Française en Afghanistan, 1959.

Nath, R. *History of Sultanate Architecture*. New Delhi: Abhinav Publications, 1978.

Page, J.A. *An Historical Memoir on the Qutb: Delhi*, vol. 22. Calcutta: Memoirs of the Archaeological Survey of India, 1926.

Welch, Anthony, Hussein Keshani, and Alexandra Bain. "Epigraphs, Scripture, and Architecture in the Early Delhi Sultanate." *Muqarnas, an Annual on the Visual Culture of the Islamic World* 19 (2002): 12–43.

R

RANIRI, AL-, NUR AL-DIN (D. 1658)

Nur al-Din Muhammad ibn 'Ali ibn Hasanji ibn Muhammad al-Raniri (d. 1658) was a scholar and religious reformer who was influential in the religious affairs of the Malay Peninsula and the Indonesian Archipelago. He was born in the port city of Rander in Gujarat, India, in the late 1500s to a father of South Arabian and Indian ancestry and probably to a Malay mother. Little is known of al-Raniri's early life, but he was likely already studying in Arabia when he performed the hajj in 1620. He was a member of the Shafi'i rite, of the Ash'ari theological school, and of the Rifa'iyya Sufi order.

In 1637, al-Raniri arrived in Acheh, North Sumatra, the most important sixteenth- and seventeenth-century Southeast Asian center of Islam since the fall of Malacca in 1511. Acheh's ruler, Sultan Iskandar Thani (r. 1637–1641), appointed al-Raniri to the highest religious office, and al-Raniri immediately set about to purge heterodox Sufi pantheistic ideas (wujudiyya), which had been popularized by the Malay poet Hamza Fansuri (fl. 1550–1600) and by his followers Shams al-din of Pasai (d. 1629) and 'Abd al-Ra'uf al-Singkili (d. c. 1693). Al-Raniri had holders of heretical views banished and some possibly burned at the stake.

During his time in Acheh (and, later, Pahang on the Malay Peninsula), al-Raniri wrote eighteen of his twenty-one works. The *al-Sirat al-Mustaqim (Straight Path)*, in which he itemizes rules of orthodox belief, contributed to the Islamization of Kedah (on the peninsula), and it continues to be popular in Southeast Asia. The polemical *Hujjat al-Siddiq li-Daf' al-Zindiq (Proof of the Veracious in Refutation of the Mendacious)*, was written between 1638 and 1641, and the *al-Tibyan fi ma'Rifat al-Adyan (The Exposition on Knowledge of Religions)* was commissioned by Iskandar Thani's successor, Queen Taj al-'Alam (r. 1641–1675). The Malayo-Arab scholar and polemicist S.M. Naquib al-Attas has characterized al-Raniri's critique of Hamza's teachings as distortions and the *Hujjat* as proof of al-Raniri's appetite for power. However, others view the issues taken up by al-Raniri against the backdrop of the religious and intellectual debates taking place in India, especially the ideas of Sirhindi.

Al-Raniri's longest work, the encyclopedic *Bustan al-Salatin fi Dhikr al-Awwalin wa-l-Akhirin (Garden of Kings Concerning Beginning and Ending)*, is the one that has begun to receive the most widespread attention. Commissioned by Iskandar Thani in 1638 and something of a "mirror for princes," it is divided into seven parts: (1) creation; (2) prophets and rulers; (3) just kings and wise ministers; (4) ascetic rulers and pious saints; (5) unjust rulers and oppressive ministers; (6) noble and generous people and brave men; and (7) intelligence, science, and the like. Because al-Raniri drew from numerous Arabic sources when compiling this work, it reveals a great deal about what was available in Acheh at the time.

Popular reaction to al-Raniri's measures was probably the reason he left Acheh for Rander in 1644. He died on September 21, 1658, but, a quarter century after his death, in 1684, a fatwa (legal opinion)—possibly sought by 'Abd al-Ra'uf al-Singkili—was issued in Medina condemning al-Raniri and his views.

SHAWKAT M. TOORAWA

See also Ibn 'Arabi; Malay Peninsula; Reform, or Islah; Sufism and Sufis; South Asia

Further Reading

al-Attas, Syed Muhammad al-Naquib. *A Commentary on the Hujjat al-Siddiq of Nur al-Din al-Raniri*. Kuala Lumpur: Ministry of Culture, Malaysia, 1986.

Azra, Azyumardi. "The Transmission of Islamic Reformism to Indonesia. Networks of Middle Eastern and Malay-Indonesian 'Ulama' in the Seventeenth and Eighteenth Centuries." PhD dissertation. New York: Columbia University, 1992.

Iskandar, Teuku, ed. *Bustanu's-Salatin of Nur al-Din al-Raniri*. Kuala Lumpur: Dewan Bahasa dan Pustaka, 1966.

Vakili, Abdollah. "Sufism, Power Politics, and Reform: Al-Rânîrî's Opposition toHamzah al-Fansûrî's Teachings Reconsidered." *Studia Islamika* 4 (1997): 113–35.

RASHID AL-DIN

Rashid al-Din Fadl Allah Hamadani was a physician, historian, scholar, and chief administrative official to a series of Mongol Ilkhan rulers in Iran during the late thirteenth and early fourteenth centuries.

Biography

Born in 1248, Rashid al-Din grew up among the relatively prosperous Jewish community of medieval Hamadan in western Iran. From this time forward, Iran would be under the full control of the Mongol Ilkhan dynasty (1265–1335), and its somewhat ecumenical policies allowed assertive Christians and Jews to pursue professional careers with the Mongols as patrons. It is within this context that it must be understood how a Jewish convert to Islam would ultimately rise to the highest echelons of administrative power in the Mongol empire. Information about Rashid al-Din's early life is somewhat scant, but it is known that his father was an apothecary and that Rashid al-Din himself pursued medical studies as a young man. He received his first employment, serving as the court physician for the Ilkhan Abaqa (r. 1265–1282); little is heard of him again until the reign of Arghun (1284–1291). It would appear that Rashid al-Din continued to practice medicine during this time, but historical sources describe his increasing consultation with Mongol amirs and other elites about political and governmental matters.

The historian Ahmad b. Husain b. Ali Katib describes how Rashid al-Din was an extensive traveler during these early years of his career; indeed, his detailed taxonomy in the *Athar wa Ahya* of trees, plants, and other botanical features from Iran and Central Asia point to a scholar–doctor who traveled wide and far for both scholarly and pharmacologic interests. Some of these peregrinations are likely connected to Rashid al-Din's decision to flee the Ilkhanid court in 1295 because of the paralyzing fiscal crisis and ensuing courtly strife, which resulted when the vizier Sadr al-Din introduced a paper currency (ch'ao) that was based on an earlier Chinese banking initiative.

Rashid al-Din subsequently reappeared during the late 1290s as a recent convert to Islam and an administrator of great promise in the court of Ghazan Khan (r. 1298–1305). Rashid al-Din was approached by the Mongol ruler to replace Sadr al-Din Zanjani—who had been executed for his aforementioned currency debacle—as the chief vizier of the Ilkhan empire. He appears to have enjoyed a meteoric rise from this time forward both among the Mongol ruling elite as well as in the administration. By 1299, he had been named as the sahib-divan (chief of administration) as well as na'ib (deputy), and he had also quickly arranged diplomatic marriages of his sons to daughters of a number of prominent nobles, Turco-Mongol amirs, religious scholars, and high-profile administrators. According to Rashid al-Din's personal correspondence (the veracity of these epistles has been debated extensively; see Morton, 2000, 155–199), these included, among others, Majd al-Din Isma'il b. Yahya b. Isma'il al-Fali (a famous religious scholar), 'Ala al-Din (atabeg of Yazd), Ali b. Muhammad Shah b. Pahlavan (atabeg of Azarbaijan), and Maudud Shah b. Ala al-Din (nephew of Firuz Shah, a Indian Tughluq ruler). He was also reportedly well connected through marriage to persons of quality in the city of Yazd, most notably Nizam al-Din Ali ibn Mahmud ibn Mahfuz ibn Nizam. Rashid al-Din is believed to have amassed a personal fortune during this time, and much of this was channeled toward the purchase of land and the development of this property for waqf (endowment) purposes.

According to the *Waqf Nama-i Rab'-i Rashidi* (compiled in 1310), it appears that Rashid al-Din owned property throughout central-western Iran and Azarbaijan: Yazd, Isfahan, Shiraz, Abarquh, Mawsil, Maragha, Hamadan, Sultaniyya, and Tabriz. The largest waqf complex established by Rashid al-Din was the Rabi'-i Rashidi in Tabriz. Admittedly there was a certain cupidity here, but it would appear that Rashid al-Din was genuinely alarmed by the detrimental effects of Mongol coercion and corruption on the peasantry and land. In addition to revenues from these properties being used for charitable purposes (madrasas [schools], hospices, public works), Rashid al-Din also founded and developed a number of villages and settlements in the Hawiza area.

There is little doubt that Rashid al-Din played a pivotal role in a series of dramatic administrative and agricultural reforms instituted by Ghazan Khan during the early 1300s. Excessive and haphazard taxation, in combination with governor-related and bureaucratic avarice, had resulted in considerable peasant flight from agricultural regions which—although once prosperous—had never fully recovered from the initial Mongol invasions. Ghazan Khan's interdiction against many unhelpful practices by tax collectors and strict admonitions to henceforth survey, assess, and document taxation practices are preserved in a series of yarlighs (decrees), which were included by Rashid al-Din in his monumental *Jami' al-Tavarikh (The Collection of Histories)*. The most famous yarligh is that of 1304, when Ghazan Khan declared that governors were no longer allowed to collect taxes in their respective territories; henceforth, scribes (bitikchis) were being sent in to respective provinces to properly assess and record taxation levels. As a result of his reforms, Ghazan Khan boasted, the revenues for the Mongol treasury had doubled, and Muslim peasants and townspeople alike could now enjoy justice and responsible government.

However, the Mongol era was by and large an unsafe one for chief administrators, and many viziers and mustaufis (chief financial officers) often found themselves victims of court intrigue and false allegations. Rashid al-Din was no exception to this rule, and, during his later years, he was forced to contend with considerable rivalry and opposition from his co-vizier, Taj al-Din Ali Shah, after Ghazan's successor, Oljeitu, came to power in 1305. These machinations would intensify to such a point that Oljeitu decreed that they should divide the empire so as to provide them with respective administrative bailiwicks; Rashid al-Din was given control of Luristan, Kirman, Fars, and Iraq'-i 'Ajam. Rashid al-Din would survive his seventh consecutive Mongol coronation in 1317—no small feat indeed—but he ultimately fell prey to the intrigues of Taj al-Din in July 1318, when he was accused, convicted, and executed for poisoning his previous liege Oljeitu.

His Work

Rashid al-Din was a scholar of tremendous energy and industry, and, although he produced various treatises on theology, medicine, epistolography, administration, and agronomy, his most enduring and well-recognized work is the *Jami' al-Tavarikh (The Collection of Histories)*. In the spectrum of medieval Perso-Islamic histories, the *Jami' al-Tavarikh* is arguably unsurpassed with respect to its scope, depth, and historical methodology for understanding the Turco-Mongolian world of the thirteenth and early fourteenth centuries. This work first began as a commissioned history for Ghazan Khan, who hoped to establish and record a legacy of his rule in Iran. When this text *(Tarikh-i Mubarak-i Ghazani)* was presented formally to Ghazan's brother and successor, Oljeitu, it was decided that this historical project should be extrapolated to include a general history of the Mongol invasions and the establishment of one of the largest land empires to date in Eurasia. Thus, the *Jami' al-Tavarikh* comprises a series of histories of China, India, pre-Islamic Iran, Central Asia, and the Steppe while also focusing on the respective history of the Jews, the Muslim ummah under Muhammad and the Rightly Guided Caliphs *(al-Khulafa al-Rashidin)*, and the Christian infidel Franks (Europeans). Rashid al-Din brought a formidable palette of languages to this project—Persian, Arabic, Hebrew, Turkish, and Mongolian—and his historiographical approach was such that he provided names and sources for much of the material for earlier parts of the *Jami' al-Tavarikh*. For this reason, Rashid al-Din can be considered one of the first world historians in the medieval Perso-Islamic historical tradition. Specialists of Mongol administrative history have always been enamored with Rashid al-Din because of his decision to include the full texts—some of which were written by him—of every single decree (yarligh) that was issued during Ghazan Khan's reform initiatives in the early 1300s.

Although much of the material in the *Jami' al-Tavarikh* is borrowed directly from Juvaini's earlier *Tarikh-i Jahan-gusha*, Rashid al-Din was able to bring one particularly valuable source to bear in his own history: the *Altan Debter (Golden Book)*. This peculiar text—of which there are no extant copies—was an indigenous Mongolian history that enjoyed near-holy status in the Kara Korum court of the Great Khan. No non-Mongols were permitted to see or touch it, but it is known that Rashid al-Din was able to have its contents orally transmitted to him, most likely by Boland Chingsang, the official envoy of the Great Khan in Tabriz. As the Mongol historian David Morgan cautions, it must be appreciated that Rashid al-Din's presentation of Mongol history was skewed in such a way as to present his first sponsor, Ghazan Khan, in as positive a light as possible. As a result, there is a less-than-subtle juxtaposition of the detrimental rule of earlier Mongols with the enlightened and visionary policies of Ghazan Khan himself. Nonetheless, there is no mistaking that this massive history is the product of an unrivaled erudition and industriousness, and medieval historians appreciate the authoritative status of Rashid al-Din's section about the reign of Ghazan Khan and his reforms.

COLIN PAUL MITCHELL

See also Agriculture; Bureaucrats; Horticulture; Irrigation; Mongols; Oljeitu; Tax and Taxation; Viziers

Primary Sources

Rashid al-Din Fadl Allah Hamadani. *Athar wa Ahya'*, eds. I. Afshar and M. Sotoodeh. Tehran, 1989.
————. *Jami' al-Tavarikh*, 3 vols., ed. B. Karimi. Tehran, 1959.
————. *Lata'if al-Haqa'iq*, 2 vols., ed. Ghulam Riza Tahir. Tehran, 1976.
————. *Mukatabat-i Rashidi*, ed. M. Shafi'. Lahore, 1945.
————. *Oghuz-nama*, ed. R. Shukiurova. Moscow, 1991.
————. *Tanksuq-nama*, ed. M. Minovi. Tehran, 1972.
————. *Tarikh-i Mubarak-i Ghazani*, ed. K. Jahn. La Haye, 1957.
————. *Vaqf-nama-i Rab'-i Rashidi*, eds. M. Minovi and I. Afshar. Tehran, 1977.

Further Reading

Blair, Sheila. "Patterns of Patronage and Production in Ilkhanid Iran: The Case of Rashid al-Din." In *The Court of the Il-khans 1290–1340*, eds. J. Raby and T. Fitzherbert, 39–62. Oxford, UK, 1997.
Bloom, Jonathan, and Sheila Blair. *A Compendium of Chronicles: Rashid al-Din's Illustrated History of the World*. London, 1995.
Boyle, J.A. "Juvaini and Rashid al-Din as Sources on the History of the Mongols." In *Historians of the Middle East*, ed. B. Lewis, 133–7. New York, 1962.
————. "Rashid al-Din and the Franks." *Central Asiatic Journal* 14 (1970): 62–7.
Gray, B. *The World History of Rashid al-Din: A Study of the Royal Asiatic Society Manuscript*. London, 1978.
Hoffman, B. "The Gates of Piety and Charity: Rashid al-Din Fadl Allah as Founder of Pious Endowments." In *L'Iran Face à la Domination Mongole*, ed. Denise Aigle, 189–202. Paris, 1997.
Lambton, A.K.S. "The *Athar wa Ahya'* of Rashid al-Din Fadl Allah Hamadani and His Contribution as an Agronomist, Arboriculturist and Horticulturist." In *The Mongol Empire and Its Legacy*, eds. R. Amitai-Preiss and D.O. Morgan, 126–54. Leiden, 1999.
————. *Continuity and Change in Medieval Persia: Aspects of Administrative, Economic and Social History, 11th–14th Century*. Albany, 1988.
Morgan, D.O. "Cassiodorus and Rashid al-Din on Barbarian Rule in Italy and Persia" *BSOAS* 44 (1977): 302–20.
————. *The Mongols*. London, 1986.
————. "Persian Historians and the Mongols." In *Medieval Historical Writing in the Christian and Islamic Worlds*, ed. D.O. Morgan, 109–24. London, 1982.
————. "Rashid al-Din and Gazan Khan." In *L'Iran Face à la Domination Mongole*, ed. Denise Aigle, 179–88. Paris, 1997.
Morton, A.H. "The Letters of Rashid al-Din: Ilkhanid Fact or Timurid?" In *The Mongol Empire and Its Legacy*, eds. R. Amitai-Preiss and D.O. Morgan, 155–99. Leiden, 1999.
Rashid al-Din Fadl Allah Hamadani. *The History of the Seljuq Turks from the Jami' al-Tawarikh: An Ilkhanid Adaptation of the Saljuq-nama of Zahir al-Din Nishapuri*, ed. C.E. Bosworth, transl. K. Luther. Richmond, 2001.
————. *Rashiduddin Fazlullah's Jami'u't-Tawarikh (Compendium of Chronicles)*, transl. W.W. Thackston. Cambridge, UK, 1998.
————. *The Successors of Genghis Khan*, ed. and transl. J.A. Boyle. New York and London, 1971.
Richard, Francis. "Un des Peintres du Manuscrit *Supplément Persan 1113* de l'Histoire des Mongols de Rashid al-Din Identifié." In *L'Iran face à la Domination Mongole*, ed. Denise Aigle, 307–19. Paris, 1997.
Rührdanz, K. "Illustrationen zu Rashid al-Dins *Ta'rih-i Mubarak-i Gazani* in den Berliner Diez-Alben." In *L'Iran Face à la Domination Mongole*, ed. Denise Aigle, 295–305. Paris, 1997.
Soudavar, Abolala. "In Defense of Rashid-ol-din and His Letters." *Studia Iranica* 32 (2003): 77–122.
Spuler, B. *Die Mongolen in Iran*. Berlin, 1985.
Togan, Z.V. "The Composition of the History of the Mongols by Rashid al-Din." *Central Asiatic Journal* 7 (1962): 60–72.
————. "Still Missing Works of Rashid al-Din." *Central Asiatic Journal* 9 (1964): 113–22.
Van Ess, J. *Der Wesir und Seine Gelehrten*. Wiesbaden, 1981.

RASULIDS

The Rasulid dynasty that ruled in Yemen from 1229 to 1454 started out as a family of officers of Turkmen origin that was comprised of a patriarch, 'Ali ibn Rasul, and his four sons, who were attached to the Ayyubid army that conquered Yemen from Egypt in 1173 and 1174. Their rise within the Ayyubid administration culminated in the appointment of Nur al-Din 'Umar ibn 'Ali ibn Rasul as deputy to the departing Ayyubid governor, al-Mas'ud ibn al-Kamil. When a new appointment from Cairo failed to materialize, Nur al-Din 'Umar wasted little time taking possession of the most strategic forts and towns, replacing loyal Ayyubid officials with his own followers and arranging a truce with the Zaydis. He also managed to avert a military confrontation with the Ayyubids in Yemen, and, by 1234 or 1235, he had received formal recognition of his sultanate from the 'Abbasid caliph in Baghdad. For the next two centuries, Nur al-Din 'Umar and his successors succeeded in turning Yemen into a regional power, primarily through their control of the east–west trade and their interest in cultivating diplomatic ties with the rulers of Egypt, India, Persia, Africa, and China.

The dominions of the Rasulid dynasty extended over the same territories conquered by the Ayyubids:

the central and southern highlands and the Tihama coastal plain. Ta'izz, a former Ayyubid fortress and stronghold, was chosen by the second Rasulid sultan, al-Muzaffar Yusuf, as the dynasty's political capital because of its strategic location and its proximity to the great emporium of Aden. Alternatively, the Rasulids had little control over northern and eastern Yemen beyond San'a'; both of these areas remained under the control of the Zaydis, the Rasulids' political and religious rivals. Furthermore, San'a', which continued to serve as the outpost of the Rasulid northern frontier, remained the focus of both Rasulid and Zaydi aspirations but was ultimately lost to the Zaydis by 1323. The Hadramawt, on the other hand, continued to be ruled by small local dynasties that paid tributes to the Rasulids. Trade and taxes levied on merchandise transiting through the port of Aden were the most important source of revenue for the Rasulid state. For this, they developed the port and its administration system, and they ensured the safety of merchant ships with a fleet of patrol ships. Agriculture was another source of revenue developed by the Rasulids, particularly in the Tihama region, the administrative capital of which (Zabid) became their winter residence.

In these towns and others, the Rasulids constructed a large number of secular and religious monuments. As staunch Shafi'is, they favored the construction of madrasas, which attracted many Sunni scholars from all over the Islamic world. These scholars, as well as other officials, were often offered posts in the Rasulid administration, such as Sadr al-Din al-Shirazi, who arrived in Yemen in 1394 and was appointed as chief judge (Qadi al-qudat) by Sultan al-Ashraf Isma'il, who also gave him his daughter in marriage. The sultans were learned men in their own right who not only had important libraries but who also wrote treatises on a wide array of subjects, ranging from astrology and medicine to agriculture and genealogy. They also played an active role in the religious debates between the Sufis and the faqihs with regard to the works of Ibn 'Arabi; these debates polarized opinions, but most favored the former over the latter.

The Rasulids modeled much of their administration on that of the Mamluks, despite their recurrent difficult relations because the latter considered them as a vassal state. Their competition centered at first over the Hijaz and the right to provide the kiswa (covering) of the Ka'ba, each supporting a rival faction among the ruling sharifs of Mecca. Despite the strong Rasulid–Mamluk antagonism surrounding the internal politics of the Hijaz, traditional diplomatic channels remained open, and embassies and gifts were exchanged. However, official gifts to Cairo came

to be regarded as tributes from the Rasulid side. The ultimate crisis resulted in the arrest of Sultan al-Mujahid Ali in 1352 (while he was on pilgrimage in Mecca) and his subsequent dispatch to Cairo; he was released a few months later upon payment of a large ransom. Taxation and commercial monopolization were two other major factors around which Rasulid–Mamluk rivalry revolved. Accusations against the Rasulid sultans' imposing of heavy taxes on merchants became a paramount dispute between al-Nasir Ahmad and Barsbay. By the end of the second quarter of the fifteenth century, the economic situation of the Rasulids suffered considerably as a result of Sultan Barsbay's trade monopoly, al-Nasir Ahmad's heavy taxes levied in Aden, and the emergence of Jedda as the new favored port of the Red Sea.

The Rasulid state became increasingly threatened by periodic tribal revolts, particularly those of the Tihama region, which rebelled against heavy taxes. These tribes cultivated major agricultural areas and reared stock animals (mainly horses), which became, during the Rasulid period, a major export item to the Indian subcontinent. Rasulid rule was periodically challenged by disgruntled family members over the problem of succession. It was during their frequent revolts that many Rasulid women family members played active roles in supporting one faction against another. During the last twelve years of Rasulid rule, the country was torn between several contenders for the sultanate, each supported and manipulated by different power groups. Ultimately, they lost out to the Tahirids, their own governors in Aden.

NOHA SADEK

See also Aden; Zaydis

Primary Sources

Al-Khazraji, 'Ali ibn al-Hasan. *Al-'Uqud al-lu'lu'Iyya fi Ta'rikh al-Dawla al-Rasuliyya (The Pearl Strings: A History of the Resuliyy Dynasty of Yemen)*, transl. J.W. Redhouse, 5 vols. Leiden: E.J.W. Gibb Memorial Series, 1906–1918.

Further Reading

Daum, Werner, ed. *Yemen: 3000 Years of Art and Civilisation in Arabia Felix*. Innsbruck and Frankfurt/Main: Pinguin, 1988.
Sadek, Noha. "Patronage and Architecture in Rasulid Yemen, 626–858 A.H./1229–1454 A.D." PhD dissertation. Toronto, Canada: University of Toronto, 1990.
Sadek, Noha. "Ta'izz, Capital of the Rasulid Dynasty in Yemen." *Proceedings of the Seminar for Arabian Studies* 33 (2003): 309–13.
Smith, G.R. *The Ayyubids and Early Rasulids in Yemen*, 2 vols. London: E.J.W. Gibb Memorial Series, 1974–1978.

RAZI, AL-, FAKHR AL-DIN

Fakhr al-Din al-Razi was one of the most prominent theologians, jurists, and Qur'an commentators of Sunni Islam who lived at a time when Muslim theology was trying to come to grips with the impact of the Aristotelian philosophical tradition (falsafa). Fakhr al-Din al-Razi was born around 1149 in Ray (today, Tehran), Iran. His father was a famous preacher who had studied *Kalam* at the Nizamiyya madrasa of Nishapur. Fakhr al-Din studied in Ray and in Maragha, the intellectual center of northeastern Iran. Like his father, Fakhr al-Din became an Ash'arite in theology and a Shafi'ite in Islamic law. After the conclusion of his studies, he went to Khwarizm in Transoxiana (today, Uzbekistan) to dispute with the Mu'tazilites, who were prominent there. He failed, however, to convert them to Ash'arism and was expelled. He continued to travel and teach in Iran, Central Asia (Bukhara and Samarkand), Afghanistan (Ghazna), and the Indus Valley, until he settled in 1203 in Herat (Afghanistan), where the local ruler founded a madrasa to accommodate his teaching activity. Fakhr al-Din was a controversial teacher, and Herat seemed to have been evenly divided in friends and foes. His most fierce enemies were a group of traditionalist Karramites, and it was rumored that they played a role in his death. However, Fakhr al-Din died of natural causes in 1210.

Al-Razi's theological doctrine is the result of the epistemological conflict between divine revelation (Qur'an and hadith [tradition]) and the scientific principle of demonstration (burhan; Greek *apodeixis*). After the Arabic translation of the works of Aristotle during the eighth and ninth centuries, the Muslim philosopher al-Farabi (d. c. 950) had made the Aristotelian technique of demonstration the yardstick of all knowledge in the sciences and in falsafa. If an argument is formally correct and if its premises are already proven, its conclusion is necessarily true and must be accepted. Later, Ibn Sina (d. 1037) had refined the technique of the demonstrative argument in the Arabic sciences and in falsafa. Since the beginning of the twelfth century, Ibn Sina's works had become part of the curriculum of studies at the Ash'arite madrasas in Iraq and Iran. Fakhr al-Din studied the books of Ibn Sina thoroughly, and he wrote an influential commentary about Ibn Sina's most theological work, *Pointers and Reminders*.

Al-Razi generally accepted the findings of the scientists and Muslim philosophers (falasifa) wherever they are based on demonstrative arguments. Where the views of the falasifa are not based on demonstration or where al-Razi does not accept that their arguments are truly demonstrative, he considered other sources of knowledge, most importantly the literal wording of the Qur'an and the hadith corpus. On the question of whether the place of the intellect ('aql) is within the brain or the heart, for instance, al-Razi opted for the latter; his conclusion was based on the many verses in the Qur'an that locate insight and knowledge in the heart. These clear indications in revelation cannot be overruled by the physicians' arguments for the location of the intellect in the brain, which al-Razi did not accept as being demonstrative.

Despite being a deeply pious man, Fakhr al-Din was unusually rationalistic in his theology, even for his time. He often abandoned the school tradition of the Ash'arites in favor of the philosophical system of Ibn Sina. Ash'arite theology, for instance, emphasized that the moral values of a person's actions, namely good and bad, can only be understood through revelation (rather than reason); only the fact that God recommends or condemns an action can make it good or bad. Fakhr al-Din al-Razi abandoned this principle in favor of the rationalist position that it can be determined whether an action is morally good or bad independent of revelation. This view had a profound impact on Fakhr al-Din's reasoning in Islamic law. Although al-Ghazali (1058–1111) had cautiously introduced the idea that a jurist should consider the benefit (maslaha) of society in his judgments, Fakhr al-Din al-Razi thoroughly aimed to establish maslaha as a source of Islamic law. Because the well-educated jurist knows what is best for the individual and the society, he should apply the principle of expediency in his rulings, even if such application overturns the judgments of earlier jurists.

Fakhr al-Din's most influential work is his voluminous commentary on the Qur'an, which he wrote close to the end of his life. Although its official title is *The Keys to the Unknown*, the work is often known as *The Grand Commentary (al-Tafsir al-Kabir)*. It combines Fakhr al-Din's rationalist teachings in theology with a precise philological analysis of the text and a deeply pious, often mystic interpretation. The book is known for its many digressions into the sciences, philosophy, and mysticism; Ibn Taymiyya (1263–1328), one of Fakhr al-Din's conservative adversaries, claimed it contains everything *but* a commentary of the Qur'an. Fakhr al-Din's followers, however, responded that it contains everything *and* a commentary of the Qur'an.

Fakhr al-Din's *Grand Commentary* became a yardstick for all later commentaries on the Qur'an and had a lasting influence. It was, for instance, widely read by modernist Muslim reformers in the late nineteenth and early twentieth centuries and thus shaped all modern Muslim Qur'an commentaries.

FRANK GRIFFEL

Further Reading

Anawati, George. "Fakhr al-Din al-Razi." In *Encyclopeadia of Islam*, 2nd ed., vol. 2, 751–55. Leiden and London: Brill/Luzac & Co., 1963.

Kholeif, Fathalla. *A Study on Fakhr al-Razi and his Controversies in Transoxania.* Beirut: Dar El-Mashreq, 1984.

Kraus, Paul. "The 'Controversies' of Fakhr al-Din al-Razi." *Islamic Culture* 12 (1938): 131–53.

Mafisumi, M. Saghir Hasan. "Imam Fakhr al-Din al-Razi and His Critics." *Islamic Studies* 6 (1967): 355–74.

Muhibbu-Din, Murtada A. "Imam Fakhr al-Din al-Razi's Philosophical Theology in al-Tafsir al-Kabir." *Hamdard Islamicus* 27 (1994): 55–84.

Nasr, Seyyid Hossein. "Fakhr al-Dın Razi." In *The Islamic Intellectual Tradition in Persia*, ed. M.A. Razawi, 107–21. Richmond: Curzon, 1996.

RAZI, AL-, OR RHAZES

Abu Bakr Muhammad ibn Zakariyya' al-Razi was born and died in al-Rayy (classical Rhagai; on the southern outskirts of today's Teheran) (1 Sha'ban 251–5 Sha'ban 313/28 August 865–26 October 925). He was a physician, a scientist, and a philosopher, and he was a prolific author in medicine (including ancillary subjects), alchemy, logic, and philosophy.

Life

The times of al-Razi's life and his places of residence—mostly far distant from the caliphal capital, Baghdad—as well as his nonreligious vocation removed him from the focus of attention in the extant bio-bibliographical sources of classical and medieval Islam; nevertheless, the relative importance that his birthplace al-Rayy then enjoyed and, more to the point, his own scholarly reputation there and in Baghdad, did perpetuate his memory as a person apart from his works. Although his treatise *The Philosophical Life* (*Kitab al-Sira al-Falsafiyya;* also called *Apologia* [Arberry]) is short on concrete detail, a broad outline of his life can be sketched by combining information contained in it and other works of his with carefully sifted secondary evidence.

The precise transmission of the dates of his birth and death would seem to credit his family with a certain level of education and affluence, which subsequently may have facilitated his access to the scholarship that his works amply attest. Further, comfortable circumstances would easily explain the report about his initial occupation as a moneychanger. His own station in life would later have ensured the recording of his death. As alluded to above, al-Razi spent most of his life in his hometown of al-Rayy; however, medical studies and practice more than once occasioned years of absence from al-Rayy. He is said to have sojourned in Baghdad as a student and, later, as the director of its hospital. In Nishapur and Bukhara, he attended Samanid dynasts.

Before taking up medicine (as late as in his thirties), al-Razi is alternatively said to have been a lute player and poet or a practitioner of alchemy. Because his alchemical writings show a far more empirical bent than those of the *Corpus Jabirianum* (see below), such reports would seem credible enough; however, they also function as an etiological legend, deriving his—indubitably attested—poor eyesight and eventual blindness in old age from the noxious effects of alchemical experiments; a variant and no less suspect explanation would link his eye condition to excessive predilection for the broad bean. Clearly, both accounts impugn his reliance on secular science in that they construe an otherwise inexplicable organic ailment as its consequence and, by inference, as divine retribution.

Although al-Razi came to embody Galen's ideal that the excellent physician also be a philosopher, the relationship—if any existed—between his medical and philosophical interests and the circumstances of his philosophical studies cannot be ascertained. Al-Razi himself mentions as his teacher Abu Zayd Ahmad b. Sahl al-Balkhi (i.e., the man from Balkh, classical Bactra), but he also conducted epistolary debates with two of Abu Zayd's fellow townsmen, Abu l-Qasim 'Abdallah ibn Ahmad al-Ka'bi and Abu 'l-Husayn Shahid. Actually, he thus addressed an impressive number of earlier and contemporaneous scholars—physicians, scientists, philosophers, theologians (e.g., Ahmad ibn al-Óayyib al-Sarakhsi, al-JahiÛ, al-Kindi, Abu Sahl al-Rasa'ili, al-Nashi', and the Manichean Sisinnius). Whereas al-Razi's own accounts of philosophical controversies are, with one exception, lost, disputations with the Isma'ili Abu Hatim al-Razi (d. 322/933–934) left an echo in the latter's, fortunately extant, writings; *Doubts Concerning Galen* (see below) demonstrates al-Razi's critical attitude toward classical authorities. With regard to students of al-Razi's, the only name to be transmitted is Yahya ibn 'Adi, who was later a prominent disciple of al-Farabi's.

Al-Razi's medical writings would seem to confirm the biographers' reports about his heading the hospitals of al-Rayy and of Baghdad, respectively. As some sources would have it, he was so much sought after by students and patients alike that he attended only to the most intractable cases, referring all others, by degree of severity, to his junior and senior students and assistants. In any case, he generously cared for indigent patients (as witnesses attest) and dedicated a special treatise to the needs of those who had to do without expert treatment (*Everybody His Own Doctor*—Arberry's version of *Man la yahduruhu al-tabib*). On the other hand, his medical acumen could not fail to attract the attention of the powers that be; indeed, his familiarity with princes aroused criticism for violating the principles of the philosophical life, which was here defined along cynic, ascetic lines.

Al-Razi's self-statement of indefatigably pursuing knowledge and scholarship, both for his own benefit and for that of his fellow humans, is fully borne out by the extent and quality of his literary production; the debilities of age, cataracts, and failing hand muscles did not stop him nor apparently embitter him—he merely employed help. Beyond study and writing, he strove after human perfection by practicing the philosophical life, which he saw embodied in Socrates; by honoring Socrates as "our imam"—thus applying the title of supreme Muslim leadership to a pagan philosopher—al-Razi implicitly rejected all religiously based claims of authority.

Al-Razi's outline of the good life in *Apologia* includes gainful occupation, procreation of the species, and, generally, measured enjoyment of worldly goods; he specifically rejects rigorous self-mortification on the model of Hindu, Manichean, and Christian asceticism. As for his own conduct of the philosophical life, other than study and writing, he expressly names his general moderation in material acquisitions; the pursuit of legal claims; in food, drink, entertainment, dress, mount, and slaves (eunuchs and concubines); the implied premise of a certain wealth illustrates that moderation was to be relative to one's station in life and not to be measured by some absolute standard. His reticence about his private life otherwise conforms to the conventions of his age except that male offspring would normally have been mentioned.

Works

Al-Razi's autobibliography runs close to two hundred titles. Subsuming his entire work under philosophy, he, in turn—and along established Aristotelian lines—divides philosophy into natural and metaphysical science on the one hand and mathematics on the other. However, deviating from the tradition of Islamic Aristotelianism, he depreciates mathematics and, on the other hand, includes both medicine and alchemy within natural philosophy; logic is apparently not assigned a separate place.

In trying to understand al-Razi's epistemology—learning as open-ended, infinite progress—and,

specifically in medicine and alchemy, his attitude toward book learning versus empirically acquired knowledge, care has to be taken to distinguish his programmatic statements (e.g., *Doubts Concerning Galen*) and his actual practice. In his much celebrated but understudied monograph *On Smallpox and Measles*, he is quite reluctant to impute to Galen the neglect—let alone ignorance—of these devastating transmissible diseases. A proper assessment of al-Razi's own contribution to their symptomatology and differential diagnosis is still wanting, notwithstanding the impact of his treatise on later medicine; its Greek and Latin translations were printed repeatedly (and not for antiquarian reasons) right through the middle of the nineteenth century.

Continens, the most voluminous of al-Razi's works, is a posthumous compilation of his medical notebooks and files that was never meant for publication; rather, they were mainly to serve his (as he proudly proclaims, in Islam, unprecedented) project of a medical encyclopedia—apparently consisting of a series of thematically related but separate monographs—under the title *al-Jami'* (*Colligens;* not to be confused with the nearly synonymous *al-Hawi*). However, even as they stand gathered in *Continens,* al-Razi's notes convincingly fulfill his requirement of a thorough command of existing scholarship; in the given case of medicine, this extended—beyond Greek, Sanskrit, Syriac, and early Islamic traditions—to unattributed hospital practice and that of "wise women." Finally, he recorded his own—at times contrasting—clinical experience.

The immense volume of *al-Hawi* could not but affect its manuscript transmission. However, interest in it transcended religious boundaries, as attested to, for example, by a copy in Hebrew characters and, in Europe, by its Latin translation in 1279.

Plausibly the single most influential of al-Razi's books was his medical compendium *Book for Mansur,* one hefty volume that combined theory and practice. Its success is illustrated by a large number of manuscripts in the original Arabic, in Hebrew, and in Gerard of Cremona's Latin version of 1175 (several printed editions) and by a series of Arabic and Latin commentaries.

Corresponding with the format of al-Razi's medical writings—ranging from encyclopedias to the briefest of monographs, which were designed as handy references for far-flung practitioners—his envisioned audiences run the gamut from fellow scholar to layman. His equally comprehensive thematic interests include everything from anatomy to specific disorders; to dietetics (including sexual medicine), materia medica, and pharmacy; to deontological questions; and to lay people's attitudes toward medicine and its practitioners. In addition, al-Razi engaged authoritative texts of his discipline—especially Hippocrates and Galen—in commentaries, revisions, and emulations. Monographic treatments of (in the broad medieval sense) philosophical interest include discussions of allergic reactions to flowering roses; of the strictly physiological causation of pathicism (passive anal eroticism); of the public's frequent preference for quacks over qualified doctors; and of physicians' curative failures and, conversely, of the success of wise women and their ilk.

Al-Razi's epistemological open-mindedness led him to devote a treatise to the (occult) properties (khawass) of mineral, vegetable, and animal substances. Alternatively, his work in alchemy, betraying a similar attitude, dispenses with magic in the attempted transformation of bodies, such as base metals into gold. The implications of his work, calling into question the traditional doctrine of four elemental qualities (among others), were not to be lost on al-Ghazali and other later thinkers.

Al-Razi stands out among Islamic philosophers for his ethics and his metaphysical and physical doctrines, although he did not ignore logic (in Aristotelian terms, philosophy's indispensable implement). Conspicuously, he rejects one of Islam's basic dogmas—prophecy—and with it all revealed religion. Reason being the creator's equal gift to all humankind, there was no need for divine dispensations through the mouth of prophets; to the contrary, such (in reality) demonically induced self-delusions had invariably proven pernicious in leading to sanguinary strife. Human beings' apparent inequality in philosophical potential resulted from the wide variance of their interests and preoccupations.

Further religious and philosophical disagreements of al-Razi with his contemporaries concern creation as such and man's destiny in the hereafter. He posits the pre-eternal existence of five entities: (1) God; (2) universal soul; (3) absolute time; (4) absolute space; and (5) matter. By defining, in contradiction to Aristotle, time and space as absolute and infinite, he expressly relies on the uncanny certainty of inferences from straightforward sensory perception. Al-Razi's concept of matter is atomistic in a generally Democritean way, which is in contrast to the notion of dimensionless atoms that was prevalent in Muslim dialectic theology (kalam).

In al-Razi's cosmological myth, creation is occasioned by God's accession to Soul's desire of embodiment in matter; the resulting chaos is mitigated by God's further gift of intelligence—his own—to creation and to Soul. Intelligible order is thus imparted to the universe and, in humankind, self-awareness to Soul; conscious of her incorporeal origin, she strives after liberation from imprisonment in this life to return to her primal abode. Thus, al-Razi premises the afterlife on Soul's incorporeal substantiality alone, rejecting the Qur'anic resurrection of the flesh. Generally taking, like the Gnostics and Manicheans, a dim view of Soul's embroilment with matter, al-Razi yet insists on the creator's wisdom and mercy. Creation's ultimate end, however, is its dissolution after Soul's liberation from bondage to matter.

Central to al-Razi's ethical theory are his concepts of pleasure, which exists only as release from and in proportion with previous discomfort and of the fear of death as a motive force. The attempt to silence such fear—irrational, whether or not death terminates the soul's sentient existence—impels humans to indulge their natural appetites for power, food, or sex. In an effort to predicate his ethical theory on unfounded assumptions—given the impossibility of rationally demonstrating the reality of the beyond—he bases it on the finality of death. Because the appetites, feeding on gratification, ever forestall the achievement of the desired pleasure, they are to be reduced by judiciously denying them gratification to approximate a modicum of contentment: the maximum attainable in this life.

From among al-Razi's physical works, his treatise about vision deserves special mention for his rejection of Galen's extromission theory and excessive reliance on Euclid.

LUTZ RICHTER-BERNBURG

Further Reading

Bar Asher, M.M. "Quelques Aspects de l'Éthique d'Abu Bakr al-Razi." *Studia Islamica* 69 (1989): 5–38; 70 (1990): 119–47.

Bungy, Gholam Ali, et al. "Razi's Report About Seasonal Allergic Rhinitis (Hay Fever) from the 10th Century AD." *International Archives of Allergy and Immunology* 110 (1996): 219–24.

Escobar Gomez, S. "De un Predecesor Árabe de Bentham en la Defensa de los 'Derechos de los Animales'." *Anaquel de Estudios Árabes* 8 (1997): 87–99.

Goodman, Lenn E. "Muhammad ibn Zakariyya' al-Razi." In *Routledge History of World Philosophies, Vol I, History of Islamic Philosophy*, eds. Seyyed Hossein Nasr and Oliver Leaman, 198–215. London and New York: Routledge, 1996.

———. "al-Razi, Abu Bakr Muhammad." In *Encyclopaedia of Islam*, vol. VIII, 474a–7b. Leiden: E.J. Brill, 1994.

Jacquart, Danielle. "Note sur la Traduction Latine du *Kitab al-ManÒuri* de Rhazes." *Revue d'Histoire des Textes* 24 (1994): 359–74.

Kitab al-ManÒuri fi al-Òibb, ed. Hazim al-Bakri al-Ñiddiqi. Kuwait: Publications of Institute of Arab [sic] Manuscripts, Arab League Educational Cultural & Scientific Organization, 1987.

Kitab Sirr al-Asrar (Secret of Secrets), ed. M.T. Daneshpazhuh. Tehran: Unesco, 1964 (*Nashriya-i*

Kumisyun-i Milli-i Yunisku dar Iran; 25); J. Ruska, German trl., as *al-Razi's Buch Geheimnis der Geheimnisse*, Berlin 1937.

Kitab al-Shukuk 'ala Jalinus, ed. M. Mohaghegh. Tehran: Mu'assasa-i Mutala'at-i Islami, 1372/1993.

Kitab al-Taqsim wa-l-Tashjir (as Taqasim al-'Ilal), ed. S.M. Hammami. Aleppo, Syria: University of Aleppo, Institute for the History of Arabic Science, 1412/1992.

Kraus, Paul, and Shlomo Pines. "al-Razi, Abu Bakr Muhammad." In *Encyclopaedia of Islam*, vol. III, 1134a–6b. Leiden: E.J. Brill, 1936.

Mahdi, Muhsin. "Remarks on al-Razi's Principles." *Bulletin d'Études Orientales* 48 (1996): 145–53.

Meier, Fritz. "'Urknall' bei . . . a. Bakr al-Razi." *Oriens* 33 (1992): 1–21.

Muhaqqiq [Mohaghegh], Mahdi. *Filsuf-i Rayy*. Tehran, 1970.

Pines, Shlomo. "al-Razi." *Dictionary of Scientific Biography*, vol. XI, 323a–6b. New York: Scribner, 1975.

———. *Beiträge zur Islamischen Atomenlehre*. Berlin, 1936. (Muhammad 'Abd al-Hadi Abu Rida, Ar. trl. as *Madhhab al-dharra 'inda l-Muslimin*, Cairo 1946; Michael Schwarz, Engl. trl. as *Studies in Islamic Atomism*, Jerusalem: The Magnes Press 1997).

———. "What was Original in Arabic Science?" In *Scientific Change—Historical Studies: Symposium. . . Oxford. . .1961*, ed. A.C. Crombie, 181–205. London, 1963. 1–205 [repr. in *The Collected Works of Shlomo Pines* II: *Studies in Arabic versions of Greek texts and in medieval science*, Jerusalem: Magnes and Leiden: Brill 1986, pp. 329–53].

Richter-Bernburg, Lutz. "Abu Bakr Muhammad al-Razi's (Rhazes) Medical Works." *Medicina nei Secoli Arte e Scienza* VI (1994): 377–92.

———. "al-Hawi." In *Encyclopædia Iranica*, vol. XII, 64b–7b. New York: Encyclopædia Iranica Foundation, 2003.

Rosenthal, Franz. "Al-Râzî on the Hidden Illness." *Bulletin of the History of Medicine* 52 (1978): 45–56.

Ruska, Julius. "Die Alchemie al-Razi's." *Der Islam* 22 (1935): 281–319.

Sezgin, Fuad. *Geschichte des Arabischen Schrifttums*, vol. III: Medizin [etc.]; vol. V: Mathematik; vol. VII: Astrologie [etc.]. Leiden: Brill, 1970, 1974, 1979, respectively.

Stroumsa, Sarah. *Freethinkers of Medieval Islam: Ibn al-Rawandi, Abu Bakr al-Razi and Their Impact on Islamic Thought*. Leiden: Brill, 1999. (*Islamic philosophy, theology and science. Texts and studies*; v. 35).

Ullmann, Manfred. *Die Medizin im Islam*. Leiden, etc.: Brill, 1970. (*Handbuch der Orientalistik*, 1. Abtlg., Ergänzungsbd. VI, 1), esp. pp. 128–36.

———. *Islamic Medicine*. Edinburgh: UP, 1978. (*Islamic Surveys*; 11), esp. pp. 109, 112, 129 (ns. 3–6, 14).

RAZIA SULTANA

The daughter of Iltutmish, the second of the so-called "Slave Kings" of Delhi, Razia ruled the Delhi Sultanate from 1236 to 1240, thus becoming the first woman to rule a Muslim state in India. On his death bed, Iltutmish had expressed his wish that he be succeeded by Razia, whom he thought more capable for the position than any of his sons. In the intense competition among the various factions of the court to fill the political vacuum left by Iltutmish's death, however, Razia was passed over in favor of her half-brother, Rukn ad-Din Firuz, Iltutmish's eldest surviving son. Rukn ad-Din Firuz turned out to be a ruler who was given to pursuing a life of pleasure and satisfying his lust, being content to leave the affairs of state in the hands of his mother, Shah Turkhan. Shah Turkhan used her newly acquired power to settle old insults she had suffered in Iltutmish's harem by either putting to death or humiliating some of Iltutmish's wives. Rukn ad-din Firuz's debauchery, as well as Shah Turkhan's machinations, provoked further hostility at the court when they blinded Iltutmish's infant son, Qutb ad-Din, so that he could no longer be a contender for the throne. When Shah Turkhan began making arrangements to execute Razia because she deemed her to be a threat to her son's authority, the people of Delhi and some officers of the army revolted. Because of the high esteem with which they regarded her, they raised Razia to the throne. Rukn ad-Din and his mother were put to death. At the time there were apparently no religious objections to a woman ruling a state. Only in the seventeenth century does a theologian, Abdulhaqq Dihlawi (d. 1624), deem Razia's appointment to be contrary to the shari'a.

Although Razia came to power on the basis of popular support in Delhi, the confederacy of nobles and regional governors who had been responsible for excluding her from the throne in the first place refused to acknowledge her authority. Through astute diplomacy and complex intrigues, she was able to create dissension and mistrust in the ranks of the opposition, even managing to convince some of the nobles to support her cause. Having consolidated a shaky support base, she began appearing in public unveiled and in male attire. The chronicler Minhaj as-Siraj reports that she was a wise and just ruler, possessing all of the attributes and qualifications necessary for a king. She conducted affairs of state in an open court, marching in person with her armies when engaged in battles. Early in her reign Razia, however, managed to arouse a great deal of hostility and jealousy among the predominantly Turkish nobility when she appointed Jalal ad-Din Yaqut, an Abyssinian slave, to the post of master of the stables, a position traditionally reserved for a distinguished Turk. Her partiality for Yaqut has led later historians to speculate whether there had been a sexual relationship between them, but contemporaneous sources do not indicate that this was necessarily the case. In a society in which ethnicity and race (i.e., Turkish ancestry) were the prime qualifications for holding office, Razia's advancement of Yaqut was deemed to be not only scandalous and improper but also insulting to the Turkish oligarchy. It is very likely that, by appointing Yaqut, Razia was attempting to cultivate a cadre of non-Turkish officers and courtiers to counter the power held by nobles of Turkish ancestry at the court.

As a result of the Yaqut affair, Razia encountered powerful opposition at the court in Delhi as well as from the governors of the provinces. The governor of Punjab revolted but was subdued by Razia's forces. Fatal to Razia's rule was the revolt of Ikhtiyar ad-Din Altuniyya, the governor of Bhatinda. On April 3, 1240, Razia set out with her army to subdue him. However, as the army reached Bhatinda, some officers killed Yaqut and handed over Razia to Altuniyya. The confederacy of nobles in Delhi proclaimed Muiz ad-Din Bahram, Razia's half-brother, to be the new ruler. In the meantime, Ikhtiyar ad-Din Altuniyya, feeling left out of the power sharing taking place at the court in Delhi, released Razia from prison, and, after marrying her, proceeded to Delhi to promote the claims of his wife to the throne. Altuniyya's army was defeated by Bahram's forces, and, on October 14, 1240, both Razia and Altuniyya were killed.

ALI ASANI

Further Reading

Haig, W., ed. *Cambridge History of India*, vol. 3, 56–60.
Nizami, K.A. *Some Aspects of Religion and Politics in India during the 13th Century*. Bombay, 1961.

REFORM, OR ISLAH

The Concept, Historical Development, and Main Views

Islah is an infinitive form derived from the root *s-l-h* and has the sense of "to improve, to better, or to put something into a better position." It may be seen as the Arabic counterpart of reform. The word *islah* occurs in forty verses of the Qur'an in the sense of "to restore oneself or to reconcile people with one another, to make peace." *Muslih*, the active participle of *islah*, is used to describe people who favor peace and order against wickedness, disorder, and anarchy. In the Qur'anic terminology, *islah* is the opposite of *ifsad* (corruption), and *muslih* is the opposite of *mufsid* (practicing corruption). The term *islah* also occurs in hadith (tradition) collections.

The term *islah* has acquired a systematic sense imbued with a Salafi tendency within religious thought owing to the ideological contributions of Muhammad 'Abduh and M. Rashid Rida. Modern view of islah aims at the revivification of Islamic values and is based on the principle of "commanding the good and forbidding the evil" of the Qur'an (3:104, 110). Champions of the islah movement also emphasize the Qur'anic verse that reads, "I only wish to reform you as best as I can" (11:88). Another point of reference for them is a hadith that heralds that God will bring about people in each century who are able to accomplish religious and moral reformation. Although past reform attempts stressed the adherence to the Prophet, modern reformist movements viewed the Qur'an as the most important source of reference. Those who thought it necessary to adhere to the Sunnah of the Prophet were of the opinion that innovative practices (bid'ah) penetrated the spheres of religious beliefs and worship. In their view, the articles of faith have gained a speculative outlook thanks to kalam (Islamic theology) discussions. Another reason for the increasing number of innovative ideas were the esoteric (batini) interpretation of the scripture and the views of the extreme branches of the Shi'ah. As for the domain of worship and prayers, they believed that excessive asceticism and mystic practices that stemmed from some Sufi movements and that run contrary to the *Sunnah* were indications of practices that opposed the essence of Islam. Innovations that were thought to be within the domain of belief and prayer were each deemed threatening to the creedal, political, and moral unity of Islam.

The political and moral turmoil that followed the wars of Siffin (AH 37/657 CE) and Nahrawan (38/658) resulted in political and religious controversies between the political authority and the Kahrijites and Shi'i groups. This schism played an effective role in the development of the sects that the Sunni view called ahl al-bid'ah (the people of innovation). At the end of the seventh century, the Muslim community gained a heterogeneous outlook. Theological controversies surrounding issues such as predestination, freedom of the will, the problem of evil, divine attributes, and whether or not the Qur'an was created became determining factors in sectarian identities. However, dominant official Sunnism did not appear to retain sufficient unifying force and vitality to mold the religious and moral conducts of new generations. It also diminished, to some extent, the religiously and culturally determinant power of the Sunnah (the sociological bases of which had already been weakened) within the state, which had a diverse ethnic structure and expanded borders.

The community in which early Muslims (the Companions and the generation after them) practiced the true meaning of the Sunnah was gradually disappearing. The famous discussion that took place between Hasan al-Basri (d. 110/728) and Wasil b. 'Ata' and their disagreement marked the beginning of the resystematization of the Sunni and Salafi schools against the schools that are considered by the Sunnis as the people of innovation, such as the Shi'a, Kharijiyyah, Jahmiyyal, and Mu'tazilah. The work of Ahmed b. Hanbal (d. 855/241 H) entitled *al-Radd 'ala al-Zanadiqa wa al-Jahmiyyah* is a good example of Sunnism prepared to battle the newfangled movements. The main impetus for the reformists who rejected the innovations was the desire to fight against the sects that brought innovative ideas into the social and individual lives of the believers and to revive the Sunnah with a view to guiding people back to the authentic faith.

It is in this sense that Rashid Rida refers to Ibn Hazm (fifth/eleventh century), Ibn Taymiyya (seventh/thirteenth century), Ibn Hajar al-Asqalani (ninth/fifteenth century), and Shawqani of Yaman (twelfth/eighteenth century) as the reformists and renewers (mujaddid) of their own centuries. Opposing the political authorities of their own eras, these scholars committed themselves to preserving the continuity of the Sunnah tradition as well as the original values of Islam through it. As a result of historical and cultural development, the modern Salafi movement of the Egyptian roots marks the last and the most productive phase in terms of the reformist stance. Among the prominent leading figures of this movement are Jamal al-Din al-Afghani, Muhammad Abduh, and Abd al-Rahman al-Kawakibi.

In the Muslim/Arab world, one may find many factors that have contributed to the development of the notion of islah. In an attempt to restore the Islamic way of living in accordance with the pristine state of Islam that the first generations lived, the Wahhabiyah advocated the idea of clinging to the Scripture and the Sunna and of shunning innovations and superstitions. One of the factors contributing to the Arab renaissance from 1822 on is the Bulak Printing House in Egypt, through which Egyptian, Syrian, and Lebanese intellectuals spread the doctrines of the movement. In the Ottoman Empire, by inaugurating *Tanzimat* (a policy of reforms) with the Gulkhane Khatt-i Humayun on November 3, 1839, the Sultan 'Abd al-Majid lay the foundations for the notion of liberal administration. With the Declaration of Reforms in 1856, the reforms launched under the influence of the West were gradually enforced in society, and thus the thought and impact of the West were transmitted to the Near East. Moreover, as Joseph Hajjar points out, the facts that the Eastern churches were exposed to Western thought and that missionary activities effected a reactionary movement on the part of the Muslims helped establish an intellectual infrastructure in the Muslim world.

Furthermore, since the beginning of the nineteenth century, Muslims familiarized themselves with Western science, culture, and technology via translations and travels. They had on their agenda discussion of the causes of—and solutions to—the backwardness of the Muslim world, which was the main theme of the writings of Muhammad Abduh and Rashid Rida in *al-Urwa al-Wuthqa* and *al-Manar*. Ernest Renan's conference on "Islam and Science" at the Sorbonne on March 29, 1883, and the subsequent discussions that took place between Renan and al-Afghani led the reformists to struggle against the thesis that Islam clashed with science and that it was the reason that the Muslim world is backward. The main driving force and motivation of the reformists to put an end to the cultural and social stagnation was the following Qur'anic verse: "God does not change the state of a people until they change themselves" (13:11). The proponents of islah held that it was necessary to combat the Sufi orders and conservative and traditionalist forces to improve the situation. The problems on which they concentrated most were education, law, and the Sufi orders. The improvement of Islamic education in traditional institutions and the *Azhar* in particular was considered to be related to the improvement of the mosques and religious foundations. The idea was that, if these were administered well enough, new resources could be obtained for the educational system.

This general reform movement at the end of the nineteenth century and the beginning of the twentieth century appeared in Arabic and Turkish media. After a while, islah became a movement that was attractive to those who strive for their cultural and social freedom. However, interest in islah that grew in the minds of young generations and intellectuals faced some difficulties. This new movement drew the suspicions of many countries, because it meant cultural and political inclinations toward the exaltation of Arabism and Pan-Islamism. Because of its social and political aspect, it caused reactions on the part of the authorities representing the status quo. Moreover, the reformists' uncompromising notion of divine oneness that viewed certain beliefs and practices of people as possessing idolatrous elements also drew criticisms of those who considered traditions and some rituals as complementary parts of religion. Lacking the patronage of a spiritual authority (e.g., one resembling the reformist church), the Salafiyya was apt to be accused of altering and even destroying the sacred Sunni tradition.

Furthermore, making constant references to the early period of Islam and to primary sources was one of the salient characteristics of the movement. According to the reformists, to be loyal to Islam amounted to the adherence to the Qur'an and the Sunna. The saying attributed to Malik b. Anas saying that "the later (generations) of this *ummah* will only improve through that by which the first (generations) improved" is a good example that indicates the historical connection of islah.

The reformists refused to accept the subjective forms of interpretation that claimed to find out the symbolism that lies deep beneath or beyond the visible images of the external meaning of the Qur'anic verses. Rashid Rida's comment that "interpretation *(ta'wil)* is a typical example of innovation *(bid'ah)*" epitomizes the reformist position. The reformist understanding of interpretation tended to reject ta'wil in favor of mere tafsir (commentary) and embraced the view that the Qur'anic revelation was as comprehensible to modern Muslims as it was to the salaf (first generations), except for certain verses concerning divine attributes and the hereafter. For them, the fundamental aim of tafsir was to explicate the moral values that would invigorate the religious sentiment and hence guide the believer. The Sunna is of the same significance as the Qur'an, and the former explains the latter. However, the reformist doctrine ascribes more importance to the Qur'an than to the Sunna.

Being aware of the significance of preaching and guidance in mosques and other environments, the reformists disseminated their doctrines by issuing journals (e.g., Rashid Rida's *al-Manar* in 1898–1935 and Ibn Badis' *al-Shihab* in 1925–1939). What the reformists attempted to do was to warn people against beliefs and practices that seemed religious but that in fact did not have reliable proofs in the Sunna of the Prophet, such as reciting Qur'anic verses over graves, saying prayers loudly, the mawlid celebrations, and some other practices that modern Salafiyya deems idolatrous, such as excessive veneration of the awliya' (the saintly men) and appealing to the dead for help.

Theoretically, the logical consequence of the principle of returning to the first and essential sources was the rejection of taqlid (following blindly) and the subsequent search for new ways in the practice of ijtihad (independent judgment). For example, Rashid Rida viewed ijtihad as the "vital energy of the religion." According to the reformists, ijma' (consensus) is neither the general consensus of the Muslim community nor the agreement of Muslim scholars on a given issue. For the reformists, ijma' is restricted to the consensus of the Companions of the Prophet only.

The intellectual infrastructure of the reformists is based on such notions as the universality of Islam, freedom of reason, and summoning people to God and religion. Summoning to God amounts to attempts at reverting to the Islamic sphere those Muslims who have been intoxicated by modern scientific knowledge and who have been in a position of ridiculing the injunctions of Islam.

On these foundations, the development of islah consists of three significant phases. The first phase is the period in which Jamal al-Din al-Afghani, Muhammad 'Abduh, and 'Abd al-Rahman al-Kawakibi lay the foundation of the islah project. The second one is the period covering the years from 1905 to 1950, in which Rashid Rida and Ibn Badis played crucial roles and which witnessed the emergence of the doctrinal system of the movement. Among the prominent figures of this period were Farid Wajdi, who composed a commentary on the Qur'an with a reconciliatory perspective; Mustafa al-Maraghi, who was the Shaykh of the Azhar; Mahmud Shaltut; and Ahmad Amin, who tried to give a Mu'tazilite direction to the movement through his writings in the *Journal of al-Thaqafa*. Muhammad Tahir b. Ashur in Tunisia and Abd al-Hamid b. Badis in Algeria were leading reformists during the second half of the nineteenth century. There are also many reformist activities in Turkey, Iran, and India. The third phase covers the period after World War II.

Consequently, the idea of islah—although it does not appear to be a religious and cultural movement as strong and unified as it was between the two world wars—continues its existence in different forms that are extreme in some cases and moderate in others. Whether it is considered the liberal reformism of the moderate intellectuals who advocate tolerance and freedom of inquiry, who wish to deliver people by way of education, and who maintain the optimistic view that man will evolve through reason and science; the radical reformism of Ikhwan al-Muslimin, who desired to maintain the existence of Islam in the world; or the reformism of the idealist youth that was activated by demands for social justice and political morality and articulated with concepts characteristic of the left, each of these tendencies represents one of the main preferences that were provided by al-Afghani, 'Abduh, and al-Kawakibi and that were disseminated by their followers throughout the East and West.

MÜFIT SELIM SARUHAN

Further Reading

Abduh, Muhammad. *Risalat al-Tawhid*, ed. Rashid Rida, 7, 15, 101, 103, 124–5, 139, 169, 172, 195–9, 202. Cairo, 1379/1960.
Abu al-Hasan al-Nadwi. *Rijal al-Fikr wa al-Da'wa fi al-Islam*, 25–60. Damascus, 1379/1960.

Amin, Ahmad. *Zu'ama' al-Islah fi al-Asr al-Hadith*. Cairo, 1368/1949.

Al-Afghani. Jamal al-Din. *al-Radd 'ala al-Dahriyyin*. Beirut, 1886.

Al-Afghani, Jamal al-Din and Muhammad Abduh. *Al-'Urwa al-Wuthqa*, 65–128. Cairo, 1958.

Brockelmann, Gal. *Tarikh al-Adab al-Arabi*, transl. A. Halim al-Najjar, vols. i and vi; vol. iii, 310–355. Cairo, 1983.

Halaf Allah, Ahmad. *al-Qur'an wa Mushkilat Hayatina al-Mu'asirah*, 63–5. Cairo, 1967.

Hourani, Albert. *Arabic Thought in the Liberal Age, 1798–1939*, 11, 46. Oxford, 1962.

Ibn Hazm. *Al-Ihkam*, ed. Ahmad Shakir, vol. i, 121–2; vol. iv, 132 ff. Cairo, 1345/1927.

Ikbal, Muhammad. *The Reconstruction of Religious Thought in Islam*, 89, 164. Oxford, UK, 1934.

Keddie, N.R. *An Islamic Response to Imperialism: Political and Religious Writings of Sayyid Jamal al-Din Afghani*. Berkeley, 1968.

Kerr, M. *Islamic Reform and the Political and Legal Theories of Abduh and R. Rida*, 179. Berkeley and Los Angeles, 1966.

Kudsi Zadeh, A. Albert. *Sayyid Jamal al-Din al-Afghani, An Annotated Bibliography*, 80. Leiden, 1970.

Merad, Ali. "Islah." In *Encyclopedia of Islam*, vol. iv, 141, 167. Leiden: Brill, 1978.

Rida, Rashid. *Tafsir al-Manar*, vols. i, x, xii. Cairo, 1353–1354.

Schacht, J. *The Origins of Muhammadan Jurisprudence*, 122. Oxford, UK, 1950.

Al-Shatibi. *Al-I'tisam*, ed. M. Rashid Rida, vol. i, 1–19. Cairo, 1332.

Wensinck, A.J. *al-Mu'jam al-Mufahras li-Alfaz al-Hadith al-Nabawi*, vol. viii, "slh." Leiden, 1936–1969.

RENEWAL (TAJDID)

Tajdid is an Arabic word that means "renewal" and that is usually coupled with *din* to mean "renewal of the religion." A similar but less common expression is *ihya' al-din,* which may be translated as "revival of the religion." Other phrases that occur less frequently in the literature are *ihya' al-sunna* (revival of the custom [of the Prophet]); *tajdid al-islam* (renewal of Islam); and *iqamat al-din* (the [proper] establishment of the religion). The "renewer" and the "reviver" of the religion are referred to as *mujaddid* and *muhyi al-din,* respectively.

These terms and their specific significances are not to be found in the Qur'an, although the general concepts of renewal and revival are part of Qur'anic prophetology, according to which God sent various prophets through time to various communities to cleanse and revitalize the primordial religion of Islam in the sense of submission to God. The concept of tajdid and the term *mujaddid* come rather from the famous hadith (tradition) recorded by Abu Da'ud in his *Sunan*, one of the six authoritative Sunni collections of the Prophet's statements, in which Muhammad foretells, "At the beginning [or possibly end] of every [Islamic] century, [there will come] someone who will renew the faith in it." The concept of tajdid is essentially an optimistic one, expressing the belief that the religion is always capable of regenerating itself through the insights and labors of its most gifted and morally excellent adherents.

The first such designated mujaddid for the second century by popular consensus (there is no formal mechanism for such a designation) is the Umayyad Caliph 'Umar ibn 'Abd al-'Aziz (d. AH 101/720 CE), who was lionized as the only righteous ruler among the Umayyad coterie of perceived godless tyrants. Every century since his time has henceforth been assigned a renewer of the faith, who tended to be drawn mainly from among the most prominent scholars of the time and, less frequently, from among pious rulers. Among scholars are the celebrated jurist Muhammad ibn Idris al-Shafi'i (d. 204/820), acknowledged for his groundbreaking contributions to jurisprudence, and, more famously, the theologian and prolific author with Sufi leanings, al-Ghazali (d. 505/1111); these men were acknowledged as the renewers of the second and sixth centuries, respectively. The latter is specifically given the title Muhyi al-Din, no doubt because of his magnum opus entitled *Ihya' 'Ulum al-Din (The Revivification of the Religious Sciences)* and for his seminal role in making Sufi thought part and parcel of the religious and intellectual mainstream. Other religious scholars who have been recognized as centennial renewers are al-Ash'ari (d. 324/935) and al-Baqillani (d. 403/1013), both stalwart defenders of Sunni orthodoxy during their time. One source is of the opinion that the 'Abbasid caliph al-Ma'mun (d. 218/833) was the renewer of the second century rather than al-Shafi'i, but this is clearly a minority opinion.

The Shi'i have their own list of mujaddids that are drawn from the descendants of the Prophet. Among the Sufis, the Naqshbandiyya in particular have their own tradition of mujaddids. It is from among this Sufi order that the well-known Indian Muslim scholar Shaykh Ahmad Sirhindi (d. 1034/1624) emerged as the acknowledged mujaddid of the eleventh century. Sirhindi is called, in Persian, *mujaddid-i alf thani* (renewer of the second millennium) and *Imam-i Rabbani* (the Divinely Appointed Leader). His disciples, dispersed throughout Central Asia and Afghanistan, are known as Mujaddidis, after the order established by him.

The title of mujaddid al-din was sometimes coveted by ambitious individuals, who tried to canvass for themselves as the promised renewer of their centuries. One such person who failed in this enterprise was the scholar and jurisprudent Jalal al-Din al-Suyuti

(d. 911/1505), who expressed hope in one of his works that he would be awarded this title for the tenth century. His irascible disposition and consequent general unpopularity militated against this possibility.

The tradition has persisted to the present day. For the thirteenth/nineteenth century, the erudite and charismatic Egyptian reformer Muhammad 'Abduh (d. 1323/1905), who served as the rector of Sunni Islam's premier educational institution, al-Azhar University in Cairo, is sometimes declared to be the reviver of the faith, but this is not a universally held opinion. So far, no one has emerged as the undisputed renewer of the fourteenth/twentieth century. The Iranian cleric and revolutionary Ayatullah Khomeini's (d. 1409/1989) name has been advanced as a possible contender, but this has by no means gained widespread recognition.

ASMA AFSARUDDIN

Further Reading

Jansen, J.J.G. Art. "Tadjdid." In *The Encyclopaedia of Islam, New Edition*, ed. P.J. Bearman et al., vol. 10, 61–2. Leiden and London, 2000.

Lazarus-Yafeh, Hava. "*Tajdid al-Din*: A Reconsideration of Its Meaning, Roots and Influence in Islam." In *Studies in Islamic and Judaic Traditions*, eds. William M. Brinner and Stephen D. Ricks. Atlanta, Ga, 1986.

Van Donzel, E. Art. "Mudjaddid." In *The Encyclopaedia of Islam, New Edition*, ed. C.E. Bosworth et al., vol. 7, 290. Leiden and London, 1993.

Voll, John O. "Renewal & Reform in Islamic History: *Tajdid* and *Islah*." In *Voices of Resurgent Islam*, ed. John L. Esposito, 32–47. New York and Oxford, 1983.

RHETORIC

An interest in rhetorical practice and theory has been an aspect of Islamic civilization since its inception. The Prophet Muhammad received his calling in a cultural environment in which various kinds of verbal arts, including poetry and oratory, were taken seriously and held in high esteem, and the art of public speaking and oratory has played a very important role in the history of Islam ever since. However, because the word *rhetoric* may have different meanings in different contexts in Western languages, there is no precise notional equivalent in Arabic. The closest equivalents are *al-balagha* and *al-khataba*, which are frequently used in compounds such as *'ilm al-balagha* (the science of eloquence) and *fann al-khataba* (the art of public speaking), respectively. *'Ilm al-balagha* parallels rhetoric in Western traditions in the sense that it deals with tropes and figures of speech, thus corresponding with what is called *elocutio* in Latin rhetoric. In general, however, *'ilm al-balagha* shows little similarity with rhetoric in the sense of public speaking and oratorical art. In this respect, *fann al-khataba* is a closer counterpart to rhetoric.

To a significant degree, early preachers and orators in Islam inherited their profession and position in society from the pre-Islamic orator (khatib), soothsayer (kahin), and poet (sha'ir), and from traditions of rhetoric current in the Near East in late antiquity and the early Middle Ages. Speeches and sermons attributed to leading personalities during the first centuries of Islam—including the Prophet, the caliphs, governors, generals, and others—were subsequently recorded in writing and preserved in the classical works of adab (edifying literature), such as the *Kitab al-Bayan wa-l-Tabyin* of al-Jahiz (d. 868) and *'Uyun al-Akhbar* by Ibn Qutayba (d. 889); in chronicles such as *The History of al-Tabari* (d. 923); and, in the case of Muhammad's sermons, in the hadith literature and biographies of the prophet. These recorded speeches served as models for later orators. Another important source in this respect, particularly in Shi'i circles, was the book *Nahj al-Balagha*, which purportedly contained the speeches and letters of 'Ali, the Prophet's son-in-law (d. 661). During subsequent centuries, sermons by eloquent preachers and learned scholars ('ulama) were also preserved in writing to form part of this corpus of exemplary models, which have continued to exert an influence up to modern times. Among the most important of these are the collections attributed to the Hanbali scholar 'Abd al-Rahman bin 'Ali Abu 'l-Faraj Ibn al-Jawzi (d. 1200), who was also the author of a well-known handbook for preachers and admonishers (see below).

Different names are applied to various kinds of oratory or preaching in the sources: for example, khutba (official sermon in the mosque, referring specifically to the Friday sermon), qasas (a "free" sermon based on edifying narratives) and wa'z (admonition, exhortation). Although the term *khutba* tends to be reserved for official preaching in the mosque by a preacher (khatib) approved by the authorities, qasas and wa'z were applied to less-regulated kinds of preaching. As such, the latter were the focus of much controversy during the Middle Ages. Qasas came under particular attack, because its practitioners, the qussas, were accused of leading people astray by transmitting false hadiths, thus creating political turmoil and social unrest among the ordinary people. Several well-known scholars contributed to this criticism, including Abu Hamid al-Ghazali (d. 1111), who based his arguments on those of Abu Talib al-Makki (d. 996). More generally, there was a tendency on the part of the scholarly community to make a distinction between undesirable forms of unofficial preaching (qasas) on the one hand

and praiseworthy or at least tolerable forms of the same practice (wa'z) on the other. Although there may be little difference between these genres in reality, the term *wa'z* thus came to be the preferred designation for a more respectable kind of "free" preaching, whereas the term *qasas* fell into disrepute and subsequently acquired the meaning of popular "storytelling." One example of a collection of sermons that has been variously described as wa'z or qasas is *al-Rawd al-Fa'iq (The Splendid Garden)*, attributed to Shu'ayb al-Hurayfish (d. c. 1400).

The rhetorical science called 'ilm al-balagha developed through exegetical as well as linguistic and rhetorical practices. As a scholastic discipline, it acquired a certain maturity during the thirteenth century, epitomized in *Talkhis al-Miftah (Epitome of the Key)* and *al-Idah (The Clarification)* by Muhammad bin 'Abd al-Rahman al-Qazwini (1268–1338). Al-Qazwini had important precursors, particularly 'Abd al-Qahir al-Jurjani (d. 1078) and Abu Ya'qub Yusuf al-Sakkaki (d. 1229). However, al-Qazwini provided a systematic presentation of the subject that came to be most influential during subsequent centuries, including, for instance, the common tripartite division of 'ilm al-balagha into the following categories: (1) 'ilm al-ma'ani (the science of meanings); (2) 'ilm al-bayan (the science of clarification); and (3) 'ilm al-badi' (the science of embellishments). Although the first of these may be seen as dealing with pragmatic issues of language use, such as the distinction between informative statements and performative speech acts, the second concerns the use and interpretation of metaphorical language to clarify rather than obscure. The third is about the art of embellishing an utterance with various modes of beautification, including figures of meaning and figures of speech.

To a significant degree, the development of 'ilm al-balagha was shaped by theological concerns, first and foremost the interpretation of the Qur'an. Many of its illustrative cases and examples are taken from the Qur'an, and there is a clear emphasis on the possibility of reconstructing the intentions of the speaker, who in the case of the Qur'an is God Himself. For this reason, it might be argued that 'ilm al-balagha is a hermeneutic discipline and an auxiliary to Qur'anic exegesis rather than rhetoric proper. Apart from this, various forms of rhetorical theory and practice were cultivated by bureaucrats and courtiers in more profane settings. In the bureaucracies and erudite circles of the caliphate, it was important to be able to master elegant prose as well as poetry in the composition of official letters and documents. Over the centuries, handbooks and guides were written about these subjects to serve a practical purpose, including, for instance, the *Subh al-a'Sha fi*

Sina'at al-Insha', al-Qalqashandi's (d. 1418) famous manual for bureaucrats and clerks in the Mamluk administration. In addition, the art of public speaking and oratory, including the art of preaching, was discussed and practiced in terms of al-khataba rather than al-balagha. The former was commented upon theoretically by the medieval Muslim philosophers, such as al-Farabi (Alfarabius; d. 950), Ibn Sina (Avicenna; d. 1037), and Ibn Rushd (Averroes; d. 1198), who treated it in the context of their studies of the Aristotelian *Organon* (the corpus of texts dealing with the various tools of logical reasoning to be used in all the sciences). However, the philosophers were not the only ones to take an interest in the art of public speaking. Quite naturally, the subject of al-khataba also attracted the attention of Muslim preachers and theologians for other, more practical reasons than those that motivated the philosophers. The primary concern here was homiletic practice (the preaching of religious truths and values) rather than philosophical and logical debates. In addition to the collections of sermons, a few books with rules and guidelines for preachers have also survived from the medieval period, such as 'Ala' al-Din Ibn al-'Attar al-Dimashqi's (d. 1324) *Kitab Adab al-Khatib (The Book of the Preacher's Etiquette)* and 'Abd al-Rahman bin 'Ali Abu'l-Faraj Ibn al-Jawzi's (d. 1200) *Kitab al-Qussas wa-l-Mudhakkirin (The Book of the Storytellers/Admonishers and Those Who Remind)*.

The medieval Muslim works of 'ilm al-balagha, like those devoted to the art of public speaking (fann al-khataba), show significant similarities with rhetoric as discussed and practiced in European traditions. Several concepts and notions are similar, such as the distinction between figures of meaning and figures of speech. With regard to the art of public speaking proper (fann al-khataba), it should be remembered that the translation into Arabic of the Aristotelian *Organon*, including the book on rhetoric, was a complex process that went through several phases, from the early works based on Syriac translations of the editions current in late antiquity to the final phase as represented in the scholarship of Christian and Muslim Aristotelians in 'Abbasid Baghdad. The commentaries that were subsequently composed by Muslim philosophers are important contributions in the history of rhetoric: not only did they provide the Muslim world with a knowledge of Aristotelian rhetoric, they also came to have significance in the West, where they were translated into Latin and provided with commentaries by Christian scholars during the later Middle Ages. This process provided an important impetus to the cultural development in Europe known as the Renaissance.

PHILIP HALLDÉN

Primary Sources

Aristotle. *Ars Rhetorica: The Arabic Version*, 2 vols., ed. Malcolm C. Lyons. Cambridge: Pembroke Arabic Texts, 1982.

al-Farabi. *Deux Ouvrages Inédits sur la Rétorique*, eds. Jacques Langhade and Mario Grignaschi. Beirut: Dar El-Machreq, 1971.

al-Hurayfish, Shu'ayb. *al-Rawd al-Fa'iq fi'l-Mawa'iz wa'l-Raqa'iq*, ed. Khalil al-Mansur. Beirut: Dar al-Kutub al-'Ilmiyya, 1997.

Ibn al-'Attar al-Dimashqi. *Kitab Adab al-Khatib*, ed. Mohamed Ibn Hocine Esslimani. Beirut: Dar al-Gharb al-Islami, 1996.

Ibn al-Jawzi. *Kitab al-Qussas wa'l-Mudhakkirin*, ed. Merlin L. Swartz. Beirut: Dar El-Machreq Éditeurs, 1971.

Ibn Rushd. *Averroes' Three Short Commentaries on Aristotle's 'Topics,' 'Rhetoric,' and 'Poetics'*, ed. and transl. Charles E. Butterworth. Albany, NY: State University of New York Press, 1977.

Ibn Sina. *Al-Shifa': al-Khatabah*, vol. 1, pt. 8, rev. I, ed. Muhammad Salim. Cairo: Imprimerie Nationale, 1954.

al-Qazwini, Muhammad bin 'Abd al-Rahman. *Talkhis al-Miftah fi'l-Ma'ani wa'l-Bayan wa'l-Badi'*. Cairo: Mustafa al-Babi al-Halabi, 1938.

Further Reading

Berkey, Jonathan P. *Popular Preaching & Religious Authority in the Medieval Islamic Near East*. Seattle and London: University of Washington Press, 2001.

Black, Deborah. *Logic and Aristotle's* Rhetoric *and* Poetics *in Medieval Arabic Philosophy*. Leiden and New York: E.J. Brill, 1990.

Bohas, George, Jan-Patrick Guillaume, and Djamel Eddin Kouloughli. *The Arabic Linguistic Tradition*. London and New York: Routledge, 1990.

Butterworth, Charles E. "The Rhetorican and his Relationship to the Community: Three Accounts of Aristotle's *Rhetoric*." In *Islamic Theology and Philosophy. Studies in Honor of George F. Hourani*, ed. Michael E. Marmura. New York: State University of New York Press, 1984.

Halldén, Philip. "What is Arab Islamic Rhetoric? Rethinking the History of Muslim Oratory Art and Homiletics." *International Journal of Middle East Studies* 37 (2005): 19–38.

Heinrichs, Wolfhart. "Poetik, Rhetorik, Literaturkritik, Metrik und Reimlehre." In *Grundriss der Arabischen Philologie*, vol. 2, ed. Helmut Gätje. Wiesbaden: Reichert, 1987.

Jenssen, Herbjorn. *The Subtleties and Secrets of the Arabic Language: Preliminary Investigations into al-Qazwini's* Talkhis al-Miftah. Bergen: Centre for Middle Eastern and Islamic Studies, 1998.

Larcher, Pierre. "Quand, en Arabe, on Parlait de l'Arabe... (I): Essai sur la Méthodologie de l'Histoire des 'Metalangages Arabes'." *Arabica* 35 (1988): 117–42.

Larcher, Pierre. "Quand, en Arabe, on Parlait de l'Arabe... (II): Essai sur la Catégorie de *Isha'* (vs *Khabar*)." *Arabica* 38 (1991): 246–73.

Larcher, Pierre. "Quand, en Arabe, on Parlait de l'Arabe... (III): Grammaire, Logique, Rhétorique dans l'Islam Post-classique." *Arabica* 39 (1992): 358–84.

Larcher, Pierre. "Eléments de Rhétorique Aristotélicienne dans la Tradition Arabe Hors la *Falsafa*." In *Traditions de l'Antiquité Classique*, eds. Gilbert Dahan and Irène Rosier-Catach. Paris: Vrin, 1998.

Larkin, Margaret. *The Theology of Meaning: 'Abd al-Qahir al-Jurjani's Theory of Discourse*. New Haven, Conn: American Oriental Society, 1995.

Mehren, August F. *Die Rhetorik der Araber*. Hildesheim, New York: G. Olms, 1970 (1853).

Pedersen, Johs. "The Criticism of the Islamic Preacher." *Die Welt des Islams* II (1953): 215–31.

Simon, Udo Gerald. *Mittelalterliche Arabische Sprachbetrachtung Zwischen Grammatik und Rhetorik: 'ilm al-Ma'ani bei as-Sakkaki*. Heidelberg: Heidelberger Orientverlag, 1993.

Smyth, William. "Rhetoric and *'Ilm al-Balagha*: Christianity and Islam." *The Muslim World* LXXXII (1992): 242–55.

Swartz, Merlin L. "The Rules of the Popular Preaching in Twelfth-Century Baghdad, According to Ibn al-Jawzi." In *Preaching and Propaganda in the Middle Ages: Islam, Byzantium, Latin West*, eds. George Makdisi, Dominique Sourdel, and Janine Sourdel-Thomine. Paris: Presses Universitaires de France, 1983.

Swartz, Merlin L. "Arabic Rhetoric and the Art of the Homily in Medieval Islam." In *Religion and Culture in Medieval Islam*, eds. Richard Hovannisian and Geroges Sabagh. Cambridge, UK: Cambridge University Press, 1999.

Wansbrough, J. 1968. "Arabic Rhetoric and Qur'anic Exegesis." *Bulletin of the School of Oriental and African Studies* xxxi (1968): 469–85.

ROAD NETWORKS

The roads of the medieval Middle East were largely a continuation of the preexisting road systems of the Roman and Partho-Sasanian empires, which in turn were often continuations of more ancient routes. Although paved streets had existed in towns before the Roman period, paved roads between settlements were a Roman innovation. Under the Romans, the development of the road network was dictated by military and, to a lesser extent, commercial considerations. During the Islamic period, the existing road system was supplemented by new routes that were developed to provide easy access to Mecca and Medina.

Principal Hajj routes ran from Damascus (Darb al-Hajj al-Shami), Cairo (Darb al-Hajj al-Misri), and Baghdad (Darb Zubayda), with subsidiary routes from Yemen and Oman and trans-Saharan routes from West Africa. The majority of these routes were unpaved (except in places where they used preexisting Roman roads), although they were provided with facilities such as milestones, wells, cisterns (burak), caravansaries, and mosques. The best-documented route is the Darb Zubayda, which was constructed by the 'Abbasid caliph Harun al-Rashid during the eighth century and which included palatial residences in addition to the usual facilities. The Syrian pilgrimage route via Medain Saleh and Petra is of the greatest antiquity and was of primary importance during the Umayyad period and later under the Ottomans. Some idea of the political importance of this route can be gauged by the fact that the 'Abbasid revolution was organized from Humayma, a small town on the road midway between Damascus and Medina. The Egyptian route via Aqaba/Ayla is the least well-known route, although it appears to have been the most important for much of the Medieval Period, when it was used by the Mamluk sultans.

There is little evidence that major new roads were constructed during the Islamic period, although improvements were made to existing routes, such as the construction of bridges, rock cut passes, and the provision of milestones. One of the earliest known examples of road improvements is a rock cut pass near Lake Tiberias in Palestine, which is recorded on a milestone (now in the Israel Museum) dated to the reign of the Umayyad Caliph 'Abd al-Malik. Other examples of rock cut passes include two at Aqaba/Ayla: one on the Arabian side dated to the tenth century and one on the Egyptian side dated to the Mamluk period.

Numerous bridges are known both through historical sources and through archaeology. Bridges were of two types: arched masonry structures (qantara) and wooden floating structures (jisr). The former were used for rivers of limited span, whereas the latter were used on wide rivers or where there was a significant variation in seasonal water levels. Often caravansaries or khans were located next to bridges, such as at al-Harba south of Samarra in Iraq and at Lajjun in Palestine. Rivers also functioned as routes in their own right; the Tigris and Euphrates rivers provided important links between Anatolia and the [Persian] Gulf, just as the Nile connected upper Egypt with the Mediterranean.

One innovation of the Islamic period was the increased use of camels for transport (c.f. Bulliet), which opened up trans-desert routes for commercial use but which also meant that roads did not have to be maintained to the same standards that were needed for wheeled vehicles. There was, however, some revival of wheeled transport in the eastern Islamic world during the thirteenth century, when the Mongols established an imperial road network.

Also during the thirteenth century, the Mamluk rulers of Egypt and Syria revived and improved the postal routes of early Islamic times. The revival took place in two stages. During the first phase, the route was provided with khans that could be used both by the members of the official postal service and by merchants traveling the route. During the later period, special postal stations were built where horses and

riders could be exchanged. The most important route was the road linking Cairo with Damascus, the so-called Via Maris, which was provided with a number of bridges, the most famous of which is Jisr Jindas in Palestine, which carries carvings of panthers. Other routes included a special road into the Lebanon mountains to bring ice to Damascus.

As in other cultures, settlements often developed around road systems. Thus, the caliphal city of Samarra was built along a main arterial route leading north from Baghdad to Mosul. Similarly, the city of Ramla in Palestine, founded during the early eighth century, was built at the intersection of the Cairo–Damascus route (Via Maris) and the Jaffa–Jerusalem roads.

ANDREW PETERSEN

See also Hajj; Silk Roads; Travel; Transport; Ibn Khurradadhbih; Yaqut

Primary Sources

Ibn Khudadhbih. *al-Masalik wa-l-Mamalik (The Book of Routes and Provinces)*.

Further Reading

Birks, J.S. *Across the Savannas to Mecca: The Overland Pilgrimage Route from West Africa*. London, 1978.
Petersen, A.D. "Early Ottoman Forts on the Darb al-Hajj." *Levant* 21 (1989): 97–118.
al-Rashid, S.A. *Darb Zubayda*. Riyadh, 1980.
Sauvaget, Jean. "Les Caravanserais Syriens du Hadjdj de Constantinople." *Ars Islamica* 4 (1937).
———. *La Poste aux Chevaux dans l'Empire des Mamelouks*. Paris: Adrien-Maisoneuve, 1941.

ROMANCE LANGUAGES AND LITERATURES OF IBERIA

For centuries after the settlement of Muslims in parts of the Iberian Peninsula (beginning in 711 CE), the vernacular literature produced by Christians in Spain displayed various signs of cross-fertilization with Arabic. Contact with Arabic occurred not only through actual Muslim kingdoms on the peninsula but also through Muslim minorities living at different times under Christian rule. There is much debate today, especially among Hispanists, regarding the extent of the influences brought about by this contact. Although some consider the role of Islamic civilization central to the literary history of medieval Spain, others interpret it as a marginal detail; other opinions cover the vast range in between. To consider the nature of the contact between Arabic and Romance literatures, one naturally has to raise questions about the appropriate ways to gauge how one culture affects another and what the actual definition of *influence* is; such issues are increasingly being addressed by scholars.

Attention must be paid to the fact that the languages of the Iberian Peninsula are not limited to Castilian (commonly referred to as Spanish): Basque (not a Romance language), Catalan, and Gallego-Portuguese enjoy a rich heritage in the literary history of Spain. However, because of its frequent contact with Muslim communities, Castile appears to show the stamp of encounter more visibly.

Certain facts about the interaction between Castilian literature and the cultural world of Islam are clear. Castilian contains numerous words of Arabic origin. In the realm of nonfiction, the constant movement of Arabic medical, philosophical, and scientific treatises into the vernacular, enabled by events such as the massive translation projects of King Alfonso X of Castile (r. 1252–1284 CE), embedded Arabic terms into Castilian vocabulary and even syntax, much of which is visible today.

In the realm of fiction, literature produced in Castilian by Christian authors of the Middle Ages provides evidence of intimate engagement with the Islamicate cultures that coexisted on the Peninsula for centuries. The tradition of prose narrative in Castilian was enriched by translations or close retellings from Arabic and other non-Western languages (e.g., the tales of Kalila and Dimna). The didactic narratives of Don Juan Manuel (14 CE) and Petrus Alfonsus (12 CE) show ample evidence of Indian, Persian, and Arabic sources, among others. The early popular lyric of Castilian, often expressing the laments of a young lovesick girl, is injected with Arabic words and metrical sensibilities.

The question of Arabic poetics as an integral part of Castilian literary history becomes more complex in cases in which the works being studied are no longer obvious retellings or translations. Here, scholarship is divided with regard to the Western or Eastern derivation of medieval masterpieces such as Juan Ruiz's *El Libro de Buen Amor* (c. 1330 CE), Fernando de Rojas' *La Celestina* (1499 CE), and mystical poetry. Much debate has been generated by questions of a strong Islamic versus Western and Latin presence in the motifs, patterns of composition, and general thematics in these and other works. No consensus has been achieved, but a useful discussion about the nature of the fundamental hybridity of Spanish culture—transcending mere categories of Eastern or Western identification—has been generated. At the same time, increasing attention is being paid to Spain's intricate ties to Islamic civilization.

LEYLA ROUHI

See also Folk Literature, Arabic; Kalila wa Dimna; European Literature, Perception of Islam

Further Reading

Brann, Ross, ed. *Languages of Power in Islamic Spain.* Bethesda, Md: CDL Press, 1997.
Cacho Blecua, Juan Manuel, and María Jesús Lacarra, eds. *Calila e Dimna.* Madrid: Castalia, 1984.
Castro, Américo. *De la Edad Conflictiva.* Madrid: Taurus, 1961.
Constable, Olivia Remie, ed. *Medieval Iberia: Readings from Christian, Muslim, and Jewish Sources.* Philadelphia: University of Pennsylvania Press, 1997.
Hook, David, and Barry Taylor, eds. *Cultures in Contact in Medieval Spain: Historical and Literary Essays Presented to L.P. Harvey.* London: King's College Medieval Studies, 1990.
Khadra Jayussi, Salma, ed. *The Legacy of Muslim Spain.* Leiden: Brill, 1992.
López Baralt, Luce. *Huellas del Islam en la Literatura Española: de Juan Ruiz a Juan Goytisolo.* Madrid: Hiperión, 1985.
Márquez Villanueva, Francisco. "The Alfonsine Cultural Concept." In *Alfonso X of Castile: The Learned King (1221–1284): An International Symposium: Harvard University 17 November 1984*, eds. Francisco Márquez Villanueva and Carlos Alberto Vega, 76–109. Cambridge, Mass: Department of Romance Languages, Harvard University, 1990.
Menocal, María Rosa. *Shards of Love: Exile and the Origins of the Lyric.* Durham, NC: Duke University Press, 1994.
Rouhi, Leyla. "Trotaconventos, Doña Garoça and the Dynamics of Dialectical Reasoning in the *Libro de Buen Amor*." *Bulletin of Hispanic Studies* 76 (1999): 21–33.
Smith, Colin. *Christians and Moors in Spain*, 3 vols. Warminster: Aris and Philips, 1988.

ROSEWATER

The manufacture of rosewater (ma' al-ward or ma' ward; sometimes contracted to maward) was an important industry with centers in Damascus, Jur (in Fars, southern Iran), and other places, including Muslim Spain. An historian of the early tenth century, quoting a document from the time of Harun al-Rashid (r. 786–809), mentions that the caliphs in Baghdad used to receive thirty thousand flasks of rosewater from Fars annually. The technique of its distillation using steam or hot air ovens is described in several medieval treatises; sublimation was another method used.

Rosewater was normally made from red roses (the damask rose was particularly popular) using fresh or dried petals, and it was usually blended with herbs and aromatic substances such as saffron, musk, or camphor. It was used medicinally: it was deemed good for the stomach and the eyes and was used for a variety of diseases. It was also very popular in dishes and lotions, as a refreshing ingredient and a scent, and it was used as a mouthwash, a deodorant, and in ointments. Rosewater could, by vaporization, be turned into a scented powder, which could be used in various ways. Julanjabin (from the Persian *gol-angabin* [rose honey]) was a kind of preserve made from roses and honey.

Rosewater is included among the ingredients of countless recipes in, for instance, the anonymous Arabic Mamluk cookery book *Kanz al-Fawa'id fi Tanwi' al-Mawa'id (The Treasure-Trove of Things Delicious for the Diversification of the Table's Dishes)*. The same source also gives recipes for various kinds of rosewater. These may differ in color (i.e., pale, red, or glaucous), provenance (i.e., from Jur, Damascus, Nasibin, or Persia), or composition (i.e., with saffron and musk, with camphor and musk). The Persian word for rosewater, *gol-ab*, adopted in Arabic as *jullab* (sometimes *julab*), was in turn borrowed by many European languages as *julep,* in the meantime acquiring the sense of various kinds of sweet drink. The popularity of rosewater is not unconnected with the greet esteem in which the rose, chief of flowers, was held; this is obvious, for instance, from the countless poems in Arabic (at least in Islamic times) and even more in Persian, in which the rose is associated with love. Strange though it may seem, the Arabic word for roses, *ward,* the Persian/Turkish *gol/gül,* and the several European words (Greek *rhodon*; English *rose*) are all related etymologically, going back to an Old Iranian word.

GEERT JAN VAN GELDER

See also Perfume

Further Reading

al-Hassan, Ahmad Y. and Donald R. Hill. *Islamic Technology: An Illustrated History*, 140–3. Cambridge, UK: Cambridge University Press, 1986.

Johnstone, Penelope C. "Ward." In *Encyclopaedia of Islam, New Edition*, vol. 11, 144–5. Leiden: Brill, 2002.

Rodinson, Maxime, A.J. Arberry, and Charles Perry. *Medieval Arab Cookery*. Totnes, Devon: Prospect Books, 2001.

Sanagustin, F. "Ma' al-Ward." In *Encyclopaedia of Islam, New Edition*, Supplement, fasc. 7–8. Leiden: Brill, 2003.

S

SA'ADYAH GAON

Born in Egypt in 882 CE, Sa'adyah ben Joseph al-Fayyumi emigrated to Palestine around the beginning of the tenth century, studying with a leading Hebraist in Tiberias before migrating to Iraq. His incisive mind, erudition, and forceful personality were early apparent and his intervention on behalf of Iraqi Jewish authorities in a calendar dispute with the Palestinian Jewish leadership (921–922) brought him wide recognition. In 928, the Exilarch, or Head of the Babylonian Jewish community, David ben Zakkai, appointed him *Gaon* (Head) of the *Yeshiva* (academy) of Sura in Baghdad. Within two years, however, Sa'adyah and the Exilarch became embroiled in a politico-economical dispute that quickly escalated into a community-wide affair, with each side issuing bans of excommunication. When reconciliation between the parties was effected some six years later, Sa'adya again became the undisputed Gaon of Sura, continuing in this post until his death in 942.

Styled "the first and foremost of scholars everywhere" by the twelfth-century polymath Abraham Ibn Ezra, Sa'adyah pioneered many disciplines. Immersed from an early age in such traditional Jewish subjects as Bible and Talmud, he was also well versed in Muslim and Christian scholarship. Indeed, his greatest innovation was to synthesize many different areas of Jewish and Arabic learning. Impressed by Arab grammarians, he composed the first Hebrew lexicon, *Sefer ha-'Egron* (902) and wrote a pioneering work on Hebrew grammar, *Kutub al-Lugha (Books of the Language)*, which bears the imprint of Arabic linguistic theory. He translated the Bible into Arabic to make it more accessible to Jewish readers; noted for its idiomatic qualities, this translation (Ar. *tafsir*) served as the basis for numerous other Arabic versions, some of them Christian. Sa'adyah also wrote Arabic commentaries on many, if not all, of the books of the Bible. These commentaries, which have only survived in part, are notable for their long, programmatic introductions, their attention to thematic and structural issues, and their incorporation of Arabic exegetical terminology. A gifted liturgical poet, he also edited the Jewish prayer book. Sa'adyah tirelessly defended rabbinic Judaism, polemicizing against the Karaites, a Jewish sect that denied the authority of the Oral Tradition, and refuting the freethinker, Haywayhi of Balkh (ninth century). Sa'adyah's *chef d'oeuvre* is his *Kitab al-amanat wa'l-i'tiqadat (Book of Doctrines and Beliefs)*, composed toward the end of his life. One of the earliest Jewish works of systematic theology, it is firmly grounded in the Bible and rabbinic literature on the one hand, and the Mu'tazilite *kalam* on the other, while incorporating certain philosophical doctrines. From the outset, Sa'adyah argues that knowledge is grounded in revelation and reason, and that these two sources are complementary. The book covers such topics as creation, the proof of God's existence and unity, divine revelation, divine command and prohibition, obedience to God and rebellion, human merits and demerits, the essence of the soul and the afterlife, resurrection, redemption, reward and punishment, and ethics. It was translated into Hebrew by Judah Ibn Tibbon (Provence, 1186).

DANIEL FRANK

See also Baghdad; Freethinkers; Hebrew; Judeo-Arabic; Kalam; Polemics and Disputation; Scriptural Exegesis, Jewish

Primary Sources

Gaon, Sa'adyah. *The Book of Beliefs and Opinions*. Transl. Samuel Rosenblatt. New Haven, CT: Yale University Press, 1948.

Sa'adyah ben Joseph al-Fayyumi. *The Book of Theodicy: Translation and Commentary on the Book of Job*. Transl. L.E. Goodman. New Haven, CT: Yale University Press, 1988.

Further Reading

Brody, Robert. *The Geonim of Babylonia and the Shaping of Medieval Jewish Culture*. New Haven, CT: Yale University Press, 1998.

Malter, Henry. *Saadia Gaon: His Life and Works*. New York: Hermon Press, 1969.

Stroumsa, Sarah. "Saadya and Jewish *Kalam*." In *The Cambridge Companion to Medieval Jewish Philosophy*, eds. D.H. Frank and O. Leaman, 71–90. Cambridge: Cambridge University Press, 2003.

SACRED GEOGRAPHY

Sacred geography refers to notions of the world centered on the Ka'ba in Mecca [q.v.] with the specific purpose of finding the *qibla* [q.v.], or direction toward the Ka'ba, without any calculation whatsoever, that is, with the framework of folk science. It is quite distinct from the Islamic tradition of mathematical geography [q.v.], in which the qibla was calculated from available geographical coordinates using a complicated trigonometric formula. Sacred geography was developed by Muslim scholars working exclusively in the folk astronomical tradition.

Some twenty different schemes of this kind of sacred geography—sometimes beautifully illustrated in manuscripts, sometimes described in words—are known from some thirty different medieval sources. In most of the illustrations, the Ka'ba is accentuated and its various features identified. The world is divided in sectors around the Ka'ba that are defined by specific segments of its perimeter. The qiblas for each sector are then defined in terms of specific astronomical horizon phenomena, such as the risings and settings of the sun and various qibla-stars. In some schemes the qibla is defined in terms of the winds, whose limits were defined in Islamic folklore in terms of such horizon phenomena.

This tradition began in Baghdad in the ninth century. It was particularly popular in the medieval Yemen, not least because a *faqîh* of Basra of Yemeni origin named Ibn Surâqa proposed three serious schemes with eight, eleven, and twelve sectors around the Ka'ba. In various later works, such as the geographical writings of Yâqût (Syria ca. 1200 CE) and al-Qazwînî (Iraq ca. 1250), the information on the qibla in twelve sectors, sometimes eleven, is suppressed. In yet later works, such as the nautical atlas of Ahmad al-Sharafî al-Safâqusî (Tunis ca. 1550) and various other Ottoman compilations, forty or seventy-two sectors are uniformly distributed on a ring around the Ka'ba with no specific qibla values.

Underlying all of these schemes is the notion that to face the Ka'ba in any region of the world, one should face the same direction in which one would be standing if one were directly in front of the appropriate segment of the perimeter of the Ka'ba. Since that sacred edifice is itself aligned in astronomically significant directions, the directions adopted by the legal scholars for the qibla were toward the risings and settings of the sun at the equinoxes or the solstices or of various significant qibla stars. The astronomical orientation of the Ka'ba—major axis aligned with the rising of Canopus, and minor axis toward summer sunrise and winter sunset—is implicit in statements about the directions of the winds by a series of medieval Muslim scholars.

The various directions adopted for the qibla in these schemes would necessarily be different from the qiblas that were calculated by the Muslim astronomers. Indeed, the various qibla directions proposed in the medieval sources account for the wide range of orientations of religious architecture in each region of the Muslim world.

DAVID A. KING

See also Astronomy

Further Reading

———. "The Orientation of Medieval Islamic Religious Architecture and Cities." *Journal of the History of Astronomy* 26 (1995): 253–274.

King, David A. *World-Maps for Finding the Direction ad Distance to Mecca*. Leiden: Brill and London: Al-Furqan Islamic Heritage Foundation, 1999.

———. *In Synchrony with the Heavens*. 2 vols. Leiden: Brill, 2004–2005, esp. vol. 1, Parts VIIa–c.

———. *The Sacred Geography of Islam*. Leiden: Brill, in press. [A summary is in the article "Makka. iv. As centre of the world" in Enc. Islam.]

King, David A., and Gerald S. Hawkins. "On the Orientation of the Kaaba." *Journal for the History of Astronomy* 13 (1982): 102–109. [Reprinted in King. *Astronomy in the Service of Islam*. Aldershot: Variorum, 1993, XII.]

SAFAVIDS

The Safavids are the longest ruling of Iran's Islamic period's dynasties. The dates of the Safavids are often given as 1501 CE, from the capture of Tabriz by the first shah, Isma'il I, to 1722, the Afghan capture of the capital of Isfahan.

Within ten years of the former, Safavid forces, spearheaded by a confederation of Turkic tribal forces called the Qizilbash (Turkish, meaning "red heads") after their distinctive red headgear, secured territories previously ruled by eight different rulers and roughly contiguous with modern-day Iran. The allegiance of these tribal elements with which Isma'il—himself of both Christian and Turkic noble descent—had already intermarried, was further bolstered with the allotment of key territories and military–political posts. The much-needed support of the Tajik, native Iranian, administrative class, many of whom had served the region's earlier polities, was secured by appointing them to key posts at the central and provincial levels and by patronage of distinctly Persian cultural traditions. A complex spiritual polemic identified Isma'il with the region's key Christian and Muslim, Tajik, Persian, Shi'i, and Turkish and Sufi discourses and traditions; indeed, although Twelver Shi'ism was the new realm's established faith, Isma'il was also the latest head of the Safavid Sufi order, whose militantly messianic appeal to his tribal followers he also promoted. Sunnism also was tolerated following a nominal conversion to Shi'ism. The strong attachment of Turk and Tajik to Isma'il and to each other ensured the polity's survival in the face of both internal challenges and military defeat by the Ottomans at Chaldiran in 1514. So based was the polity on the person of Isma'il, however, that at his death in 1524, the confederation's members, and their Tajik allies, fell to fighting among themselves for dominance of Isma'il 's son and heir, Tahmasp.

After a twelve-year civil war that encouraged repeated Uzbek and Ottoman invasions, a new Turkish-Tajik hierarchy established itself around Tahmasp. The center repelled the Uzbeks and sued for peace with and ceded territory to the Ottomans, and projected a heterodox spiritual–cultural discourse that, as under Isma'il, both spoke to and legitimized the interests of the polity's key constituencies, including Georgian and Circassian elements to the north, and promoted Tahmasp as representing each and leader over all. Tahmasp's death in 1576, which again removed the focal point of this alliance, engendered an eleven-year struggle between and among the Qizilbash tribes and their Tajik and Northern supporters, in support of Tahmasp's sons, Isma'il II (r. 1576–1577) and Khudabandah (r. 1578–1587) and, again, left the polity vulnerable to Ottoman and Uzbek attacks. Even with the enthronement in 1587 of the latter's son, 'Abbas I (d. 1629) [q.v.], backed by a new alliance, the future of the polity was threatened by ongoing internal military-political and spiritual-religious challenges, as well as foreign occupation.

A 1590 treaty ceding further territories to the Ottomans allowed 'Abbas to secure victory over his internal rivals and commence a series of military campaigns that, by the end of his reign, recovered territories lost to the Ottomans and Uzbeks.

The new alliance secured these victories by expanding the center's core constituencies to include *ghulam* or *qullar* corps—non-Qizilbash Arab and Persian tribal volunteers and captured Georgian, Circassian, and Armenian youth converted to Islam—at both the central and provincial military and political levels, albeit subordinate to the Qizilbash and Tajik elites, and, more importantly, by expanding the Qizilbash confederation. The center also reinvigorated its heterodox, spiritual–cultural discourse, further emphasizing the dynasty's Shi'i, Sufi, and distinctly Persian associations, and undertook to develop the realm's spiritual, secular, and economic infrastructure, the latter including the removal of eastern Turkey's Armenians, especially its long-distance merchants, to the new capital of Isfahan, and projecting the center's credentials at all these levels. New efforts were undertaken to construct an anti-Ottoman alliance by expanding contacts with European political, commercial, and religious interests.

The prominence of this expanded Turk-Tajik-*ghulam* alliance at the center remained a feature of Safavid politics for the remainder of the period, even if specific personnel changed. While the 1639 treaty of Zuhab with the Ottomans, and the access to the overland route to Mediterranean ports for Iran's silk it guaranteed, produced growing economic prosperity and increasingly smoother accessions; struggles for preeminence between factions at the courts of 'Abbas' grandson Safi (r. 1629–1642) and great-grandson 'Abbas II (r. 1642–1666) did not assume the proportions of the civil wars thta marked the earlier deaths of Isma'il and Tahmasp.

In the middle and late seventeenth century, a series of natural disasters—disease, famine, and drought—together with a growing drain of specie, exacerbated the economic decline of urban craft and artisanal and other marginal elements, and contributed to a rising interest among these in Sufi-style messianic discourse and a corresponding growth in anti-Sufi and anti-philosophical polemics. The center, although occasionally scapegoating minority communities, adopted a variety of economic and social welfare measures in response to these crises, and further promoted the identification of successive shahs with Shi'i religious orthodoxy, other alternative messianic or otherwise 'popular' spiritual and cultural discourses, and other religious traditions, and combined with continued patronage of the realm's spiritual and secular infra-structure, further asserted the legitimacy of the center's authority. The smooth accessions of 'Abbas II's elder son Sulayman (r. 1666–1694) and the latter's eldest son Sultan Husayn (r. 1694–1722), aided by an otherwise relatively healthy economy, attest to the overall success of such efforts.

In 1722, the Afghan seizure of Isfahan did not immediately dent the Safavids' popular standing. For example, tribal contingents stationed throughout the realm rushed to the shah's rescue, and even Nadir Shah (d. 1747), a member of one of the original Qizilbash tribes, as commander of the army of Sultan Husayn's son, placed the latter on the throne in Isfahan in 1729 and married into the Safavid house before himself seizing power in 1736. The political, especially cultural, achievements of the period were key points of reference for later generations.

ANDREW J. NEWMAN

See also 'Abbas I

Further Reading

Newman, forthcoming.

SAINTS AND SAINTHOOD, CHRISTIAN

The rapid Arab conquest of the eastern Byzantine provinces and the Sasanian empire resulted in the acquisition of vast territories that, over the course of the preceding centuries, had been mapped by the lives and deaths of Christian saints. The landscape was dotted with monasteries, churches, and shrines where apostles, martyrs, and a variety of holy men and women were remembered, their remains venerated, and their patronage and intercession sought. Itineraries of pilgrimage connected many of the dots. Already in the late fourth century CE, the Western pilgrim Egeria visited not only what was being constructed as a Christian "Holy Land" in Palestine, but also monastic sites in Egypt and Sinai—Edessa with its *martyrion* of the apostle Thomas, and the shrine of the martyr Thecla in Seleucia. The two centuries that followed were a period of intense church building and of growth in the cult of the martyrs, which is to some extent reflected in the account of the "Piacenza Pilgrim" (ca. 570): In addition to his visit to the biblical sites in Palestine, he reports an excursion south and west (to Mt. Sinai, the cave of Paul, the first hermit near the Red Sea, the pilgrimage center of the martyr Menas outside of Alexandria, and the church of the evangelist and martyr Mark in Alexandria itself), and another north and east (to Antioch and its martyrs, the shrine of the martyr Bacchus at Barbalissus, and nearly to the frontier shrine of the martyr Sergius at Rusafa).

The Qur'an itself alludes to stories of Christian saints and martyrs whose commemoration contributed to the construction of this Christian sacred geography. *Surat al-Buruj* (85) refers to the martyred "men of the pit," probably the Christians massacred by Dhu Nawas around 520 in Najran in South Arabia. Their *martyrion* became a pilgrimage center that, for a time, rivaled Mecca to the north. *Surat al-Kahf* (18) presents a version of the legend of the Seven Sleepers of Ephesus, whose cult spread through the Islamic world as well as the Christian world. Of course, a large number of biblical figures appear prominently in the Qur'an, including Jesus Christ, the Virgin Mary, and John the Baptist.

The Christian map of holiness underwent continual reconfiguration under Islamic rule. Not all shrines fared well, however. The Christian community of Najran was uprooted under the caliph 'Umar, while the Church of St. John the Baptist in Damascus was converted into a mosque under the Umayyad caliph al-Walid. At the shrine of St. Sergius in Rusafa, however, a mosque was constructed *alongside* the existing Christian buildings. While some pilgrimage centers suffered slow decline because of changing political and demographic realities, new cults sprang up, as they continue to do in the present day.

At the time of the Arab conquest, the Christian communities that suddenly found themselves within the *Dar al-Islam* all possessed extensive hagiographical literatures in their original languages (Syriac, Greek, Coptic, and others). These literatures continued to grow after the Arab conquest, but with the passage of time many Christians came to adopt the Arabic language. In a process that began in the monasteries of Palestine in the eighth century, many *Lives* and *Martyrdoms* were translated into Arabic, while others were composed directly in that language. In some communities the *Lives* and *Martyrdoms* of the principal saints were collected together, in abbreviated form, in *synaxaria* that served their daily commemoration in the liturgy.

The hagiographical literatures of the Christian *dhimmi* communities were enriched by the stories of the neomartyrs, Christians who were executed by Muslim authorities while confessing their Christian faith; the grounds for execution are normally apostasy from Islam, converting others from Islam, or invective preaching against Islam. A particularly rich literature of this kind, much of it composed in Arabic, sprang up in the Melkite communities of Syria and Palestine in the early Islamic centuries. The phenomenon of voluntary martyrdom sometimes found in these stories was controversial among Christians and puzzling to Muslims. Occasionally, voluntary martyrdoms would come in waves, as in the case of the "martyrs of Córdoba" during the 850s, or the Forty-Nine Martyrs in Egypt during the patriarchate of Matthew I (1378–1408). Such phenomena must be interpreted against a background of rapid Arabization and/or Islamization.

The example of the martyrs, old and new, was an important element in preaching and catechesis that urged Christians to cling to their faith, regardless of the consequences. The hagiographical production of the Christian churches under Islam, however, was by no means restricted to stories of martyrs. Holy men and women regularly emerged from communities that eagerly recognized them as "saints"—one notes the informality of the process—and that recorded and read their *Lives* and *Miracles*. Some of these saints were consulted by Muslim authorities and notables, and on occasion played the role of mediator between them and the Christian community. The Coptic *synaxarion* records, for example, that Barsum the Naked (d. 1317) had a role in persuading the Mamluk sultan al-Nasir Muhammad to reopen the churches of Cairo, after he had ordered them closed in 1301.

It will be apparent that the commemoration of the saints (including the regular retelling of their stories, visiting their shrines, and participating in their feasts) was an important element in forming and reinforcing the specific identities of Christian communities over their Islamic environment. At the same time, the cult of saints and martyrs could be a meeting place for Christians and Muslims. The sharp edges of particular figures could blur, as when the martyrs Sergius and George were confused not only with one another but also with the mysterious Qur'anic figure Khidr. In many places, Christians and Muslims were ready to seek healing and protection wherever it could be found, whether from Christian or from Islamic saints. From early in the Islamic period to the present day, the annual festivals of certain much-beloved saints have been fairlike events at which Christians and Muslims alike have sought entertainment, as well as blessing.

MARK N. SWANSON

See also Apostasy; Christians and Christianity; Churches, Coptic; Copts; Dhimma; Greek; Syriac; Seven Sleepers

Further Reading

Fowden, Elizabeth Key. *The Barbarian Plain: Saint Sergius between Rome and Iran.* Berkeley, Los Angeles, and London: University of California Press, 1999.
Frankfurter, David, ed. *Pilgrimage and Holy Space in Late Antique Egypt.* Leiden, Boston, and Köln: Brill, 1998.
Graf, Georg. *Geschichte der christlichen arabischen Literatur, I: Die Übersetzungen* [*The History of Arabic Christian Literature, I: Translations*]. Vatican City: Biblioteca Apostolica Vaticana, 1944, esp. part four, "Hagiographie."
Griffith, Sidney H. "Christians, Muslims, and Neo-Martyrs: Saints' Lives and Holy Land History." In *Sharing the Sacred: Religious Contacts and Conflicts in the Holy Land, First–Fifteenth Centuries CE.* Ed. Arieh Kofsky and Guy G. Stroumsa, 163–207. Jerusalem: Yad Izhak Ben Zvi, 1998.
Hoyland, Robert G. *Seeing Islam as Others Saw It: A Survey and Evaluation of Christian, Jewish and Zoroastrian Writings on Early Islam.* Princeton: The Darwin Press, 1997, esp. Chap. 9, "Martyrologies."
Meinardus, Otto F.A. *Coptic Saints and Pilgrimages.* Cairo and New York: The American University in Cairo Press, 2002.
O'Leary, De Lacy. *The Saints of Egypt in the Coptic Calendar.* London and New York: Church Historical Society, 1937. Reprint, Amsterdam: Philo Press, 1974.
Segal, J.B. *Edessa, "the Blessed City."* Oxford: Oxford University Press, 1970. Reprint, Piscataway, NJ: Gorgias, 2001.
Swanson, Mark N. "The Martyrdom of 'Abd al-Masih, Superior of Mount Sinai (Qays al-Ghassani)." In *Syrian Christians under Islam: The First Thousand Years*, edited by David Thomas, 107–129. Leiden, Boston, and Köln: Brill, 2001.
Wilkinson, John. *Jerusalem Pilgrims before the Crusades.* Warminster, England: Aris and Phillips, 1977.
Wolf, Kenneth B. *Christian Martyrs in Muslim Spain.* Cambridge and New York: Cambridge University Press, 1988.

SALADIN, OR SALAH AL-DIN

Salah al-Din Yusuf b. Ayyub (d. 1193 CE) was a Kurdish warrior who established the Ayyubid confederation that dominated Egypt, Syria, and the Jazira (upper Iraq) from the late twelfth to the mid-thirteenth centuries. The career of Saladin (as his name was rendered by Europeans) was marked by concerted military campaigns against the Crusader states of the Syrian littoral. These military activities culminated in his decisive victory over Crusader forces at the Horns of Hattin on July 4, 1187, which brought about the near elimination of the Frankish states centered around Jerusalem, Tripoli, and Antioch.

Little is known of Saladin's early life. His father Ayyub (the Arabic form of the prophetic name Job) was for a time in the military service of Zangi (d. 1146), the Turkish military leader who controlled Mosul and Aleppo. In 1152, at age fourteen, Saladin joined his uncle Shirkuh in Aleppo in the service of Zangi's son, Nur al-Din. Nur al-Din had emerged by then as the most powerful figure of the Muslim opposition to the Crusader states. When the Fatimid caliphate of Egypt was troubled with succession struggles and threatened by several Frankish invasions, Nur al-Din sent armies under the command of Shirkuh to aid the Fatimids. Saladin accompanied his uncle, and thus was in Egypt when Shirkuh died in 1169. Taking advantage of the internal chaos of the Fatimid state, Saladin took control of Egypt, first as a vizier of the Fatimids and subsequently, in 1171, by displacing the Fatimids and ruling in the name of his sovereign, Nur al-Din. Saladin's relations with Nur al-Din grew strained, however, and when the latter died in 1174, Saladin quickly marched to Damascus to take that city from Nur al-Din's heirs. By May 1175, Saladin was invested by the 'Abbasid Caliph al-Mustadi' (r. 1170–1180) as the Sultan of Egypt and Syria. Over the next decade, Saladin's forces were frequently engaged with fighting the Franks. Saladin was also concerned, however, with solidifying his rule (by 1175 he had survived two assassination attempts) and expanding the land under his control. In 1183, Aleppo submitted to him, and in 1186, Mosul recognized him as well. Having thus brought the collective resources of Egypt, Bilad al-Sham (Syria), and the Jazira under his control, Saladin renewed his efforts against the Crusaders. His campaign in the summer of 1187 resulted in the surrender of Jerusalem three months after his victory at Hattin. Saladin's subsequent campaigns left the Crusader states reduced to the coastal enclaves of Tyre, Antioch, and Tripoli.

Saladin's capture of Jerusalem resulted in the call for the Third Crusade in Europe. Those Crusader forces, including Kings Richard I of England and Phillip II of France, arrived on the Syrian coastal plain in the summer of 1191. While Phillip soon departed, over the next year Richard's forces engaged those of Saladin in a series of military maneuvers. Two Crusader marches on Jerusalem failed, yet the two significant battles—at Arsuf in 1191 and Jaffa in 1192—resulted in Frankish victories. A truce was negotiated between Saladin and Richard in September 1192, and Richard left the Levant a month later, the Third Crusade having thus expanded and strengthened the Crusader kingdom of Jerusalem so weakened by Saladin in 1187–1189. Saladin died a few months later in March 1193. His Ayyubid relatives who succeeded him in control of Egypt and Syria were unable to duplicate his degree of success against the Franks.

The life of Saladin has resonated for many audiences since his death. Members of his administration penned biographies celebrating his achievements, and eulogists commemorated him as the epitome of a *mujahid fi sabil allah*, a fighter for the cause of God. A dissenting view, however, is found in the works of Ibn al-Athir (d. 1233), who wrote in the service of Nur al-Din's descendants displaced by Saladin. His struggles against Richard became the stuff of chivalry in medieval Europe and the fodder for Sir Walter Scott's historical fiction in the nineteenth century. More significantly, Saladin's unification (forcibly or otherwise) of the Muslim lands surrounding the Crusader states, as well as his success against those states, are major reasons why he has been celebrated by many subsequent Muslim authors and rulers, and his example has been appropriated into the ideas of twentieth-century Arab nationalism and contemporary Islamist thought. Within modern Western scholarship about Saladin, a dissenting interpretation of his achievements is found in the biography by Ehrenkreutz.

WARREN C. SCHULTZ

See also 'Abbasids; Ayyubids; Caliph; Fatimids; Nur al-Din; Sultan

Primary Sources

Ibn Shaddad, Baha' al-Din. *The Rare and Excellent History of Saladin.* Transl. D.S. Richards. Crusade Texts in Translation 7. Aldershot: Ashgate Publishing, 2001.
Al-Maqrizi. *A History of the Ayyubid Sultans of Egypt.* Transl. R.J.C. Broadhurst. Boston: Twayne Publishers, 1980.

Further Reading

Ehrenkreutz, Andrew S. *Saladin.* Albany: State University of New York Press, 1972.
Gibb, H.A.R. *The Life of Saladin.* Oxford: Clarendon Press, 1973.
Hillenbrand, Carole. *The Crusades: Islamic Perspectives.* Chicago: Fitzroy Dearborn, 1999.
Lyons, Malcolm Cameron, and D.E.P. Jackson. *Saladin: The Politics of Holy War.* Cambridge: Cambridge University Press, 1982.

SALMAN AL-FARISI

Salman al-Farisi was a Persian companion of Muhammad who plays a large role in the self-image of the nascent Shi'i, and later a cosmic role for some of the *ghulat* extremists; little is known about his life before his arrival in Medina. Hagiographies describe his provenance from a courtly family in Isfahan, who dissatisfied with the religion of his ancestors sought the "true" religion. This account may have some roots in the religious conflicts of the later Sasanian period in which Mazdaian orthodoxy was under threat. Having tried out other religious options such as Nestorian Christianity in Iran, Mosul, and Chalcis, Salman was sold as a slave into Arabia, where he ended up in Medina. Meeting the Prophet, he became a Muslim, recognizing the seal of prophecy on Muhammad's back. He later became famous as the one who devised the strategy of building a ditch (khandaq) to defend Medina.

After the death of the Prophet, he was a staunch supporter of the rights of 'Ali and was regarded as one of the four pillars of the early Shi'i. The Prophet is reported to have honored him by describing him as a member of his family. Following Abu Bakr's selection at Saqifa Bani Sa'ida, he was reported to have said to the Quraysh, "kardid o nakardid" ("They have selected a successor to the Prophet but failed to recognize the true successor, 'Ali"). This phrase is a key example of New Persian fragments in early Islamic texts. Popular Twelver tradition commemorates his death on AH 9 Safar 35/17 August 655 CE. In some forms of later extremist Shi'ism, Salman became the part of the tripartite divine hypostasis, along with Muhammad and 'Ali.

SAJJAD H. RIZVI

See also Abu Bakr; 'Ali ibn Abi Talib; Islam; Muhammad; Shi'ism

Primary Source

Ibn Ishaq. *Sirat Rasul Allah [The Life of Muhammad]*. Transl. A. Guillaume. Karachi: Oxford University Press, 1955, 95–98.

Further Reading

Crone, P. "Kavad's Heresy and Mazdak's Revolt." *Iran* 29 (1991): 21–42.
Kosky, A., and M. Bar-Asher. *The 'Alawi-Nusayri Religion*. Leiden: Brill, 2002.
Massignon, L. *Salman Pak et les prémices spirituelles de l'islam iranien*. Tours: Arrault et die, 1934.
Stroumsa, G.G. "Seal of the Prophets: The Nature of a Manichean Metaphor." *Jerusalem Studies in Arabic and Islam* 7 (1986): 61–74.

SAMANIDS

The Samanids were a semiautonomous eastern Iranian dynasty, based in Bukhara, that ruled Transoxiana, Khurasan, Tabaristan, and Tukharistan between 819 and 999 CE. They are largely recognized for ushering in the New Persian linguistic and literary renaissance of the tenth and eleventh centuries.

Dynastic History

The origins and early history of the Samanids as familial governors of Transoxiana on behalf of 'Abbasid Baghdad are far from clear, but most near-contemporary historians are fond of repeating the tradition that Saman-Khuda—a prominent *dihqan* (Iranian noble landowner) and eponymous founder of this governorial dynasty—was a direct descendant of the Sasanian hero-cum-general Bahram Chubin. It would appear that Saman-Khuda and his son, Asad, served the 'Abbasid authorities efficiently in Transoxian, and in recognition of their campaigns against local rebels, a number of prestigious posts in the region were appointed to the four sons of Asad: Nuh received Samarqand; Ahmad was appointed to Farghana; Yahya received control of Shash; and Ilyas was granted the city of Herat. It would appear that Samanid control of the southern reaches of Herat could not contend with the rise of another local regional power, the Saffarids under Ya'qub al-Laith, and Ilyas was defeated and captured in 867. By 875, Ahmad's son, Nasr I, was more or less the sole governor of all of Transoxiana, a reality that was ceremonially acknowledged by the 'Abbasid caliph in 875 when he named Nasr as governor of the region. Samanid control of the region extended to Bukhara thanks to the campaigns of Nasr's brother, Isma'il, but fraternal civil war soon ensued. By 892, Isma'il had displaced Nasr as the sole Samanid governor of Transoxiana. The emergence of a centralized Samanid state with a lively court culture, consistent bureaucracy, and efficient provincial administrations is typically dated to the reign of Isma'il (892—907). This might be at least partially rationalized by the fact that Isma'il is touted by later scholars—most notably Nizam al-Mulk—as a paragon of justice and responsible rule. He invested considerable energy toward building up the urban infrastructure of Bukhara, and numerous traditions describe his equitable treatment of artisans, peasants, and sharecroppers. However, we must acknowledge that Isma'il was also an efficient military campaigner, and no doubt his exemplary status as a Muslim ruler was bolstered by his defeat of the disruptive Saffarid dynasty in 900 and his extension of control into central Iran, along with his *jihad* against the pagan Turkic areas north of Samarqand.

After the death of Isma'il in 907, and the assassination of his immediate successor, Ahmad, in 914, the Samanid house was placed under control of eight-year-old Nasr b. Ahmad (Nasr II). Politically, the Samanids were at their most vulnerable as various familial rebellions, revolts, and external invasions dominated much of the 910s and 920s. By 926, however, Nasr II was able to consolidate control of his territory, and mounted a number of successful expeditions against central Iran and Tabaristan. Despite these menaces, the reign of Nasr II is widely acknowledged as the apogee of Samanid literary and cultural activity. This is undoubtedly explained by Nasr's decision to appoint two key Persians—Abu 'Abd Allah al-Jaihani and Abu al-Fadl Muhammad al-Bal'ami—to the office of vizier. Henceforth, we see the development of a centralized administration—based largely on its Baghdadi counterpart but with some interesting influences from Sasanian Iranian and Central Asian culture—with various offices for land assessment, tax collection, financial accounting, bureaucratic correspondence, agronomical improvements, and military maintenance. This administrative confidence was only reinforced by the fact that Transoxiana was no longer the subordinate, weaker province to the great region of Khurasan and henceforth was considered a productive and culturally sophisticated component of the *Dar al-Islam*. Indeed, the *Siyasat nama* holds up Samanid administration as a model for the Seljuks to emulate in their own administrative organization. Religiously, there is no substantial evidence to suggest that the Samanids were anything but orthodox Hanafi Sunnis; it should be noted that there was a brief flirtation by certain elements of the Samanid military (particularly a general named al-Husain al-Marwazi) with Isma'ili Shi'i preachers in the 920s, but by and large Shi'is and heterodox groups were considered anathema by the authorities.

Medieval geographers such as Ibn Hawqal, who had extensive experience traveling across Spain and the Maghrib, presents a Samanid Bukhara replete with legal scholars, Qur'anic exegetes, tradition compilers, Arab grammarians, philosophers, and other classes of intellectuals. The relative proximity of Bukhara to eastern Asia and the increased access to paper and papermaking technology (especially in Samarqand), fostered a certain bibliophilia among the Samanids; Ibn Sina (Avicenna), originally from the region of Balkh, talked glowingly of the library in Bukhara, noting that it was there he had been first introduced to the political philosophical writings of al-Farabi. The infusion of scholarly and courtly Arabic—at the expense of local idioms of Soghdian and Khwarazmian—is attested to by the large number of poets listed in the *Yatimat al-dahr* by Abu Mansur al-Tha'alibi and the *Lubab al-albab* by Muhammad 'Aufi. Nonetheless, the majority of the subject population was unable to digest such highbrow Arabic, and many translation projects were initiated under Nasr II, most notably the monumental Persian translation of the history of al-Tabari by al-Bal'ami (son of the aforementioned vizier).

The remaining years of the Samanid dynasty were occupied chiefly with contending with the Buyid "heretical" threat to the west and the restoration of the 'Abbasid caliph in Baghdad to nominal Sunni

control. However, overextension in Tabaristan and financial mismanagement only exacerbated the devolution of power that had begun to characterize the Samanid court under the amir-ships of Nuh I (r. 943–954) and 'Abd al-Malik (r. 954–961). Like the 'Abbasid caliphs, Samanid military commanders had begun to look to the vibrant slave trade of Samarqand and Bukhara, and the arrival of prodigious numbers of Oghuz Turks into the Farghana and Zarafshan valleys, as new and skilled sources of military power. By the 960s and 970s, Turks had risen to considerable levels of military and courtly power, so much so that rivalries and competing claimants began soliciting the political support of these recently empowered Turkish military elite. A good example of this trend is the career of the Turkish general Alp Teghin, who had manipulated court machinations to secure an appointment as governor of Khurasan and developed ultimately sufficient prestige to relocate to Ghazna and establish the first independent Turkic dynasty in Central Asia: the Ghaznavids. Samanid impairment was at its highest during the reign of Nuh II (976–997) who, in addition to contending with the Shi'i Buyids and a politically precocious Turkish elite, was now attempting to fight off numerous invasions from the north by the Qarakhanid Turks of Kashgar and Balasghun. Their leader, Bughra Khan, would conquer Bukhara temporarily in 992, and by 997, Samanid dominion had shrunk considerably. The *coup de grace* invasion of 999 by the Qarakhanids was so quick and successful that some historians have suggested that key personages of the Samanid court might have collaborated with the Qarakhanids.

Ascendancy of New Persian Language and Literature

While the Samanid court and administration was ostensibly conducted in Arabic, nonetheless, we see the emergence of a new and stylized Persian language that, in turn, replaced local Iranian idioms of Soghdian and Khvarazmian. This New Persian fused older vocabulary and concepts of pre-Islamic Sasanian and Achaemenian Iran with the energetic and robust stylistic motifs and imagery found not just in the Qur'an but also in traditions of the Prophets, hagiographies of Companions, and of course the popular poetic Bedouin tradition. The eminent Iranologist Richard Frye has always contended that it was the New Persian "renaissance" under the Samanids and other eastern Iranian states—all beneficiaries to millennia of pre-Islamic Zoroastrian,

Manichean, Buddhist, and Nestorian Christian traditions—that "liberated" Arab, Bedouin-dominated Islam from its parochial roots and brassbound worldview. The bulk of what was produced in New Persian for this period were translations of key Arabic texts (al-Tabari's history or translations of the Qur'an, for example), but within time we see the rise of an independent and vigorous Persian literary tradition. In its infancy, New Persian was established and cemented in the increasingly famous court of Bukhara by such legendary poets as Abu 'Abd Allah Ja'far b. Muhammad Rudaki (d. 940) and Abu Mansur Muhammad b. Ahmad Daqiqi (d. 977). Rudaki spent much of his professional career in Bukhara, under the auspices of the ruler Nasr b. Ahmad, and is widely recognized for developing the panegyric form of poetry *(qasida)*; indeed, Rudaki was the foundation for later great panegyrists of the thirteenth and fourteenth centuries such as 'Unsuri, Mu'izzi, and Anvari. Likewise, Daqiqi's lyrical poetry is considered to be a forerunner of Ferdowsi's *Shahnama*, and historians of Persian literature agree that many of the great literary accomplishments of the Ghaznavid and Seljuk periods would not have been possible if not for the Samanid program of encouraging New Persian at both the elite and popular levels.

COLIN PAUL MITCHELL

See also 'Abbasids; Bukhara; Buyids; Epic Poetry; Epics, Persian; Ibn Sina; Khurasan; Libraries; Nizam al-Mulk; Paper Manufacture; Persian; Persians; Poetry, Persian; Samarqand; Transoxiana

Primary Sources (in Arabic and Persian)

'Abd al-Malik Tha'alibi. *Yatimat al-dahr.* Ed. M.M. Qumyhah. 6 vols. Beirut, 2000.
Abu 'Abd Allah Ja'far b. Muhammad Rudaki. *Asar-i manzum.* Ed. I.S. Braginskii. Moscow, 1964.
Abu Mansur Muhammad b. Ahmad Daqiqi. *Daqiqi va ash'ar-i u.* Ed. M. Dabir-Siyaqi. Tehran, 1964.
Ibn Hawkul. *Kitab surat al-'ard.* Ed. J.H. Kramers. Leiden, 1938.
Muhammad ibn Ja'far Narshaki. *Tarikh-i Bukhara.* Ed. M. Razavi. Tehran, 1972.

Further Reading

Bartold, W. *Turkestan Down to the Mongol Invasion.* London, 1928.
Bosworth, C.E. "Samanids—History, Literary Life and Economic Activity." In *Encyclopedia of Islam.* 2d ed. Vol. 9, 1025–1029.
Browne, E.G. *A Literary History of Persia.* 4 vols. Cambridge, 1958.
Frye, Richard. *Bukhara: The Medieval Achievment.* Norman, 1965.
———. *The Golden Age of Persia: the Arabs in the East.* London, 1975.
———. "The Samanids." In *Cambridge History of Iran.* Ed. R. Frye, 136–161. Vol. 4. London, 1975.
Muhammad ibn Ja'far Narshaki. *The History of Bukhara.* Transl. R. Frye. Cambridge: 1954.
Paul, Jürgen. *Herrscher, Gemeinwesen, Vermittler: Ost Iran und Transoxanian in vormongolischer Zeit.* Stuttgart, 1996.
Rypka, Jan. *History of Iranian Literature.* Ed. K. Jahn. Dordrecht, 1968.
Soucek, Svat. *A History of Inner Asia.* Cambridge, 2000.
Spuler, B. *Iran in der früh-islamischer Zeit: Politik, Kultur, Verwaltung und öffentliches Leben 633–1055.* Wiesbaden, 1952.

SAMARQAND

Samarqand has always been the leading city *(misr al-iqlim)* of Transoxiana (Ma-wara al-nahr: the land beyond the Oxus River in Arabic). Its importance is explained chiefly by its position at the junction of the main trade routes crossing Central Asia (the name "Silk Road" was coined in the nineteenth century by Baron Ferdinand von Richthofen), and its situation on the banks of the Zarafshan (Sughd) River *(nahr)*. The elaborate irrigation system *(ariq)* that watered the city and its environs caused many people to settle in the district of Samarqand.

As the Soghdanian word *kand* (settlement) attests, the place was an urban center long before the coming of Islam. The traditional historiography of the Islamic conquests narrates that in the early Umayyad period, Muslim armies penetrated the Zarafshan River Valley. The Arabs, the people of Sogdia *(sughd)*, and the Turks fought over the territory. The fighting ended when Sa'id Ibn Uthman seized the castle *(quhnduz)* of Samarqand. Muslim chronicles narrate, in line with the Islamic conquest *(futuhat)* literary genre, that Kutham Ibn 'Abbas, the Prophet's cousin and companion, died during this raid (AH 56/676 CE). Even if this event actually took place its importance would be marginal, since other historical traditions describe later Islamic onslaughts against the city. In this narrative a second person plays a role: Umm Muhammad bint 'Abd Allah joined the armies of Islam and by doing so gained fame as the first Muslim woman to cross the Oxus River.

When Qutayba Ibn Muslim arrived (in 87/706), Samarqand was governed by a local chief, named by the Arab source as Ghurak, who bore the title Ikhshid. The victorious Muslim commanders did not remove him from his post—they accepted his surrender and were satisfied with his payments, an arrangement that lasted until his death in 737. As in other quarters of Transoxiana, this local force served as a buffer between the caliphate and the indigenous inhabitants. Hoping to take advantage of the crisis in the Umayyad administration, the people of Samarqand joined forces with the Turks (Targesh) and fought the Muslim armies. It was only during the term in office of Nasr b. Sayyar (738–748) that the authority of the Umayyad caliphate was firmly reinstalled.

With the emergence of the 'Abbasid caliphate, Samarqand, like other settlements in the Zarafshan Valley, was deeply affected by the revolt of the al-mubayyida (safid jamgan; the white-clad ones). This was a coalition of heretical forces led by a person nicknamed al-Muqanna' (the Veiled). A generation after the suppression of this revolt Rafi' ibn Layth killed the governor of Samarqand and seized the territory (190/806). The difficulties of the central government in Baghdad to control the remote frontier lands in Central Asia and the relationships that al-Mam'mun established between the periphery and the caliphate paved the way for the Samanids.

Nuh b. Asad b. Saman became the ruler of Samarqand in 204/819. On his death the city passed to his brother Ahmad (227–250/842–858). His son Nasr was virtually the independent ruler of Ma-wara al-Nahr (Transoxiana, 260–279/874–892). Samarqand served as the capital of Islamic Central Asia until Isma'il b. Ahmad removed the province's headquarters to Bukhara (279–287/892–907). Following the disintegration of the Samanid dynasty, Samarqand fell into the hands of the Qarakhanids (382/992). Under Ali Tegin (d. 1034) it served as the center of the western khanate of this dynasty.

Following their defeat at Katwan (536/1141), Samarqand came under the lordship of the Kara Khitay, who installed a collaborating force as governor of the city. They lost it to Khwarazm Shah (in 608/1212), who failed to defend it against the Mongols (Chingiz/Genghis Khan 617/1220). After Chingiz Khan died, his son Chagatay inherited the city. Samarqand was the capital of his offspring (the Chagatay ulus). The fighting and siege devastated the city. It was not until the days of Timur Leng (Tamerlane) that Samarqand reemerged as the major city of Central Asia. It then became the seat of the Timurid dynasty (1370–1507).

It seems that only after the successes of Abu Muslim and the emergence of the 'Abbasids that Islam able to gain ground in Samarqand, driving out Buddhism and Nestorian Christianity. From the biographies collected by 'Umar al-Nasafi it seems that Islam then became firmly established in the city and the countryside. He mentions scholars who originated in villages and towns, and illuminates a local tradition of Islamic learning and transmission of knowledge and history, a process facilitated by the diffusion of a new material: paper. Samarqand became a center of Islamic studies, as attested to by biographies of many Muslim scholars.

The economy of Samarqand was strongly connected to the central Islamic lands. The city served as an emporium for goods, including furs from Inner Asia and Eurasian slaves. The Qarakhanids further developed it as a cultural center. Descriptions of the city are preserved in geographical and travel literature. They tell of a fortified city populated with scholars. Another source that bears evidence to the past glory of Samarqand are several illustrious buildings including mausoleums, schools, mosques, and an observatory. From the late 'Abbasid period the tomb of Kutham b. al-'Abbas in Afradiyab attracted pilgrims to the shrine of Shah-i zinda (the living prince; also called Shah-i javanan, or the prince of the youth).

YEHOSHUA FRENKEL

Further Reading

Collins, B.A. Al-Muqaddasi—The Best Divisions for Knowledge of the Regions. Reading, 1994.
Le Strange, Guy. The Lands of the Eastern Caliphate. London, 1905.
Najm al-Din Umar b. Muhammad al-Nasaf (d. 1142). Al-Qand fi dhikr 'ulama Samarqand. ed. Y. al-Hadi. Tehran, 1420/1999.
Paul, J. "The Histories of Samarqand." Studia Iranica 22 (1993): 69–92.

SAMARRA

Samarra is a city on the East bank of the middle Tigris River in Iraq, situated 125 kilometers north of Baghdad, with a present-day population of about two hundred thousand. Between AH 221/836 CE and 279/892, Samarra, the seat of the 'Abbasid caliphs, expanded to a built-up area of 58 square kilometers, the largest ancient city in the world whose plan has survived.

Before Islam, Samarra was not much more than a village, in an area that was only lightly occupied in antiquity along the banks of the Tigris River. However, the digging of the Qatul al-Kisrawi in the sixth century, by the Sasanian king Khusraw Anushirwan (r. 531–578), as a feeder to the Nahrawan canal, irrigated the area east of Baghdad, stimulated interest in the area, and led the Sasanians to build a hunting park east of modern-day al-Dur, and a monumental tower (Burj al-Qa'im). The 'Abbasid caliph Harun al-Rashid (r. 170–193/786–809) dug a supplementary canal, the Qatul Abi al-Jund, and commemorated it by an unfinished octagonal city (modern-day Husn al-Qadisiyya), called al-Mubarak by al-Hamadhani, and left unfinished in 180/796. The plan is one of two surviving imitations of the Round City of Baghdad.

Minaret of the mosque at Samarrah. Abbasid dynasty, 848–852 CE. Credit: SEF/Art Resource, NY. Great Mosque (Mosque of al-Mutawakkil), Samarra, Iraq.

Probably in 220/834–845, the caliph al-Mu'taṣim left Baghdad in search of a new site for the court and army, a move explained by the sources as due to conflict of the Turkish guard with the population of Baghdad. Although there are different versions of al-Mu'taṣim's journey, all agree that a start was made on a city near Rashīd's unfinished foundation, a site identified east of Ḥuṣn Qīdisiyya. Then he stopped work and moved on to Samarra.

The caliph's city was formally called *Surra Man Ra'ā* ("He who sees it is delighted"). Although Yāqūt (*Mu'jam sv Samarra*) suggests that the present name is a shortened form of *Surra Man Ra'ā*, it is clear that *Samarra* is in reality the Arabic version of the pre-Islamic toponym, *Sumere* in Latin, *Šumrā* in Syriac, and *Souma* in Greek.

Surra Man Ra'ā was founded by al-Mu'taṣim in 221/836, with the palace on the site of a monastery. The plan was composed of a caliphal palace complex, called in the sources variants on the theme of "House of the Caliphate": *Dār al-Khilāfa*, *Dār al-Khalīfa*, *Dār al-Sulṭān*, and *Dār Amīr al-Mu'minīn*. The interior was divided into two major units: the official palace, *Dār al-'Āmma*, where receptions and public business were conducted, and the residence, *al-Jawsaq al-Khāqānī*, intended for family life, where four of the caliphs are buried. The site was excavated by Viollet (1910), Herzfeld (1913), and most recently by the Iraq Directorate-General of Antiquities.

From the south gate of the palace, an avenue, later referred to by al-Ya'qūbī as Shāri' Abī Aḥmad, was laid out over seven kilometers parallel to the river, with a single bend, where the original mosque of al-Mu'taṣim and the markets were located. Otherwise, the plan was composed of subunits (Ar. *qaṭā'i*) dedicated to the military leaders and their troops, and composed also of a palace, avenue, and a grid of houses. North of the bend, the cantonments of the Turks under Waṣīf were located on the east side, and possibly the Farāghina (from the Farghāna valley in Uzbekistan) on the west side. South of the markets were situated the cantonments of the Maghāriba from Egypt, the Iranian Arabs, and the Khurāsānī troops from Baghdad. On the north side of the palace, two quarters, one of which was under the Turk Khāqān 'Urtūj, appear to have been dedicated to the palace servants. Two further principal military cantonments were located outside the city, that of the Central Asian Iranians under al-Afshīn Khaydar b. Kāwūs al-Ushrūshanī at al-Maṭīra, a mainly Christian village south of Samarra (modern-day *al-Jubayriyya*), and that of the Turks under Ashinās at al-Karkh, that is, Karkh Fayrūz (modern-day *Shaykh Walī*), ten kilometers north of Samarra. The area east of the city was walled as a hunting park *(al-Ḥayr)*, in imitation of the earlier Sasanian parks.

Al-Muʿtaṣim died in 227/842. His successor, al-Wāthiq (r. 227–232/842–846), stayed in Samarra and built a new luxurious palace called al-Hārūnī, identified at the unexcavated site of al-Quwayr, now an island in the Tigris, to the west of the Caliphal Palace. The main feature of the short reign of al-Wāthiq was the consolidation of settlement—the people are said by al-Yaʿqūbī to have been more convinced of the permanence of the settlement and to have turned a camp *('Askar al-Muʿtaṣim)* into a real city.

The reign of al-Mutawakkil (232–247/847–861) had a great effect on the appearance of the city, for the size of the city doubled in his reign. A list of his building projects has survived in various versions, the new congregational mosque and twenty other construction projects that totaled in cost between 258 and 294 million dirhams. The congregational mosque of al-Mutawakkil with its spiral minaret was built between 235 and 237 (849 and 852) and constituted part of an extension of the city to the east. Two new hunting palaces were built in the south, al-Iṣṭablāt, identified as al-ʿArūs, and al-Musharraḥāt, identified as the palace of al-Shāh.

The palace of Balkuwārā, excavated by Herzfeld in 1911, was also built in the south as the kernel of the cantonment of a new army of Arabs under al-Muʿtazz, second son of al-Mutawakkil. An important feature of al-Mutawakkil's reign was a sixty-six percent increase in the size of the military cantonments, suggesting extensive new recruiting of Arabs and others to balance the Turks of al-Muʿtaṣim.

In this period, the city center reached its greatest extent, and was described by the geographer al-Yaʿqūbī (Buldān 260–263). There were seven parallel avenues. *Shāri' al-Khalīj*, adjacent to the Tigris, accommodated the quays for the river transport supplying the city, and the cantonments of the Maghāriba. The principal avenue of al-Yaʿqūbī, *al-Shāri' al-Aʿẓam*, or *al-Sarīja*, followed an irregular line passing by the tax registry *(Dīwān al-Kharāj)*, the stables, the slave market, the police office, the prison, and the main markets, before reaching the *Bāb*

al-'Āmma (Gate of the Public) of the caliphal palace. The third avenue, *Shāri' Abī Aḥmad*, the original avenue of the time of al-Muʿtaṣim, terminated at the south gate of the palace and housed the leading Turks of the period. The remaining avenues, *Shāri' al-Ḥayr al-Awwal, Shāri' Barghāmish al-Turkī, Shāri' al-Askar*, and *Shāri' al-Ḥayr al-Jadīd*, were the quarters of disparate military units, the Shākiriyya, Turks, Farāghina, Khazar, and Khurāsānis.

Al-Mutawakkil began a final new project in 245/859: the replacement of the caliphal city of Surra Man Ra'ā by a new unit called al-Mutawakkiliyya, though also referred to as al-Jaʿfariyya and al-Māḥūza. The main palace, al-Jaʿfarī, was located at the entrance to the Qāṭūl, and the city plan is a variant of the already existing models at Samarra: a central avenue leading past the Abū Dulaf Mosque, and subunits allocated to military units. After the death of al-Mutawakkil in 247/861, the site was abandoned, and has survived virtually untouched until the present day.

The reign of al-Mutawakkil was the climax of the city. Vast architectural projects were undertaken—though using inexpensive techniques—and large numbers of troops were recruited to balance the political power of different ethnic units, thus stimulating the economy of the city. However, the financial drain was fatal to the survival of the city; disturbances stemming from revenue shortages led to the unmaking of four caliphs up to 256/870.

In the following decade, under al-Muʿtamid, the army was removed from Samarra, but the city remained the official residence of the court until 279/892. Al-Muʿtamid himself appears to have left in 269/884, though he was buried there in 279/892. Reports of looting of the city occur between 274 and 281 (887–888 and 894–895) and suggest a depopulation in these years. Nevertheless, the area around the markets continued to be occupied, together with the settlements of al-Maṭīra and al-Karkh. The two imams, 'Alī al-Hādī (d. 254) and al-Ḥasan al-ʿAskarī, had a house in the center of the city on the Shāri' Abī Aḥmad, and were buried there. The twelfth imam disappeared in a cleft there in 260/874. The shrine was first developed in 333/944–945 by the Hamdanids, and later by the Buyids. The shrine was frequently rebuilt, notably by the 'Abbasid caliph al-Nāṣir li-Dīn Allah in 606/1209–1210. Consequently, Samarra became a pilgrimage and market town, but it remained an open city until a wall was built in 1834.

ALASTAIR NORTHEDGE

Further Reading

Al-Yaʿqūbī, Aḥmad b. Abī Yaʿqūb b. Wāḍiḥ. *Kitāb al-Buldān*. Ed. de Goeje, 255–268. *BGA* 7, Leiden, 1892.

Creswell, K.A.C. *Early Muslim Architecture*. 1st ed, vol. II. Oxford, 1940.

Directorate General of Antiquities. *Hafriyyat Samarra' 1936–1939*. 2 vols. Baghdad, 1940.

Gordon, M.S. *The Breaking of a Thousand Swords: A History of the Turkish Military of Samarra (AH 200–275/ 815–889 CE)*. Albany, NY, 2001.

Herzfeld, E. *Ausgrabungen von Samarra VI, Geschichte der Stadt Samarra*. Hamburg, 1948.

Leisten, T. *Excavation of Samarra*, vol. I, *Architecture: Final Report of the First Campaign 1910—1912*. Mainz. 2003.

Northedge, A. "An Interpretation of the Palace of the Caliph at Samarra (Dar al-Khilafa or Jawsaq al-Khaqani)." *Ars Orientalis* 23 (1993): 143–171.

———. *The Historical Topography of Samarra*. Samarra Studies 1, British Academy Monographs in Archaeology/British School of Archaeology in Iraq, 2005.

Robinson, C., ed. *A Medieval Islamic City Reconsidered: An Interdisciplinary Approach to Samarra, Oxford Studies in Islamic Art*. Vol 14. Oxford, 2001.

Rogers, J.M. "Samarra, a Study in Medieval Town-Planning." In *The Islamic City*, eds. Hourani and Stern, 119–155. Oxford, 1970.

SASANIANS, ISLAMIC TRADITIONS

Islamic civilization's Sasanian inheritance runs broad and deep. The conquest of the Sasanian empire, which began in 638 CE but was not completed until 651, with the death of the Sasanian king, Yazdgird III, provided the victorious Arabs with a ready-made imperial structure and administration that had overseen the area stretching from the eastern borders of Syria into present-day Turkmenistan in Central Asia. The conquest also made the Arabs heirs to a rich and ancient cultural tradition, for Sasanian civilization was the culmination of more than a millennium of religious and artistic traditions in Iranian and neighboring lands.

Administration and Government

A well-organized state with an efficient bureaucracy, the Sasanian empire provided a class of qualified administrators and scribes to administer the conquered territories. The introduction of royal etiquette and ceremonial practices that closely imitated the elaborate court ritual of the Sasanian kings fulfilled the need of the newly established caliphate to proclaim its legitimacy to the diverse peoples who came under its rule. The prime minister of the Sasanian state, the *vuzurg framadar* ("Great Commander"), was replaced by the chief official of the caliphate, the *Wazir* (vizier), which as a title seems to be derived from the Middle Persian *vičir* (decision). To serve an increasingly centralized government, specialized *diwan*s or bureaus were created, based on the Sasanian model, among which were the *diwan al-khatam* (office of the seal, or chancellery) and the *diwan al-barid* (postal service), which took over the network of roads with rest stations (Ar. *Ribat*) that had been developed by the Sasanians. Under the Sasanians, priests *(mobads)* had directed many administrative activities; the Muslim *qadis* continued this function. The endowment of fires for the Zoroastrian fire temples may have influenced the system of Islamic *waqfs* (Ar. pl., *auqaf*).

The continuity of Sasanian court ceremony is attested to not only in Islamic art (see the section on art below) but also in literature. Well into the later Middle Ages, Muslim chroniclers were drawing upon such Middle Persian literary works as the counsels *(andarz)* or "mirrors for princes," addressed to aristocrats or to rulers, which contributed to the development of Arabic *adab* literature. Besides presenting stories to illustrate the wisdom of the sixth-century Sasanian king, Khosrow Anoshirvan, or of the third-century founder of the dynasty, Ardashir, these works describe Sasanian court practice and rules of conduct and strongly influenced the conduct of Muslim rulers. Such "advice" literature was also known in the Byzantine world, but it was not as widespread as in Persia. Arabic books based on this literature about Sasanian administrative practices and government were produced well into the twelfth century (AH sixth century) as far west of the former Sasanian lands as Sicily and Spain. These works were adapted to reflect Islamic precepts and practices.

Literature, Mathematics, and Science

In addition to *andarz* literature, oral and written narratives about the Sasanian and earlier kings and heroes had a valued place in Islamic culture and for centuries inspired artists and writers throughout Muslim lands. In particular, the *Shahnama,* or *Book of Kings,* written down by the Persian Ferdowsi around 1000, provided specific incidents about the mythic and historic Iranian past, as well as the courtly themes of feasting, drinking, and hunting for both Persian and Arab painters and poets; among such stories are the exploits of the hero Rustam, and the Sasanian hunting king, Bahram Gur.

The Sasanians also gave the Arabs a wealth of medical, mathematical, astronomical—as well as astrological—and other scientific writings (partly of Indian origin); these were co-foundations of many of the Muslim contributions to science, such as the astrolabe and other instruments for measuring the circumference of the earth. Such Sasanian traditions carried into the early centuries of Islam and, indeed, many of the great mathematicians and scientists in the early centuries of Islam were of Iranian origin, among them the ninth-century mathematician and astronomer Muhammad b. Musa al-Khwarazmi, who wrote on algebra; the polymath Abu 'l-Rayhan al-Biruni, who in the eleventh century produced treatises on geography, geology, astronomy, and history; and the eleventh-century poet 'Umar Khayyam, who was also a mathematician and astronomer.

Religion and Philosophy

It is of some scholarly dispute whether the Zoroastrian religion of Sasanian Iran influenced the development of Islam. It seems possible that Zoroastrian dualism with its ethical doctrine of the struggle of good against evil, as well as the use of myth or mythical language to express religious thoughts, influenced early Islamic thinkers, especially those of Iranian origin. Some scholars have noted the similarities between specific Zoroastrian and Muslim practices and beliefs: the five times daily prayer, the reading of holy texts as part of the funeral rite, and the significance of the number thirty-three. Similarly, there may be a connection between Zoroastrian thought and some Islamic philosophies; for example, the Illuminationist or Ishraqi school of philosopher-mystics (founded by Suhrawardi) parallels such Zoroastrian doctrines as concern the function of angels and the symbolism of light (goodness) and darkness (evil).

Art and Architecture

Perhaps the greatest impact the Sasanians exerted on Islamic civilization was in the visual and building arts. Although it had its unique stylistic and iconographic characteristics, Sasanian monumental and decorative arts also partook of the many earlier cultures that had flourished for millennia in Iran and Mesopotamia. This Sasanian heritage, not surprisingly, was strongest in Iran, continuing with the Qajar dynasty well into the nineteenth century, although aspects of the Sasanian legacy can be found as far west as the Maghreb.

The Sasanian architectural legacy consists of building techniques and architectural forms. The main techniques are squinches to support a dome on a square base and brick or rubble construction coated with plaster; a key building form is the *chahar taq*, a domical room or structure resting on four pillars with arches in between, which characterized Zoroastrian fire temples and served as the prototype for the *kushk* or kiosk mosque, with its vaults and domes. Of pre-Sasanian origin but put to spectacular effect in the great Sasanian palace at Ctesiphon (the *Taq-i Kisra*) in Iraq was the iwan *(aiwan)*, a vaulted hall open on one end—when joined to the domed kiosk, it influenced religious architecture from Egypt to Central Asia. These architectural forms were also used for palatial structures, as their association with the Ctesiphon audience hall imbued them with the power and ceremony of kingship and conferred legitimacy upon the ruler who held audience within. This was certainly the intent of the late thirteenth-century Mongol ruler who built a palace at Takht-i Suleiman in northwestern Iran by incorporating surviving Sasanian palatial and religious buildings and thus presented himself symbolically as the heir of the Sasanian dynasts.

Plaster or stucco, a material not used in pre-Islamic architecture west of Iran but a major decorative medium in Sasanian architecture, became widely used, as it was well-suited for carrying the rich vocabulary of decorative motifs—geometric, floral, vegetal, faunal, and even human—required for the interiors of religious and secular buildings. Many of these motifs, mainly of Sasanian origin (though some derived from the classical Mediterranean world)—the stepped merlon, rosette, palmette, the fantastical Senmurv, griffin, and harpy—were transferred across Islamic territories through highly portable small-scale works of art, such as metalwork and textiles; in particular, richly patterned silks were an important means of transmittal.

The conquering Arabs readily adopted other Sasanian motifs bound up with imperial imagery and iconography. The winged crown, topped by a crescent and globe, which from the fifth century was worn by every Sasanian emperor to symbolize his divine fortune, was the typical headgear worn by enthroned, feasting, and even hunting kings in Islamic works of art. Abstracted into a crescent and globe between a pair of wings, the motif became a generic symbol of royal power and legitimacy; abstracted further, it is a decorative design that appears as far west as the ninth-century Great Mosque in Qairouan, Tunisia.

Other motifs taken from Sasanian royal iconography include the ribbons that flutter to either side of the crown or from the necks of various animals, and the crescent (Ar.: *hilāl*), an emblem closely associated with Islam to the present day; its pairing with a star, also widespread in Islamic contexts, occurs on

Arab–Sasanian coins and is a continuation of late Sasanian coin designs. Although winged animals (griffins, horses, bulls, and lions) have a long history in the art of the ancient Near East, they are ubiquitous in Sasanian art and are taken into Islamic design; similarly, the lion-bull combat comes from this long tradition as both an astronomical symbol and one of royal power and as such was transferred through Sasanian into Islamic art.

The image of the Sasanian ruler holding court or engaged in the pleasures of the banquet and the hunt, as depicted in a variety of artistic media, was readily adopted by the Muslim rulers to illustrate their power and greatness. Despite the prohibitions against figural art, Muslim rulers and their well-to-do subjects perpetuated these pictorials, as well as a range of literary themes, through commissioned works in metal, ceramic, fabric, and paint.

Further Examples of the Sasanian Legacy

Such games as backgammon, chess, and polo were developed or invented under the Sasanians. Backgammon, ubiquitous in Islamic lands, and chess were brought (probably in the sixth century) from India to Iran, where they became an important part of princely education. The earliest treatises on the games are in Middle Persian and date from this period of late Sasanian rule. As a training game for elite cavalry, polo may be a Persian invention. Considered the sport of kings, it was played in much of the Islamic world and was often associated with a royal architectural complex (for example, Timurid Samarkand, Safavid Isfahan, and Mughal Agra).

Finally, the Islamic garden, both a heavenly and earthly creation, is based on Sasanian and much earlier Iranian designs; in fact, "paradise" derives from Old Persian *pairidaeza*. The typical "four garden" plan *(chahār bāgh)*, in which intersecting streams or avenues divide the enclosed area into quarters that are planted with trees and flowers, informs not only actual gardens in the Islamic world but also some carpet designs. Indeed, the numerous mentions of the celestial garden in the Qur'an reflect this garden design.

JUDITH LERNER

See also Al-Biruni; Al-Suhrawardi, Shihab al-Din 'Umar; Angels; Architecture, Religious; Architecture, Secular: Palaces; Archives and Chanceries; Astrolabes; Astronomy; Backgammon; Bureaucrats; Carpets; Ceramics; Chess; Epics, Persian; Ferdowsi; Frescoes; Gardens and Gardening; Hospitals; Hunting; Intellectual History; Mathematics; Medical Literature, Arabic; Medical Literature, Persian; Medicine; Metal Work; Mirrors for Princes; Mosques; Murals; Mythology and Mythical Beings; Painting, Miniature; Painting, Monumental and Frescoes; Poets; Post (Barid); Sculpture; Shahnama; Silk Roads; Textiles; Translation, Pre-Islamic Learning into Arabic; Viziers; Waqf; Zoroastrianism

Further Reading

Arnold, Thomas W. *Survivals of Sasanian and Manichaean Art in Persian Painting*. Oxford: The Clarendon Press, 1924.
Baer, Eva. *The Human Figure in Islamic Art: Inheritance and Islamic Transformations*. (Bibliotheca Iranica. Islamic Art and Architecture Series, 11). Costa Mesa, CA: Mazda Publishers, 2004.
Bier, Lionel. "The Sasanian Palaces and their Influence in Early Islam." *Ars Orientalis* XXIII (1993): 57–66.
Daryaee, Touraj. "Mind, Body, and the Cosmos: Chess and Backgammon in Ancient Persia." *Iranian Studies* 35/4 (2002): 281–312.
Ettinghausen, Richard. "Hilal, ii.—In Islamic Art." In *Encyclopaedia of Islam*, new ed., vol. III. Leiden: Brill, 1971, 381–385. Reprint, *Islamic Art and Archaeology: Collected Papers [of] Richard Ettinghausen*. Prepared and edited by Myriam Rosen-Ayalon. Berlin: Gebr. Mann Verlag, 1984, 269–280.
———. *From Byzantium to Sasanian Iran and the Islamic World: Three Modes of Artistic Influence*. (L. A. Mayer Memorial Studies in Islamic Art and Architecture, 3). Leiden: Brill, 1972.
Frye, Richard N. *The Golden Age of Persia: The Arabs in the East*. London: Weidenfeld and Nicolson, 1975.
Grabar, Oleg. "Notes sur les cérémonies umayyades." In *Studies in Memory of Gaston Wiet*, edited by Myriam Rosen-Ayalon, 51–60. Jerusalem: Institute of Asian and African Studies, Hebrew University of Jerusalem, 1977.
———. *The Formation of Islamic Art*. Revised and enlarged ed. New Haven and London: Yale University Press, 1987.
Hartner, Willy, and Richard Ettinghausen. "The Conquering Lion, the Life Cycle of a Symbol." *Oriens* 17 (1964): 161–171. Reprint, *Islamic Art and Archaeology: Collected Papers [of] Richard Ettinghausen*. Prepared and edited by Myriam Rosen-Ayalon. Berlin: Gebr. Mann Verlag, 1984, 693–711.
Hillenbrand, Robert. *Islamic Architecture: Form, Function and Meaning*. New York: Columbia University Press, 1994.
Irwin, Robert. *Islamic Art in Context: Art, Architecture, and the Literary World*. New York: Harry N. Abrams, Inc., 1997.
Kröger, Jens. "Vom Flügelpaar zur Flügelpalmette. Sasanidische Motive in der Islamischen Kunst." *Bamberger Symposium: Rezeption in der Islamischen Kunst vom 26.6–28.6.1992*. Ed. Barbara Finster, Christa Fragner, and Herta Hafenrichter, 193–203. Beirut: Franz Steiner Verlag Stuttgart, 1999.
Lerner, Judith. "A Note on Sasanian Harpies." *Iran (Journal of the British Institute of Persian Studies* XIII (1975): 166–171.
Melikian-Chirvani, Assadullah Souren. *Islamic Metalwork from the Iranian World 8th–18th Centuries*. London:

Victoria and Albert Museum; Her Majesty's Stationery Office, 1982.

———. "*Rekāb*: the Polylobed Wine Boat from Sasanian to Saljuq Times." In *Au Carrefour des religions mélanges offerts à Philippe Gignoux*. ("Res Orientales, VII), edited by Rika Gyselen, 187–204. Bures-sur-Yvette: Groupe pour l'Étude de la Civilisation du Moyen-Orient, 1995.

Pinder-Wilson, Ralph. "The Persian Garden: Bagh and Chahar Bagh." In *The Islamic Garden*. (Dumbarton Oaks Colloquium on the History of Landscape Architecture, 4, 1974). Ed. Elisabeth B. MacDougall and Richard Ettinghausen, 69–85. Washington: Dumbarton Oaks, Trustees for Harvard University, 1976.

Simpson, Mariana Shreve. "Narrative Allusion and Metaphor in the Decoration of Medieval Islamic Objects." In *Pictorial Narrative in Antiquity and the Middle Ages*. (Studies in the History of Art, 16). Ed. Herbert L. Kessler and Marianna Shreve Simpson, 131–149. Washington, D.C.: National Gallery of Art, 1985.

Sims, Eleanor, with Boris I. Marshak and Ernst J. Grube. *Peerless Images. Persian Painting and Its Sources*. New Haven and London: Yale University Press, 2002.

SCHOLARSHIP

Scholars

The word for scholar in the Arabic Islamic tradition is *'alim* (pl. *'ulama'*, meaning wordly, "knowing," learned). It denotes scholars of almost all disciplines: traditions of the Prophet and his Companions; traditionist (*muhaddith*), Qur'anic exegesis; exegete and other Qur'anic fields like variant readings; reader (*muqri'*); jurisprudence: jurist (*faqih*), and connected areas like successions; specialist of successions, or the one who is recognized as a mufti (that is, having the competence of delivering juridic or theological decisions), or judicial power; judge (*qadi*); dialectic theology: dialectic theologian (*mutakallim*); grammar, lexicography, and philology; knowledge of poetry and poets; learned in (ancient) poetry and poets (*'alim bi-l-shi'r wa-l-shu'ara'*); tribal traditions of the ancient Arabs, such as "the days of the Arabs" (*ayyam al-'Arab*, above all their battles); genealogy: genealogian; chronology and historiography and related disciplines such as prosopography; learned in the "men," that is, in the biography of traditionists or others; belles-lettres; man of letters (*adib*); and later, philosophy and medicine, astronomy, mathematics, and other sciences. Those last five disciplines are usually called "foreign sciences," most having their origin in the Greek legacy.

However, the term *'alim* refers more specifically to the scholars of religious sciences, considered as Islamic, because in this religious realm the central component of science is the knowledge of religious precepts and duties. In the Indo-Iranian world, and especially but not exclusively in the Shi'i environment, the scholars in religious sciences are called "Molla," a word derived from Arabic *mawla* (master). The word *scholars (*'ulama'*)* to denote a group devoted to religious sciences compelled recognition only progressively, as scholars recognized as such succeeded in occupying a favored rank in the society, and even in the various governments in the Islamic countries. In the two first centuries of Islam they consisted of a relatively small number of people engaged in the elaboration of jurisprudence (*fiqh*) on the basis of the Qur'an and its exegesis, and the traditions of the Prophet and his Companions (also local customs, often presented as coming from the Prophetic Tradition). They were concentrated in Medina, in the South of Irak (Basra, Kufa), then in Baghdad after its construction. However, they had a consciousness of their identity that marked them as a distinct group.

As a general tendency was to be observed in the practitioners of religious sciences to consider as certain knowledge only that transmitted (or attributed) to the Prophet, that is, Qur'an and Sunna (transmitted in the Hadith), traditions were attributed to Muhammad, which emphasized the precedence of knowledge and the scholars, most of them dating probably from a period in which the influence and prestige of the latter were not yet well established. Therefore Muhammad is supposed to have declared: "Scholars are the heirs of the prophets," or that they are superior to "martyrs" (*shuhada'*, those who are killed in the Holy War), or that the best of his community are the scholars and among the latter the jurists.

Indeed, the scholars were progressively constituted as such by the practice of jurisprudence; however, the notion of "heirs" was very important in their self-consciousness, because their essential characteristic was definitely the knowledge of hadith, this being the science *par excellence* in that religious representation and imaginaire, because it was transmitted (inherited) from the Prophet (like the Qur'an). All the scholars studied the Qur'an and the Sunna, but not all were specialists in law, and those engaged in theology were fewer still.

The 'Abbasids, with the exception of the caliph al-Ma'mun, preferred to have the scholars and the army on their side, rather than with bureaucracy. During the first five centuries of Islam the scholars developed their own practices and organization independent of the state. It is a fact that the Umayyads, then the 'Abbasids, had recourse to scholars and employed them as judges, but they did not found lasting institutions with personnel dedicated to the study of religion and law.

The political traumas of the AH fourth/tenth CE centuries and the eighth/eleventh centuries, and the disintegration of the 'Abbasid state, contributed not a little to the consolidation of the power of scholars. Whereas they had been essentially a religious elite, scholars also became a social and political elite. This evolution and the creation and development of new institutions of learning, such as the "higher colleges" (*madrasas*) from the fifth/eleventh century onward, and pious foundations *(waqfs)*, resulted in a certain professionalization of scholars, at least of groups among them. In Cairo, for instance, between the second half of the eighth/thirteenth century and the eleventh/seventeenth century, appointments to post in the education were often controlled by the Mamluks or by the intellectual elite itself. Concerning that, some have spoken of the scholars at this time as an intermediate class. Despite the evidence of social mobility, this scholarly elite experienced certain forms of self-reproductions, if not inbreeding, and this led to the emergence of veritable dynasties of scholars. Evolution toward professionalization reached its culminating point under the Ottomans, who among other things established a hierarchy of muftis, presided over by the senior mufti in Istanbul.

Scholarship and Scholars

Given the importance of the Qur'an in Islamic culture, the Qur'anic disciplines have played a great role in education, activities, and works of scholars, first of all exegesis. We can distinguish several periods in this huge production. During the formative period three types of exegesis emerged. The first type was paraphrastic, such as the Meccan Mujahid b. Jabr (d. 104/722), the Kufan Sufyan al-Thawri (d. 161/778), the Kufan then Meccan Sufyan b. 'Uyayna (d. 196/811); most of these people were also traditionists and jurists. The second genre was the narrative exegesis. It featured edifying narratives, generally enhanced by folklore from the Near East, especially that of the Judeo-Christian milieu. To this genre belongs the exegesis of al-Dahhak b. Muzahim (d. 105/723), who delivered moral lessons to the young warriors of Transoxiana, that of the genealogian and historiograph al-Kalbi (d. 146/763). The third genre was legal exegesis, like the exegesis of Ma'mar b. Rashid (d. 154/770) in the recension of the Yemenite 'Abd al-Razzaq al-San'anî (d. 211/827). An intermediary and decisive stage was the introduction of grammar and the linguistic sciences, with works such as *The Literary Expression of the Qur'an* of the Basran Abu 'Ubayda (d. 210/825) or *The Significations of the Qur'an* of the Kufan grammarian al-Farra' (d. 207/822). A latter development was represented by the constitutive exegetical corpora, such as *The Sum of Clarity Concerning the Interpretation of the Verses of the Qur'an* of the Sunnite Abu Ja'far al-Tabari (d. 310/923), or *Unveiling the Elucidation of the Exegesis of the Qur'an* of the Shafi'ite of Nishapur al-Tha'labi (d. 427/1035), or the commentary of the Cordoban Malikite al-Qurtubi (d. 671/1272), which is especially oriented in legal matters.

This type of exegesis includes all the elements of the different exegetical production of the previous period: exegetical traditions coming from ancient exegetes, historical and legendary material, grammar, variant readings, poetry of the ancient Arabs, legal exegesis, and so on.

Scholars of all theological and/or "sectarian" orientations were active in this realm: Mu'tazilites, such as Abu 'Ali al-Jubba'i (d. 303/915) and Abu l-Qasim al-Ka'bi al-Balkhi (d. 319/931); Kharijite Ibadites such as Hud b. Muhakkam (living in the second half of the third/tenth century); Shi'is such as 'Ali al-Qummi (still alive in 307/919); Shi'is who were also Mu'tazilites in theology, such as Abu Ja'far al-Tusi (d. 460/1067); and Sunnites who were Ash'arites in theology, such as Fakhr al-Din al-Razi (d. 606/1210). Of course, the Qur'anic disciplines do not constitute the whole of Islamic scholarship, but it is a mirror of many of its components: grammar and philology, poetry, hadith and traditions of the ancient Muslims, law, and theology.

The sciences of traditions *('ulum al-hadith)* were matters necessary in the formation of every Muslim scholar. Some of them, however, became more specialized in this field, such as Ibn Hanbal (d. 241/855), whose Summa of prophetical traditions *(Musnad)* contains approximately thirty thousand traditions, and al-Bukhari (d. 256/870), whose Summa of traditions is the second book in Sunni Islam after the Qur'an. This book, like others of the same type, has been often commentated on.

It should be noted that the different genre of the commentary and gloss in almost every field of knowledge is one of the characteristics of Islamic scholarship: in poetry, grammar, law, traditions, theology, and so forth. To give only two examples, the compendium on Arabic grammar, a poem in a thousand verses *(Alfiyya)* of the Andalusi grammarian Ibn Malik (d. 672/1274) has been commented on several hundreds of times; that has also been the case for the *Creed* of Abu Hafs al-Nasafi (d. 537/1142).

In Islamic scholarship the oral transmission of knowledge has played a great role: memorizing the Qur'an and vast quantities of traditions, as well as poems and stories, was of major importance. However,

Muslim civilization was a civilization of the written word. Both aspects, orality and literacy, are present together in several ways of the transmission of knowledge from masters to students, for instance, in the "license of transmission" (ijaza), by which an authorized guarantor of a text or of a whole book (his or her own book or a book received through a chain of transmitters) gives the person the authorization to transmit it in his or her turn. To the institutions of Islamic scholarship belong also the journeys for seeking knowledge.

CLAUDE GILLIOT

See also Education; Seeking Knowledge

Primary Sources

Marçais, William (Trans and annot). *Le Taqrîb de en-Nawawî.* Paris: Imprimerie Nationale, 1902.
al-Qabisi, Abu l-Hasan. *Epitre détaillée sur les situations des élèves, leur règles de conduite et celle des maîtres,* edition of the Arabic text and translation by Ahmed Khaled. Tunis: Société Tunisienne de Diffusion, 1986.

Further Reading

Gilliot, Claude. *Exégèse, langue et théologie en islam.* L'exégèse coranique de Tabari. Paris: Vrin (Études Musulmanes, XXXII), 1990.
———. "La transmission des sciences religieuses." In *États, sociétés et cultures du monde musulman médiéval Xe-XVe siècle,* II, edited by Jean-Claude Garcin et al, 327–351. Paris: PUF (Nouvelle Clio), 2000.
——— et al. "'Ulama'." *EI,* X, 801–10: Joseph E. Lowry, Devin J. Stewart, and Shawkat M. Toorawa (Eds). *Law and Education in Medieval Islam.* Studies in memory of Professor George Makdisi. Warminster: E. J. W. Gibb Memorial Trust, 2004.
Makdisi, George. *Rise of Colleges. Institutions of Learning in Islam and the West,* Edinburgh: EUP, 1981.
Melchert, Christopher. "The Etiquette of Learning in the Early Islamic Study Circle." In *Law and education,* edited by Lowry et al., 33–44.
Rosenthal, Franz. *Knowledge Triumphant. The Concept of Knowledge in Medieval Islam.* Leiden: Brill, 1970.
———. *The Technique and Approach of Muslim Scholarship.* Roma: Pontificum Institute Biblicum (Analecta Orientalia), 24, 1947.
Weisweiler, Max. "Das Amt des mustamli in der arabischen Wissenschaft." *Oriens* IV (1951): 27–57.

SCHOOLS OF JURISPRUDENCE

Schools of jurisprudence (*madhahib,* sing. *madhhab*) of law; literally means "a way," and in the context of Islamic law, a legal opinion attributed to a particular individual or group.

Islamic law was largely the product of efforts of private scholars operating in the major urban centers of Islamdom, such as Kufa, Basra, Makka, Medina, and Damascus. By the third century of the Islamic era, legal opinions of these scholars began to be attributed explicitly to individual authorities (*mujtahid or imam*), for example, the opinion of Malik (*madhhab Malik*), rather than generically to a particular locale, such as the opinions of the people of Madina (*"madhhab ahl al-madina" or "ara' ahl al-madina"*). Because of the generally deferential relationship that characterized post–third-century jurists to the opinions of the various mujtahids, legal specialists, beginning in this era, generally became known as followers (*muqallidun;* sing. *muqallid*) of the teachings of a particular mujtahid, for example, the followers of Malik (*ashab Malik*). Eventually, legal specialists who deferred to the doctrines of a particular mujtahid, such as Malik, became known simply by their affiliation to that mujtahid (a Maliki). Although Islamic legal history produced numerous authorities universally recognized as mujtahids, only four of the Sunni schools had adherents in numbers sufficient to guarantee them an institutional role in the governance of Islamicate societies—the Maliki, Hanafi, Shafi'i, and Hanbali madhhabs.

The Maliki madhhab is affiliated with the teaching of Malik b. Anas, who lived in Medina and was thought to represent the legal opinions of the Medinese. The Hanafi madhhab is affiliated with the teaching of Abu Hanifa, who for most of his life lived in Kufa, Iraq. Both Malik and Abu Hanifa lived in the second Islamic century.

The Shafi'i madhhab is affiliated with the teaching of Muhammad b. Idris al-Shafi'i. Al-Shafi'i studied with many authorities throughout Islamdom, including Malik b. Anas in Medina, and Muhammad b. al-Hasan al-Shaybani and Abu Yusuf in Baghdad (the two leading disciples of Abu Hanifa), before he settled permanently in Egypt, where he died at the beginning of the third Islamic century. The Hanbali madhhab is affiliated with the teaching of Ahmad b. Hanbal. Like al-Shafi'i, Ibn Hanbal's teaching was not associated with any particular geographical school. Although Ibn Hanbal was reported to have traveled extensively in pursuit of hadith, his scholarly career was centered in Baghdad. Ibn Hanbal died in the middle of the third Islamic century.

Unlike the Maliki and Hanafi schools, which succeeded to the geographically based schools of the Hijaz and Iraq, respectively, the Shafi'i and the Hanbali schools were to a much greater degree defined by their self-conscious adherence to an explicit method of systematic legal reasoning. In particular, al-Shafi'i is credited with an attempt to transcend the differences of the geographical schools that had developed in the Islamic world by developing an explicit methodology for legal argumentation set forth in his Epistle *(al-Risala)*. Central to al-Shafi'i's methodological innovation was his insistence that the provenance of proof texts be subject to objective corroboration. Accordingly, a hadith of the Prophet Muhammad that was supported by an explicit and uninterrupted chain of transmitters *(isnad)*, all of whom were known to be reliable because of their knowledge and piety, and which is expressly attributed to the Prophet Muhammad, is a more reliable indicator *(dalil)* of the divine will than the opinion of a Companion of the Prophet—no matter how prominent—or a hadith whose isnad was formally defective, either because the chain of authority was incomplete, or because one or more of the reporters in the isnad was not reliable. *A fortiori*, a validly corroborated hadith of the Prophet Muhammad is weightier than any analogy or other argument based on legal reasoning *(ijtihad)*.

Despite the influence of al-Shafi'i on the form of legal argumentation, however, his conviction that consistent methodology could lead to legal uniformity proved to be misplaced. Ibn Hanbal, unlike the other three mujtahids, had greater influence in his capacity as a scholar of hadith rather than for his legal opinions, and indeed, many of his contemporaries and near contemporaries did not even consider him a jurist. Nevertheless, Ibn Hanbal's conservative approach to law and theology was retained by his followers, and the Hanbali madhhab gained a reputation as rigorous adherents to the apparent sense of revelatory texts. Because they accepted ijtihad, their scripturalism is distinct from the defunct Zahiri madhhab, which rejected any ijtihad that attempted to go beyond the apparent sense of revelation's texts.

In response to the centrality that the Shafi'is (and to a lesser extent, the Hanbalis) afforded methodology, the Malikis and the Hanafis were forced to reconstruct the "methodology" that lay behind the ijtihad of their founders. In so doing, the Malikis and the Hanafis developed methodological doctrines that justified the doctrines of their predecessors while at the same time acknowledging the basic proposition of al-Shafi'i—ijtihad was not applicable in the face of conclusive textual evidence. For example, the Hanafis introduced the interpretive concept of *'umum al-balwa*, which was used to justify ignoring the apparent rule communicated by a hadith in circumstances where the alleged rule would be one of general (or near general) applicability, but the practice of the community as documented in the opinion of a Prophetic Companion or prominent scholars was not in conformity with the teaching of that hadith. The Maliki concept of "the practice of the people of Madina *('amal ahl al-madina)* also served to preserve normative practices that appeared to conflict with formally authentic

hadiths. In each case, the Hanafi and the Maliki doctrines functioned to reinforce the authority of Prophetic sunna, while at the same time challenging Shafi'i's thesis that hadiths with formal isnads were the most reliable historical source for discovering normative Prophetic practice, especially when solitary transmissions *(khabar al-wahid)* conflicted with well-known and widespread religious practices. In any case, the Malikis and the Hanafis developed theories regarding the manner by which sunna should be documented that distinguished their approach to the Prophet's sunna from that of the Shafi'is and the Hanbalis without challenging the supremacy of the Prophet's practice in determining Islamic normativity.

In addition to their differences vis-à-vis the Prophetic sunna, it also appears (at least from interschool polemics) that the Malikis and the Hanafis were more willing to give practical reason, often in the form of direct or indirect appeals to utility (sometimes called *istihsan, maslaha mursala,* or *sadd al-dhari'a*), a greater role in the derivation of legal rules than the Shafi'is and the Hanbalis. Thus, whereas the Shafi'is deprecated these techniques as little more than arbitrary personal opinion, the Malikis and the Hanafis deemed them to be central to the development of Islamic substantive law. These differences can be exaggerated, however. Prominent Shafi'is, for example, played an important role in articulating the jurisprudential theory of the five universal ends of revealed law, with its attendant doctrines of primary, secondary, and tertiary goods *(masali')* secured by the law, and the principle that, in the event of any conflict among various commands or goals of the law, the law commanded the maximization of net legal benefits. Accordingly, the law would never command the performance of an act designed to achieve a tertiary good if it would preclude the satisfaction of a primary good. Likewise, prominent Shafi'i jurists writing in the area of public law advanced arguments rooted in utility despite their Shafi'i affiliation.

Historically, the Hanafi madhhab has had the greatest institutional impact of all the madhhabs, as a result of its close relationship first with the 'Abbasids and then with the Ottomans. To the extent that Islamic law is still applied in modern jurisdictions, it is often Hanafi law, subject to legislative reforms in particular areas. Geographically, Hanafism spread from Iraq to Iran, Central Asia, the Indian subcontinent, and Eastern Europe. Malikis dominated the political and social life of Islamic Spain, North Africa, and Islamic sub-Saharan Africa, and in earlier periods of Islamic history, were influential in Egypt. Today they are a distinct minority of Egyptian Muslims, largely confined to Upper Egypt. Shafi'is historically have been predominant in Cairo and lower Egypt, Syria, and Palestine and, prior to the Mongol invasion, Iran. Shafi'is dominated the judicial administration during the Ayyubid and Mamluk periods and continued to predominate in Egypt, Syria, Palestine, and Yemen. They have also become the dominant school of law followed by the Muslims living on the East African coast and Southeast Asia. The Hanbalis, prior to the modern period, were politically the least significant of the madhhabs, both in terms of their impact on the administration of the law and in numbers of adherents. They have enjoyed a renaissance in the modern era, however, as a result of their relationship with the Kingdom of Saudi Arabia, where the Hanbali madhhab is recognized as the official law of the Kingdom.

In the modern era, as a result of multiple factors that included colonialism, the rise of mass literacy, and ideals of egalitarianism, the traditional madhhabs have lost much, if not all, of their currency.

MUHAMMAD H. FADEL

Further Reading

Coulson, Noel. *A History of Islamic Law*. Edinburgh University Press, 1964.
Hallaq, Wael B. *Authority, Continuity and Change in Islamic Law*. Cambridge University Press, 2001.
Melchert, Christoper. *The Formation of the Sunni Schools of Law, 9th–10th Centuries C.E.* Leiden: Brill, 1997.
Schacht, Joseph. *An Introduction to Islamic Law*. Oxford: The Clarendon Press, 1964.
———. *The Origins of Muhammadan Jurisprudence*. Oxford University Press, 1950.

SCRIBES, COPYISTS

One of the most important occupations in medieval Muslim society was that of the scribe. This was due primarily to the centrality of the Qur'an in Islamic civilization and the resultant culture of the book.

As the need for copies of the Qur'an increased, and new disciplines emerged, the corpus of Islamic literature grew rapidly, as did the number of educated people. The search for religious knowledge became a hallmark of Islamic society. This, in turn, created a demand for numerous copies of existing works. With this increased intellectual activity there coincides the introduction and later the widespread usage of a new writing surface: paper.

Although many manuscripts were copied by scholars for their private use, the role of the professional scribe *(warraq)* was significant throughout the manuscript period. Indeed, the profession, called *wiraqah*, came to characterize the intellectual life of the period and was a cultural phenomenon of not only the AH third/ninth CE and fourth/tenth

centuries but throughout the medieval period as well. The *warraq* was a copyist, stationer, and bookseller at the same time. Professional scribes and calligraphers became much-respected members of Muslim society. Indeed, they formed a distinct class of people.

Normally, the scribe was responsible for the copying of the text itself. However, sometimes this function was shared with those who specialized in orthography and vocalization. This practice goes back to the early period of copying Qur'ans and is evident in the later periods. On the other hand, the same person often did this and other functions. The most common phenomenon encountered in illuminated books is one where the scribe was also the illuminator/limner. Quite often, indeed, the scribe was a jack-of-all-trades.

Many scribes were secretaries in the state chancery, as well as famous scholars or other professionals, such as imams, qadis, and the like, who practiced this trade to earn their living. Indeed, to be engaged in this profession was regarded as a mark of distinction and manliness. Thus a saying is attributed to the Kufan traditionalist and lawyer Ibrahim al-Nakha'i (d. ca. 69/717), "an aspect of manliness is to see ink stains on man's clothes and lips." It is also related of the vizier 'Ubayd Allah ibn Sulayman (d. 288/901) that when he saw a yellow stain on his clothes, he took ink, covered the stain with it, and said: "saffron is the perfume of young maidens, whereas ink is the perfume of men." This, of course, does not mean that the profession was the exclusive preserve of men. On the contrary, medieval texts have preserved for us several names of women scribes and calligraphers.

Since Islamic books are fundamentally products of a religious culture, their makeup, that is, their internal and external structure, clearly reflects Muslim piety. It is important to bear in mind that these books, first the copies of the Qur'an, but also works on hadith and jurisprudence *(fiqh)*, were regarded as sacred objects. It is not surprising, therefore, that the copying of books was seen an act of worship *('ibadah)* or that the conduct of the scribe came to be governed by a well-defined set of rules, the religious etiquette *(adab)*. The reverent attitude toward books, but especially copies of the Qur'an, is also reflected in the way in which worn-out books were disposed.

This religious etiquette of the scribe incuded such standards as a pure intention *(niyah)*, the state of ritual purity *(taharah)*, observation of the *qiblah*, having a clean body, and wearing clean clothes. The copyist or calligrapher was instructed always to begin his or her work by writing the *basmalah* ("In the name of God, the Merciful, the Compassionate"), followed by the *hamdalah* ("praise be to God") and *tasliyah* ("prayer for the Prophet"), even if these formulae were not in the exemplar. Furthermore, it was believed that an elegant, clear handwriting, but especially an elegantly executed *basmalah*, would earn the scribe forgiveness of his or her sins.

All throughout the manuscript age there was a tendency on the part of the scribe to preface his or her name (normally in the colophon) with adjectives of humility, such as servant *('abd)*, poor *(faqir)*, wretched *(haqir)*, sinner *(mudhnib)*, or humble *(miskin)*. The name was usually followed by pious invocations and prayers for longevity, God's grace, and the forgiveness of sins.

From the early years of Islam the traditional writing instrument was a reed pen or calamus *(qalam)*. This word appears in the Qur'an several times, and one chapter, namely *surah 68*, bears its name *(surat al-qalam)*. Before the reed was ready to be used as a pen it had to be pared or trimmed to create a nib by cutting off at an angle one of its extremities. The nib was then slit at its end, usually once in the middle, but for large scripts twice or even three times. In most cases, however, the nib was halved to create two half-nibs.

The most important aspect of nibbing was the cutting of the point of the nib. Thus, for instance, in the Middle East (Mashriq) the point was usually cut either straight or at an angle, obliquely. The thickness and the manner of cutting the nib had a direct impact on the calligraphic style or script. The nibbing was done on a nibbing block *(miqattah)* made either of ivory or hard wood or animal bone. The pens were kept either in a writing case or in a pen box.

The ink was often kept in its solid state, especially when used by itinerant scribes. Inks were made either for writing on paper or for writing on parchment. The two types of inks used were carbon (soot) ink and gallnut (tannin) ink. The soot was traditionally suspended in gum arabic, honey, and water. The gallnut ink, on the other hand, was made by mixing galls (pulverized or fermented), vitriol, and gum arabic. When mixed properly, it made a fine permanent black ink, but when improperly mixed it produced a highly acidic or encaustic ink that, over a period, could cause burns in parchment or paper.

Inks were sometimes perfumed using camphor and musk. Other ingredients sometimes added to ink were aloe (to ward off flies and worms), honey, salt, vinegar, or yoghurt to act as preservatives and to prevent or slow down the formation of mold. To dry the ink on the freshly written surface the scribe would use sand or sawdust.

Among other important implements used by scribes were the ruler or straight edge, ruling board *(mistarah)*, scissors, and a burnisher for paper and gold leaf. Arabic sources also mention a paperclip used both for a roll and a codex, compass, or a pair of dividers. Supports for copying paste or wooden boards were also used.

Unlike the Western scribe who worked behind a desk, Muslim scribes sat with one leg folded under and the other bent. They held a sheet of paper (or a quire) on their right or left knee. For a support, they may have used the palm of their left hand or a pasteboard. Their calamus, when not in use, rested behind their right ear or on a support, and they followed the ancient custom of keeping their writing case stuck in their girdle.

Scribes tried to reproduce the arrangement of the original text and even imitate their teachers' handwriting. The imitation of the handwriting of holy people and scholars carried with it an inherent blessing. A scribe's attitude was expected to be marked by humility and reverence toward books, knowledge, and teachers.

Medieval literature provides many accounts of the daily or lifetime output of famous scholar scribes and calligraphers. Even though some of these accounts may be exaggerated or embellished, they certainly give us a picture of great activity consistent with the prevailing preoccupations in literary and scholarly circles. Thus, Ibn al-Jawzi (d. 597/1200), one of the most prolific authors in the Arab world, is said to have written or recopied, according to his own account, two thousand volumes in all, that is, fifty to sixty volumes per year (four quires per day = forty folia = eighty pages). The great calligrapher Yaqut al-Musta'simi (d. 698/1298) is reported to have copied two sections *(juz')* of the Qur'an every day, two Qur'ans every month, and 1001 Qur'ans in his lifetime.

Although some scribes certainly enjoyed a good standard of living, especially when working for wealthy patrons, many others were underpaid to say the least. Abu Mansur 'Abd al-Malik al-Tha'alibi (d. 429/1038), for instance, included the following passage in his *Kitab khass al-khass*:

"A *warraq* was asked, 'What is pleasure?' He answered, 'parchments, papers, shiny ink and a cleft reed pen.' And when asked about his condition, he replied, 'my livelihood is narrower than an inkwell, my body more slender than a ruler, my rank (standing) more delicate than glass, my face darker than vitriol, my lot more concealed than the slit of a nib, my hand weaker than a reed, my food comes from gall nuts, and bad luck clings to me like gum arabic.'"

Libraries were often not just repositories of books but also centers of learning where new works and translations were created, and the copying and correction of books was a regular activity. Indeed, the medieval library was a privileged place for the copying of books. Although a *scriptorium* (a place where the copying of books is done in a structured way), in the Western sense of the word, did not exist, libraries throughout the manuscript age, by providing paper and pens for copyists, were an important factor in the dissemination and transmission of texts. Major libraries employed scribes to copy manuscripts for their collections. On the other hand, workshops (ateliers) bringing together painters, illuminators, and calligraphers flourished under the Ilkhanids, Timurids, Mughals, Safavids, and Ottomans.

ADAM GACEK

Further Reading

Beg, M.A.J. "Warrā." *Encyclopaedia of Islam*. New ed. 11: 150–151.

Déroche, François et al. *Manuel de codicologie des manuscrits en écriture arabe*. Paris: Bibliothèque nationale de France, 2000, 112–167, 198–215.

———. "Copier des manuscrits: remarques sur le travail du copiste."*Revue des Mondes Musulmans et de la Méditerranée* 99–100 (2002):133–144.

SCRIPTURAL EXEGESIS, ISLAMIC

The exegetical literature written to elucidate the Qur'an, called *tafsir* in Arabic, was the product of a highly cultivated discipline of the religious sciences. Tafsir became a cherished mode of self-articulation for most of the sects in medieval Islam. In the classical phase these works show a remarkable uniformity across the different sects and Islamic languages (whether Arabic, Persian, or Turkish). A tafsir work usually commented on the whole of the 'Uthmanic codex in its canonical sequence. The verses of the Qur'an were commented on word by word, or phrase by phrase, depending on the preference of the commentator. More often than not these works were sprawling, multivolume compositions that reflected the significance and attention given to articulate the meaning of the word of God.

Origins of Tafsir

The study of the early phase of tafsir has long engaged modern scholars, yet there is no consensus as to how far back we can push the beginning of this genre. There is, however, enough evidence that some form of exegetical activity was well advanced by the early second/eighth century. The most significant groups of works that stem from this period are two: the works that have their origins in the school of Ibn 'Abbas (d. 69/688), and the work of Muqatil Ibn Sulayman (d. 150/767). The works stemming from the school of Ibn 'Abbas do not comment on every word or verse in the Qur'an, but do that rather selectively. Most of these early works are lost and can now be studied only to the degree that they are quoted in later works. Muqatil's work comments on almost all of the Qur'an, and it set the tone for subsequent commentaries.

The early phase of tafsir ended with the emergence of a fully articulated grammatical theory that explained the workings of Arabic language in a scientific way. The publication of the work of Sibawayhi (d. ca. 180/798) changed the course of the development of tafsir, for it made possible an independent analysis of the language of the Qur'an uncontrolled by dogma. The publication of this book brought out into the open the latent tension between a dogmatic polemical reading of the Qur'an and a philological reading that gave little heed to doctrinal considerations. This tension became characteristic of the history of tafsir. The creative impulse behind tafsir is thus a paradoxical conflict between two mutually exclusive axioms, both of which are central to the experience of tafsir and were both held and affirmed at the same time throughout the subsequent history of tafsir. The first is that the Qur'an has to encompass everything because it is the word of God eternal, and as such it was spoken above history. In other words, the Qur'an was made to justify later developments in dogma and theology. The second axiom is philological, the realization that language can only mean one thing at any moment. When they lacked a philological backing, dogmatic interpretations soon had to be legitimized through the process of giving precedence to earlier authorities; thus the interpretations of scholars who were part of the early phase of tafsir came to enjoy a sort of canonical status in the Sunni camp, while the Shi'i imams came to enjoy that status for the Shi'is.

Pre-Classical Phase

This is the phase that saw the rise of the grammatical approach to the language of the Qur'an. Many works stemming from this period concentrated on the linguistically interesting parts of the Qur'an: difficult constructions, unusual phraseology, rare and difficult words, and possible variations in grammatical case endings. Like the early phase, grammatical works were selective in what they commented on. The written 'Uthmanic codex, with its lack of vocalization, has given rise to different readings of various Qur'anic words, which became known as qira'at, or variant readings. The new grammatical science was used to justify, accept, or dismiss such readings. As such, grammar was starting to act as a judge on some of the traditional methods developed to safeguard the transmission of the Qur'an. The battle was being drawn now between the two camps, grammarians on one hand and the Qur'an specialists on the other. Eventually some sort of resolution to these issues would come about, but the threat that philology posed to traditional interpretation was always latent. It is also important to draw attention to the fact that philology was not unaffected by religious dogma. The Arabic lexicon shows remarkable sensitivity to theological issues, and at certain points is willing to avoid conflict by siding with theology. Thus the interplay between the two was far more complex a phenomenon than might first appear. The major works stemming from this period are those of Abu 'Ubaydah (d. 209/825) and al-Farra' (d. 207/822).

This pre-classical phase of the exegetical tradition culminated in the publication of the monumental work *Jami' al-bayan* of al-Tabari (d. 310/923). *Jami' al-bayan* is nothing short of a consolidation of two centuries of exegetical Sunni tradition. It sought to collect, sift, and prescribe the most orthodox meanings to the Qur'an. One virtue—and it has many— was its attempt to be catholic in its taste. Material from the formative period was wedded to the grammatical exegetical tradition and although al-Tabari would more often than not weigh in to tell the reader which of the many interpretations offered to a certain verse was more valid than others, he nevertheless made available to the reader the spectrum of various interpretations current in the tradition of tafsir. Thus the work remains one of our most complete registers of lost early material. This marriage between the two streams of the Sunni exegetical tradition came with a heavy price, however, and a great license. Sunni scholars admitted to the main premise of the philological school: that divine speech, no matter how divine it was held to be, was still comprehensible because it was using conventional human language. In other words, the language of the Qur'an was transparent and decipherable through philology. The main premise of Sunni hermeneutical theory is that the literal meaning of the text is the divine meaning. The text as such is transparent—and as it happens the Sunni dogmatic reading of the Qur'an was also claimed to be nothing but its literal meaning—or such was the premise. Yet, having allowed philology to be the bedrock of Sunni hermeneutics, the exegetes negated this all-too-powerful restriction on their craft by allowing for a polyvalent Qur'an. A philological reading of the text did not mean one reading only. The Qur'an was deemed to be capable of offering more than one meaning to any verse at any single time.

The other important aspect of al-Tabari's work is that it introduced its material with a chain of transmitters, in Arabic isnad. The science of exegesis was now donning the mantle of a traditional science: isnad. Soon this appearance would shield the traditional material from any criticism and thus obscure its true origins: All exegetical material is based on nothing more than the personal reflections of the respective exegetes. As Sunnism moved to consolidate its grip on what is orthodox and what is not, it attempted to limit the scope of meanings by enshrining the older layer of exegetes as authoritative.

Meanwhile, other Islamic sects and intellectual currents were busy issuing their own commentaries. The most important of these were the Shi'is, the Mu'tazilites, and the Sufis. The early Shi'i hermeneutical practice was based on two premises, both formulated in contradistinction to the Sunnite theory. The first is that the language of the Qur'an has an inner meaning (a *batin*), in addition to the literal meaning (a *zahir*). The second premise was that this inner meaning can only be made manifest through the interpretations offered by the imams (the divinely guided presumptive leaders of the community). The major two figures in early Shi'i exegesis are al-Kufi (d. ca. AH 310/922 CE) and al-Qummi (alive around 260/873). When read thus, the Qur'an spoke of the truth of the claims of the Shi'is against the Sunnis.

Little has survived of the exegetical material from the early Mu'tazilites, and we still await a study of one of the major medieval Mu'tazilite commentaries to survive: the Qur'an commentary of al-Jushami (d. 494/1101), which has early material now otherwise lost. The mystical approach to interpreting the Qur'an reached a stage of high development by the time of al-Tustari (d. 283/896). The premise of this approach was not unlike the Shi'i method of stipulating two levels of meaning in the Qur'an, one literal, which was of little concern to the mystics, and one inner, the layer they were confident they could unearth. Invariably the mystics saw the inner meaning of the Qur'an to cluster around two major themes: God's ineffable majesty, and the quest for a sort of human perfection and connection to God.

Classical Phase

The emphasis in modern scholarship has been shifting to the study of the better-documented classical period. Indeed, what we know about the six hundred years of the later history of the medieval exegetical tradition is sketchy at best. Thus the Qur'an commentary of the Mu'tazilite al-Zamakhshari (d. 538/1144), the closest we will come to a household name in this field, is usually described in the secondary literature as a philological and Mu'tazilite commentary. There is, however, no study available that elaborates on such broad characterizations. Moreover, no one seems to be puzzled by the fact that al-Zamakhshari's Mu'tazilite commentary was preserved and highly esteemed by the Sunni scholars.

The work of al-Tha'labi (d. 427/1035) ushered in the high classical phase of Qur'anic commentary. Al-Tha'labi enlarged and perfected the trends started by al-Tabari. First, he decided to collect independently of al-Tabari the early material, in addition to the material that had accumulated since al-Tabari's work. To allow space for this enlargement al-Tha'labi dropped the use of isnad. He used no fewer than seventy works as basis for his commentary. Thus the work is our second most important source for the early period, and for the fourth/tenth century. Moreover, al-Tha'labi decided to include Shi'i and Sufi material in his commentary. This catholic encyclopedic spirit was hardly unique to Sunnism of this period. The Shi'i exegetes were busy making their commentaries more mainstream, thus swamping their Shi'i sympathies with a normative philological discourse. Sufism, in the person of al-Qushayri (d. 465/1063), attempted to give the literal sense a reverential nod. The Mu'tazilite al-Zamakhshari produced what for all practical purposes was a Sunnite mainstream commentary. Finally, the exegetical tradition could no longer ignore scholastic theology and philosophy, and it would offer us the most important response in the work of Fakhr al-Din al-Razi (d. 606/1210).

The encyclopedic spirit that was behind the classical exegetical tradition came with a drawback. Works were becoming unwieldy and soon the need arose for more manageable works that could offer a summary of the debates in those encyclopedic commentaries. The rise of what I have termed the *Madrasa* (college)-style commentary was a major development and allowed the field to continue to grow and respond to different intellectual developments. Finally, the rise of Madrasas (colleges) after the fifth/eleventh century produced a new genre of commentaries, the glosses.

Two major reactions to the Sunnite encyclopedic approach should be mentioned. The first is philological, the second is dogmatic. Soon after the work of al-Tha'labi appeared, his student al-Wahidi (d. 468/1076) would publish his magnum opus, *al-Basit* (published 446/1054), in which he attempted to align Sunnism with a thorough philological reading of the Qur'an. The attempt horrified even its author. But having sounded the alarm for the disaster awaiting the Sunnite neglect of the challenge of philology, orthodoxy soon mustered a far more daring response: jettison philology and keep dogma. A reexamination of the foundations of Sunnite hermeneutics became thus inevitable, and having offered it, Ibn Taymiyya (d. 728/1328) would challenge the field and reinvigorate it. His radical hermeneutics would claim that only Muhammad and his Companions knew what the Qur'an meant. His call for purifying tafsir would have to await the indefatigable al-Suyuti (d. 911/1505). Luckily for us no one kind of tafsir was able to negate the others, and medieval exegetical tradition is one of the most intellectually interesting of the medieval disciplines.

WALID SALEH

See also al-Suyati; al-Tabari; Fakhr al-Din al-Razi; Hadith; Ibn Taymiyya; Madrasa; Mu'tazilites; Qur'an; Shi'is; Sibawayhi; Sufis

Further Reading

For a medieval exemplar of Islamic scriptural exegesis see: Beeston, A.F.L. *Baidawi's Commentary on surah 12 of the Qur'an: text, accompanied by an interpretative rendering and notes.* Oxford: Clarendon Press, 1963.

For the formative period see: Versteegh, C.H.M. *Arabic Grammar and Qur'anic Exegesis in Early Islam.* Leiden: Brill, 1993; see also the relevant parts of Wansbrough, John. *Quranic Studies.* Oxford: Oxford University Press, 1977. For early Shi'i exegetical tradition see: Bar-Asher, Meir M. *Scripture and Exegesis in Early Imami Shiism.* Leiden: Brill, 1999.

For Sufi and mystical tradition see: Bowering, Gerhard. *The Mystical Vision of Existence in Classical Islam: The Qur'anic Hermeneutics of the Sufi Sahl at-Tustari (d. 283/896).* Berlin: Walter de Gruyter, 1980.

For classical period see: Saleh, Walid A. *The Formation of the Classical Tafsir Tradition: The Qur'an Commentary of al-Tha'labi (d. 427/1035).* Leiden: Brill, 2004.

SCRIPTURAL EXEGESIS, JEWISH

Background

Because the Hebrew Bible is the Jewish scripture, its interpretation has determined the shape of Judaism. Biblical exegesis, therefore, has always been central to Jewish religious and intellectual activity. Scholars active in Islamic lands during the Middle Ages played a key role in developing a rationalistic, philologically based approach to scripture.

Jewish interpretation of the Bible dates to antiquity, when various exegetical approaches emerged, including the prognostic *pesher* of the Qumran community and the philosophical allegory of Philo Judaeus (25 BCE–50 CE). Most widespread and enduring was Rabbinic *midrash*, which literally means "searching" scripture. *Midrash* seeks to discover apparent difficulties or contradictions in the Bible, which it then resolves through further scrutiny of the text. The method demonstrates scripture's perfection, the significance of its every detail, and its eternal relevance. Midrashic literature encompasses a variety of genres, including expansive Aramaic translations *(targumim)*, exegetical compilations, and anthologies of homilies. The midrashic method is also used throughout the Babylonian and Palestinian Talmuds. Like all classic rabbinic writing, this literature preserves the oral character of preaching or teaching. Interpretations, comments, or discussions are ascribed to ancient rabbis, and sometimes, short chains of transmission are given. But the compilers who arranged the material remain anonymous, revealing nothing of their editorial methods and motivations. In certain respects, then, classic rabbinic literature resembles early Islamic writings, such as *hadith* (tradition) collections, which do not yet betray the imprint of Greco-Arabic scholarship.

Rabbanites and Karaites in the East (Tenth–Eleventh Centuries)

During the late ninth century and tenth century, Jews began composing full-fledged Bible commentaries. Writing in Arabic, they drew upon Christian models, while borrowing from the terminology and methodology of Qur'anic exegesis. Dawud Ibn Marwan al-Muqammas (middle to late ninth century), an Iraqi Jew who converted to Christianity and then reverted to Judaism, wrote commentaries on Genesis and Ecclesiastes that drew heavily upon older Syriac works. Little of this work remains, but much of the exegetical oeuvre of Sa'adyah Gaon (882–942) and Samuel ben Hophni Gaon (d. 1013), and such Karaites as Ya'qub al-Qirqisani (d. after 938), Japheth ben Eli (d. after 1006), and Abu'l-Faraj Ibn Asad (mid-eleventh century) survives. Although these commentaries remain rooted in rabbinic midrash, they also evince familiarity with contemporary Islamic, Christian, and philosophical texts. Like the non-Jewish works that inspired them, they include extended introductions that discuss theological, methodological, and literary problems. They also feature full Arabic translations of the biblical text, detailed philological comments, and lengthy digressions on many different topics.

Three main factors prompted this outburst of exegetical activity. First, by the tenth century, many eastern Jews knew Arabic better than Hebrew or Aramaic, the traditional national languages. For them, new Arabic translations and commentaries made scripture accessible again. Although Sa'adyah's rendering—the first Arabic version of the entire Hebrew Bible—is faithful to the original, it avoids anthropomorphisms, resolves syntactic ambiguities, and identifies obscure toponyms. It often circulated independently of his commentaries. By contrast, the Karaite translation's extreme literalism defies good Arabic usage; likely, they aimed at conveying the original Hebrew as faithfully as possible. Second, as Jews acculturated and gained an appreciation for Islamic modes of thought and expression, they sought to produce Jewish works on Islamic models. At the same time, they responded to Muslim cultural and religious claims for the superiority of the Arabic language and the inimitability of the Qur'an, by striving to demonstrate the excellence of Hebrew and the perfection of the Bible. Consequently, they developed the fields of Hebrew grammar and lexicography in order to study the Bible scientifically. Finally, the Rabbanite–Karaite debate revolved around biblical exegesis—who was authorized to interpret scripture and how it was to be interpreted. Here, too, Islamic notions shaped the arguments. Rabbanites maintained, for example, that legal ambiguities (Ar. *mutashabbihat*; Q 3:7) in the Bible are all resolved by the authoritative traditions preserved in the Talmud. Karaites, however, insisted upon the interpreter's autonomy in determining the details of the Law.

Legal passages aside, Karaites and Rabbanites alike strove to interpret the Bible contextually. Sa'adyah and Japheth ben Eli both insisted that every passage in scripture must be understood according to its plain meaning, unless this would contradict sense perception, human reason, or the evidence of another passage. (Sa'adyah adds a fourth category: tradition.) Like their Muslim contemporaries, therefore, they sought to identify and explain figurative language (Ar. *majaz*) and parables (Ar. *amthal*) in scripture whose literal meaning would be absurd or even blasphemous. For example, the statement that Eve was "the mother of all living" (Genesis 3:20) cannot be taken literally, since she was not the ancestor of lions or oxen; nor is God really "a devouring fire" (Deuteronomy 4:24), since fire can be created and extinguished, whereas God is eternal and immutable. Consequently, these exegetes distinguished between the literal/exoteric (Ar. *zahir*) and the hidden/esoteric (Ar. *batin*) meanings of biblical expressions. According to Sa'adyah, the plain sense of Proverbs 24:27 is that a man should have a profession before he marries; the hidden meaning is that he must attend to the demands of this world before addressing the concerns of the next.

A striking feature of Karaite exegesis from tenth-century Jerusalem is its prognostic approach to biblical prophecies. Referring many passages to recent or contemporary events, these sectarians found allusions to the Fatimids (Numbers 24:21), the Carmathian assault on Mecca (Daniel 11:31), and the Buyids (Daniel 11:40). Like the *pesher* of the ancient Qumran sectarians, this type of exegesis was fostered by an apocalyptic worldview.

The Andalusian School

During the late tenth and early eleventh centuries, Andalusia emerged as a leading Jewish cultural center and Hebrew studies progressed dramatically. Grammarians such as Menahem ben Saruq, Judah Hayyuj, Abu'l-Walid (Jonah) Ibn Janah, and Moses Ibn Chiquitilla set biblical Hebrew philology on a sound basis by using their thorough knowledge of Arabic and Aramaic effectively. At the same time, exegetes such as Ibn Chiquitilla and Judah Ibn Bil'am produced concise, philologically oriented commentaries on many biblical books. Rationalistically inclined, Ibn Chiquitilla offered naturalistic explanations for certain biblical miracles, and referred many biblical prophecies to events that transpired in antiquity. Other Andalusians sought to discover philosophical notions in the Bible. The jurist and religious poet Isaac Ibn Ghiyath (1038–1089) composed a Neoplatonic commentary on Ecclesiastes in Arabic; within two generations, Bible commentaries would become important conduits for the dissemination of philosophical ideas. Commentaries were not the only works dedicated to biblical interpretation. The poet and philosopher Moses Ibn Ezra (ca. 1055–ca. 1135) devoted his *Treatise of the Garden* to figurative and literal expressions in scripture and much of his *Book of Discussion and Conversation* to biblical poetics. Also, Moses Maimonides (1135/38–1204) wrote his *Guide of the Perplexed* (see later in this entry) for philosophically informed readers of the Bible.

During the mid-twelfth century, the greatest Andalusian exegete, Abraham Ibn Ezra (ca. 1089–ca. 1164), composed Hebrew commentaries in Christian Europe incorporating both the grammatical advances and philosophical outlook of the Spanish school. Since he also drew heavily upon the interpretations of eastern Rabbanite and Karaite scholars, Ibn Ezra became an important conduit for the transmission of Judeo-Arabic learning in Latin Europe. (An extremely important, but largely independent, exegetical school in northern Europe lies outside the scope of this article.)

Maimonides and Later Exegetes

Completed in Egypt around 1190, Maimonides' *Guide of the Perplexed* was intended for scholars who found certain biblical expressions to be incompatible with philosophical truth. Drawing upon the rabbinic dictum "the Torah speaks in human language," Maimonides declared that biblical anthropomorphisms and anthropopathisms must be understood metaphorically. References to God's sitting or standing, for example, connote His immutability (*Guide* 1:11, 13); conversely, "seeing" or "beholding" God means apprehending Him intellectually (*Guide* 1:5). Maimonides also interprets extended passages as philosophical parables whose plain meaning (Ar. *zâhir*), intended for the uneducated masses, masks their true, esoteric significance (Ar. *bâtin*). His philosophical outlook, moreover, leads him to naturalize certain miraculous events, such as Abraham's encounter with the three angels (Genesis 18), which he explains as a prophetic vision (*Guide* 2:42). He also rationalizes ceremonial commandments, insisting that they are not arbitrary enactments (*Guide* 3:28–49).

Jewish intellectual life in the East declined after Maimonides' death. To be sure, his direct line included several important scholars, notably his son Abraham (1186–1237) and his descendant, David II Maimuni (fl. 1335–1415), both of whom composed Bible commentaries imbued with Sufi notions. Another exegete deserving of notice is Tanhum ben Joseph ha-Yerushalmi (ca. 1220–1291), who commented on the entire Bible. Philologically rigorous, he drew upon Arabic grammar and lexicography for his explanations. A committed rationalist, he allegorized certain biblical narratives, such as Jonah, which he viewed as a parable about the soul.

Finally, a school of philosophically informed exegetes developed in the Yemen during the fourteenth through sixteenth centuries. Favoring a homiletical style—they called their commentaries *midrashim*—commentators such as Nethaneel ben Isaiah, Zechariah the Physician, and Sa'adyah ben David drew upon rabbinic literature, Maimonidean theory, and Ismaili notions for their unusual readings of the Bible. For them, as for other exegetes living in Islamic lands, Arabic furnished an important tool for scriptural exegesis.

DANIEL FRANK

See also Baghdad; Education, Jewish; Hebrew; Judeo-Arabic; Karaites; Moses Maimonides; Sa'adyah Gaon

Primary Sources

Abraham Ibn Ezra. *Ibn Ezra's Commentary on the Pentateuch.* Vol. 1. Transl. H. Norman Strickman and Arthur M. Silver. New York: Menorah, 1988.

Japheth ben Eli. *A Commentary on the Book of Daniel by Rabbi Jephet the Karaite.* Ed. and transl. by D.S. Margoliouth. Oxford: Clarendon Press, 1889.

Moses Maimonides. *The Guide of the Perplexed.* Transl. S. Pines. Chicago: University of Chicago Press, 1963.

Saadiah ben Joseph al-Fayyumi. *The Book of Theodicy: Translation and Commentary on the Book of Job.* Transl. L.E. Goodman. New Haven: Yale University Press, 1988.

———. *Rabbi Saadiah Gaon's Commentary on the Book of Creation.* Transl. Michael Linetsky. Northvale, NJ: Jason Aronson, 2002.

Further Reading

Frank, Daniel. *Search Scripture Well: Karaite Exegetes and the Origins of the Jewish Bible Commentary in the Islamic East.* Leiden: Brill Academic Publishers, 2004.

Langermann, Yitzhak Tzvi. *Yemenite Midrash: Philosophical Commentaries on the Torah.* New York: Harper Collins, 1996.

Polliack, Meira. *The Karaite Tradition of Arabic Bible Translation: A Linguistic and Exegetical Study of Karaite Translations of the Pentateuch from the Tenth to the Eleventh Centuries.* Leiden: E. J. Brill, 1997.

Sæbø, Magne (Ed.). *Hebrew Bible/Old Testament I/1-2.* 2 vols. Göttingen: Vandenhoeck & Ruprecht, 1996–2000, esp. Chaps. 25, 31, 33.

Simon, Uriel. *Four Approaches to Psalms: From Saadiah Gaon to Abraham Ibn Ezra.* Albany: SUNY Press, 1991.

Strack, H.L., and Günter Stemberger. *Introduction to the Talmud and Midrash.* 2nd ed. Minneapolis: Fortress Press, 1996.

SCULPTURE

Among the forms of art produced in medieval Islamic cultures, sculpture is frequently overlooked and its prevalence is generally underestimated. Nevertheless, sculpture, comprising the techniques of carving, casting, molding, and modeling and the work of art produced by those techniques, was part and parcel of the late-antique visual culture and continued for centuries after the rise of Islam. Sculpture can be divided into two modes. The first is work in low or high relief used as surface decoration on architecture and objects, with figural and nonfigural representation, made of stone, stucco, ceramic, wood, ivory, and rock crystal. The second mode consists of freestanding statues and figurines of human and animal forms, often with potentially utilitarian functions, made of cast metal, modeled or molded ceramic, and probably also of carved wood and stone. The focus here will be on freestanding and high-relief figural sculpture, which, in contrast to low-relief nonfigural sculpture, has received little attention.

For the early period, copious examples of very high-relief stucco sculpture have been found in the eighth-century Umayyad country estates of Qasr al-Hayr al-Gharbi (Syria) and Khirbat al-Mafjar (Jordan). Most of these may be said to derive from the late-antique artistic tradition employed in the Byzantine and Sasanian realms, with representations of enthroned rulers, dancers, attendants, and hunters applied to walls and domes. Beyond contributing to the aura of princely pleasure in the court, the iconographic programs of these works were probably keyed into Umayyad cultural and imperial ambitions.

Similar ambitions may have motivated the placement of statues that turned with the wind over the domes of the four gates and the palace complex of the Round City of Baghdad founded in the mid-eighth century by the 'Abbasids. As reported in the sources, the Green Dome of the palace was surmounted by the statue of a horseman carrying a lance that was believed to point toward the enemy. This public spectacle of wind-powered statues had its private counterpart in the 'Abbasid palaces where automata of various types were prominently displayed. The taste for conspicuous displays of statuary survived the slow disintegration of the 'Abbasid empire. In particular, animal statues in metalwork designed as fountains—attributable to Fatimid Egypt and to caliphal and post-caliphal Spain—reveal the ongoing fascination with "animated" statues. Such playful statues were produced in both small and large scale, the latter exemplified by the famously mysterious Pisa griffin, as well as the fountain lions of the Alhambra.

In the eastern Islamic world, stucco continued to be used for high-relief sculpture of figural subjects. A number of nearly life-size stucco figures of attendants have been attributed to twelfth- and thirteenth-century Iran, but the precise nature of their architectural contexts remain unknown. In contemporary Anatolia and northern Mesopotamia, stone was the primary medium for high- and low-relief figural sculpture that adorned city gates and walls. At the same time, there was a rise in the production of small figurines in metal and ceramic. Many of these were conceived as vessels or incense burners, but it was the figural form rather than potential functionality that had primacy in design. Thus the famous Hermitage bull—cast in bronze with its suckling calf and a predatory if diminutive feline on its back—could have contained liquid, but such a function was secondary to its visually engaging overall design. Other forms produced in ceramic include equestrian figures and more remarkable vessels in the form of breastfeeding women, or objects in the form of courtyard dwellings with an assembly of figures. The lack of knowledge about the contexts of such objects has hindered meaningful interpretation, although they are less puzzling if they are considered as part and parcel of the contemporary rise in figural art in general. The display of figural statues as fountains also continued to be appreciated in this period, as evidenced by three ceramic examples found in Raqqa, which depict a rooster, a sphinx (David Collection, Copenhagen), and a horseman spearing a serpent (National Museum, Damascus).

In addition to extant examples of medieval Islamic sculpture, there is considerable textual evidence for a cultural interest in famous sculptural works, which can be gleaned from moralizing and entertaining discourse on images and image making. The high-relief Sasanian sculpture of Khusraw Parviz on horseback at Taq-i Bustan, for example, appealed to the popular imagination as an epitome of artistic skill and functioned as a didactic motif in edifying stories. Ultimately, medieval Islamic sculpture may be better understood as an integrated, rather than a discrete, art form that partook of various cultural products ranging from ceremonial and propaganda to folklore, literature, and the other visual arts, especially painting.

OYA PANCAROGLU

See also Architecture, Secular: Palaces; Ceramics; Marvels and Wonders; Metal Work; Painting

Further Reading

Baer, Eva. "A Group of Seljuq Figural Bas Reliefs." *Oriens* 20 (1967): 107–124.

Ettinghausen, Richard. *From Byzantium to Sasanian Iran and the Islamic World. Three Modes of Artistic Influence.* Leiden: E. J. Brill, 1972.

Gibson, Melanie. *The Enigmatic Figure: Islamic Glazed Ceramic Sculpture 1100–1250.* Ph.D. dissertation, University of London, forthcoming 2005.

Gierlichs, Joachim. *Mittelalterliche Tierreliefs in Anatolien und Nordmesopotamien.* Tübingen: Ernst Wasmuth Verlag, 1996.

Grabar, Oleg. *The Formation of Islamic Art.* Rev. ed. New Haven: Yale University Press, 1987.

Grube, Ernst J. "Islamic Sculpture. Ceramic Figurines." *Oriental Art* 12 (1966): 165–175.

Hamilton, R.W., and Oleg Grabar. *Khirbat al-Mafjar. An Arabian Mansion in the Jordan Valley.* Oxford: Clarendon Press, 1959.

Hillenbrand, Robert. "La Dolce Vita in Early Islamic Syria: The Evidence of Later Umayyad Palaces." *Art History* 5 (1982): 1–35.

Lassner, Jacob. *The Topography of Baghdad in the Early Middle Ages.* Detroit: Wayne State University Press, 1970.

Loukonine, Vladimir, and Anatoli Ivanov. *Lost Treasures of Persia. Persian Art in the Hermitage Museum.* Washington, DC: Mage Publishers, 1996, esp. cat. nos. 84, 87, 92–93, 100–101, 103, and 127.

Melikian-Chirvani, A.S. "Les taureaux à vin et les cornes à boire de l'Iran islamique." In *Histoire et cultes de l'Asie centrale préislamique*, edited by Paul Bernard and Frantz Grenet, 101–125. Paris: Editions du Centre Nationale de la Recherche Scientifique, 1991.

———. "The Wine Birds of Iran from Pre-Achaemenid to Islamic Times." *Bulletin of the Asia Institute* 9 (1995): 41–97.

Otto-Dorn, Katharina. "Figural Stone Reliefs on Seljuk Sacred Architecture in Anatolia." *Kunst des Orients* 12 (1978–1979): 103–149.

Pancaroglu, Oya. "Signs in the Horizons: Concepts of Image and Boundary in a Medieval Persian Cosmography." *Res: Anthropology and Aesthetics* 43 (2003): 31–41.

Redford, Scott. "The Seljuqs of Rum and the Antique." *Muqarnas* 10 (1993): 148–156.

Rice, Tamara Talbot. "Some Reflections Aroused by Four Seljukid Stucco Statues." *Anatolica* 2 (1968): 112–121.

Riefstahl, Rudolf M. "Persian Islamic Stucco Sculptures." *The Art Bulletin* 8 (1931): 439–463.

Rogers, J.M. "On a Figurine in the Cairo Museum of Islamic Art." *Persica* 4 (1969): 141–179.

Schlumberger, Daniel. *Qasr e-Heir el-Gharbi.* Paris: Librairie Orientaliste Paul Geuthner, 1986.

Soucek, Priscilla P. "Farhad and Taq-i Bustan: The Growth of a Legend." In *Studies in Art and Literature of the Near East in Honor of Richard Ettinghausen*, edited by Peter J. Chelkowski, 27–52. New York: New York University Press, 1974.

———. "Solomon's Throne/Solomon's Bath: Model or Metaphor." *Ars Orientalis* 23 (1993): 109–134.

SEDENTARISM

Within the civilizatory process in the *Old World Dryland Belt*, where nomads/pastoralists and sedentists/agriculturalists practice antipodal lifestyles, *sedentarism* exists when agricultural or artisanal activities become the primary factor governing the rhythm of life and the organization of time (Herzog 1954). In this context, empirical nomadism studies and practical experience generally assume an evolution from full nomadism, seminomadism/mountain nomadism to transhumance/alpine cattle breeding (farming) to agriculture. Regarding the underlying process, a distinction is made between *sedentization* (based on free and independent decision) and *sedentarization* (the forced result of external intervention).

There are two contending approaches in the civilization theory debate. In Ibn Khaldun's three-generation theory, *umran badawi* (nomadic mobility) and *umran hadari* (sedentary cultivation), are the (primitive) beginning and (civilized) peak/outcome of a general pattern of social evolution (Alafenish 1982). By contrast, the theory of nomadism as a socioecological mode of culture sees nomadism and sedentarism as (the only) meaningful and interchangeable alternatives. Throughout the *Old World Dryland Belt*, ecological and/or political constraints caused these survival strategies to recur and/or alternate in time and space (Scholz 1995, 2001). This contention is corroborated by ethnoarchaeological (Cribb 1991; Francfort 1990) and historical studies attributing the shift between sedentarism and mobility to changes in the ecological, social, and political settings (see Scholz 1995). Drought, famine, disease, animal deaths, the rise and fall of empires, population pressure, raiding, tribal conflicts, and wars are regarded as governing factors.

Roman rule on the Arabian peninsula (second century CE), Arab incursions into the fertile lands of the Nile (seventh century), the migration of the Beni Hilal tribes in North Africa (eleventh century) or the Mongol invasions of Western Asia (thirteenth century) triggered a wave of Bedouinization (Caskel 1953; Planhol 1975: "medieval Bedouinization"). However, similarly significant sedentization processes were activated (Ehlers 1980; Leidlmair 1965), and the invaders were assimilated (Herzog 1954). This is documented by many place names in North Africa and Western Asia indicating a nomadic-tribal origin, such as *bani/ beni* (tribe) or *bilad* (brother) (for example, Bilad Bani Bu Ali/Oman). According to Oppenheim (1939–1952), similar processes occurred in what are now Syria and Iraq and caused the invasions of Anatolia by Timur (fourteenth century) and the Turkmen (sixteenth century) (Braudel 1990), where nomadism was replaced by sedentary agriculture in the West, yet burgeoned again in the East. Sedentization also occurred in Inner Oman, for example (after the ninth century approximately), where former Bedouin immigrants from southern and central Arabia used water in the wadis of Jabal Akhdar or Wadi Batha and became sedentary oasis farmers (Wilkinson 1972). Nomads also settled on the floodplains of the Tigris and Euphrates rivers, the alluvial fans at the foot of the Zagros Range, the water-rich wadis at the southern edge of the Atlas and the northern edge of the Hindu Kush (Afghanistan), or the lowland bays of the southern Taurus (Antalya, Cukurova) on the Anatolian Peninsula, and the Kithar Range (Las Bela, Kachhi) in Baluchistan. Similarly, it is likely that the nomadic Baluchi who entered the Indus valley from the west (ninth century) soon adopted a semisedentary or sedentary way of life (Wissmann, 1961), like the Seraikis who advanced into the floodplains of the Punjab from the Cholistan Desert in the east.

Even the foundation of towns or oases such as Agades, Kanem, Bilma, and Kufra in North Africa; Nizwa, Ibri, Kuwait, Doha, and Liwa on the Arabian Peninsula; or Kalat, Kharan, and Panjgur in Baluchistan was the outcome of nomadic settlement or semisettlement. The town of Meknes (eleventh century) was founded by former Berber nomadic herders; Timbuktu resulted from the sedentization of Tuareg nomads in the eleventh century (Herzog 1954). The horizontal social pattern typical of Islamic-oriented towns, that is, their division into quarters according to ethnic groups (Bobek 1950–1951), is both the expression and the result of the incursion of nomadic groups into urban settlements.

Not infrequently, sedentarism of nomadic tribes led to the creation of empires (Klengel 1972). For instance, Westermann (1949) attributes the empires of western Sudan to the activities of Berber tribes, who—as Herzog (1954) concludes—lived at least a partly nomadic life. The Brahui confederation in Baluchistan can be interpreted as the outcome of partial sedentization of the Dravidian nomads in Sarawan and Jhalawan (eastern Iranian mountains/ Baluchistan) (Scholz 2002). Also —not least owing to partial sedentarism in the valleys in the southern arc of the central mountain massif (Hindu Kush)— Pashtunization (the settling of nomadic/Pashtun groups in areas belonging to other tribes) enabled the Pashtun Durrani (the predominant nomadic group in the area of present-day Afghanistan) to create an empire stretching from Seistan west of the Iranian mountains to the Indus lowlands in the east during the eighteenth and nineteenth centuries (Grötzbach 1990). Nor should we forget the Fertile Crescent of northern Syria, where Cherkessian farmers were settled to defend the land against nomads in the nineteenth century (sedentarization; Wirth 1963).

Sedentarization and sedentization of nomads/ Bedouins—sedentarism—have prevailed throughout the *Old World Dryland Belt* since the end of the nineteenth century. Settlement processes were initiated by Ottoman rulers (Al Wardi 1972), closely followed by the colonial powers with the aim of controlling and making political use of the nomadic tribes. Today, sedentarism is demanded/imposed and promoted by national governments. By contrast, the traditional nomadic mode of culture as an ecologically adapted subsistence strategy is considered outdated and is being consistently eliminated by sedentarization policies.

FRED SCHOLZ

Further Reading

Alafenish, Salim. "Die Beduinen in Ibn Khalduns Wissenschaft." In *Nomadismusein Entwicklungsproblem? Abhandlungen des Geographischen Instituts—Anthropogeographie*. Band 33. Ed. Fred Scholz and Jörg Janzen, 119–129. Berlin, 1982.

Al Wardi, Ali. *Soziologie des Nomadentums*. Neuwied: Darmstadt, 1972.

Bobek, Hans. *Soziale Raumbildungen am Beispiel des Vorderen Orients*. In Abhandlungen d. 27. deutschen Geographentages München. Landshut 1948, 193–206.

Braudel, Fernand. *Das Mittelmeer und die mediterrane Welt in der Epoche Philipps II*. I. Band, Frankfurt a.M., 1990.

Caskel, W. "Die Bedeutung der Beduinen in der Geschichte der Araber." In *Arbeitsgemeinschaft für Forschung des Landes Nordrhein-Westfalen, Geisteswissenschaften*. Vol. 8. Köln: Opladen, 1953, 7–26.

Cribb, Roger. *Nomads in Archaelogy*. New York, Port Chester, Melbourne, Sydney. Ehlers, Eckard. "Die Entnomadisierung iranischer Hochgebirge—Entwicklung und Verfall kulturgeographischer Höhengrenzen in vorderasiatischen Hochgebirgen." In *Höhengrenzen in Hochgebirgen*, edited by Ch. Jentsch and H. Liedtke, 311–325. Arb. A, d. geogr. Inst. D. saarlandes, Bd. 29, Saarbrücken, 1980.

Francfort, H.-P. (Ed). *Nomades et sédentaires en asie centrale*. Paris: Apports de l'archéologie et de l'ethnologie.

Grötzbach, Erwin. *Afghanistan*. Darmstadt, 1990.

Herzog, Rolf. "Veränderungen und Auflösungserscheinungen im nordafrikanischen Nomadentum." In *Paideuma, Mitteilungen zur Kulturkunde*, Bd. Vi, H. 1. Wiesbaden, 1954, S. 210–223.

Klengel, Horst. *Zwischen Zelt und Palast. Die Begegnung von Nomaden und Sesshaften im alten Vorderasien*. Wien, 1972.

Leidlmair, Adolf. "Umbruch und Bedeutungswandel im nomadischen Lebensraum des Orients." *Geogr. Zeitschrift* 53, 85–100.

Oppenheim, Max v. *Die Beduinen*. Band 1–3. Leipzig, 1939–1952.

Planhol, Xaver de. *Kulturgeographische Grundlagen der islamischen Geschichte*. Zürich, München, 1975.

Scholz, Fred. *Nomadismus. Theorie und Wandel einer sozioökologischen Kulturweise*. Stuttgart, 1995.

———. "Nomads/Nomadism in History." In *Intern. Encyclopedia of Social and Behavioral Sciences*. Amsterdam, Paris, New York, Oxford, 2001, Article-Nr. 3.7.108, 10650–10655.

———. *Nomadism and Colonialism. A Hundred Years of Baluchistan 1872–1972*. Oxford/Krachi, 2002.

Westermann, Dietrich. *Die Volkwerdung der Hausa*. Sitzungsberichte der Deutschen Akademie der Wissensachaften zu Berlin, Jahrgang 1949, 12.

Wilkinson, John, C. "The Origin of the Omani State." In *The Arabian Peninsula: Society and Politics*, edited by Hopwood, Derek, 67–88. London, 1972.

Wirth, Eugen. "Die Rolle tscherkessischer 'Wehrbauern' bei der Wiederbesiedlung von Steppe und Ödland im osmanischen Reich. *Bustan*, 4, H. 1, 16–19.

Wissmann, Hermann v. "Bauer, Nomade und Stadt im islamischen Orient." In *Die Welt des Islam und die Gegenwart*, edited by Rudi Paret. Stuttgart, 1961.

SEEKING KNOWLEDGE

Knowledge and faith are equated in the Qur'an. This identification, however, was not left undiscussed by subsequent generations of Muslim scholars. "Seeking/searching for knowledge" *(talab al-'ilm)* does not necessarily refer to extensive journeys, but it is the case when the context indicates it or in the expression "The journey for seeking knowledge." This knowledge is usually equated with traditions of Muhammad (and his Companions), that is, the Hadith.

The specialists of hadith, like al-Khatib al-Baghdadi (d. AH 463/1071 CE) in his book *The Journey for seeking hadith*, base themselves on a well-known tradition attributed to Muhammad: "Search for knowledge even as far as China, for this is incumbent upon every Muslim." It is a spurious tradition, also from the point of view of hadith criticism among Muslim scholars; only they label it "weak," as far as its chain of authorities *(isnad)* is concerned, and "sound" in its signification. It was probably put into circulation circa 150/767. What it may be, there are lengthy discussions in books of the import of the statement that knowledge is a duty *(farida)*, whether or not it is a duty in the legal sense, and which types of knowledge are individual duties and which are community duties (that is, not incumbent upon every member of the Muslim community).

Other traditions were attributed to Muhammad on the same matter, such as: "He who sets out searching for knowledge, verily the angels joyfully spread their wings to which he is searching for, he sets out on a path that leads to paradise."

The feverish desire to know what Muhammad had said and done in every thing increased in intensity. The enormous mass of traditions attributed to him became bigger still in the first/seventh century and the first half of the second/eighth century. They had been accumulated by Companions and Followers, and followers of the Followers, who were scattered throughout the Islamic world, or they were forged. Some of the "searchers for knowledge" displayed an enormous activity, undertaking long and hazardous journeys from the Guadalquivir to the Oxus in order to hear a hadith from the lips of one who claimed to have it in succession of Muhammad. According to al-Darimi (d. 255/869), a man came from Medina to Damascus to hear a tradition from the Companion Abu l-Darda'; this tradition was the following: "Whoso travels a road in search of knowledge will God lead in a road to paradise. Verily the angels joyfully spread their wings over him who is seeking knowledge. All creatures in heaven and earth and even the fishes in the depth of waters pray for the learned man (or scholar, 'alim). His superiority over the worshiper is as that of the full moon over the stars. The learned men (or scholars) are the heirs of the prophets. They do not herit a dinar and not a dirham, but they herit knowledge...."

This statement atttibuted to Muhammad is a putting together of different declarations, also known in other contexts. It has its origins in a period in which debates took place concerning the best knowledge or the best scholars. One of the weapons in this "war" consisted in prophetical hadith and/or traditions from the early generations of Muslims. Was the best knowledge one of the Qur'anic disciplines, the hadith, the biography of the Prophet, or jurisprudence and connected matters *(fiqh)*? For instance, the son-in-law of the great exegete Muqatil b. Sulayman, Abu 'Isma (Nuh b. a. Maryam, d. 173/789), a student of Abu Hanifa (d. 150/767) and a judge in Marv, was asked on traditions that he transmitted from the Companion Ibn 'Abbas about "the excellencies of the Qur'an sura by sura," although transmitters of 'Ikrima, one of the students of Ibn 'Abbas, did not possess them. He replied: "I saw that people had turned away from the Qur'an and occupied themselves with the *fiqh* of Abu Hanifa and *The Military Campaigns of the Prophet (maghazi)* of Ibn Ishaq, so I forge this tradition seeking reward in the next world."

It seems that the predominant characteristic of the various centers in which in early Islam traditions were collected and recorded, was their regionalism. So we should distinguish between "seeking knowledge" and "traveling in quest of knowledge."

This last activity became a general practice at a relatively late date. The first scholars who are said to have practiced it are people who died between between 150/767 and 180/796. Sometimes 'Abd Allah b. Mubarak (d. 181/797) is said to have been the first of them. He is a well-known traditionist of Marv, who wrote a book in which he collected traditions on the Holy War, a community duty in which he took part in Syria against the Byzantines. He was a rich tradesman who enterprised journeys to Iraq, Syria, Egypt, and Yemen, not only for the purpose of seeking knowledge but also for his own business. Many scholars in the following generations were also tradesmen. For a lot of them, the pilgrimage to Mecca was the occasion of very extensive journeys, especially students or scholars coming from Muslim Spain or from Northern Africa.

The example of the exegete, traditionist, jurist, and historian al-Tabari (d. 310/923) is representative, among thousands of others, of what traveling in quest of knowledge practically means. After having learned the Qur'an by heart at the age of seven and studied traditions of the Prophet since he was age nine, al-Tabari left his hometown of Amol in Tabaristan, and his parents, at the age of twelve in 236/850. He received his further schooling in Rayy (site of present-day Teheran), where he remained almost five years; there he was formed in the Hanafi law and the historiographical traditions of Ibn Ishaq transmitted to him by Muhammad b. Humayd al-Razi, who was also one of his masters in hadith and Qur'anic exegesis.

Then he left for Baghdad, where he wanted to attend the lessons of Ibn Hanbal in hadith, but when he arrived in the caliphal capital (241/855), the master was dead. However, he could attend there the lessons of other masters, not only in hadith but also on Shafi'ite law (the ancient doctrine of al-Shafi'i; he then became acquainted with "the new doctrine of al-Shafi'i" in Egypt). Rather soon, he left Baghdad to continue his study in Basra and Kufa, including Wasit on the way, attending other lessons on Qur'anic exegesis, hadith, life of the Prophet, and so on. He returned to Baghdad about 244/858, where he became the tutor of the young son of a wazir.

In 248/962, al-Tabari was in in his late twenties and an acknowledged scholar, when he again left Baghdad, this time to Egypt. This journey included visits to Syria and Palestine. In Beirut, for instance, he had the opportunity to study the variant Qur'anic readings of the Syrian school and the legal views of al-Awza'i (d. 157/774), Syria's most prominent jurist.

He had attended lessons also in Homs (Emesa), Ramlah, Damascus, and Jerusalem, among others. He arrived in Egypt in 253/867, and perhaps again in 256/870, after being returned to Syria, and probably having performed the pilgrimage. In Fustat he profited from the knowledge of Yunus b. al-A'la al-Misri (d. 264/877), a leading scholar in the field of hadith and Qur'an reading. But the greatest boon that he reaped during his sojourn in Egypt was an increased understanding of the Maliki and Shafi'i legal system. For the second one, his main authority was al-Rabi' b. Sulayman al-Muradi (d. 270/884), from whom he learned "the new doctrine of al-Shafi'i"; but in the same time al-Tabari could teach there "the ancient doctrine of al-Shafi'i," which he had learned in Baghdad. Among his many contacts in Egypt, the most important was probably the one with the eminent Ibn al-Hakam family, whose members had been intimately connected with al-Shafi'i himself. They were also outstanding representatives of the Maliki legal system.

On his return to Baghdad, after 256/870, he had fifty years of scholarly activity there. He appears never to have married. The tremendous volume of work he accomplished evoked the admiration of all scholars. It is said that he used to write fourteen (or up to forty!) folios every single day.

Given the importance of "seeking knowledge" and "traveling in quest of knowledge," the relation between masters and students, and also the importance of a so-called sure continuity of transmission of hadith and other matters, one should not be astonished of a great literary production in the field of prosopography. Toward the second half of the third/ninth century, traditionists began to write special books, often arranged alphabetically as dictionaries, on the masters they had encountered during their studies and journeys for the research of science, meaning with that above all hadith, and including especially those masters from whom they had received a certificate *(ijaza)* to transmit "science" to others. These books could have different titles, such as *The Masters (mashyakha)* or *Dictionary of the Masters of....* Some of them contain very precise dates or data (the place where the lessons were held, the number and/or the names of participants). We may mention here the case of the great Alexandrian traditionist Abu Tahir al-Silafi (d. 576/1180). He wrote a *Dictionary* on his masters in Baghdad and *The Dictionary of Journey*, in which he assembled entries on scholars whom he had met outside Baghdad and Isfahan, and more specifically in Alexandria (Egyptians, Maghribis, among others).

Others wrote indexes of disciplines, genres and books, or bio-bibliographical dictionaries. The oldest and most important is the *Index* of the Baghdadian copyist and bookseller *(warraq)* Ibn al-Nadim (d. 380/990 or 385/995). Mention should be made of the *Index of Books and Masters* of Ibn Khayr of Seville (d. 575/1179), and of the *Well Established Confluent of the Alphabetical Index* of the Egyptian Ibn Hajar al-'Asqalani (d. 852/1449).

Scholars wished to be very accurate in the correct pronunciation of proper names: names of transmitters and authors *(rijal)*, ethnic names *(ansab)*, geographical names, and so on. For this reason many of them devoted themselves also to the writing of special books in these fields, also a branch of prosopography. The great traditionist of Marv, Abu Sa'd al-Sam'ani (d. 562/1166), for instance, composed the *Book of Genealogies and Proper Names* and two *Dictionaries of Masters*, in which we also find precise data on the localities he has visited. Special books were also written on "different and connected" names, for example, *The Connected and Different* (in the names of transmitters and the like) by al-Daraqutni (385/995), which was completed by the *Reshaping of Achievement of the Connected and Different*, by al-Khatib al-Baghdadi. Another Baghdadian, Ibn Makula (d. 486/1093, or other dates) wrote the *Perfect for Removing Doubt about the Connected and Different Proper Names or Names of Relation.*

We have, above all, spoken here of seeking knowledge in religious sciences that appear in the "direct formation" of scholars, but many of them had also what we have called elsewhere an "indirect formation," which was more personal, not passing by the usual ways of learning and not always recognized, for instance, in the "foreign sciences," coming from the Greek and Syrian legacies: philosophy, medicine,

astronomy, and so on. Tabari, for instance, was acquainted with arithmetics and algebra. He had a certain mastery of logic, dialectics, and, indeed Greek philosophy *(falsafa)*. Medicine was one of his great interests. The important medical encyclopedia the *Paradise of Wisdom*, by 'Ali b. Rabban (viv. 2nd/ninth century), a Christian who converted to Islam, became Tabari's medical Bible.

Of course, it was not the case of every scholar, because many of them—often qualified as "Hanbali in theology" *(hanbali al-usul)*, that is, not only people pertaining to the Hanbali law school—were not only opposed to the knowledge of the foreign sciences but also to the practice of speculative theology *(kalam)*.

Seeking knowledge remained a principle and a reality during the different periods of classical Islam. But the practice of traveling in quest of knowledge disappeared in the course of time. At the end of the Mamluk period a lack of enthusiasm for it has been noticed, and it is difficult to find a single Egyptian scholar who practiced it after Shams al-Din al-Sakahawi (d. 902/1497).

CLAUDE GILLIOT

See also Scholarship

Primary Source

Marçais, William, trans. and annot. *Le Taqrîb de en-Nawawî*. Paris: Imprimerie Nationale, 1902.

Further Reading

Dickinson, Eerik. *The Devlopment of Early Sunnite Hadith Criticism. The Taqdima of Ibn Abi Hatim al-Razi (240/854/327/938)*. Leiden: Brill, 2001.
Gilliot, Claude. *Exégèse, Langue et Théologie en Islam. L'exégèse coranique de Tabari*. Paris: Vrin (Études Musulmanes, XXXII), 1990.
———. "Prosopography in Islam. An Essay of Classification." *Medieval Prosopography*. 23 (2002): 19–54.
Grandin, Nicole, and Marc Gaboriau, Marc (under the direction of). *Madrasa. La transmission du savoir dans le monde musulman*. Paris: Edition Arguments, 1997.
Guillaume, Alfred. *The Traditions of Islam*. Oxford, 1924.
Juynboll, Gautier H.A. *Muslim Tradition. Studies on chronology, provenance and authorship of early Îadîth*. Cambridge: Cambridge University Press, 1983.
Lowry, Joseph E., Devin J. Stewart, and Shawkat M. Toorawa (Eds). *Law and Education in Medieval Islam. Studies in memory of Professor George Makdisi*. Warminster: E.J.W. Gibb Memorial Trust, 2004.
Mez, Adam. *The Renaissance of Islam*. Transl. Salahuddin Khuda Bukhsh and D.S. Margoliouth. London: Luzac, 1937.
Rosenthal, Franz, trans. and annot. *The History of al-Tabari*, I. *General introduction and from the Creation to Flood*. Albany: SUNY, 1989.
———. *Knowledge Triumphant: The concept of knowledge in medieval Islam*. Leiden: Brill, 1970.

Toorawa, Shawkat M. "A Portrait of 'Abd al-Latif al-Baghdadi's Education and Instruction." In *Law and Education in Medieval Islam*, edited by Lowry et al., 91–109.

SELIMIYE MOSQUE, EDIRNE

The Selimiye Mosque complex was built in AH 976–982/1569–1575 CE by the architect Sinan for Sultan Selim II in Edirne, the Ottoman empire's European gateway. The new architectural foundation celebrated the recent conquest of Cyprus and was financed by its rich spoils. Regarded by most modern historians as the culminating achievement of Sinan's distinguished fifty-year career as chief architect to the Ottoman court, Sinan himself (according to the "autobiography" that he wrote with Sa'i Mustafa Čelebi) undertook the Selimiye project in a competitive frame of mind. He stated, "Those who consider themselves architects among Christians say that in the realm of Islam no dome can equal that of the Hagia Sophia... [but] in this mosque, with the help of God and the support of Sultan Selim Khan, I erected a dome six cubits higher and four cubits wider than the dome of the Hagia Sophia" (Kuran). He was determined both to outdo the size and grandeur of that venerable Byzantine monument (finished in 537) and to continue a dialogue with his own Suleymaniye Mosque that was built twenty years earlier.

The Selimiye has a magnificent presence on the skyline of Edirne—its hilltop position and imposing profile were intended to overwhelm and to suggest, through architectural grandeur, the imperial majesty of the patron. It stands on a high platform and, unlike comparable Ottoman *külliyes* (religious complexes), has few dependent buildings. The complex consists of a large enclosure with a centrally placed mosque, and a *medrese* (theological college) and Qur'an school of equal size symmetrically filling the southeast and southwest corners of the greater enclosure. The complex was entirely symmetrical until a covered market was added on the west side of the enclosure in the 1580s to provide rental income.

The mosque consists of a rectangular prayer hall and rectangular courtyard of equal size (sixty by forty-four meters) with an ablution fountain in its center. A large, single central dome dominates the prayer hall; from the prayer hall's corners rise four exceedingly slender fluted minarets that at approximately seventy meters are taller than any others in the Ottoman realm. Their soaring verticality provides a marked contrast to the massive and imposing domical structure of the prayer hall and provides a spatial frame that both draws attention to the mosque in Edirne's skyline and sets it apart. Sinan wished to make the central dome higher than the Hagia Sophia (which he had not quite outstripped in the Suleymaniye). Although from floor level the Hagia Sophia rises to 55.60 meters while the Selimiye rises to only 42.25 meters, if calculated from the base of the dome, the latter's profile is indeed steeper and higher.

The dome rests on eight enormous piers, which is a departure from Sinan's earlier four-pier plans at the Shahzade and Suleymaniye mosques. Each pier rises from a fluted, then faceted shaft that transitions, without a capital to mark the shift in architectonic function, to a great arch that springs from *muqarnas*. The piers are ingeniously pushed toward the walls of the prayer hall so that, rather than permitting their manifest architectonic function to obstruct interior space, they seem to frame and articulate it. The consequence is an extraordinarily unified interior in which there is no perceptible distinction between the space beneath the central dome and the auxiliary spaces below the half domes that fill the corners of the hall. The equidistant positioning of the piers also diminishes the sense of lateral axiality that such a rectangular space might have provoked, and the side arcades bearing galleries are pushed to the far walls, where they do not interrupt or intrude on the open interior. Instead, the dominant axis runs from the mosque's northern entrance, through the courtyard, into the prayer hall, and culminates at the mihrab. Indeed, the axis is slightly prolonged by the spatial recession of the mihrab apse. The sole interruption in the mihrab axis is a platform for Qur'an reading *(dikka)*, poised above a fountain, which temporarily shifts the visual focus from the horizontal axis to the vertical, directing vision upward to the great dome overhead.

The airy interior is flooded with light from the rows of windows encircling the base of each dome and semidome. Furthermore, enormous arches of alternating red and white voussoirs relieve the supportive function of the mosque's walls so that instead of wall mass, the space is filled by thin tympana with windows. The recessed mihrab is likewise lined on both the *qibla* and side walls, with windows that filter light through windows with ornate mullions. Beautiful Iznik glazed ceramic covers much of the *qibla* wall, reflecting light and giving the interior a gleaming luminosity. A band of inscription in blue and white tile runs around the upper part, while below there are panels with floral designs that were probably intended to suggest paradise, a common theme in mosque ornament.

The brilliance of Sinan's design appears not only in the spatial plasticity of the manipulation of domes, semidomes, and arches within the prayer hall but also in the clarity of the design's structural logic from

Sinan the Great (1489–1588). Interior of dome. Built for Selim II, Ottoman sultan. 1568–1575. Credit: Vanni/Art Resource, NY. Selimiye Mosque, Edirne, Turkey.

without. Although from afar the building appears as a single mountainous dome surrounded by elegant spires, at middle distance the eight piers, capped by small cupolas and descending into mighty buttresses, have clear presence on the building's exterior, revealing a well-composed, symmetrical, and geometrically conceived figure of discrete geometrical units subordinated to a harmonious whole. The Selimiye is a tour de force of interior and exterior space.

D. FAIRCHILD RUGGLES

See also Istanbul; Suleymaniye Mosque

Further Reading

Bates, Ülkü. "Architecture." In *Turkish Art*, edited by Esin Atıl, 44–136. Washington, D.C., and New York, 1980.
Blair, Sheila and Jonathan Bloom. *Art and Architecture of Islam, 1250–1800.* New Haven: Yale University Press, 1994.
Goodwin, Geoffrey. *A History of Ottoman Architecture.* London: Thames and Hudson, 1971.
Kuban, Doğan. "The Style of Sinan's Domes Structures." *Muqarnas* 4 (1987), 72–98.
———. "Architecture of the Ottoman Period." In *The Art and Architecture of Turkey*, edited by in Ekrem Akurgal, 137–169. New York, 1980.
Kuran, Aptullah. *Sinan, The Grand Old Man of Ottoman Architecture.* Washington, D.C., and Istanbul, 1987.
Sa'i, Mustafa. *Tezkiretü'l-Bünyan (Istanbul, 1897).* Transl. M. Sözen, and S. SaatçI, Mimar Sinan, and Tezkiret-ül Bünyan. Istanbul, 1989.

SELJUKS

The Seljuk dynasty was a Turkish dynasty that ruled much of the Middle East from the late eleventh through the twelfth century CE. The eponymous Seljuk ibn Duqaq was the chief of a confederation of Oghuz Turkmen tribes that migrated in search of land, perhaps pressured by other tribes, from the area between the Caspian and Aral seas to Transoxiana in the mid-tenth century. Settling in Jand on the left bank of the Jaxartes (Syr Darya), Seljuk and the Oghuz became Muslims. In the early eleventh century, these Oghuz were caught between the expansionist ambitions of the Qarakhanids from the north and the Ghaznavids from the south. In 1040, Seljuk's grandsons, Chaghri Beg and Toghril Beg, defeated the Ghaznavids at Dandanqan near Merv. This victory opened the Middle East to large-scale Turkish immigration. Thus began the long-term movement, laden with enormous social, economic, and political consequences, of Turkish peoples from Central Asia to the Middle East, changing the linguistic and cultural zones of that region from Arabic and Persian to Arabic and Turko-Persian.

Having taken the title of sultan and proclaiming himself the protector of the 'Abbasid caliph and defender of Sunni Islam, Toghril entered a politically fragmented Muslim world. Many areas were ruled by Shi'i dynasties. One of them, the Buyids, held sway over the 'Abbasid caliphs in Baghdad. From Cairo the Fatimid caliphs claimed authority over the entire Muslim world. Toghril attempted to put an end to these Shi'i dynasties and reunite Muslims under Sunnism. In 1055, he entered Baghdad and destroyed the Buyids. In 1058, the caliph al-Qa'im formally acknowledged him as sultan and later gave him a daughter in marriage. Toghril consolidated his power in Iraq, destroying pro-Fatimid forces in 1060, while keeping the caliph under tight control, and sending various family members to conduct further conquests. The empire in turn was parceled out to these family members. Toghril thus laid the foundation of the Great Seljuk Empire. He died in 1063 at Rayy, his capital.

Toghril had no children. His nephew, Alp Arslan, succeeded him in 1064 after a brief struggle for the throne. Alp Arslan reorganized the government and appointed the brilliant Nizam al-Mulk as grand vizier. Nizam ran the empire and tried to mold the state along traditional Persian lines. Alp Arslan was continuously in the field suppressing revolts and campaigning on the frontiers. In 1071, he defeated the Byzantine emperor Romanus Diogenes at Manzikert. Byzantine defenses collapsed and Anatolia was open to Turkmen tribes, who streamed into it. Also in 1071, another Turkmen army under Atsiz captured Jerusalem from the Fatimids. These two victories reverberated in Europe where Pope Urban II eventually called for a crusade in 1095. After Manzikert, Alp Arslan marched east to Transoxiana, where he faced a crisis with the Qarakhanids. There he was murdered in 1073.

Alp Arslan was succeeded by his son Malikshah, during whose reign the Great Seljuk Empire reached its height. Malikshah made Isfahan his capital and kept Nizam as grand vizier. Besides settling various family quarrels, he further expanded Seljuk power by bringing the Qarakhanids to terms and extending his authority down the west coast of Arabia to Yemen. Furthermore, in the early years of his reign an independent Turkmen chief, Sulayman ibn Qutulmish (r. 1081–86), founded the Seljuk Sultanate of Anatolia. In 1092, shortly after Nizam was assassinated, Malikshah died. The empire, stretching from Khwarazm to the Mediterranean, was then torn by struggles for succession. His sons Muhammad I Tapar (r. 1105–1118) and Sanjar (r. 1118–1157) were more or less able to keep the core of Iraq and Iran together, although the latter's reign ended in disaster in 1153, when the Oghuz revolted and took him captive. While Anatolia had been independent from the beginning (1081–1307), other regions of the empire broke away: Kirman (1048–circa 1188) and Syria (1078–1117). The last of the Great Seljuks, Toghril III, was killed in 1194 in the east, fighting the Khwarazm-Shah Tekish.

The major reason for the disintegration of the empire was the lack of a well-ordered means of succession. The Seljuks followed the custom whereby the state was considered the common property of the dynasty. Consequently, each member of the dynasty could claim to be the ruler. This resulted in a struggle for the throne with each passing sultan. These struggles in turn provided opportunities for the 'Abbasid caliphs to try to reassert their worldly authority and also allowed the *atabegs*, the guardians and tutors of various princes, to take local power into their own hands. Some, like the Zankids, established their own dynasties. All of this contributed to the further fragmentation of the empire.

GARY LEISER

See also Byzantine Empire; Muslim–Crusader Relations; Nomadism and Pastoralism; Seljuk Warfare; Shi'ism; Sultan; Turks; Vizier

Primary Sources
Ibn al-Athir. *The Annals of the Saljuq Turks.* Transl. and annot. D.S. Richards. London: Routledge Curzon, 2002.
Zahir al-Din Nishapuri. *The History of the Seljuq Turks.* Transl. Kenneth Luther. London: Curzon, 2001.

Further Reading
Bosworth, C.E. "The Political and Dynastic History of the Iranian World (A.D. 1000–1217." In *The Cambridge History of Iran, vol. 5, The Saljuq and Mongol Periods*, ed. by J.A. Boyle, 1–202. Cambridge: Cambridge University Press, 1968.
Cahen, Claude. "The Historiography of the Seljuqid Period." In *Historians of the Middle East*, edited by B. Lewis and P.M. Holt, 59–78. London: Oxford University Press, 1962.
Lambton, Ann K.S. "The Internal Structure of the Saljuq Empire." In *The Cambridge History of Iran, vol. 5, The Saljuq and Mongol Periods*, ed. by J.A. Boyle, 203–202. Cambridge: Cambridge University Press, 1968.
———. *Continuity and Change in Medieval Persia.* Albany, NY: Bibliotheca Persica, 1988.
Leiser, Gary. *A History of the Seljuks: Ibrahim Kafesoğlu's Interpretation and the Resulting Controversy.* Carbondale, IL: Southern Illinois University Press, 1988.

SEVEN SLEEPERS

The legend of the Seven Sleepers of Ephesus, in its earliest form, relates the fabulous experience of seven (or eight) Christian soldiers who are saved from the persecution of the Roman Emperor Decius (r. 249–251) by a miraculous sleep, from which they awake only during the reign of the Christian Emperor Theodosius II (r. 408–450). The Seven Sleepers of the Christian legend appear in the Qur'ān as the "Companions of the Cave" of Chapter Eighteen (named accordingly "the Cave" *[al-kahf]*), a chapter in which narratives based on the Jewish legend of Joshua ben Levi and the Christian Romance of Alexander also appear. Louis Massignon, pointing to the fact that the recitation of this chapter is encouraged every Friday at Islamic common prayer, describes the legend of the Seven Sleepers as a point of mystical and eschatological meeting between Islam and Christianity.

The origins of the legend, however, are unclear. Although some reports credit Steven, bishop of Ephesus during the Second Council of Ephesus (449), with compiling the original version in Greek, T. Nöldeke and P. Huber argue that the legend was originally written in Syriac. Indeed, the first extant form thereof appears in two Syriac homilies of Jacob of Sarug (d. 521), while Gregory of Tours (d. 594), author of the first Latin version, employed the services of a Syriac translator for the job. In any case, the spread of the legend into numerous languages (it entered later into English, German, Nordic, French, and Spanish literature) testifies to its attraction. Popular Christian devotion to the Sleepers, embraced as saints by both Catholic and Orthodox tradition, spread as well. Feast days were devoted to them. Chapels and shrines were dedicated to them, not only in Ephesus itself but also throughout the Middle East and Europe, including the Church of the Seven Sleepers in Rome, which is decorated with vivid paintings of the seven heroes.

The attraction of the story in the Christian context lies in the fact that it is at once edifying and didactic. On one hand, it celebrates the devotion of Christian martyrs and, more generally, the victory over paganism. On the other hand, it serves as a proof for the resurrection, as the sleep of the seven saints in most recensions is only a metaphor for death (see John 11:11 and I Thessalonians 4:13), from which they are raised by God.

In the Qur'ān, meanwhile, certain details of the Christian legend remain: the Cave as a refuge (Q 18:10) from unbelief (Q 18:14–15), the sensation of the sleepers that only a day had passed (Q 18:19), their plan to buy food with a coin they had preserved (Q 18:19), and the building of a shrine above the spot where they slept (Q 18:21). Other elements of the Qur'ānic narrative are novel: a watch dog (Q 18:18; on the model of the Greek Cerberus, protecting the domain of the dead), the insistence on "pure" food (Q 18:19), confusion over the number of sleepers (Q 18:22), and 309 years as the duration of sleep (Q 18:25; early Christian sources state 372 years). Still other elements of the Qur'ānic account present a mystery to Muslim interpreters, not least of which is the introductory line, which speaks of the "Companions of the Cave" and al-raqīm. This latter word is interpreted variously as: tablet, inscription, name of the sleepers, their ancestry, their religion, the thing from which they fled, the town from which they came, the mountain of their cave, or the name of their dog.

Most important, perhaps, is the particular tone with which the Qur'ān relates the legend of the cave. While in the Christian legend the Emperor Decius closes up the cave in order to kill the saints, in the Qur'ān there is no protagonist other than God Himself, and it is He who shuts in the "Companions of the Cave" (Q 18:11). In the Christian legend it is shepherds stumbling across the site of the sleepers that causes their awakening. In the Qur'ān it is God

Himself who awakens them, in order to test them, by seeing if they are able to calculate the duration of their sleep (See Q 18:12, 18:19). Ultimately (Q 18:19), one of the sleepers shouts out the pious solution to the test: "Your Lord knows best how long you have tarried." In its Qur'ānic form the legend of the Seven Sleepers becomes an affirmation of human limitation before an omnipotent, and omniscient, God. Thus if this legend indeed serves as a point of contact between Christianity and Islam, it also manifests the uniqueness of each tradition.

GABRIEL SAID REYNOLDS

Further Reading

Avezzù, Guido. *I Sette Dormienti: Una leggenda fra Oriente e Occidente*. Milano: Medusa, 2002.
Coleridge, Mary. *The Seven Sleepers of Ephesus*. London: Chatto & Windus, 1893.
Huber, P. Michael. *Die Wanderlegende von den Siebenschläfern*. Leipzig: Harrassowitz, 1910.
Massignon, Louis. "Les 'Septs Dormants' Apocalypse de l'Islam." In *Opera Minora*, edited by Y Moubarac. 3 Vols. Beirut: Dār al-Ma'ārif, 1963, 3:104–118.
Torrey, Charles. *The Jewish Foundation of Islam*. New York: KTAV, 1967, esp. Chap. 5.

SEVILLE

Seville (Ar. *Ishbiliyya*, a derivation from the Latin place name *Hispalis*) was a major town of al-Andalus on the bank of the Guadalquivir River (an Arabic name, *Wadi 'l-kabir*, meaning "The Wide River"). It was the capital of the *kura* that bore its name, a *kura* being the basic territorial division of al-Andalus.

History

Seville was conquered around 713 or 716 CE in the first wake of the Muslim occupation of the Iberian Peninsula. Subsequently, contingents of mainly Yemeni warriors settled in the city and its outskirts, and formed the core of its ruling classes until the end of the Muslim-ruled period, when the city was conquered by the Castilian king, Ferdinand III, in 1248. Overt or more concealed Islamic lifestyles, however, continued to be conducted in Seville, as in other parts of Spain, until the expulsion of the Moriscos (converted-to-Christianity Muslims) from Spain in 1609–1610, that is to say, almost four centuries after the Christian conquest of the city.

The Arab warrior elite of Seville often revolted against the central power based in Cordoba during the time of the first Umayyad ruler, al-Andalus Emir

'Abd al-Rahman I (756–788). He was succeeded in the throne by Hisham I (r. 788–796) and al-Hakam I (r. 796–822). Both reigns were periods of relative peace for Seville, according to the sources. In 844, under the Emir 'Abd al-Rahman II (r. 822–852), Seville was stormed by the Normans (named *Majus* in the Arabic chronicles). Normans pillaged the whole of Western Andalusia for almost a month and a half, until they were driven out by an army dispatched from the Andalusi capital of Cordoba.

The following years under the ruling of Emir 'Abd Allah I (844–912) saw a widespread outburst of rebellions all over Al-Andalus, including in Seville. A *de facto* autonomous state was established by the local powerful clan of the Banu Hajjaj from 889 to 913.

Seville was sieged and pacified by the first Andalusi caliph, 'Abd al-Rahman III, in 913. The period of the caliphate (929–1031) was one of certain prosperity for the city. Only an uprising instigated by the Banu Hajjaj family in 974 troubled to some extent the stability of the period.

With the downfall of the caliphal regime and the outburst of the *fitna* (civil war) in Al-Andalus from 1009 to 1031, Seville became the capital of one of the *taifa* (party) kingdoms into which Al-Andalus had split. The new dynasty of the Banu 'Abbad or 'Abbadids (1013–1090) seized power, leading the town into what is generally considered to be its cultural and economic peak. It was, objectively speaking, the moment when the greatest territory was ruled from Seville.

The most celebrated 'Abbadid ruler was Muhammad bin 'Abbad al-Mu'tamid (1069–1090), who is still widely regarded as one of the finest classical Arab poets. His verses about his concubine Rumaykiyya have never ceased to be a part of the common Arab poetic curriculum.

In the political sphere, the 'Abbadid rulers were forced to pay *parias* (levies) to the Castilian kings. This forced al-Mu'tamid and many other *taifa* sovereigns to seek the help of the Almoravid sultan, Yusuf bin Tashufin, whose territorial base was in the current territory of Morocco. In 1086 and 1088, Yusuf bin Tashufin disembarked in the Iberian Peninsula in assistance of his coreligionists. Sources tell us that he—motivated by Islamic religious scholars *(fuqaha)* and with popular spur—resolved to seize power of Iberian Muslim-ruled lands and depose the *taifa* rulers, including al-Mu'tamid. In 1090, Yusuf bin Tashufin conquered Seville and sent al-Mu'tamid to exile.

Seville remained under Almoravid rule for more than half a century. Aspects of daily life during this period can be deduced by reading Ibn 'Abdun's *hisba* (market policing) treatise. During the Almoravid period, Seville was transformed into a key port where troops were disembarked. Seville also became a gathering point for the army. Archaeological evidence implies that the last wall ring of Seville was built by the Almoravids as a compound crowned by eight fortified towers.

In 1132, the King of Castile, Alphonse VII, sacked the region of Seville and even killed the Almoravid governor. In 1147, Seville was incorporated into the Almohad caliphate, which had before replaced the Almoravids. An Almohad governor of Seville, Abu Ya'qub Yusuf, was proclaimed caliph and made his second (with Marrakesh, in Morocco) capital in the town since 1171/1172. He conducted a full public works program that included an improvement to the fortifications of the town, a new palace outside the walls, a new pontoon bridge over the Guadalquivir River that linked the town and the Triana quarter at the other side of the river, and a new Friday mosque. Construction of this new central mosque began in 1172. Its minaret is a twin of the famous Kutubia minaret in Marrakesh. After the Christian conquest, the whole site of the great mosque was dedicated to the new cathedral. The minaret is today the "Giralda" bell tower, which is recognized as the major symbol of the city throughout the world.

Frequent Castilian raids threatened the safety and stability of Seville during the Almoravid period. Additionally, the periodic floods of the Guadalquivir contributed to the unease of the population.

Since 1220, the Almohad power approached its final decline. Following a number of unsuccessful revolts, the people of Seville turned to the Ibn Hud family against the Almohads in 1229. In 1248, the Castilian King Ferdinand III conquered the city after seventeen months of siege. Soon after, the Moroccan Marinid dynasty attempted to seize control of the city, but they could only pillage the outskirts, and in 1275 made an unsuccessful siege on the city.

Islamic Heritage in Modern Seville

Although Seville was counted among the richest cities of al-Andalus, its extant Islamic built heritage is not abundant, since a myriad of new buildings in the Renaissance and Baroque styles were commissioned in the prosperous period—which lasted from the sixteenth to the seventeenth centuries—as a result of Seville's key role in economic exchange with the Spanish colonies in America.

The walls that defended the city against attacks both from the navigable Guadalquivir and from the surrounding plains are a major extant that remains.

Numerous accounts in extant sources report building and repair work being conducted in the Umayyad and subsequent periods. In 1220–1221, a new angled defensive outwork was built, ending in a twelve-sided stronghold, the "Golden Tower" (*Torre del Oro* in its current Spanish denomination), which is still a landmark of the city. Originally standing three stories high, only the two lower ones have been preserved, as the upper lantern was modified after the Christian conquest.

A compound of residential palaces, known as the *Reales Alcázares*, is still the official residence for the Spanish royals when they are in Seville. It is, together with the Alhambra and the ruins of Medina Azahara in Cordoba, a fine example of Andalusi architecture. Its foundations were laid in the time of Umayyad Emir 'Abd al-Rahman II (822–852).

Before the construction of the current cathedral, the third largest cathedral in the world, the Friday or central mosque, occupied the same site. The mosque was itself a building of considerable size, probably measuring 150 meters by 100 meters. Its most relevant feature was the aforementioned minaret. In its present form, the belfry is 16.1 meters wide and 50.85 meters high.

JESÚS DE PRADO PLUMED

See also 'Abd al-Rahman III; Al-Ghazali; Al-Idrisi, or Dreses; Al-Maqqari; Almohads; Almoravids; Andalus; Berbers; Cordoba; Gibraltar; Granada; Ibn Battuta; Ibn Ezra; Ibn Gabirol; Ibn Khaldun; Ibn Quzman; Ibn Rushd, or Averroes; Ibn Tufayl; Malik ibn Anas; Mediterranean Sea; Party Kingdoms: Iberian Peninsula; Umayyads

Primary Source

Ibn 'Abdun, Muhammad bin Ahmad al-Tujibi. *Sevilla a Comienzos del Siglo XII: el Tratado de Ibn Abdun.* 1st ed. Transl. Emilio García Gómez and Evariste Lévi-Provençal. Sevilla: Servicio de Publicaciones del Ayuntamiento de Sevilla, 1981. Reprint, 1948.

Further Reading

Arberry, Arthur John. *Moorish Poetry.* 1st ed. Cambridge, UK: Cambridge University Press, 1953.
Burkhardt, Titus. *Moorish Culture in Spain.* 1st ed. London: Allen and Unwin, 1972.
Kennedy, Hugh. *Spain Muslim and Portugal: A Political History of Al-Andalus.* 1st ed. London: Longman, 1996.
Latham, John Derek. *From Muslim Spain to Barbary.* 1st ed. London: Variorum Reprints, 1986.
Wasserstein, David. *The Rise and Fall of the Party-Kings.* 1st ed. Princeton, NJ: Princeton University Press, 1985.
Whishaw, Bernhard. *Arabic Spain: Sidelights on Her History and Art.* 1st ed. Reading: Garnet, 2002 Reprint, 1912.

SHADOW PLAYS

Terminology

Many Western and Arab scholars have assumed that the Arabic term for the shadow play *(khayal al-zill)* is tautological, since both *khayal* and *zill* mean "shadow" in Arabic. The assumption is that it is a vulgar coinage, and that it should really be termed *zill al-khayal* (shadow of the vision or shadow fantasy). The term *khayal*, appearing alone, has been routinely explained or translated as "shadow play." The German Orientalist Theodore Menzel, however, objected that in Arabic, Persian, and Turkish the term is puzzling; he argued that it cannot mean shadow play unless it occurs in its complete form, that is, *khayal al-zill* in Arabic and *zill-i-khayal* in Persian.

In Arabic literature and historiography, the term *khayal* or *khiyal* was used in the Jahiliyya (pre-Islamic times) and in the first centuries of Islam in the sense of "figure" and "statue," and was given to the figure of the hobbyhorse *(kurraj)* as well (*see* Theater, Arabic). During the eighth century it came to mean "imagination," "phantom," and "fantasy," and finally it became synonymous with the term *hikaya* (imitation or pantomime, as in Hebrew *hikkuy*). When, during the ninth century, the term *hikaya* came to mean strictly "story" or "storytelling," the term *khayal* replaced it to denote "live play" or "live theatrical performance." It seems that this is the main reason that led to the conclusion that the Arabs performed only shadow plays and puppet theater, and neglected live theatrical performance because of religious restrictions. When Gypsies and Muslim merchants from southeast Asia to the Muslim world imported the shadow play during the late tenth century, the word *zill* (shadow) was added to the already established term for acting and theater, and the new term *khayal al-zill* was coined.

Performance Practice

The earliest discussion of the technique of the shadow play occurs in a scientific work on optics, *Kitab al-manazir* (Latin, *Thesaurus Opticus*), by the Arab mathematician and physicist Ibn al-Haytham (Alhazan) (Basra, ca. 965 CE, Cairo, 1039, *see* Mathematics and Optics). His description of *khayal* recalls modern cinematographic techniques: He speaks of translucent figures of characters and animals "which the performer *(mukhayyil)* manipulates so that their

Shadow play figures, translucent colored camel-leather figures from Istanbul. On the right Karakoz (30 cm × 8 cm), and on the left Hajibad (28 cm × 8.5 cm). Private collection of Shmuel Moreh, Jerusalem.

shadows appear upon the wall which is behind the curtain and upon the curtain itself" (*Kitab al-manazir* 1983:408). Other descriptions of shadow plays state that figures made of colored, translucent camel leather were held against the screen with one stick, while the limbs of the figures were moved with another. The performer, accompanied by music and singing, recited the dialogue between the *dramatis personae*. The light of candles or lamps cast the shadow of the figures upon the screen *(sitara, izar)*, which was made of muslin *(shash)*.

Significance

The extant prose and verses composed by Sufi scholars such as al-Ghazali (d. 1111), Ibn al-'Arabi (d. 1240) and Ibn al-Farid (d. 1235), as well as introductions to shadow plays, describe the hidden philosophical and religious significance of this art. They argue that "God has presented it as a parable" to this world. The presenter represents God who is the *muharrik* (prime mover); the curtain represents the hidden and secret foreordained future. The first figure represents Adam, who describes the images that will

follow him as depicting the generations of mankind, who behave according to God's will and predestination. The characters of the plot are arranged according to role, in a box on the right-hand side, which stands for the womb, while the box on the left, in which the figures are placed after ending their role, represents the tomb. It is this moral parable that induced poets to use the shadow play as a symbol of this world in Arabic literature and historiography. Even the three indecent shadow plays composed by the oculist Ibn Daniyal (Mosul, 1248; Cairo, 1311) at the request of a shadow puppeteer who complained that the art had became tedious and trivial emphasize moral admonition.

According to the Egyptian historian Ibn Iyas (d. 1524), who recorded the Ottoman occupation of Egypt in 1517, shadow players used to represent actual political and social events, such as the hanging of the defeated Mamluk sultan by Sultan Selim. The latter was pleased with the plot of the performer, rewarded him, and took him to Istanbul to entertain his son. On the other hand, E. W. Lane indicates that a reversed direction of influence occurred later on. In his *Manners and Customs of the Modern Egyptians* (1836), he says that the shadow play "Kara Gyooz," as he calls it, "has been introduced into Egypt by the Turks, in whose language the puppets are made to speak... They are conducted in the manner of the 'Chinese shadows', and therefore exhibited only at night."

Historians and scholars of the shadow play have criticized the pornographic and frivolous aspects of this popular art. Some plays, however, satirized the tyranny of rulers, administrators, and religious officials, and it seems that this is the main reason why some Mamluk sultans and scholars prohibited the shadow play and even burned the puppets and made the performers sign an undertaking not to practice it.

SHMUEL MOREH

See also Theater, Arabic

Further Reading

And, Metin. *A History of Theatre and Popular Entertainment in Turkey*. Ankara: Forum, 1963–1964.
———. *Karagoz, Theatre d'ombres Turc*. Ankara: Editions Dost, 1977.
Hamada, I. *Khayal al-zill wa-tamthiliyyat Ibn Daniyal (Shadowplay and the Plays of Ibn Daniyal)*. Cairo, 1963.
Ibn Daniyal, Muhammad. *Three Shadow Plays*. Edited by Paul Kahle, with a critical apparatus by Derek Hopwood. Prepared for publication by Derek Hopwood and Mustafa Badawi. Cambridge: E. J. W. Gibb Memorial, 1992.
Ibn al-Haytham. *Kitab al-manazir (The Book of Optics), al-Maqalat*: 1-2-3, fi 'l-ibsar 'ala al-istiqama. Ed. 'Abd al-Hamid Sabra. Kuwait, 1983.

Jacob, G. *Geschichte des Schattentheaters im Morgen-und Abendland.* Osnabruck, 1972.

Kahle, P. *Zur Geschichte des arabischen Schattentheaters in Ägypten.* Leipzig, 1909.

Kahle, P. E. Zur geschichte des arabischen Schattentheaters in Agypten. Leipzig, 1909.

———. "The Arabic Shadow Play in Medieval Egypt (Old Texts and Figures)." *The Journal of the Pakistan Historical Society.* (April 1954): 85–115.

Kayyal, Mounir. *Mu'jam babat masrah al-zill, karakuz wa-'Iwaz fi nusus muwaththaqa. (Dictionary of the Plays of Shadow Theatre, Arabic, Arabic).* Beirut: Librairie du Liban Publishers, 1995.

Menzel, Theodore. *Meddah, Schattentheater und Orta Ojunu.* Prague, 1941.

Moreh, S. "The Shadow Play *(khayal al-zill)* in the Light of Arabic Literature." *Journal of Arabic Literature* 18 (1987): 46–61.

———. "Shadow-play." *Encyclopedia of Arabic Literature.* Ed. J. Scott Meisami and P. Starkey. Vol. 2, 701–702. ADD UNDER Encyclopedia of Arabic Literature: "Ibn Daniyal" (E. K. Rowson), I, 319–320.

Sa'd, Faruq. *Khayal al-zill 'inda al-'Arab (Arabic Shadow Play).* Beirut, 1991.

SHAFI'I, AL-, ABU ABDALLAH MUHAMMAD IBN IDRIS

Al-Shafi'i (767–820 CE) ranks among the most influential jurists in the history of Islamic law by virtue of his contributions to substantive legal doctrine, elaboration of hermeneutic concepts and techniques, and his jurisprudential legacy as preserved in the Shafi'i School of Jurisprudence. Al-Shafi'i was probably born in Palestine and studied law first in Mecca and then in Medina, where he became a pupil of the celebrated jurist Malik ibn Anas. He also studied with at least one prominent student of the important Iraqi jurist Abu Hanifa.

Although al-Shafi'i taught and wrote for a period of years in Baghdad, only scattered references to his doctrines from this period survive. After relocating to Egypt (ca. 814), however, he authored (or his students compiled) a number of works that became authoritative. His massive *Kitab al-Umm (The Exemplar)* covers the standard topics found in a work of Islamic law. Traditionally published with the *Umm* are a number of shorter works, including some that preserve doctrines of earlier jurists with critical evaluations of these by al-Shafi'i.

What is new in al-Shafi'i's writings is the self-conscious concern with adherence to hermeneutical principles. Al-Shafi'i insists that laws be derived exclusively from revealed sources, namely the Qur'an and Hadith. In particular, al-Shafi'i emphasizes the special importance of Hadith from the Prophet, both as a supplement to the Qur'an and as an independent source of law. Thus, al-Shafi'i sought to ground law

exclusively in revelation, making Islamic jurisprudence (for him, anyway) into a field more dependent on textual analysis than on the handing down of traditional authority. This feature of al-Shafi'i's thought entailed a further development in his hermeneutics, namely the elaboration of a series of techniques for sorting through and resolving apparent contradictions in the revealed sources of the Shari'a. Al-Shafi'i's most detailed discussion of his hermeneutical principles is contained in his *Risala (Epistle)*, but they also figure prominently in his *Ikhtilaf al-Hadith (Contradictory Hadith)*, in several shorter works, and in the context of discrete problems dealt with in the *Umm*.

Recent scholarship, however, has cast doubt on the attribution of all works traditionally ascribed to al-Shafi'i. Scrutiny of the works bearing al-Shafi'i's name has led some to conclude that the *Umm* and the *Risala* were subject to a process of organic growth and redaction, and it has also been argued that hermeneutical approaches found in both works fit more easily into the intellectual world of the later ninth century. These studies raise important questions that are, for a variety of reasons, difficult to resolve definitively.

Al-Shafi'i's two Egyptian students, al-Rabi' ibn Sulayman al-Muradi (d. 883) and al-Muzani (d. 877), preserved, developed, and transmitted his doctrines. It is on the basis of their efforts to preserve al-Shafi'i's teachings that the Shafi'i School of Jurisprudence was founded and began to flourish, especially in Baghdad (c. 900). In time, the Shafi'i School spread to and remains important, in Arabia, Egypt, East Africa, and Malaysia.

JOSEPH E. LOWRY

See also Ibn Hanbal; Imam; Knowledge; Madrasa; Scholarship; Theology

Primary Sources

Al-Shafi'i. *Kitab al-Umm.* 8 vols. Beirut: Dar al-Fikr, 1990.

———. *Al-Risala.* Ed. A.M. Shakir. Cairo: al-Halabi, 1940.

Further Reading

Al-Shafi'i. *Islamic Jurisprudence: al-Shafi'i's Risala Translated with an Introduction, Notes, and Appendices.* Transl. Majid Khadduri. Baltimore: Johns Hopkins University Press, 1961.

Calder, Norman. *Studies in Early Muslim Jurisprudence.* Oxford: Clarendon Press, 1993.

Chaumont, Eric. "Al-Shafi'i." In *Encyclopaedia of Islam.* New Ed. Leiden: E. J. Brill, 1954–2002.

Coulson, N.J. *A History of Islamic Law.* Edinburgh: Edinburgh University Press, 1964.

Hallaq, Wael B. *A History of Islamic Legal Theories: An Introduction to Sunni usul al-fiqh.* Cambridge: Cambridge University Press, 1997.

Lowry, Joseph E. "Does Shafi'i Have a Theory of Four Sources of Law?" In *Studies in Islamic Legal Theory*, edited by B.G. Weiss. Leiden: Brill, 2001.

Schacht, Joseph. *The Origins of Muhammadan Jurisprudence*. Oxford: Clarendon Press, 1950.

SHAH 'ABBAS I (1571–1629), FIFTH SHAH OF IRAN'S SAFAVID DYNASTY (1501–1722)

'Abbas was the great-grandson of the first Safavid shah Isma'il I (r. 1501–1524), grandson of the second, Tahmasp (r. 1524–1576), and son of the fourth, Khudabandah (r. 1578–1587), and was enthroned by an alliance dominated by elements of the Ustajl, one of the preeminent tribes of the Qizilbash tribal confederation that had provided the military backbone of the dynasty to this period.

Tahmasp's death had caused splits among different tribal factions, Tajik (native Persian), Georgian, and Circassian, at court around his sons Isma'il II (r. 1576–1577) and Khudabandah (1578–1587). These left the polity vulnerable to Ottoman and Uzbeg invasions and, accentuated by Isma'il II's flirtation with Sunnism in an effort to bolster his own position, engendered considerable domestic spiritual unrest. The alliance that deposed Khudabandah and enthroned 'Abbas in 1587 collapsed soon thereafter as key Turk and Tajik elements coalesced around other Safavid princes, including 'Abbas' two younger brothers. Further foreign invasions resulted, and certain Sufi (and especially Nuqtavi and other) elements openly challenged 'Abbas' spiritual legitimacy.

'Abbas' 1590 purchase of peace with the Ottomans by ceding them key territories allowed him to move successfully against internal rivals and, thereafter, commence a series of campaigns that by the end of his reign regained territories lost to the Ottomans and Uzbegs since Tahmasp's death.

These military–political victories were achieved by forces composed of both tribal elements but also *ghulam* or *qullar* forces—non-Qizilbash Arab and Persian tribal volunteers and captured Georgian, Circassian, and Armenian youth converted to Islam whose presence in smaller numbers predated 'Abbas—who were now incorporated at the central and provincial military and political levels, albeit in positions subordinate to existing Qizilbash and Tajik elites and, more importantly, elements of Kurdish, Lur, and Chagatay tribes whose presence attests to the widening of the Qizilbash confederation.

Like his predecessors, 'Abbas further strengthened his personal position by using marriages to cement alliances with Qizilbash tribal elements, local political notables, and especially and more so than earlier shahs, prominent Tajik sayyids. The latter, including some of 'Abbas' relatives by marriage, were particularly prominent at the central and provincial administrative levels.

'Abbas' reign also witnessed a reinvigorated effort to identify the shah with the agendas and discourses of each of the realm's key component constituencies and project himself as transcendent ruler over all. Isfahan, which 'Abbas designated the capital soon after his accession, was home to many manifestations, including more secular projects such as Naqsh-i Jahan Square, whose construction created a new city center southwest of the traditional one. Isfahan's more spectacular religious projects included the 1599 'Abdallaah Shushtari school and the Lutfallah Maysi (1602 to 1618–1619) and Shah mosques (1611 to 1630–1631), the latter two both on 'Abbas' new square, but the provincial cities of Mashshad, the former capital Qazvin, and Kashan received similar attention. 'Abbas' special identification with Twelver Shi'ism was further attested to by his close association with such prominent philosopher–clerics as Mir Damad (d. 1630–1631), Mulla Sadra (d. 1640), and Shaykh Baha'i (d. 1621), the capital's *shaykh al-Islam*, his patronage of the Shi'i shrine cities of Najaf and Karbala after their 1624 capture, and his patronage of the Hijazi Shi'a. 'Abbas also carefully cultivated his image as head of the Safavid Sufi order and associated himself with such manifestations of "popular" religious feeling as the Muharram ceremonies, commemorating the martyrdom in 680 of the third Shi'i Imam Husayn, and the commemoration of the 661 martyrdom of Imam 'Ali. He also sponsored public, displayed clashes between the Ni'mati and Haydari factions, which were Iran's traditional urban factions. The commission of a never-completed, illustrated *Shahnama* attests to the center's atttentiveness to traditional Tajik Persian cultural discourse.

The development of Isfahan and the realm, aided by the center's restoration of road security, facilitated marked economic expansion, the more so in the aftermath of the forced importation to Isfahan of Armenians from war-torn eastern Anatolia beginning circa 1604, including many long-distance merchants who dominated the east–west trade routes through Iran, and the appearance in the Gulf of the Western commercial interests interested in expanding trade with the East, particularly in Iranian silk. These, with Western missionaries and political envoys, were welcomed by 'Abbas in his effort to construct an anti-Ottoman alliance.

ANDREW J. NEWMAN

Entrance to room of Qur'an students to the east madrasah (religious school). Built by Shah Abbas I, Sufavid dynasty. 1611–1638. Credit: SEF/Art Resource, NY. Masjid-I Shah, Isfahan, Iran.

See also Safavids

Further Reading

Newman, Andrew J. *The Formative Period of Twelver Shi'ism: Hadith as Discourse Between Qum and Baghdad.* Richmond: Surrey, 2000.
———. *Between Medieval and Modern: Iran in the Safavid Centuries.* London, forthcoming.

SHAHNAMA

Sometimes referred to as the Iranian National Epic, the *Shahnama (Book of Kings)* is the life's work of the Persian poet Abu 'l-Qasem Ferdowsi, from Tus in Khorasan, northeastern Iran. It is a work of heroic scale and heroic character, consisting of between fifty and sixty thousand lines *(beyt)*, each containing two rhyming couplets *(mesra')* in the same meter: u - -/u - -/ u - -/u -, known as the *bahr-e motaqareb*.

Ferdowsi was born around 935 CE and died around 1020 CE. He was thus writing approximately four centuries after the fall of the ancient Persian empire and the coming of Islam. The final version was completed in 1010, dedicated to the most powerful ruler of the time, Sultan Mahmud of Ghazna (modern Afghanistan, r. 999–1020). Ferdowsi conceived his work as a memorial to Iran's glorious past at a time when its memory was in danger of disappearing for good under the twin assaults of Arabic and Islamic culture and the political dominion of the Turks. His literary masterpiece has since been used by many subsequent regimes, both imperial and provincial, to assert their rightful place in the political traditions of the country, and to legitimize their dynasty. As a result, the text survives in countless manuscript copies, often lavishly illustrated in princely court ateliers. The earliest, however, was copied two hundred years after the poet's death, making it impossible to establish with certainty exactly what he wrote.

The *Shahnama* narrates the history of Iran (Persia) from the creation of the world and the first king, Kayumars, who established his rule at the dawn of time, to the conquest of Persia by the Muslim Arabs in the early seventh century CE. The poem follows the structure of a king-list, with altogether fifty reigns described in sequence, though at greatly differing length. Therefore it has the appearance, at least, of a chronicle and is often cited as such by later medieval Persian historians as a source of information about the pre-Islamic past. This formal structure also emphasizes the centrality and importance of the role of the king (Shah) in Persian political culture, a characteristic also noted by Herodotus. Many of its early figures are mentioned in the *Avesta*, especially the *Zamyad Yasht* (on the *khwarnah*, or Divine splendor), dealing with those who held and those who sought it.

Nevertheless, the *Shahnama* is more than a straightforward celebration of the monarchical and imperial tradition in Persian history. In the first place, much of its material is ahistorical. The reigns are grouped according to four major dynasties, the Pishdadians, Kayanians, Ashkanians, and Sasanians, an ancient division that became entrenched in Persian historiography. In parallel with these divisions, the poem is generally divided into mythical, legendary, and historical sections. The first includes the formation of human society, the discovery of fire, the domestication of animals, the struggle with the forces of evil (represented by *divs*, or devils), and the definition of Iranian territory. The distinction between the mythical passages and the following legendary sections is rather fluid; the collapse of time, the pervasive presence of the supernatural, of the fantastic, magic, dragons, and heroic endeavors give a strong continuity across these prehistorical chapters.

Secondly, a significant proportion of the narrative is taken up with a discrete cycle of stories concerning the local rulers of Sistan (southeast Iran), which is grafted onto the main structure of the poem. Olga Davidson has challenged the opinion that the "Sistan cycle" represents a separate textual tradition, suggesting that both these stories and those of the royal Kayanian line entered the National Epic together, as a conflation of a "book of kings" with an "epic of heroes," both drawn from oral sources. The chief subject of these stories is the heroic exploits of Rostam, son of Zal, who was the champion of successive Iranian monarchs. Indeed, Rostam is the Iranian epic hero *par excellence*, and his adventures encapsulate more than anything else the spirit and the popular appeal of the *Shahnama*. As discussed by Davidson and by Dick Davis, the role of the hero is intrinsic to the epic, and the bravery, reliability, and loyalty of the hero form a counterpoint to the behavior of the Shahs. Davis even regards the poem as a denunciation of kingship, as increasingly unjust rulers provoke even their loyal commanders to revolt against them. Throughout the poem, however, despite his frank depiction of the shortcomings of various Shahs, Ferdowsi's didactic intentions are clear from his comments on the consequences of poor judgment, tyranny, or rashness. The misfortunes of rulers are shown to be the result of their failings, and in contrast, success and prosperity come from wisdom and justice. Many later Persian historians claimed the same exemplary purpose in their works, but few showed Ferdowsi's integrity and rigor in denouncing the bad. Rather, as noted by Shahrokh Meskoob, flattery and praise of rulers became standard.

Sohrab looking again for the tent of Roustem. Ferdowsi, Shahnama (Book of Kings). Ms. 607–1144, fol. 11v. Moghul dynasty, sixteenth century CE. Credit: Bridgeman-Giraudon/Art Resource, NY. Musée Condé, Chantilly, France.

Rostam and the Shahs he served take part primarily in the endless cycles of wars with Turan (approximately Turkestan or modern Central Asia), Iran's traditional foe throughout the first sections of the poem. The episodes that have attracted most attention are the stories of Rostam and Sohrab and of Seyavosh, both ending in the tragic death of sons due to their domineering and intransigent fathers. Both of these, and the equally powerful confrontation between Rostam and Esfandiyar, son of the tyrannical Shah Goshtasp, are available in modern verse translations. These episodes reveal the strength of Ferdowsi's poetry and his stark exposure of the human condition. Caught up in their own preoccupations and trapped by their sense of honor, obedience, pride, and ambition, the protagonists are unable to extricate themselves from the net that circumstances have made for them. Despite the importance and, indeed, his convincing portrayal of human motivations, Ferdowsi always implicates blind, remorseless Fate for the actual outcome. When one's time is up, no human action can alter events. Shortly after killing Esfandiyar, Rostam too is killed, the price to be paid for accepting the help of the mythical Simorgh to overcome his foe. Rostam's death marks the end of an era, and with it the impetus goes out of the epic narrative of the Kayanians.

The historical section, that is, when known historical events can be identified, starts only with the story of Alexander the Great, also treated as legend. It is remarkable, for example, that there is no reference to the reigns of Cyrus the Great, Darius, or the Achaemenid dynasty that preceded the appearance of Philip of Macedon on the scene. The reasons for this silence lie in the sources available to the poet. Ferdowsi followed an eastern Iranian narrative tradition, which evidently knew nothing of the separate traditions of southwest Iran and the Tigris–Euphrates valley. It is only with the coming of the Parthians (Ashkanians, Arsacids), whose long history (247 BCE to 224 CE) is treated in barely twenty verses, and during which time memory of earlier events in the southwest must have been lost, followed by the Sasanian dynasty (224–651), that Fars becomes the focus of events.

Ferdowsi provides a long account of the Sasanians, based on written sources that were also used by early Islamic historians in Arabic translations from Pahlavi (Middle Persian). The main conflicts are now with Iran's western neighbor, the Byzantine empire. Some passages, particularly in the reign of Anushirvan ("the Just") and the exchanges with his vizier, Bozorjmehr ("Great light"), are the vehicle for much moral and political wisdom. The stories of Bahram Gur and Bahram Chubina (Bahram V and VI) to some extent maintain the epic aspect of the *Shahnama*, with their heroic hunts, romantic adventures, dragon-slayings, and martial prowess. The final episode is the murder of the last Sasanian ruler, Yazdagird III (r. 632–652). Its ending echoes with the gloomy predictions of the Persian general, Rostam—killed at the battle of Qadisiyya by the Arab commander Sa 'd b. Waqqas—of the disasters about to befall Iran.

The *Shahnama* is ultimately a story of defeat, yet Ferdowsi has contrived to turn this disaster into a triumph for Persian civilization. It encapsulates and expresses, as no other work of Persian literature has been able to, the Iranians' view of themselves and their rightful place in the world.

CHARLES P. MELVILLE

Further Reading

Clinton, Jerome W. *The Tragedy of Sohrab and Rostam from the Persian National Epic, The* Shahname *of Abol-Qasem Ferdowsi*. Washington, D.C.: Mage, 1987.

———. *In the Dragon's Claws. The Story of Rostam & Esfandiyar from the Persian Book of Kings by Abolqasem Ferdowsi*. Washington, DC: Mage, 1999.

Davidson, Olga M. *Poet and Hero in the Persian Book of Kings*. Ithaca and London: Cornell University Press, 1994.

Davis, Dick. *The Legend of Seyavash*. London: Penguin, 1992.

———. *Epic and Sedition. The Case of Ferdowsi's* Shahnameh. Fayetteville: The University of Arkansas Press, 1992.

———. *Stories from the Shahnameh of Ferdowsi*. 3 vols. Vol. 1, *The Lion and the Throne* (by Ehsan Yarshater, transl. Dick Davis); vol. 2, *Fathers and Sons*; vol. 3, *Sunset of Empire*. Washington, DC: Mage, 1998, 2000, and 2004.

Hillmann, Michael C. *Iranian Culture: A Persianist View*. Lanham, NY and London: University Press of America, 1990, 13–41.

Khaleghi-Motlagh, Djalal. "Ferdowsi, Abu'l-Qasem i. Life." In *Encyclopaedia Iranica*, vol. 9. New York, 1999, 514–523.

Meisami, Julie Scott. *Persian Historiography to the end of the Twelfth Century*. Edinburgh: University Press, 1999, 37–45.

Meskoob, Shahrokh. *Iranian Nationality and the Persian Language*, transl. Michael C. Hillmann, 78–79. Washington, DC: Mage, 1992.

Robinson, B.W. *The Persian Book of Kings: An Epitome of the* Shahnama *of Firdawsi*. London and New York: Routledge Curzon, 2002.

Shahbazi, A. Shapur. *Ferdowsi: A Critical Biography*. Costa Mesa, CA: Mazda, 1991.

Yarshater, Ehsan. "Iranian National History." In *The Cambridge History of Iran*, vol. 3. Cambridge: University Press, 1983, 359–477.

SHAJAR AL-DURR

Shajar al-Durr, a Turkish slave and concubine of the Ayyubid sultan of Egypt, al-Salih Ayyub (d. 1249), became his wife after bearing him a son. The son,

Khalil, soon died, but Shajar al-Durr retained the sobriquet Umm Khalil (Mother of Khalil) for the remainder of her life. Her name can be rendered in English as "Spray of Pearls."

Shortly before al-Salih Ayyub's death in 1249, during the Fifth Crusade's invasion of Egypt, he appointed his wife and two others to safeguard the transition to the sultanate of al-Mu'azzam Turanshah, his son by another woman. Shortly after his arrival in Egypt and assumption of rule, Turanshah was murdered by his father's Bahri mamluks (military slaves), whom he had alienated. This murder took place on May 2, 1250, and two days later, Shajar al-Durr was proclaimed sultana (the feminine form of sultan) of the Ayyubid dominions, although this was not recognized by the Syrian Ayyubid princes. Shajar al-Durr subsequently ruled Ayyubid Egypt in her own name for a period of three months. The legends on coins minted in her name bore the legend *malikat al-muslimin* ("Queen of the Muslims"). Her claim to royal authority was buttressed by her status as widow of al-Salih and as mother of his son. Shajar al-Durr's assumption of rule was a rare occurrence within the medieval Dar al-Islam. Although women had exercised positions of power, usually as wives of rulers or as regents (such as the Ayyubid Dayfa Khatun, regent for her grandson al-Nasir Yusuf—see later in this entry—during his minority in Aleppo), only Radiyya, the sultana of Dehli (r. 1236–1240), preceded Shajar al-Durr as an autonomous head of a state.

Her short reign came to an official close by the end of July 1250, when she abdicated in favor of a leader of her husband's Mamluks, the amir Aybak al-Turkumani. This move was likely taken in the face of increasing Syrian Ayyubid pressure, most notably from al-Nasir Yusuf, ruler of Damascus and Aleppo. Aybak himself abdicated shortly thereafter in favor of a young Ayyubid prince named al-Ashraf Musa. Both Shajar al-Durr and Aybak, who had married at some point after al-Ashraf Musa came to the throne, were the true powers behind the child. By 1254, Aybak deposed al-Ashraf Musa and assumed the sultanate in his own name. When Aybak took steps to strengthen his position by marrying a daughter of Badr al-Din Lu'lu, the ruler of Mosul, this exacerbated his already estranged marriage with Shajar al-Durr. She arranged Aybak's murder on April 10, 1257. In the power struggle that ensued, the forces loyal to al-Mansur 'Ali, Aybak's son by another wife, emerged victorious. Shajar al-Durr was arrested, and her corpse was subsequently found lying outside the Cairo citadel on April 28, 1257. Tales of her life and death were later embellished with myriad details not found in the earliest accounts.

WARREN C. SCHULTZ

See also Ayyubid, Mamluks, Sultan

Primary Source

Al-Maqrizi. *A History of the Ayyubid Sultans of Egypt.* Transl. R.J.C. Broadhurst. Boston: Twayne Publishers, 1980.

Further Reading

Holt, P.M. *The Age of the Crusades: The Near East from Eleventh Century to 1517.* London: Longman, 1986.

SHAWKANI, AL-, MUHAMMAD IBN 'ALI

A Yemeni scholar, judge, and reformer, Muhammad Ibn 'Ali al-Shawkani was born in the village of Hijrat Shawkan in 1760 and died in Sanaa in 1834 CE. Shawkani saw himself as the heir of the Sunni- and hadith-oriented school that arose in Yemen with Muhammad ibn Ibrahim al-Wazir (d. 1436 CE) and came to full prominence with Shawkani himself in the late eighteenth century. Drawing heavily on the teachings of the Sunni Traditionists *(ahl al-hadith)*, Shawkani was a prolific author (more than two hundred words are attributed to him) in virtually every field of the Islamic sciences. The thrust of his reformist message was to inveigh against the evils of strict adherence to the teachings of the established schools of law (sing. *madhhab*)—a practice he labeled *taqlid*. Instead, Shawkani argued that Muslims had to reform themselves by reverting to an unmediated interpretation of the sources of revelation, namely the Qur'an and the Sunna (the latter being encapsulated in the canonical Sunni hadith collections). His interpretive approach stresses the practice of independent judgment *(ijtihad)* and focuses on the explicit meaning of the texts (strict constructionism). He rejected most forms of analogical reasoning, as well as the principle of juristic consensus *(ijma')*. This amounted to a radical revamping of the traditional system of law with the claim of obtaining greater certainty of God's will. Shawkani's most influential book is his multivolume *Nayl al-awtar fi sharh muntaqa al-akhbar (Attaining the Aims in Commenting on the Choicest Traditions)*. This consists of a legal manual based on the Prophet Muhammad's traditions *(hadith)* and is the principal source for Sayyid Sabiq's *Fiqh al-sunna*, perhaps the most widely used legal text among modern Sunnis. Other works by al-Shawkani that have attained prominence include his commentary on the Qur'an, entitled *al-Fath al-qadir (Victory of the Almighty)*; his work on the principles of jurisprudence, entitled *Irshad al-fuhul (Guidance to the Luminaries)*; a legal work entitled *al-Sayl al-jarrar (The Raging Torrent)*; and a biographical dictionary entitled *al-Badr al-tali' (The Rising Moon)*. His works, especially on the Qur'an and on hadith-based law, are taught widely throughout the Islamic world today. For modern Muslim reformers, al-Shawkani is a towering figure, not only because of his clear and synthesized writing style but also because he was successful with his reformist project in Yemen. The dominant sect and school of law in eighteenth-century highland Yemen was Zaydism, one of the branches of Shi'ism. Al-Shawkani attacked the Zaydis in his writings, arguing that many of their theological and legal teachings had no basis in revelation and therefore had to be rejected. The aforementioned work, *The Raging Torrent*, is a point-by-point critique of the Zaydis' principal legal text, the *Kitab al-azhar (The Book of Flowers)* by the fifteenth-century imam al-Mahdi Ahmad ibn Yahya al-Murtada (d. 1436 CE). The Qasimi imams, who ruled Yemen from 1635 until the 1850s CE, had by the mid-eighteenth century established a dynastic state and began patronizing scholars like Shawkani. The Qasimis saw in Shawkani a jurist who would both legitimize their rule and lead a centralized judicial system. This is because Shawkani advocated a quietist political view that rejected the Zaydi teachings that rulers had to be exemplary men who satisfied rigorous qualifications for the position of imam and that unjust rulers had to be removed, by force if necessary. Shawkani was appointed to the position of chief judge of the state, a post he held from 1795 until his death in 1834 CE. As chief judge, he was able to push through his reformist agenda and teach several generations of like-minded scholars and jurists, many of whom were given posts in the state's bureaucracy. Shawkani's success was such that the Zaydis were never able to recover, intellectually or politically, from the onslaught waged against them by these Sunni-oriented reformers. The Zaydis claimed that Shawkani's efforts amounted to nothing more than the founding of a new school of law, with him as the ultimate authority, and that they preferred to follow their own imams, who as members of the Prophet's family *(ahl al-bayt)* were more worthy of emulation. The most forceful exponent of this position was Muhammad ibn Salih al-Samawi (d. 1825), who was executed by the Qasimi state for his criticism of the conjuncture of knowledge and power that was represented in the alliance between Shawkani and Qasimi imams. Shawkani's life and work are perhaps best appreciated if they are understood as forming a key link between premodern and modern Islamic reformist thought and action.

BERNARD HAYKEL

Further Reading

Al-'Amri, Husayn 'Abdullah. *The Yemen in the 18th and 19th Centuries: A Political and Intellectual history*. London: Ithaca Press, 1985.

Haykel, Bernard. *Revival and Reform in Islam: The Legacy of Muhammad al-Shawkani*. Cambridge: Cambridge University Press, 2003.

SHI'I LAW

The juristic traditions of the three Shi'i groups (the Zaydis, the Imamis, and the Ismailis) are best treated separately; although their traditions did influence one another, the jurists of each tradition perceived themselves as quite different from their fellow Shi'is. In general terms, however, the Zaydis and the Imamis concentrated more of their intellectual effort on the elaboration of the Shari'a, and consequently, their legal structures were more sophisticated than those of the Ismailis. All Shi'is trace the beginnings of their juristic heritage to the sayings of 'Ali, the cousin and son-in-law of the Prophet Muhammad. For Shi'is, 'Ali was not merely the rightful leader of the Muslims, he was also the supreme interpreter of Islam. His decrees hold the same authority as those of the Prophet. Indeed, except for a section of the Zaydis, Ali's decrees have a quasi-revelatory status, not being a book (like the Qur'an) but equal to the *sunna* of the Prophet.

Imami and Ismaili jurists have also reserved a pioneering role for Imam Ja'far al-Sadiq (d. AH 148/785 CE), a fifth-generation descendant of 'Ali and a widely respected scholar. Ja'far supposedly "founded" the Shi'i legal school, and his legal statements are taken by Imamis, Ismailis, and even some Zaydis as indicators of the Shari'a. For example, most of the legal positions in Qadi al-Nu'man's (d. 363/974) *Da'a'im al-Islam* concur with the reported positions of Imam Ja'far. This work, together with the same author's *Ikhtilaf usul al-madhahib* (a work of legal theory) represent the major Ismaili legal sources. For two reasons, there is little Ismaili legal scholarship after this date. First, the Ismaili Fatimid dynasty collapsed in 567/1171 and the Ismailis had already become less interested in the implementation of the law, and more interested in philosophical and mystical enquiry. Second, the Fatimid descendants led the Ismailis as present Imams, who could answer all legal questions due to their perfect legal knowledge. There was no need for jurisprudence because theoretically all legal issues could be answered by the Imam.

Imamis, on the other hand, believed their Imam to be in occultation since 329/941, and hence there was plenty of scope for scholars to study and develop legal arguments in defense of their own opinions. In the tenth century, Muhammad al-Kulayni (d. 328 or 329/940 or 941) collected *al-Kafi*, the first significant compendium of Imami Shi'i hadith. This was supplemented soon after by Ibn Babuya's (d. 381/992) *Man la yahduruhu al-faqih* and then by al-Shaykh al-Tusi's (d. 460/1067) two works, *al-Istibsar* and *al-Tahdhib*. Together these became known as "the four books" and were used as the sources for the legal manuals (*fiqh*) written by subsequent Imami jurists. Ibn Babuyah himself wrote a legal manual (entitled *al-Muqni'*), and was followed in this by a succession of Imami scholars in the eleventh century. Around this time, there emerged Imami works of legal theory (*usul al-fiqh*), the earliest extant being al-Sharif al-Murtada's (d. 436/1044) *al-Dhari'a*.

The centers of Imami learning were Baghdad and Qum. In the twelfth and thirteenth centuries, the town of Hilla in southern Iraq also became an important center of Imami scholarship. Two jurists in particular further developed a distinctive Shi'i *usul al-fiqh*. In Shi'i *usul*, as in Sunni legal theory, there were four sources. The first was *al-Kitab* (*The Book,* that is, the Qur'an), though it was best understood when interpreted by the Imams. The second was *Sunna* (the example of the Prophet), though this included the example of the Imams, since they were the embodiment of the Prophet's will. The third was *ijma'* (consensus), though this was only valid if the Imam's opinion was included. The final source was *al-'aql* (reason), the natural human faculty that recognizes good and evil. The Imamis rejected the Sunni principle of *qiyas* (analogy), labeling it a "tool of Satan." Early Imamis also rejected *ijtihad*, the exegetical effort of the individual jurist to find an answer to a legal problem. There was no need to perform *ijtihad*, because there were sufficient statements of the Imams (*akhbar*) to guide the community. As time passed, Imami jurists realized that the *akhbar* were not really sufficient for developing the law, and so they introduced *al-'aql* as the fourth source of law and legitimized *ijtihad*. The jurists could not do without these tools in their search for the law. Imami law manuals (*mukhtasars* and more expansive works of *fiqh*) outlined the law in a manner very similar to that found in Sunni works. There are some significant differences though. The fact that Fatima, the Prophet's daughter, was the line through which the Prophet's descent was traced meant that the agnate and cognate relatives were considered equal in Imami inheritance law. The Imamis permitted a form of temporary marriage (*mut'a*, the "marriage of pleasure") disallowed by the Sunnis. There was to be no *jihad* during the occultation, as there was no Imam to lead it. The validity of Friday prayers, the collection of taxes, and the implementation of legal punishments were matters of

dispute among Imamis well into the modern period. In the fourteenth century, al-Shahid al-Awwal ("the First Martyr," d. 786/1384) wrote his *al-Lum'a*, an extremely brief summary of Imami law. His advocacy of juristic authority and the right of scholars to interpret the revelatory texts was challenged by Imamis in the seventeenth century, but his approach continues to dominate Imami legal curricula today.

The Zaydis also developed a sophisticated tradition of legal literature. In particular, the Yemeni Zaydi state, formed by al-Hadi ila al-Haqq in the late ninth century, served as a center for Zaydi legal development. Al-Hadi was the grandson of the great Zaydi scholar al-Qasim b. Ibrahim (d. 246/860), and he developed his grandfather's teachings into a school of law, himself writing works of *fiqh*. The "Hadawi" school, as it became known, remains authoritative for Yemeni Zaydis today, and central to its teaching is the work of *fiqh Kitab al-Azhar* by Ibn al-Murtada (d. 840/1437). This latter work and its commentary serve as reference points for Yemeni law, even after the end of the Imamate in 1962. For Zaydis, any member of the *ahl al-bayt* who is a scholar can rise up and become Imam. The Imam is a legal authority because he has had political success. This is in contrast to the Ismaili and Imami views, for whom the Imam is a legal authority whether or not he holds political power.

ROBERT GLEAVE

See also al-Allama al-Hilli; al-Tusi; Ja'far al-Sadiq; Muhammad b. al-Hasan; Qadi Nu'man; Shi'i Thought; Shi'ism

Further Reading

Hossein Moddarressi Tabataba'i. *An Introduction to Shi'i Law*. London: Ithaca, 1984.
Kohlberg, Etan. *Belief and Law in Imami Shi'ism*. London: Variorum, 1991.
Stewart, Devin. *Islamic Legal Orthodoxy*. Salt Lake City: University of Utah Press 1998.

SHI'I THOUGHT

It is commonly said that Twelver Shi'ism is based on five principles. The first three, called "principles of the religion," are fully shared with the Sunnis: to believe in the uniqueness of God; to believe in the mission of the prophets and, in particular, in the mission of Muhammad; and to believe in the existence of reward and punishment in the afterlife. The two remaining principles, the so-called principles of the school (that is, of Twelver Shi'ism), are to believe in Divine Justice and to believe in the principle of the imamate. This list, however, comes not only from a later date (seventeenth or eighteenth century) but is also extremely reductive. A look at ancient texts and at the founding sources of Shi'ism shows that things are far more complex.

Scriptural Sources

Like the Sunnis, Shi'is recognize two scriptural sources: the Qur'an and the Hadith, but definitions differ greatly in both trends. In Sunnism, the Hadith is what is called "the prophetic tradition" (that is, the sayings, sentences, and, at times, behaviors attributed to Muhammad), conveyed through texts of varying lengths and transmitted via a chain of transmitters made up essentially by the Companions of the Prophet. These traditions are collected in a number of compilations, which the Sunnis concluded to be "authentic."

For Shi'is, the Hadith is not limited to the Prophet. It is made up of the sayings and attitudes attributed to the "Fourteen Impeccables," that is, Muhammad, his daughter Fatima, and the Twelve Imams. Thus the Shi'i Hadith is broader than the Sunni Hadith. Further, when it comes to transmitting the hadith, Shi'is heed no one but the Impeccables. They therefore reject the testimony of the Companions and the authenticity of the Sunni compilations. The hadith can be transmitted only by an Impeccable, particularly an Imam. Moreover, the Shi'is began to create their own compilations of hadith; the oldest to reach us were written between AH 250 and 350/864 and 961 CE. The corpus thus created is enormous, with thousands of pages and hundreds of thousands of traditions. Obviously, the hadith collections played a key role in the creation, consolidation, and development of the doctrines. Their authors are regarded as champions of the faith and are highly respected. It is, for the most part, thanks to them that Shi'ism was able to become one of the most powerful religious trends of Islam. It is worth noting that the majority of these ancient compilers came from the two great Iranian cities of Qumm and Rayy: al-Barqi, Saffar al-Qummi, 'Ali ibn Ibrahim al-Qummi, al-Kulayni al-Razi, al-Nu'mani, and Ibn Babawayh al-Razi.

As for the Qur'an, Sunnis recognize as official vulgate the Qur'an we know today, the one that Muslim tradition eventually introduced as having been written under the reign of the third caliph 'Uthman (r. 24–35/644–656).

For the Sunni "orthodoxy," this "'Uthman Collection" represents (chronology of the revelations aside) the faithful and complete reproduction of the divine Word "descended" upon Muhammad. For Shi'is, however, as shown through texts as sacred as the hadith of the Imams, the 'Uthmanian vulgate is but a falsified, altered, and censored version of the Revelation made to Muhammad. The original, complete version, which was three times bigger than the known vulgate, included explicit passages on the holiness of 'Ali's rank and the Imams who descended from him. Those who pushed him away from power, in this case the first three caliphs and their followers, could not tolerate this original version, which they rejected because they denied 'Ali to be the only legitimate successor of the Prophet. The "integral Qur'an" thus stayed with 'Ali and was secretly transmitted from Imam to Imam, up to the last one who took it with him in his Occultation. Therefore it will only be revealed to all, as will the original version of the other Holy Scriptures, with the coming of the Mahdi at the End of Times.

Following the definitive introduction of Islamic orthodoxy and orthopraxy by the end of the third/ninth century, and the fact that from rite to institutions, including basic dogma, the foundations of the religion were from then on justified by the 'Uthmanian vulgate, the belief in its falsification was becoming truly dangerous. Indeed, from the mid-fourth/eleventh century, Shi'is would start abandoning the falsification doctrine *(tahrif)* by questioning the authenticity of the traditions that supported it and by adopting a stance similar to that of the Sunnis with regard to the official Qur'an. Ibn Babawayh (d. 381/991) seemed to have been the first great author to have adopted this stance, which would become the prevailing one in Shi'ism. Yet there still were some important but isolated authors who supported the veracity of the hadith about the falsified nature of the vulgate, from Ibn Shahrashub and Tabrisi in the sixth/twelfth century, Majlisi and Sharif 'Amili in the eleventh to twelfth/seventeenth to eighteenth centuries, up to the great religious authority of modern times, Mirza Husayn Nuri (d. 1902).

Doctrinal Specificity of Shi'ism

What is the doctrinal specificity of Shi'ism, as it appears through the teachings going back to the Imams or through the citations of the "complete Qur'an," which is found in the enormous corpus of the hadith? What makes Shi'ism stand out within the many religious trends of Islam? Its characteristic lies in the notion of the person of the "guide" represented by the Imam. The person of the Imam is the true hub around which revolves the entire Shi'i doctrine. From theology to ethics, from law to Qur'anic exegesis, and from cosmology to rites and eschatology, all the articles of faith are determined and given meaning only by the Imam. Shi'ism specifically developed around a double vision of the world. The person of the Imam, in its many meanings, is ubiquitous.

Dual Vision

Any reality, from the highest to the most trivial, has two levels: a manifest, exoteric level *(zahir)* and a secret, esoteric level *(batin),* which is hidden under the manifest level. This fundamental creed operates within the different religious disciplines. First, in theology: God Himself has two levels of being. First is the level of the Essence, forever elusive. This is the absolute Unknowable, the forever hidden face of God. If things were to remain on that level, no relation would ever be possible between the Creator and the created. So God, in his Goodness, hatched another level within His own Being: that of the Names and Attributes through which He reveals Himself. This is the exoteric level of God, of the Unknown that yearns to be known. The Divine Names act in creation through "vehicles," "divine Organs" that are as many places of God's manifestations, as many theophanies.

The theophany par excellence, the highest point of the revelation of the Names of God, is a metaphysical being that Shi'i literature (depending on authors and eras) has called Imam in heaven, 'Ali in heaven, Imam of Light, Cosmic Man, among others. It is the Imam (with a capital letter) in its full and universal ontological meaning. Knowing its reality is thus equivalent to knowing what can be known in God, since the true revealed God, that which manifests all that can be manifested in God, is the cosmic Imam. In turn, he too has a hidden dimension and a manifest level. His esoteric level is precisely his metaphysical, cosmic aspect. His exoteric, or apparent level, his point of manifestation, is the historical imams (with a lower case letter) from the different cycles of the Sacred History. Here we are getting into prophetology.

For Shi'is, each great prophet is accompanied in his mission by one or more Imams. They all make up the long chain of the Friends of God *(wali, pl. awliya'),* who carry and transmit the divine Covenant *(walaya),* a key word in Shi'ism that refers among other things to the nature and function of the Imamate. They are the points of manifestation of the cosmic Imam, his revealed face. Knowledge of God thus begins with knowledge of the man of God or, more precisely, of the Man–God because theophanic man, the ultimate mystery of the Shi'i doctrine.

The Word of God, the Revelation, also has a double dimension. Its exoteric dimension, its letter *(tanzil),* is brought by the Prophet to the faithful. Its hidden, esoteric dimension, its spirit, or, more exactly, its spiritual hermeneutics *(ta'wil),* is taught by each prophet's Imam to a minority of initiates. Those initiates of the Imam's teachings thus make up the "Shi'is" of each religion. The historical Shi'is, in Islam, are therefore presented as the last link of a long initiatory chain that goes back to Adam, first man and first prophet.

Dualistic Vision

Next to this dual vision of the world also lies a dualistic vision of History. The history of creation is that of a cosmic battle between the forces of knowledge and the forces of ignorance. Since the primeval battle between the cosmic Intelligence and the cosmic Ignorance described in the cosmogonic traditions, this war has been waged from age to age, opposing the imams and their initiates on one side to the "enemies of the imams" and their followers on the other. This universal fight will end only with the coming of the Mahdi at the End of Times and his definitive victory over the powers of Evil. Indeed, according to the Shi'i Hadith, because of the usurpation of power by the "imams of injustice," the birth of each religion is accompanied by the formation in each community of a "majority" that, while being subjected to the letter of this religion, refuses even to believe in a spirit hidden behind the letter. This majority, ruled by ignorant people, thus amputates the religion from its most profound element. The enemy is then not necessarily the pagan or the nonbeliever, but the pseudo-faithfuls who reject the esoteric of the religion, the People of the exoteric *(ahl al-zahir)* who reject the initiatory teachings of the Imam. Complex cyclical reasons mean that contemporary humanity is still ruled by the forces of ignorance and that the initiates are but a threatened minority. This explains the need for discretion, for "keeping the secret" *(taqiyya),* canonical duty for the Shi'i initiate, to protect the mysteries of the teachings from those who are not worthy.

These two visions of the world determine the two constants of Shi'i thought: the permanent initiation, provided by the Imams of each era to their faithful, and the perpetual fight between the Imams and their initiates on one hand and the forces of ignorance on the other. The first constant shows the spirituality of humanity; the second characterizes its history. The role of the Imam proves to be fundamental everywhere.

These doctrines are ubiquitous in the ancient corpus of the hadith and the different doctrinal chapters. They are inevitably tinged with esotericism, initiatory and mystical teachings, and even magical themes. They characterize what could be called the "nonrational original esoteric tradition," the prevailing tradition in Shi'ism up to the fourth/tenth century, which marked a great turning point in the historical evolution of Twelver Shi'ism. This century was indeed a crossroads for Islam in general and for Shi'ism in particular, because of two great events. The first great event is that it became the "Shi'i century" of Islam. With the Buyids in Baghdad (then the center of the 'Abbasid empire), the Fatimids in Egypt and in North Africa, the Hamdanids in Iraq and Syria, and the Qarmatians in Arabia and in the South of Iran, the most important regions of the Islamic empire were under Shi'i rule. To keep the then largely Sunni public opinion on their side, Shi'is (particularly the Buyids, who kept the 'Abbasid caliphs in place) attempted to move closer to Sunni orthodoxy, expunging or at least redefining the Shi'i doctrines deemed "heretic" or "heterodox." The second great event is that the fourth/tenth century was the century of the "rationalization" of Islam. Greek and Alexandrine works translated in Arabic during the third/ninth century were now assimilated by Muslim intellectuals seduced mostly by the logic and dialectical reason of Aristotelian tradition. Theologians and lawmakers found in it the best "weapon" for their endless arguments. The Shi'is, left without an Imam since the Occultation of the twelfth and last imam in 329/941, and with their sacred texts having many doctrines now deemed "irrational," were in an embarrassing position. Consequently, Shi'i theologian–jurists of the Buyid era, such as Shaykh al-Mufid and his followers al-Radi, al-Murtada, and Shaykh al-Tusi (fourth to fifth/tenth to eleventh century), who were inspired by the Mu'tazili (see Mu'tazilites) thought and collaborated more or less closely with the power in place, slowly took their distance from the original esoteric tradition up to its marginalization and the creation of the "rational, theologico-judicial tradition." It is within this tradition that the theologian-jurist, the Doctor of the Law, would gradually fill the empty space left by the imam, acquiring the privileges that were until then exclusive to the imam or his named delegate (that is, to lead collective prayers, apply legal sanctions, collect some religious taxes, and also declare holy war). This increasing power of the theologian-jurist on the political, social, and economic levels was done through the elaboration of three basic doctrines: the criteriological science of the hadith (which allowed them to do away with the ideologically embarrassing traditions by accusing them of

inauthenticity), the practice of *ijtihad* (personal interpretation of matters of faith by the jurist, a concept explicitly forbidden by the Imams but rehabilitated by the scholars from the school of al-Mufid), and the concept of "collaboration with authority" (*al-'amal ma'a l-sultan,* theological definitions and justifications that allowed political activity also forbidden by the imams). This rationalist trend would be further developed by the scholars from the School of Hilla in Iraq, before and after the Mongol invasion of the seventh and eighth/thirteenth and fourteenth centuries. It would reach its peak with the Shi'i "clergy" set up in Iran during the Safavid era (tenth/sixteenth century) and the proclamation of imamate Shi'ism as state religion. The doctrine of the "charismatic power of the jurist" *(walayat al-faqih)*, the central thesis of Khomeynism and the Iranian Islamic revolution, can thus be considered as the issue of a millennial process going from the rationalization of the Buyid era to the ideologizing of the modern era.

The original esoteric tradition was marginalized but did not disappear. Many of its doctrinal elements can be found in Ismailism, as well as in other Shi'i esoteric trends or even in Sufism. In Twelver Shi'ism, it had isolated important representatives during the Middle Ages: Ibn Shahrashub, Ibn Tawus, Irbili, Rajab al-Bursi, the philosophers from the school of Bahrayn, and the jurists from the traditionalist School (Akhbariyya). The Safavid era also saw the emergence of several trends of thought that proclaimed themselves to be faithful to the ancient tradition: some great names from the philosophical School of Isfahan and Shiraz (Mir Fendereski, Mulla Sadra, Muhsin Fayd Kashani), from the traditionalist theologians (al-Jaza'iri, al-Bahrani), and from the masters of the great mystical Shi'i brotherhoods, which are still alive and active (Ni'matullahiyya, Dhahabiyya, Khaksr, Shaykhiyya).

MOHAMMAD ALI AMIR-MOEZZI

See also Imam; Shi'ism

Further Reading

Amir-Moezzi, M.A. *Le Guide divin dans le shi'isme originel. Aux sources de l'ésotérisme en Islam.* Paris, 1992. English translation: *The Divine Guide in Early Shi'ism.* Albany, NY, 1994.
Amir-Moezzi, M.A. et C. Jambet. *Qu'est-ce que le Shi'isme.* Paris, 2003.
Bar-Asher, M.M. *Scripture and Exegesis in Early Imâmî Shi'ism.* Leiden, 1999.
Corbin, H. *En Islam iranien.* Paris, Vols. I, II, et IV, 1971–1972.
———. *Histoire de la philosophie islamique.* Paris, 1974, esp. Chap. 2.
Friedlaender, I. *The Heterodoxies of the Shiites According to Ibn Hazm.* New Haven, 1909.

Halm, H. *Die Schia*. Darmstadt, 1988.

Kohlberg, E. *Belief and Law in Imâmî Shî'ism*. Aldershot, 1991.

Lalani, A.R. *Early Shi'i Thought. The Teachings of Imam Muhammad al-Bâqir*. London, 2000.

Le shî'isme imâmite. colloque de Strasbourg (6-9 mai 1968), Paris, 1970.

Madelung, W. *Religious Trends in Early Islamic Iran*. Albany, NY, 1988. Modarressi, H. *Crisis and Consolidation in the Formative Period of Shi'ite Islam*. Princeton, 1993.

Newman, A.J. *The Formative Period of Twelver Shî'ism*. Richmond, 2000.

Sachedina, A.A. *Islamic Messianism: The Idea of the Mahdi in Twelver Shi'ism*. Albany, NY, 1981.

Sander, P. *Zwischen Charisma und Ratio. Entwicklungen in der frühen imâmitischen Theologie*. Berlin, 1994.

Shi'ism. Ed. E. Kohlberg. Ashgate (The Formation of the Classical Islamic World), 2003.

SHI'ISM

Shi'ism is the oldest religious trend of Islam, given that what can be considered its early core goes back to the time when the problem of Prophet Muhammad's succession arose. The main minority of Islam, it is considered by the Sunni majority—also called "orthodox"—as the main "heterodoxy," if not "heresy," of the religion. Shi'is, on the other hand, regard their doctrine as the "orthodoxy" par excellence.

The Arabic term *shî'a* (party, members, faithfuls) got increasingly applied by antonomasia to what would have been the first of the religious-political parties of Islam, a party that was made up of those who claimed for 'Alî b. Abî Tâlib, cousin and son-in-law of Muhammad, and for 'Alî's descendants, the exclusive right to guide the community, on the spiritual level, as well as on the secular level. Indeed, after the death of the Prophet in AH 11/632 CE, two conflicting views of the crucial question of his succession clashed. A majority of Muslims, claiming that Muhammad never clearly named anyone to succeed him, resorted to the ancestral tribal tradition of electing a chief by which a counsel, made up of a few Companions of Muhammad plus the influential members of the most powerful Meccan tribes, chooses a wise man of respectable age. The choice fell on Abû Bakr, old Companion and one of the Prophet's fathers-in-law, who thus became the first caliph of the new community. His followers became the ancestors of those who would later be called Sunnis.

Opposite the Sunnis were the Alids, followers of 'Alî *(Shî'at 'Alî)*, who claimed that Muhammad had clearly and often named him as his successor, both by alluding to it and explicitly. They believed it could not be otherwise: How could the Prophet have left the question of his succession unsolved? Is it conceivable that he would have been so indifferent to the direction of his community to the point of leaving it in a state of hazy confusion? It would be contrary even to the spirit of the Qur'an, in which the great prophets of the past had their successors elected among the closest of their kins, those with the most privileged blood ties and who were initiated to the mysteries of their religion. It is true that the Qur'an calls for consultation in some cases, but never when it comes to the succession of the prophets, which remains an election of divine order. For those who would later be called Shi'is, 'Alî was the chosen heir, named by Muhammad and supported by the Qur'an. In this case, his youth, which was a dissuasive handicap for the beholders of the ancestral tribal customs, was of no importance. 'Alî is thus seen by the Shi'is as their first *imam* (leader, commander, chief). Referring to the true leader of the community, even if he does not hold the power, the person of the imam would become the key concept of the Shi'i religion, which never used the word "caliph" to refer to their Guide.

Shi'ism is thus as old as the dispute about the succession of the Prophet. Still, it cannot be reduced to it. Alid legitimism can only be seen as the beginning of vast doctrinal developments during which the key concept of the imamate as "prophetic legacy" would find multiple, complex meanings and would lead to the creation of varied branches within Shi'ism. These branches are characterized mostly by the line of historical imams, descendants of 'Alî, whom they regard as legitimate. New schisms and divisions would appear almost every time an imam died, and more than one hundred Shi'i sects and trends appeared during the first centuries of Islam. Three of them, still active today, can be thought of as the main spiritual families of Shi'ism: Zaydiyya, Isma'iliyah, and Twelver Shi'ism, which is by far the main branch.

Twelver Shi'ism (with twelve imams) is first of all based on the doctrine of the holiness of the Fourteen Impeccables (*ma'sûm*, as in "pure of sin," "infallible"): Muhammad, his daughter Fâtima, and the twelve imams. This group is where the Cosmic Imam manifests, as he himself manifests the Names and Attributes of God. The line of imams of the Twelver Shi'is is as follows. (The presumed sites of their grave are mentioned only to present the main holy places of Shi'ism.)

1. 'Alî b. Abî Tâlib (d. 40/661; mausoleum in Najaf, Iraq)
2. Al-Hasan b. 'Alî (d. 49/669; mausoleum in Medina, destroyed by the Wahhabites)
3. Al-Husayn b. 'Alî (d. 61/680; emblematic martyr of Shi'ism; killed and buried in Karbalâ, Iraq)

4. 'Alî Zayn al-'Âbidîn b. al-Husayn (c. 95/174; mausoleum in Medina, destroyed by the Wahhabites. Zayd, eponym of the Zaydiyya, was the son of the fourth imam)

5. Muhammad al-Bâqir (c. 115/732; mausoleum in Medina, destroyed by the Wahhabites)

6. Ja'far al-Sâdiq (d. 146/765; mausoleum in Medina, also destroyed. The fifth and sixth imams played a key role in the creation and development of Shi'ism. Ja'far is the father of Ismâ'il, eponym of the Isma'iliyya)

7. Mûsâ al-Kâzim (d. 183/799; mausoleum in Baghdad)

8. 'Alî al-Ridâ (d. 203/818; mausoleum in Mashhad, Iran)

9. Muhammad al-Jawâd (d. 220/835; mausoleum in Baghdad)

10. 'Alî al-Hâdî (d. 254/868; mausoleum in Sâmarrâ, Iraq)

11. Al-Hasan al-'Askarî (d. 260/874; mausoleum in Sâmarrâ)

12. Muhammad al-Mahdî, the hidden imam and expected Savior of the End of Times. (According to the tradition, he occulted a first time after his father's death in 260/874. During this "Minor Occultation," which lasted until 329/941, he communicated with his faithfuls via four "representatives." At this latter date, he declared in a letter that he would never again have a representative and that the time of the "Major Occultation" had begun. For the Twelvers, this Occultation is still going on and will last until the eschatological coming of the hidden imam, the living imam of our time.)

There are four great eras in the history of Shi'ism, as follows:

1. The first era, from the first to fourth/seventh to tenth centuries, is that of the historical imams, who succeeded each other from father to son, and of their disciples—some of whom were the first Shi'i thinkers. It ends with the beginning of the major Occultation. The end of this era is marked by the beginning of the systematic compilations of the hadîth in the main "hadîth schools" *(dâr al-hadîth)* of Qumm, Rayy (Iran), Kûfa, and Baghdad (Iraq), and especially by the compilers from the two Iranian cities.

2. A second era extends from 329/941 (end of the historical imams' era) to the Mongol invasion in the mid-seventh/thirteenth century. The beginning of this era sees the continuation of the production of the great compilations

and the development of the School of Baghdad, that of the rationalist jurist–theologians of the Buyid era: al Shaykh al-Mufîd and his disciples (Sharîf al-Radî and al-Murtadâ, al-Shaykh al-Tûsî). It is also the era of the great scholars of the sixth and seventh/twelfth and thirteenth centuries, such as Ibn Shahrâshûb, Fadl al-Tabrisî, and Ibn Tâwûs. It ends by the time of the great Iranian philosopher Nasîr al-Dîn al-Tûsî (672/1273) and his disciple, al-'Allâma al-Hillî (726/1326), key figure of the theologico-judicial school of Hilla in Iraq.

3. The third era begins with Nasîr al-Dîn al-Tûsî, during the Safavid era, and the proclamation of Shi'ism as state religion in Iran, and ends at the very beginning of the tenth/sixteenth century. The development of many schools of thought during this era heralded what would be called the Safavid Renaissance: the continuators of the school of Hilla, the philosophers from the School of Bahrayn, and also the great mystic thinkers, nourished by a Shi'ism enriched with classic Sufism and the mysticism of Ibn 'Arabî (Sa'd al-Dîn Hamûnyî, Haydar Âmulî, Rajab al-Bursî, and Ibn Abî Jumhûr al-Ahsâ'î).

4. The fourth and last era extends from the accession of the Safavids to today. This era saw the creation of a Shi'i theocracy, gradually organized into a true "clergy," initially set up by the Doctors of the Law invited from Syria or Bahrayn to legally justify Safavid power. Members of this clergy came from the ancient rationalist school of jurists *(mujtahid usûlî)*. They slowly gained great social, political, and economic powers through the gradual exercise of privileges traditionally reserved exclusively for the imams and their delegates namely designated (religious justice and enforcement of legal sanctions, leading of collective prayers, declaration of holy war, and collection of some religious taxes such as *kharâj* and *khums*). The 1978 victory of Khomeynism in Iran and the effective rise to power of the jurist–theologian is the direct consequence of this evolution.

In parallel, the Safavid Renaissance led to the emergence of powerful philosophy schools in the main Iranian cities (Isfahan, Shiraz, Sabzewar, Tehran) represented by eminent thinkers, such as Mîr Dâmâd (1041/1631) or Mullâ Sadrâ, and continuing until the thirteenth/nineteenth century. The traditional philosophy still has a few notable representatives today: Hâ'irî Yazdî, Mutahharî, Abdol Karîm Sorûsh, and Mujtahid Shabistarî.

This is also the time of the compilation of the famous and enormous encyclopedia of Shi'i hadîth, *Bihâr al-anwâr*, by Majlisî the Second (d. 1111/1699) and of the emergence of the traditionalist judicial school of the Akhbâriyya in the twelfth/eighteenth century. Lastly, mystic Shi'i societies began to develop in the eleventh/seventeenth century. First came the Ni'matullâhiyya and the Dhahabiyya, followed by the Khâksâr and the Shaykhiyya in the thirteenth/nineteenth century. Out of the schisms of the latter school came Babism, which in turn, after some division, led to the Baha'i faith. Despite the repression they endured during the first years of the Islamic revolution of 1978 in Iran, these societies still remain popular and active.

Today, Twelver Shi'is amount to about 120 or 150 million people, an uncertain number due to the unreliability of statistics in Sunni countries. Still, an estimate is not too difficult to assess: There are more than sixty million in Iran and almost as many, if not more, on the Indian subcontinent across India and Pakistan, who at times hide their doctrinal allegiance and are almost absent from official statistics. They also form a majority in Azerbaijan, Iraq, and Bahrayn. Communities of varied sizes can be found in almost all Sunni countries, especially in the Near and Middle East, Central Asia, and Afghanistan. Thus one can see that the number of 100 million touted by the media as being the total number of Shi'is, all faiths included, does not rest on solid ground. To obtain the total number of Shi'is, one would have to add to the Twelvers not only the Isma'iliyah and the Zaydiyya but also all other Shi'i groups that do not always reveal their names: Nusayris–Alaouites from Syria, Bektashis and Alevis from Turkey, and Kurdish Ahl-i Haqq. The correct number would seem to approximate 200 million.

MOHAMMAD ALI AMIR-MOEZZI

See also Imam; Shi'i Thought

Further Reading

Amir Arjomand, S. *The Shadow of God and the Hidden Imam*. Chicago, 1984.
Amir-Moezzi, M.A., et C. Jambet. *Qu'est-ce que le Shi'isme?* Paris, 2003.
Corbin, H. *Histoire de la philosophie islamique*. Paris, 1964.
Gobillot, G. *Les Chiites*. Turnhout (Belgique), 1988.
Halm, H. *Die Schia*. Darmstadt, 1988.
Jafri, S.H.M. *The Origins and Early Development of Shi'a Islam*. London, 1979.
Laoust, H. *Les schismes dans l'Islam: introduction à une étude de la religion musulmane*. Paris, 1965.
Momen, M. *An Introduction to Shi'i Islam*. New Haven, 1985.
Richard, Y. *Le Shi'isme en Iran. Imam et révolution*. Paris, 1980.
———. *L'Islam Shi'ite*. Paris, 1991.
Shi'ism. Ed. E. Kohlberg. Ashgate (the Formation of the Classical Islamic World), 2002.

SHIPS AND SHIPBUILDING

The ship occupies a unique position in the Islamic tradition. The *Qur'an* counts it among the *ayat* (miracles) of God and devotes twenty-eight verses enumerating its benefits to mankind. The generic Arabic words for "ship" that appear invariably in the classical Arabic sources are *markab* (lit., a conveyance or riding vessel), *safina*, and *law* (lit., a board or plank of wood); *fulk* (Ark), which is another term to denote a ship, is Qur'anic. It may be surmised that some of the variations are more linguistic than physical and that professional sailors and experienced sea travelers could appreciate the actual sailing characteristics of each type of vessel. A typical seagoing merchant vessel had to carry on board many anchors, appropriate hawsers and ropes, canvas and/or cotton sails, masts, oars, rudders, and draw bridges (for greater ease in embarking and debarking), in addition to nautical instruments, pilot books, and charts. Oversized vessels had to have service boats on board for the transport of goods to the quayside. Identical rules applied to ship sales and purchase contracts. Both parties to the contract had to specify the vessel's tackle and navigational instruments in the bill of sale. When signing a contract to lease a specific vessel for the conveyance of cargo, shippers were most concerned with the seaworthiness of the ship, besides other considerations such as the freight tariff. Seaworthiness of a ship was associated with the equipment and amount and proficiency of the crew it was required to carry. The design, structure, condition, and equipment of the ship had to be suitable for carrying goods of a particular kind and bringing them safely to their destination. Meaning, it had to be technically able to encounter the ordinary perils of the voyage. Concerning the crew, bringing the carriage into completion required a lessor to recruit a competent master and professional complement to navigate the vessel under various circumstances; a ship that was powered by unskilled mariners could certainly be regarded as unseaworthy.

The office of Islamic *muhtasib* (market superintendent) supervised, among other duties, the construction of ships at the shipyard and carriage by sea. The *muhtasib* was helped by assistants called *'urafa' al-sina'a* (arsenals' inspectors), whose main task was to insure the shipwrights' observance of technical standards and prevent them from using inferior and

Anonymous. Turkish ship with passengers. Codex Cicogna. Credit: Cameraphoto Arte, Venice/Art Resource, NY.

inadequate raw materials. Exacting and thorough inspections were carried out to avoid human and financial losses. Whoever violated these regulations was punished. While the ship was still in the yard, a comprehensive technical inspection had to be carried out by the *muhtasib* (*see* Markets), the captain, and the ship's scribe. Islamic law entitled sailors and lessees to not honor a leasing contract if a technical defect was discovered in the ship. The working hours of carpenters, including shipwrights, began late in the morning and ended before evening. Thus the inspection of commercial ships took place between sunrise and sunset, but not in the evening and prior to the loading processes. The amount of cargo the ship could properly carry was determined by the *muhtasib*. When the cargo was stowed and placed appropriately and the ship was ready to depart, an official examination to prevent overloading was requested by the *muhtasib*, or his representative, and the captain. The *hisba* manuals plainly state that "a

ship can be freighted with cargo as long as the water-line (plimsoll) alongside the outer hull is visible." Islamic law requires that each ship be marked with a load line to indicate how deeply the ship could legally be submerged. The waterline mark along the outer hull could not lie more than a certain depth below the surface of the water. The provision against overloading was intended to prevent not only sinking but also the overexertion of the rowers.

Types, dimensions, and technical constructions of ships varied in accordance with their purposes and bodies of waters they plied. Nukhayli counts more than 150 nautical crafts, including river crafts, coasters, and oceangoing and seagoing vessels that differed in their structures. Recent underwater archaeological excavations off the Palestinian, Turkish, and French coasts have shed further light on the Islamic technology of shipbuilding from the seventh century CE onward. Material and written evidence show that the length-to-beam ratios of a typical size of commercial vessel were usually 3:1 or 4:1, with a shallow keel and rounded hull; the wide beam relative to the length aimed to provide maximum storage for cargo. Shipwrights in the Islamic Mediterranean employed the skeletal-building method in all stages of the hull's construction. All the frames were in place before the wales and upper side planks were added. At some point after side planking began, the open area between the bottom and sides was covered with an odd configuration of strakes, at least three of which did not run the full length of the hull. When planking was completed, they were caulked with a mixture of pitch or tar. After all the floor timbers were in place, the keelson was bolted between the frames and through the keel at irregular intervals with two-centimeter-diameter forelock bolts. Then stringers were added to the floor of the hold, on which a removable transverse ceiling was placed. Next came the side ceiling, clamps, and deck beams. The major difference in the construction techniques and methods between the Islamic Mediterranean and the eastern part of the empire is in reference to planking. The ship's planks in the Red Sea and Indian Ocean were sewn together with ropes, while in the Mediterranean, iron nails were used. The lateen sail was a distinctive feature of the rig of Islamic ships in the Mediterranean.

The materials needed for shipbuilding were found within the Islamic domain. For instance, Egyptian shipwrights used different types of timber—lebek, acacia, fig, palm, and lotus, which were abundantly found in Egypt—in their arsenals. Later. and due to deforestation processes, cedar, pine, and other timbers were imported from Palestine, Lebanon, Asia Minor, and Europe. Furthermore, a closer look at the arsenals' locations prove that beyond strategic considerations, they were situated near forests and areas rich in mining.

HASSAN KHALILEH

Further Reading

Baghdadı, 'Abd al-Latif (557–629/1162–1231). *Al-Ifada wa'l I'tibar*. Translated into English and edited by Kamal H. Zand et al. London: George Allen & Unwin, 1965.

Bass, George, and Frederic H. van Doornick. "An 11th Century Serçe Liman, Turkey." *The International Journal of Nautical Archaeology and Underwater Exploration* 7, no. 2 (1978): 119–132.

Christides, Vassilios. "Byzantine Dromon and Arab Shini: The Development of the Average Byzantine and Arab Warships and the Problem of the Number and Function of the Oarsmen." *Tropis* 3 (1995): 111–122.

———. "New Light on the Transmission of Chinese Naval Technology to the Mediterranean World: The Single Rudder." In *Intercultural Contacts in the Medieval Mediterranean*, edited by Benjamin Arbel, 64–70. London: Frank Cass, 1996.

Constable, Olivia R. *Trade and Traders in Muslim Spain: The Commercial Realignment of the Iberian Peninsula 900—1500*. Cambridge: Cambridge University Press, 1994.

Delgado, Jorge L. *El poder naval de Al-Andalus en la época del Califato Omeya*. Granada: Universidad de Granada, 1993.

Dickson, H.R.P. *The Arab of the Desert*. London, 1959.

Fahmy, Aly M. *Muslim Naval Organisation in the Eastern Mediterranean from the Seventh to the Tenth Century A.D.* Cairo: National Publication & Printing House, 1966.

Flecker, Michael. "A Ninth-Century A.D. Arab or Indian Shipwreck in Indonesia: First Evidence for Direct Trade with China." *World Archaeology* 3, no. 32 (2001): 335–354.

Goitein, Shelomo D. *A Mediterranean Society: The Jewish Communities of the Arab World as Portrayed in the Documents of the Cairo Geniza, Economic Foundations*. Berkeley: University of California Press, 1967.

Hocker, Frederick M. "Late Roman, Byzantine, and Islamic Galleys and Fleets." In *The Age of the Galley: Mediterranean Oared Vessels since pre-Classical Times*, edited by Robert Gardiner, 86–100. London: Naval Institute Press, 1995.

Hornell, James. "A Tentative Classification of Arab Sea Craft." *The Mariner's Mirror* 28, no. 1 (1942): 11–40.

Ibn 'Abdun, Muhammad Ibn Ahmad al-Tujibi (12th century CE). *Seville Musulmane au debut du XIIᵉ Siècle*. Traduit avec une introduction et des notes par: E. Lévi-Provençal. Paris, 1947.

Ibn Bassam al-Muhtasib, Muhammad Ibn Ahmad (d. 884/1479). *Nihayat al-Rutba fi Talab al-Hisba*. Baghdad: Matba'at al-Ma'arif, 1968.

Ibn al-Ukhuwwa, Muhammad Ibn Muhammad (648–729/1250–1329). *Ma'alim al-Qurba fi Ahkam al-Hisba*. Cairo: Al-Hay'a al-Misriyya al-'Amma lil-Kitab, 1976.

Joncheray, M.J.P. "Le navire de Bataiguire." *Archeologia* 85 (1975): 42–48.

Kahanov, Yaakov. "The Tantura B Shipwreck: Preliminary Hull Construction Report." In *Down the River to the Sea*, edited by Jerzy Litwin, 151–154. Gdansk: Polish Maritime Museum, 2000.

Kaplan, Marion. "The History and Construction of the Dhow." Available online at http://nabataea.net/ships.html, 2002.

Kindermann, H. "*Safina*." In *The Encyclopaedia of Islam*. Leiden: E. J. Brill, 1995, vol. 8, 808–809.

Kreutz, Barbara M. "Ships, Shipping and the Implications of Change in the Early Medieval Mediterranean." *Viator* 7 (1976): 79–109.

Lichtenstadter, Ilse. "Origin and Interpretation of Some Qur'anic Symbols." In *Studi Orientaliststici in Onore di Giorgio Levi Della Vida*. Roma: Instituto per l'Orient, 1956, vol. 2, 58–80.

Makrypoulias, Christos G. "Muslim Ships through Byzantine Eyes." In *Aspects of Arab Seafaring: An Attempt to fill in the Gaps on Maritime History*. Ed. Yacoub Y. al-Hijji & Vassilios Christides. Athens, 2002: 179–190.

Manguin, Pierre-Yves. "Late Mediaeval Shipbuilding in Indian Ocean: A Reappraisal." *Moyen Orient and Océan Indien* 2 (1985): 1–30.

Moreland, W.H. "The Ships of the Arabian Sea about A.D. 1500." *Journal of the Royal Asiatic Society of Great Britain and Ireland* (1939): 63–74 and 173–192.

Nicolle, David. "Shipping in Islamic Art: Seventh through Sixteenth Century A.D." *The American Neptune* 49 (1989): 168–197.

Nukhayli, Darwısh. *Al-Sufun al-Islamiyya 'ala Huruf al-Mu'jam.* Alexandria: Alexandria University Press, 1974.

Pryor, John H. "From Dromon to Galea: Mediterranean Bireme Galleys A.D. 500–1300." In *The Age of the Galley: Mediterranean Oared Vessels since pre-Classical Times,* edited by Robert Gardiner, 101–116. London: Naval Institute Press, 1995.

Rezq, 'Assem M. "The Craftsmen of Muslim Egypt and Their Social and Military Rank during the Medieval Period." *Islamic Archaeological Studies* 3 (1988): 3–31.

Saqati, Abu 'Abd Allah Muhammad Ibn Abu Muhammad. *Un manuel hispanique de Hisba (Adab al-Hisba).* Ed. G. S. Colin and E. Lévi-Provençal. Paris: Librairie E. Leroux, 1931.

Shihab, Hasan S. *Al-Marakib al-'Arabiyya, Tarikhuha wa-Anwa'uha.* Kuwait, 1987.

Steffy, J. Richard. "The Reconstruction of the 11th Century Serçe Liman Vessel: A Preliminary Report." *The International Journal of Nautical Archaeology and Underwater Exploration* 11, no. 1 (1982): 13–34.

Van Doornick, Frederick. "The Medieval Shipwreck at Serçe Limani: An Early 11th Century Fatimid-Byzantine Commercial Voyage." *Graeco-Arabica* 4 (1991): 45–52.

Wachsmann, Shelley and Yaakov Kahanov. "Shipwreck Fall: The 1995 INA/CMS Joint Expedition to Tantura Lagoon, Israel." *The INA Quarterly* 24, no. 1 (1997): 3–18.

Yajima, Hikoichi. *The Arab Dhow Trade in the Indian Ocean.* Tokyo: Institute for the Study of Languages and Cultures of Asia and Africa, 1976.

Zayyat, Habib. "Mu'jam al-Marakib wal-Sufun fi al-Islam." *Al-Mashriq* 43 (1949): 321–364.

SIBAWAYHI

Abu Bishr 'Amr ibn 'Uthman ibn Qanbar, known as Sibawayhi, is the founder of Arabic grammatical science. Of Persian origin, he attached himself in the middle of the second/eighth century to a number of early authorities on the Arabic language in Basra, notably al-Khalil ibn Ahmad and Yunus ibn Habib. The dates of his birth and death are not known: He died perhaps in his early forties in around AH 180/796 CE, before Yunus (d. 182/798) but after al-Khalil, who died between 160 and 175/776 and 791.

His untitled treatise on Arabic grammar, known only as *Kitab Sibawayhi (Sibawayhi's Book),* or simply "the Book", is the first systematic description of the language, and retains its unsurpassed authority to this day. It probably owes its survival to one of Sibawayhi's few students, al-Akhfash al-Awsat (d. between 210 and 221/825 and 835), who had his own copy of the work, which would become the basis of all subsequent versions, with one possible exception.

The *Kitab* falls into four sections, a group of seven introductory chapters setting out the main theoretical assumptions, then a long treatment of syntax (Chapters 8–284, completing the first volume as it is conventionally divided), with morphology occupying the bulk of volume two (Chapters 285–564), and concluding with seven chapters on phonetics (Chapter 565–571). The borderline between the last two is not as precise as it might be in modern linguistics and, in fact, many earlier chapters deal with what would now be called morphophonology.

The arrangement of the material, proceeding from syntax to phonology, is itself a statement of position, namely that language must first be described in its surface realization, as connected speech, *kalam,* before it can be further decomposed into its constituents in successively smaller units. Speech is therefore analyzed pragmatically as a social activity (the word *nahw,* "way [of speaking]", used frequently in the *Kitab,* later became the name of the science of grammar, but is ultimately only a synonym of *Sunna,* or "the [Islamic] way of behaving"). Hence the criteria for correctness are ethical in origin: an utterance is acceptable when it is both well-formed (*hasan,* lit. "morally good") and successfully conveys the intended meaning (*mustaqim,* lit. "morally right"). Only three parts of speech are formally identified: noun *ism,* verb *fi'l,* and meaningful particle *harf ja'a li-ma'na,* and their syntactical relationship is referred to as "operation" *('amal),* in binary units consisting (mostly) of an active element (*'amil,* "operator") that assigns case to a passive element (*ma'mul fihi,* "operated on"). Sibawayhi names more than seventy such speech operations, and the concept is entirely unconnected with the Western notion of "governing." His morphological chapters cover the range of word patterns so thoroughly that scarcely anything has had to be added since, and his treatment of the articulation of Arabic sounds remains an invaluable source for the pronunciation of early Arabic.

Although Sibawayhi's debt to his masters is clear on almost every page, his originality is beyond question; as the first of its kind the *Kitab* is literally unprecedented, and we depend on it for our knowledge of grammar before Sibawayhi. After his death it took a couple of generations for the importance of the work to be recognized, but then its descriptive contents were quickly adapted for the prescriptive grammars needed to sustain Arab culture in its Islamic manifestation.

MICHAEL G. CARTER

See also Grammar and Grammarians

Primary Sources

Le livre de Sibawaihi. 2 vols. Ed. Hartwig Derenbourg. Paris: Imprimerie Nationale, 1881–1889. Reprint, Hildesheim: Georg Olms, 1970.

Kitab Sibawayhi. 2 vols. Cairo: Bulaq Press, 1898–1900. Reprint, Baghdad: Muthanna, 1965.

Kitab Sibawayhi. 5 vols. Ed. 'Abd al-Salam Muhammad Harun. Cairo: Dar al-Qalam et al., 1968–1977; 2d ed, 1977; 3rd ed, 1983.

Further Reading

al-Bakka, M.K. *Manhaj Kitab Sibawayhi fi l-taqwim al-nahwi.* Baghdad: Dar al-Shu'un al-Thaqafiyya al-'Amma, 1989.

Bernards, M. *Changing Traditions. Al-Mubarrad's Refutation of Sibawayhi and the Subsequent Reception of the Kitab.* Leiden, New York, and Köln: Brill, 1997.

Bohas, G., J.-P., Guillaume, and D.E. Kouloughli. *The Arabic Linguistic Tradition.* London and New York: Routledge, 1990.

Carter, M.G. "Sibawayhi." In *Encyclopaedia of Islam.* new ed, edited by H.A.R. Gibb et al., vol. 9, 524a–531a. Leiden: Brill, 1960.

———. "Patterns of Reasoning: Sibawayhi's Treatment of the *hal.*" In *Proceedings of the 20th Congress of the Union of European Arabists and Islamicists, Part One, Linguistics, Literature, History,* edited by K. Devenyi. Budapest, 2002, [*The Arabist,* vols. 24–25], 3–15.

Humbert, G. *Les voies de transmission du Kitab de Sibawayhi.* Leiden, New York, and Köln: Brill, 1995.

Mosel, U. *Die syntaktische Terminologie bei Sibawaih.* Diss. Munich, 1975.

al-Nassir, A.A. *Sibawayh the Phonologist,* London and New York: Kegan Paul International, 1993.

Reuschel, W. *Al-Khalil ibn Ahmad, der Lehrer Sibawaihs, als Grammatiker.* Berlin: Akademie-Verlag, 1959.

Semaan, K.I. *Linguistics in the Middle Ages, Phonetic Studies in Early Islam* Leiden: Brill, 1968.

Sezgin, F.M. *Geschichte des Arabischen Schrifttums.* Leiden, 1984, vol. 9, 51–63, 241–242.

Talmon, R. *Eighth-Century Iraqi Grammar. A Critical Exploration of Pre-Khalilian Arabic Linguistics.* Winona Lake, 2003.

Troupeau, G. *Lexique-Index du Kitab de Sibawayhi.* Paris: Klincksieck, 1976.

'Udayma, M. 'A. *Faharis Kitab Sibawayhi wa-dirasa lahu.* Cairo: Matba'at al-Sa'ada, 1975.

Versteegh, Kees C. H. M. *The Arabic Linguistic Tradition, Landmarks in Linguistic Thought III.* London and New York: Routledge, 1997.

Web Editions

Complete text on www.alwaraq.com.

Partial Editions

Matveev, A., M. G. Carter, and L. Edzard (Eds). Chapters 1–7 and 565–571, Oslo, 1999–2002, available online at www.hf.uio.no/east/sibawayhi/HomePage.

Translation

Carter, M.G. *Sibawayhi.* Delhi: Oxford University Press, 2004.

Jahn, Gustav. *Sibawaihi's Buch über die Grammatik, übersetzt und erklärt.* Berlin: Reuther und Reichard, 1895–1900. Reprint, Hildesheim: Georg Olms, 1969.

SIBT IBN AL-JAWZI, SHAMS AL-DIN ABU'L-MUZAFFAR YUSUF B. QIZUGHLI

Sibt was a celebrated preacher and voluminous historian. He was born in Baghdad in AH 581 or 582/1185 or 1186 CE. His Turkish father was a freedman of 'Awn al-Din Ibn Hubayra, the long-serving vizier of the 'Abbasid caliphs al-Muqtafi and al-Mustanjid. His mother was a daughter of the famous Iraqi preacher and writer Ibn al-Jawzi, for whom Sibt (grandson) was named Sibt Ibn al-Jawzi (grandson of Ibn al-Jawzi).

Sibt is predominantly associated with Ayyubid Damascus, where he moved from Baghdad in AH 600/1203 CE, although circumstances sometimes forced him to leave Damascus for lengthy periods. In AH 603/1206 CE, he moved to Aleppo, apparently drawn by the patronage that the Ayyubid ruler al-Malik al-Zahir extended to religious and literary scholars. Sibt remained in Aleppo for two years, breaking his stay in AH 604/1208 CE to make his first pilgrimage to Mecca via Mosul and Baghdad.

Two years after his return to Damascus, Sibt began his lengthy and significant association with al-Malik al-Mu'azzam 'Isa, then nominal ruler of the city for his father, al-Malik al-'Adil. Sibt's first meeting with al-Mu'azzam took place in the wake of his celebrated *da'wa li'l-jihad* (call to holy war), which he delivered in the Umayyad Mosque in Damascus on AH Rabi' II 5, 607/September 26, 1210 CE. Producing a quantity of horses' hobbles made from human hair, he roused a number of the men present to cut their own hair, in a conventional gesture of ardent religious commitment. A military force was raised, with Sibt in the vanguard. After being met by al-Mu'azzam outside Nabulus in Palestine, the Muslims went on to the coast, where they pillaged some Frankish villages. Sibt remained in al-Mu'azzam's retinue for the next four years, accompanying him to Egypt in AH 609/1212 CE.

Sibt was not uncritical of his patron. In AH 615/1218 CE, after al-Mu'azzam had become ruler of Damascus, Central Syria, Transjordan, and Palestine on the death of al-'Adil, Sibt had occasion to rebuke al-Mu'azzam for his treatment of another scholar and friend of Sibt's. Nevertheless, Sibt left the Hanbali *madhhab* (Islamic legal school) for the Hanafi *madhhab*, which was the *madhhab* that al-Mu'azzam himself promoted. In AH 623/1226 CE, a year before his death, al-Mu'azzam appointed Sibt *mudarris* (professor) in the (Hanafi) Madrasa Shibliyya al-Barraniyya in Damascus.

Al-Mu'azzam was not the only Ayyubid ruler whose confidence Sibt gained. In AH 612/1215 CE, he went to Akhlat in Armenia, at the request of al-Mu'azzam's brother al-Malik al-Ashraf, who deputized for their father east of the Euphrates River. Al-Ashraf wanted Sibt to look at a work written by the 'Abbasid caliph, al-Nasir. He then sent Sibt on a mission to al-Zahir in Aleppo. In AH 614–615/1217–1218 CE, he traveled extensively on behalf of al-Ashraf, who had tasked him with the supervision of the *khanqah*s (Sufi hospices) in his territory.

Sibt did not escape becoming embroiled in the disputes and rivalries that beset the Ayyubids after the death of Saladin. In AH 626/1229 CE, the new ruler of Damascus, al-Mu'azzam's son al-Malik al-Nasir Da'ud, asked Sibt to preach in the Umayyad Mosque against al-Malik al-Kamil, the ruler of Egypt, for treatising with the Holy Roman Emperor, Frederick II, and against al-Ashraf for acquiescing in al-Kamil's policy. Sibt delivered a stirring oration and issued a *fatwa* (religious ordinance) commanding the Damascenes to take up arms against the two Ayyubids. As a result, when al-Ashraf laid siege to Damascus and ousted al-Nasir from the city, Sibt followed al-Nasir to al-Karak, which the defeated prince had been given under the terms of surrender. He remained there until AH 633/1235 CE, when relations with al-Ashraf improved, and he was able to return to Damascus.

More trouble befell Sibt after the death of al-Ashraf in AH 635/1237 CE, and the accession to rule in Damascus of his immediate successor, al-Malik al-Salih Isma'il. The latter saw Sibt as belonging to the Egyptian camp, which was opposed to Damascus. For al-Salih Isma'il believed (erroneously) that, while in al-Karak, Sibt had persuaded al-Nasir to release from custody al-Kamil's son al-Malik al-Salih Ayyub. Al-Salih Isma'il was encouraged in this belief by his vizier, al-Samiri. Sibt left Damascus, apparently returning to al-Karak, where he remained for the next four years, with periods in Jerusalem and Nabulus.

In AH 639/1241 CE, he moved to Egypt, where he enjoyed good relations with the ruler al-Salih Ayyub, whom he had met in Jerusalem after al-Salih Ayyub's release from prison in al-Karak. Sibt returned to Damascus two years later, and resided in his adopted city until his death in AH 654/1256 CE.

While Sibt was soundly schooled in *hadith* (Prophetic Tradition), Qur'anic reading, and Arabic grammar, he was particularly esteemed as a *wa'iz* (preacher), and it is here that his career sheds revealing light on the intellectual procedures of the age, as well as on the man himself. A preacher would hold a *majlis al-wa'z* (preaching session) in the towns through which he passed, attracting and keeping audiences by means of a variety of skills: familiarity with the stories of ascetics and pietists; declamatory skill; ability to speak in *saj'* (rhymed prose); knowledge of *hadith*; knowledge of metonymy; repartee; and above all, a stirring voice. By all accounts, Sibt was well versed in each of these. The Damascenes would spend Friday night in the mosque, so that they might be assured of a place at the discourse, which Sibt used to deliver a session early on Saturday morning. His audiences would frequently be moved to tears by his words.

Sibt's most important written work is the *Mir'at al-zaman fi ta'rikh al-a'yan (The Mirror of Time in the Matter of the History of Notables)*. It is a lengthy, universal chronicle in eight parts. Where possible, the account of the events of each year concludes with the obituaries of people who died in that year. In this, Sibt followed the format of a chronicle written by his famous grandfather. The *Mir'at* is most valuable for its coverage of the events of the tenth and eleventh centuries, for which the sources include works that have been lost; and for the period of Sibt's own lifetime, where it offers an eyewitness view, especially of events in Ayyubid Syria, in which the author was often personally involved. The *Mir'at* was much drawn on as a source for subsequent histories.

The text of the *Mir'at* has survived in two ways: in manuscripts containing or based on parts of Sibt's own working draft; and in the manuscript of an abridgement of the work made by a Syrian historian of the next generation, al-Yunini. Printed editions have been published of that part of the *Mir'at* covering the years AH 448–480/1056–1087 CE, and of the period between AH 495/1101 CE and Sibt's death. Part of the latter has been translated into French.

DAVID MORRAY

See also Ayyubids; Damascus; Historical Writing; Madrasa

Primary Sources

Sibt Ibn al-Jawzi. *Mir'at al-zaman fi ta'rikh al-a'yan*.
1. Edited and and translated in *Recueil des historiens des croisades. Historiens orientaux*. Vol. 3. Paris: 1884. Extracts from years AH 492–532/1099–1137 CE.
2. Hyderabad, 1952. 2 vols. Covers years AH 495–654/1101–1256 CE.
3. Ali Sevim (Ed). Ankara, 1968. Covers years AH 448–480/1056–1087 CE.

Further Reading

Ihsan 'Abbas. Introduction to vol. 1 of *Mir'at al-zaman fi ta'rikh al-a'yan*, by Sibt Ibn al-Jawzi. Beirut, 1985.
Humphreys, R. Stephen. *From Saladin to the Mongols: the Ayyubids of Damascus, 1193–1260*. Albany: State University of New York Press, 1977.

SICILY

The history of Muslim Sicily begins at the court of
Ziyadatallah in 827, the autonomous Aghlabid ruler
of Ifriqiyya. Faced with a restless and rebellion-prone
army, opposition from Kharijite Berber tribes, a disen-
franchised urban poor, and a hostile and critical ulema,
Ziyadatallah found a solution to his problems, in the
form of an external enemy. Using information from a
renegade Sicilian Byzantine general (Euphemius)
concerning Muslim soldiers being illegally held captive
in Sicily, and galvanized by his chief judge, Asad Ibn
al-Furat, eminent jurist and politically astute advisor,
Ziyadatallah invaded Sicily with all the legal justification and military pageantry of jihad he could muster.

The Muslim era of Sicilian history, until the
Norman Conquest was completed in 1091, was dominated by jihad. The first hundred years witnessed
offensive jihad against the Byzantine forces supported
by the emperors in Constantinople and the local
Christian population. The latter years were marked
by a defensive jihad as the Sicilian Muslims resisted
the armies of the North. Jihad also had a major
impact on the economy. The massive flow of booty,
gold, silver, slaves, horses, and land made Muslim
Sicily a powerful and wealthy state where trade and
local industries, shipbuilding, arms manufacturing,
textiles, and agriculture flourished. Politically, jihad
was the dominant issue in acquiring, maintaining, or
losing the power and legitimacy to rule.

The dynastic history of Muslim Sicily may be
divided into the Aghlabid, Fatimid, and Kalbid
periods. The Aghlabid period (827–909) is characterized by the long and difficult process of offensive
jihad and close ties and dependence on the rulers of
Ifriqiyya for manpower, arms, and logistic support.
The invading army, under the command of Asad Ibn
al-Furat, arrived in Mazara in 827 and captured
Palermo in 831. The following decades were spent
consolidating control over the central and southeast
of the island where the Byzantines relocated their
headquarters in Enna and Syracuse. The Northeast
would not fall into Muslim control until after the
fall of the Aghlabids. The Fatimid period of Sicily
(909–944) saw no discernible change in the thrust,
direction, and policies of the jihad movement. The
new Shi'i rulers of Ifriqiyya expended vast resources
on Sicily as a base to expand their naval and mercantile powers in the Mediterranean. They appointed
trusted servants to rule the island, especially among
the Kutama Berbers, and made efforts to spread the
doctrines of their mission (al-da'wa) to a predominantly Maliki Sunni Sicilian populace. A violent four-
year insurrection (937–941) launched by the Sicilian
Muslims against their Fatimid governor, Salim Ibn
Rashid, and his Ifriqiyyan-appointed backup, Khalil

Ibn Ishaq, coincided with Fatimid efforts to conquer
Egypt in their quest for the grand prize of Baghdad.
Gradually, the island was granted greater autonomy
in the appointment of al-Hasan ibn 'Ali al-Kalbi,
whose father died during the uprisings in Agrigento
in 938. When al-Hasan was recalled to al-Mahdiyya
in 953, he left the duties of ruling Sicily to his
son Ahmad, creating a dynastic process that would
remain intact throughout the rest of the century.

The Kalbid period of Sicily (944–1044) enjoyed
a period of political stability, economic expansion,
cultural florescence (architecture, poetry, and scholarship), and military security. The Byzantines were held
in check and the last Christian strongholds in the
northeast of the island, not to mention fortress
towns in Calabria and Apulia in southern Italy, fell
under Muslim control. Kalbid success reached a high
point in the rule of Abu al-Futuh Yusuf (989–998).
But a stroke left him partially paralyzed in 998, and
the rule of his son and successor, Ja'far, was
challenged by Yusuf's second son, 'Ali, with the support of Kutama Berber factions and the slave corps.
Ja'far crushed the revolt, executed 'Ali and the slaves,
and expelled the Berbers from the island. As a precaution against further disturbances, Ja'far rebuilt his
military forces conscripting only Sicilian troops.
Ja'far's harsh policies, his illegal taxation on Muslim
land and produce, and his mistreatment of members
of his own family—princes themselves who were
supported by entourages of wealthy and influential
clients—eroded his base of support in Palermo. The
Sicilians deposed him and would have executed him
had it not been for the intercession of Yusuf.

A third son, Ahmad al-Akhal, pitted the Sicilians
against each other, reopening festering wounds between the Arabs of Palermo and the Berbers of Agrigento on the one hand, and the old-guard "Sicilian"
landed gentry against the more recent generations
of "North African" immigrants on the other. This
wrought devastating results, drawing energy and
resources away from the jihad and tearing the threads
of unity that held the Muslim Sicilians together. The
political fragmentation of the island paved the way
for the Norman invasion. Despite attempts by the
Zirid Court in Ifriqiyya to rescue Muslim Sicily
from the clutches of the Christian Reconquest, the
enmity among the island's petty warlords was too
strong. Abu al-Futuh Yusuf's fourth son, Hasan
al-Samsan, was deposed in 1044, and in 1055, Ibn
al-Thumna, warlord of Syracuse and Noto, offered
the Normans a deal to deliver the island to them in
exchange for their assistance in avenging his enemies.
This final act of treason, reminiscent of the Byzantine
renegade Euphemius two centuries earlier, who
opened the way for the Muslim entry into Sicily,

paved the way for the Normans to take their turn as Sicily's new rulers.

The intellectual and cultural history of Islamic Sicily developed along the lines of those in Ifriqiyya and al-Qayrawan. Sicilian religious life was predominantly of the Sunni-Maliki sect, and its secular culture imitated the Arabo-Islamic mainstream, sharing features with both North African and Andalusian cultures. An "indigenous" Sicilian Islamic specificity came into its own and flourished at the Kalbid court in the middle of the tenth century. The academic journey *(al-rihla≈)* played a pivotal role in Sicilian Muslim scholarship and, along with commerce, war, and pilgrimage to Mecca, was instrumental in the import and export of knowledge and cultural influences to and from the island. The later Norman synthesis, the historical appellation for the great cultural eclecticism of the courts from Roger II to Frederick II in the eleventh and twelfth centuries, sprouted in good part from the seeds of Arabo-Islamic institutions that were sown in this period.

The education of Sicilian Muslims was based upon a tripartite of Arabic language, religion and ethics, and Islamic law. Sicily resembled Ifriqiyya in the composition and diversity of its religious and scholarly life. As military society evolved into a more civilian society, Sicily's institutions developed in new directions. It expanded beyond the fortress or fortified monastery to include private homes with extended mosque complexes for worship and education, pleasure palaces, and government complexes with adjoining shops and factories. Islamic legal studies, as elsewhere, evolved into a complex of subjects including methodological literature and speculative theology that assumed a degree of rationalist thinking. The study and practice of piety and asceticism gave way to a more sophisticated Sufism as a field of inquiry.

Language studies branched out into its many subsets, and poetry as entertainment became the subject of linguistic, historical, and aesthetic investigation. In the tenth and eleventh centuries, Arabic language and linguistic studies (Ibn al-Birr, Ibn Makki, Ibn al-Qattafi), as well as poetry and *belles-lettres,* competed with the traditional Qur'anic disciplines. This cultural florescence owes a great deal to the Fatimids who, through political acumen, tolerance, farsightedness, and patronage of learning, allowed the natural processes of Sicilian Islam to follow natural courses.

WILLIAM GRANARA

Further Reading

'Abbas, Ihsan. *al-'Arab fi Siqilliya.* Cairo: Dar al-M'arif, 1959.

Ahmad, Aziz. A History of Islamic Sicily. Edinburgh: University Press, 1975.

Amari, Michele. *Biblioteca arabo-sicula*. Lipsia: Brockhaus, 1857.

———. *Storia dei Musulmani di Sicilia*. 2d ed. Ed. C. A. Nallino. Catania: Romeo Prampolini, 1933.

Granara, William. "Islamic Education and the Transmission of Knowledge in Medieval Sicily." In *Law and Education in Medieval Islam: Studies in Honor of George Makdisi*. London: E. J. W. Gibb Memorial Trust, 2004, 150–173.

Rizzitano, Umberto. *Storia e Cultura nella Sicilia Saracena*. Palermo: S. F. Flaccovio, 1975.

Talbi, Mohamed. *L'Emirat Aghlabide*. Paris: Librairie d'Amerique et d''orient Adrien-Maisonneuve, 1966.

SILK ROADS

Silk Roads was a popular name for the premodern system of trade routes by which goods, ideas, and people were exchanged between major regions of Eurasia, mainly between China, Central Asia, the Middle East, and Europe. The name can denote both land and sea routes, but this survey concentrates on the land routes (for sea routes, see Trade, Indian Ocean).

More specifically, the term *Silk Roads* denotes the roads leading from North China via the Gansu corridor westward. In the Gansu corridor the road is divided in two—the northern route, passing north of the Tianshan to Semirechye, and the southern route, leading from south of the Tianshan via the Tarim basin, again splitting into two routes passing north or south of the Taklamakan Desert. The northernmost route went either west to Khwarazm and Eastern Europe, or southwest via Transoxiana to Khurasan and Iran. Of the southern routes, one led via Farghana to Transoxiana and Iran, and the other through Balkh to India or Iran. From Iran the Silk Roads continued either to Iraq and the Middle East or to the Black Sea, Anatolia, and Western Europe.

Silk was a major good carried along these roads, due to its high value and small weight, but many other goods also traveled along the way. These included other kinds of cloth and clothing; precious metals and stones; furs, hides, and animals; porcelain; glass vessels; foods of various kinds; spices; exotica; and slaves. While the lucrative items often traveled the whole route, an important segment of the trade was in necessities, usually carried for shorter distances, often along north–south routes between nomads and sedentaries. This was made possible as the commerce was normally one of multiple resales, and up to the Mongol period individuals rarely traversed the whole route. A major part in the trade was therefore taken by people living not in its ends (China, Europe, the Middle East) but along the way, mainly in Central Asia. With the gradual political and religious expansion of Islam into Central Asia, Muslim merchants became major actors in the Silk Roads trade, supplanting the Soghdians, Jews, and Uighurs who were active in the early centuries of Islam. The profit was lucrative enough to bring prosperity to the medieval cities of Central Asia and to cause numerous wars for control of the region.

Despite the importance of the Silk Roads exchange to the history of the civilizations bordering it and to world history in general, we know little about the actual commerce, as both literary and archaeological sources are scanty. Yet camels were the main vehicles of the merchant caravans, who traveled at a pace of 12–30 kilometers per day, staying the night in the caravanserais, which supplied lodging, food, and a place for negotiations. The building and maintenance of the routes and the caravanserais was often the work of individuals, but sympathetic governments who helped to secure the roads did much to enhance the trade. While barter was not unknown, most of the trade was monitarized, and credit letters and cheques were highly developed, at least from the tenth century. Most traders worked as individuals but enjoyed connections with their coreligions or coethnics along the roads. Some used different kinds of partnership to secure capital and minimize the risk to their investments.

Chronological Survey

The Silk Roads had been active long before Islam appeared in the Middle East. The rise of Islam coincided with one of the flourishing periods of the Silk Roads, initiated by the rise of the Turkic empire (sixth to eighth centuries), and accelerated with the consolidation in China of the Tang dynasty (618–906), known for its cosmopolitanism. Tang China, whose elite was enthusiastic for Iranian and Central Asian foodstuff, clothing, furniture, and entertainment, maintained close connections with the Sasanid empire. Indeed, the last Sasanid rulers tried to find refuge there when the Arabs conquered Iran in the mid-seventh century. In the seventh to mid-eighth centuries, Tang China also controlled important segments of the Silk Road, mainly the Tarim basin and Semirechye, and extended certain sovereignty even to Transoxiana, mainly on the expense of the Western Turks. Yet most of the commercial relations by the rise of Islam were conducted by the Soghdians, an Iranian people originating in Soghd (Transoxiana), who at least from the fourth century AD built trade diasporas along the roads: in Semirechye, the different oasis of the Tarim basin, in China proper, and even in North India.

Islamic expansion into the Silk Roads began with the campaigns of Qutayba b. Muslim, the Umayyad governor of Khurasan (705–715), who conquered Transoxiana and Farghana with their commercial centers. It is uncertain whether Qutayba tried (but failed) to reach Kashgar, one of Tang's westernmost strongholds and a major station on the Silk Roads, but apparently he initiated the sending of embassies to China, which continued throughout the Umayyad period. Though probably not initiated by the caliphs themselves, these embassies had both commercial and diplomatic functions. The mid-eighth century saw the one military clash between China and Islam. The battle of Talas (near modern-day Awlia-Ata, in Kazakhstan) in 751, a skirmish initiated by local interests of the governors of the newly established 'Abbasid empire and of Tang China, became in retrospect a turning point that determined the future orientation of Central Asia as part of the Muslim and not of the Chinese world. Whether paper arrived to Central Asia earlier with Buddhist missionaries, or only with the paper makers the Muslims took captives in Talas, certainly the battle was influential in initiating a paper industry in Samarqand. The diffusion of this Chinese technology contributed significantly to the expansion of culture and knowledge in the Muslim world and, since it rendered bookkeeping much easier, it also promoted all branches of trade and banking.

The establishment of the 'Abbasid dynasty (750–1258), whose center was in Iraq (as opposed to Umayyad Syria), combined with a growing demand for luxuries in Baghdad and Samarra, enhanced the importance of the eastern trade in the Muslim empire, though much of it was conducted by sea. The eighth and ninth centuries were also the time of the mysterious Rāhdāniya, Jewish merchants who allegedly traveled along the whole Silk Routes from Europe to China but specialized in connecting Europe and the Near East. Another profitable channel of this age was the commerce via Khwarazm with the Rus and Khazars in Eastern Europe, where Muslim silver *dirhams* were traded for northern furs, foods, and slaves. The demand for (mostly Turkic) slaves, who from the ninth century onward played an ever-growing role in Muslim armies, enhanced the land route traffic again. Its height was under the Samanids (888–999), who, from their capital in Bukhara, conducted trade networks that reached both China and Scandinavia. The Samanids closely controlled the extremely profitable slave markets, licensed slave traders, and levied dues on all sales. Muslim geographical works describe the fruitful commerce with Baghdad, the Turks north of the Jaxartes, and Eastern Europe via Khwarazm. Trade further East seemed to have been still conducted mainly by Soghdians or Uighurs (Turks who after 840 migrated from Mongolia to Gansu and the

Caravan crossing the Silk Road. Detail of the map of Asia, from the Catalan Atlas. Spain, Majorca. Fourteenth century CE. Photo: Dietmar Katz. Credit: Bildarchiv Preussischer Kulturbesitz/Art Resource, NY. Kunstbibliothek, Staatliche Museen zu Berlin, Berlin, Germany.

Tarim basin), though there is evidence of several embassies from the fringes of China that reached the Samanid court. Samanid military, economic, and cultural prestige, combined with their missionary efforts, also resulted in the expansion of Islam eastward into the Silk Roads, and in the mass conversion of whole Turkic tribes, later known as the Qarakhanids and the Seljuks.

The fall of the Samanids, and the division of their territory between the Qarakhanids and Ghaznavids, is usually considered the beginning of a decline in the Silk Roads trade, which continued until the rise of the Mongols. Yet cross-cultural contacts continued during this period, and with quite a significant scope, though the political fragmentation and the nature of the sources make it harder to follow them closely. The Qarakhanids (ca. 992–1213), who now ruled over significant parts of the trade routes (from Transoxiana to the Tarim Basin), maintained commercial and diplomatic relations with the contemporary Sinitic states, which rose after the fall of the Tang, especially with

the Northern Song dynasty (960–1127), to which they sent a first commercial mission already in 1008, and with the Khitan Liao dynasty (907–1125), with whom in the early eleventh century they even concluded matrimonial relations (unlike the Ghaznavids, who refused a similar offer of the Liao). Khotan, a city on the southern Silk Road in the Qarakhanid realm, also took an important part in the trade with the Tangut Xi Xia dynasty (1038–1227), who took over the Gansu corridor. It was in this period that Muslim merchants replaced the Soghdians as the dominant Silk Road traders. Under the rule of the non-Muslim Qara Khitai (1124–1218), fugitives from the Liao dynasty who took over Central Asia and became the Qarakhanids' and Uighurs' overlords, the commercial relations with the Xi Xia improved, and certain connections existed also with the more eastern states in China, among which at least the Southern Song dynasty (1127–1279) also had maritime connection with the Middle East. Central Asian Muslim traders also had contacts with Genghis Khan's forefathers in

Mongolia, and many gained considerable wealth from the long-range trade.

The rise of the Mongol empire in the early thirteenth century begins the most flourishing and best-documented period in the history of the Silk Roads. The Mongols united the whole Silk Roads under their rule and protected them, but their contribution to its prosperity went much further. As shown by Thomas Allsen, the process of state formation among the nomads in itself stimulates trade through an increased demand for luxuries, especially fine cloth, needed to assert the new empire's authority. Genghis Khan was certainly aware of the benefits of commerce (which initiated his invasion into the Muslim world), and Muslim merchants were among his earliest supporters. Moreover, after the early conquests, Mongol elites, the main benefactors of the conquests' booty, became extremely wealthy. They provided both enthusiastic consumers for the best products of the sedentary world and major investors, who recycled their wealth by entrusting it as capital in the hands of their mostly Muslim commercial agents (ortogh). The establishment of a Mongol capital, Qara Qorum, also promoted trade as the resources of Mongolia could hardly support such a big city (in Mongolian terms). It also led to the growing importance of the northern route of the Silk Roads, now shifted to include Qara Qorum. Even after the dissolution of the empire into four khanates in 1260, Mongol governments continued to promote both local and international trade, which provided taxes, markets, profits, and prestige. The khanates competed for commerce specialists, provided infrastructure for transcontinental travel, sometimes even by building new cities, and were actively involved in the manipulation of bullion flow. Yet traders were only part of the lively traffic along the Silk Roads in Mongol times. The formation of the empire, its continued expansion, and the establishment of its administration required a huge mobilization of soldiers and specialists throughout the empire. Mongol policy of ruling through strangers (for example, bringing Muslims to China and Chinese to Iran), originating in Mongol numerical inferiority and in their fear of potential local resistance, also promoted mobilization and cross-cultural exchanges. To secure the loyalty of these foreign strata, the Mongols aspired to give them "a taste of home," and therefore brought foreign food, medicine, and entertainment into different parts of their empire. Moreover, the Genghisids regarded human talent as a form of booty, and the different khanates competed for specialists and exchanged them to enhance their kingly reputations. The wide-range mobilization and the expanding trade led to frequent and continuous movement of people, goods, ideas, plants, and viruses throughout Eurasia. This in turn not only encouraged integration but also created means that facilitated further contacts, such as maps, multilingual dictionaries, and travel literature, and helped the diffusion of information and technologies, such as gunpowder and alcohol distilling. In the Muslim world the fruitful exchange of commodities, scientific knowledge, and artistic techniques, mainly between Iran and China, was widely felt. Mongol policies led to a considerable infiltration of Muslims into China, creating a firm basis for the modern Chinese Muslim community. Moreover, the Islamization of the Mongols in Iran, South Russia, and Central Asia brought about a massive expansion of Islam and made it by far the dominant religion along the Silk Roads.

With the collapse of the Mongol khanates from the mid-fourteenth century, the Silk Roads never regained their former importance. Indeed, they strived again under Tamerlane (r. 1370–1405), who from his base in Transoxiana tried to revive the Mongol empire and made concerted efforts to shift the trade routes into his realm (mainly on the expense of the more northern routes passing through the Golden Horde). Spanish, Ottoman, Mamluk, and Chinese ambassadors reached Timur's Samarqand, and the gunpowder technology was brought back to the East from Europe and the Ottomans. Yet the new political boundaries of the fifteenth and sixteenth centuries, combined with the opening of a direct sea route to India and China by Western Europeans, the rise of Europe in general, and the waning of the nomads' power, initiated the decline of the Silk Roads. The land routes between China and the Middle East were marginalized, though new channels, mainly on the north-south axis connecting India, Central Asia, and Russia, as well as a fruitful regional trade, retained certain importance until the eighteenth century.

The Silk Roads were a major channel through which the medieval Muslim world enriched itself by purchasing Eurasian—but mostly East Asian—goods, knowledge, and technologies, most important among which were paper and gunpowder. They were also a major path for the expansion of Islam, which became the dominant religion along the Silk Roads.

MICHAL BIRAN

See also Bukhara; Camels; Cartography; Central Asia; China; Genghis Khan; Merchants, Christian; Merchants, Jewish; Merchants, Muslim; Mongols; Nomadism and Pastoralism; Road Networks; Samarqand; Slaves and Slave Trades, Eastern Islamic World; Spices; Tamerlane; Trade, African; Trade, Indian Ocean; Trade, Mediterranean; Transport; Transoxiana; Travel; Turkestan; Turks

Primary Sources

Anonymous. "Ḥudūd al-"ālam." Ed. M. Sitūdah. Tehran, 1340/1961; *The Regions of the World*. Translated and annotated by V. Minorsky. 2d. ed. London, 1970.

Gardīzī, Abū Saʻīd, ʻAbd al-Ḥayy. *Zayn al-akhbār*. Ed. ʻA. Ḥabībī. Tehran, 1347/1968.

Ibn Khurdādhbah. *Kitāb al-masālik wa'l- mamālik*. Ed. M. J. de Goeje. BGA, 6. Leiden, E. J. Brill, 1889.

Marwazī, Sharaf al-zamān. *Ṭabāʼiʻ al-Ḥayawān*. Edited and translated by V. Minorsky as *Sharaf al-Zamān Ṭāhir Marvazī on China, Turks and India*. London, 1942.

Al-Muqaddasī, Muammad b. Aḥmad. *Kitāb aḥsan al-taqāsīm fī maʻrifat al-aqālīm*. Ed. M.J. de Goeje. BGA, 3. Leiden: E. J. Brill, 1877. Transl. Basil A. Collins as *The Best Divisions for Knowledge of the Regions*. Reading, UK: Garnet Publishing Limited, 1994.

Rashīd al-Dīn, FaÃlallāh Abū al-Khayr. *Jamiʻuʼt-tawarikh [sic] Compendium of Chronicles*. Transl. W.M. Thackston. Cambridge, MA: 1998–1999. 3 vols.

Yāqūt al-Rūmī. *Muʻjam al-buldān*. 5 vols. Beirut, 1955–1958.

Yule, H. (Tr). *The Book of Ser Marco Polo*. 2 vols. London, 1903.

Yule, H. (Tr and comp). *Cathay and the Way Thither*. Rpt. Taibei, 1966. 2 vols.

Further Reading

Allsen, Thomas T. "Mongolian Princes and Their Merchant Partners, 1200–1260." *Asia Major* 3d series, 2 (1989): 83–127.

———. *Commodity and Exchange in the Mongol Empire*. Cambridge: Cambridge University Press, 1997.

———. "Ever Closer Encounters: The Appropriation of Culture and the Apportionment of Peoples in the Mongol Empire." *Journal of Early Modern History* 1 (1997): 2–23.

———. *Culture and Conquest in Mongol Eurasia*. Cambridge: Cambridge University Press, 2001.

Ashtor, Eliyahu. *A Social and Economic History of the Near East in the Middle Ages*. London: Collins, 1976.

Bentley, Jarry H. *Old World Encounters: Cross-Cultural Contacts and Exchanges in Pre-Modern Times*. Oxford: Oxford University Press, 1993.

Christian, David. *A History of Russia, Central Asia and Mongolia,. Vol. 1*. Oxford: Blackwell, 1998.

———."Silk Roads or Steppe Roads? The Silk Roads in World History." *Journal of World History* 11 (2000): 1–26.

De La Vaisserie, Éttiene. *Histoire des marchands sogdiens*. Paris: Collège de France, 2002.

Gunder Frank, Andre. "Central Asia's Continuing Role in the World Economy to 1800." *Toronto Studies in Central and Inner Asia* 3 (1998): 14–38.

Noonan, Thomas F. *The Islamic World, Russia and the Vikings 750–900: The Numismatic Evidence*. Aldershot, Hampshire: Ashgate, Variorum, 1998.

Richards, Donald S. (Ed). *Islam and the Trade of Asia*. Oxford: Bruno Cassirer Ltd., 1970.

Rossabi, Morris. "The Decline of the Central Asian Caravan Trade." In *Ecology and Empire*, edited by G. Seaman, 81–102. Los Angeles, 1989.

The Silk Road Foundation website: www.silk-road.com.

SINAN (1490–1588)

Sinan was the chief architect of the Ottoman court from 1538 until his death in 1588. He is known to have designed more than 450 buildings throughout the Ottoman empire, although the majority of buildings cluster around the imperial Ottoman capital of Constantinople (Istanbul).

Although other Ottoman architects are known by name, the number and quality of buildings attributed to Sinan make him preeminent not only among Ottoman architects but also a major figure in the history of world architecture. Sinan's significance as an architect was greatly enhanced by the fact that for most of his career he worked for the most famous Ottoman sultan, Sulayman the Magnificent (r. 1520–1566), whose career saw the expansion of the Ottoman empire throughout the Middle East and North Africa, and saw the Eastern Mediterranean becoming effectively a Turkish lake.

In view of Sinan's undoubted significance for the Turkish and Muslim culture, it is ironic that he was born in Salonika and brought up as a Greek Christian until the age of twenty-one, when he was recruited into the Janissary core. Nevertheless, it is clear that he embraced Islam wholeheartedly once he had entered Ottoman service. During these early years of service Sinan worked as a military engineer building and repairing bridges, forts, aqueducts, and cisterns. During the winter and when he was not on military campaigns, Sinan was involved in the construction of mosques, madrasas, and other religious buildings in the Ottoman capital. From the early 1530s, it is clear that Sinan had become an architect, and from 1538, the main architect of the Ottoman court. The list of buildings attributed to Sinan comes principally from three sixteenth-century works; *Tadhkirat al-bunyan* and *Tadhkirat al-abniya* by Mustafa Saʻi, and an anonymous work, *Tuhfat al-miʻmarin,* that may have been written by Sinan himself. It is likely that for some of the buildings in this list, Sinan supplied no more than drawings and written instructions and that he did not oversee the work himself. It is unlikely that he was directly involved in the construction of Sulayman's pilgrimage complex (1554–1555) in Damascus and the Melek Ahmad Pasha in Diyarbakir.

Sinan's first major work was the construction of a mosque and *turbe* (mausoleum) commemorating Sulayman's son Mehmed, who died in 1543. The most remarkable part of the complex was the mosque, which, though employing traditional Ottoman forms based on a square domed box and derived ultimately from Orthodox churches, was revolutionary in its construction. The most notable feature of the Shehzade mosque was that it was flanked by four

Sinan the Great (1489–1588). Exterior. 1550–1577. Credit: Vanni/Art Resource, NY: Suleymaniye Camii (Mosque), Istanbul, Turkey.

semidomes instead of the usual two seen in mosques, such as the Bayazid II mosque (1501–1505), also in Constantinople. The Shehzade Cami was not the first mosque to use four semidomes, as this formula had been used previously by the Fatih Pasha Mosque (1516–1520) in Diyarbakir. However, the Shehzade was a different order of scale and sophistication. In the first place, Sinan pierced the supporting walls with successive tiers of arched windows, compensating for this with thick internal and external buttresses. This created a large, light, interior space that marked a departure from the mysterious dark interiors of many earlier Ottoman mosques. The change in architecture was also apparent on the exterior where the roof has a pyrimidical appearance with a high central dome flanked by semidomes, which in their turn are supported by smaller semidomes, each one tier lower. The massing of the domes is complemented by the four corner towers or minarets, which enhance the upward thrust of the building and detract from the heaviness of the roof system. Other early works by Sinan were the Mirimah Sultan Mosque at Uskudar (1540–48) and another mosque dedicated to Mirimah

Sultan at Edirnekapi, also built during the 1540s. All three mosques share the same basic design principle of a central dome descending in curved surfaces (domes and semidomes) to near ground level, presenting a hierarchical order. Also, all three mosques have multiple fenestration set between tall relieving arches that admit plentiful light to the interior and on the exterior reduce the heavy appearance of the roofing system.

These three early mosques (the Shehzade, Edirnekapi, and Uskudar Mirimah Sultan mosques) may be seen as a preparation for Sinan's most famous building, the Suleymaniye, which was built between 1550 and 1567. The vast complex, built on a high hill overlooking the harbor, comprised more than fourteen different buildings arranged around the mosque, which still dominates the skyline of Istanbul. Sinan's first problem was to produce a design that overcame the sloping nature of the site without compromising the unity and order required in a complex of this size. The fact that Sinan was able to accomplish this is a testament not only to his architectural abilities but also to his skills as a civil engineer acquired during his earlier military career. The mosque that forms the centerpiece of the complex was built to rival the former cathedral of Hagia Sophia, which had served as the architectural nucleus of Constantinople/Istanbul for more than a thousand years. Sinan's mosque adopted the same principle of a large central dome flanked on two sides by a series of smaller (and lower domes), though semidomes are used on the north and south (qibla) axis. Although the span of the central dome is slightly less than on the Hagia Sophia (twenty-six meters instead of thirty-two meters), the internal area appears larger because of the size of the flanking domes, which produce a vast covered area only interrupted by the corner piers supporting the main dome.

While the Suleymaniye is probably Sinan's most famous building, his masterpiece is probably the Selimiye in Edirne, built between 1564 and 1575. Like the Shehzade and the Suleymaniye mosques, the design of the Selimiye was characterized by the desire to achieve the maximum interior space. With the Selimiye, Sinan adopted a novel approach to increasing the internal space by supporting the vast central dome (thirty-six meters) on an octagonal system of eight piers. Sinan had already experimented with hexagonal plans in buildings such as the Sinan Pasha mosque in Besiktash (1555), the Semiz Ali Pasha mosque at Basaeski (1561–1565), and the Sokollu Mehmet Pasha Mosque (1570–1571) at Kadirga in Istanbul. The main advantage of the octagonal plan was that it was possible to build a larger dome spreading the downward thrust on eight piers instead of four. The other advantage of this system was that the weight resting on the curtain walls could be reduced, allowing an even larger number of windows creating a vast area lit by natural light. One of the problems of this design was that it reduced the emphasis on the qibla axis. Sinan compensated for this by setting the mihrab within a deep recess. The exterior of the mosque is equally impressive, with its four slender minarets, which attain a height never surpassed in Ottoman architecture. Also notable is the polychrome stonework of the exterior (in particular, the projecting mihrab recess), which provides a change from the somber stonework of the Sulemaniye.

The Selimiye was Sinan's last major work, although he continued to build a number of mosques that are evidence of his continuing architectural creativity. Examples of Sinan's later mosques include the Sokullu Mehmet Pasha Mosque at Azakapi (1578) and the Mesih Mehmet Pasha (ca. 1580), both of which use the octagonal base first used in the Selimiye.

Although from the 1540s, Sinan's name is mostly associated with mosques, he is also known to have designed secular and functional buildings such as the aqueduct at Maghlova that, with its two-tier design and diamond-shaped piers, displays unusual elegance.

Sinan is buried in a small plot decorated with a small, domed monument near the Suleymaniye mosque in Istanbul.

ANDREW PETERSEN

Further Reading

Goodwin, G. *A History of Ottoman Architecture*. 1971.
———. *Sinan. Ottoman Architecture and Its Values Today*. 1993.
Kuran, A. *Sinan, the Grand Old Master of Ottoman Architecture*. 1987.
O'Kane, B. "Sinan." In *Encyclopaedia of Islam*. New ed. 629–630.

SINDH

The word *Sindh* comes from the Sanskrit *sindhu*, with the meaning of "river, ocean." In the Middle Ages, Sindh was the southern part of the valley of the Indus River, which included the present-day province of Sindh, as well as the southern part of Punjab. Sindh was the first Indian territory to be conquered by a Muslim army led by Muhammad bin Qasim in 710–711.

When Muhammad bin Qasim invaded Sindh, he defeated Raja Dahir, son of the Hindu usurper Chach. According to architectural remains and Chinese pilgrims, southern Sindh was dominated by the Buddhists, while the north was under the control of the Shivaite school of the Pashupatas. The history of medieval Sindh is usually divided according to the different dynasties who ruled it. Up to the eleventh century, Sindh was ruled by governors sent by the 'Abbasids from Baghdad, and after 372/983, by Fatimid governors from Cairo who settled in the city of Multan.

In 1010, a Somra leader, apparently from the Rajput stock, put an end to the Arab rule. The Somra dynasty, which may have converted to Isma'ilism, was succeeded in 1352 by the Sammas, another Rajput clan. The resistance of both the Somras and the Sammas opposed to the sultans of Dihli, for instance, 'Ala' al-Din Khalji in 697/1297, was to be the core of Sindhi literature. The sultan Muhammad Shah Tughluq, while in pursuit of a rebel governor, arrived in Sindh in 1351, where he died. He was buried in the *darbar* of La'l Shahbaz Qalandar. His cousin and successor Firuz Shah Tughluq (d. 1388) invaded Thatta twice, in 1365 and 1367. In the fifteenth century, after Tamerlane's (*see* Tamerlane [Timur]) invasion of the Indian subcontinent, Sindh was ruled by Central Asian dynasties, the Arghuns and the Tarkhans. The sixteenth century saw many disturbances in Sindh. First is the sack of the wealthy city of Thatta by the Portuguese in 1555. Secondly, the Mughul emperor Akbar (1556–1605) sent his army to secure his control on Sindh, which was achieved in 1593. It is only in the seventeenth century that a new Sindhi dynasty seized power, the Kalhoras, replaced in 1783 by a Baluch dynasty, the Talpurs, which was to be defeated by the British in 1843.

There is no evidence the population of Sindh converted to Islam before the thirteenth century, when the Sufi *tariqa*s became well organized and efficient. More relevant is the question as to whether the people really converted to Islam when one knows that many Hindus were still affiliated to Muslim *pir* at the time of the British colonization. The main cleavage was more between Sharif (from external origin) and Desi (indigenous), than between Muslims and Hindus. The study of La'l Shahbaz Qalandar's pilgrimage, a thirteenth-century Sufi saint, in Sehwan Sharif, gives evidence that a consensus based on the *qalandar*'s charisma was reached among the different communities of Sindh, including the Hindus and the Muslims, as well as the Animists, and also the Sayyids and non-Sayyids. The Sufis, following the Ismailis, can be named as the great integrators who gave birth to Sindhi culture.

Persian was the language used by the chroniclers in Sindh. Vernacular literature appeared through the devotional poetry of Qazi Qazan (d. 1551). Even if the Ismailis claimed their own *pir* have composed their canticles *(ginan)* in the fourteenth century, Sindhi literature really began to flourish with Shah 'Abd al Karim (d. 1624), and his great-grandson Shah 'Abd al Latif (d. 1753). In his compiled work *Shah jo Risalo*, 'Abd al Latif uses Sindhi folk narratives for symbolizing the mystical quest. For him, there is no difference between the Hindu yogis and the Sufis, who are both seekers on the path of God. Makla, located in the neighborhood of Thatta, can be seen as a conservatory of the cross-cultural legacy of medieval Sindh. The mausoleums built by the different dynasties give a last evidence of the location of Sindh at a crossroads among Persia, Central Asia, and India.

MICHEL BOIVIN

Further Reading

Boivin, Michel. "Le pèlerinage de Sehwân Sharîf: territoires, protagonistes, rituels." In *Les pèlerinages dans le monde musulman*, edited by S. Chiffoleau and A. Madoeuf. Damas: IFPO, 2004.
Chachnama (ca. third/ninth century). Translated from Arabic into Persian in the year 613/1216 by 'Ali ibn Hamid al-Kufi. Ed. Umar ibn Muhammad Da'udpota. Delhi: Matba'at Latif, 1939.*Chachnama (the), an Ancient History of Sind, Giving the Hindu Period Down to the Arab Conquest*. Translated from the Persian by Mirza Kalichbeg Fredunbeg, Karachi: Commissioner's Press, 1900.
Cousens, Henry. *The Antiquities of Sind with Historical Outline*. Karachi: Department of Culture, Government of Sindh, 1998 [first ed., 1929].
Kervran, Monique. "Entre l'Inde et l'Asie Centrale: les mausolées islamiques du Sind et du sud Penjab." *Cahiers d'Asie Centrale* 1–2 (1996): 133–171.
Khan, Ansar Zahid. *History and Culture of Sind. Study of Socio-Economic Organization and Institutions during the 16th and 17th centuries*. Karachi: Royal Book Company, 1980.
MacLean, Derryl. *Religion and Society in Arab Sind*. Leiden: E. J. Brill, 1989.
Shah 'Abd al Latif. *Shah jo Risalo. Kalam Shah 'Abd al-Latif Bhita'i*. Ed. 'Allama Mustafa Qasmi. Shikarpur: Mehran Akademi, 1999 [first ed. 1951].

SINGING

The voice has always been central in Middle Eastern music. Very little is known about preIslamic singing or the songs of the common people, but early medieval Arabic texts describe the contemporary elite (court) tradition of vocal music in detail. Legal texts on the permissibility of singing and music and on the regulation of markets provide glimpses of the musical practices of the common people. (In Islamic tradition, recitation of the Qur'an and the call to prayer fall outside the category of "singing.")

The origins of the court tradition of music-making go back to pre-Islamic Bedouin songs (such as camel-drivers' chants) and other types of folk singing on the one hand, and to a lighter, more refined urban style performed by slavegirls on the other. In the Umayyad period, singers from the Hijaz assimilated elements of Sasanian, Byzantine, and possibly other traditions felt to be compatible with the Arabic musical idiom and the Arabic poetry, which furnished the lyrics. Singing became an art practiced by men and women, generally slaves or of humble origin, and appreciated by members of the ruling elite, including some caliphs. Vocal technique became more sophisticated, and singers took to accompanying themselves on the lute. Light-hearted love poems like those of 'Umar ibn Abi Rabi'a (ca. AH 23–93/644–712 CE) provided ideal lyrics for songs, and singers and poets often associated closely with each other.

With the music-loving caliph al-Mahdi's (158–169/775–785) invitation to singers to perform in Baghdad, vocal music acquired an established place at court. The singer, or *mughanni* (a term that also includes composition and accompanying oneself on an instrument), was expected to have an all-around culture and, in particular, to be well versed in the Arabic language and poetry, as well as being an agreeable and entertaining companion. He should possess a fine, trained voice, have a good grounding in the theory of rhythmic and melodic modes, and be thoroughly familiar with the repertoire of songs. One key to success was the capacity to improvise; the modes of a setting were given, but skill in improvising on them and inducing a feeling of ecstasy *(tarab)* among the audience was an individual gift. The training of singers was very demanding, as can be seen from Ishaq ibn Ibrahim al-Mawsili's (150–235/767–850) account of his education. Some members of the governing elite were noted amateur singers and composers, as were a few rulers; the first such royal music-maker was the Umayyad caliph al-Walid ibn Yazid (d. 126/744 CE), the last the Ottoman sultan Selim III (d. 1808 CE).

Whereas most leading singers in the 'Abbasid period were men, a few women were also famous composers. Most women singers, however, belonged to the category of singing-girls *(qaynas)*, who simply performed other people's songs. The best women musicians were acquired by the caliph, governors, or eminent dignitaries and lived a secluded life at court; less gifted ones entertained music lovers of humbler status. The owners of *qaynas* often derived profit not only from the girls' musical skills but also from their physical charms, and the dividing line between singing-girl and prostitute was not always clear. Women singers played an important role in preserving and handing down the repertoire.

Songs were performed in contexts from the highly ritualized to the informal. Singers might be summoned to the caliph's formal audience and asked to perform in turn; often a prize would be offered for the song that most appealed to the caliph. Or a singer would be expected to attend court on one particular day each week. The most informal gatherings, by contrast, were those of singers entertaining themselves and their friends. While many songs celebrated love, poems of praise and congratulation, elegies, wine poems, descriptions of nature, and even the occasional satires were also set to music. Regardless of theme, however, the lyrics never exceeded more than a handful of lines.

From the 'Abbasid period on, singing was a part of court culture, with rulers and their ministers patronizing singers and writers of music. Some dynasties, such as the Fatimids, were particularly noteworthy for their patronage of singers. Where a class of wealthy merchants emerged, they, too, often encouraged forms of art music and singing. Regional traditions developed, for instance, in al-Andalus, where a suite form, the *nuba*, evolved with vocal pieces incorporating strophic *muwashshahat* and *zajals*. In the East the 'Abbasid and Mongol court musician and theoretician Safi al-Din al-Urmawi (d. 693/1294 CE) was the author of an authoritative compendium on music, reflecting practice in Iraq and Persia, which

was translated into Persian and Turkish. He mentions different kinds of songs, simple and more sophisticated, the latter being combined in suites *(nawbas)*. Safi al-Din's writings became the basis for musical practice in Persia and later the Ottoman court, which developed differently from that found in Egypt and Syria. One can thus speak of Persian and related Turkish traditions of singing distinct from the Arabic one in the later medieval period.

Besides the court and wealthy urban classes, certain Sufi brotherhoods that appeared from the twelfth century on preserved, transmitted, and contributed to the elite musical tradition. Mystical poetry, or poetry that lent itself to mystical interpretation— whether anonymous or by poets such as Ibn al-Farid (576–632/1181–1235 CE), Hafiz, Saadi, Rumi, or the Turkish Yunus Emre (d. 720/1320–1321 CE), was set to music and sung during *dhikr* ceremonies or "spiritual concerts," with the aim of inducing in the hearers a state of mystical ecstasy, the *hal*; the most famous ceremonies were and still are those of the Mevlevis. This Sufi musical tradition guaranteed continuity in the art of singing even during times of political instability, and in the Ottoman empire the Mevlevis played a role comparable to that of the court in fostering art music.

Finally, a specifically Iranian phenomenon was the chanting of Ferdowsi's *Shahnama* during physical-training sessions in what became known as the *Zurkhana,* or "house of strength."

HILARY KILPATRICK

See also Adab; Ferdowsi; Music; Musical Instruments; Mystical Poetry; Poetry; Women Poets

Further Reading

Al-Hasan ibn Ahmad ibn 'Ali al-Katib. *La perfection des connaissances musicales. Kitâb kamâl adab al-∞inâ'.* Translation and commentary by Amnon Shiloah. Paris: Paul Geuthner, 1972.

Farmer, Henry George. *A History of Arabian Music To the XIIIth Century.* [1929], Repr. by London: Luzac & Co., 1973.

Feldman, Walter. "Ottoman Turkish Music: Genre and Form." In *The Middle East.* The Garland Encyclopedia of World Music Volume 6, edited by Virginia Danielson et al. New York: Routledge, 2002.

Guettat, Mahmoud. "The Andalusian Musical Heritage." In *The Middle East.* The Garland Encyclopedia of World Music Volume 6, edited by Virginia Danielson et al. New York: Routledge, 2002.

Sawa, George Dimitri. *Musical Performance Practice in the Early 'Abbâsid Era 132/320 A.H./750–932 A.D.* Toronto: Pontifical Institute of Medieval Studies, 1989.

Shiloah, Amnon. *Music in the World of Islam. A sociocultural study.* Aldershot: Scholar Press 1995.

Wright, O. "Music and Verse." In *Arabic Literature to the end of the Umayyad Period,* edited by A.F.L. Beeston et al. Cambridge: Cambridge University Press, 1983.

SIRA

Sira, meaning "the way," is, for the student of Islam, synonymous with biography, and particularly the biography of the Prophet Muhammad. The *Kitab sirat rasul Allah*, which tells of the life of Muhammad from birth to death, is the title given by Ibn Hisham (d. AH 218/834 CE) to his edition of three compilations of traditions regarding ancient legends, Muhammad's birth, early life and mission, and the expeditions of Muhammad (d. 11/632) right up to the moment of his death, that had been brought together by the greatest compiler of 'Abbasid times Muhammad ibn Ishaq (d. 150/767) under the titles, *Mubtada', Mab'ath*, and *Maghazi*. On the other hand, biographical narratives on other historical personalities, such as *Sirat Mu'awiya*, were also written, but these postdate the *Sirat rasul Allah* by Ibn Hisham and have never commanded as much interest.

Orientalists have disputed the exact meaning of the term *sira*. Writing in 1899, Hartmann concluded that, "Ibn Ishaq hat keine sira geschrieben." Nevertheless, they were Ibn Ishaq's compilations that were brought together by Ibn Hisham as *Sirat rasul Allah*. Importantly, the *Maghazi* portion of the Prophet's biography is considered most significant, for it is this portion that tells us, through more recognized traditions, of Muhammad's last years and his achievements in Yathrib/Medina. Indeed, the earliest traditions concerning the life of the Prophet are believed to come from *Maghazi* works, those compiled by 'Urwa ibn al-Zubayr (d. 643/710) and Wahb ibn Munabbih (d. 654/728): In this regard, the *Kitab al-maghazi* by al-Waqidi (d.207/823) has won a considerable reputation, as is indicated by the fact that the two most significant sources cited by al-Tabari (d. 310/923) for his narrative concerning the life of the Prophet, in his *History of Prophets and Kings*, come from the compilations of al-Waqidi and Ibn Ishaq. It seems to me that the title *Sira*, first used by Ibn Hisham, applies, in particular, to biographical material that progresses from birth to death. It does not take away from the premise that *Maghazi* compilations tell of the life of the Prophet, as well, albeit only the last ten years after his emigration from Mecca.

The significant issue raised by biographical literature on the Prophet concerns its reliability. Is this information historical and verifiable? Does it, for instance, provide the necessary context for understanding the Qur'an? Importantly, such compilations are based on a system of transmission that communicates both the piece of information *(matn)* and the names of those who communicated it *(isnad)*. Regarding the traditions communicated by Ibn Ishaq, Ibn Hanbal (d. 241/855) is reported to have condemned his handling of isnads; Ibn Hanbal's denunciation of

al-Waqidi as a liar is probably based on the same grounds. Yet, several of these traditions are found among the exegetical compilations on the Qur'an.

Modern historians such as I. Goldziher, J. Schacht, and J. Wansbrough have rejected the majority of early Islamic traditions as unreliable: They suggest that these are the prejudiced creation of a later generation of believers. More recently, Marsden Jones has exposed the numerous chronological discrepancies that exist in *Sira-Maghazi*, while P. Crone opines that many of these narratives are the result of a desire to explain Qur'anic verses. As obvious are the parallels to the New Testament stories of miracles performed by Jesus. Nevertheless, scholars such as Montgomery Watt, Alford T. Welch, and H. Motzky continue to insist that these materials may be used to extract a basic biography of Muhammad. On the other hand, significant Muslim scholars, such as W. N. Arafat, have objected to the notorious tales concerning the expulsion and execution of the Jews of Medina that form an integral part of the *Maghazi* as "unislamic."

Tradition informs us that the compilations of Prophetic traditions were first arranged by Ibn Ishaq in response to a command from the 'Abbasid caliph al-Mansur. Concerned to explain the practices of the Prophet of Islam as based on teachings of the Qur'an, Ibn Ishaq informs us through his compilations that these Qur'anic revelations came to Muhammad as inspiration, from the time of his Prophethood, after his fortieth year, and especially in moments of crisis. According to Ibn Ishaq, the final verses of the Qur'an were communicated during Muhammad's pilgrimage to Mecca. The compilations include legalistic traditions, poetry, and genealogical information concerning the Prophet's Companions. Carefully learned and transmitted by his students, the books of Ibn Ishaq were soon to spread throughout the empire to be accepted and acclaimed by the Muslim community.

RIZWI FAIZER

Further Reading

Arafat, W.N. "New Light on the Story of Banu Qurayza and the Jews of Medina." *JRAS* (1976): 100–110.
Cook, M. *Muhammad.* Oxford University Press, 1996.
Guillaume, Alfred. *The Life of Muhammad: A Translation of Ibn Ishaq's Sirat Rasul Allah.* 9th ed. Oxford Univeersity Press, 1990.

SIRHINDI, AHMAD (ca. 1564–1624)

The eponymous founder of the Mujaddidi branch of the Naqshbandi Sufi order named after his title, known to posterity, '*Mujaddid-i alf thani*' (the religious renewer of the second millennium), Shaykh

Ahmad ibn 'Abd al-Ahad Faruqi Sirhindi was born in the Punjab in around 1564. From an *ashraf* family claiming descent from the second caliph 'Umar, he was given a firm education in the literary and religious sciences in Sialkot and Agra, where he joined the court, disputing with Abu'l-Fadl and collaborating with Fayzi on literary projects.

In 1600, Sirhindi met the Naqshbandi Khwaja Baqi billah and became committed to the discipline and didactic method of that order, which he now promoted at court and beyond. He became a leading master of the order, and his writings were influential in defining a new Naqshbandi path of critical engagement with the Mughal rulers and contemptuous attack upon the heterodox (such as the Shi'is) and non-Muslim Indians. Although there is a historiographical debate concerning the "Naqshbandi reaction" and his role in establishing Jahangir as the successor to Akbar, no doubt because Sirhindi (and the Naqshbandis) was hostile to Akbar's religious innovations, it is clear that Jahangir failed to live up to Sirhindi's expectations of an orthodox ruler. Following conspiracies at court, Jahangir had him imprisoned in 1619; the Naqshbandi hagiographies blamed his treatment on the Shi'i notables at court. Released the following year, Sirhindi continued preaching until his death in 1624. After his death, his son Khwaja Ma'sum succeeded him as head of the Naqshbandiyya.

The historiography pits the inflexible Naqshbandis associated with Sirhindi against the peaceable Chishtis in the "battle" for Sufism in India. But such a picture is misleading. Although Sirhindi did write polemics such as *Radd-i rawafid* against the Shi'is, attack non-Muslims in his letters, and criticize the Sufi doctrine of the unity of being *(wahdat al-wujud)* attributed to Ibn 'Arabi and his followers, a careful reading of his letters suggests a more nuanced picture. His own doctrine of *wahdat al-shuhud*, a critique of the ontological monism of *wahdat al-wujud* that instead considers there to be a unity in mystical vision, is not far removed from Ibn 'Arabi's views. His opinions on the continuing need for the role of the heirs of the Prophet are not dissimilar to Shi'i doctrines. As a thorough-going elitist, he considered all issues and texts to be read at two distinct hermeneutical levels: At the exoteric level, there could be no compromise on persecuting non-Muslims and attacking "deviant" monist Sufis; however, on the mystical level, Islam and infidelity were no longer pitted against each other but different levels on the path to God. These two levels became two trends opposed to each other in his legacy.

SAJJAD H RIZVI

See also Akbar; Mughals; Sufism

Further Reading

M. Abdul Haq Ansari. *Sufism and Shari'ah: A Study of Shaikh Ahmad Sirhindi's Efforts to Reform Sufism.* Leicester: The Islamic Foundation, 1986.
Damrel, D. "The Naqshbandi Reaction Reconsidered." In *Beyond Turk and Hindu*, edited by D. Gilmartin and B. Lawrence, 176–198. Gainesville: University of Florida Press, 2000.
Faruqi, B.A. *The Mujaddid's Concept of Tawhid.* Lahore: Institute of Islamic Culture, 1989 [1940].
Friedman, Y. *Shaikh Ahmad Sirhindi: An Outline of His Thought and a Study of His Image in the Eyes of Posterity.* New Delhi: Oxford University Press, 2000 [1971].
Rahman, F. *Selected Letters of Shaikh Ahmad Sirhindi.* Karachi: Institute of Islamic Studies, 1968.
Rizvi, S.A.A. *Muslim Revivalist Movements in Northern India in the Sixteenth and Seventeenth Centuries.* New Delhi: Munshiram Manoharlal, 1993 [1965].
Ter Haar, J.G.T. *Follower and Heir of the Prophet: Shaykh Ahmad Sirhindi as Mystic*, Leiden: het Oosters Instituut, 1992.

SLAVERY, MILITARY

Forms of military slavery have existed in the Islamic world since the early ninth century, and variations of this institution were found in many Muslim countries at different times up to the beginning of the nineteenth century. Military slaves, known variously as *ghulam*s (lit. "youths"), *mamluk*s ("owned ones"), and janissaries (from Turkish *yeni cheri*, "new army"), had a tremendous impact on the military and political life, as well as economic and social aspects, of the societies in which they were found.

There is still a significant debate among scholars as to the origins of this institution, and the reader is referred to the studies later in this entry for opinions different from that presented here. Military slavery had its origin in the convergence of factors: the withdrawal of the Arab tribes from military service (a process encouraged by the government); the perceived lack of dependability of troops from Khurasan, hitherto the bulwark of the 'Abbasid state; the precedent of hundreds, perhaps thousands of clients of slave provenance or freed prisoners of war, known as *mawali*, in the court and army, many from eastern Iran, Transoxiana, and even the Eurasian Steppe region; and contact with the Turks of the Eurasian Steppe, with their well-known military qualities, including hardiness, horsemanship, and archery. The first unit of military slaves, composed mainly of Turks, was founded by the future caliph al-Mu'tasim (r. 833–842), during the reign of his brother al-Ma'mun. Soon after his ascension to the throne, al-Mu'tasim decided to move his formation from Baghdad to Samarra, about two hundred kilometers to the north, to limit tension with other units and to keep his new formation isolated. This unit was originally envisioned as a guard corps but soon began participating in campaigns in the empire and on the frontier. It soon became the mainstay of the 'Abbasid regime. Al-Mu'tasim's son and second successor, al-Mutawakkil (r. 847–861), eventually became disenchanted with these Turkish guardsmen, their commanders (also Turks), and the power that they wielded at court, and moved to weaken them. The Turkish commanders moved first and assassinated the caliph, setting a pattern for future officers, not only of slave origin. The Turkish slave soldiers and officers played a significant role in the political unrest that characterized Iraq in the next several generations, at least until the coming of the Buwayhids in 944, and sometimes afterwards. In spite of the problems inherent in importing new Turkish slaves from the Steppe, the expenses involved, and the problems of discipline, the institution of military slavery spread throughout the eastern Muslim world. The quality of the Turkish soldiers and the loyalty, at least accorded to their original patron, evidently had enough to commend them to various rulers and generals. The basic idea of the military slave, which we will henceforth call *Mamluk* for convenience, if somewhat anachronistically, was that they were more or less cut off from the local population and its political and religious concerns, and therefore loyal primarily to their patron who bought and educated them (and continued to support them), and to each other. We have here a classic client–patron relationship, institutionalized through the mechanism of slavery.

Over the generations, we can see that this institution developed several principles, most of which were articulated in various forms by Muslim historians and other writers (see the famous statement by the fourteenth-century historian Ibn Khaldun in the translation by B. Lewis, *Islam: From the Prophet Muhammad to the Capture of Constantinople* [New York: Walker and Company, 1974], 1:97–99), as follows:

1. Young slaves (mainly Turks) were brought from pagan areas to the north of the Islamic world, mainly the Steppe region.
2. These slaves were converted to Islam and underwent several years of military training (and often religious education) in the barracks.
3. On completing training and reaching manhood, the slaves were enrolled in the army of their patron (often they were formally manumitted), mainly as mounted archers.
4. In theory, and usually in practice, this was a one-generation system, meaning that the sons of military slaves could not themselves be such slaves, but rather new military slaves had to be brought continually from the Steppe. The idea behind this principle was that the descendants of *Mamluk*s would not have the same toughness and military qualities as their fathers, as well as the lack of connections to the surrounding society.
5. Military slaves were to be loyal to their patrons, who educated and supported them, as well as to their comrades, slaves of the same patron.

It is interesting to note that the Turkish Seljuks, who came to power in the eleventh century with the assistance of the Turcoman tribesmen, soon set up a large formation of Turkish Mamluks. They realized that with all due respect to the emotional ties to the Turcomans, and their clear military skills as mounted archers, they could not always be depended upon, and therefore an alternative force that was both loyal and effective was needed. This use and dependence on Turkish Mamluks was passed on to the various successor states of the Seljuks, including that of the Ayyubid established by the Kurd Saladin. From the beginning of Saladin's reign, Turkish Mamluk units played the major role in the war against the Crusaders. The role of the Mamluks was increased by his great-nephew al-Salih Ayyub (r. 1238–1249), who established the famous Bahriyya regiment, which first came to prominence at the victory at Mansura over the Crusaders under Louis IX of France. Subsequently, this unit and other Mamluks took over the rulership directly, establishing the Mamluk sultanate, which ruled in Egypt and then in Syria until the Ottoman conquest of 1516–1517. The Mamluks gained renown for their victories over the Mongols in a war lasting more than sixty years, from the battle of 'Ayn Jalut (1260) onward, as well as eradicating the Crusader presence in Syria (1291). Even after their subjugation by the Ottomans, Mamluks continued to play an important role in Egyptian politics until they were eliminated by Muhammad 'Ali at the beginning of the nineteenth century. It should be mentioned that the Ottomans also erected an institution based on military slavery, the aforementioned Janissaries, although this was somewhat different from the classical Mamluk institution.

REUVEN AMITAI

See also 'Abbasids; 'Ayn Jalut; Ayyubids; Mamluks; Mongols; Ottomans; Warfare

Further Reading

Amitai, Reuven. "The Mamluk Institution: 1000 Years of Military Slavery in the Islamic World." In *Arming Slaves*, edited by Philip Morgan and Christopher Brown. New Haven, CT: Yale University Press, forthcoming.
Ayalon, David. "Preliminary Remarks on the Mamluk Military Institution in Islam." In *War, Technology and*

Society in the Middle East, edited by V.J. Perry and M. E. Yapp. London: Oxford University Press, 1975. Reprint, D. Ayalon, *The Mamluk Military Society: Collected Studies*. London: Variorum Press, 1979, article no. IX.

———. "Mamlūk." In *The Encyclopaedia of Islam*. New ed. 6:314–321.

Beckwith, Christopher I. "Aspects of the Early History of the Central Asian Guard Corps in Islam." *Archivum Eurasiae Medii Aevi*. 4 (1984): 29–43.

Crone, Patricia. *Slaves on Horses: The Evolution of the Islamic Polity*. Cambridge: Cambridge University Press, 1980.

Gordon, Matthew S. *The Breaking of a Thousand Swords: A History of the Turkish Military of Samarra (A.H. 200–275/815–889 C.E.)*. Albany: State University of New York Press, 2001.

Kennedy, Hugh. *The Prophet and the Age of the Caliphates: The Islamic Near East from the Sixth to the Eleventh Century*. London: Longman, 1986, 158–171.

———. *The Armies of the Caliph*. London: Routledge, 2000.

Lewis, Bernard. *Race and Slavery in the Middle East: An Historical Enquiry*. New York and Oxford: Oxford University Press, 1990, esp. Chap. 9 ("Slaves in Arms").

Pipes, Daniel. *Slave Soldiers and Islam: The Genesis of a Military System*. New Haven, CT: Yale University Press, 1981.

Shaban, M.A. *Islamic History: A New Interpretation*. Cambridge: Cambridge Press, 1976, 63–65.

Sourdel, Dominique et al. "Ghulām." In *The Encyclopaedia of Islam*. New ed. 2:1079–1091.

SLAVES AND SLAVE TRADE, EASTERN ISLAMIC WORLD

As in the Roman Empire, the slave *('abd)* was the cornerstone of the domestic workforce in medieval Islam and provided a lucrative source of revenue for Islamic infrastructure. The Prophet Muhammad accepted slavery as a fact of life, but he mitigated it by insisting upon kindness to slaves. According to the Qu'ran, anyone who mistreated his slave would be damned, something that Muhammad's early followers took seriously. The early caliph Abu Bakr, for example, ransomed slaves.

Methods of Enslavement

Muslims practiced slavery freely during the Middle Ages. Slaves were an important element in the Islamic world, one that required constant replenishment through trade, war, raids, and the birth of new slaves to old ones. A large segment of the urban population, they could also be found working the fields in some places. However, they did not make up a large section of the agricultural workforce. Slaves in Islam, as in Christian lands, tended to be skilled labor.

Legally, slaves were supposed to be war captives or the children of already existing slaves, though reality did not entirely reflect theory. Like Christianity and Judaism, Islam frowned upon enslaving coreligionists, but in practice, Muslims did occasionally enslave each other. Under Sunni law, a man could be enslaved for defaulting on his debts. Muslims enslaving Muslims, however, most frequently occurred during wars between hostile sects, or rebellions against civil authority, where women and children spared from death were sold into slavery instead, as an example to other potential rebels. In 1077 CE, for example, the women of a Berber tribe were sold in Cairo as punishment for the tribe's revolt. Frontier raiders tended not to scruple over their captives' religion either, enslaving whomever they caught in their *razzias* (raids).

A great source of Christian slaves came from these *razzias* into the Dar al-Harb, the "Land of War." In the East this area was usually the Byzantine empire or Eastern Europe. The Dar al-Harb provided the source of the most famous Muslim slaves of the Middle Ages—the Mamluk slave–soldiers of Egypt. These were Christian boys kidnapped mainly from Eastern Europe or the Steppes and raised to fight in private or state armies. Through them the slave trade had considerable influence upon local political dynasties, since slave–soldiers sometimes overthrew their masters and ruled in their place. The Mamluks, for example, overthrew the Ayyubid Egyptian sultanate in 1250 and ruled as sultans in Cairo until 1517. Another large group of male slaves (frequently Slavs from Russia) were castrated and made into eunuchs. These were usually employed as domestic servants and some wielded considerable power. Not all eunuchs lost sexual function completely. Some were able to marry and occasionally, depending on the nature and skill of the operation, could still father children.

The Slave Trade

Piracy and privateering also supplied slaves from as far west as the Iberian Peninsula. Muslims frequently found themselves enslaved by Christians, particularly in Spain, Latin Palestine, or in the Byzantine empire. In the tenth century, the Byzantine emperor had a ritual of inviting Muslim slaves to his banquet. However, increasing numbers of slaves came from Africa in the late Middle Ages. The trans-Saharan slave trade with West, Central and East Africa was the precursor to the later trans-Atlantic slave trade. This differed from that in the northern Mediterranean trade in significant ways. While some of the trans-Saharan trade resulted from raiding, much of it came from peaceful trade in slaves and other goods with local, slave-raiding tribes. These tribes sold off criminals, war captives, and debtors—the latter two categories being the same criteria for enslavement as in the Islamic world—but the desire for profit fueled the trade on both sides. Similarly, the Venetians traded lucratively in Christian slaves to the Muslim world from the eighth century onward, despite papal censure about selling coreligionists to the infidel. Christians and Muslims were not the only groups engaging in the slave traffic. Some Jewish merchants were also instrumental in the trade of Slavs (who were favored for becoming eunuchs) via Eastern and Central Europe, though how involved they were—particularly later on in the early Modern era—is subject to academic controversy.

Types and Functions of Slaves

Not all slaves had the same value. White slaves were considered more valuable than black slaves, for example, though it is difficult to say how strong this prejudice was, particularly in how it influenced the origins of the trans-Atlantic slave trade. Different slaves from different regions were favored for different functions. Women, particularly if they were young, beautiful, well educated, and skilled, were favored over men because they made good housekeepers, nursemaids, and concubines. Men could be slave–soldiers, eunuchs, bodyguards, field workers, officials, or domestic slaves. They might also transact the master's or mistress's business outside of the house, as merchants and representatives of the master's affairs, sometimes with considerable freedom. Some male slaves served their masters or mistresses sexually, just as female slaves did. This practice could be extremely dangerous for male slaves, however, since a mistress was usually committing adultery when she took a slave as a lover and the penalty was death for both partners.

Manumission

There were several roads to manumission. Muslims, Christians, and Jews all ransomed coreligionists from slavery in hostile territory. Ransoming was a lucrative by-product of the slave trade for slave owners. A slave might buy his freedom, or win it through negotiation with his master or if his master mutilated him, or if he contracted blindness, leprosy, or paralysis. A slave's master might also free and marry the mother of his child, but this was not automatic upon the birth of the child. However, if she and her child survived her master, she won her freedom at the price of her sale, taken out of her child's inheritance.

Conversion to Islam did not automatically win freedom either. The concubines of the Ottoman sultans, for example, were converted to Islam upon their sale to their royal master but remained slaves. Almost all of them were originally Christians from Central and Eastern Europe, or Russia. The frequency and acceptability of relations between masters and slaves introduced a not-inconsiderable ethnic mixing into all levels of slave-holding society, even the highest. Because the child of a slave and a free person was born free, a slave's son could therefore inherit the throne. Muslim slaves were more likely to find manumission than Christians or Jews, and conversion tended to precede freedom, particularly in the case of concubines who were freed for bearing heirs to their masters. As with so many other aspects of his or her life, the freedom of a slave depended on the whim of the master.

PAULA R. STILES

See also Mamluks; Slaves and Slave Trade, Western Islamic World; Slavery, Military; Trade, African

Further Reading

Ayalon, David. *Islam and the Abode of War: Military Slaves and Islamic Adversaries*. Aldershot and Brookfield, VT: Variorum, 1994.
Crone, Patricia. *Slaves on Horses: The Evolution of the Islamic Polity*. Cambridge: Cambridge University Press, 1980.
Goldenberg, David M. *The Curse of Ham: Race and Slavery in Early Judaism, Christianity, and Islam*. Princeton: Princeton University Press, 2003.
Pipes, Daniel. *Slave Soldiers and Islam: The Genesis of a Military System*. New Haven, CT, and London: Yale University, 1981.
Savage, E. "Berbers and Blacks: Ibadi Slave Traffic in Eighth-Century North Africa." *The Journal of African History* 33, no. 3 (August 1992): 351–368.
Segal, Ronald. *Islam's Black Slaves: The Other Black Diaspora*. New York: Farrar, Straus and Giroux, 2001.
Willis, John Ralph. *Slaves and Slavery in Muslim Africa: Islam and the Ideology of Enslavement (Slaves & Slavery in Muslim Africa)*. Portland, OR: International Specialized Book Services, 1986.

SLAVES AND SLAVE TRADE, WESTERN ISLAMIC WORLD

Legal texts are the greatest, most precise, and biggest sources of information about slavery. The predominant legal school in the Islamic West was the Maliki, providing a wealth of works of different genres: legal practice, compilations of legal opinions, legal rulings, record of notaries, and so on. These works have a great abundance of information in the chapters devoted specifically to slavery—often called Law of Slavery—whose main focus was the issue of manumission. But they also contain a number of references scattered in the other chapters that form the book.

In addition to these sources, whose contents deal with the domestic slave, more news is dispersed in historical chronicles, biographical dictionaries, and literary works. Although they are not long stories, nor is the aim of the author to describe the slave, those passages help to enhance the information about what slavery was actually like. It must be emphasized that, despite all bibliographical sources, theoretical information about slavery in the Western Islamic world during the Middle Ages and the Renaissance is far richer than the references to legal practice of this subject.

Slaves: Types and Circumstances

According to all the legal schools, anybody born as a slave, being a son of a female slave, could be considered a slave no matter whether or not he was Muslim. A war prisoner could also be enslaved given that he was not a free Muslim, but professed another faith. However, it was forbidden to enslave a member of another religion who lived in Islamic territory and therefore enjoyed the protection of the *dhimma* status. This privilege was obtained by means of paying a tax. Only if this status was lost by any reason, such as cooperating with the unfaithful enemy in a battle, might the *dhimmi* become a slave. Nor was abandonment considered a valid origin of slavery: If anybody found a deserted child *(manbudh)* and took him in, that child was considered a free person. In fact, there were Muslim slaves, both born in such condition, as well as those who wished to convert to Islam after having acquired that status. Conversion was not a reason to obtain freedom.

The Maliki school considered the same kinds of slaves as other legal schools: a common slave *('abd, jariya, ama)*; concubines *(milk al-yamin, jariya, ama)*; a concubine who gives a son to her master *(umm walad)*; a slave having completed the conditions for a manumission contract *(mukatab)*; and the slave to be released after his master's death *(mudabbar)*. Moreover, it included a new kind, the slave who was authorized to trade *(ma'dhun bi-l-tijara)*, who needed to have free movement and certain economic means to conduct business. The possibility of being manumitted in the future provided some of these slaves with a number of rights and legal obligations that placed them close to the status of free persons, thus acquiring an intermediate status between slavery and freedom.

In the Islamic world a slave could be married legally and create his own family structures with previous authorization of his master. Still, in order to perform the legal act of marriage he had some limitations that the free man lacked. According to Maliki law, a slave could have four legal wives, the same as a free man, whereas for the other legal schools, only two were allowed. On the other hand, the slaves' capacity to form their own families was restricted to the servants of very rich people, or else to those slaves who paid their manumission in installments by means of a contract signed up with their master. Both kinds of slaves had a right to enjoy a certain degree of independence in order to have a job that enabled them to pay for their freedom.

A master was not allowed to marry one of his concubines legally. However, if one of them became pregnant, she acquired a new status that provided her with certain rights common to a free woman. These *ummahat al-awlad*, or mothers with child, might not be sold and acquired freedom after their master's death. On the other hand, their children were free according to the principle on which nobody may be his father's slave, despite slavery being a condition inherited from the mother.

A slave was not considered an object of law by himself, like in Roman law, but a subject of legislation. Consequently, he had civil and criminal rights, as well as obligations. His master could not kill him nor impose any arbitrary penalty on him, although there are examples of this being made in practice. Likewise, a slave was subject to penalties that were half the amount of those imposed on a free person, because his responsibility was considered to be less.

As for property rights, law provided that the goods belonging to a slave pertained to his master, so that the slave was the usufructuary only as long as the master permitted it. Nor had he rights to inherit, even from free relatives. Nevertheless, Maliki law emphasized that a slave's manumission had to include enough possessions for the slave to survive with dignity; otherwise, to give him freedom would not be a generous deed but a concealed abandonment. When the slave was released, a client bond was established between him and his master. Although he acquired all the rights and duties of a free person, his former master and his agnates preserved the right to become heirs to the slave. Consequently, slaves were not only members of the medieval Islamic family—and must be included in every study concerning it—but after their manumission, they continued to be bound to the master's family unit through a client bow *(wala')*. In such a way, they contributed to perpetuate its patrilineal structure, a fact that had important social and economic consequences.

Maliki jurists established a number of legal principles concerning slave property, trade, and their liberation that were considered when dealing with the matters of law. First, the rights of a free person—especially property rights—were secured because, as texts repeated once and again, "slaves are goods, just as cattle is." Respect for the property of a free person might have priority over the religious element. Likewise, it was important that a manumission or sale did not damage the interests of any free person. Secondly, there were the fundamental rights of the slave to be considered: respect for his legal condition as an individual and therefore for the rights applying to that particular type of slave. Other aspects were his manumission and kind treatment; the concession of an amount of money for his use after liberation; and some sexual rights of female slaves, as the forbiddance to be rendered, rented, and so on, to another person.

Slave Trade

The most common way of acquiring slaves must have been, on the one hand, by birth at home of the children of other slaves. On the other hand, captivity at war, particularly in places such as al-Andalus, where there was continuous struggle against Christian territories throughout many centuries, provided prisoners. Since the tenth century there was an institution created for the release of captives, the redeemer *(al-fakkak)*.

Captives, such as other slaves imported from diverse places, were sold in the market. Their transaction was subject to controls in which the fulfillment of the legally established criteria were secured, the same as with other goods (cattle, luxury items). Among the many questions Maliki jurists dealt with, two were worth special attention: the slave's possible physical defects or blemishes—where the possibility of selling a pregnant female slave was included, since it might give rise to claims and conflicts between the parties involved—and possible frauds related to the legal status of the slave, which would result in the annulment of the sale once it had been carried out. The texts dealt extensively with the question of slaves owned by several masters, because the lack of whole property of a slave restricted the rights of the masters over that person. For example, during a sale or rent, there had to be a unanimous agreement among all the proprietors; or, in the case of female slaves, they could not have sexual intercourse with her.

Up to the twelfth century there existed an intense slave trade between al-Andalus and the Christian kingdoms, in which Jews living in the Christian lands played an active role. During this period, different commercial products were exported from al-Andalus to other Islamic countries, either in the West or in the East. Among the products that were in great demand Christian slaves stood out. Since the ninth century, Radhanite merchants had traded with "Andalusian slave women," who had become very popular in North Africa and the Orient. The Verdun merchants are also referred to in the sources as people trading slaves between both territories.

The drastic territorial withdrawal of al-Andalus in 1212 brought about a radical change in the commercial relationships of all the products. Al-Andalus stopped being an importer, and most of the trade is addressed to the north of the peninsula from the thirteenth century onward. In the case of Muslim slaves, the Nasrid sultans were forced to prohibit their sale to the Christians.

Most of the slaves were destined for domestic use, although their numbers are unknown. The different genres of written sources refer to privileged social groups living in an urban environment, without any information about the rural world and other urban contexts, so it is difficult to determine the absolute social and economic weight of the slave population. The use of slaves was infrequent in the armies of Western Islam, both in al-Andalus and North Africa. As for some high-ranking officers of the army whose status as slaves has been assumed, it is difficult to say whether they were so, or else they had slave origins but had been enjoying freedom for several generations already, so they would rather be clients than slaves.

Eunuchs should also be mentioned briefly. Their existence is known by means of historical chronicles. Their destination, according to these sources, was only the royal palace and some very wealthy families. They were mainly assigned to manage the harem, but some of them had high positions in the administration, and even in the army of the Umayyad court of al-Andalus.

Nowadays, one of the most debated issues in the field is the ethnic origins of the slaves in Western Islam. The confused state of terminology at some point when, for instance, the term *saqaliba*—which was used to designate only slaves of Slavic origins—started to be used to call any palace slave, makes a systematic revision of Arabic sources very necessary. It seems that the sources indicate that slaves came mainly from captivity, so in al-Andalus, Christians from the Northern Iberian Peninsula must have been abundant. On the other hand, a great number of black slaves of sub-Saharan Africa must have been acquired in North Africa, especially since the expansion of the Berber dynasties of Almoravids and Almohads, in the eleventh century. On their part, the treatises on market rules and the very few treatises of slave trade allude to ethnic origins in a merely theoretical way.

CRISTINA DE LA PUENTE

See also Andalus; Concubinage; Eunuchs; Human Geography; Land Tenure and Ownership; Law and Jurisprudence; Malikism; Markets; North Africa; Slavery, Military; Trade

Primary Sources

Al-Jaziri, 'Ali ibn Yahya (m. 585/1189). *Al-Maqsad al-mahmud fi talkhis al-'uqud. (Proyecto plausible de compendio de fórmulas notariales)*. Ed. Asunción Ferreras. Madrid, 1998.

Al-Muktabis. III. Chronique du règne du calife umaiyyade 'Abd Allah à Cordoue Al-Qism al-thalith min kitab al-Muqtabis fi ta'rikh rijal al-Andalus. Edited and introduction by M. Martínez Antuña. Paris, 1937.

Al-Muqtabas (Al-Juz' al-khamis). Ed. P. Chalmeta, F. Corriente, and M. Subh. Madrid, 1979.

Al-Muqtabas II-2. Ed. Mahmud 'Ali Makki. Beirut, 1393/1973.

Al-Muqtabas VII. Ed. 'Abd al-Rahman 'Ali al-Hajji, *al-Muqtabas fi akhbar balad al-Andalus*. Beirut, 1965; Spanish translation by E. García Gómez, *El Califato de Córdoba en "al-Muqtabis" de Ibn Hayyan. Anales palatinos del califa de Córdoba al-Hakam II, por 'Isa b. Ahmad al-Razi (360–364 H./971–975 J.C.)*, Madrid, 1967.

Al-Muwatta, Imam Malik. Transl. 'A'isha 'Abdarrahman al-Tarjumana and Ya'qub Johnson. Norwich, 1982.

Ibn Abi Zayd Al-Qayrawani (m. 386/996). *Risala/ La Risala ou Epître sur les éléments du dogme et de la loi de l'Islam selon le rite mâlikite*. Texte arabe et traduction française avec un avant-propos, des notes et trois index par Léon Bercher. Alger, 1968.

Ibn Al-'Attar (m. 399/1009). *Kitab al-watha'iq wa-l-sijillat. (Formulario notarial hispano-árabe por el alfaquí y notario cordobés Ibn al-'Attar [s. X])*. Ed. P. Chalmeta y F. Corriente. Madrid, 1983.

Ibn Hayyan. *Muqtabis II-1 (Al-Safar al-thani min Kitab al-muqtabas)*. Ed. Mahmud 'Ali Makki. Riyad, 1424/2003.

Ibn 'Idhari Al-Marrakushi. *Histoire de l'Afrique du Nord et de l'Espagne musulmane, intitulée Kitab al-bayan al-mughrib, et fragments de la chronique de 'Arib*. Vol. I–II. Ed. G. Colin and E. Lévi-Provençal. Leiden, 1948–1951; Vol. III. *Histoire de l'Espagne musulmane au XIème siècle*. Edited by. E. Lévi-Provençal. París, 1930.

———. *Al-Bayan al-mugrib fi akhbar al-Andalus wa-l-Magrib. Al-Juz' al-rabi': qit'a min ta'rikh al-murabitin*. Nouvelle édition publié d'aprés l'edition de 1848–1851 de R. Dozy par G. S. Colin and E. Levi-Provençal. Beirut, 1967, 4 vols.

Ibn Mugith, Ahmad b. Mugith al-Tulaytuli (m. 459/1067). *Al-Muqni' fi 'ilm al-shurut. (Formulario notarial)*. Introduction and edition by F.J. Aguirre Sádaba. Madrid, 1994.

Ibn Rushd al-Hafid. Abu 'l-Walid Muhammad (Averroes) (m. 595/1198). *Bidayat al-mujtahid wa-nihayat al-muqtasid*. Beirut, 1409/1988, 9th ed., 2 vols.

Ibn Rushd. *The Distinguished Jurist's Primer*. Transl. Imran Ahsan Khan Nyazee. London, 1994 (vol. I) and 1996 (vol. II).

Malik Ibn Anas. *Kitab al-Muwatta'-* Al-Suyuti, *Is'af al-Muwatta, bi-rijal al-Muwatta'*. Edition by Faruq Sa'd. Beirut, 1401/1981.

Muwatta' al-imam Malik (riwayat al-Shaybani). Ed. 'Abd al-Wahhab 'Abd al-Latif. Beirut, [1984].

Sahnun, 'Abd al-Salam ibn Sa'id. *Al-Mudawwana al-kubra*. Cairo, 1323/1905.

Crónica del califa Abdarrahman III An-Nasir entre los años 912 y 942 (al-Muqtabis V). Spanish translation by M.J. Viguera and F. Corriente. Zaragoza, 1981.

Kitab al-Muqtabas fi ta'rikh al-Andalus: 'ahd al-Amir 'Abd Allah ibn Muhammad ibn 'Abd al-Rahman ibn al-Hakam ibn Hisham. Ed. Isma'il al-'Arabi. Casablanca, 1411/1990.

Further Reading

Abd Elwahed. *Contributions à une théorie sociologique de l'esclavage*. Paris, 1931.

Aguirre Sádaba, Francisco Javier. "Notas acerca de la proyección de los "*kutub al-wata'iq*" en el estudio social y económico de al-Andalus." *Miscelánea de Estudios Árabes y Hebreos* 49 (2000): 3–30.

Ayalon, D. "On the Eunuchs in Islam." *Jerusalem Studies in Arabic and Islam* 1 (1979): 67–124.

———. "On the Term *Khadim* in the Sense of 'Eunuch' in the Early Muslim Sources." *Arabica* XXXII (1985): 288–308.

Blanc, F.P., and A. Lourde. "Les conditions juridiques de l'accès au statut de concubine-mère en droit malékite." *Revue de l'Occident Musulman et de la Mediterranée* 36 (1983): 163–175.

Bonnassie, P. "Survie et extinction du régime esclavagiste dans l'Occident du haut Moyen Âge (IVe–XIe siècles)." *Cahiers de Civilisation Médiévale* XXVIII, no. 4 (1985): 307–343.

Bresc, H. *Politique et société en Sicilie, XIIe–XVe siècles*. Aldershot, 1990.

———. (sous la direction de) *Figures de l'esclave au Moyen-Âge et dans le monde moderne*. Paris, 1996.

Brockopp, Jonathan E. *Early Maliki Law. Ibn 'Abd al-Hakam and His Major Compendium of Jurisprudence*. Leiden, Boston, Köln, 2000.

Cilardo, A. *The Slave's Inheritance. A Reconsideration* (Conference of the School of Abbasid Studies, Univ. of St. Andrews, Scotland, 31st July–5th August 1989), *Annali Istituto Universitario Orientale Suppl.* 1990.

Coello, P. "Las actividades de las esclavas según Ibn Butlan (s. XI) y al-Saqati de Málaga (ss. XII–XIII)." In *La mujer en al-Andalus. Reflejos históricos de su actividad y categorías sociales*, edited by M.J. Viguera, 201–210. Madrid, 1989.

Constable, Olivia Remie. *Trade and Traders in Muslim Spain. The Commercial Realignment of the Iberian Peninsula: 900–1500*. Cambridge, 1994.

Fischer, Allan G.B., and Humphry J. Fisher. *Slavery and Muslim Society in Africa. The Institution in Saharan and Sudanic Africa and the Trans-Saharan Trade*. London, 1970.

Fischer, Rudolf. *Gold, Salz und Sklaven. Die Geschichte der grossen Sudanreiche Gana, Mali, Songhai.* Tübingen (Germany), 1982.

Gordon, M. *Slavery in the Arab World.* New York, 1989.

Graham, C. "The Meaning of Slavery and Identity in al-Andalus: The Epistle of Ibn Garcia." *Arab Studies Journal/Majallat al-dirasat al-'arabiyya* 3i (1995): 68–79.

Granja Santamaría, F., de la. "La venta de la esclava en el mercado." *Revista del Instituto Egipcio de Estudios Islámicos (Madrid)* XIII (1965–1966): 119–136.

Handler, Andrew. "The *'abid* Under the Umayyads of Cordova and the *muluk al-tawa'if*", *Occident and Orient. A Tribute to the Memory of A. Scheiber.* Budapest and Leiden, 1988, 229–238.

Harvey, L.P. *Islamic Spain. 1250 to 1500.* Chicago and London, 1992.

Koningsveld, P.S., van. "Muslim Slaves and Captives in Western Europe During the Late Middle Ages." *Islam and Christian-Muslim Relations* VI. 1 (1995): 5–24.

Lovejoy, P.E. *Transformations in Slavery: A History in Slavery in Africa.* Cambridge, London, New York, New Rochelle, Melbourne, Sydney, 1983.

———. "Concubinage and the Status of Women Slaves in Early Colonial Northern Nigeria." *Journal of African History* 29.2 (1988): 245–266.

Marín, Manuela. *Mujeres en al-Ándalus (Estudios Onomástico-Biográficos de al-Andalus XI).* Madrid, 2000.

Meillassoux, C. (Ed). *L'esclavage en Afrique pré-coloniale.* Paris, 1975.

Meouak, Mohamed. *Pouvoir souverain, administration centrale et élites politiques dans l'Espagne Umayyade (IIe–IVe vVIII^e–Xe siècles).* Helsinki, 1999.

Miller, J.C. "Muslim Slavery and Slaving: A Bibliography." *Slavery and Abolition* 13 (1992): 249–271 and 296–297.

———. *Slavery and Slaving in World History: A Bibliography, 1900–1991.* Millwood (New York), 1993.

Müller, H. "Zur Erforschung des islamischen Sklavenwesens." *Zeitschrift der Deutschen Morgenländischen Gesellschaft*, suppl. 1, Teil 2, 611–622 (*Vorträge der Deutscher Orientalistentag vom 21–27. Juli 1968*, Würzburg, ed. W. Voigt).

———. "Sklaven." En *Handbuch der Orientalistik (Wirtschafsgeschichte des vorderen Orients in Islamischer Zeit. Teil 1)*, edited by Bertold Spuler, 53–83. Leiden, 1977.

Philips, J.E. "Some Recent Thinking on Slavery in Islamic Africa and the Middle East." *Middle East Studies Association Bulletin*, 27 (1993): 157–162.

Phillips, W.D. *Slavery from Roman Times to the Early Transatlantic Trade.* Manchester, 1985.

Puente, Cristina, de la. "Esclavitud y matrimonio en la *Mudawwana al-kubra* de Sahnun." *Al-Qantara* xvi (1995): 309–333.

———. "Slavery and the Fulfilment of the Five Pillars of Islam in Early *Maliki* Works." In *Law, Christianity and Modernism in Islamic Society.* Proceedings of the Eighteenth Congress of the Union Européenne des Arabisants et Islamisants held at the Katholieke Universiteit Leuven (September 3–September 9, 1996), special issue of *Orientalia Lovaniensia Analecta.* Ed. U. Vermeulen and J.M.F. van Reeth. Leuven, 1997, 61–70.

———. "Juridical Sources for the Study of Women: An Example of the Limitations of the Female's Capacity to Act According to Maliki Law." En *Writing the Feminine. Women in Arab Sources*, edited by M. Marin and R. Deguilhem. London, 2002.

———. "Entre la esclavitud y la libertad: consecuencias legales de la manumisión según el derecho malikí." *Al-Qantara* XXI (2000): 339–360.

Raghib, Yusuf. "Les marchés aux esclaves en terre d'Islam." En *Mercati e Mercanti nell'alto medioevo: l'Area euroasiatica e l'area mediterranea (Settimane di Spoleto XL).* Spoleto, 1993, 721–763.

Savage, E. (Ed). *The Human Commodity. Perspectives on the Trans-Saharan Slave Trade*, special issue of *Slavery and Abolition* (13.1, April 1992).

Talbi, M. "Law and Economy in Ifriqiya (Tunisia) in the Third Islamic Century: Agriculture and the Role of Slaves in the Country's Economy." In *The Islamic Middle East, 700–1900: Studies in Economic and Social History*, edited by Abraham Udovitch, 209–250. Princeton, 1981.

Toru, Miura, and J.E. Philips (Eds). *Slave Elites in the Middle East and Africa. A Comparative Study.* London and New York, 2000.

Verlinden, C. *L'esclavage dans l'Europe Médiévale. Tome I. Peninsule Iberique, France.* Brugges, 1955.

Watson, J.L. (Ed). *Asian and African Systems of Slavery.* Oxford, 1980.

Willis, J.R. (Ed). "Islamic Africa: Relections on the Servile Estate." *Studia Islamica* LII (1980): 183–197.

———. *Slaves and Slavery in Muslim Africa.* 2 vols. London, 1985.

SOCIALIZING

Socializing outside the family was not mixed. Socializing took place either in a context where one person played host to a number of guests, or else in a place where people gathered spontaneously. Examples of the former are the tribal leader's council, the ruler's court, and the prominent official or scholar's literary or academic salon; the most common Arabic term for these institutions is the *majlis.* Very little information exists about women's socializing, although it was apparently organized partly on the same lines as men's; some princesses, for instance, are known to have had their own salon.

Rules of correct behavior in social gatherings existed; they included showing proper respect to the host and to older and more important people present. Thanks to this formal etiquette, sensitive and controversial subjects, including religion, could be discussed with considerable freedom. The *majlis* were also places where reputations were made and unmade. Young secretaries (*see* Bureaucrats) who favorably impressed a ruler with their eloquence or technical knowledge, and budding poets whose odes received a patron's praise or a philologist's stamp of approval (*see* Poetry), could find themselves launched on a successful career after attending *majlis.* However, someone who betrayed ignorance, failed to parry a rival's attack, or allowed himself to be made a laughingstock might lose his position and standing (*see* Adab).

The character of the gathering was determined by the host's interests and mood; a ruler could discuss affairs of state with his courtiers and then invite musicians to sing. The host set the tone; the 'Abbasid caliph al-Mutawakkil (r. AH 232–247/847–861 CE), for instance, was known for his barrack-room sense of humor and enjoyed humiliating his courtiers. Intellectually minded rulers, such as al-Ma'mun (198–218/813–833), sometimes invited experts in various fields to give short talks on subjects they wanted to learn more about. Al-Tawhidi's (d. 411/1023) account of evenings of conversation with the vizier Ibn Sa'dan, *Delight and Entertainment*, gives an idea of the intellectual level and breadth of interests that were current in some courts.

A scholar's salon—whether at his home or in a shop or mosque—was often the setting for more or less formal teaching. Hence the existence of a genre of books, sometimes termed *majalis* (salons, or sessions), recording the pronouncements of prominent philologists on linguistic topics. The subjects of less specialized conversations among cultured people have been preserved by the Baghdadi judge al-Tanukhi (d. 384/994) in his *Table-Talk of a Mesopotamian Judge*.

Socializing served more than to affirm one's status, advance one's career, or improve one's mind. Friends would invite each other to spend a pleasant time together; this almost always involved the recitation of poetry and often, singing, with musicians being invited if necessary. Such gatherings could be accompanied by wine, and the more attractive the setting and attendants the better.

The second (spontaneous) type of socializing took place in mosques, bathhouses, or taverns. The mosque was, and is, a kind of community center where people gather not only to pray but also to chat and discuss matters in neutral surroundings, without anyone having to play host. In medieval times a stranger arriving in a city where he knew no one would make some first contacts at the mosque. Conversations were usually dignified and serious in the mosque's tranquil, meditative atmosphere, but they were not necessarily devoted to religious matters; in his *Book of Misers*, al-Jahiz (d. ca. 255/869) portrays a group of men who regularly gathered in a mosque in Basra to exchange tips on how to save money.

The public baths, too, were a socially acceptable place to meet, although unlike the mosque they were not free and therefore seldom became a regular rendezvous for friends. They offered physical relaxation, and their informal atmosphere encouraged conversation. Since ritual purification accompanies Islamic

rites, including important stages in the life cycle such as weddings (*see* Marriage), a visit to the baths was an integral part of many celebrations. Women had far fewer opportunities than men of socializing outside the house, and for them in particular going to the baths was often synonymous with a party to which they brought their own food. Baths were (and are) not mixed; they were open to women and men on separate days.

The third meeting-place, the tavern, was reprehensible from the religious point of view since it sold wine; it was also associated with gambling, sexual immorality, and unseemly behavior. Yet taverns counted poets and singers among their customers, and they offered a setting for creative artistic activity.

The coffeehouse appeared at the end of the medieval period (*see* Beverages), first in Yemen and the Hijaz and then in the wider Ottoman empire and Iran. Offering the advantages of the tavern (food and conversation) without its drawbacks, it rapidly became popular.

HILARY KILPATRICK

See also Adab; Baths and Bathing; Bureaucrats; Courtiers; Gambling; Al-Jahiz; Al-Ma'mun; Marriage; Poetry; Al-Tawhidi

Further Reading

Hattox, Ralph S. *Coffee and Coffeehouses. The Origins of a Social Beverage in the Medieval near East.* Seattle and London: University of Washington Press, 1985.

Lazarus-Yafeh, Hava, Mark R. Cohen, Sasson Somekh, and Sidney H. Griffith, (Eds). *The Majlis. Interreligious Encounters in Medieval Islam.* Wiesbaden: Otto Harrassowitz Verlag, 1999.

Margoliouth, D.S. (Trans). *The Table-Talk of a Mesopotamian Judge.* London: The Royal Asiatic Society, 1922. al-Tanukhi, *Nishwar al-muhadara.* Ed. 'A. al-Shalji (Beirut: Dar Sadir, 1971–1973), translated by D.S. Margoliouth, *The Table-Talk of a Mesopotamian Judge*, part I (London: Royal Asiatic Society, 1922), parts VIII and II, *Islamic Culture* 3–6 (1929–1932).

al-Tawhidi, Abu Hayyan. *al-Imta' wa-l-Mu'anasa.* Ed. Ahmad Amin and Ahmad al-Zayn. Cairo: Lajnat al-Ta'lif wa-l-Tarjama wa-l-Nashr, 1953.

SONGHAY EMPIRE

Origin

Islam began to spread in the Songhay empire some time in the eleventh century CE, when the ruling Za or Dia dynasty first accepted Islam. It was a prosperous region with a booming trade from the city of Gao.

In fact, a Songhay kingdom in the region of Gao had existed since the eleventh century, but it had come under the control of Mali in 1325. After the decline of Mali, the kingdom of Gao reasserted itself as the major kingdom in the *Sahel*. By the late fourteenth century, Gao reasserted itself as the Sunni dynasty, the other name of the Songhay empire.

Songhay would not fully eclipse Mali until the reign of Sunni 'Ali Ber, who reigned from 1464 to 1492. He aggressively turned the kingdom of Gao into an empire under his leadership, and the most important towns of the Western Sudan came under the Songhay empire. The great cities of Islamic learning, such as Timbuktu (captured from the Tuaregs) and Jenne, also came under his power between 1471 and 1476. The empire stretched across the Niger valley, west to Senegal and east to Agades (modern-day Niger). With his cavalry and a highly mobile fleet of ships, 'Ali Ber pushed the Berbers who had always played such a crucial role in the downfall of Sahelian kingdoms, far north.

The Sunni Kings

The *'ulama* have condemned Sunni 'Ali, the first real founder, in spite of his contribution in founding the Songhay empire. They claimed he was a nominal Muslim and compromised between paganism and Islam, although he prayed and fasted. Once he punished the famous scholar Al-Maghili—to whom is attributed the introduction of the *Qadiriyya* fraternity of Sufis in Africa—by calling him "a pagan." He believed in magical practices and local cults. This, however, was not something new in the Songhay only. Almost the same practice continued in other parts of West Africa until the time that various revivalist movements took place in the eighteenth and nineteenth centuries.

Sunni 'Ali's syncretism was soon denounced by the eminent Muslim scholars in Timbuktu. Timbuktu had an established reputation as a center of Islamic learning and civilization of West Africa. Members of the famous *Aqit* family of Berber scholars were enjoying the post of the Grand *Qadi* (Chief Justice) at the time and were known for their fearless oppositions to the rulers. Sunni 'Ali did not take such criticism lightly. In his lifetime he suppressed the scholars of Timbuktu, but after his death the situation completely changed and the Muslim scholars triumphed. Muhammad Touré, a military general, asked his successor, Sunni Barou, to make a public appearance and make a confession of his faith in Islam. When Barou refused to do so, Muhammad Touré ousted

him and established a new dynasty in his own name, called the *Askiya* dynasty. Sunni 'Ali may be compared with Sundiate of Mali and Askiya Muhammad Touré to Mansa Musa, a champion for the cause of Islam.

An ardent Muslim, when Muhammad Touré (r. 1493–1528) came to power, he established Islamic law and extensively drew upon the expertise of his Timbuktu scholars in matters of the state. He also arranged for a large number of Muslims to be trained as judges *(qadis)* and he replaced native Songhay administrators with Arab Muslims in a bid to stabilize the empire. Timbuktu gained fame as an intellectual center rivaling many others in the Muslim world. It had the credit of establishing the first Muslim university—Sankore University—in West Africa, the name of which is commemorated still today in Ibadan University, where a certain staff residential area is named Sankore Avenue. Learners from various parts of the world came to study a wide array of sciences, ranging from language and politics to law and medicine (apart from the city's more than 180 *madrasahs* where one could undertake strictly Islamic studies). Medieval Europe sent emissaries to the University of Sankore to witness its excellent libraries with manuscripts and to consult with the learned mathematicians, astronomers, physicians, and jurists whose intellectual endeavors were said to be paid for out of the king's own treasury.

Muhammad Touré continued Sunni Ali's imperial expansion by seizing the important Saharan oases and conquering Mali. From there he conquered Hausaland. He also further centralized the government by creating a large and elaborate bureaucracy to oversee his extensive empire. Merchants and traders traveled from Asia, the Middle East, and Europe to exchange their exotic wares for the gold of Songhay. As in Mali, there was a privileged caste of craftsmen, and slave labor played an important role in agriculture. Gold, kola nuts, and slaves were the main exports, whereas textiles, horses, salt, and luxury goods were the main imports.

Touré also standardized weights, measures, and currency so that culture throughout the Songhay began to homogenize. These programs of conquest, centralization, and standardization were the most ambitious and far-reaching in sub-Saharan history until the colonization of the continent by the Europeans. Songhay reached its greatest territorial expansion under Askia Dawud (r. 1549–1582), when the empire stretched all the way to Cameroon. With literally several thousand cultures under its control, Songhay was the largest empire in African history.

Touré, on his pilgrimage to Makkah, came into close contact with various Muslim scholars and rulers in the Arab countries. He visited the caliph of Egypt, who proclaimed him caliph of the whole of Sudan. Sudan, at the time, was a loose term for a large area in sub-Saharan Africa usually embracing Mali, Chad, northwest Nigeria, and Niger. In Makkah, the King accorded him great respect, turbanned him, and gave him a sword and the title of *Khalifah* of western Sudan. On his return from Makkah in 1497, he proudly used the title of *al-Hajj*. Askiya took such a keen interest in the Islamic legal system that he asked a number of questions on Islamic theology from his personal friend, Muhammad al-Maghili. Al-Maghili wrote down the answers in detail, which Askiya circulated in the Songhay empire. The questions pertained to the fundamental structure of the faith that later served as the chief source of 'Uthman Dan Fodio's revolution in Hausaland a few years thereafter.

Although most of the people in urban areas had turned Muslim, the majority of those living in the rural areas still followed African traditional religion. Some aspects of traditional religion have been preserved to this day, including the sacred drum, the sacred fire, and the old types of costume and hairstyle.

Overall, the appearance of Islam in western Sudan was important for much more than religious reasons. It introduced the culture of scholarship to countries beyond Egypt and the *Maghrib* and stabilized trade between her and the lands beyond the Sahara. It also, however, left terrible religious conflicts between the various tribes who did or did not accept Islam, and created a different kind of unrest.

Decline

After Askiya Muhammad Touré, the empire began to crumble. His sons who had shared power with him deposed him since there was no fixed law of succession to the throne. During a period of sixty years (1528–1591), eight Askiyas came to power consecutively.

Songhay had gotten too large by this time; it encompassed too much territory to control. After the reign of Askia Dawud, subject peoples began to revolt, even though Songhay had an army of more than thirty five thousand soldiers. The first major region to go was Hausaland. In 1590, al-Mansur, the powerful and ambitious sultan of Morocco, decided that he wanted control of the West African gold trade badly enough to send his army all the way across the Sahara. The spears and swords of the Songhay warriors were no match for the cannons and muskets of the Moroccan army. The Moroccan invasion destroyed the Songhay empire. It contributed, along with such other phenomena as the

growing Atlantic trade, to the decline of the trade routes that had brought prosperity to the region for hundreds of years.

Trade routes fell under local control and deteriorated beyond recovery. The Moroccans also took Timbuktu in 1591 and ruled over the city until about 1780, supervising its ultimate decline. During the early nineteenth century, Timbuktu passed into the hands of a variety of West African groups, including the Tuaregs and the Bamabra, who founded the Bamabra kingdom of Ségou farther to the south. In the late nineteenth century, as European powers invaded parts of Africa, French colonizers took over the city.

In 1612, the remaining cities of Songhay fell into anarchy and the greatest empire of African history came to a sudden close. No African nation since has risen to prominence and wealth as did the mighty Songhay.

KHALID DHORAT

Further Reading

Caillié, Réné. *Travels Through Central Africa to Timbuctoo; and Across the Great Desert to Morocco Performed in the Years 1824–1828.* Colburn and Bentley, 1830.
Davidson, Basil. *Africa in History.* Simon & Schuster, 1996.
Dubois, Felix. *Timbuctoo the Mysterious.* Transl. Diane White. Heinemann, 1897.
Gardner, Brian. *The Quest for Timbuktu.* Cassell, 1968.
Jackson, John G. *Introduction to African Civilizations.* Citadel Press, 1994.
Robinson, D., and D. Smith. *Sources of the African Past.* London: Heinemann, 1979.
Shillington, Kevin. *History of Africa.* St. Martin's Press, 1995.
Shinnie, Margaret. *Ancient African Kingdoms.* Edward Arnold, 1965.

SOUTHEAST ASIA, HISTORY AND CULTURE

Although never conceived of as a unitary region in Arabic accounts, Southeast Asia was a maritime contact zone for Indian Ocean trade with China from antiquity. The shippers who plied this route, such as Ibn Khurradadhbih, recorded the names of several of the harbors at which they called for water, victuals, and trade. The most famous of the trading ports were located in the vicinity of the Isthmus of Kra (Kalah), in the locales of North Sumatra (Ramni), East Sumatra (Zabaj), Tioman Island (Tiyuma), and the coasts of Cambodia (Qmar) and Champa (Sanf)—the last being the collective name for the Austronesian kingdoms once located in central Vietnam.

The majority of the Southeast Asian ports gained advantage from this passing India trade, and their organization and culture reflected Indic modes. The Buddhist (or at times Saivite) kingdoms of Java; Angkor in Cambodia; the Cham cities in Vietnam; and Srivijaya in the Straits of Malacca all maintained cults of divine kingship and the use of Sanskrit for official proclamations. Because of this, most medieval accounts placed Southeast Asian toponyms in general descriptions of India.

The region was not always a stable constellation of states. Eleventh-century attacks by the Tamil Cholas weakened Srivijaya and may have led the Khmers to play a stronger role on the peninsula. Further, the Mongol conquests of the twelfth century saw a reorientation of Southern Song networks involving Java as a more active agent of interoceanic trade. The Javanese state Singasari, and then its thirteenth-century successor Majapahit, exercised hegemony over Sumatra. The general view of a Java-dominated island world seems to have led to the nascence in the Arabic texts of this toponym, as in the encyclopedia of Yaqut, who stated in his *Mu'jam al-buldan* that Java was one of the first of the kingdoms of China. Ibn al-Mujawir also made reference, in his *Ta'rikh al-mustabsir* (ca. 1228), to rough passage to "the region of Jawa." When Marco Polo visited the region in 1292, he referred to Sumatra as *Java Minora*. Similarly, when Ibn Battuta returned from China circa 1345, he named Sumatra as a part of *Jawa*.

The Mongols had also invaded mainland Burma in 1258, and their impact in Asia was a catalyst for the southward movement of the Tai peoples at the expense of the mainland Mon and Khmer populations. After slow beginnings on North Sumatra, and between the exertions of Singasari and Majapahit, Islamization would spread westward to other parts of the Malay Peninsula and the spice islands before the arrival of the Portuguese, who took the port of Malacca in 1511 and attempted to monopolize the collection of spices in the region. This allowed for the rise of the Sumatran state of Aceh under 'Ali Mughayat Shah (r. 1514–1530). Whereas the Portuguese apothecary Tomé Pires, stationed in freshly conquered Malacca between 1512 and 1515, could write of a largely non-Muslim Java, by 1527, Majapahit had been defeated by the coastal sultanate of Demak, ushering in a long-term process of Islamization from above.

Muslims were also an increasingly notable presence in mainland Southeast Asian courts, such as Siam and Cambodia, but their influence was short-lived. With the rise of Atlantic commercial power in the seventeenth century, Sumatran Aceh and West Java's Banten constituted the leading Muslim competitors for trade in the region. Their territories, like those of many Southeast Asian states, were slowly being eaten away over the course of the coming centuries by Western colonialism. At the same time, Islam became ever more linked with many of the cultures of the archipelago while Theravada Buddhism became ever more entrenched as that of the mainland.

MICHAEL LAFFAN

See also Ibn Battuta; Ibn Khurradadhbih; Java; Silk Roads; Southeast Asia, Languages and Literatures; Sumatra and the Malay Peninsula; Yaqut

Further reading

Cortesão, Armando (Trans and ed). *The Suma Oriental of Tomé Pires (...) and the book of Fransisco Rodriguez (...)*. The Hakluyt Society, second series, no. 89, London, 1944.
Coedès, George. *The Indianized States of Southeast Asia*. Honolulu: East West Center Press, 1968.
Ibn Battuta. *The Travels of Ibn Battûta A.D. 1325–1354*, vol. IV. Translated and edited by H.A.R. Gibb and C.F. Beckingham. London: Hakluyt Society, 1994, 874–887.
Ibrahim, Muhammad Rabi' b. Muhammad. *The Ship of Sulaimân*. Transl. J. O'Kane. Routledge and Kegan Paul: London, 1972.
Jacq-Hergoualc'h, Michel. *The Malay Peninsula: Crossroads of the Maritime Silk Road*. Leiden: Brill, 2002.
Reid, Anthony. *Southeast Asia in the Age of Commerce*. 2 vols. New Haven, CT: Yale University Press, 1988–1993.
Tibbetts, G.R. *A Study of the Arabic Texts Containing Material on South-East Asia*. Leiden and London: Brill, 1979.
Wolters, Oliver. *Early Indonesian Commerce: A Study of the Origins of Śrîvijaya*. Ithaca: Cornell University Press, 1962.
Yule, Henry, and Henri Cordier. *The Book of Ser Marco Polo*. 2 vols. Philo Press, Amsterdam, 1975.

SOUTHEAST ASIA, LANGUAGES AND LITERATURES

Ever since Southeast Asia began to feature in the accounts of Muslim mariners, it is clear they had dealings mainly with the Austronesian peoples of the archipelago and coastal harbors of the mainland, for whom Malay served as the *lingua franca*. Ninth-century Arab accounts referred to the Malacca Straits as Salaht, from the Malay *selat* (strait), while the *'Aja'ib al-hind* of al-Ramhurmuzi (ca. 1000) made reference to the practice of sitting deferentially before a local king by using the Malay verb *bersila*. The use of Malay along the main artery of trade was often commented on by later travelers. Jean Baptiste Tavernier (1605–1689) reported that the languages of the cultured world included Malay as that "of educated people, from the flooding Indus to China and Japan, and in most of the Eastern isles, much like Latin in our Europe."

Although Malay played an important role in interethnic communication, there is a dearth of inscriptions in that language as compared to those of the cultures of Java and Cambodia, whether in the once widespread Indic-derived scripts or in the Arabic script that supplanted them in the Muslim islands of Indonesia and the Malay Peninsula. Equally, there is a paucity of manuscript holdings—again as compared with the palm-leaf texts of those kingdoms that remained substantially Hindu–Buddhist in outlook when the Europeans arrived; most notably the Southeast Asian mainland and the islands of Java and Bali.

Nonetheless, the holdings that remain indicate that the pre-Islamic Malay literature, like most of the literatures of the region, consisted of a rich selection of royal epics, declamatory poetry, and morality tales, suffused with stories from (or complete reworkings of) Indian epics, such as the Mahabharata and the Ramayana. With Islamization, these were both supplemented or replaced by Islamic tales drawn from Arabic and Persian literature, such as the *Hikayat Muhammad Hanafiyya*, and many indigenous compositions in the form of poems—sometimes brief, sometimes epic—known as *syair* (from the Arabic).

Malay also played a leading role in the inculcation of Islamic norms in the archipelago, first mystical and then primarily for the transmission of knowledge of Shafi'i *fiqh* (Islamic jurisprudence). The first known Malay author, Hamzah al-Fansuri (d. 1527), wrote in one of his poetic works that he had done so in Malay in the hope that "those of God Almighty's servants unacquainted with Farsi and Arabic will be able to discuss its contents." Again, in 1601, Shams al-Din of Pasai, wrote in his *Mir'at al-mu'min* that he had written "in the Jawi language in order to render words of the principles of religion for those unable to understand Arabic or Farsi," and al-Raniri, the chief Qadi to the Acehnese court in the late 1630s, composed his compendium on Shafi'i *fiqh*, the *Sirat al-mustaqim;* he did so in Malay.

Malay literature has also been strongly influenced by that of Java, which shares in the corpus of Indian stories that were often recast with specifically Javanese admixtures (such as the powerful clown characters or the cultural hero Panji).

Furthermore, with the Islamization of Java and closer contacts between its sultanates and those of the Malay world, there was an increasing trend toward polyglossia among Islamic scholars. Perhaps for this reason one of the great Malay exponents of the Sufi tradition, and the author of the first Malay exegesis of the Qur'an, 'Abd al-Ra'uf al-Sinkili (1615–1693), noted in his *Mir'ât al-tullâb* that he made specific recourse to *al-lisan al-jawiyya al-samutra'iyya* (the Sumatran Jawi tongue), perhaps implying that there were indeed other Southeast Asian languages.

MICHAEL LAFFAN

See also Java; Scriptural Exegesis, Islamic; Sufism and Sufis; Sumatra and the Malay Peninsula

Further reading

Collins, James T. *Malay, World Language: A Short History*. 2d ed. Kuala Lumpur: Dewan Bahasa dan Pustaka, 2000.

SPICES

When comparing the simple fare and the paucity of ingredients of pre-Islamic Bedouin (or even sedentary) Arab food with the sophistication displayed in 'Abbasid or Mamluk cookbooks, one is struck by the quantities and diversity of the spices, herbs, and condiments employed by the latter. These books reflect the aristocratic cuisine of the courts and the rich rather than the populace. It may not be superfluous to point out that the often-heard assertion that the lavish use of spices was generally meant to mask the odor of badly preserved meat is a slanderous insult to a highly refined cuisine. The choice of a particular seasoning was naturally guided by matters of taste and culinary delight, but at the same time a coherent theory of dietetics and medicine would give guidelines for the selection of ingredients appropriate to the dish, the eater, his or her circumstances, and the time of the year. Medical treatises deal with the theory and practice of this, but the cookbooks, too, may include dietary recommendations for the preservation of a balanced constitution.

Medieval Arabic texts sometimes differentiate between various categories of spices, herbs, aromatics, and condiments. The terminology is fluctuating but will usually include *abazir* (mostly seed-based), *tawabil* (other seasonings), and *afawih* (aromatic substances); *bahar* is another general term for "spice." The precise definitions often overlap, and the distinction between herbs and vegetables (Ar. *buqul*) is not strict. Some items are multipurpose: saffron, for instance, is used for its fragrance in food and as a perfume, in addition to its use as a coloring agent. In a thirteenth-century cookbook, cinnamon and coriander are used in approximately eighty percent of all dishes, followed by cumin, mastic, pepper, and ginger. An introductory chapter of the tenth-century cookbook from Baghdad, by Ibn Sayyar al-Warraq, lists the spices, herbs, and fragrances that are indispensable for any cook. They include musk, ambergris, rosewater, saffron, cinnamon, galingale, cloves, mastic, saltwort, cardamom, sugar, honey, treacle, pepper, coriander, cumin, caraway, ginger, spikenard, asafoetida, salt (allegedly called by the Prophet Muhammad "the lord of condiments"), onion, vinegar, olive oil, garlic, celery, cress, leek, dill, fennel, rue, mint, and thyme, not to mention numerous fruits, pickles, nuts, aromatics, and vegetables. Other chapters give the digestive properties of these ingredients. Almost any kind of dish, savory, sweet, or sour, including kinds of bread, pastry, and drinks, could and should be enhanced by the addition of spices and herbs. Recipes are often amazingly complex, as if simple ones were to be disdained by the wealthy. The correct use of spices and herbs was an art, and anecdotes in literary sources show the disgrace resulting from sinning against the rules, even though the consequences would not always have been as severe as in the story told in the *Thousand and One Nights* (in the story cycle of "The Hunchback"), in which a man annoys his lover by using an excess of cumin.

Naturally, the use of spices was not uniform and there are many local differences or shifts in time. Striking in all periods is the frequent use of sugar and other sweeteners in meat dishes. The various condiments and pickles, called *kawamikh*, which are used either as side dishes or as ingredients in the cooking process, are in a special category of seasoning. Among the most often mentioned of these is a briny concoction based on fish, like the Roman *liquamen* or *garum*; another is based on barley. Recipes for these relishes describe a very complicated and lengthy process taking several months. Both kinds may be called *murri*, which seems to be derived from Latin *muria*.

The spice trade, both within and beyond the Muslim territories, was a flourishing business. Pepper, ginger, cinnamon, cloves, cardamom, mace, nutmeg, and musk were among the products imported from India, China, and Black Africa. In due course, even before the time of the Crusades, Europe became greatly interested in the Eastern spices, with Venice being at the hub of the spice trade with the Middle East, with Egypt in particular. The spice trade in the Ayyubid and Mamluk periods was dominated by a group of merchants known as the Karimi, who were active in the major centers of trade and sent their fleets over the Red Sea and the Indian Ocean. Their power dwindled in the course of the fifteenth century due to the policy of the Mamluk sultans and the economic crisis in Egypt. The end of the Middle Ages coincided with the taking over of much of the spice trade by European powers.

GEERT JAN VAN GELDER

See also Food and Diet; Trade, Indian Ocean; Trade, Mediterreanean

Further Reading

Aubale-Sallenave, Françoise. "Parfums, épices et condiments dans l'alimentation arabe médiévale." In *La alimentación en las culturas islámicas*, edited by Manuela Marín and David Waines, 217–249. Madrid: Agencia Española de Cooperación Internacional, 1994.
Dietrich, A. "Afāwīh." *Encyclopaedia of Islam*. New ed. Supplement, fasc. 1–2. Leiden: Brill, 1980. 42–43.
Rodinson, Maxime, A.J. Arberry, and Charles Perry. *Medieval Arab Cookery*. Totnes, Devon: Prospect Books, 2001 (see general index s.v. caraway, cardamom, cinnamon, cloves, coriander, cumin, mace, mustard, nutmeg, pepper, pickles, spice bread, spice mixture, spice trade, spices; and see index of foreign words, especially s.v. *kamakh*, *murri*.)

SPORTS

Engagement in various types of sports was undoubtedly a favorite pastime of medieval Muslims throughout Islamic territories. However, given both the extremely scattered data and the relatively poor research on this subject the information that follows is bound to be incomplete. In addition, since our sources report next to nothing on the sport activities of the common people, this entry deals with a limited number of sports and of the medieval Islamic elite in particular.

We first learn of horseracing, an expensive pastime and a sport of princes, in the Umayyad period, although it stands to reason that it took place also in pre-Islamic Arabia. It appears from our sources that its apogee was in the eighth century CE, in the reigns of the Umayyad Hisham to the 'Abbasid Harun al-Rashid. Probably at some point after the ninth century, it went into decline, although it certainly did not disappear altogether. Being also part of equitation (*furusiyya*), horseracing was always essential for military training and an object of entertainment for the rulers, dignitaries, and others. Long hippodromes (*maydan*), sometimes stretching for several kilometers, were set apart for this purpose in major Islamic towns. Horses that participated had to undergo a period of training that lasted a few weeks. According to the rules, a race could take place only between horses of the same class, age, and other defined criteria. Prizes for winners were part of this sport activity. As for the defeated competitors, some sources tell of the custom of placing a monkey on the back of their horses with a whip to lash the horse, thus putting the masters to shame. Due to the high costs of horse breeding for competition, the common people had to satisfy themselves with alternative sorts of races, such as camel, donkey, or dog races. Especially popular was pigeon racing.

Polo (*sawlajan* and *jukan*, from Persian Chawgan), originally a Persian sport, was another pastime limited to the higher echelons of the society that became favorable under the early 'Abbasids and contemporary local dynasties. Some of the caliphs are reported playing polo with their boon companions. In later periods, polo was exercised on festive occasions such as the visit of foreign ambassadors. This was the case in AH 660/1262 CE, when the Mamluk sultan Baybars I received a Mongol delegation. When, in the last years of the Mamluk reign in Egypt, Sultan Qansuh al-Ghawri received Ottoman and Safavid delegates, he entertained them with polo games. The status of polo in the Mamluk court is demonstrated in the establishment of the post of the *jukandar*, a high official in charge of supervising polo exercises.

The wide practice of polo games among the Mamluk elite was based on the assumption that it was suitable for keeping soldiers and horses in good physical condition. Polo was usually played on horseback. Players were divided into two teams, each carrying a long-handled stick with one end bent back. One of the players started by throwing a leather ball (but sometimes a ball of silver) high into the air, another player struck it, and thereafter the ball passed from player to player. Each team tried to get the ball between two posts defended by the opponents, the posts being located at the end of a pitch so large that it gave ample freedom of movement for the mounted participants. The polo game is repeatedly reported for the Ayyubid and Mamluk courts, where it was played in special hippodromes constructed for that purpose. It appears that in the Mamluk state, at least under the reign of Barsbay (825–841/1422–1437), a special season of polo games was fixed. The favor that polo gained in the Mamluk state can be gauged from its recurrence as a theme in artistic objects. Similar to polo, and also a favorite pastime of the early 'Abbasids, was the sport of *tabtab*, which was played on horseback with a broad piece of wood or a racket to hit the ball.

Qabaq, or gourd game, entailed shooting arrows from a moving horse at a gourd target at the top of a high pole, where a pigeon was placed. It was popular in the early Mamluk period and was occasionally played during feasts for the birth of a Mamluk prince, or his circumcision. Sultan Baybars I constructed for it the grounds known as Maydan al-Qabaq, which were used till the reign of al-Nasir Muhammad ibn Qalawun (ca. 700/1300).

Finally, on equestrian sports, one should mention archery competitions. These simulated a duel between mounted horsemen with the use of imitations to shoot at from a distance of a few hundred yards. Betting was part of the game. Many manuals were written to guide participants through the numerous techniques. Shooting with the crossbow was known as *bunduq*.

Flight and target shooting with arrows was a sport as much as a basic part of military proficiency.

Wrestling matches took place at Islamic courts. A fragmentary lustre plate, probably from eleventh-century Egypt, has a painting of a wrestling match, most likely serving as a royal theme. We laconically know of popular wrestling matches in Cairo during the fourteenth and fifteenth centuries. Their referees were versatile entertainers and street performers. In the same vein one should mention weightlifting.

A report about the 'Abbasid al-Mu'tasim (218–227/833–842) notes that he lifted weights during exercise. Fencing, riverboat racing, swimming, and games with lances were also in vogue, due to their low costs. Among the sports of the 'Abbasid period, contests of animals and bird fighting were notable. The rulers and the common people alike favored them. Dogs, rams, and cocks, among others, were used in competitions, and thus Ma'mun's (198–218/813–833) servants were on one occasion busy watching cock fighting at the court. A duel of lions and buffaloes is reported for al-Mu'tasim's court.

Also related to the present discussion is the subject of falconry (hunting with trained falcons), an ancient sport practiced in different parts of the world, which was introduced into Arabia many centuries before the Christian era. It seems to have been of special appeal there. It was sanctioned in the Qur'an and after the conquests became a favorable pastime with the ruling elite and a symbol of high status. It is first associated with the Umayyad Yazid (680–683 CE) and later the 'Abbasids maintained falconers on official posts with lavish expenses. When Marco Polo, the famous Venetian traveler, visited the Mongol Khan Kublai in 1275 CE, he was astonished to see as many as ten thousand falconers. All that enormous interest resulted in sanctuaries for falcons and hawks and a flourishing literature on falconry.

One of the best descriptions of hunting practices is provided by the "aristocrat" Usama ibn Munqidh (1095–1188 CE), who was a member of an Arab petty dynasty from northern Syria. In his memoirs he describes some hunting expeditions in which he himself participated.

BOAZ SHOSHAN

See also Hunting

Further Reading

Abd al-Raziq, Ahmad. "Deux Jeux Sportifs en Egypte au temps des mamluks." *Annales islamologiques* 12 (1974): 95–130.
Ahsan, Muhammad Nanazir. *Social Life Under the Abbasids*. London: Longman, 1979.

Ali, Abdul. "Arab Legacy to Falconry." *Islamic Culture* 70 (1996): 55–63.

Ayalon, David. "Notes on the Furusiyya." *Scripta Hierosolymitana* 9 (1961): 31–62.

STORIES AND STORYTELLING

See Popular Literature

SUDAN

Bilad al-Sudan, the "land of the blacks," was the name used for the savannah regions south of the Sahara from the Atlantic to the Red Sea. It can be divided into the Western Sudan (present-day Senegal to Mali), the Central Sudan around and to the northeast of Lake Chad (today Niger, northern Nigeria, and Chad), and the Nilotic Sudan (today the northern part of the Republic of Sudan). Western Sudan was sometimes also given the generic name "Takrur."

The Muslims' relation to the Sudan was initially one of trade. The origins of trans-Saharan trade is not known, but it did predate the Arab presence in North Africa, and it must have seen a marked expansion when the Maghrib was included in an Islamic world market, at least from the eighth or ninth century. Muslim traders traveled across the desert to market towns in the Sudanic belt, such as Tadmekka, Walata, and Awdaghost, where they met with local long-distance traders that had brought gold, ivory, and slaves from forest regions of the south. Eventually these Sudanic traders also started to make the journey across the desert to the trade centers that grew up on the northern side, such as Aghmat, Sijilmasa, and Wargala.

The Muslim traders did not, by and large, make any attempt at proselytization of their faith. Instead, they kept apart in separate quarters, often somewhat outside the main Sudanic towns. But the lucrative trade did in itself attract local elites to the civilization and thus the religion of the strangers. The rules of the Shari'a formed a legal framework necessary for more elaborate commercial networks, and those Sudanic traders that wanted to insert themselves directly in the transdesert trade would find conversion a major benefit for participation in it.

The trade also led to the growth of large empires in the Sudanic region. The first was Ghana (or Wagadu). It collapsed, perhaps after an Almoravid attack, in 1076, and was succeeded by Mali on the Niger bend (early thirteenth century). Mali became famous in the Muslim world for its wealth based on the gold trade, a reputation entrenched when its ruler, Mansa Musa, made a resplendent *hajj* in 1324. In the fifteenth century, the power of Mali was overtaken by the Songhay empire (c. 1460–1591), slightly to its east, with the capital of Gao.

Unlike Ghana's rulers, those of Mali had converted to Islam. However, it was initially only a partial conversion, as they also had to retain their religious legitimacy as divinely ordained rulers according to the popular faiths of their subjects. As Islam spread among the socially dominant classes of the population, however, Muslim religiosity also became important for the ruler, and the *askiya* rulers of Songhay, such as Askiya Muhammad, sought a reputation for piety by inviting Muslim reformers from the north to deepen knowledge of Islam in his lands.

Local traders also spread Islam southward from Jenne and other riverain centers, embodied by scholarly lineages such as the Suwari teachers and traders (the Jahanke and Juula).

The western trade routes were initially the most important ones across the desert. But the first major Sudanic king to convert to Islam was not of the west, but the ruler of the Kanem empire east of Lake Chad. He had already in the eleventh century made the transition to Islam. Kanem was also the first and only Sudanic kingdom to colonize a part of the Maghreb when it invaded Fezzan (today southern Libya) and established a local capital there at Traghen in around 1258. This expansionism from the south lasted about a century before weaknesses at home caused contacts to the colony to be cut off and it eventually withered away.

The traders that first brought Islam across the desert were mostly Ibadis or other Khariji groups that dominated such northern centers as Sijilmasa and Wargala. Thus Sudanic Islam was initially an Ibadi Islam, and it may have been this school to which the Kanem king converted. However, in this period Islam was still an elite and trader religion. By the time it spread to a wider audience from the twelfth and thirteenth centuries, Malikism reigned supreme in the north, and although some Ibadi desert retreats (Ghardaia, Wargala, Ghadames) remained important trading centers, it was Maliki Islam that came to dominate the Sudan, and all traces of an Ibadi past were lost to posterity.

The history of Islam in the Nilotic region differs from the western and central ones, because the Nile River allows a continuity of population from north to south. It also differs because Christianity had gained a firm foothold in the Nile valley, such as in the Nubian kingdoms of Maris, Muqurra, and Alwa. Muqurra, with its capital of Dongola, came under Egyptian Muslim control under the Mamluks, and its cathedral was turned into a mosque in 1317. The kingdom of Alwa to the south (near modern-day Khartoum) fell apart around the same time. The immigration of Arab tribes, together with Arabization of the local population groups, made Arabic the dominant language, and Islam dominated the Nilotic Sudan by the end of the sixteenth century. At the end of this period, a dynasty of the Funj people established the kingdom of Sennar, which included most of the Nilotic Sudan and lasted until the nineteenth century.

In spite of its geographical closeness to Muslim Egypt, Islamic scholarship was much less developed in the Nilotic regions than in the western Sudan. There, desert-side centers such as Timbuktu and Walata, as well as scholarly tribes of the desert proper, produced an extensive Islamic literature and became focuses of learning that later came to influence not only their own region but also the central lands of Islam. More militant expressions of religious mobilization, such as the Almoravid movements that had some roots in the south, also showed the impact that the Sudan had on the Maghreb and beyond.

KNUT S. VIKØR

See also al-Bakri; Berber or Tamazight; Ibn Battuta; Mahmud al-Kati; Slaves and Slave Trade; Sunni 'Ali; Trade, African; Waqwaq

Further Reading

Hunwick, John O. *Timbuktu and the Songhay Empire: Al-Sa'di's Ta'rikh al-Sudan down to 1613 and Other Contemporary Documents.* Leiden: Brill, 1999, 2003.
———. *Shari'a in Songhay: The Replies of al-Maghili to the Questions of Askia al-Hajj Muhammad.* Oxford: Oxford University Press, 1985.
Levtzion, Nehemia. *Ancient Ghana and Mali.* London: Methuen, 1973.
———. "Islam in the Bilad al-Sudan to 1800," and "The Juula and the Expansion of Islam into the Forest." In *The History of Islam in Africa,* edited by N. Levtzion and Randall L. Pouwels, 63–116. Athens: Ohio University Press, 2000.
Levtzion, Nehemia, and J.F.P. Hopkins (Eds). *Corpus of Early Arabic Sources for West African History.* Cambridge: Cambridge University Press, 1981.
Lewicki, Tadeusz. "Traits d'histoire du commerce transsaharien. Marchands et missionnaires ibadites en Soudan occidental et central au cours des viiie-xiie siècles." *Etnografia polska* viii (1964): 291–311.

SUFFERING

Various discussions that relate to the theme of suffering can be found in several genres, including discussions of pain, evil, misery *(shaqa'),* affliction *(bala'),* and torment *('adhab).* Traditionally, humans (including prophets), animals, and jinn are liable to suffer, to the exclusion of God and angels. As with pleasure and happiness, suffering may be experienced in this world and the hereafter; and it is generally accepted that "the torment of the hereafter is greater" (Q 68:33). The entry discusses this-worldly suffering only.

The Qur'an and *hadith* literature approach suffering in various ways. Some suffering is explained as punishment deserved by those who commit unbelief or disobedience, and is cited to draw people toward piety. The worst cases involve the violent and humiliating annihilation of an individual or a people (for example, the peoples of Noah and Lot), leading to more severe torment in the hereafter. Those with greater prudence should perceive these cases as a warning and as lessons through example. Where the sufferer survives, he or she will have the opportunity to recognize his or her own suffering as a directive to mend his or her ways.

Equally, suffering may be cathartic and thus a reason to rejoice. It may redeem the sufferer by purging him or her of sin, bringing relief from greater torment in the hereafter. According to one *hadith,* any Muslim who suffers harm, even the prick of a thorn, will have his or her sins expiated, "shedding from him as a tree sheds its leaves." Suffering may also draw one nearer to God (Q 7:94), or serve as an ordeal that tests the individual's faith (Q 2:155–157). Another *hadith* describes the plague as representing divine punishment upon some people, and divine mercy upon the believer, who will be rewarded for his or her patience in enduring a plague-ridden town. The Qur'an presents Prophet Job as the patient believer *par excellence,* who passed the test of severe adversity.

As regards the moral and spiritual virtues associated with the experience of suffering, the main religious traditions in Islam are in general agreement but differ on details. The central cathartic virtue emphasized throughout the Qur'an is patience, which (in contrast to stoic endurance) should be based on faith in, and reliance on, God's goodness and power. This basis is explained in various ways, for example, by reference to the eventual happiness that the patient should expect, or the insignificance of mundane pain to the believer, who is absorbed in his or her relation with God. To be truly patient, one should also conceal one's suffering, turning to none but God.

A spiritually advanced person will go beyond patience and reach the station of acquiescence and approval *(rida)* of whatever God decrees. This stance led some Sufis to take the non-mainstream view that, at this stage, one should not supplicate God to relieve suffering, which would imply disapproval.

Certain rituals—most notably fasting—induce moderate suffering in the believer and are thus considered cathartic. Ascetics typically went further by undertaking forms of mortification, which serve a similar purpose. In Imami Shi'ism, great importance is attached to commemorations of the events of 'Ashura', partly as means to participating in the suffering of al-Husayn and his supporters in the battle of Karbala.

Theological Tradition

The rise of rational theology witnessed the development of systematic solutions to the problem of evil, which is essentially as follows. God is good, and good beings do not perform evil acts; yet God created the world, including at least some of the evil it contains.

According to the Mu'tazila, evil is justified rationally in the framework of their moral realism, whereby moral value can be intrinsic to acts and knowable to unaided reason. We are therefore able to make moral judgments in relation to both human and divine acts, for example, God is obligated to omit bad acts, including those that harm creatures. However, they argued, the act of creation is good, since it allows humans to attain great reward in the hereafter. Human suffering in this world, though *prima facie* bad, becomes good on account of afterlife compensation that God will provide. As for unjustified harm caused intentionally by other humans, it is their own moral responsibility (as they have free choice), not that of their Creator. It is thus incumbent upon God to deliver retributive justice by punishing wrongdoers. Though Mu'tazilism did not survive as a school, this theodicy was adopted in Zaydi and Imami Shi'ism.

By contrast, most Sunni theologians took an antirealist metaethical stance. Members of the Ash'ari school advanced an increasingly sophisticated criticism of Mu'tazili ethics and argued that ordinary moral judgments stem from emotion and social convention, rather than reason. God, therefore, is not obliged to adhere to any moral rules or duties. Though He creates everything, including human suffering and its causes, none of His acts are bad or morally justifiable. Yet God is compassionate and, out of favor, promises reward to believers who suffer patiently.

The Philosophical Tradition

According to Abu Bakr al-Razi (d. 313/925), an early maverick philosopher, pain is real, whereas pleasure, being mere relief from pain, is unreal. In reality, therefore, creatures experience only pain and anguish.

Al-Razi argues that God, being absolutely good, could not have produced such a wretched creation. Rather, this world came into being when the preeternal Soul, out of sheer ignorance, desired to unite with matter (also, in his view, preeternal). Having witnessed the result of this union, God ameliorates it as much as possible and introduces reason, which serves to emancipate the Soul from matter, gradually as it advances through metempsychosis.

By contrast, Ibn Sina (d. 429/1037), the most influential Muslim philosopher, advances a Neoplatonic, purely ontological analysis of the problem of evil, which aims to prove that God, the absolutely good First Cause, produces a good world. Evil, he argues, refers either to imperfection in an entity (such as blindness), in which case it is nonexistent, or to a cause thereof, which is a quality in another entity (such as burning in fire). Such qualities are necessary features of the best possible cosmic order and serve greater good than the harm they cause accidentally. Pain, for Ibn Sina, is ontologically insignificant and deserves little justification; time, after all, erases most memories of pain from the mind. God, therefore, should not be judged morally on account of creaturely suffering—higher causes never act for the sake of lower beings. Ibn Sina lambastes the Mu'tazila who fail to comprehend this and take the subjective human experience of pain at face value in their theodicy.

This standard Neoplatonic theodicy became influential on later philosophical Sufis, most notably Ibn 'Arabi (d. 638/1240). But Ibn Sina was seriously challenged by Fakhr al-Din al-Razi (d. 606/1210), who argues that a theodicy that disregards the human experience of suffering merely circumvents the real problem of evil, which concerns the ordinary understanding of evil in terms of pain. This world, he retorts, contains much more pain than pleasure. Yet (reiterating the prevalent Sunni view) this has no moral bearing on God.

AYMAN SHIHADEH

See also Afterlife; Ash'aris; Ethics; Mu'tazilites

Further Reading

Austin, 'Umar. "Suffering in Muslim Religious Thought., *Islamic Quarterly* 26 (1982) 27–39.
Ayoub, Mahmoud M. "The Problem of Suffering in Islam." *Alserat*, 8, no ii (1982) 11–21; and 8, nos. ii–iv (1982) 26–35.
———. *Redemptive Suffering in Islam: A Study of the Devotional Aspects of Ashura in Twelver Shi'ism.* The Hague: Mouton Publishers, 1978.
Bowker, John. "The Problem of Suffering in the Qur'an." *Religious Studies* 4 (1968): 183–202.
———. *Problems of Suffering in Religions of the World.* Cambridge: Cambridge University Press, 1970, esp. Chap. 3, "Islam."

Heemskerk, Margaretha T. *Suffering in Mu'tazilite Theology*. Leiden: E. J. Brill, 2000.

Ormsby, Eric L. *Theodicy in Islamic Thought: The Dispute over Al-Ghazali's "Best of All Possible Worlds."* Princeton: Princeton University Press, 1984.

SUFISM AND SUFIS: SOUTH ASIA

Sufism, or the mystical component of Islam, in South Asia constitutes a critical component of Muslim society in the medieval period. Alongside the religious learned class (*'ulama'*), Sufis had developed sophisticated institutions of learning, networks for merchants, charitable organizations, and contributed immensely to scholarship. In South Asia, just as their counterparts in the Middle East and North Africa, Sufis were scholars of law, philosophy, theology, literature, medicine, mathematics, and astronomy. Sufis obtained prominent political positions as advisors to statesmen on jurisprudence and on policy decisions, and they also were influential members in all of the major Islamic Sunni and Shi'i legal schools. Sufi scholars in South Asia were responsible for developing major intellectual trends, philosophical schools of thought, and devising legal interpretations that were historical in nature.

Many of the major educational institutions that taught traditional Qur'ānic, legal, linguistic, and hadith and seerah studies had incorporated Sufi studies into their curriculum. As scholars, Sufis developed new ways of defining and transmitting spiritual knowledge and authority and simultaneously devised their own methods of legitimation. By the medieval period, Sufism evolved as the main expression of Islamic piety by being patronized either by the Delhi sultanate or the Mughal dynasty. Their popular religious appeal simultaneously was connected to the intellectual growth and exuberance of Muslim scholarship.

Emperor Akbar's erudite historian, Abu Fazl, recorded in *A'in-i Akbari* that there were fourteen major Sufi orders in South Asia. In Abu Fazl's analysis of Sufism, he outlines the subbranches of each of the orders, the founding Sufi masters, the genealogies, and their primary areas of influence. The fourteen Sufi orders that were dominant in the medieval period were: Chishtī, Hubairī, Zaidī, Habibī, Karkia, Suhrawardī, Taifurī, Junaidī, Firdausī, Tasuia, Gazrunī, 'Iyazī, Adhamī, and Saqatia. Each Sufi order constituted its own rituals, meditation practices, prayer manuals, literature on Sufism, and independent institutions that lodged members and senior Sufi masters.

A review of two major Sufi orders, the Chishtis and Suhrawardīs, will illustrate the major religious practices of Sufis in South Asia. Mu'īn al-dīn Chishtī, commonly called *Khwaja Gharib Nawaz* ("The Patron Saint of the Poor") established the Chishti Sufi order in India. Mu'īn al-dīn Chishtī was born in Sijistan, an eastern province of Persia, was forced out of his town by invasions, and became itinerant until he settled in Ajmer, India. Chishtī studied in a variety of prestigious Islamic colleges (*madaris*) in Baghdad, Samarqand, Tabriz, and Bukhara, where he mastered languages, philosophy, law, and ethics and then concentrated on an internal mystical approach to religion. It is recorded that Chishtī met prominent Sufis, such as 'Abdu'l Qadir Jilānī, Najm ud-dīn Kubra, and Abdul Qadir al-Suhrawardī, and studied under the eminent Usmān Baghdadī for twenty years. Mu'īn al-dīn Chishtī reached Delhi in 1193, and then settled in Ajmer to establish his teachings and the Sufi order. Like earlier prominent Sufi masters before him, Mu'īn al-dīn Chishtī implemented a hierarchical master–disciple (*pir–murīd*) structure for spiritual training, and he also successfully assimilated local customs into the order. Chishtī understood the benefits of cross-religious exchanges and shared many Hindu *yogi* practices, such as bowing before an elder, shaving the head of new members, presenting water to guests, and the use of devotional music (*samā'*) for worship. The distinguishing features of Mu'īn al-dīn Chishtī's teachings and practices are assimilating Sufi practices within the Indian religious context, while other contemporary Sufis and legal-minded scholars were interested in maintaining boundaries between Islam and the Hindu tradition.

Mu'īn al-dīn Chishtī's beliefs were a combination of Islamic mystical beliefs with an emphasis on social reforms. Chishtī Sufi mystical practices are rooted in the theory of the unity of being (*wahdat al-wujūd*), which stressed that the presence of the Divine is manifested in everything in the universe and one is able to access the divine through spiritual exercises. In contrast to the legal-minded scholars or *'ulamā'* who claimed they had the exclusive rights to interpreting divine knowledge through the laws of the Qur'ān, Sūfī masters like Mu'īn al-dīn Chishtī emphasized that the ability for each individual, regardless of class and educational training, was to be able to experience the ecstasy of divine union. Mu'īn al-dīn Chishtī's esoteric path involved a disciple in relentless sacrifice and love to God. Like many Sufis before him, Mu'īn al-dīn Chishtī believed that the individual needed to be guided by a master in order for the disciple to be completely immersed in living for God and cultivate a special kind of inner love (*muhabbat-i khass*). This involved striving to a higher spiritual level where the disciple developed an emotional and spiritual relationship between himself or herself and the Divine. At this ideal state nothing else existed but a complete spiritual union.

The difficult social and political conditions under which Mu'īn al-dīn Chishtī lived influenced his emphasis on incorporating social services with his Sufi theosophy. With a corrupt sociopolitical and economic system under the Delhi sultanate, Chishtī's rejection of all worldly material (tark-i dunyā) was the foundation of his ideology. Any possession of property was considered a compromise of faith. According to Mu'īn al-dīn Chishtī, "The highest form of worship to God was to redress the misery of those in distress, to fulfill the needs of the poor and to feed the hungry." Chishtī Sufis lived on charity (futuh) and practiced several mystical breathing techniques, engaged in spiritual confinement in a cell for meditational purposes, and involved themselves in devotional music gatherings (samā'). The more advanced Sufis tied a rope around their feet and lowered their bodies into a well for forty days for prayer (chilla-i ma'kus). Mu'īn al-dīn Chishtī preached that fasting from food was a good method for increasing one's faith, and if one desired food it should be a vegetarian diet. The Chishtīs had a reputation of having a large section of lower classes and the dispossessed in society as members. Since the Chishtīs accepted any member without discrimination of religion, class, ethnicity, and gender, the order rapidly became eclectic. When an individual became a member of the Chishtī Sufi order, which did not require religious conversion, he or she needed first, to choose an elder as a spiritual guide and second, to commit themselves to maintain the grounds of the shrine (dargāh). Mu'īn al-dīn Chishtī's blend of a mystical life and social services for the poor profoundly changed the Islamic mystical institutions in the Indian subcontinent. His Sufi order served as an alternative form of popular spiritual expression because it empowered individuals to develop a spiritual discipline within a meaningful framework.

Another significant Sufi order in South Asia during the medieval period was the Suhrawardī Sufis, mainly located in Punjab and Sind. Baha' al-dīn Zakariyya Multanī (1181–1262) was Shihāb al-dīn 'Abū Hafs 'Umar al-Suhrawardī's (d. 1234) primary successor (khalīfa) to establish the Sufi order in Multan. Zakariyya successfully made his Sufi center (khānaqāh) an important center for both secular and religious activities as prominent royal families would visit and attend Suhrawardī rituals. A well-known poet and disciple of Zakariyya was Faqr al-dīn 'Irāqī, who wrote on the experience of divine union in his book Lama'āt (Divine Flashes). Zakariyya's son and primary khalīfa, Sadr al-dīn 'Arif (d. 1285), continued the Suhrawardī order's mission, and his conversations were recorded by his successor, Zia al-dīn. Another important Suhrawardī successor of 'Umar al-Suhrawardī was Qādī Hamīd al-dīn Nagauri, who was based in Delhi. Nagauri wrote on the principles and practices of Sufism in Usūl ut tarīqāt (The Principles of the Sūfī Path), which was widely used in most Suhrawardī centers in the Indian subcontinent. Nagauri served as Shaikh-al-Islam for the Delhi sultānate and was considered a leading scholar in his period. An extensive tafsīr is attributed to Nagauri called Tafsīr-i Para-i 'Amma. Works pertaining to Nagauri's ideas on mystical experiences connected to the larger cosmos. Another eminent Suhrawardī master and teacher was Jalāl al-dīn Bukhārī (d. 1291), who wrote Sirāj al Hidayāh (Rays of Guidance) in which he discussed the establishment of the Suhrawardī order in Ucch and in the Sind province. Most of this information is recorded by one of the major Suhrawardī chroniclers, Hamīd ibn Fazl Allāh Jamalī (d. 1536), author of Siyār al 'Arifīn.

Since its early history in Baghdad, the Suhrawardī Sufi order maintained the principle of embracing the world with the esoteric practices of Sufism. That is, the early theosophist of the Sufi order, 'Umar al-Suhrawardī, emphasized the necessity of becoming politically active and building networking alliances in order to be active members of the community. Part of al-Suhrawardī's basic creed was to adhere to and fully recognize the caliph's rule, or perhaps to obey general state authority, because this authority was a manifestation of divine authority on earth.

Suhrawardīs understood the Sufi path as the way to perfect one's devotion and the journey where one can fully embrace divine beauty; at the heart of the Suhrawardī Sufism was the reconnection with the divine the human soul had previously experienced in a preexistent time. This did not mean that Suhrawardīs could not lead a practical life; rather, they were encouraged to enjoy the benefits of this world and to not reject the world. They understood that the Prophet Muhammad established a balanced code for Sufi living, and this example was the model for Suhrawardīs. According to the Suhrawardīs, there were only a few advanced devotees who were able to pray all night and work all day. The majority of believers needed to maintain prayers and specific Sufi practices, such as meditational spiritual exercises (dhikr), as part of their daily routine. On the controversial issue of whether Sufis should maintain a celibate lifestyle, Suhrawardīs argued that only advanced Sufi masters were qualified to judge whether their disciples were spiritually equipped to take on that challenge. But there was a consensus that the lifestyle of the antinomian nomadic begging Qalandars was not acceptable in the Islamic tradition.

The overwhelming stress on proper moral conduct (adab) is mainly connected with his concern that

Sufis develop an internal and external discipline that mirrored the Prophet's life. For the Suhrawardīs the physical world is very much related to the spiritual world, and in order for Sufis to perfect their spirituality their physical customs must reflect their internal condition. Most South Asian Suhrawardī masters connected *adab* as way to obey the law completely because it was a manifestation of divine order. Some suggested that in the process of creating a perfect harmonious society, it required an intensely structured model. *Adab* was a critical element in this ideal world because all the minute details of an individual's behavior could be controlled. However, Suhrawardīs believed they were practicing more than spiritual purity, but in the larger scheme, Suhrawardī Sufis were attempting to reunite with the divine, and this required them to uphold Islamic law. One needed to be prepared to carry out this extraordinary responsibility by having one's thoughts and actions planned for every moment.

QAMAR-UL HUDA

Further Reading

Akhtar, Mohd. Saleem. "A Critical Appraisal of the Sufi Hagiographical Corpus of Medieval India." *Islamic Culture* 52 (1978): 139–150.

Buehler, Arthur. *Sufi Heirs of the Prophet: The Naqshbandiyya and the Rise of the Mediating Sufi Shaykh.* Columbia: University of South Carolina Press, 1998.

Currie, Paul. *Muin al-dīn Chishtī of Ajmer.* Delhi: Oxford University Press, 1989.

Ernst, Carl. *Eternal Garden: Mysticism, History and Politics at a South Asian Sufi Center.* Albany: State University of New York, 1992.

Ernst, Carl, and Bruce Lawrence. *Sufi Martyrs of Love: The Chishti Order in South Asia and Beyond.* New York: Palgrave Macmillan, 2002.

Dihlavi, Akhtar. *Tazkirah-o 'Auliyā'-yi Hind-o Pakistan.* Lahore: Kimiraj Printers, 1972.

Haq, Muhammad Enamul. *A History of Sufism in Bengal.* Asiatic Society of Bangladesh Publication, 30. Dacca: Asiatic Society of Bangladesh, 1975.

Haeri, Muneera. *The Chishtis: A Living Light.* Karachi: Oxford University Press, 2000.

Huda, Qamar-ul. *Striving for Divine Union: The Spiritual Exercises for Suhrawardī Sufis.* London and New York: Routledge Curzon, 2003.

Jotwani, Motilal. *Sufis of Sind.* New Delhi: K. S. Printers, 1986.

Martin, Grace, and Carl Ernst (Eds. *Manifestations of Sainthood in Islam.* Istanbul: Editions Isis, 1994.

Nabi, Mohammad Noor. *Development of Muslim Religious Thought in India from 1200 A.D. to 1450 A.D.* Aligarh: Aligarh Muslim University Press, 1962.

Nizam Ad-Din Awliya'. *Morals for the Heart.* Recorded by Amir Hasan Sijzi. Transl. Bruce Lawrence. Classics of Western Spirituality, 74. New York: Paulist Press, 1992.

Nizami, Khaliq Ahmed. *Some Aspects of Religion and Politics in India in the Thirteenth Century.* 2d ed. New Delhi: Idarah-i Adabiyat-i Delli, 1978.

Qureshi, Regula Burckhardt. *Sufi Music of India and Pakistan.* Cambridge: Cambridge University Press, 1987.

Rasool, Ghulam. *Chishti Nizami Sufi Order of Bengal till mid 15th Century and its Socio-religious Contribution.* Delhi: Idarah-i Adabiyat-Delli, 1990.

Rizvi, Saiyid Athar Abbas. *Early Sufism and its History in India to 1600 A.D.* Vol. 1. New Delhi: Munshiram Manoharlal Publishers, 1978 and, *A History of Sufism in India, from 16th Century to Modern Century.* Vol. 2. New Delhi: Munshiram Manoharlal Publishers, 1983.

Schimmel, Annemarie. *Islam in the Indian Subcontinent.* Handbuch der Orientalistik. Leiden: E. J. Brill, 1980.

———. *Mystical Dimensions of Islam.* Chapel Hill: University of North Carolina Press, 1975.

Siddiqui, Iqtidar Husain. "Resurgence of Chishti Silsila in the Sultanate of Delhi during the Lodi Period (A.D. 1451–1526)." *In Islam in India: Studies and Commentaries.* Vol. 2, *Religion and Religious Education*, edited by Christian Troll, 58–72. Delhi: Vikas Publishing House Pvt Ltd, 1985.

Troll, Christian (Ed). *Muslim Shrines in India: Their Character, History and Significance.* New Delhi: Oxford University Press, 1989.

Valiyuddin, Mir. *Contemplative Discipline in Sufism.* London: East-West Publications, 1980.

SUHRAWARDI, AL-, SHIHAB AL-DIN 'UMAR (1145–1234)

Shihab al-Din Abu Hafs 'Umar al-Suhrawardi belonged to a prominent Persian Sufi family and was responsible for officially organizing the Suhrawardi Sufi order. At an early age he was initiated into Islamic mysticism by his renowned uncle, Abu Najib al-Suhrawardi (d. 1168), and he studied jurisprudence, philosophy, law, logic, theology, Qur'anic studies, and hadith studies. He studied theology under the eminent scholar and Sufi teacher 'Abd al-Qadir al-Jilani (d. 1166), and at a young age al-Suhrawardi mastered the Hanbali and Shafi'i branches of Islamic law in Baghdad.

The 'Abbasid caliph al-Nasir li-Din Allah designated al-Suhrawardi the *Shaykh al-Islam* or Minister of Religious Affairs to supervise political and religious affairs for the 'Abbasid administration. As a political theorist, al-Suhrawardi advocated the supremacy of the caliph because he was the capstone who mastered the Islamic sciences, who commanded knowledge of law, and who was the mediator between God and creation. For al-Suhrawardi, since humanity was incapable of returning to God on its own, the caliphate was the temporal overseer and the representative of God on earth. His political theories did invite their share of criticism from legal scholars of his time, who felt he was too closely connected to legitimizing the policies of the state.

Al-Suhrawardi's legacy is primarily within Sufism, where he asserted that living according to

Sufi principles and beliefs was the perfect way for devotion and to enjoy divine beauty. According to al-Suhrawardi, the Sufi tradition was rooted in the life of the Prophet Muhammad, who embodied human perfection and divine guidance. It is the goal of Sufis to mirror the Prophet in order to discipline their entire inner and outer selves. His Sufi theosophy stressed proper moral conduct *(adab)* because the physical world is very much related to the spiritual world, and in order for Sufis to perfect their spirituality to meet the divine their physical customs must reflect their internal condition. Al-Suhrawardi's ideas on proper moral conduct stem from the belief that it is necessary to obey the law completely because it is a manifestation of divine order. *Adab* was a critical element in his ideal world because all minute details of an individual's behavior could be controlled, a practice the Sufi novice needed to master. For al-Suhrawardi, Sufis were practicing more than spiritual purity, but in the larger scheme, Sufis were attempting to reunite with the divine in their lifetime, and this required them not to abandon or neglect the law. According to al-Suhrawardi, one needed to be prepared to carry out this extraordinary responsibility by having one's thoughts and actions planned for every moment, at every place.

One of al-Suhrawardi's best extant Sufi texts, *'Awarif al-Ma'arif (The Knowledge of the Spiritually Learned)*, was one of the more popular Sufi books of his time, and posthumously it became the standard preparatory text book for Sufi novices around the Islamic world. One of the many reasons for its esteemed reputation in the Sufi world was that the manual attempted to reconcile the practices of Sufism with the observance of Islamic law. To later generations of Sufis and to a wide cross-section of Sufi orders, al-Suhrawardi's Sufi treatise became one of the most closely studied and memorized texts in the tradition. Al-Suhrawardi's contribution to Sufi thought, to Islamic piety, and to living a holy life was to ensure that Sufis fully comprehended *adab* as a transformative medium between the inner and outer worlds. For him, *adab* was grounded in theology that is less about the physical, psychological, and temporal dimensions of moral conduct; rather, it is more concerned with accentuating the constant opening of the heart that inspires a real journey toward encountering God.

QAMAR-UL HUDA

See also 'Abd al-Qadir al-Jilani; Sufis and Sufism

Further Reading

Ali Suhrawardi, Seyyed Abu Fez Qalandar. *Anwar-e Suhrawardiyya*. Lahore: Markarzi Majlis Suhrawardiyya, n.d.

Gramlich, Richard (Trans). *Die Gaben der Erkenntnisse des 'Umar as-Suhrawardi*. Wiesbaden: Steiner, 1978.
Haartmann, Angelika. *An-Nasir li-Din Allah*. Berlin: Walter de Gruyter, 1975.
Huda, Qamar-ul. *Striving for Divine Union: Spiritual Exercises of Suhrawardi Sufis*. London: Routledge Curzon, 2003.
Kalam, Muhammad din. *Suhrawardi 'Auliya'*. Lahore: Maktaba Tarikh, 1969.
Manai, Aishah Yusuf. *Abu Hafs 'Umar al-Suhrawardi: haya tuhu wa-tasawwuf*. Cairo: Dar al-Thaqafa, 1991.
Maqbul, Nur Ahmed. *Khazina-yi Karam*. Karachi: Kirmanwala Publishers, 1976.
al-Suhrawardi, 'Abu Hafs 'Umar. *'Awarif al-Ma'arif*. Cairo: Maktabat al-Qahira, 1973.
"The Light beyond the Shore in the Theology of Proper Sufi Moral Conduct (Adab)." *Journal of the American Academy of Religion* 72, no. 2 (2004): 461–484.
"The Remembrance of the Prophet in Suhrawardi's *'Awarif al-Ma'arif*." *Journal of Islamic Studies* 12, no. 2 (2001): 129–150.

SULAYHIDS

The Sulayhids, a Yemenite dynasty in close relationship with the Fatimid caliphate of Egypt, ruled Yemen between AH 439/1047 CE and AH 532/1138 CE. The earliest Fatimid base had been in Yemen when the Isma'ili da'i Ibn Hawshab Mansur al-Yaman declared his mission at Mt. Masar near San'a' in 268/881 and started conquering many parts of northern Yemen in preparation for the advent of the Fatimid caliphate there. However, the Fatimid al-Mahdi chose North Africa for the establishment of his caliphate, and Yemen, on purpose, was abandoned politically, although a mission *(da'wa)* continued to exist there. When, in the eleventh century, to face the Seljuk challenge, the Fatimids entered into a thick confrontation with the 'Abbasid caliphate, their interest in Yemen was revived as a base for its trade with India to compete with that of the 'Abbasids in that region, and also because the Fatimid Mediterranean trade declined because of the Zirid defiance in North Africa in league with the 'Abbasid–Seljuk entente. This brought the Sulayhids into prominence, helped by the Fatimids, to establish themselves in Yemen on their behalf.

'Ali ibn Muhammad ibn 'Ali, of the Sulayhi family, belonging to the Yam branch of the Hamdan tribe, was the son of a Shafi'i *qadi* in the Haraz region west of San'a'. He was converted to Ismailism by the then incumbent of the Fatimid *da'wa* in Yemen, Sulayman ibn 'Abd Allah of the Zawahi family. In 429/1038, at a pilgrimage at Mecca, 'Ali gathered enough followers to declare his mission on behalf of the Fatimids and to embark on a campaign of conquests that culminated in the taking of San'a' in 439/1047 from the Yu'firids. By 455/1063, he had conquered all of

Yemen. About this the near-contemporary historian Umara wrote: "By the end of 455 H. he had conquered all the plains and mountains; all the lands and waters of Yemen, the like of which had not been seen either in the *Jahiliyya* or Islam."

Exactly at that time, Fatimid Egypt was passing through a great crisis because of a long-drawn-out famine *(al-shidda al-'uzma)* and the ravages of a soldier of fortune, Nasir al-Dawla. 'Ali sent a prolonged embassy under his *da'i* Lamak ibn Malik al-Hammadi from 454/1062 to 459/1067 to the court of the Imam–Caliph al-Mustansir bi-Allah (427–487/1036–1094) at Cairo. Lamak was lodged at the Dar al-'Ilm (Academy of Science), the headquarters of the Chief Da'i al-Mu'ayyad fi al-din al-Shirazi (d. 470/1077). It seems that this embassy was responsible for many decisions. 'Ali wanted to visit the Fatimid court as a savior from its crisis, but he was prevented from doing so. 'Ali had wanted to control Mecca and its Sharifate. He was dissuaded from it and was instead encouraged to conquer Hadramawt. 'Ali wanted that his family would be confirmed in the *da'wa* as da'i-kings. This was agreed upon, but an autonomous *da'wa* was set up under the Sulayhid sovereigns. It is possible that the process of transferring the *da'wa* literature to the Yemen began at this time, and so also the strengthening of the *da'wa* in India under Yemeni control, thus securing the Egypt–Yemen–India trade route.

Without waiting for the Imam's permission, 'Ali started on his journey to Egypt via Mecca, where he went for pilgrimage at the end of 459 (early 1067). He was assassinated there by the forces of Sa'id, the Najahid king of Zabid. 'Ali's wife, Asma bint Shihab, was taken prisoner.

'Ali was succeeded by Ahmad al-Mukarram, his second son. His first son, Muhammad al-A'azz, had predeceased him by a year. Al-Mukarram rescued his mother by defeating the Najahid Sa'id in a battle that also resulted in his paralysis. In 467/1074, he had to retire to Dhu Jibla near Ibb, leaving the affairs of the state in the hands of his wife, al-Sayyida al-Hurra al-Malika Arwa, who resided probably in Haraz, while San'a' was put under the charge of 'Imran ibn al-Fadl al-Yami, along with Abu l-Su'ud ibn As'ad ibn Shihab, the brother of queen-mother Asma. Asma died later in the same year (467/1074).

That year also saw the establishment of the absolute power of the Armenian military leader Badr al-Jamali in Egypt. From then until his death in 470/1078, the Chief Da'i al-Mu'ayyad fi l-din al-Shirazi was probably responsible for bringing Badr al-Jamali and Queen Arwa in close collaboration with each other. Badr needed the adherence of Yemen, and the queen needed her autonomy. The maintenance of this Egypt–Yemen entente explains the acceptance by the Yemeni *da'wa* of the caliphate of al-Musta'li, the nominee of Badr's son al-Afdal after the death of the caliph al-Mustansir. The older son of al-Mustansir, Nizar, was bypassed in Fatimid succession but was supported by the Da'i Hasan ibn Sabbah who established a rival Nizari Da'wa at Alamut in Iran.

When al-Mukarram died in 477/1084, the queen faced a rivalry between the two Qadis—'Imran ibn al-Fadl and Lamak ibn Malik. Imran was stationed in San'a' and was the commander-in-chief of the Sulayhid army. However, he once insulted the memory of al-Mukarram's father and fell out of grace of the king and the queen, although he later fought with the Sulayhids against the Najahids and was killed in battle. 'Imran's family would later control San'a' and found a Hamdanid kingdom there. The queen, on the other hand, was supported by the *da'wa* under Lamak and then under his son, Yahya. Although the queen was the sole *de facto* ruler, the official ruler was her minor son, 'Ali 'Abd al-Mustansir. However, she was at this time given by Imam al-Mustansir the title of *Hujja,* making her the highest religious leader in her region. The queen was supported by two military chiefs—Amir Abu Himyar Saba ibn Ahmad of the Sulayhid family and Amir Abu l-Rabi' 'Amir ibn Sulayman of the Zawahi family—both in constant conflict with each other, thus weakening the Sulayhid state. In the years 491–492/1098–1099, the two Amirs died. The da'i Lamak ibn Malik and the queen's two sons, 'Ali and al-Muzaffar, also died about this time, leaving the queen at the mercy of another Amir, al-Mufaddal al-Himyari, who guarded her treasure at the fortress of Ta'kar but was also responsible for creating many enemies against her by his constant warfare. On his death in 504/1110, Egypt sent an Armenian commander, Ibn Najib al-Dawla, as a *da'i* to reign in the chaotic situation in Yemen. Soon the local tribes revolted against him and the authority of the queen was much constrained by him. In any case he was drowned in the Red Sea, probably at the unavowed instigation of the queen. Another administrator was appointed at this time from the Sulayhid family, 'Ali ibn 'Abd Allah, with the title of Fakhr al-khilafa. The queen, however, relied on the *Da'wa* under Yahya ibn Lamak and its military arm, Sultan al-Khattab ibn al-Hasan al-Hamdani, the baron of Jurayb in the Hajur district. He is also called a *da'i,* for many works of the Yemeni *da'wa* were authored by him. He became the queen's defender of faith and the protector of her realm. He never attained the position of a *Da'i mutlaq* under the queen as a Hujja, which went to his mentor—the Da'i Dhu'ayb ibn Musa al-Wadi'i—on Da'i Yahya's death in 520/1126.

In the meantime, in Egypt, the imam–caliph al-Mustansir was followed by al-Musta'li (487–495/ 1094–1101), and then by al-Amir (495–524/1101– 1130), who was assassinated by the Nizaris. On Amir's death, Queen Arwa recognized his minor son Tayyib as imam, thus severing her ties with the new Fatimid ruler al-Hafiz and his successors. Tayyib, in hiding, was then never heard from. Two years later, in 526/1132, the Tayyibi da'wa was declared in Yemen with da'i Dhu'ayb as the first *da'i Mutlaq*—a rank that continued to signify the headship of the da'wa in Yemen and India, independent of the Fatimid caliphate. The last years of Queen Arwa saw the disintegration of her empire. She died in 532/1138, leaving in her will a large fortune to the absent Imam Tayyib, that is, to the da'wa. Soon after, in a year's time, her chief military supporter, the da'i Khattab, also died.

The Hamdanid dynasty of San'a' and the Zuray'id dynasty of Aden supported the Hafizi da'wa of the Fatimids till all three of them were terminated by the Ayyubid conquest of Egypt and Yemen during 567–569/1171–1173. Under Ayyubid rule, the Tayyibi Ismailis remained as a community, not involved in politics, and thus survived till today in Yemen and India, preserving the *Da'wa* structure and the Fatimid literary heritage.

ABBAS HAMDANI

See also Arwa; Ismailis

Primary Sources

Al-Janadi Baha' al-din (d. 632/1332). *Al-Suluk* (relevant section trans. by Kay. See Further Reading).
Al-Khazraji (d. 812/1410). *Al-kifaya wa-l-i'lam.* (See Kay in the Further Reading section for copious English notes.)
Idris Imad al-din b. Hasan al-Anf (d. 872 H./1467 CE). *Uyun al-Akhbar*, VII (The Fatimids and their Successors in Yemen). Ed. Ayman Fu'ad Sayyid; English summary by Paul Walker, London: I.B. Tauris, 2001.
Nuzhat al-afkar, I (Ms. Hamdani coll.). Umara ibn 'Ali al-Hakami (d. 569/1174). *Ta'rikh al-Yaman*. Ed. Hasan Sulayman Mahmud. Cairo: Maktabat Misr, 1957. (See Kay in the Further Reading section for English translation).

Further Reading

Al-Hamdani, Husayn. *Al-Sulayhiyyun.* Cairo: Maktabat Misr 1955 (now the standard source for the period).
Daftary, Farhad. *The Isma'ilis: Their History and Doctrines.* Cambridge: Cambridge University Press, 1990.
Hamdani, Abbas. "The Da'i Hatim b. Ibrahim al-Hamidi (d. 596/1199) and his book *Tuhfat al-qulub*." *Oriens*, 23–24 (1970–1971): 258–300.
Kay, H.C. *Yaman: Its Early Medieval History.* London: India Office, 1892. (English translation from several Arabic sources with copious historical notes.)
Krenkow, F. "Sulaihi." In *Encyclopedia of Islam.* Old ed., 4 (1954): 515–517.
Stern, S.M. "The Succession of the Fatimid Imam al-Amir, the Claims of the Later Fatimids to the Imamate and the Rise of Tayyibi Isma'ilism." *Oriens* 4 (1951): 193–255. (The chronology of the last two titles was corrected in works published after 1954 when Fatimid sources began to be fully used.)
"The Letters of al-Mustansir bi llah." *The Bulletin of the School of Oriental Studies* 7 (1933–1935): 307–324.
"The Tayyibi-Fatimid Community of Yaman at the time of the Ayyubid Conquest of Southern Arabia." *Arabian Studies* 7 (1985): 151–160.

SÜLEYMANIYE MOSQUE

The architect Sinan (AH 895/1490 CE–996/1588) built the great Süleymaniye *külliye* (socioreligious complex) for his patron Sultan Süleyman the Magnificent (926–974/1520–1566) in the years 957–965/1550– 1557. The mosque complex dominated the eastern skyline of Istanbul, occupying the third of its seven hills. The choice of such a site was intended to enhance the building's grandeur, so that the mosque, and by identification its patron, had visual prominence in the Ottoman capital. Moreover, it commanded dramatic panoramic views from its elevated platform, which on its eastern side was raised so high that one could gaze over the rooftops of the Salis and Rabı Medreses to the Golden Horn and the Sea of Marmara below.

The architectural construction, maintenance, and the huge support staff of 748 needed for the daily running of the complex was financed, as typical for such enormous imperial Ottoman commissions, by an extensive *waqf* endowment of farms and other income-producing properties, taxes on villages, and the rents produced by the assorted shops and cafes around the perimeter of the site. The seven-hectare complex consisted of a centrally placed mosque, a courtyard, and a cemetery enclosed within a walled esplanade that was surrounded by six *medreses* (colleges), a Koran school *(mekteb)*, soup kitchen *(imaret)*, hospital *(darussifa)*, baths, a Sufi hostel *(tabhane)*, and various coffeehouses and shops. The *medreses* were self-contained schools with small rooms for students, residences for the academic directors, and lecture halls organized around large open courtyards. A residence for Sufis was a central feature of earlier *zawiya*-mosque complexes, but here, its position outside the walls of the main mosque precinct was a sign of the diminished importance of Sufi sheikhs and the imperial subordination of the Sufi orders to the orthodox and increasingly centralized Sunni state.

The centerpiece of the hilltop complex is the great domed mosque, erected on sloping ground artificially leveled at great expense. The prayer hall and mosque courtyard together form a rectangle, with a second courtyard beyond the mosque's *qibla* wall that contains the simple yet imposing, double-shell-domed, octagonal tomb of the sultan. The location of the founder's tomb here firmly and permanently attached his identity to the great *külliye*. Off center stood the smaller tomb of his favorite wife, the Haseki Hürrem Sultan (d. 1558). Surrounded by a roofed colonnade and adorned with inscriptions referring to paradise and tile panels with garden themes, Süleyman's tomb bore a resemblance to the late-seventh-century Dome of the Rock in Jerusalem, and by extension evoked an association with Solomon's Temple, which was particularly appropriate since the sultan was sometimes called "The Solomon of the Age." Although earlier Ottoman complexes, such as the Ulu Cami in Manisa (776/1374), included the founder's tomb beside the mosque, its placement directly beyond the mihrab at Süleyman's mosque followed the example of the Fatih Cami (867–875/1463–1470), an ideologically important mosque built just after the conquest of Constantinople, that trumpeted the realization of the Ottoman imperial dream.

Visually dramatic and mathematically rational, the Süleymaniye mosque is one of the sublime achievements in Islamic architecture. A peristyle *(revak)* with twenty-four domes runs around the interior of the courtyard (forty-four by fifty-seven meters), which has a central ablution fountain. The courtyard is marked by four minarets that vertically extend its dimensions, the sharp spikes contrasting and competing with the majestic dome of the prayer hall. The minarets at the courtyard's outer wall have two balconies, whereas those at the juncture of the courtyard and prayer hall are taller, with three balconies. The change in height and elaboration contributes to a sense of acceleration that culminates in the dome, a huge fifty-three-meter-high half sphere that rises above a host of smaller and lower half and full domes. The central dome is raised on a high drum buttressed at the north and south ends by great half domes, which are, in turn, supported by smaller half domes fitted neatly into the corners of the rectangle thus formed by the great central and half domes. The dome rests on four massive piers that inscribe a central area of 26.5 square meters, a dimension that is exactly half of the dome's height. To the east and west sides of the central dome, galleried secondary spaces are vaulted by a rhythmic succession of large and small domes. The result is not so much an accumulation of discrete domical units but a single, continuous space that crescendoes at its apex. Goodwin, who has traced the relative proportions of the domical units, the interior volumes of the prayer hall, and the mosque's plan, asserts that Sinan had a sophisticated understanding of mathematical and geometrical harmony: "These measurements conform absolutely to the symbol of the perfect circle in the perfect square and it is so satisfactory a definition of space that it dominates the complexities which modulate the rigid form of the rest of the mosque...." (p. 213).

The mosque was built with luxurious materials: marble, porphyry, glazed tile, gold, richly hued paints, and even ostrich eggs. The interior furnishings once included crystal mosque lamps, handsomely inlaid wooden chests, and carpets. The mihrab wall was the first of Sinan's works to be extensively decorated with red and blue Iznik tiles. The brilliantly colored glass windows on the *qibla* wall were the work of Sarhoş Ibrahim. The bright painting of the mosque's interior seen today is largely the work (recently retouched) of the Fossati brothers in the mid-nineteenth century. Between the dome's immense piers, four massive red granite columns form lateral screens that run perpendicular to the *qibla* wall. Their provenance was charged with territorial and political symbolism, for according to reports, one each came from the old Ottoman palace (the site on which the Süleymaniye was built), Kiztaşi in Istanbul, Alexandria (Egypt), and Baalbek (Lebanon), which itself was associated with a palace built by Solomon. However, modern historians point to the impossibility of obtaining four perfectly matched columns of such prodigious size from such disparate sources; although architectural spolia (reused material) was no doubt extracted from those places, it is more likely that all four of the columns were specially commissioned for the mosque from the same quarry and workshop.

If the Süleymaniye mosque made sophisticated reference to numerous earlier buildings at the symbolic level, it also was clearly the architectural progeny of the Hagia Sophia. Both are enormous religious buildings with expansive interior spaces that, through the careful massing of domes and half domes, had elongated axes in which vision was unimpeded by vertical supports. The concentration of architectonic support on corner piers liberated the walls so that they could be filled with windows, flooding the interior with light. Sinan had plenty of opportunity to study the great sixth-century Byzantine church that had been converted to a mosque immediately after the conquest of Constantinople of 857/1453, and appears to have deliberately striven to equal and eventually exceed the venerable monument. The Hagia Sophia's patron Justinian was reputed to have proclaimed, "Solomon, I have surpassed you!" at the church's inauguration, but a thousand years later Süleyman could claim to have surpassed Justinian.

D. FAIRCHILD RUGGLES

See also Istanbul; Madrasa; Sinan

Further Reading

Barkan, Ömer Lütfi. *Süleymaniye Cami ve İmareti İnşaati (15550–1557)*. 2 vols. Ankara: Türk Raih Kurumu Basımevi, 1972–1979.
Bates, Ulku. "The Patronage of Sultan Süleyman: The Süleymaniye Complex in Istanbul." In *Memoriam A. L. Gabriel, Edebiyet Fakultesi Araştırma Dergisi Özel Sayısı*. Ankara: Erzurum Atatürk Üniversitesi Yayınları, 1978, 65–76.
Goodwin, Godfrey. *A History of Ottoman Architecture*. London: Thames and Hudson, 1971.
Kuban, Doğan. "The Style of Sinan's Domed Structures." *Muqarnas* 4 (1987): 72–97.
Kuran, Aptullah. *Sinan: The Grand Old Master of Ottoman Architecture*. Washington, DC, and Istanbul, 1987.
Mainstone, R. "The Suleymaniye Mosque and Hagia Sophia." In *Uluslararas Mimar Sinan Sempozyumu Bildirileri: Ankara, 24–27 Ekim 1988*, edited by Azize Aktas-Yasa (Atatürk Kültür Merkezi Yayin, 83; Kongre ve Sempozyum Bildirileri dizisi, 3). Ankara: Türk Tarih Kurumu Basimevi, 1996, 221–229.
Necipoğlu-Kafadar, Gülru. "The Süleymaniye Complex in Istanbul: An Interpretation." *Muqarnas* 3 (1985): 92–117.
Rogers, J.M. "The State and the Arts in Ottoman Turkey: The Stones of Süleymaniye." *International Journal of Middle East Studies* 14 (1982): 71–86, 283–313.

SULTAN

The Arabic word *sultan* is derived from the noun *sulta*, defined as authority in medieval Arabic dictionaries such as Ibn Manzur's (d. 1312) *Lisan al-'Arab* or al-Fayuzabadi's (d. 1414) *al-Qamus al-muhit*. A sultan is thus one who holds authority. In the Qur'an, the word *sultan* is linked to the concept of spiritual power, but use of the term *sultan* soon spread to other aspects of the medieval Islamic world, most notably in governmental and nongovernmental areas. Thus, for example, a master of poetry or a Sufi shaykh could receive the honorific appellation of *sultan* from his devotees. However, it is the use of *sultan* in the political and governmental spheres with which this entry is concerned.

In political spheres the term was given to (or claimed by) rulers, primarily derived from the military classes, who achieved independent power and control over the regions they ruled. Its use in this context emerged during the periods of Buyid (c. 932–1062) and Seljuk (c. 1038–1194) domination of the Central Islamic lands of Iraq and Iran, although after the Seljuks it was used primarily in regions where the rulers were Sunni. A representative list of the polities who used this title for their preeminent ruler would include the Ayyubid (1169–1250), Delhi (1206–1555), Ghaznavid (977–1186), and Mamluk (1250–1517) sultanates. It was the highest title such a military warlord could claim, as titles such as caliph or imam were reserved for those who possessed religious authority. It is worth noting that while it is commonplace to mention that there is no Islamic precept similar to the Christian idea of "rendering unto Caesar that which is Caesar's and unto God that which is God's," the regnal titles *(laqab, alqab)* adopted by many of these *sultans* often took the form of a phrase such as *"sayf al-dawla wa-l-din."* While *sayf* is easily translated as sword, translations of both *dawla* and *din* are heavily dependent on context and difficult to translate into only one English word, but in a context such as this, *sayf al-dawla wa-l-din* may be rendered as "sword of the polity and the faith." Thus while sultans would not have the authority to rule on matters of faith, they would be charged with upholding Islamic belief and defending and ensuring justice for the Muslims they ruled.

In many cases, while sultans were the *de facto* rulers of their regions, they often sought the *de jure* recognition of their authority from the 'Abbasid caliphs. The decline of the actual power of the 'Abbasid caliphate and the rise of military leaders as sultans did not go unnoticed by medieval Islamic jurists. Al-Ghazali (d. 1111), al-Mawardi (d. 1058), Nizam al-Mulk (d. 1092), Ibn Taymiyya (d. 1328), and Badr al-Din Muhammad ibn Jama'a (d. 1333), to name but five, wrote normative treatises on government that discussed, among other things, the rise and power of sultans, and the impact this had on Sunni principles of Islamic government. The reader is referred to the respective entries for the first four; the remainder of this entry will briefly discuss the ideas of the last.

Prior to the Mongol sack of Baghdad and murder of the 'Abbasid caliph al-Musta'sim in 1258, most Sunni political thought had been concerned with maintaining the primacy of the caliph (the title "imam" is often used). Normative thought legitimized the authority of sultans by arguing that while the sultans held power, the caliph was suzerain, although it is probable that most jurists recognized that such suzerainty was theoretical only. After 1258, and despite the creation of the oft-called "Shadow" 'Abbasid caliphate in Cairo by the Mamluk Sultan Baybars—whose authority few jurists recognized—this theoretical suzerainty was abandoned by jurists such as Badr al-Din ibn Jama'a. In his work *Tahrir al-ahkam fi tadbir ahl al-islam*, whose title echoes the *Ahkam al-sultaniyya* of al-Mawardi, Ibn Jama'a instead "was prepared to transfer to the de-facto ruler the constitutional theories worked out by earlier jurists and to recognize [the *de facto* ruler] as imam, holding that the seizure of power itself gave

Sixteenth century CE. Courtyard. Built around 1570 by Sultan Mulay Abdullah. Credit: Erich Lessing/Art Resource, NY. Madrasa Ben Yusuf, Marrakesh, Morocco.

authority" (Lambton, p. 139). Even the seizure of power by a bad ruler, according to Ibn Jama'a (although the idea is not unique to him), was preferable to the absence of a government. In order to provide just rule and protection to his subjects, however, Ibn Jama'a wrote that the sultan should by necessity consult with the 'ulama'. In this, of course, Ibn Jama'a was following a well-developed line of Islamic thought.

WARREN C. SCHULTZ

See also 'Abbasid Caliphate; Ayyubids; Baybars; Buyids; Al-Ghazali Ghaznavids; Ibn Taymiyya; Mamluks; al-Mawardi; Nizam al-Mulk; Seljuks

Primary Source

Kofler, Hans (Ed and trans). "Handbuch des islamischen Staats- und verwaltungsrechtes von Badr-ad-Dīn Ibn Ğamā'a." *Islamica* 6 (19332934): 34914; 7 (1935): 164.

Further Reading

Lambton, Ann K.S. *State and Government in Medieval Islam*. Oxford: Oxford University Press, 1981.

Rosenthal, E.I.J. *Political Thought in Medieval Islam*. Cambridge: Cambridge University Press, 1958.

Watt, W. Montgomery. *Islamic Political Thought*. Edinburgh: Edinburgh University Press, 1968.

SUNNI ALI, SONGHAY RULER

In the thirteenth century, Mali extended its sovereignty to include the Songhay area and, according to the chronicles (most of them by African writers of the sixteenth and seventeenth centuries), took two noble hostages. One of them, Ali Kolon, escaped and returned to found the Sunni (Sonni) dynasty. Ali Kolon's far descendant, Sunni Ali (Ber), is known as a powerful and combative Songhay ruler who laid the foundations of an extensive empire, among others by conquering Timbuktu during his reign from 1463 to 1492. Islam's influence in the area, with a flourishing base in Timbuktu, appeared as an obstacle to Sunni Ali Ber's plan to exert more complete control over the entire region. According to the chronicles, he was a lukewarm Moslem at best. However, there is good reason to consider such descriptions as either biased by political points of view from regions with growing links to Islamic Northern Africa or as the product of a literary model, since both these chronicles and present-day oral traditions picture Sunni Ali in contrast to his illustrious successor Askia Muhammad.

JAN JANSEN

See also Askia Muhammad; Mali; Songhay Empire

Further Reading

Hale, Thomas A. *Scribe, Griot, & Novelist—Narrative Interpreters of the Songhay Empire*. Gainesville: University of Florida Press/Center for African Studies, 1990.
Hunwick, John O. *Timbuktu & the Songhay Empire—Al-Sa'dis Ta'rikh al-sudan down to 1613 and Other Contemporary Documents*. Leiden/Boston: Brill, 2003.

SUNNI REVIVAL

The Sunni revival occurred during the eleventh century when the 'Abbasid caliphate in Baghdad and the Turkish–Seljuk Sultans actively supported Sunnism. During this period Sunni Islam became the dominant branch in the Muslim east. Sunni Islam is based on the approved standard or practice introduced by the Prophet Muhammad, as well as the pious Muslim forefathers. Sunnism first gained prominence during the eighth century when reports on the sayings and deeds of the Prophet were collected. During its early days, Sunnism stood in opposition to the 'Abbasid caliphate, which favored more rationalist schools of thought, like the Qadarites, Murji'ites, or Mu'tazilites. The most prominent figure of early Sunnism, Ahmad ibn Hanbal (d. 855), withstood the persecution of prominent Sunni leaders during the *mihna*, the "inquisition" instituted by the Caliph al-Ma'mun (r. 813–833). After the end of the *mihna* in 848, 'Abbasid caliphs are said to have paid homage to Ahmad ibn Hanbal and his followers, but they still did not support their traditionalist Sunni views. As the 'Abbasid caliphs became more and more marginalized during the ninth and tenth centuries, the real power came into the hands of the emirs and grand-emirs of the Buyid family, who openly supported Shi'ism in Iraq and Iran.

During the beginning of the eleventh century, the twenty-fifth 'Abbasid caliph, al-Qadir, who reigned the long period between 991 and 1031, managed to pursue a religious policy in Baghdad that became increasingly independent of the Buyid grand-emir in Shiraz. Al-Qadir found support among the well-organized group of traditionalist Sunni scholars of the Hanbali school and their local militias ('ayyarun). In 1018, al-Qadir published the so-called Qadiri Creed, in which he attempts to set a standard for Muslim orthodoxy. The Qadiri Creed, inspired by Hanbali Sunnism, is the very first document of its kind and it was repeatedly read in public throughout the eleventh century. In it, al-Qadir condemns Shi'is and Mu'tazilites and declares that rationalist theological positions such as the belief in the createdness of the Qur'an are unbelief *(kufr)* and liable to punishment by the state authorities. The open alliance of the Caliph al-Qadir and his grandson and successor, al-Qa'im (r. 1031–1075), with the conservative Hanbali branch of Sunni scholars led to violent tensions between the equally powerful Sunni and Shi'i militias in Baghdad that often exploded in outbursts of civil war.

The arrival of the Seljuks in Baghdad in 1055 completely changed the balance of power in favor of the caliph and his Sunni allies. The Seljuks were Turkish nomads from the plains of Central Asia (in today's Kazakhstan) who had adopted Islam and crossed the border to the Muslim empire in about 1025. With their superior horsepower they destroyed the Buyid principalities one by one and aimed to establish amicable relations with the 'Abbasid caliph in Baghdad. In 1055, they rescued the Caliph al-Qa'im from what was almost a successful Shi'i-supported coup d'état by an Iraqi military leader. Under the leadership of their Sultan Toghilbeg (d. 1063) and his Grand Vizier al-Kunduri (d. 1065), a Hanafi jurist from Nishapur in northeast Iran, the Seljuks pursued a religious policy that favored the conservative branches of Sunnism, who were loyal to the caliph. In Baghdad and Iraq they followed a middle way that acknowledged the rights and customs of the moderate Shi'i population and made a halt to the excesses of the radical Shi'i and Sunni militias.

The politics of a middle path in order to establish moderate Sunnism as the dominant way of Islam was most forcefully pursued by al-Kunduri's successor, Nizam al-Mulk (r. 1019–1092). He served as grand-vizier over a period of almost thirty years, between 1063 and his violent death in 1092. Second in power only to the Seljuk Sultans Alp Arslan (r. 1063–1072) and Malikshah (r. 1072–1092), both of whom he served, Nizam al-Mulk formulated the religious policy for an area that stretched from Asia Minor to Afghanistan. In the big cities he founded religious *madrasas* (so-called *Nizamiyyas*) that institutionalized the teaching of Sunni jurisprudence and theology. In theology, he favored the Ash'arite school tradition of Nishapur and mentored such outstanding scholars as al-Juwayni (1028–1085) and al-Ghazali (1058–1111). His religious policy was successful because it combined tolerance toward the moderate groups of Shi'ism with intolerance toward the radicals in all camps. Under the leadership of Nizam al-Mulk, the

Seljuks continued to persecute Ismaili Shi'is, who often acted as agents of the Shi'i Fatimid caliphate in Cairo. Some Sunni groups, such as the populist Karramites, who were powerful in the province of Khorasan in Northeast Iran until the end of the eleventh century, lost much influence during Nizam al-Mulk's reign, while particularly the Ash'arites came to dominate the scholarly activities in the Muslim east.

FRANK GRIFFEL

Further Reading

Bulliet, Richard W. *Islam: The View from the Edge.* New York: Columbia University Press, 1993, 145–168.

Glassen Erika. *Der mittlere Weg: Studien zur Religionspolitik und Religiosität der späteren Abbasiden-Zeit.* Wiesbaden: Steiner, 1981.

Juynboll, G.H.A. "Sunna." In *Encyclopeadia of Islam.* 2d ed. Vol. 9, 878–881. Leiden: Brill, 1997.

Makdisi, George. "The Sunni Revival." In *Islamic Civilisation 950–1150,* edited by D.S. Richards, 155–168. Oxford: Cassirer, 1973.

———. *Ibn 'Aqil: Religion and Culture in Classical Islam.* Edinburgh: University Press, 1997.

SURGERY AND SURGICAL TECHNIQUES

The art of healing wounds, *djiraha*, was derived from the Arabic root *djurh,* meaning injury or wound. The term *'ilm al-djiraha* was used from the ninth century on, meaning knowledge of wounds, operation of ill organs, and surgical treatment and instruments. Surgical operation, *'amaliyya djirahiyya,* was expressed as *'amal bi'l-yad* or *'amal al-yad,* that is, work performed by hand. The one who treated wounds was named *djarrah*, while the bonesetter and bonehealer (Ar. *mudjabbir*) and *sınıkcı* (in Turkish) and the oculist *kahhal* were both regarded as practitioners of special fields of surgery.

Surgical development started in the ninth century following the translation of the ancient Indian, Greek, and Roman surgical works into Arabic. Hunain ibn Ishaq (d. 874) highly contributed to Arabian surgery by translating works of Hippocrates, Galen, and above all Paulus Aegineta (d. 690). We find chapters on surgery in the books of known physicians, for example, *al-Mansuri, al-Jami,* and *al-Hawi* of Zakariya' ar-Razi (d. 925); Kamil as-sina'a of 'Abbas al-Madjusi (d. 994); *Qanun fi't-tibb* of Ibn Sina (980–1037); *Tadhkirat al-kahhalin* (about 1000) of 'Ali ibn 'İsa; *Dhakhira* of İsmail al-Jurjani (d. 1136); and *al Mujiz* and *Sharh Tashrih al-Qanun* of Ibn an-Nafis (d. 1288). The first known monograph

on surgery, titled *al-'Umda fi sina'at al-djiraha,* was compiled by Ibn al-Quff (1233–1286) in the thirteenth century.

The greatest surgeon of the medieval ages was Abu' l-Qasim az Zahrawi (d. 1010), a most important representative of the Andalusian school. Called Albucasis in Europe, Zahrawi is mainly known for the thirtieth chapter on surgery, *fi'amal al-yad* in his encyclopedic book *at-Tasrif liman ajiza.* The sources of Zahrawi were classical Greek and Latin authors, Paulus Aegineta being the immediate source. However, Zahrawi inserted his own experiences, not following any author in the description of some new pathological conditions and methods of treatment, for example, ptosis and its method of cure; removal of ranula beneath the tongue; removal of a leech sticking in the throat; treatment of fracture of male and female private parts; hunchback; wounds of the neck; various pathological conditions affecting the adult uterus; and lithotomy incision in the female case; and the designs and ways of using various instruments, such as the tonsil guillotine and its use, the concealed knife for opening abscesses, the trocar for paracentesis, vaginal speculum, and obstetric forceps. The illustrations of surgical instruments and the sketches of several incision and excision techniques are the earliest addition of these operative elements to a book. In the second half of the twelfth century, Gerard of Cremona translated the chapter on surgery into Latin as *Liber Alsaharavi de cirurgia.* Zahrawi's surgery was utilized as a main source in the Islamic and European worlds through eight centuries.

From the fourteenth century on, Arabic and Persian medical books started to be translated into Turkish; consequently, Turkish medical literature began to develop. In the fifteenth century a comprehensive chapter in *Dhakhira-i Muradiye* (1437) of Mu'min b. Mukbil, and the exhaustive book *Murshid* (1483) by Mehmed ibn Mahmud of Shirvan were assigned to ophthalmology. The Turkish book on surgery, *Jarrahiyatu'l Khaniye* (1465), of Sharafaddin Sabunjuoghlu, the head physician of the Amasya Hospital in central Anatolia, is mainly a translation of Zahrawi's work *Kitabu't- Tasrif,* specifically the thirtieth chapter on surgery. However, he introduced his own experiences as well, and added two new chapters. Sabunjuoghlu was the earliest in illustrating surgeons treating patients. Certain spots of cauterization marked on the patients illustrated are similar to those used in acupuncture and moxa. Fifteenth-century Turkish surgical monographs *Kitab-ı djarrahnama* by an unknown writer (Süleymaniye Library, No. 814); *Tarcama-i hulasa fi fenni'l-ciraha* by Djarrah Mesud; and *Alaim-i djarrahin* by Ibrahim b. Abdallah are also notable.

The main surgical instruments and techniques of medieval Islamic surgery were, for example, *kayy* (cauterization by fire) used with the objective of surgical excision or as a stimulating remedy; the *mismariya* (cautery) of several forms, such as claviform, crescentic, ring, quill, and so on; the *mibda'* (scalpel) with numerous shapes and sizes for incision, scraping, extraction, separation, and opening; *fasd* (bleeding) applied by a phlebotome, the *al-fa's*, an edged and sharp pointed scalpel; *hadjm* (cupping) without or after scarification, practiced with *mahajim* (cupping vessels); *miqass* (scissors) invented for surgical purpose; *miqdah* (needles) for eye operations; several probes *(barid, misbar, mirwad)* and the fine trocar *(midass)* as exploring instruments; *sinnara* (hook) for picking up and holding tissues; instruments for circumcising, the *musa* (razor) and *falka* (spindle whorl); *anbuba* (tube) for drainage; *zarraqa* (syringe) both for aspiration and for irrigation; *mihqan* (clyster) for irrigating sinuses; *kasatir* (syringe); *al-qam* (funnel) for fumigation and irrigation; and *mus'ut* (dropper) for irrigating the nose. A great variety of *minshar* (saw), *mijrad* (raspatory), *miqta'* (osteotome), *mithqab* (trephine), *kalalib* (forceps), *jabira* (splint) devices to reduce dislocations or displace fracture ends and plaster cases were used to treat fractures and dislocations. Several instruments such as *minqash, mibrad, mishdakh* (lithotrites), and *mish'ab* (lithotriptor) were developed for extracting stones. Various kinds of suture materials for surgical purposes were utilized, such as ants' nippers; gut sutures; wool, linen, ox, or horse hair and silk in connection with the ligature *(rabt)*; gold or silver wire for wiring in the teeth. Drugs called *muhaddir* or *murkid,* such as opium, henbane, mandrake, hemlock, Indian hemp, and yellow alison, were used as anesthetics by snuffing or inhaling, especially as a soporific sponge or as local anesthetics in surgical operations.

Surgery was regarded as an art necessitating skill and experience. Though authors like Zahrawi noted anatomy as a necessary knowledge for surgeons, dissection of dead bodies as a means of training was not practiced, though there is no religious prohibition of it. Surgeons were trained by the master-apprenticeship method, usually as a family profession; they were employed as primary or secondary surgeons at hospitals, palaces, military service, or offices, and some were itinerant. The head of surgeons was called *ser-djarrahin.* Information and hints about the requirements and expectations of morality regarding surgery is found in surgical manuscripts and the deed of trusts of hospitals. The reflection of Muslim morality to surgical practice is found in judges' registries, for example, a patient's or guardian's written consent taken before surgical operation and a contract signed to certify this in order to withhold a suit for compensation against the surgeon in case of death or injury.

NIL SARI

See also Abbas al-Madjusi; Abu' l-Qasim az Zahrawi; 'Ali ibn 'Isa; Hunain ibn Ishaq; Ibn an-Nafis; Ibn al-Quff; Ibn Sina, or Avicenna; Kahhal; Medical Literature, Turkish; Paulus Aeginata; Zakariya' ar-Razi

Further Reading

Hau, Friedrun R. "Die Chirurgie Und Ihre Instrumente in Orient und Okzident Vom. 10. Bis 16. Jahrhundent." Paper presented at the Internationaler Kongress Krems An Der Donau 6. Bis 9. Oktober 1992. Österreichische Akademie Der Wissenschaften Philosophisch-Historische Klasse Sitzungsberichte, 619. Band. Wien, 1994: 307–352.

Jhonstone, Penelope (Ed). *Max Meyerhof Studies in Medieval Arabic Medicine Theory and Practice.* London, 1984.

Öncel, Öztan. "Anesthesia in Turkish-Islamic Medicine." Ph.D dissertation. Istanbul University, Istanbul Medical School, Medical Ethics and History Department. Istanbul, 1982.

Sarı, Nil. "Ethical Aspects of Ottoman Surgical Practice." *Türkiye Klinikleri.* 8, no. 1 (April 2000): 9–14.

Sarton, George. *Introduction to the History of Science.* 3 vols. Baltimore, 1927–1947.

Spink, M.S., and Lewis, G.L. *Albucasis on Surgery and Instruments.* London: The Welcome Institute of the History of Medicine, 1973.

Uzel, İlter. *Sharafaddin Sabunjuoghlu Jarrahiyatu'l Khaniye.* 2 vols. Ankara: Turkish History Society, III/15, 1992.

Yıldırım, Nuran. "A Fifteenth Century Turkish Book of Surgery." Ph.D dissertation. Istanbul University, Istanbul Medical School, Medical Ethics and History Department. Istanbul, 1981.

SUYUTI, AL-, 'ABD AL-RAHMAN

Al-Suyuti, the celebrated erudite Egyptian savant, is recognized today as one of the most prolific authors of all Islamic literature.

The family of al-Suyuti, of Persian origin, settled during the Mamluk period in Asyut, in Upper Egypt (from where they derive their name). His father, however, was established in Cairo, and it is there that al-Suyuti was born on October 3, 1445. The child followed a very thorough course in various Islamic sciences. It is shown very early on, as of eighteen years of age, that he teaches Shafi'i jurisprudence and the science of Hadith; in addition, he delivers *fatwa*s (legal consultations) in various sciences. In parallel, he writes prolific works: Before al-Suyuti reached the age of thirty, his works came to be required reading throughout the whole of the Middle

East and then soon circulated in India until they reached Tekrur in sub-Saharan Africa.

In Egypt, on the other hand, he evokes much jealousy and polemic because he claims to have reached the status of *mujtahid* (that is, a legal scholar possessing independent authority in interpreting the sources of the law) in the Shafi'i school of jurisprudence. Moreover, al-Suyuti affirms that his *ijtihad*, far from being limited to Islamic law, also applies to the sciences of Hadith and the Arabic language. Finally, al-Suyuti is announced as the *mujaddid* (renewer of Islam) (*see* Renewal, or Tajdid) for the ninth century of the *hijra*, two or three years before the year 900/ 1494. At the age of forty, al-Suyuti withdraws from public life to his house on the island of Rawda, in Cairo. He dies on October 18, 1505. The reasons that he calls upon in connection with his withdrawal are the corruption of the institution of the ulema and the ignorance that prevails among them; in fact, the decline of the cultural level at the end of the Mamluk era is manifest.

The assurance, even the claim, to which al-Suyuti testifies, comes initially from the awareness that he has of his own gifts: He has an extraordinary memory, a remarkable spirit of synthesis that enables him to write or to dictate several works at the same time. He is convinced to be invested with a mission, which prevails over any other consideration and, in particular, over the opinion that others have of him. This mission consists of gathering and transmitting to the future generations the Islamic cultural inheritance, before it disappears following the neglect of his contemporaries. In fact, he quotes in his works many old texts now lost, particularly in the field of the Arabic language. Al-Suyuti precedes the modern time by certain aspects: for example, he is partly an autodidact, and herewith to a public that he wishes to reach out to with handbooks centered on precise topics. In the same spirit of popularization, he summarizes the works of others and makes them clean. One cannot regard al-Suyuti as only a compiler. Indeed, he approaches topics usually neglected in the Islamic literature; he is the first to have introduced Sufism into the field of the *fatwa*.

Al-Suyuti wrote approximately one thousand works (981 according to a 1995 study). Hardly three hundred were published, but his manuscripts are nowadays a great success in published editions. The scientific versatility of al-Suyuti illustrates the Islamic ideal, according to which there is no really profane science; he explores geography, as well as lexicography, pharmacopoeia, dietetics, erotology. More profoundly, his approach to a subject is often multidisciplinary, and he often employs several sciences to cover a subject.

This versatility allowed al-Suyuti to free himself from a determined axis through his attachment to the Prophet (*see* Muhammad the Prophet) and his Sunna. He includes in his field of vision the most scattered sciences as long as they do not contradict the Revelation descended on Muhammad; this is why he condemns *al-mantiq* (Hellenistic logic). Among the disciplines that he says to control, that of Hadith prevails because it permeates the greatest part of his work. Sciences having been imbued with the Arabic language represent, according to him, his subject of predilection, but one very clearly notes the influence of the science of Hadith in his major work on language, *Al-Muzhir fi 'Ulum al-Lugha wa Anwa'iha*. In his other "linguistic" works, al-Suyuti follows the method of religious sciences like usul al-fiqh (foundations of jurisprudence) or the fiqh (jurisprudence). Qur'anic sciences constitute another axis of al-Suyuti's work (approximately twenty works). "Al-Itqan fi 'Ulum Al-Qur'an" makes the beautiful share with the language and rhetoric, but the principal commentary of al-Suyuti, Al-Durr al-Manthur fi al-Tafsir bi-al-Ma'thur, is exclusively based on Hadith and the words of the first Muslims. In this field, it is also necessary to mention the very practical *Tafsir al-Jalalayn*, a Qur'anic commentary started with al-Suyuti's professor, Jalal al-Din al-Mahalli, and completed by him.

If the discipline of Hadith represents in al-Suyuti's eyes the noblest "of sciences," it is imbued with the prophetic model, which for him is the only way that leads to God. In this field, al-Suyuti's working model is undoubtedly *Tadrib al-Rawi fi Sharh Taqrib al-Nawawi*, which pertains to the terminology of Hadith. The aforementioned prophetic model could not be transmitted by book science alone; it must be experienced interiorly. Al-Suyuti, who affirms to have seen the Prophet more than seventy times while in a waking state, ensures that he can maintain during a vision the validity of Hadith directly from the Prophet. As a Sufi (*see* Sufis and Sufism), al-Suyuti found in the *tariqa Shadhiliyya* (Shadhili order) the right balance between the Law and the Way. Moreover, he benefited besides from his notoriety as a scholar and jurisconsult to carry out a perspicacious apology for Sufism and its Masters: He sees in the *dhikr* (invocation of God) the highest form of worship, showing that it is necessary to interpret the words of the Sufi, and to defend the orthodoxy of Ibn 'Arabî.

Finally, al-Suyuti wrote much in the fields of history and biography, including a number of works on the theory of history (for example, *al-Shamarikh fi 'Ilm al-Ta'rikh*), in its various fields of application: the history of the caliphs, to which he was very attached *(Ta'rikh al-Khulafa')*, about the history of

Egypt *(Husn al-Muhadara)*, and a great number of biographical collections by specialty (specialists in Hadith, grammarians, poets, and so on).

ERIC GEOFFROY

See also Caliphs; Ibn 'Arabi; Renewal; Sufism; Usul al-fiqh

Primary Sources

Al-Hâwî lil-fatâwî: recueil de toutes les fatwas d'al-Suyuti (droit, langue, histoire islamique, soufisme, etc.), Beyrouth, s. d.
Al-Itqân fî 'ulûm al-Qur'ân, maintes éditions : reste un ouvrage de référence pour aborder les sciences coraniques.
Al-Tahadduth bi-ni'mat Allâh : autobiographie, éd. en arabe par E. M. Sartain. Cambridge, 1975.
Husn al-muhâdara fî akhbâr Misr wa l-Qâhira, Le Caire, 1968: sur l'histoire de l'Egypte et du Caire.
Târîkh al-khulafâ', Le Caire, 1964: sur l'histoire des califes de l'islam, depuis Abu Bakr.

Further Reading

E. Geoffroy, E. art. *al-Suyûtî* dans l'Encyclopédie de l'Islam II, tome IX, 951–954.
Garcin, J. Cl. "Histoire, opposition politique et piétisme traditionaliste dans le Husn al-muhâdarat de Suyûtî." *Annales Islamologiques* VII, IFAO, Le Caire, 1967, 33–88.
Kaptein, N.J. *Muhammad's Birthday Festival*. Leiden, 1993: présente et traduit la *fatwa* d'al-Suyuti validant la pratique du *mawlid nabawî* (célébration de l'anniversaire du Prophète).
Sartain, E.M. *Jalâl al-dîn al-Suyûtî, Biography and Background*. Cambridge, 1975: reste l'étude la plus complète en langue occidentale.

SYNAGOGUES

There were Jewish communities scattered throughout Arabia in Muhammad's time. Mecca, his hometown, does not seem to have had an organized Jewish community, but the oasis of Yathrib, to which he emigrated in 622, housed a large and well-organized community. Now known as al-Madina (from *madinat al-nabi,* or "the city of the Prophet"), it had two tribes of *Kohanim,* that is, of Priestly ancestry, a third Jewish tribe, and possibly other clans. The synagogue there was called *Midras*; the word is from the Hebrew *Bet Midrash,* or "House of Study." Islamic tradition has preserved some details about the *Midras* of the Jews in Yathrib, enough to suggest various conclusions about the building, religious services, administration, and theology, but unfortunately not to secure them.

The Qur'an itself has several terms that refer to Jewish houses of worship. It most likely refers to the Temple in Jerusalem, with the term *Masjid.* While the reference of 17:1 (*al-masjid al-aqsa,* "the farther place of prostration") is open to some controversy, the reference to the twofold destruction of the Israelites, alluding to destroyers entering the *masjid* as they had before (17:7), can hardly refer to anything else. Places of monotheistic prayer before Islam are called *sawami', bi'a, salawat,* and *masajid,* roughly translated as "cloisters," "places of petition and prayer," and "places of prostration" (Q 22:40). *Bi'a* (sing. *bi'a*) and *kanisa* (pl. *kana'is*)—a term not used in the Qur'an—came to be the most usual appellations for synagogue and church, although some authors say the one or the other ought to be used only for houses of prayer of Christians or Jews; others use both as synonyms. Jewish sources generally referred to the synagogue as *kanis* or *kanisa* in Arabic, and *bet knesset* in Hebrew. Some geniza sources use the term *majlis* (assembly) to refer to certain synagogues, especially those clearly postdating Islam.

Islamic expansion quickly brought the largest centers of Jewish life into its orbit; indeed, for several centuries, most of the world's Jews resided in areas ruled by Muslims. Islamic provisions about the status of non-Muslims in Islamic lands, including the status of their synagogues and churches, reached full expression in the form of the document usually known as the Pact of Umar. The framework of the Pact reflects reports of agreements made with non-Muslims by Umar b. al-Khattab or his generals during the Islamic conquests. The early pacts indicate that non-Muslims were allowed to retain their religion and places of worship, although the part of their houses of worship facing the *qibla* could be used by the Muslims as a place of prayer. Many more limitations are found in later legal works, such as *Kitab al-Umm* by al-Shafi'i, and the regulations do not appear in the form of the Pact of Umar earlier than the tenth century. According to this document, Jews and Christians stated:

> "We shall not found in (the town) or in the land surrounding it, a new monastery, church, cloister or monastic cell. Nor shall we renew whatever has been destroyed of them, nor revive any of them which are in Muslim quarters. We shall not prevent any Muslims from staying in our churches at night or during the day, and we shall open their gates wide to passers-by and wayfarers."

The legal prohibition of the construction of new churches and synagogues applied particularly to Muslim areas, and some of the legal traditions had no objections to synagogues in neighborhoods where there were no Muslims, or which had been Jewish prior to becoming Muslim. So, too, in the early days, establishment of synagogues to serve the Jewish community seems to have been less of a problem: Kairawan, Cairo, Baghdad, Fez, and other places established by Muslims all had synagogues, although often in neighborhoods considered to antedate Islam. A report that Umar himself established seventy Jews in Jerusalem was cited to support the synagogue there.

By the twelfth century, opinions about this became more settled, and the Pact of Umar came to be applied more stringently. Synagogues were closed in North Africa and Cairo, and there was discussion and occasional violence concerning whether synagogues in Cairo and Jerusalem were allowed to be retained or repaired; in early-fourteenth century Cairo, continuing riots led to the closure of numerous synagogues and churches and the intervention of the king of Aragon and the Byzantine emperor to reopen them. These restrictions continued into the nineteenth century, until reform attempts by Muhammad Ali and his successors in Egypt and in Palestine, by the Ottomans, and by European protectorates.

We have little information about the layout and procedures in synagogues of the Islamic world. Nathan the Babylonian gives a particularly vivid description of one synagogue service in Baghdad from the tenth century. Geniza records confirm that in addition to meeting for prayer it was the center for many other community functions. Lawsuits were brought there and persons, including women, could delay services to seek redress. Sometimes, funerals would stop outside or in the courtyard. In some, a women's entrance indicated that women attended services. Many cities had multiple synagogues, reflecting differences in custom between the traditions of the Jews of Babylonia (Iraq) and Palestine, or Rabbanite, Qaraite, and Samaritan Jews. Some synagogues were built primarily in locations of pilgrimage, such as the Dammuh synagogue in Egypt; travelers' descriptions of sacred tombs also suggest these were sometimes the locations of synagogues, although in many cases graves associated with figures from biblical history were also sacred to the Muslims and Christians, and the buildings associated with these sites could not be considered synagogues.

In some cases the few structural details of which we are aware suggest that the buildings continued the pre-Islamic basilica style, and may even have been converted from churches; in other cases, as, for example, in Benjamin of Tudela's description of the synagogue in Baghdad, the colonnaded hall and open courtyard suggest similarities to early Islamic mosques, although synagogues in Muslim areas would necessarily have had modest facades.

SETH WARD

Further Reading

Goitein, S.D. *A Mediterranean Society*. Vol II. University of California Press, 1971, 143–170.

Ward, Seth. "Taqi al-Din al-Subki on Construction, Continuance and Repair of Churches and Synagogues in Islamic Law." In *Studies in Islamic and Judaic Traditions II*, edited by W. Brinner and S. Ricks, 169–188. Atlanta: Scholars Press, 1989.

SYRIA, GREATER SYRIA

Syria, specifically Greater Syria (Ar. Bilad al-Sham), is a historical term denoting a region that comprises modern Syria, Lebanon, Jordan, Israel, the West Bank of Palestine, and the southwestern borderlands of Turkey. Geographically, Greater Syria can be divided into two sections: the mountainous coastal region in the west, which in the medieval period included Antioch (modern Antakya in southern Turkey), and the Mediterranean ports of Tripoli, Beirut, Tyre, and Acre; and the steppe and desert region in the east, of which the leading centers were Aleppo, Hama, Hims, Damascus, and Jerusalem.

Greater Syria played a major role in the development of Islam from the earliest period. The decisive battles of the *futuh* (Islamic conquests) against the Byzantines were fought there; Damascus was the capital of the first Islamic dynasty, the Umayyads; and Jerusalem quickly became the Muslims' third most important religious center after Mecca and Medina. A degree of religious and linguistic pluralism persisted in spite of Islamization: Christianity survived, although at times under duress; and neither Greek nor Aramaic was completely abandoned for Arabic.

By the start of the medieval period, the political predominance that Greater Syria had enjoyed under the Umayyads had long since gone. 'Abbasid rule over the region from Baghdad had given way successively to Tulunid and Ikshidid control, successor dynasties of the weakening 'Abbasids. In the middle of the tenth century, the decline of Ikshidid power resulted in northern Syria being given to the Bedouin Arab Hamdanids, under whom Aleppo enjoyed a period of literary and artistic inflorescence.

Even before Hamdanid rule in Aleppo had come to an end in AH 394/1004 CE, the Egyptian Fatimids had conquered Palestine and Syria. Fatimid rule over Greater Syria was weak, however, especially in the north, where a revived Byzantium regained some of its old territory, and another Bedouin dynasty, the Mirdasids, established themselves in Aleppo.

The situation in Greater Syria was altered by the advance of the Seljuk Turks during the second half of the eleventh century. By the eve of the Crusades, often mutually hostile Seljuk *amir*s (princes) ruled in Jerusalem, Damascus, Aleppo, and Hims. In AH 477/1084 CE, the Byzantines lost Antioch, their last possession in Syria. An independent Arab family of *qadi*s (Islamic judges) ruled in Tripoli, while the Fatimids remained in control of some of the coast.

There was a tension between the strongly Sunni Seljuks and the existing Shi'is and Shi'i-influenced sects. The latter included people in sympathy with the (Ismaili Shi'i) Fatimids, and more heterodox elements, such as the Nusayris and the Druze of the coastal montagne. To these would later be added the Syrian Assassins.

The map of Greater Syria changed again in the wake of the arrival of the Crusaders before Antioch in AH 491/1098 CE. By 1130, much of the region was under Frankish control: the principality of Antioch and the county of Edessa (modern Urfa in southern Turkey) in the north; the county of Tripoli in the central maritime region; and the kingdom of Jerusalem to the south. Many of the military fortifications that the Crusaders built to protect their possessions have survived, such as the impressive Krak des Chevaliers in the west of modern-day Syria. Much of the Muslim interior, meanwhile, maintained a precarious independence, with the Turkish *amir*s of Aleppo and Damascus among others paying tribute to the Crusaders in return for peace.

The Frankish possessions shrank almost as rapidly as they had grown. The Crusaders were isolated, and weakened by their unwillingness to make common cause with their coreligionists in the East, the Byzantines and the Armenians. 'Imad al-Din Zanki, a Turk who had risen to prominence in the service of the Seljuks and made himself independent of his former masters, pushed the Crusaders back west of the River Euphrates. In the middle of the twelfth century, his equally able son, Nur al-Din Mahmud, became ruler of both Aleppo and Damascus. Nur al-Din continued and emphasized the Seljuk Sunni Muslim tradition by founding *madrasa*s (Islamic schools) in which an orthodox curriculum was taught.

Outdoing the Zankids in their opposition to the Crusaders was a Kurdish lieutenant of Nur al-Din's, Saladin, the founder of the Ayyubid dynasty. Having declared himself ruler of Egypt on the death of the last Fatimid caliph, Saladin proceeded to seize Damascus from Nur al-Din's heirs. He then turned on the Crusaders. By the time of Saladin's death in AH 589/1193 CE, only Antioch, Tripoli, Tyre, and Acre remained in Frankish hands.

The following century saw the increasing dominance of Egypt as the center of the Ayyubid empire, at the expense of Greater Syria, particularly of Damascus. In AH 642/1244 CE, the Egyptian Ayyubids defeated a prudential alliance of central Syrian Ayyubids and Crusaders in southern Palestine. Aleppo, meanwhile, bought its continued independence from Egypt by helping the Egyptians to capture

Damascus. Jerusalem was also brought under Egyptian control, after a brief period in the hands of the Crusaders, to whom the Syrians had given the city in return for cooperation against the Egyptians. In AH 648/1250 CE, the Ayyubids of Egypt were ousted by the Mamluks, originally Turkish slave soldiers who would found their own dynasty. Aleppo seized the advantage and occupied Damascus. It was a short-lived triumph: Within ten years the Mongols had overrun Greater Syria and put an end to Ayyubid rule.

The Mamluks would eventually absorb Greater Syria into their empire. In AH 658/1260 CE, they defeated the Mongol armies at 'Ayn Jalut in Palestine. Damascus and Aleppo were occupied by the Mamluks, although the Mongols remained a threat to Greater Syria until the beginning of the fourteenth century. Before the end of the thirteenth century, the Mamluks had taken all the Frankish colonies still remaining in Greater Syria. It was the end of an era marked by ambivalent relations between Muslims and Crusaders: hostility punctuated by accommodation, and mutual destruction contrasting with thriving commercial links between East and West.

Mamluk rule lasted until AH 922/1516 CE, when they were defeated by the Ottomans at Marj Dabiq near Aleppo in a decisive battle that marks the end of the medieval period in Greater Syria. Damascus and Aleppo were leading cities of the Mamluk empire. Both took years to recover from the effects of the plague pandemic of the mid-fourteenth century, and of Tamerlane's ravages in AH 803/1400 CE, when they were pillaged and emptied of their populations. This notwithstanding, and in spite of the depredations of some of the governors of the Syrian *niyaba*s (Mamluk provinces), industry and trade at times resulted in a degree of prosperity that allowed intellectual and artistic life to flourish.

DAVID MORRAY

See also Architecture, Secular: Military; Black Death; Byzantine Empire; Earthquakes; Excellences Literature; Madrasa; Merchants, Christians; Dome of the Rock; Muslim–Byzantine Relations; Muslim–Crusader Relations; Muslim–Mongol Diplomacy; Silk Roads; Sunni Revival; Trade, Mediterranean; Umayyad Mosque (Damascus)

Further Reading

Gabrieli, Francesco. *Arab Historians of the Crusades*. London: Routledge and Kegan Paul, 1969.
Hitti, Philip K. *History of Syria: Including Lebanon and Palestine*. 2d ed. London: Macmillan, 1957.
Holt, P.M. *The Age of the Crusades: The Near East from the Eleventh Century to 1517*. London: Longman, 1986.
Le Strange, Guy. *Palestine under the Moslems*. London, 1890.

SYRIAC

Syriac is the name that came to be given to the Late Aramaic dialect of Edessa (modern-day Sanliurfa, southeast Turkey). The earliest texts (in Old Syriac) are pagan inscriptions of the first to third century CE, and three legal documents on skin from the early 240s. Syriac, with its own distinctive script, soon became the literary language of Aramaic-speaking Christians, both in the Eastern provinces of the Roman Empire and in the Parthian and Sasanian empires to the east. Syriac literature, which covers many secular and religious topics, constitutes by far the largest body of Aramaic literatures, spanning from the second century to the present day. Many of the earliest writings are preserved in manuscripts of the fifth and sixth centuries.

Syriac script takes on three main forms: the oldest, *estrangelo*, is the norm in manuscripts till at least the end of the eighth century, when it was largely replaced by *serto* in the west (based on an earlier cursive) and a distinctive "eastern" script. It is disputed whether Arabic script has its roots in Syriac or Nabataean script.

Syriac literature can most conveniently be divided into three main periods, second to mid-seventh centuries, mid-seventh to thirteenth centuries, and the thirteenth century onwards. Although some names are known from the second and third centuries, only a few texts survive, and it is not until the fourth century that major authors emerge: Aphrahat, writing in the Sasanian empire around 345, and the poet Ephrem (d. 373) in the Roman empire. Subsequent important prose writers of this first period include the historian John of Ephesus (d. ca. 589). Poetry is particularly well represented, with Narsai (d. ca. 500) and Jacob of Serugh (d. 521), as well as many fine anonymous authors. Among the genres developed is one that continues the ancient Mesopotamian precedence dispute; thus Syriac provides the bridge between ancient Mesopotamia and the Arabic *munazara* (debate or contest in verse or prose). A remarkable number of translations from Greek were made during this period, especially in the latter part, and include medical and philosophical texts. A few translations were also made from Middle Persian, among them the oldest version of *Kalila wa-Dimna*.

A distinctive feature of the second period is the more learned and encyclopedic character of its writings. Despite the political upheavals of the time, the seventh century witnessed a great flowering of Syriac literature, both in the Syrian Orthodox Church (notably with the scholar Jacob of Edessa, d. 708) and in the Church of the East, where several monastic authors flourished, among whom Isaac of Nineveh was to prove particularly influential (he, in fact, originated from Qatar). In the late eight and ninth centuries, Syriac scholars (the most notable being Hunayn ibn Ishaq) played an important role in the 'Abbasid translation movement, especially early on when it proved more practical to translate Greek texts first into Syriac (a task that had the benefit of several centuries of experience) and only then into Arabic. The second period comes to an end with the encyclopedic writings of the polymath Gregory Abu 'l-Faraj, better known as Bar Bar Hebraeus (Bar 'Ebroyo, d. 1286). Whereas authors of the sixth and seventh centuries had come to be greatly influenced by Greek literary culture, Bar Hebraeus draws freely on both Arabic and Persian sources.

The third period is the least known, and most texts remain unpublished. Syriac literature, however, has continuously been produced right up to the present time. Poetry in Modern Syriac is known from the seventeenth century onward, and prose from the mid-nineteenth century.

SEBASTIAN BROCK

See also 'Abbasids; Aramaic; Hunayn ibn Ishaq; Kalila wa-Dimna

Further Reading

Baumstark, Anton. *Geschichte der syrischen Literatur*. Bonn: Marcus und Weber, 1922.
Brock, Sebastian. *A Brief Outline of Syriac Literature*. Kottayam: St Ephrem Ecumenical Research Institute (SEERI), 1997.
Reinink, G.J., and H.L.J. Vanstiphout (Eds). *Dispute Poems and Dialogues in the Ancient and Medieval Near East*. Leuven, 1991.

T

TABARI, AL-

Ab-Ja'far Muhammad b. Jarar al-Tabari (d. AH 310/ 923 CE) was the most important scholar of his generation. His works exerted a profound influence on future Muslim scholarship, because of both their voluminous content and their meticulous methods of inquiry. Although many of his works have not survived, his two most famous works, his *History (Ta'rikh al-Rusul Wa'l-mul-k)* and his Qur'an commentary *(Tafsir)*, remain standard references today.

Al-Tabari was born in 224–225/839 in or near Amul, in Tabaristan near the Caspian Sea. He then spent most of his life in Baghdad, where he composed most of his works. He left his birthplace at a young age to pursue studies in Rayy and then in Baghdad, where he arrived in 241/855, shortly after the death of Ibn Hanbal, with whom he had hoped to study. His scholarly travels subsequently took him to most of the major intellectual centers in the Muslim world, including Bara, Kufa, Damascus, Beirut, and Egypt. Unlike many scholars, al-Tabari does not appear to have studied in the Hijiz, with the exception of brief pilgrimage visits. Ultimately, he returned to Baghdad around 256/870 to write and teach.

Although income from his family's estate in Tabaristan spared him the poverty many scholars suffered, he did occasionally find himself in dire financial circumstances. For a time he served as a tutor to the son of al-Mutawakkil's vizier, 'Ubaydallah b. Yahya, probably because of his own economic difficulties. Despite many later offers, this was his only stint of government employment. Payments from his many students (supplemented by income from his family's estates) sufficed to meet his modest needs.

Reports about al-Tabari's lifestyle typically emphasize his piety and moderation. Although he was not an ascetic, he did not live extravagantly or indulge in food, drink, or other diversions. He never married, and he apparently committed himself to a life of celibacy. He spent his days teaching, worshipping at the mosque, and writing. His scholarly works attracted both admirers and enemies. He condemned the usual heretical groups, including Mu'tazilites, Shi'is, Zahiris, and others. He attracted unusual enmity from the followers of Ibn Hanbal, who reportedly rioted in front of his house on at least one occasion. His dispute with the Hanbalis reportedly centered on two issues. The first was al-Tabari's decision to exclude Ibn Hanbal from his *Ikhtilaf al-Fuqaha'*; this was done because of his opinion that Ibn Hanbal was a great muhaddith but not a jurist. Ibn Hanbal's followers naturally took offense and reacted violently. The second focus of al-Tabari's feud with the Hanbalis was his interpretation of the praiseworthy position *(maqaman mahm-d'an)* that God had promised the Prophet Muhammad. Al-Tabari rejected the Hanbali interpretation that this meant Muhammad would sit on God's throne. Some reports suggest that Hanbali hostility toward al-Tabari was so extreme that, when al-Tabari died in 310/923, he had to be buried secretly at night to prevent Hanbali mobs from disrupting his funeral. Most reports, however, describe a peaceful daylight funeral instead.

Al-Tabari's works covered a broad range of topics, including law, history, Qur'anic exegesis, and hadith (tradition). His most famous and influential works are his *History* and his *Tafsir*. The *History* presents a complete history of the world from creation until just before al-Tabari's time. In the *History*, al-Tabari applied the methods of the hadith scholars to historical reports, emphasizing proper isnads and including divergent versions of events to allow the reader to decide which interpretation was most valid. His meticulous methods profoundly influenced the way in which later Muslim historians approached their craft. Modern scholars have emphasized al-Tabari's objectivity and his reluctance to impose his own interpretations on material or to insert his own narrative voice in any way. The work is also praised for al-Tabari's skillful incorporation of pre-Islamic narratives into a master narrative that places Islam at the center of world history. Although al-Tabari skillfully concealed his own agenda in his *History*, careful analysis of his treatment of pivotal events suggests that he did adhere to a theory of historical causation according to which calamity befell the Muslim community when tribal rivalries and personal greed were not sufficiently suppressed. His *History* is essentially a salvation story in which the advent of Islam is situated in God's larger plan and proper adherence to Islam raises human society to its pinnacle.

In his *Tafsir*, al-Tabari was more willing to express his own opinions about particular disputes about Qur'an interpretation. He relied extensively on grammatical analysis of the text and included divergent interpretations of particular verses. However, he ultimately offered his own judgment about which interpretation was most viable, relying on ijtihad to an extent that his Hanbali rivals could not accept. As a legal scholar, al-Tabari initially adhered to the Shafi'i madhhab, which he probably embraced during his travel to Egypt as a young man. Later, however, his followers began to consider themselves to be a separate madhhab, usually called the Jaririis. His madhhab did not survive long, and its principles were apparently not far removed from the Shafi'i school from which it sprang.

Al-Tabari's influence on later scholarship cannot be understated. His *History* became the model for many later works, some of which were merely poorly disguised abridgments. The hadith methodology he so carefully applied to historical reports became the standard procedure for scrutinizing and reporting historical akhbar. His *Tafsir* remains a crucial work for understanding the development of Qur'anic exegesis and for insight into the debates about variant readings of the Qur'anic text. In addition, his *Ikhtilaf* offers thorough comparisons of the legal theories of the orthodox madhhabs (with the exception of the Hanbalis). His reputation as a pious and exemplary scholar survived the extreme hostility of his Hanbali foes and the accusations that he was in fact a Shi'i, which stemmed from his unwillingness to condemn 'Ali with sufficient vigor. His meticulous work ultimately withstood his critics' venom and remains a vital part of Muslim scholarship to this day.

STEVEN C. JUDD

Primary Sources

Ibn 'Asakir. *Ta'rukh Madinat Dimashq*. Beirut, 1995–1999.
al-Tabari, Muhammad b. Jarar. *Ta'rikh al-Rusul Wa-l-mul-k*, ed. M.J. de Goeje. Leiden, 1879–1901.
al-Tabari, Muhammad b. Jarir. *Tafsir (Jami' al-Bayan 'an ta'Wil ay al-Qur'an)*. Cairo, 1905.
Yaq-t. *Irshad al-Arib ila ma'Rifat al-Adib*. Cairo, 1936.

Further Reading

Gillot, Claude. "La Formation Intellectuelle de Tabar." *Journal Asiatique* 276 (1988).
Khalidi, Tarif. *Arabic Historical Thought in the Classical Period*. Cambridge, UK: Cambridge University Press, 1994.
Rosenthal, Franz. *The History of Tabari. Vol. 1. General Introduction and From the Creation to the Flood*. Albany, NY: State University of New York Press, 1989.

TAJ MAHAL

During the first decade of his rule, the Mughal Emperor Shah Jahan (r. 1627–1658 CE) embellished the imperial capital of Agra with stunning white marble buildings that were metaphors of the hierarchy and order supporting the state. That huge architectural programs of this sort could be undertaken not only in Agra but also in Delhi, Lahore, Ajmer, and Allahabad reflects the wealth, artistic talent, and administrative acumen available to the Mughal rulers. They projected a developed classic style, reproducible in its elements and clear in its symbolic content. When the emperor's favorite wife Arjumand Banu Begam (or Mumtaz Mahal) died in 1631 giving birth to their fourteenth child, the grieving ruler added another massive project to those already underway, the construction of her tomb, now known as the Taj Mahal.

Built over an eleven-year period from 1632 to 1643, the tomb's form came from a rich tradition of Mughal sepulchral architecture, beginning with the tomb of the second Mughal emperor, Humayun, whose tomb was built in Delhi under the patronage of his son Akbar from 1562 to 1571. In the center of a cruciform (four-quadrant) garden *(chahar bagh)*, Humayun's tomb was a huge octagon faced in red sandstone with marble outlining the main structural elements. It supported a high double dome that glistened in white marble and reflected the influence of architecture from the Mughals' Timurid heartland in Central Asia. For the builders of the Taj Mahal, the tomb of Humayun, along with the 1636 tomb of the Khan Khanan in Delhi, was a direct prototype.

The Taj Mahal and its extensive gardens were surrounded on the east, south, and west sides by red sandstone walls measuring 305 by 549 meters in length. The main gate was on the south side and was preceded by an extensive bazaar (Mumtazabad or city of Mumtaz), the income of which, along with that from thirty neighboring villages, was assigned to the maintenance of the tomb. The gate not only controlled access to the complex; it also had a specific meaning. Its great arch is framed by white marble inlaid with a black marble inscription from the Qur'an that describes the Last Judgment and the joys awaiting the blessed who can enter Paradise; this is seen as visitors enter the tomb's garden.

Once inside the gate, visitors left behind the everyday life of Mumtazabad and entered a place of ordered quiet. A formal four-part garden stretched from the gate north to the actual tomb and provided a structured space intended to replicate paradise. Movement was controlled by paved walkways that outlined beds of flowers, flowering shrubs, and trees fed by streams of water from bubbling fountains.

The name *Taj Mahal* first appears in the writings of visiting Europeans during the seventeenth century. To the Mughals, it was known simply as "the illumined tomb." Begun in 1632, it was almost entirely complete by 1643, and much of its construction took place at the same time as the rebuilding of the Agra Fort. It was the single largest building project underway in the Mughal state, and some twenty thousand workers from India, Iran, and Central Asia were employed at the enormous cost of forty million rupees. The overall project was supervised by two distinguished architects, Makramat Khan and 'Abd al-Karim; a third architect, Ustad Ahmad, appears to have been responsible for the design of the actual tomb. Passionately interested in architecture, Shah Jahan must have carefully watched over the design and its implementation. Imprisoned by his son Awrangzeb in the Agra Fort from 1658 until 1666, he could look east to view the Taj.

The mausoleum itself is a square with chamfered corners that rests on a marble plinth that is seven meters high. Each side is dominated by a thirty-three-meter-high *pishtaq* (niche arch) that is flanked to the east and west by two smaller pishtaqs and topped by a domed and arcaded pavilion at each corner. At each corner of the plinth stands a three-storied minar. This elaborate structure of repeating identical elements is dominated by a twenty-meter-high drum and double dome. The outer dome provides the dramatic profile that defines the sky around it; the inner dome is low and comforting. Directly under its peak was the cenotaph of the deceased empress, beside her the cenotaph of Shah Jahan. Both grave markers are enclosed by an intricate marble screen inlaid with precious stones, as are the cenotaphs themselves.

The great calligrapher Amanat Khan designed inscriptions that frame the great pishtaqs, the smaller arched entrances into the tomb, the eight interior pishtaqs, the inner frieze of the drum, and the two cenotaphs themselves. Written in a majestic cursive style of script known as *thuluth,* they are inlaid in black marble into the white marble. A number of inscriptions give us completion dates, the name of the scribe, and other historical information. Most, however, are Qur'anic: admonitions to follow Islam; warnings of hell to those who do evil; evocations of the Last Judgment; references to the Resurrection; and descriptions of the joys of paradise for the righteous. The inscriptions were selected to fit the purpose of the tomb and to reinforce an image: the Taj Mahal was designed to replicate one of the houses of paradise.

Family and adherents were expected to make formal visits on birth and death anniversaries. To the tomb's west was a red sandstone and marble mosque with three glistening white domes. Its exact counterpart (*jawab*; answer) was on the east side. Mughal designers laid out gardens and buildings according to precise grids that preserved predictable proportions. A formal garden replaced natural chaos with order; although buildings might inspire awe, they should avoid surprises. The great south–north garden is divided into identical quadrants; the mausoleum creates balance through repetition, and a visitor's expectations are rewarded by dazzling elements that have already been seen before. One must remember, however, that harmony has variations, and, in its interaction with its natural setting, the tomb provides a multitude of them. The white marble facing is minutely inlaid with precious stones that only reveal their variety when a visitor is close. The marble is translucent, and the great dome absorbs and responds to every change in the sky over Agra.

ANTHONY WELCH

See also Agra Red Fort; Akbar; Architecture, Religious; Architecture, Secular: Civil; Architecture, Secular: Palaces; Babar; Baraka; Beauty and Aesthetics; Burial Customs; Dara Shikoh; Death and Dying; Delhi; Festivals and Celebrations; Funerary Practices, Muslim: Sunni; Gardens and Gardening;

God; Hadith; Horticulture; Hindus; Humayun; India; Irrigation; Lahore; Love; Mughals; Nur Jahan; Persians; Pilgrimage; Prayer; Qur'an; Scriptural Exegesis, Islamic; Timurids; Turks; Waqf; Water

Further Reading

Asher, Catherine B. "Architecture of Mughal India." In *The New Cambridge History of India*, vol. I, 4. Cambridge, UK: Cambridge University Press, 1992.

Begley, W.E., and Z.A. Desai. *Taj Mahal: The Illumined Tomb*. Cambridge, Mass: The Aga Khan Program for Islamic Architecture; and Seattle: University of Washington Press, 1989.

Brandenburg, Dietrich. *Der Taj Mahal in Agra*. Berlin: Verlag Bruno Hessling, 1969.

Crowe, Sylvia and S. Haywood. *The Gardens of Mughal India*. London: Thames & Hudson, 1973.

Gascoigne, Bamber. *The Great Moghuls*. New York: Harper & Row, 1971.

Koch, Ebba M. *Mughal Architecture*. Munich: Prestel-Verlag, 1992.

———. *Mughal Art and Imperial Ideology: Collected Essays*. Oxford, UK: Oxford University Press, 2001.

Nath, R. *The Taj Mahal and Its Incarnation*. Jaipur, 1985.

Pal, P., S. Merkel, J. Leoshko, and J.M. Dye. *Romance of the Taj Mahal*. W.W. Norton, 1989.

Wescoat, James L., and Joachim Wolschke-Bulmahn. *Mughal Gardens: Sources, Places, Representations, and Prospects*. Washington: Dumbarton Oaks Research Library, 1996.

TALISMANS AND TALISMANIC OBJECTS

The term *talisman* refers in its widest sense to an object made to protect the owner, to avert the power of evil, and to promote well-being. *Talisman* is used interchangeably with *amulet,* although Savage-Smith (1997) has drawn a distinction between an amulet, which is made from durable materials such as hard stones and which can function over time, and a talisman, which is made from more ephemeral materials such as paper and kept in amulet cases. Talismanic objects, which, by association, include magic bowls and talismanic shirts, belong therefore in the realm of magic *(sihr)*. In Arabic, this is a term that has a variety of connotations, from "that which entrances the eye" to "actions effected through recourse to demons" (Fahd, 1996). In the sphere of healing and well-being, this magic is beneficent; for the present context Dols (1992) has aptly described it as a "forceful method of supplication or a supercharged prayer."

What links talismanic objects together, irrespective of what material they are made from, is a particular vocabulary of inscriptions and designs. The most important of these elements are verses from the Qur'an, which in itself is considered the most powerful of all talismans (Hamès, 1997; Porter, 2002). Particularly powerful in talismanic contexts are, for example, the opening of the Qur'an *(Fatiha)*, which has been used in oral incantations from the time of the Prophet against the evil eye and for healing (Hamès, 1997), and Qur'an 2:255, the "throne verse" *(ayat al-kursi)*, also known as the "verse of seeking refuge" or the "verse for driving out Satan" (Canaan, 1937). The short chapters *(suras)* known as the Four Declarations (suras 109, 112, 113 and 114) and the last two suras (113 and 114) are additionally known as *al-mu'awwidhatan* (the verses that provide the antidote to superstition and fear) (Ali, 1975). In addition, there are verses that are deemed to have specific powers: for example, those that contain the Arabic root word *sh-f-y* (to heal) were used for curing sickness (Porter, 1998); those with the victory verse (61:13) were used for help in battle.

In addition to these, the names of God *(asma' al-husna')* feature prominently, particularly on amulets, as do the names of or invocations to the cherished figures in Islam, the Prophet Muhammad, and the twelve imams revered by the Shi'is. The archangels—Jibrail, who revealed the Qur'an to the Prophet and the others, such as Izrafil, Mikail, Israfil, and Uzrafil—also appear, as do the Seven Sleepers of Ephesus, whose story is told in Qur'an 18:9–26 (Porter, forthcoming).

Other important elements of the magical vocabulary—which, although they appear more esoteric, are still deeply rooted in the Qur'an—serve to strengthen the supplication (Savage-Smith, 2004). They include individual Arabic letters, which are often repeated and which are believed to be particularly powerful when written in isolated form. The "Mysterious letters of the Qur'an" (which appear singly or in groups at the beginning of twenty-nine suras of the Qur'an) are also widely used. Magic squares *(wafq)*, in which religious phrases, names of God, and so on appear are represented numerically in the abjad system (an alphanumeric system based on the old order of the Semitic alphabet) within a square. At their simplest, they are three by three, but they can extend at least as high as twenty by twenty or more, as is seen by the talismanic chart in the Khalili collection (Savage-Smith, 1997). Symbols such as the "seven signs" (see below) also feature, as well as the five- or six-pointed star known as "Solomon's seal." Solomon had power over the jinn, and it is to him that, according to the writer of the *Fihrist* (written 987 to 1010 CE), Ibn al-Nadim, licit magic can be traced (Dols, 1992). Other symbols include scorpions, lions, and magical scripts that include invented alphabets (these appear from as early as the mid-ninth-century text of Ibn Wahshiya; Savage-Smith, 2004). There are strings of numbers, meaningless Kufic letters sometimes combined with numbers, and the so-called "lunette" script, which is characterized by a group of Arabic letters with long looped forms attached (Canaan, 1937 and 1938).

Depending on the object, these elements sometimes appear on their own or in combinations: for example, Qur'anic verses with magic squares or the seven signs with magical letters. Many of these elements are first found in the influential text of Abu'l 'Abbas Ahmad ibn 'Ali ibn Yusuf al-Buni (d. 1225), author of the *Shams al-Ma'arif al-Kubra,* a treatise that draws on Hellenistic, Jewish, and other pre-Islamic magical practices. Al-Buni focuses in large part on the "beautiful names of God" and their magical properties, creating elaborate magic squares made up of the numerical value of the names. He also includes charms using the lunette script and the seven signs, which he believed denoted the "greatest name of God." As a result, it is through the proliferation of this text throughout the Islamic world that these symbols start to appear regularly on medieval talismanic objects; this practice continues to this day.

The range of objects covered by the terms *talisman* and *talismanic* in their broadest sense includes amulets, about which the largest body of material is available. Amulets are objects that are worn as protection or for warding off the evil eye, a practice that entered the life of the early Muslims (Henniger, 2004) and that was tolerated in Islamic theology. The practice continues today, although it is more prevalent in some parts of the Islamic world (e.g., North Africa, Egypt) than others. These small objects, which are made to either be worn around the neck or on a ring, are made from hard stones or metal. The material from which they are made can be significant, because particular beneficial properties are often traditionally ascribed to certain stones and are cited in textual sources. Carnelian, for example, was said by the medieval gemologist Ahmad ibn Yusuf al-Tifaschi to control fear in battle and to stop hemorrhages (Tifaschi, 1998). It was also popular because it was the stone most favored by the Prophet Muhammad. These objects are most frequently inscribed positively, although there are some that are inscribed negatively that are "activated" when they are stamped onto something.

Another important category of talismanic objects are the magic-medicinal bowls used to cure sickness, continuing a pre-Islamic tradition found in Aramaic bowls. Among the earliest datable Islamic examples are bowls made for Nur al-Din Zangi (1146–1174; Savage-Smith, 1997). These bowls can be inscribed with Qur'anic verses and invocations; very frequently magic squares are used, and they are often interspersed with strings of meaningless Kufic-style letters;

some examples have toggles attached to them that bear the Names of God. In an associated tradition, the water used to clean the wooden writing boards used by children to learn the Qur'an is believed to be rendered efficacious, and it is used to cure sickness because it contains the words of the Qur'an. Talismanic shirts made from linen or cotton and covered with magic squares, Names of God, and passages from the Qur'an were worn beneath armor in battle for protection; these are found in Ottoman, Safavid, and Mughal contexts. One of the finest is an example made for Ottoman Sehzade Selim in AH 972/1564–1565 CE (Rogers and Ward, 1988). Talismanic charts are associated with the shirts in style and are generally covered with magic squares, Qur'anic and other inscriptions, and strings of letters and numbers; these are made to carry around in times of need or to be displayed in the home.

Another powerful talismanic object is the hand. Made from brass and other materials or inscribed on paper (in the western Islamic lands), it symbolizes the hand of Fatima, the Prophet Muhammad's daughter, and it often has a blue bead in the center to ward off the evil eye. In Shi'i contexts, it symbolizes the hand of Abbas, Imam Husayn's uncle who was also killed at Kerbela. A final group of objects to be mentioned are mirrors. Magical inscriptions start to appear on the shiny side of twelfth- and thirteenth-century mirrors from Iran and Anatolia. These inscriptions were probably engraved later than the object itself. They consist of elements of the magical vocabulary mentioned above and were probably associated with a specific type of magic requiring shiny surfaces (Savage-Smith, 1997). In the case of an example in the British Museum, the names of the Seven Sleepers of Ephesus are combined with magic squares, the seven signs, letters, and numbers.

VENETIA PORTER

See also Alphabets; Angels; Numbers

Further Reading

Ali, Abdallah Yusuf. *The Meaning of the Glorious Qur'an.* London: Nadim & Co., 1975.

Canaan, T. "The Decipherment of Arabic Talismans." *Berytus* IV (1937): 69–110; V (1938): 369–97. (Reprinted in Savage-Smith, Emilie, ed. *Magic and Divination in Early Islam. The Formation of the Classical Islamic World,* vol. 42. Ashgate Publishing, 2004.)

Dols, Michael W. "The Theory of Magic in Healing." In *Majnun: The Madman in Medieval Islamic Society,* ed. Diana E. Immisch. Oxford, UK, 1992. (Reprinted in Savage-Smith, Emilie, ed. *Magic and Divination in Early Islam. The Formation of the Classical Islamic World,* vol. 42. Ashgate Publishing, 2004.)

Fahd, Toufic. "Sihr." In *The Encyclopeadia of Islam, New Edition,* vol. IX, 567–71. Leiden: Brill, 1996.

Hamès, Constant. "Le Coran Talismanique." In *Religion et Pratique de Puissance*, ed. A. de Surgy, 129–60. Paris, 1997.

Henniger, Joseph. "Belief in Spirits Among the Pre-Islamic Arabs." In *Magic and Divination in Early Islam. The Formation of the Classical Islamic World*, vol. 42. Ashgate Publishing, 2004.

Ibn al-Nadim. *The Fihrist of Ibn al-Nadim*, transl. B. Dodge, 2 vols. New York, 1970.

Porter, Venetia. "Islamic Seals: Magical or Practical?" In *University Lectures in Islamic Studies*, 2nd ed., ed. A. Jones, 135–51. Altajir: World of Islam Trust, 1998. (Reprinted in Savage-Smith, Emilie, ed. *Magic and Divination in Early Islam. The Formation of the Classical Islamic World*, vol. 42. Ashgate Publishing, 2004.)

————. "Amulets Inscribed with the Names of the 'Seven Sleepers' of Ephesus in the British Museum." Proceedings of the Conference *Word of God Art of Man*. The Institute of Ismaili Studies, forthcoming 2005.

Porter, Venetia, and Robert Hoyland. "Seals and Amulets" in "Epigraphy." In *Encyclopaedia of the Qur'an*, vol. 2. Leiden: Brill, 2002.

Rogers, J.M., and R.M. Ward. *Suleyman the Magnificent*. London, British Museum Publications, 1988.

Savage-Smith, Emilie. *Science Tools and Magic. The Nasser D. Khalili Collection of Islamic Art*, vol. XII., Part One. London, 1997.

————. "Introduction: Magic and Divination in Early Islam." In *Magic and Divination in Early Islam, The Formation of the Classical Islamic World*, vol. 42, ed. Emilie Savage-Smith. Ashgate Publishing, 2004.

Tifaschi, Ahmad ibn Yusuf. *Best Thoughts on Best of Stones*, transl. Samar Najm Abul Huda as *Arab Roots of Gemology*. Lanham and London: Scarecrow Press, 1998.

TAMERLANE, OR TIMUR

Tamerlane, or Timur, (ca. 1336–1405 CE), was the last of the great nomadic conquerors and the founder of the Timurid dynasty, which ruled in Transoxiana and eastern Iran (1405–1507). A member of the Turco-Mongol Barlas tribe, Timur was born in Transoxania and rose to power among the Ulus Chaghatay, a nomadic tribal confederation that formed the western region of the Mongolian Chaghadaid khanate. Stories about Timur's early life are rife with legend and share too-striking similarities with those of Genghis Khan; therefore, it is hard to estimate the credibility of the descriptions of his lowly beginnings. He advanced in the tribal arena through personal valor and brigandage, gathering a nucleus of supporters and offering his services to the local rulers. During one of his early battles in Iran, he got the limp that became part of his name (Persian: *Timur-i leng*, "Timur the lame"). His military genius and charismatic personality in combination with his clever manipulation of tribal politics led to his rise first to the leadership of his tribe (1361/1362) and then to the head of the whole ulus (1370). Not being a descendant of Genghis Khan, Timur could not bear the title *khan* and thus was known only as *amir* (commander). To legitimate himself, he married Genghisid princesses, took the title *küregen* (Mongolian; "son-in-law"), and appointed a puppet Genghisid as khan. He also collected a host of princes of the different Genghisid branches, portraying himself as their patron.

Another important component of Timur's legitimation was Islam. Timur respected and patronized Sufi sheikhs and ulama, with whom he often debated, and he built religious monuments. The third facet of his legitimation was his own charisma and success: Timur stressed his intimate connection with the supernatural, consciously imitated Genghis Khan, and used monumental building and court historiography to magnify his name.

From 1370 onward, Timur fought almost imminently at the head of his troops, unwilling to entrust their command to anybody but himself. He started with a series of raids into Moghulistan, the eastern part of the Chaghadaids, and into Iran, and this occupied him between 1370 and 1385. During the next decade, he was active mainly against the Golden Horde Khan and his former protégé Toktamish, in south Russia and Ukraine, achieving his major victory at 1395 when he ruined Sarai, the Golden Horde capital, thereby encouraging the rise of Muscovy. In 1398 and 1399, Timur raided India, inflicting a decisive blow on the Delhi Sultanate. In 1400, he turned westward, defeating the Mamluks in 1401 in Damascus (where he met Ibn Khaldun) and the Ottomans in 1402 at Ankara, capturing their sultan and enabling Byzantium to survive for another fifty years. In 1405, Timur was on his way to attack China, but he died near Utrar before completing his campaign.

Although Timur raided the territory between Moscow and Delhi, he established permanent administration only in Iran, Iraq and Central Asia. These sedentary territories, governed by his sons and commanders, provided him with a rich tax base and a reserve of manpower. Unlike Genghis Khan, Timur did not try to subjugate the nomads whose domains he invaded. While Timur's capital, Samarqand, became a cosmopolitan imperial city that flourished as never before, Iran and Iraq suffered devastation at a greater degree than that caused by the Mongols.

Because Timur's campaigns were a mass of unco-ordinated raids, he often conquered one place more than once. However, the constant fighting enabled Timur to engage and reward his troops, thereby preventing them from turning against him. Timur's conquests also consciously aimed to restore the Mongol Empire, and the deliberate devastation that accompanied them was a conscious imitation of the Mongol onslaught. The third aim of the conquests was the

Exterior of Tamerlane's (Timur's) mausoleum. Timurid dynasty. 1405 CE. Credit: Bridgeman-Giraudon/Art Resource, NY. S. Isidro el Real, Leon, Spain.

revival of the Silk Roads, shifting their main routes into his realm, mainly at the expense of the more northern route that passed through the Golden Horde's lands.

Timur's conquests were a high time for Transoxiana, but they weakened—although did not eliminate—nearly all of the Muslim forces of his time (Ottomans, Mamluks, Golden Horde, Chaghadaid Moghuls, Delhi Sultanate). They also led to the spread of the gunpowder weapon back eastward, from the Ottomans to China and India, thereby contributing to the subsequent decline of the nomads.

Timur's empire, which was mainly based on his personal charisma and lacked a strong institutional basis, did not survive intact after his death. However, his descendants, the Timurids, ruled over a smaller realm that was composed of eastern Iran and Transoxania for another century (1405–1501), presiding over a period of cultural brilliance. With the Uzbek conquest of Transoxania, one Timurid prince, Babur, escaped into India, where he founded the Mughal dynasty (1526–1858), the rulers of which called themselves Timurids. Under the Timurids,

Timur had become a source of legitimacy in his own right and was used as such by different rulers in Central Asia and Iran up to the nineteenth century. He was also well known in Renaissance Europe. During the late twentieth century, Timur also became the father of independent Uzbekistan, even though the Uzbeks had expelled his descendants from the territory that later became Uzbekistan.

MICHAL BIRAN

See also Architecture, Religious; Architecture, Secular: Civil; Central Asia; China; Genghis Khan; Iran; Iraq; India; Khurasan; Mongols; Mughals; Nomadism and Pastoralism; Raids; Samarqand; Silk Roads; Timurids; Turks; Warfare and Techniques

Further Reading

Primary Sources

de Clavijo, Ruy Gonzales. *Narrative of the Spanish Embassy to the Court of Timur at Samarkand in the Years 1403–1406*, transl. G. Le Strange. London, 1928.

Ibn 'Arabshah. *Tamerlane or Timur the Great Amir*, transl. J.H. Sanders. 1936; Reprint 1976.

Ibn Khaldun. *Ibn Khaldün and Tamerlane*, ed. and transl. W.J. Fischell. Berkeley and Los Angeles: Berkeley University Press, 1952.

Khwandamir. *Habib al-Siyar*, ed. and transl. W.M. Thackston., 2 vols. Cambridge, Mass: Department of Near Eastern Languages and Civilizations, Harvard University, 1994.

Shami, NiÛam al-Din. *Zafar Namah*, ed. F. Tauer. Monographie Archivu Orientalniho 5. Beirut, 1937.

Yazdi, Sharaf al-Din. *Zafar Namah*, ed. Urunbaev. Tashkent: Academy of Sciences of the Uzbek SSR, 1972.

Studies

Manz, B.F. "Tamerlane and the Symbolism of Sovereignty." *Iranian Studies* 21 (1988): 105–22.

———. *The Rise and Rule of Tamerlane*. Cambridge, UK: Cambridge University Press, 1989.

———. "Tamerlane Career and Its Uses." *Journal of World History* 13 (2002): 1–25.

Woods, John E. "Timur's Genealogy." In *Intellectual Studies on Islam, Essays Written in Honor of Martin B. Dickson*, eds. M.M. Mazzaouni and V.B. Moreen, 85–126. Salt Lake City: Utah University Press, 1990.

TAWHIDI, AL-, ABU HAYYAN

Abu Hayyan 'Ali ibn Muhammad ibn al-'Abbas al-Tawhidi was an essayist, philosopher and one of the greatest masters of the Arabic style. According to sources, his name (Tawhidi) probably derives from the variety of date *(tawhid)* that his father traded.

Al-Tawhidi was probably born in Iraq or Fars sometime between AH 310/922 CE and AH 320/932 CE, and he died in Shiraz (Iran) in 414/1023. It is not known whether he was of Arab or Iranian descent or what his mother tongue was, but he did not understand Persian. He spent his childhood in Baghdad, which was rife with clashes between the Sunnite and the Shi'i populations; despite this, it offered an intellectually rich life. In Baghdad, he studied grammar, law, the Qur'an, hadith (the traditions of the Prophet), mathematics, rhetoric, theology, and Sufism. Al-Tawhidi was familiar with Ismaili doctrines and Greek philosophy, both of which were in vogue in the intellectual circles of the time. One of his masters was in fact the Christian philosopher and theologian Yahya ibn 'Adi, follower of the famous al-Farabi and translator and commentator of Aristotle, whose lectures he attended in 361/971.

In 350/961, al-Tawhidi decided to dedicate himself to literature and began writing *Insights and Treasures*, which took him fifteen years to complete. This first, rather modest work is an anthology of anecdotes and aphorisms. The didactic aim and its sometimes serious, sometimes humorous style are typical of the adab literature of which al-Jahiz was a master. Al-Tawhidi, inspired by the latter's writings, adopts his style and later dedicates *In Praise of Jahiz* to him. For a living, he worked as a copyist, a job that was fairly common among men of learning without private means. The influence of this activity is reflected in *On Penmanship,* which talks about different handwriting techniques and tools of the trade and contains the aphorisms and sayings of famous copyists and scribes.

Al-Tawhidi, like many of his colleagues, spent much of his life in search of a patron. For this reason, he twice set out to find his fortune in Rayy (southern Iran), but he did not meet with success. He first presented himself to the Buyid vizier Abu 'l-Fadl ibn al-'Amid and later to his son, Abu 'l-Fath, who died soon after. In 367/ CE, his successor, the vizier al-Sahib ibn 'Abbad, who was also a refined man of letters, hired al-Tawhidi as a copyist. Unsuited to life at court and frustrated by his lack of intellectual success, al-Tawhidi reacts badly to the continuous humiliation that his employer inflicted on him; three years later he lost his job. He got his revenge by writing *The Characters of the Two Viziers (al-Sahib ibn al-'Abbad and Abu 'l-Fadl ibn al-'Amid)*, a virulent pamphlet that is stylistically brilliant despite its often obscene tone and that portrays al-Sahib ibn 'Abbad in a very bad light.

On his return to Baghdad, al-Tawhidi was taken under the wing of Abu 'l-Wafa' al-Muhandis, the mathematician, politician, and man of science, who introduced him to Ibn Sa'dan, a high-ranking civil servant. With him, al-Tawhidi finally found an intellectual equal who can offer him the type of intellectual relationship he had been looking for. He dedicated *Of Friendship and Friends* to him; this is an anthology of poems, prose, aphorisms, and sayings about friendship which took him thirty years to write. This encounter marks the beginning of a period of intense intellectual activity. Al-Tawhidi became a close friend of the logician Abu Sulayman al-Sijistani al-Mantiq, another philosopher formed at the school of al-Farabi and by whom al-Tawhidi was greatly influenced. The debates held under the guidance of al-Sijistani and Yahya ibn 'Adi in the circle of intellectuals that al-Tawhidi frequents are reproduced in *Conversations,* which contains 106 conversations about religious, philosophical, ethical, factual, and literary topics. This work is a precious record of the discussions between men of learning of different beliefs and origins, and it is also the main extant source of al-Sijistani's thoughts.

When, in 373/983, Ibn Sa'dan became vizier to the Buyid Prince Samsam al-Dawla, al-Tawhidi remained at his court and took part in his cultural evenings. Here, the vizier presented a wide range of philological, philosophical, and literary topics that al-Tawhidi discussed, often reflecting Abu Sulayman al-Sijistani's viewpoint. This inspired *Delight and Entertainment,* which is a detailed record of these evenings compiled at al-Muhandis' request. The work is a mine of information about intellectual life in Baghdad during the tenth century, especially with regard to the thoughts of the most important philosophers of that period. *Searching [Questions] and Compendious [Answers]* is of similar documentary value and was written together with the Persian philosopher-historian Miskawayh; it is a collection of questions put forward by al-Tawhidi about matters of philosophy, natural science, ethics, and linguistics, and it contains detailed answers given by Miskawayh. After Ibn Sa'dan's death (374/984), al-Tawhidi seeks refuge in Shiraz (central Iran) at the home of the vizier of the Buyid prince, Samsam al-Dawla. Little is known about the later years of al-Tawhidi's life other than that he burns his life works in the throes of a spiritual crisis or perhaps as a result of disappointment in the poor consideration of his writings during the preceding twenty years.

He is undoubtedly a master of style: his crystalline, elegant prose deliberately imitates that of his great predecessor and model, al-Jahiz. His encyclopedic knowledge is reflected in the layout of a brief treatise entitled *Of the Branches of Knowledge,* which deals analytically with the different sciences. Al-Tawhidi does not seem to have followed a specific doctrine, although he showed very obvious sympathy toward Sufism. This is particularly evident in *Divine Intimations,* which was written when he was older and contains homilies, prayers, and some technical references to the doctrine. A follower of the Shafiite school of Islamic law, he was opposed to Mu'tazilism and Shi'ism, but he never explicitly belonged to any theological school of thought. His varied and sometimes controversial beliefs led many Muslims to view him suspiciously: Ibn al-Jawzi (twelfth century) says that al-Tawhidi is an example of *zandaqa* (heresy), and his contemporaries probably ignored him for this reason. This was something that much surprised the biographer Yaqut al-Hamawi (thirteenth century), who describes him as "the philosopher of cultured men and a man of culture among philosophers." During the nineteenth and twentieth centuries, scholars rediscovered him and appreciated the variety of his works, the wide range of his interests, and his love of literary activities, which al-Tawhidi saw as having a noble function. Al-Tawhidi's double personality (polyhedric intellectual and refined man of letters on the one hand, hypochondriac and pessimistic on the other) is reflected in the opinions of the scholars: if some consider him to be a worthy representative of humanism,

endowed with great intellectual honesty, others consider him to be a disappointed and intellectually embittered courtier as a result of his failure at climbing the social ladder.

ANTONELLA GHERSETTI

See also Adab; Baghdad; Buyids; al-Farabi; Heresy and Heretics; Ismailis; al-Jahiz; Mu'tazilites; Shi'ism; Sufism and Sufis; Viziers

Further Reading

Bergé, Marc. *Pour un Humanisme Vécu: Abu Hayyan al-Tawhidi.* Damascus, 1979.
———. "Abu Hayyan al-Tawhidi". In *The Cambridge History of Arabic Literature. 'Abbasid Belles-Lettres,* ed. J. Ashtiany et al., 112–24. Cambridge, 1990.
Keilani, Ibrahim. *Abu Hayyan al-Tawhidi* (in French). Beirut, 1950.
Kraemer, Joel. *Humanism in the Renaissance of Islam,* 212–22. Leiden, 1986.
———. *Philosophy in the Renaissance of Islam.* Leiden, 1986.

TECHNOLOGY, MILLS: WATER AND WIND

Water and wind mills in Islam were part of a general technology involving the transport and use of water in irrigation and for power. Muslim science took great interest in hydraulic technology, particularly mills. This interest reflected the importance of irrigation in the dry climates of many Muslim regions. Reliable irrigation systems and a plentiful supply of hydraulic power were critical, because Muslim agriculture focused heavily on intensively cultivated crops such as dates, citrus fruit, and olives. In addition to structures like mills, Muslims also perfected reservoir technology, dams, above-ground irrigation systems, and underground systems like *qanats* (filtration galleries), which exploited water tables using vertical wells, and *cimbras* (riverbed galleries), which used covered trenches to transport water.

Mills provided an important source of industrial power, both for local agriculture and for more far-reaching trade products. Mill wheels refined important raw materials by grinding them down, and this made them critical machines for several industries, not all of which were food related. They were used to grind wood pulp for paper, sugarcane for sugar, grain and corn for flour, and flax for cloth. The papermaking technology fostered the explosion in Muslim books and libraries during the eighth century. Paper quickly replaced papyrus in the Islamic world and made the creation of relatively cheap and numerous books possible. This revolution was so important in al-Andalus (Muslim Iberia) that, after the

Christian King James I of Aragon conquered Muslim Valencia (with its paper mills) in southeastern Spain in 1238, the Aragonese production of documents increased exponentially.

Sugar mills were an important part of the Meccan trade in early Islam, as were grain mills. Unlike Christian European mills, which were often owned and tightly controlled for lucrative tax purposes by a feudal lord, Muslim mills were privately owned businesses in many areas. However, in al-Andalus, Muslim ownership of mills tended to be communal in nature; the mills were owned and managed by local groups. This system, called a "tribal system," allowed for more local and decentralized control. When power became more centralized in a more stratified society (e.g., in the taifa kingdoms of eleventh century al-Andalus; in the post-conquest Christian kingdoms of the next century), horizontal mills gave way to more efficient mill designs like vertical mills and windmills. This increased production but restricted the benefits of such progress to fewer people in the society.

Also important to Islamic agriculture were windmills, which date back to the time of the caliph 'Umar in the seventh century. These were used for drawing water for irrigation (like norias) and for grinding corn. The sails (six or twelve to a windmill) turned a large wheel inside the windmill house, which then turned the millstone; the system could also be set up with multiple mill wheels. Windmills were built on a height—on top of a hill or on the top of a fortress or substructure—to maximize the availability and power of the wind. Early windmills were built in two stories, with the mill wheels in the top story and the sails attached to the lower story. The sails consisted of bundles of palm leaves and resembled the sails of a European-style windmill.

Mills came in three types based on their sources of power: water-, wind-, or animal-driven. In some agricultural machines, one source was used to gain another. For example, in a noria, an animal drove a cup wheel that transported water from a river or stream to an irrigation tank or channel. Animal-driven mills were most useful in areas that lacked enough water to power a mill and in which a windmill was not feasible. Whatever the power source was, it drove a large hydraulic wheel that turned a millstone that ground raw agricultural materials into refined products. Mills could differ greatly in complexity, depending on how the power was transferred to the wheel. In the simpler horizontal mill, the water drove a current wheel that directly turned the mill wheel. In the more efficient—but also more expensive—vertical mill, the power transferred to the mill wheel via a set of gears. The advantages of the horizontal mill over the vertical were that it could be set on smaller rivers or even irrigation channels, that it was cheaper and easier to build, and that it could be used to drive multiple mill wheels. Also, in Islamic systems, the delivery tank and millrace were separate, so water could be diverted for irrigation before entry into the mill. This shows the importance of water in Islam as an agricultural tool for both harnessing power and transferring water. The separate tanks and the possibility of having multiple mill wheels also facilitated ownership and use by groups rather than individuals.

Despite the clearly industrial uses for power, a primary use was always in agricultural irrigation, of which mills were a major component. Set up on rivers, they were usually connected to a system of irrigation canals and were used to grind the products of that system. Streams or rivers often had multiple mills on them, particularly horizontal mills. The nature of ownership heavily influenced the placement of a mill. In single-owner or post-Islamic feudal systems, the mill came at the head of the agricultural system, getting the first part of the water. In communally owned systems, the mill was built downstream at the bottom of the network of irrigation channels, at a point after the water had been diverted for irrigation use; this maximized the availability of the water for both irrigation and power. Another way to maximize use was to have water schedules in which water was allocated to different parts of the system at different times. This extended to the allocation of water to the mill. In the case of a community mill, co-owners had shares (i.e., rights to use the mill at different times). Attempts to feudalize or otherwise centralize the management of such extensive systems often failed. Their structure was too inherently collective to make centralization practical, and such attempts generated hostility among those working within the older system. When centralization succeeded, older owners found themselves marginalized, losing their collective rights to irrigation and milling.

PAULA R. STILES

See also Agriculture; Andalus; Irrigation; Land Tenure and Ownership

Further Reading

Glick, Thomas F. *From Muslim Fortress to Christian Culture: Social and Cultural Change in Medieval Spain.* Manchester and New York: Manchester University Press, 1995.

—— *Irrigation and Hydraulic Technology: Medieval Spain and Its Legacy.* Aldershot: Variorum, 1996.

Hill, D.R. *Islamic Science and Engineering.* Edinburgh: Edinburgh University Press. 1993.

Long, Pamela O. *Technology and Society in the Medieval Centuries: Byzantium, Islam, and the West, 500–1300.* Washington, DC: American Historical Association, 2003.

Watson, A.M. *Agricultural Innovation in the Early Islamic World*. Cambridge, UK: Cambridge University Press, 1983.

TEXTILES

Much of the study of early Islamic textiles is overshadowed by the prominence of studies on medieval tiraz textiles that carry inscriptions following an official caliphal protocol, similar to that on coins and other official documents, with historically identifiable content referring to the patrons, places, workshops, and the year of manufacture. Scholars have tended to focus on this group of material, because it is provides a distinct and narrow enough field for historical investigation. This goes hand in hand with a general scholarly focus on Egypt, because most medieval Islamic textiles that are extant today were found there, and many of them were produced there or had been exported there from other parts of the Islamic world. Furthermore, most medieval literary sources discuss the textile industry of early Islamic Egypt rather than that of other parts of the Islamic world. Therefore, the present view of the medieval Islamic textile industry is very much dependent on what is known about Egypt and how its network of trade was linked to the Mediterranean region on the one hand and the Indian Ocean on the other.

Egypt, the Mediterranean, and the Indian Ocean

Studies Based on Literary Evidence

The first serious study of the concept of tiraz is Josef von Karabacek's *Die Arabischen Papyrusprotokolle* of 1908, which links the contents of protocolary inscriptions on papyri to those on coins and textiles.

One of the earliest studies of the literary sources of the Egyptian textile industry is Ali Bey Baghat's "Les Manufactures d'Étoffe en Égypte au Moyen Âge," which was published in 1903. It contains a number of literary references relating to the 'Abbasid and Fatimid periods, and these focus on the products and centers of the textile industry rather than the structure of its administration.

Adolf Grohmann's article about the term *tiraz* in the *Encyclopaedia of Islam* of 1934 adopts the concept of tiraz as a protocolary inscription, but he applies it exclusively to textiles. He lists the contents of a large number of tiraz textile inscriptions, but he also introduces an institutional and industrial dimension by using several historical literary sources. As a papyrologist, Grohmann also uses the documentary evidence of papyri to supplement and test the historical information contained in the inscriptions.

Gaston Wiet can be credited with raising tiraz textiles from obscurity to wider scholarly interest. He assembled the massive tiraz collection of the Museum of Islamic Art in Cairo and masterminded the publication of approximately 1140 inscribed textiles in the RCEA. In 1935, Wiet also planned a large exhibition of the collection at the Musée des Gobelins. It is to his credit that any significant scholarship of tiraz textiles exists. However, Wiet treated tiraz textiles as historical documents and did not see them as textile products, a methodology that owed debts to a scholarly interest in epigraphy since the nineteenth century and is the basis for a number of related publications (Michele Angelo Lanci's *Trattato Delle Simboliche Representanze Arabiche Della Varia Generazione de' Musulmani Carrateri Sopra Differenti Materie Operati* of 1845–1846; A.R. Guest's series of articles in the *Journal of the Royal Asiatic Society* between 1906 and 1931; Kendrick's catalog of the tiraz textile collection in the Victoria and Albert Museum; Carl Johan Lamm's articles about Swedish tiraz collections; Nancy Pence Britton's catalog of the tiraz collection at the Boston Museum of Fine Arts). The early publications of Ernst Kuhnel also show a clear interest in epigraphy and documentation rather than the artifacts themselves.

Two early attempts to study the organization of tiraz institutions were written by Muhammad Abd al-Aziz Marzouk and Etienne Combe. Both authors see textile inscriptions as historical documents without giving any consideration to the fabrics on which they are found. Their studies of the institutions rely almost exclusively on known textual sources; neither use the textile evidence in a convincing manner to support their theses.

Ugo Monneret de Villard has been one of the only scholars to devote a study to the production of court textiles in Palermo under the Normans; this was also largely drawn from literary sources. His study suggests that, until the arrival of the Normans, a tiraz workshop did not exist in Sicily despite a thriving textile industry, which is suggested by the lack of surviving specimens from Sicily, in Egypt, and in Italy and the silence of contemporary literary sources. The Arabic inscription on the coronation robe of Roger II states that it was made in the khizana al-malikiyya, suggesting that, when the Normans took control of the island, they organized a workshop within their palace. By contrast, a recent study based on the evidence of another surviving inscribed fragment from Palermo that stated in Latin that it was made in a royal workshop ("Operatum in Regio

Ergast") suggests that the Palermitan workshop was ultimately based on the ergasterion (the Byzantine court workshop).

R.S. Serjeant's *Islamic Textiles, Material for a History up to the Mongol Conquest,* reveals an entirely different approach, because it functions very much like a historical source book for textile historians. It draws from histories, administrative works, works of hisba, geographical works, dictionaries (both biographical and geographical), and agricultural treatises. The material is arranged in parts chronologically, geographically, and by subject. Encyclopedic in approach, Serjeant's work covers all main areas of the Islamic world between Spain and India.

Yadida Stillman's doctoral dissertation, *Female Attire of Medieval Egypt: According to the Trousseau Lists and Cognate Material from the Cairo Geniza,* is an important contribution to the current understanding of medieval textile terminology, both in terms of fabrics and materials but also in terms of fashion. Drawn on surviving documents from the Cairo Geniza, it puts into order and defines the meanings of the often very confusing usage of medieval Arabic terms for textiles, and it expands on the previous scholarship by S.D. Goitein.

Maurice Lombard, in his study *Les Textiles dans le Monde Musulman,* also adopts a purely literary approach, albeit with a different aim than Serjeant's work. Lombard presents an interpretative history of Islamic textiles, with particular reference to manufacture, society, and trade. It is divided into sections that deal with the materials and techniques of manufacture, aspects of the administration and patronage, and the social and economic issues of labor and technology. A large section of this work is devoted to Egypt, particularly the textile manufacturers of the Delta region and the structure and role of the textile institutions.

Irene Bierman's doctoral dissertation entitled *Art and Politics: The Impact of Fatimid Uses of Tiraz Fabrics* presents an interpretative study of the court context of inscribed textiles and their political significance, a study that takes tiraz inscriptions beyond their documentary, epigraphic, or semantic value by attempting to establish their semiotics.

Another interpretative work is Gladis Frantz-Murphy's article "A New Interpretation of the Economic History of Mediaeval Egypt: The Role of the Textile Industry 254–567/868–1171," which follows the tradition of scholarship on Egyptian economic and administrative history. Hers differs, however, from these earlier studies in that it focuses on the role of the textile industry in the economic development of Egypt under the Tulunids, a time when taxes were withheld from the central 'Abbasid authorities in Baghdad and reinvested into Egyptian agriculture to boost the production of raw materials and finished products for export.

Studies Based on the Evidence of Textiles

Although their epigraphy, decorative style, and historical and administrative contexts have been studied in some depth, the technical issues presented by tiraz textiles have hardly been addressed. Tiraz textiles have been subjected to taxonomic analysis relatively rarely. The studies by R. Pfister, Carl Johan Lamm, Louisa Bellinger, Veronika Gervers and Lisa Golombek, Mary Ballard, and Georgette Cornu are pioneering works in this area, but their value has been limited by the fact that they have drawn their evidence largely from single collections. This is also the case with Anna Contadini's study of the Fatimid textiles at the Victoria and Albert Museum, which is a relatively small collection. Although Contadini touches on vital questions such as manufacture, administration, and commerce, her findings are not checked against larger samples. Lamm was the only scholar who based his research on several collections.

Lamm's *Cotton in Mediaeval Textiles in the Near East* was one of the first studies that focused on one material that was important during the early Islamic period and traced it through the literary sources as well as the extant textile evidence. He presented a wide range of textiles from Sasanian, Umayyad, 'Abbasid, and Indian importers, most of which were found in Egypt. The material was arranged by decorative method, the technicalities of which were given great attention. A gazetteer of places that produced cotton and relevant textual sources was included as an appendix.

Lamm's contemporary, R. Pfister, was working on a series of articles that were, like Lamm's, novel in their approach and methodology. His two articles, "Matériaux pour Servir au Classement des Textiles Égyptiens Postérieurs à la Conquête Arabe" and "L'Introduction du Coton en Égypte Musulmane," were, like Lamm's work, concerned with materials and techniques. The first of the two articles evaluated the Islamic contribution to the development of Egyptian textiles. For this Pfister had the color dyes of a number of Coptic and Islamic textiles analyzed and found that, during the Islamic period, a lac dye was used; this was an insect-based substance that had reached Egypt via the Indian Ocean route from India. In his other article, Pfister linked the introduction of Z-spinning (i.e., twisting the yarn to the left) into Egypt during the 'Abbasid period to the concurrent import of Iraqi cotton textiles. The trade between Egypt and India (another important eastern trading partner of Egypt) has been the basis of a massive study by Ruth Barnes of the Newberry Collection of medieval Indian block-printed textiles.

The catalog of the tiraz collection at the Textile Museum Washington published in 1952 by Ernst Kühnel and Louisa Bellinger is to this day one of the most comprehensive surveys of early Islamic textiles available. Its trendsetting quality lay in the cooperation of an Islamic art historian with a textile specialist. While Kühnel interpreted the historical data, Bellinger analyzed materials, fabrics, and decorative techniques by using taxonomy; this correlation of historical and technical data allowed for contextualizing. Bellinger showed convincingly the various trends and developments in the making of tiraz textiles from Iran, Yemen, and Egypt, and she was able to distinguish several centers of production and put forward theories about the transmission of materials and techniques from East to West. Lisa Golombek and Veronica Gervers followed Kühnel and Bellinger's approach in their 1977 study, "Tiraz Fabrics in the Royal Ontario Museum." Although Gervers' contribution was largely a reëvaluation of the theories put forward by Lamm, Pfister, and Bellinger, Golombek attempted an interpretation of the sociological implications of materials, patronage, and the uses and significance of tiraz textiles, which were areas that had not been touched upon seriously before. However, rather than taking the literary sources as her stepping stone, Golombek decided to raise questions on the basis of the textile evidence itself. This led her to investigate what kinds of garments could be reconstructed from the textile fragments, the kinds of fabrics used, the degree of foreign influence in Egypt, and who made and ordered these textiles. Rather than providing answers, Gervers' and Golombek's article provides a forum for discussion.

Mary Ballard, a textile conservator at the Freer and Sackler Galleries in Washington, has contributed to the field a technical study of tiraz textiles based on the collection of the Detroit Institute of Arts. By analyzing mostly materials and weaving methods, she documents the technical peculiarities of this sample.

The most recent studies of tiraz have been published by Georgette Cornu. Her study "Wası Yéménite des IXe–Xe Siècles au Musée Historique des Tissus de Lyon," published in 1991, presents a new approach, because it traces one particular extant textile type through available textual sources, making constant reference to existing textiles. Perhaps more prominent—but not as ingenious in its approach as her previous article—is Cornu's catalog of the Pfister Collection of tiraz textiles held at the Bibliotheca Apostolica Vaticana in Rome. Massive in scale, this work continues the approach introduced by Kühnel and Bellinger, although it is less interpretative with regard to the historical implications of technological issues. However, every item in the catalog is meticulously recorded; each entry includes the inscription, technical data, and comparisons. In an appendix, the fabric structures of several textiles are explained with schematic drawings. Cornu's exhibition catalog of 1994, *Tissus d'Egypte, Témoins du Monde Arabe VIIIe–XVe Siècles, Collection Bouvier,* continues this approach.

The recent doctoral dissertation *Tiraz Textiles from Egypt: Production, Administration and Uses of Tiraz Textiles from Egypt Under the Umayyad, 'Abbasid and Fatimid Dynasties* has tried to overcome the existing rift between historians and textile specialists, by approaching the subject in a more unified way, taking into account the interrelationships among production, administration, and use. Rather than relying on one collection (as most previous authors have done), samples from all of the major museum collections are examined here and have been arranged in a database of 1823 items, which made it possible to analyze the properties of textiles taxonomically. By using taxonomic analysis, both material and historical information are combined, and emerging trends are tested against the historical evidence of literary sources. A major discovery lies in how the textile evidence reflects administrative changes in control of the textile industry and the wider administrative relationship between Egypt and Iraq under the 'Abbasids. Despite agreement by both textile specialists and historians that tiraz textiles were produced for court consumption, neither have considered addressing why tiraz textiles were used in burials; graves are the sources from which most surviving tiraz textiles have in fact been recovered archaeologically. This thesis approaches that subject by considering both material and literary evidence and suggests that tiraz textiles were regarded as a source of blessing for the deceased because of the caliphal association recorded in their inscriptions.

Iran

The finds of medieval Buyid silks at Rayy in Iran, which were supposedly made in tombs at Naqqareh Khaneh and Kuh-i Sorsoreh at the foot of the mountain of Bibi Shahr Banu (Aminabad), are what appear to be the only other known major Islamic burial finds of textiles outside of Egypt and have therefore aroused enormous attention from scholars and textile dealers alike. For a long time there existed a controversy about the authenticity of these finds; it is now clear that a good number of textiles that were claimed to have come from Rayy are in fact forgeries, particularly those that came on to the art market after 1930.

Some textiles, however, have been found to be genuine, particularly those that came on the market around 1925, when the tombs were excavated. Many of this latter group are now in the Victoria and Albert Museum in London and have been compared with the scant descriptions by those excavators, dealers, and scholars present in Iran in the 1920s. The Rayy textiles are, however, fundamentally different from those textiles found in Egypt with regard to materials, technique, and historical context. They are compound-woven silks (rather than linen, cotton, or wool like those found in Egypt), and there is very little contemporary literary information about the historical context in which they were produced and used.

JOCHEN SOKOLY

Further Reading

Baghat, A.B. "Les Manufactures d'Étoffes en Égypte au Moyen Age." *Bulletin de l'Institut Egyptien* IV (1903): 351–61.

Ballard, M. Paper given at the CIETA conference in September 1983. Typescript, personal communication.

Barnes, R. "From India to Egypt: The Newberry Collection and the Indian Ocean Trade." In *Islamische Textilkunst des Mittelalters: Aktuelle Probleme*, vol. V, 79–92. Riggisberg (Bern): Abegg-Stiftung, 1997.

———. *Indian Block-Printed Textiles in Egypt: The Newberry Collection in the Ashmolean Museum, Oxford*, 2 vols. Oxford, UK, 1997.

Bierman, I.A. *Art and Politics: The Impact of Fatimid Uses of Tiraz Fabrics*. PhD dissertation. Chicago: University of Chicago, Department of Near East Languages and Civilisation, 1980.

Blair, Sheila, Jonathan Max Bloom, and Anne E. Wardwell. "Reevaluating the Date of the 'Buyid' Silks by Epigraphic and Radiocarbon Analysis." *Ars Orientalis* 22: 1–42.

Bouvier. *Tissus d'Egypte, Témoins du Monde Arabe VIIIe–XVe Siècles, Collection Bouvier*. Geneva and Paris, 1994.

Britton, N.P. *A Study of Some Early Islamic Textiles in The Museum of Fine Arts Boston*. Boston, 1938.

Combe, É. "Une Institution de l'État Musulman: Le Dâr al-Tirâz, Atelier de Tissage." *Revue des Conférences Francaises en Orient* XI (1947): 85–92.

Cornu, G. "*Wasi*; Yéménite des IXe–Xe Siècles au Musée Historique des Tissus de Lyon." *Archéologie Islamique* II (1991): 47–70.

———. *Tissus Islamiques de la Collection Pfister*. Vatican City: Biblioteca Apostolica Vaticana, 1992.

Contadini, A. *Fatimid Art at the Victoria and Albert Museum*. London, 1998.

Goitein, S.D. *A Mediterranean Society, I, Economic Foundations*. Berkeley and Los Angeles, 1967.

———. *A Mediterranean Society, III, The Family*. Berkeley, Los Angeles, and London, 1978.

———. *A Mediterranean Society, IV, Daily Life*. Berkeley, Los Angeles, and London, 1983.

———. *A Mediterranean Society, V, The Individual: Portrait of a Mediterranean Personality of the High Middle Ages as Reflected in the Cairo Geniza*. Berkeley, Los Angeles, and London, 1988.

Golombek, L., and V. Gervers. "Tiraz Fabrics in the Royal Ontario Museum." In *Studies in Textile History in Memory of Harold B. Burnham*, 82–125. Toronto, 1977.

Grohmann, A. "Tiraz." In *The Encyclopaedia of Islam*, vol. IV, 785–93. 1934.

Guest, A.R., "Arabic Inscriptions on Textiles at the South Kensington Museum." *Journal of the Royal Asiatic Society* (1906): 387–99.

———. "Further Arabic Inscriptions on Textiles." *Journal of the Royal Asiatic Society* (1918) 263–5.

———. "Further Arabic Inscriptions on Textiles (II)." *Journal of the Royal Asiatic Society* (1923): 405–8.

———."Further Arabic Inscriptions on Textiles (III)." *Journal of the Royal Asiatic Society* (1930): 761–6.

———. "Further Arabic Inscriptions on Textiles (IV)." *Journal of the Royal Asiatic Society* (1931): 129–34.

Lamm, C.J. "Egyptiska Tekstiler I Nationalmuseum." *National Musei Arsbok* III (1933): 1–11.

———. "Five Egyptian Tapestry-Weavings in Swedish Museums." *Ars Islamica* I (1934) 92–8.

———. "Arabiska Inskrifter Pa Nagra Textilfragment fran Egypten." *Rhösska Konstslöjdmuseets Arstryck* (1935): 3–11.

———. "Egyptiska Dukagangsvavnader." *Kulturen En Arsbok* (1936): 258–74.

———. *Cotton in Medieval Textiles in the Near East*. Paris, 1937.

———. "Jordfundne Tekstiler fra Aegypten." *Tilskueren* (1938): 333–50.

———. "Dated or Datable Tiraz in Sweden." *Le Monde Oriental* XXXII (1938): 103–25.

Lombard, M. *Les Textiles dans le Monde Musulman du VIIe au XIIe Siècle, Études d'Économie Médiévale III*. Paris, 1978.

von Karabacek, J. *Zur Orientalischen Altertumskunde, II, Die Arabischen Papyrusprotokolle*. Vienna, 1908.

Kendrick, A.F. *Catalogue of Muhammadan Textiles of the Medieval Period*. London: Victoria and Albert Museum, 1924.

King, D. "The Textiles Found Near Rayy About 1925." *CIETA Bulletin* 65 (1987): 34–59.

Kühnel, E. "Tirazstoffe der Abbasiden." *Der Islam* XIV (1925): 82–8.

———. *Islamische Stoffe aus Ägyptischen Gräbern in der Islamischen Kunstabteilung und in der Stoffsammlung des Schlossmuseums*. Berlin, 1927.

———. "Zur Tiraz-Epigraphik der Abbasiden und Fatimiden." In *Aus Funf Jahrtausenden Morgenländischer Kultur, Festschrift Max Freiherrn von Oppenheim zum 70*, 59–65. Berlin: Geburtstage, 1933.

Kühnel, E., and Bellinger, L. *Catalogue of Dated Tiraz Fabrics, Umayyad, Abbasid, Fatimid*. Washington, DC: The Textile Museum, 1952.

Marzouk, M.A.A. "The Evolution of Inscriptions on Fatimid Textiles." *Ars Islamica* X (1943): 164–6.

———. "Alexandria as a Textile Centre 331 B.C.–1517 A.D." *Bulletin de la Société d'Archéologie Copte* XIII (1948–1949): 111–35.

———. "The Turban of Samuel Ibn Musa, The Earliest Dated Islamic Textile." *Bulletin of the Faculty of Arts Cairo University* XVI (1954): 143–51.

———. "Four Dated Tiraz Fabrics of the Fatimid Khalif az-Zahir." *Kunst des Orients* II (1955): 45–51.

———. "The Earliest Fatimid Textile." In *Akten des Vierundzwanzigsten Internationalen Orientalisten-Kongresses*

Munchen, 28. August bis 4. September 1957, ed. Herbert Franke, 356–7. Wiesbaden, 1957.

————. "The Earliest Fatimid Textile (Tiraz al-Mansuriya)." *Bulletin of the Faculty of Arts Alexandria University* XI (1957): 37–44.

————. "Five Tiraz Fabrics in the Völkerkunde-Museum of Basel." In *Aus der Welt der Islamischen Kunst, Festschrift fur Ernst Kuhnel zum 75. Geburtstag am 26. 10. 1957*, 283–9. Berlin, 1959.

————. "The Tiraz Institutions in Medieval Egypt." *Studies in Islamic Art and Architecture in Honour of Professor K.A.C. Creswell*, 157–62. Cairo, 1965.

Monneret de Villard, U. "La Tessitura Palermitana Sotto I Normanni e i Suoi Rapporti con l'Arte Bizantina." In *Miscellanea Giovanni Mercati, Volume III, Letteratura e Storia Bizantina*, 1–26. Vatican City: Biblioteca Apostolica Vaticana, 1956.

Pfister, R. "Matériaux pour Servir au Classement des Textiles Égyptiens Postérieurs à la Conquête Arabe." *Revue des Arts Asiatiques* X (1936): 1–16, 73–85.

————. "L'Introduction du Coton en Égypte Musulmane." *Revue des Arts Asiatiques* XI (1937): 167–72.

————. "Toiles a Inscriptions Abbasides et Fatimides." *Bulletin d'Études Orientales* XI (1945–1946): 47–90.

Piazza, R.V. "La Produzione di Manufatti Tessili nel Palazzo Reale di Palermo: "Tiraz" o "Ergasterion"." In *I Normanni, Popolo d'Europa 1030–1200*, 288–90. Venice, 1994.

Serjeant, R.B. *Islamic Textiles: Material for a History up to the Mongol Conquest*. Beirut, 1972.

Sokoly, J.A. "Towards a Model of Early Islamic Textile Institutions in Egypt." In *Islamische Textilkunst des Mittelalters: Aktuelle Probleme*, vol. V, 115–22. Bern: Riggisberger Berichte, 1997.

————. "Between Life and Death: The Funerary Context of Tiraz Textiles." In *Islamische Textilkunst des Mittelalters: Aktuelle Probleme*, vol. V, 71–8. Bern: Riggisberger Berichte, 1997.

————. *Tiraz Textiles from Egypt: Production, Administration and Uses of Tiraz Textiles from Egypt Under the Umayyad, 'Abbasid and Fatimid Dynasties (A Thesis Submitted for the Degree of Doctor of Philosophy at the University of Oxford.)* Oxford, UK: Faculty of Oriental Studies, University of Oxford, 2001. Typescript.

Stillman, Y.K. *Female Attire of Medieval Egypt: According to the Trousseau Lists and Cognate Material from the Cairo Geniza*. PhD dissertation. University of Pennsylvania, Faculty of the Graduate School of Arts and Sciences, 1972. (Ann Arbor, Mich: University Microfilms, 1973.)

Exposition des Tapisseries et Tissus du Musée Arabe du Caire (du VIIe au XVIIe Siècle), Période Musulmane. Paris: Musée des Gobelins, 1935.

THEATER

General Features

The answer to the question of whether live theater existed in the medieval Arab world lies in understanding the exact meaning of the terms used to describe various kinds of performances and performing artists during a long process of development.

There were no special buildings for theatrical performances in the medieval Islamic world. Troupes of actors and performing artists were invited to perform with music and dancing during feasts such as the Nawruz, the Feast of the Nile, the month of Ramadan, holy days, mawlids, weddings, and circumcision ceremonies. These performances were held in public places, markets, courtyards, rulers' palaces, orchards, taverns, inns, near the walls of citadels, on top of a hill, or on a platform.

The audience, who took an active part in the performances, would form a circle *(halqa)* around the performers, who were called by various terms in different Islamic regions and centuries (see Performing Artists). The audience would exchange sharp retorts with the performers, slapping them on the neck for amusement and lavishing coins upon them as a sign of approval. Performances took place by day with dancing and music or at night with torches or by moonlight (in medieval Egypt, actors who performed by moonlight were called *samir*). Male and female actors, comedians, and farce players used makeup with kohl on their eyes and facial makeup made of lime, soot, or flour, sometimes wearing masks *(samaja)* or false beards of various colors according to the age of the *dramatis personae*. They either improvised or performed memorized or written texts copied from various writers and poets (a method called *talfiq*; "patching pieces together"). In literary and historical works, few live theatrical plays are mentioned, and fewer still are extant in manuscript, because performers depended mainly on memorizing existing poems and literary works and on improvisation.

The main themes of plays and farces were criticism and the mockery of rivals and religious functionaries, such as Muslim scholars *('ulama')*, judges *(qadi;* pl. *qudat)*, and rulers. Actors and comedians pleased their patrons by censuring their rivals and enemies. Those actors who dared to criticize rulers by mocking their appearance, manner of speech, and behavior were sometimes severely punished, flogged, or banished to another town; some even had their houses demolished. Some comedians, jesters, and buffoons served in rulers' courts, received monthly wages, and were employed in various professions in the household besides being drinking companions to their patrons (see Wine).

Historical Development

The ruins of Greek and Roman theaters around the Mediterranean basin are clear evidence of the important role that theater played in the region during the Hellenistic period. Its influence was felt not only among pagans but also among Jews, Christians, and later on by the Muslim population in the East. Both Syriac and Hebrew employed the Greek term for theater (*te'atron* and *teatron,* respectively). Arab historians and geographers rarely used the term *tiyatir* and preferred the Arabic term *mal'ab*. On the eve of Islam, impersonators, clowns, and buffoons had replaced the classical theater in the Near Eastern provinces of the Roman Empire. The original significance of the pagan religious dramas had been long forgotten, and they became seasonal folk theater, tending toward parody and mockery of former customs and fertility rituals. Muslim scholars considered them to be ceremonies commemorating legendary or historical events.

Orientalists and Arab scholars have been divided on the issue of whether, after the Islamic conquests, there was an Arab theatrical tradition before the Arabs came into close contact with the European imperialist powers in the Middle East. There are two main schools of thought: (1) scholars who presume that the Arabs must have found their way to an oral popular entertainment with improvised mimicry performed in colloquial Arabic (however, unable to verify the exact meaning of the complicated Arabic theatrical terminology, they fail to give solid proof of the existence of Arab theater before the nineteenth century); and (2) scholars who deny that Arabs had profane live theatre in the sense of a live actor or actors reconstructing a real or legendary incident that occurred in the past, giving the audience the illusion that it is happening in the present. The underlying assumption is that theatrical performance deserves to be considered drama only if it conforms to the conventions of the ancient Greek dramatists and modern European theater. These scholars argue that there are no extant Arabic manuscripts of dramas in classical Arabic literature; that the Arabs knew only popular entertainment such as shadow plays, marionettes, storytelling and the ritual Shi'i theater known as *ta'ziya;* that Islam is a puritan religion that forbids jesting, folly, mimicry, and imitation; that Arabs in the strict sense were Bedouin (i.e., nomadic pastoralists) and theater can thrive only in urban society; and, finally, that Islam, unlike Greek paganism and modern European culture, is a monotheist religion that requires total submission to Allah's will and forbids conflict between man and his Creator—between the believer and his predestination.

During the first century after the rise of Islam, there is evidence—albeit sparse—of Arab awareness of theatrical performances in the Byzantine Empire. Hassan ibn Thabit (d. ca. 674 CE), the poet of the Prophet Muhammad, mentions the "mayamis Ghazza," where *mayamis* seems to be used in the Greek sense of *mimos* rather than alluding to the Hebrew term *meyumase 'Azza,* in the sense of *Maiumas,* the orgiastic festival celebrated on the Syrian coast from ancient times. Further evidence is found in the story of 'Amr ibn al-'As (d. 663), a rich merchant who knew Egypt well during the Jahiliyya (pre-Islamic) period from traveling there with his merchandise. In Alexandria, he attended a Byzantine theatre *(mal'ab)*, and he advised the Caliph 'Umar (d. 644) to occupy Egypt and make it the granary of Islam. There is also the story of the Jewish actor and magician from Jisr Babil near Kufa in Iraq that provides evidence that parody and mimicry continued to be performed during the Muslim caliphate. He was said to have performed "various kinds of magic, illusionistic tricks and acts of buffoonery" during the time of the third caliph, 'Uthman (d. 655), according to the tenth-century historian al-Mas'udi (Moreh, 1986).

Arabic theatrical performance was, in most cases, not based on the use of written texts (scripts), because it was an oral art and in colloquial Arabic, tending toward mockery and jest, a genre that was ignored and despised by Muslim scholars. E.W. Lane (1836), in his *Manners and Customs of the Modern Egyptians,* and other European travelers to the Middle East described theatrical performances that they witnessed as being similar to those played in Europe. A few Arabic theatrical plays are extant in manuscript, although some scholars assign them to narrative and not to theatrical genres. The most famous are the "Play (Hikaya) of Abu 'l-Qasim al-Baghdadi," composed about 1009 or 1010 by Abu 'l-Mutahhar al-Azdi; the "Short Assembly on Fifty Women" *("al-Maqama al-Mukhtasara fi l-Khamsin Mar'a")* by Muhammad ibn Mawlahum al-Khayali (thirteenth century); and "The Discourse of Umm Mujbir" *("Munadamat Umm Mujbir")* by 'Abd al-Baqi al-Ishaqi (d. 1660). Among the most interesting surviving plays are those of Ahmad al-Far, published by Woidisch and Landau (1993) in *Arabisches Vokstheater in Kairo, im Jahre 1909, Ahmad il-Far und Seine Schwanke,* which shed light on the development of Arabic theater since the 'Abbasid period as a result of the terminology used for actors and plays in popular Arabic theater. The actor al-Far is called *Ibn Rabiya* (the son of Rabiyya), a nineteenth-century nickname for actors (pl. Awlad Rabiyya). He performs the role of khalbus (comedian or/and assistant to female dancers, who were known as 'awalim [sing. 'alima]). In the introduction of one of these plays, the actor is described as a man who is invited by the Egyptian riffraff to celebrate their sons' weddings. He is accompanied by a band of musicians, such as a popular drummer and a flautist, and by a torch holder. Later on, the actor who plays the role of *khawal* (male dancer) performs *(yakhruj)* in the role *(sifa)* of a woman and starts dancing.

The Egyptian Sufi scholar of the sixteenth century, 'Abd al-Wahhab al-Sha'rani (d. 1565), in his book *Lata'if al-Minan (The Subtle Blessings)*, uses the same terms of *khalbus* and *khawal* (an actor who performs a scene of a live play *[babat al-khayal]*) (1903). These terms suggest the continuity of Arabic live theatre during the sixteenth through nineteenth centuries. According to al-Sha'rani, the khalbus performs plays *(khayal)* with itinerant actors *(muhabbazun)*. The phrase "muhabbaz of the Devil" is attested in thirteenth-century Egypt by the writer of shadow plays *(khayal al-zill)* Muhammad Ibn Daniyal (1248–1311) when, in one of his poems, Ibn Daniyal curses his wife for forcing him to entertain his child by performing plays and watching actors playing in taverns with pimps and prostitutes.

Although the term *muhabbaz* continued to be used from the time of Ibn Daniyal up to that of E.W. Lane to denote itinerant actors of farces, the earlier terms for actors in medieval Islamic civilization were quite different. The notorious scurrilous poet Ibn al-Hajjaj (ca. 940–1001) used the term *mukhannathun* to denote actors in a period when the term *muhabbazun* had not yet been coined. Since the time of the Prophet Muhammad, live performance had been called *hikaya* (live play or imitation) before the word acquired the restricted meaning of "story," and only then was it replaced with the term *khayal*. In Arabic literature, the term *mukhannath* was used from the rise of Islam to denote a live actor, musician, dancer, entertainer, or performer on the hobbyhorse *(kurraj)* (see Performing Artists, Arab). In a poem composed by the Umayyad poet Jarir (d. 733) to ridicule his opponent al-Farazdaq, he described him with his moustache looking like a masked actor riding on a hobbyhorse wearing a fur like a monkey, which might be an allusion to a kind of theatrical performance. However, the Prophet Muhammad allowed hobbyhorse performances not as entertainment but as training for combat, despite the fact that the hobbyhorse had originally been used in Persian shamanism to achieve contact with spirits through ecstasy. In Syriac, the Greek term *mimos* is given as *mimas* and *mimsa* with the corresponding Arabic meaning of *al-mukhannath al-muhaki al-maskhari* (the imitating comedian mimic; see Payne Smith, R. *Thesaurus Syriacus,* vol. II, col. 2093. 1879–1901). Another performance of pre-Islamic origin is the *Nawruz* or *Nayruz,* which was celebrated up to the nineteenth century with masks, hobbyhorse, and the play of *Amir al-Nayruz (The Lord of Nayruz)* in carnival processions of the Feast of Fools in Medieval Islam.

Arabic Theater in al-Andalus

The term for hobbyhorse in Maimonides' (d. 1204) Mishna Commentary is the Arabic *faras al-'ud* (horse-headed stick) "with which the players of wind instruments and actors play; it is well known among entertainers" (Maimonides, 1903). In addition to actors on the hobbyhorse, Maimonides refers to the actress whom he calls in Hebrew *yotset ha-huts* ("the woman who goes out"); in Arabic, *takhruju* means "she sets out" (i.e., performs). She performs khayal with masks and live plays using a gown made of fine net fabric for comical purposes, as many actors used to do at this time (Maimonides, 1903). This usage might shed light on the Arabic term *kharijat* used by Ibn Shuhayd (922–1035) in his *Risalat al-Tawabi' wa-l-Zawabi' (Epistle of Good and Evil Spirits;* see Moreh, 1986). This is the first highbrow literary work that might have been performed by actors. The author tells us of his rival, Ibn al-Iflili (b. 963), who was so miserly that "he does not try to bribe students of mosques and actresses who dwell in the caravansary *(kharijat al-khanat)* to perform his poems and plays *(rasa'il;* "epistles") by brackish ponds and heaps of dung" as their stage. This hint might indicate that Ibn Shuhayd, a generous and rich man, could employ actresses to perform his own poems and plays in orchards by brimming lakes. Ibn Shuhayd says that, failing to find respectable actresses, Ibn al-Iflili used to perform by himself "the play of the Jew" *(la'bat al-Yahudi)* and that "when he hobbled about, slightly advancing, then retreating, with staff in hand and sack on shoulder, he was the most skillful person at performing the play of the Jew." On the other hand, David ben Abraham al-Fasi (tenth century) uses the Syriac term for actor, *mutamaymis* (Greek *mimos*).

Pedro de Alcala's *Vocabolista Aravigo en Lietra Castillana* (Granada, 1505) contains various Arabic terms for theatrical performance that are still in use in modern Arab world, such as *khiyal, mal'ab,* and *masrah* for theater and *la''ab* and *mumaththil* for actor; this is a clear indication that Arabic theater existed in Muslim Spain. Moreover, the Andalusian poet Ibn Quzman (d. 1160), who composed a *zajal* (popular Arabic strophic verse) describing troupes of actors performing variety shows, is typical of what Alcala termed in Castilian *representador de comedias/tragedias* and in Arabic *sha'ir* ("poet"). Further evidence for the existence of live theater in Muslim Spain is the fact that, after the expulsion of the Jews from Spain (1492) and their settlement in the territories of the Ottoman Sultan Bayazid II, they played an important role in Ottoman popular entertainment and the Turkish *commedia dell'arte* known as *Ortaoyunu*.

SHMUEL MOREH

See also Dancing; Maimonides; Music; Nawruz; Performing Artists; Shadow Plays; Stories and Storytelling

Further Reading

Al-A'raji, Muhammad Husayn. *Fann al-Tamthil 'inda al-'Arab*. Baghdad: 1978.

Al-Azdi, Muhammad Ibn Ahmad Abu 'l-Muthhar. *Abulkasim ein Bagdader Sittenbild, mit Anmerkungen Herausgegeben*, ed. Adam Mez. Heidelberg: Carl Winter's Universitäts-Buchhandlung, 1902.

Al-Far, Ahmad Fahim. *Arabisches Volkstheaer in Kairo, im Jahre 1909, Ahmad il-Far und Seine Schwanke, Heausgegeben, Ubersetzt und Eingefuhrt*, eds. M. Woidisch und J. Landau. Beirut: Franz Steiner Verlag; Stuttgart: Bibliothca Islamica, 1993.

Al-Hajjaji, A.Sh.-D. *The Origins of Arabic Theater*. Cairo: General Egyptian Book Organization, 1981.

Al-Talib, 'Umar Muhammad. *Malamih al-Masrahiyya al-'Arabiyya al-Islamiyya*. al-Maghrib, 1987.

And, M. *Drama at the Crossroads, Turkish Performing Arts Link Past and Present, East and West*. Istanbul: The Isis Press, 1991.

———. *Culture, Performance and Communication in Turkey*. Tokyo: Institute for the Study of Languages and Cultures of Asia and Africa, 1987.

'Arsan, 'Ali 'Uqla. *Al-Zawahir al-Asrahiyya 'inda al-'Arab*, 3rd ed. Damascus: 1985.

'Aziza, M. *Le Theatre et l'Islam*. Algeri.

Brakel, C., and Shmuel Moreh. "Reflections on the Term Baba: From Medieval Arabic Plays to Contemporary Javanese Masked Theatre." In *Edebiyat*, vol. 7, 21–39.

Burgel, J.C., and S. Guth, eds. *Gesellschaftlicher Umbruch und Historie im Zeitgenössischen Drama der Islamischen Welt*. Beirut-Stuttgart: Franz Steiner Verlag, 1995.

Chelkoviwski, P.J., ed. *Ta'ziyeh, Ritual and Drama in Iran*. New York: NYUP, 1979.

Corrao, Francesca M. *Il Riso, il Comico e la Festa al Cairo nel XIII Secolo*. Rome: Il Teatro Delle Ombre di Ibn Daniyal, 1996.

Horovitz, J. *Spuren Griechischer Mimen in Orient*. Berlin, 1905.

Ibn Shuhayd al-Andalusi. *Risalat al-Tawabi' wa-l-Zawabi' (The Treatise of Familiar Spirits and Demons by Abu 'Amir ibn Shuhaid al-Ashja'i, al-Andalusi)*, ed. and transl. J.T. Monroe. Los Angeles, 1971.

Jacob, G. *Geschichte des Schattentheaters im Morgen- und Abendland*. Osnabruck, 1972.

Landau, J. "Popular Arabic Plays, 1909." *Journal of Arabic Literature* 17 (1986): 120–5.

Lane, E.W. *The Manners and Customs of the Modern Egyptians*. London, 1836.

Maimonides. *Commentaire de Maimonide sur la Mischnah*, ed. J. Derenbourg Berlin, 1903.

Malti, Habib Abla. *The Quick-Tempered Simpleton*, eds. S. Moreh and M. Shawarba. Haifa: Universiy of Haifa, Al-Karmil Publications Series 7, 1997.

Moreh, S. "Live Theatre in Medieval Islam." In *Studies in Islamic History and Civilization in Honour of Professor David Ayalon*, ed. M. Sharon, 565–611. Jerusalem and Leiden: E.J. Brill, 1986.

———. "The Meaning of the Term *Kharja* of the Arabic Andalusian *Muwashshah*." In *Litterare Judaerum in Terra Hispanica*, ed. Y. Ben-Abou. Jerusalem, 1991.

———. *Live Theatre and Dramatic Literature in the Medieval Arab World*. Edinburgh: Edinburgh University Press, 1993.

———. "Acting and Actors, Medieval." In *Encyclopedia of Arabic Literature*, eds. J.S. Meisami and P. Starkey, vol. I, 52–4. London and New York: Routledge, 1998.

———. "Theatre and Drama, Medieval." In *Encyclopedia of Arabic Literature*, eds. J.S. Meisami and P. Starkey, vol. II, 766–9. London and New York: Routledge, 1998.

Moreh, S., and P. Sadgrove. *Jewish Contributions to Nineteenth-century Arabic Theatre. Plays from Algeria and Syria, a Study and Texts*. Manchester and Oxford, UK: Oxford University Press, JSS Supplement 6, 1996.

Prüfer, C. "Drama (Arabic)." In *Encyclopaedia of Religion and Ethics*, vol. IV, 872–8. New York: C. Scribner's & Sons, 1914.

al-Sha'rani. *Lata'if al-Minan*. Cairo, 1903.

Shoshan, Boaz. *Popular Culture in Medieval Cairo*. Cambridge, UK: Cambridge University Press, 1993.

THEOLOGY

Islamic theology consists the following: (1) Qur'anic teachings, (2) theological schools, (3) sectarianism, (4) philosophical theology, and (5) Sufi theology. This article focuses on Qur'anic theology and the Sunni theological schools; there are separate articles in this encyclopedia devoted to the Mu'tazila, most sectarian groups, numerous Imami Shi'i theologians, the major philosophers, and the Sufi theologians Ibn 'Arabi and Jami. Those readers interested in the complex origins of Islamic theology should consult W. Montgomery Watt's *The Formative Period of Islamic Thought* (1998).

Qur'anic Theology

Qur'anic theology revolves around a merciful, singular God named Allah who is omniscient, omnipotent, and possesses a host of additional qualities. Allah created the heavens and the earth in six days and created Adam, the first human, as his vicegerent (*khalifa*) on earth out of wet clay. After God "taught Adam the names," He commanded the angels to prostrate to him, which they did, save for Iblis (Satan), who was one of the creatures created from fire (jinn). God allowed Satan to descend to earth and serve as the "manifest enemy" of humans until the end of time. God also sent prophets, such as Noah, Abraham, Moses, and Jesus, with the same essential message to obey Him, act righteously, and believe in the Hereafter. The "seal of the prophets" is Muhammad, to whom God revealed the Qur'an via the angel Gabriel. The Qur'an informs Muslims that on the Last Day there will be two blasts as the world is destroyed and all humans are brought forth from their graves to be judged by God and sent to either the gardens of Paradise or the blazing Hellfire. There is widespread consensus among Sunnis that the Prophet Muhammad will intercede for members of his community and that none of them will be in the Hellfire eternally, although the Qur'anic support for these beliefs is somewhat ambiguous.

Sunni Theological Schools

The major Islamic theological schools are the Mu'tazila, Ash'aris, Maturidis, and the hadith scholars (traditionalists). Most Imami and Zaydi Shi'is embraced Mu'tazili dogma, whereas most Sunnis considered only the latter three schools as orthodox. The Mu'tazila, Ash'aris, and Maturidis are distinguished from the hadith scholars through their employment of rational argumentation and adoption of philosophical concepts, such as atoms and accidents, that form the theological discourse known as *kalam*. The primary topics addressed by all four of these theological schools concern the relationship between God and His attributes *(sifat)* and between God and human agency *(qadar)*. The general Mu'tazili opinions (rejected by most Sunni theologians) about both of these topics were the denial of essential divine attributes that were "neither God nor other than God" and robust affirmation of each human's ability to create their own actions. Other topics found in theological works include the nature of prophecy, the question as to whether faith increases or decreases according to one's deeds, epistemology, the believers' vision of God in Paradise, and leadership of the community *(imama)*.

The Ash'aris, who derive their name from Abu l-Hasan al-Ash'ari (d. 935), distinguished themselves through the affirmation of seven eternal attributes that are "neither God nor other than God": (1) knowledge, (2) power, (3) life, (4) will, (5) seeing, (6) hearing, and (7) speech. The Maturidis, who derive their name from Abu Mansur al-Maturidi (d. 944), regularly added the attribute of creating *(takwin, takhliq)* to these seven attributes. The popular creed of the Maturidi theologian al-Nasafi (d. 1142)

includes the attributes of desiring, doing, and sustaining, and it states that "[God] has attributes from all eternity subsistent in His essence. They are not He nor are they other than He" (Elder, 1950). Later Ash'ari scholars, such as al-Juwayni (d. 1085) and his pupil al-Ghazali (d. 1111), reconciled the dogmatic position of the seven eternal attributes and the prophetic hadiths that enumerate God's ninety-nine names by means of the construction of categories of names, such as those names that signify God's essence or the eternal attributes and those names that relate to actions (al-Juwayni, 2000). The hadith scholar theologians, such as Ibn Khuzayma (d. 923), scrupulously affirmed all of the names and attributes by which God describes Himself in the Qur'an and in sound prophetic hadith while simultaneously insisting that none of these attributes—including God's hands, eyes, and face—is truly anthropomorphic because of the vast gulf between the natures of temporal humans and the infinite deity. Most Ash'ari and Maturidi theologians did not hesitate to apply metaphorical interpretations to Qur'anic verses that mention God's hands, eyes, and face.

Sunni theologians insisted that all human actions are created by God on the basis of the rational argument that God's omnipotence is void if additional creators exist and on the basis of Qur'anic verses such as 6:101–2 and 37:96. They also insisted that humans lack the capacity to perform any action until the action is brought into existence by God. Despite these unwavering dogmatic positions, both Ash'aris and Maturidis argued that humans are responsible for their actions through a form of acquisition, which is called *kasb* (acquisition) by the former school and *ikhtiyar* (choice) by the latter one. Daniel Gimaret (1980) has articulated the three positions adopted by Sunni theologians concerning human acts: (1) "Radical Ash'arisim" in which God creates the individual's power *(qudra)*, will, and the actual act; (2) God creates the power and will in a human, who acts as an agent for the divinely created act; and (3) God creates the act, but man "adds specific qualifications" to the act, which are uncreated. Gimaret identifies al-Ghazali as an advocate of the first position, Fakhr al-Din al-Razi (d. 1209) and the hadith scholar Ibn Taymiyya (d. 1328) as supporters of the second one, and Abu Bakr al-Baqillani (d. 1013) and later Maturidis as champions of the third one. The Hanafi hadith scholar Abu Ja'far al-Tahawi (d. 933) affirmed that "human acts are the creation of God and the acquisition of the human beings" in his famous creed, along with the comment "the principle of predetermination (or predestination) is God's secret" (Watt, 1994).

SCOTT C. LUCAS

See also Al-'Allama; Al-Farabi; al-Ghazali; Al-Hasan al-Basri; Al-Hilli; Al-Jahiz; Al-Kindi; Al-Kulayni; Al-Majlisi; Al-Razi, Fakhr al-Din Afterlife; Al-Shaykh Al-Mufid; Al-Tusi, Muhammad ibn Hasan; Al-Tusi, Nasir al-Din; Angels; Ash'aris; Caliphate and Imamate; Druze; Eschatology; God; Hassan-i Sabbah; Heresy and Heretics; Ibadis; Ibn 'Arabi; Ibn Babawayh; Ibn Hanbal; Ibn Rushd (Averroes); Ibn Sina (Avicenna); Ibn Taymiyya; Ibn Tumart; Ismailis; Ja'far al-Sadiq; Jami; Kharijis; Muhammad al-Baqir; Mu'tazilites; Mulla Sadra; Nusayris; Polemics and Disputation; Predestination; Qur'an; Shi'ism; Shi'i Thought; Sunni Revival; Zaydis

Further Reading

Al-Ghazali. *The Ninety-Nine Beautiful Names of God- al-Maqsad al-Asna fi Sharh Asma' Allah al-Husna*, transl. David B. Burrell and Nazih Daher. Cambridge: Islamic Texts Society, 1995.

Al-Juwayni, Imam al-Haramayn. *A Guide to Conclusive Proofs for the Principles of Beliefs*, transl. Paul E. Walker. Reading: Garnet, 2000.

Elder, Earl Edgar. *A Commentary on the Creed of Islam: Sa'd al-Din al-Taftazani on the Creed of Najm al-Din al-Nasafi*. New York: Columbia University Press, 1950.

Encyclopaedia of Islam, New Edition. Leiden: Brill, 1960.

Gimaret, Daniel. *Théories de L'Acte Humain en Théologie Musulmane*. Paris: J. Vrin, 1980.

Goldziher, Ignaz. *Introduction to Islamic Theology and Law*, transl. Andras and Ruth Hamori. Princeton, NJ: Princeton University Press, 1981.

Kholeif, Fathalla. *A Study on Fakhr al-Din al-Razi and His Controversies in Transoxiania*. Beirut: Dar al-Machreq Editeurs, 1966.

Madelung, Wilferd. *Religious Schools and Sects in Medieval Islam*. London: Variorum Reprints, 1985.

Makdisi, George. *Ibn Qudama's Censure of Speculative Theology*. London: Luzac & Company, Ltd., 1962.

Martin, Richard, Mark Woodward, and Dwi Atmaja. *Defenders of Reason in Islam: Mu'tazilism from Medieval School to Modern Symbol*. Oxford, UK: Oneworld, 1997.

McCarthy, Richard. *The Theology of al-Ash'ari*. Beirut: Imprimerie Catholique, 1953.

Morewedge, Parviz, ed. *Islamic Philosophical Theology*. Albany, NY: State University of New York Press, 1979.

Shahrastani, Muhammad b. 'Abd al-Karim. *Muslim Sects and Divisions: The Section on Muslim Sects in Kitab al-Milal wa 'l-Nihal*, transl. A.K. Kazi and J.G. Flynn. Boston: Kegan Paul International, 1984.

van Ess, Josef. "Mu'tazila." In *The Encyclopedia of Religion*, ed. Mircea Eliade, vol. X, 220–9. New York: Macmillan Publications, 1987.

Watt, W. Montgomery. *The Formative Period of Islamic Thought*. Oxford, UK: Oneworld Publications, 1998.

———. *Islamic Creeds: A Selection*. Edinburgh: Edinburgh University Press, 1994.

Wensinck, A.J. *The Muslim Creed: Its Genesis and Historical Development*. New York: Barnes & Noble, 1932.

Wolfson, Harry Austryn. *The Philosophy of the Kalam*. Cambridge, Mass: Harvard University Press, 1976.

TIME, CONCEPTS OF

Classical concepts of time confronted philosophers with perplexing paradoxes. Some wondered whether time altogether was nonexistent, whereas others doubted the reality of its divisibility into parts by arguing that the past ceased to be, the future does not yet exist, and the present as a moment/now that is without magnitude (i.e., like a mathematical point is not part of time). In addition, it was unclear whether time progressed smoothly or proceeded by way of discontinuous and divisible leaps.

Although inquiries about the nature of time were integrated within physical theories of motion, their broad cosmological and metaphysical bearings had an impact on speculations about creation and causation. In Plato's *Timaeus* (37d; 38a) time *(khronos)* was pictured as a moving image *(eikona)* that imitated *(mimoumenon)* eternity *(aiona)* by circling around according to number *(arithmos)* and came into existence with the generation of the heavens. In the earliest systemic investigation of the essence and existence of time, which was contained in Aristotle's *Physics* (219b3-4; 220a25-b20; 222b20-23), *khronos* was defined as the number *(metron)* of a continuous *(sunekhes)* motion *(kinesis)* with respect to the anterior *(proteron)* and the posterior *(husteron)*. Rejecting the claim that time was the movement of the whole *(holos)*, Aristotle argued that the circular, uniform, and continuous motion of the celestial sphere *(sphaira)* acts as the measure *(metron)* of time *(Physics,* 223b21). His theory subsequently received numerous responses by Neoplatonist and Hellenist exegetes; these are grouped in a monumental edition titled *Commentaria in Aristotelem Graeca*. Damascius argued that time was a simultaneous whole, Plotinus grasped it as the changing life of the soul *(Enneads,* 3.7.11-13), and Simplicius defended the thesis of the eternity of the world against doubts raised by the grammarian Philoponus, who adopted a Christian doctrine of *creatio ex nihilo*. As for the author of the *Confessions*, Augustine of Hippo, he noted that *tempus* (time) was created when the world came to be while affirming that the existential reality of time is grounded in the present *(praesens)*, which in itself is what tends not to be *(tendit non esse)*, given that only eternity was stable *(semper stans)*.

On the basis of a belief in the linear directionality of time, from Genesis to Judgment, Augustine argued that the present of things past was preserved in memory, the presence of present things was confirmed by visual perception, and the presence of things future was secured through expectation. Accordingly, the reality of time depended on an *anima* who remembers, perceives, and expects events; this is similar to

Aristotle's claim in the *Physics* (218b29-219a1-6, 223a25) that *khronos* required *psukhe* to compute its numbering *(arithmein)*. Ishaq ibn Hunayn's translation of Aristotle's *Physics (al-Tabi'a)* secured the transmission of the Aristotelian conception of *khronos* into Arabic, which subsequently inspired variegated philosophical interpretations of time in Islam. Al-Kindi held that *al-zaman* (time) had a beginning and an end and that it measured motion according to number *(Tempus ergo est numerus numerans motum)*, whereas al-Farabi and Ikhwan al-Safa' affirmed that time resulted from the movement of the created celestial sphere *(al-falak)*. Abu Bakr al-Razi claimed that the *dahr* (perpetuity) was absolute *(mutlaq)*, while taking *al-zaman* (time) to be a flowing substance *(jawhar yajri)* that is bound *(mahsur)* as well as being associated with the motion of al-falak.

In *Kitab al-Hudud*, Ibn Sina defined *al-zaman* (time) as that which resembles the created being *(yudahi al-masnu')* and acts as the measure of motion *(miqdar al-haraka)* in terms of the anterior and the posterior *(mutaqaddim wa muta'akhkhir)*. He also noted that *al-dahr* (supratemporal duration) resembled the Creator *(yudahi al-san'i)* insofar that it was stable throughout the entirety of time. In the *Isharat wa'l-Tanbihat,* he linked time to physical inquiries about motion; in *'Uyun al-Hikma,* he construed it as a quantity *(kamiyyat)* of motion that measures change *(yuqaddir)* and whose perpetuity *(dahr al-haraka)* generated temporality. Time also played a notable role in *Kitab al-Manazir (Optics;* II.3, II.7, III.7) by the polymath Ibn al-Haytham, who argued that the propagation of light rays was subject to time and consequently inferred that the velocity of light *(al-daw')* was finite despite being immense in magnitude. Moreover, he held that acts of visual discernment and comparative measure *(al-tamyyiz wa'l-qiyas)* were subject to the passage of time even if not felt by the beholder, and he cautioned that, if the temporal duration of contemplative or immediate visual perception fell outside of a moderate range, it resulted in optical errors. In addition, he listed al-zaman as one of the known entities *(ma'lumat)*, while taking duration *(mudda)* to be its essence *(mahiyya)* and the scale *(miqyas)* of its magnitude *(miqdar)* and quantity *(kamiyya)* that become knowable in reference to the motion of the celestial sphere *(al-falak)*.

Opposing the views of the peripatetic philosophers in Islam, the exponents of kalam (dialectical theology) articulated alternative conceptions of time that rested on physical theories inspired by Greek atomism. Time was grasped by the *mutakallimun* (dialectical theologians) as being a virtual *(mawhum)* phenomenon of changing appearances and renewed atomic events *(mutajaddidat)* whereby a discrete moment *(waqt)* replaced the concept of a continuous zaman. Motivated by this theory—although resisting its thrust—al-Nazzam believed in the divisibility of particles *ad infinitum,* which entailed that a spatial distance with infinitely divisible parts requires an infinite time to be crossed unless its traversal proceeded by way of leaps *(tafarat)*; this echoes the Stoic views regarding the Greek notion of *halma* (leap). When doubting the doctrine of the eternity of the world in *Tahafut al-Falasifa,* al-Ghazali attempted to show that duration *(mudda)* and time *(zaman)* were both created, and he argued that the connection between what is habitually taken to be a cause and an effect was not necessary given that observation only shows that they were concomitant. Consequently, he proclaimed that the ordering relation of an antecedent cause with a consequent effect does not necessarily rest on an irreversible directionality in time.

In defense of causation, Ibn Rushd argued in *Tahafut al-Tahafut* that the refutation of the causal principle entailed an outright rejection of reason while asserting that the eternal *(al-qadim)* was timeless and that the world was subject to the workings of a continuous zaman. Affirming the truth of Genesis, Maimonides asserted in *Dalalat al-Ha'irin* the belief that time was created, given that the celestial sphere and the motion on which it depended were both generated. Although speculations about time continued with scholars of the caliber of Nasir al-din Tusi, Fakhr al-din al-Razi, Mir Damad, Mulla Sadra, Abu'l-Barakat al-Baghdadi, al-Iji, and al-Jurjani, the elucidation of its uncanny reality remained inconclusive.

NADER EL-BIZRI

Primary Sources

Aristotle. *Physics*, ed. W. David Ross. Oxford, UK: Oxford University Press, 1998.
Augustine. *Confessions*, ed. James O'Donnell. Oxford, UK: Clarendon Press, 1992.
Ghazali. *Tahafut al-Falasifa*, transl. Michael Marmura. Provo, Utah: Brigham Young University Press, 1997.
Ibn al-Haytham. *Kitab al-Manazir*, ed. Abdelhamid I. Sabra. Kuwait: National Council for Culture, Arts and Letters, 1983.
———. *The Optics of Ibn al-Haytham*, transl. A.I. Sabra. London: Warburg Institute, 1989.
Ibn Rushd. *Tahafut al-Tahafut*, ed. Muhammad 'Abid al-Jabiri. Beirut: Markaz Dirasat al-Wihda al-'Arabiyya, 1998.
Ibn Sina. *Kitab al-Hudud*, ed. A.-M. Goichon. Cairo: Institut Français d'Archéologie Orientale du Caire, 1963.
———. *al-Isharat wa'l-Tanbihat*, 3 vols., ed. Sulayman Dunya. Cairo: Dar al-Ma'arif bi-Misr, 1957–1960.
Ikhwan al-Safa'. *Rasa'il Ikhwan al-Safa' wa Khullan al-Wafa'*, vol. II, ed. Butrus Bustani. Beirut: Dar Sadir, 1957.

Maimonides. *Dalalat al-Ha'irin, The Guide for the Perplexed*, transl. M. Friedlander. New York: Dover, 1956.

Philoponus. *Corollaries on Place and Void;* Simplicius. *Against Philoponus on the Eternity of the World*, transl. David Furley and Christian Wildberg. London: Duckworth, 1991.

Plato. *Timaeus*, transl. R.G. Bury. Cambridge, Mass: Harvard University Press, 1999.

Simplicius. *Corollaries on Place and Time*, transl. J.O. Urmson. London: Duckworth, 1992.

Further Reading

Dhanani, Alnoor. *The Physical Theory of Kalam*. Leiden: Brill, 1994.

Mallet, D. "Zaman." In *Encyclopaedia of Islam*, vol. XI. Leiden: Brill, 2001.

Massignon, Louis. "Le Temps dans la Pensée Islamique." In *Opera Minora*, vol. II, ed. Y. Moubarak. Beirut: Dar al-Ma'arif, 1963.

Rashed, Roshdi. *Les Mathématiques Infinitésimales du IXᵉ au XIᵉ siècle*, vol. IV. London: al-Furqan Islamic Heritage Foundation, 2002.

Sorabji, Richard. *Time, Creation and the Continuum*. Ithaca, NY: Cornell University Press, 1983.

Walzer, Richard. *Greek into Arabic: Essays in Islamic Philosophy*. Columbia, South Carolina: University of South Carolina Press, 1962.

TIMURIDS

The Timurids were a dynasty of Central Asian nomadic origin that dominated the Middle East and Central Asia in the AH eighth/fourteenth CE and ninth/fifteenth centuries. The founder, Timur Leng, was a Chagatai Turk of the Barlas tribe in the region of Kish, Western Turkestan. The significant period of his career began in 771/1370, when he embarked on a series of campaigns in Transoxiana that involved the Chagatai khanate in Eastern Turkestan, the Blue Horde, and the Golden Horde. In 782/1380–1301, he began his conquests in Persia, subduing the local dynasties that had assumed power after the disintegration of the Il Khanate, including the Sarbadars in northwestern Khurasan, the Karts in Herat, the Muzzafarids in central and southern Persia, and the Jalayarids centered on Baghdad. He also campaigned against the Mamluk sultanate of Egypt and defeated the Ottoman sultan Bayazid Ilderim at the battle of Ankara in 804/1402.

Timur's conquests brought about the removal of large numbers of artists and artisans to his capital, Samarqand, as a workforce to embellish and enrich his court. The lavish results of this are perhaps most vividly portrayed in the account by the Spanish ambassador, Clavijo, who visited Samarqand and Timur's palace at Aq Sarai in 1404–1406. Timur's legitimacy was established on two bases, apart from conquest and his control of the Chagatai tribes, by his marriage to a Chingissid princess that gave him the concomitant title of *guregen* (royal son-in-law [of the puppet Chingissid khan he installed in Samarqand]) and by his claim to be the true protector and upholder of Islam. It was on this basis that his campaigns in Persia, Iraq, Syria, and Anatolia were justified in contemporary accounts. He made effective use of the Chagatai nomads and their traditional military skills in his campaigns, and initially the areas that resisted him suffered considerably. Like Chingiz Khan, he punished any opposition or rebellion ruthlessly and speedily. For instance, virtually all of the Muzzafarids were executed when one of them, Shah Mansur, attempted to re-establish independent rule. Direct Timurid control of conquered territories in Persia and Khurasan was based on installing military governors (usually Timurid princes) along with garrisons of Chagatai soldiery in various cities and provinces. At the time of his death in 807/1405, Timur was embarking on the conquest of China.

After Timur's death, a series of conflicts broke out between his sons and grandsons that ended with the victory of his son Shah Rukh. The latter did not attempt any fresh conquests and indeed during the war of succession certain peripheral territories, such as those in the Caucasus, were lost. However, the heartlands of the empire remained untouched, and Shah Rukh consolidated his control of the regions of Persia (most of what is now Afghanistan and Central Asia) from his capital in Herat, with a series of Timurid princes and Chagatai khans as governors of the various provinces; the most important of these was his son, Ulugh Beg, who was the ruler of Transoxania throughout his father's reign. Both of these rulers were patrons of the arts, architecture, and literature, and Ulugh Beg was an able mathematician who drew up mathematical tables and built an observatory in Samarqand; likewise, Shah Rukh's wife, Gauhar Shad, who in particular created religious foundations, built the great mosque in Mashad, northern Persia, one of the surviving monuments of the Timurid age. Iskandar b. Umar Shaikh, who ruled Fars and was eventually imprisoned and blinded for his rebellious activities in 816/1413, was a notable patron of painting and the arts of the book. The development of historical writing under the Timurids is one of the most important intellectual aspects of the period. For example, Hafiz Abru employed different approaches to the history of the age. First, he wrote the continuation *(zayl)* of the *World History* of Rashid al-Din Tabib, then a series of provincial histories and dynastic studies, and finally the *Majma*, a general history of which the last section, the *Zubdat al-Tawarikh*, presents a dynastic history of the Timurids, all comprising a unique achievement of sophisticated and detailed historical literature. Current knowledge about the political history of the period is based on these and other works, such as Sharaf al-Din 'Ali Yazdi's biography of Timur, the *Zafarnama*, the *Matla 'al-Sa'dain* of 'Abd al-Razzaq al-Samarqandi, and the works of Mir Khwand and Khwand Amir.

Shah Rukh died on campaign in Western Persia in 850/1447 and once again conflict broke out between the Timurid princes. Other powers in the region, such as the Turkoman confederacies in Azarbaijan, also became involved in the struggle with the result that the empire was further fragmented and diminished. Timurid rule in the west was effectively ended, and, by the late fifteenth century, Transoxania had succumbed to the advances of the Uzbek Muhammad Shaibani. However, in Khurasan, the Timurid capital Herat enjoyed what was to be a final efflorescence under Sultan Husain Baiqara as a center of learning and the arts. When Shah Ismail Safavi captured the city in 916/1510, the artists of the royal ateliers were transported west to serve the Safavid court, thus perpetuating the artistic traditions that had been developed under the Timurids.

ISABEL MILLER

Further Reading

Barthold, W. *Ulugh Beg*. In *Four studies on the History of Central Asia*, transl. V. and T. Minorsky. Leiden: E.J. Brill, 1958.

Jackson, Peter, and L. Lockhart, eds. *Cambridge History of Iran, Vol. 6, The Timurids and Safavids*. Cambridge, UK: Cambridge University Press, 1986.

Lentz, Thomas W., and Glenn D. Lowry. *Timur and the Princely Vision: Persian Art and Culture in the Fifteenth Century*. Los Angeles: Los Angeles Country Museum of Art; Washington, DC: Arthur M. Sackler Gallery, 1989.

Manz, Beatrice. *The Rise and Rule of Tamerlane*. Cambridge, UK: Cambridge University Press, 1989.

Thackston, W.M., ed. and transl. *A Century of Princes. Sources on Timurid History and Art*. Cambridge, Mass: Aga Khan Program for Islamic Architecture, 1989.

TITLES

The sudden introduction of the nascent Arab Islamic community to older, more complex societal structures contained in the Sasanian and Byzantine empires of the Irano-Mediterreanean world had a profound effect on Islamic political taxonomies. Ostensibly an egalitarian sociopolitical community that eschewed privilege and rank, the politically naive Muslim umma would undergo considerable transformations as it intermingled with Syriac, Berber, Byzantine, Persian, Turkic, Indian, and Mongol traditions. By

the height of the medieval period, Islamic civilization had embraced hierarchy and social stratification, and with this is seen the emergence of a rich panobly of official titles in use by different Islamic states, from Andalusia to India.

Arabic Titles

The oldest and most important of the Arabic political titles was *khalifa* (caliph), which came into use after the death of the Prophet Muhammad. Initially, *khalifa* was understood as successor, or deputy, and the comportment of the first four caliphs—the Rightly Guided ones (Abu Bakr, 'Umar, 'Uthman, and 'Ali)—suggests that they did not interpret this title as anything other than this. However, the beleaguered Umayyad dynasty subtly altered this title to confer a sense of "God's Caliph" (khalifat Allah) while also openly circulating their status as *amir al-mu'minin* (Commander of the Faithful). The perception of *khalifa* to signify divine regent on earth was aggrandized by the 'Abbasids as they sought to diminish rival claims from the Shi'is and their veneration of the imams (see Caliphate and Imamate). Likewise, the title of *amir* dates back to the earliest days of Islamic expansion, originally denoting an all-inclusive office (*imarat*) with military and bureaucratic duties. With time, the amir was devolved of most administrative responsibilities and was expected to function solely in a military capacity. This title would develop a sense of sovereignty when 'Abbasid caliphs began conferring amir ships on the various upstart dynasts appearing on the periphery during the tenth and eleventh centuries CE; however, by the thirteenth century, *amir* had lost its sense of political preeminence. Another important Arabic title that emerged in the medieval period was *sultan*, which denoted power or dominion, and it would be the Seljuk dynasty (1038–1194) which embraced *sultan* enthusiastically. Contemporary political theorists and scholars—often in the pay of the Seljuks themselves—understood this to be the most prestigious title possible for a non-caliphal Muslim ruler. Timur would use this Arabo-Islamic title in conjunction with the Turkish *khan* as well as *amir gurgan* (son-in-law), the latter referring to his diplomatic marriage to the Mongol Chingizid line. By the time of the Ottomans' zenith during the sixteenth century, *sultan* denoted absolute political independence, but Salim the Grim dispelled any ambiguity when he decided to appropriate the title of *khalifa* after conquering the holy cities of Mecca and Medina during the early sixteenth century. Likewise, after Mehmed II defeated the Byzantine Greek Palaeologi and assumed control of Constantinople in 1453, *qaysar* (Caesar) was added to the ever-expanding list of Ottoman appellations. The other Arabic title of note, *malik* (king), was not especially popular among the Arabs during the early centuries, but it would gain currency under the Buyids (932–1062) in western Iran and the Samanids (819–1005) in Transoxiana. The adoption of this particular Arabic title is not surprising considering these dynasties' location and their familiarity with ancient pre-Islamic notions of absolute kingship.

Persian Titles

The most enduring and important Persian title—*shah* (king)—dates back to the Achaemenian and Sasanian periods, as does another related title, *shahanshah* (king of kings). These titles were not appropriated by the Arab caliphs during their initial invasions of the seventh century, but the incorporation of Persian bureaucrats in the 'Abbasid administration and the proximity of Baghdad to former centers of pre-Islamic government allowed for the revival of this title by the Buyid dynasty, specifically Adud al-Daula (d. 983) in his khutba and on his minted coins. *Sultan*, however, was the title of choice during the Turkic and Mongol eras, but *shah* would enjoy renewed importance in the courts of the Timurids, Safavids, Mughals, and Ottomans. A hybrid term—*padishah* (emperor)—was the principal sovereign title for the Timurid Mughal dynasty in India in the sixteenth and seventeenth centuries. The other principal Persian title which emerged during the fifteenth century was *mirza,* which was derived from *amir-zada* (son of an amir). This was the appellative term for royal members of the Timurid household (e.g., Shah Rukh Mirza, Mirza Baysanqur), and this practice was continued by the Aq Qoyunlus, Safavids, Mughals, as well as local independent dynasties such as the Kar Kiyas in Lahijan. Interestingly, however, *mirza* was also conferred by Safavid shahs during the sixteenth century on high-ranking Persian viziers (e.g., Mirza Shah Husain Isfahani, Mirza 'Ata Allah Isfahani).

Turkish Titles

The ascendancy of Turco-Mongol political culture during the late medieval period saw an infusion of Turkic titles into Islamic political nomenclature. The most significant of these was *khan*, introduced by the Qarakhanid dynasty (992–1211) and continued by

Seljuk and Khwarazmian rulers. *Khan* was also a key titular feature in the Mongol political tradition, and it was appended to the names of those direct descendants of Chingiz Khan who were in control of an ulus (appanage), whereas a derived title of *khaqan* referred to the Great Khan based in Qara Qorum. *Khaqan* would continue to denote imperial sovereignty in the Timurid, Ottoman, Safavid, and Mughal traditions, whereas *khan* would lose much of its distinction and was only awarded to Turkic military men of intermediate status. *Pasha,* which is more than likely derived from the Persian *padishah,* was a title of considerable political prestige with the Seljuks and their Ottoman successors. Akin to the Safavid understanding of the title *mirza,* pashas in the Ottoman empire were either military provincial governors or palatial viziers. Lastly, the title *beg*—derived from the Turkish *bäg* and comparable to the Arabic title of *amir*—was introduced by the Qarakhanids and enjoyed healthy representation in the Seljuk empire. Other titular derivations—*beglerbeg* and *atabeg*—would be used consistently throughout the medieval period until the end of the Ottoman and Safavid empires.

COLIN PAUL MITCHELL

See also Caliphate and Imamate; Political Theory

Further Reading

Ando, Shiro. *Timuridische Emire Nach dem Mu'izz al-Ansab: Untersuchung zur Stammesaristokratie Zentralasiens im 14. um 15. Jahrhundert.* Berlin, 1992.
Ashtiany, Julia, ed. *'Abbasid Belles Lettres.* Cambridge, 1990.
al-Azmeh, Aziz. *Muslim Kingship: Power and the Sacred in Muslim, Christian, and Pagan Polities.* London, 1997.
Black, Antony. *The History of Islamic Political Thought: From the Prophet to the Present.* New York, 2001.
Bosworth, C.E. "The Titulature of the Early Ghaznavids." *Oriens* 15 (1962): 210–33.
Lambton, A.K.S. *Continuity and Change in Medieval Persia: Aspects of Administrative, Economic and Social History, 11th–14th Century.* Albany, 1988.
———. *State and Government in Medieval Islam.* Oxford, 1981.
———. *Theory and Practice in Medieavel Persian Government.* London, 1980.
Lewis, Bernard. *The Political Language of Islam.* Chicago, 1988.
Madelung, Wilferd. "The Assumption of the Title Shahanshah by the Buyids and the Reign of Daylam (Dawlat al-Daylam)." *Journal of Near Eastern Studies* 28 (1969): 84–108.
Mottahedeh, Roy. *Loyalty and Leadership in an Early Islamic Society.* London, 2001.
Richter-Bernburg, L. "*Amir-Malik-Shahanshah*: Adud al-Dawla's Titulature Re-examined." *Iran* 18 (1980): 83–102.
Röhrborn, K.M. *Provinzen und Zentralgewalt Persiens im 16. und 17. Jahrhundert.* Berlin, 1966.

Rosenthal, Franz. *Political Thought in Medieval Islam.* Cambridge, 1968.

Siddiqui, A.H. *Caliphate and Sultanate in Medieval Persia.* Karachi, 1969.

Woods, John. *The Aqquyunlu: Clan, Confederation, Empire,* new and revised ed. Salt Lake City, 1999.

TRADE, AFRICAN

With the possible exception of North Africa, the adoption of Islam in Africa was largely as a result of trade networks. For convenience, the Islamic trade network in Africa may be divided into four regions: North Africa, West Africa, The Nile/Red Sea Corridor, and East Africa. Each of these is characterized by certain physical features and possesses a degree of cultural homogeneity expressed either in terms of language, ethnic composition, or historical ties. However, this division should not obscure the fact that there was a large volume of inter-regional trade and also a significant amount of trade with the non-Muslim world, particularly in pagan Africa, medieval Europe, China, and India.

Physically, North Africa may be defined as that part of Africa between the Mediterranean and the Atlas mountains and that contains a mixed Arabic and Berber population. In many ways, the trade network of North Africa continues the pattern established when the region was under Roman rule, with trans-Saharan caravan routes connecting it to West Africa and sea routes linking it into a wider Mediterranean network. As with much of Africa, the trade was dominated by precious metals, particularly gold from West Africa. For example, the power of the Fatimids (tenth and eleventh centuries) was based on the wealth derived from the trade in gold with sub-Saharan Africa, and its conquest of Egypt would have been inconceivable without this financial base. The trade of North Africa was also linked, via Egypt, to the Middle East, particularly during the Umayyad and 'Abbasid periods, when both regions formed part of a unified political entity. An interesting example of this long-distance trade can be seen in the Mosque of Qayrawan, where polychrome luster tiles made in Baghdad are incorporated into the decoration of the Great Mosque. Historical accounts indicate that marble for the mihrab and teakwood for the minbar were also imported from Baghdad at this time. Although it may be certain that the luster tiles were made in Baghdad, both the teakwood and the marble came from further afield, perhaps from India or Turkey.

For the purposes of this discussion, West Africa may be described as that part of sub-Saharan Africa dominated by the Niger and Senegal rivers and extending northward into the Sahel. The trade of West Africa was always dominated by trans-Saharan caravan routes leading to North Africa, and there is no substantial evidence for sea-borne Atlantic trade. Although it is possible that there may have been a certain amount of Roman trade with West Africa, it is likely to have been small as compared with the volume of trade during the medieval Islamic period. The principal commodity was gold from the Bambuk, Bure, and Akan areas of the rainforest. The gold trade is thought to have provided the impetus toward the development of cities and the formation of states (e.g., Ghana, Mali). The other major commodity was salt from the central Sahara, which enabled the Tuareg to exchange salt for gold, which could more easily be sent by caravan to North Africa. Other important commodities include goods such as hippopotamus teeth, which were imported to Europe via Ifriqiyya and used as ivory in Sicily.

The Nile/Red Sea Corridor links Egypt and the Mediterranean with sub-Saharan Africa, Arabia, and the Indian Ocean. The trade networks of this area are of great antiquity and precede the advent of Islam by many centuries. Despite frequent assertions concerning the difficulty of navigating from north to south in the Red Sea, it is clear that at least some trade was carried on in this way, particularly from Egypt to Yemen. One frequently used trade route involved transporting goods by boat up the Nile and then transferring them to camel caravans, which would cross the desert to one of the Red Sea ports from where they could be shipped elsewhere.

The coming of Islam had major implications for the economy and trade of this region. In the first place, the institution of the Hajj meant that thousands of African pilgrims would annually cross via the Red Sea to Arabia. In addition, the increased importance of Mecca and Medina meant that there was an increased demand for food and other commodities in the Hijaz, which could be supplied from Egypt and other parts of Africa. However, one major difference between this region and other parts of Africa is the presence of Christianity, which acted as a block to the southern extension of the Muslim overland trade networks.

In many ways, the trade of East Africa can be seen as an extension of the Red Sea trade network, although there are significant differences. Whereas the Red Sea is located in the heart of the Islamic world, the Muslim presence in East Africa is restricted to a narrow band of coast and small islands along the coast from Mogadishu in Somalia to Sofala in Mozambique. Also, the East African coast shares a common Swahili culture, which, although Muslim, is distinct from the predominantly Arabic culture of the Red Sea region.

Although Roman ceramics have been identified from as far south as Zanzibar, it is evident that the high point of East African maritime trade was during the Islamic period. East Africa's trade with the Islamic world was not restricted to Egypt and the Red Sea, and there were direct connections with Oman in southeast Arabia as well as more distant places such as Iraq via the Persian/Arabian Gulf and the Muslim communities of India via the Indian Ocean. As with West Africa, one of the principal trading commodities was gold, which came from the region of Zimbabwe in southern Africa. The gold trade contributed to the growth of Muslim trading cities such as Kilwa in southern Tanzania as well as inland non-Muslim settlements like Zimbabwe. Slaves were another highly valued commodity, and it is known that large numbers of East African slaves were imported to work in the marshes of southern Iraq during the 'Abbasid period (eighth and ninth centuries). Other precious export commodities included elephant ivory and spices such as cloves. Imports to East Africa included ceramics from Mesopotamia, Iran (Makran), India (Gujarat), and China. In some cases, these ceramics would be set into the fabric of a building, probably indicating prestige and contacts with long-distance trade.

ANDREW PETERSEN

Further Reading

A good insight into the workings of Islamic trade in Africa is given in the writings of Ibn Battuta, who traveled extensively throughout Africa.

Horton, M. *Shanga: The Archaeology of a Muslim Trading Community on the Coast of East Africa.* Nairobi: British Institute in Eastern Africa, 1996.

Insol, T. *The Archaeology of Islam in Sub-Saharan Africa.* Cambridge, 2004.

Lunde, P., and A. Porter, eds. *Trade and Travel in the Red Sea Region.* Oxford, UK: BAR International Series 1269, 2004.

TRADE, INDIAN OCEAN

The Indian Ocean during the medieval centuries became drawn into the sphere of Islamic civilization, generating a dynamic economic zone, expanding the faith far beyond its Arab homeland, and consequently producing a tremendous variety of cultural forms. The extension of Islam across the Indian Ocean was a product of commerce and conversion rather than conquest. Some have argued that this area represented a nonhierarchical world system before the fifteenth-century penetration of Europeans into the ocean. The Indian Ocean is commonly thought of as a route between east and west, complementing the transcontinental Silk Road north of the Himalayas. However, routes south along the East African coast and penetrating into Southeast Asia were equally important for long-distance trade and the spread of Islam's religion and cultures. These regions, which encompassed tremendous cultural diversity, nevertheless obtained their unity from constant economic and cultural contact.

The basis for that unity is the monsoon weather system that governs virtually the entire ocean. The seasonal monsoon winds (monsoon is derived from the Arabic *mawsim,* which means season) enabled mariners to travel long distances more efficiently with relatively simple maritime technology. The regularity of the winds also facilitated extensive contact between people of different cultures, because sailors often had to wait in distant ports for the monsoon to shift and carry them homeward. Unity is also evident in the ship technology used there until well past the arrival of European vessels. Although there were a great variety of crafts—as indicated in the description of the fourteenth-century traveler Ibn Battuta—Indian Ocean vessels all shared the characteristic that they were constructed without iron nails, because this metal was unavailable in sufficient quantities; instead, ship planking was "sewn" or "stitched" together with coconut coir rope and caulked with palm shavings, and the hulls were greased with castor or shark oils. These ships carried a large variety of goods, the markets for which bound the ocean's littorals in numerous economic relationships. A few of the commodities of Indian Ocean trade were the following: from southern and eastern Asia, silk, ceramics, sandalwood, black pepper, and other spices; from western Asia, horses, textiles, metal goods, frankincense, and products from the Mediterranean; from eastern Africa, ivory, gold, timber, and slaves. More significantly, beyond these basic features of material life, by the end of the medieval period Islam had touched virtually all of the Indian Ocean's shores. In recent years, researchers have started to investigate more intensively the role of Islam and Muslims in the complex world of the Indian Ocean; although many questions remain unanswered, the broad outlines of medieval Islamic civilization in the Indian Ocean are clear.

Historical sources about the medieval Indian Ocean are varied and include geographies, travelers' accounts, anecdotes and tales, navigational handbooks, and occasional references found in chronicle and documentary sources. Much evidence is in Arabic, but there also exist sources in the languages of the other imperial actors in Indian Ocean history, from Persia to India to China. Conceptions of the Indian Ocean are indicated by the variety of names used to identify the ocean and its parts. In Arabic, it was called both the Great Sea and the Sea of India, whereas in Persian it was called the Green Sea and in Chinese the Western Ocean. The view from the Indian subcontinent bifurcated the ocean into the Sea of Lar (the Arabian Sea) and the Sea of Harkal/Harikela, or, from tenth-century CE evidence in Bengal, the Sea of Vanga. In the Arabic geographical literature, the ocean was also identified with other adjacent lands: it was known variously as the Sea of Persia, the Sea of East Africa, and the Sea of Ethiopia, reflecting perhaps Arab scholarship's greater familiarity with the western half of the ocean. Further afield, as one would expect, the medieval Arabic conception becomes increasingly vague. To the east, the Indian Ocean merged with the Sea of China, which included what is now called the South China Sea as well as the waters on both sides of insular southeast Asia; beyond the Sea of China as well as to the far south the ocean merged into the Surrounding Ocean, also known as the Green Sea or the Sea of Darkness.

The spread of Islam and developments in medieval Indian Ocean commerce are processes that are difficult to separate. The initial Muslim penetration of the Indian Ocean world was through the expansion of the newly found Islamic empire into Yemen and Oman in the seventh century and Sind in the early eighth century. From these footholds, however, commerce, immigration, and missionary activity became the primary means of the spread of Islam and its resultant cultural forms and the basis for relationships across the Indian Ocean. The impact of the Islamic empire (whose capitals in Damascus and then, starting in the eighth century, Baghdad fueled demand for luxury goods) on the Indian Ocean was matched by the expansion of the Chinese Tang Dynasty (608–907), which generated a burst of commercial activity across the ocean. During the earliest Islamic centuries, the Arabic sources give the impression of direct trade by Muslim Arab and Persian merchants from such ports as Siraf on Iran's Persian Gulf coast and Sohar on the Arabian Peninsula's coast, with south and east Asia ports, most notably Canton (Khanfu), which was known for its large community of foreign traders, including Muslims, who constituted a large enough presence to have pillaged the city in 758. Arabic chronicle sources refer to "the Chinese ships" in Muslim harbors, probably referring to ships with Chinese merchandise. Routes across the ocean are documented as early as the ninth century by the geographer Ibn Khurradadhbih and as late as the fifteenth century in the much more thorough navigational handbook of Ibn Majid, which provided detailed nautical instructions for all the major sectors of the ocean. During the ninth century, the route eastward from such ports as Siraf to the eastern terminus in Canton included stops in Muscat or Sohar (in modern Oman), Daybul (near modern Karachi), and Calicut or Quilon/Kulam Malay on the Malabar (southwestern) coast of India. From here the ships would round the subcontinent and Sri Lanka and head directly across the Bay of Bengal, stopping at the Andaman and Nicobar Islands before passing through the Strait of Malacca (Melaka) into the South China Sea and on to Canton. Alternatively, vessels might sail from Malabar to al-Ma'bar ("the Crossing Place"), corresponding roughly with India's Coromandel (southeastern) coast, either proceeding northward to Bengal or eastward across the Bay of Bengal.

The evidence for this trade is most vividly apparent in the Chinese stoneware and porcelain that litter archaeological sites on the coast of east Africa (e.g., Sofala, Kilwa, Mogadishu) as well as the sites mentioned above in Arabia and Southeast Asia. This transoceanic pattern shifted slightly in 879, when a Chinese rebel general captured Canton and expelled members of the foreign merchant community; the Muslims then established themselves in the Hindu-Buddhist kingdom of Srivijaya in Sumatra. Despite the activity of Muslim merchants in eastern Asian trade, southern and southeastern Asian Buddhists and Hindus probably dominated the carrying trade in the eastern half of the Indian Ocean during the first Islamic centuries. However, Muslim seamen were the primary carriers of long-distance trade in the western half of the ocean, operating between the coasts of Arabia, Africa, and, especially in the eleventh century, the growing number of Muslim settlements on the western coast of India.

The activity of southwest Asian Muslims in the Far East continued until roughly the tenth and eleventh centuries, when trading patterns became oriented around emporia clustered in three interlinking regions: on the coasts of Southwest Asia and East Africa, on the Gujarat and Malabar coasts of west India, and in Southeast Asia's Sumatra and the Malay Peninsula, which formed the edge of an eastern zone of trade north across the South China Sea. This pattern shift may have been encouraged by the entry of the Chinese into Indian Ocean trade when the Sung Dynasty (960–1279) started to promote commerce and established direct trading relations with Sri Lanka. By the following century, Chinese ships dominated the trade of the eastern Indian Ocean. At roughly the same time, the Fatimid Dynasty (in Cairo, 969–1171) established its capital in Cairo and began to sponsor commercial activity in the Red Sea and western Indian Ocean; consequently, Cairo and neighboring Fustat became a dynamic emporium serving as a link between the two trading worlds of the Mediterranean and the Indian Ocean, a role the metropolis continued to hold through the medieval period. The role of Egypt in long-distance trade is vividly documented in the Judeo-Arabic Geniza letters, found in Fustat, which provide numerous details about commerce that extended from the western Mediterranean to India. It is also during this time that the Karimi merchants are first mentioned; these are a poorly defined group of merchants that played a prominent role in the long-distance trade of luxury goods until they seemed to dwindle in importance during the fifteenth century.

Also, starting in the eleventh century, Sunni and Ismaili Muslim communities began to flourish in coastal western India, often in the context of Hindu states, and from here these populations spread to East Africa and to Southeast Asia. Concerning the latter, the Khoja (derived from Persian; "master") community of western India is known to have established extensive commercial contact with East Africa. At about this time, such East African trading centers as Malindi, Mombasa, and Zanzibar became prominent. However, the links were by no means exclusively economic. Until the mid-sixteenth century, the leader of the Ismaili Bohra (derived from Gujarati; "trader") community, also of western India, resided in Yemen; members of the community traveled there on a regular basis for pilgrimage, directed their tithes there, and appealed to the leader for adjudication. Contacts were also established eastward so that, by the thirteenth century, Muslims dominated commercial activity in the eastern Indian Ocean. Although Arab and Persian merchants had been the first Muslims to establish contact with East and Southeast Asia, Indian and Southeast Asian Muslim merchants and missionaries spread Islam into insular Southeast Asia and the Philippines. The establishment of the systems of trading emporia culminated in the fifteenth century with the rise of the Malacca (Melaka) on the coast of the Malayan peninsula from an obscure fishing village to a dynamic commercial emporium. The success of the Sultanate of Malacca (c. 1403–1511) has been associated with the alliance of its Hindu Javanese founder with the neighboring Muslim sultan of Pasai and his subsequent conversion to Islam as well as the growing commercial activity of the Chinese Ming Dynasty (1368–1644). During the first decades of the fifteenth century, the Ming authorities also undertook a series of commercial expeditions, led by a Chinese Muslim named Cheng Ho, across the Indian Ocean to Calicut and then to Hormuz in the Persian Gulf, and a small detachment are said to have ventured as far as Mecca. Although of renowned size—Chinese junks could have as many as four decks and crews of a thousand—this was a foray of ultimately limited impact, because no permanent trading relations were established.

The economic relationships of Asia and the Indian Ocean have been characterized as a net of interlinking systems or, alternatively, as a unitary world system, particularly during the century after about 1250, when the Mongols imposed economic unity across the Asian land mass that may have been integrated into the Indian Ocean system. Political power is central to the notion of a world system, and, in the history of the medieval Indian Ocean, further investigation is needed into the role of states in transoceanic connections. However, it is uncontested that Islam brought to the Indian Ocean cultural hegemony, reinforcing its geographical and economic unity. The impact of Islam established during the medieval period is manifest in the modern world, from Mindanao to Zanzibar. However, this hegemony was far from a uniform and static phenomenon; rather, it engendered the cultural diversity of manifold types of Islam and the syntheses that these created with indigenous cultures.

JOHN L. MELOY

Further Reading

Abu-Lughod, Janet. *Before European Hegemony: The World System A.D. 1250–1350*. New York: Oxford University Press, 1989.

Adas, Michael, ed. *Islamic and European Expansion: The Forging of a Global Order*. Philadelphia: Temple University Press, 1993.

Chaudhuri, K.N. *Trade and Civilisation in the Indian Ocean: An Economic History from the Rise of Islam to 1750*. Cambridge, UK: Cambridge University Press, 1985.

Parkin, David, and Ruth Barnes, eds. *Ships and the Development of Maritime Technology in the Indian Ocean*. London: Routledge Curzon, 2002.

Ray, Himanshu Prabha, and Jean-François Salles, eds. *Tradition and Archaeology: Early Maritime Contacts in the Indian Ocean*. New Delhi: Manohar, 1996.

Risso, Patricia. *Merchants and Faith: Muslim Commerce and Culture in the Indian Ocean*. Boulder: Westview Press, 1995.

Tibbetts, G.R., ed. and transl. *Arab Navigation in the Indian Ocean before the Coming of the Portuguese*, Oriental Translation Fund, New Series, vol. XLII. London: Royal Asiatic Society, 1981.

Wink, Andre. *Al-Hind: The Making of the Indo-Islamic World*, 3 vols. Leiden: Brill, 1990, 1997, 2004.

TRADE, MEDITERRANEAN

During the first century of Muslim domination in the eastern, southern, and western parts of the Mediterranean, freedom of navigation and overseas commerce continued despite the wars and naval raids between Muslims and Christian countries. The Islamic military expansions in the Middle Sea were, however, not destructive and did not create an abrupt change in the material culture of the occupied countries. Instead, cultural continuity remained discernible in various life aspects for centuries despite gradual Arabization and Islamization processes. Non-Muslim subject populations retained their own socioeconomic and judicial institutions. There is no evidence to prove that the Arabs in the seventh or eighth centuries CE desired to reduce the maritime commerce in the Mediterranean to their territorial domain only. However, to what extent early Muslim merchants were involved in the Mediterranean trade remains vague. All that can be said is that, on the eve of the Islamic expansions, shipping in the Mediterranean regions was primarily controlled by the church, state, rich merchants, and middle-class entrepreneurs, including Jews. For example, the commercial ships of the church of Alexandria sailed eastward to India and Ceylon and westward to Marseilles at the time when the Byzantines still preserved maritime supremacy over the Mediterranean, and the commerce of the Mediterranean world was largely in the hands of Syrians and Egyptians. The patriarch of the church hired sailors, maintained a commercial fleet and a dockyard, and regulated maritime laws. However, written evidence about Islamic maritime trade in the Mediterranean comes from the ninth century CE onward.

The existence of a transcontinental trade, from China to the eastern and western Mediterranean, gave the countries of the Indian Ocean (see Trade, Indian Ocean) an economic unity and brought a new impetus to sea trade. The Arab achievements made it possible to unite the two arteries used since antiquity for the long-distance trade between the Indian Ocean and the Mediterranean. The twin routes of the transcontinental trade from Asia—the sea-borne traffic through the Red Sea and the combined sea, river, and overland journey across the Persian Gulf, Iraq, the Syrian desert, and Egypt—were brought under political control of a single authority: first that of the Umayyad caliphs and later that of the 'Abbasids.

The year AH 212/827 CE constitutes a turning point not only in the naval history of the Mediterranean but also in the history of maritime commerce. The establishment of the Sicilian and Cretan Arab emirates marked a new era in the Christian-Islamic international trade. Meanwhile, the breakup of Islamic Mediterranean territories into fragments motivated the ruling dynasties to found commercial hubs and ports of call to attract local and foreign merchants and expand the interregional and international commerce. Among the major Andalusian seaports on the Mediterranean were Tortosa, Valencia, Denia, Cartagena, Málaga, Algeciras, Seville, Silves, Almería, and Pechina; of western Maghrib they were Ceuta and

Badis; for Central Maghrib they were Hour, Dellys, Djidjelli, Bijaya, Bône, and Marsa al-Kharaz; for Ifriqiyya they were Tabarqa, Bizerta, Tunis, Monastir, Susa, al-Mahdiyya, Sfax, Gabes, and Derna; and for the eastern Maghrib they were Tripoli, Lebda, Surt, Bernik, Barqa, Ra's al-Tin, and Tubruk. In addition, seaports of Islamic Mediterranean islands, especially those on Sicily—Palermo, Trapani, Mazara, Messina, and Syracuse—linked Christian Europe with most Islamic territories. In these commercial centers gathered together merchants of different races, religions, and languages—indigenous and foreign Muslims, Jews, and French, Italian, Greek, and Slavic Christians—to exchange their views as well as their wares despite the prevalent enmities among the various powers. With a few exceptions, political boundaries never formed an obstacle to the freedom of movement of either persons or goods. Only during wartime and political disturbance were the visits of foreigners limited in time or confined to certain localities. The Mediterranean, divided as it was between a Christian north and a Muslim south, eventually recovered much of its economic unity through the activity of merchants and traders. Although Muslims maintained some sort of superiority at sea, neither they nor Christians could call the Mediterranean *"mare nostrum"* ("our sea").

The Islamic Mediterranean maintained direct and very frequent commercial relations with Christian Europe. Although Jews played an integral role and acted as intermediaries between Islamic coastal frontiers and Christian seaports, as early as the tenth century CE, Byzantine and Islamic sources indicate that Muslim merchants carried out commercial transactions in Christian Mediterranean trade centers. Traders from the Islamic east, including Arab Christians, were, for instance, a constant feature of the Constantinopolitan landscape throughout the late tenth, eleventh, and twelfth centuries. Their stay in the Byzantine capital was ordinarily limited to three months, although some of them resided in Constantinople for longer periods. Similarly, foreign merchants entered *dar al-Islam* (the realm of Islam) by virtue of a valid pledge of security *(aman)* and were allowed to conduct commercial transactions in any part of Islamic territories if they carried such a pledge. Sources also show that more than a *masjid* (mosque) had been built in the capital city; one of the earliest masjids was constructed during the reign of Constantine VII (913–959). Meanwhile, their commercial networks exceeded beyond the realm of Byzantium and included the Slavic territories in Eastern Europe.

Geographically, Muslim, Jewish, and Christian merchants operated within separate but overlapping commercial spheres. They all took part in Mediterranean international commerce and all did business in Syrian, Egyptian, North African, and Spanish markets, but each group was subject to different constraints. It was characteristic throughout the medieval Mediterranean world to find Jews and Christians trading with all regions, whereas Muslim merchants generally restricted their sphere of operation to Islamic markets; Muslim merchants traded freely throughout the realm of Islam. Why Muslim itinerant merchants were absent from the hinterland markets of Latin Europe has been explained by two factors. First, perhaps they found Christian cities uncongenial to their needs in terms of facilities for bathing and eating. Second, Islamic law discouraged them from trading with non-Islamic lands. Third, the hinterland markets of Latin Europe might have been less favorable to Muslim merchants.

The boom of Islamic trade in the Mediterranean was made possible as a result of the innovation of commercial techniques (see Merchants, Muslim) and the establishment of shipping laws and *responsa*. It was during the first third of the tenth century when the *Kitab Akriyat al-Sufun wa-al-Niza' Bayna Ahliha (Treatise Concerning the Leasing of Ships and the Claims Between Their Passengers and Sailors)* was promulgated. Written in the form of *responsa,* the core text of the treatise, as composed by the original author Muhammad Ibn 'Umar al-Kinani al-Andalusi al-Iskandarani (d. 310/923), consists of only nine chapters; an appendix of six jurisprudential inquiries from a later period was apparently supplemented by the compiler Khalaf Ibn Abi Firas or a later Maliki jurist. The first chapter deals with the hiring of sailors on ships. Chapter two treats the leasing of ships, forms of hire, and the freight charges. Problems that may emerge between the parties to the contract after concluding the charter agreement and preventing them from carrying out their transaction and bringing it to completion are discussed in the third chapter. However, the fourth chapter establishes the payment arrangements between the contracting parties if a technical malfunction to a ship should occur in the port of origin, en route, or after docking in the final destination. The fifth chapter is the longest, and it covers jettison, salvage, and contribution. Liability of ship owners for what they carry and for what they are not liable is addressed in the sixth chapter. The author of the treatise devotes the seventh chapter to discussing the procedures of the loading and unloading of goods. Partnership in a vessel is inadequately treated in the eighth chapter. The concluding chapter refers to profit-sharing with the person who operates the vessel. Finally, the appendix, the legal inquiries of which are dated between the second half of the tenth century and first half of the eleventh

century CE, concerns itself with the calculation of freight charges, overloading, liability of the shipowner for the transport of fixed goods to the intended destination, collision, and jettison and general average. The *Kitab Akriyat al-Sufun* is, thus, not precisely a collection of maritime laws that treats ownership and possession of ships, methods of acquisition, rights of co-owners, the relations of master and crew, and so on but rather a maritime treatise that exclusively treats mercantile and shipping matters. Despite the substantial legal data that can be derived from this unique treatise, it does not enable economic historians to draw a global view on Christian–Islamic maritime commerce in the Mediterranean region. Additionally, its geographical scope does not cover the entire Islamic Mediterranean; rather, it is confined to the major ports of Egypt, Ifriqiyya, Sicily, and Andalusia. However, the Moroccan, Syrian, and Cretan ports are not mentioned at all.

Mediterranean merchants handled an enormous range of commodities: expensive luxury goods and mundane everyday necessities, raw and manufactured, bulky and compact. Spices, medicinal drugs, aromatics, lac, brazilwood, indigo, dyestuff, and textiles were imported from the East, whereas metals, minerals, timbers, ceramics, leather, furs, and slaves arrived in Islamic ports from Christian Europe.

HASSAN KHALILEH

See also Navigation; Merchants, Muslim; Trade, Indian Ocean

Further Reading

Citarella, Armando O. "Merchants, Markets and Merchandise in Southern Italy in the High Middle Ages." In *Mercati e Mercanti Nell'Alto Medioevo: L'Area Euroasiatica e L'Area Mediterranea*, 239–84. Spoleto: Centro Italiano di Studi sull'alto Medioevo, 1993.
———. "The Relations of Amalfi with the Arab World before the Crusades." *Speculum* 42 (1967): 299–312.
Constable, Olivia R. "The Problem of Jettison in Medieval Mediterranean Maritime Law." *Journal of Medieval History* 20 (1994): 207–20.
———. *Trade and Traders in Muslim Spain: The Commercial Realignment of the Iberian Peninsula 900–1500.* Cambridge, UK: Cambridge University Press, 1994.
Christides, Vassilios. "Raid and Trade in the Eastern Mediterranean: A Treatise by Muhammad bn. 'Umar, the *Faqih* from Occupied Moslem Crete, and the *Rhodian Sea Law*, Two Parallel Texts." *Graeco-Arabica* 5 (1993): 61–102.
Delgado, Jorge L. *El Poder Naval de Al-Andalus en la Época del Califato Omeya.* Granada: Universidad de Granada, 1993.
Goitein, Shelomo D. *A Mediterranean Society: The Jewish Communities of the Arab World as Portrayed in the Documents of the Cairo Geniza: Economic Foundations.* Berkeley: University of California Press, 1967.

————. *Letters of Medieval Jewish Traders*. Princeton, NJ: Princeton University Press, 1973.

————. "Mediterranean Trade in the Eleventh Century: Some Facts and Problems." In *Studies in the Economic History of the Middle East from the Rise of Islam to the Present Day*, ed. M.A. Cook, 51–62. Oxford, UK: Oxford University Press, 1970.

————. *Studies in Islamic History and Institutions*. Leiden: E.J. Brill, 1968.

Hammam, Mohammed. "La Pêche et al., Commerce du Poisson en Méditerranée Ocidentale (Xᵉ–début XVIᵉ) In *L'Occident Musulman et L'Occident Chrétien au Moyen Age*, ed Mohammed Hammam, 151–78. Rabat, 1995.

Imamuddin, S.M. *Muslim Spain 711–1492 A.D.* Leiden: E.J. Brill, 1981.

Khalilieh, Hassan S. *Islamic Maritime Law: An Introduction*. Leiden: E.J. Brill, 1998.

Kreutz, Barbara M. *Before the Normans: Southern Italy in the Ninth and Tenth Centuries*. Philadelphia: University of Pennsylvania Press, 1991.

Labib, Subhi. "Egyptian Commercial Policy in the Middle Ages." In *Studies in the Economic History of the Middle East from the Rise of Islam to the Present Day*, ed. M.A. Cook, 63–77. Oxford, UK: Oxford University Press, 1970.

Lagardere, Vincent. "Le Commerce des Céréales Entre al-Andalus et le Maghrib aux XIᵉ et XIIᵉ Siécles." In *L'Occident Musulman et L'Occident Chrétien au Moyen Age*, ed. Mohammed Hammam, 123–50. Rabat, 1995.

Lewis, Archibald. "Mediterranean Maritime Commerce: A.D. 300–1100 Shipping and Trade." In *La Navigazione Mediterranea Nell'Alto Medioevo*, 481–501. Spoleto: Centro Italiano di Studi sull'alto Medioevo, 1978.

————. *Naval Power and Trade in the Mediterranean A.D. 500 to 1100*. Princeton, NJ: Princeton University Press, 1951.

Lombard, Maurice. *Espace et Réseaux du Haut Moyen Âge*. Paris: La Haye, 1972.

Lopez, Robert S. *The Commercial Revolution of the Middle Ages, 950–1350*. Cambridge, UK: Cambridge University Press, 1994.

————. "The Role of Trade in the Economic Readjustment of Byzantium in the Seventh Century." *Dumbarton Oaks Papers* 13 (1959): 69–85.

————. "The Trade of Medieval Europe: The South." In *The Cambridge Economic History of Europe*, eds. M. Postan and E.E. Rich, 257–354. Cambridge, UK: Cambridge University Press, 1952.

————. "Mohammed and Charlemagne: A Revision." *Speculum* 18 (1943): 14–38.

Lopez, Robert, and Irving Raymonds. *Medieval Trade in the Mediterranean World*. New York: Columbia University Press, 1990.

Monks, George R. "The Church of Alexandria and the City's Economic Life in the Sixth Century." *Speculum* 28 (1953): 349–62.

Nazmi, Ahmad. *Commercial Relations between Arabs and Slavs*. Warszawa: Wydawnictwo Akademickie, 1998.

Pirenne, Henri. *Medieval Cities: Their Origins and Revival of Trade*. Princeton, NJ: Princeton University Press, 1974.

————. *Mohammed and Charlemagne*. New York: Meridian Books Inc., 1957.

Pleguezuelo, José Aguilera. *Estudios de las Normas e Instituciones del Derecho Islámico en Al-Andalus*. Seville: Guadalquivir Ediciones, 2000.

————. "El Derecho Mercantil Marítimo en Al-Andalus." *Temas Arabes* 1 (1986): 93–106.

Reinert, Stephen W. "The Muslim Presence in Constantinople, 9th–15th Centuries: Some Preliminary Observations." In *Studies on the Internal Diaspora of the Byzantine Empire*, eds. Hélène Ahrweiler and Angeliki E. Laiou, 125–50. Washington DC: Dumbarton Oaks Research Library and Collection, 1998.

Taher, Mustafa Anwar, ed. "Kitab Akriyat al-Sufun wa-al-Niza' Bayna Ahliha." *Cahiers de Tunisie* 31 (1983): 5–54.

Udovitch, Abraham L. "An Eleventh Century Islamic Treatise on the Law of the Sea." *Annales Islamologiques* 27 (1993): 37–54.

Whitehouse, David. "Abbasid Maritime Trade: The Age of Expansion." In *Cultural and Economic Relations between East and West: Sea Routes*, ed. Takahito Mikasa, 62–70. Wiesbaden: Otto Harrassowitz, 1988.

Yusuf, Muhsin. "Sea Versus Land: Middle Eastern Transportation during the Muslim Era." *Der Islam* 73 (1996): 232–58.

TRANSLATION, ARABIC INTO HEBREW

During a period of about three hundred years, from around 1100 to 1400 CE, several dozen translators rendered more than four hundred Judeo-Arabic, Arabic, and Greco-Arabic works of grammar, law, theology, philosophy, medicine, and literature into Hebrew. The translators, who were often refugees from Islamic Spain or descendants of refugees, produced a variety of texts for patrons, students, and colleagues. Jews worked with other Jews and also collaborated with Christians, often producing Hebrew versions of the same texts that they would help render into Latin. The main centers of translation were Toledo, where Avendaut (probably Abraham Ibn Daud) worked together with the Christian Dominicus Gundissalinus; Barcelona, where Abraham Bar Hiyya collaborated with Plato of Tivoli; Southern France (Lunel, Bezier, Narbonne, Montpellier, Marseilles), where Judah Ibn Tibbon, the "father of translators," established a dynasty of translators, followed by his son Samuel, grandson Moses, and great grand-son Judah b. Makhir; and Naples, where a long line of Jewish translators found patronage, from Jacob Anatoli in the thirteenth century to Qalonymus b. Qalonymus in the early fourteenth century.

The first works translated into Hebrew were Jewish works of grammar and theology, including the writings of Isaac Israeli, Dunash b. Tamim, Sa'adyah Gaon, Judah Ibn Hayyuj, Jonah Ibn Janah, Solomon Ibn Gabirol, Bahya Ibn Paquda, Moses Ibn Ezra, Judah Halevi, and Moses Maimonides. Then the translators shifted their attention to Arabic and Greco-Arabic works of philosophy, medicine, and literature. Among the classical authors rendered from Arabic into Hebrew were Aristotle, Alexander, Themistius, Hippocrates, Galen, Archimedes, Euclid, and Ptolemy; lesser-known authors such as Appolonius, Autolycus, Geminus, Menaleus, and Theodosius; and pseudoepigraphical works of Neoplatonic or Hermetic orientation, such as the *Book of the Apple*, the *Book of Causes*, and the *Book of Istimakhus*. Al-Razi, 'Ali ibn Ridhwan, al-Majusi, Ibn al-Jazzar, Ibn Zuhr, Abu 'l-Salt, Ibn al-Muthanna, Ibn al-Haytham, al-Farghani, Jabir ibn Aflah, Ibn al-Zarqalluh, Ibn al-Saffar, al-Kindi, al-Farabi, al-Ghazali, al-Batalyawsi, Ibn Bajja, Ibn Tufayl, Averroes, and al-Bitruji were translated from among the Arabs, along with popular works such as *Kalila wa-Dimna*, *Bilawhar wa-Yudasaf*, and even al-Hariri's *Maqamat*. The most influential author translated was Averroes, many of whose writings survive only in Hebrew. Avicenna, by contrast, was made available only in his medical *Canon* and *Canticum* and in a late anthology of texts excerpted from the *Najat* and *Shifa'*.

From the very beginning of the translation movement, there were two established approaches: literary and literal. Philosophical and scientific works were generally translated word for word, producing calques and loanwords and following the original text closely even in terms of word order. Literary works, such as *Kalila wa-Dimna* and *al-Hariri*, on the other hand, were translated more loosely, often using paraphrases and replacing citations from the Qur'an and hadith (tradition) with verses from the Bible and rabbinic dicta. However, there was not always this neat division into different specialties and disciplines. Two famous controversies among the early translators helped to shape the development of the different ideologies: both Judah Ibn Tibbon and his son Samuel criticized their rival translators for subordinating meaning to language and style, failing to accurately reproduce difficult philosophical notions in their paraphrastic translations. The Hebrew terminology of the Ibn Tibbon family in particular became the standard language of philosophy and science. Their "Arabized Hebrew," as it has been called, became the accepted terminology used in original compositions as well, even by Jewish scientific authors who did not know Arabic.

The Jewish communities of Europe were changed dramatically by the translations. The traditional yeshivah student, who had previously studied only the Bible and rabbinic literature, now had access to the vast riches of the classical tradition. As a result, science and philosophy influenced every area of rabbinic Judaism. Philosophical commentaries were written about biblical texts and rabbinic legends. Legal codes and commentaries were introduced with theoretical discussions of ethics and political philosophy. Sermons with philosophical and scientific content became a common occurrence in the synagogues, whereas liturgy was framed by philosophical poems praising wisdom and describing the soul's ascent to the supernal realm or conjunction with the active intellect. The translations also stimulated the emergence of a Hebrew scientific tradition, represented by such outstanding philosophers as Gersonides, whose original astronomical investigations were recorded primarily in Hebrew. The translations served as the basis for commentaries, supercommentaries, abridgments, encyclopedias, and original compositions. They satisfied a practical need as well, creating a medical library for aspiring physicians, who were not allowed to enter into the Christian medical schools. In fact, the extensive Hebrew medical library produced during the thirteenth century made Jewish education even superior to Christian and Jewish physicians more highly sought after.

However, not every Jew was enamored of the new sciences made available through translation. From the very beginning of the translation movement, there was opposition expressed by traditional scholars and legal authorities who recognized a danger in a "foreign wisdom" that contradicted religious doctrines and presuppositions. This opposition led to three major communal controversies, which resulted in a ban on the study of philosophy and the public burning of Maimonides' *Guide to the Perplexed*. The opposition to science and translation continued into the fourteenth and fifteenth centuries as well, when the Jewish study of Greco-Arabic philosophy in Hebrew translation was even blamed for the persecutions in Spain in 1391 and the expulsion of 1492. However, the reaction to Greco-Arabic science and philosophy during the fourteenth and fifteenth centuries led to a renewed interest in translation as well: works of Arabic anti-Aristotelianism such as Ghazali's *Incoherence of the Philosophers* were translated into Hebrew for the first time. During the fifteenth century, Jews began to turn to Latin rather than Arabic sources, not out of scientific curiosity but polemical necessity: to know how to respond to the Christians. Thus, the medieval period of scientific and philosophical renaissance among the Jews began and ended with translation.

JAMES T. ROBINSON

See also Andalus; Aristotle and Aristotelianism; Astrology; Astronomy; Botany; al-Farabi; Geometry; al-Ghazali; Grammar and Grammarians: Hebrew and Judeo-Arabic; Hunayn ibn Ishaq; Ibn Ezra; Ibn Gabirol; Ibn al-Haytham (Alhazen); Ibn Rushd (Averroes); Ibn Sina (Avicenna); Ibn Tufayl; Ibn Zuhr;

Judah al-Harizi; Judah ha-Levi; al-Kindi (Historian); Maimonides; al-Majusi; Maqama; Mathematics; Medical Literature, Arabic; Medical Literature, Hebrew; Medicine; Meteorology; Plato and (Neo)Platonism; Provence; Ptolemy; al-Razi (Rhazes); Sa'adyah Gaon; Sicily; Translation, Arabic to Persian; Translation, Pre-Islamic Learning into Arabic

Further Reading

Berman, Lawrence. "Greek into Hebrew: Samuel b. Judah of Marseilles, Fourteenth-Century Philosopher and Translator." In *Jewish Medieval and Renaissance Studies*, ed. Alexander Altmann, 289–320. Cambridge, UK: Harvard University Press, 1967.

Bos, Gerrit, ed. and transl. *De Anima, Translated into Hebrew by Zerahyah b. Isaac b. She'altiel Hen*. Leiden: E.J. Brill, 1994.

Bos, Gerrit, and Charles Burnett, eds. and transl. *Scientific Weather Forecasting in the Middle Ages: The Writings of Al-Kindī*. London: Kegan Paul International, 2000.

Drossaart-Lulofs, H.J., and R.L.J. Poortman, eds. and transl. *Nicolaus Damascenus, De Plantis: Five Translations*. Amsterdam, 1989.

Filius, L.S., ed. and transl. *The Problemata Physica Attributed to Aristotle: The Arabic Version of Hunayn b. Ishaq and the Hebrew Version of Moses Ibn Tibbon*. Leiden: E.J. Brill, 1999.

Fontaine, Resianne. *Otot ha-Shamayim: Samuel Ibn Tibbon's Hebrew Version of Aristotle's Meteorology*. Leiden: E.J. Brill, 1995.

———. "Samuel Ibn Tibbon's Translation of the Arabic Version of Aristotle's *Meteorology*." In *The Ancient Tradition in Christian and Islamic Hellenism*, eds. Gerhard Endress and Remke Kruk, 85–100. Leiden, 1997.

Freudenthal, Gad. "Les Sciences dans les Communautés Juives Médiévales de Provence: Leur Appropriation, Leur Rôle." *Revue des Études Juives* 152 (1993): 29–136.

———. "Science in the Medieval Jewish Culture of Southern France." *History of Science* 33 (1995): 23–58.

Goldstein, Bernard, ed. and transl. *Ibn al-Muthannâ's Commentary on the Astronomical Tables of al-Khwârizmî, Two Hebrew Versions*. New Haven, Conn: Yale University Press, 1967.

———, ed. and transl. *Al-Bitrûjî: On the Principles of Astronomy Vol. 1, Analysis and Translation; Vol. 2, The Arabic and Hebrew Versions*. New Haven: Yale University Press, Yale Studies in the History of Science and Medicine 7, 1971.

———. "The Survival of Arabic Astronomy in Hebrew." *Journal for the History of Arabic Science* 3 (1979): 31–9.

———. "The Heritage of Arabic Science in Hebrew." In *Encyclopedia of the History of Arabic Science*, 3 vols., ed. Roshdi Rashed, 276–83. London: Routledge, 1996.

Harvey, Steven. "The Hebrew Translation of Averroes' Prooemium to his *Long Commentary on Aristotle's Physics*." *Proceedings of the American Academy for Jewish Research* 52 (1985): 55–84.

———. "Did Maimonides' Letter to Samuel Ibn Tibbon Determine Which Philosophers Would be Studied by Later Jewish Thinkers?" *Jewish Quarterly Review* 83 (1992): 51–70.

———, ed. *The Medieval Hebrew Encyclopedias of Science and Philosophy*. Dordrecht: Kluwer Academic Publishers, 2000.

Lévy, Tony. "The Establishment of the Mathematical Bookshelf of the Medieval Hebrew Scholar: Translations and Translators." *Science in Context* 10 (1997): 431–51.

Lieber, Elinor. "Galen in Hebrew." In *Galen: Problems and Prospects*, ed. V. Nutton. London: Wellcome Institute for the History of Medicine, 1981.

Schiffman, Yair. "The Differences between the Translations of Maimonides' *Guide of the Perplexed* by Falaquera, Ibn Tibbon, and al-Harizi and their Textual and Philosophical Implications." *Journal of Semitic Studies* 44 (1999): 47–61.

Shatzmiller, Joseph. *Jews, Medicine, and Medieval Society*. Berkeley: University of California Press, 1994.

Sirat, Colette. "Les Traducteurs Juifs a la Cour des Rois de Sicile et de Naples." In *Traduction et Traducteurs au Moyen Âge*, ed. G. Contamine, 169–91. Paris, 1989.

Steinschneider, Moritz. *Die Hebraischen Übersetzungen des Mittelalters und die Juden als Dolmetscher*. Berlin, 1893; Reprinted Graz, 1956.

Stern, Samuel Miklos. "Ibn Hasday's Neoplatonist: A Neoplatonist Treatise and Its Influence on Isaac Israeli and the Longer Version of the Theology of Aristotle." *Oriens* 13–14 (1961): 58–120.

Twersky, Isadore. "Aspects of the Social and Cultural History of Provençal Jewry." *Journal of World History* 11 (1968): 185–207.

Wolfson, Harry Austryn. "Plan for the Publication of a *Corpus Commentariorum Averrois in Aristotelem*." *Speculum* 36 (1961): 88–104.

Zonta, Mauro. *La "Classificazione Delle Scienze" di Al-Farabi Nella Tradizione Ebraica*. Torino, 1992.

———. *La Filosofia Antica nel Medioevo Ebraico: La Traduzioni Ebraiche Medievali dei Testi Filosofici Antichi*. Brescia, 1996.

TRANSLATION, ARABIC INTO PERSIAN

From the early Islamic centuries onward, translations have played an important role in the interaction between the Arabic and Persian languages and literatures.

Translations of the Samanid Period

The first known translations of Arabic writings into (New) Persian were produced in Eastern Iran and Transoxiana under the patronage of the Samanids (AH 204–395 CE/819–1005), who promoted extensive literary activity in both languages. Among the earliest recorded examples, Abu'l-Fadl Bal'ami (d. 329/940), vizier of Nasr II b. Ahmad (r. 301–331/914–933), translated Ibn al-Muqaffa''s Arabic version of the *Kalila wa-Dimna*, a collection of animal fables, into Persian prose, and the poet Rudaki (d. 329/941–942) rendered it into Persian verse. Some two centuries earlier, Ibn al-Muqaffa' (d. ca. 139/757) had himself translated the work from Middle Persian into Arabic, and his rendering served as the basis for numerous later versions in prose and verse in both Arabic and Persian.

The most ambitious translations sponsored by the Samanids, however, belong to the reign of Mansur I b. Nuh (350–365/961–976), who commissioned his vizier Abu 'Ali Bal'ami (d. 382–387/992–997, the son of Abu'l-Fadl) to translate the universal history of al-Tabari (d. 310/923) into Persian and also ordered a translation of al-Tabari's Qur'anic commentary. During a period of increasingly tense relations between the Samanids on the one hand and the 'Abbasids and the Buyids on the other, Mansur's initiative was almost certainly intended to strengthen the legitimacy of Samanid rule in the eastern regions. Bal'ami, who added some materials and omitted others, reworked al-Tabari's *History* into a continuous narrative that presents Islamic history from an Iranian point of view. The Persian *Tafsir (Commentary)* likewise omits portions of al-Tabari's work and introduces several elements that are not found in the Arabic original; it was perhaps intended to undermine the teachings of the many heterodox and sectarian groups, especially the Isma'ilis and Karramis, that flourished in Khurasan and Transoxania at the time and to appeal to non-Muslim communities as well. Both "translations" were probably also designed to foster the acculturation of the Turkish military elite created by the Samanids (Daniel, 1990; Meisami, 1999).

Although the Samanid period is associated with the earliest translations from Arabic into Persian, such works continued to appear throughout the premodern period across the Iranian-speaking world and indeed beyond it. For the patrons who commissioned them, translations of Arabic works could enhance legitimacy and confer prestige. At the same time, many translations served practical and instructional purposes. The range of subject matter covered by the recorded translations shows that there was a significant demand among Persian speakers for some access to the scholarship and scientific learning expressed in Arabic. Several Persian translators of the fourth/tenth and fifth/eleventh centuries stated in their prefaces that their purpose was to make their Arabic sources available to the elites and the common people alike (Lazard, 1975; Bosworth 1978–1979).

Translations of Works on Religious Subjects

Despite disagreement among religious scholars about the permissibility of translating the Qur'an, many translations into Persian appeared throughout the medieval period. Interlinear translations were especially common. When Mansur b. Nuh commissioned his translation of al-Tabari's *Tafsir*, he consulted a group of Transoxianan scholars, who declared it permissible for those did not know Arabic to read and write the Qur'anic commentary in Persian (*Tarjuma-yi Tafsir-i Tabari*, ed. H. Yaghma'i. Tehran, 1988. I:5). From the fifth/eleventh century onward, many commentators on the Qur'an chose to write in Persian so as to reach a broader audience.

Although Arabic never lost its status as the preeminent medium for the expression of religious thought and scholarship, Persian rapidly developed as an important secondary language into which works about religious subjects, including jurisprudence, theology, and mysticism, could be translated and in which, eventually, original works were written. The *Sawad al-A'zam*, a catechism formulated by the Hanafi scholar Abu'l-Qasim al-Samarqandi (d. 342/953), was translated into Arabic at the behest of the Samanid ruler Nuh II b. Mansur (r. 365–387/976–997). Among the most popular Persian translations of Arabic works were those that recorded the sayings and speeches of 'Ali, the first imam, those of the later imams, and commentaries on these materials. Arabic collections of the imams' utterances and communications included the *Hundred Words* of 'Ali, compiled in Arabic by al-Jahiz (d. 255/868–869), and the *Covenant of Ashtar*, 'Ali's letter to his governor, al-Ashtar (d. 38/658), itself also contained in the *Nahj al-Balagha*, the anthology of 'Ali's homilies and letters compiled by al-Sharif al-Radi (359–406/970–1016). Numerous Persian translations of these works were produced, including Husayn b. Muhammad Avi's version of the *Covenant of Ashtar* (ca. 729/1329) and the versions of the *Covenant* and of the *Risala al-Ahwaziyya* of Ja'far al-Sadiq, the sixth imam, recorded in the *Adab al-Wulat* of the eminent Shi'i scholar of Safavid times, Muhammad Baqir Majlisi (d. 1111/1699). The establishment of Shi'ism as the religion of the state in Iran under the Safavids stimulated a particularly large number of translations from Arabic, especially of Shi'i works.

By the fifth/eleventh century, Iranian Muslim writers frequently composed works about religious subjects in both languages. Among such bilingual scholars were the Sunni intellectual Abu Hamid al-Ghazali (450–505/1058–1111), the Shi'i theologian and scientist Nasir al-Din Tusi (d. 672/1273), and several Sufi thinkers, such as 'Abdallah Ansari (d. 481/1088), Shah Ni'matallah Wali (d. 834/1431), and 'Abd al-Rahman Jami (d. 898/1492).

Translations of Works on Scientific Subjects

As in the case of the religious sciences, Arabic remained the primary—but not the exclusive—language for the expression of scientific thought in Iran. Ibn Sina (ca. 370–428/980–1037) and Biruni (362–ca. 442/973–ca. 1050) wrote their principal works in Arabic, despite the fact that they spent their lives in Persian-speaking regions. Both scholars, however, expressed a portion of their oeuvres in Persian. Ibn Sina wrote two introductory Persian works: a short medical text, *Andar Danish-i Rag*, and a philosophical anthology, the *Danishnama-yi 'Ala'i*, both composed for his last patron, the independent ruler at Isfahan, 'Ala' al-Dawla Muhammad b. Dushmanziyar b. Kakuya (r. 398–433/1008–1041). As a further illustration of the porous nature of the two literatures even in scientific fields, the *Danishnama* was effectively rendered into Arabic in the *Maqasid al-Falasifa* of al-Ghazali. In the case of Biruni's *Kitab al-Tafhim* (420/1029), which deals with geometry, arithmetic, astronomy, and astrology, it is unclear whether the Arabic or the Persian version of the work appeared first.

Translations of Ethical and Political Works

Among the types of writing that were frequently chosen for translation from Arabic into Persian (and into other languages as well) were works dealing with statecraft, books of advice for rulers, and collections of wisdom literature. Selected sayings of Plato appear in several Persian works. The *Sirr al-Asrar (Secretum Secretorum)* ascribed to Aristotle was translated into Persian. A selection of the *Epistles* of the Ikhwan al-Safa' appeared in Persian translation in a work entitled *Mujmal al-Hikma*. Many Persian translations were made of Aristotle's letter to Alexander; among these translations was that of Muhammad b. Ahmad Zawzani, which was prepared during the fifth/eleventh century. In southern Iran, during the reign of the Muzaffarid Shah-i Shuja' (r. 765–786/1364–1384), al-Raghib al-Isfahani's widely-read treatise the *Dhari'a ila Makarim al-Shari'a* was rendered into Persian, with added counsels drawn from Islamic, Greek, and Iranian materials. In 901/1495, Yusuf b. Hasan Husayni Shafi'i Rumi (d. 922/1516) translated al-Mawardi's famous work on government, the *Ahkam al-Sultaniyya*, into Persian for Rustam Bahadur Aqquyunlu (r. 898–901/1492–1495). In India, the Arabic mirror for princes the *Siraj al-Muluk* of al-Tartushi (451–520/1059–1126) was translated into

Persian for the Mughal commander and potentate 'Abd al-Rahim Khan Khanan (d. 1036/1627).

Translations of Works of Historiography

Adaptations of Arabic historiographical works, especially those that concerned Iran, found a ready audience among Persian-speakers. The anonymous author of the *Mujmal al-Tavarikh va-l-Qisas*, compiled around 520/1126, translated some of his materials from Arabic into Persian. In 603/1206–1207, Jarbadhqani produced a Persian translation of the Arabic history of the Ghaznavids, the *Ta'rikh al-Yamini* of 'Utbi (350–427 or 31/961–1036 or 1040). A decade later, Ibn Isfandiyar, journeying in Khvarazm, came across a copy of the *Letter of Tansar*, a Sasanian work reportedly rendered into Arabic from Middle Persian by Ibn al-Muqaffa'; Ibn Isfandiyar translated the Arabic text into Persian and incorporated it into his *History of Tabaristan* (ca. 613/1216–1217). Ibn al-Tiqtaqa (d. ca. 709/1309), author of the two-part Arabic *Kitab al-Fakhri* (701/1301), revised his book after the execution in 702/1303 of its first dedicatee, Fakhr al-Din 'Isa, governor of Mosul; the second, historiographical half of the revised version was translated with significant modifications into Persian around 714/1314 as the *Tajarib al-Salaf* of Hindushah b. Sanjar Nakhjavani and dedicated to the Hazaraspid ruler Nusrat al-Din Ahmad b. Yusufshah (r. 696–730 or 733/1296–1330 or 1333). Avi translated not only the *Covenant of Ashtar* (see above) but also the Arabic *Mahasin Isfahan* as the *History of Isfahan* in 729/1329 under the patronage of the vizier Ghiyath al-Din (d. 736/1336), for whom a number of other Arabic works were translated into Persian. A manuscript dated 789/1387 and entitled *Tajarib al-Umam fi Akhbar Muluk al-'Arab wa-l-'Ajam* purports to be the Persian translation of an Arabic history composed in 75/694–695; it covers the period from Sam b. Nuh to Yazdagird III, and it is said to have been in the possession of a succession of rulers until such a time that it could no longer be read and the ruler of the age had it translated into Persian.

Bilingualism

The exchange between the Arabic and Persian literatures took several forms, not all of which involved freestanding translation–adaptations. Many authors of poetry and prose wrote in both languages; some composed independent works in each language, and some rendered their own Arabic works into Persian (and, occasionally, vice versa). The literary anthologies of al-Tha'alibi (350–429/961–1038) and his student al-Bakharzi (d. 467/1075) attest to a considerable number of poets and writers in Iran and Transoxiana who wrote equally fluently in Arabic and Persian. Another literary feature of the fourth/tenth and fifth/eleventh centuries are patchwork poems (mulamma'at), which are either Arabic poems that include Persian words or poems in which verses in the two languages alternate. The twelfth-century Khvarazmian poet Rashid al-Din Vatvat (d. 573 or 578/1177 or 1182) composed verses in Arabic and Persian and sometimes employed both languages in a single poem, and the celebrated Persian poets Sa'di (d. 691/1292) and Rumi (604–672/1207–1273) likewise wrote in Arabic as well as Persian.

Authors of prose works display a similarly high degree of bilingualism. Among many other writers, al-Ghazali wrote some works in Persian as well as many in Arabic. Although he composed his vast compendium, the *Ihya' 'Ulum al-Din,* in Arabic, al-Ghazali wrote a modified abridgment of it, the *Kimiya-yi sa'Adat,* in Persian, for the benefit of ordinary people who were unschooled in Arabic. In the *Akhlaq-i Nasiri,* his acclaimed work on ethics and political philosophy, Nasir al-Din Tusi (d. 672/1273) includes a Persian summary of the *Tahdhib al-Akhlaq* of Miskawayh (d. 421/1030), who had himself brought together Greek, Iranian, Arab, and Islamic traditions in his (Arabic) writings. The *Akhlaq-i Nasiri* became a model for later writers, including Davvani (d. 908/1502), whose *Akhlaq-i Jalali* likewise includes a Persian epitome of Miskawayh's treatise.

The sizable number of translations that are known to have been prepared undoubtedly constitute only a small portion of those that were actually undertaken. Moreover, very few works are extant in both their original Arabic and their translated versions, so the relationship of one to the other is often difficult to assess. In some instances, especially when the subject matter concerned religion, precision was essential. In other cases, it seems that translators were not necessarily required to provide complete or accurate versions of the original work but were expected to adapt the text, especially by omitting and adding materials, to suit the needs and interests of the new audience; the surviving translations of historiographical works often display a particularly free relationship with their Arabic sources, and, in several cases, they explicitly incorporate later materials to extend the narrative beyond the period covered by the original. However, the process of translation was only one medium for the reception of Arabic materials in Persian; the high frequency of bilingualism among educated Iranian Muslims facilitated various other forms of interaction between the two literatures, including abridgement in Persian, commentary in Persian, quotation, and compositions involving both languages.

LOUISE MARLOW

Further Reading

Baygi, Sh.M. "The First Available Persian Interpretation of the Qur'an Known as the *Tarjumah Tafsir-i-Tabari'.*" *Hamdard Islamicus* 19 (1996): 31–44.
Bosworth, C.E. "The Interaction of Arabic and Persian Literature and Culture in the Tenth and Early Eleventh Centuries." *al-Abhath* 27 (1978–1979): 59–75.
Daniel, E. "Manuscripts and Editions of Bal'ami's *Tarjamah-i Tarikh-i Tabari'.*" *JRAS* (1990): 282–321.
Danishpazhuh, M.T. "Fihrist-i Para-i az Kitabha-yi Akhlaq va-Siyasat bi Farsi'." *Nashriyya-yi Kitabkhana-yi Markazi-yi Danishgah-i Tihran* 1 (1961): 211–28.
———. "Chand Athar-i Farsi dar Akhlaq'." *Farhang-i Iran-zamin* 19 (1973): 261–84.
———. "An Annotated Bibliography on Government and Statecraft," transl. Andrew Newman. In: *Authority and Political Culture in Shi'ism,* ed. S.A. Arjomand, 213–39. Albany, NY, 1988.
Lazard, G. "The Rise of the New Persian Language." In *The Cambridge History of Iran, Vol. 4, The Period from the Arab Invasion to the Saljuqs,* ed. R. N. Frye, 595–632. 1975.
Lewis, F. "Persian Literature and the Qur'an." In *Encyclopaedia of the Qur'an,* ed. J.D. McAuliffe, vol. 4, 55–66. 2004.
Meisami, J.S. *Persian Historiography to the End of the Twelfth Century.* Edinburgh, 1999.
Tajarib al-Umam fi Akhbar Muluk al-'Arab wa-l-'Ajam. Istanbul: MS Aya Sofya 3115, Süleymaniye Kütüphanesi.

TRANSLATION, PRE-ISLAMIC LEARNING INTO ARABIC

According to the historian and man of letters Ibn Khallikan: "Nobody could have had access to the writings of the ancient Greeks, because nobody among the Arabs knew the Greek language." The same declaration could be made about the Persian legacy in other realms of knowledge, such as mirrors for princes. Presented here are only translations from the Greek legacy.

Several Arabic authors have given accounts at different periods about the knowledge of the Arabs about Greek legacy: al-Ya'qubi (d. ca. AH 292/905 CE) in sixty five pages of his *History;* the Christian physician and translator Ishaq b. Hunayn (d. 299/911) in his *History of the Physicians and Wise Men* (philosophers, above all, before Islam); the Baghdadi logician Abu Sulayman al-Sijistani (d. ca. 375/985) in his *Cabinet of Wisdom,* of which only an abridgment is extant and published; the bookseller and copyist of

Baghdad Ibn al-Nadim (d. 380/990 or 385/995), in his *Index* of books and disciplines; the Corduvan Ibn Juljul (d. c. 354/994), in the *Classes of Physicians and Wise Men;* Sa'id al-Andalusi (d. 462/1070–1071 in Egypt) in his *Categories of Nations,* written in Toledo; the Syrian physician Ibn Abi Usaybi'a (d. 668/1269) in the *Classes of Physicians,* parts of which have been translated into French, German, and English; and Ibn Khaldun (d. 808/1406) in his *Introduction to History.* Information is also found scattered in the huge Arabic biobibliographical productions, in marginalia of manuscripts, in commentaries, and in glosses.

The Syriac-speaking Christians have played a great role as a result of their technical skill in translation of Greek works into Syriac and Arabic. The major translators who flourished during al-Ma'mun's reign include the (probably Melkite) Christian Yahya b. al-Bitriq, who is credited with translating into Arabic Plato's *Timaeus,* Aristotle's *On the Soul, On the Heavens,* and *Prior Analytics,* the *Book of Animals,* and the *Secret of Secrets (Sirr al-Asrar),* an apocryphal political treatise of unknown authorship that was attributed to Aristotle.

However, the great translator of this caliphate was the Nestorian Hunayn b. Ishaq (d. 264/873), who was born in Hira in Iraq and, together with his son Ishaq b. Hunayn, his nephew Hubaysh, his pupil 'Isa b. Yahya, and others placed the translation of Greek medieval and philosophical texts on a sound scientific footing. The chief interests of Hunayn himself were medical, and he translated the complete medical corpus of Hippocrates and Galen. Hunayn and his associates were also responsible for translating Galen's treatises on logic, his *Ethics* (the Greek original of which is lost), and his epitomes of Plato's *Sophist, Parmenides, Cratylus, Euthydemus, Timaeus, Statesman, Republic,* and *Laws,* of which only the epitomes of the *Timaeus* and the *Laws* have survived in Arabic. The logical and ethical writings of Galen played an important role in the development of Arabic thought, and they have influenced moral philosophers from Abu Bakr al-Razi (Rhazes) (d. 313/925) to Miskawayh (d. 421/1030).

Of the works of Aristotle, Ishaq b. Hunayn is responsible for translating the *Categories, De Interpretatione, On Generation and Corruption, Physics, On the Soul, Nicomachean Ethics,* and the spurious *De Plantis,* which was written by the peripatetic philosopher Nicolaus of Damascus (first century). However, the most important Aristotelian treatise to be translated into Arabic during this period is the *Metaphysics,* which is known in the Arabic sources as the *Book of Letters* or the *Theologica (al-Ilahiyat).* According to reliable authorities, a little-known translator named Ustat (Eustathius) translated the twelve books

(excluding M and N) for al-Kindi, as did Yahya ibn 'Adi a century later. However, Ishaq, Abu Bishr Matta, and others are also credited with translating some parts of the *Metaphysics.*

Equally important is the translation by Ibn Na'ima al-Himsi (d. 220/835) of a treatise allegedly written by Aristotle and referred to in the Arabic sources as *Uthulugia* or *Theologia Aristotelis.* It consists of a paraphrase of Plotinus' *Enneads* IV–VI made by an anonymous Greek author (who could very well be Porphyry of Tyre); together with Proclus' *Elements of Theology,* known as the *Pure Good (al-Khayr al-mahd)* or *Liber de Causis,* it was largely responsible for the whole development of Arab-Islamic Neoplatonism. Al-Kindi is said to have commented on the *Theologia Aristotelis* as did Ibn Sina and others, and al-Farabi refers to it as an undoubted work of Aristotle. A series of other pseudo-Aristotelian works also found their way into Arabic, including *Secret of Secrets, De Plantis, Economica,* and the *Book of Minerals.*

Among other translators of Greek philosophical texts, the Harranean mathematician and astronomer Thabit b. Qurra (d. 288/901) should be mentioned. He translated, among other things, the *Arithmetical Introduction* of Nicomachus of Gerasa (a masterpiece of translation) and Archimedes' *The Sphere and the Cylinder.* He further revised many translations made by others, such as Euclid's *Elements* and Ptolemy's *Almagest.* Abu 'Uthman al-Dimashqi (d. 298/910) translated directly from Greek the *Topics* of Aristotle, which was translated again by Yahya b. 'Adi (d. 363/974), this time from Ishaq b. Hunayn's previous Syriac version. The Syro-Palestinian Greek physician Qusta b. Luqa (d. 300/912) was commissioned for the translation of mathematical and astronomical works, like the *Spherics* of Theodosius, the *Rising and Setting (of Fixed Stars)* by Autolycus, and the *Lifting Screw* by Hero of Alexandria. The Nestorian Abu Bishr Matta b. Yunus (d. 328/940), a skilled logician and the founder of the Aristotelian school in Baghdad, made his translations from Syriac: *The Analytica Posteriora,* with the commentary of Alexander of Aphrodisias and the paraphrase of Themistius; the book *Lamda* of *Metaphysica* with the commentary of Alexander (which was used by Averroes); and the *Ars Poetica.* His disciple the Jacobite Yahya b. 'Adi stands out as the best-known writer about Christian theological questions and ethics in Arabic. He translated logical works of Aristotle and also passages of his *Physics* and *Metaphysics,* with ancient commentaries. His translation of Themistius' paraphrase of *De Caelo* is extant in a Hebraic version. His Christian disciple 'Isa b. Ishaq b. Zur'a (d. 395/1008) was also active in translation. Such was the case also for

Ibn 'Adi's pupil Ibn al-Khammar al-Hasan b. Suwar (d. 407/1017).

CLAUDE GILLIOT

Primary Sources

al-Andalusi, Sa'id. *Science in the Medieval World, Book of the Categories of Nations*, transl. I. Salem Semaan and Alok Kumar. Austin: University of Texas Press, 1991.

Ibn al-Nadim. *The Fihrist of Ibn al-Nadim A Tenth-Century Survey of Muslim Culture*, 2 vols., ed. and transl. Bayard Dodge. New York: Columbia University Press, 1970.

Ibn Khaldun. *The Muqaddimah. An Introduction to History*, 3 vols., transl. Franz Rosenthal, vol. III, 111–70. New York: Bollingen Foundation; Princeton, NJ: Princeton University Press, 1967.

Ya'qubi. *Ibn Wadih qui Dicitur al-Ja'qubi Historiae*, 2 vols., ed. M.T.H. Houtsma, vol. I, 106–71. Leiden: Brill, 1883; reprinted, 1969. (Translated, annotated, and corrected by Klamroth, Martin. "Ueber die Auszüge aus Griechischen Schriftstellern bei al-Ja'qubi." *ZDMG* 40 (1886): 189–233, 612–38; 42 (1888): 1–44.)

Further Reading

Ayalon, Ilai. *Socrates in Medieval Arabic Literature*. Jerusalem: The Magnes Press; Leiden: Brill (IPTS, X), 1991.

Burnett, Charles, ed. *Glosses and Commentaries on Aristotelian Logical Texts. The Syriac, Arabic, and Medieval Traditions*. London: The Warburg Institute, 1993.

De Zénon d'Elée à Poincaré. Recueil d'Études en Hommage à Roshi Rashed, eds. Régis Morelon and Ahmad Hasnawi. Louvain-Paris: Peeters (Les Cahiers du MIDEO, 1), 2004.

Endress, Gerhard. "Die Wissenschaftliche Literatur." In *Grundriss der Arabischen Philologie*, vol. II, ed. Helmut Gätje, 400–506; vol. III, ed. Wolfdietrich Fischer, 3–152. Wiesbaden: Ludwig Reichert, 1987 and 1992.

Fakhry, Majid. *A History of Islamic Philosophy*. New York: Columbia University Press, 2004.

Fraenkel, Gutas Dimitri. *Greek Thought, Arabic Culture. The Greco-Arabic Translation Movement in Baghdad and Early 'Abbasid Society (2nd–4th/8th–10th Centuries)*. London and New York: Routledge, 1998.

Hugonnard-Roche, Henri. "Les Traductions du Grec au Syriaque et du Syriaque à l'Arabe (à propos de l'Organon d'Aristote)." In *Rencontres de Cultures*, 131–47.

Morelon, Régis. "Une Proposition de Lecture de l'Histoire de l'Astronomie Arabe." In *De Zénon d'Elée à Poincaré*, 237–49; *Rencontres de Cultures dans la Philosophie Médiévale. Traductions et Traducteurs de l'Antiquité Tardive au XIVᵉ Siècle*. Actes du Colloque International de Cassino, 15–17 Juin 1989, eds. Jacqueline Hamesse and Marta Fattori. Louvain-la-Neuve and Cassino, 1990.

Richter, Gustav. *Studien zur Geschichte der Älteren Arabischen Fürstenspiegel*. Leipzig: J..C. Hinrischs'sche Buchhandlung (Leipziger Semitische Studien, N.F., III), 1932.

Sezgin, Fuat. *Geschichte des Arabischen Schrifttum, Vol. VI, Astronomie*, 83–96. Leiden: Brill, 1978.

Steinschneider, Moritz. *Die Arabischen Übersetzungen aus dem Griechischen*. Graz: Akademische Druck und Verlagsanstalt, 1969.

"Religion, Learning and Science in the 'Abbasid Period." In *The Cambridge History of Arabic Literature*, 3rd ed., eds. M.J.L. Young et al., Cambridge, UK: Cambridge University Press, 1990.

TRANSOXIANA

The historical core of Central Asia was a region known as *Transoxiana,* a term that was coined by scholars to describe the location of this region beyond the River Oxus as one approached it from the classical world of Iran (more specifically from its northeastern province of Khorasan). The Oxus (or Oxiana) River, a Latinized form of an ancient Iranian word, was known to the Arabs as Jayhun. It is known today as the Amu Darya (the Amu River); this is based on a local variant, *Amu,* and the Persian word for lake or sea, *darya,* borrowed by Central Asian Turkic and with the connotation of river. Beginning east of the Oxus, Transoxiana extended even further eastward to meet the second—although relatively minor—lifeline of Central Asia, the Jaxartes or the Syr Darya. However, despite the connection of the Amu and Syr Darya with the term *Transoxiana* and the enormous significance of the two rivers in sustaining the culture of the region since ancient times, the historical center of gravity of Transoxiana lay elsewhere. This was along a third river called the Zarafshan, which originates far to the east in the Pamir Mountains, flows further to the west through the Turkestan and Zarafshan ranges, and then flows through the central lowlands of present-day Uzbekistan. Although it ultimately appears to head for a junction with the Amu Darya itself, instead it disappears into the sands of the Kyzyl Kum desert. Irrigation derived from the Zarafshan has supported dense agricultural and urban settlements in Transoxiana since antiquity, and existing cities like Samarqand and Bukhara (Uzbekistan) and archaeological sites such as Penjikent (Tajikistan) are only the best-known examples. In addition to the Zarafshan, several smaller streams such as the Kashka Darya also rise in the southern watershed of the Zarafshan range, flowing southwest and westward, somewhat parallel to the Zarafshan, toward the Bukharan oasis but again disappearing before reaching it. The Kashka Darya has, in turn, nourished historical places such as the Timurid Shahrisabz (Kesh) and Mongol Karshi (Nasaf). In cumulative effect, through the combination of pockets of great fertility (oases) created by the Oxus, the Jaxartes, the Zarafshan, and their smaller tributaries, Transoxiana was a fertile and important region—a literal gateway, bridge, and bottleneck—that led to the three fascinating worlds beyond: Greater Eurasia, China, and India.

In addition to demarcating the southern limit of Transoxiana, historically the Oxus River also represented a strong physical border separating Iran from Central Asia; this was a point of concern for all those who desired to cross to the other side, including Alexander the Great, the Sasanian monarchs, the Turks and Arabs, and even the units of the Red Army during the early nineteenth century. It is from this river that the entire surrounding tract, extending from the Amu to the Syr Darya (the Oxus to the Jaxartes), appears to have received its name. It was recorded by Darius in his inscriptions as Sugdam or Sugda, with the Avestan and Greek equivalents as Sughdha or Sogdiana. Likewise, the people who inhabited the area came to be known as the Sogdians, whereas the Zarafshan River itself came to be called the Soghd.

The Sogdians had resided in Transoxiana for several centuries before the Arab conquests. They spoke an Iranian tongue, because Sogdia, like much of Central Asia before these invasions, was an Iranian-speaking region. Although their language (called Sogdian by some scholars) is now extinct, scholars believe that traces of the rich Sogdian culture still survive in the toponomy of the several towns in the region, whose names end in -kent, -kand, -kat, or other variants of this Iranian word, which means "town." Appropriate examples are Penjikent, Uzgend, Samarqand, Numijkat (the original name for Bukhara), Tashkent, and Yarkand. In addition, a sizable component of the population of certain pockets of Central Asia still speaks Iranian or speaks both Iranian and Turkic (although some time after the Islamic conquest a shift occurred from Sogdian to Farsi, the language of Fars, a province in southern Persia, which developed into modern Persian). That the Sogdian culture was still intact in the tenth century and to some degree assimilated into the practices and beliefs of Islam is attested to by the accounts of contemporary Muslim geographers who called the country (Sogdiana) the Bilad al-Sughd (Land of the Sogdians) and the Zarafshan river the Wadi al-Sughd (Sogd river). As mentioned earlier, the Arabs used the term Mawarannahr ("that which is beyond the river [Jayhun]"), for the region of Transoxania, also following the same psycholinguistic process. Employing the Syr Darya as a demarcation line marking the northern limit of Transoxania, all of the land that lay outside of this domain was the Turkestan or the Bilad al-Turk—the abode of the Turkic nomads.

If Transoxiana was the geographical and cultural core of Central Asia, then southeast of it lay the historical territory of Bactria, home to a sophisticated urban culture, including several urban foundations established by Alexander the Great. Of these, most prominent was the capital of ancient Bactria (the Balkh of early Islamic centuries), which flourished as an important urban center until its destruction by the Mongols in 1221, briefly recovering only to yield primacy to the funerary sanctuary of Mazar-i Sharif. Today Bactria corresponds to northern Afghanistan, southern Tajikistan, and southeastern Uzbekistan and Turkmenistan.

Northwest of Transoxiana and bordering the Aral Sea lay Khwarazm, comprising the lowermost course of the Amu Darya and its sprawling delta estuary fringing the southern shore of the Aral Sea. Khwarazm had since ancient times been home to a flourishing agricultural and urban civilization, typically Iranian in style and character. Medieval Khwarazm functioned as an important commercial link between Eurasia, the Middle East, and Russia, controlling the most important trade routes between the three worlds and stimulated by the Islamization of Central Asia and the rise of Urgench as the chief city in the region from the tenth century onward.

Two other regions, Ferghana and Khorasan, which also surrounded Transoxiana, should be mentioned here. The Ferghana Valley, located east of the expanded region of Transoxiana, has been a land of an ancient agricultural civilization, colonized early by Sogdian merchants. Today most of Ferghana lies within the easternmost province of the republic of Uzbekistan, except for fringes shared by neighboring Kyrgystan and Tajikistan. To the south of Transoxiana lies the province of Khorasan. In pre-Islamic and early Islamic times, it comprised a large area, including central Turkmenistan and northwestern Afghanistan and the cities of Nisa, Merv, Nishapur, and Herat. By the Middle Ages, several of these cities lay on the Silk Road's trunk routes linking Sinkiang through Samarqand as well as routes going to Bactria, India, Khwarazm, and Russia. Khorasan was the focus of the Arab invasions before Transoxiana, and, in several ways, it set the stage for sociocultural developments elsewhere.

MANU P. SOBTI

Further Reading

Barthold, Wilhelm. *Turkestan Down to the Mongol Invasion.* London: Porcupine Press, 1928.

Frye, Richard. *The Heritage of Central Asia—From Antiquity to the Turkish Expansion.* Princeton: Markus Wiener Publishers, 1998.

Jacobson, Henry. *An Early History of Sogdiana.* Unpublished Masters thesis. Chicago: University of Chicago, 1935.

Knobloch, Edgar. *Beyond the Oxus: Archeology, Art and Architecture in Central Asia.* London: Ernest Benn Ltd., 1972.

Le Strange, Guy. *The Lands of the Eastern Caliphate.* London: Frank Cass & Co, 1966.

Pumpelly, Richard, ed. *Explorations in Turkestan—Expeditions of 1904,* Vols. 1 and 2. Washington, DC: Carnegie Institution of Washington, 1908.

Soucek, Svat. *A History of Inner Asia.* Cambridge, UK: Cambridge University Press, 2000.

Tucker, Jonathan. *The Silk Road: Art and History.* Chicago: Art Media Resources, 2003.

TRAVEL

By 750 CE, the era of the conquerors and empire builders was over in Islam. A new historical figure, as mobile but more peaceful, began to roam around: the traveler. A multifaceted figure, he may have been a merchant, a scholar, an ambassador, a missionary, or an adventurer. To this, one must add the ritual wanderer, such as the mystic. This new figure was a creation of the cities. He was a city dweller, either by choice or by origin, and, when the city was not his starting point, it became his horizon.

One traveled in the medieval Muslim world by foot or by horse, individually or collectively, by caravan as well as by boat. Some of these medieval travelers seem like true athletes. After finishing their "grand tour" *(jawla)*, they earned—deservedly—the name of "tourist" *(jawwâl)*. Such travelers did not hesitate to seek out physical challenges even if it meant risking their lives. The Iranian Abû Hâtim from Rayy (died AH 277/890 CE), who was destined to a prestigious career as transmitter of hadith, is one such example. In the travelogue transmitted by his son, he narrates: "The first time I traveled, I did it for seven years. I walked for more than one thousand parasangs [5700 kilometers] before I stopped counting. After I left Bahrayn, I walked to Egypt, from which I left on foot to Syria [...]. I did all this when I was not yet twenty years old." One of his contemporaries, an Andalusian who had accomplished a grand tour under the same circumstances, was also proud to repeat to anyone who cared to hear, "All the masters toward whom I traveled, I went to meet them on foot." Touring the central lands of Islam, the Persian philosopher poet Nâsir-î Khusrû reached Jerusalem in 1047, accompanied by his brother and a young slave via the caravan of Hârran. From the third of all holy places of Islam, he decided to go to the first two and undertook the trip on foot in the company of other travelers who shared the same resolve. The group's guide was "an energetic man, good walker, and with an agreeable physiognomy." (Safar-nâma, 106). The trip to Mecca took thirteen days. The Persian scholar seems to have undertaken this walking journey as a challenge. This was not always the case for him or for the other trekkers mentioned earlier. When the same scholar set out to travel by foot across the Arabian Peninsula to go to Basra, that was because he had no other choice; he and his brother did not have enough means to rent two camels. After having paid the guide who was to lead them, they could only afford to pay for one camel: "the Bedouin loaded my books on the camel that my brother would ride, and as for me, I followed on foot" (223). To cover more than eighteen hundred kilometers under such conditions could only make the crossing of desert lands, already perilous in itself, only more arduous: "When we reached Basra, we were in such a state of destitution and misery that we looked like madmen; we had not untied our hair for three months. Who would let us into a bath in the state we were in?" (237).

In vast territories, such as those of Islam, that are covered by some of the world's largest deserts and vast steppes, the camel is the best means of transportation. Travelers who do not depart alone or within a small group travel with a caravan. The caravan is indeed the surest link between cities. Like a city in motion, the caravan has its own emir to guide and manage it and its own troop to protect it, especially against robbers. According to Nâsir-i Khusrû, during the mid-eleventh century, the caravan that left from Cairo for the great pilgrimage (hajj) required so many soldiers that the daily expense to cover their needs and fodder was one thousand Maghribi dinars, not including the twenty dinars spent for each soldier's pay. Multiply these daily thousands of dinars by the twenty-five days it took to reach one's destination (and as many to return), add sixty thousand dinars to cover provisions for pilgrims and travelers, and it becomes clear that a caravan is a vast economic undertaking before being a means of transporting goods from one town to another or from one country to another.

One did not only travel by land, but also by sea. The traveler at times had to use a ship to go from one point to another, although it was the most feared means of transportation. The medieval Muslim world was a land-loving one that kept its back turned to the sea for most of the time. Only a few regions had established maritime traditions, including the Persian Gulf and the Gulf of Aden (al-Andalus). Everywhere else, the thought of crossing the sea conjured up images of terror and the throes of a horrible death. The great Iraqi traveler and encyclopedist, Mas'ûdî (d. 345/956) experienced it firsthand with sailors from Oman during his crossing of the Gulf of Aden on his way to Zanzibar: "I sailed on this sea leaving Sinjâr, capital of Oman, in the company of Sirafian captains [from Sîrâf, the main harbor of the Persian Gulf], including Muh. B. Zaydabûd and Jawhar b. Ahmad, also called Ibn Sîra—who later perished with his entire crew. My last sea crossing, going from the island of Qanbalû [Zanzibar] to Oman, goes back to 304/916. I was on board a ship owned by Ahmad and 'Abd'l-Samad b. Ja'far al-Sîrâfî [...]. These two brothers later disappeared body and soul in the very same sea [...]. I may have sailed on many a sea, the China Sea, the Mediterranean Sea, the Caspian Sea, the Red Sea, and the Sea of Yemen, yet I have known none more perilous than this Sea of Zanzibar" (*The Meadows of Gold*, I, 94). All those who encountered the fortune of the sea said the same thing about their own place of peril. Thus, the other great traveler of the year 1000, the Palestinian geographer Muqaddasî, said it about the Mediterranean Sea in more apocalyptic terms: "It is a difficult, tumultuous sea that continually roars, especially during the night of [Thursday to] Friday." That is because it was thought that the sea was hostile toward Muslims. This revolt from the sea of the infidels can be explained by the following tradition: "[...] When He created the sea of Shâm (Syria), God made this revelation: 'I created you, and I will hand you over my servants who, wishing to obtain some favor, will say "Glory be to God!" or "God is Holy!" or "God is great!" or "there is no other divinity but God!" 'How will you treat them?'—'Well, Lord, answered the sea, I will drown them!'—'Away from me! In truth I curse you! I will make you less beautiful and less bountiful!'" (*Ahsan al-Taqâsîm*, 43). All of the medieval travelers who have left behind tales of their "going into the sea" have compared it to a cemetery (or, more exactly, to a coffin) from which they miraculously escaped. Yet, despite all of the dread and terror (for one must add to the misdeeds of nature those of men, especially of pirates who hounded each and every sea), the travelers did not hesitate to board a ship; they had little choice if they wanted to go to India or China for commercial reasons. At times they did not hesitate to board infidel ships, as did the Andalusian Ibn Jubayr (d. 614/1217) to go on a pilgrimage to Mecca. The ulemas from al-Andalus had endorsed traveling on board of Christian ships as early as the eleventh century, although one could have gone from al-Andalus to the Orient by way of land, through the Maghreb. The reading of al-Bakrî's (d. 487/1094) *Description,* however, shows the chronic insecurity that ruled over itineraries such as those linking the Maghreb to Egypt, making it clear why the Andalusian geographer's compatriots saw traveling by sea—even aboard infidel ships—as a lesser evil.

This information about traveling during medieval times comes via writings composed mostly by the travelers themselves, especially the most learned ones. The latter, however, took a long time before deciding to write down their travel experiences. This attitude would not change until the end of the ninth century, even if the oldest travel description goes back to 851, it being the work of an Iraqi merchant who was familiar with India and China.

Why is it that the scholars of the eighth and ninth centuries, who traveled often and extensively, did not think of putting their experiences down in writing? One theory is that they did not think that the story was the prime condition of the trip. To travel and to write about it is a motion that took time to develop in Islam. Nonetheless, a look at the great traveling scholars of the ninth century shows that their travel accounts were heavily circulated within their own milieu. A chain of learned solidarity perpetuated the travelers' oral souvenirs from mouth to ear. Here and there, an attempt at literalizing oral narratives was made. Still tentative, this literary shaping borrowed its narrative expression from the khabar. Thus, the Iraqi Abû Khuzayma (d. 243/857) was able to preserve in his *Book of Science* fragments of the travel account from one of the first—if not *the* first—peripatetic scholars of Islam, Mak'hûl (d. 112/730). He had obtained the account from one of his Syrian masters, who himself had acquired it from a direct disciple of the traveler who had died in Syria (this is factually known). Other travel accounts were obtained in a similar fashion, by trusting the scholarly memory or even the family memory.

The travel khabar offers the dual characteristic of being, in its organizing principle, a reported and fragmented narrative in which the author–transmitter is not confused with the traveler–narrator. Because it is in bits and pieces, it must dramatize in a few words or sentences the entire arc of a trip; it therefore must be a story worth telling. To achieve this, it must stir strong emotional feelings that will make up for its fragmentary aspect. Where can such emotions be found? In the realm of the extraordinary and the wonderful. In the same way that the 'aj'ib (wonders), which were part of the Islamic knowledge, had been feeding the instructive as well as the entertaining literature since the ninth century, the travel khabar ran into their writing since its inception. Moreover, many travel accounts of this type are 'ajâ'ib (tales of wonder). The 'ajâ'ib found a place in the travel account as processes of the similar and dissimilar rhetoric, because they act as translators of the difference. As figures of the extraordinary, however, they do not imply that one leaves the space of Islam to go experience them and then recover them through travel writing. Similarly, the ancient Greeks did not have to leave their cultural world to go meet with the *thoma* (the wonder-curiosity), nor did the men of the medieval western world to go discover the *mirabilia.* Thus, it is understandable that a travel account that does not include any 'ajâ'ib is not really a travel account. The medieval Muslim reader always expects from the person who is relating his travels that he will tell about what he has seen and/or heard that was the most ajîb—the most curious, the most extraordinary, the most wonderful. Thus, the pseudo-Shâfi'i tells in his travel story—a work from the tenth century—about his having seen in Yemen conjoined twin sisters united within "the one body of a normal woman who, instead of having one trunk, had two distinct ones, with four hands, two heads, and two faces." After one died, "[her body] was solidly tied, from the top to the bottom, with a rope and thus kept until it rotted away; after which it was cut and buried." As for the "body left alive," she kept on "coming and going through the souks."

By the end of the ninth century, the travel account still had not found a stable and lasting literary frame. It would borrow that of the epistle, a literary genre that appeared toward the mid-eighth century and that would be its host for about two centuries. Unfortunately, the most ancient travel epistles are known to us only through allusions, citations, or fragments snatched out of oblivion and waste by the hazards of the compilation. For example, the epistle written by an Andalusian scholar at the turn of the ninth and tenth century is known only because mention is made of it in the biographical dictionaries of the Muslim west. Of its contents, only one recommendation survived from the writer who had endured many hardships away from his country and that he transmitted to his fictional, or real, addressee: never undertake a long trip! The epistle by a Hamadhan judge from the Seljuq era is also known as a result of a biographical dictionary compiled during the twelfth century. Written in 1040, this epistle allowed its writer to depict what he saw, such as the great mosque of Damascus, and the men he met. Fortunately, some travel epistles have reached us in their entirety. One of them is the epistle that the physician Ibn Butlân (d. ca. 455/1063), a Christian from Iraq, devoted to describing his itinerary from Baghdad to Cairo. Most of these travel epistles articulate their writing around what was seen and heard. The two epistles from Abû Dulaf, who traveled across India and China around 942, are the most representative of this writing with the eyes. An entire trend of travel epistle, however, kept on rendering, as was done in the ninth century, what the traveler–writer had heard. One representative epistle of this trend is that of Ibn 'Abbâd (d. 385/995) to a scholar from his hometown of Rayy, destined as he was to a political career as a vizier. During a studying trip to Baghdad around 958, the young Ibn 'Abbâd frequented the intellectual circles and the literary salons of the 'Abbâsid capital. This epistle did not survive in its entirety, but its literary success was such that a contemporary succeeded in reconstituting it by reassembling most of its membra dijecta.

When back home in Seville, after his return from the Orient, Abû Bakr b. al-'Arabî (d. 534/1148) wrote a rihla (account) and thus started a revolution in travel writing at the dawn of the twelfth century. Born four centuries earlier, the rihla, which had been sheltered until then by the inventory of masters (mashyaka or fahrasa), the biographical dictionary (tabaqât), the epistolary narrative (risâla), and the diary (rûznâmja), could finally abandon them and move into a genre in its own name: that of the travel rihla. From then on, the way is paved for the great travel narratives in which the Muslims of the Muslim west would more than excel, from Ibn Jubayr (d. 614/1217) to Ibn Battûta (d. ca. 770/1368).

HOUARI TOUATI

Further Reading

Bulliet, R. *The Camel and the Wheel*. Cambridge, Mass: Harvard University Press, 1975.
Charles-Dominique, P. *Voyageurs Arabes: Ibn Fadlân, Ibn Jubayr, Ibn Battûta et un Auteur Anonyme*. Paris, 1995.
Eikelmann, D., and Piscatori, J. *Muslim Travellers: Pilgrimage, Migration, and the Religious Imagination*. Berkeley and Los Angeles, 1990.
Fernand, G. *Relations de Voyages et Textes Géographiques Arabes, Persans et Turcs Relatifs à l'Extrême-Orient, du VIIIe au XVIIIe Siècle*, 2 vols. Paris, 1913–1914. (Reprint, Frankfurt: F. Sezgin, 1996.)
Goitien, S.D. *A Mediterranean Society: The Jewish Communities of the Arab World as Portrayed in the Documents of the Cairo Geniza*, 5 vols. Berkeley, 1967–1986.
Hadj-Sadok, M. "Le Genre de la *Rihla*." *Bulletin des Études Arabes* 40 (1948): 196–206.
Kratchkovskii, I.J. *Arabskaïa Geografitcheskaïa Literatura*, 3 vols. Moscou-Leningrad, 1957.
M'Ghirbi, S. *Les Voyageurs de l'Occident Musulman du XIIe au XIVe Siècle*. Tunis, 1996.
Miquel, A. *La Géographie Humaine du Monde Musulman Jusqu'au Milieu du XIe Siècle*, 4 vols. Paris, 1967–1975.
Netton, I.R. *Thought and Travel in the House of Islam*. Richmond, Va, 1996.
Netton, J.R., ed. *Golden Roads. Migration, Pilgrimage, and Travel in Medieval and Moderne Islam*. London, 1993.
Picard, Ch. *La Mer et les Musulmans d'Occident au Moyen Age*. Paris, 1997.
Sâlih al-Dîn and 'U. Hâshim. *Târîkh al-Adab al-Jughrâfî*, 3 vols. Beirut, 1987.
Touati, H. *Islam et Voyage au Moyen Age*. Paris, 2000.
Udovitch, A. "Time, the Sea and Society: Durations of Commercial Voyagers on the Southern Shores of the Mediterranean During High Middle Ages." *Princeton Near Eastern Papers* 31 (1981): 503–63.

TRIBES AND TRIBAL CUSTOMS

Tribal societies have played a continuous and crucial role in shaping Islamic civilization. Not only did

Islam first emerge among the tribal societies of the Arabian peninsula, but also, among others, Berber tribes in North Africa and Turkic tribes from Central Eurasia were instrumental in the founding of important medieval empires. The term *tribe* generally refers to a group or sociopolitical organization claiming descent from a common ancestor and sharing common values, customs, and a sense of identity and solidarity. In medieval Arabic and Persian historical texts, one finds the terms *qawm* and *qabila* frequently used to refer to such groups; the terms *il* and *oymak* are similarly used in Turkic Muslim texts. Anthropologists and historians use the term *tribe* to refer to a diverse variety of social organizations. Although this term is generally associated with nomads, not all tribes were nomadic, and not all nomads were tribal. Furthermore, whether nomadic, semi-nomadic or settled, tribes maintained strong connections with urban areas. For example, Arab tribes participated in trade with the Roman and Sasanian Empires, and Central Asian nomads engaged in long-distance trade along the Eurasian land route.

Despite their diversity, tribal societies share certain common characteristics. Chief among these is a belief in a common line of descent, whether fictional or real. In tribal societies, lineage functioned as a crucial source of identity and a focus of loyalty; kinship ties were political ties. In most tribal societies, wealth was acquired for distribution rather than accumulation. One's position within a tribe was not determined by how much one owned but rather by how much one shared. Wealth was more a source of tribal solidarity than a source of authority. Despite a tendency toward decentralization and egalitarianism, it should be noted that some tribes were more centralized and hierarchical than others and that, over time, tribal societies adapted to changing political and economic circumstances. Tribal nomadic societies maintained rich traditions of oral literature in the form of poetry and epics. Such literature functioned to strengthen kinship ties and provide legitimation for a tribe's social and religious identity. For example, in Central Asia, the common ancestor of the tribe was often recast as the bringer of Islam after the tribe's conversion.

From its inception, there was a close connection and interaction between tribal society and Islam. In the seventh century CE, the Arabian peninsula was largely populated by Arabic-speaking peoples organized into tribes that were themselves composed of smaller clans. Clan loyalty was the paramount principle by which society was organized. Arab tribal society was relatively decentralized, lacking authoritarian structures like jails and courts. Order was maintained largely by familial pressure and, when necessary, blood wit. However, as a result of involvement in global trade, there was an influx of wealth, which led to sedentarization and urbanization, particularly in Mecca, which resulted in increasing economic stratification. Islam arose as an explicit challenge and alternative to an increasingly anachronistic and unwieldy tribal system. Converts to Islam gave allegiance to the Prophet Muhammad and the *ummah* (Muslim community). As a member of the ummah, devotion and allegiance to one God and Islam were to become one's primary source of identity, transcending any existing tribal loyalties.

However, although Islam tended to weaken or subordinate tribal identity, it also incorporated tribal values and customs. The Prophet's success was due in part to his effectiveness within the tribal system. The Prophet Muhammad was born into the respected clan of Banu Hashim of the dominant Meccan tribe, the Quraysh. His lineage provided him protection, especially in the form of support from his uncle Abu Talib, the leader of Banu Hashim. As a young man, Muhammad gained a reputation as a mediator of tribal disputes, earning him the title of al-Amin (the trustworthy). He exemplified the tribal virtues of hospitality, forbearance, and courage, all of which were incorporated into Islam. Even the central religious ritual of the polytheistic Arabs, the Hajj, was ultimately Islamicized. Furthermore, the early Islamic state did not eradicate tribal institutions; initially it brought non-Arabs into the Islamic polity by incorporating them as clients of Arab tribes. Additionally, many of the early conflicts in Islam were rooted in lingering tribal animosities.

Although the earliest Islamic empires were founded by Arabs, from the tenth century onward, Turkic and Turco-Mongolian tribes dominated the political life of Islamic civilization, especially in Eurasia. By the end of the tenth century, the Qarluk tribal union established their regime in Transoxiana, whereas the Oghuz tribal union under the leadership of the Seljuk family established the Seljuk dynasty in Iran and Khurasan during the eleventh century. Another Seljuk dynasty was also established in Anatolia, which was succeeded by the Turkic Ottoman Empire. Similarly, the Safavid Empire in Iran and the Mughal Empire in India were originally founded by members of Turkic tribes.

The Turkic and Turco-Mongol tribes of Central Asia during the medieval period were mainly pastoral, nomadic, or semi-nomadic in background. They were organized into families, clans, and tribes, with each clan claiming descent from a common ancestor. The fifteenth-century *Book of Dede Korkut* consists of earlier oral stories produced by the nomadic Oghuz Turkic tribes, and it provides a vivid description of their tribal life and customs. In *Dede Korkut,* it is demonstrated that social hierarchies were reflected not in material terms but rather in ideological ones. In other words, one's lineage was the primary indicator of one's status within the tribe. Certain individual qualities such as generosity and military prowess were also sources of authority and status. Tribal leadership emerged from the most prestigious clans. The elders of the tribe stood as arbiters and mediators among the different members or subdivisions within a tribe or among tribes, and their authority depended more on consensus than coercion. Women also had authority and status based on their lineage and played important roles in family and tribal affairs.

Although the political structures of these dynasties initially reflected their tribal backgrounds, once established, they had to deal with the centrifugal tendencies of the tribes from which they came. In Central Asia, for example, the tension and conflict between the ruling khan who represented central state authority and the begs who were the local tribal leaders was crucial. Islamic institutions played an important role in facilitating the sedentarization of nomadic tribes and integrating tribes into the state. Rulers increasingly used Islam to legitimize their authority and to transcend the limitations placed on their power by the decentralizing tendencies of the tribal system. They thus gave increasing attention to Islamic institutions by supporting the Islamic scholars, establishing Islamic schools, constructing Sufi tombs, and seeking the support of the Sufi elite. This balancing act between tribal and Islamic sources of authority in many ways defined the political culture of Eurasian Islam during the medieval period.

NURTEN KILIC-SCHUBEL

See also Epics, Turkish; Nomadism and Pastoralism; Safavids; Trade; Transoxiana; Turkish and Turkic; Turks

Further Reading

Barfield, Thomas J. *The Nomadic Alternative.* Englewood Cliffs, NJ: Prentice Hall, 1993.
DeWeese, Devin. *Islamization and Native Religion in the Golden Horde.* University Park, Penn: The Pennsylvania State University Press, 1994.
Donner, Fred W. *The Early Islamic Conquests.* Princeton, NJ: Princeton University Press, 1981.
Khoury, Philip S., ed. *Tribes and State Formation in the Middle East.* London: Tauris, 1991.
Manz, Beatrice F. *The Rise and Rule of Tamerlane.* Cambridge, UK: Cambridge University Press, 1989.
Togan, Isenbike. *Flexibility and Limitation in Steppe Formation.* Leiden: Brill, 1998.
The Book of Dede Korkut, transl. Geoffrey Lewis. London: Penguin Books, 1974.

TULUNIDS

The Tulunids were a semi-autonomous Turkish dynasty that ruled Egypt and Syria from approximately 868 to 905 CE. These rulers served officially as 'Abbasid governors but, in fact, wielded broad authority and sometimes came in conflict with the caliphs whom they claimed to serve. They followed in this manner the example of other semi-independent families of governors, such as the Aghlabids and the Tahirids, who previously ruled in North Africa and Khurasan, respectively.

Ibn Tulun, the founder of this dynasty, came to Egypt in 868 as part of the entourage of his stepfather Bakbak, the 'Abbasid governor of Egypt. He survived the assassination of his stepfather and outmaneuvered his rivals shortly afterward to gain control of the province. He took advantage of disturbances in Syria to create a powerful personal army and campaigns against the Byzantines to extend his authority eastward. His administrative skill, moreover, established firm foundations for his successors at the time of his death in 884.

Ibn Tulun's son, Khumarawayh, who succeeded him, was able to extend the dynasty's dominions to include the Jazira. However, a reinvigorated 'Abbasid caliphate, internal dissension among his ministers, and financial exhaustion undermined his military achievements. Khumarawayh was assassinated in 896, as was his son and successor, Jaysh. Another son, Harun, ruled until 905. The 'Abbasids shortly afterward seized control.

The Tulunids mark the rise of non-Arab groups to power in the Near East and, in particular, a Turkish military elite in Egypt. The family descended from a military slave who served at the court of al-Ma'mun. Turkish military slaves were not only renowned for their fighting skills but were considered very loyal. They owed their position and privileges entirely to the caliph. They lacked the ties of kinship that divided the sympathies of Arabs and Persians.

The decline of the 'Abbasid caliphate allowed the Tulunids to establish themselves. Intrigue at the court, revolts of the Zanj in southern Iraq and the Saffarids in eastern Iran, and general financial exhaustion during this period dissipated the caliphate's energy. Ministers and generals often intervened in caliphal succession by supporting weak candidates for the benefit of their interests. Caliph al-Mu'tamid's brother, al-Muqaffaq, emerged as the predominant force behind the caliph in the 870s, but he remained preoccupied with suppressing the Zanj until the 880s.

The Tulunids posed a fundamental problem for the legitimation of government. Originally protégés of the caliph, they lacked an ethnic and ideological constituency upon which they could draw immediate support. They countered this weakness by maintaining nominal allegiance to the caliph in Baghdad, allying themselves carefully with local commercial and religious interests and recruiting slave soldiers. They inscribed the name of the caliph on their coinage, appointed important Egyptians to ministerial posts and consulted others, and bought large numbers of Sudanese slaves. In addition, they promoted campaigns against Byzantiun under the auspices of holy war against the infidel.

The quickness with which the Tulunids succumbed to 'Abbasid forces probably resulted from their inherent political weakness. However, although the 'Abbasids eventually recovered and reestablished their authority over Egypt and Syria, the precedent of the Tulunids remained for a later Turkish dynasty of semi-independent governors, the Ikhshidids, who came to power in Egypt in 935.

Egypt and the Levant appear to have prospered under the Tulunids. It has been suggested that this prosperity reflected the expenditure of taxes locally rather than their remittance to Baghdad. Ibn Tulun established an efficient bureaucracy that earned the respect of local Arabs. He also established a new quarter near Fustat, where he erected a famous congregational mosque that still stands today.

STEPHEN D. SEARS

See also Ibn Tulun

Further Reading

al-Balawi. *Sirat Ahmad ibn Tulun*, ed. Kurd 'Ali. Cairo.
Gordon, M.S. "Tûlûnids." In *The Encyclopedia of Islam*, 2nd ed., vol. X., 616–8. Leiden: E.J. Brill, 1999.
Hassan, Z.M. *Les Tulunides*. Paris, 1937.
Ibn Sa'id al-Andalusi. *Kitab al-Mughrib fi Hula al-Maghrib*, ed. K.L. Tallquist. Leiden, 1899.
———. *al-Mukâfa'a*. Cairo, 1941.
Kennedy, H. *The Prophet and the Age of the Caliphates*, 309–13. London and New York, 1986.
Randa, E.W. *The Tulûnid Dynasty*. PhD dissertation. University of Utah, 1990.
al-Tabari. *Ta'rikh al-Umam wa-l-Muluk*. Cairo, 1962.

TURKISH AND TURKIC LANGUAGES

Modern Turkish and its predecessor, Ottoman Turkish, belong to the Turkic language family, the speakers of which were and are spread over a wide area of Europe and Asia (Eurasia). Those areas and the Turkic languages spoken in those areas are Turkish and Azeri in the Middle East; Turkmen, Uzbek, Uygur, Kazak, and Kirgiz in Central Asia; Altay, Khakas, Tuvan, and Yakut in Siberia; and Tatar,

Bashkir, Chuvash, and various Turkic dialects like Gagauz in East Europe. Some of these Turkic peoples are the dominant population in their own independent countries, including the Republic of Turkey and the Turkic Republics of Central Asia, and others have their own autonomous regions within Russia and China. Other countries with substantial Turkic-speaking populations include Afghanistan, Iran, Iraq, Bulgaria, and Greece. The total number of speakers within this family may be estimated at between 150 and 170 million, with Turkish speakers making up by far the largest group of about 70 million.

According to the famous Turcologist Wilhelm Radloff, there is no other language family in the world with the same geographical magnitude as the Turkic languages. Despite the immense number of Turkic languages and dialects spread out all over the word, the linguistic difference between these languages is quite amazingly minimal, with the exception of Yakut and Chuvash. For a long time, scholars have been trying to classify the Turkic languages to no avail, because no single classification has yet been agreed on. The difficulty comes from the fact that a tremendous amount of work still needs to be done with regard to collecting and interpreting data from these languages, some of which have only recently been discovered. In addition, vastly different political concerns over the course of time have left their own mark on these efforts as well. For example, a great majority of Turcologists from Turkey still insist on a single Turkic language with numerous "dialects," with Turkish being the "Turkic of Turkey." This argument in many cases evokes an ultra-nationalist and expansionist ideology suggesting the existence of a so-called "Turkic world." In reality, despite the linguistic proximity, the speakers of the Turkic languages of the world enjoy a great diversity of history, cultures, and traditions, and they rarely identify themselves as "Turks" but rather as Tatars, Uzbeks, Kazaks, Azeris, and the like.

Despite the tremendous difficulty of classifying Turkic languages and dialects, one may consider the following picture in future attempts of classification: Turkish and the closely related Azeri and Turkmen form the Oguz group of Turkic languages. The ancestors of those who speak these languages migrated from Central Asia into the Near East beginning in the first half of the eleventh century. By 1300 CE or so, the Osman clan of the tribes had laid the foundation of what would become the Ottoman State (1299–1923). The other Turkic languages fall into several historical and linguistic groups: Karluk (Uzbek, Uygur); Kipchak (Kazak, Kirgiz, Tatar, Bashkir); Uygur (Tuvan, Yakut); and the entirely separate branch of Turkic, Ogur (Bulgar, Khazar), which is represented by the modern Chuvash.

Beginning already during the eighth century, before Turks had migrated out of East Asia and into Central Asia, several literary languages were formed. The first of these was written in the so-called Runic script and survives in a number of stone inscriptions from Mongolia and South Siberia and also in manuscripts discovered in Western China (modern Xinjiang). During the same period, a distinct literary language called Uygur took shape in the Turfan area of modern Xinjiang. That language was written in Runic, Uygur, Manichaean, and Brahmi scripts. From this language survive texts dealing with the Manichaean, Nestorian, and Buddhist religions as well as with civil and economic affairs, dating from the eighth century up to the fourteenth century, and in some areas into the eighteenth century. Meanwhile, to the west in Central Asia starting in the eleventh century, a related literary language arose. Written in Arabic script, this language came to be called Chagatay and was used by Muslim Turks not only of Central Asia but in a variant form in the Crimea and Volga regions until the twentieth century. After many of these Turkic areas were incorporated into the Soviet Union, their spoken languages became bases of national languages written first in Latin, then in Cyrillic, and today mostly in Latin alphabets again. In the case of the Uygurs of China, the literary language is written in a highly modified Arabic script.

The formation of the Turkish literary language in Anatolia (known as Old Anatolian Turkish) goes back to approximately the thirteenth century, although some so-called "mixed-language" manuscripts belong to even earlier centuries. The construction and development of written Turkish in Anatolia cannot possibly be identified and studied without dealing with perhaps the most significant cultural and political change in Turkish history: the acceptance and proliferation of Islam. Institutionalized Islam not only brought a brand new belief system and sedentary social norms to the Turkish-speaking authors but also greatly reshaped the lexical and philosophical vocabulary of their language. After converting to and/or embracing Islam (beginning approximately toward the end of the ninth century), an educated minority of the Turkish-speaking population began to develop a literary language that was enhanced with a compelling amount of borrowings from the Arabic and Persian languages. The construction process of the Old Anatolian Turkish literary language also necessitated the adaptation of the Arabic script. The infiltration of the Arabic script into the writing of Turkish was a religious, cultural, and ideological constraint. The place of the Arabic script in Turkish literary history is undoubtedly most significant, given the fact that, up until 1928, almost every single Turkish book was composed in it. Nonetheless, although the Arabic alphabet was only one among more than a dozen documented writing systems used in scripting Turkic languages throughout the centuries, it was perhaps the most unsuitable of all of them. The script was incapable of representing the phonetic needs of the Turkish language. Although a similar argument later became the foundation for the modernist revolution in Turkey, which successfully replaced the Arabic script with a new Roman-based alphabet, there is little or no doubt among linguists that the modern Turkish writing system is by far much easier to learn, more practical, and more democratic. One can argue that the use of the Arabic alphabet constituted one of the fundamental reasons for the mostly illiterate population of the Ottoman Empire. During its six hundred year lifespan, the Ottoman Empire had a very low literacy rate, due in part to the "holy script" with which no more than thirty thousand books were ever printed. It should be remembered that the literary products of the Ottoman elite were transmitted through manuscripts, and, generally speaking, only those who could afford to possess them had access to the classical works in writing.

By the end of the fifteenth century, Old Anatolian Turkish was already a refined literary language. Beginning with the sixteenth century, what is usually called Ottoman Turkish or Classical Ottoman became the Latin of the Turks. Classical Ottoman was not only a peculiar combination of the Arabic, Persian, and Turkish literary lexicons but of a particular grammatical system as well. In some cases, it manifested itself as a mixture of Arabic and Persian words that were constructed according to the Turkish language syntax. It was not used by the common (and, for the most part, illiterate) people, and it survived for hundreds of years as the symbol of the cultivated, learned, and literary members of the glorious Ottoman court. By the end of the seventeenth century, classical Ottoman authors began showing a conscious interest in the Turkification and localization of Ottoman Turkish for use in their otherwise courtly works. Especially during the eighteenth century, developments in this regard were highly significant. The spoken language (and, in some cases, the written language as manifested in thousands of surviving folk manuscripts) of the vast majority of the Turkish-speaking populations in Anatolia was vastly different. However, it should also be mentioned that, since the 1980s, postmodern scholarship on the subject and proponents of various political positions—particularly the Islamist one—have been engaging in a rather different argument regarding this linguistic and literary dichotomy, basically interpreting it as the "invention" of the modernist ideology of the early twentieth century.

KEMAL SILAY

Further Reading

Johanson, Lars, and Csato, Eva, eds. *The Turkic Languages.* London: Routledge, 1998.
Lewis, Geoffrey. *The Turkish Language Reform: A Catastrophic Success.* Oxford, UK: Oxford University Press, 1999.

TURKS

The name *Turks* generally applied to various Turkic-speaking peoples living between Eastern/Chinese Turkistan (Sinkiang) and the Balkans. The first mention of the ethnonym *Turk* may date from Herodotus' (c. 484–425 BCE) reference to Targitas (IV.5), the first king of the Scythians, or to the Iyrcai people (IV.22). During the first century CE, Pomponius Mela refers to the Turcae (I.116) in the forests north of the Sea of Azov, and Pliny the Elder (*Natural History*, VI.19) lists the Tyrcae among the people of the same area. The first definite references to the Turks come mainly from Chinese sources in the sixth century. In these sources, *Turk* appears as *T'u-chüeh* and referred to a diverse group of nomadic Turkic speakers who lived north and west of Chinese territory.

Seventh-century Chinese sources preserve the earliest legends of the origins of the Turks, saying that they were a branch of the Hsiung-nu (Huns) and living near the "West Sea" (perhaps the Caspian) or that they were from the country north of the Hsiung-nu, were descended from a man born of a wolf, and first came to the Chinese border to trade for silk. Modern research tends to indicate that their ancestors indeed lived within the state of the Hsiung-nu in the Trans-Baikal area and that they later, during the fifth century, migrated to the southern Altay.

The Turks first appear in history in 552 CE, when Bumın established the Turk Empire, a kind of tribal state, that stretched from the northern marches of China west to the Central Asian territories of Sasanid Iran. Eventually, this empire and the Sasanids clashed over control of the silk trade. In the 580s, internal strife resulted in a rift between the Eastern and Western Turks. During the first half of the seventh century, both nominally submitted to Chinese authority. In 682, the Eastern (Gök/Blue) Turks established a new empire in Mongolia and attempted to include the Western Turks, but by 711 the latter had broken away. The heartland of the Western Turks was between the Eastern Karatau Mountains and Jungaria.

The oldest extant Turkish texts, the Orkhon inscriptions found in Mongolia and dating from the mid-eighth century, shed light on these events.

On the eve of the Islamic penetration of their region, the Western Turks were overwhelmingly nomadic but had a strong interest in trade. Most were probably shamanists, whereas others were adherents of Manichaesim, Nestorian Christianity, or, especially, Buddhism. Having destroyed the Sasanian Empire (see Sasanians, Islamic Traditions) in 642, the Muslim Arab armies reached the Oxus (Amu Darya), the traditional border between Iran and Turan, by 674 and began raids into Central Asia. In 751, these armies reached Talas, near modern Dzhambul, where they defeated a Chinese army and firmly established Islam as the major political and cultural force in the area.

Although initiated by the Arabs, the conversion of the Turks to Islam was filtered through Persian and Central Asian Iranian culture. Most Turks converted through the efforts of missionaries, Sufis, and merchants. At the same time, Turks entered the Muslim world proper as slaves, the booty of Arab raids and conquests. Under the Umayyads, most were domestic slaves; under the 'Abbasids, increasing numbers were trained as soldiers. By the ninth century, Turkish commanders were leading the caliphs' Turkish troops into battle, and the caliphs' Turkish guards were making and unmaking the caliphs themselves. As the 'Abbasid caliphate declined, Turkish officers assumed more and more military and political power. They took over or established provincial dynasties with their own corps of Turkish troops. Ibn Tulun (868–884) made himself virtually independent in Egypt and Syria. This process culminated when the Turkish commander Sebuktigin (977–997), who was born a pagan, established the Ghaznavid Sultanate controlling Afghanistan, eastern Iran, and northern India.

Meanwhile, Islam made great strides among the Turks in Central Asia. Around the mid-tenth century, the Qarakhanids, a Turkish dynasty that arose from a tribal confederation in the ninth century and ruled the region from Eastern Turkistan to Transoxania, became, at least nominally, Muslim. They promoted a Turkish cultural consciousness and the first Muslim Turkish literature. Also around the mid-tenth century, a certain Seljuk, the leader of the Oghuz confederation who came from the steppes north of the Caspian and Aral seas, came to Jand on the Jaxartes (Syr Darya). Subsequently, Seljuk and the Oghuz adopted Islam. In 1040, his grandsons Chaghrı; and Toghrıl defeated the Ghaznavids at Dandanqan near Merv, establishing the Seljuk Empire and opening the Middle East to the first massive immigration of Turks.

Henceforth, until the fall of the Ottoman Empire, almost every major ruling dynasty in the Muslim world was to be of Turkish origin.

GARY LEISER

See also Epics, Turkish; Khurasan; Nomadism and Pastoralism; Ottoman Empire; Samanids; Sasanians, Islamic Traditions; Silk Roads; Slavery, Military; Slaves and Slave Trade, Eastern Islamic World

Further Reading

Barthold, W. *Turkestan Down to the Mongol Invasion*, 3rd ed. London: Luzac, 1968.
Bazin, L. et al., "Turks." In *EI²*.
Bosworth, C.E. *The Ghaznavids*, 2nd ed. Beirut: Librairie du Liban, 1973.
———. "Barbarian Incursions: The Coming of the Turks into the Islamic World." In *Islamic Civilization, 950–1150*, ed. D.S. Richards, 1–16. Oxford, UK: Cassirer, 1973.
Gibb, H.A.R. *The Arab Conquests in Central Asia*. New York: AMS Press, 1970.
Golden, Peter B. "The Karakhanids and Early Islam." In *The Cambridge History of Inner Asia*, ed. Denis Sinor, 343–70. Cambridge, UK: Cambridge University Press, 1990.
———. *An Introduction to the History of the Turkic Peoples*. Wiesbaden: Otto Harrassowitz, 1992.
Sinor, Denis. "The Establishment and Dissolution of the Türk Empire." In *The Cambridge History of Inner Asia*, ed. Denis Sinor, 285–316. Cambridge, UK: Cambridge University Press, 1990.

TUS

Tus is the name of a valley district and a town near Mashhad in Khurasan in northeast Iran. Already in pre-Islamic times, several towns existed. In early Islamic times, the main towns were Tabaran, which changed into the later town of Tus, Nawqan, and Radkan. Nawqan was integrated in the growing village of Sanabad, later called Mashhad, and since 203 AH/818 CE the burial place of the eighth Shi'i imam 'Ali al-Rida. The town of Tus was finally destroyed in AH/1389. The waters that supplied it were diverted to Mashhad, which became, in Safavid times (1501–1736), the capital of the district of Tus and of all Khurasan. However, the name of Tus was mentioned still in the seventeenth centuries on Persian astrolabes.

In the sources about Tus, it is not always clear if the authors are speaking about the district or the town. According to the historian al-Baladhuri, the Sasanian governor of Tus invited the Arab governors of the Iraqi towns Kufa and Basra to Khurasan; Tus was then conquered by the latter one. During Arab and Samanid times, Tus was involved in some civil wars but did not constitute a significant local center. The 'Abbasid Caliph Harun ar-Rashid died during one of these uprisings in Sanabad in 193/809, and he was buried near the tomb of imam 'Ali al-Rida. His tomb has vanished but was still mentioned by the traveler Ibn Battuta in the fourteenth century. The main town in Samanid times was Tabaran. The Arab geographer al-Muqaddasi mentioned in 985 its citadel, main mosque, large market, and subterranean water pipes. According to him, the Muslim people were following the Shafi'i rite. Tus was also mentioned by the later geographers like Idrisi (1154), Yaqut (d. 1229) and Ibn Battuta (fourteenth century), who did visit it.

After 995, the district of Tus became part of the Ghaznavid empire, but after 1030 the Turk Seljuks penetrated into it. Tus was conquered in 430/1038–1039, and, in 1072, it was given as a fief to the Seljuq vizier Nizam al-Mulk, who had been born there. During the second half of the twelfth century, Tus was ruled by a local dynasty, the al-Mu'aiyad family. The Mongols arrived in Tus by 1220 and raided it one year later, killing most of the inhabitants. The Mongol governor of Tus, a Buddhist by the name of Kürküz, ordered the rebuilding of the city in 1239.

In 497, the sources mention a Nestorian bishop of Tus and Abarshahr (Nishapur), but, for Islamic times, there is little information available about the plight of Christianity in that district. Only from the Mongol period is there some news about Christians: the future Jerusalem patriarch Yahballaha visited Tus during his travel to Jerusalem in 1278 and was saved by the monks and the bishop in the cloister Mar Sehyon. One year later, the bishop of Tus was ordained as the metropolitan of China. In 1381, Timur came to Tus. After revolts, the town was ravaged completely by the Timurid Miran Shah in 791/1389, and it is said that ten thousand people were killed. Although the town was ordered rebuilt by Shah Rukh in 1405 (and again by Ulugh Bek in 1407), it never did recover, and it was reduced to a small village. This decline was mainly connected with the uprising of Mashhad as a main pilgrim town for the Shi'is.

The district of Tus was the birthplace of the Persian poet Firdausi. In the town of Tus itself, Nizam al-Mulk, the polymath and astronomer Nasir ad-Din at-Tusi, and also the Shi'i scholar Muhammad bin al-Hasan at-Tusi (d. 1065 or 1067) were born.

The district of Tus was producing wheat, stone vessels, mats, and special striped clothes. It was famous for its special trouser bands, which were regarded as well as the most famous Armenian ones. During the thirteenth century, the stone vessels are still mentioned, and Idrisi also mentions mines for turquoise, silver, copper, iron, and rock crystal. Only a few archaeological monuments of the town of Tabaran/Tus survived. The city walls made from mud brick enclose an area of approximately one kilometer across, sporting nine gates and more than a hundred towers. North of the city lies the citadel, with twelve towers, and a castle with nine towers inside.

Within the city walls is the tomb of Firdausi (the modern tomb was constructed during the early twentieth century, during the Pahlavi period), and a monument with a central dome and minor cupolas remained, the so-called Haruniya Mausoleum. Its architectural and stucco decoration style recall the Sultan Sanjar Mausoleum in Merv (built 1157).

GISELA HELMECKE

See also 'Ali al-Rida; Khurasan; Nizam al-Mulk

Further Reading

Minorsky, V., and C.E. Bosworth. "Tus." In *The Encyclopaedia of Islam*, vol. 10, Leiden, 1999.
Pope, Arthur U. *A Survey of Persian Art*, vol. 2, 1072–4; tome 5, plate 380. 1939.
"Haruniya Mausoleum." Available at: http://archnet.org/library/images.

TUSI, AL-, MUHAMMAD IBN HASAN

Muhammad b. al-Hasan al-Tusi, Shaykh al-Ta'ifa (d. AH 460/1067 CE), was a Baghdad-based Twelver Shi'i jurisprudent and compiler of two well-known collections of the imams' traditions, *Tahdhib al-Ahkam (The Rectification of Judgments)* and the later *al-Istibsar fi ma Ukhtulifa Fihi min al-Akhbar (The Consideration on Those Traditions Which are Disputed)*, which, together with al-Kulayni's *al-Kafi* and Ibn Babawayh's *al-Faqih,* have come to be called "the four books" that are the key compilations of the imams' traditions that were compiled after the disappearance of the twelfth imam in 260/873–874.

Despite the tolerance of the Buwayhid regents, during this period Baghdad was experiencing yet another resurgence of Sunni traditionism and, specifically, anti-Shi'i feeling and a wave of Sunni-Shi'i "incidents." At the same time, the small Twelver community itself, one of many contemporary Shi'i groups, was accepting that the Imam's absence (occultation) from the community would be prolonged. Al-Tusi himself had studied with key rationalist and traditionist scholars who, respectively, favored increasingly less and increasingly more reliance on the imams' hadith (tradition) to adjudicate issues of

doctrine and practice in the interim (until the imam's return).

Al-Tusi, through these two hadith collections as well as other key works of theology and fiqh, charted a middle course between these two extremes. In the process, he commenced the process of devolving to the *faqih* (the jurisprudent), whom he postulated as trained in both the rationalist and traditionist sciences, and increasing responsibility for a growing number of the imam's theological and practical duties during the occultation. The latter process culminated in the doctrine of *wilayat al-faqih* (deputy-ship of the jurisprudent) as enunciated by the late Ayatallah Khomeini (d. 1989).

ANDREW J. NEWMAN

See also al-Kulayni; Ibn Babawayh

Further Reading

Momen, Moojan. *An Introduction to Twelver Shi'ism*, 79–80. New Haven, Conn: Yale University Press, 1985.

TUSI, AL-, NASIR AL-DIN (1201–1274 CE)

The continuity of philosophical and scientific inquiry in medieval Islam coupled with the material resources offered to it by official patronage owe much to the role and efforts of the Shi'i philosopher, scientist, and polymath Nasir al-Din al-Tusi during the thirteenth century. He defended Ibn Sina from the criticisms leveled against him from the direction of theology (most notably by Fakhr al-Din al-Razi), he made a significant contribution to the acceptance of metaphysical argumentation and terminology in Twelver Shi'i theology, he brought the ethical tradition of Ibn Miskawayh and the philosophers into the center of Islamic ethical discourse, and he had a lasting effect on the study of the exact sciences in Islam through both his original contributions to mathematics and astronomy and the observatory at Maraghah, which the Mongol Khan Hülegü established for him.

Nasir al-Din Muhammad ibn Muhammad al-Tusi was born in Tus in Khurasan in northwest Iran in 1201 into a Twelver Shi'i learned family. Along with his studies in jurisprudence, he developed an interest in philosophy and was attached to the Nizamiyya madrasa in Nishapur, studying with Farid al-Din Damad al-Nisaburi (d. ca. 1221), a thinker whose philosophical lineage stretched back to Ibn Sina. Damad had been a student of Fakhr al-Din al-Razi as well, and so al-Tusi became acquainted with the ideas of the famous Sunni theologian. The Mongol sack of the city in 1221 forced him to move. He proceeded to Mosul, where he studied mathematics, astronomy, and logic with Kamal al-Din Musa ibn Yunus al-Shafi'i (d. 1242). As a result of his studies, in 1233 he wrote *Asas al-Iqtibas*, a pioneering work of Avicennan logic in Persian. His intellectual and spiritual curiosity and growing renown drew him to the attention of the Nizari Isma'ilis of Quhistan. He attached himself to the court of 'Ala' al-Din Muhammad and wrote major works of Isma'ili theology and mysticism (e.g. *Rawdat al-Taslim, Sayr va Suluk*), a pioneering work of ethics entitled *Akhlaq-i Muhtashami* (later edited and renamed during his post-Isma'ili period), and his influential commentary on Ibn Sina's *al-Isharat wa-l-Tanbihat (Pointers and Reminders)*.

For about twenty years, he remained a faithful follower and contributor to the cause, despite his later allegation that he was held against his will in the fortress of Alamut. The Mongol defeat of the Isma'ilis in 1256 brought this to an end. He became a negotiator and advisor to the Mongol conquerer Hülegü at the sack of Baghdad in 1258 and was later put in charge of religious endowments. At this point, he reverted back to Twelver Shi'ism. The Mongols had a great observatory and library at Maraghah in Azerbaijan built for al-Tusi, where he led a team of scientists and mathematicians. It is clear that immense resources were put at his disposal for this project, where the teaching and study of philosophy went on hand in hand with that of the exact sciences. The codices that have survived from that period testify to the intimate complementarity of philosophy and science in the curriculum and intellectual curiosity of the time. He signaled his change of religious affiliation by writing a critique of the crypto-Isma'ili theologian al-Shahrastani (d. 1153) entitled *Musari' al-Musari' (Wrestling With the Wrestling)* and penned a short but influential metaphysical exposition of Twelver theology, *Tajrid al-I'tiqad (Sublimation of Belief)*. He trained a number of important thinkers, including the illuminationist philosopher and scientist Qutb al-Din al-Shirazi (d. 1310) and the Twelver theologian al-'Allama al-Hilli (d. 1325). He died in Baghdad in 1274, and, in accordance with his wishes, was buried in the precinct of the shrine of the seventh Imam Musa al-Kazim in Kazimayn on the southern outskirts of the city.

He made a wide-ranging contribution to the pursuit of knowledge. His commentary on Ibn Sina's *al-Isharat* was the basis of his philosophical reputation, and it was in part a refutation of the hostile commentary of Fakhr al-Din al-Razi. His major ethical work was a manual that developed from an early draft dedicated to precepts to a major work of philosophical ethics that was divided into three parts: (1) ethics (akhlaq), (2) domestic economics *(tadbir-i manzil)*, and (3) politics *(siyasat-i mudun)*. This scheme set the pattern for subsequent works about practical philosophy in the Islamic tradition. The first part on ethics is modelled on Ibn Miskawayh's *Tahdhib al-Akhlaq (Cultivation of Morals)*, of which the work was initially commissioned to be merely a Persian translation. The sources of the second part about domestic economics are the Arabic translation of Bryson's *Oikonomikos* and a text by Ibn Sina, *Kitab al-Siyasa (Book of Politics)*, whereas the third part, about politics, goes back to al-Farabi's *Kitab al-Siyasa al-Madaniyya (The Political Regime)* and *Fusul al-Madani (Aphorisms of the Statesman)*. The concern with justice and love in this work illustrates his continuing affiliation with and interest in mysticism and Twelver theology.

Throughout his life, al-Tusi was a prolific writer in mathematics and the natural sciences, and he made advances in trigonometry, mathematics, and astronomy. This aspect of his intellectual endeavor was eventually rewarded with the foundation of the Maraghah observatory. The result of the astronomical observations and calculations made there was the famous tables of the Zij-i Ilkhani (in Persian, but also translated into Arabic). The setting up of the observatory and the institutionalization of the rational sciences created a demand for teaching materials; al-Tusi was himself the author of a number of recensions *(tahrir)* of scientific texts as well as summaries and abridgments of theological, logical, and philosophical texts, which were clearly intended to supply this teaching need. Al-Tusi's lasting influence can be seen in the subsequent surge of activity in the rational sciences in the Islamic east as well as in their absorption into religious education, which in turn affected the development of theology, particularly among Shi'i scholars.

SAJJAD H. RIZVI

Primary Sources

Akhlaq-i Nasiri (The Nasirean Ethics), transl. G.M. Wickens. London: George Allen & Unwin, 1964.

"Rawdat al-Taslim (The Garden of Submission)", transl. C. Jambet. In *La Convocation d'Alamût: Somme de Philosophie Ismaélienne (Rawdat al-Taslîm: Le Jardin de Vraie Foi.)*. Paris: Éditions Verdier and Éditions UNESCO, 1996.

Sayr wa Suluk (Contemplation and Action), ed. and transl. S.J.H. Badakhchani. London: I.B. Tauris in association with the Institute of Ismaili Studies, 1997.

al-Tadhkira fi 'Ilm al-Hay'a (Nasir al-Din al-Tusi's Memoir on Astronomy), 2 vols., ed. and transl. F.J. Ragep. New York: Springer Verlag, 1993.

The Metaphysics of al-Tusi (Including Risala dar Ithbat-i Wajib, Risala dar Jabr va Qadar, Risala dar Qismat-i Majwudat), transl. P. Morewedge. New York: Society for the Study of Islamic Philosophy and Science, 1992.

Further Reading

Dabashi, H. "Khwajah Nasir al-Din al-Tusi: The Philosopher/Vizier and the Intellectual Climate of His Times." In *History of Islamic Philosophy*, eds. S.H. Nasr and O. Leaman, vol. I, 527–84. London: Routledge, 1996.

———. "The Philosopher/Vizier: Khwaja Nasir al-Din al-Tusi and the Isma'ilis." In *Medieval Isma'ili History and Thought*, ed. F. Daftary, 231–46. Cambridge, UK: Cambridge University Press, 1996.

Madelung, W. "Nasir al-Din Tusi's Ethics Between Philosophy, Shi'ism, and Sufism." In *Ethics in Islam*, ed. R.G. Hovannisian, 85–101. Malibu, Calif: Undena, 1985.

Morewedge, P. "The Analysis of 'Substance' in Tusi's Logic and in the Ibn Sinian tradition." In *Essays on Islamic Philosophy and Science*, ed. G. Hourani, 158–87. Albany, NY: State University of New York Press, 1975.

Pourjavady, N., and Z. Vesel, eds. *Nasir al-Din Tusi: Philosophe et Savant du XIIIe Siècle*. Tehran: L'Institut Français de Recherches en Iran, 2000.

U

'UMAR IBN 'ABD AL-'AZIZ

'Umar ibn 'Abd al-'Aziz was the Umayyad caliph who ruled from 717 until 720 CE. His popularity with his subjects and his pious persona make him a unique figure in the Umayyad dynasty. Before becoming caliph, he served as governor in Medina and in Mecca and Ta'if from 706 to 712. Here his leniency toward his subjects brought objections from harsher Umayyad officials, particularly al-Hajjaj ibn Yusuf, the governor of the East. He became a confidant to his predecessor as caliph, Sulayman ibn 'Abd al-Malik, who overturned his father's wishes by naming 'Umar instead of his brother Yazid as his successor. The circumstances of 'Umar's appointment were quite unusual. Sulayman conveyed his deathbed wish to substitute 'Umar for Yazid to his trusted advisor Raja' b. Haywa, who then convinced the assembled Umayyad leaders to accept Sulayman's choice without actually revealing whom he had designated. The peculiar rise of 'Umar has brought speculation that Raja' orchestrated a coup d'état, or that the Umayyad family was uncomfortable empowering the more wanton Yazid.

As caliph, 'Umar instituted significant policy changes. He severely curtailed military operations on the frontiers and abandoned the expensive and unsuccessful siege of Constantinople that was begun by Sulayman. Whether these choices reflect a different philosophy about expansion or a recognition of fiscal realities is debated. 'Umar also restructured the empire's tax regime, lightening the tax burden on new, predominantly non-Arab converts to Islam.

His "fiscal rescript" is often cited as evidence of his pious insistence that all Muslims be treated equally, regardless of financial consequences for the treasury. The ambiguity of both the existing taxation system and 'Umar's reform make it difficult to assess the degree of tax relief he provided. Some modern studies suggest that his objective was to standardize and centralize taxation rather than to lessen the burden on new converts.

Although 'Umar's reforms were short-lived, his image as a pious leader continued to grow after his death. Later 'Abbasid historians treated him as the single exception to the Umayyad tendency toward depravity and even elevated him to the ranks of the *Rashidun* (the Rightly-Guided Caliphs). Hints of messianic expectations of 'Umar also appear in the sources; the unusual nature of his rise to power, his uniquely pious persona, and the fact that he reigned during the centennial of the hijra certainly contributed to such speculation.

STEVEN C. JUDD

Primary Sources

Ibn 'Abd al-Hakam. *Sirat 'Umar ibn 'Abd al-'Aziz,* ed. Ubayd. Cairo, 1983.

al-Tabari, Muhammad b. Jarir. *Ta'rikh al-Rusul wa-l-Muluk,* ed. M.J. de Goeje. Leiden, 1879–1901.

Further Reading

Hawting, G.R. *The First Dynasty of Islam.* London: Croom Helm, 1987.

Wellhausen, Julius. *The Arab Kingdom and its Fall,* transl. Margaret Weir. Calcutta, 1927.

'UMAR IBN AL-FARID

Ibn al-Farid is one of the greatest mystical poets of Islam. He was born in Cairo, Egypt, in 1181 CE, and was raised by his father, who was a respected *farid* (an advocate for women in legal cases), hence 'Umar's title *Ibn al-Farid* or "son of the women's advocate." Ibn al-Farid studied Sufism and Arabic literature, and he memorized the traditions of the prophet Muhammad (hadith) with al-Qasim ibn 'Ali Ibn 'Asakir (d. 1203). Like his father, 'Umar was a member of the Shafi'i school of jurisprudence. As a young man, Ibn al-Farid went on pilgrimage to Mecca, where he stayed for about fifteen years. He then returned to Cairo, where he taught the traditions of the Prophet Muhammad and poetry at the al-Azhar congregational mosque.

Ibn al-Farid married and had at least two sons and a daughter. He died in Cairo in 1235 CE. Ibn al-Farid's diwan (collected poems) is composed of more than a dozen poems, including love poems and odes, together with several dozen quatrains and riddles. The spiritual dimension of this verse is suggested by Ibn al-Farid's frequent allusions to God, the Qur'an, the Prophet Muhammad, and Sufi doctrines. His *al-Khamriyya (Wine Ode)* in particular has been regarded for centuries as one of the finest Muslim allegories about mystical love. However, even more celebrated has been Ibn al-Farid's *Nazm al-Suluk (Poem of the Sufi Way)*, also known as the *al-Ta'iyya al-Kubra (Ode Rhyming in T-Major)*, the longest and most famous Arabic mystical poem. Within this poem's 760 verses, Ibn al-Farid addressed a number of religious and, especially, mystical themes centered on the love between human beings and God. Often taking the role as a guide for the perplexed, the poet offers instruction and advice on such matters as unselfish love, spiritual intoxication and illumination, the pains of separation from the beloved, and the indescribable joy of union.

Ibn al-Farid portrays creation as intimately involved with its divine creator. Thus, when seen aright, everything in life reveals a ray of supernal light. This mystical view is mirrored in the refined and sophisticated beauty of Ibn al-Farid's verse, which strongly influenced later generations of medieval Arab poets and led to his veneration as a saint known as *sultan al-'ashiqin* ("the sultan of lovers").

TH. EMIL HOMERIN

See also Al-Azhar; Sufism; Schools of Jurisprudence

Further Reading

Homerin, Th. Emil. *From Arab Poet to Muslim Saint: Ibn al-Farid, His Verse, and His Shrine,* rev. ed. Cairo: American University in Cairo Press, 2001.
Ibn al-Farid. *Diwan,* ed. 'Abd al-Khaliq Mahmud. Cairo: Dar al-Ma'arif, 1984.
———. *The Mystical Poems of Ibn al-Farid,* 2 vols., transl. A.J. Arberry. London: Emery Walker, 1952–1956.
———. *The Poem of the Way,* transl. A.J. Arberry. London: Emery Walker, 1952.
———. *'Umar Ibn al-Farid: Sufi Verse, Saintly Life,* transl. Th. Emil Homerin. New York: Paulist Press, 2001.
Nicholson, R.A. *Studies in Islamic Mysticism.* Cambridge, UK: Cambridge University Press, 1921.

'UMAR IBN AL-KHATTAB

'Umar ibn al-Khattab was the second ruler of the Islamic state after the death of Muhammad, reigning from 634 to 644 CE. Before becoming caliph, 'Umar was a close advisor to his predecessor, Abu Bakr. In fact, some sources suggest that he (rather than Abu Bakr) exercised real authority after Muhammad's death. When the ailing Abu Bakr named 'Umar his successor, there was little objection from the community. Some Shi'i sources, however, suggest that Abu Bakr and 'Umar colluded to deprive 'Ali ibn Abi Talib of power.

'Umar's reign was pivotal for the young Islamic polity. With much of the Arabian peninsula subdued during Abu Bakr's reign, 'Umar turned his attention outward, embarking on a series of successful military campaigns against the Byzantine and Sasanian empires. By the end of his reign, Muslim forces had wrested Syria and Egypt from the Byzantines and had taken the Sasanian capital at Cteisphon. 'Umar himself did not lead the troops into battle but instead directed his generals from Medina. His only foray into the field was his visit to Jerusalem in 638, when he accepted the surrender of the city personally. His refusal to pray at the Church of the Holy Sepulcher for fear that his followers would subsequently transform it into a mosque is frequently cited as evidence of his tolerance toward other faiths. Scholars debate the extent to which 'Umar coordinated the conquests. Some argue that 'Umar merely allowed the conquests as an outlet for ambitious tribal leaders to gain spoils; other scholars have found evidence of significant centralized planning, suggesting that 'Umar firmly controlled the Muslim forces.

Regardless of the extent to which 'Umar directed the conquests, the task of administering the newly created empire fell to him. His choices about the disposition of conquered lands and the treatment of non-Muslim subjects shaped the Muslim polity for centuries to come. Rather than distributing land to the troops as spoils, 'Umar opted to retain communal control over much of the conquered land, using the land's revenue to fund soldiers' stipends. He established the *diwan* (registry) to fix stipends for soldiers based on how early they had converted to Islam. The soldiers were housed in newly established garrison towns (the most notable of which were Kufa and Basra in Iraq) to ensure that the Muslim forces did not disperse and that they remained ready for combat. 'Umar also began to clarify the rights and responsibilities of the *dhimmi* (the non-Muslim natives who had submitted to his authority).

'Umar's reign was cut short when he was mortally wounded by a disgruntled slave. Before succumbing to his wounds, 'Umar selected a committee of six trusted followers to choose his successor. After their *shura* (consultation), they settled on 'Uthman ibn Affan as the next caliph. This process of consultation is cited in modern times as a precedent for democratic institutions in Islam.

Some historical sources suggest messianic undertones to 'Umar's reign, a theme some modern scholars have pursued as well. In particular, his epithet *al-Faruq,* which is similar to the Syriac term for savior, and his visit to Jerusalem have been the focus of such speculation. In addition, 'Umar appears quite frequently in Islamic legal texts as an exemplar. The fact that his conduct—rather than that of Abu Bakr or Muhammad—is often cited as a precedent reflects his role in shaping Islamic law and administration. Whether this is evidence of messianic adoration or simply a reflection of the many new issues he confronted as the leader of a larger and more complex community is difficult to ascertain.

STEVEN C. JUDD

See also Abu Bakr; Polity (Umma); Consultation (Shura); 'Ali ibn Abi Talib; Dhimma

Primary Sources

al-Baladhuri, Ahmad ibn Yahya. *Futuh al-Buldan,* ed. M.J. de Goeje. Leiden, 1866.
al-Tabari, Muhammad ibn Jarir. *Ta'rikh al-Rusul wa-l-Muluk,* ed. M.J. de Goeje. Leiden, 1879–1901.

Further Reading

Cook, Michael, and Patricia Crone. *Hagarism.* Cambridge, UK: Cambridge University Press, 1977.
Donner, Fred. *The Early Islamic Conquests.* Princeton, NJ: Princeton University Press, 1981.
Kennedy, Hugh. *The Prophet and the Age of the Caliphates.* London: Longman, 1986.
Madelung, Wilferd. *The Succession to Muhammad.* Cambridge, UK: Cambridge University Press, 1997.

Shaban, M. *Islamic History: A New Interpretation,* vol. 1. Cambridge, UK: Cambridge University Press, 1971.

UMAYYAD MOSQUE, DAMASCUS

Built between 705/706 and 715 CE, the Umayyad Mosque in Damascus was considered one of the wonders of the medieval Islamic world. The mosque was the epitome of an architectural program sponsored by the Umayyad Caliph al-Walid I (r. 705–715), son of 'Abd al-Malik (r. 685–705), who built the Dome of the Rock in Jerusalem (692). The mosque appropriated the site of the Christian cathedral of St. John, which had itself replaced a temple of Jupiter Damascenus; some of the columns reused in the mosque bear inscriptions attesting to different phases of use in temple and church.

Despite frequent fire damage and multiple restorations, the basic details of the eighth-century mosque have been preserved. The church, which probably stood at the center of the pre-Islamic sanctuary, was demolished, but the massive rectangular outer stone walls of the sanctuary were retained, as were its two southern corner towers, which formed the bases of two minarets. Access was via three monumental gates located in the centers of the eastern, western, and northern walls of the sanctuary. The space enclosed by the walls was occupied by a hypostyle mosque consisting of a courtyard surrounded on three sides by a narrow *riwaq* (arcade), which led to a prayer hall about 120 meters long that was built against the south side of the ancient enclosure wall. The façade of the prayer hall was distinguished by a monumental gabled entrance similar to the façades of earlier Syrian basilicas but comparable also to the entrance to the palace of the Byzantine emperors in Constantinople.

The prayer hall consisted of three bays running parallel to the south wall, which was approximately aligned toward Mecca, its superstructure borne on a double arcade. The aisles were bisected at their center by a wide axial nave leading from the courtyard façade to a monumental dome that preceded the *mihrab* (a concave niche). A private entrance by the mihrab led directly into the Umayyad palace, which lay behind the southern wall. The two were also connected by an extensive arcade that led from the Bab al-Ziyada, a gate at the eastern end of the south wall of the mosque that contained a monumental water clock that featured automata.

In its original form, the mosque was lavishly decorated with gilded carved marble, including a famous vine scroll and epigraphic bands. It was embellished throughout with glass mosaics, the surviving portions of which depict pastoral scenes, multitiered buildings, pavilions, bridges over rivers, and gigantic trees. Their high quality and references in the medieval sources to assistance from the Byzantine emperor have led to speculation about the involvement of craftsmen from Constantinople in the mosaic decorations. Their meaning has long been a matter of contention, with scholars split between a paradisal interpretation and one that sees them as continuing a tradition of topographic representation known from the floor mosaics of Jordanian churches.

The Damascus mosque witnesses a reconfiguration and reformulation of formal and decorative elements drawn from a local Syrian as well as an imperial Byzantine repertoire, continuing a trend begun a generation earlier in the Dome of the Rock. The introduction of common features such as the axial nave, mihrab, dome, and glass mosaics in the mosques rebuilt by al-Walid in Arabia, Syria, and North Africa amounts to the dissemination of an imperial architectural style designed to project both the ascendancy of the new religion and the political aspirations of the Umayyad dynasty.

Even after 750 CE (when the seat of the caliphate moved to Iraq), in places as diverse as Cordoba in Andalusia and Ghazna in Afghanistan, the Damascus mosque provided the standard against which many medieval mosques were measured. Moreover, its characteristic three longitudinal aisles and gabled façade set the tone for medieval mosque architecture in Syria and the Jazira. During the thirteenth and fourteenth centuries, the mosque inspired the decoration of a series of monuments built by the Mamluk sultans of Egypt and Syria.

FINBARR BARRY FLOOD

See also 'Abd al-Malik ibn Marwan; Damascus; Dome of the Rock, Mosaics; Umayyads; Syria, Greater Syria

Further Reading

Brisch, Klaus. "Observations on the Iconography of the Mosaics in the Great Mosque at Damascus." In *Content and Context of Visual Arts in the Islamic World,* ed. Priscilla P. Soucek, 13–20. University Park & London: The Pennsylvania State University Press, 1988.

Creswell, K.A.C. *Early Muslim Architecture, Volume 1, Part 1: Umayyads A.D. 622–750,* 151–210. Oxford: Clarendon Press, 1969.

Flood, Finbarr Barry. *The Great Mosque of Damascus: Studies on the Making of an Umayyad Visual Culture.* Leiden: Brill, 2001.

Georgopoulou, Maria. "Geography, Cartography and the Architecture of Power in the Mosaics of the Great Mosque of Damascus." In *The Built Surface, Volume 1: Architecture and the Pictorial Arts from Antiquity to the Enlightenment,* ed. Christy Anderson, 47–74. Aldershot: Ashgate, 2002.

Grabar, Oleg. "La Grande Mosquée de Damas et les Origins Architecturales de la Mosque." In *Synthronon: Art et Archéologie de la fin de l'Antiquité et du Moyen Age,* ed. A. Grabar, 107–14. Paris: Librairie C. Klincksieck, 1968.

Rabbat, Nasser. "The Dialogic Dimension in Umayyad Art." *Res* 43 (2003): 78–94.

UMAYYADS

The Umayyad dynasty of caliphs ruled all of the lands conquered by the Arab Muslims from 661 until 749/750 CE. Following the overthrow of the dynasty and the killing of several members of the Umayyad family, 'Abd al-Rahman, a grandson of the caliph Hisham (724–743), established himself as ruler of Islamic Spain (al-Andalus). He became the ancestor of a long line of Umayyad rulers of al-Andalus, who, between 929 and 1027, used the title of caliph.

Origins

According to the Islamic genealogical tradition, the Umayyad family was a part of Quraysh, the clan that dominated Mecca before Islam and to which the Prophet Muhammad and many other prominent early Muslims belonged. The Umayyads descend from a certain Umayya, son of 'Abd Shams of Quraysh. 'Abd Shams was the brother and rival of Hashim, the ancestor not only of the Prophet but also of the 'Abbasid family that seized the caliphate from the Umayyads in 749/750. The Umayyad family had become rich and powerful during the lifetime of the Prophet and was prominent in the Meccan opposition to him. The leaders of the family only submitted to the Prophet and entered Islam toward the end of Muhammad's life, when it had become clear to them that he was going to be victorious.

Mu'awiya, the first of the line, was generally accepted as caliph after the killing of 'Ali in 661. 'Ali, the cousin and son-in-law of the Prophet, had himself claimed the caliphate after the murder of the caliph 'Uthman in 656. Like his cousin Mu'awiya, 'Uthman had been a grandson of Umayya, and there are some grounds for seeing him as the first Umayyad caliph, although the historical tradition only begins the line with Mu'awiya. The latter had been governor of Syria since 636, and he refused to accept 'Ali's claims to the caliphate. He put himself forward as having the right to seek vengeance on those who had murdered his cousin, and a period of civil war (the *fitna*) followed the killing of 'Uthman. Mu'awiya and 'Ali fought against each other indecisively, but, when 'Ali himself

Interior view of the Great Mosque. Umayyad caliphate (Moorish). Tenth CE. Credit: Art Resource, NY. Mosque, Cordoba, Spain.

was assassinated in 661, Mu'awiya was best placed to take over the caliphate.

For the next ninety years or so, all of the caliphs were descendants of Umayya, and Muslim tradition contrasts this introduction of the dynastic principle unfavorably with the pre-Umayyad caliphate, when, it claims, caliphs were chosen according to merit and after some consultation. The Umayyad caliphs are divided traditionally into two branches. The first three caliphs (Mu'awiya, his son Yazid I, and the latter's short-lived son and successor Mu'awiya II) are referred to as Sufyanids, after Mu'awiya's father, Abu Sufyan. After the death of Yazid I in 683, another period of civil war saw the caliphate pass into the hands of Marwan I, the leader of a collateral branch of the Umayyad family. All of the remaining Umayyad caliphs were descendants of Marwan and are therefore referred to as Marwanids.

Significance

The Umayyads ruled at the crucial time when important cultural developments arising from the Arab Muslim conquest of the former Byzantine and Sasanid territories were taking effect. Those developments may be summarized as the emergence of Islam as the religion and culture of the region extending from Central Asia through North Africa into parts of southern Europe. That process was certainly not complete by the time the Umayyad caliphate was overthrown, but, in general, the period of the Umayyad caliphate can be understood as one that saw the transition from the world of Late Antiquity to that of Islam.

Essentially, the period saw the formation of a new society with an Islamic and Arabic identity in which the original separation of Arab Muslim conquerors from the non-Arab, non-Muslim subjects was broken down. Arabs and non-Arabs began to be assimilated so that the majority of people identified as Muslims, and Arabic became the dominant language of both high culture and everyday communication. That did not happen everywhere to the same extent or at the same speed, but by the end of the Umayyad period the process was under way. Its outcome was the emergence of a distinctive Arabic and Islamic civilization, many aspects of which were developed from the pre-conquest Middle East and the Mediterranean world.

Much of that occurred independently of—and even in contradiction to—the intentions of the Umayyad rulers. Originally the Arab empire had assumed the more or less complete separation of the Arab Muslim conquerors from the subject peoples; the latter were expected to contribute the taxes that would support the Arab elite. Islam was viewed as the prerogative of the Arabs, and it was not expected that many non-Arabs would enter it; however, right from the start, there were some who did.

The mechanism by which they could do so was that of clientage *(wala')*. Islam and Arab identity were so closely tied together that, in order for a non-Arab to become a Muslim, he in effect had to become an Arab. He did that by becoming the client *(mawla)* of an Arab patron and thus acquiring an Arab identity. Both the patron and the client assumed certain duties to one another and obtained certain advantages. For the client, those advantages included protection from the fiscal demands of the Umayyad authorities and employment; naturally that would make the status attractive to those among the conquered who lacked social status and economic power. As the idea grew that Islam should be open to all, regardless of ethnic origin, the attempts by the Umayyads to prevent the movement into Islam of their non-Arab subjects came to be seen as un-Islamic, and that has much to do with the reputation for impiety that they have in the Muslim historical tradition.

Alternatively, the Umayyads did much to establish the conditions necessary for the development of the new Arab Muslim civilization. When Mu'awiya took over the caliphate, Arab rule did not reach much beyond Libya in the west and the eastern parts of Iran in the east, and even much of that territory must have been held only insecurely. By the end of their caliphate, it had been extended, as a result mainly of centrally organized campaigns, from central Asia to the Atlantic. In the armies of the Umayyads, the Arabs were supported by increasing numbers drawn from the non-Arab subjects.

The territories thus conquered were controlled by an administrative system that was centered on governors and tax collectors and that intended to funnel revenues from the provinces to the center. Much of the administrative system had been taken over from the two empires that the Arabs had displaced, but, by the time of the caliph 'Abd al-Malik (685–705) and his son al-Walid (705–715), a significant Arab and Muslim character was evident. It was around that time that Arabic was adopted as the official language of the administration (although the situation did not change overnight), and a new and distinctive Islamic coinage was introduced. Those two caliphates also saw the first major achievements of a new style of architecture, with the Dome of the Rock and the Aqsa mosque in Jerusalem and the Mosque of the Prophet in Medina.

Downfall

The Umayyad caliphs saw themselves as the absolute leaders of Islam, subject only to God. The caliphal title for them meant "Deputy of God" *(khalifat Allah)*, and obedience to them was a religious duty. Their opponents, too, usually expressed their protests in religious terms, and both Kharijite and Shi'i rebels rejected the legitimacy of the Umayyads. Their overthrow, which was facilitated by rivalries within the family and factionalism in the army, was brought about by a Shi'i revolt that began in Khurasan in northeastern Iran and that aimed to establish the caliphate in the family of the Prophet. The Sunni tradition of Islam also grew out of circles that had been opposed to the Umayyads. The result, therefore, is that the Islamic historical tradition, which crystallized after the overthrow of the Umayyads, tends to look upon them with disfavor, ranging from the complete rejection of them by the Shi'is to a more ambiguous disapproval on the part of most Sunnis. This attitude has often led to the view that their rule was not a real caliphate but merely a kingship.

GERALD R. HAWTING

Further Reading

Crone, Patricia. *Slaves on Horses: The Evolution of the Islamic Polity.* Cambridge, UK: Cambridge University Press, 1980.

Hawting, G.R. *The First Dynasty of Islam,* 2nd ed. London and New York: Routledge, 2000.

Kennedy, Hugh. *The Prophet and the Age of the Caliphates: The Islamic Near East from the Sixth to the Eleventh Century.* London and New York: Longmans, 1986.

Wellhausen, Julius. *Das arabische Reich und sein Sturz.* Berlin: Georg Reimer, 1902. (English translation: *The Arab Kingdom and Its Fall.* Calcutta, 1927.)

URBANISM

The Muslim conquest occurred in two stages. The first one was led by Arab armies, assisted by Islamized Iranians or Berbers, and began in 635 CE. Within a century, Islam spread all over western Asia (with the exception of Anatolia), reaching the edges of Indian, Chinese, and Turkish territories; it also spread over the whole of northern Africa and the largest portion of the Iberian Peninsula. After 750, the massive quest to expand slowed, and then it stopped for three centuries. The second conquest, led predominantly by Turkish armies, began in about 1040 in Armenia, Caucasus, and Anatolia. It continued for five centuries, alternating between successes and failures, until the sixteenth century, when the Ottoman Empire controlled Anatolia, the Balkans, and the greatest part of the Arab-speaking countries around the Mediterranean Sea (except for Morocco). At the same time, Safavid rule dominated Persia, and the Mughals ruled the Indian Peninsula. Conversely, the Arab and the Jewish populations were driven away from the Iberian Peninsula by the Catholic kings of Castilla.

In this immense Muslim area that stretched from the Atlantic Ocean to the deserts of Central Asia, the climate was relatively homogenous: quite hot and dry. Numerous towns thrived; most of them were more or less devoted to trade. Ancient cities were Islamized or new cities were established by the Muslims; all of these were suitable to the climatic environment and moving toward a model that was unique for the time.

Usually the towns that were grouped together were protected with fortification, with convenient access to water, rivers, underground canals, springs, wells, or tanks. Until the twelfth century, towns were often protected by a great wall, but this was more symbolic than effective against invasions. A green belt of orchards, market gardens, and kitchen gardens irrigated by shrewd hydraulic techniques enclosed most of the urban territory; this ensured city dwellers a large part of their sustenance and offered them a shaded paradise for their leisure time during summer.

The town's layout was haphazard, and the most frequent layout was a great intersection of narrow lanes that crossed at the center of the town, near the Friday mosque. Between these radiating streets, which were often lined by the *souk* (market) stalls, each inside quarter was inhabited by extended patriarchal families living in single-story houses (although occasionally the houses had two or three floors) built around open courtyards. The local community was homogeneous, closely linked by blood, tribal, ethnic, linguistic, or religious relationships. Strict politeness protocols dictated the notables' inter-quarter visits to avoid clashes between passionate youth.

Close attention was paid to a family's honor, the result of a strict endogamy that forbade women to go outside of the close community neighborhood. A wooden screen *(mushrabiyya)* of intricate geometric lattice work on windows allowed a woman inside to see out without being seen. Only dead-end streets with semi-private status led from the main streets inside the quarter; this prevented anyone from crossing the quarter from one radiated lane to another. Thus, one wishing to travel from one quarter to another had to cross through the center of the town.

The inside courtyard, open to the sky, was the domain of women; here grew flowers and ornamental or fruit trees. A pond with fish provided an image of nature in the countryside. A staircase allowed a woman to climb to the flat roof *(sath)*, where she could speak to neighboring females. In the rainy countries, ridge roofs *(saqf)* were often built. In Yemen, high tower houses were devoid of this type of courtyard. In overcrowded harbors (e.g., Eastern Tripoli) and large towns (e.g., Baghdad, Basra, Mamluk Cairo), a lack of space forced inhabitants to build many-storied buildings with independent flats (Egyptian *rab'*).

In the streets, there were no carts; huge bundles were carried on camels from outside to the large khans set up near the doors in the city walls. Donkeys then carried goods from the khans to the shops, stalls, or houses. Although the lanes were tortuous, with reed hurdles, pedestrians could enjoy cool shade, and there was no dusty desert wind. Ancient Roman avenues, broad and straight, were not so suited to this dry and hot climate. As seen by a pedestrian, the city looked like a labyrinth inside blank walls; however, upon ascending a minaret, one could see many open spaces, the courtyards of mosques and houses, and dark green vegetation enveloping nearly every building.

Unlike Italian medieval towns, the street façades outside of the houses of nobles were neither high nor monumental. The owner's fortune was measured by the expanse of the plot, allowing a large family to live with an extensive household staff; this is why a long distance between the main entries of houses on a street was the sign of a wealthy quarter. In these little palaces, there were many courtyards, some being strictly domestic *(haramlik)*, whereas others were open to visitors *(salamlik)*. According to the local supplies and customs, builders used stone, mud, wood, cob, and crude or baked bricks. The frame of the building was fitted more to the comfort of the inhabitants than to an orthogonal, geometric, and symmetric pre-established drawing. Changing with the seasons, furniture (trays used as portable tables, mats, rugs, or mattresses) could be carried easily from one room to another. Roofed spaces with three walls *(iwan)* gave everyone shelter from sun or wind and opened onto the courtyard, with free access to the view, the light, and the fresh air. On the walls, one could see many kinds of artistic decorations: carved stones or stuccoes, colorful frescoes or ceramic tiles, and sometimes skillful games created with plain building materials.

The vast public square inside a city, around which was organized the Italian medieval town, was generally absent from the Muslim medieval town (apart from the courtyard in the Friday mosque). Outside of the city, near the external walls, the *maydan* was an empty area devoted to military training for the cavalry that was also suitable for the weekly animal markets and to set up camps for the caravans for a few days. This area was often located at the confluence of wadis' valleys; this area was wet and of easy use, unless an unexpected flood devastated everything. During the first centuries of Islam, this danger was sometimes forgotten, and, because of the quick expansion of cities, permanent structures were erected. Arab historians report that hundreds of inhabitants drowned during the first huge rainstorm in this type of suburb.

The nobles' houses were generally in the center, near the Friday mosque. In the souks nearby, one could find Christian or Jewish jewellers or money changers; Muslim manuscript copyists and binders; and merchants of precious goods such as medical drugs, scents, fine leather slippers, and books. In the area of town closer to the external walls, the social status was lower; cheaper goods or objects that were considered unpleasant because of the noise or the stench and pollution linked with their production were offered in these remote souks. Near the city's gates or in the suburbs, one may find prostitutes, rowdies, poor villagers, army deserters, and also Bedouins without tribe or slaves without masters. They lived in huts around large clay courts *(hawsh)* that were used for livestock farming. Near the city's doors, city inhabitants were buried in cemeteries, according to their family, tribal, religious, or Sufi affiliation. The Qarafas (vast areas allocated to the tombs around Fustat and Cairo) were often colonized by provincial families looking for work in the capital. Everywhere, nearby suburbs and cemeteries were built when the growth of the number of inhabitants forced to the walls of the city to come down and urban territory to spread.

The primary duties of a Muslim sovereign were to protect the community from outside enemies and to maintain Islamic law and public order. Alternatively, there were also minimal edilitary duties, such as water irrigation and mending the lanes and the sewage systems, which allowed city dwellers to wash themselves. These duties began to be put in the control of the private sector; the nobles held them financially through the waqf system. Out of their purses, they built schools (*kuttab* for little children, *madrasas* for students), hospitals *(bimaristan)*, convents for Sufis *(khanaqah)*, drinking fountains *(sabil)*, baths *(hammam)* public hostels for travelers, and warehouses for goods *(funduq, khan, wikala)*. In addition, they rented out houses, shops, and gardens to pay the expenses for the waqf's work. Often a waqf monument distinguished itself by having a finely wrought façade and a huge carved wood door. Until recent times, the numerous Zankid, Ayyubid, and Mamluk waqf buildings lent their charm to the ancient town centers in Damascus, Aleppo, and the Arab part of Jerusalem.

From the seventh to the seventeenth century, Muslim towns evolved significantly. During the twelfth century, political power was in the hands of the military. Huge citadels dominated towns and symbolized a new order, violent and unequal. In Cairo, under the Mamluk dynasty (thirteenth–sixteenth century), the palaces of the emirs show a beautiful façade with a high door that one can cross without coming down from his or her horse. The Friday mosque was no longer a symbol of the unity of a city's people; now, even Friday at noon, most male inhabitants prayed in their quarter mosque.

At the beginning of the sixteenth century, Muslim territories were divided into three major groups. The Turkish Ottoman Empire dominated the Balkans in Europa, Turkish-speaking Anatolia, and all Arab-speaking countries around the Mediterranean Sea (except Morocco). Here the greater mosques were built in stone and covered by high domes that were modeled on the Byzantine tradition. Slim pencil minarets dashed toward the sky; courtyards were external, around the mosque.

The Iranian Sasanian Empire overcame the Persian-speaking territories and some neighboring Turkish-speaking provinces. Here greater mosques were built with mud bricks but decorated with marvelous glazed tiles. Four high pishtaq iwans opened onto a vast inside courtyard. Minarets were as high as the Ottoman ones but quite larger and not so strictly cylindrical.

The Indian Peninsula was for the most part under the rule of the Mughal sultans. In their beautiful mosques, they skillfully mixed Persian and Indian decorating styles. Despite these differences, many of the characteristics of Muslim cities continued throughout the whole of Dar al-Islam until the middle of the nineteenth century.

THIERRY BIANQUIS

See also Primary Schools (Kuttab); Madrasa

Further Reading

Beg, M.A.J. *Historic Cities of Asia.* Kuala Lumpur, 1986.

Behrens-Abouseif, Doris, ed. *The Cairo Heritage. Papers in Honor of Layla Ibrahim.* Cairo, 2000.

Bonine, M., et al., eds. *The Middle Eastern City and Urbanism.* Bonn, 1994.

Creswell, K.A.C. *The Muslim Architecture of Egypt,* 2 vols., reprint. New York, 1978.

Garcin, Jean-Claude, dir. *États, Sociétés et Cultures du Monde Musulman Médiéval.* Paris: PUF, 1995 and 2000.

———. *Grandes Villes Méditerranéennes du Monde Musulman.* Rome: École Française de Rome, 2000.

Gaube, H., Wirth, Eugen. *Aleppo.* Wiesbaden, 1984.

Ibn Khaldun. *The Muqaddimah,* 2 vols., transl. Franz Rosenthal. Princeton, NJ, 1967.

Lapidus, Ira, ed. *Middle Eastern Cities.* Berkeley and Los Angeles, 1969.

Nicolet, Claude, dir. *Mégapoles Méditerranéennes, Géographie Urbaine Retrospective.* Rome: École Française de Rome, 2000.

Serjeant, R.B. *The Islamic City.* Paris, 1980.

Wirth, Eugen. *Die Orientalische Stadt,* 2 vols. Mainz. 2000.

USAMA IBN MUNQIDH

A twelfth-century Syrian Muslim warrior and man of letters, Usama ibn Munqidh was best known for his poetry and, above all, for his autobiographical anecdotes and his observations about the customs of the Frankish Crusaders who settled in the Levant.

Born on July 4, 1095 CE at the family castle of Shayzar in northern Syria, Usama ibn Munqidh (or Usama ibn Murshid ibn 'Ali ibn Munqidh) was the most famous member of the Banu Munqidh, a small Arab clan that became influential in the affairs of northern Syria starting in the middle of the eleventh century. Usama's early years were some of the most momentous decades in Syrian history, a period that saw the arrival of the First Crusade (1097–1099), the consolidation of Seljuk authority, and the spread of the Nizari Isma'ilis into Syria. These first decades at Shayzar were for Usama his golden years, when he learned to acquire all the manly polish expected of an amir of his day, fighting Muslim and Crusader enemies, hunting, and trying his hand at poetry. Unfortunately, Usama's uncle later exiled Usama from Shayzar in 1131, seeing in him a rival to his plans to place control of Shayzar solidly in the hands of his own sons.

After leaving Shayzar, Usama sought service in the nearby principality of Homs, which was just then under attack by the ambitious atabeg of Mosul, the warlord Zanki (see Zankids). When Homs finally fell to Zanki, Usama was captured, and it appears that he entered the service of the atabeg. In 1137, however, Usama was obliged to return to Shayzar first upon news of his father's death and later in 1138 to help defend his family home from a joint Byzantine–Crusader siege.

It was at this point, after the siege had lifted, that Usama left the service of Zanki and made for Damascus and the court of Mu'in al-Din Unur, the atabeg of the Burid prince Mahmud. One of Unur's principal concerns was establishing a truce with the Latin Kingdom of Jerusalem so that he might better focus his resources on the growing threat of Zanki in the north. As part of that goal, Usama and Unur made many visits into Crusader territory, and these form the background of his celebrated observations about the Frankish character in his later "memoirs." Usama eventually found himself caught up in the intrigues of the court in Damascus, however, and, by 1144, he had fled the city for the more sophisticated world of Fatimid Cairo.

Usama's decade of service (1144–1154) to the Fatimid caliphs of Egypt was the pinnacle of his political career. While there, his skills as a soldier, boon companion, and adviser were richly rewarded, and Usama himself experienced a level of personal influence that he had never before tasted. His diplomatic skills were also of use, as in the (failed) Fatimid attempt to enlist the support of Zanki's son and heir Nur al-Din in Damascus to fight a joint war against the Crusaders of Ascalon. However, Usama's rise to power ended in an equally abrupt fall, when, implicated in the plot to murder of the caliph al-Zafir in 1154, Usama fled with his family into the desert, abandoning most of his property to rioting troops in Cairo. After narrowly escaping capture by Crusaders, Usama made his way to Damascus, where he enlisted in the service of Nur al-Din.

In Damascus, Usama found a new patron in Nur al-Din and a position from which to reconstitute his life as best he could. He settled into a new home, served his master on campaign, ransomed captive family members, carried on poetic correspondence with friends in Egypt, and even reopened communications with his cousins at Shayzar, humbly asking them to bury old family squabbles and to have him back. As it happened, however, Usama could never return to Shayzar, because, in 1157, a massive earthquake struck northern Syria and leveled the castle; almost every member of the Banu Munqidh household was killed. Usama, exiled in Damascus, could only mourn for his kin and decry the vicissitudes of fate. In 1164, Usama joined his lord Nur al-Din in a victorious campaign against the Franks and, for reasons that remain unclear, promptly took up with one of Nur al-Din's allies, Qara Arslan, Lord of Hisn Kayfa.

Although next to nothing is known about his time spent under Qara Arslan at Hisn Kayfa, it was during this decade (1164–1174) that Usama produced most of his literary works. For Usama, Hisn Kayfa was a terribly provincial place in far northern Iraq, and his literary activity may have been some attempt to stay connected to the more urbane worlds with which he was more familiar. Of the many works that Usama composed there, only a few have survived. He seems to have specialized in topical anthologies: collections of anecdotes, poetry, hadith, and other lore organized around common themes, such as his entertaining *Book of the Staff*, devoted to famous staves and walking sticks; his *Kernels of Refinement*, a manual of ideal conduct *(adab)*; and his *Creator of High Style*, a manual about poetic criticism. He also composed works (now lost) about women, castles, dreams, rivers, and old age. His massive examination of the erotic prelude in classical Arabic poetry, the *Book of Dwellings and Abodes*, could well be considered his masterpiece.

For modern readers, Usama's greatest fame stems from his collection of poetry and above all his autobiographically inclined *Book of Learning by Example*, often inaccurately called his "memoirs." These he finished at the end of his unusually long life in Damascus, where, in 1174, he returned at the summons of his last patron, Saladin. The book is remarkable by any standards. Ostensibly a reflection upon the inevitability of fate, the work artfully uses examples drawn almost entirely from Usama's long and adventurous life and so is filled with details of daily life, high politics, and witty observations of the men and women of Usama's world. It is a compelling testament of one medieval Muslim's presentation of his world and the manner in which God's will has intersected with it.

Usama ibn Munqidh died in 1188 at the age of ninety-three, and was buried in Damascus.

PAUL M. COBB

Primary Sources

Usama ibn Munqidh. *Kitab al-I'tibar (Book of Learning by Example)*. Ed. Philip K. Hitti. Princeton, NJ: Princeton University Press, 1930. (Translated by Hitti as *An Arab-Syrian Gentleman and Warrior in the Period of the Crusades*. New York: Columbia University Press, 1929. [reprinted 2000].)

———. *Kitab al-'Asa (Book of the Staff)*, ed. Hasan 'Abbas. Alexandria: al-Hay'at al-Misrya al-'Amma li'l-Kitab, 1978. (For translated excerpts, see Cobb, *Book of the Staff*.)

———. *Lubab al-Adab (Kernels of Refinement)*, ed. A.M. Shakir. Cairo: Maktabat Luwis Sarkis, 1935. (For translated excerpts, see Cobb, *Kernels of Refinement*.)

———. *Kitab al-Manazil wa'l-Diyar (Dwellings and Abodes)*, ed. Mustafa Hijazi. Cairo: Lajnat Ihya' al-Turath al-Islami, 1968.

———. *Al-Badi' fi'l-Badi' (Creator of High Style)*, ed. A.A. Muhanna. Beirut: Dar al-Kutub al-'Ilmiya, 1987.

———. *Diwan Usama ibn Munqidh*, eds. A.A. Badawi and H. 'Abd al-Majid. Cairo: al-Matba'a al-Amiriya, 1953.

Further Reading

Cobb, Paul M. *Usama ibn Munqidh: Warrior-Poet of the Age of Crusades*. Oxford: Oneworld, 2005.

———. "Usama ibn Munqidh's *Book of the Staff (Kitab al-'Asa)*: Autobiographical and Historical Excerpts." *Al-Masaq* 17 (2005): forthcoming.

———. "Usama ibn Munqidh's *Kernels of Refinement (Lubab al-Adab)*: Autobiographical and Historical Excerpts." *Al-Masaq* 18 (2006): forthcoming.

Derenbourg, Hartwig. *Ousâma ibn Mounîdh. Un Emir Syrien au Premier Siècle de Croisades (1095–1188)*, 2 vols. Paris: Ernest Leroux, 1889.

Irwin, Robert. "Usamah ibn Munqidh: An Arab-Syrian Gentleman at the Time of the Crusades Reconsidered." In *The Crusades and Their Sources. Essays Presented to Bernard Hamilton*, eds. J. France and W.G. Zajac, 71–87. Aldershot: Ashgate, 1998.

USURY AND INTEREST

Usury and interest were initially identified with the levying of exorbitant fees for the borrowing of capital but later included more generally the taking of any unfair advantage in transactions and any unearned gains resulting from chance. These concepts are known in Arabic sources as *ribâ*. Islamic law prohibits it generally, but different jurists interpret the circumstances to which it applies in different ways. Many Muslim merchants engaged in usury or, more frequently, entered into contracts that circumvented the specific legal restrictions while serving the same purpose.

The practice was well established in Mecca during pre-Islamic times. Money lenders often offered the use of their capital at interest rates as high as twenty-five or fifty percent for periods of just a few months. Moreover, they usually forced borrowers to agree to a doubling of the interest if the capital was not repaid in time. Important companions such as 'Uthmân b. 'Affân, 'Abd al-Raìmân b. 'Awf, Khâlid b. al-Walîd, and 'Abbâs b. 'Abd al-Muttalib earned a large part of their wealth in this way.

The Qur'an first criticizes and later bans these practices. In verse 30:39, which dates to the late Meccan period, the Qur'an counsels against usury but does not forbid it. The verse declares, "What you give from usury increases in proportion to people's wealth but does not increase with God. What you give in alms seeking the countenance of God [will increase]. These are the ones who double their wealth!'' Later verses condemn it unambiguously. In 3:130, which belongs to the Medinan period, the Qur'an declares: "O You who believe do not consume usury, compounding in doubles! Fear God! Perhaps you will prosper." This is stated more strongly in 2:275–80, which also belongs to the Medinan period. The first part of this passage reads, "Those who consume usury will not stand except like one whom Satan knocks around with that touch...." It goes on to mention the collection of usury as a pretext for righteous war: "O you who believe, fear God! Give up what remains of usury—if you are true believers/If you do not, take notice of war from God and His messenger...."

Prophetic tradition contains additional prohibitions. However, many of these are not authentic and, where they are, are imprecise or contradictory. The most famous is in the prophet's "Farewell Sermon," given on the occasion of his last pilgrimage to Mecca. Much of this sermon, however, is of questionable authenticity. Another widely quoted tradition states the following: "Gold for gold, silver for silver, wheat for wheat, barley for barley, dates for dates, salt for salt, the same thing for the same thing, like for like, measure for measure; but if these things are different then sell them as you please if it is (only) done measure for measure." Other traditions prohibit any contract promising an increase over a fixed period, but they differ regarding whether the same increase would be allowable in an immediate sale.

Although they never doubted the general prohibition, jurists disagreed about many of the exact circumstances that qualified as usury. Legal schools differed, for example, with regard to the enumeration and classification of objects that are liable to usury. The Œâhirî school limited these objects to the six enumerated by the prophet; its refusal to accept the principle of analogy did not allow it to speculate further. Other legal schools took the specified objects as representative of categories of objects but differed when it came to the characterization of these categories. Mâliki and Shâfi'î jurists judged them to be precious metals and foodstuffs. Hanafîs and Zaydis described them as objects transacted by weight and measure. Although most legal schools considered the exchange of unequal quantities of the same object to be usury regardless of the term of the contract, this was not always the case. For example, the Mâliki school did not object when the transfer of possession took place immediately.

A significant part of the confusion and difficulties has to do with the fact that various pre-Islamic practices subsumed under usury continued to be an integral part of commerce in the Muslim world for many years after the Prophet. For instance, the use of muzâbana contracts (where unripe fruit on trees is bartered for dried fruit of the same kind) was widespread. Jurists, in fact, tolerated them when they stipulated the exchange of unripe dates on the palm for dried dates. The use of checks or receipts also technically contravened the prohibition against usury, because they gave an advantage to the party that carried the check rather than the goods. Checks, nevertheless, continued to serve as essential financial instruments for many centuries afterward.

Moreover, legal proscriptions became more rigid over time as piety-minded scholars conceived of Islamic law more idealistically. Although they were cognizant of ethical problems, many early discussions show ignorance of specific legal prohibitions for the collection of interest. These scholars sometimes describe contracts where "nine-tenths of the permitted amount is renounced"; later discussions do not entertain this possibility.

Jurists, in any case, developed numerous legal evasions that allowed merchants to circumvent these proscriptions. They defended them as legitimate, because man, they argued, could not know the divine wisdom behind a specific law; he needed only to observe its letter. The Œâhisrîs were among the biggest proponents of these evasions, although the Shâf'îs and later the Hanîfis and Imâmîs recognized them as well. One of the most popular evasions was the double contract of sale. With this contract, the borrower purchased an article from the lender, agreeing to pay at a future date a sum equal to the cost of the borrowed capital and interest. Simultaneously, the borrower sells the lender the same article for the immediate payment of a sum equal to the capital he wishes to borrow. Mâlikî, Hanbalî, and Zaydî schools, in general, rejected these circumventions.

STUART D. SEARS

Primary Sources

Ânis, Mâlik b. al-Muwaøøâ.
Hubayra, Yahyâ b. Muìammad b. al-Ifsah 'an Ma'ânî al-Sihâì.
Ismâ'îl al-San'ânî, Muìammad b. Subul al-Salâm al-Mûsila ilâ Bulûgh al-Marâm.
Wensinck. A Handbook of Early Muìammadan Tradition. Leiden, 1971.

Further Reading

Coulson, N. A History of Islamic Law. Delhi, 1997.
Hallaq, W. The Origins and Evolution of Islamic Law. Cambridge, UK, 2005.
Ibrahim, M. Merchant Capital and Islam. Austin, Tex, 1990.
Schacht, J. "Ribâ." In The Encyclopedia of Islam, 2nd ed., vol. VIII, 491–3.

'UTHMAN IBN 'AFFAN

'Uthman was the third caliph (644–656 CE). His personality and actions are controversial, and different groups in Islam formed conflicting views of him. He was a descendant of Umayya of the clan of Quraysh, but, unlike most of the other Umayyads, he was an early follower of the Prophet Muhammad and one of the inner circle of the Prophet's Companions. He became caliph after the deliberations of the small consultative group (shura) set up by the previous caliph, 'Umar, when he was dying.

As caliph, 'Uthman is best known for two things. First, he is generally regarded as the one who ordered the collection of the revelations made to Muhammad and the establishing of the text of the Qur'an as it has been known ever since. Second, his caliphate saw the beginning of divisions among the Muslims that were to lead to a civil war (fitna) upon his death. 'Uthman was killed by a group of Arab Muslim warriors who came to Medina from the garrison town of Fustat in Egypt with various grievances.

Their immediate grievances probably concerned pay and the allocation of land and booty, but the historical tradition preserves lists of complaints against 'Uthman of a more general sort. He is accused of favoring his Umayyad relatives when making appointments to governorships and other offices, of failing to apply Islamic law properly, and of the mistreatment of pious individuals like Abu Dharr, who warned of corruption in high places. Even what he did regarding the scripture alienated some.

For the Sunnis, 'Uthman is one of the Rightly Guided Caliphs (khulafa' rashidun). He was one of ten of the Prophet's Companions to whom the Prophet promised entry into paradise, and his death was an unjustifiable murder that warranted his designation as a martyr (shahid). For the Shi'is, 'Uthman was an illegitimate caliph who had usurped the office that rightly belonged to 'Ali and whose personal weakness opened the way for the takeover and corruption of Islam by the Umayyads. For the Kharijis, he was an unrighteous ruler whose killing was entirely justified.

Those views were mainly retrospective ones. Modern historians have argued that 'Uthman's policies and personality may have been open to criticism, but he was unfortunate in that he was caliph at a time when the swift conquests achieved under his two predecessors had begun to slow down and frustrations and tensions that had previously been suppressed came to the surface.

GERALD R. HAWTING

Further Reading

Hinds, Martin. "The Murder of the Caliph 'Uthman." *International Journal of Middle East Studies* 3 (1972): 450–69. (Reprinted in Hinds, Martin. *Studies in Early Islamic History,* eds. J. Bacharach, et al. Princeton, NJ: Darwin Press, 1996.)

Madelung, Wilferd. *The Succession to Muhammad.* Cambridge, UK: Cambridge University Press, 1997.

V

VIZIERS

The term *vizier* is derived from the Arabic term *wazir*, the core meaning of which refers to "bearing a load." This is an apt definition, because the viziers were those that headed the administrations of caliphs, amirs, and sultans throughout the continuum of medieval Islamic history. The modern studies of viziers have focused on a number of key questions: the origins of the office and its early duties; the varied roles played by viziers over the centuries; and case studies of important families of viziers ranging from the 'Abbasid period through the Ottoman era. One theme that runs throughout the history of the vizierate in Islamic history is the personal nature of the power dynamics in Islamic administrations. Viziers could rise from humble secretarial posts or even slavery to the extreme heights of wealth and power, only to be removed from office and/or killed by the whims of caliphs or sultans. This "hire and fire at will" nature of the post did not deter many from seeking it for themselves and their family members. As is seen in the examples of the Barmakids and the Banu 'l-Furat of the 'Abbasid period and the Çandarlı and Köprülü families of the Ottoman Empire, the personal nature of the vizierate also helped create dynasties of capable administrators.

The origin of the vizierate in Islam is hard to pinpoint accurately, because the sources are vague regarding the development of early Islamic administration. From the rudimentary structure of the diwan system during the Islamic conquests through the Umayyad dynasty, the officials who helped the caliphs with the running the government were often typified as being freedmen, boon companions, or *aides-de-camp*. It is not until the 'Abbasid period that clear references to the term *vizier* are found; even then key questions remain regarding whether the use of the word stemmed from traditional Persian practices or from other cultures and when exactly the 'Abbasids began to use the term exclusively. By the end of the eighth century, however, viziers were the central component of 'Abbasid administration, taking on the important tasks of overseeing the various ministries (e.g., chancellery, tax, mazalim [courts of justice]). The Barmakids, a Persian family who had converted to Islam from Buddhism, rose to prominence during the late eighth century and played a variety of roles: patronizing scholars, tutoring princes and caliphs, overseeing 'Abbasid affairs, and creating their own cadre of supporters within the government. By the beginning of the ninth century, it appeared that the Barmakids were indispensable elements of the 'Abbasid system, but their famous fall from grace in 803 CE, replete with arrests, confiscation of wealth, and executions, underscored the fact that they, as was true of all government officials, were working at the will of the caliphs. The example of the Barmakids' rise and fall would become a staple in many works written about the nature and duties of the vizierate for centuries to come.

As the 'Abbasid caliphs began to weaken in power during the ninth century, the viziers took stronger roles within the government, often rivaling the caliphs when it came to determining policies or even succession issues. Such regional dynasties as the Fatimids, Buyids, and Saljuqs, which arose during the tenth and eleventh centuries, had strong vizierates of their own, although the personal power dynamics between the ruler and his viziers in these cases were similar to those of the earlier 'Abbasids. Ibn Killis was a key vizier for the Fatimids during the ninth century, whereas Nizam al-Mulk, who worked for the Seljuk sultans Alp Arslan and Malikshah, would become the most famous vizier in Islamic history. Nizam al-Mulk, who was Persian by birth, was instrumental in developing the administrative structure of the Seljuk system in addition to helping found the state-sponsored madrasa educational institution. His ideas about government and rule are found in his work titled *Siyasat-name (The Book of Government)*, a "Mirror for Princes" guide that is akin to Machiavelli's *The Prince*. Nizam al-Mulk uses historical examples to argue his points on justice, effective rule, and the role of government in Islamic society. After his assassination in 1092 at the hands of assassins, members of his bureaucratic entourage, the Nizamiyya, played key stabilizing roles in the chaos that accompanied the gradual breakup of Seljuk control in Iraq and Iran. Another notable development in eleventh- and twelfth-century vizierial history is that there was a blending of administrations that involved viziers who would work for the revitalized 'Abbasid vizierate at one point and then work for other regional dynasties. Because viziers would often work for a variety of regional powers throughout their careers, the idea of separate or parallel administrations is undermined, whereas the personal, individualized nature of the administrative system is again underscored.

During the Ottoman period of expansion, the roles of viziers remained largely unchanged from the past; they were tutors, administrators, military figures, and confidantes. In addition, the grand viziers would often be linked to the Ottoman family through marriages to Ottoman princesses. This familial tie was not unprecedented, however; numerous examples abound from earlier centuries of viziers marrying into regional dynasties' families. The most famous vizierial families of the Ottoman eras include the Çandarlı family, who aided the fifteenth-century Ottoman sultans until the reign of Mehmed II, and the Köprülü family, who were instrumental in stabilizing Ottoman rule during periods of crisis during the late seventeenth century. Individual viziers also made their mark in history: Ibrahim Paşa rose from slavery to become the boon companion of Suleyman (r. 1520–1566) and eventually to become Grand Vizier until his fall from grace in the 1530s; Sokollu Mehmet Paşa, who at the end of Suleyman's reign attempted to stabilize the government, fought against rival factions within the imperial courts of Suleyman's successors. Their careers and those of the viziers before them clearly show that, however bureaucratized and formalized the system of Islamic administration would become, at its core the nature of the administration and delegation of power and authority from caliphs and sultans was highly personal in nature.

ERIC HANNE

See also Bureaucrats; Courts; Diplomacy; Madrasa; Mirrors for Princes; Nizam al-Mulk; Political Theory; Scribes; Ya'qub ibn Killis

Further Reading

Bravmann, Meir M. "The Etymology of Arabic Wazir." In *Islam* 37 (1961): 260–3.
Fodor, P. "Sultan, Imperial Council, Grand Vizier: The Ottoman Ruling Elite and the Formation of the Grand Vizieral *Telkhis*." *Acta Orientalia* (Budapest) 47 (1994): 67–85.
Imad, Leila S. *The Fatimid Vizierate, 969–1172*. Berlin: Schwarz, 1990.
Kennedy, Hugh. "Central Government and Provincial Elites in the Early 'Abbasid Caliphate." *Bulletin of the School of Oriental and African Studies* 44 (1981): 26–38.
———. "The Barmakid Revolution in Islamic Government." In *History and Literature in Iran: Persian and Islamic Studies in Honour of P.W. Avery*, ed. C. Melville. London: British Academic Press, 1990.
Lambton, A.K.S. *Continuity and Change in Medieval Persia: Aspects of Administrative, Economic and Social History, 11–14th Century*. London: Tauris, 1988.
Sourdel, Dominique. *Le Vizirat 'Abbâside de 749 à 936*, 2 vols. Damascus: Institut Français de Damas, 1959–1960.
Tyan, Emile. *Institutions du Droit Public Musulman*, 2 vols. Paris: Recueil Sirey, 1954–1957.

WAQF

A *waqf* is trust-like instrument created by a Muslim who designates the principle of property that he or she owns as an endowment that henceforth may not be sold, gifted, or transmitted through inheritance, with the result being that the property becomes inalienable in perpetuity. The terms of an endowment are recorded in an endowment deed *(waqfiyya)* that is drawn up with great care in an effort to eliminate any ambiguity; in the deed, the founder announces the purpose of the endowment, specifies the beneficiaries, and makes provisions for its administration. These deeds are important sources for the history of Muslim societies.

Revenues generated by endowment property are distributed among beneficiaries according to the rules specified by the founder in the endowment deed. The beneficiaries are generally of two types: (1) the founder's children and lineal descendants (i.e., a family endowment) or (2) religious institutions (e.g., a mosque or madrasa) or public endowments (e.g., a drinking fountain). Not infrequently, a founder creates a joint or shared endowment in which half of the revenues are assigned to the founder's children and descendants and half are assigned to a religious or public institution. The endowment property itself is placed in the hands of an administrator, whose duties include maintaining the property and ensuring its proper exploitation, supervising repairs, and distributing the revenues to the beneficiaries. If the purpose for which the endowment was created ceases to exist (e.g., the line of beneficiaries comes to an end or the

institution to which the revenues originally were assigned is destroyed or ceases to function), the revenues revert to some charitable purpose (e.g., the poor or travelers).

Although endowments are not mentioned in the Qur'an, the Prophet Muhammad is reported to have sanctioned the use of the institution in response to an inquiry from 'Umar ibn al-Khattab relating to valuable land acquired by the latter. When 'Umar asked the Prophet what he should do with the property, Muhammad is said to have replied, "If you wish, sequester its principle and distribute the usufruct as alms." It is believed that 'Umar did in fact create an endowment and that he stipulated that the principle "may not be sold, given away as a gift, or inherited." The revenues were used to support "the poor, kin relations, slaves, the Holy War, travelers, and guests," and guidelines were established for the use of the revenues by the endowment administrator.

The waqf is a distinctive Islamic institution that emerged during the course of the AH first/seventh century CE. It was in large part the creation of Muslim jurists who, drawing on a range of existing customs (e.g., Byzantine, Sasanian, Jewish) relating to both piety and property, brought clarity and order to this area of the law by creating the legal terms and principles that became the defining features of the system. By the end of the first century, the Umayyads had created a central waqf administration that no doubt kept registered copies of endowment deeds. By the middle of the third/ninth century, the system was fully formed, and sophisticated waqf treatises had been written by scholars such as al-Khassaf and Hilal al-Ra'y.

Endowments are a special kind of *sadaqa* (an act pleasing to God intended to bring the founder closer to Him). A key motivation for the creation of endowments is the founder's concern for salvation. The establishment of an endowment is a two-way transaction: the founder provides a regular source of income for his descendants or the means for the establishment and upkeep of a public institution, and, in return, the beneficiaries of his largesse are instructed to perform certain duties on his behalf (e.g., saying prayers, performing the pilgrimage), the reward for which is credited to the deceased. Thus, these endowments contributed to the memorialization of the founder and to the safeguarding of his or her memory, in perpetuity, by ensuring that good deeds would be performed in his or her name even after death.

The endowment system has many practical functions. By creating a family endowment, a founder removes part or all of his patrimony from the atomizing effects of the Islamic law of inheritance, shields it from taxation and confiscation by the state, and provides a regular income for children and descendants. Beginning during the twelfth century, Muslim rulers such as Salah al-Din, and, later, the Mamluk and Ottoman sultans, used the endowment system to transform the urban landscape of cities like Cairo, Damascus, Jerusalem, and Istanbul by creating madrasas for jurists, khanaqahs for Sufis, hospitals, public kitchens, arsenals, and military fortifications, to name just a few. The assets dedicated to the support of these institutions included both urban properties (e.g., apartments, shops, ovens, food stalls, bathhouses, warehouses, caravansaries) and rural properties (e.g., gardens, orchards, villages [or part thereof]). Rulers also created ribats on the frontiers of the Islamic state in which Sufis and other Muslims worked the land and contributed to the spread of Islam. The waqf system was an important source of income for scholars, Sufis, administrators, workers, and the poor. Slowly but inexorably, the volume of urban and rural properties dedicated to endowments increased greatly; at the time of the Ottoman conquest of Egypt in 1516, for example, fifty percent of Egypt's agricultural resources reportedly had been designated as endowments.

The endowment system was dynamic and diverse, responding to the changing needs of families, communities, and the Muslim state. Although endowment properties are in principle inalienable, Muslim jurists developed mechanisms for the exchange of endowment properties in response to the needs of the market. At any given point in time, large numbers of Muslims were affected by—or benefited from—endowments. The system provided Muslim society with stability; in some cases, endowments created a thousand years ago continue to function today. It also created an important connection between the beneficiaries and employees of a particular institution and the properties that were the source of its revenues.

DAVID S. POWERS

Further Reading

Amin, M.M. *Catalogue des Documents d'Archive du Caire de 239/853 à 922/1516.* Cairo, 1981.

Baer, Gabriel. "Women and *Waqf*. An Analysis of the Istanbul *Tahrir* of 1546." *Asian and African Studies* 17 (1983).

Bakhit, M.A. "Safad et sa Région d'Après des Documents de *waqf* et des Titres de Propriété 780–964 (1378–1556)." *Revue des Mondes Musulmans et de la Méditerranée* lv–lvi (1990): 101–23.

Barkan, O.L. "Les Fondations Pieuses Comme Méthode de Peuplement et de Colonisation." *Vakìflar Dergesi* 2 (1942): 59–65.

Cahen, Claude. "Réflexions sur le Waqf Ancien." *Studia Islamica* xiv (1961): 37–56.

Catten, H. "The Law of Waqf." In *Law in the Middle East*, vol. 1, eds. M. Khadduri and H. Liebesny, 203–22. Washington DC, 1955.

Deguilhem, Randi. *Le Waqf dans l'Espace Islamique. Outil de Pouvoir Socio-politique.* Damascus, 1995.

Hennigan, Peter C. *The Birth of a Legal Institution: The Formation of the Waqf in Third-Century A.H. Hanafi Legal Discourse.* Leiden: E.J. Brill, 2004.

Hoexter, Miriam. *Endowments, Rulers, and Community. Waqf al-Haramayn in Ottoman Algiers.* Leiden: E.J. Brill, 1998.

McChesney, Robert D. *Waqf in Central Asia: Four Hundred Years in the History of a Muslim Shrine, 1480–1889.* Princeton, NJ: Princeton University Press, 1991.

Pahlitzsch, J. "The Concern for Spiritual Salvation and *Memoria* in Islamic Public Endowments in Jerusalem (XII-XVI C.) as Compared to the Concepts of Christendom." In *Egypt and Syria in the Fatimid, Ayyubid and Mamluk Eras*, vol. 3, eds. U. Vermeulen and J. Van Steenbergen, 329–44. Leuven: Uitgeverij Peeters, 2001.

Petry, Carl F. "A Geniza for Mamluk studies? Charitable Trust *(Waqf)* Documents as a Source of Economic and Social History." *Mamluk Studies Review* 2 (1998): 51–60.

Powers, David S. "The Maliki Family Endowment: Legal Norms and Social Practices." *International Journal of Middle East Studies* 25 (1993): 379–406.

Rabie, Hassanein. "Some Financial Aspects of the *Waqf* System in Medieval Egypt." *al-Majalla al-Ta'rikhiyya al-Misriyya* 18 (1971): 1–24.

Verbit, Gilbert P. *The Origins of the Trust.* XLIBRIS, 2002.

WAQIDI, AL-

Born in Medina during the reign of the Umayyad caliph al-Marwan ibn Muhammad (AH 26/744–133/750 CE), just before the 'Abbasid Revolution (130/747), Abu 'Abd Allah Muhammad ibn 'Umar was better known as al-Waqidi, after his grandfather al-Waqid, *mawla* (client) to 'Abd Allah ibn Burayda of the Banu Aslam of Medina. According to Abu Faraj al-Isfahani, al-Waqidi's mother was the daughter of 'Isa ibn Ja'far ibn Sa'ib Khathir, a Persian, and the great granddaughter of Sa'ib, who introduced music to Medina.

These is no information about al-Waqidi's early education. Yaqut tells us that al-Waqidi was appointed judge over eastern Baghdad by the caliph Harun al-Rashid. In around 204/819, al-Ma'mun, son and heir to al-Rashid, appointed him to the position of qadi over the military camp of the prince al-Mahdi at Rasafa. Here he was able to accumulate a considerable collection of books and even to produce a large volume of writing, aided by his well-known amanuensis, Ibn Sa'd (d. 230/845).

Ibn al-Nadim gives a long list of the numerous works authored by al-Waqidi. The majority of his writings are devoted to excerpts from the history of Islam after the death of the Prophet, and, although none of these are extant, quotations from these works have been preserved in the works of later historians: accounts of the murder of 'Uthman are cited by both al-Tabari and Ibn Hubaysh (d. 584/1188) from the *Kitab al-Dar;* accounts from *Ta'rikh al-Kabir,* in which Waqidi listed all of the important events of history in the form of annals up to the year 179/795, have been cited by other scholars. As for his *Kitab al-Tabaqat,* it served as the basis of Ibn Sa'd's biographical dictionary and provided information about the Companions of the Prophet and their descendants.

Al-Waqidi is best known for his compilation, the *Kitab al-Maghazi,* which is his only work that survived. It tells of the last ten years of the Prophet's life and is an important source for the historical writings of al-Baladhuri (d. 279/892) and al-Tabari (d. 310/923), entitled *Futuh al-Buldan* and *Ta'rikh al-Rusul wa-l-Muluk,* respectively. Al-Waqidi wrote his *Kitab al-Maghazi* roughly a generation after Ibn Ishaq had composed his. According to al-Tabari, al-Waqidi had read Ibn Ishaq's biography of the Prophet and had gone so far as to commend his knowledge of the maghazi and ayyam al-'Arab. Nevertheless, al-Waqidi never cites even one of Ibn Ishaq's traditions in his compilation.

Sadly, al-Waqidi was a spendthrift by nature and generous to a fault. He died a pauper during the fourth year of his judgeship at the age of seventy-eight, in Baghdad, in the year 207/822 or 823, and he was buried at the Khayzuran cemetery. It is said that even the shroud for his burial had to be purchased by the caliph al-Ma'mun, whom al-Waqidi had appointed as executor of his will.

RIZWI FAIZER

Further Reading

Abbas, Ihsan, et al., eds. *The History of al-Tabari*, vols. 6–9. SUNY Press, 1985.
Rippin, Andrew. *Muslims: Their Religious Beliefs and Practices.* Routledge, 2001.

WEATHER

One of the most neglected aspects of medieval Islamic and Middle Eastern history is the role of the physical environment in economic and demographic issues important to the affected societies. In any serious study of the environment, weather and the fluctuations of the weather can be regarded as an obvious issue for the researcher or the analyst. Even the most cursory examination of the chronicles—whether Syriac, Arabic, or Persian—offers ample evidence of the role played by weather events or disturbances in the Near East and in neighboring Islamic lands, such as Spain and North Africa.

The evidence afforded by these sources describes damage or destruction that was wrought by four major types of weather disturbance: (1) damaging winds and/or dust storms; (2) severe cold and/or freezing precipitation in the form of hail, sleet, or snow; (3) rainstorms or inundations; and (4) droughts and excessive heat. The remainder of this article will address the nature and effects of such inclement weather.

Numerous windstorms, occasionally bearing damaging dust, struck at the core lands in the Middle East, such as Iraq, Egypt, and greater Syria, throughout the period from 600 to 1500 CE In some cases, hot, dusty winds withered crops, disrupted cultivation and commerce, and uprooted valuable trees (e.g., in Iraq and Iran in 848–849). In other instances, strong winds even sank boats (e.g., on the Tigris) and destroyed buildings (e.g., Iraq in 1051). The great windstorms thus ruined goods and infrastructure and thoroughly disrupted normal life, even causing apocalyptic reactions (e.g., end of the world or Resurrection fears in Mosul in 931 and in Egypt in 1038) among the affected populations.

Although popular perceptions of the Middle East have focused on desert heat and associated aridity, the fact is that one can find numerous examples of devastating hailstorms, damaging cold outbreaks, and even of snow and sleet (especially in Iraq in 748/49, Iran in 1014, and greater Syria in 682/83). The hailstorms could be especially dangerous, because they destroyed crops, damaged houses, and occasionally killed people and animals. Freezing temperatures and ice or snow wrought havoc on agricultural enterprises (e.g., in the case of ruined vineyards and olive groves in Syria in 748/49), killed

859

animals, and caused mortality from apparent hypothermia or cold-related maladies (e.g., in Syria in 768).

The rain associated with severe thunderstorms also contributed to loss of life and property. Flooding rains, which could cause tremendous damage, ravaged houses, shops, orchards, and crops. In particularly severe downpours, people were killed by raging waters (e.g., in Khuzistan in 904), collapsing buildings, or even by mud slides (e.g., in Mecca in 894). Water, which was always a precious commodity in the Middle East, became a deadly foe when severe storms battered such areas as Iraq, Arabia, and Egypt. Not surprisingly, the destruction from these storms was compounded by lightning strikes, wind, and hail (e.g., lightning damage in Mosul in 1130).

Less-surprising weather-related disasters in the context of the Middle East were, of course, the numerous episodes of excessive heat and severe drought that swept through the region and occasionally through Andalusia. The most obvious consequence in these instances was food shortage and, in severe cases, famine. Although numbers of people perished at times from heat exhaustion or thirst, the most common form of mortality associated with drought was either outright starvation during famines or mortality associated with epidemics sparked by drought-related food shortages. As is indicated elsewhere (see Secondary Sources below), nutritional deficiencies can be especially dangerous, subverting health and causing sickness or death. In this respect, one sees an important feature of climatic and other disasters: they tend to frequently occur in clusters and in related sequences—the common nexus of drought, food shortage, and famine, followed by disease epidemic.

More than thirty years ago, the French social historian Emmanuel Le Roy Ladurie published the seminal work *Times of Feast, Times of Famine: A History of Climate Since the Year 1000,* in which he amply demonstrated the importance of climate and weather disturbances throughout human history. Obviously, much of Le Roy Ladurie's work specifically addressed French climate history and thus had a more limited applicability for Middle Eastern societies. However, it clearly demonstrated the decisive role of environmental conditions in shaping the evolution of human societies, whatever the region.

WILLIAM F. TUCKER

Primary Sources

Anonymous. *Tarikh-i Sistan*, transl. Milton Gold. Rome, 1976.
Bar Hebraeus, Gregory. *Chronography*, transl. E.A.W. Budge. London, 1932.
Dionysus of Tell-Mahre. *Chronique*, transl. J.B. Chabot. Paris, 1895.
Ibn al-Athir, 'Izz al-Din. *al-Kamil fi al-Tarikh*, VIII. Beirut, 1966.
Ibn al-Dawadari. *Kanz al-Durar wa Jami' al-Ghurar*, VI. Cairo, 1961.
Ibn Hajar al-Asqalani. *Inba' al-Ghumr bi-Abna al-'Umr.* Bibliotheque Nationale Ms. Arabes, 1602.
Ibn Iyas. *Histoire des Mamlouks Circassiens*, II. transl. Gaston Wiet. Cairo, 1945.
Ibn al-Jawzi. *al-Muntazam fi Tarikh al-Muluk wa al-Umam*, V. Beirut, 1967.
Ibn Kathir. *al-Bidayat wa al-Nihayat*, XII. Cairo.
Michel le Syrien. *Chronique*, transl. J.B. Chabot. Beirut, 1963.
al-Nuwayri, Muhammad. *Kitab al-Ilman.* Hyderabad, 1970.
Sibt ibn al-Jawzi. *Mir'at al-Zaman.* British Library Ms. Or. 4619.
al-Suyuti. *Husn al-Muhadara fi Akhbar Misr wa al-Qahira*, Pt. 2. Cairo, 1981.
al-Tabari. *Tarikh al-Rusul wa al-Muluk*, X. Cairo, 1965.

Secondary Sources

Le Roy Ladurie, Emmanuel. *Times of Feast, Times of Famine: A History of Climate Since the Year 1000*, transl. Barbara Bray. New York, 1971.
Melville, Charles. "Meteorological Hazards and Disasters in Iran: A Preliminary Survey to 1950." *Iran* 22 (1984): 113–50.
Rabie, Hassanein. "Some Technical Aspects of Agriculture in Medieval Egypt." In *The Islamic Middle East, 700–1900: Studies in Social and Economic History*, ed. A.L. Udovich. Princeton, NJ: Darwin Press, Inc., 1981.
Tawwa, Fadi Ilyas. *al-Manakh wa al-As'ar wa al-Amrad fi Bilad al-Sham fi 'Ahd al-Mamalik (642–922 H./1250–1516 M.).* Beirut, 1998.
Tucker, William F. "Natural Disasters and the Peasantry in Mamluk Egypt." *JESHO* XXIV (1981): 215–24.
———. "Environmental Hazards, Natural Disasters, Economic Loss, and Mortality in Mamluk Syria." *Mamluk Studies Review* III (1999): 109–28.

WINE

The Arabic word for wine, *khamr/khamra*, is very common in early Arabic poetry and is probably a loanword from Syro-Aramaic *(hamra)*. Arabia and the Syrian desert—as opposed to Palestine and Mesopotamia—are not composed of soil that is fit for the growing of grapes. However, there are some exceptions, such as the Ta'if and several parts of Yemen, and wine is also referred to Medina. Usually wine was imported from Syria and Iraq, and, in early Arabic poetry, the wine trade is chiefly connected with Jews or Christians.

Wine is praised in the Qur'an (16:67): "And of the fruits of the date-palm, and grapes, whence ye derive an intoxicant *(sakar)* and a provision fair. Lo! therein is indeed a portent for people who have sense."

However, the configuration of the poetic genre of the wine song *(khamriyya)* of the Islamic period is believed to have originated in the town of Hira, from such sources as the Christian Tamimite 'Adi b. Zayd. In *The Cheery Companion, On the Prohibition of Old Wine,* the lexicographer al-Firuzabadi (d. 817/1415) collected an alphabetical list of approximately 357 "names of the wine," the majority of which are descriptive or allusive terms, like "golden," "cock's eye," "mother of vices," and a qualification taken from a tradition attributed to Muhammad, "the one which is drunken in the morning."

However, the intoxicant that the Arab of the Peninsula drank most was the *nabidh* (liquor, "spirit of wine"), a designation that does not appear in the Qur'an as a name for intoxicating drinks, several of which were produced in early Arabia from barley, honey, spelt, or different kinds of palms. Muhammad is said to have drunk nabidh, but he put water from the sacred source of Zamzam in it. In modern Syria, Lebanon, Palestine, Jordan, and other Arabic countries, the word *nbid* (dialectal pronunciation) is used to refer to any kind of intoxicating drink (especially wine), whereas, in Egypt, *khamr* and *nibid* have the same meaning.

The legal status of wine in the Qur'an has seen an evolution (2:219): "They question thee about strong wine [or strong drink] *(khamr)* and game of chance. Say: In both is great sin, and (some) utility for men; but the sin of them is greater than their usefulness." It is also mentioned in verse 4:43: "O ye who believe! Draw not near unto prayer when you are drunken…." Finally came the absolute prohibition (5:90): "O ye who believe! Wine *(khamr)* and game of chance and idols and divining arrows are only an infamy of Satan's handiwork. Leave it aside in order that ye may succeed." As compensation for abstaining, the believers will enjoy a pure wine in Paradise (83:25): "They are given to drink of a pure wine *(rahiq)*, sealed."

The prohibition of wine did not prevent a members of the higher classes, caliphs, viziers, men of letters, poets, and many others from enjoying it (e.g., in Iraq). The genre of the wine song reached its high point with poets like the Umayyad Caliph al-Walid b. Yazid (r. 125–126/743–744) and, above all, Abu Nuwas (d. ca. 200/815).

CLAUDE GILLIOT

See also Alcohol

Further Reading

Fulton, A.S. "Firuzabadi's 'Wine-list'." *BSOAS* 12 (1948): 579–85.
Goitein, S.D. *A Mediterranean Society. The Jewish Communities of the World as Portrayed in the Documents of the Cairo Geniza,* 6 vols., I, 1224; IV, 253–61. Berkeley, Calif: University of California Press, 1967–1993.
Heine, Peter. "Nabidh." In *EI*, VII, 840.
———. *Weinstudien. Untersuchungen zu Anbau, Produktion und Konsum des Weins im Arabisch-Islamischen Mittelalter.* Wiesbaden: Otto Harrassowitz, 1982.
Kueny, Kathryn Mary. "A Drink of Many Colors. Altered States of Wine in Islam." PhD dissertation. Chicago: University of Chicago Divinity School, 1995.
———. *The Rhetoric of Sobriety. Wine in Early Islam.* Albany, NY: State University of New York, 2001.
McAuliffe, Jane D. "The Wines of Earth and Paradise: Qur'anic Proscriptions and Promises." In *Logos Islamikos. Studia Islamica in Honorem Georgii Michaelis Wickens,* ed. Roger M. Savory and Dionisius A. Aguius, 159–74. Toronto: Pontifical Institute of Medieval Studies, 1984.
Wensinck, A.J., and J. Sadan. "Khamr." In *EI*, IV, 994–7. (Part reprinted: "Wine in Islam." *MW* 18 (1928): 365–73.)

WOMEN, JEWISH

Until the late Middle Ages, most of the world's Jewish population lived in Islamic lands such as Babylonia (Iraq), Persia (Iran), Syria-Palestine, and Egypt, and they also lived in the non-Arab Islamic countries of Spain and Sicily. The major sources of information about their lives in general—and about women's lives in particular—were the Geniza (Storage) documents, which were discovered in 1896 in a synagogue in Cairo. These documents reflect international commercial, intellectual, and family connections throughout the Muslim world. Later documents from Ottoman archives and shari'a court records were added to the various Hebrew preliminary sources, thus expanding modern knowledge of social and family life.

Jews and Muslims in Islamic lands shared a common urban cultural world. Jewish customs were influenced by the frequent social interaction between the two ethnic groups. There was great similarity between Muslim and Jewish wedding ceremonies, and polygamy was practiced by both Muslim and Jews, even being adopted by Ashkenazi and Sephardic Jews who immigrated to Muslim lands during the fifteenth and sixteenth centuries from Christian countries where polygamy was outlawed. In addition, both Jews and Muslims kept concubines. Child marriage—especially of young girls—was normal in both cultures, designed to ensure the girl's chastity and for social and economic reasons; however, unlike what was seen in Muslim society, the Jewish *kidushin* (wedding ceremony) was considered a sacred act, and it was very difficult to release a girl from its bonds if a marriage was unsuccessful. Because the commercial character of Jewish families and their frequent migration, marriages between individuals from different countries, which were contracted to extend and strengthen contacts between business partners, were common. Another phenomenon resulting from the mobility of Jewish society was the voluntary or involuntary neglect of wives. The problem of *agunot* (deserted wives) caused many *halakhic* (legal) discussions throughout the Middle Ages. Alternatively, husbands' absences, which sometimes extended over very long periods of time, enabled women to enjoy relative independence in managing their households and their children's educations. Jewish and Muslim women shared popular customs and beliefs, frequented the same holy places, and practiced the same methods and formulas to ensure safe pregnancy and childbirth.

Unlike those that were seen in Muslim homes, there were no separate quarters for women in Jewish homes. The "Geniza women," as described in Shlomo D. Goitein's monumental works, were expected to look after their young children and do the household chores, but these duties were apparently not very demanding: almost all households consisted of more than one female adult, and most urban middle-class families employed at least one maidservant. Older women were often assisted by their daughters-in-law, because, as was also done in Muslim society, newly-wed brides usually moved in with the husbands' families. Women of well-to-do families passed their time sewing or embroidering textiles for their homes. The daily routine of lower-class women included communal cleaning, laundering, cooking, and baking. Accordingly, women's education normally did not exceed the essential domestic skills. Although there are a few examples of women teachers during the Middle Ages, their activities caused personal and halakhic controversies, and they did not represent the norm. A girl's education depended entirely on her father's whim, and, even among the upper classes, most women were illiterate. Among thousands of letters from the Geniza, only a couple of dozen were sent by women; these were probably dictated to a professional scribe or a male acquaintance, and they deal with personal matters.

There is no single document about any spiritual or religious subject written by a woman. In addition to the halakhic restrictions, it seems that the crucial reason for women's illiteracy was the prevailing view that women do not need scholarly education, because they were meant to dedicate themselves to looking after their husbands and homes and to enable their menfolk to study. Halakhic and kabbalistic writings about this matter promised the ideal wife—the "Woman of Valor" (Proverbs 31:31)—a share in the world to come. However, in daily life, women's illiteracy maintained their dependency and ensured men's supremacy.

In external appearance, Jewish women were not distinguishable from their Muslim counterparts. They even wore a veil, in accordance with local customs, although women of the non-Muslim minorities (*dhimmi*) were not required—and were sometimes even forbidden—to do so. According to Jewish and non-Jewish travelers, all women were so heavily draped that even their husbands could not recognize them; the exposure of even a tiny bit of flesh was considered a disgrace.

Alternatively, as revealed by lists of trousseaus, wills, and inventories, middle-class Jewish women had a variety of weekday and Sabbath dresses, as well as gowns, veils, scarves, belts, and jewelry. One gets the impression that the objects were so thoroughly itemized mainly because of their investment value. The beautiful costumes and other items were not displayed outdoors, not only because women were covered with gowns but also for fear of inciting the authorities' attention. During the late Middle Ages, Jewish communal regulations went so far as to forbid excessive extravagance. From time to time, dhimmis—both male and female—were required to wear a distinctive color or sign.

Although modesty was required of Jewish women and women lived in relative seclusion, they were allowed freedom of movement, and they routinely took advantage of it. They worshipped at the synagogue; visited relatives; attended funerals, weddings, and other celebrations; and made pilgrimages to holy sites. Their outings led to many "immoral" incidents, which were often denounced by local sages. Regulations enacted by Jewish communities in Cairo, Damascus, Aleppo, Jerusalem, Safed, and other Jewish centers tried to prevent women from mingling with men on such occasions. A regulation from Jerusalem, for instance, instructed women to leave the synagogue a while before the ceremony ended to prevent them from encountering men on the way out. In Cairo, a pre-Ottoman regulation was reinstated during the mid-sixteenth century: "Men and women embroiderers are henceforth forbidden to sit at the same working table. . .only older women, aged forty or over, are allowed" (Rabbi David ben Zimra, *Responsa*, III, no. 919).

Usually, aside from philanthropy, women's economic activities in Islamic lands were restricted to money lending and real estate transactions. These financial activities enabled them to preserve both the value of their money and their modesty, and they were common even among the more secluded Muslim women of the Middle Ages. However, Jewish women were also active in business and commercial transactions outside of their homes. They traded textiles, precious stones, perfumes, spices, foodstuffs, wine, and other items. Those who had no property or money to finance such enterprises took to crafts and other professions, becoming weavers, embroiderers, wine and cheese producers, brokers, cosmeticians, healers, and town criers. The majority of working women, however, were widows and divorcees.

Jewish women were aware that, in some aspects of marital and inheritance laws, the Islamic legal system was more favorable to women than Jewish halakha. For fear that women would seek justice in non-Jewish courts, a regulation (enacted already by the late seventh century) enabled women to receive a divorce upon their request; this procedure was otherwise most difficult according to Jewish law. Over the years, this legal "breach" became more and more popular, especially among upper-class women. Shari'a court records testify that Jewish women applied to the qadi in matters concerning inheritance, divorcing recalcitrant husbands, family disputes, collecting *ketuba* (marriage contract) money, guardianship of children, and ensuring commercial transactions and the priority of a wife as compared with other creditors or debtors. Quite often, these women appeared personally in court to demand their rights.

Goitein described women in the early geniza period as living in a "world within a world," meaning that, within a world dominated by men, there was another, secluded world that was created by women for themselves. As far as Jewish women were concerned, their world was much more complicated: not only were they living as dhimmis in an Islamic traditional society, they were also subjected to Jewish halakhic and moral obligations. There was, however, a gap between theory and reality. It seems that many Jewish women found ways not only to lead a parallel world but also to take an active part in the economy and in social activities and to insist on their legal rights.

RUTH LAMDAN

See also Jews; Marriage, Jewish

Further Reading

Assis, Yom Tov. "Sexual Behaviour in Mediaeval Hispano-Jewish Society." In *Jewish History, Essays in Honour of Chimen Abramsky*, eds. A. Rapoport-Albert and S.J. Zipperstein, 25–59. London, 1988.

Bashan, Eliezer. *Studies in the History of the Jews in the Orient and North Africa*, 147–67. Lod, 1996.

Ben-Ami, Issachar. "Customs of Pregnancy and Childbirth among Sephardic and Oriental Jews." In *New Horizons in Sephardic Studies*, eds. Y.K. Stillman and G.K. Zucker, 253–67. New York, 1993.

Cohen, Amnon. *Jewish Life Under Islam*. Cambridge, Mass, 1984.

Friedman, Mordechai A. "The Ethics of Medieval Jewish Marriage." In *Religion in a Religious Age*, ed. S.D. Goitein, 83–102. Cambridge, Mass, 1974.

———. *Jewish Polygyny in the Middle Ages*. Jerusalem, 1986.

———. "Marriage as an Institution: Jewry Under Islam." In *The Jewish Family, Metaphor and Memory*, ed. D. Kraemer, 31–45. New York and Oxford, 1989.

Gil, Moshe. *In the Kingdom of Ishmael: Studies in Jewish History in Islamic Lands in the Early Middle Ages*, vol. I. Israel, 1997.

Goitein, Shlomo D. *Jews and Arabs*. New York, 1955.

———. *A Mediterranean Society, Volume III: The Family*. Berkeley, 1978.

Grossman, Avraham. "Changes in the Status of Jewish Women in 11th Century Spain." In *Me'ah She'arim, Studies in Medieval Jewish Spiritual Life in Memory of Isadore Twersky*, ed. E. Fleischer et al., 87–111. Jerusalem, 2001.

Guthrie, Shirley. *Arab Women in the Middle Ages, Private Lives and Public Roles*, 209–17. London, 2001.

Kraemer, Joel. "Spanish Ladies from the Cairo Geniza." *Mediterranean Historical Review* 6 (1991): 237–66.

Lamdan, Ruth. *A Separate People, Jewish Women in Palestine, Syria and Egypt in the 16th Century*. Leiden, Boston, and Köln, 2000.

———. "Female Slaves in the Jewish Society of Palestine, Syria and Egypt in the 16th Century." In *The Days of the Crescent*, ed. M. Rozen, 355–71. Tel-Aviv, 1996.

Levine, Melammed Renée. "Sephardi Women in the Medieval and Early Modern Periods." In *Jewish Women in Historical Perspective*, ed. J. Baskin, 115–34. Detroit, 1991.

Lewis, Bernard. *The Jews of Islam*. Princeton, NJ, 1984.

Marmer, David. "Patrilocal Residence and Jewish Court Documents in Medieval Cairo." In *Judaism and Islam, Boundaries, Communication and Interaction, Essays in Honor of William M. Brinner*, ed. Benjamin H. Hary et al., 67–82. Leiden, Boston, and Köln, 2000.

Stillman, Yedida K. "Attitudes Toward Women in Traditional Near Eastern Societies." In *Studies in Judaism and Islam Presented to S.D. Goitein on the Occasion of His 80th Birthday*, ed. S. Morag et al., 345–60. Jerusalem, 1981.

WOMEN, PATRONS

Some of the greatest Islamic works of art and architecture were commissioned by women. The most prolific patrons were usually members of the royal family: the mothers, wives, daughters, and sisters of rulers who built handsome mosques and tombs as public signs of dynastic and political power and amassed personal wealth in the form of art objects and coin. Members of the elite class, possessing wealth and social connections, could likewise commemorate themselves and their family members while performing an act of public charity to benefit their community. For relatively well-to-do women, property might consist of land and a house, a commercial venture, or farmland; at any economic level, it might include household goods such as jewelry, pots, bedding, and especially textiles (the Cairo Geniza documents show that textiles were one of most traded and collected items in the medieval Mediterranean). Although any woman with sufficient funds and autonomy could commission public and private art and architecture, generally the acts of patronage deemed important enough for historic record were those of politically prominent women whose names were inscribed on the works themselves.

The mothers, wives, and concubines of rulers were the most prolific patrons, both because they might have inheritance, state stipends, and gifts and because their construction of mosques, schools, hospitals, and communal fountains was a public demonstration of the ruling family's piety and generosity. Thus, in Ayyubid Damascus and Aleppo, numerous *madrasas* (theological colleges) and *khanqahs* (Sufi convents) were built by the regent queen Dafiya Khatun. In Cordoba, neighborhood mosques and a leper hospital were built by women of the Umayyad house. Because Islamic law protected a woman's right to inheritance and to the ownership of her dowry, in theory any women could own land and buildings and gain income from it by leasing her land or operating a business. Such rental income might go towards a *waqf* (perpetual endowment) for providing a mosque or public institution with support for upkeep and management. Thus, a woman's patronage could take the form of building a structure, collecting valuable objects, or creating endowments for charitable activities that might include building maintenance for a mosque, Qur'an recitation, alms, or providing dowries for orphan girls. Of course, in practice, not all societies within the medieval Islamic world granted women sufficient autonomy to exercise this right.

In regions in which male mortality was high as a result of war (e.g., Ayyubid and Mamluk Egypt), the family wealth was often held by women, because women provided stability and continuity for the transfer of wealth from one generation to the next. Female patronage typically benefited the family more than the women as individuals, and probably some buildings that were attributed to individual women patrons were in fact collaborative enterprises in which the woman's name, as a representative of her family, was more prominent than her actual financial or architectural contribution. This was also true of smaller works of art. For example, the inscription on an ivory game box from tenth-century Cordoba states that it was made for the daughter of 'Abd al-Rahman III. However, the name of the woman is not given, and, because that ruler had numerous daughters, the specific recipient of the box remains unknown. Furthermore, if she received it as a gift, the commission reflected little or nothing of her artistic taste.

In Islamic societies that engaged in diplomatic marriage between parties of equal status, the wife built in her own name, identifying herself by her paternal genealogy. Hence, at the madrasa/mausoleum/mosque complex (completed in 1438 CE in Herat) of Gawhar Shad, the powerful wife of Shah Rukh, the dedication inscription names her as the daughter of her father, a prominent noble from an allied clan. However, in the case of a slave-concubine, a woman might identify instead with her "adopted" family, which gave her status and rank as the mother of sons that would continue the family line. This was the case in the Ottoman Empire, where monumental mosques were typically built by the sultan's mother in her official capacity as *valide sultan* (queen mother). These concubines were not Muslim by birth, because the law forbade the enslavement of Muslims; however, they became politically powerful women, especially when they gave birth to an heir. Although the royal concubine mothers in the Ottoman and Mughal Empires and Umayyad al-Andalus came from ethnic and religious backgrounds that differed from those where they came to live, rarely can any cultural difference be discerned in their built works.

In general, female patronage must be contextualized within familial politics and the diverse cultural milieux in which choices were limited by the skills of the available artisans and the state of architectural technology. However, there are several outstanding instances of women whose patronage was remarkably innovative, evincing unusual personal taste that changed the history of Islamic architecture. For example, the women of the Timurid royal family built a series of diminutive mausolea at the Shah-i Zindeh complex (ca. 1350–1450) in Samarkand with lively tile revetment. Because these were small, quickly built works of individual commemoration, they reflected the various tastes of individuals rather than an official architectural style, and thus they were sites for experimentation in architectural ornament. Perhaps the most innovative early female patron was Shajar al-Durr, who, after the death of her consort, the Ayyubid Sultan Negm al-Din, in 1249, ruled as the legitimate sultan of Egypt for several months. Her major work was the addition of a monumental tomb to the mosque/madrasa complex of Negm al-Din (1250, Cairo). Standing prominently at one end of the façade of this complex, the tomb firmly linked the identity of the sultan with his major foundation, and thereafter the addition of the patron's tomb to an endowed complex became standard practice.

All patronage can be viewed as a reification of family and especially dynastic identity; however, because women and men played distinctly different roles within the family structure, their motivations for commissioning art and architecture differed accordingly.

D. FAIRCHILD RUGGLES

See also Family; Women, Muslim; Women Rulers

Further Reading

Atil, Esin, ed. "Patronage by Women in Islamic Art." *Asian Art* 6:2 (1993).

Hambly, Gavin, ed. *Women in the Medieval Islamic World: Power, Patronage, and Piety.* New York: St. Martin's Press, 1998.

Humphreys, R. Stephen. "Women as Architectural Patrons of Religious Architecture in Ayyubid Damascus." *Muqarnas* 11 (1994): 35–54.

Petry, Carl. "Class Solidarity Versus Gender Gain: Women as Custodians of Property in Later Medieval Egypt." In *Women in Middle Eastern History: Shifting Boundaries in Sex and Gender*, ed. Nikki Keddie and Beth Baron, 122–42. New Haven: Yale University Press, 1991.

Ruggles, D. Fairchild, ed. *Women, Patronage, and Self-Representation in Islamic Societies.* Albany, NY: State University of New York Press, 2000.

Woman writing. Courtier of Abbas I during a picnic. Sufavid mural, 1640s. Credit: SEF/Art Resource, NY. Chihil Sutun (Pavilion of 40 Columns), Isfahan, Iran

WOMEN POETS

Women poets of classical times were far fewer in number than their male counterparts, and their poetic domain was relatively restricted. Women were largely excluded from the "high" poetic genres of panegyric and satire, probably because of their social roles: mandatory seclusion in the case of freeborn women, and the providing of entertainment in the case of slave girls. The majority of extant women's poems are in the genres of elegy *(ritha')* by the former group and of erotic love song *(ghazal)* by the latter. In addition, there are some Sufi poems composed by women and sporadic compositions of nostalgia verses, wisdom verses, and children's lullabies; these last are often in the rajaz meter, which is generally not considered suitable for true poetry. The restriction of genre simultaneously denotes a restriction of form, whereby women's poetic production has usually been in the form of the more informal monothematic *qit'a* (short piece) generally used in elegies and love songs rather than the long, formal, polythematic *qasida* (ode) that is reserved mostly for the panegyric. It also denotes simplicity of language, which is a hallmark of the genres of elegy and love song.

The poetry composed by pre-Islamic women was almost wholly limited to *marathi* (sing. marthiya; elegy). Suzanne Stetkevych (1993, 161–6) argues that this limitation of poetic domain reflects the limitation of the role played by women in the public (which is equated with male) ritual life of the tribe, of which it was the function of poetry to record; this meant that there was limited occasion—the death of a warrior kinsman—upon which free women were allowed public voice. Indeed, at these occasions, it was their obligation to lament their fallen warriors and incite their remaining kinsmen to vengeance *(tahrid)*; it was their duty to shed ritual, poetic tears to redeem their fallen menfolk, just as it was the men's duty to redeem the death of kin by shedding blood.

Al-Khansa' (d. 24/645) was a preeminent mukhadrama poetess (one who straddled the pre-Islamic and early Islamic periods) who excelled in the genre of elegy. She composed more than a hundred short or medium-length elegies in which she elegized her brothers Sakhr and Mu'awiya and incited her tribesmen to take blood vengeance. A large number of her opening lines, and, indeed, the opening lines of most elegies by women, contain the "eyes shedding tears" motif, often in an exhortation by the poetess to herself to weep. The medieval anthologist Ibn Sallam al-Jumahi placed al-Khansa' second within the four great poets of ritha'; she was the only woman to make it into his ranks of 110 outstanding poets of pre-Islam and early Islam.

Layla al-Akhyaliyya (d. ca. AH 85/704 CE) was an Umayyad poetess whom critics often ranked close to al-Khansa'. Layla composed almost fifty short poems, particularly elegies for her slain kinsman and her lover, Tawba ibn Humayyir. She also composed an elegy for 'Uthman ibn 'Affan. However, "challenging gender-prescribed literary norms" (al-Sajdi, 143), Layla also exchanged some lewd satires with the poet al-Nabigha al-Ja'di and composed a few panegyrics for the Umayyad governor al-Hajjaj and the Umayyad Caliphs Marwan I and 'Abd al-Malik ibn Marwan. Her panegyric about 'Abd al-Malik is particularly noteworthy for its tripartite nasib-rahil-madih qasida form, traditionally a form that was squarely in the male poetic domain but that was reworked by her into a female version.

The other important genre of women's poetry was the love lyric. During the Umayyad and 'Abbasid periods, there were large numbers of professional singing slave girls (qiyan; sing. qayna) who often composed the love songs that they sang to the accompaniment of musical instruments. The line between musical and sexual entertainment was not always clearly drawn—singing girls were courtesans—and many eventually became concubines of the ruling elite. In his treatise about singing girls entitled *Risalat al-Qiyan (Epistle of the Singing-Girls)*, al-Jahiz (d. 255/868–869) stated, without referring to composition of poetry, that an accomplished singing girl had a repertoire of more than four thousand songs. Abu al-Faraj al-Isfahani (d. ca. 363/972) composed a different kind of treatise about singing girls entitled *al-Ima' al-Shawa'ir (Slave-girl Poets)*, in which he focused on their poetry. On the basis of this text, Hilary Kilpatrick (1991, 175) explains that three genres of poetry were preeminent among singing girls: (1) love poetry *(ghazal)*; (2) verse-capping competition with fellow poets, particularly other singing girls; and (3) short, informal panegyric verse for their masters. Three early 'Abbasid singing girls were particularly famous for their poetry: 'Inan (paramour of al-Rashid, r. 786–809), al-'Arib (concubine of al-Ma'mun, r. 813–817), and Fa-dl (concubine of al-Mutawakkil, r. 847–861). Additionally, literary anthologies attribute some courtly love poetry (most likely spuriously so) to Layla, who was the beloved of Majnun.

The 'Abbasid princess 'Ulayya (d. 210/825), daughter of al-Mahdi and half-sister of Harun al-Rashid, was also a singer-poet, although her social status was far above that of the singing girls. Her poetry and songs dealt mostly with the themes of courtly love and wine. She was trained by her mother, Maknuna, who, before being purchased by al-Mahdi,

had been a professional singing girl. 'Ulayya, in turn, trained singing girls for al-Rashid's palace.

Also said to have had her origins in the world of the singing girl was the famous mystic and poet of Basra, Rabi'a al-'Adawiyya (d. 185/801). She transmuted the love poetry of the singing girls to Sufi love poetry. Rabi'a is believed to have secured her freedom through her sanctity and, from that point on, to have lived an ascetic and teaching-oriented life. Several short pieces of Sufi love poetry are attributed to her.

Almost eight centuries later in the Mamluk period flourished another female Sufi master and poet named 'A'isha al-Ba'uniyya (d. 922/1517). A'isha, who lived in Syria and Egypt, belonged to the 'Urmawi branch of the Qadiriyya order and came from the distinguished Ba'uni family of judges and scholars. She composed more than a dozen books in prose and poetry, and was, according to Emil Homerin, the most prolific woman author before the twentieth century. More than 300 of her long poems have been collected in a yet unpublished anthology entitled *Fayd al-Fadl wa Jam' al-Shaml*. In them, she described mystical states and praised variously the Prophet Muhammad, the founder of her order 'Abd al-Qadir Jilani, and her own Sufi shaykhs. She used technical Sufi terminology and typical Sufi poetic motifs such as wine and love in her poems, sometimes in the strophic form and once in an eminent badi'iyya (long poem in which each verse uses a different rhetorical trope to praise Muhammad).

In addition to the East, women poets also composed love lyrics in the Muslim West. One such Andalusian poet is the Umayyad princess, Wallada (d. 484/1091), daughter of al-Mustakfi (r. 1024–4) and lover of the renowned poet Ibn Zaydun. Wallada was a literary force in Cordoba and hosted an important literary salon. Her extant oeuvre is made up of two short love poems for her lover and several obscene verses of invective addressed to him that were composed after their relationship had ended. Her models are believed to be not Western but Eastern, particularly Abu Nuwas. Anthologies also contain several poems by other Andalusian women, such as the courtesan Nazhun bint al-Qala'i (fifth/eleventh century), the teacher Hafsa bint al-Hajj (d. 585/1191), and the Jewish lady Qasmuna bint Isma'il (sixth/twelfth century); these were written in a similarly popular love-lyrical and satirical vein.

The classical Arabic library features three (extant) anthologies of poetry dedicated to women that provide their biographies and cite their poetry: Abu al-Faraj's above mentioned *al-Ima' al-Shawa'ir*; al-Marzubani's (d. 384/994) *Ash'ar al-Nisa' (Verses by Women;* this volume is partially extant, with works by thirty-eight mostly obscure ancient women); and al-Suyuti's (d. 911/1505) *Nuzhat al-Julasa' fi Ash'ar al-Nisa' (Recreation for Boon-Companions a propos Poems by Women,* a collection of works by forty "modern" women). The citation of women's poetry in the general medieval anthologies is sporadic and sparse. The earliest anthologists either ignored women poets or made disparaging remarks about them (see Ibn Sallam's upbraiding of Ibn Ishaq for citing women's poetry in his *Sira—Tabaqat Fuhul al-Shu'ara',* vol. 1, 8. Cairo, 1974.). However, most of the later anthologists—such as al-Jahiz, Abu Tammam, Ibn al-Mu'tazz, and Abu al-Faraj in the East and Ibn Bassam and al-Maqqari in the West—do cite some poetry by women. In addition, historians such as al-Tabari, Yaqut, and Ibn 'Asakir cite verses by women—such as elegies for the Prophet Muhammad by his daughter Fatima al-Zahra' and his aunt Safiyya bint 'Abd al-Muttalib—as part of their historical narratives. Most anthologies of classical women poets are modern compilations and rather short. In modern times, Arabic scholars have put together from the medieval sources several anthologies dedicated to women's poetry.

In his introduction to the *Nuzhat al-Julasa',* al-Suyuti refers to a large (at least six-volume) anthology—now lost—of "ancient" women's poetry by an anthologist named Ibn al-Tarrah (d. 720/1320) and titled *Akhbar al-Nisa' al-Shawa'ir (Accounts of Women Poets).* It would seem from this that women poets may have formed a more dynamic part of the poetic landscape, at least in the earliest classical period, than is generally believed.

TAHERA QUTBUDDIN

See also Poetry, Arabic; Elegy; Love Poetry; Concubinage; Singing; Women Ascetics and Mystics; Sufism and Sufis; Mystical Poetry

Primary Sources

Diwan al-Bakiyatayn: al-Khansa', Layla al-Akhyaliyya, ed. Yusuf 'Id. Beirut, 1992.
Diwan Fatima al-Zahra', ed. Kamil Salman al-Juburi. Beirut, 1999.
Diwan al-Khansa', ed. Ibrahim Shams al-Din. Beirut, 2001.
Diwan Layla al-Akhyaliyya, eds. Khalil al-'Açtiyya and Ibraim al-'Atiyya. Baghdad, 1967.
Diwan Rabi'a al-'Adawiyya wa Akhbaruha, ed. Muwaffaq Fawzi al-Jabr. Damascus, 1999.
Al-Isfahani, Abu al-Faraj. *Al-Ima' al-Shawa'ir,* ed. Jalil al-'Atiyya. Beirut, 1984.
Al-Marzubai. *Ash'ar al-Nisa',* eds. Sami Makki 'Ani and Hilal al-Naji. Baghdad, 1976.
Shi'r-Safiyya bint 'Abd al-Muttalib, ed. Muhammad al-Basyuni. Cairo, 2002.
Al-Suyuti, Jalal al-Din. *Nuzhat al-Julasa' fi Ash'ar al-Nisa',* ed. Salah al-Din al-Munajjd. Beirut, 1984.

Modern Anthologies

Garulo, Teresa, ed. *Diwan de las Poetisas de al-Andalus.* Madrid, 1985.
Al-Hayali, Layla Muhammad Nazim, ed. *Mu'jam Diwan Ash'ar al-Nisa' fi Sadr al-Islam.* Beirut, 1999.
Mardini, Raghda. *Shawa'ir al-Jahiliyya: Dirasa Naqdiyya.* Damascus, 2002.
Muhanna, 'Abd, ed. *Mu'jam al-Nisa' al-Sha'irat fi al-Jahiliyya wa al-Islam.* Beirut, 1990.
Saqr, 'Abd al-Badi', ed. *Sha'irat al-'Arab.* Doha, 1967.
Al-Wa'ili, 'Abd al-Hakim, ed. *Mawsu'at Sha'irat al-'Arab (min al-Jahiliyya hatta Nihayat al-Qarn al-'Ishrin),* vol. 1. Amman, 2001.
Wannus, Ibrahim, ed. *Sha'irat al-'Arab.* Antelias, Lebanon, 1992.

Further Reading

Di Giacomo, Louis. *Une Poetesse Grenadine du Temps des Almohades: Hafsa bint al-Hajj.* Paris, 1949.
Homerin, Th. Emil. "Living Love: The Mystical Writings of 'A'ishah al-Ba'uniyah (d. 922/1516)." *Mamluk Studies Review* 7 (2003): 211–34.
Khulayf, Yusuf. *Al-Shi'r al-Nisa'i fi Adabina al-Qadim.* Cairo. 1991.
Kilpatrick, Hilary. "Women as Poets and Chattels. Abu l-Farağ al-Isbahani's 'al-'Ima' al-Šawa'ir'." *Quaderni di Studi Arabi* 9 (1991): 161–76.
Nichols, J.M. "Wallada, the Andalusian Lyric, and the Question of its Influence." *Literature East and West* 21 (1977): 289–91.
———. "Arabic Women Poets in al-Andalus." *Maghreb Review* 4 (1979): 114–7.
Al-Sajdi, Dana. "Trespassing the Male Domain: The Qasidah of Layla al-Akhyaliyyah." *Journal of Arabic Literature* 31:2 (2000): 121–46.
Shamsi, Mas'ud Hasan. "'Ulayya: A Less Known 'Abbasid Princess." *Islamic Culture* 21 (1947): 114–22.
Smith, Margaret. *Rabi'a the Mystic and her Fellow Saints in Islam.* Cambridge, 1928.
Stetkevych, Suzanne. "The Obligations and Poetics of Gender: Women's Elegy and Blood Vengeance." In *The Mute Immortals Speak: Pre-Islamic Poetry and the Poetics of Ritual,* 161–205. Ithaca, NY, and London, 1993.
See entries on al-Khansa, Layla al-Akhyaliyya, Rabi'a al-'Adawiyya, 'Ulayya, and Wallada in the *Encyclopaedia of Islam,* 2nd ed., and the *Encyclopedia of Arabic Literature.*

WOMEN WARRIORS

In pre-Islamic Arabia, women are said to have customarily taken part in warfare, infrequently as combatants themselves but more often as inciters of the men of their tribes and as providers of succor and aid to the wounded. This situation continued through the early period of Islam. Biographical works document the presence of women on the battlefield during the time of the Prophet, including some of his wives. Ibn Sa'd (d. AH 231/845 CE), in his famous *al-Tabaqat al-Kubra (The Great Generations),* records the activities of some of these remarkable women, including their martial exploits in some cases, as does Ibn Hisham (d. 218/833) in his celebrated biography of Muhammad. More frequently, the women companions accompanied the men to battle to nurse the wounded and feed the thirsty. For example, Umm Ayman, the nurse and freedwoman of the Prophet, was present at the battle of Uhud in 4/625, at Khaybar in 7/628, and at Hunayn in 8/630, primarily in her capacity as a nurse. The pre-Islamic custom of goading the men to battle, especially by uttering imprecations on the enemy, appears to have been discouraged during the Islamic period. Ibn Sa'd mentions that, when Umm Ayman invoked God's curse on the opposing army, she was gently reprimanded by Muhammad. Several other women companions, such as Umm Sinan al-Aslamiyya and Ku'ayba bt. Sa'd al-Aslamiyya, are mentioned as having been present during a number of battles, primarily to tend to the sick and the wounded. The latter is said to have set up a tent in the mosque at Medina to serve as a makeshift hospital for the wounded.

There were actual female combatants as well: Safiyya bt. 'Abd al-Muttalib, for example, is reported to have descended on the battlefield at Uhud with a weapon in her hand. However, the most famous female warrior of the early Islamic period is the Ansari woman Nusayba bt. Ka'b, also known as Umm 'Umara. She was present at Uhud, al-Hudaybiyya (9/630), Khaybar, Hunayn, and al-Yamama (12/633–34). At Uhud, she valiantly defended Muhammad (along with her mother, according to some accounts) when the tide began to turn against the Muslims. She fought with a sword and a bow and arrow, sustaining severe injuries in the process. Her assailant was a man named Ibn Qumi'a from the opposing Makkan side, who had loudly declared his intention to kill the Prophet. Umm 'Umara would later proudly state that she had managed to strike at Ibn Qumi'a, ruing, however, the fact that "the enemy of God had on two suits of armor." She would later lose a hand at al-Yamama during the battle against the false prophet Musaylima after the fall of Mecca in 9/630.

The early biographers speak approvingly of these heroic women; for example, Ibn Sa'd gives a fulsome and laudatory account of Umm 'Umara's martial feats. The twelfth-century memoirs of Usama b. Munqidh (584/1188), a Syrian notable, contain references to women combatants during his own time, including his mother, which indicates that this practice had not become completely extinct during the later medieval period. However, Mamluk biographers like Ibn Hajar (d. 852/1449) tend to display ambivalence toward the martial activities of early women warriors. Ibn Hajar, in fact, considers the case of an obscure woman companion by the name of Umm Kabsha, who is said to have been denied permission to accompany Muhammad to an unspecified battle, as rescinding the earlier permission given to women to participate in battles, either as active combatants and/or as providers of humanitarian services. Ibn Hajar's opinion is to be regarded as being in accordance with the changed sensibilities of the Mamluk period, which involved a much more circumscribed public role for women.

ASMA AFSARUDDIN

Primary Sources

An Arab-Syrian Gentleman and Warrior in the Period of the Crusades: Memoirs of Usama ibn Munqidh, transl. Philip K. Hitti. New York, 2000.

Ibn Hajar, Ahmad b. 'Ali. *Al-Isaba fi Tamyiz al-Sahaba*, vol. 8. Beirut.

Ibn Sa'd, Muhammad. *Al-Tabaqat al-Kubra*, vol. 8, ed. Muhammad 'Abd al-Qadir 'Ata. Beirut, 1997.

Further Reading

Afsaruddin, Asma. "Reconstituting Women's Lives: Gender and the Poetics of Narrative in Medieval Biographical Works." *The Muslim World* 92 (2002): 461–80.

Ahmed, Leila. *Women and Gender in Islam: Historical roots of a Modern Debate*. New Haven and London: Yale University Press, 1992.

Lichtenstadter, Ilse. *Women in the Aiyam al-'Arab: A Study of Female Life During Warfare in Pre-Islamic Arabia*. London: The Royal Asiatic Society, 1935.

Y

YA'QUB IBN KILLIS

Abu 'l-Faraj Ya'qub ibn Killis—statesman, administrator, and intellectual—was born a Jew in Baghdad in 930 CE and died in Cairo in 991. During his youth, his family settled in Ramle, Palestine, where he engaged in commerce, achieving the important post of *wakil al-tujjar* (representative of the merchants). Bankruptcy forced him to flee to Egypt, where he entered the service of the regent Kafur and worked his way up to chief financial administrator. After Kafur remarked that, were Ibn Killis a Muslim, he would be worthy of being vizier, Ibn Killis converted to Islam in 967 and became an avid student of scripture and law. However, his patron's death the following year and the jealousy of the vizier Ibn al-Furat caused him to seek refuge in the Maghreb, where he entered the service of the Fatimid caliph al-Mu'izz. Ibn Killis's firsthand knowledge of Egyptian affairs proved invaluable to the Fatimids, who were planning an invasion of Egypt.

After the conquest and transfer of the seat of Fatimid power to the new capital of Cairo, Ibn Killis reorganized the financial administration of the country. He instituted a highly successful monetary reform that greatly increased state revenues and made the Fatimid dinar the standard currency of the Mediterranean. In 977, he became vizier under the young Caliph al-'Aziz. During his administration, the Fatimid Caliphate reached the height of prosperity and power. On his deathbed, Ibn Killis advised al-'Aziz to keep peace with Byzantium and to eliminate the unruly Bedouin in Palestine; this policy was followed. When Ibn Killis died in February 991, the young caliph himself led the funeral prayers and openly wept.

In addition to being an architect of Fatimid administration, Ibn Killis was a patron of scholarship and the arts. He conceived of making the Azhar mosque into a great institution of higher learning and was himself an expert on Isma'ili jurisprudence.

NORMAN A. STILLMAN

See also Al-Azhar; Fatimids; Ikhshidids

Further Reading

Fischel, Walter J. *Jews in the Economic and Political Life of Mediaeval Islam,* 2nd ed. New York: Ktav Publishing House, 1969.

YAQUT

The word *yaqut,* via the Syriac Arabicized Greek *(hyakinthos),* means corundum. It became the name of at least five well-known Muslim scholars who were slaves that were taken into captivity by Muslims during the Holy War; two of them became famous. The first is Yaqut al-Mu'tasimi (d. AH 698/1298 CE), who was native of Abyssinia or a Greek of Amasia. His "noun of relation" *(nisba)* al-Mu'tasimi, is derived from his master, the last 'Abbasid caliph in Baghdad, al-Mu'tasim, who had him educated; he became a librarian and a famed calligrapher.

The second of these slaves is the celebrated encyclopedist Yaqut al-Rumi al-Hamawi (575–626/

1179–229). He was born in Byzantine territory (hence his ethnic *al-Rumi*). He was captured as a boy and purchased by a merchant of Hama in Syria, who added to his name the ethnic *al-Hamawi*. Al-Rumi's master sent him to school so that he could help the master in his trade in the Persian Gulf. After his master died, al-Rumi settled in Baghdad and became a bookseller.

Al-Rumi traveled to many lands: Syria, Mosul, Egypt, Khorasan, and others. He benefited also from the assistance of important personalities, like the vizier Ibn al-Qifti in Aleppo. As a result of his journeys, he met a lot of scholars and came across many libraries, and he was very active in the copying of books. Of his numerous works, two should be mentioned. First, *The Dictionary of Learned Men*, which contains, in alphabetical order, biographies of grammarians, philologists, men of letters, poets, and so on. The second one is the *Geographic Dictionary*, which contains not only geographical information but also, under each place name, historical data, a list of eminent natives of the place, and other pertinent information.

CLAUDE GILLIOT

Further Reading

Canby, Sheila. "Yakut al-Mu'tasimi." In *EI*, vol. XI, 265.
Gilliot, Claude. "Yakut al-Rumi." In *EI*, vol. XI, 265–66.

YAZIDIS

Yazidiyya is a syncretistic sect, mainly made up of Kurdish speakers, whose adherents live mostly in Iraq (in the Jabal Sinjar and Sheikhan regions, north of Mosul). Small communities of Yazidis live also in northern Syria, southern Turkey, and Armenia. The size of the sect is estimated to be around two hundred and fifty thousand. Apart from Iraq, the derivation of the sect's name is obscure; the prevalent view among Western scholars is that it is related to Yazid ibn Mu'awiya, the second caliph of the Umayyad dynasty (r. 680–683 CE). Others believe the name to have been derived from the Persian word *yazad* ("divine being").

The Yazidis consider the founder of their religion to be a certain Shaykh 'Adi b. Musafir (of Umayyad descent), who is reported to have settled in the Kurdish mountains of northern Iraq at the beginning of the twelfth century.

Despite some external resemblance to Islam, the Yazidi cult shows no real affinity to Muslim beliefs or rituals. Its terminology and imagery both point to the mainly Iranian nature of this religion. The Yazidis believe in one God, who, after having created the world, delegated it to seven archangels, known also as "The Seven Secrets" *(haft sirr)*, the most powerful of whom is the Peacock Angel *(ta'us-e malak)*. Adversaries of the sect claimed that the latter was identical to the devil; it is from this that the abusive appellation "Devil worshippers" *('abadat al-shaytan)* came to be used by which the sect's opponents.

The syncretistic nature of the Yazidiyya cult is reflected in its rich mythology, which is made up of elements of Iranian, Jewish, Christian, and Muslim origins.

The sacred scriptures of the Yazidis include two major books, the *Mashaf-a Rash* and the *Kitab-i Jilwa*. These texts are commonly believed to have been composed by non-Yazidis who nevertheless relied on Yazidi traditions.

MEIR M. BAR-ASHER

Further Reading

Ebied, R.Y., and Young, M.J.L. "An Account of the History and Ritual of the Yazidis of Mosul." *Le Museon* 85 (1972): 481–522.
Guest, J. *Survival Among the Kurds: A History of the Yezidis.* London and New York, 1993.

YEMEN

Yemen's early Islamic history continues to suffer from a dearth of information. During the first two centuries AH (seventh and eighth CE), the administration of Yemen was directly dependent on the central caliphate, first in Medina and then in Damascus and Baghdad. The country was divided into three *mikhlafs* (administrative regions), each of which was overseen by a governor appointed by the caliph (the senior governor was the one appointed to San'a'): the mikhlaf of San'a', which included a large part of highlands from Sa'ada and Najran in the north to al-Janad; the mikhlaf of al-Janad, which included the southern region as well as the coastal plain of Aden and Lahij; and the mikhlaf of Hadramawt, which was limited to the district bearing that name, with Shibam as its principal town.

The weakening of the 'Abbasid caliphate during the ninth century led to the rise of several local and foreign dynasties in Yemen, with conflicting territorial, political, and religious interests. The first of these dynasties was the Ziyadids (819–1012), whose founder Muhammad ibn Ziyad was sent by the caliph al-Ma'mun to quell a rebellion in the Tihama region. There, he founded the city of Zabid, which became his capital and that of his descendants. During the same period, a local dynasty known as the Yu'furids (847–997), which was centered in Shibam-Kawkaban and occasionally in control over San'a', reigned over the territory extending south until al-Janad. However, parts of the northern highlands escaped all control until the arrival of Yahya ibn al-Husayn in 897, who came from Tabaristan at the invitation of several tribes. He chose Sa'ada in north Yemen as his capital, where he established the Zaydi imamate. However, for several centuries, the authority of his descendants did not go beyond the region of Sa'ada.

From the beginning of the eleventh century until the middle of the twelfth century, Yemen continued to be fragmented among several competing dynasties. The Najahids (1021–1156), who took over Zabid, were opposed to the Sulayhids (1047–1138), who held close relations with their co-religionists, the Isma'ili Fatimids of Egypt, and who were able to impose a certain political unity over southern Yemen, the Tihama, and the Hadramawt. Reigning at first from San'a' and then from their new capital in Dhu Jibla, the Sulayhids were able to restore commerce between the Orient and the Mediterranean basin, which became a source of prosperity for the country. Thus, the port of Aden, which was run by the Zuray'ids (1080–1173) in the name of the Sulayhids, became an important center for international commerce. The Sulayhids lost control over San'a' at the end of the eleventh century to the sultans of Hamdan, the local tribal leaders of that region; the Hadramawt was ruled by a number of local dynasties of tribal origins (e.g., the Banu Rashid in Tarim, the Banu Daghar in Shibam, and the Banu Iqbal in the port of al-Shihr).

The conquest of Yemen in 1173 and 1174 by the Ayyubids, who were successors of the Fatimids in Egypt, included the Hadramawt, where they succeeded briefly in eliminating the mini states of that region; the inhabitants of the highlands of the north, who were generally loyal to the Zaydis, rebuffed them. The Tihama and the southern parts of Yemen formed a single political unit after their regional dynasties were eliminated. San'a', which fell under their hegemony for a while, reverted to the control of Banu Hatim, a branch of the Hamdan, whereas the north continued to be loyal to the Zaydis. Equipped with an efficient army and a competent administration, the Ayyubids introduced numerous reforms, most notably in the fields of agriculture and commerce. They also brought to Yemen the institution of the madrasa, which their successors, the Rasulids, developed further in an effort to counter the Zaydi doctrine. Having arrived in Yemen with the Ayyubid army, the Rasulids (1229–1454) gained control of the country and established their authority as far as San'a'. They chose Ta'iz in the southern highlands as their capital, and Zabid became their winter residence. Under their impetus, the capital of the Tihama became a major center for the teaching of the Sunni doctrine.

The weakening of the Rasulids presented the opportunity to the Tahirids, the governors of Aden, to take over and establish themselves as the new rulers of southern Yemen in 1454. They were also keen builders (as were their predecessors), allocating much of their building activity to their capital, al-Miqrana, and to Rada', Juban, and Zabid. The Tahirids were equally interested in developing the agriculture of the area, and they established new palm groves in the irrigated regions of the coastal plains. They also tried to extend their authority over the Hadramawt, where political instability continued. Their hold on that region, much like that of their predecessors, was short lived, because they were faced with strong opposition from local dynasties, who would accept only nominal allegiance. Thus, the Al Yamani dynasty that was established in Tarim in 1224 remained on the political scene until the sixteenth century (it ended in 1714) before it was eliminated by the Kathiris. At the beginning of the sixteenth century, a new political power appeared in the region: the Yafi'is, a large tribe from the northeast of Aden whose influence extended over the ports of Mukalla and Shihr. They created a new sultanate, first under the name of the Qasidis and then under that of the Qu'aytis, whose seat of power was in Qatn.

After the demise of the last Tahirid sultan in 1517, a group of mercenaries from Egypt, known as the Lewend, became the rulers of lower Yemen during a brief period (1521–1538) before the Ottomans put an end to their presence. The arrival of the Portuguese in the Indian Ocean and the Red Sea also had strong repercussions throughout the country. Increasingly worried about the security of the Holy Cities of Arabia as well as about maintaining control of the international trade between the East and the Mediterranean, the Ottomans, who had conquered Egypt in 1517, decided to take hold of Yemen in 1538. However, their presence there rapidly provoked revolts, led by the Zaydi imams of the Qasimi dynasty, who were able to liberate the country in 1635; they then extended their control to most of Yemen from Najran to the Hadramawt.

NOHA SADEK

See also Aden; Arwa; Sulayhids; Rasulids; Zaydis

Further Reading

Daum, Werner, ed. *Yemen: 3000 Years of Art and Civilisation in Arabia Felix.* Innsbruck: Pinguin, 1988.
Kay, H.C. *Yaman. Its Early Mediaeval History.* London: Edward Arnold, 1882.

Al-Mad'aj, 'Abd al-Muhsin M. *The Yemen in Early Islam, 9–233/630–847: A Political History.* London, 1980.

Serjeant, R.B., and Lewcock, R., eds. *San'a', an Arabian Islamic City.* London: Festival of Islam Trust Foundation, 1983.

Schuman, L.O. *Political History of the Yemen at the Beginning of the 16th Century.* Groningen, 1960.

Z

ZANKIDS

The Zankids were a Turkmen dynasty, several branches of which ruled in Jazira and Syria between 1127 and 1251 CE. Zanki, the founder of the dynasty, was the son of Aqsunqur, a military slave of the Seljuk sultan Malikshah and ruler of Aleppo between 1087 and 1094. In 1127, Sultan Mahmud made Zanki ruler of Mosul and atabeg (guardian and tutor) for his two sons. In 1129, the sultan appointed him malik (king) of the West. Zanki took advantage of the struggles for succession of the Seljuk sultans and their problems with the 'Abbasid caliphs to solidify his own base of power in Mosul. By 1128, he controlled Aleppo and then campaigned in Syria, attacking the atabeg state of the Burids in Damascus and seizing territory in southeastern Anatolia. He won his greatest fame in 1144, when he conquered the Crusader County of Edessa, which provoked the Second Crusade.

When Zanki was murdered in 1146, his two sons divided his realm. Ghazi took Mosul and the territories in Jazira, whereas Nur al-Din Mahmud took Aleppo and the territories in Syria. Zanki's most renowned descendant was Nur al-Din, in whom he inspired a Sunni religious zeal against both the Shi'is and, especially, the Crusaders. In 1154, Nur al-Din captured Damascus, putting an end to the Burids and uniting most of Syria against the Crusaders. His army entered Egypt several times, and, in 1169, its commander, Shirkuh, became vizier to the greatly weakened Fatimid caliph. Shirkuh's nephew Saladin abolished the Fatimid caliphate in 1171 and acknowledged the authority of Nur al-Din. Around the same time, Nur al-Din conquered Jazira and established suzerainty over Mosul. He died in 1174 at the height of his power.

Nur al-Din's state did not long survive him. Saladin immediately invaded Syria and took Damascus. By 1183, he had conquered all of the Zankid territory in Syria. The descendants of Ghazi managed to retain Mosul somewhat longer. Saladin attacked Ghazi in 1175–1176, and he invaded Jazira in 1182–1183 and 1185–1186. This fragmented the Zankid territory into five principalities that acknowledged Saladin's suzerainty. Saladin's Ayyubid successors maintained supremacy in that region. In 1209, his brother al-'Adil annexed part of Jazira. In 1211, Mas'ud II became atabeg of Mosul. Mas'ud's father had chosen a military slave, Badr al-Din Lu'lu', to serve as regent. Badr al-Din eventually became so powerful that he could depose the Zankid atabegs while keeping the Ayyubids in check. In 1233, the last Zankid claimant to Mosul died, and the caliph recognized Badr al-Din as the new ruler of that city. Minor branches of the Zankids at Sinjar and Jazirat Ibn 'Umar fell under Ayyubid dominion in 1220 and 1251, respectively. The branch at Shahrazur was destroyed by the Mongols in 1245.

The Zankids did much to encourage the economic and cultural revival of Jazira and Syria. They rebuilt cities, established such institutions as hospitals and madrasas, ensured the supremacy of Sunnism over Shi'ism in their territory, and played a critical role in repelling the Crusaders.

GARY LEISER

See also 'Abbasids; Ayyubids; Fatimids, Jihad; Muslim–Crusader Relations; Seljuks; Shi'ism; Slavery, Military

Primary Sources

Ibn al-Qalānisī. *The Damascus Chronicle of the Crusades,* transl. H.A.R. Gibb. London: Luzac, 1932.

Further Reading

Alptekin, Coşkun. *The Reign of Zangi (521–541/1127–1146).* Erzurum, Turkey: Atatürk University Press, 1978.
Elisséeff, Nikita. *Nūr ad-Dīn, un Grand Prince Musulman de Syrie au Temps desCroisades,* 3 vols. Damascus: Institut Français de Damas, 1967.
Patton, Douglas. *Badr al-Dīn Lu'lu': Atabeg of Mosul, 1211–1259.* Seattle: University of Washington Press, 1991.

ZAYD IBN THABIT

Zayd ibn Thabit was a Medinan, born in 611 CE, who served as the Prophet Muhammad's scribe after the Hijra. Since he was only eleven years old at the time of the Hijra, he must have become Muhammad's scribe while he was a mere teenager. Zayd gained this prestigious position in part because of his knowledge of Hebrew and/or Syriac script.

Zayd played a particularly important role in the collection and codification of the Qur'anic text. Reports vary in their descriptions of when the Qur'an was first collected and committed to writing. Some reports assert that the impetus to create a standard, written text came after the death of many of the qurra' in the battles of the Ridda wars after Muhammad's death. Abu Bakr and 'Umar feared that the divine revelation would be lost if too many of those who knew it were killed in battle; they therefore urged Zayd to collect and compile the revelation. Other accounts place the establishment of a standard Qur'an text earlier, during the last year of Muhammad's life, when he edited a final copy of the Qur'an that Zayd had written down. Still other reports suggest that there was not an agreed-upon text until the reign of 'Uthman, when the caliph assigned Zayd and three other companions to collect variant readings and establish a canonical text. In each of these versions of the compilation and codification of the Qur'anic text, Zayd ibn Thabit was the central figure.

During the strife at the end of 'Uthman's reign, Zayd was one of the few prominent Medinans (Ansar) to remain loyal to the caliph and to refuse to support 'Ali ibn Abi Talib. He had been a loyal servant to Uthman and remained loyal to his kinsman Mu'awiya after he came to power in 41/661. Various reports indicate that Zayd served as a qadi, as head of the treasury, as keeper of the diwan, and in other capacities. He was also recognized as an expert in the distribution of inheritance (fara'id), which required both a familiarity with Qur'anic rules and considerable mathematical skill.

Zayd's young age and the prestige associated with his position as Muhammad's scribe made him a particularly important hadith transmitter. He had many students, and the veracity of his hadith transmissions was not questioned by later commentators. This is to be expected, because questioning his competence as a muhaddith implicitly cast doubt upon the veracity of his recording of the Qur'an itself. Even pro-'Alid sources do not malign Zayd's compilation of the Qur'an, although some explain his loyalty to Uthman as a consequence of the considerable wealth he accumulated while serving the caliph. Zayd's death date is uncertain, but it is likely sometime between 42/662 and 56/675.

STEVEN C. JUDD

Primary Sources

Ibn 'Asakir. *Ta'rikh Madinat Dimashq,* ed. al-'Amrawi. Beirut, 1995–2001.
Ibn Sa'd. *Kitab al-Tabaqat,* ed. E. Sachau. Leiden: Brill, 1904–1940.

Further Reading

Burton, John. *The Collection of the Qur'an.* Cambridge, Mass: Cambridge University Press, 1977.
Nöldeke, Theodor. *Gesschichte des Qorans.* Leipzig, 1938.

ZAYDIS

Zaydi is a branch of Shi'i Islam that emerged in support of the abortive revolt of Zayd ibn 'Ali in Kufa against Umayyad rule in 740 CE. Unlike the Twelver or Imami Shi'is, Zaydis do not unconditionally condemn the first three caliphs who preceded 'Ali ibn Abi Talib to the leadership of the Muslim community after the Prophet's death, and they do not consider Sunni Muslims to be infidels. As such, they are often considered moderates. In political terms, however (and again unlike the quietist Twelvers), the Zaydis are militant and insist on armed rebellion against unjust Sunni rule as a religious obligation. They also seek to establish righteous rule under a qualified *imam* (supreme leader) from the Prophet's family *(ahl al-bayt)*. Thus, the Zaydi doctrine of the imamate is one of the group's most distinctive features, and their history is dominated by a number of hugely influential imams.

Zaydi law has set a number of rigorous qualifications for the imamate, the most important of which are religious knowledge *(ijtihad)* and descent from either of 'Ali ibn Abi Talib's two sons, al-Hasan or al-Husayn. Zaydis hold that 'Ali was the most excellent of men after the Prophet and that he and his two sons were designated by the Prophet as his legatees. After al-Husayn, the imamate could only be established through a summons to allegiance *(da'wa)* and the armed rising *(khuruj)* by a qualified candidate. Over the course of time, Zaydis were able to establish several states in two distinct geographical locations: (1) in the Caspian regions of Tabaristan, Daylam, and Gilan; and (2) in the highlands of Yemen. The Zaydis do not follow the legal teachings of the imam after whom they are named (i.e., Zayd ibn 'Ali) but rather those of certain later imams, two of whom established states. In matters of theology, Zaydis are antideterminist and anti-anthropomorphist. In the Caspian, the first Zaydi state was established in 864 by al-Hasan ibn Zayd, and the last ended in 1526–1527 in eastern Gilan with the conversion of its ruler to Twelver Shi'ism. Here two rival schools of law emerged: the *Qasimiyya* (followers of al-Qasim ibn Ibrahim [d. 860]) and the *Nasiriyya* (followers of al-Nasir al-Hasan ibn 'Ali al-Utrush [d. 914]). These were ultimately reconciled doctrinally through the adoption of the principle that all mujtahids were correct regardless of their differences.

It is in the Caspian that Zaydi scholars developed a theology that was heavily influenced by Mu'tazilism, and, through their close connections with the Zaydis of Yemen, they were able to transmit these to the latter community. In the Yemen and at the invitation of the local tribes, Imam al-Hadi Yahya ibn al-Husayn (d. 911; grandson of the aforementioned al-Qasim b. Ibrahim) established a state in Sa'da in 897, and this lasted, under varying conditions of expansion and contraction, until 1962, with the emergence of the modern republic of Yemen. Al-Hadi's teachings in law became dominant among the Zaydis of Yemen and ultimately even among the Caspian Zaydis. During the reign of the last great Zaydi state, the Qasimis (1635–1850s), dynastic rule became the norm, and a group of influential Sunni-oriented reformist scholars emerged under Qasimi patronage, causing a Sunnification of the religious and political environment. The most prominent Sunni-oriented scholar who helped effect this change was Muhammad al-Shawkani (d. 1834).

BERNARD HAYKEL

Further Reading

Haykel, Bernard. *Revival and Reform in Islam: The legacy of Muhammad al-Shawkani.* Cambridge, Mass: Cambridge University Press, 2003.

Khan, M.S. "The Early History of Zaydi Shi'ism in Daylaman and Gilan." *Zeitschrift der Deutschen Morgenländischen Gesellschaft* 125: 301–14.

Madelung, Wilferd. *Der Imam al-Qasim ibn Ibrahim und die Glaubenslehre der Zaiditen.* Berlin: Walter De Gruyter, 1965.

———. "Zaydi Attitudes to Sufism." In *Islamic Mysticism Contested,* eds. Frederick De Jong and Bernd Radtke. Leiden: Brill, 1999.

ZIRYAB, ABU 'L-HASAN 'ALI BIN NAFI'

Abu 'l-Hasan 'Ali bin Nafi' Ziryab was an Iraqi musician born around 790 CE who died in Cordoba (Al-Andalus) in 852. His figure became the embodiment of the Andalusi classical musical style, and he was allegedly the arbiter of fashion in Cordoba under the reign of the Umayyad Emir 'Abd al-Rahman II (r. 822–852). He is historically better known by his nickname *Ziryab* ("Jay") than by his full name.

Extant sources tell us that Ziryab was forced to flee Baghdad after his musical mentor Ishaq al-Mawsili became jealous of him when Caliph Harun al-Rashid showed the young musician an esteem that might jeopardize al-Mawsili's position in the court. Ziryab subsequently settled down in Qayrawan, Tunisia, where he served the Aglabid rulers until he fell in disgrace. He then gained the Spanish shores and entered the service of the Umayyad emir (the *de facto* independent ruler) of Muslim Iberia, 'Abd al-Rahman II. Sources indicate that, until Ziryab's death and that of the emir himself (which occurred in the same year), the Andalusi sovereign treated Ziryab with the highest consideration.

Ziryab has traditionally been credited with introducing the refinements of the Oriental metropolis of Baghdad to Cordoba. He is said to have influenced the spread of cooking, clothing, hairdressing, and other arts and crafts fashions by introducing Eastern styles to the western Islamic world. However reliable this account is, it is true that a whole array of culture and etiquette principles that formed the bulk of Andalusi (and, later, North African) sophistication are ascribed to his merit. Modern scholarship has contested Ziryab's real influence, identifying later figures as initiators of the practices and styles that have been previously attributed to Ziryab's influence.

Ziryab is said to have founded a music-teaching institution in the Andalusi capital, Cordoba, where he taught the principles of the Baghdadi school to his sons and daughters. His songs were apparently collected in *Kitab fi Agani Ziryab (Ziryab's Songbook)*, which is no longer in existence. Ziryab endorsed several innovations that had an effect on the fundamental instrument of Arab music, the lute *('ud)*. He is reported to have added a fifth, red-colored string to the lute; this string would correspond with the soul, following the Arab idea that each string influences *(ta'thir)* a particular organ of the human body. (It has also been claimed that the philosopher and humanist, al-Kindi, as well as Ziryab's mentor, Ishaq al-Mawsili, introduced the five-stringed lute.)

Ziryab's alleged novelties include exchanging the traditional wooden plectrum used for plucking the lute for a vulture quill. He is also said to have made the two lower strings of his instrument out of wolf gut, and he may have introduced a new way of cleaning the silk of the higher strings. He claimed that his lute weighed a third less than most other lutes.

More importantly, Ziryab assumed the continuity of Oriental musical practices in the Islamic Occident. His performances began with a measured song with an unmeasured recitative. He closely followed the modes of the East; his songs increased in lightness and tempo in lyrics and tune, thereby favoring the consolidation of the *nawba* (vocal suite) genre, which later became the paramount Andalusi musical genre.

More than anything else, it is the Andalusi/Maghribi *nawba* that justifies the musician's fame. As previously mentioned, tradition credits Ziryab with the composition of the integral collection of Andalusi nawbas. One must bear in mind that a compilation featuring all eleven of the Moroccan nawbas requires a total of seventy three compact discs.

Historical reality does seem to have evolved rather differently, according to French musicologist Christian Poché in his work on Andalusi music. A thirteenth-century work by al-Tifashi (1184–1253) gives an account of the evolution of the so-called classical Arab music through the portrayal of its greatest performers. According to his report, the main figure who helped this type of music to acquire its structure was the twelfth-century Andalusi philosopher Ibn Bajja (Latinized as *Avempace)*. Ibn Bajja was the first to merge the singing techniques of the East with those of the western Islamic world. In Al-Andalus and North Africa, a diatonic scale is used; this is in opposition with the musical practice of the Orient. Moreover, Andalusi and Maghribi music does not include the quarter tones that are featured in Eastern styles. Ziryab seems to have historically been used as a narrative excuse rather than with any regard for his actual historical integrity.

A nawba is a highly structured vocal and instrumental piece based on a principal mode *(tab')*, along with some secondary ones. It fuses Arabic rhythms with ancient Greek music modes. Each nawba adopts a suite structure, usually in a binary or ternary form, thereby allowing little scope for rhythmic variation as compared with music from the East. Every two movements are linked with a brief musical phrase that is called *kursi* (chair) in Arabic. A vocal solo can be substituted for this instrumental link; this style allows the singer to sing alone and demonstrate his or her vocal ability. The singer can also take this moment to move emotions in the audience by interpreting the most beautiful poetic passage of the lyrics.

A certain mystical content has traditionally been associated with the Andalusi nawba; this has led to the idea that each nawba is linked to a certain moment of the day. Thus, there may be twenty-four nawbas, one for each hour of the day. Subtle disparities can be found between the modern musical genres of Morocco's tarab al-a'la, hawzi, and malhun; Algeria's maluf, gharnati, and sana'a; and Tunisia's maluf; however, they can all still be recognized as branches of the single musical form of the nawba.

JESÚS DE PRADO PLUMED

See also 'Abd al-Rahman III; Aghlabids; Al-Farabi (Alfarabius or Avennasar); Al-Kindi; Al-Maqqari; Andalus; Harun al-Rashid; Ibn Quzman; Mystical Poetry; Music; Nawruz; Performing Artists; Poetry, Arabic; Qayrawan

Primary Sources

Al-Makkari, Ahmed ibn Mohammed. *The History of the Mohammedan Dynasties in Spain,* 1st ed., transl. Pascual de Gayangos. London: RoutledgeCurzon, 2002.

Further Reading

Greus, Jesús. *Ziryab: La Prodigiosa Historia del Sultán Andaluz y el Cantor de Bagdad,* 1st ed. Madrid: Swan, 1987.
Kennedy, Hugh. *Muslim Spain and Portugal. A Political History of Al-Andalus,* 1st ed. London: Longman, 1996.
Parsons, David, producer. *Music of Islam, vol. 7: Al-Andalus, Andalusian Music, Tetouan, Morocco* (CD). Tucson, Ariz: Celestial Harmonies, 1998.
Poché, Christian. *La Musique Arabo-andalouse,* 1st ed., with accompanying CD. Arles: Actes Sud, 1995.

ZOROASTRIANISM

Designations

Medieval Zoroastrians referred to their religion by the Middle Persian or Pahlavi phrase *den i Mazdesn* (religion of Mazda), because they regarded Ahura Mazda (Wise Lord) as the Creator. The expression *Zardushtig den* (Zoroastrian religion) was also used, because they regarded their devotions as having originated from the preachings of a devotional poet named Zarathushtra (Middle Persian: Zardukhsht, Zardusht; New Persian or Farsi: Zardosht). Therefore, they called themselves *Mazdesnan* (Worshipers of Mazda) and *Zartoshtiyan* (Zoroastrians).

Medieval Muslims writing in Classical Arabic and New Persian designated all Zoroastrians as *al-Majus* (Magians) on the basis of the technical term for Zoroastrian priests or magi (Middle Persian: maguk, mowbed, mowmard; New Persian: mobed). Zoroastrian acts of worship customarily were conducted in the presence of fires on altars inside fire temples (Middle Persian: atakhshkadag; New Persian: ateshkade), so the New Persian term *atashparast* (fire worshipper), picked up from Christians, become an insult directed by Muslims at Zoroastrians, despite the latters' protesting that their actions were similar to Muslims facing prayer niches and the Ka'ba. Another New Persian designation that came to be used by Muslims to deride Zoroastrians as nonbelievers in God was *gabr* (hollow, empty, one lacking faith, infidel), despite the latter sect's claim that their scripture—the Avesta—was a holy book just like the Bible and the Qur'an.

Conversion to Islam, Minority Status, and Doctrinal Interaction

The Arab Muslim conquest of Zoroastrian Iran and overthrow of the Sasanian dynasty (224–651 CE) during the seventh century came to be associated with apocalyptic and prophetic expectations. Zoroastrian apocalypticism alluded to doom and the final days of humanity. Islamic prophecy highlighted triumph, presenting the Prophet Muhammad (ca. 570–632) and the Muslim caliphs as successors to Zarathushtra and the Sasanian monarchs. Because people believed those statements, they acted on their beliefs. Many despondent Zoroastrians, concluding that a true deity would not have forsaken them or their religion, chose to accept the faith that had demonstrated its ascendance through political victory. Urban Irani Zoroastrians adopted Islam between the eighth and tenth centuries CE, and that faith spread among rural folk from the tenth through thirteenth centuries CE. As residents' confessional alliance shifted to Islam, there was a diminishment of contributions to pious foundations that supported the magi. Consequently, many Zoroastrian ecclesiastical institutions, such as fire temples and *herbedestans* (seminaries), were either transformed into Islamic mosques and Sunni madrasas, respectively, or abandoned and destroyed by the fourteenth century. The *chahar taq* (four arch) style of the Zoroastrian fire precinct, with its domed roof, passed into Muslim architecture as domed mosques.

Zoroastrianism initially represented the dominant faith numerically—although no longer politically—in those regions of the Islamic empire that were seized from the Sasanians and the princes of western Central Asia. To facilitate peaceful governance, medieval Muslim scholars drew upon hadith (traditions) attributed to Muhammad and caliphs like 'Umar I (d. 644) and 'Ali ibn Abi Talib (598–661) for incorporating Zoroastrians into the ahl al-dhimma (protected communities). Not all Muslims recognized Zoroastrians as a dhimmi community, but the Umayyad (661–750) and 'Abbasid (750–1258) caliphates did.

Because dhimmi status provided at least nominal safety to the Zoroastrians as a religious minority, magi facilitated the Zoroastrian claim to that position by making copies of the Avesta and its Zand (exegesis). Zarathushtra's hagiography was augmented to reshape him as a Near-Eastern prophet who had preceded Muhammad. Ahura Mazda was gradually transformed into the Zoroastrian God. Angra Mainyu (Angry Spirit), who had originally been Ahura Mazda's spiritual opposite, became the Devil. Zoroastrianism influenced Islam as well, with Iranian traditions of afterlife—including the imagery of a bridge leading to a heaven filled with pleasure and notions of an apocalypse at the end of time, followed by an eschaton—entering both Sunnism and Shi'ism.

Medieval Migrations

The Arab Muslim conquest of Iran triggered migrations by Zoroastrians. Some Zoroastrians, especially Sasanian nobles and military personnel, immigrated to China. Zoroastrians survived in China as late as the middle fourteenth century, after which time they were completely assimilated into the local population. The situation proved different for those who went to India in the tenth century and formed the Parsi (Persian) community there.

The Zoroastrian migration to India is recorded as the Parsi community's founding legend, known as the New Persian *Qessa-e Sanjan (Story of Sanjan)*. According to that text, during the reign of the Samanid kings (892–1005), groups of Zoroastrians left the northeastern Iranian province of Khorasan to avoid forced conversion to Islam. Their descendents finally reached Gujarat in western India via the sea in 936. About five years after their arrival, the Parsis consecrated an *ātesh behrām* (victory fire, the highest level of ritual fire), called Iran Shah (King of Iran), which remained their main flame for more than eight hundred years. Most religious rituals were performed using *dadgah* (hearth) fires. The *jizya* (poll tax) was imposed on Parsis in 1297, when the Delhi Muslim sultanate conquered Gujarat. Economic hardship created by payment of the jizya, plus the stigma of designation as dhimmis, resulted in the conversion of portions of the Parsi population to Islam. However, the community persisted in their beliefs and praxes, with the result being that early European travelers began to encounter them; for example, in 1350, the Dominican friar Jordanus commented on the exposure of Parsi corpses. When their Indian religious stronghold at Sanjan was sacked by the Muzaffarid Sultan Mahmud Begath (Begada; r. 1458–1511) around the year 1465, Parsi magi transferred the Iran Shah atesh behram to a mountain cave for twelve years to ensure that it continued to burn unhindered by Muslims. Eventually, in 1479, the flame was moved to the Parsi city of Navsari to once again become the main locus of Zoroastrian piety in India.

Medieval Iran

Between the eighth and fifteenth centuries, the lives of Zoroastrians as members of a dhimmi community were governed by religious tenets and by a sectarian society dominated by Muslim men. Realizing that cross-communal contacts threatened the traditional way of life, magi outlawed sex, marriage, and most forms of interaction by Zoroastrians with Muslims unless such contact was vital for a Zoroastrians livelihood or safety. Likewise, Muslim jurists such as Malik ibn Anas (716–795) ruled that Zoroastrians should not be permitted to marry Muslims unless Islam was adopted. However, intermarriage across confessional boundaries became increasingly frequent, with Zoroastrian spouses experiencing rejection from their co-religionists. In response to this, they adopted Islam and raised their children as Muslims. Because Zoroastrians were regarded as unclean, Muslims initially were not supposed to eat food prepared by Zoroastrians. Traditions attributed to various early caliphs, including 'Ali and an ex-Zoroastrian companion of the Prophet Muhammad named Salman al-Farisi (d. 656), developed to overcome that barrier, eventually resulting in Muslim jurists such as Ahmad ibn Hanbal (780–855) decreeing that meals prepared by Zoroastrians could be consumed by Muslims.

Such social interactions between Muslims and Zoroastrians notwithstanding, their minority status resulted in considerable hardship for followers of Zoroastrianism. For example, the powerful Seljuk vizier Nizam al-Mulk (d. 1092 CE) enjoined that Zoroastrians, like other dhimmis, should not be appointed to positions of authority over Muslims, and he even equated them with Muslim groups that he regarded as heretical. Even more problematic was that Zoroastrians' standing under Islamic law was secondary to members of the majority confessional group, thereby affecting the equitable resolution of commercial and social disputes. The jizya was usually collected by community leaders rather than paid directly to Muslim officials by each Zoroastrian; here, too, however, there was an impact of legal inequality. Mahmud ibn 'Umar al-Zamakhshari (1075–1144), an important Muslim theologian, suggested that Zoroastrians be publicly humiliated each time the jizya was paid. After 850 CE, Zoroastrians were required to wear yellow caps, shawls, belts, and badges so that Muslims could easily identify them, and the use of horses and saddles by Zoroastrians was forbidden by Muslim authorities.

Conquest and rule of Iran by the Mongols (1219–1256), Ilkhanids (1256–1335), and Timurids (1370–1507) resulted in violence against urban Zoroastrians residing in city quarters that had been specifically designated for them. Those seeking to avoid harm often sought protection through reaffiliating their faith to Islam. Those Zoroastrians who survived sought refuge by moving to out-of-the-way locales within the Fars, Yazd, and Kerman provinces of Iran. There the magi attempted to maintain Zoroastrian rites and beliefs by compiling religious literature known as the *Pahlavi Books* in Middle Persian and the *Revayats (Treatises)* in New Persian.

JAMSHEED K. CHOKSY

Further Reading

Boyce, Mary. *Zoroastrians: Their Beliefs and Practices.* London: Routledge and Kegan Paul, 1979.

Choksy, Jamsheed K. *Conflict and Cooperation: Zoroastrian Subalterns and Muslim Elites in Medieval Iranian Society.* New York: Columbia University Press, 1997.

———. "Hagiography and Monotheism in History: Doctrinal Encounters Between Zoroastrianism, Judaism, and Christianity." *Islam and Christian-Muslim Relations* 14 (2003): 407–15.

Kreyenbroek, Philip G. "The Zoroastrian Priesthood After the Fall of the Sasanian Empire." In *Transition Periods in Iranian History,* 151–66. Louvain: Peeters, 1987.

de Menasce, Jean. "Zoroastrian Literature After the Muslim Conquest." In *Cambridge History of Iran,* vol. 4, ed. Richard N. Frye, 543–65. Cambridge: Cambridge University Press, 1975.

Morony, Michael G. *Iraq After the Muslim Conquest.* Princeton, NJ: Princeton University Press, 1984.

Shaked, Shaul. *From Zoroastrian Iran to Islam.* Aldershot: Ashgate-Variorum, 1995.

INDEX

INDEX

INDEX

INDEX

INDEX

INDEX

INDEX

INDEX

W

Wadi al-'Allaqi, 505
Wadi al-kabir, *See* Guadalquivir River
Wadi al-Khaznadar, 510
Wadi al-Sughd, 829
Wadi Batha, 713
Wadi Fas, 257
Wahb ibn Munabbih, 358, 476, 754
Wahdat al-wujud, 290, 620
Wahdat ash-shuhud, 290
Wahhabis, 434
Wahidi, al-, 708
Wajib, 157, 171
Walashama dynasty, 12
Walayat al-faqih, 735
Wali, 620
Walid, al-, 3, 514, 520, 525, 845, 848
Walid ibn 'Abd al-Malik, al-, 50, 191
Walid ibn Yazid, al-, 753
Walid II, 480
Wall painting, 588–589
Wallada, 866
Wallada Bint al-Mustakfi, 308
Waqf, 145–146, 857–858
Waqf deeds, 66
Waqf Nama-i Rab'-i Rashidi, 666
Waqidi, al-, 366, 452, 754, 858–859
Waqifiyya, 35
Waqwaq, 549
War of Ajnadayn, 59
Waraqa, 527
Warfare
    Mongol, 508–511
    Muslim-Byzantine relations, 537–539
Washsha', al-, 161
Wasil ibn Ata, 99, 544, 676
Wasiti, al-, 116
Wasiyya, 387
Water mills, 799–801
Wathiq, al-, 11, 356, 403, 438
Wattasids, 479
Wayfarers, 635
Weak and Geminate Verbs, 301
Weapons
    composite bow, 510
    Mongol use of, 510
Weather, 859–860
Weddings
    Islamic, 481
    Jewish, 481
Weeping over the Ruins, 618
Weightlifting, 769
Well Established Confluent of the Alphabetical Index, 716
Well of Zamzam, 429, 431
Well-Preserved Pearl, The, 548
What Is Desirable in the Pursuit for the History of Aleppo, 341
What is Sufficient in the Knowledge of the Faith, 443
White Mosque, 480
Wiet, Gaston, 801
William of Rubruck, 540
Wind mills, 799–801
Wind's Breeze on the Juicy Andalusian Branch, The, 478
Windstorms, 859
Wine, 10, 26, 860–861
Wine Ode, 844

Wine poems, 27
With the Prophets in the Glorious Qur'an, 645
Wizarisn i Catrang ud Nihisn i New-Ardaxsir, 88
Women
    circumcision of, 156–157
    clothing worn by, 181
    cosmetics use by, 177
    dancing by, 192
    economic activities of, 862–863
    education of, 862
    equality for, 278
    in Geniza period, 862–863
    jewelry worn by, 416–417
    Jewish, 861–863
    legal system effects on, 863
    license to issue legal opinions, 203
    as patrons, 863–865
    as poets, 865–867
    poverty among, 635
    segregation of, 330
    veiling of, 160
    as warriors, 867–868
Wonders of Created Things and the Oddities of Existing Things, The, 651–652
Wonders of Creation, The, 651–652
Wonders of Regions, 548
Wonders of the Lands, The, 651–653
Wrestling, 769
Wrestling With the Wrestling, 840
Writers, 201
Writing
    "cursive" form of, 134
    forms of, 134
    "monumental" form of, 134
    tools for, 134
Wu Zixian, 120
Wula al-harb, 591
Wuzurgmihr, 88, 148

X

Xenophon, 328
Xenopsylla cheopis, 113
Xerxes, 604
Xi Xia dynasty, 280, 747

Y

Yahudiyya, 399
Yahyâ al-Shabihi, 274
Yahya Bey, 97
Yahya ibn 'Adi, 68, 377, 610, 827
Yahya ibn al-Husayn, 871
Yahya ibn 'Umar, 39
Yahya ibn 'Umar al-Lamtuni, 39
Yahya ibn Yaya al-Laythi, 468
Yahya II, 382
Yamama, 55
Yamin al-Dawla Mahmud, 142
Yang, 280
Ya'qub al-Laith, 691
Ya'qub al-Qirqisani, 709
Ya'qub ibn akhi Hizam, 45
Ya'qub ibn Killis, 623, 869
Ya'qub Lais, 603